8974

INTRODUCTION TO FEDERAL TAXATION

INTRODUCTION TO

FEDERAL TAXATION

William L. Raby
The Raby Report on Tax Practice

Victor H. Tidwell
Arizona State University

Richard A. White
University of South Carolina

1991

EDITION

PRENTICE HALL, ENGLEWOOD CLIFFS, N.J. 07632

A Division of Simon & Schuster, Inc.
Englewood Cliffs, New Jersey 07632

Editorial/production supervision: *Patrick Reynolds*
Text design: *Alice Erdman*
Interior design: *Linda Conway*
Cover design: *Bruce Kenselaar*
Manufacturing buyers: *Bob Anderson and Trudy Pisciotti*

ISSN: 0731-7905

Printed in the United States of America

10 9 8 7 6 5 4 3 2 1

ISBN 0-13-481664-1

PRENTICE-HALL INTERNATIONAL (UK) LIMITED, *London*
PRENTICE-HALL OF AUSTRALIA PTY. LIMITED, *Sydney*
PRENTICE-HALL CANADA INC., *Toronto*
PRENTICE-HALL HISPANOAMERICANA, S.A., *Mexico*
PRENTICE-HALL OF INDIA PRIVATE LIMITED, *New Delhi*
PRENTICE-HALL OF JAPAN, INC., *Tokyo*
PRENTICE-HALL OF SOUTHEAST ASIA PTE. LTD., *Singapore*
EDITORA PRENTICE-HALL DO BRASIL., LTDA., *Rio de Janeiro*

CONTENTS

PART TWO

PART TWO

THE TAXPAYER IN BUSINESS

PREFACE

to the student

The tax collector (IRS) is a silent partner in every business deal. And not just in business, for IRS is also involved with marriage, divorce, birth, and death.

If the system operated automatically, and if what you did individually made little difference, then the ubiquitous presence of the IRS might be interesting and nothing more. Like the weather.

But what you do does make a difference. Your federal tax life is like a hockey game, with IRS guarding the goal while you try to score with your tax planning decisions. If you're smart, you study the rules of the game first, before you get out on the ice and start moving the puck around for real money. Especially since it's your real money.

Of course, you can plan the tax game on a strictly defensive basis. Then the best you can do is to stop IRS from scoring. That's the traditional approach to teaching taxes. Avoid this trap, sidestep that pitfall! Our approach to federal taxes goes beyond the defense, for the taxpayer can also take the initiative. Planning what happens is the taxpayer's competitive edge.

In this book we walk you through some basic moves and some simple plays. Our goal? To take you from a starting position of not knowing anything about anything to the point where you'll know a little bit about almost everything—and quite a bit about the most important things. This course may be the only tax course you'll take as an undergraduate, or you may be taking the course as a graduate student who never had a formal tax course before. Either way, it must lay the foundation for graduate work and for continuing professional education after you're out of school, and must also give you the basics you'll need without another tax course to function as a businessperson, taxpayer, and concerned citizen. This book will be your best shot at a total immersion, concentrated crash course in successful tax tactics.

When you finish the course, you should understand how tax rules can advantageously be taken into account in your personal, investment, and business decisions. You should also have an idea of how to cope with federal tax problems administratively, how to get answers to tax questions, and where to get tax help. And you should have a foundation that will help you to understand anything you read about taxes, whether in the professional literature or in general-interest writings.

to the teacher

"The antithesis between a technical and liberal education is fallacious. There can be no adequate technical education which is not liberal, and no liberal education which is not technical: that is, no education which does not impart both technique and intellectual vision."

—Alfred North Whitehead

Why is it important to know a thing or two about taxes? Because you can do something about them. That is the great lesson of this book, and the reason that we wrote it.

None of your students will have had much or any tax background or experience. The accounting background of many students may not be too strong, either, so we start with the assumption that they know nothing—and we go from there. We move from the known to the unknown, taking little steps at the beginning rather than great leaps. As the semester progresses, and a foundation of concepts and vocabulary takes shape, our pace picks up.

We assume that few of your students will ever take a second course in taxes. This is it. So we select judiciously and pare with care, using our judgment and experience in making trade-offs between detailed coverage of major topics and an adequate breadth of survey for a one-semester, terminal course. By the end of the semester, the student understands the tax concepts of income; appreciates the impact of tax factors on individual, family, and business decision making; and has some rudimentary feel for tax research and for the relationships between the taxpayer and IRS.

Thus, every student will have a foundation of tax knowledge for career decisions, for turning points in personal life, and for action as responsible citizens. Those who will go on are ready for graduate work in taxes as well as for on-the-job and professional training programs.

Tax rules could be all-encompassing and simple, with no choice. Then, knowing taxes would mean being able to look up the rule to apply to what happened. The complexity would lie in figuring out what happened.

In reality, tax rules are neither simple nor all-encompassing. Similar situations may produce different tax results. Thus, knowing taxes involves understanding the structure of the rules, knowing how to find the appropriate specific rule, but, most important realizing that the tax results are shaped by how what is to be done will fit within the rule. Tax dollars are not so much saved when returns are being prepared as when what is to be done is being planned.

There is, however, a pedagogical advantage to using tax forms and return situations in teaching an introductory course. For most students, the tax form framework is easier to grasp than any alternative. A tax form is like a picture, and "a picture is worth a thousand words." But, as you will see as you peruse the book, we will continually underscore the planning aspects. In fact, our criterion for including or excluding material has been whether it can be used in a planning context.

In addition to an instructor's manual, a student workbook has been prepared to accompany this text. The workbook allows you to assign a variety of supplemental problems, and can be used to bring the student much closer to a programmed learning experience. But you can also teach a good course without the workbook, since each text chapter has a complete repertoire of questions and problems. Questions that require resources outside the text are marked with an asterisk (*). Plan 1040, available from the publisher, allows you to bring the computer into the course with problems cross-referenced to this book. See the Fall 1985 *Journal of the American Taxation Association,* p. 89.

The book is revised annually. Your comments, corrections, and suggestions directed in care of the publisher will be gratefully received.

While this book has been designed on the assumption that the majority of those taking a first tax course will not go on to a second course, it provides an excellent foundation for a second course that is oriented toward tax research, planning, and practice. The instructor's manual that accompanies this text contains sample assignment schedules for the first course, sample test questions, problem solutions, etc., and also discusses materials and approaches for teaching a second course that follows a first course using this text.

The drawings are the work of the gifted Margot Sheehan.

William L. Raby
Victor H. Tidwell
Richard A. White

INTRODUCTION TO FEDERAL TAXATION

PART ONE

THE NONBUSINESS TAXPAYER

Kindly Old Gent:
"And what do you want to be when you grow up, little girl?"
Little Girl:
"A high-bracket taxpayer, sir!"

1

taxes and choices

People *can* do something about the federal income tax they pay. That is the main reason individuals and businesses spend time and money gaining an understanding of the tax law. You, too, can learn how to save money on taxes. To do so, you must understand how the tax system operates.

1.1 Life-style and Taxation

There is a trade-off between activities that produce taxable income and other activities, such as sitting on a park bench all day. For some people, $10,000 of additional income, which would result in only $6,700 after taxes, may not be worth the extra effort or risk to earn it. Ask yourself whether it would be worthwhile for you? For your parents? For others you know?

There is also another kind of trade-off that affects taxable income. If you repair your own car, no taxable income results from doing the work. Ditto for mowing your own lawn, painting your own house, and preparing your meals at home or at the homes of friends instead of eating in restaurants. One person works in a city but lives on enough acreage to raise most of her family's food. A couple reside on a yacht and make their living chartering it out of St. Thomas in the Virgin Islands. A handyman enjoys the avocation of fixing up run-down residences. Every few years he sells a house in tip-top shape for a tip-top profit which he reinvests in another run-down house and starts over again. Each of these persons has selected a life-style with different tax consequences.

Income for tax purposes does not include the value of services rendered to yourself; neither does it include the increase in net worth resulting from the passage of time, such as the increase in value of stocks or bonds or of a residence. If they are sold, however, gain or loss may result for tax purposes. But in the case of a principal residence, there may be no tax if the proceeds are invested in another residence (see Chapter 6). The food you raise creates no income if you consume it. If it is sold for cash, or traded for something else, there is income, of course. There is no income imputed to one who enjoys one's work, such as a person who lives on a yacht that also results in income when the yacht is rented. But the rent is income. Because of some special tax rules, a person whose employer furnishes meals and lodging may not have income. For example, a hotel manager might be required to occupy a suite in the hotel as a condition of employment. The fair rental value of the suite may not be income to the employee. In other occupations, the employee might have to pay tax on the fair rental value of the lodging and the fair market value of the meals furnished by an employer. Thus, a person might be motivated to seek employment under conditions where lodging and/or meals would be furnished in such a way as to result in no additional tax.

Thus, one way to avoid tax is to refuse to accept the sort of job or life-style in which you need to earn money to buy all the goods and services that you want. If money has to be earned before food can be purchased, then what is earned is taxable, but the cost of the food is not deductible. Obviously, there are limits. The dentist may well be capable of doing his own carpentry and building

FIGURE1–1 Gross collections of tax dollars for fiscal year ended September 30, 1988.

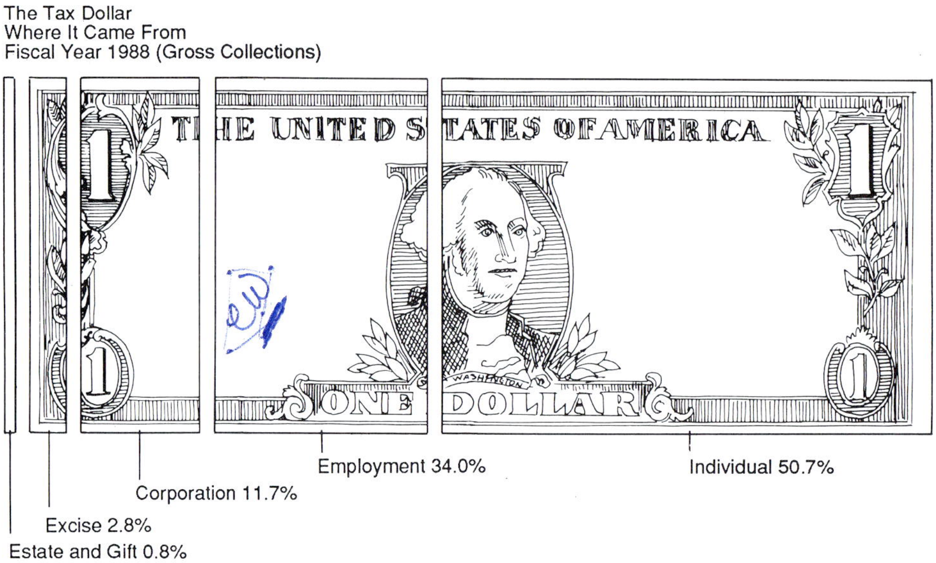

Source: *Statistics of Income Bulletin,* Vol. 8, No. 4 (U.S. Treasury Department) Spring, 1989, p. 111.

himself a bookcase, but it is unlikely that the carpenter will be able to fix his children's teeth. Thus, even reflecting the tax they would both pay, it may be more efficient for the dentist to fix the teeth of the carpenter's children and the carpenter to build a bookcase for the dentist. Even if they were to decide to barter for each other's services, thus avoiding cash as an interim step, there would still be a taxable event. It is only the performance of services for yourself that escapes a tax impact.

You can see why those who must buy everything that is needed in a money economy—food, clothing, shelter, entertainment, education, etc.—may not only get less real after-tax income than those who operate in a more self-sufficient manner, but may also build less net worth, all other things being equal. The question is: How many things do you *want* to make or do for yourself? How many of your needs would you rather satisfy with things you can buy, even though the income it takes to buy them will be taxed?

The point to remember is that almost all decisions have tax implications, even those that do not show up on tax returns.[1] But now we turn our attention to what does show up on the individual income tax return, how that return is put together, and how planning can reduce the portion of income that goes to pay taxes.

1.2 Different Income, Different Taxes

The individual income tax is a primary source of funds for the U.S. government. For fiscal 1988 (October, 1987 to September, 1988), it accounted for 50.7% of the total taxes collected by the federal government (see Fig. 1-1). Another 11.7% came from the corporate income tax. Of more importance to you is the fact that the individual income tax is also a major drain on the personal budgets of the majority of Americans. The Tax Reform Act of 1986 was designed to shift a significant portion of the tax burden from individuals to businesses, especially to corporations. This shift began with taxes for calendar 1986, but the full impact will not be realized until 1991. Also, the Tax Law of 1987 (Omnibus Budget Reconciliation Act of 1987) became law on December 22, 1987, and the Tax Law of 1988 (Technical and Miscellaneous Revenue Act of 1988) was enacted on November 10, 1988. Some of the results of these changes will not be reflected on tax returns until 1992 and later. More recently, the Omnibus Budget Reconciliation Act of 1989 was signed by President Bush and became effective on December 19, 1989. While this latter change in rules did not change the tax rates, it made many technical changes of importance to individuals as well as businesses.

Let's consider the impact of the tax laws on someone who is still a student, Billy Barnes. An unmarried college senior, Billy, who earned $8,000, and was self-dependent, paid $437 of federal tax, for 1989.

As we will see later, had Billy been someone's dependent, then the tax could have been more.

The sample Form 1040EZ in Fig. 1-3 shows the tax liability on line 7. Where that number came from will be explained later. Also, the deduction of $5,100 on line 4 is the sum of $3,100 for a

[1] As Sherlock Holmes remarked, "The significant fact was that the dog did *not* bark."

"standard deduction" and $2,000 for a personal exemption. These will be explained later. Other than those calculations, everything on this 1040EZ is simple and straightforward. The $8,000 salary is on line 1, the tax of $437 on line 7 has been partially paid in advance (the $426 on line 6), and the balance due of $11 on line 9 will be paid with a check to the Internal Revenue Service.

Millions of taxpayer returns are just this uncomplicated.[2] But while all of Billy's earnings are taxed, not every dollar that everyone receives is income for tax purposes. Nor is all income taxed at the same rate. Also, some expenditures can be deducted in arriving at the amount of income subject to tax. Certain types of transactions and situations even generate a *credit,* which reduces the final tax payable.[3] These all complicate the otherwise simple and straightforward job of figuring the amount of income tax that is due.

Further, these "complicators" affect personal financial decisions of individuals. All other things being equal, people tend to seek income that is not subject to income tax rather than income that is; they tend to prefer expenditures that are deductible to expenditures that are not. They tend to avoid behavior that will provide the government with a greater part of their resources than is required under the law.

Types and amounts of income, nature and size of potential deductions, and even marital status also affect which tax return forms can even be filed by an individual:

> Form 1040EZ, discussed above for Billy Barnes, can only be used by single persons who are not age 65 or older, or blind, have no dependents, have no dividend income, have $400 or less of interest income, have taxable income of less than $50,000, and have no other income except wages, salaries, or tips (not reported to the employer).
>
> Form 1040A can be used regardless of marital status, but does not provide for claiming such itemized deductions as medical expenses, interest paid, theft losses, state or local income or property taxes, or expenses of producing income (such as union dues) or for reporting income other than wages, interest, dividends, taxable scholarships, and unemployment compensation.
>
> Form 1040 is the workhorse of the individual tax forms. With its various supplementary schedules, it is used by everyone who uses neither the 1040EZ nor the 1040A.[4]

The three forms do not represent three different systems of taxing individuals. Rather, the 1040EZ and the 1040A represent attempts to simplify the return preparation process for those who cannot benefit from the more complicated tax law provisions.

1.3 Figuring Taxes: The Choices at Each Step

People often think of taxes as being a "number-crunching" subject. Certainly, number skills are important in tax work. But an understanding of taxes requires an understanding of words—of many words that often do not mean exactly what they appear to mean. Tax words frequently are like words used in writing computer programs—that is, they mean what they are defined to mean for a specific purpose. Sometimes the definition is very precise; sometimes it is quite broad. Like other words, a tax word's meaning can also depend on the context in which the word appears.

While the purpose of this text is not to teach how to fill out forms, a review of the forms can be instructive. Take a look at the Form 1040A in Fig. 1-4. Some of the words seem quite simple, such as "single" on line 1. But if "single" means unmarried, and "married" means the opposite, then what about the caption on line 4: "head of household"? (That will be discussed in Chapter 4.)

Although the concept of income may seem intuitively clear, what is "gross income," which is implicit in the caption "Adjusted gross income" on line 13, and by what has "gross income" been "adjusted"?

Modifying the 1040EZ numbers we used before for Billy Barnes may provide a preliminary idea of some key words and how they fit together. We will assume now, as is reflected in the 1040A (Fig. 1-4) that Billy had $225 of dividend income. Note the circumstances under which additional schedules (see Appendix 1-H) would be necessary to accompany Form 1040A:

a. Interest income of more than $400

b. Dividend income of more than $400

c. Credit for child/dependent care (discussed in Chapter 4)

[2] For calendar 1987, 18.7 million taxpayers filed Form 1040EZ, out of 107.1 million total individual tax returns filed. *Statistics of Income Bulletin,* Vol. 8, No. 4 (U.S. Department of Treasury) Spring, 1989, p. 93.

[3] For tax purposes, the word "credit" means a reduction in the amount of tax otherwise due. This term is contrasted to "deduction," which means a reduction in the amount that is subject to tax, and to "exclusion," which means an amount that is omitted from the tax computation altogether.

[4] For 1987, 66.1% of the individual tax returns filed were on Form 1040 and 16.5% on Form 1040A. *Statistics of Income Bulletin,* Vol. 8, No. 4 (U.S. Department of Treasury), Spring 1989, p. 93.

Billy's income is now:

Salary	$8,000
Dividends	225
Gross income (also Adjusted Gross Income)	$8,225

Note that the $225 of dividends that were taxed increased Billy's 1989 tax from $437 to $469, an increase of $32. In evaluating the return on that investment, Billy should consider the amount of tax. Thus, the return is $193, not $225.

Completing the look at Form 1040A (Figure 1-4(b), note that the interest income, which had no income tax withheld as does salary, caused Billy to have additional tax due of $43 (line 28) instead of a tax due of $11.

So what is the definition of "adjusted gross income"? Gross income is the number derived after excluding from income certain items, such as scholarships (equal to tuition, books, and supplies) interest received from municipal and state bonds and some employee fringe benefits. Certain specific items (called "deductions") are then subtracted from gross income to arrive at "adjusted gross income." These deductions, such as contributions to an Individual Retirement Account (see line 12(a) on Form 1040A) or alimony (see line 29 on Form 1040, Appendix 1-D) are set out in the tax law. Adjusted gross income is on line 13 of Form 1040A. Some specific kinds of income and some kinds of deductions require that Form 1040 rather than Form 1040A or Form 1040EZ be filed.

Billy Barnes was single, had only one exemption (which resulted in a $2,000 deduction for 1989), and thus had $3,125 of taxable income on line 19 of the 1040A in Fig. 1-4. Billy's 1989 tax liability can be determined by reference to a tax table (Appendix 1-A at the end of the chapter). Look at that table now. Opposite $3,125 under the column headed "single" is Billy's tax of $469.

Earlier we said that we would explain the $3,100 deduction which is a part of line 4 of Form 1040EZ and appears on line 16 of Form 1040A. It is called the "standard deduction," and represents a *minimum* amount (in addition to the "exemption amount," explained later) to which most taxpayers are entitled. The standard deduction consists of two parts, a "basic" standard deduction and an "additional amount." The basic standard deduction depends upon both filing status and the year, as shown in Figure 1-2.

FIGURE 1-2 Basic standard deduction chart

	1989	*1990*
Single person	$3,100	$3,250
Married persons filing a joint return	5,200	5,450
Married persons filing separate returns	2,600	2,725
Head of household	4,550	4,750

The difference between the 1989 and 1990 amounts in Figure 1-2 is due to an inflation adjustment factor that was applied to the 1989 numbers to arrive at the 1990 numbers. The adjustment factor was determined by a comparison of the Consumer Price Index for 1988 with that for 1989, with the adjustment then being rounded *down* to the nearest multiple of $50 (except for married filing separately which was rounded down to the nearest multiple of $25). Similar adjustments were made in the rate schedules for 1990 as compared with 1989 (compare Appendix 1-B with Appendix 1-C). There is a similar inflation adjustment factor applied to the personal exemption deduction amount. The 1990 amount is $2,050, representing an increase from $2,000 for 1989, and $1,950 for 1988.[4-a]

If a taxpayer has reached age 65 by the end of the year 1990, or is blind, modification of the basic standard deduction is made by adding an "additional amount." The additional amount is $650 for a married person and $800 for a single person. Thus, if a married couple are both age 65, and not blind, the additional amount for them is $1,300, and the total 1990 standard deduction (if they file jointly) is $6,750. If they are both age 65, and both blind, the 1990 standard deduction is $8,050. A single person age 65, and not blind, has a 1990 standard deduction of $4,050. If Billy Barnes, not age 65, is blind the 1990 standard deduction is $4,050.

The inflation factor adjustment described above was applied to the "additional amount" standard deduction for 1988 also. However, due to the *rounding down* procedure (to the lowest $50 multiple), there was no change between the 1988 and the 1989 amounts which were $600 and $750, respectively.

The standard deduction (basic plus additional, if any) is used by taxpayers only where the sum of "itemized deductions" (explained in Chapter 4) is less than the standard deduction. For example, in our 1989 example for Billy Barnes, a standard deduction of $3,100 was used. (Note that it made no difference if Form 1040EZ or Form 1040A were used. The $3,100 would also have been used if Form 1040—the so-called "long form"—had been used.) If Billy's 1989 itemized deductions had been more than $3,100 then the itemized deductions would have been used. (That would have required the use of Form 1040 and an accompanying Schedule A. See Appendix 1-D.)

[4a]While this may appear to be an increase of $50 each year, the 1990 adjustment was the result of the increase in the average Consumer Price Index (CPI) for the 12-month period ending August 31, 1989, over the same figure for the previous year.

Not everyone is entitled to the full standard deduction. You may have noticed the question at line 4 on Form 1040EZ and the instruction on line 15b of Form 1040A. If a person can be claimed as a dependent on someone else's tax return (also explained in Chapter 4) then the amount of the basic standard deduction is limited to $500, or the amount of "earned income" if larger.

However, there is a special rule for the standard deduction for a person who is a dependent of another person AND who is either blind or at least 65. Since we discuss the qualifications for having a dependent in Chapter 4, we will discuss that special provision in Chapter 4 also.

This reduced basic standard deduction can apply in several different circumstances, but the most common occurrence is that of a child who is a dependent of his or her parent(s). Assume that a child, age 17, is the dependent of his or her parents. Income (and adjusted gross income) for the year is $5,000, all from interest and dividends (called "unearned income"). The amount of the standard deduction is limited to $500.

In a different family, a child is age 17, a dependent of his or her parents, and has income of $2,000 from wages ("earned income") and $3,000 from interest and dividends ("unearned income"). Adjusted gross income is $5,000. The standard deduction, however, is $2,000. Why $2,000 instead of $500? Remember that the standard deduction is the *larger* of $500 or earned income (but not more than the amount shown in Fig. 1-2) for a person who can be claimed as a dependent by someone else. The tax law uses a somewhat strange definition of "earned income." It is income from salary, wages, or a proprietorship business. All other income, such as interest or dividends, is "unearned."

For 1989 the amount of the personal exemption was $2,000. That amount will be adjusted each year for changes in the price level as explained above for the standard deduction. The issue of how many "exemption amounts" can be deducted will be covered in Chapter 4. However, we need to point out that not every taxpayer is entitled to the deduction. We noted that Billy (a student in the examples for Forms 1040EZ and 1040A) was "self dependent" for 1989. This meant that Billy was not eligible to be claimed as a dependent on someone else's tax return. If Billy could have been claimed as a dependent on someone else's tax return—the most likely eligible person(s) for a student would be his or her parent(s)—then there would be no deduction for the exemption amount. If that had been the case for the 1989 example in Figure 1-3, then the $2,000 deduction would not have been claimed and taxable income would have been $4,900 instead of $2,900. This would have increased the tax from $437 to $739, a difference of $302. (See Appendix 1-A.)

It should be clear that even if Billy is a dependent of someone else, the standard deduction will be more than $500, so long as earned income is in excess of $500. In both of the following examples *for 1990,* Billy is a dependent of someone else.

Example 1: Earned income = $1,200
Unearned income = $3,000
Personal exemption deduction = 0
Standard deduction = $1,200
Taxable income = $3,000

Example 2: Earned income = $4,000
Unearned income = $3,000
Personal exemption deduction = 0
Standard deduction = $3,250 (maximum for 1990)
Taxable income = $3,750

Note the following concerning the loss of the deduction for personal exemption:

(a) Unlike the standard deduction, where there is still a minimum of $500 even where the balance of the basic deduction is lost, there is no minimum personal exemption. A deduction for the full amount ($2,050 for 1990) is available, or nothing is available.

(b) Unlike the standard deduction, the loss of the exemption amount deduction is not a function of the amount or kind of income. Rather, the exemption deduction is denied to anyone who can be claimed as a dependent (per the five tests which are described in Chapter 4) of someone else.

(c) The age of the taxpayer makes no difference. We will see later that if a person has not reached the age of 14 by the end of the year, there can be an impact upon the *rate* of tax paid.

Let's change the facts. Assume that Billy, not qualifying as someone's dependent, became an accountant during 1989 with a salary of $20,000 and spent money during 1989 in ways that provided deductions *from* adjusted gross income as follows:

Interest on home mortgage	$2,100
Real estate taxes	950
Donations to charities	450
Total	$3,500

These deductions totaled $3,500, which was $400 more than the (1989) $3,100 standard deduction. Billy was not entitled to *both* the $3,100 and the $3,500, but only to the larger amount. Thus:

FIGURE 1-3

Form **1040EZ**

Department of the Treasury - Internal Revenue Service

Income Tax Return for Single Filers With No Dependents **1989**

OMB No. 1545-0675

Name & address

Use the IRS mailing label. If you don't have one, please print.

LABEL HERE

BILLY B. BARNES
Print your name above (first, initial, last)

1219 E. LOYOLA DRIVE
Home address (number and street). (If you have a P.O. box, see back.) Apt. no.

HAMPTON ARIZONA 85235
City, town or post office, state, and ZIP code

Please print your numbers like this:

9876543210

Your social security number

332 00 0001

Instructions are on the back. Also, see the Form 1040A/1040EZ booklet, especially the checklist on page 14.

Presidential Election Campaign Fund
Do you want $1 to go to this fund?

Note: *Checking "Yes" will not change your tax or reduce your refund.* ▶

Report your income

1 Total wages, salaries, and tips. This should be shown in Box 10 of your W-2 form(s). (Attach your W-2 form(s).) 1 — 8 000 00

Attach Copy B of Form(s) W-2 here.

2 Taxable interest income of $400 or less. If the total is more than $400, you cannot use Form 1040EZ. 2

3 Add line 1 and line 2. This is your **adjusted gross income.** 3 — 8 000 00

4 Can your parents (or someone else) claim you on their return?

Note: You ***must*** *check Yes or No.*

☐ **Yes.** Do worksheet on back; enter amount from line E here.

☒ **No.** Enter 5,100. This is the total of your standard deduction and personal exemption. 4 — 5 100 00

5 Subtract line 4 from line 3. If line 4 is larger than line 3, enter 0. This is your **taxable income.** 5 — 2 900 00

Figure your tax

6 Enter your Federal income tax withheld from Box 9 of your W-2 form(s). 6 — 426 00

7 **Tax.** Use the amount on **line 5** to look up your tax in the tax table on pages 41-46 of the Form 1040A/1040EZ booklet. Use the **single** column in the table. Enter the tax from the table on this line. 7 — 437 00

Refund or amount you owe

8 If line 6 is larger than line 7, subtract line 7 from line 6. This is your **refund.** 8

Attach tax payment here.

9 If line 7 is larger than line 6, subtract line 6 from line 7. This is the **amount you owe.** Attach check or money order for the full amount, payable to "Internal Revenue Service." 9 — 11 00

Sign your return

(Keep a copy of this form for your records.)

I have read this return. Under penalties of perjury, I declare that to the best of my knowledge and belief, the return is true, correct, and complete.

Your signature — X Billy B Barnes

Date — 3-14-90

For Privacy Act and Paperwork Reduction Act Notice, see page 3 in the booklet.

Form 1040EZ (1989)

H732

FIGURE 1-4 (a)

Form **1040A** Department of the Treasury—Internal Revenue Service

U.S. Individual Income Tax Return 1989

OMB No. 1545-0085

Step 1 Label

Use IRS label. Otherwise, please print or type.

LABEL HERE

Your first name and initial: BILLY B.	Last name: BARNES	Your social security no.: 332 00 0001
If a joint return, spouse's first name and initial	Last name	Spouse's social security no.
Home address (number and street). (If you have a P.O. box, see page 15 of the instructions.): 1219 E. LOYOLA DR.	Apt. no.	
City, town or post office, state and ZIP code. (If you have a foreign address, see page 15.): HAMPTON ARIZONA 85235		

For Privacy Act and Paperwork Reduction Act Notice, see page 3.

Presidential Election Campaign Fund

Do you want $1 to go to this fund? . . . . ☐ Yes ☒ No

If joint return, does your spouse want $1 to go to this fund? ☐ Yes ☐ No

Note: *Checking "Yes" will not change your tax or reduce your refund.*

Step 2 Check your filing status

(Check only one.)

1 ☒ Single (See if you can use Form 1040EZ.)

2 ☐ Married filing joint return (even if only one had income)

3 ☐ Married filing separate return. Enter spouse's social security number above and spouse's full name here. ______

4 ☐ Head of household (with qualifying person). (See page 16.) If the qualifying person is your child but not your dependent, enter this child's name here. ______

5 ☐ Qualifying widow(er) with dependent child (year spouse died ▶ 19____). (See page 17.)

Step 3 Figure your exemptions

(See page 17 of instructions.)

6a ☒ **Yourself** If someone (such as your parent) can claim you as a dependent on his or her tax return, do not check box 6a. But be sure to check the box on line 15b on page 2.

6b ☐ **Spouse**

No. of boxes checked on 6a and 6b: 1

c **Dependents:**

1. Name (first, initial, and last name)	2. Check if under age 2	3. If age 2 or older, dependent's social security number	4. Relationship	5. No. of months lived in your home in 1989

If more than 7 dependents, see page 20.

No. of your children on 6c who:
- lived with you ______
- didn't live with you due to divorce or separation (see page 20) ______

No. of other dependents listed on 6c ______

Attach Copy B of Form(s) W-2 here.

d If your child didn't live with you but is claimed as your dependent under a pre-1985 agreement, check here . . . . ▶ ☐

e Total number of exemptions claimed.

Add numbers entered on lines above: 1

Step 4 Figure your total income

Attach check or money order here.

7	Wages, salaries, tips, etc. This should be shown in Box 10 of your W-2 form(s). (Attach Form(s) W-2.)	7	8,000 —
8a	**Taxable** interest income (see page 24). (If over $400, also complete and attach Schedule 1, Part II.)	8a	
b	**Tax-exempt** interest income (see page 24). (DO NOT include on line 8a.) 8b		
9	Dividends. (If over $400, also complete and attach Schedule 1, Part III.)	9	225 —
10	Unemployment compensation (insurance) from Form(s) 1099-G.	10	
11	Add lines 7, 8a, 9, and 10. Enter the total. This is your **total income.**	▶ 11	8,225 —

Step 5 Figure your adjusted gross income

12a	Your IRA deduction from applicable worksheet. Rules for IRAs begin on page 25. 12a		
b	Spouse's IRA deduction from applicable worksheet. Rules for IRAs begin on page 25. 12b		
c	Add lines 12a and 12b. Enter the total. These are your **total adjustments.**	12c	
13	Subtract line 12c from line 11. Enter the result. This is your **adjusted gross income.** (If this line is less than $19,340 and a child lived with you, see "Earned Income Credit" (line 25b) on page 37 of instructions.)	▶ 13	8,225 —

H732

FIGURE 1-4(b)

Step 6

Figure your standard deduction, exemption amount, and taxable income

14	Enter the amount from line 13.	14	8,225 —
15a	Check if: ☐ **You** were 65 or older ☐ Blind ☐ **Spouse** was 65 or older ☐ Blind } **Enter number of boxes checked** . ▶ 15a ☐		
b	If someone (such as your parent) can claim you as a dependent, check here . . . ▶ 15b ☐		
c	If you are married filing separately and your spouse files Form 1040 and itemizes deductions, see page 29 and check here . . . ▶ 15c ☐		
16	**Enter your standard deduction. See page 30 for the chart (or worksheet) that applies to you. Be sure to enter your standard deduction here.**	16	3,100 —
17	Subtract line 16 from line 14. Enter the result. (If line 16 is more than line 14, enter -0-.)	17	5,125 —
18	Multiply $2,000 by the total number of exemptions claimed on line 6e.	18	2,000 —
19	Subtract line 18 from line 17. Enter the result. (If line 18 is more than line 17, enter -0-.) This is your **taxable income.**	▶ 19	3,125 —

If You Want IRS To Figure Your Tax, See Page 31 of the Instructions.

Step 7

Figure your tax, credits, supplemental Medicare premium, and payments (including advance EIC payments)

Caution: If you are under age 14 and have more than $1,000 of investment income, check here . . . ▶ ☐
Also see page 31 to see if you have to use Form 8615 to figure your tax.

20	Find the tax on the amount on line 19. Check if from: ☒ Tax Table (pages 41–46) or ☐ Form 8615	20	469 —
21	Credit for child and dependent care expenses. Complete and attach Schedule 1, Part I.	21	
22	Subtract line 21 from line 20. Enter the result. (If line 21 is more than line 20, enter -0-.)	22	
23	**Supplemental Medicare premium.** See page 35. Complete and attach Schedule 2 (Form 1040A).	23	
24	Add lines 22 and 23. Enter the total. This is your **total tax** and any supplemental Medicare premium.	▶ 24	
25a	Total Federal income tax withheld—from Box 9 of your W-2 form(s). (If any is from Form(s) 1099, check here ▶ ☐ .) 25a 426 —		
b	**Earned income credit,** from the worksheet on page 38 of the instructions. Also see page 37. 25b		
26	Add lines 25a and 25b. Enter the total. These are your **total payments.**	▶ 26	426 —

Step 8

Figure your refund or amount you owe

27	If line 26 is more than line 24, subtract line 24 from line 26. Enter the result. This is your **refund.**	27	
28	If line 24 is more than line 26, subtract line 26 from line 24. Enter the result. This is the **amount you owe.** Attach check or money order for full amount payable to "Internal Revenue Service." Write your social security number, daytime phone number, and "1989 Form 1040A" on it.	28	43 —

Step 9

Sign your return

(Keep a copy of this return for your records.)

Under penalties of perjury, I declare that I have examined this return and accompanying schedules and statements, and to the best of my knowledge and belief, they are true, correct, and complete. Declaration of preparer (other than the taxpayer) is based on all information of which the preparer has any knowledge.

Your signature Date Your occupation

X

Spouse's signature (if joint return, both must sign) Date Spouse's occupation

X

Paid preparer's use only

Preparer's signature Date Preparer's social security no.

X

Firm's name (or yours if self-employed) Employer identification no.

Address and ZIP code Check if self-employed ☐

Adjusted gross income		$20,000
Less: Itemized deductions[5]	$3,500	
Exemption amount	2,000	5,500
Taxable income		$14,500

The 1989 tax on taxable income of $14,500 from the table (Appendix 1-A) was $2,179. With $20,000 of income and only the exemption and standard deduction as deductions, Billy's taxable income would have been $14,900, with a tax of $2,239. Thus, "itemizing deductions" (as it is called) saved Billy $60. Billy could plan accordingly.

Another way to obtain the $60 tax savings would be to multiply the difference in deductions by the 15% tax rate (see Appendix 1-B). Note, however, that the 1989 tax rate for a single person was 28% rather than 15% if taxable income was more than $18,550.

TAX PLANNING TIP: Carefulness in record keeping and retention of receipts for expenditures that qualify as itemized deductions (such as medical insurance premiums, interest, taxes, charitable contributions, and nonreimbursed casualty or theft losses) can result in itemized deductions that total more than the standard deduction for the year.

Let's consider the same income and deductions for Billy for the year 1990, in order to illustrate the changes:

Adjusted gross income		$20,000
Less: Itemized deductions	$3,500	
Exemption amount	2,050	5,550
Taxable income		$14,450

Note that the deductions will be itemized because the total is more than the standard deduction despite the increased amount of the standard deduction for 1990. As before, the *larger* of the standard deduction or the total of itemized deductions will be claimed. Since $3,500 is more than the 1990 standard deduction of $3,250, that amount will be deducted. (Another way of stating the rule is that the standard deduction represents a *minimum* deduction.) Also, the 1990 personal exemption is $2,050 as compared with $2,000 for 1989.

The 1990 tax on taxable income of $14,450 is $2,168. As this book goes to press, there is no tax table for 1990 similar to that which is in Appendix 1-A for 1989. Therefore, it is necessary to use the rate schedule, which appears in Appendix 1-C.

Compare the tax rate schedules in Appendix 1-B with those in Appendix 1-C. Note that the amount of taxable income at which the rate changes from 15% to 28% is different. This is due to an adjustment that was made in the 1990 schedules based on an inflation factor similar to that explained earlier for the standard deduction. Do not attempt at this time to compare the *table* in Appendix 1-A with the *rate schedule* in Appendix 1-B. This comparison will be made later when we explain how the *table* numbers were derived.

Billy probably has choices, at least in the long run, about how income is spent. Itemizing deductions, however, means that Billy must switch to Form 1040 instead of using 1040A. (There are some other factors that dictate which form is to be used. The details are mechanical and, hence, are omitted from this text.)

In determining Billy's taxable income for 1989 and 1990 a deduction was taken for an "exemption amount." The only difference was that the amount was $50 larger for 1990. Generally, a taxpayer gets to claim such a deduction for himself and an additional one for each "dependent." The amount of the deduction was explained earlier. However, the tax reduction resulting from the deduction will begin to phase out for persons who have a taxable income above a certain level. For single persons for 1989, that amount of taxable income was $93,130. For 1990, that level will be $97,620. Each year that level will be adjusted upward by an inflation factor similar to the adjustment explained earlier for the standard deduction and the rates. The arithmetic for this phase-out, the level at which the phase-out begins for married persons and heads of household, and the qualifications for taking an exemption amount deduction for "dependents" are explained in Chapter 4.

In figuring Billy's taxes, we have used all the basic elements of tax computation for most individuals. Figure 1-5 presents them in graphic form. The amount of tax is determined by reference to the tax table. (The status of single, married filing jointly, married filing separately, or head of household is discussed in Chapter 4.) The process is not complete at this point, however, because credits (see lines 41 through 47 of Form 1040, Appendix

[5] It would be necessary to file Form 1040, and Schedule A. See Appendix 1-D. A close look at Schedule A (Appendix 1-D(c)) will reveal other deductions possibly available to Billy. Most states and some cities impose deductible income taxes. In the interest of simplicity we have purposely omitted any of these at this time. Schedule B is on the back side of this IRS form. It provides for a listing of interest and dividend income mentioned above.

FIGURE 1-5 Basic elements of tax computation for most individuals

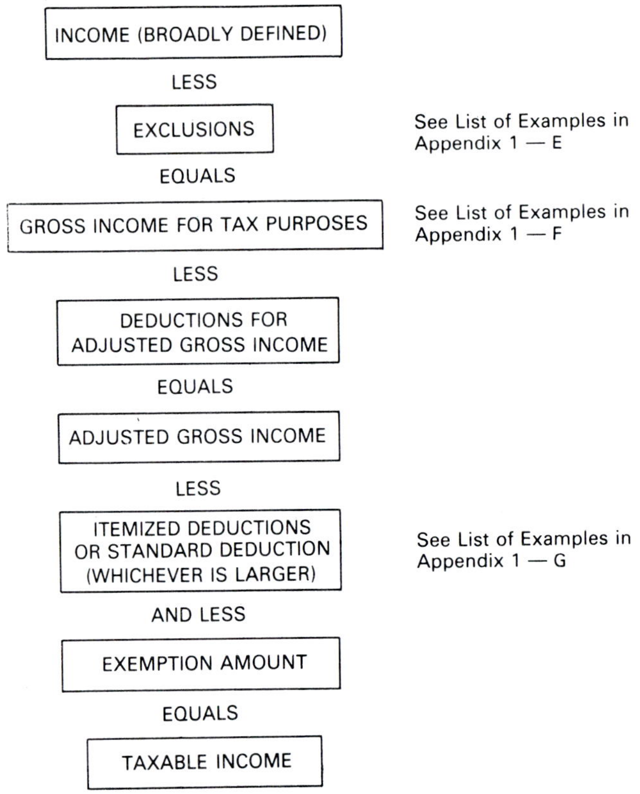

1-D) and payments (lines 56 through 63) must be subtracted before the amount still due, or the amount of refund, can be determined.

Minimizing tax liability involves some combination of maximizing exclusions from gross income, maximizing deductions *for* adjusted gross income, maximizing itemized deductions, maximizing personal exemptions ("exemption amount"), using the most advantageous tax table, and taking all available tax credits.

TAX PLANNING TIP: Sometimes a person has control over the timing of expenditures that are deductible. It may be possible to control the timing in such a way as to ensure getting the standard deduction as a deduction in one year and the "itemized deductions" in the following year. This can result in more deductions for the two years combined than if the expenditures were spread more evenly over the two years.

1.3.1. Income Exclusions

The items that are excluded from the tax concept of income include interest on obligations of states and their subunits, such as cities; certain life insurance proceeds; social security receipts (limited); scholarships (limited); and some employee fringe benefits, such as health insurance premiums paid by an employer. Chapter 2 deals with income and exclusions in more detail.

1.3.2. Exclusion versus Deduction

Why draw a distinction between an exclusion from income and a deduction for adjusted gross income? Both appear to accomplish the same purpose, that is, a reduction in adjusted gross income. The difference is a conceptual one rather than a difference in result. An exclusion is by definition not a part of income. Some exclusions are not income because they represent recovery of an investment. For example, if Billy Barnes had loaned a friend $600, there would be no income upon receipt of principal when repaid. (If the friend paid interest on the debt, however, the interest would be income.) Other exclusions are statutory, such as certain money received from a scholarship. Generally, exclusions do not have to be reported on the tax return, whereas deductions are required to be entered. Further, all deductions are statutory, which means that they are specifically provided by the rules written by Congress.

TAX PLANNING TIP: In negotiating for a pay increase, an employee might request that the employer pay for some fringe benefit (such as medical insurance premiums) that will provide additional economic income to the employee but which will be excluded from income for federal income tax purposes. The employer will get the deduction for the cost, whether the employee is paid directly or is paid with a nontaxable fringe benefit.

1.3.3. Deductions for Adjusted Gross Income versus Itemized Deductions

Chapters 3 and 4 deal with deductions and credits in detail. The difference between a deduction *for* adjusted gross income (AGI) and an itemized deduction (sometimes called a deduction *from* AGI) is mainly that a deduction for AGI can be taken even though only the standard deduction is taken as a deduction from AGI.

Example. A single person who has $19,000 of 1990 gross income pays $2,000 alimony. Itemized deductions total only $1,400. If alimony had to be treated as an itemized deduction (which it does not), there would be total itemized deductions of $3,400 and taxable income would be $13,550:

Gross income (also AGI)	$19,000
Less:	
Itemized deductions	3,400*
	$15,600
Exemption amount	2,050
Taxable income	$13,550

The 1990 tax would be $2,033.

However, alimony is, in fact, a deduction *for* AGI and *not* an itemized deduction. Thus, 1990 taxable income is really $11,700:

Gross income		$19,000
Less: Alimony		2,000
Adjusted gross income		$17,000
Exemption amount	$2,050	
Standard deduction	3,250	5,300
Taxable income		$11,700

The 1990 tax is $1,755. This $1,850 difference in taxable income results from the way in which the alimony payment is classified. The taxpayer here gets the benefit of both the alimony *and* the full standard deduction.

* Note that itemized deductions exceed the standard deduction.

The fact that alimony is a deduction for AGI rather than an itemized deduction made a $278 tax difference in this case. Note, however, that the basic standard deduction ($3,250 for a single person for 1990) is a deduction regardless of most other facts which may exist for the taxpayer. (The exception, which results in a lower standard deduction, was explained earlier.)

If a person has no deductions for AGI, the gross income and adjusted gross income are the same.

As discussed further in Chapter 4, the amount of some deductions (e.g., medical expenses, casualty losses, and miscellaneous deductions) may be affected by the size of adjusted gross income. Whether an item is classified as a deduction "for" or "from" AGI will thus affect those other deductions as well.

COMPUTER FORMULAS: If you were to set up the above example on a computer spreadsheet the formulas would look this.

	A	*B*	*C*
1	Gross income		19,000
2	Less:		
3	Itemized deductions		3,400
4			———
5			+C1 − C3
6	Exemption amount		2,050
7			———
8	Taxable income		+C5 − C6
9			
10	Tax		.15(C8)
11			═══
12			

Note that even the underlines must be placed in their own cell. The tax formula will change as income increases, and as we shall see, the computer can be instructed to select the correct tax rate for a particular level of income.

1.3.4. Rate Schedules

Appendix 1-A includes the tax tables for 1989. Appendix 1-B and 1-C presents the rate schedules (X, Y, and Z) for 1989 and 1990. The purpose of the tables, which, at first glance, often confuse, is to simplify the tax computation process. The tables allow most persons to calculate their tax by one quick reference to the appropriate column. Individuals who have $50,000 or more of taxable income, as well as some others, have to calculate tax liability using the appropriate *schedule*.[6]

[6] The term "schedule" may refer to the tax rates that appear in Appendix 1-B and 1-C, but it can also refer to a tax form, as illustrated by Schedule A in Appendix 1-D(c).

TAX PLANNING TIP: The tax rates for head of household may be lower than are those for a single individual. Careful planning can sometimes result in a person's qualifying for head-of-household rates, whereas otherwise he or she would have to pay tax at the rates for a single person.

Understanding the relationship between the tax table and rate schedule will explain why $1 more in income *can* result in more than a $1 increase in tax in some limited situations. More important, it will illustrate how the rate schedules were used to create the tax tables. Except for slight alterations in arithmetic (i.e., rounding) the two would result in the same tax determination.

Assume that Billy (single) had 1989 taxable income of $19,999. This is at the top bracket in the tax table (Appendix 1-A). ("Bracket" refers to the amount "At least $19,950, but less than $20,000.") The $3,182 tax for that bracket actually represents the tax on the midpoint of that bracket ($19,975) as it would be calculated using Schedule X (Appendix 1-B). Thus, with $19,999, Billy would not pay tax, in effect, on $24 of income. By the same token, had Billy's taxable income been $19,950, the tax would still have been $3,182. In that event, Billy would have paid tax on $25 that was never received. This may seem unfair, but because the tax impact is small, there is no relief from this slight injustice. Except for the midpoint calculation, and arithmetic rounding, use of the rate schedule would result in exactly the same amount of tax as use of the tax table.

The calculation of the 1989 tax of $3,182, using the rate schedule from Appendix 1-B, is as follows:

Tax on $19,975 = $2,782.50 + 28% (19,975 − $18,550) = $3,181.50
Rounded = $3,182

The entire Tax Table (Appendix 1-A) was constructed in that manner. In the latter part of 1990, the IRS will issue a 1990 Tax Table that will have been constructed by using the above procedure and the rates that are contained in the 1990 rate schedules of Appendix 1-C

How could $1 of additional taxable income result in more than $1 additional income tax? Let's continue with the illustration above with Billy, who had 1989 taxable income of $19,999. With $1 more taxable income (total of $20,000) the tax would have been calculated on $20,025. The 1989 tax on $20,000 (from Appendix 1-A) was $3,196, which is $14 more than the tax on $19,999. Thus, $1 more income could cost $14 more in income tax. On the other hand, $50 more in income (taxable income of $20,049) would also have cost $14 more in tax. Additional income of $100 (taxable income of $20,099) would have resulted in $28 of additional tax.

Where taxable income is too large to use the tax tables (i.e. $50,000 or more), the amount of additional tax from $1 of income is easier to determine. Thus, if Billy had 1989 taxable income of $51,600 the tax [Appendix 1-B] would have been $10,160.50 + 33% ($51,600 − $44,900) which is $12,372. The 33% is called the "marginal rate." With it, the impact of increases, or decreases, can be more easily calculated. Additional income of $100, with no changes in deductions, would result in $33 more tax. Thus, the after-tax effect of $100 more income would be $67. Clearly, the answer changes as the marginal tax rate changes. The calculation is not so easy if the income change puts the taxpayer into a different marginal tax rate.

Earlier we mentioned that recent changes made by Congress shifted a substantial burden of the tax from individuals to businesses, especially corporations. Let's compare 1987, 1988, 1989, and 1990 tax for a single person given the same amount of gross income for each of those four years, $55,000. We will assume that the only deductions were the standard deduction and one personal exemption. The 1987 and 1988 taxes are shown here, although tax schedules are not included in this text.

	1987	*1988*	*1989*	*1990*
Gross income	$55,000	$55,000	$55,000	55,000
Standard deduction	(2,540)	(3,000)	(3,100)	(3,250)
Personal exemption	(1,900)	(1,950)	(2,000)	(2,050)
Taxable income	$50,560	$50,050	$49,900	$49,700
Tax	$13,550	$12,039	$11,811	$11,520

We will leave it up to you to decide if that reduction is "substantial."

Even though the tax table must be used to determine tax where taxable income is under $50,000, the rate schedule reflects the "marginal tax rate" for any given amount of taxable income.[7] For example, for 1990, the marginal tax rate for a

[7] The marginal tax rate is that percentage of tax which was paid on the last dollar of taxable income or will be paid on the next dollar of taxable income.

single person with taxable income of $27,500 is 28%. See Appendix 1-C for the rate schedules. Starting with 1989, both the tax tables and the rate schedules are modified each year to reflect the impact of changes in the purchasing power of the dollar as reflected by the Consumer Price Index. Thus, we have the rates, the standard deduction, and the exemption amount altered each year to reflect changes in the purchasing power of the dollar as reflected by the Consumer Price Index. If inflation continues, the rates will go down, and the deductions will increase each year.

Before leaving the discussion of rate schedules and marginal tax rates, we need to discuss one matter which you may have already noticed. For many, many years the federal income tax rates have been "progressive," which means that the marginal tax rate increases when the amount that is being taxed (taxable income) increases. A look at Appendix 1-C, for example, will show that the 1990 marginal tax rate for a single person goes from 15% to 28% when taxable income increases above $19,450. This does not mean that *all* taxable income is taxed at the 28% rate, but only that the 28% rate applies to taxable income in excess of $19,450. If taxable income were $30,000, for example, the tax would be calculated as:

Tax on $19,450 at 15% =	$2,917.50
Tax on $10,550 at 28% =	2,954.00
Total tax	$5,871.50

Note that the 1990 marginal rate increases to 33% for taxable income over $47,050, and then decreases to 28% (except for the specific 5% surtax which will be explained later) for taxable income in excess of $97,620. Why?

One way to look at the rate schedule—the way Congress chooses to look at it—is to think in terms of a rate of 13% (the difference between 15% and 28%) that a single taxpayer does *not* pay on the first $19,450 of taxable income. That's $2,528.50.

If the tax rate were a "flat" 28%, tax on $30,000 would be $8,400. The difference between $8,400 and $5,871.50 is $2,528.50. That's 13% of $19,450.

Congress decided to remove the tax benefit of the lower 15% rate for certain persons. They decided that the way to increase the tax by all or part of the $2,528.50 would be with a 5% surtax added to the 28% rate. The other variable, then, was the question, to what level should the surtax first apply? Apparently, the choice of $47,050 (for single persons) was completely arbitrary. Note, however, that the 5% applies to taxable income between $47,050 and $97,620.

$97,620 − $47,050 = $50,570
50,570 × 5% = 2,528.50

Therefore, the highest rate is still 28%, but the tax reduction from the 15% rate is eliminated when taxable income is $97,620 or more. The year 1988 was the first year that the tax calculation was designed to remove the effect of the lower rates.

This still leaves the question of the second 5% surtax, that applies to taxable income that is in excess of $97,620. If taxable income were exactly $97,620, the tax would be $27,333.60, which is a "flat" 28%. In other words, the impact of the 15% lower rate has been completely removed. After it has been removed, why is there a second 5% surtax? The answer is that the purpose of the second 5% surtax is to remove the tax reduction from the *deduction* for personal exemptions ($2,050 each for 1990). This will be explained briefly here and then more fully in Chapter 4.

What is the tax benefit of a $2,050 deduction for a personal exemption? At a tax rate of 28%, a $2,050 deduction reduces tax by $574. When this benefit has been eliminated, the tax rate goes back to 28%. A problem arises because a person may have more than one of the personal exemption deductions of $2,050 each. Assuming, however, that Billy Barnes (single) has 1990 taxable income of $98,000, which includes *one* deduction of $2,050 for a personal exemption, the tax (determined from using the schedule at Appendix 1-C) will be as follows:

Tax at 28% on $98,000 =		$27,440
Plus lesser of:		
(a) 28% ($2,050) =	$574	
or		
(b) 5% ($380) =	19.00	
		+ 19.00
Total tax		$27,459.00

Note that Billy still receives *part* of the benefit of the $2,050 deduction. How much? Since the benefit of the entire deduction would have been $574, and the above calculation indicates that $19 has been added to the tax, the benefit is still $555. We will leave it up to you to determine the level of taxable income at which the entire $574 tax reduction disappears.

It still remains important to recognize that the *effective* marginal tax rate can be 33%. Thus, if you are single and your 1990 taxable income is going to be $70,000, for example, another $1,000 of income will increase your tax by $330. Using the same analysis, another $1,000 of deductible expenditures (e.g. charitable contributions to your alma mater) will reduce your taxes by $330 and cost you $670 after-tax.

One further point:

Having been through the analysis of the elimination of the "tax benefit" of the lower 15% rate for single taxpayers, we will leave it up to you to determine the amount of the tax benefit which results from the 15% rate for taxpayers other than single persons *and* the level at which the elimination of that benefit begins.

1.4 Conclusion

This chapter has focused on selected aspects of individual tax returns. Forms 1040EZ and 1040A are simpler but can be used only by taxpayers with limited types of transactions. Form 1040, and its numerous related schedules, will be filed by all other individual taxpayers. The purpose of illustrating with sample returns is not to set out rules for filling in forms. Understanding the tax return format provides better understanding of the tax implications of a given situation or transaction. Such understanding facilitates control of the transaction or situation so as to minimize the amount of tax that will have to be paid. Tax dollars are not so much saved when returns are being prepared as they are saved in the planning that happens before a financial transaction occurs. Tax consulting represents a substantial portion of the professional services provided by many CPAs and attorneys. Several of the largest multi-national CPA firms, for example, report that as much as one-third of their revenues are generated from tax related services provbided to clients, the other services being auditing and non-tax consulting. Many individual CPA practitioners realize a higher percentage of their receipts from tax related services.

Chapters 2 through 6 explore the individual income tax return, its problems, and its opportunities in more detail.

TRUE-FALSE QUESTIONS

State whether each of the following statements is true or false. For each *false* answer, reword the statement to make it *true.*

T F 1. If a taxpayer plants a garden and raises vegetables for his or her own consumption, the fair market value of the items grown must be included in gross income.

T F 2. Minimizing one's federal income tax liability can be accomplished by maximizing the exclusions from gross income, maximizing the deductions for adjusted gross income, maximizing the deductions from adjusted gross income, planning to be eligible for the most advantageous tax rate schedule, and maximizing credits.

T F 3. In tax law, a credit is a reduction in the amount that is subject to tax.

T F 4. Adjusted gross income refers to all the income that a person earns during the year plus all income that is received from investments.

T F 5. If a single taxpayer has 1990 taxable income that exceeds $47,050, then the entire benefit of the 15% tax rate is lost for the first $19,450 of taxable income.

T F 6. The standard deduction for 1990 for a person filing a tax return as an unmarried (single) person under age 65 and not blind is $3,250.

T F 7. Taxable income is the number that must be derived in order to determine the tax liability from the tax tables or the rate schedules.

T F 8. If 1990 taxable income was over $50,000, a taxpayer could not use the tax tables, but was required to calculate tax from the rate schedule.

T F 9. A taxpayer who is a head of household and who is otherwise eligible to take a deduction in 1990 for an "exemption amount" but who will have taxable income in excess of $97,620 will have an effective reduction in the amount of the "exemption amount" deduction.

T F 10. If it is desired to claim itemized deductions greater than $3,250 in 1990 for a single individual under age 65 and not blind, neither of the short forms (1040EZ or 1040A) can be used.

T F 11. The "marginal tax rate" is the percentage of tax that will be paid on additional taxable income.

T F 12. Interest from bonds issued by a state or local government will not be subject to federal income tax under present rules.

T F 13. The "standard deduction" is a minimum amount of deduction to be claimed in 1990 where married taxpayers filing a joint return do not have itemized deductions which are greater than $3,250.

T F 14. The only difference between adjusted gross income and taxable income is the deduction for the "exemption amount."

T F 15. The amount of the "exemption amount" and "standard deduction" were price level adjusted in 1990.

T F 16. A person will "itemize deductions," and will complete a Form 1040 along with its related Schedule A, if his or her itemized deductions are greater than the amount of the applicable "standard deduction."

T F 17. A person seeking to reduce taxes would presumably prefer to spend money on an item that is deductible rather than to spend it for something that is not deductible.

T F 18. A single person filing a tax return for 1989 had a tax liability (before credits) of $1,346 if his or her taxable income were exactly $9,000.

T F 19. A single person who is a dependent of someone else will have a minimum standard deduction of $500 for purposes of 1990 federal income tax.

T F 20. The amount of 1990 tax on taxable income of $24,725 is less if a person qualifies as a head of household rather than being single.

DISCUSSION QUESTIONS

1. What is the definition of "adjusted gross income"?
2. Distinguish between a deduction and a credit.
3. What is meant by the "marginal rate of income tax"? What is its significance?
4. Is the "exemption amount" really a deduction? Explain.
5. What is the difference between "taxable income" that is used to calculate tax liability using the rate schedule and "taxable income" that is used to determine tax liability from the tax table?

PROBLEMS

(*Note:* Many of the problems require determination of tax liability. The tax tables (Appendix 1-A) that are available are for the year 1989, although you may be using this book in 1990 or 1991. We are concerned with the method for determining tax rather than a technically correct final number.)

Problem 1-1. a. For each of the following taxpayers, determine the amount of the tax (before credits) given the amount of taxable income: (Use 1990 rate schedules).

b. Identify which taxpayers will use the tax table (when it is available) rather than the rate schedule.

c. Identify which taxpayers lose part of the benefit of the 15% tax bracket.

	Taxable Income	
	A	*B*
Single	$12,443	$61,730
Married-joint return	$41,634	$55,289
Married-separate return	$67,840	$57,370
Head of household	$38,990	$77,167

Problem 1-2. Harry and Alma Mite will file a joint return. Harry's salary is $31,000. In addition to Harry's salary, the Mites have taxable interest income of $900. Alma had $500 of consulting income. Their 1990 itemized deductions total $5,600. They have three preteenage children, who receive all their support from Harry and Alma. (Note that there will be five "exemption amount" deductions.)

Required:

(a) What was the Mites' federal income tax liability for the year?

(b) What would be the tax if their taxable income were reduced by $900?

(c) Suggest a way for the family to reduce their tax while keeping the same amount and sources of family income and not changing expenditure patterns. (*Hint:* The children can be taxpayers, but will not have to pay any tax if their income is under $500 each.)

Problem 1-3. Mr. and Mrs. Flowers have been told by their physician that they will not be able to have children. Consequently, they are considering adoption proceedings. At the present time they are both employed and their combined gross income is $33,350. They have no other gross income. They have $2,000 of deductions for AGI and $6,000 of itemized deductions. (For purposes of the exemption amount deduction, adopted children are treated the same as children born to the taxpayers.)

Required:

(a) Assuming that Mr. and Mrs. Flowers do not adopt a child before the end of 1990, calculate their tax liability. (On a joint return, a husband and wife are *each* counted as one exemption for a total of two.)

(b) If they do complete adoption proceedings before the end of the year, they will be entitled to claim the child as an exemption. If that happens, what will their federal tax liability be for the year?

(c) How much federal income tax will be saved by the couple if they can claim the child as a dependent?

Problem 1-4. Clif Jones is single but qualifies as a head of household for 1990. Clif has one child, a son age twelve, who lives with him and who qualifies as Clif's dependent (i.e. there will be two "exemption amounts"). Clif's salary was $39,000. His only other income was a dividend of $400 from a domestic corporation. He had expenditures of $4,800 that qualified as itemized deductions. He had no deductions for adjusted gross income. Clif's neighbor, an elderly widow, wanted him to paint her house during his vacation last summer. She offered him $900 for the job. Clif declined and took his son fishing instead.

Required:

(a) Calculate Clif's tax liability using 1990 rates and exemption amounts.

(b) If Clif had accepted the offer to paint his neighbor's house, what would have been the after-tax earnings from painting the house? (Note that deductions would not change.)

Problem 1-5. It has been proposed in Congress that the Internal Revenue Code be amended to remove the exemption amount deduction and replace it with a tax credit. Obviously, this would have a different impact upon different taxpayers.

Required:

(a) What amount of tax credit would be necessary for each of the following taxpayers in order for the tax effect to be equal to that of one exemption amount of $2,050? (Use the 1990 rate schedules despite the fact that a taxpayer's situation may fit the tax tables.)

Taxpayer	*Filing Status*	*Taxable Income (Before E.A. Deduction)*
A	Single	$ 8,000
B	Head of household	60,000
C	Married—joint return	35,000
D	Married—separate return	40,000

(b) At what level of *taxable income* would the tax effect of a $400 credit or a $2,050 deduction be exactly the same for a single individual for 1990? Explain.

Problem 1-6. Jim Mitchell is an employee of Home Real Estate Corporation. Jim and his wife, Janet, will properly claim five exemptions on a joint return for 1990, and will have taxable income of $35,500. Jim's employer has recently told him that the corporation is considering the payment of premiums for group term life insurance coverage of $50,000 on his life, and Jim will have the opportunity to name the beneficiary. The tax rules permit the employer to take a deduction for the premium paid, but Jim does not have to include any additional amount in his gross income. Jim has recently talked with his insurance agent and was told that at his age he can purchase a $50,000 five-year term life insurance policy for an annual premium of $650. Jim has concluded that the effect of the employer's recent offer is an annual raise of $650. Except for any change discussed here, taxable income will be the same each year. (*Note:* There is no deduction available to an individual for the cost of premiums paid to purchase life insurance.)

Required:

Explain why Jim's effective salary increase is more than $650.

Problem 1-7. Indicate the *total* amount of standard deduction (basic and additional amount if applicable) for each of the following taxpayers for 1990:

(a) Megan and Fred file a joint return. They are less than age 65.

(b) Missy, age 20, is a full-time student and is claimed as a dependent by her parents. This year, Missy earned $1,200 of wages during the summer.

(c) Helen, age 66, is single and semi-retired. This year she earned $12,000 of income.

(d) Keith, age 74, is single. Although he has limited vision with corrective lenses, he is considered blind for tax purposes.

Problem 1-8. Harriett Laidlaw earned a 1990 salary of $26,235, and had $3,700 of income tax withheld, and is single. She will not itemize deductions. She has no deductions to arrive at adjusted gross income.

(a) What is the amount of her 1990 refund or additional tax due?

(b) Hank Berry had a salary of $27,000, out of which $3,800 was withheld for federal income tax. He has only the minimum deductions also. What is his tax refund or additional amount due? (He is single.)

(c) Would Laidlaw and Berry end up paying more or less tax for the year if they were to get married on December 31? (As we will see in a later chapter, marital status is determined as of the last day of the year, so that a wedding on December 31 would result in a tax situation that is the same as if they had been married for the entire year. The standard deduction for a married couple for 1990 is $5,450. They will get two "exemption amounts." The filing status will be "married-joint.")

(d) Explain what factors operate to cause their tax to be greater as a married couple than the combined tax if they remain single.

Problem 1-9. "It just doesn't pay for me to work," sighs Mrs. Portly, resigned to the fate of a childless housewife caring for a one-bedroom apartment. Her husband earns $95,000 a year and they do not itemize deductions. "The income tax destroys all incentive," she complains. (Note that a married couple will get two "exemption amount" deductions and will use the tax rate schedule for filing jointly.)

(a) How much additional tax would Mr. and Mrs. Portly have to pay for 1990 if Mrs. Portly took a job paying $10,000 per year? (Assume their deductions would not increase.)

(b) Commuting, clothes, lunches, etc. (all nondeductible) would cost Mrs. Portly an additional $1,900 per year if she worked. At what level of income for Mrs. Portly would she net $10,000 after tax and expenses? (Again, assume that their deductions would not increase.)

Problem 1-10. Charitable contributions are presently an itemized deduction. However, Congress has considered changing them to a deduction *for* adjusted gross income (AGI). Ms. Jones has $32,000 of gross income and itemized deductions of $6,000, of which $2,000 was charitable contributions. She is single.

(a) How much of a tax difference will it make to Jones if charitable contributions were deductible to arrive at AGI rather than *from* AGI? (Use 1990 rates.)

(b) If Jones has, instead, $3,000 of itemized deductions, of which $2,000 are charitable contributions, with all other facts the same, what difference will the proposed change make?

(c) Assume that you are the treasurer of a church. Do you feel that the proposed change will substantially benefit your ability to obtain contributions? Would it make a difference if your members were largely well-to-do homeowners? Largely less-well-off apartment renters? Mainly married people with two or three dependents who earn less than $12,000 a year?

Problem 1-11. Clara Chatter is employed part time as a salesclerk and is a part-time student at Hippodrome University. She is single. Her income for 1990 will consist only of her wages of $11,000. She plans to make 1990 expenditures as follows: (Each of the following will be included as itemized deductions.)

Charitable contributions	$450
State income taxes	500
Real estate taxes	500
Interest on home mortgage loan	1,500
Personal property tax	350
Total	$3,300

(a) If all goes according to plan, will Clara "itemize" deductions for the year 1990 or use the standard deduction? Explain.

(b) Assume that for the next year Clara expects to have the same amount of income and the same pattern of expenditures. Suggest a way for her to change the situation so that her federal income tax for the two years together will be reduced. (Ignore the changes in rates and amount of personal exemption deduction which will be made from 1990 to 1991.)

Problem 1-12. Jerry J. Jones earned a salary of $47,500 in 1990. In addition, Jerry received dividend income of $3,000. Itemized deductions would total $6,000. You have the following data from Jerry's file:

Marital status: single

Dependents: none

Required:

(a) Calculate Jerry's tax liability.

(b) Calculate the tax savings that would have resulted if Jerry had incurred $1,000 of additional home mortgage loan interest expense, which would increase itemized deductions to $7,000.

(c) What would have been the after-tax cost of borrowing the money?

(d) Calculate Jerry's tax liability from part (a) and part (b) if everything remains the same except his salary, which is increased to $67,500.

(e) What would be the after-tax cost of incurring $1,000 of deductible interest expense in part (d)?

Problem 1-13. As we will see in Chapter 4, a single person can qualify for "head of household" filing status by having his or her child living in the household even if that child is not a dependent. "Head of household" filing status allows a taxpayer to use the rate schedule by that name even if the amount of taxable income is the same as it would be if the single person rate schedule had to be used.

Alfredo Santiago is a single person. His 1990 taxable income will be $32,500 as a single person or as a head of household. If he can qualify as a head of household, how much federal income tax will be saved?

COMPUTER PROBLEM

At the end of several chapters there is a problem which has been designated as a "computer problem." The purpose of these problems is to integrate the use of a personal computer, using a spreadsheet program, into the tax instruction process. The problems are progressive, starting with very simple situations and progressing to those which are more complex. The problems are designed to be adaptable to almost any of the standard spreadsheet software packages. Students who have only a fundamental working knowledge of the spreadsheet software should be able to work these problems with minimum time required.

Problem 1-14. For purposes of this problem, assume that the federal income tax rate which will apply to "taxable income" for a single person will be 15%. Ms. Jones is single. Her social security number is 111-22-3333. She is employed with a salary of $22,000. Her only other source of income is interest from corporate bonds of $3,000. She will have a deduction *to arrive at adjusted gross income* of $1,000. She will have total itemized deductions of $5,000. The year is 1990, so her "exemption amount" is $2,050. The amount of federal income tax withheld from her salary for the year was $2,400.

Required:

Create a spreadsheet which will calculate the amount of federal income tax for Ms. Jones. The spreadsheet should be designed so that changes in the amount of income, deductions, exemptions, or tax rate will automatically reflect the correct amount of tax liability *and* the amount of additional tax due or refund.

When creating the spreadsheet, include the following in your plan:

1. The first four lines of the spreadsheet should be reserved for a heading which will include the taxpayer name, social security number, and date.
2. Column A should be used for labels, with column B used for the dollar amounts.
3. Line 5 should be salary income. Line 6 should be interest income. Line 7 should be dividend income and line 8 should be income from other sources. For Ms. Jones, lines 7 and 8 will be zero in this problem. Other lines should be as follows:
   9: Total income (sum of 5B to 8B)
   10: Deductions to arrive at AGI
   11: Adjusted gross income (9B − 10B)
   12: Itemized deductions
   13: Exemption amount
   14: Total deductions (12B + 13B)
   15: Taxable income (11B − 14B)
   16: Tax rate
   17: Tax liability (15B times 16B)
   18: Federal income tax withheld
   19: Tax due or (−) refund (17B − 18B)

Later, as we progress, the spreadsheet will be modified to do the following:

1. Add more lines for different kinds of income,
2. Create a subsidiary worksheet to show the detail of deductions to arrive at adjusted gross income,
3. Deduct the standard deduction rather than itemized deductions, if the latter is smaller,
4. Create a subsidiary worksheet to show the detail of itemized deductions,
5. Expand the rate schedule to include more than one tax rate,
6. Calculate the tax using different rate schedules, i.e., married filing a joint return, or head of household,
7. Reduce tax liability by credits.

When you are finished with this problem, be sure to save the results on your floppy disk. We will return to the data for the computer problem at the end of the next chapter.

1989 Tax Table

Use if your taxable income is less than $50,000. If $50,000 or more, use the Tax Rate Schedules.

Example: Mr. and Mrs. Brown are filing a joint return. Their taxable income on line 37 of Form 1040 is $25,300. First, they find the $25,300–25,350 income line. Next, they find the column for married filing jointly and read down the column. The amount shown where the income line and filing status column meet is $3,799. This is the tax amount they must write on line 38 of their return.

At least	But less than	Single	Married filing jointly *	Married filing sepa-rately	Head of a house-hold
		Your tax is—			
25,200	25,250	4,652	3,784	5,051	3,833
25,250	25,300	4,666	3,791	5,065	3,847
25,300	25,350	4,680	(3,799)	5,079	3,861
25,350	25,400	4,694	3,806	5,093	3,875

If line 37 (taxable income) is—		And you are—			
At least	But less than	Single	Married filing jointly *	Married filing sepa-rately	Head of a house-hold
		Your tax is—			
$0	$5	$0	$0	$0	$0
5	15	2	2	2	2
15	25	3	3	3	3
25	50	6	6	6	6
50	75	9	9	9	9
75	100	13	13	13	13
100	125	17	17	17	17
125	150	21	21	21	21
150	175	24	24	24	24
175	200	28	28	28	28
200	225	32	32	32	32
225	250	36	36	36	36
250	275	39	39	39	39
275	300	43	43	43	43
300	325	47	47	47	47
325	350	51	51	51	51
350	375	54	54	54	54
375	400	58	58	58	58
400	425	62	62	62	62
425	450	66	66	66	66
450	475	69	69	69	69
475	500	73	73	73	73
500	525	77	77	77	77
525	550	81	81	81	81
550	575	84	84	84	84
575	600	88	88	88	88
600	625	92	92	92	92
625	650	96	96	96	96
650	675	99	99	99	99
675	700	103	103	103	103
700	725	107	107	107	107
725	750	111	111	111	111
750	775	114	114	114	114
775	800	118	118	118	118
800	825	122	122	122	122
825	850	126	126	126	126
850	875	129	129	129	129
875	900	133	133	133	133
900	925	137	137	137	137
925	950	141	141	141	141
950	975	144	144	144	144
975	1,000	148	148	148	148
1,000					
1,000	1,025	152	152	152	152
1,025	1,050	156	156	156	156
1,050	1,075	159	159	159	159
1,075	1,100	163	163	163	163
1,100	1,125	167	167	167	167
1,125	1,150	171	171	171	171
1,150	1,175	174	174	174	174
1,175	1,200	178	178	178	178
1,200	1,225	182	182	182	182
1,225	1,250	186	186	186	186
1,250	1,275	189	189	189	189
1,275	1,300	193	193	193	193
1,300	1,325	197	197	197	197
1,325	1,350	201	201	201	201
1,350	1,375	204	204	204	204
1,375	1,400	208	208	208	208
1,400	1,425	212	212	212	212
1,425	1,450	216	216	216	216
1,450	1,475	219	219	219	219
1,475	1,500	223	223	223	223
1,500	1,525	227	227	227	227
1,525	1,550	231	231	231	231
1,550	1,575	234	234	234	234
1,575	1,600	238	238	238	238
1,600	1,625	242	242	242	242
1,625	1,650	246	246	246	246
1,650	1,675	249	249	249	249
1,675	1,700	253	253	253	253
1,700	1,725	257	257	257	257
1,725	1,750	261	261	261	261
1,750	1,775	264	264	264	264
1,775	1,800	268	268	268	268
1,800	1,825	272	272	272	272
1,825	1,850	276	276	276	276
1,850	1,875	279	279	279	279
1,875	1,900	283	283	283	283
1,900	1,925	287	287	287	287
1,925	1,950	291	291	291	291
1,950	1,975	294	294	294	294
1,975	2,000	298	298	298	298
2,000					
2,000	2,025	302	302	302	302
2,025	2,050	306	306	306	306
2,050	2,075	309	309	309	309
2,075	2,100	313	313	313	313
2,100	2,125	317	317	317	317
2,125	2,150	321	321	321	321
2,150	2,175	324	324	324	324
2,175	2,200	328	328	328	328
2,200	2,225	332	332	332	332
2,225	2,250	336	336	336	336
2,250	2,275	339	339	339	339
2,275	2,300	343	343	343	343
2,300	2,325	347	347	347	347
2,325	2,350	351	351	351	351
2,350	2,375	354	354	354	354
2,375	2,400	358	358	358	358
2,400	2,425	362	362	362	362
2,425	2,450	366	366	366	366
2,450	2,475	369	369	369	369
2,475	2,500	373	373	373	373
2,500	2,525	377	377	377	377
2,525	2,550	381	381	381	381
2,550	2,575	384	384	384	384
2,575	2,600	388	388	388	388
2,600	2,625	392	392	392	392
2,625	2,650	396	396	396	396
2,650	2,675	399	399	399	399
2,675	2,700	403	403	403	403
2,700	2,725	407	407	407	407
2,725	2,750	411	411	411	411
2,750	2,775	414	414	414	414
2,775	2,800	418	418	418	418
2,800	2,825	422	422	422	422
2,825	2,850	426	426	426	426
2,850	2,875	429	429	429	429
2,875	2,900	433	433	433	433
2,900	2,925	437	437	437	437
2,925	2,950	441	441	441	441
2,950	2,975	444	444	444	444
2,975	3,000	448	448	448	448
3,000					
3,000	3,050	454	454	454	454
3,050	3,100	461	461	461	461
3,100	3,150	469	469	469	469
3,150	3,200	476	476	476	476
3,200	3,250	484	484	484	484
3,250	3,300	491	491	491	491
3,300	3,350	499	499	499	499
3,350	3,400	506	506	506	506
3,400	3,450	514	514	514	514
3,450	3,500	521	521	521	521
3,500	3,550	529	529	529	529
3,550	3,600	536	536	536	536
3,600	3,650	544	544	544	544
3,650	3,700	551	551	551	551
3,700	3,750	559	559	559	559
3,750	3,800	566	566	566	566
3,800	3,850	574	574	574	574
3,850	3,900	581	581	581	581
3,900	3,950	589	589	589	589
3,950	4,000	596	596	596	596
4,000					
4,000	4,050	604	604	604	604
4,050	4,100	611	611	611	611
4,100	4,150	619	619	619	619
4,150	4,200	626	626	626	626
4,200	4,250	634	634	634	634
4,250	4,300	641	641	641	641
4,300	4,350	649	649	649	649
4,350	4,400	656	656	656	656
4,400	4,450	664	664	664	664
4,450	4,500	671	671	671	671
4,500	4,550	679	679	679	679
4,550	4,600	686	686	686	686
4,600	4,650	694	694	694	694
4,650	4,700	701	701	701	701
4,700	4,750	709	709	709	709
4,750	4,800	716	716	716	716
4,800	4,850	724	724	724	724
4,850	4,900	731	731	731	731
4,900	4,950	739	739	739	739
4,950	5,000	746	746	746	746

* This column must also be used by a qualifying widow(er).

Continued on next page

1989 Tax Table—*Continued*

If line 37 (taxable income) is—		And you are—			
At least	But less than	Single	Married filing jointly *	Married filing sepa-rately	Head of a house-hold
		Your tax is—			
5,000					
5,000	**5,050**	754	754	754	754
5,050	**5,100**	761	761	761	761
5,100	**5,150**	769	769	769	769
5,150	**5,200**	776	776	776	776
5,200	**5,250**	784	784	784	784
5,250	**5,300**	791	791	791	791
5,300	**5,350**	799	799	799	799
5,350	**5,400**	806	806	806	806
5,400	**5,450**	814	814	814	814
5,450	**5,500**	821	821	821	821
5,500	**5,550**	829	829	829	829
5,550	**5,600**	836	836	836	836
5,600	**5,650**	844	844	844	844
5,650	**5,700**	851	851	851	851
5,700	**5,750**	859	859	859	859
5,750	**5,800**	866	866	866	866
5,800	**5,850**	874	874	874	874
5,850	**5,900**	881	881	881	881
5,900	**5,950**	889	889	889	889
5,950	**6,000**	896	896	896	896
6,000					
6,000	**6,050**	904	904	904	904
6,050	**6,100**	911	911	911	911
6,100	**6,150**	919	919	919	919
6,150	**6,200**	926	926	926	926
6,200	**6,250**	934	934	934	934
6,250	**6,300**	941	941	941	941
6,300	**6,350**	949	949	949	949
6,350	**6,400**	956	956	956	956
6,400	**6,450**	964	964	964	964
6,450	**6,500**	971	971	971	971
6,500	**6,550**	979	979	979	979
6,550	**6,600**	986	986	986	986
6,600	**6,650**	994	994	994	994
6,650	**6,700**	1,001	1,001	1,001	1,001
6,700	**6,750**	1,009	1,009	1,009	1,009
6,750	**6,800**	1,016	1,016	1,016	1,016
6,800	**6,850**	1,024	1,024	1,024	1,024
6,850	**6,900**	1,031	1,031	1,031	1,031
6,900	**6,950**	1,039	1,039	1,039	1,039
6,950	**7,000**	1,046	1,046	1,046	1,046
7,000					
7,000	**7,050**	1,054	1,054	1,054	1,054
7,050	**7,100**	1,061	1,061	1,061	1,061
7,100	**7,150**	1,069	1,069	1,069	1,069
7,150	**7,200**	1,076	1,076	1,076	1,076
7,200	**7,250**	1,084	1,084	1,084	1,084
7,250	**7,300**	1,091	1,091	1,091	1,091
7,300	**7,350**	1,099	1,099	1,099	1,099
7,350	**7,400**	1,106	1,106	1,106	1,106
7,400	**7,450**	1,114	1,114	1,114	1,114
7,450	**7,500**	1,121	1,121	1,121	1,121
7,500	**7,550**	1,129	1,129	1,129	1,129
7,550	**7,600**	1,136	1,136	1,136	1,136
7,600	**7,650**	1,144	1,144	1,144	1,144
7,650	**7,700**	1,151	1,151	1,151	1,151
7,700	**7,750**	1,159	1,159	1,159	1,159
7,750	**7,800**	1,166	1,166	1,166	1,166
7,800	**7,850**	1,174	1,174	1,174	1,174
7,850	**7,900**	1,181	1,181	1,181	1,181
7,900	**7,950**	1,189	1,189	1,189	1,189
7,950	**8,000**	1,196	1,196	1,196	1,196

If line 37 (taxable income) is—		And you are—			
At least	But less than	Single	Married filing jointly *	Married filing sepa-rately	Head of a house-hold
		Your tax is—			
8,000					
8,000	**8,050**	1,204	1,204	1,204	1,204
8,050	**8,100**	1,211	1,211	1,211	1,211
8,100	**8,150**	1,219	1,219	1,219	1,219
8,150	**8,200**	1,226	1,226	1,226	1,226
8,200	**8,250**	1,234	1,234	1,234	1,234
8,250	**8,300**	1,241	1,241	1,241	1,241
8,300	**8,350**	1,249	1,249	1,249	1,249
8,350	**8,400**	1,256	1,256	1,256	1,256
8,400	**8,450**	1,264	1,264	1,264	1,264
8,450	**8,500**	1,271	1,271	1,271	1,271
8,500	**8,550**	1,279	1,279	1,279	1,279
8,550	**8,600**	1,286	1,286	1,286	1,286
8,600	**8,650**	1,294	1,294	1,294	1,294
8,650	**8,700**	1,301	1,301	1,301	1,301
8,700	**8,750**	1,309	1,309	1,309	1,309
8,750	**8,800**	1,316	1,316	1,316	1,316
8,800	**8,850**	1,324	1,324	1,324	1,324
8,850	**8,900**	1,331	1,331	1,331	1,331
8,900	**8,950**	1,339	1,339	1,339	1,339
8,950	**9,000**	1,346	1,346	1,346	1,346
9,000					
9,000	**9,050**	1,354	1,354	1,354	1,354
9,050	**9,100**	1,361	1,361	1,361	1,361
9,100	**9,150**	1,369	1,369	1,369	1,369
9,150	**9,200**	1,376	1,376	1,376	1,376
9,200	**9,250**	1,384	1,384	1,384	1,384
9,250	**9,300**	1,391	1,391	1,391	1,391
9,300	**9,350**	1,399	1,399	1,399	1,399
9,350	**9,400**	1,406	1,406	1,406	1,406
9,400	**9,450**	1,414	1,414	1,414	1,414
9,450	**9,500**	1,421	1,421	1,421	1,421
9,500	**9,550**	1,429	1,429	1,429	1,429
9,550	**9,600**	1,436	1,436	1,436	1,436
9,600	**9,650**	1,444	1,444	1,444	1,444
9,650	**9,700**	1,451	1,451	1,451	1,451
9,700	**9,750**	1,459	1,459	1,459	1,459
9,750	**9,800**	1,466	1,466	1,466	1,466
9,800	**9,850**	1,474	1,474	1,474	1,474
9,850	**9,900**	1,481	1,481	1,481	1,481
9,900	**9,950**	1,489	1,489	1,489	1,489
9,950	**10,000**	1,496	1,496	1,496	1,496
10,000					
10,000	**10,050**	1,504	1,504	1,504	1,504
10,050	**10,100**	1,511	1,511	1,511	1,511
10,100	**10,150**	1,519	1,519	1,519	1,519
10,150	**10,200**	1,526	1,526	1,526	1,526
10,200	**10,250**	1,534	1,534	1,534	1,534
10,250	**10,300**	1,541	1,541	1,541	1,541
10,300	**10,350**	1,549	1,549	1,549	1,549
10,350	**10,400**	1,556	1,556	1,556	1,556
10,400	**10,450**	1,564	1,564	1,564	1,564
10,450	**10,500**	1,571	1,571	1,571	1,571
10,500	**10,550**	1,579	1,579	1,579	1,579
10,550	**10,600**	1,586	1,586	1,586	1,586
10,600	**10,650**	1,594	1,594	1,594	1,594
10,650	**10,700**	1,601	1,601	1,601	1,601
10,700	**10,750**	1,609	1,609	1,609	1,609
10,750	**10,800**	1,616	1,616	1,616	1,616
10,800	**10,850**	1,624	1,624	1,624	1,624
10,850	**10,900**	1,631	1,631	1,631	1,631
10,900	**10,950**	1,639	1,639	1,639	1,639
10,950	**11,000**	1,646	1,646	1,646	1,646

If line 37 (taxable income) is—		And you are—			
At least	But less than	Single	Married filing jointly *	Married filing sepa-rately	Head of a house-hold
		Your tax is—			
11,000					
11,000	**11,050**	1,654	1,654	1,654	1,654
11,050	**11,100**	1,661	1,661	1,661	1,661
11,100	**11,150**	1,669	1,669	1,669	1,669
11,150	**11,200**	1,676	1,676	1,676	1,676
11,200	**11,250**	1,684	1,684	1,684	1,684
11,250	**11,300**	1,691	1,691	1,691	1,691
11,300	**11,350**	1,699	1,699	1,699	1,699
11,350	**11,400**	1,706	1,706	1,706	1,706
11,400	**11,450**	1,714	1,714	1,714	1,714
11,450	**11,500**	1,721	1,721	1,721	1,721
11,500	**11,550**	1,729	1,729	1,729	1,729
11,550	**11,600**	1,736	1,736	1,736	1,736
11,600	**11,650**	1,744	1,744	1,744	1,744
11,650	**11,700**	1,751	1,751	1,751	1,751
11,700	**11,750**	1,759	1,759	1,759	1,759
11,750	**11,800**	1,766	1,766	1,766	1,766
11,800	**11,850**	1,774	1,774	1,774	1,774
11,850	**11,900**	1,781	1,781	1,781	1,781
11,900	**11,950**	1,789	1,789	1,789	1,789
11,950	**12,000**	1,796	1,796	1,796	1,796
12,000					
12,000	**12,050**	1,804	1,804	1,804	1,804
12,050	**12,100**	1,811	1,811	1,811	1,811
12,100	**12,150**	1,819	1,819	1,819	1,819
12,150	**12,200**	1,826	1,826	1,826	1,826
12,200	**12,250**	1,834	1,834	1,834	1,834
12,250	**12,300**	1,841	1,841	1,841	1,841
12,300	**12,350**	1,849	1,849	1,849	1,849
12,350	**12,400**	1,856	1,856	1,856	1,856
12,400	**12,450**	1,864	1,864	1,864	1,864
12,450	**12,500**	1,871	1,871	1,871	1,871
12,500	**12,550**	1,879	1,879	1,879	1,879
12,550	**12,600**	1,886	1,886	1,886	1,886
12,600	**12,650**	1,894	1,894	1,894	1,894
12,650	**12,700**	1,901	1,901	1,901	1,901
12,700	**12,750**	1,909	1,909	1,909	1,909
12,750	**12,800**	1,916	1,916	1,916	1,916
12,800	**12,850**	1,924	1,924	1,924	1,924
12,850	**12,900**	1,931	1,931	1,931	1,931
12,900	**12,950**	1,939	1,939	1,939	1,939
12,950	**13,000**	1,946	1,946	1,946	1,946
13,000					
13,000	**13,050**	1,954	1,954	1,954	1,954
13,050	**13,100**	1,961	1,961	1,961	1,961
13,100	**13,150**	1,969	1,969	1,969	1,969
13,150	**13,200**	1,976	1,976	1,976	1,976
13,200	**13,250**	1,984	1,984	1,984	1,984
13,250	**13,300**	1,991	1,991	1,991	1,991
13,300	**13,350**	1,999	1,999	1,999	1,999
13,350	**13,400**	2,006	2,006	2,006	2,006
13,400	**13,450**	2,014	2,014	2,014	2,014
13,450	**13,500**	2,021	2,021	2,021	2,021
13,500	**13,550**	2,029	2,029	2,029	2,029
13,550	**13,600**	2,036	2,036	2,036	2,036
13,600	**13,650**	2,044	2,044	2,044	2,044
13,650	**13,700**	2,051	2,051	2,051	2,051
13,700	**13,750**	2,059	2,059	2,059	2,059
13,750	**13,800**	2,066	2,066	2,066	2,066
13,800	**13,850**	2,074	2,074	2,074	2,074
13,850	**13,900**	2,081	2,081	2,081	2,081
13,900	**13,950**	2,089	2,089	2,089	2,089
13,950	**14,000**	2,096	2,096	2,096	2,096

* This column must also be used by a qualifying widow(er).

Continued on next page

1989 Tax Table—*Continued*

If line 37 (taxable income) is— At least	But less than	And you are— Single	Married filing jointly *	Married filing sepa-rately	Head of a house-hold
		Your tax is—			
14,000					
14,000	14,050	2,104	2,104	2,104	2,104
14,050	14,100	2,111	2,111	2,111	2,111
14,100	14,150	2,119	2,119	2,119	2,119
14,150	14,200	2,126	2,126	2,126	2,126
14,200	14,250	2,134	2,134	2,134	2,134
14,250	14,300	2,141	2,141	2,141	2,141
14,300	14,350	2,149	2,149	2,149	2,149
14,350	14,400	2,156	2,156	2,156	2,156
14,400	14,450	2,164	2,164	2,164	2,164
14,450	14,500	2,171	2,171	2,171	2,171
14,500	14,550	2,179	2,179	2,179	2,179
14,550	14,600	2,186	2,186	2,186	2,186
14,600	14,650	2,194	2,194	2,194	2,194
14,650	14,700	2,201	2,201	2,201	2,201
14,700	14,750	2,209	2,209	2,209	2,209
14,750	14,800	2,216	2,216	2,216	2,216
14,800	14,850	2,224	2,224	2,224	2,224
14,850	14,900	2,231	2,231	2,231	2,231
14,900	14,950	2,239	2,239	2,239	2,239
14,950	15,000	2,246	2,246	2,246	2,246
15,000					
15,000	15,050	2,254	2,254	2,254	2,254
15,050	15,100	2,261	2,261	2,261	2,261
15,100	15,150	2,269	2,269	2,269	2,269
15,150	15,200	2,276	2,276	2,276	2,276
15,200	15,250	2,284	2,284	2,284	2,284
15,250	15,300	2,291	2,291	2,291	2,291
15,300	15,350	2,299	2,299	2,299	2,299
15,350	15,400	2,306	2,306	2,306	2,306
15,400	15,450	2,314	2,314	2,314	2,314
15,450	15,500	2,321	2,321	2,321	2,321
15,500	15,550	2,329	2,329	2,335	2,329
15,550	15,600	2,336	2,336	2,349	2,336
15,600	15,650	2,344	2,344	2,363	2,344
15,650	15,700	2,351	2,351	2,377	2,351
15,700	15,750	2,359	2,359	2,391	2,359
15,750	15,800	2,366	2,366	2,405	2,366
15,800	15,850	2,374	2,374	2,419	2,374
15,850	15,900	2,381	2,381	2,433	2,381
15,900	15,950	2,389	2,389	2,447	2,389
15,950	16,000	2,396	2,396	2,461	2,396
16,000					
16,000	16,050	2,404	2,404	2,475	2,404
16,050	16,100	2,411	2,411	2,489	2,411
16,100	16,150	2,419	2,419	2,503	2,419
16,150	16,200	2,426	2,426	2,517	2,426
16,200	16,250	2,434	2,434	2,531	2,434
16,250	16,300	2,441	2,441	2,545	2,441
16,300	16,350	2,449	2,449	2,559	2,449
16,350	16,400	2,456	2,456	2,573	2,456
16,400	16,450	2,464	2,464	2,587	2,464
16,450	16,500	2,471	2,471	2,601	2,471
16,500	16,550	2,479	2,479	2,615	2,479
16,550	16,600	2,486	2,486	2,629	2,486
16,600	16,650	2,494	2,494	2,643	2,494
16,650	16,700	2,501	2,501	2,657	2,501
16,700	16,750	2,509	2,509	2,671	2,509
16,750	16,800	2,516	2,516	2,685	2,516
16,800	16,850	2,524	2,524	2,699	2,524
16,850	16,900	2,531	2,531	2,713	2,531
16,900	16,950	2,539	2,539	2,727	2,539
16,950	17,000	2,546	2,546	2,741	2,546

If line 37 (taxable income) is— At least	But less than	And you are— Single	Married filing jointly *	Married filing sepa-rately	Head of a house-hold
		Your tax is—			
17,000					
17,000	17,050	2,554	2,554	2,755	2,554
17,050	17,100	2,561	2,561	2,769	2,561
17,100	17,150	2,569	2,569	2,783	2,569
17,150	17,200	2,576	2,576	2,797	2,576
17,200	17,250	2,584	2,584	2,811	2,584
17,250	17,300	2,591	2,591	2,825	2,591
17,300	17,350	2,599	2,599	2,839	2,599
17,350	17,400	2,606	2,606	2,853	2,606
17,400	17,450	2,614	2,614	2,867	2,614
17,450	17,500	2,621	2,621	2,881	2,621
17,500	17,550	2,629	2,629	2,895	2,629
17,550	17,600	2,636	2,636	2,909	2,636
17,600	17,650	2,644	2,644	2,923	2,644
17,650	17,700	2,651	2,651	2,937	2,651
17,700	17,750	2,659	2,659	2,951	2,659
17,750	17,800	2,666	2,666	2,965	2,666
17,800	17,850	2,674	2,674	2,979	2,674
17,850	17,900	2,681	2,681	2,993	2,681
17,900	17,950	2,689	2,689	3,007	2,689
17,950	18,000	2,696	2,696	3,021	2,696
18,000					
18,000	18,050	2,704	2,704	3,035	2,704
18,050	18,100	2,711	2,711	3,049	2,711
18,100	18,150	2,719	2,719	3,063	2,719
18,150	18,200	2,726	2,726	3,077	2,726
18,200	18,250	2,734	2,734	3,091	2,734
18,250	18,300	2,741	2,741	3,105	2,741
18,300	18,350	2,749	2,749	3,119	2,749
18,350	18,400	2,756	2,756	3,133	2,756
18,400	18,450	2,764	2,764	3,147	2,764
18,450	18,500	2,771	2,771	3,161	2,771
18,500	18,550	2,779	2,779	3,175	2,779
18,550	18,600	2,790	2,786	3,189	2,786
18,600	18,650	2,804	2,794	3,203	2,794
18,650	18,700	2,818	2,801	3,217	2,801
18,700	18,750	2,832	2,809	3,231	2,809
18,750	18,800	2,846	2,816	3,245	2,816
18,800	18,850	2,860	2,824	3,259	2,824
18,850	18,900	2,874	2,831	3,273	2,831
18,900	18,950	2,888	2,839	3,287	2,839
18,950	19,000	2,902	2,846	3,301	2,846
19,000					
19,000	19,050	2,916	2,854	3,315	2,854
19,050	19,100	2,930	2,861	3,329	2,861
19,100	19,150	2,944	2,869	3,343	2,869
19,150	19,200	2,958	2,876	3,357	2,876
19,200	19,250	2,972	2,884	3,371	2,884
19,250	19,300	2,986	2,891	3,385	2,891
19,300	19,350	3,000	2,899	3,399	2,899
19,350	19,400	3,014	2,906	3,413	2,906
19,400	19,450	3,028	2,914	3,427	2,914
19,450	19,500	3,042	2,921	3,441	2,921
19,500	19,550	3,056	2,929	3,455	2,929
19,550	19,600	3,070	2,936	3,469	2,936
19,600	19,650	3,084	2,944	3,483	2,944
19,650	19,700	3,098	2,951	3,497	2,951
19,700	19,750	3,112	2,959	3,511	2,959
19,750	19,800	3,126	2,966	3,525	2,966
19,800	19,850	3,140	2,974	3,539	2,974
19,850	19,900	3,154	2,981	3,553	2,981
19,900	19,950	3,168	2,989	3,567	2,989
19,950	20,000	3,182	2,996	3,581	2,996

If line 37 (taxable income) is— At least	But less than	And you are— Single	Married filing jointly *	Married filing sepa-rately	Head of a house-hold
		Your tax is—			
20,000					
20,000	20,050	3,196	3,004	3,595	3,004
20,050	20,100	3,210	3,011	3,609	3,011
20,100	20,150	3,224	3,019	3,623	3,019
20,150	20,200	3,238	3,026	3,637	3,026
20,200	20,250	3,252	3,034	3,651	3,034
20,250	20,300	3,266	3,041	3,665	3,041
20,300	20,350	3,280	3,049	3,679	3,049
20,350	20,400	3,294	3,056	3,693	3,056
20,400	20,450	3,308	3,064	3,707	3,064
20,450	20,500	3,322	3,071	3,721	3,071
20,500	20,550	3,336	3,079	3,735	3,079
20,550	20,600	3,350	3,086	3,749	3,086
20,600	20,650	3,364	3,094	3,763	3,094
20,650	20,700	3,378	3,101	3,777	3,101
20,700	20,750	3,392	3,109	3,791	3,109
20,750	20,800	3,406	3,116	3,805	3,116
20,800	20,850	3,420	3,124	3,819	3,124
20,850	20,900	3,434	3,131	3,833	3,131
20,900	20,950	3,448	3,139	3,847	3,139
20,950	21,000	3,462	3,146	3,861	3,146
21,000					
21,000	21,050	3,476	3,154	3,875	3,154
21,050	21,100	3,490	3,161	3,889	3,161
21,100	21,150	3,504	3,169	3,903	3,169
21,150	21,200	3,518	3,176	3,917	3,176
21,200	21,250	3,532	3,184	3,931	3,184
21,250	21,300	3,546	3,191	3,945	3,191
21,300	21,350	3,560	3,199	3,959	3,199
21,350	21,400	3,574	3,206	3,973	3,206
21,400	21,450	3,588	3,214	3,987	3,214
21,450	21,500	3,602	3,221	4,001	3,221
21,500	21,550	3,616	3,229	4,015	3,229
21,550	21,600	3,630	3,236	4,029	3,236
21,600	21,650	3,644	3,244	4,043	3,244
21,650	21,700	3,658	3,251	4,057	3,251
21,700	21,750	3,672	3,259	4,071	3,259
21,750	21,800	3,686	3,266	4,085	3,266
21,800	21,850	3,700	3,274	4,099	3,274
21,850	21,900	3,714	3,281	4,113	3,281
21,900	21,950	3,728	3,289	4,127	3,289
21,950	22,000	3,742	3,296	4,141	3,296
22,000					
22,000	22,050	3,756	3,304	4,155	3,304
22,050	22,100	3,770	3,311	4,169	3,311
22,100	22,150	3,784	3,319	4,183	3,319
22,150	22,200	3,798	3,326	4,197	3,326
22,200	22,250	3,812	3,334	4,211	3,334
22,250	22,300	3,826	3,341	4,225	3,341
22,300	22,350	3,840	3,349	4,239	3,349
22,350	22,400	3,854	3,356	4,253	3,356
22,400	22,450	3,868	3,364	4,267	3,364
22,450	22,500	3,882	3,371	4,281	3,371
22,500	22,550	3,896	3,379	4,295	3,379
22,550	22,600	3,910	3,386	4,309	3,386
22,600	22,650	3,924	3,394	4,323	3,394
22,650	22,700	3,938	3,401	4,337	3,401
22,700	22,750	3,952	3,409	4,351	3,409
22,750	22,800	3,966	3,416	4,365	3,416
22,800	22,850	3,980	3,424	4,379	3,424
22,850	22,900	3,994	3,431	4,393	3,431
22,900	22,950	4,008	3,439	4,407	3,439
22,950	23,000	4,022	3,446	4,421	3,446

* This column must also be used by a qualifying widow(er).

Continued on next page

1989 Tax Table—*Continued*

If line 37 (taxable income) is— At least	But less than	And you are— Single	Married filing jointly *	Married filing sepa-rately	Head of a house-hold
		Your tax is—			
23,000					
23,000	**23,050**	4,036	3,454	4,435	3,454
23,050	**23,100**	4,050	3,461	4,449	3,461
23,100	**23,150**	4,064	3,469	4,463	3,469
23,150	**23,200**	4,078	3,476	4,477	3,476
23,200	**23,250**	4,092	3,484	4,491	3,484
23,250	**23,300**	4,106	3,491	4,505	3,491
23,300	**23,350**	4,120	3,499	4,519	3,499
23,350	**23,400**	4,134	3,506	4,533	3,506
23,400	**23,450**	4,148	3,514	4,547	3,514
23,450	**23,500**	4,162	3,521	4,561	3,521
23,500	**23,550**	4,176	3,529	4,575	3,529
23,550	**23,600**	4,190	3,536	4,589	3,536
23,600	**23,650**	4,204	3,544	4,603	3,544
23,650	**23,700**	4,218	3,551	4,617	3,551
23,700	**23,750**	4,232	3,559	4,631	3,559
23,750	**23,800**	4,246	3,566	4,645	3,566
23,800	**23,850**	4,260	3,574	4,659	3,574
23,850	**23,900**	4,274	3,581	4,673	3,581
23,900	**23,950**	4,288	3,589	4,687	3,589
23,950	**24,000**	4,302	3,596	4,701	3,596
24,000					
24,000	**24,050**	4,316	3,604	4,715	3,604
24,050	**24,100**	4,330	3,611	4,729	3,611
24,100	**24,150**	4,344	3,619	4,743	3,619
24,150	**24,200**	4,358	3,626	4,757	3,626
24,200	**24,250**	4,372	3,634	4,771	3,634
24,250	**24,300**	4,386	3,641	4,785	3,641
24,300	**24,350**	4,400	3,649	4,799	3,649
24,350	**24,400**	4,414	3,656	4,813	3,656
24,400	**24,450**	4,428	3,664	4,827	3,664
24,450	**24,500**	4,442	3,671	4,841	3,671
24,500	**24,550**	4,456	3,679	4,855	3,679
24,550	**24,600**	4,470	3,686	4,869	3,686
24,600	**24,650**	4,484	3,694	4,883	3,694
24,650	**24,700**	4,498	3,701	4,897	3,701
24,700	**24,750**	4,512	3,709	4,911	3,709
24,750	**24,800**	4,526	3,716	4,925	3,716
24,800	**24,850**	4,540	3,724	4,939	3,724
24,850	**24,900**	4,554	3,731	4,953	3,735
24,900	**24,950**	4,568	3,739	4,967	3,749
24,950	**25,000**	4,582	3,746	4,981	3,763
25,000					
25,000	**25,050**	4,596	3,754	4,995	3,777
25,050	**25,100**	4,610	3,761	5,009	3,791
25,100	**25,150**	4,624	3,769	5,023	3,805
25,150	**25,200**	4,638	3,776	5,037	3,819
25,200	**25,250**	4,652	3,784	5,051	3,833
25,250	**25,300**	4,666	3,791	5,065	3,847
25,300	**25,350**	4,680	3,799	5,079	3,861
25,350	**25,400**	4,694	3,806	5,093	3,875
25,400	**25,450**	4,708	3,814	5,107	3,889
25,450	**25,500**	4,722	3,821	5,121	3,903
25,500	**25,550**	4,736	3,829	5,135	3,917
25,550	**25,600**	4,750	3,836	5,149	3,931
25,600	**25,650**	4,764	3,844	5,163	3,945
25,650	**25,700**	4,778	3,851	5,177	3,959
25,700	**25,750**	4,792	3,859	5,191	3,973
25,750	**25,800**	4,806	3,866	5,205	3,987
25,800	**25,850**	4,820	3,874	5,219	4,001
25,850	**25,900**	4,834	3,881	5,233	4,015
25,900	**25,950**	4,848	3,889	5,247	4,029
25,950	**26,000**	4,862	3,896	5,261	4,043

If line 37 (taxable income) is— At least	But less than	And you are— Single	Married filing jointly *	Married filing sepa-rately	Head of a house-hold
		Your tax is—			
26,000					
26,000	**26,050**	4,876	3,904	5,275	4,057
26,050	**26,100**	4,890	3,911	5,289	4,071
26,100	**26,150**	4,904	3,919	5,303	4,085
26,150	**26,200**	4,918	3,926	5,317	4,099
26,200	**26,250**	4,932	3,934	5,331	4,113
26,250	**26,300**	4,946	3,941	5,345	4,127
26,300	**26,350**	4,960	3,949	5,359	4,141
26,350	**26,400**	4,974	3,956	5,373	4,155
26,400	**26,450**	4,988	3,964	5,387	4,169
26,450	**26,500**	5,002	3,971	5,401	4,183
26,500	**26,550**	5,016	3,979	5,415	4,197
26,550	**26,600**	5,030	3,986	5,429	4,211
26,600	**26,650**	5,044	3,994	5,443	4,225
26,650	**26,700**	5,058	4,001	5,457	4,239
26,700	**26,750**	5,072	4,009	5,471	4,253
26,750	**26,800**	5,086	4,016	5,485	4,267
26,800	**26,850**	5,100	4,024	5,499	4,281
26,850	**26,900**	5,114	4,031	5,513	4,295
26,900	**26,950**	5,128	4,039	5,527	4,309
26,950	**27,000**	5,142	4,046	5,541	4,323
27,000					
27,000	**27,050**	5,156	4,054	5,555	4,337
27,050	**27,100**	5,170	4,061	5,569	4,351
27,100	**27,150**	5,184	4,069	5,583	4,365
27,150	**27,200**	5,198	4,076	5,597	4,379
27,200	**27,250**	5,212	4,084	5,611	4,393
27,250	**27,300**	5,226	4,091	5,625	4,407
27,300	**27,350**	5,240	4,099	5,639	4,421
27,350	**27,400**	5,254	4,106	5,653	4,435
27,400	**27,450**	5,268	4,114	5,667	4,449
27,450	**27,500**	5,282	4,121	5,681	4,463
27,500	**27,550**	5,296	4,129	5,695	4,477
27,550	**27,600**	5,310	4,136	5,709	4,491
27,600	**27,650**	5,324	4,144	5,723	4,505
27,650	**27,700**	5,338	4,151	5,737	4,519
27,700	**27,750**	5,352	4,159	5,751	4,533
27,750	**27,800**	5,366	4,166	5,765	4,547
27,800	**27,850**	5,380	4,174	5,779	4,561
27,850	**27,900**	5,394	4,181	5,793	4,575
27,900	**27,950**	5,408	4,189	5,807	4,589
27,950	**28,000**	5,422	4,196	5,821	4,603
28,000					
28,000	**28,050**	5,436	4,204	5,835	4,617
28,050	**28,100**	5,450	4,211	5,849	4,631
28,100	**28,150**	5,464	4,219	5,863	4,645
28,150	**28,200**	5,478	4,226	5,877	4,659
28,200	**28,250**	5,492	4,234	5,891	4,673
28,250	**28,300**	5,506	4,241	5,905	4,687
28,300	**28,350**	5,520	4,249	5,919	4,701
28,350	**28,400**	5,534	4,256	5,933	4,715
28,400	**28,450**	5,548	4,264	5,947	4,729
28,450	**28,500**	5,562	4,271	5,961	4,743
28,500	**28,550**	5,576	4,279	5,975	4,757
28,550	**28,600**	5,590	4,286	5,989	4,771
28,600	**28,650**	5,604	4,294	6,003	4,785
28,650	**28,700**	5,618	4,301	6,017	4,799
28,700	**28,750**	5,632	4,309	6,031	4,813
28,750	**28,800**	5,646	4,316	6,045	4,827
28,800	**28,850**	5,660	4,324	6,059	4,841
28,850	**28,900**	5,674	4,331	6,073	4,855
28,900	**28,950**	5,688	4,339	6,087	4,869
28,950	**29,000**	5,702	4,346	6,101	4,883

If line 37 (taxable income) is— At least	But less than	And you are— Single	Married filing jointly *	Married filing sepa-rately	Head of a house-hold
		Your tax is—			
29,000					
29,000	**29,050**	5,716	4,354	6,115	4,897
29,050	**29,100**	5,730	4,361	6,129	4,911
29,100	**29,150**	5,744	4,369	6,143	4,925
29,150	**29,200**	5,758	4,376	6,157	4,939
29,200	**29,250**	5,772	4,384	6,171	4,953
29,250	**29,300**	5,786	4,391	6,185	4,967
29,300	**29,350**	5,800	4,399	6,199	4,981
29,350	**29,400**	5,814	4,406	6,213	4,995
29,400	**29,450**	5,828	4,414	6,227	5,009
29,450	**29,500**	5,842	4,421	6,241	5,023
29,500	**29,550**	5,856	4,429	6,255	5,037
29,550	**29,600**	5,870	4,436	6,269	5,051
29,600	**29,650**	5,884	4,444	6,283	5,065
29,650	**29,700**	5,898	4,451	6,297	5,079
29,700	**29,750**	5,912	4,459	6,311	5,093
29,750	**29,800**	5,926	4,466	6,325	5,107
29,800	**29,850**	5,940	4,474	6,339	5,121
29,850	**29,900**	5,954	4,481	6,353	5,135
29,900	**29,950**	5,968	4,489	6,367	5,149
29,950	**30,000**	5,982	4,496	6,381	5,163
30,000					
30,000	**30,050**	5,996	4,504	6,395	5,177
30,050	**30,100**	6,010	4,511	6,409	5,191
30,100	**30,150**	6,024	4,519	6,423	5,205
30,150	**30,200**	6,038	4,526	6,437	5,219
30,200	**30,250**	6,052	4,534	6,451	5,233
30,250	**30,300**	6,066	4,541	6,465	5,247
30,300	**30,350**	6,080	4,549	6,479	5,261
30,350	**30,400**	6,094	4,556	6,493	5,275
30,400	**30,450**	6,108	4,564	6,507	5,289
30,450	**30,500**	6,122	4,571	6,521	5,303
30,500	**30,550**	6,136	4,579	6,535	5,317
30,550	**30,600**	6,150	4,586	6,549	5,331
30,600	**30,650**	6,164	4,594	6,563	5,345
30,650	**30,700**	6,178	4,601	6,577	5,359
30,700	**30,750**	6,192	4,609	6,591	5,373
30,750	**30,800**	6,206	4,616	6,605	5,387
30,800	**30,850**	6,220	4,624	6,619	5,401
30,850	**30,900**	6,234	4,631	6,633	5,415
30,900	**30,950**	6,248	4,639	6,647	5,429
30,950	**31,000**	6,262	4,650	6,661	5,443
31,000					
31,000	**31,050**	6,276	4,664	6,675	5,457
31,050	**31,100**	6,290	4,678	6,689	5,471
31,100	**31,150**	6,304	4,692	6,703	5,485
31,150	**31,200**	6,318	4,706	6,717	5,499
31,200	**31,250**	6,332	4,720	6,731	5,513
31,250	**31,300**	6,346	4,734	6,745	5,527
31,300	**31,350**	6,360	4,748	6,759	5,541
31,350	**31,400**	6,374	4,762	6,773	5,555
31,400	**31,450**	6,388	4,776	6,787	5,569
31,450	**31,500**	6,402	4,790	6,801	5,583
31,500	**31,550**	6,416	4,804	6,815	5,597
31,550	**31,600**	6,430	4,818	6,829	5,611
31,600	**31,650**	6,444	4,832	6,843	5,625
31,650	**31,700**	6,458	4,846	6,857	5,639
31,700	**31,750**	6,472	4,860	6,871	5,653
31,750	**31,800**	6,486	4,874	6,885	5,667
31,800	**31,850**	6,500	4,888	6,899	5,681
31,850	**31,900**	6,514	4,902	6,913	5,695
31,900	**31,950**	6,528	4,916	6,927	5,709
31,950	**32,000**	6,542	4,930	6,941	5,723

* This column must also be used by a qualifying widow(er).

Continued on next page

1989 Tax Table—*Continued*

If line 37 (taxable income) is— At least	But less than	And you are— Single	Married filing jointly *	Married filing separately	Head of a household
		Your tax is—			
32,000					
32,000	**32,050**	6,556	4,944	6,955	5,737
32,050	**32,100**	6,570	4,958	6,969	5,751
32,100	**32,150**	6,584	4,972	6,983	5,765
32,150	**32,200**	6,598	4,986	6,997	5,779
32,200	**32,250**	6,612	5,000	7,011	5,793
32,250	**32,300**	6,626	5,014	7,025	5,807
32,300	**32,350**	6,640	5,028	7,039	5,821
32,350	**32,400**	6,654	5,042	7,053	5,835
32,400	**32,450**	6,668	5,056	7,067	5,849
32,450	**32,500**	6,682	5,070	7,081	5,863
32,500	**32,550**	6,696	5,084	7,095	5,877
32,550	**32,600**	6,710	5,098	7,109	5,891
32,600	**32,650**	6,724	5,112	7,123	5,905
32,650	**32,700**	6,738	5,126	7,137	5,919
32,700	**32,750**	6,752	5,140	7,151	5,933
32,750	**32,800**	6,766	5,154	7,165	5,947
32,800	**32,850**	6,780	5,168	7,179	5,961
32,850	**32,900**	6,794	5,182	7,193	5,975
32,900	**32,950**	6,808	5,196	7,207	5,989
32,950	**33,000**	6,822	5,210	7,221	6,003
33,000					
33,000	**33,050**	6,836	5,224	7,235	6,017
33,050	**33,100**	6,850	5,238	7,249	6,031
33,100	**33,150**	6,864	5,252	7,263	6,045
33,150	**33,200**	6,878	5,266	7,277	6,059
33,200	**33,250**	6,892	5,280	7,291	6,073
33,250	**33,300**	6,906	5,294	7,305	6,087
33,300	**33,350**	6,920	5,308	7,319	6,101
33,350	**33,400**	6,934	5,322	7,333	6,115
33,400	**33,450**	6,948	5,336	7,347	6,129
33,450	**33,500**	6,962	5,350	7,361	6,143
33,500	**33,550**	6,976	5,364	7,375	6,157
33,550	**33,600**	6,990	5,378	7,389	6,171
33,600	**33,650**	7,004	5,392	7,403	6,185
33,650	**33,700**	7,018	5,406	7,417	6,199
33,700	**33,750**	7,032	5,420	7,431	6,213
33,750	**33,800**	7,046	5,434	7,445	6,227
33,800	**33,850**	7,060	5,448	7,459	6,241
33,850	**33,900**	7,074	5,462	7,473	6,255
33,900	**33,950**	7,088	5,476	7,487	6,269
33,950	**34,000**	7,102	5,490	7,501	6,283
34,000					
34,000	**34,050**	7,116	5,504	7,515	6,297
34,050	**34,100**	7,130	5,518	7,529	6,311
34,100	**34,150**	7,144	5,532	7,543	6,325
34,150	**34,200**	7,158	5,546	7,557	6,339
34,200	**34,250**	7,172	5,560	7,571	6,353
34,250	**34,300**	7,186	5,574	7,585	6,367
34,300	**34,350**	7,200	5,588	7,599	6,381
34,350	**34,400**	7,214	5,602	7,613	6,395
34,400	**34,450**	7,228	5,616	7,627	6,409
34,450	**34,500**	7,242	5,630	7,641	6,423
34,500	**34,550**	7,256	5,644	7,655	6,437
34,550	**34,600**	7,270	5,658	7,669	6,451
34,600	**34,650**	7,284	5,672	7,683	6,465
34,650	**34,700**	7,298	5,686	7,697	6,479
34,700	**34,750**	7,312	5,700	7,711	6,493
34,750	**34,800**	7,326	5,714	7,725	6,507
34,800	**34,850**	7,340	5,728	7,739	6,521
34,850	**34,900**	7,354	5,742	7,753	6,535
34,900	**34,950**	7,368	5,756	7,767	6,549
34,950	**35,000**	7,382	5,770	7,781	6,563

If line 37 (taxable income) is— At least	But less than	And you are— Single	Married filing jointly *	Married filing separately	Head of a household
		Your tax is—			
35,000					
35,000	**35,050**	7,396	5,784	7,795	6,577
35,050	**35,100**	7,410	5,798	7,809	6,591
35,100	**35,150**	7,424	5,812	7,823	6,605
35,150	**35,200**	7,438	5,826	7,837	6,619
35,200	**35,250**	7,452	5,840	7,851	6,633
35,250	**35,300**	7,466	5,854	7,865	6,647
35,300	**35,350**	7,480	5,868	7,879	6,661
35,350	**35,400**	7,494	5,882	7,893	6,675
35,400	**35,450**	7,508	5,896	7,907	6,689
35,450	**35,500**	7,522	5,910	7,921	6,703
35,500	**35,550**	7,536	5,924	7,935	6,717
35,550	**35,600**	7,550	5,938	7,949	6,731
35,600	**35,650**	7,564	5,952	7,963	6,745
35,650	**35,700**	7,578	5,966	7,977	6,759
35,700	**35,750**	7,592	5,980	7,991	6,773
35,750	**35,800**	7,606	5,994	8,005	6,787
35,800	**35,850**	7,620	6,008	8,019	6,801
35,850	**35,900**	7,634	6,022	8,033	6,815
35,900	**35,950**	7,648	6,036	8,047	6,829
35,950	**36,000**	7,662	6,050	8,061	6,843
36,000					
36,000	**36,050**	7,676	6,064	8,075	6,857
36,050	**36,100**	7,690	6,078	8,089	6,871
36,100	**36,150**	7,704	6,092	8,103	6,885
36,150	**36,200**	7,718	6,106	8,117	6,899
36,200	**36,250**	7,732	6,120	8,131	6,913
36,250	**36,300**	7,746	6,134	8,145	6,927
36,300	**36,350**	7,760	6,148	8,159	6,941
36,350	**36,400**	7,774	6,162	8,173	6,955
36,400	**36,450**	7,788	6,176	8,187	6,969
36,450	**36,500**	7,802	6,190	8,201	6,983
36,500	**36,550**	7,816	6,204	8,215	6,997
36,550	**36,600**	7,830	6,218	8,229	7,011
36,600	**36,650**	7,844	6,232	8,243	7,025
36,650	**36,700**	7,858	6,246	8,257	7,039
36,700	**36,750**	7,872	6,260	8,271	7,053
36,750	**36,800**	7,886	6,274	8,285	7,067
36,800	**36,850**	7,900	6,288	8,299	7,081
36,850	**36,900**	7,914	6,302	8,313	7,095
36,900	**36,950**	7,928	6,316	8,327	7,109
36,950	**37,000**	7,942	6,330	8,341	7,123
37,000					
37,000	**37,050**	7,956	6,344	8,355	7,137
37,050	**37,100**	7,970	6,358	8,369	7,151
37,100	**37,150**	7,984	6,372	8,383	7,165
37,150	**37,200**	7,998	6,386	8,397	7,179
37,200	**37,250**	8,012	6,400	8,411	7,193
37,250	**37,300**	8,026	6,414	8,425	7,207
37,300	**37,350**	8,040	6,428	8,439	7,221
37,350	**37,400**	8,054	6,442	8,453	7,235
37,400	**37,450**	8,068	6,456	8,467	7,249
37,450	**37,500**	8,082	6,470	8,484	7,263
37,500	**37,550**	8,096	6,484	8,500	7,277
37,550	**37,600**	8,110	6,498	8,517	7,291
37,600	**37,650**	8,124	6,512	8,533	7,305
37,650	**37,700**	8,138	6,526	8,550	7,319
37,700	**37,750**	8,152	6,540	8,566	7,333
37,750	**37,800**	8,166	6,554	8,583	7,347
37,800	**37,850**	8,180	6,568	8,599	7,361
37,850	**37,900**	8,194	6,582	8,616	7,375
37,900	**37,950**	8,208	6,596	8,632	7,389
37,950	**38,000**	8,222	6,610	8,649	7,403

If line 37 (taxable income) is— At least	But less than	And you are— Single	Married filing jointly *	Married filing separately	Head of a household
		Your tax is—			
38,000					
38,000	**38,050**	8,236	6,624	8,665	7,417
38,050	**38,100**	8,250	6,638	8,682	7,431
38,100	**38,150**	8,264	6,652	8,698	7,445
38,150	**38,200**	8,278	6,666	8,715	7,459
38,200	**38,250**	8,292	6,680	8,731	7,473
38,250	**38,300**	8,306	6,694	8,748	7,487
38,300	**38,350**	8,320	6,708	8,764	7,501
38,350	**38,400**	8,334	6,722	8,781	7,515
38,400	**38,450**	8,348	6,736	8,797	7,529
38,450	**38,500**	8,362	6,750	8,814	7,543
38,500	**38,550**	8,376	6,764	8,830	7,557
38,550	**38,600**	8,390	6,778	8,847	7,571
38,600	**38,650**	8,404	6,792	8,863	7,585
38,650	**38,700**	8,418	6,806	8,880	7,599
38,700	**38,750**	8,432	6,820	8,896	7,613
38,750	**38,800**	8,446	6,834	8,913	7,627
38,800	**38,850**	8,460	6,848	8,929	7,641
38,850	**38,900**	8,474	6,862	8,946	7,655
38,900	**38,950**	8,488	6,876	8,962	7,669
38,950	**39,000**	8,502	6,890	8,979	7,683
39,000					
39,000	**39,050**	8,516	6,904	8,995	7,697
39,050	**39,100**	8,530	6,918	9,012	7,711
39,100	**39,150**	8,544	6,932	9,028	7,725
39,150	**39,200**	8,558	6,946	9,045	7,739
39,200	**39,250**	8,572	6,960	9,061	7,753
39,250	**39,300**	8,586	6,974	9,078	7,767
39,300	**39,350**	8,600	6,988	9,094	7,781
39,350	**39,400**	8,614	7,002	9,111	7,795
39,400	**39,450**	8,628	7,016	9,127	7,809
39,450	**39,500**	8,642	7,030	9,144	7,823
39,500	**39,550**	8,656	7,044	9,160	7,837
39,550	**39,600**	8,670	7,058	9,177	7,851
39,600	**39,650**	8,684	7,072	9,193	7,865
39,650	**39,700**	8,698	7,086	9,210	7,879
39,700	**39,750**	8,712	7,100	9,226	7,893
39,750	**39,800**	8,726	7,114	9,243	7,907
39,800	**39,850**	8,740	7,128	9,259	7,921
39,850	**39,900**	8,754	7,142	9,276	7,935
39,900	**39,950**	8,768	7,156	9,292	7,949
39,950	**40,000**	8,782	7,170	9,309	7,963
40,000					
40,000	**40,050**	8,796	7,184	9,325	7,977
40,050	**40,100**	8,810	7,198	9,342	7,991
40,100	**40,150**	8,824	7,212	9,358	8,005
40,150	**40,200**	8,838	7,226	9,375	8,019
40,200	**40,250**	8,852	7,240	9,391	8,033
40,250	**40,300**	8,866	7,254	9,408	8,047
40,300	**40,350**	8,880	7,268	9,424	8,061
40,350	**40,400**	8,894	7,282	9,441	8,075
40,400	**40,450**	8,908	7,296	9,457	8,089
40,450	**40,500**	8,922	7,310	9,474	8,103
40,500	**40,550**	8,936	7,324	9,490	8,117
40,550	**40,600**	8,950	7,338	9,507	8,131
40,600	**40,650**	8,964	7,352	9,523	8,145
40,650	**40,700**	8,978	7,366	9,540	8,159
40,700	**40,750**	8,992	7,380	9,556	8,173
40,750	**40,800**	9,006	7,394	9,573	8,187
40,800	**40,850**	9,020	7,408	9,589	8,201
40,850	**40,900**	9,034	7,422	9,606	8,215
40,900	**40,950**	9,048	7,436	9,622	8,229
40,950	**41,000**	9,062	7,450	9,639	8,243

* This column must also be used by a qualifying widow(er).

Continued on next page

1989 Tax Table—*Continued*

If line 37 (taxable income) is— At least	But less than	And you are— Single	Married filing jointly *	Married filing sepa-rately	Head of a house-hold
		Your tax is—			
41,000					
41,000	**41,050**	9,076	7,464	9,655	8,257
41,050	**41,100**	9,090	7,478	9,672	8,271
41,100	**41,150**	9,104	7,492	9,688	8,285
41,150	**41,200**	9,118	7,506	9,705	8,299
41,200	**41,250**	9,132	7,520	9,721	8,313
41,250	**41,300**	9,146	7,534	9,738	8,327
41,300	**41,350**	9,160	7,548	9,754	8,341
41,350	**41,400**	9,174	7,562	9,771	8,355
41,400	**41,450**	9,188	7,576	9,787	8,369
41,450	**41,500**	9,202	7,590	9,804	8,383
41,500	**41,550**	9,216	7,604	9,820	8,397
41,550	**41,600**	9,230	7,618	9,837	8,411
41,600	**41,650**	9,244	7,632	9,853	8,425
41,650	**41,700**	9,258	7,646	9,870	8,439
41,700	**41,750**	9,272	7,660	9,886	8,453
41,750	**41,800**	9,286	7,674	9,903	8,467
41,800	**41,850**	9,300	7,688	9,919	8,481
41,850	**41,900**	9,314	7,702	9,936	8,495
41,900	**41,950**	9,328	7,716	9,952	8,509
41,950	**42,000**	9,342	7,730	9,969	8,523
42,000					
42,000	**42,050**	9,356	7,744	9,985	8,537
42,050	**42,100**	9,370	7,758	10,002	8,551
42,100	**42,150**	9,384	7,772	10,018	8,565
42,150	**42,200**	9,398	7,786	10,035	8,579
42,200	**42,250**	9,412	7,800	10,051	8,593
42,250	**42,300**	9,426	7,814	10,068	8,607
42,300	**42,350**	9,440	7,828	10,084	8,621
42,350	**42,400**	9,454	7,842	10,101	8,635
42,400	**42,450**	9,468	7,856	10,117	8,649
42,450	**42,500**	9,482	7,870	10,134	8,663
42,500	**42,550**	9,496	7,884	10,150	8,677
42,550	**42,600**	9,510	7,898	10,167	8,691
42,600	**42,650**	9,524	7,912	10,183	8,705
42,650	**42,700**	9,538	7,926	10,200	8,719
42,700	**42,750**	9,552	7,940	10,216	8,733
42,750	**42,800**	9,566	7,954	10,233	8,747
42,800	**42,850**	9,580	7,968	10,249	8,761
42,850	**42,900**	9,594	7,982	10,266	8,775
42,900	**42,950**	9,608	7,996	10,282	8,789
42,950	**43,000**	9,622	8,010	10,299	8,803
43,000					
43,000	**43,050**	9,636	8,024	10,315	8,817
43,050	**43,100**	9,650	8,038	10,332	8,831
43,100	**43,150**	9,664	8,052	10,348	8,845
43,150	**43,200**	9,678	8,066	10,365	8,859
43,200	**43,250**	9,692	8,080	10,381	8,873
43,250	**43,300**	9,706	8,094	10,398	8,887
43,300	**43,350**	9,720	8,108	10,414	8,901
43,350	**43,400**	9,734	8,122	10,431	8,915
43,400	**43,450**	9,748	8,136	10,447	8,929
43,450	**43,500**	9,762	8,150	10,464	8,943
43,500	**43,550**	9,776	8,164	10,480	8,957
43,550	**43,600**	9,790	8,178	10,497	8,971
43,600	**43,650**	9,804	8,192	10,513	8,985
43,650	**43,700**	9,818	8,206	10,530	8,999
43,700	**43,750**	9,832	8,220	10,546	9,013
43,750	**43,800**	9,846	8,234	10,563	9,027
43,800	**43,850**	9,860	8,248	10,579	9,041
43,850	**43,900**	9,874	8,262	10,596	9,055
43,900	**43,950**	9,888	8,276	10,612	9,069
43,950	**44,000**	9,902	8,290	10,629	9,083

If line 37 (taxable income) is— At least	But less than	And you are— Single	Married filing jointly *	Married filing sepa-rately	Head of a house-hold
		Your tax is—			
44,000					
44,000	**44,050**	9,916	8,304	10,645	9,097
44,050	**44,100**	9,930	8,318	10,662	9,111
44,100	**44,150**	9,944	8,332	10,678	9,125
44,150	**44,200**	9,958	8,346	10,695	9,139
44,200	**44,250**	9,972	8,360	10,711	9,153
44,250	**44,300**	9,986	8,374	10,728	9,167
44,300	**44,350**	10,000	8,388	10,744	9,181
44,350	**44,400**	10,014	8,402	10,761	9,195
44,400	**44,450**	10,028	8,416	10,777	9,209
44,450	**44,500**	10,042	8,430	10,794	9,223
44,500	**44,550**	10,056	8,444	10,810	9,237
44,550	**44,600**	10,070	8,458	10,827	9,251
44,600	**44,650**	10,084	8,472	10,843	9,265
44,650	**44,700**	10,098	8,486	10,860	9,279
44,700	**44,750**	10,112	8,500	10,876	9,293
44,750	**44,800**	10,126	8,514	10,893	9,307
44,800	**44,850**	10,140	8,528	10,909	9,321
44,850	**44,900**	10,154	8,542	10,926	9,335
44,900	**44,950**	10,169	8,556	10,942	9,349
44,950	**45,000**	10,185	8,570	10,959	9,363
45,000					
45,000	**45,050**	10,202	8,584	10,975	9,377
45,050	**45,100**	10,218	8,598	10,992	9,391
45,100	**45,150**	10,235	8,612	11,008	9,405
45,150	**45,200**	10,251	8,626	11,025	9,419
45,200	**45,250**	10,268	8,640	11,041	9,433
45,250	**45,300**	10,284	8,654	11,058	9,447
45,300	**45,350**	10,301	8,668	11,074	9,461
45,350	**45,400**	10,317	8,682	11,091	9,475
45,400	**45,450**	10,334	8,696	11,107	9,489
45,450	**45,500**	10,350	8,710	11,124	9,503
45,500	**45,550**	10,367	8,724	11,140	9,517
45,550	**45,600**	10,383	8,738	11,157	9,531
45,600	**45,650**	10,400	8,752	11,173	9,545
45,650	**45,700**	10,416	8,766	11,190	9,559
45,700	**45,750**	10,433	8,780	11,206	9,573
45,750	**45,800**	10,449	8,794	11,223	9,587
45,800	**45,850**	10,466	8,808	11,239	9,601
45,850	**45,900**	10,482	8,822	11,256	9,615
45,900	**45,950**	10,499	8,836	11,272	9,629
45,950	**46,000**	10,515	8,850	11,289	9,643
46,000					
46,000	**46,050**	10,532	8,864	11,305	9,657
46,050	**46,100**	10,548	8,878	11,322	9,671
46,100	**46,150**	10,565	8,892	11,338	9,685
46,150	**46,200**	10,581	8,906	11,355	9,699
46,200	**46,250**	10,598	8,920	11,371	9,713
46,250	**46,300**	10,614	8,934	11,388	9,727
46,300	**46,350**	10,631	8,948	11,404	9,741
46,350	**46,400**	10,647	8,962	11,421	9,755
46,400	**46,450**	10,664	8,976	11,437	9,769
46,450	**46,500**	10,680	8,990	11,454	9,783
46,500	**46,550**	10,697	9,004	11,470	9,797
46,550	**46,600**	10,713	9,018	11,487	9,811
46,600	**46,650**	10,730	9,032	11,503	9,825
46,650	**46,700**	10,746	9,046	11,520	9,839
46,700	**46,750**	10,763	9,060	11,536	9,853
46,750	**46,800**	10,779	9,074	11,553	9,867
46,800	**46,850**	10,796	9,088	11,569	9,881
46,850	**46,900**	10,812	9,102	11,586	9,895
46,900	**46,950**	10,829	9,116	11,602	9,909
46,950	**47,000**	10,845	9,130	11,619	9,923

If line 37 (taxable income) is— At least	But less than	And you are— Single	Married filing jointly *	Married filing sepa-rately	Head of a house-hold
		Your tax is—			
47,000					
47,000	**47,050**	10,862	9,144	11,635	9,937
47,050	**47,100**	10,878	9,158	11,652	9,951
47,100	**47,150**	10,895	9,172	11,668	9,965
47,150	**47,200**	10,911	9,186	11,685	9,979
47,200	**47,250**	10,928	9,200	11,701	9,993
47,250	**47,300**	10,944	9,214	11,718	10,007
47,300	**47,350**	10,961	9,228	11,734	10,021
47,350	**47,400**	10,977	9,242	11,751	10,035
47,400	**47,450**	10,994	9,256	11,767	10,049
47,450	**47,500**	11,010	9,270	11,784	10,063
47,500	**47,550**	11,027	9,284	11,800	10,077
47,550	**47,600**	11,043	9,298	11,817	10,091
47,600	**47,650**	11,060	9,312	11,833	10,105
47,650	**47,700**	11,076	9,326	11,850	10,119
47,700	**47,750**	11,093	9,340	11,866	10,133
47,750	**47,800**	11,109	9,354	11,883	10,147
47,800	**47,850**	11,126	9,368	11,899	10,161
47,850	**47,900**	11,142	9,382	11,916	10,175
47,900	**47,950**	11,159	9,396	11,932	10,189
47,950	**48,000**	11,175	9,410	11,949	10,203
48,000					
48,000	**48,050**	11,192	9,424	11,965	10,217
48,050	**48,100**	11,208	9,438	11,982	10,231
48,100	**48,150**	11,225	9,452	11,998	10,245
48,150	**48,200**	11,241	9,466	12,015	10,259
48,200	**48,250**	11,258	9,480	12,031	10,273
48,250	**48,300**	11,274	9,494	12,048	10,287
48,300	**48,350**	11,291	9,508	12,064	10,301
48,350	**48,400**	11,307	9,522	12,081	10,315
48,400	**48,450**	11,324	9,536	12,097	10,329
48,450	**48,500**	11,340	9,550	12,114	10,343
48,500	**48,550**	11,357	9,564	12,130	10,357
48,550	**48,600**	11,373	9,578	12,147	10,371
48,600	**48,650**	11,390	9,592	12,163	10,385
48,650	**48,700**	11,406	9,606	12,180	10,399
48,700	**48,750**	11,423	9,620	12,196	10,413
48,750	**48,800**	11,439	9,634	12,213	10,427
48,800	**48,850**	11,456	9,648	12,229	10,441
48,850	**48,900**	11,472	9,662	12,246	10,455
48,900	**48,950**	11,489	9,676	12,262	10,469
48,950	**49,000**	11,505	9,690	12,279	10,483
49,000					
49,000	**49,050**	11,522	9,704	12,295	10,497
49,050	**49,100**	11,538	9,718	12,312	10,511
49,100	**49,150**	11,555	9,732	12,328	10,525
49,150	**49,200**	11,571	9,746	12,345	10,539
49,200	**49,250**	11,588	9,760	12,361	10,553
49,250	**49,300**	11,604	9,774	12,378	10,567
49,300	**49,350**	11,621	9,788	12,394	10,581
49,350	**49,400**	11,637	9,802	12,411	10,595
49,400	**49,450**	11,654	9,816	12,427	10,609
49,450	**49,500**	11,670	9,830	12,444	10,623
49,500	**49,550**	11,687	9,844	12,460	10,637
49,550	**49,600**	11,703	9,858	12,477	10,651
49,600	**49,650**	11,720	9,872	12,493	10,665
49,650	**49,700**	11,736	9,886	12,510	10,679
49,700	**49,750**	11,753	9,900	12,526	10,693
49,750	**49,800**	11,769	9,914	12,543	10,707
49,800	**49,850**	11,786	9,928	12,559	10,721
49,850	**49,900**	11,802	9,942	12,576	10,735
49,900	**49,950**	11,819	9,956	12,592	10,749
49,950	**50,000**	11,835	9,970	12,609	10,763

* This column must also be used by a qualifying widow(er).

50,000 or over—use tax rate schedules

APPENDIX 1-B

1989 Federal Income Tax Rate Schedules

Schedule X—For Unmarried Persons (Other Than Surviving Spouses and Heads of Households)

If Taxable Income Is:	The Tax Is:
Not over $18,550	15% of taxable income
Over $18,550 but not over $44,900	$2,782.50, plus 28% of the excess over $18,550
Over $44,900 but not over $93,130	$10,160.50, plus 33% of the excess over $44,900
$93,130 and over	28% of taxable income, plus lesser of (a) 28% times the total deduction for personal exemptions or (b) 5% times the taxable income in excess of $93,130.

Schedule Y-1—For Married Persons Filing Jointly or Qualifying Widow(er)

If Taxable Income Is:	The Tax Is:
Not over $30,950	15% of taxable income
Over $30,950 but not over $74,850	$4,642.50 plus 28% of the excess over $30,950
Over $74,850 but not over $155,320	$16,934.50 plus 33% of the excess over $74,850
$155,320 and over	28% of taxable income, plus lesser of (a) 28% times the total deduction for personal exemptions or (b) 5% times the taxable income in excess of $155,320

Schedule Y-2—For Married Individuals Filing Separately

If Taxable Income Is:	The Tax Is:
Not over $15,475	15% of taxable income
Over $15,475 but not over $37,425	$2,321.25 plus 28% of the excess over $15,475
Over $37,425 but not over $117,895	$8,467.25 plus 33% of the excess over $37,425
$117,895 and over	28% of taxable income, plus lesser of (a) 28% times the total deduction for personal exemptions or (b) 5% times the taxable income in excess of $117,895

Schedule Z— For Head of Household

If Taxable Income Is:	The Tax Is:
Not over $24,850	15% of taxable income
Over $24,850 but not over $64,200	$3,727.50 plus 28% of the excess over $24,850
Over $64,200 but not over $128,810	$14,745.50 plus 33% of the excess over $64,200
$128,810 and over	28% of taxable income, plus lesser of (a) 28% times the total deduction for personal exemptions or (b) 5% times the taxable income in excess of $128,810.

APPENDIX 1-C

1990 Federal Income Tax Rate Schedules

Schedule X—For Unmarried Persons (Other Than Surviving Spouses and Heads of Households)

If Taxable Income Is:	The Tax Is:
Not over $19,450	15% of taxable income
Over $19,450 but not over $47,050	$2,917.50, plus 28% of the excess over $19,450
Over $47,050 but not over $97,620	$10,645.50, plus 33% of the excess over $47,050
$97,620 and over	28% of taxable income, plus lesser of (a) 28% times the total deduction for personal exemptions or (b) 5% times the taxable income in excess of $97,620.

Schedule Y-1—For Married Persons Filing Jointly or Qualifying Widow(er)

If Taxable Income Is:	The Tax Is:
Not over $32,450	15% of taxable income
Over $32,450 but not over $78,400	$4,867.50 plus 28% of the excess over $32,450
Over $78,400 but not over $162,770	$17,733.50 plus 33% of the excess over $78,400
$162,770 and over	28% of taxable income, plus lesser of (a) 28% times the total deduction for personal exemptions or (b) 5% times the taxable income in excess of $162,770

Schedule Y-2—For Married Individuals Filing Separately

If Taxable Income Is:	The Tax Is:
Not over $16,225	15% of taxable income
Over $16,225 but not over $39,200	$2,433.75 plus 28% of the excess over $16,225
Over $39,200 but not over $123,570	$8,866.75 plus 33% of the excess over $39,200
$123,570 and over	28% of taxable income, plus lesser of (a) 28% times the total deduction for personal exemptions or (b) 5% times the taxable income in excess of $123,570

Schedule Z— For Head of Household

If Taxable Income Is:	The Tax Is:
Not over $26,050	15% of taxable income
Over $26,050 but not over $67,200	$3,907.50 plus 28% of the excess over $26,050
Over $67,200 but not over $134,930	$15,429.50 plus 33% of the excess over $67,200
$134,930 and over	28% of taxable income, plus lesser of (a) 28% times the total deduction for personal exemptions or (b) 5% times the taxable income in excess of $134,930.

APPENDIX 1-D (a)

Form **1040** Department of the Treasury—Internal Revenue Service
U.S. Individual Income Tax Return **1989**

For the year Jan.–Dec. 31, 1989, or other tax year beginning , 1989, ending , 19 OMB No. 1545-0074

Label

Use IRS label. Otherwise, please print or type.

LABEL HERE

Your first name and initial | Last name | **Your social security number**

If a joint return, spouse's first name and initial | Last name | **Spouse's social security number**

Home address (number and street). (If a P.O. box, see page 7 of Instructions.) | Apt. no.

City, town or post office, state and ZIP code. (If a foreign address, see page 7.)

For Privacy Act and Paperwork Reduction Act Notice, see Instructions.

Presidential Election Campaign
Do you want $1 to go to this fund? . . . . Yes No
If joint return, does your spouse want $1 to go to this fund? . Yes No
Note: *Checking "Yes" will not change your tax or reduce your refund.*

Filing Status

Check only one box.

1 ☐ Single
2 ☐ Married filing joint return (even if only one had income)
3 ☐ Married filing separate return. Enter spouse's social security no. above and full name here. ______
4 ☐ Head of household (with qualifying person). (See page 7 of Instructions.) If the qualifying person is your child but not your dependent, enter child's name here. ______
5 ☐ Qualifying widow(er) with dependent child (year spouse died ▶ 19). (See page 7 of Instructions.)

Exemptions

(See Instructions on page 8.)

6a ☐ **Yourself** If someone (such as your parent) can claim you as a dependent on his or her tax return, do not check box 6a. But be sure to check the box on line 33b on page 2 . .

b ☐ **Spouse** . . . .

No. of boxes checked on 6a and 6b ____

c **Dependents:**

(1) Name (first, initial, and last name)	(2) Check if under age 2	(3) If age 2 or older, dependent's social security number	(4) Relationship	(5) No. of months lived in your home in 1989

If more than 6 dependents, see Instructions on page 8.

No. of your children on 6c who:
- **lived with you** ____
- **didn't live with you due to divorce or separation (see page 9)** ____

No. of other dependents on 6c ____

d If your child didn't live with you but is claimed as your dependent under a pre-1985 agreement, check here ▶ ☐
e Total number of exemptions claimed . . . .

Add numbers entered on lines above ▶ ☐

Income

Please attach Copy B of your Forms W-2, W-2G, and W-2P here.

If you do not have a W-2, see page 6 of Instructions.

Please attach check or money order here.

7 Wages, salaries, tips, etc. *(attach Form(s) W-2)* 7
8a **Taxable** interest income *(also attach Schedule B if over $400)* 8a
b **Tax-exempt** interest income (see page 10). DON'T include on line 8a | 8b |
9 Dividend income *(also attach Schedule B if over $400)* 9
10 Taxable refunds of state and local income taxes, if any, from worksheet on page 11 of Instructions . . 10
11 Alimony received 11
12 Business income or (loss) *(attach Schedule C)*. 12
13 Capital gain or (loss) *(attach Schedule D)* 13
14 Capital gain distributions not reported on line 13 (see page 11) 14
15 Other gains or (losses) *(attach Form 4797)* 15
16a Total IRA distributions . . | 16a | 16b Taxable amount (see page 11) 16b
17a Total pensions and annuities | 17a | 17b Taxable amount (see page 12) 17b
18 Rents, royalties, partnerships, estates, trusts, etc. *(attach Schedule E)* 18
19 Farm income or (loss) *(attach Schedule F)* 19
20 Unemployment compensation (insurance) (see page 13) 20
21a Social security benefits. . | 21a | 21b Taxable amount (see page 13) 21b
22 Other income (list type and amount—see page 13) ______ 22
23 Add the amounts shown in the far right column for lines 7 through 22. This is your **total income** ▶ 23

Adjustments to Income

(See Instructions on page 14.)

24 Your IRA deduction, from applicable worksheet on page 14 or 15 | 24
25 Spouse's IRA deduction, from applicable worksheet on page 14 or 15 | 25
26 Self-employed health insurance deduction, from worksheet on page 15 | 26
27 Keogh retirement plan and self-employed SEP deduction . . | 27
28 Penalty on early withdrawal of savings . . . . | 28
29 Alimony paid. **a** Recipient's last name ______ and **b** social security number. . . | 29
30 Add lines 24 through 29. These are your **total adjustments** . . . . ▶ 30

Adjusted Gross Income

31 Subtract line 30 from line 23. This is your **adjusted gross income.** *If this line is less than $19,340 and a child lived with you, see "Earned Income Credit" (line 58) on page 20 of the Instructions. If you want IRS to figure your tax, see page 16 of the Instructions* . . . . ▶ 31

H732

Form 1040 (1989) Page **2**

Tax Computation

32 Amount from line 31 (adjusted gross income) . . . 32

33a Check if: ☐ **You** were 65 or older ☐ Blind; ☐ **Spouse** was 65 or older ☐ Blind.
Add the number of boxes checked and enter the total here . . . ▶ 33a

b If someone (such as your parent) can claim you as a dependent, check here . . ▶ 33b ☐

c If you are married filing a separate return and your spouse itemizes deductions, or you are a dual-status alien, see page 16 and check here . . . ▶ 33c ☐

34 Enter the **larger** of:
- Your **standard deduction** (from page 17 of the Instructions), **OR**
- Your **itemized deductions** (from Schedule A, line 26).

If you itemize, attach Schedule A and check here . . ▶ ☐ 34

35 Subtract line 34 from line 32. Enter the result here . . . 35

36 Multiply $2,000 by the total number of exemptions claimed on line 6e . . . 36

37 **Taxable income.** Subtract line 36 from line 35. Enter the result (if less than zero, enter zero) . . 37

Caution: If under age 14 and you have more than $1,000 of investment income, check here ▶ ☐ and see page 17 to see if you have to use Form 8615 to figure your tax.

38 Enter tax. Check if from: a ☐ Tax Table, b ☐ Tax Rate Schedules, or c ☐ Form 8615.
(If any is from Form(s) 8814, enter that amount here ▶ d ______ .) . . . 38

39 Additional taxes (see page 18). Check if from: a ☐ Form 4970 b ☐ Form 4972 . . . 39

40 Add lines 38 and 39. Enter the total . . . ▶ 40

Credits

(See Instructions on page 18.)

41 Credit for child and dependent care expenses *(attach Form 2441)* 41

42 Credit for the elderly or the disabled *(attach Schedule R)* . . . 42

43 Foreign tax credit *(attach Form 1116)* . . . 43

44 General business credit. Check if from:
a ☐ Form 3800 or b ☐ Form (specify) ______ . . . 44

45 Credit for prior year minimum tax *(attach Form 8801)* . . . 45

46 Add lines 41 through 45. Enter the total . . . 46

47 Subtract line 46 from line 40. Enter the result (if less than zero, enter zero) . . . ▶ 47

Other Taxes

(Including Advance EIC Payments)

48 Self-employment tax *(attach Schedule SE)* . . . 48

49 Alternative minimum tax *(attach Form 6251)* . . . 49

50 Recapture taxes (see page 18). Check if from: a ☐ Form 4255 b ☐ Form 8611 . . . 50

51 Social security tax on tip income not reported to employer *(attach Form 4137)* . . . 51

52 Tax on an IRA or a qualified retirement plan *(attach Form 5329)* . . . 52

53 Add lines 47 through 52. Enter the total . . . ▶ 53

Medicare Premium

54 Supplemental Medicare premium *(attach Form 8808)* . . . 54

55 Add lines 53 and 54. This is your **total tax** and any supplemental Medicare premium . . . ▶ 55

Payments

Attach Forms W-2, W-2G, and W-2P to front.

56 Federal income tax withheld (if any is from Form(s) 1099, check ▶ ☐) 56

57 1989 estimated tax payments and amount applied from 1988 return 57

58 Earned income credit (see page 20) . . . 58

59 Amount paid with Form 4868 (extension request) . . . 59

60 Excess social security tax and RRTA tax withheld (see page 20) 60

61 Credit for Federal tax on fuels *(attach Form 4136)* . . . 61

62 Regulated investment company credit *(attach Form 2439)* . . 62

63 Add lines 56 through 62. These are your **total payments** . . . ▶ 63

Refund or Amount You Owe

64 If line 63 is larger than line 55, enter amount **OVERPAID** . . . ▶ 64

65 Amount of line 64 to be **REFUNDED TO YOU** . . . ▶ 65

66 Amount of line 64 to be **APPLIED TO YOUR 1990 ESTIMATED TAX** ▶ 66

67 If line 55 is larger than line 63, enter **AMOUNT YOU OWE.** Attach check or money order for full amount payable to "Internal Revenue Service." Write your social security number, daytime phone number, and "1989 Form 1040" on it . . . 67

68 Penalty for underpayment of estimated tax (see page 21) . . . 68

Sign Here

(Keep a copy of this return for your records.)

Under penalties of perjury, I declare that I have examined this return and accompanying schedules and statements, and to the best of my knowledge and belief, they are true, correct, and complete. Declaration of preparer (other than taxpayer) is based on all information of which preparer has any knowledge.

Your signature	Date	Your occupation
Spouse's signature (if joint return, BOTH must sign)	Date	Spouse's occupation

Paid Preparer's Use Only

Preparer's signature	Date	Check if self-employed ☐	Preparer's social security no.
Firm's name (or yours if self-employed) and address		E.I. No.	
		ZIP code	

SCHEDULES A&B (Form 1040)
Department of the Treasury
Internal Revenue Service

Schedule A—Itemized Deductions

(Schedule B is on back)

▶ Attach to Form 1040. ▶ See Instructions for Schedules A and B (Form 1040).

OMB No. 1545-0074
1989
Attachment Sequence No. **07**

Name(s) shown on Form 1040 | **Your social security number**

Medical and Dental Expenses (Do not include expenses reimbursed or paid by others.) (See Instructions on page 23.)	**1a** Prescription medicines and drugs, insulin, doctors, dentists, nurses, hospitals, medical insurance premiums you paid, etc.	1a			
	b Other. (List—include hearing aids, dentures, eyeglasses, transportation and lodging, etc.) ▶	1b			
	2 Add the amounts on lines 1a and 1b. Enter the total here	2			
	3 Multiply the amount on Form 1040, line 32, by 7.5% (.075)	3			
	4 Subtract line 3 from line 2. If zero or less, enter -0-. **Total** medical and dental ▶			4	
Taxes You Paid (See Instructions on page 24.)	**5** State and local income taxes	5			
	6 Real estate taxes	6			
	7 Other taxes. (List—include personal property taxes.) ▶	7			
	8 Add the amounts on lines 5 through 7. Enter the total here. **Total** taxes ▶			8	
Interest You Paid (See Instructions on page 24.)	**9a** Deductible home mortgage interest (from Form 1098) that you paid to financial institutions. Report deductible points on line 10.	9a			
	b Other deductible home mortgage interest. (If paid to an individual, show that person's name and address.) ▶	9b			
	10 Deductible points. (See Instructions for special rules.)	10			
	11 Deductible investment interest. (See page 25.)	11			
	12a Personal interest you paid. (See page 25.) 12a				
	b Multiply the amount on line 12a by 20% (.20). Enter the result	12b			
	13 Add the amounts on lines 9a through 11, and 12b. Enter the total here. **Total** interest ▶			13	
Gifts to Charity (See Instructions on page 25.)	**14** Contributions by cash or check. (If you gave $3,000 or more to any one organization, show to whom you gave and how much you gave.) ▶	14			
	15 Other than cash or check. (You must attach Form 8283 if over $500.)	15			
	16 Carryover from prior year	16			
	17 Add the amounts on lines 14 through 16. Enter the total here. **Total** contributions ▶			17	
Casualty and Theft Losses	**18** Casualty or theft loss(es) (attach Form 4684). (See page 26 of the Instructions.) ▶			18	
Moving Expenses	**19** Moving expenses (attach Form 3903 or 3903F). (See page 26 of the Instructions.) ▶			19	
Job Expenses and Most Other Miscellaneous Deductions (See page 26 for expenses to deduct here.)	**20** Unreimbursed employee expenses—job travel, union dues, job education, etc. (You MUST attach Form 2106 in some cases. See Instructions.) ▶	20			
	21 Other expenses (investment, tax preparation, safe deposit box, etc.). List type and amount ▶	21			
	22 Add the amounts on lines 20 and 21. Enter the total.	22			
	23 Multiply the amount on Form 1040, line 32, by 2% (.02). Enter the result here	23			
	24 Subtract line 23 from line 22. Enter the result. If zero or less, enter -0-. ▶			24	
Other Miscellaneous Deductions	**25** Other (from list on page 26 of Instructions). List type and amount ▶			25	
Total Itemized Deductions	**26** Add the amounts on lines 4, 8, 13, 17, 18, 19, 24, and 25. Enter the total here. Then enter on Form 1040, line 34, the LARGER of this total or your standard deduction from page 17 of the Instructions ▶			26	

For Paperwork Reduction Act Notice, see Form 1040 Instructions. **Schedule A (Form 1040) 1989**

H732

APPENDIX 1-E

Abbreviated List of Items That Are Exclusions from Gross Income

Accident and disability benefits
Allowance for parsonage for clergy
Amounts received as an agent (note that this is income of the principal)
Amounts received under a worker's compensation act
Appreciation in value of property
Benefit payments to blind persons
Bequests
Board and lodging supplied by employer for employer's convenience
Bonus payments to ex-service personnel by the state
Campaign contributions
Certain death benefits received by beneficiary of an employee
Combat-related injuries
Contributions by employer to accident and health plans (e.g., hospitalization insurance)
Contributions to the capital of a corporation
Cost of living allowances to U.S. civilian employees outside the United States
Damages for personal injury or sickness
Educational assistance program payments
Employee stock-purchase plans
Employee achievement awards (limited)
Gifts
Group legal services plans
Group life insurance premiums paid by employer (limited)
Improvements made by lessee
Inheritance
Interest-free loans up to $10,000
Interest from state and local government bonds
Life insurance proceeds
Living expense reimbursements necessitated by fire or other casualty damage to taxpayer's home
Medical-care expense reimbursements
Mileage allowance to parents to transport children to school
Military disability pensions
Military moving expenses
Military mustering-out pay
Military reenlistment allowance
Repayment of principal on loan
Scholarships (limited)
Strike benefits
Supper money
Trade discounts
Unemployment training benefits
Welfare benefits (limited)

APPENDIX 1-F

Abbreviated List of Items That Are Included in Gross Income

Administrator's fees
Advances from:
  commissions
  fees
  rentals
  royalties
Alimony
Awards
Bank deposit interest
Bargain purchases from employer
Beneficiary's share of distributable net income of estate or trust
Bonuses
Business profits
Compensation for services rendered
Contest awards
Damages for employment discrimination
Damages for personal reputation
Death benefits over $5,000
Debt cancellations
Deposits on containers
Dismissal pay
Dividends
Embezzlement proceeds
Employee annuities
Executor's fees
Extortion proceeds
Fees for personal services
Fellowship grants
Gain from surrender of life insurance
Gambling gains
Gratuities
Honorarium
Interest (except on state and local bonds)
Jury fees
Mileage allowance
Overtime pay
Payment for agreement not to compete
Payoffs
Per diem allowance for expenses
Prizes won in contest
Profits from illegal businesses
Punitive damages
Reimbursement for moving expenses
Rent
Royalties
Salary
Sale of expected inheritance
Self-employment income
Severance pay
Suggestion awards
Tips
Trustee's fees
Vacation payments

APPENDIX 1-G

Abbreviated List of Items That Are Deductible as Itemized Deductions

Ambulance hire (limited)
Artificial limbs and teeth (limited)
Casualty damages (in excess of $100 and in excess of 10% of AGI)
Contributions to charitable organizations
Dental expenses (limited)
Diagnosis fees (limited)
Education expenses (some)
Employee business expenses (limited)
Eye examination expenses (limited)
Fees paid for income tax return preparation (limited)
Fire loss (limited, see casualty damages, above)
Flood loss (limited, see casualty damages, above)
Gambling losses (to the extent of gambling gains, but limited)
Health and accident insurance premiums (limited)
Hearing devices (limited)
Income tax (state and local)
Interest on mortgage of personal residence
Interest on personal (consumer) loans (limited)
Interest (except interest incurred to produce tax-free income)
Investment advice fees (limited)
Medical fees (limited)
Prescription drugs (limited)
Property taxes
Safe deposit box used to store income-producing assets (e.g., bonds) (limited)
Safety equipment required on the job (limited)
State and local property taxes
Tax return preparation fees (limited)
Theft losses (limited, see casualty damages, above)
Transportation costs in connection with medical treatment (limited)
Union dues (limited)
Work clothing not appropriate for street wear (limited)

1989 Schedule 1 (Form 1040A)

OMB No. 1545-0085

Name(s) shown on Form 1040A | Your social security number

You MUST complete and attach Schedule 1 to Form 1040A only if you:

- Claim the credit for child and dependent care expenses (complete **Part I**)
- Received employer-provided dependent care benefits (complete **Part I**)
- Have over $400 of taxable interest income (complete **Part II**)
- Have over $400 of dividend income (complete **Part III**)

Part I

Child and dependent care expenses (see page 32 of the instructions)

- If you are claiming the child and dependent care credit, complete lines 1 through 12 below. But if you received employer-provided dependent care benefits, first complete lines 13 through 20 on the back.
- If you are not claiming the credit but you received employer-provided dependent care benefits, only complete lines 1 and 2, below, and lines 13 through 20 on the back.

Note: *If you paid cash wages of $50 or more in a calendar quarter to an individual for services performed in your home, you must file an employment tax return. Get* ***Form 942*** *for details.*

1 Persons or organizations who provided the care. You MUST complete lines 1 and 2. (See page 33.)

a. Name	b. Address (number, street, city, state, and ZIP code)	c. Identification number (SSN or EIN)	d. Amount paid (see instructions)

(If you need more space, attach schedule.)

2 Add the amounts in column d of line 1 and enter the total. 2

3 Enter the number of qualifying persons who were cared for in 1989. You must have shared the same home with the qualifying person(s). (See the instructions for the definition of a qualifying person.) 3

Note: *See the instructions to find out which expenses qualify.*

4 Enter the amount of **qualified** expenses you incurred and actually paid in 1989. See the instructions for the amount to enter. DO NOT ENTER MORE THAN $2,400 ($4,800 if you paid for the care of two or more qualifying persons). 4

5 Enter the **excluded benefits,** if any, from line 19 on the back. 5

6 Subtract line 5 from line 4. Enter the result. If line 5 is equal to or more than line 4, STOP HERE; you cannot claim the credit. 6

7 You **must** enter your **earned income.** (See page 34 of the instructions for the definition of earned income.) 7

8 If you are married filing a joint return, you **must** enter your spouse's earned income. (If spouse was a full-time student or disabled, see the instructions for the amount to enter.) 8

9 If you are married filing a joint return, compare the amounts on lines 7 and 8. Enter the **smaller** of the two amounts here. 9

10 • If you are married filing a joint return, compare the amounts on lines 6 and 9. Enter the **smaller** of the two amounts here.
• All others, compare the amounts on lines 6 and 7. Enter the **smaller** of the two amounts here. 10

11 Enter the decimal amount from the table below that applies to the amount on Form 1040A, line 14.

If line 14 is: Over—	But not over—	Decimal amount is:	If line 14 is: Over—	But not over—	Decimal amount is:
$0	10,000	.30	$20,000	22,000	.24
10,000	12,000	.29	22,000	24,000	.23
12,000	14,000	.28	24,000	26,000	.22
14,000	16,000	.27	26,000	28,000	.21
16,000	18,000	.26	28,000		.20
18,000	20,000	.25			

11 ×

12 Multiply the amount on line 10 by the decimal amount on line 11. Enter the result here and on Form 1040A, line 21. 12 =

1989 Schedule 1 (Form 1040A)

OMB No. 1545-0085

Name(s) shown on Form 1040A. (Do not complete if shown on other side.) | Your social security number

Part I (continued)

Complete lines 13 through 20 only if you received employer-provided dependent care benefits. Be sure to also complete lines 1 and 2 of Part I.

13 Enter the total amount of employer-provided dependent care benefits you received for 1989. (This amount should be separately shown on your W-2 form(s) and labeled as "DCB.") DO NOT include amounts that were reported to you as wages in Box 10 of Form(s) W-2. 13

14 Enter the total amount of **qualified** expenses incurred in 1989 for the care of a qualifying person. (See page 34 of the instructions.) 14

15 Compare the amounts on lines 13 and 14. Enter the **smaller** of the two amounts here. 15

16 You **must** enter your **earned income.** (See page 34 of the instructions for the definition of earned income.) 16

17 If you were married at the end of 1989, you **must** enter your spouse's earned income. (If your spouse was a full-time student or disabled, see page 34 of the instructions for the amount to enter.) 17

18
- If you were married at the end of 1989, compare the amounts on lines 16 and 17 and enter the **smaller** of the two amounts here.
- If you were unmarried, enter the amount from line 16 here. 18

Note: *If you are also claiming the child and dependent care credit, first fill in Form 1040A through line 20. Then complete lines 3-12 of Part I.*

19 Excluded benefits. Enter here the **smallest** of the following:
- The amount from line 15, or
- The amount from line 18, or
- $5,000 ($2,500 if married filing a separate return). 19

20 Taxable benefits. Subtract line 19 from line 13. Enter the result. (If zero or less, enter -0-.) Include this amount in the total on Form 1040A, line 7. In the space to the left of line 7, write "DCB." 20

Part II

Interest Income (see page 24 of the instructions)

Complete this part and attach Schedule 1 to Form 1040A if you received over $400 in taxable interest.

Note: *If you received a Form 1099-INT or Form 1099-OID from a brokerage firm, enter the firm's name and the total interest shown on that form.*

1 List name of payer		Amount
	1	
2 Add amounts on line 1. Enter the total here and on Form 1040A, line 8a.	2	

Part III

Dividend Income (see page 24 of the instructions)

Complete this part and attach Schedule 1 to Form 1040A if you received over $400 in dividends.

Note: *If you received a Form 1099-DIV from a brokerage firm, enter the firm's name and the total dividends shown on that form.*

1 List name of payer		Amount
	1	
2 Add amounts on line 1. Enter the total here and on Form 1040A, line 9.	2	

*U.S. GOVERNMENT PRINTING OFFICE: 1989 245-151

2

income

> Minimizing tax liability involves some combination of maximizing exclusions from gross income, maximizing deductions *for* adjusted gross income, maximizing itemized deductions, maximizing personal exemptions, using the most advantageous tax table, and taking all available tax credits.
> —Chapter 1

This chapter concentrates on recognizing what is and what is not required to be included in gross income and on the effort to plan to maximize exclusions from gross income. This effort involves, first, gaining an understanding of the concept of income on which income taxes are based. Then we survey the various sorts of receipts besides "wages, salaries, tips, and other employee compensation" that the tax law requires to be included as income. Finally, we see what can be excluded from gross income, noting throughout the choices that an individual can make to maximize these exclusions. A glance at Form 1040, lines 7 through 23 [Appendix 1-D(a)], will reveal some of the items that are included in gross income. Appendix 1-E is a partial list of exclusions from gross income.

WHAT IS INCOME?

Everybody uses the word "income," but they do not all mean the same. What one economist means by income may be different from what another economist means; and probably neither of them would mean the same as an accountant would mean. Sections 2.1 through 2.3 of this chapter review these different approaches to defining income.

In taxation, income is what it is made to be, like sausage. What you get in the sausage casing depends on what you feed into the grinder. The ingredients, and their proportions, can vary from batch to batch. In the same way, the items that are put into income and left out of it for tax purposes change as new statutes are passed by Congress, interpreted by the U.S. Treasury Department and its collection arm, the Internal Revenue Service, and modified by hundreds of court decisions each year. Section 2.4 picks up the discussion of the tax concept of income. If you have a fair idea of the meaning of "income" in economics and in accounting, you can skip 2.1 through 2.3 and go directly to 2.4.

2.1 An Economist's Concept of Income—Changes in Net Worth

A widely accepted definition of income among economists is: the amount of money that could be consumed by an individual, or distributed by a business to its owners, and still leave the person or the business as well off financially at the end of the year as at the beginning. If a person has no debts and $10,000 in cash on January 1, spends $15,000 during the year for consumption, and has a total of $13,000 in cash and no debts on December 31, what is income for the year? A net worth increase of $3,000, plus consumption of $15,000, means that income must have been $18,000, using that definition of "income."

2.2 Another Economist's Concept of Income—Consumption

At the opposite pole in economic theory from the net worth approach to income is an approach emphasizing "satisfaction" or "consumption." Money is viewed as merely a convenient mechanism for allocation of real wealth. The amount spent on consumer goods and services is the amount of real wealth actually consumed and hence is a person's income. (To this must be added the value of *using* durable goods that are owned. Thus, not the purchase, but the use, of a house or a car would be income.) The source of what is spent is immaterial. Because a business cannot consume anything (for all its size, General Motors cannot even eat a toasted cheese sandwich), only people have income under such a definition.

In a consumption approach, if the year was started with $10,000 net worth, represented by cash in the bank, there is $13,000 of salary, and net worth is a $13,000 bank account at year end, consumption *expenditures* must have been $10,000. If the fair rental value of the owner-occupied home was an additional $4,000, "income" under this approach was $14,000.

2.3 The Accountant's Concept of Income

The problem of determining income exists entirely independently of tax considerations.

Some concept of income must be agreed upon whenever two or more people join together to conduct any enterprise for profit. In a simple, one-shot venture, the problem is not acute. If X and Y pool their resources, rent an empty lot in early December, buy some Christmas trees, and burn whatever trees remain on January 2, they can figure their profit quite easily on January 2. Theirs is a self-liquidating venture. They start with cash and end with cash. But few modern businesses are one-shot endeavors.

A one-sentence definition of *income,* as the financial accountant might see it, would probably be something like this: Income for a period is the excess of the consideration received, in completed transactions involving the furnishing of goods or services, over the sum of (1) the costs of the assets consumed in providing those goods or rendering those services and (2) any losses sustained during that period. Losses, in this context, would be the using up of assets without the receipt of a full consideration, as, for instance, through a fire that was only partially compensated by insurance.

The financial accountant's concept of income differs substantially from the economist's. The economist deals with value, which is essentially a speculation about the *future.* The concern is with the ways of allocating scarce resources. Money is used as a measure of value. The accountant deals with transactions and events that have occurred. Thus, financial accountants deal with the *past.* Money is used as a symbol. Money (dollars in the case of the United States) provides the accountant with a common denominator for the diverse components of transactions.

The financial accountant is concerned with measuring the flow of transactions through the individual enterprise. The objective is to reflect fairly the contractual rights of the various claimants to income and assets, so that those who are responsible for the assets of the firm can report on the performance of their stewardship. This is not all of modern accounting, but this aspect of accounting, as ancient in its origin as the separation of ownership and control, still underlies the concepts employed by practicing accountants.

Let us contrast the net worth approach of the economist and the transactional approach of the accountant. A factory building is purchased at a cost of $110,000, including $100,000 for the building itself and $10,000 for the land on which it stands. In the accountant's symbolism, one building equals $100,000; land equals $10,000. When half the utility of the building (based on estimates of useful life) has been used, the accountant's symbolism might show: one-half building equals $50,000; land equals $10,000. Note that the $10,000 representing the land has not been changed because land is not consumed.

By this time, the fair market value of the building may be $70,000 and that of the land $40,000. To date, however, accountants in the United States have not made it a general practice to measure and account for current market value or replacement cost, and thus this information would not affect the primary financial statements.

If the property is sold for $100,000, the economist might say that before the sale the property had a value of $110,000, whereas after the sale there was only $100,000, and therefore a loss of $10,000 was sustained. The accountant, however, deals with the symbols derived from the original transactions—not with the constantly changing values. The transaction would be reported as $50,000 (one-half building) plus $10,000 (land) exchanged for $100,000 cash, resulting in a gain of $40,000.

This "historical cost" concept used by most accountants can be contrasted with a "future cost" concept opined by other accountants. Under the latter notion, the building, in our example, represents some capacity for production of goods and services in the future. Therefore, the theory goes, what should be accounted for is the expected cost needed to replace that building when it is no longer physically or technologically capable of providing the productive capacity. Such a theory contains, in part, an idea that one of the goals of conducting business currently, is to provide for replacement of the capacity to continue to conduct that business in the future.

Because the accountant deals with transactions, not with speculative values, the records will report *the transaction* of purchasing the property. A derivative of the original transaction is the necessity of recording the periodic expiration of part of the cost of the building, since the original transaction included an expenditure of $100,000 for the use of a building for an estimated number of years. Except for recording the periodic estimated consumption of the building (depreciation), the accountant's record is unaffected by happenings that were not transactions—that did not involve exchanges between the particular accounting entity and the outside world. Thus, the changing property values will not have been recorded because they were not evidenced by any such transactions. Finally, when a sale occurs, its effect is measured relative to the previous transactions. Thus, the flow of transactions, rather than value changes, is measured. At any time, the financial records also allow management to fulfill its stewardship function. The responsibility, assumed as the result of the basic transaction, was to account for one building plus some land. From this point of view, the fluctuating values of land and building were irrelevant. However, once the land and building were disposed of, a new accountibility—for purchasing power or cash—was created.

It should be noted that in this "historical cost" use of money as a symbol, the fact that a dollar at one point in time does not equal a dollar at another point in time disturbs many accountants. Although they would retain the use of the dollar as a symbol, some would like to adjust the dollar to represent a more constant common denominator. To date, such adjustments for the changing purchasing power of the dollar have been mostly experimental or supplemental. In the preceding chapter, we mentioned three such changes, based on the Consumer Price Index, that are now part of the tax rules: annual changes in (1) the exemption amount, (2) the standard deduction, and (3) the amount of taxable income to which different rates of tax apply.

2.4 Tax Concept of Income

The tax concept of income is a result of the pressure of administrators toward specific, workable rules and of taxpayer groups toward special treatment for themselves and their problems. The tax law adopts the accountant's transactional approach for the determination of taxable income. This means that revenue and expenses are to be determined on the basis of completed transactions between a taxpayer and an outside party. Increments in value not realized through transactions are not income. Declines in value, not actually sustained as losses through transactions or other readily identifiable events, are not deductible.

Even though the tax law's approach is essentially the transactional approach of the accountant, there are numerous differences between accounting concepts of income and tax concepts of income. In fact, much of this book—indeed, much of the study of taxation—is devoted to the study of the areas where commercial accounting and tax accounting do not coincide. The reason is that those responsible for creating tax rules and those responsible for creating accounting rules are different groups with different goals.

Added to the transactional approach to taxes in the United States is a basic point of view: All inflows of assets, except to the extent of recoveries of amounts invested, constitute income unless the law specifically provides otherwise. Similarly, no outflows or consumption of assets result in deductions unless specifically authorized by the law. This view places the burden of proof on the taxpayer to show that he or she is entitled to exclude from income something that has been received. It also requires the taxpayer to prove that he or she is entitled to any deductions that are claimed.

The excess of includable income over allowable deductions, then, constitutes taxable income. Taxable income is thus whatever the Congress says it is; or whatever the administrators say that Congress said or intended to say; or whatever the courts say the Constitution, rules of judicial construction of statutes, and requirements for protection of the revenue may finally determine it to be. Hence, we say that tax law originates in all three branches of government: the legislative, the administrative, and the judiciary.

2.5 Income versus Inheritance

The tax law could impose an income tax on the value of inherited property, but it does not.[1] It does impose an estate tax at the time somebody dies—and this is discussed in Chapter 15.[2] The tax

[1]IRC Sec. 102.

[2]IRC Sec. 2001(a). The tax is an excise tax on the transfer of property.

must be paid by the estate so that the amount received by the heirs is only after-tax amounts. Generally, the federal estate tax calculation begins with the value of all assets owned by a person at the time of his or her death.[3] The income tax, on the other hand, is levied annually and levied upon the income from property, or the gain from its disposition, but not on the property itself.[4] Of course, other income is taxed also, such as salaries for personal services rendered.

If a person inherits $200,000 from a relative, the $200,000 is not income to the heir. If a person receives $12,000 of interest income from investing the $200,000, the $12,000 is part of gross income.[5] (The $12,000 interest is not subject to tax, of course, if the investment is in state or local government bonds.)[6]

2.6 Income versus Gift

Gifts, like inheritances, are not income subject to income tax.[7] They may result in gift tax, as discussed in Chapter 15, but as a general rule the gift tax is upon the donor (the giver) rather than upon the donee.[8] It is, however, sometimes not too easy to tell what is and what is not a gift.

One such classic question arises when a parent transfers certain kinds of property to a child. It is generally regarded as part of the parental responsibility to furnish a dependent child with transportation for school, entertainment, etc. When a child obtains a driver's license and the parent purchases a very expensive sports car for the child, the question arises as to whether the parent has made a gift or is merely continuing to provide normal support in a different way. Income would not result to the child in any event. But change the facts. A corporation gives a car to a person who referred a large customer. Gift? Income? Since the "gift" was a reward for a service rendered, it would likely be held to be income, even though the corporation never agreed in advance to pay anything and even though the individual had no expectation of reward when he made the referral.[9]

2.7 Return of Capital

If one person loans another $10,000 and is repaid $10,800 at a later date, only the $800 difference (interest) is includable in gross income. If stock in a corporation is purchased for $10,000 and is later sold for $10,800, only the $800 (gain) is includable in gross income. If a retail merchant buys an item of inventory for $600 and later sells it for $1,000, there is $400 of income. The $600 "cost of goods sold" is a return of capital.

Although the idea that a person is entitled to a tax-free return of capital seems straightforward in such a situation, there are other applications of the same basic idea that are somewhat more complicated. The taxation of annuities, discussed later in this chapter, is one example. Another is the discussion, in Chapter 9, of how the tax law allows capital recovery on long-lived assets that are consumed with the passage of time (depreciation).

INCOME INCLUSIONS

2.8 Compensation

Whether paid in cash or in property, the general rule is that compensation for services is taxable.[10] This includes such items as wages, commissions, fees, and tips. The two questions are normally "when" and "how much." If certain conditions or restrictions are attached to the property, taxability normally occurs when the conditions are removed. The amount taxable is normally the fair market value at the time "when" it is taxable.[11] Thus, an executive may receive stock of the corporate employer as a bonus, but subject to forfeiture if employment does not continue for three more years. The *general rule* is that the employee is taxed only at the end of the three years, and the amount taxable is the value of the stock at the end of the three years.

If an employee does not have to wait in order to acquire ownership rights to noncash compensation, the amount of income is the fair market value of the asset received. For example, if an employee were paid $20,000 cash salary and were given a piece of property worth $5,000, his or her gross income would be $25,000. If the employee paid $1,000 for the property, the additional gross income would be the bargain element, $4,000. Also, the noncash compensation can be in the form of a benefit other than property. For example, an employee has gross income equal to the fair rental

[3]IRC Sec. 2031(a).
[4]IRC Sec. 61.
[5]IRC Secs. 102(b) and 61(a)(4).
[6]IRC Sec. 103. As will be explained in Sec. 2.28 of this chapter, otherwise tax-exempt interest income will, in some cases, cause part of social security receipts to be subject to taxation.
[7]IRC Sec. 102(a).
[8]IRC Sec. 2501(a).
[9]*Comm.* v. *Duberstein* (S. Ct. 1960), 363 U.S. 278, 60-2 USTC 9515, 5 AFTR2d 1626.

[10]Treas. Reg. 1.61-2(d).
[11]IRC Sec. 83. This section taxes the bargain element when property is transferred in exchange for services. However, its use by a taxpayer can have favorable tax consequences even when there is no bargain element in the transfer. See *Alves*, 79 TC No. 55.

value of an automobile where an employer provides the employee with an automobile that is used by the employee for personal (nonbusiness) purposes. (An example of the calculation of the fair rental value of an employer's car used by an employee is discussed later at section 2.24.) Employee fringe benefits that can be excluded from gross income are discussed later in this chapter.

Persons other than employees are subject to receipt of compensation that is includable in gross income. For example, prizes and awards are included in gross income.[12] Thus, a contestant on a TV quiz program is required to include in gross income the fair market value of items won in the contest. Note the difference between this situation and a gift, discussed earlier.

One apparently widespread, but erroneous, belief among U.S. taxpayers is that no gross income results for tax purposes from "bartering." Bartering is the exchange of goods or services for other goods or services with no cash involved. For example, assume a mechanic repairs the automobile for a house painter in exchange for which the painter paints the mechanic's house. Both are required to report income for tax purposes. The mechanic's income is the fair market value of the paint job on his house. The painter's income is the fair market value of the mechanical services received. They may agree that these two sets of services are of equal value, but such an agreement does not necessarily determine the values, or make them equal. For example, they might agree that the two services are of equal value and are $100 each, perhaps because the services are performed during hours when they would not otherwise be working. If, in fact, the mechanic would normally charge $1,000 for the repair work on the car, and the painter would charge $1,200 for painting the house, then the mechanic's income is $1,200 and the painter's income is $1,000.

Some people apparently attempt to justify a different tax result by claiming they have made a gift of goods or services and then received a gift of goods or services from the other party. This concept is erroneous because a gift, by definition, cannot be made if there is commitment or expectation for receipt of goods or services *in return.* (For more on the matter of what constitutes a gift, see Chapter 15.)

2.9 Deferred Compensation

If income tax can be avoided currently, it is possible to invest with before-tax dollars rather than with after-tax dollars. That, in turn, should produce a larger investment fund at some point in the future. That is part of the rationale for many types of deferred-compensation agreements between employers and employees. There is another advantage to deferred compensation. If the tax is expected to be lower in the future, which may be the case if the future total income per year will be less, an employee can avoid present tax at high rates in exchange for future taxation at lower rates. Chapter 18 discusses this topic. The basic income questions as to deferred compensation remain "when" and "how much."

For example, assume that a corporation's financial vice-president has negotiated an agreement whereby her employer pays her $10,000 per year less than it otherwise would. Assume that the $10,000 is invested by the employer and it is recorded as a liability to her on the corporate books. The earnings on those investments are similarly credited as owed to her. The balance due her will be paid when she terminates employment or retires. Assume that she is in a 33% tax bracket and that investments will earn 9% before tax. She will receive $557,645 before tax, or $373,622 after tax twenty years hence. If the $10,000 were taxable each year, there would be only $6,700 to invest. In addition, the earnings from the investment would be taxed, resulting in a slower growth. (An earnings rate of 9% before federal income tax equals 6% after-tax if the taxpayer is in the 33% bracket.) Thus, the accumulation at the end of the same period of time would be $261,251. The deferral increases her after-tax yield by $112,371, which is 30%.

TAX PLANNING TIP: A corporate executive might be able to negotiate for a deferred compensation plan and keep total compensation at an acceptable level but reduce income tax. A corporation might be able to acquire the services of an employee with less in cash payments if there is an attractive deferred-compensation plan that is acceptable to the employee.

2.10 Sales and Taxable Exchanges

Chapter 5 discusses the tax treatment of gains on the sale or exchange of property. In taxable exchanges of property, the value of property received is treated as part of the proceeds of sale in calculating gain. Since most property has involved an investment, a taxpayer is allowed to recover that investment tax-free—and only the gain on the sale will be subject to tax. For example, if Billy Barnes

[12] IRC Sec. 74.

purchased a piece of raw land for $6,000 and later exchanged the land for $2,000 cash and a sports car valued at $7,000, Billy's gain would be $3,000, all includable in gross income. There are special rules for determining gain or loss from the sale of property acquired by gift or inheritance. These will be discussed in Chapter 5.

2.11 Rents and Royalties

Rental income, royalty income, and other amounts received for the use of property are part of gross income.[13] However, there has usually been an investment made in property. If the property will be consumed through time or usage, a deduction for part of the investment is allowed in figuring taxable income. Thus, rent received from a vacant lot would not involve any consumption of the property. Income would not be reduced by depreciation. Rent from a warehouse would be reduced by depreciation because the warehouse will wear out eventually.[14] Capital recovery is discussed in Chapter 9. It is a terminological oddity in the tax rules that the recovery of an investment in property that is sold is an exclusion from income, whereas the periodic recovery (depreciation) of property that is used in business is a deduction.

2.12 Dividends

Dividends are includable in income to the extent that they are paid out of a corporation's current or accumulated earnings.[15] If dividends are not out of earnings, then they are out of capital and are treated by the taxpayer receiving them as a partial recovery of the investment. Once the investment in the stock is fully recovered in this way, additional dividends not from earnings will be treated as the proceeds of a partial sale of the stock.

Note that so-called dividends on insurance policies issued by mutual insurance companies are not dividends for tax purposes. These are refunds of premiums paid on the related policies and, hence, are totally excluded from income. The payment of such premiums is not a deduction to the policy owner.

For example, assume that Billy Barnes decided to purchase a life insurance contract from a mutual insurance company. For the stated coverage, Billy paid premiums of $1,000 each year.

[13]IRC Secs. 61(a)(5) and 61(a)(6).

[14]Depreciation deductions are allowed by IRC Sec. 167 for property placed in service before 1981 and by IRC Sec. 168 for property placed in service after 1980. See Chapter 9.

[15]Dividends are defined by IRC Sec. 316.

These payments are not deductible. After five years Billy receives a check marked "dividends" from the insurance company in the amount of $250. This is not gross income, but a return of part of the premiums previously paid. Thus, Billy's cost for the insurance for the five-year period has been $4,750, not $5,000.

Note also that "dividends" paid to depositors by mutual savings banks, some savings and loan associations, and credit unions are not dividends for income tax purposes. They constitute interest income to the depositor.

If a stockholder receives additional shares (stock dividend) and does not have an option to receive cash, there is no income. On the other hand, if a stockholder has the option of receiving cash or additional stock as a dividend, the stock dividend will be taxable.[16] The amount of the dividend will be the fair market value of the stock.

For example, assume that Billy Barnes owns 1,000 of National Chewing Gum, Inc. (NCG) common stock. NCG has a 10% stock dividend, and Billy receives 100 new shares, with no alternative to receive cash or any other property instead. Billy has no gross income. On the other hand, if Billy had been given an alternative of receiving 100 additional shares or $700 in cash, there would have been $700 of additional gross income regardless of which alternative was selected.

TAX PLANNING TIP: An investor should consider purchasing stocks that will grow in value without producing dividend income. The goal might be to invest in a company that has growth potential by reinvesting its earnings rather than paying the earnings out as dividends. Thus, the taxpayer could gain some control over the timing of payment of tax by deciding whether to sell the stock or not. Sale of stock in a year of lower total taxable income could result in less tax.

2.13 Interest

Interest income is subject to tax whether received on a bank account, a corporate bond, a personal note, or a U.S. or foreign government note or bond. Generally, interest on bonds issued by a state or local government (so-called "municipal interest") is not taxable.[17]

[16]IRC Sec. 305(a), (b).

[17]IRC Sec. 103.

Interest is taxable when available to the taxpayer, even though not actually withdrawn.[18] Some discount obligations produce interest that is taxable when the bond matures—a major exception being U.S. discount savings bonds, the interest on which is taxable when the bond matures *unless* the taxpayer elects otherwise.[19]

There is sometimes confusion over the taxability of interest on federal government bonds because such interest is not subject to state income tax. It is only interest on *state or local* bonds that is excluded from federal income tax.

There is one special, and new, exception to the general rule that interest received from the federal government must be included in gross income. This change was included as part of the Technical and Miscellaneous Revenue Act of 1988.[19a] Starting in 1990, some individuals will be able to exclude from gross income some interest received on "qualified United States savings bonds." Such bonds must have been issued after 12-31-89, issued at a discount (e.g., Series EE bonds), and purchased by a person who was at least age 24 at the time of the purchase. In order to obtain an exclusion for the entire amount of the interest on the redemption of the bonds, the owner must spend, during that same year, an amount equal to the redemption price for "qualified higher education expenses" (tuition and fees). Such expenses must be for the taxpayer, the taxpayer's spouse, or someone who is a dependent of the taxpayer. The exclusion will not be available to someone who did not purchase the bonds. Thus, if the bond owner received the bonds as a gift, there can be no interest exclusion. Also, the amount of the exclusion is phased-down when adjusted gross income exceeds a certain level. That level is $40,000 for single persons (including head of household) and $60,000 for married persons who file jointly. The exclusion is not available for married persons who file separately.

This federal bond interest exclusion rule can be explained with some examples:

Example 1: Fred and Wilma, both age 40, purchased qualified bonds at the time their daughter, Pebbles, was age 10. When Pebbles is 18 (but still their dependent) and a college student, they redeem the bonds for $5,000, which includes interest income of $2,200. During that year they spend $6,000 for qualified college tuition and fees. Their adjusted gross income is $50,000. The entire $2,200 of interest is excluded from their gross income.

Example 2: Same facts as in Example 1 above, except that Fred and Wilma spend $4,500 on qualified college tuition and fees. Since their expenditures are less than the *proceeds* from the bond redemption, only part of the $2,200 interest income can be excluded. The portion excluded is determined by the fraction:

$$\frac{\text{Qualified education expenses paid during the year}}{\text{Total redemption proceeds for the year}} =$$

$$\frac{\$4{,}500}{\$5{,}000} = 90\% \text{ (excluded interest)}$$

Thus, 90% of the $2,200 interest income can be excluded and 10% will be included in gross income for federal tax purposes.

Example 3: Same facts as in Example 1 above, except that Fred and Wilma have adjusted gross income (AGI) of $64,000. Because AGI is "excess," i.e., over $60,000 for a married couple filing jointly, the phase-down begins.

Excess AGI is $4,000. The phase-down occurs over a range of $30,000 (for a joint return). Thus, there will be no exclusion if AGI is $90,000 or more. The fractional part of the interest that cannot be excluded is the "excess AGI" divided by the $30,000. Thus:

$$\frac{\text{“Excess AGI”}}{\$30{,}000} = \frac{\$4{,}000}{\$30{,}000} = 13.33\%$$

(Note that this formula results in the amount of the interest that must be *included* in gross income.) Therefore, 13.33% of the exclusion is lost. The result is that the exclusion is $1,907, which is 86.67% of the $2,200 interest received. Gross income will include $293, which is 13.33% of the $2,200 interest received.

For single taxpayers, the phase-down of the exclusion not only begins at $40,000 instead of $60,000, but the range over which it occurs is $15,000 rather than $30,000. Thus, if a single person had AGI of $45,000 (excess AGI of $5,000), then 1/3 of the interest would be subject to tax and 2/3 would still be excluded. (This assumes, of course, that there is no further reduction in the exclusion as the result of not spending an amount equal to or greater than the proceeds for college tuition and fees.)

TAX PLANNING TIP: The interest exclusion for qualified U.S. savings bond interest is available only to the owner of such bonds who was also the over-age-23 purchaser. Therefore, anyone who will not be eligible to claim the college student as a dependent but who wishes to provide money for future college expenses should not buy bonds and give them to the child. Neither should he give

[18] A cash-basis taxpayer may be required to include in gross income certain amounts not actually received if the money or property was available to the taxpayer "merely for the asking." This is known as the doctrine of "constructive receipt."

[19] IRC Sec. 454. Series EE federal bonds, for example, are purchased at a discount. The government does not pay interest periodically, but the maturity value (face) exceeds the issue price.

[19a] IRC Sec. 135

cash to the child who in turn would purchase his or her own bonds, unless he or she has reached the age of 24. Instead, money can be given to the parents (or whoever else will be able to claim the dependency exemption) who in turn can purchase the qualified bonds and redeem them in the year when money is spent on college tuition and fees.

A lender may have interest income even if no interest is actually received. This results from rules that tax the economic advantages of low or no-interest loans and other forms of bargain financing. If a bargain loan is between family members, the lender will be considered to have made a taxable gift (see Chapter 15) equal to the amount of the "imputed" interest on the loan. Second, the lender is considered to have interest income equal to the "imputed" interest. Third, the borrower is considered to have interest expense of an amount equal to the "imputed" interest.[20] There are exceptions to the above rules, the most useful being that interest will not be imputed if the total loans between the borrower and lender do not exceed $10,000 on any one day. Similar rules will also apply to debt obligations issued at a discount (original issue discount).[21]

The imputed interest rate will be the rate of interest that the U.S. government pays in order to borrow money. Where the loan is made at an interest rate that is lower than that which the government pays to borrow, the imputed interest is the difference between the federal rate and the amount charged by the lender to the family member borrower.

For example, assume that Billy Barnes loans a friend, Lynn Larsen, $20,000 for one year and does not charge any interest. If the applicable rate that the U.S. government is paying at that time is 12%, then the imputed interest on Billy's loan will be 12%. Thus, Billy will have interest income of $2,400. The interest is actually compounded semiannually, but we use a simple interest calculation here. If Billy charged Lynn at least 12%, then there would be no imputed interest. If Billy charged Lynn only 8%, for example, then Billy would have income of $1,600 for the actual interest received plus $800 of imputed interest income. Lynn may or may not have a deduction for interest paid. The deduction depends upon the purpose of the loan. Deductions are discussed in Chapter 4.

[20]IRC Sec. 7872.
[21]IRC Sec. 1272.

2.14 Alimony, Child Support, and Property Settlements

1Alimony or separate maintenance payments must be included in the gross income of the recipient and are deductible by the payor.[22] But what is alimony for income tax purposes? The answer depends on whether the divorce settlement was reached before 1985 or after 1984. First, consider the rules which apply where the settlement was reached before 1985.

Alimony is *not* child support. For example, if a father is required to provide $300 per month as child support payments to his ex-wife, that $300 is not income to her because it is not alimony. Amounts that a divorce decree or related instrument or agreement specify as child support are not includable in the income of the recipient. On the other hand, such payments are not deductible, as such, by the payor. However, child-support payments are counted as support from the payor in determining whether more than half of the support is provided for purposes of the dependency exemption. Thus, a mother may receive child-support payments, that are excludable from her income, while the father may be able to claim dependency exemptions for the children. (The deduction for dependents is discussed in Chapter 4.) Child support payments must have been specifically labeled as such in the divorce decree in order to be so treated. Even if the amount to be paid will be reduced as children grow up, payments are not treated as child support unless labeled as such. For example, assume that payments of $800 per month are to be made until the only child reaches age 21, at which time the payments are to be reduced to $300 per month. It might *appear* that the intent of the parties in this instance was that $500 of the $800 was for child support and the other $300 was alimony. However, in a pre-1985 divorce, unless an amount was *specifically* labeled as child support it cannot be treated as such. Needless to say, the designation in the divorce decree regarding spousal support and child payments had some important tax consequences.

Second, alimony is *not* a property settlement. Property settlements, in their simplest form, occur when a married couple splits, each taking certain properties, with no future payments to be made. A variation of this is where one party pays the other in cash or in installments for the other person's rights in noncash properties. Where it is clear that

[22]For post-1984 divorce settlements, the parties can agree that such payments will not be deducted by the payor and will not be gross income to the recipient. IRC Sec. 71(b)(1)(B).

a payment is for the release or surrender of property rights, it is not alimony.

Property settlement proceeds are not, as such, income to the recipient or deductible by the payor. This is true even if the property settlement is paid in installments, if the installments are for a period of ten years or less.

Alimony is often not called "alimony." The label attached for state purposes is not controlling for federal tax purposes, although it tends to create a presumption.

In addition, in order for payments under a pre-1985 divorce to be alimony for federal income tax purposes, a "periodic payment" test must be met. A payment is not alimony unless it is a "periodic payment." There are two ways in which a payment can be "periodic." The first is where the *total* amount to be paid is uncertain. This is perhaps the most common. For example, if one party is to make payments of specified amounts to the other until some uncertain event occurs, such as death or remarriage, then the payments are periodic because there is no way of determining how long the payments will be made. Another example is where the amount of the payments might change, such as where a decrease could occur if the payor's income is reduced. The second way a payment can be periodic is where the payments are to extend over a period of more than ten years.

Obviously, if an amount is paid in *equal* installments over a period of more than ten years, each annual payment will be less than 10% of the total. In such case, the full amount of each payment will be gross income to the recipient because the tax rules defined such payments as alimony. There is a slight problem where payments are to be over a period of more than ten years but are unequal, so that in one or more years an amount greater than 10% of the total is paid. This problem is solved with a rule that provides that the amount includable in the gross income of the recipient (and allowable as a deduction to the payor) for any one year cannot be greater than 10% of the total payment. For example, assume that John is to pay Jane, his ex-wife, a total of $100,000. Payments are to extend over a period of twelve years. However, in one year the payment is $18,000. Jane's gross income for that year will be only $10,000 because of this "10% rule." For any year in which the payment is $10,000 or less, all of it will be gross income because the total period of the payments is greater than ten years and the amount received that year is equal to or less than 10% of the total.

The rules are different for divorce decrees entered into after 1984.[23] Some concepts remain the same, however. Child support payments, and a property settlement are not included in gross income. Also, it is still true that the payor gets a deduction only if the recipient is required to include the amount as gross income.

In order for alimony to exist (for tax purposes) there must be no obligation on the part of the payor to continue payments after the death of the recipient.[24] Also, the payments must be in cash. The "periodic" requirements discussed earlier do not apply.

An option is available to taxpayers in a divorce settlement. They can agree in the settlement that payments will not be included in the gross income of the recipient and will not be deductible by the payor. Thus, some tax planning should take place in any negotiation concerning a divorce which will result in such payments.

TAX PLANNING TIP: Income tax savings might result from agreeing not to include alimony in gross income and not to take the deduction. For example, if the payor will be in a lower tax bracket than the recipient, the tax savings from the deduction will be less than the tax on gross income of the recipient. Also, the recipient might agree to lower payments if they are not subject to tax. The parties have a choice, rather than being forced to construct their agreement in such a way as to satisfy an inflexible tax rule.

For post-1984 divorces it is not necessary to make child support payments a specific item in order to have such payments be treated as child support. Where there is a total payment, for example, and that payment is to be reduced in the event of a child's reaching a certain age, the amount of the reduction in the payment will be treated as child support and not as alimony even though a specific amount or portion of the payment is not labeled as "child support."[25]

Despite the fact that the "periodic" requirement is no longer a part of the rules, there is no deduction by the payor (and no income to the recipient) where there is a property settlement, such as an initial one-time or lump-sum settlement shortly after the divorce. Thus, if Fred and Wilma are divorced and each takes part of their total assets, there is no alimony. A

[23]IRC Sec. 71.

[24]IRC Sec. 71(b)(1)(D).

[25]IRC Sec. 71(c). In the example provided earlier, the $500 will be treated as child support in the post-1984 divorce despite the absence of a specific label as such.

problem exists, however, where there is a combination of a property settlement (not alimony) and a series of future payments (alimony). How can one be distinguished from the other? A payor might even be motivated to attempt to disguise the property settlement as alimony in order to obtain a deduction for the former. Such an attempt, whether motivated by expected tax savings or not, is called "front loading." For example, a payment of $50,000 might be made in the year of the divorce followed by payments of $5,000 each year thereafter. The payor, desiring a deduction for the $50,000 would claim that such payment was part of the alimony obligation and, hence, take a deduction. Also, the recipient, treating it as alimony, would have included the entire amount in gross income. The portion of the payment that is deemed to have been "front loaded" is not eligible for tax reduction. However, it may not be possible, until a later year, to determine if "front loading" occurred. The problem, then, becomes one of "correcting" the treatment. The rules do not provide for filing amended tax returns for the prior years. Instead, the rules use the term "excess alimony" for the "front loaded" amount. The "excess alimony" is "recaptured."

"Recapture" means that the payor, who formerly took a deduction for the payments, must include the amount of the "excess alimony" in gross income. Likewise, the recipient, who formerly included the receipts in gross income, will get a deduction for the same amount. "Recapture" will occur only in the third year because only then can it be determined if there was any "excess alimony." Thus, for example, if Fred and Wilma were divorced in 1989, and payments were first made in 1989, it would be 1991 before it could be determined if "recapture" would occur.

How is the amount of recapture determined? It is beyond the scope of this text to discuss all possible situations but an example will suffice. Assume that Fred and Wilma are divorced and that Fred makes payments of $60,000 during that year, and $40,000 in each of the second and third years. Each year Fred would take a deduction for the payments and Wilma would include the receipts in her gross income. It will not be possible to determine if there has been front loading until the amount of the payments for all three years has been determined. (It is the amount of the actual payment that is used for the determination and not the amount required or agreed upon by the parties.)

"Excess alimony," if any, is determined first for the second year. It is the amount by which the payments in the second year exceed the sum of the payments in the third year plus $15,000. In our example, there is no "excess" for the second year because the payments in the second and third years were the same. The purpose of the $15,000 is to permit *some* reduction in the amount of the payments in the third year without causing recapture. For example, assume that the payment in the second year was $40,000, but the payment in the third year was $27,000. Since the payment in the second year did not exceed the payment in the third year by more than $15,000, there was no "excess" and, hence, no front loading for the second year.

Determination of the "excess" for the first year is more complex. It is the amount by which the first year payments exceed:

a. $15,000 (which is an amount provided by Congress), plus

b. The average of (1) payments in the second year reduced by any second year excess, and (2) payments in the third year.

Therefore, our example ($60,000 in first year and $40,000 in each of the next ten years) results in:

Payments in the first year		$60,000
Less:	$15,000	
$\frac{\$40,000 + \$40,000}{2}$	40,000	55,000
Excess		$ 5,000

The recapture is the sum of the "excess alimony" for years one and two. In this example, there is only excess in year one and that amount is $5,000. Thus, Fred will be required to include $5,000 in gross income in the third year. Note that Fred also will deduct $40,000 for the third year (the amount actually paid) so that the net effect is a reduction of $35,000 in taxable income, although both the income and the deduction will have to be reported on the tax return. Likewise, Wilma will include $40,000 in income for the third year and deduct $5,000, for a net effect of $35,000 increase in taxable income.

There is an exception to the alimony recapture provisions. Where fluctuating alimony payments result from a requirement that a portion of business income or salary be paid to the ex-spouse, any changes in the amount of alimony will be deemed to be out of the control of the payor and, hence, not subject to the recapture provisions.[26]

[26]IRC Sec. 71 (f)(5)(c). For divorces entered into in 1985 and 1986, recapture will occur where payments in any one year are $10,000 (or more) less than the previous year.

TAX PLANNING TIP: Where the parties to a divorce want payments to decrease, recapture can be avoided by structuring the plan so that there is only a relatively small reduction between year 1 and year 2 and again between year 2 and year 3. Reduction in payments after year 3 will not result in recapture.

Major tax planning opportunities exist in a divorce. The basic goal is to be sure that both taxpayers understand the tax consequences of what they are doing and that they then file their tax returns on a consistent basis. If one deducts the amount paid but the other does not report it as income, an expensive tax controversy may ensue. The usual result is that no one wins—not even the IRS. The typical IRS attitude in such a situation is to disallow the deduction to the payor, tax the receipt as income to the other party, and let both taxpayers fight it out in court.

TAX PLANNING TIP: The parent receiving custody of a child in a divorce proceeding might prefer to receive child-support payments rather than alimony, since they are not gross income whereas alimony is gross income. The recipient of such payments might be willing to accept less money, since it is not taxable. The opposite strategy would apply to the payor, since alimony is a deduction (for adjusted gross income) and child-support payments are not a deduction.

2.15 Prizes and Awards

Prizes and awards are included in gross income.[27] Such receipts can range anywhere between the many thousands of dollars in cash and property that a person might win on a TV game show to a large sum of money from one of the internationally recognized awards (e.g. Nobel) to a small sum in recognition of a minor local achievement (e.g. undergraduate academic advisor of the year). The applicable tax rule is the same: the cash and fair market value of noncash property are included in gross income.

There is a minor exception. If the award is made in recognition of achievement (religious, charitable, scientific, educational, artistic, literary, or civic), without any action on the part of the winner and without any requirement that substantial future services be rendered, *and* the recipient designates a government or charity to receive the proceeds, then the recipient is not required to include the amount in gross income. Note that this merely avoids having to include the amount in gross income and taking a deduction for the charitable or governmental contribution.[28]

2.16 Forgiveness of Debt

Whether debt forgiveness produces income depends upon the circumstances. The general rule is that cancellation of debt results in gross income to the taxpayer whose debt was canceled.[29] There are some exceptions. If a gift is intended, there is no income.[30] If the debt being forgiven is owed by a corporation to one of its shareholders, there is no income to the corporation if the debt is forgiven.[31] It is treated as a contribution to the corporation's capital account to the extent of the debt principal.[32] If the debt cancellation is an adjustment of the purchase price of property, no income results merely because the "adjustment" is retroactive.[33]

Debt discharged in bankruptcy or to an insolvent debtor after the debt adjustment does not create taxable income.[34]

2.17 Gambling Gains

Gambling gains must be included in gross income.[35] Gambling losses are deductible but only as itemized deductions (i.e., from AGI) and only to the extent of gains.[36] Thus, a taxpayer who does *not* itemize deductions, and does any gambling, may find tax due on winning transactions even though losses exceeded gains. A

[27]IRC Sec. 74(a).

[28]IRC Sec. 74(b). Certain "employee achievement awards" are excluded from gross income by IRC Sec. 74(c). Generally, the maximum exclusion is $400 if the award is made pursuant to a nonqualified plan and $1,600 if made pursuant to a qualified plan. See IRC Sec. 274(j) and Chapter 7.
[29]IRC Sec. 61(a)(12) and IRC Sec. 108.
[30]IRC Sec. 102(a).
[31]Rev. Rul. 72-464, 1972-2 CB 214.
[32]Treas. Reg. 1.61-12.
[33]*Hirsch* v. *Comm.* (CA7 1940), 25 AFTR 1038, 40-2 USTC 9791, 115 F.2d 656.
[34]IRC Sec. 108(a)(1)(A), (B).
[35]*Joseph Carmack* (CA5 1950) 183 F.2d 1, 39 AFTR 620, 50-2 USTC 9360, *cert. denied,* 340 U.S. 875.
[36]IRC Sec. 165(d). Such losses would be part of the "miscellaneous" category of itemized deductions. As explained in Chapter 4, the total "miscellaneous" category must be reduced by 2% of adjusted gross income in order to obtain the amount which can be claimed as a part of itemized deductions.

contemporaneous record of losses is necessary to support amounts claimed as a deduction on the tax return.

SPECIFIC INCOME EXCLUSIONS

2.18 State and Local Bond Interest

As a general rule, interest received on obligations of states and their subdivisions need not be reported as income for federal income tax purposes.[37] Thus, obligations of the State of New York or of the City of New York are excludable. But what about the New York Housing Finance Agency? Excludable. What about revenue bonds issued to finance industrial development? Some are and some are not excludable.[38] Offering circulars of the sellers of such bonds always contain legal opinions as to tax treatment of the interest.

Note that the New York bond interest will be excludable from taxable income for federal and New York state income tax purposes—but will be subject to state income tax if received by residents of other states with income taxes. U.S. government bond interest, on the other hand, is not subject to state income taxes but is included in federal gross income.[39] State and local bond interest can cause part of social security receipts to be taxed, however. See Sec. 2.28 of this chapter.

TAX PLANNING TIP: In evaluating the attractiveness of an investment, the after-tax effect should be considered. Thus, although a bond issued by a state or local government may pay less interest than a bond issued by a corporation, the former is tax-free income and the latter is not. This difference becomes more important as a taxpayer's marginal tax rate becomes higher.

2.19 Prior Years' Deductions

Gross income can result from recovery or disallowance of deductions claimed in a prior year. For example, if a person takes a moving expense deduction (see Chapter 3) and later does not satisfy the requirement for the deduction, gross income can be increased for the second year. (An alternative is to file an amended return for the year the deduction was claimed.) Also, a person might claim a deduction for state income tax (also discussed in Chapter 3). If in the following year a refund of all or part of the state tax is received, the refund must be included as gross income for the year received to the extent that a "tax benefit" was derived from the deduction.[40] In this instance, the amended return route is not an alternative. However, the amount of refund will not have to be included in gross income if the deduction in the prior year did not reduce taxes for that prior year.[41]

The "tax benefit" rule can be illustrated as follows. Assume that Billy Barnes (single) filed a 1989 federal income tax return with the following items:

Gross income	$25,000
Exemption (1989)	(2,000)
Itemized deductions	(4,000)
Taxable income	$19,000

Included in the itemized deductions was state income tax of $500, withheld from Billy's salary during 1989. Early in 1990, Billy filed the appropriate state income tax return for 1989 on which it was determined that the correct amount of state income tax was $400. Thus, a $100 refund of 1989 state income tax was received in 1990. The entire $100 must be included in Billy's 1990 federal gross income because the 1989 federal taxable income was reduced by $500, and the itemized deductions would have been more than the 1989 standard deduction ($3,100) *even if* there had been no deduction for state income tax.

Change the 1989 facts as follows:

Gross income	$25,000
Exemption (1989)	(2,000)
Itemized deductions	(3,160)
Taxable income	$19,840

As before, the itemized deductions include the $500 of state income tax withheld during 1989. As before, Billy received a $100 state tax refund in 1990. However, Billy's 1990 federal gross income will increase by only $60. Note that the 1989 standard deduction would have been $3,100. The itemized deductions were only $60 more than the standard deduction. Thus, Billy only received the benefit of $60 additional deduction as the result of the deduction for state income tax. Consequently, only $60 of the $100 refund received in 1990 will be included in 1990 federal gross income.

[37]IRC Sec. 103(a). Volunteer fire departments can also issue tax-exempt bonds. IRC Sec. 103(i).

[38]IRC Sec. 103(b). Details of "industrial development bonds" and other "private activity" obligations are beyond the scope of this text.

[39]Treas. Reg. 1.61-7(b)(3).

[40]IRC Sec. 111.

[41]For computation of the recovery exclusion, see Rev. Rul. 79-15, 1979-1 CB 80.

The same concept applies to other deductions that may be recovered in a later year. For example, as we shall see in Chapter 4, "itemized deductions" include medical expenses to the extent the total amount spent exceeds 7.5% of adjusted gross income. Assume the Billy Barnes itemized deductions for 1989, that adjusted gross income was $20,000 and that medical expenses paid totaled $1,700. Therefore, the deductible portion of medical expenses was $200. If Billy received $300 from medical insurance benefits in 1990, only $200 of that $300 would be included in 1990 gross income because the balance of the expense did not result in any 1989 income tax reduction.

2.20 Life Insurance Proceeds

Life insurance premiums buy one or both of two things. The first is life insurance protection. The second is an investment.

Pure life insurance protection is reflected in term insurance policies, which have no cash values and no provision for any payoff during the life of the insured. They provide only for payments if the person dies during the term of the contract. Universal life, whole life, and endowment policies, on the other hand, provide for life insurance protection plus an accumulation (cash surrender value) that the owner of the policy may obtain by cancellation of the policy.

Life insurance proceeds from either type of policy, if paid because the person who was insured dies, are generally excluded from the gross income of the recipient.[42] The amount of the receipt does not matter. Thus, if Billy Barnes receives $1,000,000 as the result of having been named the beneficiary of a life insurance policy of someone who died, the entire $1,000,000 is excluded from Billy's gross income. There is no requirement that the decedent must have been related to Billy in any way. (Naturally, of course, most persons who are beneficiaries of life insurance have some family relationship to the person whose life is insured, but there is no such requirement in the tax rules.)

There is usually no tax deduction for the premiums paid on life insurance. This is true for persons who purchase life insurance as a personal matter and for corporations that may purchase life insurance on key executives as a business matter where the corporation is the beneficiary of the policy. However, if an employer pays the premiums on a life insurance policy where an employee is insured and the employer is not the beneficiary, then the employer gets to take a deduction. (This is covered more fully in Chapter 7.) Such cost is part of the total cost of hiring an employee. Whether the employee has gross income because of employer-paid premiums is a separate issue covered later in this section.

There is an exception to the general rule that life insurance proceeds paid because of the death of the insured are excluded totally from gross income. A person can have income if he or she purchases an already existing policy.[43] For example, assume that Lynn Larson owes $5,000 to Billy Barnes and is unable to make cash payment. Lynn owns a paid-up life insurance policy and is willing to transfer it to Billy in payment of the debt. If this is done and later Lynn dies, Billy will receive the proceeds of the insurance policy. Billy is treated as having purchased the policy from Lynn for $5,000. Billy will be permitted to exclude only $5,000 from gross income, since that was the amount paid. If the insurance payment to Billy is more than $5,000, Billy will have gross income to the extent of the excess.

When a person buys a life insurance contract other than term insurance, there is an investment element in the premiums paid. The investment portion of the policy earns a return. This return can be received by the owner of the policy in one of three ways. First, the owner may receive a periodic cash "dividend." This is not treated as gross income but as a reduction in the premiums that were or will be paid. It is perhaps unfortunate that the term "dividend" is used for such premium-refund payments because a dividend normally must be included in gross income.

The second possibility is that the return on the investment portion of the contract will not be paid in cash, but an adjustment will be made in the amount of future premiums to be paid by the insured. The tax result is the same as where cash is received (i.e., a reduction in premiums). The only difference is that the cash does not flow through the hands of the policy owner.

The third possibility is that the return on the investment portion of the contract will increase the amount of the insurance coverage and the cash surrender value of the policy. As this occurs from time to time, the policy owner's value in the policy goes up, but the policy owner has no gross income unless he or she cashes in the policy.

Where a life insurance policy is redeemed for its cash surrender value, there will be a taxable gain measured by the amount received less the total of premiums paid. If the redemption amount is less than the total premiums that have been paid

[42] IRC Sec. 101(a)(1).

[43] IRC Sec. 101(a)(2).

on the policy, there will be no deduction for the difference. The reason for this conclusion, as we shall see in the next chapter, is that there is no deduction for any expenditure or decline in value of property resulting from personal, family, or living expenses.

Except for term insurance, insurance premiums pay for both protection and investment. Any amount received under a policy, other than as the result of death, reflects only the investment portion. There is a tax advantage to the extent that the cost of protection reduces the taxable income from the investment.

For example, assume that Billy Barnes is faced with two alternatives. On the one hand, Billy can purchase a universal life insurance policy. On the other hand, Billy can purchase the same coverage under a term policy without spending as much, and can invest the difference in a mutual stock fund.

Assume that the premiums on $100,000 of term life insurance will aggregate $5,200 over a twenty-year period. Premiums on a $100,000 universal life policy for that same twenty years might be $26,500. Thus, over the twenty years Billy would have available the $21,300 difference to invest in the mutual fund. Which way will Billy be better off if, while still alive, the investment is cashed in at the end of the twenty years? Which way would be most advantageous if Billy were to die during the twenty years?

If the investment is cashed in at the end of the twenty years, the ordinary life policy might have a cash surrender value of $27,900. Since $26,500 was paid in premiums, Billy would have $1,400 of income. Assume $392 of tax on that, and there remains $27,508 in hand. What about the mutual fund alternative?

First, of course, there is much less certainty as to amounts. The investment in the mutual fund would be made at the rate of $1,065 a year. If it were strictly a growth fund, with no current distributions, and appreciated at the rate of 6% a year, the value of the investment would be approximately $40,000 at the end of twenty years. Cashed in, this would produce tax on $18,700 of gain—which might be, let us assume, $5,200. Thus, net cash would be $34,800. Compared with the $27,508 of the ordinary life alternative, this is $7,292 better. In both alternatives, Billy also had $100,000 of life insurance coverage during the twenty years.

Or the mutual fund might lose money, in which case the net cash would be less than the $21,300 paid in over the twenty years. The loss would provide some tax benefit, of course, since it would be deductible. (See Chapter 5.)

If the mutual fund and the insurance company produced the same investment results, there would be a slight advantage to the insurance company because the cost of the insurance coverage would be part of the tax basis of the investment—and Billy would be ahead at the end of the twenty years by the amount of tax that would be imposed on the portion of the premium in the universal life alternative that reflected the $100,000 of coverage.

What if Billy dies during the twenty years? With the term life plus mutual fund, Billy's heirs will receive $100,000 of life insurance proceeds plus the mutual fund investment in whatever amount it is then worth. With the universal life policy, the heirs will receive $100,000 of life insurance proceeds.

What if Billy still wants $100,000 of life insurance after twenty years? With the universal life policy, there is no problem—and the premiums are based on Billy's age at the time the policy was purchased. With the term life, Billy may have to pass a new physical exam and pay much higher premiums for coverage based upon the attained age at that time.

The point here is not to advocate universal life insurance over a combination of term insurance plus other investments, or vice versa, but rather to indicate that there are tax *and* financial effects of different investment alternatives that require analysis. In the end, what a particular taxpayer decides is the best approach will depend in large part upon that person's own goals, values, and expectations for the future.

The assumption so far has been that proceeds from a life insurance contract, paid because of the death of the insured, were paid in a lump sum. Another possibility is that the beneficiary would elect to receive the proceeds in installments. Naturally, the total of the installments will be more than the lump sum because the insurance company will pay interest. Interest must be included in gross income.

For example, assume that Billy Barnes is the beneficiary of a life insurance contract. Under the payment options, Billy could receive $50,000 cash in a lump sum or leave the proceeds with the insurance company and receive $12,000 a year for five years. If the latter option is chosen, the $50,000 gross income exclusion is prorated over the series of payments. Thus, each year the $12,000 received results in $10,000 tax-free and $2,000 of interest income.

2.21 Annuities

An annuity is a series of payments, usually of equal amounts. Frequently, but not necessarily, an

FIGURE 2–1 Annuity exclusion ratio formula

INVESTMENT IN ANNUITY CONTRACT

DIVIDED BY

EXPECTED RETURN UNDER THE CONTRACT

EQUALS

EXCLUSION RATIO

annuity contract is purchased in connection with retirement. For example, a person might purchase a retirement annuity that will pay $500 per month for ten years, starting at age sixty-five. The purchase price might be paid in a lump sum (unlikely) or paid in installments during the "working years." In either event, at the time the annuity payments begin (age 65) the annuitant has an investment in the contract. As an example, assume that the investment is $47,400. The return will be $500 × 12 × 10, or $60,000. Thus, the investment is 79% of the amount that will be received. As the annuity payments are received, 79% is a return of the original investment and 21% is interest. The 79% is called an "exclusion ratio," or the portion of each receipt that is excluded from gross income.[44] The balance is included in gross income. Figure 2-1 shows the exclusion ratio formula.

There is an obvious economic problem with the fixed term annuity. If the annuitant outlives the period of receipts, the economic situation could be serious. Therefore, it is common for a contract to provide for payments for the life of the annuitant. For example, the $500 monthly payment might be made for as long as the annuitant lives. Calculating an exclusion ratio then requires a different approach. The *expected* return on the contract is estimated by looking at the annuitant's life expectancy at the time the annuity payments begin. If the life expectancy of a sixty-five-year-old person in the example given is ten years, the result is the same (i.e., an exclusion ratio of 79%). In fact, the life expectancy of a sixty-five-year-old person is twenty years. (See Table 1 in Appendix 2-A.) Thus, the denominator of the fraction is $500 × 12 × 20, or $120,000. Using the same cost for the contract, the exclusion ratio is $47,400/$120,000, or 39.5%. For each $500 received, $197.50 will be excluded from gross income and $302.50 will be included.

The total amount of the annuity that may be excluded is limited to the total investment in the annuity contract.[45] For example, assume the annuitant in the previous example lived to be older than 85 (age 65 at the time the annuity began plus the 20 years life expectancy used in the formula). After 20 years, the total amount excluded from gross income will have been $47,400 ($2,370 per year for 20 years). Thereafter, there will be no exclusion and the full amount received each year will be included in gross income. Prior to the Tax Reform Act of 1986 there was no limit, and the exclusion continued to apply even if the annuitant lived longer than expected and consequently received more money than expected.

COMPUTER FORMULAS: The above example can be illustrated by the following formulas.

	A	B
1	Investment	47,400
2	Return	120,000
3	Exclusion ratio	+B1/B2
4		
5	Receipt	*x*
6	Excluded	+B5*B3
7	Taxable	+B5−B6
8		

The amount received is left as a variable, *x*.

2.22 Joint Annuities

Where a married couple, for example, purchases an annuity, the contract may provide for payments to be made until both have died. The only extra problem this presents is that of estimating how long the payments will be made to both of them and then to the survivor. Table II (Appendix 2-A) provides this estimate. Thus, if a husband and wife are both age sixty-seven at the time the annuity payments begin, it is expected the payments will be received for 23.2 years. This is the "expected return" multiple used in the denominator of the exclusion ratio fraction.

Another variation is that the annuity payments may be at one rate while both are alive, but at a reduced rate to the survivor of the first to die. For example, payments might be at the rate of $500 per month while both are alive and reduced to $400 per month for the survivor. The expected return can be estimated with the use of Tables II and IIA combined. Table IIA (not provided in the appendix) estimates that for persons both age

[44] IRC Sec. 72.

[45] IRC Sec. 72(b)(2).

sixty-seven, *one* will die in 13.5 years. Since the estimate (from Table II) of the time before both die is 23.2 years, the survivor is expected to live 9.7 years. Thus the expected return would be $\$500 \times 12 \times 13.5$ plus $\$400 \times 12 \times 9.7$, which is \$127,560.

With life insurance, the insured "wins" financially by dying early. The proceeds of the policy would be much greater than the premiums paid. The purchaser of an annuity, on the other hand, will "win" by outliving the life expectancy when the annuity began. Payment is made "up front" for the annuity—which in its simplest form is a contract obligating the insurance company to pay an agreed amount per month starting at a particular age and continuing for the rest of the annuitant's life.

Two economic facts stand out. If a person dies at age sixty-six, for example, after purchasing an annuity that started to pay at age sixty-five, hindsight reveals that buying the annuity turned out to be a loss. If a person dies after having excluded part of the cost of the annuity but before the entire cost has been deducted, then the balance can be deducted (assuming no refund by the insurance company) on the final income tax return of the decedent.[46] On the other hand, if the insurance company calculated the cost of the annuity by using a life expectancy table which indicated that the annuitant would live to be eighty-two, the annuity contract will be quite profitable for the annuitant who lives to be ninety-seven.[47]

Insurance companies complicate the annuity calculations by selling contracts that are not pure annuities. Thus, a contract may cover both husband and wife for joint lives plus the life of the survivor but have an insurance payment for the first to die. Furthermore, most annuity contracts provide for a minimum payout so that if an annuitant dies too early there will be a partial refund of the annuity cost to the heirs. Such a provision requires a modification in the multiple found in the actuarial tables. The details of this calculation are not as important as the basic concept. Also, there are annuity contracts written by universities, churches, other nonprofit organizations, and even private individuals, especially within a family group. The basic principles are still the same, but the applications can differ because of greater uncertainty as to whether the payments will all be made and the possibility that the annuity is purchased with property rather than cash.

Annuities are often a part of retirement plans, that are discussed in detail in Chapter 18. Funding of a retirement plan may be made by both the employer and the employee. Where a plan is "qualified" the portion funded by the employer is not currently included in the employee's gross income. For purposes of determining the amount which the annuitant will ultimately receive, the total amount contributed by the employee and the employer is counted. For purposes of determining the annuitant's cost in the contract, only the employee's contribution is counted, since the employee paid that with after-tax dollars and was not taxed on the employer's portion. On the other hand, if the employer paid the entire premium on a qualified retirement annuity, then the retired employee has not paid any income tax on any part of the investment. The result is that the retired employee must include all of the receipts in gross income. Another way of looking at it is that the exclusion ratio is zero because the numerator of the exclusion ratio fraction (Figure 2-1) is zero. This point emphasizes that the numerator, which we called "investment in the annuity contract," means the *employee's after-tax investment* rather than the total amount which may have been paid to the annuity company by all parties.

This discussion should not lead to the conclusion that the numerator of the exclusion ratio fraction will always be after-tax dollars. That need not be the case. For example, assume that a spouse dies while covered under a life insurance policy with a maturity value of \$100,000. The beneficiary is the surviving spouse who elects to take the proceeds in the form of an annuity to be paid during the remainder of her life. The \$100,000 "cost" or "investment in the annuity contract" is both a before-tax and an after-tax number because the proceeds from the life insurance policy were excluded from gross income. That does not change the tax result of the annuity. The annuity exclusion ratio for the survivor will be determined just as if the life insurance proceeds had been taxable and there was \$100,000 left after-tax to invest in the contract.

2.23 Damages for Personal Injury or Illness

Just as life insurance proceeds paid by reason of death are not taxable, damages awarded for the loss of life are also excludable from income.[48] There is no limit if the damages are paid pursuant to a tort action. For example, damages might be paid by an employer whose negligence caused the

[46] IRC Sec. 72(b)(3). As we shall see in a later chapter, a person's taxable year ends with the date of his or her death.

[47] Treas. Reg. 1.72-4(a)(4).

[48] IRC Sec. 104(a)(2). Such damages are not gross income by definition.

death of an employee.[49] Similarly, damages received for personal injuries or sickness are excludable.[50] For example, assume that Billy Barnes received $50,000 as the result of loss of a leg in an automobile accident. Tax result: no gross income to Billy.

The Omnibus Budget Reconciliation Act of 1989[51] changed the rule concerning exclusion from gross income for punitive damages received as the result of *nonphysical* injury. Previously, punitive damages such as amounts awarded for "mental" or "emotional" damages (e.g., defamation of character or alienation of affections) could be excluded from gross income.[52] Generally, an amount received after July 10, 1989, must be included in gross income unless it is paid as the result of physical injury or sickness. An amount received for injury to business reputation must also be included in gross income.[53]

Amounts paid to an employee as reimbursement for medical expenses are not gross income.[54] Also, amounts paid to an employee, or spouse, or family member, for permanent loss of a part or function of the body are not gross income.[55]

It is thus of tax planning importance when a claim is settled (either in a lawsuit or an out-of-court settlement) to specify what amount is being awarded for which specific injuries. For example, a suit alleging both physical damages and damages to the mental health of an employee caused by inhaling toxic fumes from the work environment might also seek reimbursement for the lost earnings during the period of absence from work. An agreement settling that suit might produce better tax results for the recipient if the amount paid was clearly labeled as for the physical suffering alone, since any part attributable to back pay and to nonphysical injuries might constitute taxable income to the employee.[56]

TAX PLANNING TIP: Under certain circumstances an amount received might be payment for both personal injuries and loss of wages and nonphysical injuries. To get the payment labeled compensation for physical injury will result in tax-free income, whereas any amount designated as reimbursement for lost wages for nonphysical injury will result in taxable income.

2.24 Employee Fringe Benefits

A whole range of employer-paid employee benefits gets excluded from income—some because of statute, some because of long-standing practice, and some because of administrative laxity in enforcing the rules. The following employer-paid items are specific statutory exclusions from gross income providing that the employer provides the (fringe) benefits to all employees on a nondiscriminatory basis. This means that the participants and coverage must not be more favorable to key employees than to others. Key employees are those who are either highly paid, are shareholders of the corporate employer, or are officers of the employer company.

1. Premiums for group term life insurance, up to $50,000 of coverage.[57] This is life insurance that has no cash surrender value, provides only protection, and is a contract providing for insurance for a group of persons, such as all of the employees of a company. Members of an employee's family also can be covered with insurance up to $2,000 each with no income to the employee for the premium. Where an employer-paid group-term life insurance policy provides for coverage in excess of $50,000, Treasury Regulations contain a table that provides the amount to be included in gross income. It is this amount rather than the actual cost that is taxable to the employee.
2. Hospitalization, medical, and accident insurance premiums or employer plans providing for reimbursement of such expenses or providing benefits without the formality of insurance.[58]
3. Up to $5,000 of death benefits paid to an employee's beneficiaries by the employer.[59]
4. Meals provided for an employee on the employer's premises if the employee is required to be on duty during the meal period or if the employee is a food service employee.[60]
5. Lodging provided on the employer's premises providing the employee must accept the lodging as a condition of employment (e.g., a hotel man-

[49]IRC Sec. 104(a).
[50]IRC Sec. 104(a)(2).
[51]Enacted 12-19-89.
[52]See, for example, *C. A. Hawkins,* 6 BTA 1023.
[53]For example, *Agar* v. *Comm.,* T.C. Memo 1960-021; *Wolfson* v. *Comm.* (CA6 1981), 48 AFTR 2d 81-5351. But see *Paul F. Roemer, Jr.* v. *Comm.* (CA9), 52 AFTR 2d 83-5954 and *Wade E. Church* v. *Comm.,* 80 T.C. 1104, for a contrary result.
[54]IRC Sec. 105(b). Such a payment plan cannot discriminate in favor of highly compensated employees. See IRC Sec. 89.
[55]IRC Sec. 105(c).
[56]See Rev. Rul. 58-418, 1958-2 CB 18, and Rev. Rul. 75-230, 1975-1 CB 93 for the pre-7-10-89 rules. See also Rev. Rul. 85-98, 1985-2 CB 51.

[57]IRC Sec. 79. Retired employees are also eligible for this tax-free benefit.
[58]IRC Sec. 106.
[59]IRC Sec. 101(b).
[60]IRC Sec. 119(a)(1).

ager).[61] A specific statutory provision also allows a member of the clergy to exclude the rental value of a dwelling furnished, or cash housing allowances paid for the rent or purchase of a home.[62]

6. Tuition reductions allowed by an educational institution for undergraduate (or below) study by an employee, spouse, or member of the employee's family.[63]
7. Dependent-care assistance programs paid for an employee by an employer. There is a limit of $5,000 upon the amount that can be excluded from gross income. Thus, if an employer paid $500 per month for a full year ($6,000) under such a plan, the employee benefiting from such an arrangement would include $1,000 in gross income.[64]
8. "No-additional-cost service" benefits.[65] These are services that an employee can receive from an employer and which result in no substantial additional cost to the employer. Such service is ordinarily that which is offered by the employer to customers. An example would be an airline that allows an employee to travel at no cost where there would otherwise be an empty seat on the airplane.
9. "Qualified employee discounts."[66] These are discounts from the regular price at which merchandise or services are offered by the employer to customers. The amount of the discount for merchandise is limited to the "gross profit percentage" that the employer would normally realize. Such discounts are commonly granted by retail stores to their employees. In the case of a discount for services, the amount of the discount is limited to 20% of the amount normally charged to customers.
10. "Working condition fringe" benefits.[67] These are benefits provided by an employer to an employee, but for which an employee would be entitled to a deduction if he or she had paid for such property or services. For example, the cost of an employer-provided automobile would be excluded from the employee's gross income if the conditions were such that the employee would have been entitled to a deduction for the costs of the automobile usage if he or she had paid for it. (Deductions are discussed in Chapter 4.)
11. "De minimus fringe" benefits.[68] These are employer-paid benefits of property or service the cost of which is so small that accounting for them is unreasonable or impractical. Examples would include employee use of employer-owned copying machine, an employer-paid holiday party, or occasional supper money paid to an employee working overtime as well as employer-operated eating facilities, located on or near the employer's premises, where the employee is charged a fee for food and services such that the employer's gross receipts are equal to or greater than the direct costs of operating the facility. The term specifically includes employer-provided parking near the employer's place of business.
12. Use of athletic facilities provided on the employer's premises if such facilities are operated by the employer and are used mostly by employees, their spouses, and dependent children.[69]
13. Educational assistance programs paid for an employee by an employer. Payments or reimbursements of employee educational costs of up to $5,250 per year per employee are excluded from the employee's income. However, the exclusion does not apply to graduate level courses. The Omnibus Budget Reconciliation Act of 1989 extended this exclusion to amounts paid by the employer on or before September 30, 1990.
14. Employer contributions to a qualified group legal services plan. In addition, the legal services actually provided under the plan are excludable by the recipient. This fringe benefit was also extended to September 30, 1990 by the Omnibus Budget Reconciliation Act.

TAX PLANNING TIP: Some of the fringe benefits are easier to arrange if the employer and employee are two separate tax entities. A family business conducted as a proprietorship or partnership may be less attractive from this point of view than having the same business organized as a corporation.

While all fringe benefits provided to an employee by an employer are included in the employee's gross income unless specifically excluded by Congress, there is one such benefit which requires specific mention. It is a fairly common practice for employers to provide employees with an automobile that is available for personal use. If the car is not available for personal use by the employee, there is no gross income. However, if the car is available for nonbusiness use, the employee must report gross income under one of two methods.

The first method is called the "lease value method," and is used where the car is available for use over an extended period of time. The amount of gross income is the amount that a car of equal

[61]IRC Sec. 119(a)(2). There is a special rule for lodging furnished by certain educational institutions. See IRC Sec. 119(d).
[62]IRC Sec. 107.
[63]IRC Sec. 117(d).
[64]IRC Sec. 129(a).
[65]IRC Sec. 132(b).
[66]IRC Sec. 132(c).
[67]IRC Sec. 132(d).
[68]IRC Sec. 132(e).
[69]IRC Sec. 132(h)(5).

value could be leased for the same time period. For example, assume that Billy Barnes' employer provided Billy with a car for one year and the value of the car was $10,000. According to a table provided by the IRS, Billy would have $3,100 of income for the year.[70] Note that the amount of gross income is not related to the amount of expense incurred by the employer in providing the use of the car to the employee. Where the car is *available* to the employee for unlimited personal use, the amount of gross income under this method is not dependent upon the extent to which the employee actually used the car for personal purposes. (The lease value method does not include gasoline, under the assumption that the employer provides the use of the car but not the gas. Therefore, if the employer provides the gasoline, the amount of gross income would be the sum of the lease value method plus $0.055 per mile for gasoline.)

Where the use of an employer's automobile is available to an employee for a continuous period of 30 days or more but less than a full year, the annual lease value is prorated. Thus, if the car in the above example had been available to Billy for nine months of the year, Billy's gross income would have been 75% of $3,100, which is $2,325.

The second method is a "cents-per-mile method" and can be used where the personal usage mileage is so small that the amount of gross income is less than under the lease value method and where the availability for use is less than 30 days. The current rate is 25½¢ per mile for the first 15,000 miles. For example, assume that the employer-provided car was not available to Billy on a continuous basis but that Billy used the car for 2,000 miles of personal transportation during the year. The gross income would be 2,000 times 25.5 cents, or $510. The rate changes to 11 cents for miles in excess of 15,000. Thus, if Billy used the car 16,000 miles for personal purposes, this method would result in gross income of $3,935 (15,000 miles times $0.255 times plus 1,000 miles times $0.11). If a car is used to commute to and from the employment site, such miles are personal use miles even though all other miles driven may be related to the employer's business. Under present regulations, the "cents-per-mile" method cannot be used if the value of the car exceeds $12,800. (Also, the use of the $0.255 rate assumes that the employer has provided the gasoline. If the employee provides the gasoline, the rate is reduced by $0.055 to $0.20 per mile.) All of these numbers are adjusted periodically by the IRS to take into account the change in the Consumer Price Index.

[70]The table is provided in Reg. 1.61-21(d). These regulations also discuss the methodology to be used to determine the amount of gross income from other employer-provided transportation, such as a personal trip on an employer-provided airplane.

The availability of employee benefits, even more than their tax treatment, should be of major interest to people as they pick a career. Retirement plans are discussed in Chapter 18. Where cash compensation, employee benefits, etc., are about equal in value, tax treatment may well improve the attractiveness of some occupations as compared with others. Although no one would become a member of the clergy just to obtain tax benefits, compare the tax difference for two persons, one clergy and one not. The member of the clergy receives $30,000 in salary plus a $6,000 housing allowance, whereas the other person receives a salary of $36,000 and must provide for housing with after-tax dollars. Clearly, the clergy person is financially better off by virtue of the $6,000 exclusion from gross income.

TAX PLANNING TIP: Employers can maximize the after-tax compensation to employees by providing the maximum allowable fringe benefits which are excludable from the gross income of the employees. This could result in less cash outflow for the employer since an employee might demand larger amounts of cash income in order to have after-tax income with which to purchase the benefit individually. Example: group term life insurance coverage.

2.25 Scholarship Grants

Scholarships provide funds for studies by a person who is a candidate for a degree. Degree candidates have no dollar limits on how much they can exclude so long as the stipend is a "qualified scholarship."[71] That means a grant of money equal to or less than the combined costs for tuition, fees, books, supplies, equipment and other related expenses. A stipend in excess of those specific items will be included in the gross income of the recipient. Thus, that part of a scholarship covering housing and meal costs will result in gross income to the recipient.

For example, assume that Billy Barnes has enrolled in college and is a candidate for an undergraduate degree. Billy received a scholarship of $8,000 for the first year. The total cost for tuition, books, fees, supplies, and equipment nec-

[71]IRC Sec. 117(a) and (b).

essary for school was $6,000. Billy has gross income equal to the difference of $2,000.

Degree candidates who are required to perform teaching, research, or similar services in order to receive their grants will find that the portion of the grant that is attributable to the services performed will be taxable income—even if the teaching or the research is a requirement for the degree. Taxability also results, for degree candidates and others, if the research, etc., is primarily to benefit the grantor's interests (e.g., to develop a specific product or process). Incidental benefits to the grantor, such as increasing the supply of potential employees in a particular field, do not affect taxability.

2.26 Tax-Free Exchanges

Certain exchanges of property for similar property (particularly real estate exchanged for other real estate) do not result in immediate taxability.[72] These will be discussed in more detail in Chapter 6.

2.27 Foreign Earned Income

Most developed countries do not tax their nonresident citizens on their salaries (or professional fees) from services rendered abroad. The United States allows some exclusion. Qualified U.S. taxpayers can elect to exclude up to $70,000 of "foreign earned income."[73] The exclusion applies to compensation for services (e.g., salary).[74] In order to qualify for the exclusion, the taxpayer must be present in a foreign country (or countries) during at least 330 full days out of any 12 consecutive months or be a bona fide resident of a foreign country (or countries).[75] For example, assume that Billy Barnes worked in a foreign country during 1990 for a sufficient number of days to qualify for the exclusion. Foreign earned income was $125,000. The number of days during which Billy was out of the United States during 1990 was 335. The maximum exclusion at the annual rate of $70,000 must be allocated on a daily basis. $70,000/365 = $191.78. Billy's maximum exclusion for 1990 is 335 × $191.78, or $64,246.30.

For purposes of the 330 day period (called the "physical presence test") it is not necessary for the 12 consecutive months to coincide with the taxpayer's taxable year. In addition, it is not necessary that the 330 days of absence from the U.S. fall within the same taxable or calendar year. Assume Billy's 335 days out of the U.S. consisted of 100 days during 1989 and 225 days during 1990. Billy's maximum exclusion for 1989 would be $19,178 and the maximum exclusion for 1990 would be $43,151. Naturally, if Billy's salary were less than $191.78 per day, then the entire salary would be excluded.

Persons who qualify for the exclusion above can also qualify for an exclusion and/or deduction for a "housing cost amount."[76] This is an amount (but not a lavish or extravagant amount) that is determined as follows: reasonable expenses paid for housing (including that for spouse and dependents) less $7,775 (for 1989).[77] The exclusion must be calculated on a daily basis ($21.30) where such expenses are incurred for only part of a year. This exclusion/deduction is limited to foreign earned income in excess of the flat foreign earned income exclusion noted above.

As we will discuss in Chapter 4, an employee is entitled to deduct reasonable costs of lodging and 80% of the cost of meals when he/she is "away from home overnight" in connection with employment. Where a person takes the exclusion from gross income under the foreign earned income rules discussed here, he is not eligible to claim also a deduction for the costs of lodging and meals incurred while away from home.

TAX PLANNING TIP: When considering the possibility of employment in a foreign location, an employee might find that the after-tax effect makes a prospective employment offer more attractive than the initial face amount offer might appear. Similarly, employers find it easier to recruit employees by emphasizing the after-tax compensation and adopting "equalization" policies that adjust for any tax disadvantage of being abroad. Thus, an employer may be able to pay less because employees' salaries may be nontaxable.

[72] IRC Secs. 1031–1040.

[73] IRC Sec. 911.

[74] The exclusion is not available for amounts paid by the U.S. government or any agency of the U.S. government.

[75] IRC Sec. 911(d). This second test (called the "bona fide residence test") requires that the taxpayer must have been a bona fide resident of another country or countries for an *uninterrupted* period that included a complete taxable year.

[76] IRC Sec. 911(a)(2), and 911(c).

[77] The exclusion is based on 16% of the federal employee pay at step 1 of grade GS-14. Hence, the amount will change as such pay changes.

2.28 Governmental Social Benefit Payments

Generally, prior to 1984, social benefit payments received from the United States for old age, as part of Medicare, or as a form of public assistance (e.g., because of blindness) were excludable from income.[78] Similar payments received from the states, including payments for industrial accidents or illness (i.e., workers' compensation) are excluded.

Starting in 1984, up to one-half of monthly social security receipts and certain railroad retirement benefits are included in gross income under certain circumstances. The amount included in gross income is the *lesser of* (a) one-half of the amount of benefits received or (b) one-half of ("modified" adjusted gross income, plus one-half of the social security receipts, less a "base amount").[79]

"Modified" adjusted gross income is adjusted gross income (computed without the exclusion for certain foreign income) plus tax-exempt interest. The "base amount" is $25,000 for single persons, $32,000 for married persons filing a joint return, or zero for married persons filing a separate tax return (unless living apart from the other spouse for the entire year).

For example, assume that a single taxpayer receives $6,600 in social security receipts during 1990. Adjusted gross income is $23,000. "Modified" adjusted gross income is $33,000 because of $10,000 of tax-exempt interest.

(a) one-half of the social security benefits is $3,300;

(b) "modified" AGI, plus one-half of social security less $25,000 is $11,300 ($33,000 + $3,300 − $25,000);

(c) one-half of $11,300 = $5,650.

Therefore, $3,300 of the social security benefits will be taxable.

[78]Rev. Rul. 70-217, 1970-1 CB 12; Rev. Rul. 73-87, 1973-1 CB 39; Rev. Rul. 75-271, 1975-2 CB 23; Rev. Rul. 76-395, 1976-2 CB 16; Rev. Rul. 70-280, 1970-1 CB 13; Rev. Rul. 73-154, 1973-1 CB 40; Rev. Rul. 76-131, 1976-1 CB 16.
[79]IRC Sec. 86.

If "modified" adjusted gross income had been $24,000, then (b) above would have been $1,150 [½ ($24,000 + 3,300 − $25,000)] and $1,150 of the social security would have been included in gross income. If "modified" adjusted gross income had been $21,700, or less, then (b) above would have been zero, and none of the social security receipts would have been taxable. This is because (b) above would have been zero, or less.

2.29 Unemployment Benefits

Gross income includes amounts received as unemployment compensation or unemployment benefits.[80]

2.30 Summary

This chapter has been concerned with some of the specific items of income that are included in the computation of federal tax liability. There are some items, such as return of capital, gifts, and inheritances, that are not taxable because they do not satisfy the definition of "income." There are other receipts which satisfy some definition of "income" but which the Congress has decided should be excluded. One example is scholarships. In other instances, Congress has created some arbitrary rules for the determination of income. These rules were created for the purpose of administrative convenience or to help alleviate some social or economic hardship. For example, the exclusion of up to $5,000 paid to a surviving spouse by a deceased employee's employer helps to alleviate the hardship created as the result of death. More of these rules, which are a part of the determination of tax liability, have been created in connection with deductions. Some of the deductions have a readily explainable purpose; others do not. Chapter 3 is about deductions.

[80]IRC Sec. 85.

TRUE-FALSE QUESTIONS

State whether each of the following statements is true or false. For each *false* answer, reword the statement to make it *true*.

T F 1. If a person who is receiving social security benefits has adjusted gross income which is larger than a "base amount" ($25,000 for single persons and $32,000 for married persons filing a joint return), then one-half of his or her social security receipts will be subject to federal income tax.

T F 2. Under one theory of economics, income is measured by the amount of consumption during the year, without regard to the source of money that is spent.

T F 3. Municipal bond interest is excludable from gross income.

T F 4. An employee's gross income does not include a fringe benefit provided by the employer if the employer did not incur any substantial additional cost as the result of providing that benefit.

T F 5. If an employer pays the cost of hospitalization insurance for an employee and family, the employee must include the value of the insurance coverage in gross income.

T F 6. If a taxpayer borrows money by placing a mortgage on property that is already owned, the transaction is nontaxable.

T F 7. Federal income tax rules require that income from all scholarship grants must be included in gross income in full.

T F 8. The annuity exclusion ratio is a fraction determined by dividing the investment in the annuity contract by the total payments which are expected to be received from the annuity.

T F 9. Generally, accountants deal with transactions rather than with speculative valuations.

T F 10. For federal income tax purposes, all inflows of cash constitute income except for those inflows which represent recoveries of amounts invested.

T F 11. If a person receives an award for a scientific achievement without any action on her part, and not requiring any future services, the amount of the award will not be included in her gross income unless she designates that a charity or government shall receive the stipend.

T F 12. Although inheritances and gifts may be taxed by an excise tax, the federal income tax does not include either as a part of gross income.

T F 13. Gross income includes the full amount of any unemployment benefits received during the year.

T F 14. A person who is employed overseas by a U.S. corporation during the entire year of 1990 can exclude all "earned income" from gross income.

T F 15. Gross income includes amounts received by a divorced parent as child support from the former spouse.

T F 16. If the face amount of a life insurance policy is paid to a beneficiary because the person who was insured died, the recipient must report one-half of the amount as gross income.

T F 17. If the beneficiary of a life insurance policy leaves the proceeds with the insurance company and receives interest income, that interest income can be excluded from gross income each year.

T F 18. The annuity exclusion ratio is a means of providing an exclusion from gross income for an estimated amount of return of investment.

T F 19. Damages received for personal injury as the result of a tort action suit are excludable from gross income.

T F 20. Although the general rule is that alimony is included in the gross income of the recipient and is a deduction to the payor, the parties to a post-1984 divorce can agree that alimony will not be taxed to the recipient and will not be deductible by the payor.

PROBLEMS

Problem 2-1. Mike Horn works for Cast Iron Metal Corporation. His 1990 wages and other financial considerations resulted in his having taxable income of $26,000 on a joint return. Mike did not receive a wage increase and is disgruntled. He recently told his employer that he would have to have a $1,000 increase in salary or he would quit and seek employment elsewhere. Cast Iron has not had company-paid medical insurance coverage. Mike is considering the purchase of an individual medical reimbursement plan at a cost of $600 per year. Cast Iron has refused any adjustment in Mike's salary but has indicated that it plans to purchase a group medical plan and pay 100% of the premium. Mike has reviewed the plan's benefits and has concluded that the proposed plan is equal in coverage to that which he could purchase individually. How does the company's proposal compare with Mike's request on an after-tax basis? Assume that Mike and his wife do not itemize deductions. Use the 1990 tax rates.

Problem 2-2. Mr. Jacks died last year leaving, among other assets, a life insurance policy of $100,000 on his life with his wife named as beneficiary. Mrs. Jacks received the proceeds from the policy and immediately invested the amount in securities which will produce dividend income. The dividend income for the current year will be $8,500. Mrs. Jacks will have taxable income of $20,000 from other sources. She will file a return as a single person for the current year.

(a) What will be her federal income tax liability? (Use the 1990 rate schedule.)

(b) What would her federal income tax liability have been if she had invested the $100,000 in state or local municipal bonds and had earned $8,500 of interest income?

Problem 2-3. Bill Meyer and his wife, April, manage an apartment house for Apex Corporation. They are paid a fee of $8,000 per year. One of the reasons the corporation was interested in hiring them was because they live in a house in the neighborhood and can be reached easily if the tenants need help. Bill holds down a job as a mechanic during the day and April answers any calls from tenants. Bill takes care of the apartment building during evenings and weekends. Bill makes $25,300 annually as a mechanic. They do not "itemize" deductions. The Meyers have no children. They rent their present residence for $300 per month.

(a) What is their 1990 federal income tax liability?

(b) If the corporation were to require them to live in the apartment building and supply them with an apartment worth $500 per month, plus a cash salary of $2,000, what would be the after-tax advantage of the second alternative as compared with the first? Explain.

Problem 2-4. Bill and Betty Smith were divorced in 1988. The divorce settlement required Bill to pay Betty for her marital rights a total settlement of $100,000 as follows: $25,000 to be paid at the time the divorce became final plus fifteen annual installments of $5,000 each beginning one year later. All payments are required to be made in cash and will not be paid if either dies.

(a) Did Betty have any gross income in 1988 as the result of the payments from Bill? Each year after 1988?

(b) If you had been an advocate for Betty in drafting the divorce decree, what provisions would you have requested in the document? What if you were an advocate for Bill?

(c) Assuming that all payments are made as agreed, what tax implications are there for the year 1990? Discuss.

Problem 2-5. Jane Plain's husband died last year, leaving her as beneficiary of a life insurance policy that paid her $100,000 cash. After consultation with other family members, she purchased an annuity contract that will pay her $12,000 for the rest of her life. At that time her life expectancy was sixteen years. Last year, and again this year, she received the $12,000 annual payment.

(a) How much gross income does Jane have each year?

(b) What will be the tax effect if Jane dies after only ten years? (Assume no refund from the annuity company.)

Problem 2-6. In each of the following cases, indicate the amount of gross income for federal income tax purposes:

(a) Bill Bates invested $40,000 in an annuity contract that is to pay him $6,000 a year for ten years in equal monthly installments of $500. This year he received $3,500.

(b) Wanda Fritz invested $80,000 in an annuity contract that is to pay her $5,000 per year for life. At the time the payments started, Wanda's nearest birthday was her sixty-third. (*Note:* See Appendix 2-A, Table I.)

(c) Larry Lance was the beneficiary of a life insurance policy on his son Vince, who was killed in a motorcycle accident. The policy would have paid $48,000 in a lump sum, but Larry elected to leave the proceeds with the insurance company and receive annual payments of $8,000 for the next fifteen years. The first payment was received this year.

(d) Ron and Lynda Roe purchased an annuity contract for $50,000. The contract provided for annuity payments of $300 per month for as long as either Ron or Lynda was living. At the time the payments began, September 1, this year, Ron and Lynda were both age sixty-six. (*Note:* See Appendix 2-A, Table II.)

Problem 2-7. Marilyn Maze is employed by Allied Eraser Corporation. She participates in a group term life insurance plan which will provide benefits of $50,000 to her beneficiaries upon her death. Allied Eraser pays all the premiums for this life insurance coverage. Each employee is permitted to name the beneficiary who shall receive payment in the event of death. Marilyn has named her husband, Fred, as the beneficiary. Recently, Allied Eraser has been negotiating with the insurance company to increase the benefits. One of the proposed changes in the coverage is to provide life insurance coverage on the lives of each member of the immediate family (i.e., spouse and children) of each employee. If such a change occurs, each employee will be the beneficiary of the life insurance coverage for members of his or her family. It has been proposed that each employee's family would be covered by $5,000 of life insurance per person. Marilyn and Fred have three children. This would mean that Fred and each of the three children would have $5,000 of life insurance coverage under the Allied Eraser plan at no cost to Marilyn.

(a) Assuming that this plan is adopted and the insurance on Marilyn's life is not increased in amount, will Marilyn have any gross income as the result of the payment of the premiums by Allied Eraser? Explain.

(b) What if the life insurance coverage on family members were $2,000 per person?

(c) Assume that the proposed plan is not adopted but that the amount of the life insurance coverage on each of Allied's employees is raised to $60,000. Will Marilyn have any additional gross income? If so, how can she determine the amount?

Problem 2-8. Virginia Peck, a calendar-year taxpayer, purchased an annuity contract for $30,000 that would pay her $500 per month beginning January 1. Her life expectancy as of the annuity starting date was 15.0 years.

(a) How much of this annuity is includable in gross income in the first year?

(b) Assume that any gross income which Virginia has from this investment will be taxed at a marginal rate of 28%. What would be the result if Virginia had invested her $30,000 in grade AAA municipal securities which paid 9% interest?

(c) What would be the result if Virginia had invested her $30,000 in corporate stocks which paid her annual dividends of 12% on her original investment?

Problem 2-9. Larry McFarland earns a salary of $50,000 per year as the regional personnel manager for a company. Recently, his employer has started an incentive plan whereby certain employees can receive a year-end bonus payable in stock of the corporation. This year Larry expects to receive 100 shares of stock, which is selling for $25 per share. The stock is no-par common, with a stated value of $10 per share.

(a) If Larry receives the stock under this plan, which is not subject to any special tax-deferral provisions, what is his gross income for the year?

(b) Assume Larry is told that he has "earned" the stock bonus but with a restriction. Larry will not be able to acquire title to the stock if he voluntarily leaves his job within five years. Should he be fired, be forced to quit because of health reasons, or retire, he will not receive the stock. If he remains employed for five years, he will receive the stock *at that time*. Larry checks the tax law and finds (Code Sec. 83) that he has an election to make. He can include the current fair market value in his gross income or he can wait until the restriction lapses, in which case he must include the fair market value *at that time* in his gross income. If he does elect to pay tax on the value of the stock now and never acquires the stock because of the restrictions, he cannot deduct the amount upon which he has already paid tax. What are some of the factors that he should consider in deciding whether to make the election?

Problem 2-10. Brenda Farr has an opportunity to transfer to the Madrid, Spain, office of her employer. At present her salary is $50,000. She has no other income and her itemized deductions are $10,000. She is single and has no dependents. If she accepts the position in Spain, her job will begin on January 1, and she will receive a salary of $40,000. She anticipates that her deductions will be the same as if she were to stay in the United States. Assume that she will remain in Spain long enough to qualify for the foreign income exclusion. Further, assume no change in tax rates between the two years. (Use 1990 rates.)

(a) What is her present after-tax income?

(b) How much would her U.S. salary have to be in order to provide her with the same after-tax income as the job in Spain?

Problem 2-11. Mr. and Mrs. Philip Rasmussen are both over age 65 and received social security benefits for the entire year 1990. You have collected the following data from them:

Total social security receipts for the year	$8,000
Adjusted gross income (all from investments)	30,000
Tax-exempt interest received	4,000
They will file a joint tax return for 1990.	

(a) How much, if any, of the social security receipts will be subject to tax for 1990?

(b) Would it have made any difference if the $4,000 of tax-exempt state and local governmental bond interest had been additional interest from corporate bonds? Explain.

(c) What difference would there have been if their adjusted gross income had been $28,000 and they did not have any tax-exempt interest income? Explain.

Problem 2-12. Indicate which of the following activities would produce income that would be subject to the income tax, and the reasons why or why not:

(a) Mother cuts father's hair and that of the children.

(b) Mother cuts the hair of Mr. Heard, the next-door neighbor, and he reciprocates by mowing her lawn. If the lawn requires mowing when Mr. Heard's hair does not need cutting, Mother pays him $5.00.

(c) Ginny owns a residence that increased $20,000 in value during the year. As a result, she was able to take out a $15,000 second mortgage.

(d) Jules leased a two-bedroom apartment. Alan moved in with Jules and paid Jules one-half of the rent each month. Would your answer differ if Jules and Alan leased the apartment, each paying the landlord one-half of the rent each month?

(e) Jason and Stephanie decided to build their own house. When they finished, they had invested $100,000 in actual cash, but the home was appraised as being worth $140,000. Would your answer differ if they had taken out a $90,000 loan to finance the construction of the home and related living expenses?

PROBLEMS WITH AN ASTERISK REQUIRE ADDITIONAL RESEARCH.

Problem 2-13.* The Wattage Electric Company required that certain of its corporate officers attend the annual convention and trade association meetings of the industry. The corporation reimbursed the employees for their travel and other expenses incurred to attend. It was also the custom for the corporation to reimburse the employees for expenses incurred by a spouse who might also attend the convention. Mr. Watts, a vice-president, attended the meeting and took his wife along. Upon return, he requested and received full reimbursement for his expenses as well as his wife's expenses.

(a) Will Mr. Watts be required to include any of the reimbursement in taxable income?

(b) What if the corporation required Mrs. Watts to attend the meetings?

(c) Would there be a different tax result if the corporation did not require Mrs. Watts to go, but made it clear that her presence at the meetings was desirable and had a business purpose?

Problem 2-14.* Jerry Lambert has entered into an employment agreement with Fast Food, Inc. Fast Food has agreed that it will pay Jerry a salary of $2,000 per month and that at some unspecified future time it will pay into a retirement plan fund $200 for each month Jerry has worked. Fast Food's promise to contribute to the retirement plan is unsecured.

(a) How much gross income does Jerry have per month?

(b) Would it make any difference in Jerry's tax treatment of his compensation if Fast Food purchased an insurance contract to assure that funds would be available to meet the pension plan payment obligation?

(c) Would Jerry have recognized income if Fast Food agreed to provide death and disability payments although Fast Food did not pay premiums to an insurance company to provide such benefits?

COMPUTER PROBLEM

Problem 2-15. This problem consists of two separate parts, each of which is a modification or addition to the spreadsheet which was developed in the Computer Problem at the end of Chapter 1.

Part I. In the previous spreadsheet, line 12 was "itemized deductions." Enter a new line which will be the "basic standard deduction," (BSD). BSD (which means the deduction for a person who is not blind and under age 65) for the year 1990 is $3,250. Thus, the amount to be deducted to arrive at adjusted gross income (in addition to the exemption amount) will be either (a) the BSD or (b) the total of itemized deductions, whichever is larger. Thus, you might choose to leave line 12 as "itemized deductions" and change the following lines as follows:

Line and Column	*Description*	*Column B*
13	BSD	$3,100
14	Deduction	If 12B > 13B, then 12B If 12B < 13B, then 13B If 12B = 13B, then 13B
15	Exemption amount	(same as before)
16	Total deductions	14B plus 15B
17	Taxable income	11B-16B

Balance of lines as in Problem 1-14.

Depending upon the spreadsheet software which you are using, you may be able to insert the additional lines so that taxable income will automatically be moved forward and it will not be necessary to change the formula for the taxable income line.

Part II. In the previous spreadsheet, line 8 was left blank and was labeled "income from other sources." Change that label (cell 8A) to read "annuity income," and enter the amount in column B to equal 36B.

Ms. Jones now has an annuity which pays her $200 per month. She received the annuity for three months during the current year. Her life expectancy, from the annuity tables, as of the beginning of the annuity payout, was 20.0. Her investment in the annuity contract was $16,000.

Move the cursor on the spreadsheet to line 30 and enter the following:

Line	*and Column*	*Description*	*Column B*
30	A	Investment in annuity contract	$16,000
31	A	Expected return	32B
32	A	Life expectancy × annual receipt	20.0 × $2,400
33	A	Exclusion ratio	30B/32B
34	A	Receipts this year	$600
35	A	Exclusion	34B × 33B
36	A	Taxable annuity income	34B − 35B

When finished with the problem, save the results on your disk.

APPENDIX 2-A
TABLE I

Ordinary Life Annuities—One Life—
Expected Return Multiples

Age	*Multiple*	*Age*	*Multiple*	*Age*	*Multiple*
5	76.6	42	40.6	79	10.0
6	75.6	43	39.6	80	9.5
7	74.7	44	38.7	81	8.9
8	73.7	45	37.7	82	8.4
9	72.7	46	36.8	83	7.9
10	71.7	47	35.9	84	7.4
11	70.7	48	34.9	85	6.9
12	69.7	49	34.0	86	6.5
13	68.8	50	33.1	87	6.1
14	67.8	51	32.2	88	5.7
15	66.8	52	31.3	89	5.3
16	65.8	53	30.4	90	5.0
17	64.8	54	29.5	91	4.7
18	63.9	55	28.6	92	4.4
19	62.9	56	27.7	93	4.1
20	61.9	57	26.8	94	3.9
21	60.9	58	25.9	95	3.7
22	59.9	59	25.0	96	3.4
23	59.0	60	24.2	97	3.2
24	58.0	61	23.3	98	3.0
25	57.0	62	22.5	99	2.8
26	56.0	63	21.6	100	2.7
27	55.1	64	20.8	101	2.5
28	54.1	65	20.0	102	2.3
29	53.1	66	19.2	103	2.1
30	52.2	67	18.4	104	1.9
31	51.2	68	17.6	105	1.8
32	50.2	69	16.8	106	1.6
33	49.3	70	16.0	107	1.4
34	48.3	71	15.3	108	1.3
35	47.3	72	14.6	109	1.1
36	46.4	73	13.9	110	1.0
37	45.4	74	13.2	111	.9
38	44.4	75	12.5	112	.8
39	43.5	76	11.9	113	.7
40	42.5	77	11.2	114	.6
41	41.5	78	10.6	115	.5

The annuity tables shown in Tables I and II are so-called "unisex" tables and are to be used where the investment in the contract contains any post-1986 investment. (See Treas. Reg. 1.72-9.) Where the investment was made entirely before July 1986, different tables (also in Treas. Reg. 1.72-9) can be used. These reflect different life expectancies for men and women.

APPENDIX 2-A (CONT.)
TABLE II

Ordinary Joint Life and Last Survivor Annuities Two Lives—
Expected Return Multiples

Ages	65	66	67	68	69	70	71	72	73	74
65	25.0	24.6	24.2	23.8	23.4	23.1	22.8	22.5	22.2	22.0
66	24.6	24.1	23.7	23.3	22.9	22.5	22.2	21.9	21.6	21.4
67	24.2	23.7	23.2	22.8	22.4	22.0	21.7	21.3	21.0	20.8
68	23.8	23.3	22.8	22.3	21.9	21.5	21.2	20.8	20.5	20.2
68	23.4	22.9	22.4	21.9	21.5	21.1	20.7	20.3	20.0	19.8
70	23.1	22.5	22.0	21.5	21.1	20.6	20.2	19.8	19.4	19.1
71	22.8	22.2	21.7	21.2	20.7	20.2	19.8	19.4	19.0	18.6
72	22.5	21.9	21.3	20.8	20.3	19.8	19.4	18.9	18.5	18.2
73	22.2	21.6	21.0	20.5	20.0	19.4	19.0	18.5	18.1	17.7
74	22.0	21.4	20.8	20.2	19.6	19.1	18.6	18.2	17.7	17.3
75	21.8	21.1	20.5	19.9	19.3	18.6	18.3	17.8	17.3	16.9
76	21.6	20.9	20.3	19.7	19.1	18.5	18.0	17.5	17.0	16.5
77	21.4	20.7	20.1	19.4	18.8	18.3	17.7	17.2	16.7	16.2
78	21.2	20.5	19.9	19.2	18.8	18.0	17.5	16.8	16.4	15.9
79	21.1	20.4	19.7	19.0	18.4	17.8	17.2	16.7	16.1	15.8
80	21.0	20.2	19.5	18.9	18.2	17.8	17.0	16.4	16.9	15.4
81	20.8	20.1	19.4	18.7	18.1	17.4	16.8	16.2	15.7	15.1
82	20.7	20.0	19.3	18.8	17.9	17.3	16.8	16.0	15.5	14.9
83	20.6	19.9	19.2	18.5	17.8	17.1	16.5	15.9	15.3	14.7
84	20.5	19.8	19.1	18.4	17.7	17.0	16.3	15.7	15.1	14.5
85	20.5	19.7	19.0	18.3	17.6	16.9	16.2	15.6	15.0	14.4
86	20.4	19.6	18.9	18.2	17.5	16.8	16.1	15.5	14.8	14.2
87	20.4	19.6	18.8	18.1	17.4	16.7	16.0	15.4	14.7	14.1
88	20.3	19.5	18.8	18.0	17.3	16.6	15.9	15.3	14.6	14.0
89	20.3	19.5	18.7	18.0	17.2	16.5	15.8	15.2	14.5	13.9
90	20.2	19.4	18.7	17.9	17.2	16.5	15.8	15.1	14.5	13.8
91	20.2	19.4	18.6	17.9	17.1	16.4	15.7	15.0	14.4	13.7
92	20.2	19.4	18.6	17.8	17.1	16.3	15.7	15.0	14.3	13.7
93	20.1	19.3	18.5	17.8	17.1	16.3	15.6	14.9	14.3	13.6
94	20.1	19.3	18.5	17.8	17.0	16.3	15.6	14.9	14.2	13.6
95	20.1	19.3	18.5	17.8	17.0	16.3	15.6	14.9	14.2	13.5
96	20.1	19.3	18.5	17.7	17.0	16.3	15.5	14.8	14.2	13.5
97	20.1	19.3	18.5	17.7	17.0	16.2	15.5	14.8	14.1	13.5
98	20.1	19.2	18.5	17.7	16.9	16.2	15.5	14.8	14.1	13.4
99	20.0	19.2	18.5	17.7	16.9	16.2	15.5	14.7	14.1	13.4
100	20.0	19.2	18.4	17.7	16.9	16.2	15.4	14.7	14.0	13.4
101	20.0	19.2	18.4	17.7	16.9	16.1	15.4	14.7	14.0	13.3
102	20.0	19.2	18.4	17.6	16.9	16.1	15.4	14.7	14.0	13.3
103	20.0	19.2	18.4	17.6	16.9	16.1	15.4	14.7	14.0	13.3
104	20.0	19.2	18.4	17.6	16.9	16.1	15.4	14.7	14.0	13.3
105	20.0	19.2	18.4	17.6	16.8	16.1	15.4	14.8	13.9	13.3
106	20.0	19.2	18.4	17.6	16.8	16.1	15.3	14.8	13.9	13.3
107	20.0	19.2	18.4	17.6	16.8	16.1	15.3	14.8	13.9	13.2
108	20.0	19.2	18.4	17.6	16.8	16.1	15.3	14.8	13.9	13.2
109	20.0	19.2	18.4	17.6	16.8	16.1	15.3	14.8	13.9	13.2
110	20.0	19.2	18.4	17.6	16.8	16.1	15.3	14.8	13.9	13.2
111	20.0	19.2	18.4	17.6	16.8	16.0	15.3	14.8	13.9	13.2
112	20.0	19.2	18.4	17.6	16.8	16.0	15.3	14.8	13.9	13.2
113	20.0	19.2	18.4	17.6	16.8	16.0	15.3	14.8	13.9	13.2
114	20.0	19.2	18.4	17.6	16.8	16.0	15.3	14.8	13.9	13.2
115	20.0	19.2	18.4	17.6	16.8	16.0	15.4	14.8	13.9	13.2

3

deductions from income

One way of minimizing tax liability, as mentioned in Chapter 2, is to minimize gross income—that is, to make use of all available exclusions so as to reduce the amount classified as income in the first place. Then, once this amount is determined, the fact that not all of it is necessarily subject to tax opens up another way of minimizing tax liability. This way—maximizing *deductions* from income—is the subject of this chapter. Many taxpayers have important opportunities to reduce their taxable income, and thus the taxes they will ultimately pay, through understanding what types of decisions result in deductions and what they must do to obtain these deductions.

3.1 Substantiation Requirements

It is not up to the government to prove that the taxpayer did not pay the amount claimed or to prove that it was not deductible. Proof is up to the taxpayer. If the taxpayer cannot establish the facts so as to come within the statutory authorization, and establish the amount deductible, the IRS will be supported by the courts in disallowing the deduction.[1] The IRS audit process will be explored in more detail in Chapter 19. The point here is that knowledge of what is deductible is of limited value if the taxpayer fails to maintain adequate records, receipts for paid bills, and contemporaneous explanations of facts that support claimed tax deductions.

[1] *New Colonial Ice Co.* v. *Helvering* (S. Ct. 1934), 13 AFTR 1180, 4 USTC 1292, 292 U.S. 435.

3.2 Deductions versus Exclusions

As noted in Chapter 2, exclusions from income include items that are not within the definition of income, such as the recovery of an investment and items that are specifically excludable because of provisions in the tax law. Deductions, on the other hand, are all statutory in their source. This means that nothing is deductible unless specific tax law authorization can be found for the deduction. It is often said that "deductions are by the grace of Congress."

3.3 Costs of Producing Income

Expenses of producing income are generally deductible. These tend to follow an accounting approach. Thus, a business proprietor can deduct salaries paid to employees, property taxes paid on business equipment and premises, utilities, supplies, rent, and any other "ordinary and necessary" business expenses.[2]

Students who have taken at least one college level accounting course are familiar with the concept of a "capital" business expenditure. It means an expenditure that initially increases an asset rather than increases an expense. (Some assets are subject to depreciation—discussed in Chapter 9 of this text—and some are not, i.e., land.) As used in the term "ordinary and necessary," the word "ordinary" is used in contrast to "capital," rather than as the antonym for "extraordinary," according to

[2] IRC Sec. 162(a). Chapter 7 is concerned with proprietorships.

the Supreme Court.[3] However, the IRS and the lower courts sometimes seem to put the taxpayer under the burden of showing that the expense is of a type common in the trade or industry.[4] "Necessary" is used more in the sense of "appropriate" than as meaning "indispensable" or "unavoidable."[5] Thus, while a security dealer's fraudulent activity would not be "ordinary" or "necessary" in the literal meaning of those words, the legal expenses in unsuccessfully defending against criminal fraud charges were nevertheless deductible as "ordinary and necessary" within the tax meaning of those words.[6]

Business expenses are discussed in more detail in Part Two. In this chapter we generally consider the deductions that are not connected with a trade or business. Thus, except for some employee business-related expenses, the deductions discussed here do not need to meet the "ordinary and necessary" requirement, but are allowed because Congress has written the rules to permit qualifying individuals to reduce their income tax liability. The original reasons for allowance of some of these deductions often disappear, or are forgotten, as time goes by.

3.4 Philosophy of Individual Tax Deductions

The income of an individual follows a financial accounting approach. Costs of producing income can generally be deducted. However, as we shall see, some of the costs of producing investment income or other (earned) income can only be deducted to the extent that they exceed a certain percentage of adjusted gross income or to the extent of income generated by investments.

Some concept of "ability to pay" the tax is involved for many of the deduction provisions that apply to individuals. People with extra large medical expenses, people who give money or property to charities, people who pay state and local taxes, people who suffer unreimbursed casualty losses (fire or theft, for example), people who have other people to support, people who are blind or over age sixty-five—all these people get some sort of tax break.

One problem is that huge amounts of tax dollars are involved whenever an individual deduction or credit of general applicability is permitted.[7] The rules are thus replete with limitations and restrictions, and the taxpayer needs to check a reference book to see whether a specific deduction or credit is available or not. Tax administrators, in turn, have to deal with the law as it is—which generally means that they will allow a deduction or credit only when the law unmistakably grants it to the taxpayer and the taxpayer has clearly established the facts bringing himself or herself within the law.

Another problem is that Congress changes the law from time to time in response to social and economic circumstances, and some changes involve a phase-in period so that it takes several years to reach the new stage.

3.5 Child-Care Example

The child and dependent-care credit is an example.[8] The original idea was simple when a child-care deduction was added to the law in 1954. Working parents were allowed a tax *deduction* for amounts spent to care for children when such care was necessary to enable the parent to work.

But wait! An increasing percentage of families have two working parents. Congress did not really want to give a deduction to *all* those people. So the deduction was limited to working women and widowers. But what if a man's wife was disabled rather than dead? The deduction was made available to husbands with disabled wives. What about a working wife? If both parents were working, they should have enough income to afford the babysitter. But, alas, not always. So a married couple, both working, could qualify for the deduction, but with the provision that the fee paid to the babysitter would have to be reduced by the amount their combined income exceeded $6,000.[9] (The same rule applied to husbands with incapacitated wives.) Then, to make sure these deductions did not get out of hand, in terms of revenue loss to the government, a maximum amount was created for the deduction—not more than $600 if there was one child and not more than $900 if there were two or more children.

Questions still came up. Why a deduction just for expenses for care of a child? What about the

[3]*Welch* v. *Helvering* (S. Ct. 1933), 12 AFTR 1456, 3 USTC 1164, 290 U.S. 111.

[4]See, for example, *Sanford Reffett* (1963), 39 TC 869 (dismissed CA 4). Also, *Consumers Water Co. et al.* v. *U.S.* (DC Me. 1974), 33 AFTR2d 74-566, 74-1 USTC 9189, 369 F. Supp 939.

[5]*Comm.* v. *Heininger* (S. Ct. 1943), 320 U.S. 467, 31 AFTR 783, 44-1 USTC 9109; *Welch* v. *Helvering* (S. Ct. 1933), 343 U.S. 90, 12 AFTR 1456, 3 USTC 1164; *Lilly* v. *Comm.* (S. Ct. 1952), 290 U.S. 111, 41 AFTR 591, 52-1 USTC 9231.

[6]*Comm.* v. *Tellier* (S. Ct. 1966), 383 U.S. 687, 17 AFTR2d 633, 66-1 USTC 9319.

[7]For example, the 1986 Tax Reform Act repealed the deduction for state sales tax for individuals. The expected increase in federal tax collections for 1988 from this one change was almost $4.9 billion.

[8]IRC Sec. 21(a). The current rules are discussed in Chapter 4.

[9]This rule was in effect for years through 1972.

expense of caring for other dependents? After all, the whole idea was to allow the taxpayer to be gainfully employed. So the definition of qualified expenses was broadened to cover not only children under thirteen but also other dependents incapable of caring for themselves.[10]

What is meant by a married woman? How about people who are separated but not divorced? The law was made more specific and provided that a woman would not be treated as married for this purpose if she was legally separated from her husband. Then what about deserted wives without a legal separation? They are still legally married. So a deserted wife *who did not know the whereabouts* of her husband *at any time during the year* was not to be considered as a married woman for this purpose.[11] And so forth, on and on, with rules and exceptions to rules. And when all was done, the law still had not achieved absolute fairness. For example: A deserted wife could get the maximum child-care deduction, even though her income exceeded $6,000 for the year, if she did not know the whereabouts of her husband *at any time during the taxable year.* A woman's husband who was in jail during the early part of the year provided no financial help in supporting the children. As soon as he was released, he took off for parts unknown. She argued that she should be able to deduct the amount that she paid to have her children cared for in order that she could go to work, even though her income was too high to get a deduction if the $6,000 test applied.

The Tax Court commented that "because of her unfortunate circumstances throughout the year, we would be happy to be able to extend benefits to her." But she *did know* where her husband was during part of the year (he was in jail—some help!), and thus did not meet the "standards specifically attached by Congress." The Court had to deny the deduction.[12]

A male taxpayer who had never been married claimed the deduction for expenses incurred for care of his invalid mother. On appeal from the Tax Court, the 10th Circuit held that the benefit must be extended to the taxpayer because the attempted limitation under the statute to women alone was unconstitutional insofar as it made an "invidious discrimination" premised on sex.[13] So Congress made some more changes. Sex discrimination was eliminated. The allowable deduction went to $400 per month but was reduced by 30% of any adjusted gross income over $13,000 per year.[14] This $13,000 figure was later increased to $35,000 per year.[15] The age of an eligible dependent child was raised to fifteen.

Still there were problems. The 1976 Tax Reform Act changed the deduction to a credit (with limits), eliminated any reduction related to size of income, allowed students to qualify, and even allowed payments to a grandparent to be eligible for the credit under limited circumstances. The 1978 change allowed grandparents to receive the babysitting fee under less restrictive rules. The 1981 Economic Recovery Tax Act made some further alterations in the child and dependent-care credit, generally increasing the amount of the credit. But, should babysitting expenses, for example, incurred while having a child cared for *outside* the home be treated on a par with those same expenses incurred *at* the parent's home? After all, a babysitter working in the home might be required to perform other duties, such as house cleaning or preparation of meals for the parents. Also, should all qualifying taxpayers, regardless of their income, receive the same credit? The credit was changed to a maximum of 30% with a sliding rate scale reducing to 20% as the taxpayer's income increased. The 1984 Tax Reform Act contained a provision that the noncustodial divorced parent of a child could take the exemption amount deduction for that child if the custodial parent agreed. However, the rule that only the custodial parent could qualify for the child-care credit was retained. The 1986 Tax Reform Act increased both the maximum amount of the credit and the adjusted gross income level at which the credit begins to be phased down. Also, the credit calculation shall be adjusted each year for cost-of-living inflation, similar to the adjustment that was explained earlier for the standard deduction and the personal exemption deduction. We defer detailed treatment of the current rules until Chapter 4.

This is just one provision affecting individuals. It is cited here as an example of how Congress and the courts attempt to react to changing economic and social circumstances. Note that the evolution took 34 years. Similar trails could be traced for most other tax provisions. The point is that most of the tax rules have a reason for being, even though space and time limitations prevent going through the evolution of each of them.

[10]The expense has to be incurred for the purpose of allowing the taxpayer to be gainfully employed full time. Later the statute was revised to allow students to claim the credit where the child care was for the purpose of allowing a parent to attend school.

[11]Effective for year 1974 and thereafter.

[12]*Marcia W. Seaman* (CA9 1973), 31 AFTR2d 73-1181, 73-1 USTC 9408.

[13]*C. E. Moritz* v. *Comm.* (CA10 1972), 469 F.2d 466, 31 AFTR 2d 73-308, 72-2 USTC 9759, *cert. denied,* 412 U.S. 906.

[14]Effective for the year 1973.

[15]Beginning in the year 1976.

3.6 Deductions to Arrive at Adjusted Gross Income

In Chapter 1 we noted the general preferability of a deduction taken in arriving *at* adjusted gross income over a deduction *from* adjusted gross income (an itemized deduction). The major deductions that can be taken in arriving at adjusted gross income are: alimony,[16] certain employee business expenses,[17] contributions to Individual Retirement Accounts (IRAs),[18] contributions to retirement plans by a self-employed person (H.R. 10),[19] and the limited capital loss deduction.[20]

Alimony was discussed at some length in Chapter 2. The same criteria apply in determining whether alimony is deductible as in deciding whether it is includable in income.[21] If the recipient is required to include such a payment in gross income, the payor gets a deduction. If the amount is not taxable to the recipient, the payor gets no deduction. The same result occurs if the parties agree that the payments will not be income to the recipient. As also discussed in Chapter 2, there is alimony "recapture" where the payments are deemed to have been "front loaded." Where that occurs, and the payor is required to include an amount in gross income in the third year, the payee will receive a deduction for the same amount.[22] Such a deduction is also *to arrive at* adjusted gross income.

3.6.1. Employee Transportation and Travel Expenses

These expenses are divided into three categories. The first (called "tier 1" expenses) is that set of qualifying expenses for which the employee has been reimbursed by his or her employer.[23] (Also included in this first category are expenses paid by a qualifying performing artist in connection with the performance of services as an employee in the performing arts, *whether or not* reimbursed.[24]) These expenses are a deduction *to arrive at adjusted gross income* (AGI). Thus, with the exception of the nonreimbursed expenses of the performing artist, the deduction merely removes from AGI the amount, but no more than the amount, that was included in gross income.

Other employee expenses are part of the "itemized" group of deductions. They consist of two sets of expenses. The distinction between these two sets is that the total amount of the first set is deductible as part of the itemized deductions without being reduced by a portion of adjusted gross income. The sum of the second set must be reduced by 2% of adjusted gross income. Any balance remaining is then part of the itemized deductions. Appendix 1-D(c) illustrates how these two categories were reported on Schedule A for 1989. Those expenses that did not get reduced by 2% of adjusted gross income were recorded on line 25 of that form. The expenses that were reduced by 2% of adjusted gross income were entered on lines 20 and 21. Only a relative few taxpayers claim a deduction for the expenses that do not get reduced by 2% of adjusted gross income, and the list of those expenses is short. They are:

- Gambling losses, but only to the extent that gambling winnings are part of gross income.
- Deductions allowable in connection with personal property used in a short sale. (Short sales are discussed in Chapter 5.)
- Federal estate tax on income in respect of a decedent. (Estate tax is discussed in Chapter 15.)
- Amortizable bond premium.
- Adjustments when a taxpayer restores amounts held under a claim of right.
- Impairment-related work expenses of handicapped persons.

The discussion of those expenses that are included in the "itemized" category after reduction by 2% of adjusted gross income is in this chapter at Section 3.8.10.

3.6.2. Individual Retirement Accounts

There are two advantages to contributing to an Individual Retirement Account.[25] First, subject to the limitations discussed below, there is a deduction. This means that no income tax is paid currently on that portion of salary or wages.[26] Second, the interest or dividends that are earned by the investment are not subject to income tax until the funds are withdrawn. It should be noted that the contribution is limited to earned income (salary,

[16]IRC Sec. 215.
[17]IRC Secs. 62(2) and 162.
[18]IRC Sec. 219.
[19]IRC Secs. 62(b), 404, and 405(c). See Chapter 18.
[20]IRC Sec. 1211(b). See Chapter 5.
[21]IRC Secs. 71 and 215.
[22]IRC Sec. 71(f).
[23]IRC Sec. 62(a)(2).
[24]In order to get the deduction, the artist must have performed services for two or more employers, must have had expenses in excess of 10% of gross income, and must have taxable income of $16,000 or less.

[25]IRC Sec. 408. See lines 24 and 25, Form 1040 for 1989, Appendix 1-D.
[26]IRC Sec. 219(b).

wages, and self-employment income). Investment income (i.e., interest, dividend, rent) is never eligible for contribution to an IRA.

Who is eligible for the maximum benefit? First, any employee or self-employed person can contribute to an IRA and take a deduction if he or she is not a participant in another qualified retirement plan at any time during the year. (Retirement plans are discussed in Chapter 18.) Second, a person can contribute and deduct the maximum ($2,000, or earned income if less) even if he or she is a participant in another plan *if* adjusted gross income (before considering the deduction) is below a certain level. That level is $40,000 for a married couple filing a joint return and $25,000 for a single person.

For example, if Billy Barnes (a single person) has a salary of $22,000 for 1990, and no other income, then $2,000 could be contributed to an IRA. It would not make any difference if Billy were a participant in another retirement plan or not.

If Billy were not a participant in another qualified retirement plan, then the size of AGI would make no difference as far as the amount that could be contributed to an IRA and deducted. In that case, Billy's AGI could be any amount (so long as earned income was at least $2,000), and the full $2,000 could be contributed and deducted. (We should point out that it is not necessary to contribute and deduct the maximum. For example, Billy may decide that other needs for money are so pressing that only $800 is available for the IRA. As long as the $800 is paid into the IRA account, a deduction for $800 can be taken.)

If AGI is above the given level, *and* if the individual is a participant in another qualified retirement plan, then the maximum will be reduced, called a phase-out. At some point, therefore, there can be no deductible contribution. The phase-out occurs over an AGI spread of $10,000. Thus, if Billy (single) had a salary of $35,000 or more, and was a participant in another plan, there could be no deductible contribution. However, if the salary were $27,000, for example, the allowable contribution and deduction would be reduced from $2,000 to $1,600:

Salary (also AGI)	$27,000
Phase-out begins at	25,000
Excess	2,000
Excess as % of $10,000	20%
Reduction in maximum: 20% × $2,000 =	$400
Maximum IRA deduction: ($2,000–$400) =	$1,600

For a married couple, if either is a participant in a qualified retirement, pension, or profit sharing tax deferred plan, the phase-out works the same way but begins at AGI of $40,000 rather than $25,000. The phase-out range is the same, i.e., $10,000, so that there will be no deduction if AGI is $50,000 or more. For example, assume AGI is $47,000:

Adjusted gross income	$47,000
Phase-out begins at	40,000
Excess	7,000
Excess as % of $10,000	70%
Reduction in maximum: 70% × $2,000 =	$1,400
Maximum deductible contribution:	$600

If both spouses are employed and neither is a participant in another retirement plan, then they can each contribute up to $2,000 (assuming that each earns at least $2,000) to an IRA, for a total maximum deduction of $4,000.

If both spouses are employed and *either* is a participant in another qualified plan, then each will determine the phase-out separately using the $40,000 level of AGI as the starting point. For example, Fred and Wilma are both employed, combined AGI is $44,000, and one or both participate in another qualified retirement plan:

	Fred	*Wilma*
Excess AGI	$4,000	$4,000
Excess as % of $10,000	40%	40%
Reduction in maximum (40% × $2,000)	800	800
Maximum contribution and deduction	1,200	1,200

Where only one spouse works, and is not a participant in another retirement plan, there can be a deduction for a contribution by the nonworking spouse, but the maximum is $250. Thus, together they could deduct $2,250.

TAX PLANNING TIP: Adjusted gross income in excess of $25,000 (for a single person) will result in a reduction of the amount which can be deducted for a contribution to an IRA if that person is a participant in another qualified retirement plan. If the excess AGI that causes a reduction in the IRA is investment income, a shift in the investment to tax-exempt securities will increase the amount that can be contributed to the IRA. For example, a taxpayer who has earned income (salary) of $24,000 and dividends/interest of $3,000 will have AGI of $27,000 which will reduce the allowable contribution to an IRA. By shifting part of the investment to tax-exempt securities, AGI can be $25,000 or less and the maximum contribution to an IRA can be made and deducted.

Although Chapter 7 deals with accounting methods and the *timing* of gross income and deductions in general, we should point out a specific timing issue with regard to IRA contributions. An IRA contribution does not have to be made during the same year for which the deduction will be taken so long as it is made *for* that year. The contribution needs to be made only by the due date for that tax return (not including extensions). The due date for tax returns for individuals on a calendar taxable year is April 15 of the following year. Thus, if Billy wants to make an IRA contribution that will be deductible for 1990, the actual payment of money into the plan can be made at any time during 1990 or at any time up to April 15, 1991. If Billy should make the payment early in 1991, the trustee of the plan may not know if the intention is for the amount to be a 1990 or a 1991 contribution. Therefore, Billy should take care to identify the year for which the contribution is intended.

TAX PLANNING TIP: One of the advantages of contributing to an IRA account is the fact that the earnings (i.e., dividends and interest) on the investment accumulate free of current taxation. The earlier money is contributed the longer it can earn a return. Therefore, contributions early in the year will result in greater after-tax savings than contributions made later.

Even if there is no deduction for a contribution to an IRA, an amount can be contributed in order to obtain the second advantage, tax-free accumulation of IRA earnings. The maximum which can be contributed for that purpose is also $2,000, which is not subject to reduction because of income level or participation in another retirement plan. The advantage of the contribution is that it can accumulate tax-free earnings.

3.6.3. Retirement Plans for Self-employed Persons

Persons who are self-employed may also contribute to a retirement plan and take a deduction for adjusted gross income.[27] These plans are called H.R. 10 plans, Keogh plans or self-employed retirement plans. The amount that may be contributed to the plan and deducted for AGI is limited. We discuss the tax treatment of self-employed persons in Chapters 7 and 18. IRA plans, H.R. 10 plans, and other deferred compensation arrangements will be discussed in more detail in Chapter 18.

For now we will provide a simple example. Assume that Billy Barnes was self-employed and had no employees for 1989. The net profit from the business was $45,000 and Billy decided to open a self-employed retirement plan and to contribute 10% of the net profit to the plan. See the 1989 Form 1040 at Appendix 1-D(a). The $45,000 gross income would have appeared on line 12, and the $4,500 deduction would have been reported on line 27.

3.7 Limits on Deductions

Some specific items have specific limits on deductibility. In many instances, the limits are different for married people filing separate returns. But some limits apply in a different way.

One type of limit exists because it is sometimes hard to distinguish an investment activity or a business from a hobby.[28] Vacation homes that are occasionally rented out are a prime example. Is the vacation home being held for the production of rental income, with only incidental personal use? Or is it primarily for personal use, with any rental income merely being an incidental offset to the costs of ownership? Even the owner may not really know the answer to such questions. The same problems come up with boats that are owned primarily for personal use but on occasion are rented. Similarly, with airplanes and some other assets.

3.7.1. Vacation Homes

The tax law limits deductions related to vacation homes (except for those itemized deductions discussed later in the chapter to which every property owner is entitled) to the amount of gross rental income.[29] In other words, a net loss from owning the home cannot be deducted against other income. If the vacation home is rented less than fifteen days during the year, *no* rental property deductions are allowed (except those deductions, such as property taxes and interest, that are generally available anyway). However, the rental income need not be reported either.[30]

For example, assume that Billy Barnes owns a condominium in a mountainous ski resort area.

[27]IRC Sec. 62(7).

[28]IRC Sec. 183 provides that there shall be no deduction allowed for an activity that is not engaged in for profit. Although the statute does not contain the term "hobby," it is generally referred to as the "hobby-loss" provision of the Code.

[29]IRC Sec. 280A.

[30]IRC Sec. 280A(g). This is also discussed in Chapter 9.

Billy rents the condo to a friend for one week for $700. The $700 is not gross income to Billy. However, no deduction can be claimed for the expenses incurred. This rule does not prohibit Billy from claiming the expenses that would be deductible even if the property were not rented, such as interest on a mortgage and state and local real estate property tax. These latter items are discussed later in this chapter.

Assume that Billy rents the property for a total of three months during the winter. The gross rental income is $8,400. Billy will be allowed to deduct up to $8,400 of expenses, including depreciation, in connection with the three month period. However, if the expenses exceed $8,400, the excess is not a deduction.

If the property is not a vacation home, which means that Billy can show that the purpose for ownership was "profit seeking" (even if a profit is not obtained) and that any personal use was only incidental, then the deductibility of any loss will be subject to some special rules. For example, assume that Billy owns the ski resort and attempted to rent it during the entire year but only succeeded in renting it for three months for a gross rental income of $8,400. The expenses, including depreciation, were $10,000 for the year so that there was a $1,600 loss. Can Billy deduct the loss? At this point we will say "yes," but there are special rules that could change that answer to "no." We will discuss this problem in Chapter 7 (concerning proprietorship businesses) and in Chapter 17 (concerning investments that are classified as "tax shelters"). Note that if there is a deduction for a loss on rental property., it is not part of the "itemized" deductions but would be reported on line 18 of Form 1040 (see Appendix 1-D) as a negative number.

TAX PLANNING TIP: A person who owns a vacation home can have tax-free rental income by renting the property for a period not to exceed 14 days during the year.

3.8 Itemized Deductions

For most individual taxpayers, itemized deductions will be larger in total amount than the deductions for adjusted gross income. To maximize this source of tax savings, a person needs to know what is deductible and to keep good records of those deductible items. Itemized deductions are reported on Schedule A of Form 1040. See Appendix 1-D(c).

3.8.1. Moving Expenses

In order to be deductible, moving expenses must be in connection with a change of jobs or the beginning of a new job, either as an employee or as a self-employed person.[31] A person graduating from college, for example, can deduct the nonreimbursed costs of a work-related move to a new location. The job itself does not have to be new; transfer from one location to another of the same employer can qualify, as can a change of jobs. To get the deduction, a person must be employed on a full-time basis in the new area for at least thirty-nine weeks in the twelve-month period that follows the relocation,[32] but not necessarily at the same job. (Self-employeds have to work as such for at least seventy-eight weeks in the twenty-four-month period following relocation.)

TAX PLANNING TIP: Assume that a person is considering retirement and a move to a warmer climate. Moving costs to a retirement area would be personal and not deductible. To make the move in connection with a change in employment, and to satisfy the thirty-nine-week employment requirement, can result in a deduction for the moving expenses. The tax effect of the deduction will, in effect, increase the compensation received for the thirty-nine weeks of work.

In addition to the length of employment, there is also a minimum distance requirement. For someone who has not been working, the distance between the new workplace and the former residence must be at least thirty-five miles. For someone who has been working, the distance between the new workplace and the former residence must be thirty-five miles greater than the distance from the former workplace to the former residence.[33] This is shown in Fig. 3-1. This is confusing at first but there is a reason for the rule. Assume that someone works fifty miles from home and commutes each day to work. There is no deduction for commuting expenses. She changes employers, per-

[31]IRC Sec. 217. There are some special rules for foreign moves and for retirees who were working abroad. They are not discussed here.

[32]IRC Sec. 217(c)(2).

[33]IRC Sec. 217(c)(1).

FIGURE 3–1 Allowable moving expenses

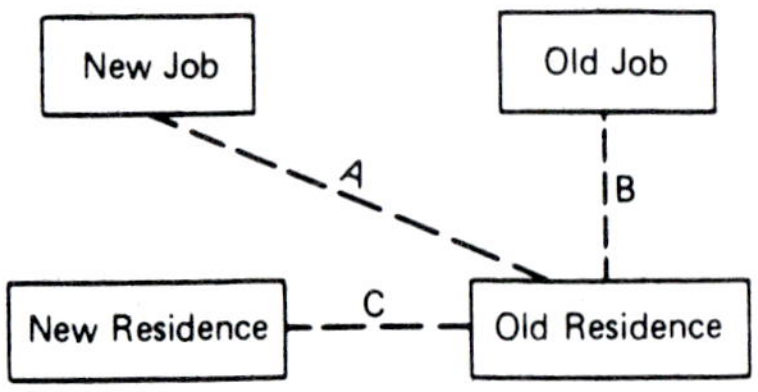

Moving expenses are allowable for the cost of moving distance C only if distance A is 35 miles greater than distance B.

haps only changing the place of employment by a few blocks, but decides this would be an ideal time to change the residence because of the deduction. It won't work. The distance requirement will not be satisfied and there will be no deduction.

What is deductible? Direct expenses, such as amounts paid to move household and personal items to the new residence and one-way costs of travel for the taxpayer and family to the new place, are deductible. There is no overall dollar limitation on the amount of this portion of the deduction. However, there is a limitation; the expenses must be reasonable and not extraordinarily large or extravagant. In addition, but subject to dollar limits, some indirect expenses such as (1) premove househunting expenses (a round trip, short-term visit to the new job location), if the job at the new location has been secured first, (2) lodging and 80% of the cost of meals for up to thirty days (after obtaining employment) in temporary quarters at the new location, and (3) some of the expenses of selling the old or buying the new residence (or comparable lease expenses) can be claimed. Not more than $1,500 can fall into the first two indirect categories, premove and temporary quarters; the total deductible amount for all three *indirect* expenses cannot exceed $3,000.[34] The only limit on the total deduction is that the amount cannot be "unreasonable." Thus one is required to use the shortest reasonable route between the two locations.

Meal costs can be incurred in connection with (a) the move from the old to the new location, (b) the "househunting" round trip, and (c) temporary (up to 30 days) living expenses incurred at the new location before moving into a permanent residence. In all three instances, the includable expense for meals is limited to 80% of the amount actually spent. The rationale for this reduction is explained later in connection with job related meals and entertainment which are also part of the "itemized deductions."

TAX PLANNING TIP: Some moving expenses could be considered either moving expenses or expenses in connection with the sale of the old or purchase of the new residence. Careful identification of such expenses, and documentation, can result in a moving expense deduction. If they are a part of the determination of gain from the sale of the former residence, or part of the cost of the new residence, the tax benefit is deferred, as discussed in Chapter 6.

To illustrate, assume that Billy Barnes has been employed as an accountant. Billy resigned to take a position as a controller in a city some 1,120 miles away. Billy's moving expense deduction is $3,190, as shown in Fig. 3-2. Billy contracted with a moving company to pack and move household goods and personal effects. The cost was $2,048, including insurance Billy purchased for the goods while in transit. Note, again, that there is no specific dollar limitation on this component. The amount, however, must be reasonable. The $228 represents the cost of driving Billy's car, 1,120 miles at 9 cents per mile, plus $127 for lodging and 80% of meals while en route. (The 9¢ rate is an allowance established by the Internal Revenue Service.) Also, the nine-cent rate is not mandatory. Billy can deduct that amount or the actual out-of-pocket costs of operating the car, whichever results in the larger deduction. Prior to actually moving, but after the new job had been secured, Billy took a trip to the new city for the purpose of looking for housing. The deduction for the two-day trip is $624, including *round-trip* airfare and lodging and 80% of meals for those two days. (This part of the deduction is limited to *one* such round trip.) After Billy moved, it took two days before the new house was ready to move into because the former tenants had not moved out. Lodging plus 80% of meals totaled $140, which is deductible. (Note that the deduction for these two items would be limited to $1,500.) Billy had been renting an apartment in the former city and had signed a one-year lease. The penalty for breaking the lease agreement was $100. Billy purchased the residence in the new city, incurring $50 in legal fees. All other costs of the purchase were paid by the seller. Note that there is an option as to tax treatment of some of the expenses incurred in connection with the purchase of a residence. For example, this $50 could be added to the cost of the residence and would be used in calculating gain in the event of a future sale. (See Chapter 5.) Billy felt that such a sale might be a

[34] IRC Sec. 217(b).

FIGURE 3-2 Moving expense deduction

Transportation of household goods and personal effects		$2,048
Travel, meals, and lodging expenses during the move		228*
Pre-move "househunting" trip expenses*	$624**	
Temporary living expenses (up to 30 days)*	140	
Total	764***	
Costs of selling former residence or settling an unexpired lease	100	
Expenses of buying a new residence or obtaining a lease on a residence	50	
Total of above three items		914****
Grand total deduction		$3,190

*Includes only 80% of the cost of meals.
**This part of the deduction is available only if the trip took place *after* having secured a new job.
***The sum of the "househunting" expenses and the temporary living expenses cannot be more than $1,500.
****This total cannot be greater than $3,000.

COMPUTER FORMULAS: The above example on a spreadsheet would look like this.

	A	B	C	D	E	F	G
1	Transportation			2048			
2	Travel, 80% meals, lodging			228			
3	Pre-move househunting		624				
4	Temporary living		140				
5			___				
6	Total		@ IF (@ Sum (C3..C4)>1500, 1500, @ Sum (C3..C4))				
7							
8	Selling residence		100				
9							
10	Buying residence		50				
11			___				
12	Total			@ IF (@ Sum (C6..C10) > 3000, 3000, @ Sum (C6..C10))			
13				___			
14	Grand Total			@ Sum (D1..D12)			
15				===			
16							

Note that the formula may be much longer than the cell width. Only the number represented by the formula will show on any printout unless you specifically instruct the computer to display a formula. Note that the formula could be written to allow input for the full cost of meals, with the 80% limit then being multiplied in order to arrive at the proper deduction.

long time off, while there would be an immediate tax reduction by claiming the fee as a moving expense. By year end, Billy had not yet satisfied the thirty-nine-week requirement, but since the intention was to stay at the new job for an extended time, the deduction is available for the year the expenses were incurred. If Billy should fail to satisfy the thirty-nine-week work requirement, an amended return would have to be filed with no deduction for the moving expenses. Alternatively, the $3,190 that was claimed as a deduction could be added to gross income for the following year when it was determined that the qualifications had not been met.

TAX PLANNING TIP: Some people, in connection with a change of employment and residence, decide that it is too expensive to hire a moving company. They would rather save money by moving their own household goods. After considering the tax effect of the deduction for moving expenses, the cost of having someone else do the work may be substantially less. Their decision might be, then, that the saving from doing the job themselves is not worth the extra effort. (Note however, that out-of-pocket costs, such as truck or trailer rentals, are deductible even if you move yourself.)

3.8.2. Medical Expenses

Medical and dental expenses are deductible to the extent they exceed 7.5% of adjusted gross income.[35] Medical expenses cover almost everything that is paid for the prevention or alleviation of a physical or mental defect or illness.[36]

Appendix 3-A is a checklist of *some* common items that are includable as medical expenses. The list is not intended to be all-inclusive. Part of tax planning may involve the classification of expenditures into deductible categories. Thus, amounts paid for medical insurance (including the medical portion of automobile insurance) and unreimbursed amounts to medical doctors, dentists, and hospitals can be counted. Basic Medicare insurance (Medicare A) cannot be included. In addition, some expenditures not routinely considered "medical" can qualify.[37] For example, a swimming pool added to a residence for the purpose of providing medically necessary physical therapy can be deducted to the extent that the cost of the pool does not increase the market value of the property.[38] Likewise, special equipment to allow a physically handicapped person to operate an automobile will qualify.[39] The costs of *prescription* medicines and of insulin are also includable.

For example, assume that Billy Barnes has adjusted gross income of $15,000 for 1990 and will itemize deductions. Nonreimbursed medical and dental expenses including medical insurance for the year totaled $1,200. Of that amount $1,125 will not be deductible and $75 will be included as part of the itemized deductions. (See Appendix 1-D(c), lines 1 to 4.)

TAX PLANNING TIP: The timing of some medical or dental expenses can be controlled. This might be done in such a way as to maximize the deduction. For example, if a taxpayer has already incurred medical expenses in excess of 7.5% of adjusted gross income then he/she might incur additional expenses for the same year (rather than wait until a later year—such as some dental repairs) in order to get a deduction. Those same expenses, postponed to the following year, might not result in a deduction because the 7.5% "floor" will apply again in the second year. There is no deduction for medical expenses paid in advance. However, expenses incurred in one year and paid in a later year are includable. For example, a doctor bill incurred in December will not result in a deduction if total medical expenses are under 7.5% of AGI. That same bill, paid in January, will result in a deduction for the second year if total medical expenses for the second year are more than 7.5% of AGI. Medical bills charged to a credit card such as VISA or MasterCard are deductible when charged rather than when the credit card bill is paid.

Medical expenses include amounts paid for the taxpayer, spouse, and dependents. They also include the medical expenses paid for someone who is not a dependent so long as the *only* reason the person is not a dependent is the failure to meet the gross income test.[40] Also, a divorced parent may deduct the medical expenses paid for his or her child despite the fact that the parent may not be able to claim the dependency exemption deduction for the child because of failure to provide more than 50% of his or her total support.[41]

TAX PLANNING TIP: Instead of giving substantial amounts of cash to a parent who needs help with making ends meet as the result of injury or illness, arrange to pay their medical insurance and other medical expenses for them. If you thus furnish over half of their total support, their medical expenses can then be added to your own and give you a larger medical expense deduction.

Transportation to and from a doctor's office, hospital, or other site of medical care will count as part of the medical expense.[42] Where a person uses a personal automobile for such transportation, the current acceptable deduction allowance is 9 cents per mile.[43] Also, lodging will count (subject to a maximum of $50 per night) where a person is away from home for medical care, such as an outpatient at a licensed hospital.[44] A person accompanying the patient may also deduct lodging (same $50 limitation) if that person's presence was required, such as a parent accompanying a minor child.

[35] IRC Sec. 213(a). The rules were different prior to 1984.
[36] IRC Sec. 213(d).
[37] Rev. Rul. 55-261, 1955-1 CB 307.
[38] *Ferris* v. *Comm.* (CA7 1978), 582 F.2d 1112, 42 AFTR2d 78-5674, 78-2 USTC 9646.
[39] Rev. Rul. 66-80, 1966-1 CB 57.
[40] See Chapter 4 for the five tests which must be satisfied in order to claim a person as a dependent.
[41] IRC Sec. 213(d)(5).
[42] Rev. Rul. 63-91, 1963-1 CB 54; Rev. Rul. 76-80, 1976-1 CB 71.
[43] Rev. Proc. 80-32, IRB 1980-29, 27.
[44] IRC Sec. 213(d)(2).

TAX PLANNING TIP: Divorced parents should consider having only one parent pay the medical expenses of a child of that marriage, perhaps the parent with the smaller adjusted gross income. Since medical expenses are deductible to the extent that they exceed 7.5% of adjusted gross income, there might not be a deduction if the parents split the costs, or if the parent with the larger AGI were to pay the costs. It is not necessary for the divorce decree to provide which parent shall pay such costs.[45]

Major medical expense planning probably involves trying to push nonreimbursed medical expense payments into alternate years so as to exceed the 7.5% of AGI limit by the maximum possible.

Assume that the cost of doctors, dentists, and hospitals is about $1,200 per year, for a family with three children. If adjusted gross income is $40,000 per year, there is no deduction because the annual expense is less than 7.5% of AGI. If the medical expenses are bunched so that $2,400 is paid *every other* year the deduction *every other* year would be $2,400 – (7.5% of $25,000), or $525. This could produce $147 or more of tax savings.[46]

The IRS will probably disallow medical payments *made in advance*.[47] But if a payment is made on January 1 for last year's expenses, and this year's expenses are paid as incurred, the bunching can be accomplished.

3.8.3. State and Local Taxes

Deductible taxes include income, real estate, and personal property taxes.[48] In general, almost any state or local tax (except sales tax and gasoline tax[49]) that is imposed on the individual will be deductible—while no federal tax will be.[50] Certain state taxes are a part of the retail price of an item and not separately stated (e.g., cigarette tax and excise tax on gasoline). There is no deduction for such taxes. Other nondeductible state taxes are rarely encountered by the average taxpayer—estate, inheritance, legacy, succession, and gift taxes.

Deductible taxes do not include payments for services rendered by local governments even though the label of "tax" may be applied to the payment. For example, fishing, hunting or driving licenses may be taxes in some locations, but since the buyer of such a license is considered to benefit directly, no deduction is allowed.[51]

The deductibility of taxes contrasts with the nondeductibility of services of the same sort that are rendered by private organizations in other locations. For example, a condominium development might assess owners of the units for amounts to pay private security police, garbage collection, etc. Such payments are not deductible, although in many cities such services are financed by property taxes. In the case of the condominium development, the property owners could convert nondeductible payments into deductible taxes by incorporating the condominium complex as a village under state law and imposing property taxes instead of assessments to finance the common services.

No deduction is available for the amount of a tax paid by one person which is really someone else's liability.[52]

Record-keeping requirements for the state and local tax deduction are probably less tedious than for some other deductions. The amount of state and local income tax paid can be determined by looking at the amount of withholding from salary checks plus the state and local income tax returns. Real estate taxes are normally paid once each year. In the case of mortgaged property, the usual procedure is for the mortgage holder to pay the tax from an escrow fund created by the owner as a part of the periodic mortgage payment. Personal property taxes are also paid annually in most jurisdictions. Thus, a statement and one cancelled check will take care of the recordkeeping requirements. In some states there is a personal property tax imposed on automobiles, with the payment made at the same time and as a part of the auto license fee. A look at the registration statement might reveal the amount. In some cases the state provides a formula whereby the total cost of the license can be divided between the tax and the price of the license. There is no deduction, for federal income tax purposes, for that part of the cost of the auto tax which is a license.[53]

[45] If the parents do split the costs, each parent can claim only the amount spent.

[46] The $147 is an estimated figure, based upon an assumed marginal tax rate of 28%. Of course, the savings could be more, or less, depending upon the applicable tax rate.

[47] See, for example, *Robert S. Bassett et al.*, 26 TC 619 (1956).

[48] IRC Sec. 164.

[49] Until 1979 the state excise tax on gasoline was a deduction for individuals. Until 1987, state sales taxes were deductible.

[50] The deductible taxes being discussed here are part of the "itemized" group for individuals. Any tax, including federal taxes other than income tax, can be deducted as a business expense if incurred for a business purpose.

[51] Another common example is a sewer or water tax. See Rev. Rul. 75-346, 1975-2 CB 66.

[52] See *El Paso National Bank* v. *U.S.* (DC Tex. 1971), 29 AFTR2d 72-745, 72-1 USTC 9392, *aff'd.* 72-1 USTC 9393, 453 F2d 1313 (CA5).

[53] Generally, a distinction is made between a tax and a fee. The latter is a charge made for a particular act or service and is not deductible.

As we shall see in Chapter 9, when a state or local sales tax is paid on an asset used in a trade or business, the total cost of the asset, including the sales tax, is capitalized. Normally, that cost will be written off over some future time period as depreciation deductions.

3.8.4. Interest

For purposes of this explanation, we will divide interest into four categories. The first, interest incurred for business purposes (i.e., where a person operates a proprietorship and a loan is made for acquisition of business assets or services) results in a deduction *for* adjusted gross income.[54] Interest and other business expense deductions are discussed in Chapter 7.

The second category includes "investment interest" and interest incurred in connection with a "passive activity." The former is interest expense that is incurred for a loan to purchase investment property. The latter is interest in connection with a rental activity or a business activity with respect to which the taxpayer is not a material participant. "Investment interest" and interest in connection with a "passive activity" have some special rules that limit their deductibility. These limitations are discussed in Chapter 17.[55] Until then, we will be satisfied with a statement of the general rule, which is that interest on loans incurred to provide money for investments is deductible to the extent of investment income. Where the amount of such interest expense is larger than the amount that can be deducted for the current year, there is a carryover to future years of the nondeductible amount. Thus, the amount may be deductible in the following year(s). For example, assume that Billy Barnes incurred interest expense of $3,000 in 1991 on a loan made for capital to invest in the stock market. If Billy's income from interest and dividends for the year totaled $3,000 or more, then the entire $3,000 interest expense can be included as part of the itemized deductions. On the other hand, if Billy's interest and dividend income were only $2,500 for the year, $2,500 of the interest expense could be deducted and the remaining $500 carried over to 1992. The amount carried to 1992 will be treated *as if* it had been spent during 1992 and any 1992 deduction will be determined using the same rules as described here for 1991. However, interest expense incurred to purchase or carry tax-exempt bonds is never deductible. Likewise, interest expense on money borrowed to purchase life insurance usually is not deductible. There are some other exceptions that are beyond the scope of this introductory discussion.

The third category is interest expense on a person's residential mortgage. Subject to the limitations discussed below, such interest is deductible as part of the itemized deductions.

Generally, if a taxpayer incurs interest expense in connection with his or her principal residence, or a second residence—such as a vacation home—the interest is deductible.[56] The deductibility of interest on residential mortgage(s) is subject to a limitation.

For residential indebtedness incurred after 10/12/87 there is a distinction between "acquisition indebtedness" and "home equity indebtedness." The former means debt incurred to buy, construct, or substantially rehabilitate a principal residence or a secondary residence. The latter means debt such as a second (or third) mortgage. The significance of the difference is the tax treatment of the interest expense paid on each type of debt. For example, assume that Billy Barnes purchases a home for $200,000, paying $40,000 down and taking a mortgage for $160,000. The debt is "acquisition indebtedness." Lynn Larsen owns a residence that is valued at $150,000 but Lynn's mortgage on the property is $70,000. Lynn borrows an additional $50,000, using the residence as collateral. None of the $50,000 is used for capital improvements of the house. Lynn's "acquisition indebtedness" is $70,000 and "home equity indebtedness" is $50,000. Any part of the $50,000 used to improve the residence would result in an increase in "acquisition indebtedness" and a decrease in "home equity indebtedness."

The limitation on deduction for "acquisition indebtedness" interest is the interest on $1 million of such debt ($500,000 each for a married couple filing separately). Any interest on debt in excess of the $1 million limit is consumer interest. The limitation on deductibility of consumer interest is explained later. Note that the $1 million limit is *not* per residence, but for the sum of taxpayer's principal residence and a second residence.[57] For example, if a person owns a principal residence that has an $800,000 mortgage and buys a vacation home, putting a $400,000 mortgage on it, there is $1,200,000 in debt, but the "acquisition indebtedness" is subject to the $1 million limit.

There is also a limitation on the deduction for interest on "home equity indebtedness." Generally, the interest on such debt in excess of $100,000 ($50,000 for married-separately) is treated as con-

[54]IRC Sec. 162 and Sec. 163.

[55]IRC Sec. 163(d).

[56]IRC Sec. 163(h). In order to qualify as a second residence, the taxpayer must live in the residence for part of the year.

[57]Mobile homes and boats can qualify as second residences.

sumer interest. For example, assume that Billy Barnes' home is worth $600,000 and that the "acquisition indebtedness" is $400,000. (Note that "acquisition indebtedness" is reduced as payments are made on the debt. Once reduced, the only way to increase such debt is to make substantial improvements to the property.) Billy borrows $120,000, placing a second mortgage on the property. None of the loan proceeds are used to improve the property. Billy's debt is as follows:

Acquisition indebtedness	$400,000
Home equity indebtedness (maximum)	100,000
Personal (consumer) indebtedness	20,000

Note that the importance of these classifications is related to the tax treatment of the *interest* paid on each of the three categories of debt.

There is another limit: The sum of "acquisition indebtedness" and "home equity indebtedness" cannot exceed $1,100,000. Any interest on debt in excess of $1,100,000 is personal (consumer) interest.

Residential mortgage debt incurred before 10/13/87 is treated as "acquisition debt" regardless of whether it is a first or second mortgage, the result of an original purchase, or a refinancing. Also, the $1 million limit does not apply. Thus, interest on such debt is fully deductible. *However,* such debt does reduce the $1 million limit on new (after 10/12/87) acquisition debt. For example, assume that a person has debt on a principal residence mortgage of $800,000, incurred prior to 10/12/87. A vacation home is purchased and a mortgage of $250,000 is placed on that property. The "new" acquisition debt is limited to $200,000 because the $1 million limit is reduced by the first debt of $800,000.

The fourth category is called "consumer interest." All such interest was deductible for 1986 and prior years as part of the itemized deductions. Starting in 1987, there was a phase-out of the deduction so that only part of the expense was deductible.

Consumer interest, such as interest on credit cards, car or boat loans, loans for education or medical expenses (unless part of the loan on a personal residence), vacation loans, loans to pay taxes, and interest on residential mortgages that exceeds the limits identified above, and the like, will not be deductible after 1990. In the meantime, part of such interest is deductible each year as reflected in the following table:

Year	*Percentage Deductible*
1987	65
1988	40
1989	20
1990	10

The above limitation applies regardless of when the loan was originated. For example, assume Billy Barnes borrowed money to purchase a car. It makes no difference if the debt was incurred in 1988 or 1987 or some other year. Assume that the interest expense for 1988 was $1,500. Only 40%, which is $600, was deducted for 1988 even if Billy itemized deductions. There is no carryover for the amount which is not deductible. If the interest expense for 1989 was $1,000, then only $200 (20%) was included in itemized deductions.

TAX PLANNING TIP: After 1990, car and other personal consumption interest will not be deductible. In the meantime, only a portion of such interest will be deductible. However, interest is deductible on a residential mortgage up to the sum of the original acquisition indebtedness plus $100,000. It is possible that a residential mortgage could be increased in order to obtain the money to purchase a car or for other purposes. In fact, some lending institutions are actively marketing such "home equity" loans. Such a loan might be particularly attractive to people who have owned their home for several years and have "paid down" the mortgage resulting in substantial equity in the property. Assume that you purchased a home for $100,000, and the existing mortgage balance is $60,000. If you can borrow up to $40,000 more by increasing the mortgage, you will be able to deduct all of the interest on the entire residential debt. You can borrow the money for any purpose, including the purchase of a car. A loan that is not secured with a residential mortgage will result in "consumer interest" which will only be partially deductible, depending upon the year. On the other hand, some people feel that it is too risky to place a lien on their personal residence for a loan the proceeds of which will be used for some other purpose, such as the purchase of an automobile.

Not all interest is clearly labeled as such; thus, careful tax planning dictates ferreting out those expenses that may be deductible. Property purchased under a deferred payment plan may not have stated interest, but an imputed interest amount may be determined.[58]

"Points" is a term used to describe a fee charged to a borrower either for loan processing or for loan origination. It is not uncommon for a seller, particularly the seller of residential property, to pay points, such as a fee to obtain an FHA mortgage for the buyer. In that case, the points are not treated as interest but as a reduction in the net sales price of

[58]IRC Sec. 483.

FIGURE 3-3 Summary of rules applicable to deduction for various kinds of interest expense

Type of Interest or Loan	*Tax Treatment*
Loans, the proceeds of which are used to buy life insurance or to invest in tax-exempt bonds	Not deductible
Business loans	Deductible to arrive at AGI
Loans, the proceeds of which are used to purchase investments, particularly securities	Itemized deduction to extent of investment income, with carryover of excess
Interest on a "passive activity"	Limited (see Chapter 17)
Interest on residential loan(s)	Itemized deduction subject to limits on the size of the *debt*
Interest on consumer loans (which includes interest on residential loans in excess of limitations)	Itemized deduction 1989: 20%; 1990: 10%; after 1990: none; no carryover

the property, thus changing the amount of the gain or loss from the sale. "Points" paid by a mortgagor-borrower as a premium to obtain a conventional mortgage loan constitutes deductible interest, although the loan documents themselves may not label the amount as interest.[59] Other "points," paid as a service charge on a loan, such as a VA loan, are not deductible as part of a residential loan.[60] Points paid to refinance a residential mortgage are amortizable over the term of the mortgage.

Figure 3-3 summarizes the tax treatment of the various kinds of interest expense discussed thus far.

TAX PLANNING TIP: An educational loan, such as a loan made to finance college expenses, will result in "consumer interest" unless the loan is secured by a mortgage on the taxpayer's first or second residence. The limitation on "consumer interest" deduction will apply. If such a loan is secured with a residential mortgage, then there will be a deduction, so long as total debt does not exceed the lesser of original cost plus improvements or $100, 000. Parents, for example, finding it necessary to borrow money to finance a child's education should consider the after-tax cost of borrowing with a home equity loan. Even persons who do not need to borrow such funds should consider the possibility of doing so if they qualify because the after-tax costs of borrowing will be less than the costs of borrowing if there is no deduction for interest expense.

In Chapter 2 we discussed the imputed interest income required to be included in the gross income of a person who makes certain below-market-rate-interest loans. The borrower also has imputed interest expense that is deductible, subject to the limitations discussed above. The tax treatment of the interest will depend upon the reason for the loan, i.e., a loan made for the purpose of having money to invest in the stock market as compared with a loan made for the purpose of obtaining money to purchase a pleasure boat.

TAX PLANNING TIP: Persons who rent their personal residence get no deduction for any part of the rent. Persons who purchase a residence, paying interest on a mortgage, can deduct the interest expense. Also, property taxes on a personal residence are deductible. Comparing the after-tax effect of renting and purchasing may result in a decision that purchasing is more economical.

If an installment contract for purchase of personal property (i.e., something other than real estate) or educational services has no interest element stated or ascertainable, the tax law imputes interest at 6% of the average unpaid balance on the contract as the interest.[61] Such interest is "consumer interest."

Another provision of the tax law imputes interest when interest is not specified in a property purchase contract of more than $3,000 that has some payments due more than a year later.[62] Interest is imputed if no interest is charged in the contract. If interest is charged, but the rate is less than 9% (on debt of $2.8 million or less), interest will be imputed at 9%. There are some exceptions.[63] If debt is more than $2.8 million, the interest rate will be a function of the average yield rate for U.S. government obligations. However, the maximum rate of imputed interest will be 6% on the sale of land between family members as long as the total sales for a year are under $500,000.

[59] Rev. Rul. 69-188, 1969-1 CB 54; Rev. Rul. 69-582, 1969-2 CB 29.

[60] Rev. Rul. 67-297, 1967-2 CB 87; Rev. Rul. 68-650, 1968-2 CB 78.

[61] IRC Sec. 163(b).

[62] IRC Sec. 483.

[63] IRC Sec. 483(e), and Sec. 1274A.

For example, assume that in September 1989, Billy Barnes sold an apartment building for $5,000,000 to an unrelated party under an installment sales contract that provided for payments to be made over a period of twelve years. The interest rate stated in the contract was 7% annual. The "applicable federal rate" for long-term debt (i.e. the average yield for marketable U.S. securities with a maturity of more than nine years) for the month of September 1989, was 8.20%. Therefore, there was 1.2% unstated interest in the sales contract. In addition to the 7% interest actually received by Billy, gross income will include interest at the imputed rate of 1.2%. The buyer will also treat part of the payments as imputed interest and may be able to deduct that amount as interest expense.

One rather interesting sidelight on interest and property tax deductions has to do with apartment living. A rentor may be paying, as a part of the monthly rent, both interest and property taxes, which are expenses of the landlord. There is no deduction to the tenant. Should the building be converted into a condominium and that person decide to purchase the apartment, the mortgage interest and property taxes would become deductible. Some states are trying to pass the real estate tax through to the tenant by requiring the rental payments to specify the amount or percentage for tax and having the landlord serve as an agent for the government in the collection of the tax. The landlord would also be responsible for the tax even if it were not collected from the tenant. The IRS has ruled that such a New York law does not provide tenants a tax deduction.

Another interesting sidelight on interest deduction has to do with the changes in taxpayer behavior that we might expect to see regarding timely payment of income tax. We discuss timely payment of taxes, interest on underpayments, and penalties for late payment or nonpayment in Chapter 19. Prior to 1987, interest on late payment of federal income tax was a deduction. Penalties have never been deductible. Thus, some taxpayers viewed a delayed payment of income tax, even if an interest charge was incurred, as a form of borrowing from the government. Since the interest was a deduction, the after-tax cost of such borrowing was assessed in the decision to postpone payment. Starting in 1987, such interest is considered part of "consumer interest" only part of which is deductible and, after 1990 none of which will be deductible.

Planning hint: It is better to pay a few dollars more for interest, which is deductible, and pay less in purchase price when buying something that will not be deductible anyway. For example, in buying a house, the seller may offer to carry a second mortgage at 15%. The buyer might be able to obtain a mortgage on the entire property at 10% interest. If the principal amount of the second mortgage can be proportionately reduced, so that the actual dollar payments come out the same, the buyer will be better off to take a smaller 10% first mortgage and take on the 15% second mortgage, because the extra interest is deductible. Of course, the seller may have opposing goals, as when more interest income, which will be taxed, is not desired. Sometimes it will make no difference to the seller, and sometimes the seller is eager enough to make the sale that adverse tax consequences will be acceptable.

3.8.5. Charitable Contributions

Cash contributions to qualified charitable organizations can be deducted,[64] with a maximum deduction for any one year of 50% of the adjusted gross income.[65] If contributions exceed the deduction limit, there is a carryover of the nondeductible portion for five years. Qualified donees include churches, hospitals, medical research organizations, art museums, nonprofit civic groups (such as a local symphony), and federal, state, and local governments.[66] The IRS publishes a list of qualified donees, which is about as large as a big city telephone directory. In addition, the IRS issues individual determination letters to the organizations themselves.

Although the basic idea of a "donation" is that no benefits are received by the donor, the actual line between deductible donations and nondeductible payments is difficult to draw. Dues paid for an athletic membership in the YMCA, for example, are clearly not a deductible contribution, even though the "Y" is a qualified donee for a bona fide donation. The reason is that the contributor can receive certain benefits as a member. Contributions to a church, on the other hand, are deductible, even though the church provides a number of social or educational amenities, Sunday school facilities, etc.

Noncash charitable contributions require some special rules. Generally, noncash charitable contributions can be placed in one of two categories, personal property or investment property. The deduction for contributions of personal property (i.e., used clothing, books, games and household appliances) is the *lower* of the original cost or the fair market value of the property at the time of the donation.[67] The theory underlying this rule is that

[64] IRC Sec. 170(a).
[65] IRC Sec. 170(b).
[66] IRC Sec. 170(c).
[67] IRC Sec. 170(e). There is a limited exception to this rule that applies to inventory contributions of corporations. IRC Sec. 170(e)(3).

personal satisfaction was derived from the consumption of part of the original cost of the property and there should be no deduction for that part of the value that has already been consumed.

The deduction for property that is held as an investment (i.e., shares of stock of a publicly traded company) and that has increased in value is the fair market value at the time of the donation.[68] It is not possible to make a profit by making a contribution of property to charity. However, a person can donate appreciated property, that is, property that has increased in value and that would have resulted in a taxable gain if sold (see Chapter 5), and obtain a deduction for the amount for which the property would have been sold. There is no income tax imposed on the excess of the value of the property over its original cost. The difference between the original cost and the higher fair market value is a "tax preference item" which will increase the alternative minimum tax, if that applies. See Chapter 16.

Assume that Billy Barnes has some shares of stock purchased as an investment several years ago at a cost of $10,000. Today the stock is worth $16,000 and it is transferred to a qualified charity. The deduction, assuming that the limitations are not exceeded, is $16,000. The $6000 "gain" is not subject to tax. This is a substantially different tax result from what would occur if the stock had been sold and then the proceeds donated to charity. The $6000 gain would then be taxed to Billy.

Where property that has increased in value is donated, and sale of the property would have produced long-term capital gain (discussed in Chapter 5), the 50% (of adjusted gross income) ceiling on contributions changes to 30%.[69] However, the 50% limit will remain if the taxpayer is willing to reduce the contribution deduction to an amount equal to the investment in the property.[70]

In our previous example, Billy's deduction limitation would have been 30% of adjusted gross income rather than 50%. Billy could choose to use the 50% ceiling, but in exchange for that privilege would be required to reduce the deduction to $10,000. In either event there is a carryover available for nondeductible amounts. Carryovers are limited to five future years. Note that where the 50% of AGI limit is elected, the *amount* of the contribution is reduced so that the amount of the carryover is also reduced. If the 30% limitation is used, the "full" amount of the contribution may be deductible by waiting until future years and using the carryover. For example, assume that Billy's AGI is $30,000. Of this amount, 50% is $15,000; 30% is $9,000. If Billy chooses the 30% limitation, only $9,000 can be deducted currently, but the $7,000 difference can be carried forward to next year (subject again to deduction limits). If the 50% limitation is elected, the deduction is $10,000 currently, but there is no carryover because there is no remaining amount.

On the other hand, if investment property has declined in value, the deduction is also for its fair market value. This prevents a tax deduction for the decline in value of the property. It also suggests a tax savings idea. A person should not donate investment property that has decreased in value since its original purchase. Rather, the property should be sold. (Deduction for loss on sale of such property is discussed in Chapter 5.) The proceeds of the sale can then be donated to charity as a cash contribution. The result is the deduction for what was the fair market value of the property *plus* the deduction for the loss from the sale.

Most individual taxpayers can take advantage of the charitable contribution deduction in small ways—such as by keeping an accurate record of the value of books, clothing, and similar items donated to charities, and claiming reasonable amounts for their unsubstantiated cash donations during the year. The amount claimed for donated used items is what would have to be paid to replace them in their used condition, not what a dealer in used merchandise would pay for them.[71]

TAX PLANNING TIP: Charitable contributions, unlike some other personal expenditures, are almost totally within the control of the taxpayer as to both amount and time. For those persons whose itemized deductions and standard deduction are close to the same amount each year, making charitable contributions every other year instead of each year could result in using the standard deduction one year and itemizing deductions the next year. Total charitable giving would not have to be increased.

[68] Treas. Reg. 1.170A–1(c). A qualified appraisal must be obtained and included with the tax return, where property with a value of more than $5,000 (other than traded securities) is deducted. Also, if the total non-cash charitable contributions for a year exceed $500, there is a special form (Form 8283) which the IRS requires be attached to the tax return. The purpose is to report additional information which is not reported otherwise. The additional information includes the name of the organization to which property was given, description of the property, date of contribution, date the property was acquired, how the property was acquired, the donor's cost, the fair market value at the date of contribution, and the method which was used to determine the fair market value. If the value of property is under $5,000, an independent appraisal is not required.

[69] IRC Sec. 170(b)(1)(C).

[70] IRC Sec. 170(b)(1)(C)(iii).

[71] Treas. Reg. 1.170A-1(c)(2).

Very few persons contribute to charity in amounts in excess of 30% or 50% of their adjusted gross income. It is possible, of course, particularly where a person may have a great deal of wealth but only a moderate amount of current income. If donations do exceed the limits, any excess may be carried forward as a deduction in following years, with a limit of five years on the carryover. Gifts of cash to a limited class of qualified donees, called private foundations, are subject to a 30% of adjusted gross income limit and with a carryover available for amounts contributed in excess of the limit.[72]

Personal services provided to qualified donees cannot be deducted.[73] But the out-of-pocket expenses of such services can be.[74] This includes an optional 12-cent-per-mile deduction for use of a personal car.[75] Where actual out-of-pocket operating costs exceed 12 cents per mile, then the larger amount can be deducted for use of a personal car for charitable purposes.

If Billy Barnes is a Scout leader, for example, there is no deduction for the time devoted to the activity. This is true no matter what Billy's time may be worth. If Billy buys supplies for the troop, the cost of such supplies is deductible. If a personal automobile is used in connection with scouting activities, a 12-cent-per-mile (or actual gas and oil cost) deduction is available.

3.8.6. Casualty and Theft Losses

Casualties and thefts may result in deductions.[76] It is important to distinguish between losses that occur to business assets and losses that occur to personal assets. The former are deductible *for* adjusted gross income. The amount of the deduction is the undepreciated cost of the asset reduced by any insurance reimbursement. This will be discussed more in Chapter 7. Here the concern is with losses of nonbusiness and noninvestment property.[77]

A casualty is the destruction (totally or partially) of property by a sudden, unexpected, or unusual event.[78] Hurricanes, floods, fires, lightning, and earthquakes are examples of casualties. Questions often arise regarding the deductibility of losses that occur from events that may or may not be sudden or unexpected. Examples are losses from infestation of insects, losses from drought, or losses from unusual freezing. Each case must be evaluated on its own merits relative to the criteria of "suddenness" and "unexpectedness." A casualty does not have to be a natural event—automobile accidents are included.[79] However, there is no deduction if the taxpayer purposely destroyed his/her property.

The loss calculation starts with the difference between the value of the property before and after the casualty.[80] In some cases these values are not easily determinable, so it may be necessary to use a substitute measure of loss, such as repair cost.[81] The loss, however determined, cannot be more than the cost of the property. The lower of (1) the decline in value or (2) the cost, is then reduced by any insurance recovery, then by $100, and then by an amount equal to 10% of AGI.[82] The amount left is the loss deduction. Each casualty or theft loss during the year must be reduced by the $100. The reduction of 10% of AGI applies to the total losses during the year rather than to each event.

Assume that Billy Barnes owned a car that was totally destroyed in a windstorm. Billy had no insurance. The original cost of the car to Billy was $7,000 and it was estimated to have a value of $4,000 before the casualty. Billy's loss deduction starts with the lower of $7,000 or $4,000. The $100 "floor" is then subtracted from the $4,000. Then (assuming no other casualties or thefts during the year) an amount equal to 10% of AGI is subtracted. If AGI is $15,000, Billy's deduction is $2,400 ($4,000 − $100 − $1,500). The reason Billy gets no deduction for the other $3,000 is because that decline in value is viewed as a personal expense that took place prior to the casualty. If Billy had received insurance proceeds of $800 because of the casualty, the deduction would be $1,600.

Assume that Billy's car was an antique that had increased in value since purchase. The original cost was $7,000, but immediately prior to the casualty it was worth $12,000. The casualty loss deduction, assuming no insurance proceeds, would be $7,000 less the $100 "floor," less the 10% of AGI, or $5,400. The reason Billy gets no deduction for the $5,000 increase in value is because that amount was never income subjected to tax. If there had been insurance proceeds of $2,000, Billy's deduction would have been $3,400.

[72]IRC Sec. 170(b)(1)(B).

[73]Treas. Reg. 1.170A-1(g).

[74]Rev. Rul. 55-4, 1955-1 CB 291.

[75]IRC. Sec. 170(j). Parking and toll road costs are additional deductions.

[76]IRC Sec. 165.

[77]IRC Sec. 165(c)(3). Business losses will be reported on Schedule C, Fig. 7-2.

[78]*Fay* v. *Helvering* (CA2 1941), 27 AFTR 432, 41–2 USTC 9494.

[79]*Shearer* v. *Anderson* (CA2 1927), 6 AFTR 6483, 1 USTC 210.

[80]Treas. Reg. 1.165-7(b).

[81]Repair cost can be used to measure the casualty loss only if repairs are actually made. *Marjorie Blackburn,* TC Memo 1982-529, 44 CCH Tax Court Memo 1121 (9–15–82).

[82]IRC Sec. 165(c).

TAX PLANNING TIP: One of the biggest problems with a deduction for casualty or theft losses is the substantiation of the amount. Careful record keeping, appraisals, and contemporary documentation can result in a tax deduction that would otherwise be denied. The taxpayers must prove (1) that there was a casualty or theft and (2) the dollar amount of the loss.

Where property, such as an automobile, is used both for personal purposes and business purposes, a casualty or theft loss will be treated as if two assets were involved—one a personal asset and one a business asset. The allocation between the two will be based upon the ratio of personal use and business use.

For example, assume that Billy Barnes uses a car 70% for business and 30% for personal purposes. The car was destroyed in a fire and there was no insurance coverage. The original cost was $10,000, but depreciation deductions of $2,800 had been taken for the business portion. The tax term for the original cost less depreciation is "adjusted basis," a term that accountants know as "book value." Since no depreciation can be taken on the non-business portion, the adjusted basis does not change.

Adjusted basis of business portion ($7,000 – $2,800)	$4,200
Adjusted basis of non-business portion	3,000

The casualty loss deduction (for adjusted gross income) will consist of $4,200 for the business portion. (See Chapter 7.) Billy's itemized deduction for the casualty will be based upon the personal use portion of the car and will be $3,000 less ($100 + 10% of adjusted gross income). If adjusted gross income is $20,000, for example, then this deduction will be $900.

If insurance coverage had provided reimbursement, then it, too, would be allocated in the 70–30 ratio. If Billy received insurance proceeds of $4,000 (allocated $2,800 to the business portion and $1,200 to the non-business portion) then the loss would have been:

Adjusted basis of business portion less insurance	$1,400
Adjusted basis of non-business portion less insurance	1,800

The deduction to arrive at adjusted gross income would be $1,400. The itemized deduction would be $1,800 less ($100 + 10% of AGI). If AGI were $20,000, there would be no deduction for this portion of the loss. (We assume, of course, no other casualty or theft losses for the year so the entire 10% of AGI reduction applies to this loss only.)

A theft is the illegal taking of property, including burglary, robbery, and embezzlement. The calculation is the same as that for a casualty. There are two significant administrative differences. First, it may be more difficult to prove a theft than to prove a casualty.[83] Frequently, in the case of a casualty, there are some "remains" or ruins that provide visual evidence of damage or destruction. In the case of a theft, the property is gone. Thus, the taxpayer must establish that the property, in fact, existed (e.g., that the purse contained $800 at the moment it was snatched) and also that the missing item was stolen rather than lost, buried by the dog, or mistakenly thrown out with the garbage. A theft is not the same as a mysterious disappearance. If a wallet is gone, how can a person "prove" that it was stolen and not just carelessly misplaced?

Second, measurement of the amount of loss may be more difficult in a theft than in a casualty. A casualty loss may be estimated by the repair cost. This is not possible with a theft loss.

Property valuation and appropriateness of the theft or casualty classification are the main problem areas with these deductions. Photographs, appraisals, original invoices, repair estimates, etc., are of great help in documenting what was taken or damaged and how its value was determined. Police reports, newspaper stories, and affidavits from friends and neighbors are all useful in establishing what happened—especially in a theft situation.

If for some reason a person could have been reimbursed for a casualty or theft, but does not request the reimbursement, the tax deduction is questionable. The IRS has taken the position that there should be no deduction in pre-1987 years, but the Tax Court, in one recent case, has allowed the deduction.[84] For years after 1986, the law disallows any deduction for an insured loss unless a timely insurance claim is filed.

3.8.7. Taxes and Insurance

After-tax benefits from the misfortunes of casualties and thefts can be obtained by recognizing that the losses can be deducted but insurance premiums cannot be. Thus, self-insurance makes good sense, at least up to a point. If a person can bear the risk of a $500 deductible automobile

[83] *Edwards, Adm. (Allen)* v. *Bromberg* (CA5 1956), 49 AFTR 856, 56-1 USTC 9448.
[84] *Hills*, 76 TC 484, *aff'd* 82-2 USTC 9669 (CA11), distinguishing *Axelrod* v. *Comm.*, 56 TC 248 (1971). See also, *Grigsby*, TC Memo 1983–744.

policy, for example, and such a policy saves appreciable premium money, then part of a casualty loss (e.g., an auto accident) may be deductible. The tax reduction plus the long-run reduction in premiums for the insurance could be greater than the $500 casualty loss.

Assume that a married taxpayer in the 28% marginal tax bracket drives a $10,000 automobile, trading for a new one each year. Collision insurance ($50 deductible) costs $700 per year, which is not deductible. Should he decide to be uninsured, an accident, even one that is his fault and results in the total loss of his car, will provide a $6,400 deduction, with a $1,792 tax savings (assuming that the accident occurred shortly after having acquired a new car and AGI is $35,000). If he has one such accident every 11.7 years, the after-tax cost of the two alternatives is the same. Note that there is no tax advantage to going without insurance for public liability and property damage or hospitalization for others in an auto accident. This is the case because any such losses suffered by a taxpayer are not deductible.

3.8.8. Education Expenses

Earlier, in Section 3.6.1, we discussed the treatment of employee expenses that can be deducted to arrive at adjusted gross income (called tier 1 expenses) and those that are deductible from adjusted gross income if the taxpayer itemizes deductions (called tier 2 expenses). Tier 2 expenses in total must be reduced by 2% of AGI before there will be any deduction. Education expenses might fall in either group. If the employee is reimbursed for such expenses, then gross income includes the reimbursement and there may be a deduction (to arrive at AGI) for the same amount.

It is possible that the reimbursement will be included in gross income and there will be no deduction. An employee must qualify for the deduction (see below). If an employer pays for education expenses of an employee and the employee gets no deduction, then the result is additional tax to the employee. The law does not provide that an employee automatically gets a deduction for any expenditures for which he or she is reimbursed by an employer. (For example, assume that an employer provides an "expense allowance" of $55 per day for lodging while an employee is out of town on business. The employee stays in an economy motel for $39 per night. The $55 is included in gross income, and the deduction (to arrive at AGI) is $39 so that the employee's taxable income is increased by $16.) If the employee is not reimbursed, then qualified education expenses become part of the tier 2 (also called "miscellaneous") group. This will result in a deduction if the total exceeds 2% of AGI.[85] The question, then, becomes one of which expenses can be included in the tier 2 group.

The qualified (deductible, after the 2% floor) expenses include those incurred for the purpose of maintaining or improving the skills necessary to keep a job. They do not include the expenses incurred to meet the qualifications to obtain a job. However, a person can include those expenses incurred to *keep* one's job, if the education requirement changed after employment began. No deduction is allowed if the purpose of education is to meet the minimum requirements for a new job or profession or if the purpose is to obtain a different job or promotion. Obviously, the line between deductible and nondeductible education expense is very unclear.

In deciding whether and how to go on to graduate school, the deductibility of at least some education expenses may be a factor. Suppose that an accounting major takes a job in the tax department of a CPA firm and enrolls in evening courses leading to a law degree. The courses are paid for by the individual. Tax result? The IRS takes the position that the cost of law school courses is not deductible because the degree could lead to a new profession.[86]

Some states require a certain minimum number of days of continuing professional education by CPAs and other professionals. Such expenses more clearly will result in a deduction. The result is not as clear where the continuing education requirement is satisfied by taking graduate courses which can lead to an advanced degree. A taxpayer seems to be in a better position to deduct educational expenses if he or she is not a candidate for a degree. In rapidly changing fields such as computers, an employee may find it necessary to incur educational expenses for short courses, just to "keep up" with developments. Such expenses are normally deductible, unless incurred for the purpose of getting a promotion or a different job.

Note that the 2% of AGI floor (an amount which is not deductible) does not apply *only* to education expenses. Education expenses, if deductible, are part of the miscellaneous (tier 2) group. It is the *total* of that group that is reduced by 2% of AGI to determine the amount of the deduction.

3.8.9. Entertainment

All deductions are subject to a requirement of substantiation by the taxpayer, but business travel

[85] Prior to 1987, all such qualified expenses were deductible.
[86] See Rev. Rul. 72-450, 1972-2 CB 89.

and entertainment expenses require substantial documentation to be deductible.

Entertainment records must show the amount, the time, the place, the business purpose of the entertainment, and the business relationship of the persons entertained. Receipts have to be obtained for lodging and for other expenses of $25 or more.[87] The IRS has an understandable concern that personal expenses not be claimed as tax deductions under the guise of being business-related unless there is a real business purpose. As explained below, these expenses are part of the tier 2 group, *but only* after being reduced by 20%.

3.8.10. Miscellaneous Deductions

Education expenses and entertainment expenses (both discussed above) are part of "miscellaneous" deductions. (See Appendix 1-D(c), lines 20-25.)

A whole range of additional items, mainly expenses related to employment or to the holding of investment assets, can also be deducted, but only as part of the tier 2 group. Tier 2 deductions include the second and third categories of employee transportation and travel mentioned at section 3.6.1 above.

The second category is employee nonreimbursed entertainment expenses and business-related meals. Only 80% of such expenses can be counted. The rationale behind allowing only 80% of such expenses to be deductible is based upon a concept known as the "two martini lunch." Congress felt that some people may have a more expensive meal, or more expensive entertainment, when the total amount is deductible. The government views any deductible expenditure as an expense that is being paid in part by the government because of the tax reduction. Hence, denial of part of an expenditure as a deduction will reduce the government's "payment."

The third category is all other nonreimbursed employee business expenses. This includes such expenditures as:

- Transportation
- Dues to trade and professional organizations and union dues[88]
- Subscriptions to professional journals
- Employment-related education
- Employment agency and counseling fees[89]
- Uniforms and other allowable work clothing,[90] (including costs of cleaning them)
- Allowable expenses of looking for a job
- Allowable office-in-home expenses
- Required tools[91]

The third category also includes expenses incurred in connection with the production of income, that may or may not also be in connection with being an employee. These include:

- Legal and accounting fees
- Fess paid to collect income
- Investment counsel fees
- Tax return preparation and tax advice fees[92]
- Hobby expenses (up to the amount of hobby income)
- Rental on safe deposit box used to store non-tax-exempt securities and other income-producing assets[93]

"Tier 2 miscellaneous" expenses must be in excess of 2% of AGI in order to result in a deduction, and it is only the amount which exceeds 2% of AGI which can be deducted. ("Tier 1 miscellaneous" expenses, discussed earlier, do not have to be reduced by 2% of AGI.)

Note that the 20% reduction for meals and entertainment applies *before* the 2% AGI reduction.

For example, assume that Billy Barnes (not a performing artist) incurred the following expenses:

Reimbursed employee travel/ transportation	$1,000
Nonreimbursed employee entertainment	800
Nonreimbursed other miscellaneous employee expenses	600

Billy's gross income is $21,000, including the reimbursement for travel/transportation. Therefore, AGI is $20,000 after the deduction for reimbursed expenses. Assuming that Billy will itemize deductions, the result is:

80% of entertainment	$ 640
Other miscellaneous employee expenses	600
Total	1,240
Less 2% of AGI	400
Deduction for tier 2 misc. expenses	$ 840

This category presents another example of how ordinary English words are used in a very specific and technical way for income tax purposes.

[87] IRC Sec. 274(d) and Treas. Reg. 1.274-5.
[88] Rev. Rul. 72-463, 1972-2 CB 93.
[89] Rev. Rul. 75-120, 1975-1 CB 55; Rev. Rul. 77-16, 1977-1 CB 37.
[90] Rev. Rul. 70-474, 1970-2 CB 34.
[91] IRS Publ. 17.
[92] IRC Sec. 212(3).
[93] *Daniel S. W. Kelly*, 23 TC 682 (1955), *aff'd* 228 F2d 512 (CA7 1956), 228 F.2d 512, 56-1 USTC 9170.

Many people might use the terms "travel" and "transportation" interchangeably. That would be a mistake for tax purposes. Let's take "transportation" first.

As mentioned before, there is no deduction for commuting expenses.[94] The tax law presumes that taxpayers will live next door to their work and will not incur any expense to get to work. If a taxpayer decides to live in the suburbs and commute, that cost must come out of pocket with no benefit from a related tax reduction. However, certain persons are required to move about from one place to another in connection with their work. For example, a construction supervisor in a city might supervise more than one job at a time and be required to spend part of each day at each location, although returning home at day's end. Another example would be where a person takes a short trip in connection with employment but does not get too far away to return home at the end of the day. This type of transportation expense is generally deductible *for* AGI if reimbursed and *from* AGI if not reimbursed and the total miscellaneous deductions exceed 2% of AGI. However, the mileage from home to the first stop each day, and from the last stop each day back to home, is considered commuting mileage and, hence, not deductible. The costs that are characterized as "transportation" refer only to the cost of moving the human body from one location to another. "Transportation" does not include meals, lodging, or any other incidental costs.

"Travel," on the other hand, is a broader term and includes transportation costs plus some other items, such as lodging and 80% of meals.

Reimbursement for an employee's expenses might be equal to, less than, or greater than the amount of the actual expenses. We will consider the tax effect of each possibility.

Many employees are required, as a part of their work, to incur travel and/or transportation costs. For some, the amount of the expenditure is offset in full by the reimbursement. As mentioned earlier, the reimbursement will be included in gross income as part of the salary/wage or as a miscellaneous income item. In either event, where the amount received as reimbursement is equal to the expense, the employee comes out even. AGI has not increased or decreased. The employer can deduct the amount paid to the employee (except for 20% of meals and entertainment) so the tax benefit of the expense deduction impacts the employer rather than the employee.

An employee will "come out ahead" if the reimbursement exceeds the actual expense. The reimbursement is included in gross income, and the deduction is limited to the actual expense. Thus, AGI is increased by the excess and the employee's tax will increase as well. This can happen, for example, where the employer pays the employee a "per diem" amount for travel but the employee spends less than that amount. For example, assume that Billy Barnes has an employer who pays $60 per day while Billy is in travel status. Billy stays in economy motels and spends only $48 per day. The extra $12 per day will increase Billy's AGI, as well as taxable income and tax liability.

Another example of how an employee can "come out ahead" is where the employer "reimburses" for use of the employee's car for business transportation at a rate that exceeds the amount of the employee's deduction. At present, the IRS allows a deduction for business use of a personal automobile at the rate of 25.5 cents per mile for up to 15,000 miles during a year and 11 cents per mile for mileage in excess of 15,000 (called the "optional" allowance). Parking and toll fees can be deducted in addition to this optional standard mileage allowance.[95] (If actual expenses for operation—including depreciation, which is discussed in Chapter 9—exceed the standard optional mileage allowance, the actual expenses can be deducted. However, all receipts and documentation will have to be kept by the employee, and, if the car is used for any nonbusiness trips, it is necessary to prorate between business and nonbusiness use. Even where the standard mileage allowance is used for the deduction, a clear and accurate record of business mileage does have to be kept by the employee in order to substantiate the deduction.) The 25.5 cent rate includes a depreciation portion. There is no depreciation deduction for an asset once it has been fully depreciated. An automobile is treated as having been fully depreciated when a total of 60,000 miles has been claimed using the standard mileage allowance. After 60,000 business miles, the standard allowance is 11 cents per mile.

For example, assume that Billy's employer pays for business use of a personal automobile at the rate of 30 cents per mile. Billy drove 12,000 miles for business purposes during the year and decides to use the optional standard mileage allowance for the deduction. Gross income includes the $3,600 received, and the deduction is $3,060. AGI and taxable income are increased by the $540 difference.

The IRS has announced that the optional standard mileage deduction rate for 1990 will be

[94]IRC Sec. 262 provides, "Except as otherwise expressly provided in this chapter, no deduction shall be allowed for personal, living, or family expenses." Commuting costs are personal expenses.

[95]IRC Publ. 17, an explanatory document issued each year by IRS to assist taxpayers in preparing their individual income tax returns.

$0.26 per mile and the rate will be applicable to all miles, rather than just the first 15,000, so long as a car is not fully depreciated.

Where an employer's reimbursement is less than the allowance or actual expenses, the excess is part of the "tier 2 miscellaneous" group. As mentioned earlier, there is a deduction for "second tier miscellaneous" expenses only if the employee itemizes deductions and if the total of "second tier miscellaneous" exceeds 2% of AGI. Thus, the excess might not be deductible. For example, assume that Billy's employer pays for business use of a personal automobile at the rate of 22 cents per mile and that Billy drove 12,000 miles and decides to use the standard mileage allowance. Gross income includes the $2,640 received. Billy can deduct the $2,640 to arrive at AGI. However, the standard mileage allowance at 25.5 cents is $3,060. The excess of $420 is a deduction only if Billy itemizes deductions *and* the total "second tier miscellaneous" deductions exceed 2% of AGI.

Prior to 1987, the miscellaneous deductions could include a "quiet business meal," i.e., one held in an atmosphere conducive to business even though business was not actually discussed during the meal. That is no longer the rule. Instead, 80% of the cost of a business meal can be included as part of the tier 2 group only if it is "directly related" or "associated with" the taxpayer's employment. This rule perhaps is more applicable to self-employed persons than to employees. As we have mentioned, Chapter 7 of this text is devoted to the taxpayer who is self-employed. However, it is not uncommon for a person who is salaried to be required to pay for some meals and entertainment even though there will be no reimbursement. In particular, a person who is in sales, for example, may be an employee but the amount of his or her compensation is based upon a commission rather than a fixed salary. It is clearly "ordinary and necessary" for such a person to incur such expenses. What about a deduction?

First, as we have seen, any includable expense for meals and entertainment must be reduced by 20%. Only the balance of 80% can be included in the tier 2 group, which is reduced by an amount equal to 2% of adjusted gross income in order to arrive at the amount of the deduction. For example, assume that Billy Barnes has 1990 AGI of $30,000, all of which is commission income. Billy incurred $2,000 of meal and entertainment expenses. There are no other tier 2 expenses. Only 80% of the $2,000 can be included in the tier 2 group. That $1,600 must then be reduced by $600 (2% of AGI) to arrive at a deduction of $1,000. There is no carryover for the nondeductible expenses.

How did an expense become qualified to be included as part of Billy's $2,000? In other words, what does it mean that the expenses must be "directly related" or "associated with" Billy's employment? For a business meal to be included, it means that business must have been discussed at the table or that the meal came just before or after a substantial and bona fide business discussion. Also, the costs are limited to the meals and entertainment of the taxpayer, guest or guests, and their spouses. The part of the cost of any meals or entertainment which is "lavish and extravagant" cannot be included. Naturally, that is a very subjective standard for which contemporaneous record keeping is a must.

If the itemized deductions exceed the standard deduction (discussed in Chapter 1), the tax return should be filed with the deductions itemized. Many taxpayers may not go to the trouble of totaling all of their possible deductions—and thus needlessly pay larger amounts of income taxes.

3.8.11 Expenses Related to Exempt Income

A fee paid to an investment adviser may be deductible.[96] However, to the extent that the investment advice (or other expenses) relates to securities producing exempt municipal bond interest, the fee is not deductible.[97] Similarly, the interest paid to borrow money to buy or to continue to own tax-exempt bonds is not deductible, even though interest expense incurred for other purposes may be deductible.

3.9 Maximizing Itemized Deductions

Just as the timing of medical expense payments can affect the tax deductibility of medical expenses (see Section 3.8.2), so, too, the timing of itemized deductions generally can influence tax benefits. The basic technique, as with the medical expenses, is to put the itemized deductions into alternate years to the maximum extent possible. The techniques are similar to those used with medical expenses—delay payments on, for example, real estate taxes, so that in 1990 both the 1989 and the 1990 real estate taxes are paid.

If a single taxpayer incurs 1990 deductible expenses for interest, real estate taxes, and medical expenses of $2,600, deductions would not be itemized because the basic standard deduction ($3,250) is greater. If this taxpayer wanted to contribute $700 to charity each year, deductions would be itemized since the result would be a deduction of

[96] IRC Sec. 212 and Sec. 67.

[97] IRC Sec. 265.

$3,300, which is $50 more than the 1990 standard deduction. However, by contributing $1,400 to charity every other year, the standard deduction could be deducted in alternate years and $4,000 itemized in alternate years. This advantage can be increased, of course, by lumping interest, taxes, and other itemized deductions into alternate years as well.

Timing of other transactions can also impact deductions. An expense paid for someone to whom you are not married, such as a medical expense, might not be deductible. Such expenses, if paid for someone to whom you *are* married, might result in a deduction. Tax planning calls for postponing the payment until after you are married.

Living in an owned residence normally generates tax deductions for real estate taxes and interest, whereas living in a rented apartment or house does not. Certain exclusions are available to taxpayers living and working abroad that are not available to those who live and work in the United States. Some locales within the United States offer extensive services (libraries, concerts, garbage collection, water, police and fire protection, etc.) covered by state and local taxes, that are deductible, whereas other communities charge user fees, which are not deductible, for the same services. Some states finance heavily through sales taxes, which are not deductible, while others rely heavily on income taxes, which are. So where a person lives makes a difference in the federal income tax that is paid.

Whether a person leases or buys—a car, a television set, an apartment full of furniture, or whatever—can make a tax difference. An installment purchase will contain an interest element (part of which is deductible, at least until 1990), but rent is not part of interest for tax purposes—hence, no deduction.

In some types of jobs, a person may spend personal money without any real chance of reimbursement. A schoolteacher may buy supplies to use to enrich classroom discussions. A staff accountant may want a personal copy of a professional magazine, and understand that the firm will not reimburse the cost. The loan officer for a small bank may use her personal car on occasion to visit bank customers. An IRS agent may decide to get a personal copy of the IRS Manual because the office copy is never kept up to date.

In any situation where an expense might be reimbursable but is not, the individual should be in a position to prove that it was not reimbursable as well as that the expense was an ordinary and necessary expense of getting the job done, in order to get a tax deduction. One good method of establishing such proof is to apply for reimbursement and be turned down—and then write a confirming memo about the refusal and retain a copy with the tax file. With such a groundwork laid, the chances improve for successfully getting a tax deduction for such an item.

Of course, to get the expense reimbursed is better. Even if it takes a corresponding salary adjustment, it is generally better for an expense item to be reimbursed by the employer than for the individual to claim a deduction for something that the employer was not willing to reimburse.

3.10 Summary

This chapter has dealt with some of the expenditures that are deductible for federal income tax purposes. Chapter 2 was concerned primarily with those items that must be included in gross income. Chapter 4 is concerned with the calculation of the tax liability, the different rate schedules, and tax credits.

TRUE-FALSE QUESTIONS

State whether each of the following statements is true or false. For each *false* answer, reword the statement to make it *true.*

T F 1. Since a person is presumed innocent until proven guilty, a taxpayer's claimed deductions are presumed to be correct until the government proves that they are not.

T F 2. A taxpayer is entitled to claim as tax deductions the same items that have been claimed by other taxpayers he knows. These would be referred to as "ordinary" expenses.

T F 3. A business manager's legal expenses in unsuccessfully defending herself on a criminal charge growing out of her business activities could not possibly be either an "ordinary" or a "necessary" expense and hence could not be deductible.

T F 4. Even though remaining alive involves expenses that would seem to be both "ordinary" and "necessary," personal living costs are not generally deductible.

T F 5. An employee's business related transportation costs are deductible to arrive at adjusted gross income if reimbursement was received and the reimbursement is included in gross income.

T F 6. The deduction that is allowed individuals for charitable contributions includes not only cash contributions but also the fair market value of certain noncash property.

T F 7. If a single taxpayer is not a participant in a retirement plan of his or her employer, and earns at least $2,000, then *any amount*, up to $2,000, can be deposited in an Individual Retirement Account and deducted to arrive at adjusted gross income.

T F 8. Expenses of an activity which is not a business (i.e., a hobby) can only be deducted to the extent of revenue generated by that activity.

T F 9. Taxpayers may take a deduction for moving expenses if they move from one state to another.

T F 10. A moving expense deduction can only be taken if the taxpayer was employed in his old location as well as being employed in his new location for the requisite time period.

T F 11. Where a taxpayer claims a deduction for moving expenses as part of the itemized deductions, that deduction can include only 80% of the costs of meals which were purchased during the trip, during a "house hunting" trip and, during the 30-day "temporary living expense" period.

T F 12. State income tax, sales taxes, and property taxes are all deductible if a taxpayer itemizes deductions.

T F 13. A portion of medical insurance premiums paid can be deducted without regard to the 7.5% of AGI rule applicable to medical expenses.

T F 14. The timing of payment of deductible items can have an impact on the tax benefit received from the deduction.

T F 15. Henry is employed by a CPA firm that treats his time as being worth $50 per hour when figuring the amount to charge clients for the firm's services. He gives 300 hours a year to charitable organizations and can thus take a deduction for $15,000 of charitable contributions (300 × $50).

T F 16. Alimony is one of the deductions available even if the payor does not itemize deductions.

T F 17. Alimony is deductible by the person who pays it only if the person who receives it is required to include it as part of gross income.

T F 18. A person who rents an apartment by the month can obtain a deduction for her pro-rata share of interest and property taxes on the building if she can obtain a written statement from the owner of the apartment as to the appropriate amount.

T F 19. A person can deduct the cost of collision insurance on her personal automobile because any casualty loss would be deductible anyway.

T F 20. Qualified "tier 2" expenses must be reduced by 2% of adjusted gross income to determine the amount of the itemized deduction.

PROBLEMS

Problem 3-1. (a) In each of the following situations, indicate whether the taxpayer would be entitled to a deduction for the cost he or she incurs for the clothing, assuming they itemize deductions and the clothing costs exceed 2% of AGI.

(a) Nurse Smith, who works in the Memorial Hospital, is required to wear a white dress, white shoes, and white hose.

(b) Slugger Jones, who plays first base for the Giant City Bums, is required to wear the team uniform and baseball shoes.

(c) Speedy Williams, the city motorcycle policeman, is required to wear the local policeman's uniform and a safety helmet.

(d) Toots Manigan, a professional drummer, is required to wear a tuxedo while his band plays dinner music at a resort hotel.

(e) Hank Hardhat, a construction worker, is required by city ordinance to wear safety-toed shoes while on the job.

(f) Red Dare, must wear heat-resistant clothing while working near the blast furnace at National Steel Company.

(g) Ace McDonnell, works on the flight line at the Nome, Alaska, airport and must have a parka and lined boots in the winter.

(h) Bill Goodwrench, an auto mechanic, is not required to wear any particular uniform or color except that his shirt must have the name of the dealership on the back and his name over the front pocket.

(i) Jock Belt, a professional model and fashion coordinator, purchased clothing to be worn only at style shows and meetings of fashion experts.

(j) Ace Flight, an airline pilot, was required by his employer to lose weight and consequently had to replace his entire personal off-duty wardrobe.

(b) What tax planning implications exist for an employer or employee in this area?

Problem 3-2. Carl Horn has been a resident of the state of Florida for eight years. He recently accepted a new position in Portland, Oregon, for a different employer. Carl's total expenses in connection with the move were as follows:

Plane fare for Mr. Horn	$ 400
Car for Mrs. Horn and children (at standard mileage rate)	220
Cost of moving furniture	2,200
Meals and lodging for Mrs. Horn and children en route (The $250 includes $80 for meals)	250
Cost of breaking apartment lease in Florida	100
Real estate commissions on the sale of their Florida residence	2,000
Total	$5,170

(a) How much may the Horns deduct for moving expenses? (Assume they itemize deductions.)

(b) How long must Mr. Horn stay employed by the Portland employer in order to remain eligible for the deduction?

(c) If you were preparing the tax return for the Horns, would you ask about other items of expenditure that might have been incurred in the move which could be claimed as a deduction? If so, what items?

Problem 3-3. In November last year, Edna Moser's son was involved in an accident while racing the family outboard. Damage to the boat was estimated at $2,000. Moser was not insured for the damage. She had the boat repaired at her own expense at a cost of $2,000. Her adjusted gross income is $16,000.

(a) If Moser is entitled to a casualty loss deduction, how much would it be?

(b) How much is saved in taxes as the result of the deduction? (Moser is a head of household, has two exemptions including herself, and $4,550 of itemized deductions in addition to the casualty loss. Use 1990 rates.)

Problem 3-4. John Petit, a CPA for a national firm, had the following items of income and expense for 1990:

Salary	$30,000
Interest income	1,200
Travel expenses	100

John made a claim and received reimbursement for the travel expenses.

(a) What is his adjusted gross income?

(b) What is the maximum amount John could contribute to an IRA and deduct for adjusted gross income? (He is not a participant in another retirement plan.)

(c) Assuming that John contributed the maximum allowable amount, and that his itemized deductions are less than the standard deduction, what was the after-tax cost of the investment in the IRA?

(d) What amount could John, who is single, have contributed to the IRA and deducted if he were a participant in his employer's retirement plan?

Problem 3-5. Mary Biagioni uses her automobile 75% for business and 25% for personal matters. While driving down the street in a windstorm, a tree limb fell across the hood. It cost Mary $4,000 to get the damage repaired. When she made application to the insurance company for reimbursement she discovered that her coverage had lapsed due to an oversight resulting in her failure to pay the semiannual premium. Her adjusted gross income is $10,000.

(a) Is Mary entitled to a deduction for the loss, and if so, how much?

(b) Does it make any difference if the car was being driven for business or personal use when the accident occurred?

(c) What would be the tax effect if use of the car had been 25% for business and 75% for pleasure?

(d) Assume that in addition to part (a) above, Mary had a $1,000 nonbusiness camera stolen this year. What is her total deduction?

Problem 3-6. Betty Silverwing is married. Her husband is unemployed. They will file a joint income tax return. Her salary will be $44,000 for the year. They have no other income, no children or other dependents, and they will not itemize deductions.

(a) How much can they contribute to Individual Retirement Accounts and deduct for the year assuming that Betty is not a participant in her employer's retirement plan?

(b) Assuming that they contribute and deduct the maximum, what will be the tax savings for the year? (Assume 1990 rates.)

(c) Assume that Betty is a participant in her employer's retirement plan. Also, she decides not to make any contribution to an IRA for her husband. What is the maximum IRA contribution which she can make and deduct?

Problem 3-7. Helen Helper will have adjusted gross income of $20,000 for 1990. During the year she made a contribution to a recognized public charitable organization as follows:

Common stock: 1,000 shares of Fairview, Inc., at $9 per share fair market value on date of gift

The stock had been purchased five years earlier at a cost of $6 per share. It is a long-term capital asset to Helen. She will itemize deductions.

(a) What is Helen's charitable contribution deduction? (Note that there are two possible answers.)

(b) What difference would there be in the tax effect in part (a) if Helen had sold the Fairview stock for $9,000 and contributed the proceeds to charity? Is there any advantage from doing this?

(c) Assume that in part (a), Helen contributed the stock, and that its value was $14,000. Explain the deduction and carryover if any. As in part (a), there are two possible answers.

Problem 3-8. Julius Greenburg (who is single) will itemize deductions because he will have a total, not counting a charitable contribution, of $3,500. His AGI is $26,000. He is thinking of contributing $200 cash to his alma mater, Easygrade Vocational University. (Assume the year is 1990.)

(a) How much may Julius deduct if he makes such a contribution?

(b) What will be the after-tax cost of such a contribution?

Problem 3-9. Jeff Boyd is a collector of rare coins. This year thieves broke into his home and stole his coin collection, which was valued at $10,000, although Jeff's investment in the coins was $7,000. They also stole his watch, which had an original cost of $400 and a fair market value of $200 at that time. Neither was insured against theft. Jeff's adjusted gross income is $40,000.

(a) How much may Jeff claim as a deduction for federal income tax purposes? Is it a deduction for AGI or from AGI?

(b) Would Jeff be able to increase his deduction if he could prove that the coin collection activity was a business rather than a hobby?

(c) How would Jeff go about proving there was a theft and proving the amount of his loss?

Problem 3-10. Jane Pratt is a sales representative for a major national corporation. In connection with her work, she is required to travel about 40% of the time. Jane's employer has agreed to reimburse her for all of the reasonable transportation, hotel and meal expenses for which she submits vouchers. During the year she submitted vouchers for $4,960 of reimbursable expenses and received that amount from her employer. In addition, she has receipts for ordinary and necessary business entertainment expenses of $800 and other ordinary and necessary employee business expenses of $660. The latter consists of dues to professional organizations, subscriptions to professional journals, and education expenses incurred to sharpen her sales skills. Her adjusted gross income *before* taking into consideration any of these items is $23,000. Her itemized deductions *before* consideration of any of these items total $3,500. She is single and has only herself to claim as an exemption. The year is 1990. Determine her taxable income with full explanation of the tax treatment of the reimbursed and nonreimbursed employee business expenses.

Problem 3-11. Bud Borg is a twenty-one-year-old college student with adjusted gross income of $4,000, all from wages. Bud's parents, who have adjusted gross income of $50,000, pay over half of his expenses and thus claim a dependency exemption for him. Bud incurred $1,700 of unreimbursed dental expenses this year. No other member of the family incurred any unreimbursed medical expenses. Bud's parents normally itemize deductions since their home mortgate interest and property taxes exceed the standard deduction allowed on a joint return. The year is 1990.

(a) If Bud's parents pay his dental expenses, can they claim a deduction? (Assume that they have no other medical expenses for the year.)

(b) If Bud pays the dental bills, could he take a deduction? (Assume that his other itemized deductions equal $2,000.) Explain fully.

(c) Who would get the deduction, if any, if Bud's parents paid the bill and Bud signed a negotiable promissory note payable to his parents and due within one year?

(d) Could Bud take a deduction if he arranged with the dentist to pay a year later?

Problem 3-12. Janet Marshall incurred $5,000 of unreimbursed medical expenses during the year. By arrangement with her physician, she agreed to pay one-third of the expenses this year and the balance next year. Her adjusted gross income this year is $20,000 and is expected to be $30,000 next year.

(a) How much may Janet deduct each year for medical expenses?

(b) If Janet borrowed enough money to be able to pay the full bill this year, would there be any tax advantage and, if so, how much?

(c) Is there any disadvantage to alternative (b)? Explain and make a recommendation to Janet.

Problem 3-13. Brenda Duke has been employed as a systems analyst for PEG Corporation for five years. This fall she decided to enroll at Bo Didley Tech for two courses, one in advanced statistics and one in modern dance. The first course meets on Monday nights and the second on Wednesday nights. The tuition fee is $25 per semester hour. Both courses are three-semester-hour credits. There were no books required for the dance class, but she spent $80 on required texts for the statistics class. Brenda drives home each night after work, then drives forty miles in the opposite direction to get to campus. She is not a candidate for a degree, having completed her B.S. in engineering six years ago. Her employer knows that she is taking the courses, but they are not required and PEG has no program for reimbursement of educational fees paid by employees, whether the courses are related to the job or not.

(a) May Brenda take a deduction for her educational expenses? Explain.

(b) Would it make any difference if PEG reimbursed her for the costs of courses that were job related? Explain.

(c) Would it make any difference if Brenda did not have a B.S. degree and these two courses would complete her degree requirements? Explain.

(d) Would it make any difference if Brenda has other employee business expenses equal to 2% of her adjusted gross income?

(e) What *one fact* is significant in the determination of the deductibility of Brenda's education expenses?

Problem 3-14. For each of the following independent situations, determine whether a deduction would be allowed for education expense, assuming that the total miscellaneous expenses exceed 2% of adjusted gross income.

(a) Professor Limeric, who teaches romance languages, took a summer trip to France to maintain and improve her linguistic skills, but was unable to prove that this was the primary purpose of the trip.

(b) Chuck Ledger, a CPA, attended law school in order to further his ability to provide professional tax service to his clients. Chuck's employer encouraged, but did not require, him to go.

(c) Minnie Meddler, an attorney, incurred tuition, travel, and room and board expenses for one week while attending the New York University Annual Institute on Federal Taxation.

(d) Lance Lens, a newspaper photographer, who also operated free lance on his own time, incurred costs of flying lessons. His employer did not require the new skill but Lens can prove that his ability to fly would improve his opportunities to get newsworthy pictures.

(e) Neil Float, a career naval officer, whose primary duties were personnel management, obtained a master's degree in Personnel Administration.

(f) Page Harp, a professional music instructor, took courses to learn to make minor repairs on musical instruments.

(g) Ann Jetson, a copilot for a regional airline, took additional lessons to learn to fly the Boeing 747 and thereby qualify as a pilot for an international airline.

(h) Re Fu Miur was an immigrant from the Republic of Korea. He obtained a job as a claims adjuster for State-Wide Insurance Company. Later he incurred the costs of courses to improve his English and to better understand U.S. government and finance. State-Wide did not require that he take the courses.

Problem 3-15. Sybil Serrer is a registered nurse. She had always lived in Ohio. Last summer she took a one-week trip to San Diego to visit a friend. A month after getting back to Ohio she decided that she was tired of the cold and snow during the winters and could not bear the thought of going through another one. Since she had accumulated some money, she quit her job and moved without first obtaining another job. After arriving in San Diego, she found an apartment within one week and started looking for employment. One week later she found a part-time job as a private-duty nurse. After six weeks she found a full-time job at one of the hospitals and began work immediately. Her total costs incurred to move from Ohio to California were $1,600. That did not include any meals. After arriving in San Diego, she spent $430 on meals and lodging while looking for the apartment. Of that amount, $120 was for food. She found a suitable apartment and moved in within eight days. She did not incur any expenses in connection with leaving her Ohio apartment and did not incur any expenses in connection with obtaining the California apartment. She will itemize deductions.

(a) Can Sybil take the position that it was her trip to California that convinced her to move there and, therefore, that she should be entitled to the cost of that trip as part of her moving expenses? Explain.

(b) How much, if any, may she claim as moving expenses for the temporary living costs?

(c) Assuming that Sybil continues her job as a nurse, will she satisfy the thirty-nine-week test? Explain.

(d) Assume that Sybil had found employment during her first visit to California and had also looked for an apartment but did not find one. Could she then claim the expense of that trip as a house-hunting trip, which would be a part of the deductible moving expenses? Explain.

(e) Assume that Sybil had not found employment during her first visit to California and not until after four months after she had moved to San Diego. Would she be entitled to any moving expense deduction? Explain.

Problem 3-16. Ronna Hastings is an employee of Bonkers, Inc., which has no retirement plan for its employees. Ronna's salary is $24,000 for the year and that is her only income. She is thinking about contributing some money to an Individual Retirement Account, but has the following questions concerning the tax impact of doing so:

(a) What amount can be contributed to such a plan and deducted for federal income tax purposes?

(b) There is a possibility that a bonus of $2,000 will be received before the end of the year. If that should happen, what impact will there be on the amount of the contribution and deduction?

(c) If there is not a bonus, but Bonkers starts a retirement plan for its employees, what impact will that have on the IRA contribution and deduction?

Problem 3-17. Buck Staghorn purchased a car during 1990 and took a personal loan at his employee credit union to pay for it. The interest expense for 1990 will be $2,200. Buck does not have any other interest expense and does not own a residence.

(a) For 1990, what will be the amount which Buck can include as part of his itemized deductions as the result of the interest expense?

(b) If the year were 1991 instead of 1990, what would be the amount of the deduction?

(c) Assuming that Buck owns the house in which he lives, might there be a way for him to arrange to be able to claim the entire interest expense as a deduction? Explain, including identification of the necessary conditions.

Problem 3-18. For each of the following taxpayers, indicate the total amount of debt that qualifies in 1990 as residential debt for purposes of the residential mortgage interest deduction. Break down your answer into acquisition debt and home equity indebtedness.

(a) Helen and Frank remodeled their home in 1989. They took out a $120,000 second mortgage. During 1990, the average debt balances of the first and second mortgages were $150,000 and $115,000, respectively. The fair market value of the home was approximately $300,000.

(b) Big Bucks purchased the house of his dreams in 1986. He paid $2 million, of which he financed $1.6 million. The average principal balance of the debt in 1990 was $1.4 million.

(c) Refer to question (b). In 1991, Big Bucks added $30,000 of landscaping to his dream house. He took out a second mortgage of $45,000 in which $15,000 of the loan proceeds was used to buy an automobile. During 1991, the average debt balances of the first and second mortgages were $1.3 million and $45,000, respectively.

(d) Beth and Keith own a home in the city and a home in the mountains. They spend the summer months and part of the winter in the mountain home. The 1991 average debt balances of the two homes were $800,000 and $400,000, respectively. The first debt was acquired in 1983 while the second debt was acquired in 1989.

Problem 3-19. Ebby Scrooge figured out that he paid $12,400 in taxes during 1990. Quite upset, he asks you, his accountant, to compute the amount of federal income tax he will save as a result of his total tax payment. Assume that he is in the 33% marginal tax rate. An itemization of the $12,400 is as follows:

Federal income tax withheld	$5,000
Federal estimated tax payments	1,000
State income tax withheld	2,000
Excise taxes	600
State sales taxes	1,400
Gift taxes	300
Real estate taxes	1,100
Personal property tax on auto	900
Hunting license	100

As a result of the above tax payments, compute the amount of federal income tax saved during 1990.

PROBLEMS WITH AN ASTERISK REQUIRE ADDITIONAL RESEARCH

Problem 3-20.* Barry Newhouse is an air traffic controller at Bigtown International Airport. Because of the heavy responsibilities and strain of the job, the employer requires that the controllers take a week's vacation every three months. In fact, the controllers are required to leave town on these vacations, and the employer provides reimbursement for a portion of the travel costs of such trips.

(a) Is Barry permitted a deduction for the costs of such travel since it is a requirement of his job? Explain.

(b) Would it make any difference if Barry were a foreign service employee (not necessarily an air traffic controller) who is required to return to the United States periodically in order to keep his job? Explain.

Problem 3-21.* In September, Bill Jordan accepted a new job in Memphis. At that time he lived and worked in Milwaukee. The new job began on April 1 of the following year. Bill and his wife, Janet, were in Memphis in October and found a house which they dearly loved, so they purchased it. Somewhat anxious to leave the cold climate, they talked about moving in mid-December so that they could be settled and enjoy the holidays in their new house. That arrangement would work out for the children, too, because they could be in their new school for the second half of the school year and have a minimum of absent days from school. Bill did not quit his former job until March 1. He commuted on weekends from Milwaukee to Memphis during January and February. Bill and Janet incurred $200 of expenses in connection with the purchase of the house in Memphis.

(a) Do they qualify for the moving expense deduction? Explain.

(b) Assuming that they will qualify for the moving expense deduction, will the $200 spent in October in connection with the purchase of the new house be deductible?

(c) Assuming that they will qualify for the moving expense deduction, will the commuting expenses for Bill qualify as part of the moving costs?

(d) Would it make any difference if all the facts were the same except that Bill is self-employed and decided to move his business from Milwaukee to Memphis? Explain.

Problem 3-22.* Charles Grady signed an $80,000 note to purchase a personal residence. The loan is secured by a 9½% mortgage on the property. Charles, a cash-basis taxpayer, had to pay $2,000 as a loan fee and this was deducted from the note, so that his proceeds were $78,000.

(a) Can Charles deduct the $2,000 as interest for the year?

(b) Would it make any difference if the lender had written him a check for $80,000 which Charles deposited in his bank checking account, following which Charles wrote a $2,000 check to the lender as a loan fee?

Problem 3-23.* Patrick McKenna is a conductor for the Topside Railroad. He pays monthly assessments as follows:

National union dues	$14
International union dues	8
Local union dues	6

Of the amount collected by the local union, $2 is earmarked as a funding for death benefits of members. The balance of the local dues, plus all of the national and international dues, are used to pay expenses of labor union activities. (For purposes of the following questions, assume that McKenna has other miscellaneous "tier two" employee business expenses which are more than 2% of his adjusted gross income and that he will itemize deductions.)

(a) How much is McKenna entitled to deduct? What is the nature of the deduction?

(b) Assume that McKenna paid an initiation fee to join the union. Is it deductible?

(c) What is the tax consequence if McKenna goes out on a legal strike and the union funds are used to pay him benefits?

Problem 3-24.* Betty and Bart Beaty live in a residence that has a basement. The walls of the basement and the foundation of the house are poured concrete. Last summer there was severe subsoil shrinkage as the result of unusually dry weather. The house "settled" and there was considerable damage from cracked walls.

(a) In filing their tax return, may Betty and Bart claim a casualty loss deduction?

(b) What critical element must exist in order for a casualty loss deduction to be sustained?

(c) What advice would you give to Betty and Bart relative to their tax return for the year? (Assume that the Beatys can expect the IRS to audit their return.)

(d) What would be the result if the Beatys took a casualty loss deduction but kept no documentation concerning the casualty or the amount of their loss?

COMPUTER PROBLEM

Problem 3–25 This problem is an addition to the computer problem that was completed at the end of Chapter 2. The purpose of this exercise is to modify the program to provide for a deduction for an IRA contribution (Part I) and to provide for a deduction for moving expenses (Part II).

Part I Line 10 of your spreadsheet should be (from the problem in Chapter 1) "deductions to arrive at AGI." Create a "go to" at line 10, column B. The "go to" will be 7AA. We will assume for this problem that Ms. Jones is a participant in her employer's retirement plan and is single. You can see that the program could be modified to include filing status (single, married, etc.), and the level at which the phase-out of deductible IRA contribution begins could be tied to that cell designation. Here, we just assume that she is single so that the phase-out begins at AGI of $25,000.

Line	*Column*	*Description*	*Column AB*
1	AA	Individual Retirement Account Deduction	
2	AA	Amount contributed to IRA	
3	AA	Limit on IRA deduction	2000
4	AA		If 2AA < 3AA, then 2AA If 2AA > 3AA, then 3AA If 2AA = 3AA, then 3AA
5	AA	AGI	Cell 11B
6	AA		If 5AA < 25000 then 4AA If 5AA = 25000 then 4AA If 5AA > 35000 then 0 If 5AA = 35000 then 0 If 5AA > 25000 < 35000 then 2000 − [(11B −25000/10000) * (2000)]
7	AA	IRA deduction	If 2AA = 6AA, then 2AA If 2AA > 6AA, then 6AA If 2AA < 6AA, then 2AA

Part II Line 12 (from the problem at Chapter 1) is itemized deductions. Modify this line with a "go to" command. Create itemized deductions in a separate schedule, e.g., starting at column AB. Part of this schedule will be the moving expense deduction. Using the illustration that follows Figure 3–2, and starting at cell 1AB, create a schedule for moving expense deduction for Ms. Jones. Keep in mind that the other itemized deductions will be added to the moving expense schedule later. Also remember that the itemized deductions will not be used if less than the standard deduction.

APPENDIX 3–A

EXAMPLES OF DEDUCTIBLE MEDICAL EXPENSES

Abortions
Acupuncture
Air conditioning used for alleviation of illness
Ambulance fee
Artificial limbs and teeth
Braces
Braille books
Chiropodist fees
Chiropractor fees
Christian Science practitioner's fees
Clinic costs
Crutches
Dentist's fees
Diagnostic fees
Diathermy
Eyeglasses
Face lift
Guide dogs (and cost of maintaining them)
Gynecologist
Hair transplants
Halfway house residency
Hearing aid (and batteries)
Hospital
Insulin
Insurance premiums for health, accident, hospitalization
Lab fees
Lip-reading lessons (for deaf)
Medicare supplementary insurance
Midwife
Nurse
Obstetrician
Oculist
Ophthalmologist
Optician
Optometrist
Osteopath
Oxygen and oxygen equipment used for relief of illness
Pediatrician
Physical examination
Physical therapist (including whirlpool bath)
Plastic surgery
Podiatrist
Prenatal care
Prescription medications
Psychiatrist
Psychoanalyst
Psychologist
Psychotherapy
Surgeon

Tuition at special schools for the handicapped
Vasectomy
Wheelchair
Wigs (if necessary for mental health)
X-ray

4

tax calculation

Expanding on Chapter 1, which presented an overview of simple individual tax returns, Chapter 2 looked more closely at income and Chapter 3 at deductions. This chapter covers the calculation of tax liability, then goes on to discuss the tax credits provided by the law and to explain some ways of planning to minimize taxes.

4.1 Tax Calculation Steps

The final tax or refund due is the result of the following steps:

1. A deduction is taken *from* adjusted gross income for either the total amount of itemized deductions *or* the applicable "standard deduction," whichever is *larger*.

Adjusted gross income and itemized deductions have been discussed in previous chapters—and use of the tax table and rate schedule was illustrated in Chapter 1.

2. A deduction is taken for exemption amounts (personal and dependent exemptions).
3. The result is taxable income, which is taken into the appropriate tax table or rate schedule to determine the amount of tax.
4. The tax liability as initially calculated is then reduced by (a) credits and (b) payments already made.

4.2 Standard Deduction

The deduction from AGI will be either (a) the standard deduction or (b) the total amount of itemized deductions, whichever is larger.[1] The standard deduction consists of a "basic" standard deduction plus an "additional" standard deduction.[2] As explained in Chapter 1, the latter applies only to persons who are blind[3] or who have reached age 65 before year end.

In Chapter 1 we were primarily concerned with the standard deduction for a single person, not age 65 and not blind. Consider the 1990 standard deduction for a single taxpayer age 66:

Basic standard deduction	\$3,250
Additional amount for over age 65	800
Total	\$4,050

If that person were also blind, the 1990 standard deduction would be \$4,850 (\$4,050 + \$800).

The 1990 standard deduction for a single, blind person under the age of 65 is \$4,050, consisting of the basic amount (\$3,250) plus one additional amount of \$800.

The 1990 standard deduction for a married couple filing a joint return is \$5,450 if neither is blind and neither is age 65. The standard deduction increases as follows:

If one is age 65 or older	\$6,100
If one is blind	\$6,100

[1] IRC Sec. 63(b).

[2] Starting in 1990 both the "basic" and the additional standard deduction may change each year as the result of a cost-of-living factor determined by the Consumer Price Index. IRC Sec. 63(b)(4).

[3] IRC Sec. 63(f). Total blindness is not required. Blindness is defined as a condition such that the central visual acuity does not exceed 20/200 in the better eye with correcting lenses, or the widest diameter of the visual field subtends an angle no greater than 20 degrees.

If both are age 65 or over	6,750
If one is age 65 or over and the other is blind	6,750
If both are under age 65 and both are blind	6,750
If both are age 65 or over and one is blind	7,400
If both are age 65 or over and both are blind	8,050

There is *not* an increase in the standard deduction as the result of the fact that any dependent has reached age 65 or is blind.

The rules for determining head of household (HOH) status are discussed at Section 4.5 of this chapter. The basic 1990 standard deduction for a HOH is $4,750 (see Figure 1-2). Since HOH persons are single, the additional 1990 standard deduction for age and/or blindness is $800 each rather than the $650 for married persons.[4]

Certain taxpayers are not entitled to either the basic or the additional standard deduction. They are:

A married person filing a separate tax return if the other spouse itemizes deductions.

Individuals who are nonresident aliens

Individuals who file a tax return for a "year" that is less than 12 months

Fiduciaries (see Chapter 14).

Any person who can be claimed as a dependent of another has a limited standard deduction.[5] The standard deduction for such a person will be $500, or the amount of earned income, if larger (but not more than the "basic standard deduction"). "Earned income" is income from salary or wages. "Unearned income" is income from investments, such as dividends and interest. This was explained in Chapter 1.

4.3 Exemptions

Generally, each taxpayer who is not someone's dependent has an "exemption amount" for himself or herself.[6] Thus, married taxpayers filing a joint return are entitled to two exemptions. In addition, one exemption amount can be claimed for each "dependent." The amount of the "exemption amount" is as follows:[7]

For 1987	$1,900
For 1988	$1,950
For 1989	$2,000
For 1990	$2,050

As explained earlier, the number is adjusted each year for inflation as measured by the Consumer Price Index.

Thus, if Billy Barnes is single, under age 65, not blind, has no dependents, will not itemize, and has a salary of $20,000, 1990 taxable income will be:

Gross income (also AGI)	$20,000
Standard deduction	(3,250)
Exemption amount	(2,050)
Taxable income	$14,700

If Billy had a dependent, then 1990 taxable income would be reduced by another $2,050 to $12,650.

A married couple, under age 65, not blind, filing jointly, not itemizing deductions, with three dependent children (none of whom has unearned income) with 1990 adjusted gross income of $25,000, will have taxable income as follows:

AGI	$ 25,000
Standard deduction	(5,450)
Exemption amounts (5 × $2,050)	(10,250)
Taxable income	$ 9,300

As explained in Chapter 1, if a person can be claimed as a dependent of someone else, then the only exemption amount deduction available is for the person claiming the dependency. There is none for the dependent himself or herself. For example, assume Lynn is a college student whose parents qualify to claim her as a dependent, but who has a summer job with wages of $3,600. She will not be able to claim the deduction for herself. Thus, her 1990 taxable income is $350 as follows:

Gross income (also AGI)	$ 3,600
Standard deduction	(3,250)*
Exemption amount	0
Taxable income	$ 350

* As explained earlier, she will be allowed the full amount of the standard deduction because her "earned income" is equal to or greater than the standard deduction.

On the other hand, assume that Lynn's income of $3,600 was entirely from interest and dividends. Since she can be claimed as a dependent by her parents, her standard deduction will be limited to $500. Her taxable income will be:

Gross income	$3,600
Standard deduction	(500)
Exemption amount	0
Taxable income	$3,100

[4]IRC Sec. 63(f).

[5]The deduction for a dependent is called an "exemption amount" and is discussed in the next section. It makes no difference whether the person entitled to claim the exemption amount deduction for the dependent did so or not. So long as he or she *could have* done so, the dependent's standard deduction is limited.

[6]IRC Sec. 151. There are exceptions noted later.

[7]IRC Sec. 151(d).

If her $3,600 of income consisted of earnings of $1,700 plus interest and dividends of $1,900, her taxable income would be:

Gross income	$ 3,600
Standard deduction	(1,700)
Exemption amount	0
Taxable income	$ 1,900

The additional standard deduction, discussed earlier in Section 4.2, is allowed even if the taxpayer is claimed by another taxpayer as a dependent. For example, assume that Mildred, age 70, qualifies as a dependent of her daughter. Her income is $1,800 from dividends and interest. Her taxable income is:

Gross income	$1,800
"Regular" standard deduction	(500)
Extra standard deduction	(800)
Exemption amount	0
Taxable income	$ 500

The tests for determining dependency are:[8]

1. Support
2. Relationship
3. No joint return by dependent
4. Citizenship
5. Gross income

All five tests must be satisfied in order to claim someone as a dependent.

The *support test* requires that the taxpayer must have provided over half of the support for the dependent. "Support" for this purpose means, but is not limited to, the following: food, shelter, clothing, medical and dental care, education, contributions to charity, child care expenses, transportation, and a reasonable amount of entertainment. Where no one person has provided more than half of the support of someone who meets the other tests, an *agreement* (called a "multiple-support agreement") can be filed designating which of the supporting persons is entitled to the exemption.[9] Thus, for example, if three adult children support an aged parent equally (and meet the other four tests), none has provided half of the support, but they can sign a multiple-support agreement so that one of them can claim the exemption amount. Such an agreement is effective only for one year so a different person can claim the deduction the following year if desired. A multiple support agreement can*not* be used if any one person has provided more than one-half of the support. In effect, the multiple support agreement is a declaration on the part of the persons who sign it—and each person who provided more than 10% of the support must sign one or the arrangement will not be valid—that they will not claim the supported person as a dependent but will agree that another qualified person can do so.

Where parents are divorced, the parent who has custody of the child during most of the year usually gets the dependency deduction for the child.[10] The other parent can, however, get the deduction if the custodial parent signs a written declaration that he or she will not claim the deduction, and the parent who claims the deduction attaches a copy of that declaration to his or her tax return. Also, a multiple-support agreement, as explained above, could be used. For divorces executed before 1985, the noncustodial parent can claim the deduction if the decree so provided and the noncustodial parent provides at least $600 toward the support of that child for the year.

The *relationship* test requires that the person being claimed as a dependent must be related in specific ways to the taxpayer.[11] Most of the categories are relationships by blood or marriage, including ancestors, descendants, siblings, and nephews and nieces. Adopted and step-children are generally treated as children by blood.[12] In-law relationships, once created, are not destroyed by divorce or by a spouse's death.[13] A child who was alive during the year qualifies, even though he or she only lived momentarily, as long as the birth was a "live" birth. In addition to relatives, any person other than the taxpayer's spouse can qualify if living in the taxpayer's home and a member of the taxpayer's household for the *entire* year.[14] Such may be the case, for example, for foster children.

The *no-joint-return test* requires that the person being claimed as a dependent cannot file a joint return with his or her spouse, unless there is no tax for the year, and the sole purpose of filing the return is to obtain a tax refund (for example, if

[8]Dependents are defined in IRC Sec. 152.

[9]IRC Sec. 152(c). All persons who contributed over 10% of the support must sign the multiple-support agreement. This permits the contributors to decide among themselves who will claim the exemption amount for the dependent. Of course, all the other requirements for dependency must also be satisfied.

[10]IRC Sec. 152(e)(1).

[11]The following are considered relatives of the taxpayer:
a. A son or daughter, or a descendant of either.
b. A stepson or stepdaughter.
c. A brother, sister, stepbrother, or stepsister (half-brothers and half-sisters also count).
d. A father or mother, or an ancestor of either.
e. A stepfather or stepmother.
f. A son or daughter of a brother or sister (i.e., nieces and nephews).
g. A brother or sister of the father or mother (i.e., aunts and uncles).
h. A son-in-law, daughter-in-law, father-in-law, mother-in-law, brother-in-law, or sister-in-law.

[12]IRC Sec. 152(b)(2).

[13]Treas. Reg. 1.152-2(d).

[14]IRC Sec. 152(a)(9). The other tests (e.g., over 50% support) would have to be satisfied, of course, for the deduction to apply.

amounts were withheld from their wages to cover income taxes).[15] This is frequently a problem with married college students who still receive support from parents. If the young married couple file a joint income tax return, the parents may not be entitled to claim one or both as dependents.

The *citizenship test* requires that a dependent must be a citizen *or* resident of the United States, Canada, or Mexico during some part of the year.[16] An alien child adopted by and living with a U.S. citizen as a member of his or her household for the entire year can be claimed as a dependent even though the U.S. citizen is residing abroad.

TAX PLANNING TIP: Parents who support a married son or daughter may be able to claim an exemption amount for the child if he or she does not file a joint tax return. The tax savings to the parents from another exemption amount may be more than the extra tax that the married child would have to pay by filing as married—separate.

The *gross income test* requires that a dependent's gross income for the calendar year be less than the "exemption amount," ($2,050 for 1990). Dependents who are children (including stepchildren and foster children) of the taxpayer, and who are either under age nineteen, or are full-time students during at least five months of the year (even if over age nineteen), are exceptions.[17] They can have $2,050 or more of gross income, although the parents still have to meet the other dependency tests, *including* the 50% support test. This exception to the gross income test does not apply if the child-student has reached age 24 by the end of the year.

What this exception means is that a child who is under age 19, or who is a full-time student if between the ages of 19 and 24, can still be claimed by his or her parents (or other person) if the first four tests are satisfied even if the child has income of more than the exemption amount. Another way of looking at it is that the fifth test is waived for a dependent who is a child of the taxpayer and is either under age 19 or a full-time student under the age of 24. As explained earlier, however, that child will not be able to claim an exemption amount for himself or herself.

[15]IRC Sec. 151(e)(2).
[16]IRC Sec. 152(b)(3).
[17]IRC Sec. 151(c).

TAX PLANNING TIP: If a potential dependent satisfies all of the tests except the gross income test, consider having that person plan to reduce gross income so that the fifth test will also be met. For example, assume that someone other than your child would be your dependent except that he or she has $3,000 of interest income. By converting their investments into state or local government bonds, the interest from which is not included in gross income as explained in Chapter 2, their gross income will be less than the exemption amount and the gross income test will be satisfied.

On the other hand, the gross income test does have to be satisfied for other dependents. For example, assume that a man, age 55, satisfies all of the first four tests for claiming his mother as a dependent. His mother, however, has gross income of $2,200. The gross income test is failed and he may not deduct the exemption amount for his mother.

TAX PLANNING TIP: Grandparents may be able to claim an exemption amount for a grandchild, even if the grandchild does not live with them. For example, John and Mary are both college students. They are married and have a small child. Mary's parents provide financial support, but not enough to claim either John or Mary as a dependent. John and Mary have a small income so that the exemption amount deduction for their child will save little or nothing in tax. If the financial support that Mary's parents provide were designated and used for the support of their grandchild, they would provide over one-half of the support of the child. Mary's parents could then take a deduction for their grandchild. Careful record keeping is advised in such a situation. Note that John and Mary must provide less than one-half of their child's support. Otherwise, they could *claim the deduction. Note, also, that support includes housing. Thus, if John and Mary rent an apartment, part of that expense is treated as support for the child.*

4.3.1 Reduction of Tax Benefit of Personal Exemption Deduction for Certain "High Income" Persons

In Chapter 1 we explained how the tax benefit of the lower (15%) rate is removed by a 5% surtax, which is added to the 28% "normal" tax. Thus, for example, a single person with 1990 taxable income of $97,620 pays a tax of $27,334, which is an average rate of 28% on all taxable income. There is no need to perform a special calculation. So long as the arithmetic of the tax rate schedule is followed correctly, the right amount of tax will be determined. In Chapter 1 we explained why the marginal tax rate went up to 33% and then back down to 28%, i.e., to remove the effect of the 15% rate.

As 1990 taxable income exceeds $97,620 (for a single person) the tax reduction from the personal exemption deduction is phased out.[18] The idea is the same as that for the removal of the 15% rate, i.e., to remove the tax reduction resulting from the exemption deduction, but only for certain "high income" persons. The way the tax benefit is removed is with a 5% surtax that is added to the "normal tax." However, this 5% surtax does not take effect until *after* the tax benefit of the 15% rate has been completely removed.

For example, assume that Billy Barnes has 1990 taxable income of $98,000. Taxable income means that all deductions (including the exemption amount) have been taken. To arrive at taxable income of $98,000, Billy claimed one such exemption, which was a deduction of $2,050. Since Billy is in the 28% tax bracket, the tax on $98,000 *without* any phase-out of the exemption amount would be $27,440. If that were the amount of the tax, then Billy's tax reduction from the $2,050 deduction would be $574 (28% × $2,050). However, since taxable income is more than $97,620, part of that $574 is removed. Billy's tax is increased by the *lesser* of:

a. 28% of the $2,050	= $574
or	
b. 5% of (taxable income − $97,620)	= 19

Thus, Billy's tax is:

28% ($98,000)	= $27,440
+ partial removal of tax benefit of exemption	19
Total	$27,459

Note that Billy still has a tax reduction from the $2,050 exemption of $555, which is the difference between $574 and $19.

What if Billy's 1990 taxable income (with one exemption amount) were $120,000?

Tax at 28% on $120,000		= $33,600
Plus lesser of:		
(a) 28% ($2,050)	= $574	
or		
(b) 5% ($120,000 − $97,620)	= $1,119	
		+ 574
Total		$34,174

[18]IRC Sec. 1(g).

Thus, the total tax reduction from the $2,050 exemption amount deduction has been removed.

Let's check it. If the $2,050 deduction were removed, taxable income would be $122,050 instead of $120,000. Tax at a "flat" 28% on $122,050 would be $34,174. Thus, the full amount of the $574 tax reduction has been phased out. Note, however, that because the phase out is at the rate of 5%, it will take $11,480 of taxable income (above the point at which the phase out begins) to remove the tax reduction from *each* $2,050 deduction. So while the $574 tax advantage is completely phased out at taxable income of $120,000, it also would have been completely phased out at taxable income of $109,100 ($97,620 + $11,480).

The phase-out applies to the total amount of the deduction for personal exemptions not just to one such amount of $2,050. Thus, if Billy had another exemption amount because of a dependent, and taxable income were $117,950 ($120,000 − $2,050), then the tax would be:

28% ($117,950)		= $33,026
Plus the lesser of:		
(a) 28% ($4,100)	= $1,148	
or		
(b) 5% ($117,950 - $97,620)	= 1,016.50	
		+ 1,016.50
Total		$34,042.50

Again, only part of the tax benefit of the two exemptions has been removed. As before, it is possible that the entire benefit will disappear. Thus, if Billy's taxable income were $140,000 after two exemptions of $2,050 each, the tax would be:

28% ($140,000)		= $39,200
Plus lesser of:		
(a) 28% ($4,100)	= $1,148	
or		
(b) 5% ($140,000 - $97,620)	= 2,119	
		+ 1,148
Total tax		$40,348

A glance at the rate schedule (Appendix 1-C) will show the level of taxable income at which the phase-out of the exemption amount deduction begins for each filing status. Figure 4-1 shows these amounts.

FIGURE 4-1
1990 Taxable income levels at which phase-out of exemption amount deduction begins

Married—filing jointly	$162,770
Head of household	134,930
Single	97,620
Married—filing separately	123,570

What amount of taxable income above the amounts in Figure 4-1 will be required for a complete phase-out of the exemption deduction? That depends upon the number of exemptions that are claimed and the filing status. The answer for 1990 can be obtained from the following formula:

$$\frac{.28\ (\text{number of exemptions} \times \$2{,}050)}{.05}$$

Assume a married couple claims four exemptions (themselves plus two dependents) on a joint return. The above formula results in $45,920. Added to $162,770 results in taxable income of $208,690. Thus, there will be *some* benefit from the exemption amounts so long as taxable income is less than $208,690. At that amount or above, there is no benefit from the exemption amount deduction.

Check:

Tax on $208,690:		
28% ($208,690)		= $58,433.20
Plus lesser of:		
(a) 28% ($8,200)	= $2,296	
or		
(b) 5% ($208,690 − $162,770) =	2,296	
		+ 2,296
Total		$60,729.20

Without the exemption amount deductions, taxable income would have been $216,890 ($208,690 + $8,200). Tax on $216,890 at 28% is $60,729.20.

4.4 Tax Calculation

Calculating the tax from the tax tables and rate schedules was covered in Chapter 1.

As noted earlier, the rate schedules must be used if taxable income is $50,000 or more.

If you have not examined the rate schedule in Appendix 1-B and 1-C do so now. Assume that Billy Barnes (single) had taxable income of $40,000 for 1990. The tax calculation is as follows:

$2,917.50 + 28% ($40,000 − $19,450) = $8,671.50

Note that the marginal tax rate is 28%. The effect of the 15% tax rate does not begin to be phased out (for a single taxpayer) until taxable income is over $47,050.

Compare the 1989 tax for Billy Barnes (single) with the 1990 tax assuming that the 1989 taxable income was also $40,000. The 1989 tax was:

$2,782.50 + 28% ($40,000 − $18,550) = $8,788.50

Note that there is a 1990 tax reduction of $117 on the same amount of taxable income for 1989. You might enjoy experimenting with some different taxable income numbers for a single taxpayer for 1989 and 1990 to see the amount of difference in tax between the two years. Such an experiment is not completely realistic, however, if the taxable income numbers are the same because of the changes in the amounts of the standard deduction and exemption deduction. You might want to make your exerise more realistic by using a 1990 taxable income that is $150 less for the increased 1990 standard deduction and is $50 less for *each* personal exemption deduction than the 1989 number.

For a married couple filing a joint return with 1990 taxable income of $40,000, the tax calculation will be:

$4,867.50 + 28% ($40,000 − $32,450) = $6,981.50

COMPUTER FORMULAS: The computer can be instructed to pick out which tax rate will apply to a particular income level. A simple way to do so is by using the @ IF function, as shown below, using the 1990 rates for a single person.

	A	B
1	Taxable income	x
2	Number of exemptions	y
3	Tax	MAX(A5,A6,A7,A8)
4		
5	@IF(B1<19450,A12,A6)	
6	@IF(B1<47050,A13,A7)	
7	@IF(B1<97620,A14,A8)	
8	@IF(B1>97620,A15,A9)	
9	(error message)	
10		
11		
12	0.15*B1	
13	2917.50+.28*(B1-19450)	
14	10645.50+.33*(B1-47050)	
15	.28*(B1)+A18	
16	.28*(B2)	
17	.05*(B1-97620)	
18	@MIN(A16,A17)	

Taxable income is entered in cell B1, shown as x, and the number of exemptions is entered in cell B2, shown as y. The tax will appear in cell B3, based on the calculations shown in A5 through A8. The formula in A5 says that if taxable income (B1) is less than $19,450, the tax will be 15% of taxable income. If it is not less than $19,450, the computer will look at A6, and so on. The entire rate schedule is entered on A12 to A18 (with A15 through A18 being the phase-out of the exemption amount deduction), and the @IF formulas at A5 to A8. We have left lines 4 and 9 through 11 open for use should the rate schedule or formulas need to be changed for future years. Naturally, the program could be expanded to provide similar instructions for each of the other filing status. A command could be entered to identify the appropriate filing status with the computer, then, another command to go to the related set of schedules to compute the tax.

4.4.1 Surviving Spouses

You may have noticed from Appendixes 1-B and 1-C that the tax rate schedules for married persons filing jointly also include persons who are "surviving spouses." That is also the case for the tax table (Appendix 1-A). Comparison of tax with the same amount of taxable income for a single person and a "surviving spouse" clearly shows that persons in the latter category pay less tax. What is a "surviving spouse"?

As a general rule, when a taxpayer dies, his or her taxable year ends. However, if the spouse who is still alive has not remarried by the end of the year, a joint return can still be filed although technically the survivor is "single" on December 31. The tax return will include all the income and deductions for the deceased spouse from January 1 to the date of death, and all the income and deductions for the survivor for the entire year. The standard deduction and exemption amounts will be determined *as if* the deceased person had not died. For example, assume that Fred died on August 1, 1990, with his wife Wilma surviving. Neither was blind or age 65. Wilma can file a joint tax return for 1990 (providing she has not remarried by December 31). The return will show a standard deduction of $5,450 (unless itemized deductions are larger) and two exemptions (one for Fred and one for Wilma) at $2,050 each. If Fred was at least 65 at the time of death, and Wilma was not age 65 by the end of the year, the standard deduction would be $6,100.

The surviving spouse may be able to use the "joint" tax rates for the year *following* the year of death *and* for the next year. In order to do so, the survivor (still not remarried) must have a dependent child. Note that the use of the joint rate schedule for the year after the year of death and the second year after the year of death does *not* mean that the survivor can claim an exemption deduction for the deceased spouse for either of those years. The exemption amount for the deceased spouse is available only for the year of death.

Using the example where Fred died in 1990, Wilma could use the joint ("surviving spouse") rate schedule for 1991 and for 1992 if she has a dependent child. Of course, she could have a child who qualifies as a dependent for 1991, but does not qualify as a dependent for 1992. In that case, she could use the joint rate schedule for 1991, but not for 1992. It is also possible that she would not qualify for 1991, but would qualify for 1992. The determination of filing status is made each year independent of the filing status for another year.

What if she still has a dependent child in 1993 and has not remarried? Then she may be able to qualify as a head of household for 1993. The determination may depend upon whether the child lives in her household. (See Section 4.5 of this chapter.)

4.4.2 Taxation of Unearned Income of Dependents and Certain Minor Children[19]

We mentioned earlier that where a person is eligible to be claimed as a dependent by another person, the person *being claimed* cannot deduct an "exemption amount" for himself. This rule applies regardless of age and regardless of the relationship between the two persons.

Example 1. Jane Smith is a full-time college student, age 23. Because her parents meet all five requirements discussed earlier, they are eligible to claim Jane as a dependent. Note, again, that the fifth requirement—the gross income test—does not apply to Jane's parents because Jane is a full-time student and not yet age 24. Jane has enough income so that she is required to file a tax return. Note that it does not make any difference whether the income is from earnings or from investments. In calculating her taxable income, Jane will not be able to deduct an "exemption amount" for herself. She will be able to use either the standard deduction or to itemize deductions, and she will be able to calculate tax starting with the lowest rates applicable for her. The amount of her standard deduction will depend upon whether her income is "earned" or "unearned," as explained earlier.

Example 2. Harry Gordon is retired and age 72. Harry's son, James, is eligible to claim Harry as a dependent because James meets all five of the requirements to do so. Harry's 1990 gross income is $1,900, which is less than the amount that would cause James to fail the "gross income" test (#5 on our earlier list) for claiming his father as a dependent. Harry will file a tax return.

Harry can claim a "regular" standard deduction of $500, plus an additional standard deduction of $800 (as the result of being over age 65 and a dependent of someone else). He cannot claim any exemption amount. Thus, Harry's taxable income is:

$$\$1,900 - (\$500 + \$800) = \$600$$

In addition to being unable to claim their own "exemption amount" deduction, children under 14 with "net unearned income" and who have a

[19]IRC Sec. 1(j). These rules apply if *either* parent of the child is alive.

parent who is alive will be taxed on that "net unearned income" at the parent's top marginal tax rate *as if* the parent had received the income instead of the child. This rule has become known as the "kiddie tax." It applies only to children who have not reached the age of 14 by the end of the year.

Example 3. Jerry Shepherd was age 14 on December 28, 1990. Because Jerry reached the age of 14 before the end of the year, the "kiddie tax" will not apply. Instead, Jerry will be taxed at his own tax rates. For that purpose, it does not make any difference if the income is "earned" or "unearned." However, for purposes of the standard deduction, it does make a difference if the income is "earned" or "unearned." The full standard deduction can be taken to reduce "earned" income, but only $500 can be deducted from "unearned" income.

Example 4. Ellen Dooley will not be age 14 before the end of 1990. One of her parents is still alive. Ellen earned $3,360 at a summer job. She had no "unearned" income. Her taxable income will be $110 (i.e., $3,360 minus the standard deduction of $3,250). Ellen will not be subject to the "kiddie tax," explained below, because she had no unearned income. Note that Ellen would be able to itemize deductions if she could demonstrate that the total was more than the standard deduction.

Example 5. Brian Jefferson will not be age 14 before the end of 1990. His parents are still alive. He will have $3,200 of income from interest and dividends for the year. As explained below, Brian will not be allowed the full standard deduction of $3,250. Instead, the standard deduction will be $500. In addition, as explained earlier, if Brian is eligible to be claimed as a dependent by his parents, he will not be able to take a deduction for the "exemption amount." We assume in this example that Brian can be claimed as a dependent by his parents. Thus, Brian's taxable income is $2,700, which is $3,200 less the reduced standard deduction of $500. Brian will be subject to the "kiddie tax," explained below.

Note that it does not make any difference when or how Brian acquired the assets which resulted in the "unearned" income. The only two requirements for this special tax computation are that the child not be age 14 by the end of the year and that at least one of the child's parents is alive. Thus, the rule will apply to a child living with someone other than his or her parent just the same as if the child were living with a parent.

What is "unearned income" that is subject to the "kiddie tax"? It is income from investments, such as dividends, interest, capital gains, rents, and royalties. As we will see in Chapter 14, a person also can have such income by being a beneficiary of a trust as well as by owning the asset which generated the income.

What is "net unearned income?" It is unearned income minus the sum of

(a) $500 *and*

(b) the greater of
  (1) $500 of the standard deduction or $500 of itemized deductions *or*
  (2) the child's allowable deductions directly connected with the unearned income.

What is the "net unearned income" of Brian, from Example 5 above? Note that *taxable income* is $2,700, which is gross income of $3,200 less the standard deduction of $500. Assuming that Brian will not itemize deductions and has no deductible expenses in connection with the $3,200 of income, his "net unearned income" is:

Unearned (passive) income		$3,200
Less (a) and	$500	
(b) the greater of (1) $500 or (2) itemized deductions	500	1,000
Net unearned income		$2,200

The tax that Brian will pay on taxable income of $2,700 will be his tax on the first $500 (15% for 1990) plus the amount of tax his parents would have paid if they had received the net unearned income. If Brian's parents are in the 28% marginal tax bracket for 1990, Brian's tax is:

15% ($500)	=	$ 75
28% ($2,200)	=	616
Total		$691

If Brian's parents are in the 33% bracket, then Brian's tax is:

15% ($500)	=	$ 75
33% ($2,200)	=	726
Total		$801

Since there is a $500 standard deduction, and the child's own rate (15% at 1990 levels) will apply to the next $500, it should be clear that the "kiddie tax" does not have any impact until a child's income is in excess of $1,000.

As explained earlier, the standard deduction will be more than $500 where there is earned income greater than $500. This is true for a dependent child under age 14 as well as for other persons who are dependent.

Example 6. Leroy Washington, age 13, is a dependent of his parents who are in the 28% tax bracket. Leroy has $800 of earned income and $3,500 of unearned income for 1990. Gross income is, thus,

$4,300 and taxable income is $3,500. Leroy's tax will be $850, which is the sum of 28% × $2,500 plus 15% × $1,000.

There are some problems which arise with respect to the "kiddie tax." The solutions are beyond the scope of our discussion, but we will identify some of the problems.

How is the child who has net unearned income taxed if his or her parents do not file a joint return and have different marginal tax rates? Note that two parents who are married can file separate returns. Also, the parents might be divorced, in which case each will file his/her own tax return. (Generally, it is the custodial parent's income that is used, but what if there is not a custodial parent, such as where the child lives with a grandparent, a guardian, or a foster parent?)

What is the calculation to determine the amount of additional tax a parent would have had to pay if there is more than one child with net unearned income in the family?

What is the calculation if the child has both unearned and earned income during the sameyear?

As we explained earlier, the amount of the "exemption amount" deduction(s) is phased out where a person has income above a certain level. Does a child's net unearned income get added to a parent's income for purposes of determining if the parent is subject to the "exemption amount phase-out?" (Generally, the answer is "yes," but how is the calculation made?)

Does the child's net unearned income get added to a parent's income for purposes of determining the amount of any deduction or credit? For example, does the parent have a larger AGI which will decrease the amount of medical expenses which can be claimed as an itemized deduction? (Generally, the answer is "no.")

Some of the computational questions are answered by the proper completion of Form 8615, which is required to be filed by a child who is subject to the kiddie tax.

TAX PLANNING TIP: The problems associated with an under-age-14 child having net unearned income can be avoided by having the child's assets invested so as not to generate current or taxable income. Some possibilities are:

> *Investment in Series EE government bonds where the interest will not be taxed until the bonds mature at which time the child will be at least age 14.*
>
> *Investment in state or local government bonds the interest on which is not included in gross income.*
>
> *Investment in securities which do not pay interest or dividends but which will increase in value. The child can sell the asset for a gain after he or she has attained the age of 14.*

Also, because of the standard deduction, a child can have up to $500 of unearned income and will not incur any income tax liability to himself or the parent.

If a child under age 14 has gross income of more than $500 but less than $5,000 and it is only from dividends and interest, an election can be made to include the child's income in the gross income of the parent rather than have the child file a tax return. The amount of the income tax will be the same as if the child filed a tax return, but the process is simplified by not having to complete a tax return for the child. Form 8814 contains detailed instructions for this process. Also, see line 38 of Form 1040, Appendix 1-D(b).

4.5 Head of Household

The head-of-household tax is less than that for a single taxpayer but more than on a joint return. A comparison, using 1990 rates and taxable income of $35,000, will show the difference:

Filing Status	*Tax*
Married, joint return	$5,581.50
Single	7,271.50
Head of household	6,413.50

In addition to being unmarried,[20] not a "qualifying widow or widower" ("surviving spouse" as discussed above) and not a nonresident alien, a head of household must:

1. Maintain a household in which a "qualified" person lives for more than one-half of the year. A "qualified" person is either (a) an unmarried child of the taxpayer's or (b) a married child or any other relative who is a dependent of the taxpayer. A person who qualifies as a dependent as the result of living with the taxpayer for the entire year, but who is not a relative (and not the taxpayer's spouse), will not qualify the taxpayer for head-of-household status. Relatives here, as before, are defined by Congress[21] and do not include some

[20]IRC Sec. 2(b). An exception exists for a taxpayer who is still legally married although his or her spouse has disappeared, and has been gone for at least the last six months of the year. Such a person may also qualify as "head of household," if a child or other dependent lived in the household more than half the year.

[21]IRC Sec. 2(b). See footnote 11 above. A married nondependent child can still qualify the parent as head of household if the parent agreed to allow the other parent to take the exemption amount for the child as discussed above.

who might otherwise be thought of as related, such as cousins.

2. Contribute over half the cost of maintaining the home. Costs of maintaining a home include, for example, rent, utility charges, upkeep and repair, property taxes, mortgage interest, property insurance, and food. Generally, the taxpayer and child or dependent relative must live in the same household. An exception exists where the dependent is a parent of the taxpayer. In that event, the parent can live in a different household provided that the taxpayer provides over half of its cost.

TAX PLANNING TIP: If an unmarried taxpayer's child lives in the taxpayer's household and the taxpayer provides over one-half of the cost of the household, the taxpayer will qualify as a head of household even if the child is not a dependent. For example, Betty is divorced and has custody of her daughter Jan. Jan is not a dependent of Betty's because Jan's father provides over one-half of Jan's support. As long as Betty provides over one-half of the cost of maintaining the household, Betty will qualify as a head of household.

To have head-of-household status for tax purposes requires that the qualifying child or dependent live with the taxpayer for more than six months. A child or dependent who moves in on January 14, and out on July 10, for example, will not result in head-of-household status because the requirement of more-than-six months will not have been satisfied.[22]

TAX PLANNING TIP: In the case of a dependent who is a parent of the taxpayer, it is not necessary for the dependent to live in the same household as the taxpayer for the taxpayer to qualify as head of household. For example, Larry, single and age forty, provides financial support for his mother, who lives in a different town. If his mother is a dependent and *if Larry provides over half of the cost of maintaining his mother's household, Larry can get the exemption amount deduction for his mother* and *qualify for the head-of-household rates.*

[22]Where death or birth occurred during the year, however, the six-month requirement is considered satisfied. Also, temporary absences, such as those that may occur when a child is away at college or is on vacation, will not disqualify the taxpayer for head-of-household status.

4.6 Filing Statuses

The following table shows the level of taxable income at which the marginal tax rate changed from 15% to 28% for taxpayers with different filing statuses:[23]

	Year	
	1989	*1990*
Single taxpayer[24]	$18,550	$19,450
Joint return	30,950	32,450
Separate returns	15,475	16,225
Head of household	24,850	26,050

Let us examine the alternatives. Schedule Y-1 (Appendix 1-C), for example, is entitled "Married Taxpayers and Qualifying Widows and Widowers." We know what it means to be married, but the timing is important. What about persons who were not married all year, but got married on December 31? The answer is that marital status is determined as of the last day of the year. Thus, a couple who are married on December 31 will be treated as if they had been married all year for tax purposes. Similarly, someone who is divorced during the year, and who does not remarry, is considered single for the entire year, for tax purposes.

Tax planning, as we noted earlier, includes planning to qualify for the most advantageous rate schedule. As a general rule, a head of household (HOH) will be a single person. There is a requirement, as noted above, that HOH status requires that (a) an unmarried child of the taxpayer's or (b) a dependent live with the taxpayer.

Assume that Carmen Smith has an unmarried, nondependent 20-year-old daughter who has lived in her house for five months of the year 1990. Carmen has provided over one-half of the costs of the household. The daughter plans to marry and move out. By staying in Carmen's house for another month (plus one day) she will have lived there "more than six months" and Carmen will qualify as HOH for the year. Carmen's 1990 taxable income in either event will be $50,000. HOH status will save Carmen $1,005 in tax:

Tax on $50,000 (single)	$11,619
Tax on $50,000 (HOH)	10,614
Difference	$ 1,005

Note that it is not necessary for Carmen's daughter to be her dependent in order for Carmen to qualify as HOH. We have assumed that her daughter will not be her dependent in either event, therefore Carmen's taxable income will be the

[23]Taxable income does not mean the same number for each of the two years because the deductions are different.
[24]Definitions for filing status are in IRC Sec. 2.

same. The difference is tax is due *solely* to the difference in filing status. Note, also, that the extra tax will result even if her daughter moved out one day too soon.

Assume that Clair Green's wife died in 1988. Clair will qualify as a "surviving spouse" (joint return rates) for 1990 if he can claim his son as a dependent. Clair's taxable income will be $70,000 if he does not qualify to claim his son and $67,950 if he does qualify, because of the extra exemption amount.

1990 tax on $70,000 (single)	$18,219
1990 tax on $67,950 (joint)	14,808
Difference	$ 3,411

Assume that the only difficulty Clair has in claiming an exemption amount for his son is the "more than 50% support" test. By spending another $3,411 for his son's support, Clair will pass the test with room to spare, plus save $3,411 in tax. Is there a father who would rather pay $3,411 more in taxes instead of spending it on a child?

Or perhaps Clair's problem is one of record keeping and documentation. With adequate records he can demonstrate qualification for the exemption amount and the joint rate schedule. Most people will go to a lot of trouble to maintain adequate records for that much tax savings.

The status of married but filing separate tax returns is discussed and illustrated later.

Tax planning involves awareness and *thought.*

4.7 Credits

In tax terminology, a credit is a reduction in the amount of tax which would otherwise have to be paid. Some credits are "personal" meaning that they do not have any connection with a taxpayer's business activities. These will be discussed here. Other credits can result from a person's business activities and are referred to as business credits. These will be discussed in Chapter 7.

There are three personal credits discussed here that are available to certain taxpayers. They are:

A credit for part of the cost of child or dependent care

A credit for certain elderly persons or persons who have retired under a public employees' retirement program (See Appendix 1-D(b), lines 41 and 42.)

A credit for "earned income" where the taxpayer has a dependent child (See Appendix 1-D(b), line 58.)

The first two are "nonrefundable." That means that the credit can reduce the tax liability to zero but not less. The third credit is "refundable" which means that a refund can be received even if the amount of tax has already been reduced to zero. For example, assume that Billy Barnes has a tax liability before credits of $300, but has a "refundable" credit of $400. Billy will have no tax liability for the year and will still receive a refund of $100.

There is also a credit against U.S. income tax for taxes paid to foreign countries and to possessions of the U.S. Discussion of this credit is beyond the scope of this introductory text.

As we will see in Chapter 7, certain business credits (even if they are nonrefundable) that cannot be used in their entirety to reduce taxes for the current year can be carried forward to reduce taxes of a future year. For example, a business credit might be $900 with the tax before credit of $800. The unused credit of $100 might be carried forward to the following year. However, none of the credits discussed here will result in a carryover. If either of the two nonrefundable credits is greater than the before-credit tax for the year, the excess is unusable.

TAX PLANNING TIP: If there will be a nonrefundable credit for the current year that will be in excess of tax, plan to increase taxable income for the year because this can be done without increasing the tax to be paid. This can be especially beneficial if income that would increase next year's tax, if collected next year, can be accelerated to the current year.

4.7.1. Child- and Dependent-Care Credit

As explained earlier, a credit is a direct reduction in tax liability, whereas a deduction only reduces the amount that is subject to tax.

Taxpayers who incur expenses to have a child or a dependent cared for in order to allow the payor to be employed or to be a full-time student can get a credit against income tax for part of that expense.[25] The percentage varies with adjusted gross income. If AGI is $10,000 or less, the credit is 30% of the dependent/child-care expense. That percentage is reduced by one percentage point for every $2,000, or fraction thereof, that AGI exceeds $10,000. Table 4-1 shows the percentage based on adjusted gross income. Note that the percentage is never less than 20%.

[25]IRC Sec. 21.

TABLE 4-1

Percentage of Child-Dependent Care Expenses Which Can Be Used for the Credit, Based Upon Amount of Adjusted Gross Income

AGI over—	But not over—	Percentage
$0—	10,000	30%
10,000—	12,000	29%
12,000—	14,000	28%
14,000—	16,000	27%
16,000—	18,000	26%
18,000—	20,000	25%
20,000—	22,000	24%
22,000—	24,000	23%
24,000—	26,000	22%
26,000—	28,000	21%
28,000		20%

For example, assume that a married couple are both employed and that they have one child. One spouse earns $700 per month and the other earns $500 per month; child-care expenses are $175 per month for one child. The expense is used to calculate the credit because it is less than the income of either spouse. Their adjusted gross income is $14,400. The credit is calculated as follows:

Child care: 12 × $175 =	$2,100
Rate (from Table 4-1)	× 27%
Total	$ 567

The percentage will never be lower than 20%, but the *amount* to which that percentage is applied is sometimes limited. Since a provision for child care might be abused, the rules concerning its availability are a little complex:

1. While the credit can be taken even when one spouse works or is a student, the expenses to be counted cannot exceed the person's earned income for the year. For a married couple, the expenses cannot exceed the income of the spouse who earned the least. If one spouse is a full-time student, or has no income and is incapable of self-care, the law imputes earned income of $200 a month for that spouse, if there is one dependent, or $400 per month if there are two or more dependents.[26] By imputing income in this manner, the rule provides for some credit even though the student spouse, for example, had no income. Thus, in the previous example, the same credit would have resulted if one spouse was unemployed but was a full-time student the entire year.

The amount of child/dependent-care expense which can be used to calculate the credit is limited, regardless of which percentage is used to determine the credit. Where one person is being cared for, the amount of the expense in excess of $2,400 for the year will not result in any additional credit. Where two or more persons are being cared for, the maximum amount which can be counted is $4,800. Thus, if in the previous example, where both spouses were employed, the child care expense had been $225 per month ($2,700 total), the credit would have been 27% of $2,400, which is $648, not 27% of $2,700, which is $729.

When the child care is incurred over a period of less than a full year, monthly calculations are made. For example, if one spouse goes to school full time for six months and is unemployed for the balance of the year, and child care of $230 per month (for the six months of school) for one child was incurred, the credit would be computed as follows:

(a) Child-care expense: 6 × $230	$1,380
(b) Imputed earnings of student spouse: $200 × 6	1,200

Lower of (a) or (b) multiplied by 30% (assuming AGI is $10,000 or less) yields:

$1,200 × 30% = $360

2. For this purpose, a qualifying dependent child must be under age thirteen or (if other than a child) incapable of self-care because of a physical or mental disability.[27] The disability need not be permament.

3. The expenses must be incurred to enable the taxpayer to be gainfully employed or to be a student. Day nursery and similar care center facility expenses are allowed, if incurred for the care of a spouse or a dependent who spends at least eight hours per day in the taxpayer's household.[28]

4. Payments to a relative can qualify, as long as the relative does not qualify as a dependent.[29] Payments to a taxpayer's parent can even be counted.

Example 1. Mary Murphy is a single person with a ten-year-old dependent son. She is employed. During the school year she does not incur child-care expenses because her son goes to school. However, assume her son is out of school three weeks because of an illness and Mary hires a sitter to be at home during the day. The expense will qualify for the credit.

Example 2. Brad Staple supports his father, who is eighty-five years old. The senior Mr. Staple is not capable of self-care, so Brad moved him into a nursing home where around-the-clock attention

[26] IRC Sec. 21(d)(2).

[27] IRC Sec. 21(b)(1).

[28] IRC Sec. 21(b)(2). The entire cost of sending a child to camp was allowed in *Edith Zoltan*, 79 TC No. 31 (1982).

[29] IRC Sec. 21(e)(6).

would be available if necessary. The cost will not qualify for the credit since it is out-of-home and Brad's dependent is over age fifteen but does not spend at least eight hours per day in Brad's home. (Incidentally, the nursing home cost *might* qualify as a medical expense deduction.[30] Also, the arrangement might result in Brad's being able to qualify for head of household.)

Example 3. Martha Reed pays her sister to babysit with her three-year-old daughter while Martha and her husband Ron are both employed. The payments will qualify for the credit as long as Martha's sister does not qualify as a dependent of Martha's.

Example 4. Steve Adams pays his nineteen-year-old dependent daughter to babysit with his two-year-old son during the summer when neither child is in school but Steve is employed. Steve's payments to his daughter will not qualify for the credit. Note that the expense might qualify if the nineteen-year-old were not Steve's dependent.

Example 5. Barbara Allen pays her mother to babysit in Barbara's home while Barbara is employed. Barbara's child is age four. Barbara's payments to her mother will qualify for the credit if her mother is not a dependent for whom Barbara claims the exemption amount.

Example 6. Tim and Tonja are married. During the year Tonja injured her back in a fall. After being released from the hospital she was confined to their home for six weeks during which time she was incapable of caring for herself. Tim was not able to stay at home and care for her because of his job. They hired someone to stay with Tonja during the day while Tim was away. This cost will qualify for the credit, providing the cost does not exceed the *imputed* income level ($200 per month) for Tonja.[31]

5. No deduction is allowed a married couple unless they file a joint return. However, this rule is waived for an abandoned spouse if the deserting spouse is not a member of the household for the last six months of the tax year.[32]

As mentioned earlier, the child-dependent care credit is nonrefundable. That means that the credit cannot exceed the tax liability for the year (after reduction by other credits). In addition, there is no carryback or carryforward if part or all of the credit is not used. For example, assume that Billy Barnes has a tax liability of $200 before a child-dependent care credit of $250. The tax liability will be reduced to zero. The extra $50 of unused credit cannot be carried back to a prior year or forward to a future year to reduce tax.

TAX PLANNING TIP: When planning to spend money to have a child or other dependent cared for so that you can be gainfully employed or be a student, the "after-tax" cost of the care should be considered. Thus, a cost of $2,000 for the year is really only $1,400 if the credit will be $600.

Also, the credit may be increased by proper planning concerning AGI. The applicable percentage can be increased by reducing AGI. For example, if the applicable percentage will be 20% because AGI is more than $28,000, and if AGI includes investment income, conversion of investments to state and local government bonds—the interest from which is excluded from gross income—could increase the credit.

4.7.2. Elderly

A credit of 15% of all types of income is available to people sixty-five or over (limited to a "base amount").[33] The credit is also available to permanently and totally disabled persons who are not yet 65. The "base amount" is as follows:

$5,000 for single persons and on a joint return where only one spouse qualifies;

$7,500 on a joint return where both spouses qualify;[34]

$3,750 for a married person filing a separate return.

In other words, the maximum credit is $750, $1,125, and $562.60, respectively.

The credit is not as valuable as it may first appear, because of an offset feature. Part of the purpose of the credit is to equalize the situation of people receiving tax-free social security benefits and those providing for their own retirement in taxable ways. The base amount used to calculate the maximum credit is reduced by social security benefits and other tax-exempt pensions before multiplying by the 15%. That eliminates the credit for many retired people, and substantially reduces it for most of the rest. If the nontaxable portion of

[30] *W. B. Counts*, 42 TC 755, *acq.* 1964–2 CB 4; Rev. Rul. 67–185, 1967–1 CB 70, and Rev. Rul. 76–481, 1976–2 CB 82.

[31] See Treas. Reg 1.44A-2(b)(3).

[32] IRC Sec. 21(e)(2), (4).

[33] IRC Sec. 22.

[34] Some critics cite this as a penalty upon marriage since two unmarried persons age sixty-five or older could get a credit of as much as $750 each. The maximum for a married couple is $1,125.

social security receipts plus other tax-exempt pension income averages $416.67 or more per month for the entire year, the credit base for a single person is zero ($5,000/12 = $416.67). The possibility that part (maximum of one-half) of social security receipts may be taxable was discussed in Chapter 2.

TAX PLANNING TIP: Gross income includes withdrawals from Individual Retirement Accounts. This increases adjusted gross income, which could result in a reduced elderly credit. Persons who may be able to obtain benefit from the credit should evaluate the impact of an IRA withdrawal on the amount of the credit. Perhaps IRA money can be withdrawn in alternative years rather than every year, with the result of obtaining more credit in years with no IRA withdrawal.

Persons who are semiretired (i.e., over age sixty-five but still working), and persons with investment income, may also see this benefit eroded because of another reduction. The $5,000 (or other) base is also reduced by one-half of adjusted gross income above $7,500 (above $10,000 on a joint return).[35] Thus, for married persons filing jointly (both age sixty-five or older), the credit base is reduced to zero if their adjusted gross income is $25,000 or more.

Example 7. Mabel Murphy is age sixty-seven. She still works part time as a librarian, although she receives social security of $375 per month. Her adjusted gross income for the year consisted of $5,000 from salary plus $3,000 in taxable interest from investments. Her credit is calculated as follows:

Credit base	$5,000
Reduced by social security:	
12 × $375	4,500
Balance	500
Reduced by ½ AGI over $7,500:	
½($8,000 − $7,500)	250
Balance	250
Rate	× 15%
Credit	$ 37.50

Example 8. Jim Brock is age sixty-seven and his wife is sixty-six. They have an income of $15,000 from his consulting fees as an attorney. They do not receive social security and have no other source of tax-free pension benefits. They receive $3,000 of taxable dividends per year. (Adjusted gross income is $18,000.)

Credit base	$7,500
Reduced by ½($18,000 − $10,000)	4,000
Balance	$3,500
Rate	× 15%
Credit	$ 525

Persons who receive little or no social security benefits, ministers who have elected not to be covered by social security, and people who did not become U.S. residents until late in their working lives are among the main beneficiaries of the credit. The credit may result in more benefit for the year a person first receives social security because the benefits will have been received for less than a full year.

TAX PLANNING TIP: Deferral of income might result in maximizing the credit. For example, assume that a single taxpayer has had $7,500 of adjusted gross income for the current year and will receive a credit. Additional income (whether earned or unearned) received in the current year would reduce the credit. Deferral of additional income until the following year will preserve the maximum credit for the current year. Income can be deferred, for example, by investing in securities which are expected to increase in value rather than paying current interest or dividends.

4.7.3 Earned Income

Certain eligible persons can reduce their tax by a credit as the result of *earned income*.[36] For 1989, the credit was 14% of *earned income* up to a maximum credit of $910. The $910 resulted from the fact that the maximum amount subject to the 14% rate was $6,500. The maximum credit will change each year because of price level adjustments (based on the Consumer Price Index as explained earlier). Although the 14% rate will remain constant, the amount to which it will apply will be adjusted. Thus, the maximum 1990 credit will be 14% of $6,810, or $953. To get the credit, the taxpayer must maintain a household for himself and at least one child who is under age nineteen or a student, or for a disabled child of any age for whom a dependency exemption

[35] IRC Sec. 22(d).

[36] IRC Sec. 32.

is allowable.[37] For a married couple, the child must qualify as the taxpayers' dependent in order for the taxpayers to be eligible for the credit. Also, married couples who file separate tax returns will not be eligible for the credit. The maximum credit is reduced when adjusted gross income (or earned income if greater) goes over a certain level.[38] Thus, the maximum credit of $910 (for 1989) was reduced if either earned income or adjusted gross income exceeded $10,250, and became zero if earned income or adjusted gross income reached $19,340.

This feature of the credit is called "phase-down." Although the credit rate is 14%, the phase-down rate is 10% and *begins* at a level of earned income or adjusted gross income that is also price level adjusted. While the phase-down began at a level of $10,250 for 1989, it will begin at a level of $10,730 for 1990, which means that it will be reduced to zero at $20,264.

For example, assume that a qualifying taxpayer had 1990 adjusted gross income of $6,300, all from wages. The earned income credit is 14% of $6,300, or $822. Another qualified taxpayer had 1990 earned income (and adjusted gross income) of $14,000. The credit is:

Maximum credit (14% of $6,810)	$953
Phase-down 10% ($14,000 – $10,730)	327
Credit	$626

A third qualified taxpayer had 1990 earned income of $14,000, but adjusted gross income of $16,000 because of interest and dividend income ("unearned income"). The credit is:

Maximum credit (14% of $6,810)	$953
Phase-down 10% ($16,000 – $10,730)	527
Credit	$426

A fourth qualifying person had 1990 earned income of $6,200 plus interest and dividend income of $11,000, for a total of $17,200 AGI. The credit is:

14% of $6,200	$868
Phase-down 10% ($17,200 – $10,730)	647
Credit	$221

The point of this example is that unearned income can reduce the amount of the credit if adjusted gross income exceeds the level at which the phase-down begins.

TAX PLANNING TIP: Conversion of interest income that is included in gross income to interest income that can be excluded from gross income (i.e. state and local goverenment bond interest) can result in an increase in the amount of the earned income credit, if the credit would otherwise be reduced because of the "phase-down" provision.

The most significant difference between this and other credits is that it is "refundable."[39] That means that the taxpayer is entitled to the credit, even though no income tax may have been due or paid.[40] For example, if no tax is due and the credit is $220, a $220 "refund" will be received. If total tax is $100 and the credit is $350, a $250 "refund" will be received. The way this credit is treated on the tax return is to record it as if it were a prepayment of income tax rather than a reduction in tax. (See, for example, line 58 of Form 1040, page 2, Appendix 1-D(b)).

Other tax credits are available to taxpayers who are in business. These will be considered in later chapters.

4.8 Advance Tax Payments

Employers must withhold, and pay to the government, income tax on compensation paid to their employees.[41] The amount of tax so withheld is reported on the individual's tax return as an advance payment of the tax liability remaining after the subtraction of the various tax credits discussed.[42]

Another way to have a prepayment of income

[37]The credit is still available to a custodial parent even though he or she allowed the other parent to claim the child as a dependent as explained in Section 4.3.

[38]It is not necessary to calculate the credit. Each year the IRS calculates the new maximum credit, the phase-down range, and provides a table which shows the correct amount of the credit to be taken according to the amount of income. The "earned income credit table" is provided as a part of the income tax package which the IRS sends to taxpayers at the beginning of the year.

[39]The congressional rationale for the "refundable" nature of the credit is that it represents a recoupment of part of the social security taxes (withheld for employees or paid by self-employed persons) on earned income. Since social security tax rates have reached record highs in recent years, it is felt that an undue burden rests on low-income persons with a dependent child.

Another feature of this credit is unique. IRC Sec. 3507 provides for an eligible employee to receive advance payments of the earned income credit from his or her employer. The employer, in turn, reduces the income tax withholding and FICA tax, which is payable to the government, by the amount of the advance payment made to the employee. The advantage of this feature, from the employee's point of view, is that it is not necessary to wait until after the end of the year to have the "cash in pocket." It is beyond the scope of this text to cover any further details of this interesting concept.

[40]Prior to 1985, the earned income credit was not reduced by the alternative minimum tax, discussed in Chapter 16. Starting in 1985 the credit is reduced by the alternative minimum tax. IRC Sec. 32(h). See Chapter 16.

[41]IRC Sec. 3402.

[42]Except for the earned income credit which is *treated* as a prepayment because it is a "refundable" credit.

tax is to have paid more than the maximum of social security during the year. For 1990, the maximum social security base is $51,300 and the social security tax withholding rate is 7.65%. Thus, the maximum that an employee will have to pay for 1990 is $3,924.45. If more is paid (withheld), the excess is refunded by treating it as a prepayment of federal income tax. For example, assume that Billy Barnes had two different employers during 1990 and each paid Billy a salary of $27,000. Since each employer is required to withhold the social security tax, Billy will have had $4,131 withheld. The $206.55 excess will be treated as a prepayment of income tax. (See line 60 of page 2 of Form 1040 (Appendix 1-D(b).) The refund due is treated as a prepayment of the income tax. Note that Billy may or may not receive a check for the $206.55. It all depends upon the amount of income tax for the year and the total amount of income tax prepayments for the year.

Employers are required to pay to the Social Security Administration not only the amount that is withheld from employees but an amount equal to that for the employer's share of the tax. Each of the two employers in the above example, in addition to the amount withheld from Billy's salaries, would have paid $2,065.50 (7.65% of $27,000) for a total of $4,131. There is no provision in the tax law for a refund to Billy or to either of the employers for this amount which could be considered an overpayment. The reason is that it is not considered to be an overpayment. *Each* employer has a tax liability of 7.65% of the first $51,300 paid to each employee.

As we will see in Chapter 7, self-employed persons must pay the social security tax also. The maximum that is subject to the tax for 1990 is also $51,300. The rate is 15.3% (2×7.65%) but it is based on self-employment income rather than wages. This suggests another way that a person could have excess social security that would be refunded by being treated as a prepayment of income tax. Assume that Billy was both self-employed and an employee during the year 1990. As a self-employed person, Billy earned more than $51,300 and thus paid the maximum of $7,848.90 in tax. If Billy's salary during the year was $10,000, then $765 would have been withheld by the employer as FICA tax. Billy will treat the $765 as if it were a prepayment of income tax, as explained above.

People who receive income that is not subject to income tax withholding (such as income from self-employment and dividends, interest, rent, or royalties), and those for whom the withholding tax does not cover the tax liability,[43] are required to pay "estimated income tax" on a quarterly basis.[44]

There are two ways to handle the estimated income tax calculation.

1. The taxpayer may use the prior year's tax as the estimated tax for the current year.
2. The taxpayer may examine all of the anticipated income and deductions for the current year and compute the tax on that amount.

The estimated tax payments are reported as prepayments, the same as withholding.

The four estimated tax payments are due on April 15, June 15, and September 15 of the current year and January 15 of the following year.[45] Taxpayers who do not prepay at least 90% of their income tax through withholding and estimated tax payments may be subject to a penalty on the amount by which the prepayments are less than 90% of the tax.[46] The penalty will not apply if prepayments equal at least 100% of the prior year's tax, if there was a tax return filed for the prior year, and it was a taxable year of twelve months. This penalty is actually calculated as of each of the quarterly tax payment dates. The calculation is like that for interest, but the penalty is not interest, hence there is no deduction for amounts paid.

The social security tax does not apply to income from investments (i.e., dividends, interest, and royalties), but only to income from self-employment. Obviously, a self-employed person does not have an employer to withhold the social security tax from wages or salary and pay it to the government. Therefore, a self-employed person is required to pay it, and the mechanism for paying it is to add the social security tax (called "self-employment tax"— to the income tax for the year. (See line 48 of page 2 of Form 1040, Appendix 1-D(b).) The requirement for prepayment of taxes, discussed in the preceding paragraph, *includes* both the income tax and the self-employment tax. Thus, if Billy Barnes is self-employed and expects to have taxable income of $40,000 for 1990, the required prepayments will be 90% of the *sum of* the expected income tax and the self-employment tax.

4.9 Tax Planning

The discussion through this point has covered a broad area and has mainly set forth details

[43]For example, a person might be both an employee and self-employed. Withholding would apply to the wages or salary but not to self-employment income.
[44]IRC Sec. 6654.
[45]IRC Sec. 6654(c)(2).
[46]IRC Sec. 6654(d). The penalty rate is adjusted twice a year to the prime rate quoted by commercial banks to large businesses. IRC 6621. This is discussed further in Chapter 19.

and rules. The rest of this chapter will focus primarily on some aspects of individual tax planning.

As we will see in Chapter 5, a taxpayer can deduct losses from sales of "capital assets," but the loss deduction is limited to $3,000 in any one year. Losses in excess of $3,000 can be carried forward to future years. This is a deduction *for* AGI and not a part of the itemized deductions.

Gains and losses from capital assets are combined to arrive at a net gain (includable in gross income regardless of the amount) or a net loss (deduction limited to $3,000).[47]

These rules give rise to some important tax planning opportunities. For example, assume that Billy Barnes has sold an asset during 1990 and has capital gain of $20,000. The year is not over. Billy can still sell another asset for a loss and reduce taxable income. In the absence of a loss deduction, the $20,000 gain could result in tax of 33%, or $6,600. A $20,000 loss which would reduce the ***net*** gain to zero will result in $6,600 of tax savings.

Assume that Lynn Larsen (single) will have 1990 taxable income of $55,000 without any further losses or deductions. Sale of a capital asset for a loss of $3,000 (fully deductible) will reduce taxable income to $52,000 and save $990 in tax.

4.9.1. Installment Sales

The financial terms of a sale may encourage reporting a portion of the gain each year over several years as collections are made. When part of the proceeds of a sale will be received in a year subsequent to that of the sale, the gain on the sale will be reported as payments are received unless the taxpayer elects to report it all in the year of sale.[48] Spreading the income over several years can reduce taxes, as illustrated below. Our example will start with 1990. We also assume that the 1990 tax rate schedule will be in effect for four years.

For example, Billy Barnes has taxable income of $17,000 each year. The tax on $17,000 is 15%, which is $2,550. Billy sold an asset in 1990 for a gain of $10,000, receiving 25% of the sales price that year and 25% in each of the next three years. If the entire gain were taxable for 1990, taxable income would be $27,000. Tax on $27,000 is $2,917.50 + 28% ($27,000 − $19,450), which is $5,031.50. That's an increase of $2,481.50 in tax. By using the installment sales method, Billy's taxable income will be increased *each year* by $2,500 to $19,500. The tax on $19,500 is $2,917.50 + 28% ($19,500 − $19,450), which is $2,931.50, an increase of $381 over the amount if no sale had been made. Since that increased tax will result in each of four years, the total additional tax will be $1,526. By spreading the tax over the four years, Billy saved $956 in taxes. The tax savings could be more dramatic for a taxpayer in a higher tax bracket. The installment sales method could be particularly advantageous where its use will keep taxable income below the level where the 5% surtax will apply in the elimination of the 15% rate and the elimination of the "exemption amount" deduction for high income taxpayers as explained earlier.

The above example ignores the interest that would probably be charged by Billy in consideration of the buyer's deferral of payment. This would compensate the seller for the delay in having the cash in hand. Any interest received by a seller would be income and subject to income tax.[49] It also ignores any tax rate changes, changes in the exemption amount, as well as the time value of tax dollars which are deferred.

4.9.2 Keeping Records

Robert Frost, a leading American poet, wrote:

Never ask of money spent
Where the spender thinks it went.
Nobody was ever meant
To remember or invent
What he did with every cent.[50]

He may have written this shortly after a session with his Form 1040. The tax law does make it worthwhile to keep a good record of what you did with some of those cents. Knowing *what* you need to keep track of can save a lot of needless work.

Good tax records allow a person to show what was spent, when, with whom, and why it falls into a deductible category. While good tax records will take a little effort, they probably save most taxpay-

[47] IRC Sec. 1211. The nondeductible amount is carried forward to the following year.

[48] IRC Secs. 453, 453A, and 453B. Because the installment sales method is used by both individuals and businesses, we postpone discussion of the topic in detail until Chapter 8.

[49] IRC Sec. 483 provides for imputed interest where an installment sales contract does not include interest. This will be discussed in a later chapter. Our purpose here is just to emphasize the tax savings potential that can result from using the installment sales method when it is available. We would be remiss if we implied that the installment method is always advantageous. A large gain might produce less tax if recognized all in one year. For example, deductions in that year could reduce the amount subject to tax. Under the installment method, more tax could result if the taxpayer will be in higher tax brackets in future years.

[50] "The Hardship of Accounting." Reprinted by permission of Holt, Rinehart and Winston, Publishers.

ers more for the time involved, hour for hour, than those people earn at their jobs. For example:

> A taxpayer attended church every Sunday and deposited $10 cash in the collection plate. When he prepared his Form 1040, he estimated that he might have missed church on two Sundays. Since he itemized deductions, he took a deduction for charitable contributions of $500. This deduction reduced his income tax by $140. An IRS office auditor disallowed the $500 deduction because of inadequate records. Using pledge envelopes or writing a check for the $10 each week so that a record of the contributions would be available could have saved $140 in taxes.

Another example will demonstrate a longer-range impact:

> A taxpayer made an addition to his residence, purchasing the materials from lumberyards and hardware stores and doing the work himself. He did not keep receipts for any of the items, but estimated that he had spent $6,000. When he sold the house five years later he reported that his "cost" (original purchase price plus additions) was $60,000. Since the sales price was $80,000, his taxable gain was $20,000. An IRS auditor examined the return and decreased the cost to $54,000 because of lack of receipts for the additions. The additional $6,000 gain from the sale cost the taxpayer $1,980 in additional income tax.[51]

How much work would have been required to keep receipts, perhaps just stuffing them in an envelope appropriately labeled? If the receipts (or canceled checks or credit card slips) did not clearly show what they were for, how much work *at the time* would have been involved in making some notations to clarify what was being purchased and that it was for the addition?

Note that phrase "at the time." It is almost impossible to keep good tax records if details are not recorded "at the time." Human memory, no matter how well intentioned, too frequently fails us when it comes to specific details.

4.9.3. Marriage and Taxes

Getting married can increase the tax burden. Marriage can also pay—after taxes. The increase or decrease in tax is due mainly to the difference in the standard deduction amount and use of different schedules.

For 1990, for a single taxpayer, the basic standard deduction is $3,250 and the exemption amount is $2,050. This means that no tax will be payable if 1990 income is $5,300 or less.[52] A married couple filing jointly has $5,450 as the basic standard deduction. This, plus two exemptions at $2,050 each, results in no tax if income is $9,550 or less.[53]

The difference in standard deduction for single and married persons can create a peculiar situation when two people with approximately the same income are thinking of getting married. Assume that Billy Barnes meets that "special someone," who is also employed. They each have a salary of $20,000 and minimum deductions, consisting of a standard deduction of $3,250 and an exemption of $2,050. If they remain single, *each* will pay a tax of $2,205 (on 1990 taxable income of $14,700), for a total of $4,410. If they get married and file a joint return (for 1990), their taxable income will be $30,450 ($40,000 less a standard deduction of $5,450 and an exemption of $4,100).

$$\text{1990 tax} = 15\%\ (\$30{,}450) = \$4{,}568$$

This is an increase in tax of $158, sometimes called the "marriage penalty." There are two reasons for a change in tax as the result of getting married. First, tax is increased by the loss of $1,050 of standard deduction. (Two at $3,250 if they are single versus one at $5,450 if they are married.) That is all that happened in the example above; hence the additional tax of 15% times the $1,050 in lost deduction. An additional possibility is that the combined taxable income could put them in a higher (28% or 33%) tax bracket than they would have been in as single persons.

The newlyweds might think of using the "married—filing separately" status. Let us look at the result. Each will report taxable income of $15,225, which is $20,000 less one exemption and the standard deduction of $2,725. Each will have tax of $2,283.75, for a total of $4,568. Thus, the tax is the same as if they use the "married—joint return" status. (We should point out that the result of a married couple filing separately will not always be the same as if they file jointly. There are some special rules and limitations that apply to the deductions for married-filing-separately status. A detailed calculation and comparison should always be made before making the decision.)

[51]Gain or loss from the sale of property will be discussed in a later chapter. A taxpayer is under the burden of proving his or her cost for property just the same as the burden of proving entitlement to a deduction.

[52]This assumes that the taxpayer is not a dependent of someone else. A taxpayer who is a dependent of someone else can only claim the standard deduction from "earned" income.

[53]The standard deduction amounts are contained in IRC Sec. 63(c).

The tax result of marriage could be favorable with different facts. Assume that Jack had $40,000 of income and married Jill who had no income. As a single person, the tax (for 1990) would be:

Gross income (also AGI)		$40,000
Less: exemption amount	$2,050	
standard deduction	3,250	5,300
Taxable income		$34,700

Tax on $34,700 = $2,917.50 + 28% ($34,700 − $19,450) = $7,188

For a married couple, filing jointly, the tax would be $4,568, as we saw earlier.

Thus, getting married would reduce the tax by $2,620. This is due to the differences noted earlier (i.e., the difference in the standard deduction and the difference in marginal tax rates). Here, there is also a third factor, an additional exemption. Jill would get no benefit from the exemption amount as a no-income single person. As a taxpayer, the $2,050 deduction for Jill is worth $574 in direct tax saving.[54]

Jack and Jill's marriage would save $2,620 in income tax. An income boost of $3,639 would be needed to produce $2,620 after paying tax on the added income if Jack remained single.[55] They might decide that getting married before the end of the year, and using the $2,620 to honeymoon in Mazatlan over New Years is better than paying $2,620 in taxes.

TAX PLANNING TIP: Marriage or divorce can have substantial tax effects due to the shift from single to joint return, or vice versa. Marital status is determined as of the last day of the year, December 31 for most people. Postponement or acceleration of a divorce or marriage, particularly one that would come close to the end of the year anyway, can result in significant savings.

4.9.4 Joint or Separate Returns

Why would any married couple not file a joint return? Some possible reasons are the following:

1. One spouse does not want the other to know about the family finances—while one refuses to sign anything he or she has not read first. The result is a stand-off. They each file their own return.
2. By not signing the return, a spouse is not liable for any resulting deficiencies.[56] A wife, or husband, might not want to share in any future tax problems for any number of reasons, including suspicion of tax return improprieties or contemplation of divorce.[57]
3. Both have income, but one has substantial medical expenses while the other has none. Medical expenses, as discussed in Chapter 3, can be deducted only to the extent they exceed 7.5% of adjusted gross income. Thus, a deduction not available on a joint return might result in tax savings on separate returns. The same is possible for a casualty loss or miscellaneous deductions. However, if one spouse "itemizes" deductions then the other must do so also.
4. Finally, of course, there are married people who are no longer living together, without being legally separated or divorced, and who have lost touch with each other.[58]

If married taxpayers are considering filing separately they should know the tax cost, if any. Where the couple will itemize deductions with either the joint or separate returns, the combined tax could be the same with separate filing as with a joint return. However, if one spouse does not have itemized deductions in excess of the standard deduction ($2,725 for 1990) and files using the standard deduction, then the other spouse cannot itemize deductions. Thus, some potential deductions will be lost. Also, one spouse may have substantially more income than the other. This can result in the low-income spouse being in the 15% bracket but forcing the high-income spouse into a bracket higher than they would be if a joint return were filed.

For example, assume the following facts for Mr. and Mrs. Adam for 1990:

	Mr. A	*Mrs. A*
Income	$70,000	$ 5,000
Itemized deductions	(6,000)	(2,600)

On a joint return, the above would appear as follows:

[54]Frequently, the tax results of a proposed transaction can be determined, or estimated closely, without a complete calculation of tax under different sets of assumptions. If the marginal tax rate is 33%, for example, an additional deduction of $1,000 will reduce taxes by $330. Similarly, a transaction that would increase income by $1,000 would increase tax by $330, for an after-tax increase in income of $670.

[55]Tax on $3,639 more income will be $1,019 at the 1990 marginal rate of 28%.

[56]Penalties are covered by IRC Secs. 6671–6708.

[57]See, e.g., *In re Pomponio* (DC Va.), 79-2 USTC 9585, 44 AFTR2d 79-5778, where the husband apparently forged the wife's signature to a joint return.

[58]Such a person might, if a child is living with him or her, qualify for the head-of-household rate schedule, as discussed in Section 4.5.

Gross income (also AGI)		$75,000
Itemized deductions	$8,600	
Exemptions (2)	4,100	12,700
Taxable income		$62,300

Tax on $62,300 = $4,867.50 + 28% ($62,300 − $32,450) = $13,225.50. On tax returns as married-separate, the above would appear as follows:

		Mr. A		*Mrs. A*
Gross income (also AGI)		$70,000		$5,000
Itemized deductions	$6,000		$2,600	
Exemption	2,050	8,050	2,050	4,650
Taxable income		$61,950		$ 350

Tax on $61,950 = $8,866.75 + 33% ($61,950 − $39,200)	= $16,374
Tax on $350 at 15%	= 53
Total tax	$16,427

Cost of filing separately = $16,427 − $13,226 = $3,201.

Where taxable income is large enough that the 15% tax rate has been phased out and the phase-out of the exemption deduction begins with a 5% surtax (as explained earlier), a married person filing separately must calculate the added surtax *as if* the taxpayer were claiming an exemption for his or her spouse. This presents an additional impact upon some married taxpayers who file separately.[59]

4.9.5 Year-End Timing

Timing of a transaction at year end may sometimes affect tax payments for two years. Assume that the taxpayer could realize a large gain in December 1990. By postponing realization of the gain until January 1991, the following tax payment results may be accomplished:

[59]IRC Sec 1(g)(2) as amended by the Technical and Miscellaneous Revenue Act of 1988.

1. The 1991 tax (to be paid by April 15, 1992) may be less. (The reverse could happen depending upon other income and acts of Congress.)
2. The estimated tax for 1991 can be based on the 1990 tax without any penalty for underestimation. This will keep the 1991 cash disbursements (quarterly payments) at a lower level than if the gain had been realized in 1990.
3. There could be a substantial alternative minimum tax impact. This is discussed in Chapter 16.

4.9.6. Controlling Tax Liability

There are some general principles that can assist in controlling tax liability:

1. Learn how to find the tax rules in some detail, since the general rules often have exceptions. A book like this, which is intended as a textbook rather than a reference book, cannot cover every twist and turn of the tax law—and so should not be relied upon for research purposes. Tax research is discussed in Chapter 20.
2. The higher the tax bracket, the more likely it is that a taxpayer can benefit from obtaining tax-free or tax-sheltered income.
3. Timing (of deductions or of gains, for example) can affect total taxes paid.
4. Splitting income among lower-bracket taxpayers (including family trusts and family corporations) can reduce the overall tax burden of a family unit especially after a child is age 14. This is discussed more fully in Chapters 14 and 15.
5. Almost any transaction, financial or not (e.g., a divorce or marriage), offers tax trade-offs and planning opportunities.
6. Tax-exempt income can result in substantial savings, such as (a) where the taxpayer is in a high tax bracket, (b) where the "kiddie tax" will apply and (c) where the surtax will apply to eliminate the tax benefit of the "exemption amount" deduction.

TRUE-FALSE QUESTIONS

State whether each of the following statements is true or false. For each *false* answer, reword the statement to make it *true.*

T F 1. The only way to satisfy the "relationship" test (which is one of the five tests which must be satisfied in order to claim an exemption amount for a dependent) is for the dependent to be a legal relative of the taxpayer.

T F 2. The earned income credit is available only to married persons who have at least one dependent child.

T F 3. The earned income credit is 15% of the amount of earned income or the amount of adjusted gross income, whichever is smaller.

T F 4. A taxpayer who can be claimed as a dependent of someone else will be allowed to take a deduction for his or her own exemption amount but will also only be allowed a standard deduction of $500.

T F 5. The installment sales method is a device used to lower taxes by spreading gain over more than one year.

T F 6. The so-called "kiddie tax" is a set of rules which provides that any child who can be claimed as a dependent by his or her parents will be required to pay a tax at the parents' tax rate on any income which is taxable to the child.

T F 7. Where the "kiddie tax" rate applies to a child, that child will not be allowed to claim either an exemption amount for himself or any standard deduction.

T F 8. A married couple must always file a joint income tax return in order to obtain the maximum advantages of all deductions.

T F 9. For purposes of filing a federal income tax return, a person's marital status is determined on the last day of the year, except for a person whose spouse died during the year.

T F 10. The exemption amount deduction allowed for 1990 for a dependent who has reached age sixty-five before the end of the year is $2,050.

T F 11. In order for any person, other than a child of the taxpayer, to be claimed as a dependent for 1990, such a person must have under $2,050 of gross income for the year.

T F 12. A taxpayer must always supply more than one-half of the support of any person for whom an exemption amount is claimed.

T F 13. The elderly credit is available to a taxpayer if he or she is over age sixty-five and is based upon 15% of all income reduced by certain items such as social security receipts.

T F 14. A multiple-support agreement is an agreement among all of the persons who supplied at least 10% of the support of a person, but none of whom supplied over 50% of the support, as to which of them shall claim the exemption amount for the person supported.

T F 15. A head of household is defined only as an unmarried person who has a dependent child living in his or her household.

T F 16. The child- and dependent-care credit allows a reduction in taxes for 20% of the cost of certain babysitting or dependent-care fees, limited to $480 if one child or dependent is cared for and if adjusted gross income is $30,000.

T F 17. The only way to reduce federal income tax liability is to avoid the recognition of gross income.

T F 18. For 1990, the exemption amount consists of a basic amount for the taxpayer plus an extra amount if that taxpayer has reached the age of 65 before the end of the year or is blind.

T F 19. The marginal rate of tax is that percentage of tax which was paid on the last dollar of taxable income.

T F 20. The child- and dependent-care credit is available only if the purpose of the expenditure was to allow the taxpayer to be gainfully employed, and consequently is not permitted if the expenditure was for the purpose of allowing the taxpayer to attend school.

PROBLEMS

Problem 4-1. Mike M. and Sybil S. Canning will file a joint income tax return. They are both employed. They had income as follows:

Mike's salary	$26,000
Sybil's salary	21,300
Interest from corporation bonds	390
Dividends from U.S. corporation stock owned jointly	350
Interest from State of New York bonds	1,000
Sybil's earnings as the church choir director	800
Mike's outside consulting income	600
State's income tax refund on taxes claimed as a deduction the previous year	200

The Cannings have two children who are dependents, Douglas and Donald. Mike paid deductible alimony of $1,800. They will file a joint return. The following information is available:

State income tax withheld from salaries	$ 900
Real estate taxes	475
Medical and dental expenses	4,150
Personal property tax	120
Consumer interest	400
Home mortgage interest	2,400*
Includable employee business expenses (Mike)	500**
Charitable contribution to church (the Cannings have receipts)	1,700
Federal income tax withheld	9,000

* Debt does not exceed limitation

** Any 20% reduction for meals and entertainment has already been subtracted.

Required:

(a) Compute their income tax liability for 1990.

(b) Sybil has a strong interest in amateur drama. She is active in the Midtown Little Theater. Contributions to this organization are deductible for federal income tax purposes. What would have been the after-tax impact to the Cannings of a $500 cash contribution to Midtown Little Theater?

(c) Assume that the Cannings were influenced by the tax benefit in making a $500 contribution. In your view, does that result in a federal subsidy to the Midtown Little Theater? Why?

Problem 4-2. Mr. and Mrs. Harvey Cousins are in the process of getting a divorce. They are negotiating over the terms of the settlement. Mrs. Cousins believes that she should be entitled to alimony. Mr. Cousins is opposed in principle to the payment of alimony but would agree to more child-support payments for their three children if alimony is not required. He understands that in any event the amount of child support that he will pay will permit him to claim the children as dependents, and Mrs. Cousins does not disagree with that result. Mr. Cousins is faced with two alternatives. He can pay $200 per month per child in child support plus $600 per month in alimony, or he can pay child support of $400 per child per month with no alimony. His taxable income, after deductions for the exemption amounts, but before any alimony payments, will be $80,000 per year, all from investments. Use 1990 tax rates.

(a) Which alternative is better for him for the first year?

(b) What other factors must be taken into consideration?

(c) Why should Mrs. Cousins care about the result?

Problem 4-3. Richard Rice is single. His mother lives in a nursing home. She received social security payments of $4,800 for the year. She also received $700 of interest during the year. As these amounts are received they are deposited into a joint bank account of Richard and his mother. During the year, Richard withdrew $3,500 from the account to pay medical expenses for his mother. His mother withdrew $2,400 from the account to pay for other personal expenses during the year. The $5,900 thus expended was the entire cost of his mother's support for the year. Answer the following questions assuming that the year is 1990.

(a) May Richard claim the exemption amount deduction for his mother? Why or why not?
(b) May Richard claim medical expenses paid for his mother as a deduction on his tax return?
(c) Assume that Richard paid the medical expenses from his own funds and left the $3,500 in the bank account. Will this permit him to claim his mother as a deduction?
(d) If he can claim the exemption amount for his mother, what other tax advantage might Richard realize as the result?
(e) What difference would there be in the answer to parts (a), (b), and (c) if his mother's interest income had been $2,100?

Problem 4-4. Sam Gibb has a twenty-one-year-old son, Bill, who is not a student. During the year, Bill was injured in an automobile accident and was unable to work for the remainder of the year. Up to the time of the accident, Bill had earned $2,500. Bill's accident insurance paid $3,000 toward his medical bills, but Sam paid an additional $2,000. Sam also incurred $3,700 in additional support for Bill after the accident. Bill provided all of his own support from his income prior to the accident. The total amount of Bill's support for the year was $11,200. The year is 1990.

(a) Is Sam entitled to an exemption amount deduction for Bill? Why or why not?
(b) Is Sam entitled to deduct any of the costs that he paid as the result of Bill's injuries? Explain.
(c) What if the additional support paid by Sam for Bill had been $2,900 instead of $3,700? Explain the different tax result if any.

Problem 4-5. Mr. and Mrs. M. E. Stock are both employees and members of their respective credit unions, where they have savings accounts. Mr. Stock has recently learned that his credit union will loan him money at 12% annual simple interest. It will pay interest on deposits at the rate of 10% annual simple interest. The Stocks have one child, Susan, age fifteen. They have been thinking of opening a savings account in her name, since up to $500 interest income would not be taxable. The interest which the Stocks would pay on the loan would be deductible because the security for the loan would be their residence, and the debt would be less than their cost.

(a) Assume that the Stocks borrow $5,000 and deposit it in an account for Susan. Calculate the savings if their combined federal and state marginal income tax bracket is 40%.
(b) What if they borrowed $20,000 for Susan's account? Assume that Susan would be subject to regular federal income tax plus state income tax at 2% on gross income. (The state income tax deduction will not be deductible by Susan.)
(c) Explain the consequences if Susan is not age 14.

Problem 4-6. Marsha and John Daniels have been married for three years. John is a full-time student at Goody University and Marsha works as a secretary for a local advertising firm. John is not otherwise employed. Marsha earns a monthly salary of $780. The Daniels have a one-year-old son, David. Marsha takes David to the Jack and Jill babysitter each day. The babysitting service costs $250 per month. The Daniels will not have any deductions from gross income and will use the standard deduction. The year is 1990.

(a) Calculate the tax liability, after credit for the child-care expense. (Ignore earned income credit.)

(b) Marsha and John are considering a divorce. What would be the combined tax liability if they get a divorce before the end of the year, assuming that Marsha gets custody of David? Who is eligible for the earned income credit?

(c) If they do not get a divorce, will Marsha and John be eligible for the earned income credit? If so, how much? Calculate their refund, assuming no withholding on Marsha's salary.

Problem 4-7. Dave Benson is twenty-one years old, married, and attending college. He and his wife, Joan, have no children. Dave's parents provide him with enough money for his college and living expenses even though Joan, who is also a full-time student, earned $2,500 during the year. Dave has no income other than his parents' support. All persons are resident U.S. citizens.

(a) May Dave's parents claim the exemption amount for him? Explain the circumstances under which they could claim him.

(b) May Dave's parents claim Joan as a dependent? Are there any circumstances under which they could claim her? Explain.

(c) In general, what tax planning advice might be given to parents with children in college?

Problem 4-8. Vic and Ann Johnson provide $200 per month support for Vic's mother, Helen, who is unemployed and a widow. Helen's only other income consists of $100 per month which she receives from her deceased husband's employer, and $120 per month (average) which she receives in dividend income. Helen uses all of the money which she receives from these three sources for her living expenses. Helen is age fifty-eight and unable to work because of physical disabilities. The $100 from her deceased husband's employer is paid under the Railroad Retirement Act and is a continuation of disability payments which he was receiving prior to his death last year. These receipts are not gross income. Last year, Helen filed a joint income tax return. This year she will be unable to file a joint return under the surviving spouse rules because she does not qualify with a dependent child living with her. Helen lives in a separate residence from her son and daughter-in-law. The year is 1990.

(a) Will Vic and Ann be able to claim the exemption amount for Helen? Explain.

(b) Will Vic and Ann be able to use the head-of-household rate status?

(c) What would be the effect if Helen were to sell her stocks and purchase state and local government bonds?

(d) Suggest another possible tax savings plan for Vic and Ann. (Assume that their gross income consists in large part of investment income.)

(e) Would the situation be any different if Helen were age sixty-five? Explain.

Problem 4-9. Herbert Adams is a junior at State University. During the summer he earned $2,000 in wages on a construction job. During the year he received $2,500 in interest from corporate bonds which were bequeathed to him by his grandmother four years ago. Herbert has no deductions from gross income. If he were to itemize his deductions, they would total $1,000. He has no dependents. His parents provide more than one-half of his support for the year and will claim him as a dependent.

(a) What is Herbert's federal income tax liability for the year 1990?

(b) What would be the tax liability if Herbert's unearned income had been interest from state and local government bonds?

Problem 4-10. Bill Gomez is eighteen years of age and has just completed high school. He plans to enter college in the fall. He has an opportunity for a summer job which would pay approximately $3,000. Bill was never employed during high school and does not plan to hold a job while in college. Bill's father has assured him that it will not be necessary for Bill to help finance his own schooling since there is adequate family income to take care of all reasonable college expenses. Bill's family will provide $7,000 toward Bill's support for the year.

(a) Bill has asked his father if there might be any adverse income tax effects if Bill should take the summer job. What do you think?

(b) Would Bill's age have an effect on the answer?

Problem 4-11. Martha Ring is entirely supported by her three sons, Bill, Bart, and Barry, who provide support as follows:

Bill	8%
Bart	47%
Barry	45%

Martha had gross income of $725 for the year.

(a) May any of the brothers claim the "exemption amount" for their mother? (Assume that all tests except the support test are satisfied.)

(b) Suggest a plan that will result in one of the boys being able to claim Martha as a dependent.

(c) Is there any possible tax advantage to one or more of the sons paying Mrs. Ring's medical expenses directly rather than providing her with money which she uses to pay the bills?

Problem 4-12.

(a) Which of the following persons will qualify as a "relative" for purposes of the exemption amount?

1. Your wife
2. Your uncle
3. Your grandmother
4. Your cousin
5. Your brother
6. Your father
7. Your ex-mother-in-law
8. Your uncle's mother-in-law
9. Your stepsister
10. Your stepson
11. Your foster father
12. Your half-sister
13. Your husband's brother
14. Your nephew by blood
15. Your sister's legally adopted daughter
16. Your wife's brother's wife

(b) How might you plan legally to take an exemption amount deduction for any of the persons in part (a) who are not relatives?

Problem 4-13. Joe Patten has adjusted gross income of $12,000. He is age sixty-eight and single. He received $2,000 of social security benefits for the year 1990. In calculating his tax liability there were no other excludable pension or annuity receipts.

(a) What is the amount of Joe's "credit for the elderly"?

(b) Joe's adjusted gross income consisted of $8,000 from investments and $4,000 from a part-time job. What would be the effect on the credit if he had quit the part-time job last year so he would only have had $8,000 of AGI this year?

(c) Joe had asked Mary Pollen to marry him. Mary is a widow, age sixty-four, and has social security income of $2,000 per year plus taxable dividend income of $3,000. If Joe and Mary get married on December 31, what will be the amount of their joint credit? (His AGI is $12,000.) Consider both the year of marriage and the following year. Assume that in the second year their combined social security will be $3,000.

(d) Assume they get married on December 31 and that Joe quit his part-time job last year so he has no earnings for the next year except the $8,000 of interest. Mary has $3,000 of taxable dividends. Combined social security is $3,000. What will be the elderly credit this year and next year?

Problem 4-14. Lisa Kline, single and age sixty-four, had the following income during the year 1990:

Interest from U.S. government bonds	$1,400
Dividends from U.S. corporations	10,200
Interest credit to passbook by the Third National Savings and Loan Association	2,000

Lisa also sold some corporate stocks during the year and realized a capital loss of $2,600. The stocks that were sold had been held for three years. (The income tax rules permit a deduction for adjusted gross income for the amount of a long-term capital loss with a maximum deduction in any one year of $3,000.) Lisa's itemized deductions would be less than the standard deduction. Lisa's eyesight is failing, but her ophthalmologist has determined that her condition does not meet the legal definition of blindness. She is not retired under a public retirement system.

(a) What is Lisa's federal income tax for the year?

(b) What difference would it make if her ophthalmologist had determined that she was legally blind?

(c) Assume that Lisa has the same amount of income and losses for 1990 as above, but that her 65th birthday is in November and that she received one month's social security check for $250. She is not blind. What is her federal income tax for 1990?

(d) Assume that Lisa converted her investments so that she had $5,000 less in dividends, but $4,600 more in interest from state and local government bonds. Recalculate the 1990 tax liability as in part (c).

Problem 4-15. Don Pitts is sixty-seven years old; his wife, Ronda, is sixty-one. They are sole supporters of Don's father, who is eighty-five and blind. Don and Ronda have itemized deductions of $4,650. Their income consists of the following:

Don's salary	$26,500
Dividends (joint)	380
Interest (joint)	620

They live in a noncommunity-property state.

(a) What is their federal income tax liability for 1990?

(b) Would they save any tax by transferring all of their investments to Don's father? Would they lose the exemption amount for Don's father? Explain.

Problem 4-16. Roxie Roth is a public school teacher whose annual salary is $18,000. She has been divorced for five years. Roxie has three teenage children by her former marriage, but none are dependents because her ex-husband provides child support and the divorce decree provides that he will be entitled to the exemption amount deductions for the children. Roxie does provide over one-half of the cost of the household and, therefore, qualifies as a head of household. Her itemized deductions are $1,500. The child-support payments are not part of her gross income.

Melvin Grey is the superintendent of schools. Melvin has also been divorced for several years, but his children are adults and have left home. Melvin's annual salary is $27,000 and he receives $6,000 per year in interest income and $10,000 in consulting fees, after deductions for expenses incurred in his consulting practice. His itemized deductions are $5,000. Melvin and Roxie are thinking of getting married. It is late in the year and they could get married before the end of the year or wait until after December 31.

(a) What is their combined tax for the year 1990 if they remain single?

(b) What is their total tax for the year if they get married before the end of the year?

(c) Explain the reasons for the difference.

(d) If Roxie and Melvin get married before the end of the year, will it be more advantageous for them to file as married—joint or married—separate? Explain the difference in tax liability.

Problem 4-17. Jane and Jim Davison both graduated as accounting majors from Playground University three years ago. They are both CPAs and are employed by different CPA firms. Jane's salary is $26,000, and Jim's is $26,500. Jane and Jim have a daughter, Lisa, age two. Their deductions from gross income amount to $2,000 for a contribution to an Individual Retirement Account (IRA). Itemized deductions totaled $6,000. In addition to her salary, Jane has $600 interest income from cash which she inherited two years ago and deposited in a savings and loan account. Babysitting expense is $225 per month.

(a) Calculate the tax liability for the Davisons (1990).

(b) Jane has been thinking of quitting work and staying at home with Lisa until Lisa reaches school age. None of their expenses except child care would change in the event Jane stopped work. What would be the net decrease in cash flow if she stopped? How much of that is attributable to the tax difference? (Assume she would have quit at the beginning of 1990.)

(c) What would be the tax savings from putting the savings and loan deposit in Lisa's name? If the current rate of return on the savings and loan deposit is 8%, what is the after-tax rate of return if Jane keeps the account in her own name? (Assume simple interest, compounded annually.)

Problem 4-18. Mr. and Mrs. Herman Agnew have filed joint income tax returns for the past several years. Mr. Agnew runs his own consulting business, from which he reports $45,000 of net income, all of which is from his personal services. He has no other sources of income. Mrs. Agnew has interest income of $5,000 from corporate bonds which she inherited three years ago. She has no other source of income. For 1990, Mrs. Agnew has said that she intends to file a separate tax return because she is convinced that her husband is not reporting all of his business income, and if he gets caught, she has no intention of being a party to the consequences. Also, Mrs. Agnew incurred $3,000 of dental expenses, which she paid from her own income. In addition, their itemized deductions for the year are as follows:

Mr Agnew:	
State and local taxes	$2,000
Interest (all deductible)	1,200
Charitable contributions	700
Total	$3,900
Mrs. Agnew:	
State and local taxes	$ 300
Charitable contributions	200
Total	$ 500

She knows that to file separately will force Mr. Agnew to do the same.

(a) Calculate the cost, in additional tax to be paid, of Mrs. Agnew's decision to file separately.

(b) What will be the tax difference if they get divorced before the end of 1990?

Problem 4-19. Marvin Fuggel is a single man with one dependent, his mother. Marvin pays all the costs of the house where he and she live and therefore qualifies as a head of household for federal income tax purposes. Marvin's income consists of the following:

Salary	$40,000
Interest and rent	25,000
Long-term capital gain	15,000

Marvin's itemized deductions, none of which result from providing over one-half of his mother's support, total $8,000.

(a) Calculate Marvin's federal income tax liability for 1990.

(b) How much tax does Marvin save as the result of having his mother as a dependent and qualifying as a head of household?

Problem 4-20. Mr. Jones and Mr. Smith met at a convention for managers. They discovered they had a lot in common. For example, Mr. Jones is the manager of a hotel. He has approximately 500 employees working for him. His current operating budget is about $20 million. Mr. Smith has about the same responsibility in terms of number of employees and budget, but he is the manager of a manufacturing company. Both are employees and own no stock in the companies they run. Mr. Jones has an annual salary of $80,000 and was surprised to learn that Mr. Smith's salary is $100,000. Jones is required by his employer to live in the building, which includes the hotel. The employer requires that he have his meals there also, unless he is away for official business or on vacation. Both lodging and meals are furnished at no cost to Jones. Smith has no such requirement and can live and eat any place he wants. Jones estimates that the value of the meals and lodging furnished by his employer is about $9,000 per year. Both men are married and have two dependent children. Both file joint income tax returns and have itemized deductions of $10,000.

Who earns the most after taxes (1990)? Explain.

Problem 4-21. Mr. and Mrs. Harold Zinser have been married for twelve years and have always filed a joint income tax return. Mr. Zinser has been steadily employed while Mrs. Zinser has been a homemaker. This year, Mrs. Zinser decided to take a full-time job and her salary was $18,000. Mr. Zinser's salary was $25,000. Their other income consisted of interest of $500. There is no deduction to arrive at AGI. Their itemized deductions will be $7,000. They have three exemption amounts, including themselves.

(a) What is their taxable income for 1990?

(b) What is the "after-tax" amount of Mrs. Zinser's salary? (Note that this will require calculation of tax *as if* she had not been employed.)

Problem 4-22. Roosevelt Haines (married, filing a joint return) will have 1990 taxable income (all ordinary income) of $80,000. He owns some property which he is in the process of selling. The sale will result in a long-term capital gain of $60,000. The buyer has indicated that she would be willing to pay the entire amount at the close of the sale (late in the year 1990) or pay one-half of the sales price at the date of closing and the remaining one-half by January 5, 1991.

(a) If Roosevelt receives the entire sales price in 1990, what will be his 1990 federal tax liability?

(b) If Roosevelt receives one-half of the sales price in 1990, only one-half of the gain will be taxed in 1990. He will have $80,000 in ordinary taxable income again in 1991 without the gain. How much tax will be saved (if any) by selling the property under the proposed installment arrangement? (Ignore the time value of money, and any interest on the installment sale. Use 1990 rules and rates for 1991.)

Problem 4-23. Mr. and Mrs. O'Hearn will have their first baby in 1990. Without the additional exemption amount deduction for the baby, their taxable income will be $170,000. In arriving at that number, they have two other exemption amounts, one each for themselves.

(a) Calculate their tax liability on taxable income of $170,000, i.e., without the additional exemption deduction.

(b) How much tax benefit do they get from the two exemption amounts of $2,000 each? Explain.

(c) Calculate their tax liability with the additional exemption deduction, i.e., a total of three.

(d) How much tax benefit will they get from the additional exemption amount? Explain.

Problem 4-24. Betty Hunt is single, but is a head of household for federal income tax purposes. She will have 1990 taxable income of $60,000 not counting the possible sale of a capital asset. If she sells the asset before the end of 1990, her taxable income will increase by $20,000. She has calculated her before-tax rate of return on the asset as follows:

$$\frac{\text{Profit on sale}}{\text{Cost}} \quad \frac{\$20{,}000}{\$100{,}000} = 20\%$$

(a) Calculate her after-tax rate of return on the sale.

(b) Suggest a way for Betty to avoid the 33% marginal tax rate.

Problem 4-25. Mr. and Mrs. Stillwater will have four exemption amount deductions of $2,050 each on their 1990 joint tax return. Taxable income will be $170,000. They are aware of the fact that they will not receive a tax benefit for the entire $8,200 deduction for exemptions, but have asked you to calculate (a) the amount of tax savings from exemptions, and (b) how much of the deduction they effectively lost.

PROBLEMS WITH AN ASTERISK REQUIRE ADDITIONAL RESEARCH

Problem 4-26.* June Lockburn, who is a widow, had adjusted gross income of $20,000 for 1990. In order to be gainfully employed, she had to obtain help in caring for her five-year-old daughter, Lisa, who attended first grade beginning in September. Expenses were as follows:

Period	*Payee*	*Cost*
January–May	Day Care Nursery	$125 per month
June–August	Mary Fillen	$200 per month
September–December	Grace School	$100 per month

Mary Fillen is a neighbor girl and a high school junior. In addition to caring for Lisa all day five days a week, Mary cleaned June's house, washed clothing and dishes, and began the preparation of the evening meal before June returned home. Grace School is a private elementary school with grades K through 6. Lisa was in school from 9:00 A.M. until 5:00 P.M., but June's mother stopped by to care for Lisa during the mornings and get her off to school. June did not pay her mother for this service.

(a) What amount may June claim as a credit for child-care expenses for 1990? (Does the amount paid to Mary Fillen have to be allocated between a child-care amount *per se* and an amount paid for non-child-care household or maid chores with only the former being eligible for the credit?)

(b) What if June had paid her mother $100 per month from September to December to care for Lisa between the hours when school was over and June got home from her job? Explain the effect on the credit.

5

taxable property transactions

The general format for calculating the federal income tax of an individual was discussed in Chapters 1 through 4. As you have learned, some types of income are not subject to income tax, and there are special provisions in the law, such as the exclusion of part of social security receipts, that affect certain other types of income. This chapter and the next deal with the special rules applicable to gains and losses on the sale or exchange of property.

5.1 Brief Historical Review

The tax treatment of capital gains and losses in the United States has varied over the years. Before 1922, capital gains were taxed the same as other income. Later, capital gains were separated into long term (held at least two years) and short term (held less than two years), with the long-term capital gains subject to a maximum rate of 12½% while short-term gains were taxed at the same rates as other income.[1] Next, the law was changed so that a varying percentage of the capital gain, depending on how long the asset had been held, was treated as ordinary income. If an asset was held for a required minimum time, the portion of the gain that was taxed was less than otherwise. The required holding period for long-term capital gains (or losses) was changed to "more than one year." In 1984, it was changed back to "more than six months" and again back to "more than one year" for property acquired after 1987. Currently there is no favorable tax treatment for long-term capital gains. However, the holding period still will be important because of the combining of capital asset transactions and the limits on capital loss deductions which will be explained later.

President George Bush proposed that favorable tax treatment for long-term capital gain be reinstated as part of the tax law with the "Omnibus Budget Reconciliation Act of 1989." That proposal did not become part of the law change that was enacted on December 19, 1989. However, some observers predict that the proposal will be made again and may become a part of the 1990 tax law changes.

The tax treatment of capital gains and losses as set forth in this chapter, began to develop in the late thirties and has been continuously modified over the years. From 1922 to 1942 preferential treatment was given to capital gains for individuals but not for corporations. From 1942 through 1987, both individuals and corporations had some kind of special tax treatment, but not necessarily the same. For many years, individuals paid tax on only half of long-term capital gains by taking a deduction for one-half of such gain. A major change, increasing the long-term capital gain deduction for individuals from 50% to 60%, was enacted in 1978.[2] The Economic Recovery Tax Act of 1981 resulted in a reduction of the maximum rate on long-term capital gains from 28% to 20%. The Tax Reform Act of 1986 repealed the basic

[1] J. S. Seidman, *Seidman's Legislative History of Federal Income Tax Laws (1851–1938)* (Englewood Cliffs, N.J.: Prentice-Hall, 1959).

[2] Revenue Act of 1978 (H.R. 13511), which amended IRC Secs. 1201 and 1202.

distinction between capital gain and ordinary gain with both being taxed at the same rates after 1987.

The treatment of capital losses has gone from nonrecognition, to full allowance against any income regardless of classification, to limitations upon the amount of loss that can be deducted.[3]

The great concern over the taxation of capital gains, as represented by the various approaches that have been tried, and the emotion with which many commentators approach the subject, may help to underscore the crucial role played by investors in maintaining the vigor of the economy from which we all draw our sustenance. When Congress repealed the rules which provided for favorable tax treatment of long-term capital gains, there was no repeal of the definition of capital assets, nor of the distinction between short-term and long-term gains and losses.[4] This has led some commentators to suggest that Congress could reenact a differential tax rate system quite easily since the basic statutory language is still in place.

5.2 A Brief Look at Pre-1988 Capital Gain Classification

Prior to 1987, the favorable (long-term) capital gains treatment resulted from a deduction—which was a deduction to arrive at adjusted gross income—equal to 60% of net long-term capital gains. Thus, only 40% of long-term capital gain was subject to taxation. This resulted in a favorable tax treatment for persons with long-term capital gain, regardless of their marginal tax rate.

The capital gain provisions allowed taxpayers to pay an effective rate of income tax that was substantially lower than the structure of the individual tax rates. According to the tax rate structure in effect for 1986, a single taxpayer with taxable income of $100,000 paid $36,981 in tax. This was an *average* rate of almost 37%, although the maximum or marginal rate was 50%. Married taxpayers with $100,000 of taxable income paid an average rate of about 31½% and a marginal rate of 45%. However, the average real tax rate actually paid by individual taxpayers with capital gain income was probably substantially less.[5]

We hasten to point out, however, that it was not just high-income taxpayers who benefited. At any income level, a dollar of long-term capital gain was preferable to a dollar of ordinary income.[6] It was a tax savings device for persons at all levels of income because only 40% of the net gain was taxed. A strong justification for the repeal of the favorable tax treatment for long-term capital gains (i.e., the 60% deduction) was that the highest tax rate for individuals was being reduced from 50% to 28% (not counting the phase-out of the 15% rate and the phase-out of the exemption amount deduction as explained earlier).

Before going any further into the tax treatment of capital assets transactions, let us pause to look at those kinds of assets which, if sold, produce capital gain or loss.

As you read the section on capital assets, keep in mind the following two points:

1. The distinction between capital gain/loss and noncapital gain/loss applies equally to *all* taxpayers (i.e. individuals, corporations, and fiduciaries) even though we will not discuss the latter two until later chapters.
2. The distinction is still important to individual taxpayers because of the limitation that applies to the deduction for a loss that is a capital loss.

Capital gain or loss arises from the sale or exchange of certain kinds of property. In abstract tax theory, if a taxpayer owns a citrus grove, the income derived from the sale of fruit is ordinary income. If, however, the grove is sold, any gain on the sale is treated as a capital gain. While dividends on stock are ordinary income, both gains *and* losses on sale of that stock are capital.[7]

Suffice it to say at this point that the U.S. income tax law does not deal with "pure" capital assets. In fact, the law does not define capital assets in a positive way. Rather, it provides us with a negative definition.

5.3 Definition of Capital Assets

Capital assets are all assets *except:*

1. Stock in trade or other inventory property.
2. Property held primarily for sale to customers in the ordinary course of business.
3. Depreciable or real property used in a trade or business.

[3]At present, capital losses are not deductible against ordinary income by corporations. Individuals are limited to a maximum deduction of $3,000 per year. IRC Sec. 1211.

[4]See IRC Secs. 1221 and 1222.

[5]The average tax rate, which is determined by dividing the tax by taxable income, is sometimes called the *nominal* rate. The *real* tax rate can be determined by dividing the tax by gross income.

[6]An obvious exception, of course, exists where the taxpayer did not pay *any* tax because income was too low or deductions too large.

[7]Technically, the citrus grove would not qualify as a capital asset under IRC Sec. 1221, but the gain would still be treated as capital under IRC Sec. 1231 even though a loss on sale would be ordinary.

4. The normal notes or accounts receivable derived by a business from the sale of goods or services.
5. A copyright; a literary, musical, or artistic composition; or a letter or memorandum or similar property in the hands of the author, composer, or someone whose tax basis is determined by reference to the author.[8]

The operational result is that gains and losses from the sale or exchange of such assets must *first* be combined or netted. If there is a net gain, that gain is included in gross income. If there is a net loss, however, the maximum deduction for individuals is $3,000. The deduction is *to arrive at* AGI. Should other income be less than $3,000, then the deduction is limited to the sum of other income.[9] Were it not for this netting and the deduction, consideration of capital assets would be relatively unimportant under the current rules. The mechanics of calculating net capital gains or losses is discussed in greater detail later in this chapter.

5.3.1. Holding Period

There is one other requirement for the determination of the tax treatment. Generally, if a "capital asset" is held for more than one year, the capital gain is considered long term. Capital assets held one year or less produce short-term capital gain or loss, which causes some special rules to apply, but generally not to the taxpayer's advantage. The distinction between short-term and long-term gain is also important for corporations, as we will see when we consider the loss carryover rules.

5.4 Basis for Gain or Loss

The concept of gain implies that the selling price or proceeds of property is not what is subject to tax. For purchased property, the taxpayer is entitled to a tax-free recovery of cost. For property not purchased, "cost" relates to the "cost" of other property exchanged[10] or the "cost" of the same property to someone else.[11] Thus, instead of talking about "cost," a broader phrase, "tax basis," is used to mean the amount that is the tax equivalent of cost in calculating gain or loss on disposition.[12] Gain is selling price less the tax basis of the property.[13] Loss results if the basis of the property is larger than the selling price. Where property is exchanged, gain or loss is measured by the difference between the fair market value of property received and the tax basis of the property transferred.

5.5 Purchased Property

The tax basis of purchased property starts with its original cost.[14] It is increased by additions or improvements, but not by ordinary maintenance and repairs.[15] Thus, the basis of a pickup truck would include its original price. If a camper body were later added, its cost would also be added. If the truck were repainted and the engine overhauled after four years, that cost would not be an addition to tax basis.[16] If the truck were used in a business and depreciation taken as a tax deduction (see Chapter 9), the tax basis would be reduced by the depreciation.[17] Introductory financial accounting texts frequently refer to the difference between the original cost of an asset and the sum of the depreciation deductions as "book value." In most cases of property that is used in a business, "book value" and "adjusted basis" are the same.

Tax basis can be viewed as a type of fund that is used only as tax deduction benefits are obtained and is finally written off as an offset to selling price in calculating taxable gain (or tax loss).

TAX PLANNING TIP: Create and maintain a home improvement book that records the capital improvement expenditures made over the years. These expenditures will increase the basis of the home and reduce the taxable gain when the property is ultimately sold in a taxable transaction. Keep a large envelope with the book, in which you save paid bills and cancelled checks, substantiating these items.

Property that is held for personal use rather than as an investment requires some special

[8]IRC Sec. 1221. For an interesting Supreme Court analysis of the definition of a "capital asset," see *Arkansas Best Corp. v. Comm.*, 61 AFTR2d 88-655.

[9]IRC Sec. 1211. There is a carryover for losses that are not deductible currently.

[10]For example, if property A is exchanged for property B in a nontaxable exchange (discussed in Chapter 6), the "cost" of property B is the same as the "cost" of property A prior to the exchange.

[11]When a taxpayer determines the "cost" of a property by reference to the cost of that same property to someone else, we sometimes refer to a "substituted" basis. IRC Sec. 1016(b). This will occur when property is acquired by gift. See Sec. 5.6 of this chapter.

[12]The terms "basis" and "adjusted basis" are used in place of "cost" whether the asset was purchased or acquired by other means.

[13]The rules for the determination of tax basis depend upon how the property was acquired.

[14]IRC Sec. 1012.

[15]IRC Sec. 1016(a).

[16]The repairs expenditure might or might not be a deduction for tax purposes. Business expenses are discussed elsewhere.

[17]IRC Secs. 167, 168, and 1016.

consideration. The tax law prohibits deduction of personal living expenses.[18] Yet a purely personal[19] pickup truck, after several years of use, will almost always sell for less than its original cost. The loss on sale of such a personal asset is not deductible. The same is true for other personal assets, such as a residence, boat, camera, etc. Note that this result occurs despite the fact that the asset is a "capital asset" under the definition previously discussed. A gain from such a sale would be taxable, however.

Is this inequitable? The answer depends upon your definition of inequitable. The reason such losses are not deductible is because they are considered to have resulted from a decline in value, which in turn resulted from personal use of the asset. An alternative to the present law would permit both gains and losses on the sale of personal use assets to go unrecognized for tax purposes. Many people would find this even more inequitable.

Note that we are talking about personal use assets. Where an asset is used in a trade or business, the *general rule* is that a gain *or* loss that results from a sale or exchange will be recognized for tax purposes. Nontaxable exchanges are discussed in Chapter 6.

There exists a tax incentive to convert personal use assets into business or investment assets if a loss is to be incurred. Thus, if a vacation home, which was sold for a loss, could be treated as a piece of rental property held for investment, the loss would be deductible. Generally, the tax rules prohibit a deduction for such a loss. Because there are some special rules that deal with such situations, they will be discussed later (see Chapter 9).

On the other hand, it might be possible to obtain a tax advantage by converting business property into nonbusiness property. Consider the following example. A traveling salesman buys a new car for $10,000. It is driven 100% for business, and after two years $5,200 of depreciation deductions have been taken. The adjusted basis of the car is $4,800. If it were sold for $5,300, there would be a $500 taxable gain.[20] Instead, the salesman turns the car over to his wife for her personal use, buying himself another new car. After two more years of use (personal use, for which no depreciation deductions are allowed) the car has declined in value to $3,700. Its basis is still $4,800. A sale of the car for $3,700 will produce no gain and no loss.[21] Thus, conversion of a business asset to personal use can sometimes generate a type of tax saving.

5.6 Gift Property

Property acquired by gift has what is called a "carryover" or "substituted" basis.[22] The person receiving the gift stands in the tax shoes of the person making the gift. For gifts made *after* 1976, if the donor paid a gift tax, the donee can add a *portion* of the gift tax to basis.[23] That portion is computed by multiplying the gift tax paid by a fraction in which the numerator is the excess of the property's value at the date of the gift over the tax basis of the property to the donor, while the denominator is the value of the gift. (For gifts made *before* 1977, the rules were the same except that the donee could increase basis by the *total* amount of gift tax as long as the basis was not increased to more than the fair market value on the date of the gift.) However, the basis cannot be raised to an amount greater than the fair market value of the property at the time of the gift.

If the value of the property at the time of the gift is less than the donor's tax basis, the tax basis *for gain* will be the donor's tax basis, but the tax basis *for loss* will be the value at the date of the gift.

For example, assume that Billy Barnes receives a current gift of 100 shares of General Aircraft Corporation common stock. The donor's gift tax was $18,500, which was based upon the fair market value of the stock at the time of the gift, $50,000. Billy ascertains that the donor purchased the stock for $30,000 several years ago. Therefore, Billy's basis is $30,000 plus a fractional part of the $18,500 gift tax:

$$\$30{,}000 + \left[\$18{,}500 \times \frac{\$50{,}000 - \$30{,}000}{\$50{,}000}\right] = \$37{,}400$$

There is an adjustment in basis by ⅖ of the $18,500 gift tax, or $7,400. The ⅖ comes from the fact that ⅖ of the current fair market value represents the appreciation in value of the property while held by the donor.

[18] IRC Sec. 262.

[19] Personal, as used here, should not be confused with the legal term "personal property" or "personalty," which refers to any property other than land (and things permanently attached to land) regardless of how used and by whom. Personal, as used here, means nonbusiness *use*.

[20] The gain would be subject to ordinary tax rates. It is called "depreciation recapture," which is included in the Chapter 9 discussion.

[21] If the car were sold for a loss, such a loss would not be deductible as explained above.

[22] The basis of property received as a gift is covered by IRC Sec. 1015.

[23] The federal gift tax is discussed in Chapter 15. As a general rule, the tax is based upon the value of the property on the date of the gift. Gift tax is imposed upon the donor, not the donee, of property. There is no tax, however, until after the donor has given away a total of $600,000 in value during his or her lifetime.

TAX PLANNING TIP: Taxable gain can be spread among family members by making gifts prior to a sale. For example, a parent owns stock that has appreciated in value by $20,000. If the parent's marginal tax rate is 28%, the tax on a sale would be (28%) ($20,000), or $5,600. A gift of the stock could be made to a child over age 14 who has a lower marginal tax rate. Since the donor's basis and holding period is attributed to the donee, the child's gain would be the same as if the parent had sold the property. (In fact, the child's recognized gain might be less if the parent incurred a gift tax which resulted in a basis adjustment to the child.) A dependent child with no other 1990 income would pay a tax of $2,932 on $20,000 gain (see Chapter 4). Even if the parent incurred a gift tax, the income tax saving is likely to be greater than the gift tax liability. Care must be taken to establish a purpose for the gift other than just tax savings. Otherwise, the transfer may not be valid. Care must also be taken to show that the parent had not in fact made the sale, or committed to make the sale, prior to the gift transfer to the child.

In the preceding example, if the fair market value on the date of the gift had been $30,000 or less, Billy would not be able to increase basis by any of the gift tax paid.[24] This result follows because the donor's basis, $30,000, results in Billy's basis (for gain) being equal to or more than the fair market value anyway. Assume that the fair market value at the time of the gift was $20,000. If Billy later sells the stock for $18,000, there would be a $2,000 loss recognized by Billy.[25] On the other hand, if the stock value goes up to $27,000, Billy faces a dilemma. If the stock is sold for a gain, the rules recited provide for a basis of $30,000 (the donor's basis). That results in a conclusion that a $3,000 loss occurred. On the other hand, if a loss occurred, the basis should be $20,000 (fair market value on date of gift) and the result is a $7,000 gain. The tax law eliminates this problem with the simple conclusion that Billy has neither a gain nor a loss for tax purposes.[26]

Since different taxpayers are in different tax brackets, imaginative use of gifts within the family group can often cut overall family income tax burdens. Of course, the gifts have to be bona fide. But $50,000 of gain removed from one family member who would pay $16,500[27] in tax, for example, and taxed to a different family member who would pay $11,454 would save the family entity $5,046. The gift tax paid by the donor might be considerably less than the $5,046 of income tax savings. Indeed, as Chapter 15 will reveal, substantial gifts can be made without incurring a federal gift tax liability. Hence, the carryover of basis for gift property is a useful device for shifting the tax burden within the family.

TAX PLANNING TIP: A person making a gift of property that has declined in value may lose a possible deduction by not selling the property instead and gifting the proceeds. If a sale would result in a recognized loss, the taxpayer will get a deduction that would not be available to the donee if the donee were to sell it.

5.6.1. Property Settlement from Divorce Agreement

As discussed in Chapter 2, no gain or loss is recognized from the division of property resulting from a divorce settlement. However, there is a catch. The basis of the property remains the same as it was prior to the divorce. Thus, as in the case of gifts of appreciated property, the carryover basis rule applies. When deciding how the property is to be divided, the potential tax consequences associated with each property should be examined.

For example, assume that John and Mary own $50,000 of ABC stock and $50,000 of XYZ stock. The bases of the stocks are $60,000 and $40,000 respectively. John and Mary currently are involved in a divorce proceeding and it is proposed that John receive all of the ABC stock and Mary receive all of the XYZ stock. Is this equitable? From a fair market value perspective, each will have received $50,000 of assets. However, the ABC stock has a "built-in loss" of $10,000 whereas the XYZ stock has a "built-in gain" of $10,000. Thus, if the stocks are sold in the near future, John will be better off because he will recognize a loss deduction while Mary will recognize a taxable gain.

To save taxes and benefit both parties, one planning strategy would be to transfer the more highly appreciated assets to the taxpayer in the

[24]The amount of the gift tax paid by the donor would have been less because the value of the gift was less. The amount is not relevant for the point being made here.

[25]This results from the rule which provides that the basis *for loss* is the value of the property on the date of gift, or the donor's basis, *whichever is lower*. See IRC Sec. 1015 (d).

[26]Note the rare set of facts that would have to exist for this result to occur. First, the property would have to have declined in value while held by the donor. Second, the property would have to have increased in value after the gift, but not to a value greater than the basis to the donor.

[27]Based upon 1990 marginal rate of 33%.

lower tax rate. Referring to the above example, if Mary were in the lower tax rate, it would be more beneficial to transfer the XYZ stock to her. Because she potentially is bearing a higher tax burden, the divorce agreement could "compensate" Mary for the extra tax burden by transferring somewhat more than one-half of the assets to her.

5.6.2. Holding Period

Another point that needs to be emphasized relates to the holding period of gift property. Sale or exchange of a capital asset results in long-term gain or loss if the asset has been held for *more than* one year or *is treated as if* it has been held for more than one year. Otherwise, short-term capital gain or loss results.

The holding period of property received as a gift depends upon two factors, the holding period of the donor and whether the donor's dollar basis or the fair market value on the date of gift is used to determine the donee's dollar basis.[28] Using the same rules as were discussed, if the donor's dollar basis is used as the donee's basis, the donor's holding period is added to that of the donee. If the fair market value on the date of the gift is used as the donee's dollar basis,[29] the donee is considered to have owned the property only since the date of the gift.[30]

Continuing with the previous example, if Billy received the property when it had a value of $50,000 and a basis to the donor of $30,000, the dollar basis would be the donor's basis of $30,000. Thus, Billy's holding period would include that of the donor. If the donor had already held the property for more than one year, then Billy could sell the property immediately and the result would be long-term. On the other hand, if the donor had held the property for exactly ten months, for example, then Billy would have to hold the property for more than two months so that the *combined* holding period would be more than one year in order to obtain long-term treatment.[31] On the other hand, if Billy's dollar basis were $20,000 because the rules required that the fair market value on the date of gift be used, the asset would be a short-term capital asset to Billy. Billy would have to hold the asset for more than one year from the date of the gift to obtain long-term capital asset treatment. Of course, if there is no recognized gain or loss, the holding period is irrelevant.

[28]Holding-period requirements are contained in IRC Sec. 1223.

[29]As discussed above, the fair market value (FMV) at the date of gift will be used as the donee's basis if the property decreased in value so that the FMV at the date of gift was *less* than the donor's basis.

[30]The holding-period rules are not affected by whether or not an adjustment is made to the donee's basis for any gift tax paid by the donor.

[31]The holding period need only be in excess of one year to have gain or loss classified as long term. The term "tack on" is sometimes used to designate the addition of the donor's holding period to that of the donee in order to determine if the "more than one year" requirement has been satisfied.

5.7 Inherited Property

Recipients of inherited property receive what is called a "step-up" in basis. The basis of property is the value placed on the property for estate tax purposes. As a general rule, this value is the fair market value on the date of death. However, under certain circumstances an alternative valuation date can be used.[32] This will be covered in Chapter 15.

The term "step-up" comes from the fact that property which has increased in value while owned by the decedent will not be subjected to federal income tax on the appreciation. For example, if a person had acquired real estate for $1,000 many years before and died in 1990 when it had a value of $50,000, the $49,000 increase in value is never subject to income tax. The heir who acquires the property will only pay income tax on the amount by which the selling price exceeds the $50,000 stepped-up basis. If the selling price is less than the fair market value that was used for the estate valuation, there is a loss. There is no basis adjustment as the result of any estate tax that might be paid on the real estate.

The term "step-up" in basis is used even though property may have declined in value. Thus, if a decedent paid $25,000 for property and still owned it at death when its value was $10,000, the heir's basis will be $10,000. No loss deduction will be available for the $15,000 decline in value.

The income tax planning advice given to elderly people by such a rule should be quite clear. "Continue to hold property that has appreciated in value. Remember that to sell it will cause taxable gain and to give it away will only mean that the donee takes your low basis. On the other hand, sell property that has declined in value so as to obtain all possible deductions for losses."

There is one exception to the step-up basis rules. It can be explained best by an example. A daughter transfers property with a low basis and a high current value to her ailing father. When father dies she reacquires the property with a basis equal to the fair market value on his death. Thus, she still owns the property, but having made the gift followed by the inheritance, she has

[32]The alternative valuation date for estate tax purposes is six months after death.

a stepped-up basis. That used to work. However, for transfers after August 13, 1981, such a step-up in basis will apply only if the decedent (who was the donee) lives more than one year from the date of receiving the gift.[33] Note that the "price" to be paid to get a step-up in basis in a situation such as this may be some gift tax. (See Chapter 15.)

5.7.1. Holding Period

The holding period rules for inherited property are simple. Inherited capital assets are automatically long-term assets. It is not necessary for the heir, or the decedent, to have held them for over one year, nor for the combined holding period to be more than one year.

5.8 Property Acquired in an Exchange

In Chapter 6 we discuss "tax-free" exchanges. These are not so much tax-free, however, as tax-deferred. The gain that is not recognized at the time of the exchange transaction reduces the tax basis of the property received in the exchange.[34] Thus, the deferred gain ultimately achieves taxation if the second property is sold.

As we will see in Chapter 6, not all exchanges are nontaxable. Where the exchange is a taxable transaction, the basis of the property acquired can be determined in either of two ways, each of which results in the same answer. First, the basis of the acquired property can be viewed as the basis of the property transferred, plus the gain recognized. Secondly, the basis of the acquired property can be viewed as equal to its fair market value. For example, assume that Billy Barnes exchanges Property A for Property B, in a transaction that does not qualify as a nontaxable exchange. Billy's basis for Property A is $30,000, and the fair market value of Property B is $40,000. Billy will recognize a $10,000 gain. The basis of Property B to Billy is $40,000 determined either way:

Basis of A ($30,000) + gain recognized ($10,000) = $40,000

Basis of B = fair market value = $40,000

Suppose that a piece of real estate with a tax basis of $20,000 and a current value of $60,000 is traded for another piece of real estate worth $90,000—and $30,000 cash is also paid. The transaction qualifies as a nontaxable exchange. The tax basis of the newly acquired real estate would be:

"Cost" (fair market value)	$90,000
Less the deferred gain on "old" real estate traded ($60,000 less $20,000)	(40,000)
Tax basis of "new" property[35]	$50,000

Another way of reasoning through to the same result is to take the $20,000 tax basis of the "old" property and add to it the "boot" of $30,000 paid in the transaction—thus getting a total of $50,000 again.

Of course, the "new" piece of property may itself become involved in a tax-free exchange. The carryover basis of the third property would be determined in the same fashion.

Transactions resulting in the receipt of "boot" will be considered in Chapter 6.

5.8.1. Holding Period

The holding period for property received in a nontaxable exchange includes the holding period of the property that was transferred. Thus, a new piece of property acquired in a nontaxable exchange need not be held for more than one year to qualify as a long-term capital asset if the holding period of the former property plus the holding period of the new property combined is more than one year.

TAX PLANNING TIP: Property acquired in a nontaxable exchange has a basis equal to the property given up (plus "boot" paid, if any). It is important to keep adequate records to verify and substantiate the basis of the property transferred in a nontaxable exchange because that basis becomes the basis of the property received.

5.9 Property Used as Taxpayer's Residence

The same general approach applies to the tax basis of a personal residence as applies to a nontaxable exchange. The difference, in most cases, is that the "old" residence is not directly exchanged for a "new" one. Instead, as discussed in Chapter 6, the proceeds of the sale of the old residence are reinvested in a new residence. When this is done within a prescribed time period (generally, two years), gain on the sale of the first residence is not

[33]IRC Sec. 1014(e).
[34]IRC Sec. 1031(d).

[35]The reader should understand that the *realized* (economic) gain on the trade is $40,000 while the *recognized* (taxable) gain is zero.

taxed. However, the cost of the new residence is reduced by the amount of the deferred gain on the sale of the old residence to determine its basis.[36] Chapter 6 will also cover some special elective rules for persons who are at least fifty-five years of age at the time of sale of a residence.

5.10 Property Transferred to a Corporation

Sometimes property is exchanged for stock in a corporation.[37] In order for nonrecognition of gain to occur, the taxpayer must "control" the corporation immediately after the transfer of property in exchange for stock. "Control" here means owning at least 80% of the voting stock and at least 80% of all nonvoting stock. Thus, if a person transferred property to General Motors in exchange for some GM stock, the nontaxable rules would not apply.[38] The nontaxable provision was put into the law to permit incorporation of a proprietorship or partnership without a resulting tax liability. Where the transaction is nontaxable, the tax basis of the stock received will be the same as the tax basis of the property transferred to the corporation.[39] Basis is reduced by any liabilities that the corporation assumes. If some gain is recognized on the exchange, the tax basis of the stock received will be increased by the gain recognized.

For example, assume that Billy Barnes has a small CPA practice organized as a proprietorship. Billy owns land, an office building, office equipment, supplies, etc. These assets can be transferred to a new corporation tax-free. Billy's basis in the corporate stock will be the same as the basis in all of the assets. If Billy's basis in the assets is $60,000 and 100% of the stock of the corporation is received, the basis for the stock will be $60,000.

Since Billy and the corporation have just exchanged places as far as the basis is concerned, what is the corporation's basis for the assets acquired? The corporation's basis will be the same as Billy's basis immediately before the transfer.

If we change the assumption to include the fact that Billy has a mortgage of $10,000 on the land and the office building, and the corporation assumes the mortgage (or took the land and building subject to the mortgage), then Billy's basis will be $50,000.[40]

[36]IRC Sec. 1034(e).

[37]IRC Secs. 351 and 368(c).

[38]Assuming, of course, that after the exchange the person would own less than 80% of the total GM stock outstanding.

[39]IRC Sec. 358.

[40]In effect, Billy gives up $50,000, the basis of property reduced by the $10,000 debt which the corporation, rather than Billy, will pay.

On such a transaction, gain will be recognized if the mortgage on the property exceeds its basis. Assume now that the only assets transferred to the corporation were the land and building. The basis in land and building is $60,000, but Billy has a $65,000 mortgage on the property. Transfer of the property and mortgage to the corporation will result in a $5,000 recognized gain to Billy.[41]

What is Billy's basis in the stock after the last transaction above? The amount of Billy's debt that the corporation will now pay is treated by Billy *as if* cash had been received in the amount of $65,000. The basis of the stock is adjusted from the $60,000 (basis of land and building) as follows:

1. Reduce the basis by the amount of money ($65,000) that is treated as having been received.
2. Increase the basis by the amount of gain taxable on the exchange ($5,000).

Thus, Billy's basis in the corporate stock is zero.

Now the corporation's basis for the assets is $65,000. This result can be obtained in either of two ways. First, the corporation has paid $65,000 for the assets by taking the mortgage, which it must ultimately pay, of course. Alternatively, the corporation's basis can be viewed as Billy's former basis of $60,000 plus the $5,000 gain taxable to Billy.

5.11 Stock Dividends, Stock Splits, and Stock Rights

Corporations sometimes pay a stock dividend, or "split" the stock. In either case, the shareholder receives stock rather than cash. Such ways of increasing the shares owned by a stockholder usually do not result in taxable income to the stockholder.[42] However, what about the tax basis of the new shares received? The reality of what has happened is that the shareholder's ownership interest in the corporation merely has been divided into more pieces. In at least some senses, therefore, the shareholder has actually received nothing more. The *aggregate* tax basis is the same as it was—but it must be spread over more shares of stock.[43]

Thus, if Billy owns 1,000 shares of RTW

[41]IRC Sec. 357(c). Note that if Billy had sold the land and building for $65,000 there would have been a $5,000 gain. This rule prevents Billy from mortgaging the property immediately prior to transfer to the corporation and pocketing the extra $5,000 tax-free.

[42]Nontaxable stock dividends are limited. For example, if an owner of common stock receives a dividend of convertible preferred stock, the result may be taxable income in the amount of the value of the preferred stock received. IRC Sec. 305(b), (c).

[43]Basis of stock received as a "dividend" or in a split is covered by IRC Sec. 307.

Corp., which cost $10,000 and paid a 5% stock dividend, Billy will have 1,050 shares after the dividend. The same $10,000 basis ($10 per share) must now be spread over 1,050 shares ($9.52 per share). If 100 shares are sold, the tax basis for calculating gain or loss on the sale will be $952.

The holding period of stock received as a stock dividend or in a stock split includes the holding period of the stock which resulted in the dividend or split. Thus, if stock has been held more than one year and additional shares are received as a stock dividend, those "new" shares can be sold immediately and still result in long-term capital gain or loss.

Instead of giving Billy additional stock, RTW Corp. may offer its shareholders the right to buy additional shares of stock at a bargain price. The bargain price is obtainable through exercise of "rights" (also called "warrants") which are transferred to all shareholders. Since these rights have a value, they may also be sold, or they may expire unused. If the value of the rights is 15% or more of the value of the stock, the basis of the stock must be allocated between the stock and rights. For purposes of calculation, the value of both is measured on the date the rights are distributed to shareholders. If the value of the rights is less than 15% of the value of the stock, an election is available.[44] The rights can have a basis of zero, with the basis of the stock remaining unchanged. Alternatively, at the election of the stockholder, the basis of the stock can be allocated between the rights and the stock. If the stock basis is allocated—either because it must be or because the shareholder elects to do so—the allocation is made in the ratio of the value of the rights and stock.

For example, assume that Billy receives 1,000 rights in RTW Corp. (one right for each share owned). The current value of a share of RTW Corp. stock is $14. Billy can buy an additional share of stock for $10 plus 4 rights. Thus, the rights have a value of $1 each. (Note that this is a theoretical value and we are ignoring any commissions or other expenses of exercising or selling the rights. In actuality, the stock market will quote a value for rights just as it does for stock.) The current value of Billy's rights is $1,000, which is 7.1% of the value of the stock. Billy can elect to allocate or not to allocate basis. If an election is made to allocate, the $10,000 original basis in the stock will be divided as follows:

Value of stock	$14,000
Value of rights	1,000
Total value	$15,000

[44]The election is provided in IRC Sec. 307(b).

The value of the rights is 6.67% of the value of the two assets combined. (Note that this ratio is used and not the 7.1% that was determined for purposes of the 15% test.)

Basis of rights: 6.67% ($10,000) =	$ 667
Basis of stock: 93.33% ($10,000) =	9,333
Total basis	$10,000

If Billy had been required to allocate basis, the same procedure would be used; that is, the basis would be allocated in the ratio of the current value of the rights to the current value of both securities combined.[45]

Note that the rules described above apply whether the stock and rights are publicly traded or not. The difference is that the value of both the stock and the rights will be determined in the market place if they are publicly traded. If the stock is "closely held" the same rules will apply but there may be more ambiguity involved in determining the value of the securities.

If stock rights are sold rather than exercised, the holding period of the rights is considered to be the same as the holding period of the stock which resulted in the receipt of the rights. Thus, if a person received stock rights and decided to sell them, long-term or short-term gain or loss might result. If the stock had been held more than one year prior to receipt of the rights, the rights would be long-term assets. If the stock had been held one year or less at the time the rights were received, but the rights were sold later, when the holding period of the stock *was* greater than one year, the rights would be considered long-term assets.

A different rule applies if the rights are exercised. When the second block of stock is acquired, the holding period of that block begins at the date of purchase. It makes no difference whether the dollar basis of the original block of stock has been partly allocated to the rights or not. Thus, it might be possible to have two blocks of stock with the first block being a long-term capital asset and the second block being a short-term capital asset. The dollar basis of a second block of stock is its cost, plus the basis, if any, for the exercised rights. Thus, if Billy purchased a second block of stock for $10,000 and had allocated $667 to the rights, the basis of the second block would be $10,667. If no basis had been allocated to the rights, the second block of stock would have a basis of $10,000.

[45]If rights are sold and they have no basis because basis was not required to be allocated and the taxpayer did not elect to allocate, the full selling price will be gain.

TAX PLANNING TIP: Stock rights may be received on stock that is a short-term asset because it has been held for one year or less. If the rights are to be sold, postponement of the sale until the stock *is a long-term capital asset will result in long-term gain treatment for the rights.*

5.12 Capital Gains

Capital gain—short-term, long-term, or a combination of both—must be included in gross income.[46] Hence, adjusted gross income and taxable income will be increased accordingly.

The calculation requires that short term (generally one year or less) be separated from long term (over one year). Then all capital asset transactions for the year are combined as follows:

1. Short-term losses offset short-term gains. An excess of short-term losses over short-term gains will offset long-term gains.
2. Long-term losses, and any excess short-term losses, are deducted from long-term gains. What is left, if anything, is net long-term gains.

In the examples that follow, the following abbreviations will be used:

STCG = short-term capital gain
STCL = short-term capital loss
NSTCG = net short-term capital gain; STCG and STCL have been combined and gains were greater than losses
NSTCL = net short-term capital loss; STCG and STCL have been combined and losses were greater than gains
LTCG = long-term capital gain
LTCL = long-term capital loss
NLTCG = net long-term capital gain; LTCG and LTCL have been combined and gains were greater than losses
NLTCL = net long-term capital loss; LTCG and LTCL have been combined and losses were greater than gains
NCG = net capital gain; NSTCG or (L) and NLTCG or (L) have been combined and gains were greater than losses
NCL = net capital loss; NSTCG or (L) and NLTCG or (L) have been combined and losses were greater than gains

[46]IRC Sec. 61(a)(3). Where capital asset transactions result in a net loss for the year, a *capital loss* deduction may be taken. See the next section. Obviously, it is not possible to have both a net capital gain and a net capital loss in the same year.

Here are five examples that all result in NCG, though each in a different way.

Example 1

STCL	0	LTCL	0
STCG	$10,000	LTCG	0
NSTCG	$10,000	NLTCG	0
NCG		$10,000	

Example 2

STCL	0	LTCL	0
STCG	0	LTCG	$10,000
NSTCG	0	NLTCG	$10,000
NCG		$10,000	

Example 3

STCL	($1,000)	LTCL	($3,000)
STCG	$5,000	LTCG	$9,000
NSTCG	$4,000	NLTCG	$6,000
NCG		$10,000	

Example 4

STCL	($17,000)	LTCL	($ 1,500)
STCG	$ 5,000	LTCG	$23,500
NSTCL	($12,000)	NLTCG	$22,000
NCG		$10,000	

Example 5

STCL	($ 1,700)	LTCL	($3,800)
STCG	$13,700	LTCG	$1,800
NSTCG	$12,000	NLTCL	($2,000)
NCG		$10,000	

In all five examples, the result is the same, i.e., net capital gain that must be included as part of adjusted gross income. Note that there is no limit upon the amount of capital loss which can be used to offset capital gains, e.g., example 4.[47]

5.13 Capital Losses

What if a net capital loss results for the year? Up to $3,000 of such loss can be deducted in any one year, *from gross income.*[48] To the extent that it is not deductible it can be carried over for use in later tax years.[49] Short-term losses and long-term losses

[47]It is much easier to keep in mind that a capital loss deduction refers to a reduction of ordinary income rather than to a reduction of capital gain.
[48]IRC Sec. 1211(b). This is for individual taxpayers. As noted earlier, the capital loss deduction is limited to the amount of other income if other income is less than $3,000. Corporations are not permitted any capital loss deduction.
[49]Capital loss carryover rules are contained in IRC Sec. 1212. Corporations are subject to different rules, discussed in Chapter 12.

get the same treatment. However, in connection with the $3,000 deduction and any possible carryover, their separate identity must be maintained.

The treatment of capital losses is illustrated by Examples 6 through 18. In all cases it is assumed that other ordinary gross income is sufficiently large to permit the deduction and taxable income is still a positive number. The result where taxable income is zero or negative is explained later.

Example 6

STCL	($2,000)	LTCL	0
STCG	0	LTCG	0
NSTCL	($2,000)	NLTCG	0
NCL		($2,000)	

Example 7

STCL	0	LTCL	($2,000)
STCG	0	LTCG	0
NSTCG	0	NLTCL	($2,000)
NCL		($2,000)	

Example 8

STCL	($2,500)	LTCL	0
STCG	500	LTCG	0
NSTCL	($2,000)	NLTCL	0
NCL		($2,000)	

Example 9

STCL	0	LTCL	($7,000)
STCG	0	LTCG	$5,000
NSTCL	0	NLTCL	($2,000)
NCL		($2,000)	

Example 10

STCL	($200)	LTCL	($2,000)
STCG	0	LTCG	200
NSTCL	($200)	NLTCL	($1,800)
NCL		($2,000)	

Example 11

STCL	($6,000)	LTCL	($7,000)
STCG	11,000	LTCG	0
NSTCG	$ 5,000	NLTCL	($7,000)
NCL		($2,000)	

Example 12

STCL	($1,000)	LTCL	($2,000)
STCG	500	LTCG	500
NSTCL	($ 500)	NLTCL	($1,500)
NCL		($2,000)	

In each of these examples, the deduction is $2,000. The rather belabored point is that the deduction for a net capital loss is available (up to $3,000) *regardless* of the nature or the composition of the gains and losses. If the net capital loss exceeds $3,000, however, then the excess can be carried forward to the next year *but* the source of the loss must be traced. This is necessary in order to be able to go through the netting or combining process of long-term gain or loss and short-term gain or loss for the following year. The distinction continues to be irrelevant after 1987 unless special tax treatment for long-term capital gain is re-enacted into law.

Example 13

STCL	($5,000)	LTCL	0
STCG	0	LTCG	0
NSTCL	($5,000)	NLTCG	0
NCL		($5,000)	

In examples 13 and 14 the tracing is easy. The loss is short-term. Thus, the $3,000 deduction leaves $2,000 STCL to be carried to the next year. The exact same result occurs in Example 15. There, however, the tracing of the loss to its source is slightly more complex.

COMPUTER FORMULAS: Example 13 can be calculated using the following formulas:

	A	B	C
1	STCL	−5000	
2	STCG	0	
3	LTCL	0	
4	LTCG	0	
5	NSTCL	+B1+B2	
6	NLTCG	+B3+B4	
7	NCL	+B5+B6	
8	Deduction	@IF (B7 < −3000, −3000, B7)	
9	Carryover	@IF (B8 > −3000, 0, B7−B8)	
10			

B1 is actually $-x$, but in the example $-x = -5000$. Note that in the formula at B9 if the deduction (B8) is less than $3,000, the carryover will be zero. If it is greater than or equal to $3,000, the carryover will be the total (B7) less the amount deducted (B8).

Example 14

STCL	($9,000)	LTCL	0
STCG	4,000	LTCG	0
NSTCL	($5,000)	NLTCG	0
NCL		($5,000)	

Example 15

STCL	($11,000)	LTCL	($2,000)
STCG	4,000	LTCG	4,000
NSTCL	($ 7,000)	NLTCG	$2,000
NCL		($5,000)	

Note in Example 15 that the NCL of $5,000 is attributable to the NSTCL side. This leaves a $2,000 STCL carryover.

If the loss results from the long-term side, the deduction is still limited to $3,000, but the carryover is for a long-term loss. In Example 16 the carryover is $4,000 of long-term loss.

Example 16

STCL	($4,000)	LTCL	($10,000)
STCG	5,000	LTCG	2,000
NSTCG	$1,000	NLTCL	($ 8,000)
NCL		($7,000)	

What happens if both the short-term and the long-term side result in losses? That was no problem in Example 12 because the full amount of the NCL was deductible. But consider the following:

Example 17

STCL	($7,000)	LTCL	($6,500)
STCG	5,000	LTCG	4,000
NSTCL	($2,000)	NLTCL	($2,500)
NCL		($4,500)	

The deduction is $3,000, but what is the carryover? The solution is found in a simple rule: deduct the NSTCL first. Thus, the deduction consists of $2,000 of NSTCL plus $1,000 of NLTCL. That leaves $1,500 of NLTCL to be carried to the next year.

There is one further possibility:

Example 18

STCL	($9,000)	LTCL	($2,500)
STCG	5,000	LTCG	1,000
NSTCL	($4,000)	NLTCL	($1,500)
NCL		($5,500)	

The same rule applies. Deduct the short-term loss first. Thus, there are *two* carryovers, (1) a NSTCL of $1,000 and (2) a NLTCL of $1,500.

We have stated repeatedly that the deduction for capital losses is limited to $3,000. That $3,000 limit is the same regardless of whether the taxpayer is single, head of household, or married filing a joint return. In Chapter 4, we mentioned that there are some special rules that apply to married taxpayers who file separate tax returns. One of those special rules is that the capital loss deduction is limited to $1,500 for each. Thus, a married couple filing separately will only be able to deduct a total of $3,000 if *each* were to have a deduction of $1,500.

Note that corporations are not subject to these rules but are covered by some other special provisions discussed in Chapter 12.

If a person has a very large capital loss, the limitation on the amount of the deduction may mean that the capital loss carryover will be made to several future years. Unlike the fifteen-year limit on net operating loss carryovers (Chapter 7), there is no limit on the number of years to which capital losses can be carried. However, if a person dies while still holding capital loss carryovers, no other taxpayer gets the benefit and the potential deduction is gone forever.

TAX PLANNING TIP: Taxpayers who are terminally ill and taxpayers who are elderly should consider arranging their financial affairs so as to avoid any capital loss carryovers because the potential deduction for such losses cannot be used by their heirs or their estate.

If taxable income is zero or negative, then the full amount of the capital loss deduction is not subtracted from the net capital loss to determine the carryover. For example, assume the following for a married couple for 1990:

Salary	$11,200
NSTCG	2,000
NLTCL	(7,000)
Adjusted gross income	8,200
Itemized deduction + exemptions	(12,400)
Taxable income	($4,200)

Applying the rules as stated above, we would conclude that the capital loss carryover was $2,000 long-term ($5,000 NCL less the $3,000 deduction). That is not the result, however. The carryover is $2,200 long-term. This is obtained by treating, only for purposes of calculating the amount of the carryover, the STCG as the actual amount of $2,000 *plus* the lesser of (a) the $3,000 deduction or (b) "adjusted taxable income" of $2,800. Adjusted taxable income (ATI) is taxable income plus the capital loss deduction plus the deduction for exemptions.[50] Thus, ATI is ($4,200) + $3,000 + $4,000 = $2,800. The carryover is $7,000 NLTCL less the *recalculated* NSTCG of $4,800.

5.14 Planning Capital Gains and Losses

For many taxpayers, the timing of recognition of gain or loss from a sale or exchange of a capital asset is controllable. Thus, a person might choose to wait until a year in which he or she expected to be in a lower tax bracket in order to sell such an asset and pay tax on the gain. As suggested earlier, an elderly person might decide not to sell an asset which has appreciated substantially in value in order to allow an heir to benefit from the "step up" in basis.

On the other hand, some opportunities to enter into a transaction are just too good to pass by even if the transaction will result in recognition of gain. Where some capital asset transaction has already occurred during the year, there may be very advantageous planning opportunities which arise. Assume, for example, that a capital loss of $20,000 has already occurred during the year. As you can tell from review of the previous examples, the tax impact—except for the carryover—is the same if the loss was short-term or long-term. The deduction will be $3,000 (assuming other income is at least $3,000) and the carryover will be $17,000 if there are no other capital asset transactions for the year. However, if a sale of an asset for a gain of $17,000 should occur, the deduction will still be available and the gain will be tax-free. At what price? There will be no capital loss to be taken into consideration for the following year. That *may* increase next year's tax, but consider the unknowns:

1. It may not be possible to forecast next year's financial activities with a great deal of certainty.
2. It may not be possible to forecast next year's marginal tax rate with much certainty.
3. Even if both of the above forecasts are acceptable, next year's tax benefit should be discounted to its current value in the decision-making process. (An expected tax savings of $1,000 next year has a present value of $909 if the discount rate is 10%.)

On the other hand, assume that a capital gain has already occurred. In the absence of any further transactions, that gain will be taxed this year. Sale or exchange of an asset that will result in a recognized loss of equal amount will convert the net gain to zero. The tax savings can be calculated if the marginal tax rate is known or can be estimated satisfactorily.[51]

Even if a capital gain has not already occurred during the year, recognition of a capital loss can result in almost immediate dollar savings. For example, assume that Billy Barnes will have a marginal tax rate of 33% for 1990. A recognized capital loss of $3,000—even late in the year—will reduce taxable income $1 for $1 and produce a tax savings of $990. That amount, presumably, would have to have been paid by April 15 of the following year. Even the "present valuing" of the tax savings could alter a previous decision by Billy to hold the property because of the expectation for a recovery of the value.

TAX PLANNING TIP: Timing a capital asset transaction is very important. If a capital loss has already occurred during the year, either a short-term or long-term gain can be executed to offset the loss. This accomplishes two purposes: (1) it removes the effect of the $3,000 limitation on the loss deduction against ordinary income and (2) it allows the loss to be utilized for the current year rather than postponed for some possible future benefit.

A reader of financial newspapers and magazines will notice that the analyses of public financial market transactions and conditions late in the year usually contain some disclaimer to the effect that market conditions may have been impacted by abnormal transactions engaged in by traders and investors for tax purposes. The implication seems to be that such year-end trading may have been different were it not for the tax result facing many investors.

5.15 Special Capital Gain Situations

When capital assets were defined earlier in the chapter, we mentioned that some assets normally thought of as capital assets are not defined as such for tax purposes, whereas others might be. It is now time to discuss some of these categories more specifically.

Many assets are treated as capital assets even though they are specifically excluded from the capital asset category under the tax law. The reasons for this treatment are:

[50]IRC Sec. 1212 (b)(2).

[51]"Wash sale" limitations are discussed later in this chapter.

1. It was felt by Congress that certain types of income should not bear the full burden of income taxation, or
2. Congress wanted to provide an incentive for certain types of transactions, such as allowance of loss deduction beyond the $3,000 limit.

5.16 Property Used in a Trade or Business

The "negative" definition of a capital asset provides, for example, that land used in a trade or business is not a capital asset (see Section 5.3). However, a special provision in the law provides the LTCG treatment on the sale of certain kinds of property, such as land, held for use in a trade or business, if the sale produces a gain, even though the gain was not a capital gain.[52] On the other hand, should the sale of such property result in a loss, the loss is ordinary—fully deductible.[53] For example, if such an asset were sold for a gain of $10,000, the $10,000 would be treated as LTCG and, thus, would become a part of the combining process as explained in the 18 previous examples. The reason is that, technically, the asset is known as a "Sec. 1231 asset." However, an asset is a "Sec. 1231" asset only if it has been held for more than one year. If the asset has not been held for more than one year, it is not a "Sec. 1231 asset." Thus, it will not be treated as *either* a STCG or a LTCG. Instead, the gain will be fully taxed without combining it with capital asset transactions.

A restatement of the rules is as follows:

> An asset that is *not* a capital asset by reason of being either (1) land used in a trade or business or (2) depreciable property used in a trade or business will be a "Sec. 1231 asset" only if it has been held for more than one year.
>
> A gain from the sale of a "Sec. 1231 asset" will be treated as long-term capital gain (subject to an exception called "recapture," discussed in the next section).
>
> A loss from the sale of a "Sec. 1231 asset" will be deducted in full without combining it with capital asset transactions incurred during the year.

As explained at the beginning of this chapter, net long-term capital gain recognized prior to 1987 received favorable tax treatment in the form of a deduction equal to 60% of the net gain. Net Sec. 1231 gain was similarly treated. Net Sec. 1231 losses were fully deductible. However, a net Sec. 1231 gain and a net Sec. 1231 loss could not occur in the same year because all Sec. 1231 asset transactions first had to be combined for the year. These rules motivated a taxpayer to arrange to have these "Sec. 1231" transactions such that gains would occur in different years from losses. Consequently, since 1985, there has been a "lookback" provision.[54] Under this rule, a Sec. 1231 gain will result in ordinary gain (rather than be treated as capital gain) to the extent of Sec. 1231 losses in any of the five previous years.

For example, assume that Billy Barnes has a $20,000 gain from a 1990 sale of land which was a Sec. 1231 asset. If Billy had no Sec. 1231 losses during any of the five previous years, the $20,000 gain will receive capital gains treatment. However, assume that in 1986 Billy had deducted a Sec. 1231 loss of $8,000. The result would be that the 1990 $20,000 gain would be divided into an $8,000 ordinary gain and a $12,000 gain which is treated as a long-term capital gain.

Clearly, the distinction between "Sec. 1231 assets" and capital assets, and the distinction between the treatment of such gain with or without the "lookback" provision is not as important today as it was when there was a significant difference in the tax rates which applied to LTCG and gain *treated as* LTCG. However, the distinction is still important because of the limitation upon the deduction for capital losses. If it is possible to offset a loss with a gain, then the $3,000 limitation does not apply. On the other hand, a net loss which is subject to a $3,000 deduction limitation, even when there is a carryover for the excess loss, has less tax benefit than a loss that is fully deductible for the current year. Planning opportunities still exist.

5.16.1. Depreciable Property

Property that is used in a trade or business and is subject to depreciation is not a capital asset, by definition. But when the predecessor of Sec. 1231 was put into law, it became possible to obtain capital gain treatment on the sale of such property. Prior to 1962, gains from the sale of depreciable *personal property* were so treated, just as land, as explained. However, this became a tax loophole.

Depreciation is deductible against ordinary income.[55] Since the methods of accelerated depreciation in use since 1954, and especially those in effect from 1980 to 1986 (see Chapter 9), make it likely that many assets will be overdepreciated

[52] IRC Sec. 1231.

[53] In other words, the $3,000 loss limitation does not apply.

[54] IRC Sec. 1231(c).

[55] IRC Secs. 167 and 168. Depreciation is discussed in Chapter 9. Business expenses in general are discussed in Chapter 7.

(relative to their value) in the early years of life, treating gains on the sale of such assets as capital gains seemed inconsistent. Thus, the law was amended so that such a gain on personal property, to the extent of the depreciation deductions allowed since January 1, 1962, results in ordinary income. The ordinary income resulting from such sales is referred to as "Sec. 1245 income" or sometimes as "depreciation recapture." It is still possible to obtain some capital gain treatment on personal property (machinery, equipment, vehicles, etc.), but only if the gain is greater than the sum of the depreciation deductions since 1961 and the "lookback" rule permits.

TAX PLANNING TIP: Where a taxpayer has two Sec. 1231 assets to sell, one resulting in a gain and one in a loss, the sequence of sale, and getting the transactions into two different years, can make a big difference. Assume that the two transactions will result in a $100,000 gain and a $100,000 loss, respectively. Further, assume that there were no Sec. 1231 transactions in the five prior years. If they are sold in the same year, the loss and gain net out and there is no deduction or capital gain treatment. If the loss asset is sold this year and the gain asset is sold next year, the capital gain treatment on the gain asset is lost because of the "lookback" rule. However, if the gain asset is sold this year and the loss asset is sold next year, there will be capital gains treatment for the gain asset and an ordinary loss deduction for the loss asset.

For example, assume that a depreciable machine was purchased several years ago for $30,000. The depreciation deductions have been $18,000. Thus, the adjusted basis of the asset is $12,000. If the asset were sold for $20,000, the $8,000 gain would all be taxed as ordinary income. If the asset were sold for $33,000, the gain would be $21,000. Of that amount, $18,000 would be taxed as ordinary income and $3,000 would be *treated as if* it were capital gain—technically, Sec. 1231 gain. (Again, we assume here that the gain would not be ordinary gain because of "lookback.") Note that in order to get any capital gain treatment, the asset will have to be sold for more than its original cost.

Where the property is depreciable real property, such as a building, some part of the gain may also be treated as ordinary income (called Sec. 1250 income) rather than as Sec. 1231 (long-term capital) gain. This is covered more fully in Chapter 9.

TAX PLANNING TIP: A taxpayer contemplating the sale of a Sec. 1231 asset should review the result of the prior five years for any Sec. 1231 losses. If such a loss had been deducted in the fifth prior year, for example, a gain during the current year would result in ordinary income to the extent of the ordinary deduction five years earlier. By postponing the gain transaction to the next year, where the then-five-year prior period has no Sec. 1231 losses, the Sec. 1231 gain will receive long-term capital gains treatment.

5.17 Timber

If fruit trees are producing, sale of the fruit produces ordinary income. If land is used to raise timber, the timber that is cut and sold is analogous to the fruit (i.e., it is a crop). But timber as a crop differs from fruit in one crucial respect. Fruit will be produced each year. However, it takes a long time before a sapling matures to the point where it is marketable as timber. Congress felt that it was unfair to tax the gain from timber as ordinary income all in one year.

Further, it seemed unfair to allow capital gains on the sale of standing timber while treating the proceeds of the sale of cut timber as ordinary income. A timber owner could merely sell a section of land containing standing timber and then buy back the land after the timber had been cut, leaving him in roughly the same economic position as if he had contracted to have the timber cut (with some differential in the expenses).

As a result, income from the cutting of timber is entitled to long-term capital gain treatment.[56] As with property used in a trade or business, losses from the cutting of timber are ordinary losses.

5.18 Coal and Iron Ore Royalties

Royalties received on coal and iron ore leases are treated as capital gains.[57] Two main arguments in favor of this particular tax peculiarity are discernible. One argument is that, because timber owners are allowed to get capital gains, owners of coal and iron deposits should receive equal treatment. To the extent that there is logic in this type of "me-too" argument, it may explain how each

[56]IRC Sec. 1231(b)(2). Again, the distinction today is important only insofar as it changes any loss deduction and/or carryover.
[57]IRC Sec. 1231(b)(2).

exception put into the tax law helps lay the groundwork for the next exception.

The strongest argument for capital gain treatment for coal and iron ore royalties appears to be the economic one. Owners of coal and iron lands are (or were) in a relatively weak economic condition. This is a way of helping them with a modest amount of tax relief which may provide an incentive for extracting coal and iron.[58]

5.19 Livestock

Livestock has some of the aspects of property used in a trade or business and some of the aspects of property held for sale to customers (i.e., inventory). After many years of controversy and uncertainty, the tax rules are now relatively clear cut. Livestock (excluding poultry) held for draft, breeding, dairy, or sporting purposes may receive capital gain treatment.[59] However, a *twenty-four-month* holding period is required for horses and cattle. Other livestock must be held for twelve months or more to qualify. In the case of depreciable livestock, purchased rather than raised, gains equal to prior depreciation deductions are taxed as ordinary income. The depreciation recapture rules of Sec. 1245 apply to livestock the same as they do to other personal property.

5.20 Patents

The proceeds from the sale of a patent, whether paid in a lump sum or through royalties, constitute capital gains to the inventor or to the financial backer of an inventor.[60] It matters not whether the inventor is a professional or an amateur.

Note the difference in the case of copyrights in literary, musical, or artistic works.[61] When General (later President) Eisenhower sold the rights to his book, *Crusade in Europe,* he was able to obtain capital gain treatment for the proceeds on the ground that he was an amateur writer. Since 1950, however, this has been impossible. Congress changed the law. Neither amateurs nor professionals can get capital gain treatment on disposal of the works they have created. This is true for artists, sculptors, and composers as well as authors. Note item #5 in the definition at Section 5.3. Contrast these rules with the ease of obtaining capital gain treatment on patents! Note, however, that a copyright or composition held by an investor can be a capital asset. (See note #60 below.)

5.21 Small Business Corporations and SBICs

As a general rule, an investment in corporate stock is a capital asset. The tax law allows a taxpayer to treat the loss on the sale of stock in a small business corporation as an ordinary loss rather than a capital loss.[62] There is a limit of $50,000 per year ($100,000 on a joint return). The stockholder must have acquired the stock directly from the corporation. During the five years immediately preceding the loss year, more than half the corporation's gross receipts must have come from operating income, as distinguished from royalties, rents, dividends, interest, annuities, and sales of securities. Only the first $1 million of common stock issued by a corporation may qualify for this special Sec. 1244 treatment.

TAX PLANNING TIP: Newly organized corporations should always make provision for the use of Sec. 1244. If the business fails, this will assure the stockholders of some ordinary loss deduction for their investment in the stock rather than a capital loss which may be limited to a $3,000 deduction each year.

There is another type of corporation, called a small business investment corporation (SBIC), that is of tax interest at this point.[63] Loss on the stock of an SBIC is an ordinary loss, without limit. The corporations that qualify are those operating under the Small Business Investment Act of 1958; a list of them can be obtained from the Small Business Administration, Washington, D.C. It matters not where or how the taxpayer acquired the SBIC stock. These provisions are more favorable than those governing Sec. 1244 stock on two points: (1) there is no limit on the amount of loss deductible in any given year, and (2) there is no restriction of benefits to stock acquired directly from the corporation. Because some of these stocks are publicly traded, they constitute interesting trading vehicles for almost any taxpayer. It is more favorable than the Sec. 1231 rule because there is no 5-year "lookback" rule.

The following example illustrates the tax benefit of SBIC stock. Assume that a taxpayer is in

[58]Incentives for the extractive industries generally take a different form. These are discussed in Chapter 9.

[59]IRC Sec. 1231(b)(3).

[60]This results from the "negative" definition of capital assets found in IRC Sec. 1221. Since patents are not among the list of assets that are not capital assets, they are capital assets. See also Sec. 1235.

[61]IRC Sec. 1221(3).

[62]IRC Sec. 1244.

[63]IRC Sec. 1242.

a marginal tax bracket of 33%. There is $10,000 of gain on some SBIC stock held for more than one year, an $11,000 loss on other SBIC stock, and a capital loss of $10,000. Not a good year, you would say. Before the tax effect, there is an $11,000 net loss. But the $10,000 gain from SBIC stock offsets the other capital loss. That leaves the $11,000 loss from SBIC stock fully deductible rather than limited to $3,000 with a carryover of $8,000. The fully deductible loss provides a tax reduction of $3,630.

Originally, the $11,000 loss year may have looked as if it would result in a $3,000 deduction and an $8,000 carryover.[64] Not so. Because of the way in which the gains and losses are combined, the result is a deduction of $11,000 with no carryover. That results in a tax savings of $3,630. What appeared to be a current tax benefit of only $990 (33% × $3,000) plus a carryover is really a current tax benefit of $3,630.

Note the difference between this and the sale of Sec. 1231 assets discussed earlier. Here the gain and loss are treated *separately* even though they occurred in the same year. Had the two SBIC transactions been Sec. 1231 transactions, it would have been necessary to combine them first. The result would have been a net Sec. 1231 loss of $1,000, which would have been deductible along with the $3,000 maximum from the capital loss. The resulting $4,000 deduction would have saved $1,320 (33% × $4,000) in taxes and there would have been a loss carryover of $7,000. In the case of the sale of Sec. 1231 assets, the transactions would have to be in different years in order to obtain separate treatment. Even then the five-year lookback rule could result in loss of the desired tax benefit.

TAX PLANNING TIP: Where two separate business ventures are being pursued, it may be advantageous to incorporate them separately rather than to have one corporation conduct both operations. If one results in a gain and the other a loss, the stock of the loss corporation can be sold with an ordinary loss deduction available to the shareholders under Sec. 1244. Otherwise, the loss and gain will get netted at the corporate level.

5.22 U.S. Bonds

Certain types of U.S. bonds (Series E, F, and J) are sold on a discount basis: for example, a $100 Series E bond will cost $75. Cash-basis taxpayers owning such bonds can elect to report each year's increase in value as income of that year.[65] The alternative is to wait until the maturity of the bond and report the entire increase in value as interest income at that time. This alternative was discussed in the previous chapter as a planning device to overcome the impact of the "kiddie tax" which imposes a tax at the parents' marginal tax rate on a dependent child under age 14 who has investment (unearned) income. Series E and J bonds, and some Series F bonds, can be exchanged for Series H bonds with no tax incurred on the exchange.[66] Although these provisions allow deferral of the time of taxation, they do not allow a taxpayer to escape taxation altogether, even by dying. The person who ultimately receives the value increment will be considered to have interest income, even if the bonds were acquired via the estate of a deceased taxpayer. Note the contrast with the general rule on "step up" in basis, discussed earlier.

The U.S. bonds traded in the over-the-counter market are of more interest as investment vehicles with tax overtones. Since the Federal Reserve System terminated its support of the U.S. bond market in 1951, these bonds have sold at varying percentages of their redemption value. As U.S. obligations, the only difference between them and money is that they are interest bearing and will mature at some future time. Money (Federal Reserve notes) bears no interest and is a demand obligation. (Take a look at your paper money and you will see that it is actually a demand note payable by a Federal Reserve bank!)

The market price of the already outstanding U.S. bond tends to equalize the difference between its interest rate and the current market interest rate on U.S. obligations. If newly issued U.S. obligations are being sold to yield 12%, an already outstanding U.S. obligation paying 8% and maturing in 1995 may be selling at only about 85% of its maturity value. The taxpayer buying the already outstanding $100,000 bond will receive taxable interest each year. On the $85,000 investment, $8,000 of fully taxable interest will be received each year. On maturity of the bond in 1995, the face amount of $100,000 will be received. The $15,000 increment will be capital gain. Purchase of a new $100,000 bond at par would have resulted in $12,000 interest each year and no capital gain upon maturity.

Although generally beyond the scope of this introductory discussion, we would be remiss if we

[64]For purposes of illustration and simplification, it is assumed that income or loss will not move the taxpayer to a different tax bracket.

[65]IRC Sec. 454(a). A taxpayer should consider carefully before making this election since it is irrevocable and will remain in effect for the remainder of the taxpayer's life.

[66]IRC Sec. 1037.

did not point out the distinction between the tax treatment of "original issue discount" on U.S. government bonds discussed above, and "original issue discount" on other bonds. In the case of the latter that were issued after July 1, 1982, it is necessary to include in gross income each year the pro rata portion of the discount. That amount then increases the owner's basis in the obligation. For example, assume that Billy Barnes purchased a corporate bond with a face amount of $50,000 and a term of ten years at an original issue discount of $5,000. Each year, a portion of the discount will be included in Billy's gross income and the basis will be adjusted upward from its original $45,000. The amortization of the discount is based upon its current value rather than upon a straight-line allocation of the discount over the term of the debt.[67]

5.23 Sales to Related Taxpayers

There is a general principle in tax law that a transaction that is a sham (i.e., has no economic substance) will be disregarded for tax purposes. Because of the possibility that persons who are related to each other may decide to manipulate their respective tax liabilities by engaging in a transaction without substance, there are some specific statutory rules that apply to related taxpayers.[68] It certainly may be the case that members of a family will engage in transactions that have economic substance and which are derived from arm's-length bargaining. Nevertheless, the rules designed to prevent persons from taking unfair advantage of the law apply regardless of motivation.[69]

5.23.1. Sales Resulting in Gain

Ordinary income rather than capital gain will result if property that will be depreciable in the hands of the buyer (because held for investment or for the production of income) is sold:

1. to a more-than-50% controlled corporation, or
2. by a corporation or partnership to its more-than-50% owner, or
3. between two corporations, two partnerships, or a corporation and partnership that are more than 50% owned by the same person or
4. to a trust in which the taxpayer or spouse have a beneficial interest.[70]

To illustrate the foregoing situation, assume that Billy Barnes purchased a copyright as an investment. The copyright is a capital asset to Billy since it was purchased and is not used in Billy's trade or business. Billy wants to sell the asset to an 85%-owned corporation that will use the copyright in its business. Therefore, the copyright will be subject to depreciation (amortization) by the corporation.[71] Billy will not be able to obtain capital gain treatment from the sale.[72]

5.23.2. Sales Resulting in Losses

For the same reasons, losses will not be deductible if property is sold to a given set of related persons.[73] These include sales to members of a family,[74] sales between individuals and more-than-50% owned corporations, and in some cases sales between a partner and a partnership and sales between a fiduciary and the beneficiary of the trust or estate.

Where a loss has been disallowed in a sale between related parties, a later sale of the same property for a gain will result in a modification of the recognized gain.[75] The unrecognized loss from the first sale can be used to reduce the recognized gain on the second sale. This can be illustrated as follows.

Assume that Billy Barnes sold a tract of investment land to a corporation in which Billy owns 55% of the stock. The sales price is $50,000 and Billy's basis was $60,000. Billy is not permitted to recognize the $10,000 loss. The corporation's basis in the property is $50,000. Should the corporation later sell the property for $58,000, for example, there will be no gain recognized to the corporation despite the fact of $8,000 economic gain. The previously disallowed loss to Billy can be

[67]IRC. Secs. 1271-1275.
[68]IRC Sec. 267.
[69]IRC Sec. 267 also applies to transactions involving certain expenses (including interest) between a person and a corporation which is controlled, directly or indirectly, by that person.
[70]IRC Sec. 1239. For purposes of the 50% ownership requirement, a person is treated as being the owner of stock that is owned by other persons to whom he or she is related as well as stock that is owned directly. The term "constructive ownership" is used to designate stock that a person is deemed to own for this purpose because it is owned by a related party.
[71]Patent applications are subject to the same treatment. See IRC Sec. 1239(e).
[72]Note that the same result could occur even if Billy does not own directly *any* of the stock. Billy's sister might own all the stock, for example. Billy constructively owns the stock that is owned directly by related persons. Where some stock is owned directly and other stock is owned constructively, the stock interests are added for purposes of applying the 50% test.
[73]IRC Sec. 267.
[74]Care must be taken as to the definition of "family." See Sec. 267 (c). Note the dissimilarity between this and the definition of family for purposes of determining who can be a dependent. Here, for example, an aunt or uncle is not considered part of a person's family.
[75]IRC Sec. 267(d).

used by the corporation to offset its gain. If the corporation later sold the property for $60,000, it would still have no gain recognized. However, if the corporation sold the property for $62,000, then $2,000 of the $12,000 gain would be taxable.

It is important to note in the example given that the corporation's basis is not adjusted upward for the seller's disallowed loss. This has an impact in at least two areas. Should the property be subject to depreciation by the corporation, the basis for depreciation would be $50,000, not $60,000. Also, if the corporation should later sell the property for $45,000, for example, the loss for tax purposes would be $5,000, not $15,000.

Finally, it must be clear that not all loss sales will result in a deduction for tax purposes even if the sale is to an unrelated party. Property that is used for personal purposes (i.e., a personal automobile or a personal residence) will not result in a tax deduction if sold for a loss. The reason is that the decline in value of the property (as reflected by the realized loss) is presumed to have resulted from personal consumption of the asset, and there is no deduction for any personal consumption item. This is true despite the fact that such an asset may satisfy the definition of a capital asset and produce taxable gain if sold for a gain.

5.24 Short Sales

Investors who buy securities presumably anticipate that the value will rise rather than fall. An investor who holds a security is said to be "long" in that security or to have taken a "long position." In the stock market, such persons are referred to as "bulls." It should be obvious that there are investors who may from time to time think that certain securities will decline in value. These people may sell a security they do not own and thus take a "short position" in the security. Such persons are called "bears." A short seller must borrow the stock in order to deliver certificates to the buyer. The borrowing, incidentally, is normally done by a broker on behalf of the investor rather than directly by the investor.

Thus, if an investor who does not own any College Education common stock decides that at a price of $90 a share the stock is too high, she might instruct her broker to sell 100 shares of the stock at $90. She would be "short" 100 shares. Her broker would borrow 100 shares for delivery to the buyer. Assume that the price of the stock does drop from 90 to 80 to 70. At that point, the investor instructs her broker to close her short position.[76] The broker does this by buying 100 shares at 70 in order to return the stock to the party from whom it was borrowed. The investor thereby realizes a profit of $2,000 (100 shares at $20), not counting the commissions and costs of borrowing.

In a "long" transaction, the investor buys property (stock, in our example) and later sells it. If the stock is held for over one year, a long-term capital gain or loss results. In a "short" sale, however, the investor sells the stock and later buys it. The holding period is zero days. The gain or loss will, therefore, be short term.[77] Some special rules apply where a taxpayer sells short some stock where substantially identical stock is already owned.[78] Also, a taxpayer might sell short, later purchase substantially identical stock, but not use the new purchase to "cover" the previous short sale. Another aspect of short sales is the treatment of payments which the borrower of stock in the short-sale transaction makes to the seller in lieu of dividends.[79] These detailed rules are not covered in this book.

5.25 Wash Sales

Frequently, a taxpayer has *unrealized losses* in a security, meaning that the market price has fallen but the securities have not been sold. For example, assume that Billy purchased College Education common at $90 and it is now selling at $70. Billy still has faith in College Education as a long-run investment but would like to get some tax benefit from this $20 per share market decline. If the stock could be sold, and then bought back at the same price, the loss could be recognized, and Billy would still own the stock. The tax rules place a limit upon this kind of transaction, called a "wash sale."[80]

The purpose of the wash sale provisions of the tax law is to prevent a taxpayer from deducting a loss while maintaining the investment from an economic point of view. If substantially identical stock is purchased within thirty days before or after the loss sale, the loss will be disallowed. This rule applies only to stock and other securities. "Substantially identical" means, normally, the same security, or one convertible into it. Thus, a sale of General Motors common stock at a loss would not be disallowed even though American Motors common stock (both are automobile manufacturers) was purchased within the sixty-day period.

[76]This is referred to as "covering" the short sale.

[77]Gain and loss from short sales are covered by IRC Sec. 1233.

[78]The term used for this type of transaction is "a short sale against the box."

[79]See IRC Sec. 263(h).

[80]IRC Sec. 1091. The arrangement as described will work if Billy is a "dealer" in securities.

TAX PLANNING TIP: Earlier we mentioned that it might be advantageous to recognize a loss in a year in which a gain has already been incurred. The purpose of such a plan would be to offset the loss against the gain so that the gain would not be taxed. Since capital gains and losses from all sources *are combined for the year, a gain from an asset other than a security can be offset with a loss from a security. Where securities are sold for a loss but the taxpayer wants to continue to hold the same securities, the waiting period for reacquisition is just more-than-30-days. Even a significant price shift within that waiting period might be more than counterbalanced by the tax savings from "sheltering" the previous gain.*

If a taxpayer does engage in a wash sale, the tax benefit of the loss is not gone altogether. The disallowed loss on the wash sale will increase the basis of the stock that was purchased. Thus, the loss recognition is deferred. A subsequent gain will be lower, or a subsequent loss larger, because basis is higher.

For example, assume that Billy sells the 100 shares of College Education at $70, realizing a loss of $20 per share, or $2,000. A few days later Billy buys 100 shares of the same stock.[81] The $2,000 loss on the sale will not be recognized for federal income tax purposes, but the basis of the second block of stock is increased by the $2,000 disallowed loss. Thus, Billy's basis in the second block is $9,000. The same result would have occurred if Billy had purchased the second block of 100 shares within 30 days *before* the sale of the first block.[82]

TAX PLANNING TIP: Wash sale rules do not apply to gain. If a taxpayer sells stock that results in a gain, immediate reacquisition of the same stock has no impact on the gain which must still be recognized. This can be advantageous where gain is desired for use as an offset against losses which would otherwise have a $3,000 deduction limitation.

The following points are of particular note relative to the wash sale provisions: First, although the rules are called "wash sale" rules, it is the *purchase* of replacement securities that causes the rules to become operational. Secondly, the rules apply *only* to sales that resulted in a loss. There is no comparable provision that applies if a sale resulted in a gain. Thirdly, there can be a partial wash sale. For example, assume that Billy Barnes owned 100 shares of RTW Corp. common stock and sold those for a loss of $20 per share for a total loss of $2,000. Further, assume that sometime during the period from 30 days before the sale to 30 days after the sale Billy purchased 30 shares of RTW Corp. common stock. (The price paid for the 30 shares is irrelevant for purposes of the application of the wash sale rules.) The purchase of 30 shares of RTW makes the loss on 30 shares of RTW a wash sale loss. Thus, the loss on 70 shares ($1,400) can be recognized, but the loss on 30 shares ($600) is unrecognized. On the other hand, the basis of the 30 shares of RTW is increased by the $600 unrecognized loss.

Even the wash sale rules might be used advantageously. Assume that Billy Barnes sells some shares of stock late in the year for a loss. Billy later decides that the loss transaction was a tax mistake. If substantially identical shares are purchased within thirty days of the previous sale, even if in the next year, the effect is to negate the previous loss and increase the basis of the second block of stock.

5.26 Puts and Calls

"Puts" and "calls" are merely options to buy or to sell. A wealthy investor, who owns a substantial number of shares of College Education common stock, for example, may not care too much whether 100 shares are sold or retained at the current price of $90. The investor may be willing, on the other hand, to sell someone the *right* to buy 100 shares of College Education at any time during the next several months at a price of $90. The buyer might be willing to pay $15 per share for this option. If the price of College Education goes above $105, the option holder can exercise the option, then sell the stock, and have a profit. The seller of the option will have received $105 per share, consisting of $90 for the stock plus $15 for the option. If the price of College Education falls below $90, the option holder most probably will not exercise the option. Thus, the seller of the option will still have the stock and the $15. The buyer of the option will have lost $15 per share.[83]

[81]We assume no change in price during those few days.
[82]The rule is not "all or nothing." A partial wash sale can be made. Assume that Billy sold the 100 shares for a loss of $2,000 but a few days later purchased 30 shares. The result is that the loss on 30 shares is disallowed, but the loss on the remaining 70 shares can be recognized. Basis of the "new" block of stock is increased by the disallowed loss on the 30 shares.

[83]It should be readily apparent that this arrangement will permit a person to speculate on future price increases by making a smaller initial investment than would be required to purchase the stock outright.

The amount received for the option is not income to the owner of the College Education stock until the option is exercised or is allowed to lapse. If the option is exercised, the option fee is simply part of the selling price, which in the example is actually $105 per share. If the option lapses, the fee constitutes ordinary income.[84]

Why would anyone want to buy an option? Some people use options for leverage. A given amount of money can control more shares of stock by being invested in an option than in the stock itself. At a price of $90, a person wishing to speculate on the price of College Education would have to invest $9,000 in order to control 100 shares of College Education outright. There would be a potential risk of losing the $9,000 as well. With our example, an option can be purchased for $1,500. This controls 100 shares of College Education. The most that can be lost will be $1,500. There is no limit to the possible gain. If College Education soars to $180 per share, the option buyer will have a profit of $7,500 on a $1,500 investment! Purchase of the stock would have resulted in a profit of $9,000, but would have required an investment of $9,000. Incidentally, it should be pointed out that, although specific individuals have made substantial sums speculating in options, apparently the only ones who consistently make a good profit are the people who sell them and the brokers who act as middlemen.

Another use of option contracts is to provide insurance. A person sells short 100 shares of College Education. There will be a gain if College Education moves down, but a loss, perhaps a substantial loss, if it moves up. Such a person might buy an option to purchase 100 shares of College Education at $90 (or some other price) simply to protect against a potential loss when the short sale is covered. By so doing, the potential loss is limited to the amount paid for the option.

The options we have been talking about are "call" options. The holder of the option contract has the right to call on the writer of the contract to sell certain securities at a previously agreed price. The holder normally will exercise the option only if the stock price has increased. A "put" option works similarly, but the holder of a put option has the right to force the writer of the contract to buy certain securities at a set price. Thus, where the price of stock has decreased, the holder of a "put" option can require that the writer buy the stock at the previously agreed price. Naturally, the holder normally would exercise this opportunity only if the value of the property has decreased so that the sales price to the writer of the option is greater than could be obtained in the market.[85]

5.27 Tax Straddles

The Economic Recovery Tax Act of 1981 and the Tax Reform Act of 1984 sought to prohibit a variety of transactions in commodities and government securities which had been perceived as abusive tax avoidance techniques.[86] Such techniques grew out of a taxpayer's ability to take market "positions" with offsetting economic effects. Thus, while an unrealized profit might develop on one contract, the offsetting contract would show an equivalent loss. By manipulating the time of sale for each contract, a profit or loss could be timed to the taxpayer's best advantage. The 1981 Act, therefore, imposed two restrictions. (1) It restricted the recognition of losses in excess of unrealized gains as to offsetting interests in actively traded personal property (other than actively traded stock and short-term options). Thus, losses in excess of gains can no longer be created to offset other income for the year.[87] (2) It closed all "regulated futures contracts" at year end, recognizing all gains or losses based on the year-end market price (i.e., "marked to market") even though the contract was not sold. Thus, the holder of a regulated futures contract, who is on a calendar taxable year, will be treated as if he or she sold the contract on December 31 with the resulting gain or loss recognized. Such a person would then be treated as if the same contract had been repurchased (at the same price) on the following day which is the first day of the new taxable year. This helps to discourage taxpayers from engaging in arbitrage transactions in the futures market for the purpose of shifting a tax burden to a different year.

[84]Rules for the tax treatment of options to buy and sell stock are contained in Treas. Reg. 1.1234-1(a).

[85]IRC Sec. 1233(c) covers options.

[86]IRC Sec. 1092.

[87]IRC Sec. 1092(a).

TRUE-FALSE QUESTIONS

State whether each of the following statements is true or false. For each *false* answer, reword the statement to make it *true*.

T F 1. Any asset, including land, that is held for the purpose of sale to customers in the ordinary course of business is not a capital asset.

T F 2. If depreciable property or real estate is used in a trade or business, it will be a capital asset.

T F 3. The difference between the tax treatment of a loss from a capital asset and a loss from a non-capital asset is that the latter is deductible from gross income without the $3,000 limitation.

T F 4. If an individual sells trade accounts receivable for a loss, the capital loss deduction rules will limit the deduction to $3,000.

T F 5. If an individual sells his personal pleasure motor boat for a loss, the capital loss deduction rules will limit the deduction to $3,000 in any one year.

T F 6. If a donor's basis for property which was gifted was $25,000, the fair market value of the property on the date of the gift was $27,000, and the amount of the gift tax paid by the donor was $12,000, then the donee's basis for the property will be $27,000.

T F 7. For a year during which some short-term capital assets are sold and some long-term capital assets are sold, there must be a netting or combining of all such sales to determine if the result was a gain or loss.

T F 8. The adjusted basis of business property that was purchased a few years ago is its original cost.

T F 9. The adjusted basis of property that was acquired by gift is always the same as the adjusted basis to the grantor of the gift.

T F 10. The adjusted basis of property that was inherited is the same as the decedent's basis.

T F 11. In a tax-free exchange, where no boot is received or given, the basis of the property acquired is the same as the basis of the property given up.

T F 12. In order to have a tax-free exchange of property transferred to a corporation in exchange for its stock, the transferor must own at least 80% of the corporation after the exchange.

T F 13. A person who receives a stock dividend may elect as to whether the basis of the original stock is allocated between the original stock and the "new" stock received as a dividend.

T F 14. When a person receives stock rights, or warrants, the basis of the original shares *must* be allocated between the stock and the rights if the value of the right exceeds 15% of the value of the stock.

T F 15. If a person has both a short-term capital gain and a long-term capital gain during 1990, the total will be taxed at the same marginal tax rate(s) as if he or she had non-capital gain equal to the same amount.

T F 16. If a person has other income of $30,000 for the year and only one capital asset transaction, and that transaction resulted in a long-term capital loss of $5,000, there would be a $2,500 deduction from gross income.

T F 17. If a person has other income of $30,000 for the year and has one capital asset transaction resulting in a $10,000 short-term capital loss, there will be a capital loss deduction of $3,000 and a $7,000 short-term capital loss carryover to the following year.

T F 18. If depreciable personal property which is used in a trade or business (Sec. 1245 property) is sold for a gain, only the gain which is equal to or less than the total previous depreciation deductions on that property will be taxed.

T F 19. A "wash sale" is a sale of securities which resulted in a loss and where the taxpayer acquired substantially identical securities within thirty days before or after the sale.

T F 20. The holding period for a capital asset which is inherited is always considered to be more than one year.

PROBLEMS

Problem 5-1. Mr. Linhardt already has a long-term capital loss of $5,000 incurred this year. It is near the end of the year. He does not anticipate any other capital asset transactions for the year. However, he does have an investment in shares of common stock which has increased in value. Sale of those shares before the end of the year would result in a $3,000 short-term capital gain. For next year, he expects to have an $8,000 long-term capital gain from different stock. Other taxable income for each year will be about $40,000. Would you recommend sale of the stock this year in order to recognize the $3,000 short-term capital gain? Show calculations and explain. (Use the 1990 single taxpayer rate schedule for both years.)

Problem 5-2. Janet Baines is a manager of a retail store that sells gifts and novelties in a resort community. Her salary is $40,000 per year. Janet will have a deduction for adjusted gross income for $2,000 which she contributed to her (IRA) retirement plan. Her itemized deductions normally run about $1,000 more than the standard deduction. She has one dependent other than herself. Several years ago Janet inherited some stock from her mother. She is interested in the stock market, follows it closely, and trades occasionally. For 1990, she has had the following results:

Short-term capital gains	$ 5,000
Short-term capital losses	(3,000)
Long-term capital gains	4,000
Long-term capital losses	(11,000)

(a) Assuming that the ordinary income and deductions will be the same as in recent years, compute Janet's taxable income and any loss carryovers if there are no further capital asset transactions for the year.

(b) If Janet were to incur another short-term capital gain of $6,000 in 1989, what difference would there be in her taxable income? In the amount of any carryovers?

(c) If Janet does not expect any capital losses next year, would you advise her to recognize the $6,000 short-term capital gain [from (b) above] this year or wait until next year? Explain. (Assume that other income and deductions will be the same each year. Use the same rates for both years.)

(d) Assume that Janet had a block of stock that would produce $6,000 of short-term capital gain if sold. Does the tax law prohibit her from recognizing the gain if she were to sell the stock and immediately buy it back at the same price? Explain.

Problem 5-3. Barry McDonald will have the following items of income and deductions for 1990:

Salary	$36,500
Interest income	2,500

Dividend income	1,700
Itemized deductions (total)	6,500
Exemption amount (1)	himself only

Barry is single and not a head of household. He owns some shares of stock that have appreciated in value $6,000 since he purchased them five months ago. (Ignore commission costs in selling the stock.)

(a) What will be Barry's tax liability if he does not sell the stock?

(b) What will be Barry's tax liability if he does sell the stock immediately?

(c) Explain the tax treatment to Barry if he were to exchange his stock for a pleasure boat rather than sell it.

Problem 5-4. For 1990, Mr. Day had $25,000 of ordinary taxable income. In addition, he had the following capital asset transactions:

$1,800 net long-term capital loss
$1,500 net short-term capital loss

(a) How much may Mr. Day deduct?

(b) Does Mr. Day have a capital loss carryover to next year?

(c) Mr. Day had intended to sell the property that resulted in a loss of $1,800 sooner, but through an oversight the property was sold two days too late and was a long-term capital loss. Explain the difference, if any, between the treatment of short-term capital loss and long-term capital loss.

Problem 5-5. On October 1, 1983, Fran Beaty loaned $5,000 to her friend, Betty Fox. The loan was of a nonbusiness nature and was to be repaid on September 30, 1990. During 1990, Betty filed for bankruptcy and was declared bankrupt. The loan was determined to be totally worthless and uncollectible. Ms. Beaty has taxable income of $30,000 each year and has no capital asset transactions. She files her tax return as a single person. The tax law requires a taxpayer to treat nonbusiness bad debts the same as short-term capital losses. Business bad debts are fully deductible, however.

(a) How much may Ms. Beaty deduct for 1990?

(b) Will Ms. Beaty have any capital loss carryover? If so, how much and how will it be treated?

(c) Is the tax law treatment of nonbusiness bad debts more advantageous or less advantageous to the taxpayer than the treatment of long-term capital losses? Explain.

(d) Would there be any tax advantage to Ms. Beaty if she could show that the loan was a business debt rather than a nonbusiness debt? Explain.

Problem 5-6. From the discussion of capital asset definition in this chapter, it should be clear that there are situations where a person may not be sure if an asset is a capital asset or not. One such instance arose with Mr. Ned Wane, who owns and operates a retail store dealing in art objects, particularly oil and watercolor paintings, all originals by beginning artists. One such artist caught Mr. Wane's attention about ten years ago. Mr. Wane purchased three of the artist's paintings and took them home to hang in his den, both because he liked them and because he was sure that they would appreciate substantially in value over the years. Mr. Wane paid for the paintings with his personal, nonbusiness funds. Mr. Wane also purchased some other work by the same artist, using business funds, and put the paintings in the store for resale. Later the artist was killed in a tragic accident. His life story became the subject of a book and movie and his paintings have skyrocketed in value. The producer of the movie asked Mr. Wane for his permission to use one of the three paintings in the movie. Mr. Wane consented for a fee of $500. The painting was used and safely returned. Now the movie producer has approached Mr. Wane with an offer to buy that painting. None of the three paintings has ever been displayed for sale in Mr. Wane's store.

(a) Do you think Mr. Wane can demonstrate that the three paintings in his den are capital assets even though he has other similar paintings which he holds as inventory?

(b) Explain the circumstances under which it could make a difference whether the paintings are capital assets or not.

Problem 5-7. For the following independent situations, classify each asset as either a (1) capital asset, (2) trade or business asset, (3) ordinary income asset, or a combination of one or more of the preceding categories.

(a) Becky owns six acres of land a few miles out of town. She has been holding on to the land for speculation.

(b) Alan is a real estate developer. He owns six acres of land that he is in the process of subdividing into 20 residential lots.

(c) Joe, a salesperson, uses his personal auto for out of town business travel. This year he determined that the car was used 70% for business.

(d) Ivan, an investor, purchased 1,000 shares of XYZ common stock.

(e) Tom, an electrical distributor, uses 20% of his home as an office and a storage facility for his electrical wire.

Problem 5-8. In January last year, Matt Luther sold 200 shares of Apple Blossom Corp. common stock to his brother, Marvin. Matt's basis in the stock was $52,000. He had owned the stock for three years prior to the sale. Marvin agreed to pay the current fair market value of $48,000. After Marvin had owned the stock for five months, he sold it to his neighbor for $54,000, its fair market value on that date.

(a) Can Matt take a deduction for any long-term capital loss?

(b) What, if any, is the tax consequence to Marvin when he sells the stock? Compare the result if Matt had held the stock and sold it for $54,000.

Problem 5-9. This year, Mable Dunn, who is single, had an ordinary taxable income of $40,500 (marginal tax rate of 28%). In addition, she had a short-term capital loss of $1,000 and a long-term capital loss of $4,000.

(a) What amount may Mable deduct for her capital losses and what amount may be carried forward as a potential deduction next year?

(b) What would be the difference if Mable had timed her $4,000 long-term capital loss to be recognized in the second year? (Assume that she will have about the same amount of ordinary income each year.)

(c) How would the result in (a) above be different if the short-term capital loss had been $4,000 and the long-term capital loss $1,000?

Problem 5-10. This has been a bad year in the stock market for Brad Malone. In a December review of his stock portfolio, Brad finds that his transactions thus far during the year have produced the following:

Short-term capital gains	$15,000
Short-term capital losses	2,000
Long-term capital gains	8,000
Long-term capital losses	65,000

Brad's other taxable income will be $50,000.

(a) If Brad has no further capital asset transactions for the year, what will be his maximum capital loss deduction and capital loss carryover?

(b) Assuming that Brad has in his portfolio securities which have appreciated in value, should he sell them in order to recognize gain? Explain why or why not.

Problem 5-11. John Ritz's salary for 1990 will be $14,500. He and his wife, Pat, received interest of $290 and dividends of $360. On June 19, John sold 25 shares of Perfume Corp. stock for $900 which he had purchased on January 15 for $550. John and Pat are under age sixty-five, have no dependents, and have good eyesight.

(a) What is their federal income tax liability for the year?

(b) What changes, if any, would there be in tax liability if the capital gain had been long-term? Explain.

Problem 5-12. Roger Thompson sold 100 shares of stock of Wink Incorporated for $18,000. Determine his basis and his gain, or loss, in each of the following independent cases:

(a) Roger purchased the stock in 1962 at a cost of $2,000.

(b) Roger's grandmother gave him the stock as a birthday present in 1975. She had purchased it in 1972 for $10,000. On the date of gift it had a fair value of $11,000. She paid $4,510 in federal gift tax as the result of the gift.

(c) Same as part (b) except there was no gift tax due as the result of grandmother's gift.

(d) Roger's uncle died in 1984 and bequeathed the stock to Roger. The uncle had purchased it in 1978 at a cost of $12,000. There was $1,000 of estate tax paid by the uncle's estate as the result of the stock, which was valued at $19,000.

(e) Roger's aunt died in 1985 and left the stock to Roger. She had inherited the stock from her father in 1958. At the time of her father's death the stock had a value of $1,000. At the time of her death the stock was valued at $15,000.

(f) Roger's father gave him the stock in 1981, at which time it had a value of $17,000. His father had purchased the stock in 1974 for $5,000 and paid a gift tax of $6,970 on the transfer to Roger.

(g) Roger's mother left the stock to Roger in her will when she died in 1982. She had acquired it as a gift from her aunt in 1970. No gift tax was paid on that gift. The aunt had purchased it in 1965 at the cost of $500. In 1970 it was valued at $14,000. On the date of Roger's mother's death, it was worth $19,000.

(h) Roger's brother willed him the stock upon his death on June 30, 1982, at which time it had a value of $17,000. The brother had purchased the stock five years prior to his death at a cost of $13,000. The executor of the estate has informed Roger that the alternative valuation date was used for the estate tax return and that the stock was valued at $16,000 on the estate tax return.

(i) Roger's sister gave him the stock in 1987. Her basis was $24,000 and it was worth $20,000 at the time of the gift.

Problem 5-13. Mary Fisher inherited some U.S. Treasury bonds from her grandmother, who died on April 18, 1980. At that date, the bonds, par value $100,000, had a fair market value of $98,000. On October 18, 1980, the bonds had a fair market value of $97,000.

(a) What is the basis of the bonds to Mary if the optional valuation date was not used by the estate?

(b) What is the basis of the bonds to Mary if the optional valuation date was used by the estate and the estate distributed the bonds to her on December 14, 1980, when the value was $97,600?

Problem 5-14. Bill Seagram has a long-term capital loss carryover from last year of $12,000. He owns a substantial portfolio of securities but does not make it a practice to trade. So far this year he has not recognized any capital gains or losses. Bill's taxable income is about the same each year and is expected to be $31,000 this year, not counting any capital asset transactions or capital loss deduction. Bill qualifies for head-of-household status.

(a) If there are no other capital asset transactions, what will be his tax liability and capital loss carryover to next year?

(b) If he sells some stock for a long-term capital gain of $12,000, what will be the result this year? If everything else remains the same, what will be the tax liability next year?

(c) Explain the disposition of any capital loss carryover if Bill should die.

Problem 5-15. Stan Parrot purchased 1,000 shares of Colorful Corporation common stock at $5 per share in 1980. On September 1, 1990, he received 1,000 stock rights entitling him to buy 250 additional shares of Colorful Corporation common stock at $10 per share. On the day that the rights were issued, the fair market value of the stock was $9 per share without rights attached. The fair market value of the rights was $1 each.

(a) Is Stan required to allocate the basis of his stock between the stock and the rights? Explain.

(b) If Stan is required, or elects, to allocate basis, what will be the basis of his stock and his rights after allocation?

(c) If Stan sells the rights on January 15, 1991, for $1.25 each, what is the amount and kind of gain he will recognize? (Consider both allocation and nonallocation of basis.)

(d) If Stan exercises the rights, what will be the dollar basis and the date basis of the new shares of stock? (Consider both allocation and nonallocation of basis.)

(e) What would be the tax effect of allocating basis to the rights and then letting the rights expire unexercised?

Problem 5-16. Jonathan Lee sold an antique automobile on May 15, this year, for $12,000. He had purchased it on August 1, 1971, for $7,000. He also sold a racing boat for $8,000 on July 10. The boat cost him $10,000 on February 12, 1976. He used both the car and boat exclusively for his personal pleasure. No other personal assets were sold during the year.

(a) What amount of gain or loss will Mr. Lee recognize for the year?

(b) Would it have made any difference, assuming everything else remained the same, if he had arranged for the two sales to be in different tax years rather than in the same year?

PROBLEMS WITH AN ASTERISK REQUIRE ADDITIONAL RESEARCH.

Problem 5-17.* Kris Kelly and Lou Lode have been operating a retail store as partners. They plan to transfer all of the assets of the store to a corporation in exchange for which each will receive 50% of the stock of a new corporation which they have formed. Since the assets have appreciated in value, the fair market value of the stock which they will receive will be more than the basis of the assets which they will transfer to the corporation. Will each have capital gain to include in gross income for the year of the exchange? Explain.

6

nontaxable property transactions

In the previous chapter we discussed the federal income tax that results from the sale or exchange of certain assets.[1] Accumulating wealth is easier if it can be managed without having to pay any income tax. The tax law does not tax increases in property value until they are "recognized" for tax purposes. So the challenge frequently is how to plan what is done so as to legally avoid a taxable event. Put another way, to be a taxwise investor requires some knowledge of the tax deferral potentials inherent in:

1. mortgaging property;
2. direct exchange of property for similar property;
3. transfers to partnerships and corporations, which will be discussed in Chapters 10 and 12, respectively;
4. corporate reorganizations and liquidations, which will be discussed in Chapter 13;
5. sale and purchase of personal residence; and
6. involuntary conversions.

6.1 Mortgaging versus Selling

As real estate increases in value, an investor is faced with the problem of putting the increased value to income-producing use. One obvious solution is to sell the appreciated property once the outlook for any further increase in value seems less bright. Some investors may find sale of the property unattractive because of the tax bite that will be incurred. This is especially true of the active speculator in real estate.

A speculator in the 33% tax bracket with a piece of rental property having an adjusted basis of $30,000 and a present value of $100,000 would incur an income tax expense of $23,100 upon the sale of the property.[2] The future potential income from the property would be lost and there would be only $76,900 to reinvest. By borrowing against the property, it might be possible to obtain up to $80,000 in cash without relinquishing the property itself and without incurring any tax.[3] Because the borrowed cash is balanced by an obligation to repay, there is no exchange transaction to produce an income tax at the time money is borrowed. The loan proceeds can be used as a full or down payment to purchase another piece of rental property. In time, as the properties appreciate in value, the remortgaging process can be repeated, and additional property can be purchased, without incurring any income tax.[4] In fact, as we saw previously, the interest expense incurred by borrowing may be partly offset by reduced taxes, if the interest is deductible. Thus, the after-tax cost of borrowing may be less than the stated rate of interest.

[1]It should be noted that there is a tax consequence, i.e., a change in amount of potential carryover, even if a recognized gain results in no tax because of a loss offset.

[2]The tax rate of 33% would apply to a gain of $70,000. Clearly, the concept is equally valid for taxpayers in lower tax brackets, although the amounts may be less dramatic.

[3]The $80,000 is merely an example, based on 80% of present value. Bankers are commonly willing to loan as much as 80% of the fair market value of property, which in this case would be $80,000.

[4]As we will see in the next section, the tax can be avoided by a qualified exchange of one piece of real estate for a different "like–kind" piece of real estate.

Borrowing money does not result in gross income to the borrower and interest expense may be deductible.

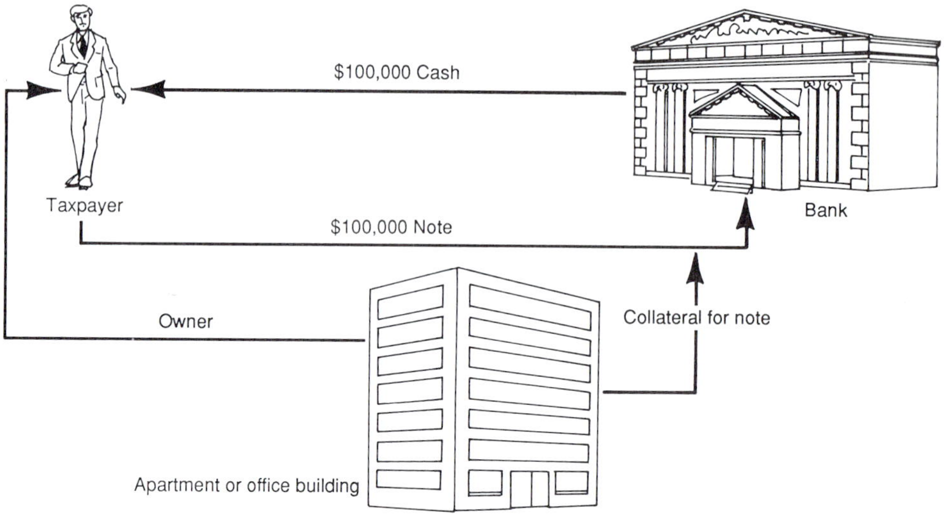

While we have used real estate as an example of appreciated property used as collateral for a loan, the concept is not limited to real estate. A lender might be willing to accept other property as collateral, such as securities. The borrower could use the proceeds of a loan to purchase additional securities, or to purchase a non-security investment.

6.2 Exchange of Property for Like-Kind Property

Tangible property that is held for productive use in a trade or business or for investment can generally be exchanged tax-free for property of a "like kind" to be similarly held.[5] However, property held primarily for sale cannot be exchanged tax-free. Thus, a real estate subdivider normally could not exchange a lot that was held for sale (inventory) for some other piece of real estate and have the exchange be tax-free.[6]

This general rule covers the tax-free trade-in of depreciable business personal property of "like-kind." For example, a business truck with an adjusted basis of $2,000, plus $8,000 cash (boot), can be exchanged tax-free for a new (or used) business truck. Unlike the treatment for financial statement purposes, there is no gain on the transaction, and the adjusted basis of the newly acquired truck is $10,000, regardless of what its cash only purchase price (fair market value) might have been.

Real property (e.g. land and buildings) can also qualify for a tax-free like-kind exchange. For example, a New York City warehouse can be swapped tax-free for an Arizona cattle ranch (sans cattle).[7] Almost any real estate held for investment or to produce income is "like kind" with almost any other real estate.[8] Assets other than real estate (i.e., personal property as distinguished from real property) have a stricter like-kind test to pass.[9] A truck for a truck is "like kind," but a truck exchanged for cattle, for example, would not be of like kind, even though both are personal property.[10]

The exchange of two properties that do not qualify for nontaxable treatment will result in taxable gain (or loss) just as if the properties had been sold for cash. Each party to the transaction will measure the amount of gain (or loss) by comparing the fair market value of what was received with the adjusted basis of what was transferred. For example, assume that an oil painting held by an investor is exchanged for 100,000 shares of High Flyer, Inc. common stock, also held by an investor. Each asset has a fair market value of

[5]IRC Sec. 1031. The term "like kind" refers to the nature or character rather than to the grade or quality of property.
[6]IRC Sec. 1237, which is beyond the scope of this text, may apply to a real estate subdivider.

[7]Receiving cash boot may result in a tax liability even in an otherwise nontaxable transaction. This will be covered in more detail later.
[8]See, for example, *E. R. Braley*, 14 BTA 1153. However, exchange of improved rental real estate for unimproved real estate to be used for subdivision purposes was not an exchange of like-kind property. *Stanley H. Klarkowski*, TC 1965-328 (*aff'd.* CA7 1967), 67-2 USTC 9649, 20 AFTR2d 5482. The Omnibus Budget Reconciliation Act of 1989, which was enacted on December 19, 1989, changed the law so that for transfers after 7-10-89, real estate located in the U.S. and real estate located in a foreign country will no longer qualify as "like kind" and, hence, will not be subject to the nontaxable exchange rules.
[9]An exchange of real property for personal property is not a like-kind exchange. *Comm.* v. *Crichton* (CA5 1941), 27 AFTR 824, 41-2 USTC 9638.
[10]IRC Sec. 1031(e) specifically provides that the exchange of livestock of different sexes will not qualify as a like-kind exchange.

$700,000. If the basis of the painting were $100,000, then the resulting taxable gain to its former owner would be $600,000. If the basis of the stock were $740,000, then there would be a recognized loss of $40,000 to its former owner.

Use of a like-kind exchange of real estate can be illustrated as follows. Assume that the owner of a motel in Massachusetts decides to sell out and go to Florida. Assume that the selling price for the motel would be $400,000, but the sale would create a sizable income tax liability because of a low tax basis for the property. The motel owner would like to use the proceeds to buy an apartment building in Miami. Instead of selling, therefore, a swap is arranged. The apartment building in Miami is exchanged for the motel.[11] Some realtors specialize in this type of three-way deal. Such a realtor might buy the apartment building in Miami for his own account, then trade it for the motel, and finally sell the motel, in order to facilitate the swap transaction. The realtor is willing to take an economic risk in exchange for the commissions earned.

Note that the transaction is tax-free to both parties. Let's analyze the transaction from the standpoint of each party. The fair market value of the motel was $400,000. Therefore, we assume that the apartment building was also worth $400,000. (Receipt or payment of boot will be covered in the next section.) Each party will compare the fair market value of what was received with the adjusted basis of what was transferred. Thus, if the adjusted basis of the motel was $150,000, the former motel owner has a *realized* (meaning economic) gain of $250,000. No gain is ecognized for tax purposes. However, the former motel owner (now the apartment building owner) has a basis for the apartment building of $150,000. This is why we say that the rules provide for a deferral of gain rather than a permanent forgiveness of tax on the gain. If the apartment owner were to sell the property for $400,000, then the $250,000 gain will be recognized. Also, the basis of $150,000 for the apartment building means that $150,000 (or the part thereof that is allocated to the building rather than the land) becomes the starting figure for calculation of depreciation deductions. (See Chapter 9.)

The former apartment owner will also compare the fair market value of the property received (the motel) with the adjusted basis of the property that was transferred (the apartment). If the adjusted basis of the apartment was $370,000, there is a $30,000 *realized*, but not recognized, gain:

Fair market value of property received	$400,000
Less adjusted basis of property transferred	370,000
Realized gain	$ 30,000

The adjusted basis of the motel is $370,000. Thus, neither party has recognized gain for tax purposes, and the adjusted basis of the property that is owned is the same as the adjusted basis of the property formerly owned.

The nonrecognition applies to a loss as well. Thus, if one or both parties had a loss, there would be no deduction for the loss, just as there was no tax that resulted from a gain.

For example, if the adjusted basis of the apartment building had been $450,000, the former apartment building owner would have a $50,000 realized loss but no deduction. Again, the adjusted basis of the property now owned will be the same as the adjusted basis of the property previously owned.

Note that these rules are not elective. Where there is an exchange of "like-kind" property, there is no gain or loss recognized and no election for alternative treatment. If such a transaction is not satisfactory, the transaction should be structured in another way, such as an outright sale.

The words "realized" and "recognized" may need some clarification. "Realized" gain is the amount of economic or accounting gain. It is measured by the difference between the fair market value of what was received and the basis of what was given up. "Recognized" gain is that part of the realized gain (if any) that is subject to tax currently.

TAX PLANNING TIP: Business assets such as trucks, automobiles, and office equipment, for example, are often "traded-in" on replacement assets, with the seller taking the old asset in partial payment for the new asset. Where the asset qualifies as "like-kind" the result is a nontaxable exchange to the buyer. Such a buyer should consider the tax impact of selling the old asset and buying the new asset without a "trade-in." (1) The sale might result in a recognized loss. (2) Even if the sale results in a gain, the gain might not result in any tax because it can be offset by a loss from another transaction. (See Chapter 5.) (3) The depreciation deductions will be different because the new asset will have a different basis under each of the two alternatives.

[11] See, for example, *W. D. Haden Co.* v. *Comm.* (CA5 1948), 48-1 USTC 9147, 36 AFTR 670. An extreme example of a multiple-party swap can be found in *T.J. Starker* (CA9), 79-2 USTC 9541, 44 AFTR2d 79-5525. See IRC Sec. 1031(a)(3)(A) for limitations on the time period between transfer and receipt of properties in a nontaxable exchange.

In addition to tangible property (real estate and personal property), insurance policies (which are intangible property) can be exchanged tax-free.[12] Ordinary life insurance can be exchanged tax-free for an endowment or an annuity contract; an endowment contract can be exchanged tax-free for another endowment contract or for an annuity contract; and an annuity contract can be exchanged tax-free for another annuity contract. Other intangible properties (such as stocks and bonds) are not eligible for tax-free exchanges.

TAX PLANNING TIP: When a disposition of appreciated property is being contemplated, consider the possibility of acquiring another piece of property in a nontaxable exchange rather than selling and purchasing the second property. Tax savings from the resulting deferral can be very large. When a disposition of property that has declined in value is being contemplated, consider a sale if the resulting loss will be a deduction for tax purposes.

Prior to enactment of the Omnibus Budget Reconciliation Act of 1989, it was possible to manipulate the nontaxable exchange rules to the taxpayer's advantage in connection with certain exchanges between related parties. The following example is oversimplified, but will illustrate the planning strategy used. Assume that father owned Greenacre with a basis of $25,000 and a fair market value of $50,000, and that daughter owned Brownacre with a basis of $45,000 and a fair market value of $50,000. Richman, an unrelated person, wanted to buy Greenacre but such a sale would have resulted in $25,000 taxable gain to father. If father and daughter exchanged properties under the nontaxable exchange rules, then daughter would own Greenacre with a basis of $45,000. She could sell it to Richman for $50,000 and recognize a gain of only $5,000. Father would not recognize any gain until he sold Brownacre.

Congress felt that this kind of arrangement should not be permitted. The answer was to amend the rules for exchanges occurring after July 10, 1989.[13] There is now a two-year waiting period before the exchanged property can be sold. If *either* of the two related parties to a nontaxable exchange should sell their property within two years of the date of the exchange, then *both* parties will recognize gain or loss. However, the recognition will be in the year of the second transaction and not in the year of the nontaxable exchange. For example, assume that father and daughter, from the above example, exchanged their properties on August 4, 1990. Assume that on June 1, 1992, daughter sells Greenacre. (Note that it will not make any difference if she sells it to Richman or to someone else. Also, the amount of the selling price will not make any difference either.) The result will be that both father and daughter will recognize gain or loss *for the year 1992*, and the amount of the gain or loss will be determined *as if* the August 4, 1990, transaction had been a taxable exchange rather than a nontaxable exchange.

What if the deal were restructured so that Richman bought Brownacre from daughter and then entered into an exchange with father for Greenacre before expiration of the two year waiting period? That will not work either because the rules provide for denial of the nontaxable exchange treatment if an exchange is part of a series of transactions entered into in order to avoid the related party nontaxable limitation.

The two year waiting period will cease to run, thus allowing the second transaction to take place without negating the nontaxable status of the first transaction, where (a) either party dies, (b) the property becomes subject to an involuntary conversion (discussed at Sec. 6.6 which follows), or (c) the IRS is satisfied that there was not a tax avoidance purpose for the original exchange or the subsequent disposition.

This leaves the question of who or what is a related party for this purpose. The answer is:

1. family members (spouse, brothers, sisters, ancestors, and lineal descendants),
2. a corporation and a more-than-50% individual shareholder,
3. two corporations that are part of the same controlled group (see Chapter 13),
4. two "S" corporations (or one "S" corporation and one "C" corporation) where the corporations have the same more-than-50% owner (see Chapter 11),
5. a corporation and a partnership if the same persons own more than 50% of the corporation's stock and more than 50% interest in the partnership (see Chapter 10),
6. a grantor and a fiduciary of a trust; a fiduciary of a trust and a beneficiary of another trust if the same person is grantor of both trusts; a fiduciary of a trust and a corporation if more than 50% of the corporation is owned by the trust or its grantor (see Chapter 14).

6.3 Boot

The situation in which the two properties involved in an exchange are equal in value is

[12]IRC Sec. 1035.
[13]IRC Sec. 1031(f).

unusual, of course. This does not eliminate the possibility of achieving a tax-free trade.[14] It simply requires that the investor take advantage of the fact that borrowing money against a piece of property has no immediate income tax effect. Similarly, paying down a mortgage on such property produces no tax.

Even in a nontaxable exchange some tax may result where "boot" is received. "Boot" is any property (including cash) which is not "like" the property which was transferred.

For example, assume that you have a piece of real estate with an adjusted basis of $30,000. You exchange it for another piece of real estate (like-kind) with a fair market value of $40,000, and you also receive cash of $5,000. Your realized gain is $15,000 because the fair market value of *everything* you received is $15,000 greater than your adjusted basis. You are only required to recognize (pay tax on) $5,000 of gain, however, because taxable gain is limited to the boot received. The balance of $10,000 is called *"unrecognized"* gain.

On the other hand, let's change the facts so that the boot received is more than the realized gain. Assume that the piece of real estate that you are transferring still has an adjusted basis to you of $30,000. However, you exchange it for another piece of real estate (still like-kind) with a fair market value of $26,000 and you also receive cash of $5,000. Now your realized gain is $1,000, which is the difference between the $31,000 that you received and your basis of $30,000. Your recognized gain is also $1,000 even though you received cash of more than $1,000.

The determination of adjusted basis for property acquired in a nontaxable exchange where boot is paid or received is a little more involved than where there is no boot. That issue will be explained later. In the meantime, let's consider a situation where exchanged property is subject to a mortgage and the exchange involves transferring the mortgage as well as the property.

Assume that Billy Barnes owns a piece of property free and clear. Its basis is $100,000, but it has increased in value to $700,000. Billy would like to part with that property and acquire another piece, which has a fair market value of $1,000,000. The owner has a present mortgage of $400,000 on it, leaving an equity of $600,000. Naturally, Billy would not want to sell the property in order to acquire the other property because that would result in a $600,000 recognized gain. The plan should be to keep the transaction tax-free if possible. Obviously, Billy would not be willing to accept an even trade of equity for equity because this would result in a $100,000 economic loss. But if the other property owner were to pay Billy $100,000 of cash as "boot," the transaction would be fair. However, that also is not the best deal. The reason is that the transaction will result in recognized gain to the extent of boot received.[15] Billy's recognized gain would be calculated as follows:

Fair market value of property received		$1,000,000
Cash received		100,000
Total		$1,100,000
Amount given up:		
Basis of property	$100,000	
Mortgage assumed by Billy	400,000	
Total		500,000
Realized gain		$600,000

As before, only $100,000 of the gain would be recognized, namely, an amount equal to the boot received.

There is another way to structure the transaction. The owner of the other property will pay $100,000, just as before. However, instead of transferring the money to Billy, the $100,000 will be paid to the mortgage holder to reduce the mortgage to $300,000 prior to the exchange. His equity becomes $700,000, the same as Billy's. The swap is both fair and tax-free. Here is Billy's calculation:

Fair market value of property received		$1,000,000
Amount given up:		
Basis of property	$100,000	
Mortgage assumed by Billy	300,000	
Total		400,000
Realized gain		$600,000

However, since Billy received no "boot," none of the gain will be taxable. If Billy would like to get the $100,000 in cash, that may be accomplished by waiting until after the new property is received and then borrowing $100,000 against it. As noted before, borrowing money does not produce a tax at that time.

As long as an investor continues to own a parcel of real estate, an increase or decrease in the mortgage liability to which such property is subject has no effect upon the tax basis or upon the tax liability. When the property is sold, however, the amount of any outstanding debt that is transferred to the buyer along with the property is a part of the selling price. This, in turn, affects the investor's

[14] Realized gain is measured by the difference between the fair market value of property received and the tax basis (cost) of property given. In a Sec. 1031 exchange where boot is also received, gain is recognized only to the extent of boot received.

[15] Treas. Reg. 1.1031(b)(1). In this illustration the boot received is cash. The same result would occur if Billy were to receive any other property not of a like kind (i.e., boot), that had a fair market value of $100,000.

gain realized on the sale. For example, assume that John owns a piece of property which has a basis of \$60,000 and a current fair market value of \$100,000. The property is mortgaged for \$20,000. John transfers the property, together with the mortgage, to Mary, who transfers a like-kind piece of property worth \$80,000 to John. Mary's property was not mortgaged. John has received (1) property worth \$80,000 and (2) relief from future mortgage payments of \$20,000, or a total of \$100,000. John gave up property with a basis of \$60,000. Thus, John's *realized* gain is \$40,000, but his *recognized* gain is \$20,000, the amount of the mortgage. It is *as if* Mary had paid John \$20,000. Here "boot" is the relief of mortgage debt.

TAX PLANNING TIP: If "A" receives "boot" in an otherwise nontaxable exchange, gain will be recognized to the extent of the boot received. If the party that is to pay the boot ("B") will apply the money against any debt which "A" would otherwise assume in the transaction, "A" will not receive boot and will not have to recognize gain.

Imaginative rearranging of a transaction can produce interesting tax results in realty trades. One trap to watch out for, however, is the situation where you exchange properties with mortgages attached and the indebtedness on your property exceeds the other party's indebtedness. Where such a situation exists, the excess (or "net mortgage") will be treated as money received by you ("boot") and will be taxable.[16] For example, assume that you have a piece of property with a value of \$500,000 but subject to an indebtedness of \$300,000 and that your basis is \$220,000. You plan to trade for a piece of property with a value of \$350,000 but subject to an indebtedness of \$150,000. You and the other party each have equity of \$200,000, so the deal is fair. The tax result may not be what was expected. You will have a realized gain of \$280,000 determined as follows:

Fair market value of property received		\$350,000
Indebtedness transferred to other party		300,000
Total "received"		\$650,000
Adjusted basis of property given up	\$220,000	
Indebtedness assumed by you	150,000	
Total "given"		370,000
Realized gain		\$280,000

[16]Treas. Reg. 1.1031(d)(2).

Since your mortgage liability after the transaction is \$150,000 less than before, you are treated as if you had received the \$150,000 in cash and then paid down your mortgage. Therefore, you have \$150,000 of recognized gain. Gain is recognized to the extent of boot received. In this case, the "net mortgage" is the same as cash.

TAX PLANNING TIP: The nontaxable exchange treatment is a two-way street. Where losses occur, such losses are not recognized for tax purposes. Therefore, if a loss is to be realized in an exchange, the transaction might be restructured so that the nontaxable exchange rules will not apply. This could be done by (a) causing the exchanged properties to fail to meet the "like kind" requirement, or (b) selling the first property and buying the second property rather than entering into an exchange.

Note that by combining the mortgage transfers, the result may be no boot received. Thus, for example, assume that the facts are changed to the following:

Fair market value of property received		\$350,000
Indebtedness transferred to other party		200,000
Total received		\$550,000
Adjusted basis of property given up	\$220,000	
Indebtedness assumed by you	240,000	
Total "given"		460,000
Realized gain		\$ 90,000

Note that the "net boot" has been "given," not received. Therefore, there is no recognized gain from this transaction. In addition to netting mortgages, boot given is netted against boot received only if the latter were generated by the reduction of debt. For example, assume that a taxpayer is relieved of \$100,000 debt, assumes a \$60,000 debt, and pays \$25,000 cash as part of a like-kind exchange. The boot received is only \$15,000, not \$40,000. This is because the \$100,000 debt relieved is reduced by the \$25,000 cash payment for the purpose of calculating boot received (\$100,000 − \$25,000 − \$60,000 = \$15,000 boot). The other party to the exchange may not net the increase in debt (boot given) against the cash received (boot received). Thus, the other taxpayer would have \$25,000 boot received.

It is only where *mortgages* are both received and given as boot that the "net boot" concept can be used. If, in a real estate transaction, you received a car as boot and also gave shares of stock as boot, the value of the car and the value of the stock will not be combined or netted to arrive at a "net boot" given or received.

For example:

Fair market value of like-kind property received		$100,000
Boot (fair market value of car)		15,000
Total received		$115,000
Adjusted basis of property given up	$80,000	
Adjusted basis of stock given up	10,000	
Total amount "given"		90,000
Realized gain		$ 25,000

The "net boot" is $5,000. However, because the boot received and the boot given are not mortgages, they cannot be "netted" for determining the tax result. Instead, gain of $15,000 is recognized, that being the full value of the boot received. Unrecognized gain is $10,000

"Boot" can be received in cash, or in the form of debt against the property being given in excess of the debt against the property being received, or even in the form of other property. Thus, an exchange of unimproved land for a motel would involve the receipt of boot to the extent of the value of the furniture, equipment, and other non-realty assets that came along with the motel. Gain in the transaction would be recognized up to the value of the boot received. Thus, if realized gain were $150,000 and $30,000 of boot were received, gain of $30,000 would be recognized.

The recognized gain is not always equal to the amount of boot received, however. Consider the following example:

Fair market value of like-kind property received	$100,000
Boot received (cash or any other non-like-kind asset)	10,000
Total	$110,000
Basis of property transferred to other party	106,000
Realized gain	$ 4,000

Here, the recognized gain is $4,000 and not $10,000. The reason is that recognized gain will not be greater than realized gain although it can be less than realized gain.

TAX PLANNING TIP: In the process of modernizing its equipment, a business might sell old assets and buy new assets. The result will be recognized gain on the sale of the old assets if the selling price exceeds the basis. Trading in the old assets for the new ones can be a nontaxable exchange, thereby avoiding tax on the gain.

An example may help clarify the tax-free exchange of equipment. A sole proprietor in the 33% tax bracket will be purchasing new business machinery in the near future. Two alternatives are being considered:

1. Sell the old machinery for $12,000 and use the cash from the sale plus other funds to acquire new machinery for $19,000.
2. Trade in the old machinery and receive a $14,000 trade-in allowance on the $22,000 list price of the new machinery and pay cash boot of $8,000.

If the old machinery which originally cost $10,000 has an adjusted basis of $2,000, the recognized gain of $10,000 will result in $3,300 of tax.*

The net cash outflow will be:

Sell			*Trade in*	
Cash in		$12,000	Cash in	0
Cash out:			Cash out	$8,000
Purchase	$19,000			
Taxes	3,300	$22,300		
Net outflow		$10,300	Net outflow	$8,000

*The recognized gain of $10,000 is actually $8,000 of Sec. 1245 gain (depreciation recapture) and $2,000 of Sec. 1231 gain (treated as long-term capital gain as explained in the previous chapter). However, if the taxpayer had any capital losses, or Sec. 1231 losses, in the same year, there would be a combining of such transactions first. In such event, the result could be different from the $3,300 of additional tax which is assumed here.

6.4 Tax Basis

In the example above, the trade-in saves $2,300 in cash this year. But the basis for depreciation after the trade-in is only $10,000 ($8,000 boot paid plus $2,000 adjusted basis on the old machinery), while the basis in the sale-purchase alternative would be the $19,000 (cash) cost of the new machine. The trade-in alternative will result in $9,000 less depreciation over the life of the new machine. This will mean $2,970 more tax ultimately to pay, assuming the rate remains at 33%.

It is important to understand that in a nontaxable exchange, the "realized" gain that is not subject to taxation is merely a deferral and not necessarily a permanent forgiveness of tax. The amount of realized gain that is not subject to tax currently (the "unrecognized gain") is a reduction in the basis of the property which was received in the exchange.

Generally, the tax basis of property received in a "tax-free" transaction is the same as the basis of the property given up, plus any boot given.[17] The same number can be derived by taking the value of the property acquired and reducing it by the nontaxable portion of the gain (unrecognized gain) on the transaction.

Assume that a new business truck would cost $15,000. A trade-in is arranged. An old truck valued at $9,000 is traded in and $6,000 cash is paid. The old truck has a tax basis of $2,000. The tax basis of the new truck is that of the old truck ($2,000) increased by the boot given ($6,000), or $8,000. Since the old truck was worth $9,000 although its tax basis was $2,000, the unrecognized gain is $7,000. Subtracting this $7,000 from the new truck's cost of $15,000 also produces an $8,000 tax basis for the new truck.

Summary of Basis of Property Received in a Nontaxable Exchange

Adjusted basis =		
Basis of property given	*or*	Fair market value of property received
+ Boot given		+ Loss not recognized
+ Gain recognized		− Gain not recognized
− Boot received		
− Loss recognized		

What is the impact on the tax basis of the "new" property when boot is received for the old? None. For example, consider the following:

Fair market value of property received	$20,000
Boot received	29,000
Total	$49,000
Adjusted basis of property "given"	10,000
Realized gain	$39,000

Only $29,000 of the gain (the amount equal to the boot) is currently taxable. The other $10,000 is deferred. The tax basis of the new property is $10,000. Note that $10,000 was also the tax basis of the old property. Under our alternative statement of the basis rule in the previous paragraph, the tax basis of the new property is the basis of the old ($10,000) plus the boot given ($0), or a total of $10,000. If the boot exceeded the gain, there would be no deferred amount, no tax-free transaction, and the basis of the new property would be the value used in determining the gain.

[17]The rules for basis of property acquired in a nontaxable exchange are contained in IRC Sec. 1031(d).

6.5 Sale of Personal Residence

As a general rule, gain on the sale of a personal residence will be taxable while a loss will not be deductible.[18] There are two major exceptions to the taxability of such gains, however:

1. Qualifying reinvestment, which will defer part or all of the gain, called "residential rollover."[19]
2. Exclusion of up to $125,000 of gain for taxpayers age fifty-five or over.[20]

Gain on sale of a personal *principal* residence is deferred to the extent that the adjusted selling price of the sold residence is reinvested in another *principal* residence within a given time frame. That time frame starts twenty-four months before sale of the old residence and ends twenty-four months after.[21] For example, assume that you sold your residence on August 1, 1990. The period of time during which you could make a qualifying replacement purchase runs from August 1, 1988, to July 31, 1992. For U.S. taxpayers living in a foreign country, the period for replacement is extended to a maximum of four years after the date of sale of the old residence.[22] There is no way for a taxpayer to get an extension of these deadlines for replacement.

Note that the word is "residence" and not "house." A principal residence can be an apartment (condominium or cooperative), a house trailer, or a boat as well as a single-family residence.[23] However, a taxpayer can only have one *principal* residence at a time, and the deferral rule does not apply to a secondary residence, such as a summer house in the mountains or a beach house at the shore.

As with the nontaxable exchange, the gain that is not taxed currently is reflected in an adjustment to the basis of the second residence. For example:

[18]IRC Sec. 262 provides that there shall be no deduction for personal, family, or living expenses. Where a personal residence is sold for less than its original cost, the decline in value is presumed to have resulted from use. There is no deduction. The same is true for any loss from the sale of other personal-use assets.

[19]IRC Sec. 1034.

[20]IRC Sec. 121.

[21]IRC Sec. 1034(a).

[22]IRC Sec. 1034(k). Members of the armed services are subject to a special rule in Sec. 1034(h).

[23]Rev. Rul. 64-31, 1964-1 CB 300, and Rev. Rul. 66-114, 1966-1 CB 181.

Sales price of former residence	$90,000
Adjusted basis of former residence	65,000
Realized gain	$25,000

If the cost of the second residence is $110,000, its basis is $85,000 because the nonrecognized gain is applied to reduce its basis. (Note that the $25,000 gain would be recognized, i.e., taxed currently, if a replacement residence is not purchased within the time period specified above. In that event, the basis of any replacement residence would be its cost.)

If an amount less than the adjusted selling price of the first residence is reinvested in a second residence, gain will be recognized to the extent of the "adjusted sales price" not reinvested.

Another important planning idea relates to the time frame for replacement. It is not enough that a replacement residence be purchased before expiration of the alloted time period. The residence must be occupied as a residence before the end of that period. This may become particularly important in the case of a seller who decides to build a replacement residence instead of buying an existing one. It is not only important that construction begin within the allotted time period, but the construction must be "far enough along" so that it can be occupied, and is occupied as a residence by the end of the period.

The following example will illustrate the rules.

Selling price of first residence	$69,000
Basis of first residence	30,000
Commission on sale	4,000
Fixing-up expenses on first residence	1,000[24]

The commission is subtracted from the gross selling price to determine the *amount* realized from the sale ($65,000). Thus, if a replacement residence is not purchased within the allotted time, the seller will have a taxable gain of $35,000, which is $65,000 reduced by the basis of the property. In that event, "fixing up" expenses are not considered. From a planning point of view such a seller might ask, "How much must I reinvest in another residence so as not to pay tax on any of the gain?" The answer is that an amount equal to the "adjusted selling price" must be reinvested. The "adjusted selling price" in our example is $64,000, which is the amount realized reduced by fixing-up expenses. If $64,000 or more is invested in a replacement residence, the $35,000 gain is not currently taxable. If less than $64,000 is invested in a replacement residence, the gain must be recognized to the extent of the adjusted selling price not reinvested. Thus, if the replacement residence cost $55,000, and if no improvements are added within twenty-four months from the date of the sale of the first house, there will be $9,000 of recognized gain. If $55,000 is spent for a replacement, but within twenty-four months from the date of sale of the first residence $6,000 of improvements are made, the replacement residence has cost $61,000 and the recognized gain will be $3,000.

The basis of the second residence is its cost reduced by any unrecognized gain resulting from the sale of the first residence. Thus, if the second residence cost $55,000, the *unrecognized* gain will be $26,000 and the basis of the second residence will be $29,000 ($55,000 − $26,000). If the second residence cost $90,000, the entire $35,000 of gain will be unrecognized. The basis of the second residence will be $55,000 ($90,000 − $35,000).[25]

TAX PLANNING TIPS:

1. *Purchase or build the replacement residence within twenty-four months before or after the sale.*
2. *Spend at least as much for the second residence as the adjusted sales price of the first residence. If not, make improvements within the allowed time period.*
3. *Be sure that the second residence is occupied as the principal residence, before the twenty-four month period ends.*

Chapter 3 included a discussion of the deductibility of interest expense as an itemized deduction for individuals. Interest on a mortgage on a person's personal residence, or second residence, is deductible so long as the debt does not exceed acquisition indebtedness (subject to a $1,000,000 limitation on the debt) plus the excess of fair market value of the residence over acquisition indebtedness (subject to a $100,000 limitation). The fact that the adjusted basis will be reduced by application of the "rollover" rules, will not impact the calculation of the interest deduction. The interest deduction limitation is determined by reference to the fair market value of the property rather than by reference to the property's basis.

[24]"Fixing-up expenses" are defined as expenses of work performed on the old residence in order to assist in its sale. Such expenses must be for work performed within ninety days before the date of contract to sell and paid no later than thirty days after the date of sale. Also, such expenses cannot be those which would add to the basis of the property, such as a new roof or conversion of a carport to a garage. They only go into the calculation of the amount of the gain recognized. Painting is a good example of fixing-up expenses.

[25]IRC Sec. 1034(e). Note that "fixing-up expenses" do not change the basis of the second house, and are not capitalized as part of the cost of the first residence.

Thus, if Billy Barnes lives in a house that cost \$1,800,000, but that has a basis of only \$500,000 because of previously unrecognized gain(s), the basis will have no impact upon the amount of debt or interest deduction.

The nonrecognition of gain rules have nothing to do with the cash flow from the sale of a residence and the purchase of a replacement residence. The amount of gain recognized can be greater than the amount of money which the taxpayer "puts in his pocket." Likewise, the amount of cash that a seller has after the transactions can be much larger than the amount of gain that was taxed.

For example, assume that a person sells a residence (basis of \$60,000) for \$100,000 with \$50,000 going to the mortgage company and \$50,000 going to him. At this point, realized gain is \$40,000, but cash "in hand" is \$50,000. If a replacement residence is purchased for \$90,000, \$10,000 of the gain must be recognized. If the person uses his \$50,000 cash as a down payment and takes a mortgage for \$40,000, there is no cash on hand, but \$10,000 of the gain is still taxable.

On the other hand, assume that the replacement house is purchased for \$90,000 with a \$10,000 down payment and a mortgage for \$80,000. The taxpayer has the same recognized gain of \$10,000, but has \$40,000 of cash that has not been used for the second house. Persons who sell their personal residence and buy a replacement often mistake the cash flow for the tax effect when in fact these are two different concepts.

There are some expenses associated with selling a residence that might be treated as selling expenses (treated the same as the sales commission in the example above) or as deductible moving expenses. (Moving expenses were discussed in Chapter 3.) A taxpayer who qualifies may elect to treat certain expenses of the residence sale as moving expenses rather than as a reduction in the selling price.[26] In no case, however, can an expense be treated both as a moving expense and as a cost of selling the residence.[27]

The nonrecognition of gain rules, and the related basis adjustment rules, are mandatory, not elective. You might, for example, sell your principal residence for a \$40,000 gain. Assuming that you have a capital loss from another transaction during the same year, you might decide that you would like to recognize the gain from the residence, offset it with the loss from another transaction, and pay no additional tax—or a small additional tax if the offset left you with some recognized gain—even though you purchased a qualified replacement. Your motivation might be that you want a higher basis for the replacement residence. You do not have that choice, however. For the residential rollover rule not to apply to you, it is necessary for you not to qualify. One way of not qualifying is not to replace the residence within the forty-eight month period described earlier. Another way not to qualify, even if a replacement house is purchased, is not to move in and occupy the property as your *principal* residence before the allotted time period has expired.

Although the nonrecognition of gain rules for a sale of a personal residence are mandatory, where more than one such sale takes place within a two-year period, the nonrecognition rule applies only to the last of the purchases within the two-year period following the date of the first sale.

Over a family's lifetime, the cumulative amount of deferred gain, perhaps from the sale of several homes, can become substantial. It is, of course, embodied in a lower tax basis in the latest residence. Then comes the time when the children leave for work or marriage, or the parents decide to retire, and a smaller residence or even a rental dwelling may seem appropriate. For example, a house valued at \$175,000 is sold, and the sales proceeds are not reinvested in a new residence. If the tax basis of the \$175,000 house is only \$80,000, due in part to the cumulative effect of deferrals of gain from the sale of previous residences, \$95,000 of gain results. The tax law contains a special one-time "forgiveness" of gain to take care of situations such as this.[28]

Taxpayers age fifty-five or over (on the date of sale) may elect—once in a lifetime—to exclude up to \$125,000 of gain on the sale of a principal residence.[29] That specific residence must have been the taxpayer's principal residence for three of the five years preceding the sale.[30] Married

[26]Generally, where a taxpayer qualifies for moving expense deduction, it is more advantageous to treat an expense as a moving expense rather than as a reduction in the sales price of the residence. In some cases, of course, an expense might exceed the amount allowable as a moving expense deduction. In that event, the usual optimal treatment would be to deduct the maximum allowable as a moving expense and treat the balance as a reduction of the amount realized from the sale of the residence. Naturally, persons not qualifying for a moving expense deduction would treat such an expenditure as a reduction of the selling price of the residence.

[27]IRC Sec. 217(e).

[28]IRC Sec. 121. Another Congressional motivation for forgiveness of tax on such gain is that the gain very probably resulted in large part from inflation. There are many persons currently living in a residence that they have owned for several years who would find that it would require double or triple the amount of money to purchase a replacement residence of the same size and quality. There is an argument that can be made for the "unfairness" of taxing a gain that resulted from the change in purchasing power of the dollar rather than a "real" economic gain.

[29]IRC Sec. 121(b). For a married couple, only one need be age 55.

[30]IRC Sec. 121(a).

people have only one election available—not a separate $125,000 maximum exclusion for each spouse.[31]

COMPUTER FORMULAS: THE $125,000 exclusion can be inserted into a formula by using the @IF function.

	A	*B*	*C*	*D*
1	Sales price	*x*		
2	Basis	*y*		
3				
4	Gain @IF ((*x* − *y*) > 125,000, (*x* − *y*) − 125,000, 0)			

Since the exclusion is up to $125,000, gain will only be recognized if the gain realized is *greater than* $125,000.

Thus, in the previous example where the residence with a tax basis of $80,000 was sold for $175,000 and a replacement residence was not purchased within the 48-month period, the $95,000 gain could be excluded from income if the taxpayer was fifty-five or over, satisfied all the requirements, and elected to do so.

One difficult decision can face an eligible taxpayer. When should the election be made? Assume that the taxpayer sells a home for a $60,000 gain at age fifty-five. Since the election may be made only once, should it be made now? In that case, a potential additional exclusion of $65,000 ($125,000 potential exclusion less $60,000 exclusion used now) is forever lost. Waiting and satisfying the holding-period rules for another residence could presumably result in the exclusion of a larger gain in the future. The gamble is on both the virtue of a replacement residence as an investment and the possibility of dying before the replacement residence would be sold. Death cuts off the election completely. Any decedent who has not used the election cannot pass it on to an heir. Of course, whoever inherits the residence gets a stepped-up basis anyway, as discussed in Chapter 5.

TAX PLANNING TIP: The $125,000 gain exclusion on the sale of a personal residence by a taxpayer age fifty-five or older is available only once to each taxpayer. A married couple is considered one taxpayer for this purpose. A man and a woman, each age fifty-five and each owning a home, may consider marriage. After marriage they could only get the $125,000 exclusion one time. By each selling the respective home prior to marriage, and selecting the exclusion, it is possible to exclude as much as $250,000 of gain.

The $125,000 exclusion can be used in tandem with the deferral of gain from reinvestment in a second residence.[32] For example, assume a $200,000 adjusted selling price for the old residence with a tax basis of only $50,000. The first $125,000 of the $150,000 gain may be excluded altogether under the election. The remaining $25,000 may be deferred if the taxpayer makes a qualifying reinvestment of at least $75,000. The tax basis of a $75,000 replacement residence, for example, would be $50,000. Since the $125,000 is an exclusion rather than a deferral, there is no basis adjustment for that amount. If less than $75,000 is spent for a replacement residence, gain will be recognized. The amount recognized will be the smaller of (1) $25,000 (the realized gain less the $125,000 exclusion) or (2) $75,000 minus the cost of the replacement. The basis of the replacement residence would be its cost minus the unrecognized gain resulting from the rollover, but not minus the unrecognized gain resulting from the over-age-55 exclusion election.

TAX PLANNING TIP: If a taxpayer has used the exclusion election—even if only part of the maximum $125,000 was excluded—and later marries a person who has not made the election, the latter person will not be eligible. Thus, an eligible person who has not used the election may decide to sell his or her residence, and make the election to use the exclusion before marrying a person who has already used the exclusion.

6.6 Involuntary Conversions

The rules on involuntary conversions are somewhat similar to those on reinvestment of the sales proceeds of an old residence in a replacement.[33] One important difference, however, is that the involuntary conversion rules are elective, whereas the residential "rollover" rules are not elective. Other differences have to do with the kind of

[31] Treas. Reg. 1.121-2(b). The maximum exclusion is $62,500 for a married person filing separately.

[32] Treas. Reg. 1.121-5(g).

[33] IRC Sec. 1033.

property that is eligible to be acquired to replace the original property, and the period for replacement.

An involuntary conversion results from the theft of property, its destruction by fire or storm or some other accident, or its seizure in condemnation proceedings (such as being taken by the state for the right-of-way for a new highway). The amount received as insurance recovery or as a condemnation award can be viewed as a type of selling price.[34] A realized gain will result if this "selling price" is more than the adjusted basis for the property. The taxpayer has an election. All of the gain can be recognized. Alternatively, if replacement occurs, an election can be made to recognize gain only to the extent the proceeds are not reinvested in qualified property within a given time period.[35] As in the case of residential property, if all of the proceeds are not reinvested, there will be recognized gain to the extent the proceeds are not reinvested. The gain that is not recognized reduces the tax basis of the replacement property.

The involuntary conversion rules apply only to gains. Thus, where theft, destruction, or condemnation (or threat of condemnation) occurs and the taxpayer realizes a loss, other rules must be consulted to determine if a deduction is permitted. As a general rule, such losses are deductible.[36] However, where a loss occurs because nonbusiness property is condemned (or sold under threat of condemnation), there is no loss deduction for tax purposes.[37]

Assume that Billy Barnes owns a business building with an adjusted basis of $60,000. The building is completely destroyed by a hurricane. The insurance proceeds are $110,000, resulting in a $50,000 realized gain. If Billy does all the "right" things, the $50,000 will not be taxed. The "right" things are the following:

1. Replace the building within the specified time period, which is explained later.
2. Spend $110,000 or more for the replacement.
3. Make the election on the tax return.

If all of these are done, the $50,000 becomes unrecognized gain and will reduce the basis of the replacement building. If all but (2) above are completed, and $90,000, for example, is spent on the replacement, then $20,000 of the gain (an amount equal to the unspent proceeds) will be recognized.

Because there is an election to be made, planning opportunities arise. In some cases the taxpayer might prefer to recognize the gain from such a sale even though the situation might qualify for nonrecognition.

Assume, from the example of Billy above, that the $50,000 gain will be treated as capital gain.[38] If the marginal tax rate were 33%, the tax on the gain would be $16,500. However, if Billy should have a capital loss, or a Sec. 1231 loss, from another transaction during the year, then part or all of the gain would be eliminated from current taxation by the netting process described in Chapter 5. Thus, Billy could choose to recognize the gain from the involuntary conversion without increasing the cash outflow for income tax for the year. If replacement occurs and the election to defer the gain is made, the basis of the new property will be $50,000 less than otherwise.

Thus, the choice is between (a) recognizing the gain for the current year, and having a basis for the replacement asset equal to its cost or (b) not recognizing the gain for the current year, and having a basis for the replacement asset equal to its cost minus the unrecognized gain. (A third alternative is to recognize part of the gain, but this requires spending less than the full amount of the proceeds on a qualified replacement.) In order to choose between those alternatives, Billy should know or estimate the following variables:

1. The tax impact for the current year, i.e., whether recognition of gain will result in additional tax or will be wholly or partially offset by a loss.
2. If a loss is used to offset all or part of the recognized gain, what future tax savings from deduction of that loss will be forfeited? (Expected future tax savings should be discounted to present value before comparison with current tax savings.)
3. If the property is subject to depreciation, what will be the tax effect of the difference in future depreciation deductions resulting from two alternative basis amounts.[39] (Again, future tax differences should be discounted to present value before comparison with current tax impact.)

Although the tax rules applicable to corporations are discussed in Chapter 12, it is noteworthy at this point that the involuntary conversion rules

[34] It is not necessary that cash be received, however. If a taxpayer were to receive property that is "similar or related in service or use," the involuntary conversion rules would apply as well. The "selling price" would be the fair market value of the replacement property received.

[35] IRC Sec. 1033(a)(2)(B).

[36] IRC Sec. 162 or 165. See Chapter 3 and Chapter 7.

[37] IRC Sec. 165 provides for a deduction if nonbusiness property is lost in a *casualty* or *theft*. Since condemnation is neither a casualty nor theft, no deduction is available.

[38] As mentioned in Chapter 5, depreciable property used in a trade or business does not meet the Sec. 1221 definition of capital asset. Sec. 1231 will allow the gain on real estate to be treated as capital gain, nevertheless, provided that depreciation has been taken under the straight-line method. IRC Sec. 1250 covers "depreciation recapture" on real estate that was depreciated under a method other than straight-line.

[39] Depreciation deductions are discussed in Chapter 9.

apply to corporations the same as to individuals. There is an important difference in the treatment of corporate capital losses that could impact a corporation's decision on whether to use the involuntary conversion election. First, a corporation that has a net capital loss does not get the $3,000 deduction that is available to individuals. Second, a corporate capital loss can be carried forward only five years. (There is a three-year carryback rule which will be discussed in Chapter 12.) If a capital loss is not "used" by offsetting it with a capital gain (or Sec. 1231 gain) within the three year carryback and five year carryover period, then it is lost.

For example, assume that the Billy Corporation had a $50,000 net capital loss in 1985. There were no capital gains in prior or subsequent years and it is now 1990. If there is no recognized gain in 1990, the loss will never result in a tax benefit. If there is an involuntary conversion in 1990, resulting in a $50,000 capital gain, the corporation should choose to recognize the gain because of the offsetting loss. The replacement property will have a higher basis than if the gain had not been recognized. Note that it is not necessary for the capital loss carryover and the involuntary conversion gain to be equal as in this example. Even if gain is larger than the capital loss carryover, payment of tax on part of the gain may be well worth the opportunity to use the loss rather than have it expire. Note that there is a difference in the basis for the replacement property.

Replacement of property involuntarily converted can be made by buying existing qualified property, building it, or by acquiring 80% or more each of the voting and nonvoting stock of a corporation that owns qualified property.[40] Congressional intent for nonrecognition of gain was that the taxpayer who replaces property be economically in the same position as before the conversion. In other words, the expectation is that the *proceeds*, usually cash, from the involuntary "sale" of the property should be used to acquire the replacement. Therefore, a taxpayer is not permitted to acquire replacement property by exchanging property that was owned before the involuntary conversion.

For example, assume that Billy Barnes owns two pieces of real estate, A and B. Real estate A is sold to the state under threat of condemnation. Billy wants to acquire another piece of real estate, C, as a replacement. If an amount equal to the sales price of property A is used to acquire C (and done within the time limitations), the nonrecognition of gain provisions may be elected.[41] But if property C is acquired by exchanging property B for C, the involuntary conversion provisions may not be used. This is true even if property B has a smaller value than property C so that some cash boot has to be paid.

The time limits for replacement of involuntarily converted property depend on the nature of the property and the type of conversion. The general rule is that the replacement must take place before the end of the *second* year after the end of the tax year in which any part of the gain is realized.[42] Thus, if insurance proceeds from a 1988 fire were received during 1988, the reinvestment must be by December 31, 1990, for a taxpayer who files on a calendar year basis. Note that the time of the destruction is important in terms of *beginning* the time period for replacement but not ending that time period. The ending of the qualified replacement period is two years following the end of the year that the proceeds are received. For example, assume that Billy's building was destroyed by fire on July 1, 1987. Because of differences in opinion between Billy and the insurance company over the fire insurance coverage, Billy did not collect proceeds until August 5, 1989. Thus, gain was realized on August 5, 1989. The time period for replacement began on July 1, 1987, and will end on December 31, 1991. This latter date is two years after the *end of the year* during which the gain was realized.

Where real property is involuntarily converted as the result of seizure, condemnation, etc., the taxpayer has until the end of the *third* (not second) year following the year in which any part of the gain is first realized within which to acquire replacement property.[43]

Replacement may also take place *before* the gain is realized.[44] Replacement property will qualify if acquired after the date of destruction, seizure, etc., or, in the case of condemnation, after the date when a decision has been reached by the condemning authority which creates a threat or imminence of condemnation and the taxpayer has been notified.

For example, assume that Billy owned a tract of lakeshore property in Arizona. The State planned to increase the size of the lake by increasing the height of the dam creating the lake. As a result, the expectation was that Billy's property would be flooded. On June 1, 1988, the State notified Billy of the intent (legally referred to as "threat") to have the property condemned under the "right of eminent domain." June 1, 1988,

[40] IRC Sec. 1033(a)(2)(A), (E).

[41] This assumes that property C meets the "similar or related in service or use" test discussed later.

[42] IRC Sec. 1033(a)(2)(B).

[43] IRC Sec. 1033(g)(4).

[44] IRC Sec. 1033(a)(2)(B).

becomes the starting date for the replacement period of the property regardless of how long it may take the State and Billy to arrive at the amount of condemnation proceeds that Billy will receive. If, for example, Billy receives the proceeds on August 1, 1991, then the end of the time period for qualified replacement will be December 31, 1994.

TAX PLANNING TIP: When a state or local government wants to purchase a taxpayer's land, have the authorities issue a letter to the taxpayer which expresses the intent to condemn the property if a "voluntary" sale is not made. This will qualify the taxpayer for nonrecognition of gain if a qualified replacement property is purchased within the allowed time period.

Unlike the period for replacement of a personal residence, the IRS can extend the replacement period if an application is filed before the end of the replacement period and the taxpayer shows good reason for the extension.[45] Where replacement property is constructed, the construction must be completed (not just started) by the end of the replacement period, including any extensions.

What, then, is "qualified replacement property" which must be acquired within these time limits? The replacement property must generally be "similar or related in use or service" to qualify.[46] This is a more severe test than that which applies to the nontaxable exchange of real property, discussed earlier. For an exchange to be nontaxable, the test is that the two properties must be of "like kind." The replacement property acquired to satisfy the involuntary conversion rules, on the other hand, must be functionally similar, as one vehicle would be similar to another. The "similarity" test applies to the owner of the property, so that rental realty leased to a manufacturer could be replaced by rental realty leased to a wholesaler.[47] But a billiard center that a taxpayer purchased with the insurance proceeds when his bowling alley burned would not be similar enough under the functional test and would not qualify.[48]

There is one major exception to the "functional" test. This is where real property is condemned, seized, requisitioned, sold, or exchanged due to the threat or imminence of seizure or requisition for condemnation.[49] This property, which also gets the three-year replacement period, need only pass the less severe *like-kind* test. Thus, the New York motel sold under threat of condemnation would be "like kind" with a Florida office building or an Arizona ranch.[50]

The replacement cost is not restricted to an initial amount spent for qualified property. In the previous example, Billy Barnes received $110,000 of insurance proceeds and had a realized gain of $50,000 on a destroyed building. The replacement had an initial cost of $90,000, leaving $20,000 of unspent proceeds. The result would be $20,000 of recognized gain if nothing more were done. However, it is the *total* cost of the replacement property within the allotted time period that is counted. Thus, if Billy found a suitable piece of replacement property, but it was in need of refurbishment, the amount of Billy's investment in the replacement property would be the initial cost plus any additions and improvements made within the allotted time period.

Unrecognized gain reduces basis. For example, if the replacement were to cost $145,000, its basis would be $95,000 because the gain of $50,000 would be unrecognized and would reduce the basis of the replacement building. The cost of any subsequent improvements would increase the basis but would have no impact on the amount of gain recognized, since no gain would be recognized anyway.

6.7 Conclusion

A nontaxable transaction is usually preferable to a taxable transaction even though the result includes a reduction of the tax basis of the replacement assets. This, in turn, will probably mean taxable income at some point in the future. Where it appears that the replacement assets will, in turn, be sold in a taxable transaction in a few years and at a time when the taxpayer will incur substantially higher taxes on the sale, comparison of the tax costs at the two points in time may be appropriate. Thus, if the effective tax rate on $10,000 of gain would be 15% for a taxpayer during 1990, deferral of that $10,000 to 1991, when the effective tax rate

[45] IRC Sec. 1033(a)(2)(B)(ii).

[46] IRC Sec. 1033(a)(2)(A).

[47] As another example, see *Steuart Bros. Inc.* v. *Comm.* (CA4 1958), 59-1 USTC 9143, 3 AFTR2d 318.

[48] A motel and a nightclub were not similar in *Ellis D. Wheeler*, 58 TC 459.

[49] IRC Sec. 1033(g)(1).

[50] When the Omnibus Budget Reconciliation Act of 1989 was being discussed in Congress, there was a proposal to amend the rules so that it would be necessary to meet the more narrow definition of "similar or related in use or service" test rather than the broader "like kind" test, in order to qualify for a nontaxable exchange (discussed earlier in this chapter). That proposal did not become part of the law change. However, we mention it here because there is the possibility that such a proposal will be made again and could become a change in the law at some future time.

is expected to be 33% (because of higher income), might be unwise. The use of $1,500 for two years would require the payment of $1,800 more in tax. The difference is too much to pay for borrowing $1,500 for two years in most situations.

The most frequent tax-free transaction for the majority of taxpayers is the reinvestment of proceeds of sale of a principal residence. The tax must be deferred if the statutory requirements are met, which is also the case with exchanges of property for property. Deferral is elective for involuntary conversions, however, as is the one-time gain forgiveness on the sale of a principal residence for taxpayers who have reached age fifty-five.

TRUE-FALSE QUESTIONS

State whether each of the following statements is true or false. For each *false* answer, reword the statement to make it *true*.

T F 1. Borrowing money by placing a mortgage on a piece of property is not a taxable transaction.

T F 2. Tangible personal property can not be exchanged tax-free for real estate.

T F 3. A nontaxable exchange of real estate for other real estate will remain completely nontaxable even though the seller receives cash in order to equate the fair market values of the two pieces of property.

T F 4. Certain costs incurred in connection with the sale of a personal residence might be deductible as part of the moving expenses deduction, or used to reduce the adjusted sales price of the residence, but not both.

T F 5. If you own a piece of property that is mortgaged, and you exchange the property with the buyer assuming your mortgage, you will be considered to have received boot to the extent of the amount of the outstanding mortgage.

T F 6. In a nontaxable exchange, the party who realizes a loss will be able to deduct the loss even though a gain would be nontaxable.

T F 7. The unrecognized portion of gain in a nontaxable exchange will reduce the basis of the property acquired in the exchange.

T F 8. Where a nontaxable exchange is made and you transfer boot to the other party, the basis of your new asset will be the basis of your old asset plus the amount of boot given.

T F 9. If you exchange a piece of property with a basis of $10,000 for a like-kind piece of property with a fair market value of $9,000 and you also receive cash boot of $2,000, you will have to recognize a gain of $2,000.

T F 10. In order for the nonrecognition-of-gain rules to apply to an individual on a "residential rollover," the former residence must be sold within two years before or after the replacement residence is purchased.

T F 11. For boot to exist, it must be received or paid in cash.

T F 12. The "like-kind" requirement for a nontaxable exchange of properties is a less severe requirement than the "similar or related in use or service" requirement, which must be met for the replacement of property that was involuntarily converted by a casualty.

T F 13. Where a person sells a personal residence and within twenty-four months buys another principal residence which costs at least as much as the adjusted selling price of the former residence, an election can be made to have the gain not recognized.

T F 14. A loss from the sale of a personal residence is deductible as a capital loss.

T F 15. Except for real property which is condemned, the replacement period for involuntarily converted property begins on the date of destruction and ends two years after the end of the year during which gain is first realized.

T F 16. If a taxpayer is age fifty-five or over and sells a personal residence that has been used as his or her principal residence for three of the past five years, the taxpayer may elect to have the gain unrecognized to the extent of the first $125,000 of selling price.

T F 17. If a taxpayer has unrecognized gain from the sale of a personal residence as the result of the purchase of a second residence, the basis of the second residence will be reduced by the amount of the unrecognized gain on the sale of the first residence.

T F 18. The election not to pay tax on up to $125,000 of gain from the sale of a personal residence is available to a taxpayer each time a residence is sold after the taxpayer has attained the age of fifty-five.

T F 19. Where a taxpayer suffers an involuntary conversion and replaces the property with qualified property within the allotted time period, the tax law requires that any gain from the involuntary conversion must be unrecognized.

T F 20. In an involuntary conversion, if the replacement property costs less than the proceeds of the "sale," the taxpayer must recognize all of the gain that was realized from the involuntary conversion.

PROBLEMS

Problem 6-1. Eight years ago Mary Moppet inherited $30,000 in cash. On the advice of a close friend, she used the money to purchase a tract of farmland about three miles from the edge of town. Because of the construction of a new highway in that direction, the commercial and industrial growth has been rapid. The result is that Mary's property has increased in value to an estimated $250,000. Her only income from the property is rent, $2,000 each year. Mary is single and a head of household. She has three "exemption amounts," including herself. Her other income consists solely of her salary of $25,000. Her itemized deductions each year are less than the "standard deduction."

(a) Calculate Mary's tax liability. (Use 1990 rates.)

(b) What would be Mary's tax liability if she were to sell the land for $250,000 cash? What would be her after-tax gain?

Mary does not need any more cash for her living expenses. She is interested in increasing her long-term wealth and feels that real estate is the best investment. She can buy another piece of undeveloped land for $200,000. She could borrow $200,000 at 9% interest if she mortgaged the first piece of land. The second tract is also under cultivation and would generate about $8,000 per year as farm rent.

(c) Will the mortgaging of the property be a taxable transaction?

(d) Calculate Mary's tax if she purchases the second tract of land. (You may want to review the discussion in Chapter 4 concerning the deduction of interest.)

Problem 6-2. Richard Scott owns twenty-two rental properties, mainly single-family dwellings. The buying, selling, and operation of these constitute his full-time occupation. Scott's rental properties have an aggregate cost of $600,000. He has taken a total of $290,000 in depreciation over the years. The present fair value of the properties is estimated to be $725,000. Scott wants to purchase several more dwellings with an aggregate cost of $110,000. He is thinking of raising the money by selling three of his older, appreciated units. The selling price of these houses would be $85,000. He has the difference of $25,000 already in the bank. The tax basis of the houses to be sold is $30,000. Assume that Scott is and will be in the 33% tax bracket for all relevant situations. A local lending agency has offered to loan Scott up to $90,000 at an interest rate of 9% annually.

(a) What will be the tax effect of selling the three older houses to purchase the new properties?

(b) What will be the tax effect of borrowing the money to purchase the new properties?

(c) Discuss the two alternatives.

(d) Is there a possible third alternative which would be more advantageous to Scott? Discuss.

Problem 6-3. Ken Overbrook, a real estate investor, owns an industrial building site in Chicago which he has held for twelve years. The cost was $20,000 and the value is $600,000. He wants to trade it for a motel in California. Indicate what the tax results will be to Overbrook in each of the following alternative situations. (Tax results means both the recognized gain or loss for tax purposes and the basis of the new property.)

(a) Overbrook's property is owned free and clear. The motel is mortgaged for $400,000 and Overbrook will assume the mortgage.

(b) Overbrook's property is subject to a $250,000 mortgage. The motel is mortgaged for $250,000. The two properties are exchanged, with each party assuming the mortgage of the other.

(c) Overbrook's property is subject to a $350,000 mortgage which the other party will assume. The motel is unmortgaged.

(d) What would be the difference in part (c) if Overbrook paid off his $350,000 mortgage and then exchanged for the motel, receiving cash boot of $350,000?

Problem 6-4. Jane Wilcox owns an oil painting as an investment. Its basis to her is $500, and its current value is $4,000.

(a) If Jane sells the painting, will she have recognized gain, and if so, how much?

(b) Jane has tired of the painting and would like to part with it. A friend has offered to exchange with her for another oil painting by the same artist, also valued at $4,000. If Jane makes the exchange, will she recognize a gain for tax purposes? If so, how much? What will be her basis in the second painting?

(c) Assume that Jane drives a hard bargain and agrees to exchange paintings but will receive $200 cash in addition. Will she recognize a gain, and if so, how much? What will be her basis in the second painting?

(d) What if Jane exchanged her painting for a used automobile worth $4,000 which she intends to use for personal transportation? Would she have to recognize gain? If so, how much? What would be her basis in the car?

Problem 6-5. The Miltown Corp. has owned a tract of undeveloped land for twelve years with the intention of building a new factory building. Highway and population growth has not gone as expected and the site now seems inappropriate for a factory, although it would make an excellent shopping center site. Miltown is not in the shopping center business. It would prefer to sell the land and purchase a suitable factory site. The land cost $60,000 and presently has a value of $700,000. A factory site is available at an estimated cost of $740,000. (For purposes of the nontaxable exchange rules, corporations are treated the same as individuals.)

(a) If Miltown sells its present land and reinvests in the new site within a year, will the gain be recognized?

(b) If Miltown could arrange an exchange even though it would pay $40,000 boot, would the gain be recognized or unrecognized?

(c) Assume that a suitable factory site has a mortgage of $100,000. If Miltown exchanged its property, assumed the mortgage, and received $60,000 cash in exchange for its present land, what would be the tax effect?

(d) Would it make any difference if the owner used the $60,000 to reduce the mortgage to $40,000, then traded with Miltown, giving its shopping center site in exchange for the factory site subject to a $40,000 mortgage? Explain.

Problem 6–6.

(a) The following four situations are unrelated to each other but apply to a like-kind exchange of productive use or investment property. Complete the schedule.

	Adjusted Basis of Property Surrendered	*Cash Boot Given (Received)*	*FMV of Property Received*	*Realized Gain (Loss)*	*Recognized Gain (Loss)*	*Basis of New Property*
A	$35,000	0	$31,000			
B	35,000	0	56,000			
C	17,000	($5,000)	26,000			
D	40,000	6,000	63,000			

(b) Would there be any advantage in part (a) if property A were sold for $31,000, with the proceeds used to purchase the replacement property? Explain.

Problem 6-7. Mr. and Mrs. Leaf, both age fifty-three, own the personal residence where they live. They recently had the property appraised and discovered that it was worth $120,000, although they paid $80,000 cash for it just six years ago. They have made no improvements since the original purchase. They are considering several financial alternatives relative to the house since they are going on an extended (three-year) world trip. For each of the following alternatives, determine the amount of gain recognized for federal income tax purposes.

(a) Sale of the house for $120,000 cash.

(b) Sale of the house for $50,000 cash plus a $70,000 mortgage payable over twenty years. The mortgage would be transferable and bear interest at the current market rate.

(c) Exchange of the residence for undeveloped land that would be held for long-term appreciation. The land is worth $120,000.

(d) Mortgage the house for 80% ($96,000) and let it sit idle while they are gone. Invest the $96,000 in mutual funds.

(e) Give the house to their son and daughter-in-law.

(f) Convert the house to rental property and have their son manage it while they are gone.

(g) Exchange the house for $120,000 of General Motors Corporation common stock.

(h) Exchange the house for another house valued at $90,000 and receive $30,000 cash. The new house would be used as rental property.

(i) Sale of the house for $120,000 cash with immediate reinvestment of the proceeds in two pieces of rental property worth $70,000 and $50,000, respectively.

(j) Sale of the house for $120,000 cash with immediate reinvestment of $90,000 into a house that will be considered their home even though they will be gone.

(k) Will any of the answers in parts (a) through (j) change if Mr. Leaf is at least fifty-five years of age and wants to minimize current tax liability?

Problem 6-8. Merle Pitt exchanged land he owned near Springfield, Illinois, for other land near Kansas City, Missouri. Pitt's basis in the Illinois land was $400,000; he had a $370,000 mortgage outstanding against the property. The Illinois land was valued at $600,000. Ron Jones, the other party to the exchange, assumed the $370,000 mortgage. Pitt paid Jones $205,000 cash boot. The Missouri land was valued at $435,000 and was clear of debt, although Jones's basis was $200,000. Pitt and Jones both held their original property and the second property as investments.

(a) Will Pitt recognize any gain for federal income tax purposes? Explain.

(b) Will Jones recognize any gain for federal income tax purposes? What if Jones used the $205,000 received from Pitt to reduce his (Jones's) mortgage one week after the exchange? Explain.

(c) Would the result have been any different for Pitt if he had used the $205,000 to reduce the debt on the Illinois land to $165,000 prior to the exchange? Explain.

(d) Would the result have been any different for Jones if Pitt had paid off $205,000 of the mortgage, as in part (c), before the exchange? Explain.

Problem 6-9. Bob Merrill has income each year which puts him in the 33% tax bracket. This year there was a fire at one of his manufacturing plants, completely destroying a storage warehouse. Fortunately, the warehouse was empty at the time and the building itself was insured. Merrill received insurance proceeds of $1,000,000. The basis of the warehouse was $600,000. He will build another warehouse similar to the first, but increased construction costs will result in the new one costing $1,200,000. The tax rules will permit the entire $400,000 gain on the destroyed warehouse to be treated the same as long-term capital gain (Sec. 1231 gain). The new warehouse will be depreciated over a 31.5 year life, with the deduction each year equal to the basis divided by 31.5.

(a) Will Merrill qualify for the involuntary conversion rules? Explain.

(b) Explain, in detail, the decision that he faces concerning recognition of gain and the resulting tax effects.

(c) Would the analysis be any different if Merrill had a $125,000 long-term capital loss carryover to the current year from last year?

Problem 6-10. Paul Sword inherited several acres of land in 1966. His basis in the land (fair market value on the date of decedent's death) was $1,000. The land was sold to the state government for $52,500. Paul made the sale because he had been notified on February 20, 1989, that the land would be condemned in order for the state to build a new freeway. He received the full proceeds from the sale on December 1, 1990. In each of the following alternative situations regarding replacement, compute (1) the recognized gain or loss for federal income tax purposes and (2) the tax basis of the replacement property, if any. Assume that Paul will elect to defer gain in all situations where he is eligible.

(a) Paul did not purchase replacement land that will qualify him for the involuntary conversion rules.

(b) New qualified property was purchased on July 15, 1990, for $60,000.

(c) New qualified property was purchased on August 12, 1990, for $40,000.

(d) New qualified property was purchased on December 10, 1991, for $63,000.

(e) New qualified property was purchased on July 30, 1992, for $55,000.

(f) New qualified property was purchased on January 10, 1993, for $53,000. Consider two possibilities: (1) the original land was used in Paul's trade or business and (2) it was not.

(g) New qualified property was purchased on January 10, 1994, for $60,000.

Problem 6-11. Bill and Martha Fannin purchased a $56,000 house for their personal residence in 1979. Now that the Fannins have four children, the house is too small. In June of this year, they purchased another house for $120,000. In July the first house was sold for $75,000. The real estate agent was paid a commission of $5,000 on the sale. Fixing-up expenses on the former residence were $500. The Fannins are both under age fifty-five.

(a) Assume that the Fannins had a large capital loss carryover from last year. Could they elect to recognize the gain on the sale of their residence and offset the gain with the capital loss carryover in order to reduce the tax impact?

(b) For the nonrecognition of gain rules to apply, does it make any difference that the second home was purchased before the first one was sold?

(c) What is the realized gain on the sale of the residence? What is the recognized gain?

(d) What is the adjusted basis for the new house?

(e) What is the *minimum* amount that the Fannins could have spent for a new house and not recognized any gain?

Problem 6-12. Rosalind Kartel owned a tract of land near the scenic Rush River Canyon. She had acquired the property several years ago as an investment. The state planned to build a dam in the river in order to create Rush River Lake. As a result, Rosalind's property would have been 100 feet under water. She was formally notified of these plans and told that the government expected to have the land condemned. As a result, she sold the property to the state for a $60,000 gain. She plans to replace the property by buying an apartment building which will be used as rental property. All of the proceeds from the sale will be spent for the apartment.

(a) Will Rosalind qualify for the involuntary conversion rules?

(b) Would Rosalind qualify if she were to spend the money to acquire another piece of vacant land suitable for residential construction?

(c) Assuming that Rosalind does qualify for the involuntary conversion election, what period of time will she have to acquire qualified replacement property?

(d) Assuming that the answer to part (a) is "no," would Rosalind be any better off taxwise by using the proceeds of the sale to acquire another home site, waiting a year or two, and then exchanging the home site for the apartment building? (We assume, of course, that she would still be able to make the deal after the waiting period.)

Problem 6-13. Marshall Bennett owned an apartment building that was severely damaged by a tornado. The property was beyond repair and had to be razed. Fortunately, Marshall had insurance on the building and realized a gain of $200,000 from the insurance proceeds. The site is ideal for an apartment building, so Marshall plans to rebuild, using all of the proceeds ($900,000) from the insurance, perhaps even more. He will have no problem getting the new building constructed within the time limits to qualify for involuntary conversion.

(a) If Marshall spends $930,000 for the new building and elects the involuntary conversion rules, what will be the basis in the new apartment?

(b) If he does not elect the involuntary conversion rules, what will be the basis in the new apartment building?

(c) Marshall is consistently in the highest marginal federal income tax bracket. Would it seem advisable to elect or not to elect the involuntary conversion rules? (We have not discussed depreciation yet, but assume that the apartment building costs will be subject to depreciation, which is an ordinary deduction.)

(d) Assume that Marshall did not own the destroyed apartment building directly, but owned all of the stock of Bennett, Inc., which owned the apartment building. Bennett, Inc., had a long-term capital loss of $100,000 four years ago and that loss has not been offset subsequently by recognized capital gains. The federal income tax rules provide that a corporation can carry forward a capital loss for five years. If capital gains are not recognized within that period, the loss carryover is of no tax benefit. Would it seem advisable for Bennett, Inc., to elect the involuntary conversion rules with respect to the apartment building? (The corporation would pay a tax of 34% on any recognized gain.)

Problem 6-14. Carl Winslow (age fifty-seven) sold his residence this year for $50,000. He and his wife, Winnie, had lived in the house since 1970, but she was killed in an auto accident two years ago. They originally paid $22,000 for the house, but remodeled the kitchen at a cost of $2,500 in 1972. Since that time, they did not make any capital additions to the residence, only routine repairs. Carl paid a real estate agent $3,000 commission for selling the house. Three weeks before the sale, he paid $400 in fixing-up expenses. Carl has moved into an efficiency apartment rented for $300 per month. Recently Carl met an attractive widow, Martha Rudd, and he thinks there is a possibility that they might get married later. Martha owns her house, which was purchased twenty years ago for $40,000 and is presently worth $90,000. Martha and her husband had added $6,000 in capital improvements to the house over the years. Martha is age fifty-three.

(a) If Carl were to decide to purchase another residence, what is the minimum amount that he could spend without recognizing any gain on the sale, assuming that he does not take advantage of the $125,000 exclusion?

(b) If Martha were to sell her house for $90,000, what would be her recognized gain, assuming a 6% commission on the sale? (Assume that she would not replace her residence.)

(c) Can Carl elect to exclude his gain even if he does not purchase another residence? Explain.

(d) If Martha were to sell her house now, could she elect to exclude gain without buying another residence?

(e) If Carl elects to exclude the gain from sale of his house and Carl and Martha marry and move into her house, could they later sell that house and elect nonrecognition of gain without buying another residence?

(f) Assuming that Carl and Martha plan to marry someday but are in no hurry, what tax advice would you give them relative to their respective homes?

PROBLEMS WITH AN ASTERISK REQUIRE ADDITIONAL RESEARCH.

Problem 6-15.* Melvin Champion owns a coin collection that cost him $50,000. Its present value is estimated to be $300,000. Melvin has lost interest in coins but has acquired a strong interest in stamp collecting. He knows of a person who would like to sell a stamp collection valued at $250,000. In investigating the possibility, Melvin discovers that the stamps are held by a lending institution as collateral on a $100,000 loan made by the owner.

(a) If Melvin sells his coins and immediately reinvests the proceeds in a stamp collection, can he claim an unrecognized gain for all or part of his sale?

(b) Could Melvin trade his coins for the stamps even up and avoid recognizing any gain? (The current stamp owner would repay the $100,000 loan.)

(c) If the stamp owner offers to trade and pay Melvin cash of $150,000, what would be the tax effect to Melvin? (The debt on the stamps would remain, but it would be Melvin's liability to pay off in the future.)

(d) Would it make any difference if the stamp owner paid off the lender with $100,000, then traded with Melvin, paying him $50,000 cash boot?

(e) Assume that Melvin's coins are stolen and the insurance company pays him $300,000. Could Melvin purchase the stamps with the proceeds and not pay tax on his gain?

Problem 6-16.* Forest Land owned some mountain property which included timber suitable for cutting by a lumber company, Wood Cutter, Inc. Because his property had increased very substantially in value, Forest did not want to sell and incur the resulting tax. Instead, he wanted to receive like-kind replacement property. Wood Cutter did not own any property that was acceptable to Forest in such an exchange but did agree that they would acquire acceptable like-kind property within two years and transfer such property to Forest. In the meantime, Forest was to transfer his property to Wood Cutter. All that Forest received, then, was a promise, in writing, that Wood Cutter would acquire acceptable replacement property and transfer it to Forest within two years. Will such an arrangement satisfy the tax law requirements relative to a tax-free exchange? Explain.

PART TWO

THE TAXPAYER IN BUSINESS

"George is inconsolable. His collapsible corporation collapsed and he lost his hold on his personal holding company."

7

the business individual

The first six chapters of this book dealt with types of transactions that could affect almost any individual taxpayer at some time. This chapter deals with the tax problems of a person who is the sole proprietor of a trade or business. A business activity can be a part-time activity as well as full-time.

The tax return preparer, particularly the CPA, devotes much time to this category of taxpayer. Millions of individuals report business income on their tax returns for at least some of the years of their lives. Of the 107.3 million individual income tax returns filed for 1988, 13.1 million (12.2%) reported some gross income from a proprietorship.[1] While 1987 "wages and salaries" accounted for 77.8% of the adjusted gross income reported on the 107.1 million individual tax returns filed in the United States,[2] the fifth largest dollar amount of income was "business or profession net income" (Table 7-1).[3]

The profit or loss from a nonfarm business or profession conducted as a proprietorship is reported on Schedule C (see Appendix 7-A) which is an income statement much like that presented in any introductory financial accounting text. The profit (or loss) from Schedule C is included in gross income, and shown on Form 1040. Farmers use Schedule F instead of Schedule C.

[1]IRS *Statistics of Income Bulletin*, U.S. Department of Treasury Publ. 1136, Vol. 8, No. 4 (Spring 1989), Table 19, p. 113.

[2] Ibid. Table 1, p. 19.

[3]Interest was the second-largest source of adjusted gross income, accounting for 5.9% of the total. Net capital gains ranked third. Pension and annuity income ranks fourth. See Table 7-1.

7.1 Business Net Income or Loss

There are a few differences between a profit and loss statement or income statement as might be presented for financial accounting purposes and the appearance of a Schedule C. Take, for example, Billy Barnes, who operates a retail store called the Simple Company. In summary form, for financial statement purposes, the Simple Company's income and expenses might be as shown in Fig. 7-1.

This same information would appear in roughly the same form, but rearranged, on a Schedule C. In general, *any* item that would be subject to special limitations or rules will not appear on Schedule C, even though it is business related. Such items will be reflected in other appropriate places on Form 1040 and supporting schedules. This is because any deduction taken on Schedule C is, in effect, a deduction from gross income; and any income included in Schedule C is reported as ordinary gross income. To apply special rules, such as limitations, the item needs to be reported elsewhere. For example, the $2,000 expense for contributions shown in Fig. 7-1 would not be deducted on Schedule C. Rather, it would be claimed as an itemized deduction (Schedule A of Form 1040). Generally, charitable contributions are not ordinary and necessary expenses of an unincorporated business. Note, also, that the provision for collection losses (bad debts) appears in a different place. Also, the sale of business equipment will be reported on Schedule D, as would the sale of business realty. The reason is that such gain or loss must be combined with

TABLE 7-1

Individual Income Tax Returns: Selected Income and Tax Items, 1987
[All figures are estimates based on samples—money amounts are in thousands of dollars]

Item	1987
Number of returns, total	107,070,087
Returns with taxable income	86,750,436
Adjusted gross income	$2,788,010,987
Sources of income:	
Salaries and wages	$2,169,144,134
Pensions and annuities in adjusted gross income	125,352,013
Business or profession net income less loss	103,929,657
Sales of capital assets net gain less loss	133,482,635
Dividends in adjusted gross income	66,441,562
Interest received	163,981,254
Rents and royalties net income less loss	(9,082,135)
Total adjustments	$ 29,565,013
Total itemized deductions	383,917,222
Number of exemptions	217,529,986
Taxable income	1,858,714,325
Income tax before credits	$ 376,131,913
Total credits	6,107,503
Income tax after credits	370,024,410

NOTE: Detail may not add to total because of rounding and omission of some items, such as alimony and farm income.
SOURCE: Internal Revenue Service, *Statistics of Income Bulletin,* U.S. Department of Treasury Publ. 1136, Vol. 8, No. 4, Table 1, U.S. Government Printing Office, Washington, D.C. (Spring 1989), p. 19.

other Sec. 1231 or capital gains and losses as explained in Chapter 5.

Some proprietorships pay medical insurance premiums on a policy that covers just the proprietor or both the proprietor and employees. The cost to an employer for medical insurance premiums *for employees* is an ordinary and necessary business expense and, hence, deductible. That cost will appear on Schedule C, at line 14. Starting October 1990, the cost of such insurance premium applicable to the proprietor (and family) will be part of the medical expenses reported on Schedule A (see Appendix 1-D) and will be subjected to reduction by 7.5% of AGI, or no deduction if total medical expenses are equal to or less than 7.5% of AGI (see discussion at Section 3.8.2). The theory is that a proprietor cannot be an employee of himself. For 1987 through 1989, and the first nine months of 1990, however, there is a special rule allowing 25% of the cost of the proprietor's medical insurance premium to be deducted to arrive at AGI, rather than as part of the itemized deductions. The deduction appears on line 26 of Form 1040 (see Appendix 1-D) rather than on Schedule C. This deduction is explained more fully at Section 7.9 below.

Similarly, if the taxpayer owns stock or bonds, the dividend or interest income would be reported on Schedule B, not on Schedule C. The reason is that such income is "investment income" and could impact the amount of any deduction for investment interest expense. (See Chapter 3.)

7.2 Cash versus Accrual

Chapter 8 includes a discussion of accounting methods in detail. This chapter assumes that a taxpayer reports business income on the accrual basis. That means that income is reported when it is earned, not just when it is collected in cash. Students of financial accounting are familiar with this concept. Similarly, expenses are deductible when a liability has been incurred, not when cash is actually paid. A taxpayer can report *business* income on the accrual basis but report all the other items of income and deductions on a cash basis. In fact, only a very few individuals report nonbusiness transactions on the accrual basis.

7.3 Ordinary Expenditures versus Capital Expenditures

To be deductible, expenses of a business must be "ordinary and necessary." The dictionary defines "ordinary" as some variant of "commonplace." In Chapters 4 and 5 we discussed "ordinary" income and capital gain income. Both have been subject to the same tax rates since 1987,

FIGURE 7-1

BILLY BARNES, d/b/a
THE SIMPLE COMPANY

Summary of Income and Expenses
year ended December 31, 19X1

Gross sales		$575,000
Less:		
Sales returns and allowances	$ 8,000	
Provision for collection losses	3,000	11,000
Net sales		$564,000
Cost of goods sold:		
Inventory, January 1, 19X1	$ 24,000	
Purchases	366,000	
Cost of goods available	$390,000	
Inventory, December 31, 19X1	31,000	359,000
Gross margin		$205,000
Operating expenses:		
Sales salaries	$ 52,000	
Office salaries	10,000	
Rent	8,000	
Repairs and maintenance	1,000	
Taxes (except federal income)	3,000	
Advertising	20,000	
Depreciation	5,000	
Contributions and donations	2,000	
Insurance	1,000	
Delivery expense	2,500	
Store supplies	500	
Miscellaneous	3,000	$108,000
Net profit		$ 97,000

but capital losses are subject to special treatment as discussed in Chapter 5. There is another meaning for the word "ordinary" in taxes. An expenditure of money may be "ordinary," meaning currently deductible, as where rent is paid for the use of a business building, for example. This is contrasted to an expenditure of money for a long-lived asset, such as a building, which is a capital expenditure. Unlike "capital gain," however, there is no specific statutory definition of a "capital expenditure."[4]

TAX PLANNING TIP: In most cases a current deduction is preferable to a capital expenditure even if the latter results in larger depreciation deductions. If an item can be properly claimed as a repair expense rather than a capital improvement, there is usually a tax advantage. In many cases it is not clear which treatment should be given to an expenditure.

A taxpayer may repair the roof of a store building. If this merely restores the ravages of routine wear and tear, the repair expense would be deductible as an "ordinary" expense. If a new roof is installed and it is a substantial improvement over the old, so that it increases the life expectancy of the whole building, the cost would be a capital expenditure.[5] It will still result in a deduction—but the deduction will be spread out over the useful life of the roof in

[4]Treas. Reg. 1.162-1(a) reads, in part, "No such item (capital expenditure) shall be included in business expenses, however, to the extent that it is used by the taxpayer in . . . determining the gain or loss basis of its plant, equipment, or other property."

[5]See *Illinois Merchant Trust Co., Ex.*, 4 BTA 103, and *Cotton Concentration Co.*, 4 BTA 121.

the form of a *depreciation* deduction.[6] Depreciation is discussed in Chapter 9.

7.4 Ordinary and Necessary Business Expenses

Most routine *business* expenses are deducted under the authority of Sec. 162 of the Internal Revenue Code, which allows "as a deduction all the ordinary and necessary expenses paid or incurred during the taxable year in carrying on any trade or business. . . ." An ordinary expense is one that could be expected in other similar business endeavors. In other words, there must be a generally accepted business purpose. It is important to remember that the word "ordinary" used in this context is not generic in the sense that an ordinary expense for one business will be an ordinary expense of a different business. The term is used in relationship to the overall circumstances of a particular business. Thus, an expenditure that will pass the test for one business may not necessarily pass the test for a different business. Also, in order to be "ordinary," an expenditure cannot be of a type that should be capitalized. What about "necessary"?[7] Dictionary definitions include such synonyms as "essential," "indispensable," or even "involuntary." The tax meaning is somewhat less severe.

In one sense, the tax meaning of "necessary" certainly encompasses "helpful," in the sense that a deductible business expense should *contribute* to the operation of the business or the production of its income.[8] "Necessary" in this context means that there must be a reasonable connection between the expense and the business activity. The tax concept of "necessary" does not, however, go so far as to mean that a taxpayer must get by with the least expensive alternative. For example, part of a store rental expense will not be disallowed as a deduction because a different location at a lesser rent could have been used. Nor does "necessary" mean "unavoidable" in a narrow, short-run sense. A taxpayer can, for example, deduct the cost of institutional advertising, even though it is likely that eliminating such advertising would have no short-run effect on sales, and the long-run benefit, if any, is impossible to establish.[9]

Perhaps a taxpayer could travel as well by flying economy or coach class, but a tax deduction will still be allowed for first-class fare if the trip itself is for business.[10] In applying the "necessary" standard, the IRS, with some prodding from the courts from time to time, shies away from second-guessing businesspeople when they are making business decisions on an arm's-length basis. Another way of putting it is that the IRS is not permitted to "Monday morning quarterback" with respect to business expenses.

Thus, the biggest problems with deducting business expenses tend to arise when the business deductions are not clearly just business or when the business deduction being claimed is interwoven with personal elements.[11]

Sec. 162 was quoted above as the statutory authority for taking a deduction for "ordinary and necessary" business expenses. Certainly salary and wages paid to employees (including fringe benefits) will meet the test. Most businesses hire employees at some time. Perhaps it could even be said that compensation for services of employees is the most common type of business expense, and hence "ordinary and necessary." If the deduction authorization were to stop there, we might see some abuses, such as a proprietor who would hire his high school age son or daughter to sweep the floor after school for $50 per hour. The floor needs sweeping. It is "ordinary and necessary" (a) for businesses to have the floor swept and (b) to hire someone to perform that task. But at $50 per hour? Would the proprietor pay an unrelated person that amount for that task? Probably not. Sec. 162 places two limitations upon the amount of the deduction for compensation for personal services. First, the deduction claimed must be "a *reasonable* allowance for salaries or other compensation for personal services actually rendered."[12] Thus, any deduction will be allowed only to the extent of the "reasonable" amount which would be paid for the task. That leaves the question, "what is reasonable?" The answer is probably something such as, "a reasonable amount is the amount which would be paid by other similar businesses under similar circumstances to an employee who is unrelated to the employer." Second, there is a deduc-

[6]IRC Secs. 167 and 168. The terminology used by the tax rules for depreciation is "cost recovery."

[7]For an interesting analysis of these terms as provided by the Supreme Court, see *Welch* v. *Helvering* (S. Ct. 1933), 290 U.S. 111, 78 L. Ed. 212, 54 S. Ct. 8, 12 AFTR 1456, 3 USTC 1164. Also, *Lilly* v. *Comm.* (S. Ct. 1952), 343 U.S. 90, 72 S. Ct. 497, 96 L. Ed. 769, 41 AFTR 591, 52-1 USTC 9231.

[8]See *Comm.* v. *Heininger* (S. Ct. 1943), 320 U.S. 467, 64 S. Ct. 249, 88 L.Ed. 171, 31 AFTR 783, 44-1 USTC 9109.

[9]See Treas. Reg. 1.162-14. Also, *Nat. Farmers Union Service Corp.* v. *U.S.* (DC-Colo. 1967), 19 AFTR2d 840, 67-1 USTC 9234, *aff'd.* 68-2 USTC 9653 (CA10).

[10]A further test of "reasonableness" (see discussion below) must also be satisfied for business entertainment to be deductible. See *Comm.* v. *Lincoln Elec. Co.* (CA6 1949), 176 F.2d 815, 38 AFTR 411, 49-2 USTC 9388. In general, the IRS has been more vigorous in applying the reasonableness test to entertainment expenses than to other business expenses.

[11]For example, taxpayers sometimes combine a trip so that it is partly for business and partly for pleasure. Also, learning to be a pilot can be partly business and partly personal. See *Gibson Products Co., Inc.*, 8 TC 654.

[12]IRC Sec. 162 (a) (1), emphasis added. There have been hundreds of litigated cases over the years involving the issue of "reasonable" salary.

tion only "for personal services actually rendered." This means that payment made for services will not be deductible unless the business received benefit of the services.

Illegal bribes and kickbacks provide for some special rules.[13] Unfortunately, such payments are apparently "necessary" in some situations in order for business to be conducted. However, where the recipient of such a payment is an employee of any government, or governmental agency, the payor will not get a deduction. Payments made to other persons may or may not result in a deduction. If there is some enforced legal sanction against the payor of a bribe or kickback, then the payor will get no deduction. However, such a payment will result in a deduction if the payor has not violated a law or a legal regulation of the United States or a generally enforced state law by making the payment. In all cases, as with other expenses, the payor must be able to show that such a payment was "ordinary and necessary," or there will be no deduction.[14]

7.5 Travel and Entertainment

Because of the potential for obtaining tax deductions for what are essentially personal expenses, the restrictions on the deductions for some aspects of travel and entertainment deductions go beyond the "ordinary and necessary" standard. In part, this shows up in the form of rules requiring stricter documentation of such expenses. In part, it shows up in dollar limits on,[15] or complete disallowance of, some types of expenses.

Thus, no tax deduction is allowed for the cost of any entertainment facility.[16] That includes a yacht, hunting lodge or fishing camp, swimming pool, tennis court, and so on. Note that it is not the expense of the facility itself that is disallowed. It depends on the purpose for which the facility is used. None of the cost of a *facility* is deductible if it is used for entertainment. This rule applies whether the facility is owned or leased. For example, $800 spent by an executive to rent court time so that tennis matches could be arranged with business associates would be nondeductible. However, the costs of operating a tennis court by someone in the business of leasing tennis court time would be deductible. Ironically, part of the costs of belonging to a country club with tennis courts might be deductible if the club was used primarily for business purposes.[17]

Entertainment is recognized as having a legitimate business purpose when it takes the form of business meals; theater, amusement, or sporting event tickets; and dues paid to civic or professional organizations and country clubs. Accordingly, 80% of such expenses generally are deductible.[18] The 20% disallowance (which started in 1987) applies to business meals as well as entertainment. In Chapter 4, we explained that only 80% of an employee's nonreimbursed business entertainment expenses can be included in the "tier 2" miscellaneous itemized deductions. This disallowance represents congressional reaction to assertion by the Carter administration that too many taxpayers were deducting too much for business meals and entertainment and, in effect, including some personal expenditures as deductible items. The same disallowance applies to self-employed persons. Thus, for example, if Billy Barnes—self-employed—incurs $500 of expenditures for business meals and entertainment during the year, the "ordinary and necessary" test will have to be satisfied for all such expenditures first, but even then only $400 of the expenses will be deductible. In addition to applying to the proprietor's own business related meals and entertainment, the rule applies to business related entertainment and meals of employees reimbursed by the proprietor. Thus, assume Billy Barnes has an employee, Lynn Larson, who spends $2,000 during the year for business related meals and entertainment for which Billy provides 100% reimbursement. Lynn will include the $2,000 reimbursement in gross income and deduct $2,000 to arrive at adjusted gross income. (See Chapter 3.) Billy, on the other hand, can only deduct 80% of the $2,000 or $1,600. See Schedule C (Appendix 7-A) at line 25.

There is a difference between the tax treatment of an employee and that of a self-employed person with regard to such expenses, however.

[13]IRC Sec. 162(c).

[14]The burden of proof that a payment is illegal is upon the government. In other words, the taxpayer need not prove that the payment is not illegal. For an interesting case where the bribery payments were found to be deductible, see *Murray Brizell*, 93 T.C. No. 16.

[15]IRC Sec. 274(d) and Treas. Reg. 1.274-5. For example, the deduction for business gifts is limited to $25 per donee per year. IRC Sec. 274(b).

[16]IRC Sec. 274(a)(1)(B).

[17]IRC Sec. 274(a)(2)(C). Only 80% of entertainment costs are deductible. A country club membership would qualify as entertainment if used for business purposes. On the other hand, some country club memberships, such as initiation fees or the original cost, will not be deductible, even where the use is 100% for business, because the cost must be capitalized. This result occurs where the cost will be recovered when the individual leaves the club and can sell his/her membership to someone else, or be repaid by the club.

[18]IRC Sec. 162 does not mention entertainment specifically, but the deduction is well established. See, for example, *Rodgers Dairy Co.*, 14 TC 66. Sec. 274 limits or denies certain deductions for entertainment.

Both are subject to the 20% disallowance for expense of business meals and entertainment. In order to get a deduction, an employee who receives no reimbursement must (a) itemize deductions and (b) reduce all miscellaneous "tier 2" expenses by 2% of AGI. A self-employed person deducts business expenses to arrive at business net income, which becomes part of AGI. The result is that business expenses, including 80% of business meals and entertainment, are a deduction *to arrive at* AGI. Such a person could use the standard deduction and still get the tax benefit of 80% of such expenses.

Like all expenses, the tests of "business purpose" and "ordinary and necessary" must be met. These can be very subjective standards. Special documentation requirements exist for claiming a deduction for travel or for entertainment. A taxpayer must maintain *adequate* records which will show the following:

1. The amount of the expense
2. The time and place of the travel or entertainment
3. The business purpose of the expense
4. The business relationship between the taxpayer and the other party

Your authors call these documentation requirements the five W's:

1. Who (was entertained)?
2. What (was the nature of the entertainment)?
3. When (did the entertainment occur)?
4. Where (did the entertainment occur)?
5. Why (did the entertainment occur)? i.e., the business purpose.

Contemporaneous records are not required, but the nearer the records are made to the actual time of the expense, the greater evidential weight they will have for substantiation purposes.

Even if an expense passes muster as a deduction, there is another restriction on the amount that can be deducted. The deduction is limited to amounts that are not "lavish or extravagant" under the circumstances.[19] Thus, while a cocktail party hosted by a salesperson for a group of customers might result in a deduction, the amount of the deduction will be limited to 80% of those costs which are not lavish or extravagant. Here, again, the standards are very subjective. What is lavish or extravagant for one person could be normal or even cheap for another.

A special rule also applies to the deductibility of the cost or lease of a "skybox" or private luxury box such as exists in some college football fields or other athletic arenas.[20] First, of course, the taxpayer must be able to prove a relationship between that cost and the business. Without such a relationship there can be no deduction. Even if that relationship exists, the deduction is limited to the face value of non-luxury box seat tickets for the same events. (For 1988 and 1987 there was a phase-in rule which allowed the deduction to include a portion of the cost in addition to the non-luxury price.)

In some cases it may be difficult to distinguish entertainment from business gifts. Nevertheless, there is a special limitation upon the deduction of business gifts. The deduction is limited to $25 per year per person to whom business gifts are made.[21] Thus, if Billy Barnes makes a gift of $40 to a customer, the deduction will be limited to $25. There is no limit upon the number of persons to whom gifts can be made. However, all gifts will have to pass the "ordinary and necessary" test, which means that there will have to be a business purpose. In addition to the $25, gifts of signs and other promotional materials and items costing $4 or less can be deducted so long as the donor's name is imprinted on the item, e.g., mechanical pencils.

Special rules also limit an individual's deductions for attending conventions held outside the North American area.[22] There are greater documentation requirements, *and* the taxpayer must be able to show that it was as reasonable for the meeting to be held outside of the North American area as within it. Transportation deductions for foreign conventions are limited to coach or economy air fare, and transportation to and from a foreign convention site must be prorated between business and personal unless greater than 75% of the trip days are devoted to business and the foreign travel exceeds one week. No deduction can be taken for any business meeting, seminar, or convention held aboard a cruise ship, unless the ship is a vessel registered in the United States and all ports of call are in the United States or its possessions. Even then, the deduction is limited to $2,000 per year.

The difference between the deduction for domestic (U.S.) travel and foreign travel can be illustrated as follows. Assume that Billy Barnes lives and works in Portland, Oregon. A three-day

[19]Treas. Reg. 1.274-1. This limitation applies *before* the 20% disallowances.

[20]IRC Sec. 274 (l). The cost of a ticket in excess of its fair market value cannot be deducted either.

[21]IRC Sec. 274 (b)(1). If non-cash items are given, it is the fair market value which counts.

[22]IRC Sec. 274(h). Note that the limitation only applies to foreign conventions, not to all foreign business trips. It does not apply to certain of the Caribbean countries.

business trip to Washington, D.C. was required. On the fourth day, Billy decided to stay in Washington to see a professional baseball game. Since the purpose of the trip was primarily business, the *entire* cost of the transportation can be deducted, but not the costs of meals and lodging for the extra non-business day. On another trip, Billy was required to travel to London, England, for a six-day business conference. Billy decided to stay three extra days in order to see the sights. Billy must allocate the transportation costs and deduct only two-thirds since only six out of nine days were spent on business. As with the domestic travel, none of the lodging and meals for the extra days are deductible.

Generally, if a taxpayer needs to travel for business purposes and decides to fly, the cost of a first class ticket can be deducted just the same as the lower "tourist" fare. The limitation on nondeductibility of "lavish and extravagant" amounts does not apply. However, if a taxpayer travels by ocean liner or cruise ship the amount of the deduction will be limited to a per-diem rate that is twice the per-diem rate which is paid by the U.S. government to its employees who travel by ship. For example, Billy Barnes made a business trip from Boston to Miami and traveled by ship. The trip lasted four days and cost $600. If the applicable federal per-diem rate is $60, then Billy can deduct $480, which is 2 × $60 × 4. If on-board meals and entertainment are included in the cost, then the 80% limitation does not apply. If such costs are stated separately, then the 80% limitation is applied *before* the double-per-diem limitation is applied.

Where an automobile is used exclusively for business, all of the costs, including depreciation, may be deducted. Where a car is used for business and for pleasure, the deduction can be the allocated portion of the actual costs or the "short-cut" method using a standard mileage allowance, whichever is larger. This latter deduction was 25½ cents per mile for the first 15,000 miles and 11 cents per mile for those in excess of 15,000 miles for 1989. In 1990 the rate is 26 cents per mile on all business miles. There are some additional considerations and limitations of depreciation where an automobile is used for both business and personal purposes or where the car is a "luxury automobile." These are discussed in Chapter 9.

7.6 Office at Home

One of the questions which appears on a Schedule C (Appendix 7-A (a), line H) is: "Are you deducting expenses for business use of your home?" This refers to a situation where the taxpayer has an office as part of his or her personal residence. A "yes" answer may substantially increase the likelihood that the tax return will be audited. (See Chapter 19.) Why? In an office-at-home deduction situation, the business purpose and the personal purpose overlap similar to the payment of wages to a family-member-employee. As a result, the tax rules on deductions for home offices go considerably beyond the "ordinary and necessary" test.[23] To qualify as a deduction, the home office[24]

1. must be a *specific* part of the residence,[25]
2. must be used *exclusively* for business purposes,
3. must be used for business purposes on a *regular* basis,
4. must be a *principal* place of business (such as a CPA who conducts the practice from home without another place of business), or
5. must be a place where the taxpayer meets with patients, clients, or customers (such as a CPA whose principal office is downtown but who uses an office at home exclusively and regularly for meeting with clients who are located in or near the suburb where he or she resides).

Even if these tests are satisfied, the deduction for business use of the residence cannot exceed the amount of gross income derived from that use reduced by all business expenses other than expenses directly associated with the home's business use. In essence, this "gross income" limitation is the net income from the use of the home office before deducting home office-related expenses. For example, if a physician used a portion of his residence as a home office, the cost of supplies, nursing, secretarial, and other costs incurred while using the home as an office must be subtracted from gross income. Once this net income figure is determined, the business-use portion of the home office expenses is deducted in the following order:

1. mortgage interest and real estate taxes,
2. operating expenses other than depreciation (for example, utilities and insurance on the home), and
3. depreciation on the home[26]

[23]This specific expense became so crucial that Congress added Sec. 280A to the IRC in 1976.

[24]IRC Sec. 280A(c).

[25]The Tax Court has ruled that the home office does not have to be a separate room in the home. *George H. Weightman,* TC Memo 1981-301.

[26]IRC Sec. 280A. The one exception to the exclusive-use rule is a taxpayer licensed under state law and engaged in the business of providing day care for children, for individuals sixty-five or over, or for the physically or mentally incapacitated. Depreciation and other deductions can be prorated, with the business portion being the ratio of business use (in hours) to total hours available for use.

There is a logical reason for this order. Interest and taxes are deductible as an itemized deduction whether or not in connection with the home office use. If the total home office deductions exceed the gross income from the home office use, the initial deduction of interest and taxes reduces the amount of the deduction of the other two categories, thereby lessening the overall reduction in taxable income due to the home office deduction. Depreciation is last to insure no deduction for part of the cost of the home that represents personal use when the income derived from the business activity may be very small, as in the case of a business that is conducted on a part-time basis. The following example illustrates the sequence of the deductions. For purposes of illustration, the term "gross income" has already been reduced by all other business deductions.

Assume that Billy Barnes meets all of the requirements necessary to take a deduction for an office at home. The gross income derived from the business conducted from that office is $4,000. The office occupies 15% of the total house. The following data apply:

	Total	*Business Portion (15%)*
Property taxes on residence	$2,000	$ 300
Interest on house mortgage	3,500	525
Operating expenses (utilities, insurance, etc.)	1,800	270
Depreciation	2,400	360
Step 1: Deduct pro-rata taxes and interest		
Gross income		$4,000
Less pro-rata items		825
Balance		$3,175
Step 2: Deduct pro-rata operating expenses		270
Balance		$2,905
Step 3: Deduct pro-rata depreciation		360
Net income from business conducted in home		$2,545

Neither the operating expenses (step 2) nor the depreciation deduction (step 3) can be used to create a loss. In other words, if gross income were $1,200, there would be $105 left over after step 2. Therefore, only $105 of the depreciation could be deducted. If gross income were $1,000, there would be $175 left after step 1, and only $175 of the operating expenses and none of the depreciation could be deducted. Note that the effect of requiring Step 1 (deduction for pro rata interest and property taxes) is to reduce the amount of total deductions if gross income is not greater than total expenses. As explained earlier, the reason for this is that the personal portion of interest and property taxes ($4,675 in the example) will be deducted as part of the itemized deductions (see Chapter 3) even if the taxpayer did not operate a business at home.

Where the allowable deductions do exceed the income, there is a carryover to the following year for the amount of the expense that is not deductible currently. Assume, for example, Billy Barnes meets the requirements for a deduction for office-in-home for 1990. Gross income from the business is $5,000 and allowable expenses are $6,000. Billy can only deduct $5,000 of the expenses—an amount equal to income. Prior to 1987, the rules did not allow expenses in excess of income to be deducted or carried forward. Now, however, the excess of allowable expenses over gross income can be carried forward to the following year.[27] Thus, Billy has a $1,000 expense carryover to 1991.

There is one additional requirement that must be satisfied for an employee to get a deduction for the costs of an office at home. It must be established that the employer requires the employee to maintain such an office. It is not sufficient that the employer merely tell the employee that he or she is required to maintain a home office, but such a requirement must be bona fide and for the convenience of the employer. Thus, where the employer provides office space for the employee, the latter is not likely to be able to sustain a deduction even though use of the employer-provided office may be inconvenient, such as for evening or weekend use.

TAX PLANNING TIP: A deduction for an office in the home for any *trade or business can result in substantial tax savings. Careful planning is important in order to qualify for the deduction. The deduction will not be available if the office is not used* exclusively *for business purposes. It may be worth the added inconvenience or cost to use an office exclusively for business purposes rather than partly for business and partly for personal use—in order to obtain the deduction.*

7.7 Hobbies

In some financial ventures, the taxpayer has the burden of proving that there has been a

[27]IRC Sec. 280A(c)(5).

good-faith intent to make a profit.[28] This is to prevent a deduction for a net loss from an activity that is really a hobby. When losses occur year after year, a reasonable person may become skeptical about the purpose of the activity. Continuous losses will not prove fatal to a tax deduction for those losses if the burden of proof is satisfied. The taxpayer who wishes to sustain a deduction should be ready and able to prove that the loss resulted from a business or investment venture, and not from a hobby. The rules provide a *presumption* that an activity is engaged in for profit and is not a hobby if it results in a profit in at least three out of five consecutive years (or two out of seven in the case of breeding, training, showing, or racing horses).

TAX PLANNING TIP: Some people engage in an activity both because it is fun and because it might generate some profit. Where a loss is incurred for the year, the IRS might assert that the activity is not for profit and that such loss should not be allowed as a deduction to reduce other income. Where the taxpayer has several years of losses, then he will be under the burden of proving that the activity is not a hobby. If, however, there are profits—even small profits—in at least three of five years, then the burden of proof will shift to the IRS to show that the activity is not being pursued with a profit motive.

These rules do not result in disallowance of the ordinary and necessary expenses which are less than or equal to the gross income. They only limit such deductions to the amount of gross income. For example, Billy Barnes earns a salary of $40,000 but also engages in a hobby which, from time to time, results in income. Assume that the gross income is $3,000 and the ordinary and necessary expenses related to that gross income are $2,800. The expenses can be deducted so that Billy's adjusted gross income is increased by $200, the net income from the hobby. If Billy's expenses were $3,300, then only $3,000 of the expenses would be deductible, resulting in no increase or decrease in AGI. If Billy could demonstrate that the activity was not a hobby but that a profit motive existed, then the loss could be deducted against other income.

7.8 Employee Achievement Awards

Perhaps one of the most common business expenses incurred by any business is the cost of hiring employees. Unless an employee is related to the employer, the question of the reasonableness of the amount of compensation paid to the employee hardly ever arises. Thus, compensation paid to unrelated employees is fully deductible. A special rule applies, however, where an employer makes an "achievement award" to an employee.[29] If such award is made under a plan that is "qualified," then the maximum deduction that the employer can claim for any one employee for any one year is $1,600.[30] If an award is made under a plan that is not "qualified" then any deduction is limited to $400 per employee per year.

7.9 Health Insurance Costs for Self-Employed Persons

In Chapter 3 we mentioned that an employee's gross income does not include the cost of employer paid premiums for health, accident, or hospitalization insurance. The exclusion applies even if the insurance policy covers family members and spouse of the employee as well as the employee. In Chapter 4, we mentioned that where a person pays such premiums himself, that cost is part of the total medical costs and that a deduction is allowed only for such costs in excess of 7.5% of adjusted gross income. Since, generally, a person cannot be an employee of himself, a proprietor would lose both the availability for an exclusion on the one hand and get no deduction on the other hand were it not for a special rule .[31] This provision allows a self-employed person to treat 25% of the cost of health insurance premiums that apply to himself as a business deduction. The remaining 75% becomes part of the other medical expenses the deductibility of which depends upon whether (a) the taxpayer itemizes and (b) such expenses exceed 7.5% of AGI. For example, assume that Billy Barnes is self-employed and paid the 1989 premium of hospitalization insurance covering both the proprietor (Billy) and other employees.

[28] IRC Sec. 183(d).

[29] IRC Sec. 274(j).

[30] A "qualified" award is one of tangible personal property which is transferred to an employee for length of service or for safety achievement and is awarded under an employer's written plan or program which is not disguised compensation and which does not discriminate in favor of those employees who are highly compensated. The average cost of such awards cannot exceed $400 even though the deduction for an award to any one employee is limited to $1,600. A qualified length-of-service award cannot be made during the first five years or more often than every five years. An award cannot be a "qualified" safety award if such awards are made to more than ten percent of the employees.

[31] IRC Sec. 162(m). As explained earlier, this is a temporary rule which will apply to taxable years 1987 through 1989 and the first nine months of 1990. Technically, the statute allows a person to be an employee of himself for this purpose, the same as is the case for certain retirement plans. See Chapter 18.

The insurance company told Billy that the portion of the premium applicable to the proprietor and family is $1,000. Billy can include $250 (in addition to the premium which is applicable to other employees) as a business deduction for 1989. The remaining $750 will be part of Billy's personal medical costs, which may or may not increase itemized deductions, depending upon the amount of AGI. When first enacted, this change was to expire after 1989. However, the Omnibus Budget Reconciliation Act of 1989 extended the rule so that it will not apply for taxable years beginning after September 30, 1990. Calendar year taxpayers will be required to prorate the premium cost for the year 1990. For example, assume that Billy Barnes can determine that the premium applicable to the proprietor (and family) for the first nine months of 1990 is $1,800. This means that $450 (25% of $1,800) will be deductible to arrive at AGI. The premium applicable to the last three months of 1990, plus 75% of the premium applicable to the first nine months, can become part of the medical expenses reported as an "itemized" deduction.

7.10 Depreciation

Most expenditures connected with a business are deductible. The question is: "When?" The cost of a truck or a building, and other long-lived assets, will be deductible—spread out over the period of its useful life. Most readers are probably familiar with the concept of depreciation, having studied it in a financial accounting course. The tax rules are significantly different in terms of (a) the life expectancy (called the cost recovery period) assigned to assets, (b) the methods which are available to compute the annual depreciation deductions, (c) limitations upon the depreciation deduction for certain kinds of assets and (d) alternative elections that may be available regarding the cost recovery period, method of computation and other matters. Chapter 9 includes a detailed discussion of these and related matters.

7.11 Research and Development

Most readers are familiar with the concept of "present value" as it applies to income. The concept can be applied to tax deductions. Assuming no change in the tax rates, a deduction available for the current year has a greater present value than a deduction of the same amount for some future year. The same amount of tax will be saved, but the change in value comes from the timing of the tax benefit. If Congress wants to encourage business expenditures in a given area, one way to do so is to provide a deduction for such expenditures. This reduces the after-tax cost of the expenditure. If the expenditure would be deductible anyway, but spread out over future years via depreciation or amortization, one way to encourage more expenditures is to increase the present value of the deduction by allowing a deduction in an earlier year than would otherwise be the case. This is what Congress has done with regards to expenditures for research and development. The very nature of research and development expenditures normally makes any expected benefit applicable to future years rather than the current year. Nevertheless, the rules provide that such expenditures can be deducted in the year incurred, or the taxpayer can elect to capitalize them and amortize them over not less than sixty months.[32] This is so even though the business is new and as a result has little or no current income. A taxpayer who has little current income, and who would not benefit (perhaps because of low income in those years) from carrying back a net loss,[33] might wish to capitalize such expenses so as to get the benefit of tax deductions in future years when higher income levels are expected, and the tax rate may be higher.

The election is made for the first year in which R&D expenditures are incurred, and that election is binding upon future years unless the IRS grants permission to change.[34] Normally, permission to change the method of accounting for R&D will not be granted unless there is some business purpose, other than tax reduction, for the change.[35]

Note that the option to deduct research and development expenses as incurred does not extend to expenditures for land or for capital assets, even if they are used in the research or development.[36] Of course, depreciation on any such assets (except land) can be expensed.

7.12 Net Operating Losses

What happens if a business shows a loss instead of a profit? If the loss was planned, some

[32]IRC Sec. 174.

[33]An additional deduction, such as research and development costs, can create a net operating loss. A net operating loss can be carried back and claimed as a reduction of taxable income for the three previous years. IRC Sec. 172. Thus, a refund of taxes previously paid can result from a net operating loss carryback. NOLs are discussed in the next section.

[34]IRC Sec. 174(a)(3).

[35]For information that must be included in an application for change, see Treas. Reg. 1.174-3(b)(3).

[36]IRC Sec. 174(c).

FIGURE 7-2 Sequence for carrying a net operating loss backward and forward

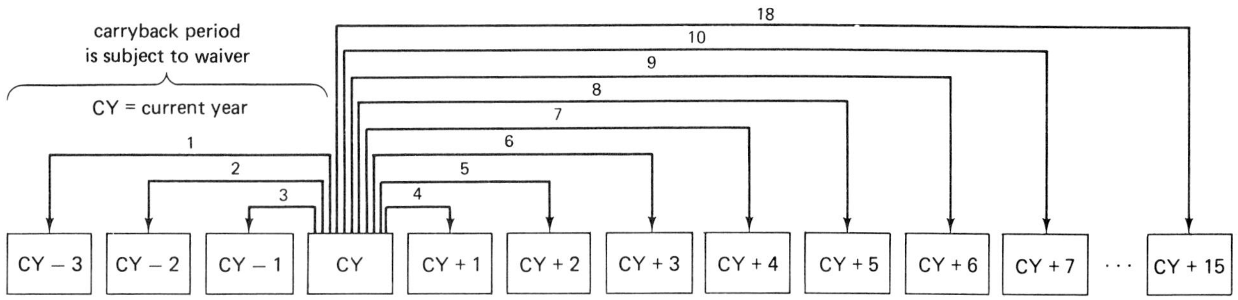

might say that the person has a tax shelter. If the loss was unplanned, the taxpayer might call it a calamity. In any event, the loss will be deducted from income from other sources in arriving at adjusted gross income and taxable income.[37]

What if the business loss exceeds other income? Then it can be carried back and taken as a deduction against taxable income of the third prior year.[38] The tax on the income of that prior year, recalculated after reduction by the carried-back loss, is then subtracted from the original tax for that year. The difference is refunded to the taxpayer. To the extent that the loss is not offset by the income of that third prior year, it can be carried to the second prior year, then the first, and then carried forward to the fifteen years following the loss year. (See Figure 7-2.) Note that the *carryback* can be waived in favor of just a carryforward.

For example, assume that the Billy Barnes Corporation has a net operating loss of $20,000 for the current year.[39] Taxable income three years ago was $30,000. The $20,000 net operating loss will reduce the taxable income of the third prior year to $10,000. The difference between the tax on $30,000 paid by the corporation, and the tax on the $10,000 recalculated taxable income, will be refunded to the corporation. If taxable income for the third previous year had been $5,000, the corporation would receive all of the tax paid for that year. The $15,000 remaining net operating loss would be carried to the second preceding year. Figure 7-2 shows the sequence for carrying a net operating loss backward and forward.

A taxpayer who has suffered a business loss can often use the cash that a tax refund would generate. A special "quickie" loss refund process allows a tentative refund to be made without IRS audit.[40] If an Application for Tentative Refund (Form 1045) is filed at or after the time the individual tax return is filed showing the loss, and if there are no omissions or computational errors, IRS must process the tax refund resulting from the loss carryback.[41] The one exception would be if the taxpayer owed taxes that had already been assessed.

A person who receives only a salary is not likely to have a tax return loss, but many businesses and individuals with business interests may have some years of profit and some of loss.

The following example will illustrate the net operating loss procedure for the Barnes Corporation. Assume that the tax return showed the following amounts of net taxable income before any net operating loss carrybacks or carryovers:

Tax Year		*Net Taxable Income Before NOL*	*Losses Applied* From 1984	*Losses Applied* From 1987
1981		$ 125,000	$125,000	
1982		75,000	75,000	
1983		25,000	25,000	
1984	Loss	(260,000)		
1985		10,000	10,000	
1986		40,000	25,000	$15,000
1987	Loss	(35,000)		
1988		5,000		5,000
1989		20,000		15,000
			$260,000	$35,000

The analysis begins with the year 1984. The 1984 net operating loss of $260,000 would first be carried back to 1981 and the balance carried over to 1982 and 1983. Refunds of the income taxes paid in each of those years would be obtained. The income of those three prior years would absorb only $225,000 of the $260,000 loss. The remaining $35,000 would be carried forward and shown as a special deduction for 1985. In 1985, only $10,000

[37]IRC Sec. 172. There is an exception where the activity is a "hobby." See Section 7.7 above.

[38]Except for the waiver of the *carryback*, discussed subsequently, the taxpayer must take the carryback and carryforward in the sequence shown in Fig. 7-2. IRC Sec. 172(b)(2).

[39]Corporation rules are discussed in Chapter 11. The basic concept of the carryback and carryforward applies to individuals and corporations alike.

[40]IRC Sec. 6411.

[41]IRC Sec. 6411(b) provides that the refund be processed within ninety days.

of the 1984 loss carryover would be used to absorb that year's profit. There would be no income tax payable for 1985. The remaining $25,000 would be carried to 1986 as a special deduction. The tax return for 1986 would show taxable income of $15,000 ($40,000 − $25,000). Tax would be paid on the $15,000. All of the 1984 loss would have been used. If not absorbed sooner, the 1984 net operating loss could be carried over through 1999. If not used by 1999 (the end of the fifteen-year carryover period), it would expire. Careful tax planning dictates not allowing a net operating loss carryover to expire.

TAX PLANNING TIP: A taxpayer who has a net operating loss carryforward should be very careful to recognize taxable income in sufficient amount to allow the NOL to be absorbed. Income could be accelerated or deductions postponed in order to have enough taxable income to use all of the NOL carryover. If the carryover is not used within the fifteen-year period, it will never result in a deduction.

In 1987 there was a $35,000 loss which could have been carried back to the third prior year. However, since that year was 1984 and there was no net taxable income that year, the loss would be carried over undiminished to 1985. Net taxable income for 1985 has been absorbed by part of the 1984 loss. Therefore, 1986 net taxable income is used next. There still remains $15,000 of net taxable income for 1986 after the 1984 loss has been applied. That $15,000 would now be absorbed, resulting in a refund of the balance of the tax paid for 1986. The $35,000 loss from 1987, reduced by the $15,000 used against 1986 income, would become a carryover of $20,000 to 1988. Since 1988 income is only $5,000, no tax would be paid for 1988. There would be a $15,000 carryover to 1989. The $20,000 taxable income of 1989 would be reduced to $5,000.

The example above was for a corporation. Whereas a corporation, by definition, has no items of income or deduction that are nonbusiness, an individual does. Appendix 7-B shows the procedure for calculating a net operating loss for an individual taxpayer. The purpose of the net operating loss provisions is to allow a tax benefit for (1) only business losses sustained and (2) only a net economic loss from taxable transactions for the year. A necessary prerequisite for an individual to have a net operating loss is to first have a negative taxable income. However, having a negative taxable income does not mean that there is a net operating loss. For example, if adjusted gross income were $10,000 and the allowable itemized deductions and exemption amount(s) were $11,000, there would be a negative taxable income of $1,000, but no net operating loss. If a negative taxable income exists, then some adjustments are necessary in order to determine if there is a net operating loss which can be carried back. It may also be necessary to make some adjustments to the taxable income of the year *to which* a net operating loss is carried in order to determine how much of the taxable income of that year may be absorbed by the loss carryback or carryforward. Some deductions affected by the amount of net income are recalculated for the various years to which a net operating loss is carried. Also, for noncorporate taxpayers, the nonbusiness deductions will be eliminated in computing the net profit absorbed by the loss, except to the extent of nonbusiness income.[42]

The objective of allowing only a net economic loss means, for instance, that no deduction will be allowed for the "exemption amount(s)." This amount represents merely an arbitrary deduction allowed by Congress in the determination of taxable income, and therefore represents no actual expense which has been incurred. Consequently, this amount as well as other adjustments will have to be made to convert a negative taxable income number into a net operating loss. The NOL carryback and carryforward for individuals can be illustrated as follows:

Assume that Billy Barnes's 1989 tax return showed the following:

Dividends	$ 3,000
Business income (loss)	(10,000)
Long-term capital gains	1,600
Standard deduction	3,100
Exemption	2,000

Thus, taxable income is a negative $10,500.

In determining the portion of the net operating loss that can be carried back to 1986, the standard deduction will be allowed, but only to the extent of the nonbusiness income. In this example it will be allowed in full, because nonbusiness income is $4,600 (dividends plus LTCG). The exemption deduction will not increase an NOL.

[42]IRC Sec. 172(d).

Business loss		($10,000)
Reduced by:		
Capital gains	$1,600	
Dividends	3,000	
Total nonbusiness income	$4,600	
Less: Nonbusiness deductions	3,100	1,500
Net operating loss carryback to 1986		($ 8,500)

Using the formula in Appendix 7-B, this amount also could be calculated by adding back the personal exemption deduction to the negative taxable income. (($10,500) + $2,000 = ($8,500)).

A similar adjustment will take place in the year *to which* the loss is carried (1986 in our example), to arrive at the amount to be carried over to the next year (1987 in our example). Of course, this latter adjustment will not be necessary if the full amount of the 1989 loss is absorbed by 1986 income.

A partnership, as such, has no net operating loss. Neither does an S corporation. Instead, the partners and stockholders, respectively, are allocated a portion of the loss. If appropriate, such business losses are deductible on their personal income tax returns. Partnerships and S corporations are discussed in Chapters 10 and 11, respectively.

A net operating loss's value depends on the effect of the tax carryback in the year to which it will be carried. The right to take a carryback can be waived by an election filed with the tax return of the loss year.[43] Such a waiver may be available when the carryback year is, for instance, one where the marginal tax rate was low, while it is anticipated that as a carryover the loss will be utilized at a high rate. Where the carryback is waived there is still a fifteen-year carry forward period.

TAX PLANNING TIP: A taxpayer with a net operating loss should consider the possibility of waiving the three-year carryback and using the loss only as a carryforward. Such a waiver could be valuable in tax savings if the marginal tax rate expected for future years is significantly higher than the marginal tax rate for prior years.

Future profits are more valuable to a business with an unused net operating loss carryover than to a business without such a carryover. This can be illustrated as follows: Assume that a corporation has a net operating loss of $50,000 with only one year left within which to deduct it. Without the loss carryover, a $50,000 profit in the following year would bear a tax of $7,500 (15% of $50,000). With the loss carryover, a $50,000 profit in the next year would result in no tax. Thus, the loss carryover can be viewed as a contingent asset. It is contingent because future profits are necessary in order for the tax savings to be realized. If profit does not result in the following year, the loss deduction will be lost forever. If at least $50,000 of taxable income does result, the full $7,500 tax which would otherwise be due is saved. This often leads corporations with NOL carryovers to acquire profitable businesses. The acquired business operation, hopefully, will still be profitable, but the NOL carryover will result in reduced tax. Such a corporation, then, may be willing to pay a higher price for a profitable business than another potential buyer without an NOL carryover. The net operating loss provision of the tax law, therefore, could be a substantial factor in the decision to rehabilitate an ailing business rather than to abandon it.

Congress felt that the concept explained here gave rise to "trafficking" in loss corporations. Consequently, in 1986 the rules were amended to place a limit upon the amount of corporate loss carryover that can be deducted after a significant ownership change. Such limitations are covered in Chapter 13.

There is a limitation upon the amount of loss deduction where the proprietor is not "at risk" with respect to the debts of the business. To be "at risk" means that the business owner will have to pay the debts of the business if there are not enough assets within the business to do so. A person will not be "at risk," for example, if the lender can collect an outstanding loan only by repossessing the property that was pledged or mortgaged rather than requiring the business owner to repay. Also, a loss is deductible by a taxpayer only if his or her interest in the business is "active" rather than "passive." (Note the question on line I of Schedule C, Appendix 7-A(a) where the terminology is "material participation," referring to active involvement in the business.) However, even though a loss from a "passive" business activity is not currently deductible, there is a carryover of that loss to a subsequent year when the taxpayer either (a) has a profit from that business or (b) sells his or her interest in the business. These matters, generally referred to as "tax shelter" considerations, are discussed in Chapter 17.

The distinction between "active" and "passive" investment also arises in connection with a person who invests in rental property, for example. The tax law defines the operation of rental property as "passive" with resulting limitations on the deductibility of any loss. There is an exception for

[43]IRC Sec. 172(b)(3)(C). Such an election is irrevocable.

losses up to $25,000 providing that the taxpayer "actively participates" in the rental activity, *and* has gross income of less than $100,000. These tax rules and the related tax planning strategies are discussed more fully in Chapter 17 also.

7.13 Inventories

As in financial accounting, taxpayers who sell merchandise (manufacturers, wholesalers, and retailers) calculate the cost of the merchandise sold by taking into account the cost of merchandise still unsold at the end of the year.[44]

The significance of inventory can be illustrated by the following example. What is the impact of decreasing the December 31, 19X1 inventory from $31,000 to $26,000? The answer: a $5,000 reduction in the net profit for the year. Because of the direct impact of the year-end inventory valuation on net profit, there are some prominent questions which are asked on the income tax return for a business. (See Appendix 7-A(a) lines E, and G and Appendix 7-A(b), Part III.) One deals with the method of valuing inventory. A taxpayer can elect to use either the cost method or the lower of cost or market method.[45] Once such a method is selected, however, a change to an alternative method is allowed only with the IRS's permission. Another question deals with method of inventory, i.e., first-in, first-out (FIFO) or last-in, first-out (LIFO) assumptions. LIFO is available only if cost is used.[46] If a taxpayer has been using FIFO and wishes to change to LIFO, such a change can be made without prior IRS approval. Any other change, such as from LIFO to FIFO, requires that the IRS grant approval for the change.

Another question on the tax return concerns any changes which were made in the determination of quantities, costs, or valuations between opening and closing inventory, since consistency of method is as important for tax purposes as is the particular method itself. Inventory is an important area of IRS audit interest because of the potential for taxpayer manipulation of profit figures.[47]

TAX PLANNING TIP: The lower of cost or market method has generally been considered a conservative method of accounting for balance sheet and credit purposes. It is not necessarily desirable for income tax purposes. Reductions in income for the current year in which inventory is reduced are offset by comparable decreases in the cost of goods sold in the following year. This is so because the ending inventory for one year must be the beginning inventory for the following year. If next year should be a year of higher marginal tax rate, the deferral of income to next year could result in more tax being paid for the two-year period as a whole. The choice should be reviewed carefully.

It is not unknown for taxpayers to estimate inventory values, or to reduce inventory valuations arbitrarily to reflect "obsolescence" or similar factors, or even to price inventories on a purely arbitrary basis.[48] The tax concept of "lower of cost or market" offers little justification for any such practices.[49] The tax concept of "market" means the "current bid price prevailing at the date of the inventory for the particular merchandise in the volume in which usually purchased by the taxpayer. . . ."[50] Inventory methods and other methods of accounting are discussed in more detail in Chapter 8.

7.14 Farmers

Although farmers are business managers, the nature of farming differs so much from other types of business that there are some special tax provisions which apply, including the following:

1. The ability to report rent received in the form of crop shares as income when converted to cash, not when received.[51]
2. Farmers receiving feed grain payments for two crop years in one year can sometimes report the second-crop-year payments in ten equal annual installments.[52]

[44]The rules for inventories are contained in IRC Secs. 471 and 472 and the Regulations thereunder.

[45]Treas. Regs. 1.471-3 and 1.471-4.

[46]The LIFO election is provided in IRC Sec. 472. The authors assume that the reader has a general familiarity with those methods from a principles of financial accounting course.

[47]There are two basic requirements under Sec. 471. Inventory accounting must (1) conform as nearly as possible to the best accounting practice in the trade or business and (2) clearly reflect income.

[48]See, for example, *Thor Power Tool Co.* v. *Comm.*, 99 S. Ct. 773, 43 AFTR2d 79-362, 79-1 USTC ¶ 9139. On occasion the IRS has attempted to change a taxpayer's ending inventory without a corresponding change in the beginning inventory. The courts have not allowed this. See, for example, *Bayne City Lumber Co.*, 10 BTA 382, and *John L. Ashe, Inc. v. Comm.* (CA5 1954), 214 F.2d 13, 45 AFTR 186, 54-2 USTC 9472. Current laws may differ. IRC Sec. 481.

[49]A taxpayer was not allowed to reduce inventory value by one-third each year even though done consistently. *Jack Rose*, 42 TC 755.

[50]Treas. Reg. 1.471-4(a).

[51]Treas. Reg. 1.61-4. If crop shares are fed to livestock, the value of the crop shares is rental income. Rev. Rul. 75-11, 1975-1 CB 27.

[52]TIR 762, Para. 55,027 P-H Fed. 1965.

3. Deduction of soil and water conservation expenses, subject to a ceiling of 25% of farming gross income (with carryovers of unused amounts).[53]
4. Estimated taxes need not be filed or paid until January 15 of the following year, or estimated taxes can be dispensed with entirely if the final 1040 is filed by March 1—but at least two-thirds of the taxpayer's gross income must come from farming or fishing.[54]
5. Deduction of fertilizer and related items when purchased without regard to when such materials will actually be applied to the land, except to the extent that prepaid expenses exceed 50% of the deductible farming expenses for the year.[55]
6. Exception to the general rule that taxpayers who are engaged in manufacturing must capitalize all direct *and* indirect costs into inventory.[56]

Some types of farming and farmers have been singled out and given less favorable tax treatment than others. For example, expenses for replanting groves, orchards, or vineyards destroyed in a natural disaster can be expensed rather than capitalized. This contrasts sharply with other types of farming activity such as raising cattle. In addition, a taxpayer who is not actively involved in farming may run into limitations on deductibility of prepaid farm expenses. However, this "limited entrepreneur" provision generally will not affect an individual farmer unless he or she does not actively participate in the farm's management or is a limited partner.[57]

7.15 Rental Property

As a general rule, the ownership and operation of rental property is a trade or business for tax purposes.[58] Rental and royalty income is usually reported on a different tax schedule (Schedule E) from that used by a business (Schedule C) or that used by a farm (Schedule F). The reason is that there are some expenses that are unique to the operation of rental property. However, Schedule E is also used to report the income or loss from a partnership (discussed in Chapter 10), income or loss from an "S" corporation (discussed in Chapter 11), and income or loss from an estate or trust (discussed in Chapter 14).

7.16 Retirement Plan Deductions

A self-employed person can create an Individual Retirement Account (IRA), contribute to the plan, and obtain a tax deduction for up to $2,000.[59] Where only one spouse is employed, the deduction can be as much as $2,250, if each has an account.[60] Self-employed persons can cover themselves to this limited extent without extending any retirement coverage to their employees.[61] Persons who are employees are also eligible to contribute to an IRA and deduct the amount, subject to the same $2,000 or $2,250 limitation, providing that they are not an active participant in an employer-financed retirement plan. Even if they are participants in another plan and their income is below a certain level, they can contribute and deduct for an IRA payment. If income is above that level, there is a phase-down of the maximum amount which can be contributed and deducted. The details of these requirements were discussed in Chapter 3.

One arrangement that a self-employed person can make for contributions to a retirement fund for employees is called a Simplified Employee Pension (SEP). Instead of maintaining a qualified plan, the employer contributes to the employees' IRA. One advantage of such an arrangement is the simplified administrative procedures that apply.

A Self-Employed Retirement Plan (sometimes called an H.R. 10, a Keogh plan or a profit sharing plan) allows a more generous retirement plan contribution. However, all of the self-employed person's employees who have three or more years of service, with some exceptions, must also be covered by the plan. Generally, such employees must be covered on a basis comparable to that of the self-employed person. There are two types of plans, defined contribution and defined benefit. Under a defined contribution plan, the amount contributed to the plan is defined, such as specific dollar amount or a percentage of salary. Under such an arrangement, the maximum that can be contributed and deducted by a self-employed person is the lesser of $30,000 or 20%

[53] IRC Sec. 175. This treatment requires that the expenditures be consistent with a plan approved by the Department of Agriculture's Soil Conservation Service.

[54] IRC Sec. 6654(i).

[55] IRC Sec. 180. and Sec. 464(f).

[56] IRC Sec. 263A(d).

[57] IRC Secs. 464 and 461(i).

[58] IRC Sec. 183 provides that there shall be no deduction for an activity if such activity is not engaged in for profit. Thus, in some cases, ownership of rental property may not result in a deduction. For example, a person renting a house to a brother for less than the fair market value may not deduct interest, taxes, operating expenses, or depreciation. Rev. Rul. 75-14, 1975-1 CB 90.

[59] IRC Sec. 219. If self-employment income is less than $2,000, a person can contribute all or part of such income to an IRA, but not more than self-employment income. There are several alternative investment opportunities available to the taxpayer for this money. Perhaps the most simple is a savings account at a bank or savings and loan association.

[60] IRC Sec. 219(c)(2). No more than $2,000 can be contributed to the account of one spouse.

[61] IRC Sec. 408.

of net earnings.[62] Under a defined benefit plan, the amount of the retirement benefits are determined and then a set of assumptions are made regarding the determination of the necessary contribution in order for the plan to have adequate funds to pay the targeted benefits. Under this latter plan, the maximum contribution is the amount needed to fund a retirement pension of not over $98,054 (for 1989). This may seem like a strange number. It started as $90,000 and has been adjusted each year for inflation.

The price for the employer's getting additional tax deductions to help fund his or her retirement is the requirement that amounts also be contributed to fund the retirement of the employees. A self-employed person can contribute to both an IRA and an H.R. 10.

The deductions for IRA plans and "Keogh" plans are from gross income to arrive at adjusted gross income. Thus, a deduction is available whether the taxpayer "itemizes" deductions or uses the standard deduction. (See Form 1040, lines 24, 25, and 27 at Appendix 1-D(a)).

A more complete discussion of employee benefit plans, including plans for self-employed persons, is presented in Chapter 18.

TAX PLANNING TIP: An employee who qualifies should consider creating an IRA account. This permits putting aside as much as $2,000 for retirement without paying currently any income tax on that amount and on its earnings. If the employee is in the 33% bracket, for example, the $2,000 would bear $660 in tax. Thus, the $2,000 investment only costs $1,340 after taxes. Of course, the retirement benefits will be taxed when withdrawn from the fund, but that could be many years away. Amounts less than $2,000 can also be contributed and deducted.

7.17 Credits

Tax credits have been used by Congress from time to time for the purpose of stimulating the economy or of enticing businesses to expend money in certain ways. For example, prior to 1987, the tax law allowed a credit of 10% of the cost of certain "qualified investments," (primarily equipment) which was purchased for use in a business. The credit was 6% for certain automobiles and light duty trucks. This investment tax credit (ITC) was based upon the cost of new property, and up to $125,000 of the cost (per year) of used property. The fundamental idea behind enactment of the ITC was to motivate businesses to purchase certain assets, which in turn would result in (a) employment for those persons who produced the assets and (b) a general modernization of America's business assets, which in turn would make U.S. businesses more competitive in the world economy. In 1986, Congress felt that those purposes were less pressing than previously, or that the credit was not the most appropriate way to achieve the goals. Also, repeal of the credit would result in an increase in tax on businesses, which was a significant goal of the Tax Reform Act of 1986 (TRA 86). Although not enacted until October, 1986, TRA 86 repealed the credit for tax years after 1985. However, because of its relationship with the depreciation deduction, we will discuss it briefly again in Chapter 9.

7.18 General Business Credit

This credit consists of the sum of the following specific credits:[63]

The targeted jobs credit

The credit for investment in low-income housing

The credit for alcohol used as fuel

There are some other components, including a credit for part of the costs of rehabilitation of older buildings, a credit for 10% of investment in solar, geothermal, and ocean thermal property, and a carryover for investment tax credit (ITC) which was unused in prior years. Again, these matters will be presented as part of Chapter 9.

Although we do not begin a specific discussion of the taxation of partnerships and corporations until later chapters, we would be remiss at this point if we did not point out that the general business credit applies to those taxpayers as well as to individuals who operate proprietorships.

There is a limitation on the amount of the general business credit with a carryover where the amount exceeds what can be used to reduce tax for the current year. That limitation is explained after we discuss each of the credits which make up the general business credit.

[62]IRC Secs. 401, 404, and 412. Some texts that say that the deduction limit is 25% of "earned income" explain that "earned income" is determined *after* the deduction. But 25% of earned income after deducting the pension contribution *is* 20% of earned income before that deduction.

[63]IRC Sec. 38.

7.18.1. Targeted Jobs Credit

Enacted to entice businesses to hire employees from among the so-called "hard core" unemployable persons, the "targeted jobs credit" was scheduled to expire after 1985. It was extended for one year. Then, TRA 86 reenacted the provision with some modifications from the earlier version.[64] The Omnibus Budget Reconciliation Act of 1989 extended the application of the credit again. It is still temporary, however, currently scheduled to apply to wages paid to qualified employees who began work before October 1, 1990. Thus, 1990 will be the last year unless Congress extends the rule again.

The credit is 40% of the first $6,000 of salary or wages paid to certain employees during the first year of employment by the employer. This one year period begins on the date of employment rather than being related to the employer's taxable year. There is no limit on the number of eligible persons who can be hired. Therefore, there is no maximum total credit.

To illustrate the credit for wages or salary paid to one eligible employee, assume that Billy Barnes—using a calendar tax year—hired a qualified person on March 1, 1989. If Billy paid at least $6,000 to that employee during 1989, Billy would have taken a credit for 40% of $6,000, or $2,400 for the year. There would be no credit for salary or wages paid to that same person for the following year. Also, if the rate of pay were such that less than $6,000 were paid during the first twelve months of employment, there would be no credit for compensation paid after the person had been an employee for twelve months. On the other hand, if Billy hired the employee on December 1, 1989, and paid $1,000 for that month, the credit for 1989 would have been $400. If the employee were paid at least $5,000 for work in 1990, Billy's 1990 credit would be $2,000. There would be no credit for any compensation paid after November, 1990, because the first year of employment would have passed. There is no credit if the person is employed less than 90 days or has completed less than 120 hours of work.[65]

As its name implies, there are certain "targeted" groups from which an employer needs to hire in order to be eligible for the credit. These are:

Vocational rehabilitation referrals

Economically disadvantaged youths, Vietnam-era veterans, and ex-convicts

Social Security (supplemental) Insurance recipients

General assistance recipients

Youths participating in a cooperative education program

Eligible work incentive employees

Involuntarily terminated CETA (Comprehensive Employment and Training Act) employees

Qualified summer youth employees

Employers are required to have made a good faith effort to determine if a new employee qualifies by coming from one of these categories.

Compensation paid to an employee is not eligible for the credit if that employee is related (a family member) to the employer. Also, if an employee had previously been hired by the same employer at a time when the employee was a member of a targeted group, salary or wages will not qualify. This latter restriction prevents an employer from firing an employee and rehiring that same person in order to get the benefit of the credit a second time.

Wages expense must be reduced by the amount of the credit. (See line 27 at Appendix 7-A(a).) Consequently, an employer is not required to take the credit and can elect to deduct all of the compensation instead. For example, assume that Billy Barnes hired one qualified employee and paid $7,000 during the year. The credit would be the maximum of $2,400 (40% of $6,000). Billy's wages expense deduction, however, would be $4,600 ($7,000 − $2,400). Consequently, Billy might elect to expense the entire compensation and not claim the credit.[66]

TAX PLANNING TIP: An election is available to take the targeted jobs credit and reduce wages expense by the credit or not to claim the credit and expense the entire amount of wages. An employer who hires a person or persons from the targeted group needs to evaluate the tax benefit of the two alternatives. The tax benefit of a credit is a given dollar reduction in income tax—but subject to certain annual limitations. The tax benefit of a deduction for wages or salaries depends upon the marginal tax rate of the employer.

[64] IRC Sec. 51.

[65] There are exceptions for certain economically disadvantaged summer youth employees.

[66] IRC Sec. 51(j). However, such an election would only make sense when other credits would bring total credits above the maximum deductible general business credit.

7.18.2. Credit for Investment in Low-Income Housing

Purchasers of residential rental property that qualified as low-income housing for 1987 were allowed a credit of 9% each year over a 10-year period.[67] The credit was available for newly constructed buildings as well as for the costs of rehabilitation. In the latter case, the rehabilitation cost per living-unit must have been at least $2,000. Where a taxpayer purchased existing low-income housing, that was placed in service more than ten years previously, there will be a credit of 4% each year even if there are no rehabilitation costs incurred.[68]

For example, assume that Billy Barnes owns some low-income housing units that were rehabilitated during 1987 at a cost of $50,000. The 1987 credit was 9% of $50,000, which is $4,500. The credit will be $4,500 in each of the following nine years as well. This is designed to provide Billy with a tax reduction which has a present value of approximately 70% of the costs incurred.

Where the construction or rehabilitation is financed with tax-exempt bonds or similar government subsidies, the credit will be 4% each for the 10-year period rather than 9%.

The credit also is available for housing projects that are placed in service during 1988, 1989, and 1990, as well as for those that were placed in service during 1987. However, for years after 1987, the credit percentages will be adjusted each month. The purpose of the adjustment is to provide a credit that will yield a present value (over a ten-year period) equal to:

> 70% of the eligible basis of new buildings that are not federally subsidized, or are substantially rehabilitated, or
>
> 30% of the eligible basis of new buildings that are federally subsidized, and for the cost of existing buildings.

For example, the percentages applicable for property placed in service in October, 1989, were:

> For a present value of 70%: 8.98%
>
> For a present value of 30%: 3.85%

Thus, if Billy rehabilitated 20 units of low-income housing (not federally subsidized) at a cost of $100,000 and placed them into service in October, 1989, the credit would be equal to 8.98% of the cost, or $8,980 each year for ten years. However, for 1989 (the first year) the credit would have to be prorated for that part of the year the units were in service. That part of the $8,980 that was not allowed for 1989 will be allowed in the eleventh year, 1999.

Where the credit is claimed for low-income housing, the unit or units must continue to qualify as low-income housing for a period of 15 years. If not, there will be recapture of the credit. Recapture means that the taxpayer will repay the amount of the credit to the IRS. For example, assume that Billy Barnes claimed a 1987 credit of $10,000 and after five years the living units no longer qualified as low-income housing. Billy would have to repay the $10,000 in that fifth year.

7.18.3 Research and Experimental Expenditures Credit

Since 1981, the tax law has allowed a credit for increasing expenditures for certain research and experimental activities.[69] Enactment of the credit was itself experimental, and it was viewed as temporary from the start. It was originally scheduled to expire at the end of 1985, but the TRA '86 extended it through 1989, and the Omnibus Budget Reconciliation Act of 1989 extended it again through the end of 1990.[70]

The key factors in determining the amount of the credit are:

1. The amount of the credit is 20% of the "qualified research expenditures."
2. The expenditures that qualify are only those that exceed a "base amount" (generally the past three-year average).
3. There is a limitation on the qualified expenditures which is tied to the average gross receipts over prior years.

[67] IRC Sec. 42. The credit will be 9% for property placed in service during 1987. For property placed in service after 1987, the credit rate will be adjusted monthly by the Department of Treasury. The percentage which a taxpayer will use will be the percentage which applied to the month during which the property was placed in service. The credit rate will be designed to provide the taxpayer with a credit which will yield, over a ten year period, a present value equal to 70% of the cost of the purchase or rehabilitation. The definition of low-income housing is somewhat complex. For example, one of the tests is that at least 20% of the living units in a project must be occupied by individuals who have income of 50% or less of the median income in the area.

[68] Where the 1987 rate is 4% (i.e., where there was governmental subsidy) the credit for post-1987 periods will be based upon the month the property was placed in service and will be designed to yield, over a ten-year period, a credit equal to 30% of the costs.

[69] IRC Sec. 41

[70] For tax years beginning before 10-1-90 and ending after 9-30-90, the credit will be prorated.

TAX PLANNING TIP: Taxpayers should (a) be aware of the kinds of expenses which will qualify for the "research credit" and (b) make provision in their accounting system to identify those costs in order to have the necessary information to claim the credit. Where a decision to incur research expenses is pending, the impact of the resulting tax reduction should be taken into consideration along with the expected "out-of-pocket" before tax costs.

For example, assume that Barnes, Inc. made qualified research expenditures during the current year of $400,000. The average such expenditures during the past three years was $300,000. Thus, there was an increase of $100,000. Normally, the credit would be $20,000, which is 20% of the increase. However, the credit may be reduced as a result of the relationship of prior such expenditures to prior gross receipts. Assume that average research expenditures for the years after 1983 was $320,000, and the average gross receipts for that same period was $15,000,000. That ratio is 2.1%.[71] The "base amount" for Barnes, Inc. is 2.1% times the average gross receipts for the previous *four* years. Assume that the average gross receipts for the past four years is $16,000,000. Thus, the "base amount" under this limitation is $336,000 instead of $300,000. The qualified expenditures for the current year exceed the "base amount" by $64,000. Thus, the credit is 20% of $64,000, which is $12,800, instead of $20,000.

"Qualified" research expenditures are:

(a) those which are paid by the taxpayer (as contrasted with expenditures which were funded by a governmental agency),
(b) paid for research conducted with the U.S.,
(c) for research and development in the experimental or laboratory sense.

In order to meet this third test, the research must rely upon principles of physical, biological, engineering, or computer science, must be experimental and related to a new or improved function, performance, reliability or quality, and must apply to a new or improved business component. Thus, research involving such matters as style, marketing, social sciences or humanities, or efficiency studies will not qualify.

[71]The ratio, called the "fixed-base percentage," cannot exceed 16%.

7.18.4. Credit for Alcohol Used as Fuel

This credit is $.60 per gallon for each gallon of alcohol which is used by a taxpayer as a fuel in a trade or business or is sold at retail by the taxpayer and placed in the fuel tank of a vehicle.[72] This credit is scheduled to expire for the sale or use of such fuel after December 31, 1992.

7.18.5. Credit Limitation

As noted above, the use of the general business credit is subject to certain limitations. The credit can be used to reduce up to $25,000 per year of income tax, plus 75% of tax in excess of $25,000. Where the credit is more than can be used in the current year, carryback and carryforward of the unused portion is allowed in a manner similar to the net operating loss carryback and carryforward discussed earlier in this chapter. However, carryback of that part of the credit that is attributable to investment in low-income housing is limited to 1987 and later.

For example, assume that Billy Barnes has a 1990 tax liability *before credits* of $90,000. The sum of the components of the general business credit, before limitations, is $76,000. The limit on the credit is:

$25,000 + 75% ($90,000 − $25,000) = $73,750

Therefore, Billy's tax liability for 1990 is $16,250, which is $90,000 − $73,750, and there is a carryback to 1987 of the 1990 unused credit of $2,250. If the 1987 tax, for example, were only $1,000, then the $1,000 would be refunded to Billy, and there would be a carryback to 1988 for the remaining $1,250 of the 1990 credit.

7.18.6. Foreign Tax Credit

The basic idea of the foreign tax credit is to allow a credit to a person who has had to pay income tax to a foreign country on income that is also subject to U.S. tax.[73] This credit is not limited to businesses, and is not subject to the limitations imposed on the general business credit. Generally, the U.S. tax is reduced by the amount of the tax

[72]IRC Sec. 40. The user credit will not apply where there was a credit for a sale at the retail level. The statute defines alcohol for this purpose as that which is at least 190 proof. Where the proof is between 150 and 190, the credit will be $.45 per gallon. A $.60 per gallon credit is also available to taxpayers who use alcohol in the production of a qualified mixture, which means a mixture of gasoline and alcohol, the so-called "gasohol."
[73]IRC Secs. 33 and 901.

paid to a foreign country. However, generalizations are hazardous in this area. There are limits on how much of the foreign tax credit can be used. These mainly reduce the usable credit when the foreign tax rate exceeds the U.S. tax rate. Also, the United States may have a treaty with a particular country which provides for special rules for income earned in that country by persons also subject to U.S. tax. In such cases, treaty law always takes preference over domestic tax law. The foreign tax credit will be discussed more completely in Chapter 13 because most taxpayers who use the credit are corporations.

7.19 Social Security

Those persons who have received a wage or salary income are familiar with the withholding that the employer is required to make for social security (FICA) taxes. For 1988 and 1989, the rate of such withholding was 7.51%. That rate applied to the first $48,000 paid to each employee during 1989. For 1990, the maximum amount an employee will have withheld is $3,924 (7.65% of $51,300). Most employees are aware of the fact that the employer is required to "match" that amount so that the total tax that is paid is double that which has been withheld from the employee's compensation. For example, if Billy Barnes has a 1990 salary of $30,000, then $2,295 will be withheld, but Billy's employer will pay a total tax of $4,590 to the Social Security Administration. (The tax is actually paid to the IRS, which transfers the funds to the Social Security Administration.)

Self-employed persons are required to pay social security tax also, but since there is no employee-employer relationship the self-employed person must pay the entire amount. However, the rate is not the same as for persons who are employees. Self-employed persons paid (for 1989) 13.02% of their self-employment income. The maximum amount that was subject to such tax was the same, i.e., $48,000. Therefore, $6,250 was the maximum a self-employed person paid for this tax in 1989.

The maximum amount subject to social security tax will increase in future years based on the Consumer Price Index. For example, the 1990 maximum rate on self-employment income is 15.3% applied to a maximum of $51,300.

The self-employment tax is paid with the income tax. See line 48 of Appendix 1-D(b). A self-employed person can deduct the social security tax that is paid for persons who are employees of the self-employed person. However, a self-employed person cannot deduct the social security tax paid on his own self-employment income, just as an employee does not get any deduction for social security tax that is withheld from salary or wages.

7.20 Unemployment Tax

Another tax (sometimes referred to as FUTA for Federal Unemployment Tax Act) that must be paid by employers is the unemployment tax.[74] This tax applies only to the employer, and many employees are not aware that this tax is part of the cost incurred by an employer to hire an employee, because there is no withholding. The purpose is to establish funds to be paid to persons during temporary periods of unemployment. The tax applies only to the first $7,000 paid to each employee each year. The maximum 1990 rate is 6.2%, which means that the maximum 1990 cost per employee is $434. Of the 6.2%, 0.8% is paid to the federal government to administer the unemployment benefits program, and the remainder (5.4%) is paid to the state to provide funds to pay benefits and for the administrative costs at the state level. The state's portion of this tax can be reduced, down to as low as 0.10%, if the employer establishes a record of not having ex-employees file for unemployment benefits. Thus, for example, an employer might pay as little as 0.90% of the first $7,000 ($63) per employee.

For 1991, the maximum rate is currently scheduled to be changed to 6.0% and 0.6% respectively, for a maximum of 6.6% of the first $7,000 of salary or wages paid to each employee. Reductions in the amount paid to the state will still be applicable.

7.21 Review

At this point, refer to the first two pages of Form 1040, which is shown in Appendix 1-D. You should by now understand the basic meaning of almost every item on those pages.

[74]IRC Secs. 3301, 3302, and 3306.

TRUE-FALSE QUESTIONS

State whether each of the following statements is true or false. For each *false* answer, reword the statement to make it *true*.

T F 1. A taxpayer who does not keep contemporaneous records is permitted to estimate the amount of the deduction for business-related travel and entertainment expenses.

T F 2. A taxpayer, who incurs $100,000 of qualified research expenditures during 1990, generally is allowed a tax credit of $20,000, assuming that the average qualified research expenditures over the past three years were $60,000.

T F 3. To obtain a deduction for an office in the home, a taxpayer must have a specific part of the residence devoted to office use and use it regularly and exclusively for business purposes.

T F 4. If a taxpayer takes a deduction for an office in the home, the deduction can be more than the gross income derived from the business conducted from that office.

T F 5. The cost of repairing a roof on a business building will be an ordinary expense if the life expectancy of the business building is increased as the result of the repair.

T F 6. No business entertainment expense deduction is available for entertainment which is lavish or extravagant, and no deduction is available for an entertainment facility.

T F 7. The deductibility of business gifts is subject to the same tax rules as business entertainment in general.

T F 8. If a taxpayer is going to take a deduction for a business convention that was held outside the North American area, he or she must prove that it was as reasonable for the convention to be held in that location as it would have been for it to be held in the North American area.

T F 9. A single person who is not a participant in an employer retirement plan and who has a profit from a proprietorship of at least $2,000 can contribute up to $2,000 into an Individual Retirement Account and can deduct that amount to arrive at adjusted gross income.

T F 10. Research and development expenditures must be capitalized and amortized over a period of not less than sixty months.

T F 11. As a general rule, a taxpayer who incurs a "net operating loss" may offset it against income of the three previous years and/or the next fifteen years.

T F 12. If a taxpayer has a net operating loss that he or she would prefer not to carry back to prior years, an election can be made to waive the carryback and to carry the loss forward only.

T F 13. A business which finds that it is ordinary and necessary to make a bribe to a local government official in order to conduct business with that government may deduct the bribe as a business expense.

T F 14. Where a proprietor hires his or her son to work in the business, the amount of the deduction for wages expense will be limited to what that son would be able to earn doing similar work for an unrelated employer.

T F 15. Congress has imposed additional documentation requirements (i.e. maintenance and retention) upon businesses which incur expense for travel and entertainment because that is an area where people might attempt to disguise personal expenses as business expenses.

John

T F 16. If a proprietor reimburses an employee for business meals and entertainment expenses incurred by that employee, then the proprietor will be able to deduct 100% of such payments as ordinary and necessary business expense.

T F 17. If a person conducts an enterprise which is determined to be a hobby rather than a "for profit" venture, that person will not be able to deduct any of the expenses incurred in connection with that activity.

T F 18. If an employer maintains a qualified "achievement award" plan, and under the terms of that plan makes an award valued at $500 to an employee, the amount which the employer can deduct will be limited to $400.

T F 19. If an employer pays hospitalization insurance premiums on a policy which covers both himself and his employees, the amount which can be claimed as a business expense deduction will be limited to 25% of the cost of the premiums applicable to the coverage on himself and his family.

T F 20. An employer who hires a "targeted jobs" employee will be able to take a credit equal to 50% of the salary or wages paid to that employee during the first year of employment.

PROBLEMS

Problem 7-1. Alice Collins operates a part-time cosmetic sales business from her home. She has a room which is used regularly and exclusively for that purpose and which is 12% of the total floor space of the house. The following data are available for the property and the business:

Net profit of business, not counting any deduction for office in home	$7,300
Interest on mortgage of house	8,200
Utilities and insurance for house	1,300
Depreciation (for entire house)	5,000
Property taxes for house	1,200

(a) What will be her deduction for office in home?

(b) What would the result have been if her net profit from the business (before deduction for the office in home) had been $1,600?

(c) Explain any carryover of nondeductible "loss."

Problem 7-2. Jim O'Neal is a sole proprietor. He operates a small real estate agency located in Los Angeles, California. Which of the following items will qualify as a deductible expense? (Identify and explain.)

(a) Cost of a fishing boat used to entertain clients

(b) Cost of a tennis country club membership

(c) Cost of professional football tickets to a game in Los Angeles attended with a client

(d) Cost of lunch by himself while working in a client's office in Seattle, Washington

(e) Cost of lunch by himself while working in a client's office in Los Angeles

(f) Cost of lunch in San Diego with a prospective client

(g) Cost of lunch in Los Angeles with an established client.

Problem 7-3. Roosevelt Harkin operates a small business which resulted in a loss of $12,000 for 1990. In addition, you have collected the following information for the year 1990 for Mr. Harkin:

Total dividends received	$2,000
Total interest received	3,000
Mr. Harkin's filing status	single

(a) To which year will Mr. Harkin's net operating loss be carried?

(b) Explain what recomputations will have to be made in the amount of taxable income for the year *to which* the 1990 NOL will be carried before the amount of tax refund can be determined.

(c) Explain the circumstances under which you might recommend to Mr. Harkin that the carryback be waived in favor of a carryforward *only*.

Problem 7-4. John Robinson is employed by the City of Megopolis as a sanitary engineer foreman. Because he is busy most of each day supervising personnel, John does the paperwork of his job at his home during the evening. He does not do this every day, but on the average he spends about eight hours per week doing such work in the spare room that he furnished as a small office. The office is used exclusively for this purpose. The city does not require that John maintain an office at home.

(a) Will John be allowed a deduction for the cost of maintaining the office, which costs him $800 for the year?

(b) Would there be a different result if John were self-employed and operating as an independent contractor with the city? (Assume that the office as described is John's only office.)

Problem 7-5. Larry Gipple incurred a net operating loss (NOL) of $40,000 in his TV repair business this year. During each of the past three years, Larry's taxable income on a joint return was $10,000, $16,000, and $14,000, respectively. Larry's chief competitor has just gone out of business. As a result, Larry is sure that his taxable income in each of the next five years will be a minimum of $45,000. (For purposes of this problem, assume that all years involved had and will have the same tax rates. Use 1990 rates.)

(a) If Larry elects to have his $40,000 NOL carried back, what will be his refund? (For purposes of the calculation, ignore the interest which the IRS would pay and assume that the $40,000 NOL is the amount determined after the adjustment explained in Sec. 7.12 of this Chapter.)

(b) If Larry elects to waive the carryback and have the loss carried forward only, how much tax will be saved next year assuming his taxable income will be $45,000?

(c) Would you advise Larry to use the NOL as a carryback or to elect to carry it forward only?

Problem 7-6. Janet March is an executive with a local advertising agency. In June of last year, Janet went to a business meeting in New York City. Her total expenses for the trip were $750. (For purposes of this problem, assume that there were no meals or entertainment.) The firm had a long-standing policy of reimbursing any employee for business trips immediately upon return and application to the company treasurer. Janet was busy after the trip and neglected to make the claim. Upon reviewing her tax records this year, in preparation for filing last year's tax return, she discovered the oversight. She filed the claim and received the $750 from her employer.

(a) May Janet claim a deduction for the business trip on last year's tax return?

(b) Must the $750 received this year be included in Janet's gross income?

(c) Would the answer be any different if Janet intentionally failed to apply for reimbursement?

(d) Assume that Janet was self-employed as an advertising consultant. Her agreement with one of her clients is that she will be paid at an hourly rate for her services and will receive reimbursement for expenses incurred on behalf of that client. She went on the New York business trip on behalf of this client. She postponed billing the client for the cost of the trip until the tax year after the trip took place. Accordingly, she did not receive reimbursement until the year after the trip. Can she deduct the cost of the trip in the year the costs were incurred? Will the reimbursement be income in the year received?

Problem 7-7. John Allen went to work as an employee for Ace Manufacturing Co. John was required to drive a new car and had to borrow the money to purchase it. The Ace sales manager promised John that Ace would reimburse him for the interest on the loan since the car was a condition of employment. During the year, John incurred and paid $600 in interest on the new car loan. He was not able to deduct the interest as an itemized expense because it is not residential interest. When John applied for the reimbursement of the interest, the company denied him the payment.

(a) Is the interest a business deduction that could be taken from gross income rather than as a part of the itemized deductions?

(b) Can John claim a bad-debt deduction?

Problem 7-8. Liz Barret owns several rental houses in addition to her primary business, which is interior decorating. Her taxable income last year was $45,000. Liz qualifies as a head of household. Liz is thinking of selling one of the houses that she owns as rental property. She would reinvest the proceeds in another house, also to be used for rental purposes. The older house would sell for $60,000 and would result in a $40,000 gain. She has no capital losses to offset the gain. (Use 1990 rates throughout.)

(a) If Liz has $45,000 of other taxable income again this year, calculate the amount of additional tax that will result from the sale of the rental property.

(b) Liz has thought about transferring the house to a corporation which she would create to own and manage some or all of her rental property. Transfer of property to a corporation that she would own would be a nontaxable exchange for the corporate stock. Since corporations pay a tax as follows, and her corporation would have no other income, it would not make any difference whether the corporation held the property for more than six months prior to sale.
Corporate tax rate:

15% on first $50,000 of taxable income
25% on taxable income over $50,000, up to $75,000
34% on taxable income over $75,000

Liz expects, even in the long run, that she would not use any gains from rental property for her own personal use. Gains both from sales and from normal rental operations will be reinvested in more rental property.

If Liz transfers the one house to the corporation, which in turn would sell it, what amount of tax would the corporation pay? (Assume that the corporation would have no operating expenses.)

(c) Would you advise Liz to form the corporation and have it sell the house? What if the corporation purchased additional rental property with the sales proceeds?

Problem 7-9. Phillip Harrell is an inventor. Over the years, he has developed several new ideas and received patents on them. At present, his income from royalties on these patents is such that he needs no other source of income and can devote all his time to further creative thinking and experimentation. A new project that he is about to undertake will require about eighty acres of land located in a remote area. He knows the owner of such a tract of land and believes that he could purchase it at a reasonable price.

(a) Assume that Phillip purchased the land and used it only for the purpose of his research and experimentation. Could he deduct the cost as a current expense?

(b) Under the same assumption as in part (a), could Phillip elect to amortize the cost of the land over sixty months?

(c) Assume that Phillip reaches an agreement with the owner of the land to lease it. Can Phillip take a deduction for the rental payments?

Problem 7-10. Larry Martin owns and operates Martin Manufacturing Co., a nonincorporated business. Last year, 1990, the first year of operations, Larry incurred $50,000 in research and development costs and this year he expects to incur another $50,000 of similar costs. The tax return for 1989 has not been filed yet and Larry must decide how to treat the R&D expenditures. His taxable income for prior years was as follows:

1986	$20,000
1987	16,000
1988	35,000

The taxable income for 1989 not including any expense for R&D is $26,000.

Larry has just signed a contract with a new customer. As a result he expects taxable income for 1990 to be $70,000, disregarding the R&D expenditures. (For the purposes of this problem, assume that any net operating loss carryback will not require any adjustment of taxable income figures. Calculate the tax from rate schedules even though the tax table might be required. Use 1990 rates throughout. Also, ignore the credit for research and experimental expenses.)

(a) Since this is a new business, can Larry elect to expense the R&D expenditures for 1989, which will result in a net operating loss carryback in 1986?

(b) What will be the amount of the refund if Larry decides to deduct the $50,000 R&D expenditure for 1989? (Assume that Larry files a joint income tax return. Ignore any interest.)

(c) What will be the effect for 1990 if Larry decides to deduct the R&D expenditures?

(d) If Larry elects to capitalize the R&D expenditures, what will be the effect for 1989 and 1990? (Assume that the amortization is to be made over the shortest allowable period of time.)

(e) May Larry elect to deduct the R&D expense for 1989, in order to get the refund that would result from the net operating loss carryback, and capitalize the R&D expenditure for 1990?

(f) Without knowing anything about the future for Martin Manufacturing, would you recommend that the R&D expenses be expensed or capitalized and amortized?

Problem 7-11. Doug Meeham is a CPA. Gross income was $40,000 from his professional practice during the year. Doug's wife was killed in an automobile accident the year before last. The Meehams have two children, Marsha and Joanne, ages nine and six, respectively. Both daughters have continued to live with their father.

Doug rents a six-room house for $550 per month. He has converted one of the bedrooms into an office that is used exclusively for that purpose. He has no other office. Doug has installed a separate telephone in the office. The telephone number is not the same as for the house. The office phone, including business long-distance calls, cost $220 last year. Other utilities cost $925 for the entire house for the year.

Doug owns an automobile. He drove 18,000 miles during the tax year. His records show that one-third of the total mileage was for business. Gas, oil, license, maintenance, insurance, and other expenses totaled $2,500 for the year. In addition, Doug paid $25 for parking and tolls, all of which were incurred while driving the car on business-related trips.

Doug attended the annual meeting of the American Institute of CPAs. He was away from home two days and spent $400 on transportation and lodging plus $137 for meals. Other expenses in connection with the practice for the year were as follows:

Office supplies	$310
Depreciation of office furniture and equipment	215
Postage	65
Malpractice insurance	600
Typing	360
Repairs to office equipment	40
Professional dues	110
Subscription to periodicals and tax services	850

During the summer (three months), Doug paid $200 per month to a neighborhood high school senior to be at his house to watch after his daughters. For the remainder of the year, he paid $100 per month to a neighbor to be there after school and during the early evening until he was finished with work. Other household expenses incurred include:

Hospitalization insurance	$ 560
Nonreimbursable doctor and dentist bills	430
Cash contributions to church	520
State income tax	1,450
Personal property tax	480

On several occasions, Doug took clients or prospective clients to lunch or dinner for the purpose of business discussions. His expenses in connection with this amounted to $850 for the year.

During the year, Doug sold some shares of stock for $5,500. The stock had been purchased four years earlier at a cost of $3,800.

Assuming that Doug has no other income or deductions, what is his 1990 federal income tax liability? (Calculate business net income first.)

Problem 7-12. Tom Inman is the president of Loose Loom, a manufacturer of men's clothing. Tom has asked you about expenses that may be deductible by his business, which is not incorporated. Are the following expenditures deductible? If so, indicate whether the deduction is for adjusted gross income or from adjusted gross income.

(a) Tom paid $1,000 to an investment counselor who showed him the advantages of investing the seasonal high cash balance in tax-exempt municipal bonds rather than in short-term taxable securities, and then arranged for the purchase. What if the investment counselor's fee were not so directly tied to the purchase of tax-exempt securities?

(b) Tom paid $15,000 in legal fees in an attempt to prevent a competitor from using a trademark very similar to that which Tom had developed several years ago.

(c) Tom paid $500 toward the political campaign of Sam Steed, who promised that, if elected, he would introduce legislation to restrict the import of men's clothing from foreign countries. (1) Steed was not elected. (2) Would the result be different if Steed had been elected and had fulfilled his campaign promise?

(d) Tom secretly paid $1,000 to the local high school band director because he was instrumental in getting the school board to order new band uniforms from Tom's company. Would it make any difference if the band director were an employee of a private school rather than a public school?

Problem 7-13. Richard Barry had taxable dividend and interest income for the year of $8,000 and $5,000, respectively. His business, operating a soft ice cream shop, resulted in a net loss of $16,000. His itemized deductions amounted to $9,000. He is single and has no dependents; therefore, his personal exemption deduction is $2,050 for 1990. Barry has financed his business through short-term borrowing for two years. It has been his hope all along to obtain a long-term loan, but he has found that prospect somewhat difficult. Following one lead, he contacted a Mr. Horse, who promised that long-term financing could be obtained in the amount of $100,000, but Mr. Horse would require a $10,000 "finder's fee" payable in advance and not refundable. Barry paid the fee, but despite repeated promises, Mr. Horse did not obtain the loan. Finally, Barry learned that Mr. Horse had moved to New Zealand. In prior years, Mr. Barry has had substantial amounts of taxable income and has paid all taxes due.

(a) What will be the effect on the net operating loss and itemized deductions if the $10,000 is part of Mr. Barry's itemized deductions?

(b) Will it make a difference if Mr. Barry can claim the $10,000 as a deduction *for* adjusted gross income? If so, how much?

(c) Would it be advisable to elect to waive the net operating loss carryback? Discuss.

Problem 7-14. Dave Rowley took a business trip from Atlanta to Richmond. On the return flight he left his briefcase in the terminal at Richmond. The briefcase had cost Dave $50 just the week before. It contained some important business papers which had no monetary value, especially since he had duplicates back at the office. It also contained his pocket calculator, which had a basis of $100 and a fair market value of $80. Dave paid $10 for an ad in the Richmond newspaper offering a reward for the return of his briefcase and contents. The reward was to be $50.

(a) If the briefcase and contents are not returned, will Dave be entitled to a deduction for the loss? Will it make any difference if Dave is an employee or is self-employed?

(b) Will Dave be able to take a deduction for the ad? Will it make any difference if Dave is an employee or is self-employed?

(c) If the briefcase is returned, will Dave be able to deduct the amount paid as a reward? Will it make any difference if he is an employee or is self-employed?

Problem 7-15. Sam Jefferson operates a retail appliance store. During the past summer Sam hired two economically disadvantaged youths to work in his store and warehouse. Over a period of ninety-two days they each worked a total of 530 hours and Sam paid each at the rate of $5 per hour. Assume the year is 1990.

(a) What is the significance of the ninety-two day period? What would have been the result if one had quit after working for seventy days?

(b) What will be the amount of the targeted jobs credit which Sam can claim for the year?

(c) Should Sam evaluate the possibility of making the election to deduct the entire wages expense rather than claim the targeted jobs credit?

1/6

46

PROBLEMS WITH AN ASTERISK REQUIRE ADDITIONAL RESEARCH.

Problem 7-16.* Ned Gilkinson operates a collection agency. Ned needed another accountant for his business. As was his practice for all new employees, Ned hired a private investigating firm to compile a background on the new employee, Bill Blake. Because Bill will have access to the accounting records and Ned did not want Bill to know about the investigation, Ned paid for the investigation by writing a check on his personal account.

(a) Will Ned be able to claim a deduction for the expense of the investigation of Bill? Explain.

(b) Assume that Ned's collection agency is incorporated. Rather than have the corporation pay for the investigation of Bill, Ned wrote the check on his personal checking account and made no entry on the corporate books. Will the corporation be able to claim a deduction? Will Ned be able to claim a deduction?

SCHEDULE C (Form 1040)

Department of the Treasury
Internal Revenue Service

Profit or Loss From Business
(Sole Proprietorship)

Partnerships, Joint Ventures, Etc., Must File Form 1065.

▶ Attach to Form 1040 or Form 1041. ▶ See Instructions for Schedule C (Form 1040).

OMB No. 1545-0074
1989
Attachment Sequence No. **09**

Name of proprietor | **Social security number (SSN)**

A Principal business or profession, including product or service (see Instructions)

B Principal business code (from page 2) ▶

C Business name and address ▶

D Employer ID number (Not SSN)

E Method(s) used to value closing inventory: (1) ☐ Cost (2) ☐ Lower of cost or market (3) ☐ Other (attach explanation) (4) ☐ Does not apply (if checked, skip line G)

		Yes	No
F	Accounting method: (1) ☐ Cash (2) ☐ Accrual (3) ☐ Other (specify) ▶		
G	Was there any change in determining quantities, costs, or valuations between opening and closing inventory? (If "Yes," attach explanation.)		
H	Are you deducting expenses for business use of your home? (If "Yes," see Instructions for limitations.)		
I	Did you "materially participate" in the operation of this business during 1989? (If "No," see Instructions for limitations on losses.)		

J If this schedule includes a loss, credit, deduction, income, or other tax benefit relating to a tax shelter required to be registered, check here. ▶ ☐
If you checked this box, you MUST attach **Form 8271**.

Part I Income

1	Gross receipts or sales	1	
2	Returns and allowances	2	
3	Subtract line 2 from line 1. Enter the result here	3	
4	Cost of goods sold and/or operations (from line 39 on page 2)	4	
5	Subtract line 4 from line 3 and enter the **gross profit** here	5	
6	Other income, including Federal and state gasoline or fuel tax credit or refund (see Instructions)	6	
7	Add lines 5 and 6. This is your **gross income** ▶	7	

Part II Expenses

8	Advertising	8		22	Repairs	22	
9	Bad debts from sales or services (see Instructions)	9		23	Supplies (not included in Part III)	23	
10	Car and truck expenses	10		24	Taxes	24	
11	Commissions	11		25	Travel, meals, and entertainment:		
12	Depletion	12		a	Travel	25a	
13	Depreciation and section 179 deduction from **Form 4562** (not included in Part III)	13		b	Meals and entertainment		
				c	Enter 20% of line 25b subject to limitations (see Instructions)		
14	Employee benefit programs (other than on line 20)	14		d	Subtract line 25c from line 25b	25d	
15	Freight (not included in Part III)	15		26	Utilities (see Instructions)	26	
16	Insurance (other than health)	16		27	Wages (less jobs credit)	27	
17	Interest:			28	Other expenses (list type and amount):		
a	Mortgage (paid to banks, etc.)	17a					
b	Other	17b					
18	Legal and professional services	18					
19	Office expense	19					
20	Pension and profit-sharing plans	20					
21	Rent or lease:						
a	Machinery and equipment	21a					
b	Other business property	21b				28	

29	Add amounts in columns for lines 8 through 28. These are your **total expenses** ▶	29	
30	**Net profit or (loss).** Subtract line 29 from line 7. If a profit, enter here and on Form 1040, line 12, and on Schedule SE, line 2. If a loss, you MUST go on to line 31. (Fiduciaries, see Instructions.)	30	

31 If you have a loss, you MUST check the box that describes your investment in this activity (see Instructions). **31a** ☐ All investment is at risk. **31b** ☐ Some investment is not at risk.
If you checked 31a, enter the loss on Form 1040, line 12, and Schedule SE, line 2.
If you checked 31b, you MUST attach **Form 6198**.

For Paperwork Reduction Act Notice, see Form 1040 Instructions. **Schedule C (Form 1040) 1989**

H732

Schedule C (Form 1040) 1989 Page **2**

Part III Cost of Goods Sold and/or Operations (See Instructions.)

32	Inventory at beginning of year. (If different from last year's closing inventory, attach explanation.)	**32**	
33	Purchases less cost of items withdrawn for personal use	**33**	
34	Cost of labor. (Do not include salary paid to yourself.)	**34**	
35	Materials and supplies	**35**	
36	Other costs	**36**	
37	Add lines 32 through 36	**37**	
38	Inventory at end of year	**38**	
39	**Cost of goods sold and/or operations.** Subtract line 38 from line 37. Enter the result here and on page 1, line 4	**39**	

Part IV Principal Business or Professional Activity Codes (*Caution: Codes have been revised. Check your code carefully.*)

Locate the major business category that best describes your activity (for example, Retail Trade, Services, etc.). Within the major category, select the activity code that most closely identifies the business or profession that is the principal source of your sales or receipts. **Enter this 4-digit code on page 1, line B.** (**Note:** *If your principal source of income is from farming activities, you should file* ***Schedule F*** *(Form 1040), Farm Income and Expenses.*)

Construction

Code

0018 Operative builders (for own account)

General contractors

0034 Residential building
0059 Nonresidential building
0075 Highway and street construction
3889 Other heavy construction (pipe laying, bridge construction, etc.)

Building trade contractors, including repairs

0232 Plumbing, heating, air conditioning
0257 Painting and paper hanging
0273 Electrical work
0299 Masonry, dry wall, stone, tile
0414 Carpentering and flooring
0430 Roofing, siding, and sheet metal
0455 Concrete work
0885 Other building trade contractors (excavation, glazing, etc.)

Manufacturing, Including Printing and Publishing

0638 Food products and beverages
0653 Textile mill products
0679 Apparel and other textile products
0695 Leather, footware, handbags, etc.
0810 Furniture and fixtures
0836 Lumber and other wood products
0851 Printing and publishing
0877 Paper and allied products
1032 Stone, clay, and glass products
1057 Primary metal industries
1073 Fabricated metal products
1099 Machinery and machine shops
1115 Electric and electronic equipment
1883 Other manufacturing industries

Mining and Mineral Extraction

1511 Metal mining
1537 Coal mining
1552 Oil and gas
1719 Quarrying and nonmetallic mining

Agricultural Services, Forestry, Fishing

1933 Crop services
1958 Veterinary services, including pets
1974 Livestock breeding
1990 Other animal services
2113 Farm labor and management services
2212 Horticulture and landscaping
2238 Forestry, except logging
0836 Logging
2246 Commercial fishing
2469 Hunting and trapping

Wholesale Trade—Selling Goods to Other Businesses, Etc.

Durable goods, including machinery, equipment, wood, metals, etc.

2618 Selling for your own account
2634 Agent or broker for other firms—more than 50% of gross sales on commission

Nondurable goods, including food, fiber, chemicals, etc.

2659 Selling for your own account
2675 Agent or broker for other firms—more than 50% of gross sales on commission

Retail Trade—Selling Goods to Individuals and Households

3012 Selling door-to-door, by telephone or party plan, or from mobile unit
3038 Catalog or mail order
3053 Vending machine selling

Selling From Showroom, Store, or Other Fixed Location

Food, beverages, and drugs

3079 Eating places (meals or snacks)
3086 Catering services
3095 Drinking places (alcoholic beverages)
3210 Grocery stores (general line)
0612 Bakeries selling at retail
3236 Other food stores (meat, produce, candy, etc.)
3251 Liquor stores
3277 Drug stores

Automotive and service stations

3319 New car dealers (franchised)
3335 Used car dealers
3517 Other automotive dealers (motorcycles, recreational vehicles, etc.)
3533 Tires, accessories, and parts
3558 Gasoline service stations

General merchandise, apparel, and furniture

3715 Variety stores
3731 Other general merchandise stores
3756 Shoe stores
3772 Men's and boys' clothing stores
3913 Women's ready-to-wear stores
3921 Women's accessory and specialty stores and furriers
3939 Family clothing stores
3954 Other apparel and accessory stores
3970 Furniture stores
3996 TV, audio, and electronics
3988 Computer and software stores
4119 Household appliance stores
4317 Other home furnishing stores (china, floor coverings, etc.)
4333 Music and record stores

Building, hardware, and garden supply

4416 Building materials dealers
4432 Paint, glass, and wallpaper stores
4457 Hardware stores
4473 Nurseries and garden supply stores

Other retail stores

4614 Used merchandise and antique stores (except motor vehicle parts)
4630 Gift, novelty, and souvenir shops
4655 Florists
4671 Jewelry stores
4697 Sporting goods and bicycle shops
4812 Boat dealers
4838 Hobby, toy, and game shops
4853 Camera and photo supply stores
4879 Optical goods stores
4895 Luggage and leather goods stores
5017 Book stores, excluding newsstands
5033 Stationery stores
5058 Fabric and needlework stores
5074 Mobile home dealers
5090 Fuel dealers (except gasoline)
5884 Other retail stores

Finance, Insurance, Real Estate, and Related Services

5520 Real estate agents or brokers
5579 Real estate property managers
5710 Subdividers and developers, except cemeteries
5538 Operators and lessors of buildings, including residential
5553 Operators and lessors of other real property
5702 Insurance agents or brokers
5744 Other insurance services
6064 Security brokers and dealers
6080 Commodity contracts brokers and dealers, and security and commodity exchanges
6130 Investment advisors and services
6148 Credit institutions and mortgage bankers
6155 Title abstract offices
5777 Other finance and real estate

Transportation, Communications, Public Utilities, and Related Services

6114 Taxicabs
6312 Bus and limousine transportation
6361 Other highway passenger transportation
6338 Trucking (except trash collection)
6395 Courier or package delivery services
6510 Trash collection without own dump
6536 Public warehousing
6551 Water transportation
6619 Air transportation
6635 Travel agents and tour operators
6650 Other transportation services
6676 Communication services
6692 Utilities, including dumps, snowplowing, road cleaning, etc.

Services (Personal, Professional, and Business Services)

Hotels and other lodging places

7096 Hotels, motels, and tourist homes
7211 Rooming and boarding houses
7237 Camps and camping parks

Laundry and cleaning services

7419 Coin-operated laundries and dry cleaning
7435 Other laundry, dry cleaning, and garment services
7450 Carpet and upholstery cleaning
7476 Janitorial and related services (building, house, and window cleaning)

Business and/or personal services

7617 Legal services (or lawyer)
7633 Income tax preparation
7658 Accounting and bookkeeping
7518 Engineering services
7682 Architectural services
7708 Surveying services
7245 Management services
7260 Public relations
7286 Consulting services
7716 Advertising, except direct mail
7732 Employment agencies and personnel supply
7799 Consumer credit reporting and collection services
7856 Mailing, reproduction, commercial art and photography, and stenographic services
7872 Computer programming, processing, data preparation, and related services
7922 Computer repair, maintenance, and leasing
7773 Equipment rental and leasing (except computer or automotive)
7914 Investigative and protective services
7880 Other business services

Personal services

8110 Beauty shops (or beautician)
8318 Barber shop (or barber)
8334 Photographic portrait studios
8532 Funeral services and crematories
8714 Child day care
8730 Teaching or tutoring
8755 Counseling (except health practitioners)
8771 Ministers and chaplains
6882 Other personal services

Automotive services

8813 Automotive rental or leasing, without driver
8839 Parking, except valet
8953 Automotive repairs, general and specialized
8896 Other automotive services (wash, towing, etc.)

Miscellaneous repair, except computers

9019 TV and audio equipment repair
9035 Other electrical equipment repair
9050 Reupholstery and furniture repair
2881 Other equipment repair

Medical and health services

9217 Offices and clinics of medical doctors (MDs)
9233 Offices and clinics of dentists
9258 Osteopathic physicians and surgeons
9241 Podiatrists
9274 Chiropractors
9290 Optometrists
9415 Registered and practical nurses
9431 Other health practitioners
9456 Medical and dental laboratories
9472 Nursing and personal care facilities
9886 Other health services

Amusement and recreational services

8557 Physical fitness facilities
9597 Motion picture and video production
9688 Motion picture and tape distribution and allied services
9613 Videotape rental
9639 Motion picture theaters
9670 Bowling centers
9696 Professional sports and racing, including promoters and managers
9811 Theatrical performers, musicians, agents, producers, and related services
9837 Other amusement and recreational services

8888 Unable to classify

APPENDIX 7-B

Adjustments to Convert Negative Taxable Income to NOL

Start with taxable income as a negative number. Add back the following items:

1. A net operating loss deduction from any other year.
2. The deduction for personal exemptions.
3. Nonbusiness capital losses in excess of nonbusiness capital gains.
4. Excess of nonbusiness deductions over nonbusiness income.
5. Contributions to a self-employed retirement plan.

A net operating loss results if there is still a negative number after these adjustments. If the adjustments convert the negative taxable income number into a positive number, there is no net operating loss.

8

tax accounting for business

What is includable in income? What is allowable as a deduction? What is a taxable year? These are some of the questions that were raised in previous chapters. Those chapters have also mentioned situations where the taxpayer can postpone the time when income will be recognized for tax purposes, such as by an exchange rather than a sale of investment property.

Tax accounting deals mainly with the "when" of taxation. Given that something is taxable income, "when" will it be taxable? Given that something is deductible, "when" will it be deductible? What can the business do to defer or postpone the time when income will be recognized while advancing or accelerating the time when a deduction can be taken?[1]

8.1 Cash versus Accrual

Most individuals are cash-basis taxpayers, at least as to everything except business income. That is, they report income when cash is received and claim deductions when cash is paid. For example, it is important to make cash payments for such items as charitable contributions before the end of the year. Pledges for future contributions are not deductible by a cash-basis taxpayer until payment is actually made. On the other hand, certain "charges" are considered as having been paid in the year that the charge is made. For example, assume that Billy Barnes paid a doctor's bill by charging the amount to MasterCard on December 31. That amount would be includible as medical expenses for the year the credit card was used. The theory is that Billy paid the doctor by borrowing from the bank that issued the credit card. Not all transactions involve cash, of course, so the cash-basis individual accounts for noncash items by converting them, for reporting purposes, to their fair market value cash equivalent.

Assume that Billy Barnes worked as a part-time real estate salesperson while in college. Upon graduation, Billy's employer sold Billy a tract of land for $5,000 less than the usual price for a comparable lot. The reason for the bargain sale was to compensate Billy for a job well done and to induce other college students to work hard so as to gain similar treatment. The $5,000 is additional gross income to Billy.[2]

Another example of noncash income is the barter transaction. An accountant keeps the financial records of a small beauty parlor. In exchange, the accountant's wife has her hair done at the shop for no cost each week. The accountant has gross income measured by the fair market value of the services received by his wife. The beauty parlor has gross income measured by the fair market value of the bookkeeping services received.[3]

[1]Generally, these are the objectives that result in lowering tax liability. As we have pointed out on occasion, the opposite strategy may be wise in some situations. For example, it may be wise to have income recognized this year rather than next year if this year's tax rate will be lower than next year's. This can be particularly critical in an "alternative minimum tax" year, as we shall see in Chapter 16.

[2]Treas. Reg. 1.61-2(d)(2)(i). The concept is called "bargain purchase."

[3]If both omit the transactions, there is no tax impact on the beauty parlor, for its additional income is offset by a deduction for bookkeeping services. The accountant has understated his

The cash basis of reporting income can be used by some business taxpayers as well.[4] It is available whenever inventories are not a material income-determining factor.[5] Thus, it is widely used by individual farmers (who are permitted the cash basis by law even though they may have substantial inventories),[6] professional persons, and a wide variety of service businesses.

What is the difference between the cash and the accrual basis? The normal financial accounting studied by students in college accounting courses is "accrual-basis" accounting. With accrual accounting, income is recognized when the business has a right to receive payment—whereas on the cash basis, income is recognized only when the cash (or equivalent) is actually received. Thus, on the accrual basis, income is recognized when the taxpayer renders a service to the customer (e.g., the dentist pulls a tooth), even though the customer (e.g., the patient) may not pay until sometime later.

The accrual of income and expenses follows what is sometimes called the "all events" test. That is, income or expense can be accrued when all of the events have occurred fixing the fact of and the size of the amount to be paid or to be received. Accrual of expenses requires a slightly different test. For tax purposes, an expense (and the related liability) cannot be accrued until "economic performance" has occurred.[7]

This concept of "economic performance" can be illustrated as follows. If Billy Barnes were to pay business casualty insurance premiums for three years in advance, a "pure" cash accounting concept would result in a deduction for the entire amount for the taxable year during which the payment was made. The "economic performance" modification of the cash accounting method will permit a deduction only for that portion of the premium that applies to the taxable year. Thus, there is a somewhat modified accrual method that is applied in the case of expenses that are paid in advance. The same principle applies to other expenses such as advertising, rent, interest, etc.

The cash method of accounting allows the accumulation of substantial assets on which no income tax has been paid. For example, a cash-basis CPA partnership might have $120,000 of accounts receivable on its books, of which $110,000 might ultimately be collectible. As compared with being on the accrual basis, the partners are allowed to build up these assets tax-free. The fact that their expenses are deducted only as paid poses little problem to these CPAs, or to most cash-basis taxpayers, because the *major* expenses (e.g., wages) are normally paid as incurred anyway. If necessary, they may borrow, using the receivables as collateral, to get the cash to pay the bills at year end. This maximizes tax deductions without requiring gross income to be reported for the receivables. Some expenses paid in advance by a cash-basis taxpayer must be prorated and are deductible only for the period to which they apply. For example, interest paid in advance by a cash-basis taxpayer is only deductible *as if* the taxpayer were on the accrual method.[8]

Tax planning for a cash-basis business generally involves controlling the time when bills are collected or suppliers and employees paid. Thus, the CPA partnership could reduce its income for a given year by not sending bills to clients toward the end of the year, or by not exerting efforts to collect bills. If the CPAs needed to increase taxable income for a year to absorb unusual expenses, the partnership could sell some of its receivables to a bank or finance company or step up the pace of its billing and collection activities.

Of course, the deferral that is inherent in the cash basis has coupled with it a possible day of tax reckoning. The receivables of the CPA partnership will be collected when the partnership is dissolved, and these collections will constitute ordinary taxable income. The day of reckoning may never come for a larger partnership that never terminates. Reckoning may come only in modified form for shareholders of a cash-basis corporation. As the corporation accumulates receivables, the value of stock may increase. This increase will be taxed to the shareholders when the shares are sold.

The concept of "constructive receipt" prohibits a cash method taxpayer from manipulating the receipt of cash near the year end in order to defer recognition of income until the following year. If the taxpayer has control over the receipt of cash, but does not exercise that control, the income will still be recognized in the year during which the cash became available. Thus, if a person could have picked up her salary check on December 31, but did not, there can be no deferral of the income until the following year. Note also, that even if the check is received there can be no postponement of income recognition under the theory that the

---

taxable income and could be charged with tax fraud. Both may, in addition, have improperly understated gross receipts for state or local sales tax purposes.

[4]The general rules for methods of accounting are contained in IRC Sec. 446. IRC Sec. 448 modifies the general rule by providing that certain taxpayers (C corporations, partnerships, and tax shelters) cannot use the cash method. Exceptions exist for farming businesses, qualified personal service corporations, and businesses which have gross receipts of less than $5,000,000.

[5]Treas. Reg. 1.446-1(c)(2)(i).

[6]Treas. Reg. 1.61-4. Certain corporations and partnerships engaged in farming must use the accrual method. IRC Sec. 447.

[7]IRC Sec. 461(h).

[8]IRC Sec. 461(g).

check is not "cash." The same is true with interest on a passbook savings account, for example. Since a person could have gone to the bank and withdrawn the interest, it must be included in income even if that control was not exercised. Constructive receipt does not apply unless the taxpayer was in control of the receipt. Thus, it would not apply where a salary check was placed in the mail on December 31 and the normal delivery would not result in receipt of the check until after the first of the year.

The result of the "constructive receipt" doctrine is that a cash basis taxpayer is required to include an amount in income as long as he/she *could have* received the income before year end. Related to that is a concept of control. That is, the tax rules do not premit a taxpayer to exercise his/her control not to receive the cash as a means of postponing payment of tax on the amount. An opposite concept is called the "claim of right" doctrine. Under this concept, an accrual basis taxpayer will be taxed on the receipt of cash (or other property) even though it has not been earned and the general principles of financial accounting would require recording the asset and related deferred income account. For example, assume that Billy Barnes uses the accrual method of accounting in connection with a business of leasing office buildings to tenants. A tenant pays Billy cash rent three years in advance. Billy is not permitted for tax purposes to include only one-third of the receipt in gross income and postpone the remaining two-thirds until the years when the income is "earned." As long as there is no unconditional obligation to return the money, even an accrual basis taxpayer will be required under this concept to recognize income when received and not when earned. If there is an unconditional obligation to return the amount, then there is a loan and, as explained in an earlier chapter, a taxpayer does not recognize income as the result of borrowing money.

8.2 Change in Method

A taxpayer can adopt either the cash or the accrual method in the first tax return for a new business.[9] Thus, an individual starting a new business can elect the cash method of accounting for that business if inventories are not a material income-determining factor. Once that election has been made, however, any change in method requires the permission of the IRS.[10] The same is true with all the other accounting methods we will discuss, except for the adoption of the LIFO method of inventory.[11] A business can adopt an acceptable accounting procedure on the first return involving a type of transaction. After adopting one method, change can only be made with the permission of the IRS.[12] The reason for this rule is to prohibit taxpayers from manipulating reported profits by changing accounting methods.

Change may come in either of two ways. The taxpayer may desire to change, or the IRS may compel the taxpayer to change to a method that more clearly reflects income.[13] Thus, an individual starting a new TV and appliance service business, for example, may adopt the cash basis. Years go by, and the business grows and alters. A large retail showroom is added and other major appliances are sold and serviced. Inventories become a major factor in calculating income, but will not appear on the tax return. An IRS agent auditing such a return would probably require the taxpayer to change to the accrual basis at least as regards accounting for inventory. The cash method may still be used for operating expenses. In making such a change, the major problem is to avoid either double counting or omitting any item of income or expense.[14]

Assume that Billy Barnes has been operating an appliance service business which has grown into a retail sales operation as described. Since substantial inventory exists, a change from the cash method to the accrual method is necessary. Assume that taxable income for the year of changeover is $40,000 calculated under the new method but without any adjustments for the beginning-of-the-year condition. Since Billy knew that the changeover was to take place, the accounts receivable, accounts payable, and inventory were counted at the beginning of the year. They were as follows:

Accounts receivable	$15,000
Accounts payable	12,000
Inventory	8,000

The correct taxable income for the year is $51,000, calculated as follows:

[9] Treas. Reg. 1.446-1(e)(1). There is a general requirement that the accounting method must "clearly reflect income." IRC Sec. 446(b).

[10] Treas. Reg. 1.446-1(e)(2).

[11] IRC Sec. 472.

[12] A "method of accounting" is not just cash or accrual. For example, the "percentage-of-completion" and "completed-contract" methods for long-term contracts are alternative methods. With some exceptions, a change in depreciation method is considered a change of accounting method.

[13] IRC Sec. 446(b).

[14] The rules for adjustments required by changes in method of accounting are contained in IRC Sec. 481 and the regulations thereunder. A taxpayer can be on an accrual method for sales and inventory and on the cash method for other expenses.

Taxable income (unadjusted accrual method)		$40,000
Add: Income not previously reported as income:		
Accounts receivable at start of year		$15,000
Deductions previously taken:		
Inventory at start of year		8,000
Total		$63,000
Deduct: Deductions not taken previously:		
Accounts payable at start of year		12,000
Corrected taxable income		$51,000

The changeover may cause taxable income to jump substantially. In this case the increase is $11,000. Both the tax law and administrative practice allow the taxpayer some relief from bunching the $11,000 into the one year.[15] This may involve recalculating the tax for the current and prior years on the assumption that the $11,000 is spread in some fashion over more than just one year, or it may involve reporting the $11,000 as income pro rata over the current and some number of future years agreed upon with the IRS.

8.3 Long-Term Contract Methods

Building and other construction contractors have a peculiar income determination problem because of the length of the contracts and uncertainties as to total cost until a contract is fully completed.

Normal accounting procedures impose serious practical problems. Costs are incurred as work progresses, of course, but these costs will build up as work-in-process inventory until the contract is completed. They are not expenses but increases in assets. At the same time, the contractor makes progress billings to customers and receives payments (less, perhaps, a percentage that is held back until the job is finally completed). These billings are not sales in the normal accounting meaning of "sales," because they usually do not integrate with any specific determinable amount of costs that have been incurred.[16]

The tax law provides that most taxpayers with income from long-term contracts (generally, contracts not completed in the taxable year in which entered into) must use the percentage of completion method if the contract was entered into on or after June 11, 1989.[17] Under this method, revenue and costs allocable to the long-term contract are recognized as the contract is being completed. The percentage of the total contract completed is estimated at the end of the year by comparing costs allocated to the contract and incurred during the year with the estimated total contract costs. The taxpayer may elect not to recognize revenue or costs allocable to a long-term contract until ten percent of the estimated total contract costs have been incurred.[18]

For example, assume that a contractor is engaged in building a $3,000,000 apartment building. Construction covers a three-year period:

	Year 1	*Year 2*	*Year 3*
Percentage completed at end of year	15%	70%	100%
Costs incurred during year	$440,000	$1,560,000	$700,000

By the percentage-of-completion method, which is analogous to the accrual method, the profit calculation would be as follows:

	Year 1	*Year 2*	*Year 3*
Percentage completed during the year	15%	55%	30%
Revenue earned (% × $3 million)	$450,000	$1,650,000	$900,000
Expenses incurred during the year	440,000	1,560,000	700,000
Gross profit	$ 10,000	$ 90,000	$200,000

After the contract is completed, the taxpayer must recompute the percentage of completion during each year based on the actual costs incurred during the applicable contract period. Interest cost or income is computed on the basis of the under- or overstated tax liability resulting from the percentage completion revisions. This procedure is known as the "look-back method" and applies to all long-term contracts except contracts completed within two years and with a gross contract price that does not exceed the lesser of (1) $1 million or (2) one percent of the average annual gross receipts of the taxpayer for the three taxable years preceding the year the contract was completed.[19]

A few taxpayers will be able to use their normal method of accounting which in most instances, will be the completed contract method. Under this method, no profit or loss resulting from the contract is reported until the contract is com-

[15]IRC Sec. 481(b). Relief is allowed if the increase in tax due to the adjustments is greater than $3,000 and the taxpayer used the old method in the two years preceding the year of change.

[16]A typical arrangement is that the architect or engineer certifies that a fractional part of the work is completed and the builder pays the contractor based upon a predetermined formula.

[17]IRC Sec. 460(a). For contracts entered into before July 11, 1989, the percentage-of-completion-capitalized-cost method was available. Under this method, 90% of the items with respect to the contract were accounted for under the percentage-of-completion method and 10% of the items were accounted for under the taxpayer's normal method of accounting (typically, the completed contract method).

[18]IRC Sec. 460(b)(5).

[19]IRC Sec. 460(b)(3)(B).

pleted. Eligible taxpayers are taxpayers with a contract for home construction, or any other construction if the estimate is that the contract will be completed within two years of the starting date and the taxpayer has average annual gross receipts of $10 million or less for the three preceding taxable years.[20]

One final exception deals with residential construction contracts. If 80 percent or more of the total estimated construction costs are attributable to residential construction other than home construction (for example, residential apartment complexes), then 70% of the contract may be reported under the percentage-of-completion method and 30% will be accounted for using the taxpayer's normal method of accounting.[21] Thus, if the taxpayer's normal method is the completed contract method, 30% of the costs and revenues will be recognized when the contract is completed. This hybrid method is known as the "percentage-of-completion-capitalized-cost" method.

Refer to the facts of the previous example. If the contractor chooses to use this method, then the $3,000,000 will be divided 70–30 as follows:

70% = $2,100,000
30% = $ 900,000

	Year 1	*Year 2*	*Year 3*
First portion (70%)			
Percentage completed during the year	15%	55%	30%
Revenue earned (% × $2.1 million)	$ 315,000	$ 1,155,000	$ 630,000
Expenses (70%)	308,000	1,092,000	490,000
Gross profit (70% portion)	$ 7,000	$ 63,000	$ 140,000
Second portion (30%)			
Revenue earned	—0—	—0—	$ 900,000
Expenses incurred	—0—	—0—	810,000
Gross profit (30% portion)	—0—	—0—	$ 90,000
Total gross profit for each year	$ 7,000	$ 63,000	$ 230,000

If the completed contract method is used, an adjustment will have to be made for the "alternative minimum tax" calculations discussed in Chapter 16. For alternative minimum tax purposes, the percentage-of-completion method is required.

8.4 Installment Sales

Taxation is not based solely on the receipt of money. It is based on other transactions as well. A sale of property will normally result in income based on the fair market value of the consideration received. But taxes are paid with cash and not with notes or other property. A hardship could result from having to pay tax before a transaction has produced enough cash to pay the tax. Thus, long ago some special rules were created to govern those sales in which only a part of the selling price is received in cash at the time of sale, with the balance of cash received later.[22] These rules now apply primarily to nondealer sales—that is, sales of personal property by someone who is not in the business of selling such property and sales of real estate by persons not deemed to be in the trade or business of selling such real estate. Note that the installment sales method does not provide relief in all cases. For example, assume that a transaction involves an exchange of properties that do not satisfy the "like kind" requirement for nontaxability as discussed in Chapter 6. Gain would be recognized, with a resulting tax liability, even though no cash was received with which to pay the tax.

8.4.1. Dealers

A business that normally sells merchandise on an installment basis is a "dealer" and may not elect to recognize gross profit on a sale as payments are received from the customer.

8.4.2. Casual Sellers

The installment sale method is available to sellers who are not dealers.[23] It applies to non-dealer sales of real estate or casual sales of personal property (i.e., property that is not real property) where proceeds will be received in a year following the year of sale. Thus, the method can be used by a non-dealer seller of investment property such as land or a piece of art work. A seller may elect *not* to report income as payments are received. The entire gain on the transaction is then taxable in the year of sale.

Where real estate is involved, the computations sometimes become complicated by the fact that mortgages may be assumed by the buyer or given by the buyer to the seller. A term that becomes significant in installment reporting in such situations is "contract price." That is the amount which will ultimately be paid to the seller in cash (whether as a down payment or in subsequent payments) plus the excess, if any, of the

[20] IRC Sec. 460(e)(1).
[21] IRC Sec. 460(e)(5).

[22] IRC Secs. 453, 453A, and 453B.
[23] IRC Sec. 453 and 453A.

mortgage assumed by the buyer over the seller's basis. For example, assume that a taxpayer owns a piece of property with a basis of $60,000 and which is subject to a $40,000 mortgage. The property is sold for $120,000, with the buyer assuming the $40,000 mortgage. The selling price is $120,000, but the "contract price" is $80,000. (In this example, the mortgage assumed by the buyer does not exceed the seller's basis, so there is not an excess.) If the seller's basis had been $30,000, the contract price would have been $90,000 ($80,000 that the buyer must pay to the seller, plus $10,000, the amount by which the mortgage exceeded the seller's basis).

TAX PLANNING TIP: *If a taxpayer who is not a dealer makes a casual sale of personal property or a sale of real estate and wants to elect not to use the installment sales method, the transaction should be analyzed carefully. Reporting all of the gain in the year of sale is irrevocable (except in the unlikely instance where the IRS grants special permission to revoke). If the entire transaction is reported in the year of sale because the taxpayer mistakenly believes the profit is small, or because there appear to be offsetting losses from other transactions, a change in the tax consequences as the result of an IRS audit will not allow the installment method to then be elected.*

The significance of the contract price is that it is used to determine the amount of subsequent payments that the seller must recognize as gain for tax purposes. The amount of gain that the seller will recognize as collections are received will be:

$$\frac{\text{Gross profit}}{\text{Contract price}} \times \text{Amount collected} = \text{Recognized gain}$$

COMPUTER FORMULAS: This above formula can easily be set up on the computer.

	A	B
1	Profit	*x*
2	Price	*y*
3	Collections	*z*
4	Gain recognized	(*x*/*y*)*z

Where a projection of gain recognized is prepared for several years the formula in B4 could be copied any number of times. If that were done it would be necessary to make *x* and *y* constants.

Assume the following facts: Billy Barnes (not a dealer) will sell a piece of real estate for $100,000. The tax basis of the property is $70,000. Thus, 30% of each payment will be gross profit to Billy. The buyer will pay $70,000 as a down payment and the balance in future years. In the year of sale, $21,000 must be recognized because $70,000 was received. Thereafter, Billy will recognize gross income equal to 30% of any cash received under the contract. There is a strategy that will postpone the recognition of tax for Billy, as follows:

Prior to the sale, Billy borrows $60,000, placing a mortgage on the property. (Note that Billy's debt immediately prior to the sale does not exceed the basis for the property.) The buyer assumes the mortgage and gives Billy $10,000 cash plus notes of $30,000 for the balance. (The buyer may or may not pay off the mortgage immediately.)

Selling price	$100,000
Tax basis (cost)	70,000
Gain ultimately to be reported	30,000
To be received *from buyer* (cash plus notes)—contract price	40,000
Gain as a percentage of contract price ($30,000/$40,000)	75%
Payments received in year of sale	10,000
Profit to be reported in year of sale (75%)	7,500
Profit to be reported in future years, based on 75% of payments received, as received	22,500

Notice that the tax basis in the property does not change as the result of Billy's borrowing money and using the property as collateral for the debt. The total $30,000 gain on which Billy will pay tax does not change as a result of borrowing, but the timing of the tax payments certainly will change. If Billy had owned the property with no debt, Billy would have to wait until the installment notes were collected to have the cash in hand. By borrowing on the property before the sale, Billy accelerated the acquisition of cash but reduced the tax impact. Tax will be paid on $7,500 instead of $21,000 in the year of sale.

There would be a different result if Billy had borrowed an amount in excess of basis. For example, assume that Billy had borrowed $80,000 on the property. Now, of course, the buyer would only pay $10,000 plus notes of $10,000 to make the total selling price of $100,000 after assuming the $80,000 mortgage. The $10,000 excess of the mortgage over Billy's basis would change the contract price to $30,000 ($10,000 down payment plus $10,000 note plus $10,000 excess of mortgage over basis). The amount of mortgage in excess of basis is treated as received in the year of the sale.

Contract price	$30,000
Gain as a percentage of contract price ($30,000/$30,000)	100%
Payments deemed received in the year of sale	20,000
Profit to be reported in sale year	20,000
Profit to be reported in future years based on 100% of payments received, as received	10,000

Notice that, where a mortgage assumption is involved, the percentage that is used to determine the profit on each installment payment is not the profit as a percentage of selling price but rather the profit as a percentage of the total cash payments to be received from the buyer (contract price). Yet Billy has accelerated the cash receipts by borrowing. Billy may have a contingent liability on the mortgage, using the method that defers tax, but even this can be eliminated by having in the mortgage note a contractual provision stating that Billy's liability ceases when the mortgage is assumed by a responsible individual satisfactory to the lender.

TAX PLANNING TIP: A taxpayer who is considering the sale of property, particularly real estate, should consider the possibility of placing a mortgage on the property prior to the sale, with the buyer assuming the mortgage. The result can be that the seller can obtain the same or more cash while reducing current income tax payments.

Use of the installment sale rules does not change the type of gain which will be recognized. Thus, if the asset was a capital asset, there will be recognized capital gain each year as the sales price is collected by the seller. Likewise, if the asset was an ordinary asset, the recognized gain will be ordinary as each installment is collected. "Recapture income," however, is not subject to the installment sales rules.[24] (Depreciation recapture under Sec. 1245—depreciable personal assets—was mentioned in Chapter 5. Depreciation recapture under Sec. 1250—depreciable real estate—will be discussed more completely in Chapter 9.) Where depreciable property that has been used in a trade or business is sold under the installment method, only the gain which will be treated as capital gain (called "Sec. 1231 gain") will receive the installment sales treatment. Also, all of the "depreciation recapture" will occur in the year of sale and will be added to the basis of the property for purposes of calculating the portion of gain realized that is reported under the installment method.

For example, assume that Billy Barnes (not a dealer in this kind of property) sold a piece of depreciable business equipment (a Sec. 1245 asset) for $5,000, under an agreement providing for the buyer to pay $1,000 each year, plus interest. The following data are related to the asset:

Original cost of the asset	$7,000
Depreciation deductions taken	4,000
Adjusted basis of property	3,000

A cash sale for $5,000 would have resulted in a gain of $2,000, which is the sales price less the adjusted basis. An installment sale would provide the same result because all of the gain is depreciation recapture. There is no advantage of gain deferral by use of the installment method.

If the same asset had been sold for $8,000, under terms where Billy would receive $2,000 each year, plus interest, for four years, there would be $5,000 recognized gain. Despite the installment sales contract, $4,000 gain (depreciation recapture) would be recognized in the year of sale. The remaining $1,000 gain ($8,000 – ($3,000 + $4,000)) will be Sec. 1231 gain (treated as capital gain) and will be recognized at the rate of $250 per year as the receipts are collected.

Some sellers might be tempted to increase the sales price of an asset in exchange for not charging the buyer any interest, or in exchange for charging only a low rate of interest. If the asset is a capital asset to the seller, an increase in the selling price would increase the recognized capital gain. If interest were charged on the installment sale, the seller would have interest income. Thus, such an attempt, if successful, would permit the seller to convert what might otherwise be interest income into long-term capital gain. To discourage this type of transaction, the rules provide that the seller must charge at least a minimum rate of interest.[25] If that is not done, the IRS can recalculate the gain on the transaction and can impute interest, changing the seller's gain to interest income to that extent. The buyer's purchase price is also adjusted downward, and the buyer has interest expense equal to the amount of imputed interest. Whether that interest is deductible or not will depend upon whether the interest is personal interest, business interest, or investment interest. These rules were discussed in Chapter 3.

[24]IRC Sec. 453(i).

[25]IRC Sec. 483. Generally, the maximum imputed interest rate is 9% where the debt is $2.8 million or less. For debt in excess of that amount the imputed interest is the average yield rate for U.S. government obligations. See IRC Sec. 1274A.

There is one exception, applicable to land transactions after June 30, 1981, involving family members. This limits the IRS to imputing no more than a 6% rate on the first $500,000 of land sales per year between siblings, spouses, "ancestors, and lineal descendants."[26]

8.4.3 Interest on Certain Amounts

Where non-farm real property used in the taxpayer's trade or business or held for the production of rental income is sold for more than $150,000, and the aggregate amount of receivables at the end of the year arising from such sales during the year exceeds $5 million, then interest is charged on the tax liability that is deferred through using the installment method of reporting gain on the property sales. Also, a taxpayer who sells residential lots or timeshares on an installment basis may elect to use the installment method and pay interest on the tax thereby deferred.

For example, assume that Billy Barnes sold such a piece of property for $8,000,000 in 1990 and the realized gain was $2,000,000 (25% of the sales price). Billy received $1,000,000 down payment. As the result, $250,000 of the gain was recognized in 1990, leaving $1,750,000 to be recognized in future years as the installment receivable of $6,000,000 is collected. At the end of 1990, Billy's situation satisfied the requirements for paying interest on the deferred tax on the $1,750,000. Assume (a) that Billy's deferred tax on $1,750,000 was $490,000 and (b) the appropriate interest rate was 12.2%. (The interest rate is the short-term federal interest rate for the last month of the year plus 3%.) Thus, the interest is $59,780, which is 12.2% of $490,000. (That amount will be prorated if the applicable period is less than one year.) In deciding between the alternatives of using the installment sales method or not, a taxpayer should consider:

1. The liquidity (or other) problems that will result from recognizing the entire gain for the year of sale without having received the cash necessary to pay the additional income tax.
2. The after-tax interest earned on the receivable compared with the after-tax interest expense that will result from the interest on the deferred tax.

8.4.4. Financial Accounting

Under generally accepted accounting principles, the accrual method is normally used for reporting sales for financial purposes. When the installment method is used for tax reporting purposes and the accrual method is used for financial statements, the "profit" is not the same for the two calculations. This results in a deferred income tax item on the financial statements, which represents the tax liability to be paid as future collections are received. Reconciliation of taxable income and accounting net income for corporations is discussed in Chapter 12.

8.5 Cost Recovery

The seller who receives a contingent price obligation of the buyer, such as a contract for deed, which does not have an ascertainable fair market value, may in rare cases use an alternative method of reporting gain.[27] This involves treating all payments received as tax-free recoveries of investment until the tax basis of the property sold has been received.[28] The entire amount received thereafter is profit.

If Billy, from a previous example, owned the property outright and had not borrowed before the sale, then sold the property for $100,000 (basis of $70,000), the gain would have been $30,000. If it could be shown that the notes had no determinable value, there would be no gain recognized until the $70,000 basis was recovered, and then all subsequent receipts would be taxable gain. The Internal Revenue Service, however, generally takes the position that it is only in a rather unusual situation that the promise of the buyer has no fair market value.[29] In the example, Billy would have to show that the $30,000 notes could not be sold for any amount. Where that is the case, the selling price of $100,000 is questionable.

TAX PLANNING TIP: Profit on sales with contingent or uncertain payments can still be reported as collections are made. It is generally better to estimate the ultimate contract price, report profit based upon that amount, and report an additional profit or deduct a loss if ultimate payments differ from the estimate. This involves less tax risk than attempting the cost recovery approach.

[26]IRC Sec. 483(e).

[27]Treas. Reg. 1.453-6(a)(2). The method originated in the Supreme Court decision of *Burnet* v. *Logan* (S. Ct. 1931), 2 USTC 736, 9 AFTR 1453.

[28]There is some authority to the effect that this method applies only to sales of real property. *Baltimore Baseball Club, Inc.* v. *U.S.* (Ct. Cl. 1973), 481 F.2d 1283, 73-2 USTC 9549, 32 AFTR2d 73-5352.

[29]Rev. Rul. 58-402, 1958-2 CB 15. See Senate Finance Committee Report on IRC Sec. 453(j) added by the Installment Sales Revision Act of 1980.

INVENTORIES

8.6 Required Capitalization of Inventory Costs

Prior to 1987, it was common practice to expense, rather than capitalize, certain indirect costs which were not related to the manufacturing process. Under rules in effect since 1986, that is no longer possible, and such costs have to be capitalized.[30] The effect of these rules is to increase inventory and defer the deductibility of certain costs until the inventory is sold. Some costs that must be capitalized under these rules include:

Costs related to the purchasing of material that will be part of inventory

Costs related to repackaging, assembly, and processing of goods in the taxpayer's possession

Costs associated with the storage of inventory, such as rent or depreciation, insurance, and taxes on warehouse facilities

A portion of the general/administrative (including pension and profit-sharing cost) expenses related to the purchasing, repackaging, etc., and storage of inventory

Certain interest costs associated with the above functions.

These rules required a significant change in the accounting procedures used by some taxpayers. For example, it had been standard practice to expense the entire accounting function (primarily wages and salaries of accountants, clerks, secretaries, etc. in the accounting department) of a business rather than to relate and capitalize some of those costs to inventory. Now it is necessary to identify those costs related to such functions as purchasing, processing, and storage and to capitalize such costs into the inventory.

Thus, assume that Barnes Manufacturing Co. incurred $100,000 in purchasing and storage costs for inventory. Other relevant data are:

Beginning inventory (using FIFO)	$200,000
Gross purchases	900,000
Ending inventory (not including storage and purchasing costs)	250,000

It cost $100,000 to purchase and store (at some time during the year) $1,100,000 of inventory. That is a ratio of 9%, or 9 cents for each dollar of inventory value. Therefore, the ending inventory must be increased by 9% of $250,000, which is $22,500, to an amount of $272,500. Instead of expensing the entire $100,000 of storage and purchasing costs for the year, only $77,500 is expensed. Similar calculations have to be made for the other costs which are listed above that must be capitalized.

These rules can make tax accounting for inventory *significantly* different from the normal procedures followed under generally accepted accounting principles.

A taxpayer using FIFO can elect either of two approaches—valuing inventory at FIFO cost or valuing it at the lower of that cost or its market value.[31] "Market" would normally be the cost of replacing the merchandise. There is no such option for a taxpayer using LIFO—the inventory must be valued at LIFO cost.[32]

Merchandise that is unsalable at normal prices because of damage, imperfections, shop wear, changes of style, or similar causes can be valued at bona fide selling prices less direct costs of disposition.

TAX PLANNING TIP: When market values are declining and a taxpayer values inventory on a lower of cost or market basis, it is important to determine whether specific items of goods may be excluded from the inventory. If they can be included at a value less than cost, the closing inventory will be reduced, the cost of goods sold increased, and the taxable income reduced. Taxpayers who must pay for merchandise that has declined in value should consider having the title transferred to them before the inventory date so that the writedown can be effective for the year.

8.7 Cost Determination

In computing taxable income, a business using the accrual method is required to compute cost of merchandise sold.[33] The cost of merchandise sold is really a return of capital rather than an expense, although the end result is the same. Sales revenue of the current year is reduced by the costs of the merchandise sold to determine gross profit. Where purchases for the year are more, or less, than the cost of goods sold, an adjustment is required for the change in the amount of inventory on hand.[34]

If a business has available for sale 150 gizmos, but actually sells only 100, its gross profit will be

[30]IRC Sec. 263A. The capitalization-of-indirect-costs rules also apply to retail and wholesale businesses which have average (over three year) gross receipts of more than $10 million per year.

[31]Treas. Reg. 1.471-4.
[32]Treas. Reg. 1.471-2.
[33]Treas. Regs. 1.446-1(c)(2)(i) and 1.471-1.
[34]Persons who have completed a financial accounting course are familiar with the procedure of calculating cost of goods sold.

the revenue derived from the sale less the cost of the 100 gizmos sold. It would make little sense to allow a deduction for the cost of all of the 150 gizmos since the unsold 50 really represent an investment to be carried over to the next year.

If gizmos always cost the same amount, the problem of determining the cost of the 100 gizmos sold and the 50 unsold would be minor. Realistically, the cost of gizmos is probably not the same each time they are purchased. The problem of valuation thus becomes more complex. The taxpayer can reason that there must be gizmos in inventory to stay in business. If a gizmo is sold, there must be a gizmo purchased to replace the one sold. Therefore, it can be argued that the cost of the gizmos sold is the cost of the gizmos bought during the year to replace those which were sold.

Alternatively, the taxpayer could conclude that the gizmos on hand are the gizmos purchased most recently, so the first ones sold must have been the gizmos on hand at the *beginning* of the year. Only after these were all gone could the gizmos bought *during* the year be sold.

If the cost for those on hand at the beginning of the year was $10 each, and during the year it cost $15 each to replenish the inventory, Table 8-1 could be prepared using that information.

The 100 gizmos sold resulted in revenue of $2,000. If these 100 were the ones purchased during the year, the gross profit would be calculated by deducting $1,500 from $2,000, which would be $500. If the gizmos sold consisted of 50 from the beginning inventory and 50 from the group purchased during the year, the cost of those sold would be $1,250 (50 at $10 + 50 at $15) and the gross profit would be $750. Which is correct?

In fact, the tax law permits either approach.[35] You may already be familiar with the first-in, first-out (FIFO) and the last-in, first-out (LIFO) concepts (Fig. 8-1) from an accounting course.[36] Under LIFO, the most recently acquired merchandise is treated as having been sold first. With the FIFO assumption, the earliest or oldest units are considered to have been sold first. While either method may be used, a taxpayer cannot switch from LIFO back to FIFO without permission. Note that a taxpayer using FIFO can switch to LIFO *without permission* by meeting certain requirements for the year of the change.[37]

TABLE 8-1
Gizmo Inventory Data

Date		*Number*	*Unit Cost*		*Total*
1/1/X1	Inventory (start of year)	50	$10	$ 500	
19X1	Purchases	100	$15	1,500	
	Available for sale	150		$2,000	
12/31/X1	Inventory (end of year)	50	?	?	$500 or $750
	Sold	100	?	?	$1,500 or $1,250

[35]IRC Secs. 471, 472, and 474.

Both LIFO and FIFO are methods for determining inventory cost flows. Inventory costs for purchased merchandise are conceptually the same for both—invoice price, plus freight and other similar charges, less trade or other discounts.[38] Cash discounts (e.g., 2/10, n/30) may either be deducted from invoice cost or reported directly as income in the year earned.[39] "Cost" is a more complex concept for manufactured goods, encompassing the purchase cost of raw materials, the cost of direct manufacturing labor, and a proportionate part of indirect (overhead) costs.[40] Also, in some cases "cost" of inventory includes the part of the costs incurred to keep the inventory on hand. Merchandising (i.e., marketing) expense is never a part of merchandise cost.[41]

So-called "variable" or "direct" costing is not an approved method of accounting for inventory for tax purposes. Students may be familiar with this method, as it is sometimes advocated as a managerial decision-making tool in cost or managerial accounting. Under such a method the inventory is valued at only the direct costs of material, labor, and overhead, with all indirect costs being charged to the current period. For tax purposes inventory value must include an allocated portion of indirect costs as well as the direct costs.

8.8 LIFO Election

The election to adopt LIFO is made at the time the tax return for the first LIFO year is filed.[42] A Form 970 will be completed and attached to the income tax return.

The use of the LIFO method is desirable in a

[36]Some financial accounting texts discuss a method of using *average* cost or *weighted average* cost for determining inventory. Such a method was disapproved by Rev. Rul. 71-234, 1971-1 CB 148. See also *Universal Steel Co.* v. *Comm.* (CA3 1931), 46 F.2d 908, 1931 CCH ¶ 9108, 9 AFTR 842. Where intermingling of various grades of grain prevented identification, FIFO was to be used. Rev. Rul. 70-541, 1970-2 CB 107.

[37]Treas. Regs. 1.472-2 and 1.472-3.

[38]Treas. Reg. 1.471-3.

[39]Treas. Reg. 1.471-3(b).

[40]Treas. Regs. 1.471-3(c) and 1.471-11.

[41]Treas. Reg. 1.471-11(c)(2)(ii).

[42]Treas. Reg. 1.472-3.

FIGURE 8-1 FIFO and LIFO inventory accounting methods (a taxpayer may use either FIFO or LIFO but may not switch back and forth from one to the other without IRS permission)

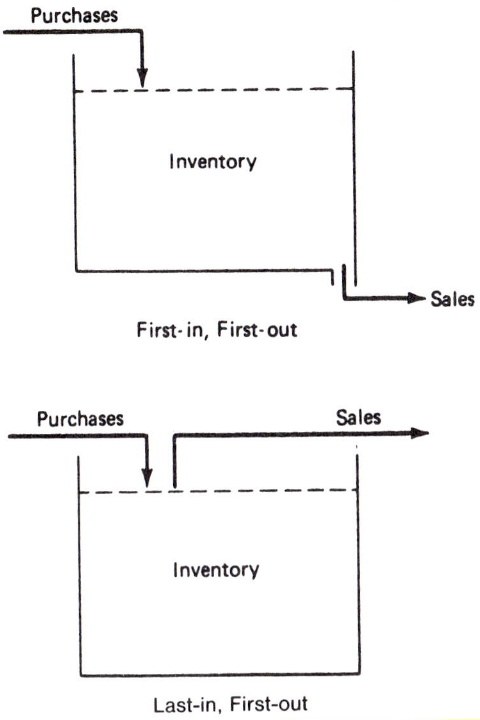

period of rising prices. It will result in smaller income than the FIFO method because it eliminates from income the effect of an increase in the market value of the inventory. In a period of declining prices the reverse will occur. A taxpayer should remember that the lower of cost or market valuation method may not be used with LIFO, and so declines in market value of inventory on hand will not be offset against taxable income.

8.9 Dollar-Value LIFO

The previous example dealt with gizmos. Many businesses do not deal with small quantities such as 50 or 75 or 150 total units in purchases or inventory. They may deal with thousands or hundreds of thousands of separate inventory items. The turnover in each item may, in turn, amount to hundreds of thousands or millions of units. Keeping track of individual units would be unmanageably expensive, even with computers.

Thus, the basic LIFO approach was modified to permit recognition that purchasing power *equivalents* were being inventoried and not merely *specific items* of merchandise. This is called "dollar-value" LIFO—and is the version of LIFO in general use by taxpayers today.[43]

[43]Treas. Reg. 1.472-8.

Possibly the simplest way to grasp dollar-value LIFO is to look at an illustration of its use.[44] Assume that a small manufacturer decided to adopt LIFO in 1989. The inventory at the start of 1989 would have been expressed in terms of December 31, 1988 prices. The company would have taken a physical inventory, showing quantities, descriptions, prices, and cost per unit. From these data, a total cost for the inventory could be calculated. Assume that the total cost was $14,000.

At December 31, 1989, a physical count of inventory would again be taken. Description, quantity, and price per unit would be listed as before. However, instead of showing only one price per unit, both the January 1, 1989 price per unit and the December 31, 1989 price per unit would be recorded. The total of quantity times price would be shown for each item. Thus, the total December 31, 1989 physical inventory would be double-extended, that is, priced at two different dollar amounts, the January 1, 1989 cost and the December 31, 1989 cost:

	Price Level	
	1/1/89	*12/31/89*
12/31/89 inventory	$20,000	$24,250

Remember that the quantity of inventory is the same. The difference in the two valuations is the result of attaching two different costs to that quantity. The quantity of inventory has increased during the year 1989. That explains why the December 31, 1988 inventory was $14,000 but the December 31, 1989 inventory at January 1, 1989 prices (just one day later) is $6,000 higher, or $20,000.

Given these figures, a December 31, 1989 "price level" can be determined for this taxpayer's merchandise. The December 31, 1989 inventory is 121.25% of the January 1, 1989 inventory ($24,250 divided by $20,000). That percentage is used to adjust the *increase* in inventory as follows:

	1/1/89 Dollars	*Factor*	*12/31/89 Dollars*
1/1/89 inventory	$14,000	100.00	$14,000
1989 inventory *increase*	6,000	121.25	7,275
Total LIFO inventory at 12/31/89	$20,000		$21,275

On the dollar-value LIFO basis, then, the value of the December 31, 1989, inventory would be $21,275. At December 31, 1990, the physical inventory would again be counted, with all items being priced at both the January 1, 1989 prices and

[44]Unfortunately, discussion of dollar-value LIFO is omitted from many financial accounting texts.

the December 31, 1990 prices. Now the inventory data are:

	Price Level		
	1/1/89	*12/31/89*	*12/31/90*
1/1/89 inventory	$14,000		
12/31/90 inventory	20,000	$24,250	
12/31/90 inventory	18,000		$27,000

This time, the relation between the current price level and the January 1, 1989 prices is meaningless for this purpose because, in terms of January 1, 1989 prices, there has been a decline in the inventory. In terms of January 1, 1989 prices, in other words, there is no inventory increase in 1990. Instead, some of the 1989 increment in inventory was sold in 1990. The valuation would therefore be:

	1/1/89 Dollars	*Factor*	*12/31/89 Dollars*
1/1/89	$14,000	100.0	$14,000
Balance of 1989 inventory increase ($18,000 – $14,000)	4,000	121.25	4,850
Total LIFO inventory at 12/31/90	$18,000		$18,850

On December 31, 1991, the physical inventory is again priced at two different amounts. The inventory data now look like this:

	Price Level			
	1/1/89	*12/31/89*	*12/31/90*	*12/31/91*
1/1/89	$14,000			
12/31/89	20,000	$24,250		
12/31/90	18,000		$27,000	
12/31/91	25,000			$30,000

In terms of January 1, 1989 prices, there has been an inventory increment of $7,000; 1991 prices are 120% ($30,000/$25,000) of January 1, 1989 prices, so that the valuation of the increment is $8,400. The inventory at December 31, 1991 contains three LIFO layers, totaling $27,250:

$ 8,400	1991 dollars
4,850	1989 dollars
14,000	1/1/89 dollars

Inventory decreases will dip into the most recently added layers (hence, LIFO), whereas inventory increases will add new layers at the price level of the year of increase.

As can be seen, this double-extension method develops a "unique" price index for a specific business. This can be an expensive process. The IRS will allow, as an alternative, the use of price indexes covering a whole industry when it is satisfied of the quality of the index.[45] A suitable index may be provided by a governmental agency such as the Bureau of Labor Statistics. The use of such indexes then obviates the necessity for the double extension and requires only that the inventory be taken at the year-end price level.[46] The index numbers are then applied to get the LIFO layers in the same manner as when double extension is used.

There is an election which can be used by some small businesses and which will simplify the use of the LIFO calculations. A taxpayer with average gross receipts (over the past three years) of $5 million or less can elect to use pools as defined by the Bureau of Labor Statistics (BLS), rather than having several "pools" for each type of inventory.[47]

Most retailers use the "retail method" of inventory.[48] Inventories are counted and priced at the marked retail price. The total thus obtained is converted into cost by applying the retailer's percentage of markup. For example, if the total retail price of items in a store is $100,000 and the average markup is 30% of cost, then the cost of the inventory must be $76,923. The type of double extension illustrated is impossible because two cost values for the closing inventory cannot be obtained. Indexes become the only practical way to utilize LIFO.[49] Where index numbers acceptable to the IRS are not available, retailers (and others) sometimes engage statisticians to help develop valid approaches to constructing their own index numbers. For instance, a sample of the merchandise inventory might be taken. A double-extension approach would be used on the sample. Although prohibitively expensive on a 100% basis, this approach may be manageable where the needed sample size is small.

TAX PLANNING TIP: Unless any decreases in inventory during the year are replaced before *the end of the year, a taxpayer may find that LIFO results in a larger tax liability than FIFO. For example, assume that beginning inventory was 1,000 units at $10 each. If 600 units were sold, but only 500 units were replaced, inventory has declined by 100 units. Assume that the replacement cost is $20. Under LIFO, the replacement of 100 units at $20 will become a part of cost of goods sold* only *if the*

[45]Treas. Reg. 1.472-8(e).

[46]See IRC Sec. 472(f).

[47]IRC Sec. 474.

[48]Treas. Reg. 1.471-8. The retail method, which involves working backward from the selling price to an *estimated* cost, can be used with either FIFO or LIFO.

[49]Treas. Reg. 1.472-1(k).

units are replaced before the end of the year. If the 100 units are not replaced until the following year, the last 100 units sold during the year will be costed at $10 each rather than at $20 each. That will cause a difference of $1,000 in reported taxable income. In such an event, acceleration of inventory purchases might be a good plan.

8.10 Tax LIFO and Accounting LIFO

From an accounting viewpoint, LIFO is a method of determining cost. If market (replacement value) is below cost, presently accepted accounting practice is to show the inventory at market rather than at cost. The inventory valuation of the preceding period becomes cost, for accounting purposes, for the current period. Accounting LIFO, then, has the tendency to show inventory valuations of LIFO users at the lowest prices that have prevailed since the adoption of LIFO. Tax LIFO, on the other hand, cannot be used in conjunction with a lower-of-cost-or-market approach, as previously noted.

Thus, in adopting tax LIFO, management should be satisfied that price levels of the pertinent inventory items are at a low point relative to the future, rather than at a high point. Depending on the nature of the business, of course, a price drop can be compensated for by year-end inventory liquidations, followed by restocking at the new and lower price level, which will then become a new LIFO layer.

If LIFO is adopted for tax purposes, the tax law requires that no other basis be used in calculating income for reports to shareholders, creditors, and so forth.[50]

This is almost the only place in the entire tax law where a specific rule requires financial accounting to conform to tax accounting. At the time that LIFO first became generally available to taxpayers in 1939, the weight of accounting thought was that LIFO was not suitable for most businesses—that it was appropriate only where it tended to correspond to the physical flow of inventory. The idea of applying LIFO to a department store would have horrified a conservative CPA of 1939. Thus, the Treasury Department had the requirement inserted in the law that LIFO must be used for reporting purposes, confident that its use would then be limited by the CPAs to those situations where it was appropriate.

However, LIFO became accepted as a way of handling cost for any business, under the rationale that it was the flow of economic utility that was being measured and not specific physical inventory items.

The "conformity requirement," the rule that provides that the financial statements must agree with the tax return as regards the use of LIFO inventory, has been relaxed somewhat in recent years.[51] Thus, footnotes and certain supplemental non-LIFO data on the financial statements are permitted and there is no requirement that interim financial statements agree with the tax treatment.[52]

8.11 Why Isn't Everyone on LIFO?

For many taxpayers, it does not matter much what inventory method they use. Inventory just is not significant. The slight advantages of adopting LIFO are more than outweighed by its inconvenience. For example, if inventories are $10,000 at year end, and cost of goods sold is $500,000 a year, with price-level changes of only 2 or 3% a year, a difference of $200 or $300 in cost of goods sold is immaterial.

Many taxpayers have felt that prices in their particular businesses are more likely to decline than to rise. Suppose that you were a television wholesaler in 1960. Television prices have tended to fall between then and now—and rather substantially. LIFO would have cost more tax dollars rather than less.

Other taxpayers simply do not understand how dollar-value LIFO operates, and have been reluctant to get involved in what seems to them a risky and expensive procedure.

Taxpayers have been concerned over the resulting financial statements if LIFO were adopted. Would stockholders understand why profits were lower? Conservatism of accountants and of the SEC has prevented use of such presentations as FIFO for inventory on the balance sheet (balanced by a noncurrent liability) and of LIFO for cost of goods sold on the income statement. Inventory can be carried on the balance sheet at FIFO (or any other method) according to IRS so long as the income disclosure rules are not violated.[53]

Sometimes, compensation of management has been based upon reported profits. Manage-

[50] IRC Sec. 472(c).

[51] For an interesting analysis, see William Roabe, Jr., "IRS Modifies LIFO Conformity Requirements," 8 *J. Corp. Tax* 132 (1981).

[52] Treas. Reg. 1.472-2(e). The LIFO conformity rule now requires that all members of the same group of financially related corporations are to be treated as one corporation. See IRC Sec. 472(g)(1).

[53] Treas. Reg. 1.472-2(e)(4).

ment faced with such a situation may be reluctant to adopt any policy that will result in lower reported profits and thus lower personal income. This is particularly true where managerial bonuses are based upon the size of reported profits. It is interesting to project the long-term effect of adopting LIFO. Imagine a taxpayer that can earn, after taxes, 7% on investment and that has an effective income tax rate of 35%. It has an inventory of $1,000,000 at the time it adopts LIFO. Prices increase in a straight line at 10% so that the inventory at the end of year 1 is valued at $1,100,000 under FIFO; at the end of year 2 it is valued at $1,200,000 under FIFO but still $1,000,000 under LIFO; and so forth. After twenty years the inventory would be $3,000,000 under FIFO, but still at $1,000,000 with LIFO. But does this mean that assets are actually worth $2,000,000 less under LIFO?

Quite the contrary! By using LIFO the taxpayer could generate tax savings of $35,000 per year. That is $35,000 more cash available to use. Invested to yield 7% after taxes and compounded annually for twenty years, it would show $1,535,264 more assets under LIFO than it would have had under FIFO. Assuming that the taxpayer will continue operating for an indefinite period into the future, it is in almost any real sense $1,535,264 better off. Certainly, its balance sheet is not only no worse off but, in fact, shows much greater liquidity and strength than if FIFO had been retained.

8.12 Miscellaneous LIFO Effects

One of the little-noticed effects of taxation on inventory decisions is that it encourages a company to recognize obsolescence and value declines in inventories. Thereby it presumably facilitates pruning of the inventory. This results from the tax deductibility of the cost of the item in the year in which it declines in value or is sold or scrapped. If the lower-of-cost-or-market approach is used, the tax benefit is obtained without the disposition of the item.[54] Otherwise, the item must be sold or scrapped for the cost to provide a tax deduction.

When LIFO is used, the management of the company acquires substantial control over the amount of profits it will earn and report, both for tax and for accounting purposes. In a year of relatively poor profits, assuming that price levels have generally been rising, management could allow the year-end inventory to decline to a substantial extent. This would have the effect of increasing profits by charging into cost of sales for the current year merchandise carried at costs based on price levels of previous years. On the other hand, if profits appear too high, they can in some LIFO applications be reduced by substantial purchases of inventory at year end.

Of course, if management does not have good control over its inventory levels, it may find that allowing inventories to decline may have an unexpected impact on profits. To a lesser extent, allowing inventories to increase beyond a reasonable level may unexpectedly reduce profits.

Example. Assume that the beginning-of-the-year inventory consists of the following LIFO layers:

Year	*1986 $*	*Factor*	*LIFO Inventory*
1986	$ 30,000	100	$ 30,000
1987	50,000	105	52,500
1988	20,000	120	24,000
1989	20,000	150	30,000
	$120,000		$136,500

The price level for specific inventory items at the end of 1990 is 200% of the 1986 price level. In terms of 1990 dollars the inventory shows $120,000 (i.e., LIFO cost is still $136,500), and the net profit before tax would be $100,000.

If management anticipated this year-end situation and wanted to increase this profit, they could allow the inventory at year end to run down (probably replacing it a few days later). If the inventory were cut in half, the result would be a change in profit of $46,000, or 46% before taxes.

Cutting the inventory in half is accomplished by reducing purchasing at year end, assuming that sales remain at a normal level. Purchases are, of course, made in current (1990) dollars. Assuming that the inventory remained at the level at which the pretax profit is $100,000, the "Cost of goods sold" section of the income statement would look like this:

Beginning inventory	$ 136,500
Purchases	2,000,000
Available for sale	2,136,500
Ending inventory	136,500
Cost of goods sold	$2,000,000

Reducing cost of goods sold increases net profit. Purchases are reduced $120,000 (in 1990 dollars). What happens? Ending inventory is reduced by allowing sales to be treated as coming from the most recently added LIFO layers.

[54]Lower of cost or market is mandatory from an accounting standpoint, except for dealers in precious metals who may use market. It is optional from a tax standpoint if any method other than LIFO is used. It is prohibited from a tax standpoint if LIFO is used.

Year	*1986 $*	*Factor*	*LIFO Cost*	*1990 $*
1986	$ 30,000	100	$ 30,000	$ 60,000
1987	50,000	105	52,500	100,000
1988	20,000	120	24,000	40,000
1989	20,000	150	30,000	40,000
	$120,000		$136,500	$240,000

If all of the 1989 and 1988 layers and 40% of the 1987 layers are sold,

Year	*LIFO Cost*
1989	$30,000
1988	24,000
1987 (40%)	21,000
	$75,000

Ending inventory consists of all of the 1986 layer and 60% of the 1987 layer:

Year	*LIFO Cost*
1986	$30,000
1987 (60%)	31,500
	$61,500

Cost of goods sold is as follows:

	Old	*New*
Beginning inventory	$ 136,500	$ 136,500
Purchases	2,000,000	1,880,000
Available for sale	$2,136,500	$2,016,500
Ending inventory	136,500	61,500
Cost of goods sold	$2,000,000	$1,955,000

Cost of goods sold is now $45,000 less ($2,000,000 − $1,955,000). Profit, before tax, is $45,000 more. The $120,000 reduction in purchases reduced the ending inventory (because of the different types of dollars involved) by only $75,000. The $45,000 profit increase is the result.

8.13 Bad Debts

Accrual basis taxpayers recognize income as goods or services are sold, not as collections arise from such sales. Most businesses other than retail cash sales businesses sell to customers from whom they realistically expect less than 100% payment. The rule of thumb for some business credit decisions is to expand sales by selling to increasingly less credit-worthy customers until the point is reached where the additional revenue from expanding sales equals the estimated credit losses such expansion will incur.

Where businesses operate this way, uncollectible accounts (bad debts) are inevitable. They are also predictable, in the sense that they can be estimated with tolerable accuracy.

The amount that can be written off for a bad debt will depend on the tax accounting employed by the business.[55] A cash-basis business will have no bad-debt deduction when it fails to collect a receivable because the sale was never reported as income.[56] This is almost always the case with service businesses such as attorneys, physicians, and CPAs. If a business uses the installment method for reporting income from sales (not likely since dealers can not use the installment method) the bad-debt expense is the cost-of-goods-sold portion in the receivable—the gross margin portion never having been reported (recognized) as income. An ordinary accrual business will have a write-off equal to the amount of the receivable, because the entire amount of the sale was reported as revenue when the sale was made.

For financial statement purposes, bad-debt losses usually are anticipated at the time of the credit sale, and those who advance credit deduct their anticipated bad-debt expenses. This is the method normally explained in an introductory financial accounting course. The amount of the estimate can be based upon a percentage of total sales, a percentage of sales on account, or can be derived by an analysis of the accounts receivable balance at the end of the year. This method has been called the "allowance" method or the "reserve" method of accounting for bad debts. When the bad debt amount is expensed, there is a corresponding entry to a *contra* account for accounts receivable. This allows the asset to be stated on the balance sheet at the amount which actually is expected to be received as collections. Since 1986, this method is not acceptable for tax purposes.[57] The alternative, called the "direct write-off" method, requires the business to wait until a specific debtor fails to pay and then expense the debt. Such a method requires no estimate.

The "reserve" method can be illustrated as follows. Assume that Billy Barnes has operated a business for one year under the accrual method. At the end of the year, accounts receivable are analyzed and it is estimated that $1,000 will never be collected. Billy thus reduces the accounts receivable by $1,000 and shows $1,000 as bad-debt expense.[58] When the fears are confirmed and

[55]The bad-debt deduction is authorized by IRC Sec. 166.

[56]In tax terminology, there is no "basis" for the receivable.

[57]IRC Sec. 166.

[58]Since Billy does not know which account(s) will not be paid, the specific receivable cannot be reduced. Therefore, a "contra" account (e.g., "Allowance for Collection Losses") is credited for

debtor Joe Doe does not pay a $600 amount due, an expense will not be reported again.

The tax rules require, except for financial institutions, that the "direct write-off" method be used.[59] This does not mean, however, that the taxpayer must wait until he believes that the debt has become entirely worthless. A deduction can be taken for that part of a debt which is deemed to be partially worthless. Thus, if Billy Barnes has an account receivable on the books from Joe Doe in the amount of $1,000, and Billy believes that Joe will not pay more than $600, Billy can take a bad debt expense deduction for the $400. It is not necessary for Billy to wait until Joe pays the $600 or to wait until there is certainty that Joe will not pay the $400.

Prior to 1987, a taxpayer had a choice between using the "reserve" method or the "direct write-off" method. Therefore, those taxpayers who used the "reserve" method are in a transition period from that into the "direct write-off" method. The transition is over a period of four years. For example, assume that a business had a "reserve" or "allowance" account balance of $12,000 at the end of 1986. This account gets eliminated by increasing income each year (for four years) by $3,000 and decreasing the account.[60] Such an adjustment, however, is *just* for tax purposes. If the financial accounts are not kept in accordance with the tax requirements, this entry will be made for purposes of determining tax liability but will not be made on the records kept for financial statement purposes.[61] Taxpayers using an accrual method of accounting for income from the performance of services can exclude from income an estimate, based on their experience, of the amounts that will not be collected.[62]

8.14 Recovery of Bad Debts

Sometimes a taxpayer will write off an account as a bad debt only to discover later that the debtor is willing to pay. The receipt of cash on a previously written off debt will be gross income.[63] An increase in taxable income normally will result in the year of the recovery by the amount of the recovery.

Assume that in the example above, Billy Barnes had been using the direct-write-off method. Bad-debt expense would have been increased by $600 when Joe Doe failed to pay the $600 debt. In a later year, if Joe paid $400, Billy would report $400 of gross income.[64]

ACCOUNTING PERIODS

The "normal" taxpayer accounting period is the calendar year. A new year starts on January 1 each year and ends on December 31.[65] Some 99.9+% of individual tax returns use the calendar year. The whole system of withholding income tax and social security tax, as well as reporting payments to individuals of such things as rent, dividends, and interest, is geared to the calendar year.

With the permission of the IRS, individuals can use an accounting year other than the calendar year.[66] They must keep books and records, and whatever year is chosen must end on the last day of a month. Individuals who are on a "fiscal" year, as it is called, are usually business proprietors.

Other business taxpayers, such as corporations and partnerships, are more likely to be on a fiscal-year basis.[67] Regular corporations can adopt a fiscal year ending at the end of any month, plus something called the fifty-two–fifty-three-week year, when they first come into being.[68] Partnerships and S corporations can adopt a fiscal year instead of a calendar year only with the consent of the IRS.[69]

$1,000. This will be netted against the gross receivable on the balance sheet. When the specific identity of the nonpayer is determined, the "allowance" account will be debited and the account to be written off will be credited. The idea is to get the expense assigned to the year when the sale was made rather than to the year when the identification of the nonpayer was made.

[59]IRC Sec. 166(a).

[60]In accounting terminology, again, this will be a debit of $3,000 to the "contra" account and a credit of $3,000 to an income account.

[61]The change from one method to the other is a "change in accounting method." As such, the adjustment is called a "Sec. 481 adjustment." See IRC Sec. 481.

[62]IRC Sec. 448(d)(5).

[63]Tax treatment of recovery of a bad debt is included in IRC Sec. 111.

[64]The tax law refers to a "tax benefit rule." Having received the tax benefit (tax reduction from the expense) in a prior year, the recovery is then gross income to Billy. Recovery of a previously deducted item will result in income only to the extent that the previous deduction resulted in a tax benefit. Thus, if Billy's taxable income had only been reduced by $300 as the result of the previous $600 deduction (this could happen if there were other deductions which caused taxable income to be reduced to less than zero), then only $300 of the $400 recovery would be taxable in the year of recovery.

[65]Taxable year is defined by IRC Sec. 441(b).

[66]IRC Sec. 441(e).

[67]There are exceptions for certain partnerships and "personal service" corporations. These will be discussed in Chapters 10 and 11, respectively.

[68]IRC Sec. 441(f). Taxpayers other than corporations can, but seldom do, use a fifty-two–fifty-three-week year.

[69]IRC Sec. 706 actually allows a partnership to also adopt a fiscal year if all of its principal partners are on that fiscal year. IRC 1378 restricts an S corporation to the calendar year. IRC Sec. 444 allows a limited election to use a fiscal year for partnerships and corporations that would otherwise have to use a calendar year.

8.15 Change of Periods

Once an accounting period has been adopted for tax purposes, it can only be changed with the permission of the IRS.[70] A change can be from a calendar year to a fiscal year, from one fiscal year to another, or from a fiscal year to a calendar year. Under some circumstances, corporations can change the year without prior IRS approval—but even then, a statement must be filed with the IRS demonstrating that certain specific requirements have been met.[71]

If a year is changed, then a "short-period" tax return will be required.[72] Thus, a change during 1990 from a calendar year to a fiscal year ending September 30 will require filing a return for the nine months ending September 30, 1990. The next return will cover the twelve months ending September 30, 1991. Although the first or final tax returns of a taxpayer do not have to be *annualized,* even though they cover less than a twelve-month period, other returns do.[73] The tax computation for the short period resulting from a change of accounting period becomes complicated by the twin objectives of neither awarding a windfall nor imposing a penalty on the taxpayer making the change. The windfall of having income taxed at lower rates is avoided by a requirement that the income be increased to reflect what twelve months income would have been. The tax is calculated on the twelve-month income, then reduced pro rata based upon the ratio of the months in the short period.[74] The purpose of this adjustment is to keep the taxpayer from avoiding higher marginal tax rates for the short year. Also, it allows for adjustment for those deductions which are intended to be for a twelve-month period, such as personal exemptions and the standard deduction.

For example, assume that Billy Barnes (single) changes from a calendar year to a fiscal year, with the result that a tax return will be filed for a tax period of eight months. Gross income for the eight-month period is $20,000. If no adjustment were made, Billy would get the full $2,050 (for 1990) personal exemption deduction and the full $3,250 standard deduction. Also, the marginal tax rate would be only 15% (see Appendix 1-C) on $19,450 taxable income. Instead, the computation will "annualize" the $20,000 income by multiplying it by 1.5, resulting in annualized gross income of $30,000.[75] The taxable income is $24,700. Tax on $24,700 is $2,917.50 + 28% ($24,700 − $19,450) = $4,388. (As can be seen, the marginal tax rate is now 28%.) The $4,388 is then divided by 1.5 to arrive at the tax liability for the eight-month period, $2,925.

The penalty impact is avoided by allowing the taxpayer to calculate actual income for the twelve months of the "old" accounting period, determining the tax on that income, and then apportioning tax to the short period on the ratio of the short-period income to the twelve-month period's income. The tax calculated in that manner cannot be less than the tax would be if calculated on the short-period income without annualizing at all.[76] This alternative calculation cannot be used for the original filing of the tax return for the short period, incidentally—but requires that the annualized tax be paid and then a refund filed based on this alternative calculation.[77] This "relief" provision will reduce the tax where the income is bunched during the period of the new short year.

8.16 Corporations and Shareholders

Corporations and their shareholders are separate taxpayers. Most shareholders in publicly held corporations generally have the receipt of dividends (and maybe occasional stock rights) as their only transaction with the corporations. Such dividends are reported by the shareholders for tax purposes on a calendar year regardless of the corporation's tax accounting period.

Shareholders of closely held corporations frequently have relationships with their corporations other than merely in their capacity as shareholders. They may lend money to the corporation, receive salaries from the corporation, rent property to the corporation, buy from and sell to the corporation. These different relationships create opportunities for tax planning as well as posing tax problems. Some of those opportunities and traps flow from the different tax years of shareholders and their corporations—while some flow from the different accounting methods they use.

Assume, for instance, that both a corporation and its sole shareholder are cash-basis taxpayers on

[70] IRC Sec. 442.
[71] Treas. Reg. 1.442-1(c).
[72] IRC Sec. 443.
[73] The *first* tax return refers to a new business (corporation or partnership) which begins during a year and selects a calendar or fiscal year that ends less than twelve months from the date business started. The *final* tax return is that one which results when a business ceases operations. Also, the last taxable year for an individual ends on the date of death and thus will be less than a full year, except for persons who die on December 31.
[74] Treas. Reg. 1.443-1(b). This process is called "annualizing" income.

[75] An easy way to "annualize" income is first to divide taxable income by the number of months in the short period. The result is the average monthly taxable income. The annual amount is then obtained by multiplying the monthly amount by 12.
[76] Treas. Reg. 1.443-1(b)(2).
[77] Treas. Reg. 1.443-1(b)(2)(v)(a).

a calendar year. The shareholder owns a building that the corporation rents. During 19X1, the corporation pays the shareholder $50,000 rent, which it deducts, and the shareholder reports the receipt of $50,000 rent. Both income and deduction are reported on 19X1 returns.

Change the facts slightly. The corporation files its tax return on a fiscal year ending January 31. In January, it pays the rent for the entire year then ending. It has a deduction of $50,000 for rent paid in January 19X2 on its income tax return for the year ending January 31, 19X2. The shareholder does not report the rent received in January 19X2 until the tax return for the *calendar year* 19X2 is filed. That could be as late as April 15, 19X3, even if no extensions are obtained. In the first example, the income and the deductions were in the same periods. By making a one-month change in the corporate fiscal year, the rent deduction is allowable in a period that ends eleven months before that in which the rent income must be reported.

Thus, where both the corporation and the shareholder are on the cash basis (e.g., a real estate sales corporation), there is a bias toward a corporate fiscal year that ends on January 31. Deductions can be claimed by the corporation more than a full year before the income must be reported from the other half of the transaction.

Because of abuses, Congress amended the rules with the Tax Reform Act of 1986. Certain corporations must now use the same taxable year as that of their owners or make an election to use a fiscal year that will prevent them from utilizing the tax deferral strategy discussed above. In most cases, this means that a calendar year will be required. The affected corporations are "S" corporations (discussed in Chapter 11) and "personal service corporations."[78] The latter are corporations which have as their principal activity the performance of personal services by the person or persons who are employee-owners. Examples of such corporations are those in accounting, engineering, law, or medical practice.

Make another slight change in the original facts. Again, both shareholder and corporation are on a calendar year. However, the corporation is an accrual-basis taxpayer while the shareholder is a cash-basis taxpayer. The corporation has not paid the 19X1 rent as of December 31, 19X1. Since the rent was due in 19X1, even though not paid, the corporation would be entitled to the expense under the accrual method. The shareholder, being on a cash basis, would not report the rent on the 19X1 return because it has not been received. This will work as long as the shareholder owns 50% or less of the outstanding stock of the corporation (including stock which is "constructively held," meaning stock which is held by certain persons to whom the stockholder is related). If a person owns more than 50% of the stock of a corporation, debt owed by the corporation to the shareholder cannot be accrued and deducted by the corporation. It can be claimed as a deduction by the corporation only when paid, just as if the corporation were on the cash method.[79]

Thus, where the corporation is on the accrual basis and shareholders with 50% or less ownership are on the cash basis, there is a bias in favor of corporate years that end on December 31. Expense items can be accrued and deducted on the corporate return, then paid to the shareholder, in the shareholder's next calendar year.

TAX PLANNING TIP: Corporations other than "personal service corporations" with one shareholder should consider having a fiscal year end January 31. Expenses such as rent, interest, and bonus can be paid by the corporation during January, resulting in a deduction by its year end. The shareholder, on the cash method, will not have to pay tax on the income until April 15 of the following year.

8.17 Conclusion

Tax accounting and financial accounting coincide for the most part. Tax accounting, however, includes some requirements and encompasses some options that would be unacceptable for financial reporting, such as the cash method; the use of the completed contract method for small businesses, even though estimates of percentage of completion can be made with reasonable accuracy; and the use of the installment method, even though collection losses can be estimated. It also requires procedures that are not permissible for financial reporting, such as carrying LIFO inventory at cost even if market is lower and capitalizing indirect costs into inventory.

There is another, more subtle, difference between tax and financial accounting when both are on the accrual basis. That difference stems from different understandings of the meaning and purpose of the word "accrue." In financial accounting, amounts accrue with the passage of time and

[78]IRC Sec. 441(i).

[79]IRC Sec. 267(a), (b), and (c).

the rendering of services. The purpose of accrual accounting is to match costs used with income produced. Being conservative, the accountant generally follows the maxim: "Never anticipate income; always provide for expenses."

For tax purposes, without a specific rule to the contrary, expense or income accrues when the amount involved becomes fixed and definite. For example, amounts received by a dance studio for lessons to be rendered at some future time would be income to the studio for tax purposes once the studio had received payment. This is true even if the taxpayer uses the "accrual method" for tax purposes. For accounting purposes the income would only accrue as the lessons were furnished.

Similarly, no tax deduction is allowed a manufacturer for warranty expenses to be incurred on consumer sales made during the current year even though warranty expenses can be estimated with reasonable accuracy. The expenses for repairs or replacements on warranties related to current year's sales will furnish a tax deduction only when the warranty service is actually rendered. Financial accounting requires recognition of the estimated warranty expense in the year the product is sold.

For financial accounting purposes, there are many administrative costs which will be deducted as an expense of the year even though the tax rules now require that part of those expenses related to the production or carrying of inventory be capitalized as part of the cost of the inventory.

A taxpayer's initial tax accounting method and reporting period can often be adopted freely from a range of alternatives. Once an election has been made, the taxpayer generally can change only with IRS permission. Thus, we have the paradox that a premium is put on a new business engaging in relatively sophisticated projections of where it may go and what sort of tax decisions would be optimum. But, right at the beginning, tax consciousness and the utilization of professional tax advisers may be limited because of the overwhelming practical problems of getting a business started. Anyone starting a business, ignoring a 34% partner and paying no attention as to how best to deal with him, would be viewed as a poor business manager. Getting competent tax advice when beginning a business is thus increasingly recognized by lawyers, bankers, and investors as one mark of a sharp businessperson.

Dollars that are "borrowed" from the tax collector through tax deferral generally bear little or no interest cost and often are not payable until many years in the future. Thus, they constitute the cheapest form of business finance available. A grasp of tax accounting methods and the proper use of tax accounting periods can help maximize the capital contribution that such interest-free tax deferral can make to the business.

TRUE-FALSE QUESTIONS

State whether each of the following statements is true or false. For each *false* answer, reword the statement to make it *true*.

T F 1. A taxpayer can deduct as an insurance expense periodic amounts credited to a reserve for self-insurance equal to the estimated premiums that would otherwise have been paid to an insurance company for business insurance.

T F 2. A cash-basis farmer may deduct on the tax return for the year 1990 an amount paid in 1990 for feed that will be consumed by livestock in 1991.

T F 3. Mr. Flour owns 100% of the Flower Manufacturing Corporation, which uses the accrual method of accounting. He also owns the Wheat Consulting Company, a proprietorship, which uses the cash method of accounting. All use a calendar year. At the end of the last year, Flower Manufacturing owed Wheat Consulting $4,000 for services rendered during the year. This bill was paid on February 1 of the current year. Flower Manufacturing may deduct the $4,000 as an expense for last year.

T F 4. Even though a method of accounting may have been acceptable when first adopted, changing circumstances may make it no longer appropriate for tax purposes and the IRS may require the taxpayer to change to another method of accounting in such a situation.

T F 5. Because the current year is the first year for Mr. Plant to be required to file a federal income tax return, he may elect to use a fiscal year ending February 15.

T F 6. Cel Mitchell sold a tract of real estate under an installment sale. The sale resulted in a loss to Cel. The loss will be recognized in part each year as the proceeds are collected.

T F 7. In making a change in accounting method, a taxpayer may often be able to spread the resulting increase in income into more than just the taxable year of change.

T F 8. A lawyer using the cash method of accounting may deduct uncollectible fees as a bad debt.

T F 9. Blank Corp., an accrual-basis company, hired an attorney in July last year to represent it on a negligence suit against Faulty Corp. The attorney's fee was to be 30% of the settlement against Faulty. As of the end of the year, the case was still in progress and the outcome was uncertain. Blank Corp. may take a deduction for this legal expense for the year.

T F 10. A dealer in personal property cannot use the installment method of accounting.

T F 11. A sale of personal property, such as a boat, for $750 could qualify for installment method reporting if the selling price will be collected in two different years by the seller.

T F 12. Mr. Smith enters into a ten-year lease to rent property to Mr. Jones. In the first year, Mr. Smith receives $3,000 for the first year's rent and $3,000 in advance as rent for the tenth year of the contract. Mr. Smith will include only $3,000 in gross income for the first year.

T F 13. If a taxpayer, who makes a casual sale of property under the installment sales method, does not charge interest of at least 10%, the IRS will impute an interest charge at 10%.

T F 14. A taxpayer uses the specific-write-off method for bad debts. In the first year of operation, the taxpayer had gross income of $10,000, a bad-debt deduction of $400, and other allowable deductions of $12,000. In the second year of operation, $150 of the debt previously written off was recovered. The recovered bad debt is includable in gross income for the second year.

T F 15. Basically, dollar value LIFO is used, rather than specific identification LIFO, in those situations where LIFO is desirable but to account for thousands or millions of individual units would be unmanageable.

T F 16. A taxpayer can change from the cash method to the accrual method of accounting automatically (i.e., without IRS approval) if the business begins to have inventories that are a material income-determining factor.

T F 17. If a taxpayer operates a manufacturing business, part of the costs which must be capitalized into inventory will be the storage costs of the inventory and the administrative costs of purchasing raw materials for inventory.

T F 18. If a taxpayer decides to begin using LIFO inventory after having used FIFO for several years, the IRS need not be asked for approval.

T F 19. A taxpayer wishing to change from a fiscal year to a calendar year must obtain the permission of IRS.

T F 20. If a taxpayer uses last-in, first-out to account for inventory, the lower of cost or "market" (where "market" means replacement cost) cannot also be used.

PROBLEMS

Problem 8-1. The Merriweather Company has counted and priced its inventory as of December 31, 1990. The valuation used was current cost. The results were as follows:

Product	*Units*	*Unit Cost*	*Total*
Gizmos	30	$3.00	$ 90
Widgets	40	$4.00	160
Things	50	$5.00	250
Total			$500

On January 1, 1990, the inventory had been priced at the "base cost" used for dollar-value LIFO purposes. The results were as follows:

Gizmos	20	$2.00	$ 40
Widgets	30	3.00	90
Things	40	4.00	160
Total			$290

It is necessary to calculate the December 31, 1990, inventory at the dollar-value LIFO amount.

(a) Under the double-extension method what is the December 31, 1990, inventory at the "base cost"?

(b) What is the increment in inventory measured in terms of "base cost" dollars?

(c) What is the inflation index which will be used to value the ending inventory?

(d) What is the increment in inventory measured in terms of "base cost" adjusted to current dollars?

(e) What is the total ending inventory value under the dollar-value method?

Problem 8-2. Lowe Plastics Company discovered shortly after taking a physical year-end inventory that some of the sheet plastic valued at $100,000 could not be sold at the current market price. This was due to a new material that had recently come on the market. A month after the end of the year, the company advertised all of that particular kind of plastic for sale at $25,000. A week later the material was placed with a commission agent for disposal. If the agent sells the plastic, the commission will be 15%. Lowe accounts for inventory under FIFO with lower of cost or market.

(a) What is Lowe's correct valuation for that inventory as of the end of last year?

(b) Would it make any difference if the company consistently used the lower of cost or market for inventory valuation?

Problem 8-3. On August 1 of last year, Jack Place sold office equipment that had been used in his insurance business on an installment contract for $4,000. The contract provided for $200 payment on delivery and the balance in monthly installments of $100 each beginning September 1. All payments were received by Jack when due. The original cost of the equipment was $3,500. The adjusted basis of the equipment was $2,800.

(a) How much gross income will Jack report for the year as the result of this sale if the installment method is used? (Assume that Jack is eligible to use the installment method for tax purposes.)

(b) Under what circumstances might it be wise for Jack to elect not to have the installment sales rules apply?

Problem 8-4. Richard Bland borrowed $5,000 for three years from the local bank on July 1, 1988. He gave the bank a note for the amount with interest at 10% per year. On December 31, he paid $250 interest to the bank. When the note matured, July 1, 1991, he paid the $5,000 plus $1,250 interest. Richard is a cash-basis taxpayer.

(a) Could Richard deduct the $250 interest he paid on December 31, 1988?

(b) Could Richard deduct any interest for the year 1989 or 1990?

(c) What if Richard had paid the remaining $1,250 interest on July 1, 1989?

Problem 8-5. Small Business Enterprises [SBI] is a construction outfit with average annual gross receipts of $4 million. On May 5, 1990, it began construction of a large metropolitan hospital. Its contract price is $10 million and it was expected to take a little less than three years to complete. In 1990 and 1991, its percentage completion was estimated at 30% and 70%, respectively. It was completed during 1992. Actual construction costs incurred during the three-year period were as follows: 1990 – $2,600,000, 1991 – $3,800,00, and 1992 – $2,400,000.

(a) Assume that SBI qualifies to use the percentage-of-completion method. Compute the gross profit recognized in years 1990, 1991, and 1992.

(b) Assume that the company decided to report the gross profit under the completed contract method. What is the major advantage of reporting under this method? What are the major disadvantages?

Problem 8-6. Dennis Compton purchased a vacant lot on January 15 last year for $37,500. The property was used as a parking lot for Dennis's customers. On August 1 the city began providing free parking facilities across the street. On December 1, Mr. Compton sold the lot for $50,000, receiving $10,000 cash as a down payment and four $10,000 11% notes due on June 1 of each of the next four years. (Assume that the 11% is adequate interest under the rules.)

(a) Assume that Mr. Compton will use the installment sales method. What will be his reported gain for last year? For this year?

(b) What if the buyer tendered, and Mr. Compton accepted, payment in full ($40,000) on July 1 of this year? How would Mr. Compton report this?

(c) What would be the nature of Mr. Compton's gain?

(d) Assuming that Mr. Compton had a net operating loss carryover of $20,000, would you advise him to use the installment sales method?

Problem 8-7. Taxpayer A is a merchandising concern. As a result of the Tax Reform Act of 1986, it must add to ending inventory a portion of the following additional costs: (1) inventory storage costs, (2) purchasing costs, (3) handling and processing costs, and (4) mixed service costs (normally indirect general and administrative costs that service both inventory and noninventory costs). A simplified method of allocation is allowed, which allocates these costs to ending inventory based on the following ratio: sum of additional costs/total purchases for the year. During 1990, it incurred $200,000 of storage costs, $500,000 of purchasing costs, $300,000 in handling and processing costs, and $200,000 of mixed service costs. Assume that the cost of purchases for the year was $10 million and beginning and ending inventory values, *exclusive of the additional costs,* were $2 million and $3 million, respectively.

(a) Assume that the company uses the FIFO method of valuation. Compute the amount of additional cost that must be added to ending inventory.

(b) Suppose instead that the company reported on a LIFO basis. Compute the amount of additional cost that must be added to ending inventory.

Problem 8-8. This year, Dale Boyd sold real estate with an adjusted basis of $76,000 to Jim Davison. The terms of the sale were that Jim was to pay $6,000 in cash, assume a $28,000 mortgage that Dale had on the property, and give Dale ten notes for $6,600 each. The notes were interest bearing at 11%, with the first note payable two years from the date of sale and each succeeding note at two-year intervals afterward. The market value of the notes was determined to be 80% of their face value. Dale will use the installment method of reporting the gain for tax purposes. (Assume that the 11% is adequate interest under the rules.)

(a) What was the "selling price" of the property?

(b) What was the "contract price"?

(c) What were the total amount of payments in the year of sale?

(d) What percentage of each payment will Dale include in his gross income *as gain from the sale?*

Problem 8-9. George Wilson owned a warehouse that originally cost $60,000. Over the years he took depreciation deductions of $40,000, using the straight-line method. He could not, of course, depreciate the land where the building was erected. The land had a basis to George of $15,000. Last summer George received an offer to purchase the land and building for $90,000 cash. If he were to sell the property, he would invest the proceeds in the stock market and retire from the warehousing business. (Use the 1990 rate schedule.)

(a) If George sells the property, what will be his additional tax liability, assuming that he would already have ordinary taxable income of $40,000 for the year and will file a joint return? [*Note:* The gain on the sale will be $55,000, which is the selling price of $90,000 less the combined adjusted basis of the building ($20,000) and the land ($15,000).]

(b) Assume that George arranges with the prospective buyer to receive a down payment plus a mortgage on the property. After considering the risk involved, George decides that the interest which the buyer is willing to pay is as high as he could earn by investing the proceeds in the stock market. The down payment would be 20% and the balance of the mortgage would be payable, over a fifteen-year period, at the rate of $4,800 per year plus interest. Ignoring interest income, which may be assumed to be the same each year whether received from the buyer or from securities investments, calculate the savings in tax from use of the installment method. Assume that all factors will remain constant for fifteen years.

(c) In what other way may George be better off by using the installment method?

Problem 8-10. Martin Collins owns a tract of undeveloped land that he acquired ten years ago for $50,000. Martin paid cash for the property, but two years ago he borrowed $100,000 from Second State Bank and put a mortgage on the land as collateral for the note. Martin has repaid $9,000 of the loan. Now Martin is considering a sale of the property. The negotiations are still in progress. Martin thinks he can sell it for $300,000, but would like to spread the gain out over several years. Assume that Martin is always in the 28% tax bracket. The buyer is willing to assume the $91,000 unpaid balance on Martin's loan. The buyer will pay Martin the market rate of interest on any unpaid balance if an installment sale is arranged. That interest rate is acceptable to Martin.

(a) If the buyer assumes the $91,000 outstanding debt, what will be Martin's recognized gain in the year of sale? (Assume no other payment in the year of sale.)

(b) Assume that Martin owns the property with no outstanding debt and that his adjusted basis is still $50,000. Could he mortgage the property for $50,000, sell the property subject to the mortgage to the buyer, receive a cash down payment of $90,000 from the buyer, and still use the installment sales provisions? (Note that Martin's cash flow would be $140,000 in the year of sale.) Explain.

Problem 8-11. Several years ago, Arthur Howitz, a calendar-year single taxpayer, purchased a tract of land at a cost of $100,000. He held the unimproved realty as an investment. The land appreciated in value and Arthur sold it on November 21, 1990, for $400,000. Arthur received $100,000 cash as a down payment. Three months later, in accordance with the sales contract, he received the second installment of $300,000 plus interest of $5,250.

(a) Explain the tax treatment of the sale.

(b) Assume that Arthur has $90,000 of other taxable income each year. Further assume that Arthur will use the installment method for tax purposes. Ignoring the "time value" of money, how much will the installment method save him in tax dollars? (Use 1990 rates.)

Problem 8-12. Al Mitchell owns 100% of the stock of Mitchell Research Associates, Inc., which uses a fiscal year ending November 30, and the accrual method of accounting. It is not a "personal service corporation." Al uses a calendar year and the cash method for his personal tax return. As of November 30, 1990, the corporation owed Al a salary of $4,000, rent of $2,000, and interest of $1,000. The corporation has adequate cash to pay these debts at any time.

(a) Should the corporation pay the debts in December? Why or why not? Explain.

(b) Under what circumstances would it be advisable for the payments to be made in December rather than January? Explain.

(c) Must the salary, rent, and interest all be treated the same, or may these items be treated differently? Explain.

(d) Explain why it would be a good idea for Mitchell Research Associates to be on a fiscal year ending January 31.

Problem 8-13. The following information has been gathered from the Flintrock Manufacturing Company for the year just completed.

Beginning inventory (using LIFO)	$150,000
Purchases of raw material for manufacturing	650,000
Ending inventory (not counting storage costs)	155,000

During the year the rent and administrative costs relative to the storage of inventory totaled $50,000. Calculate the amount of the storage costs which will have to be capitalized into the ending inventory valuation for federal income tax purposes.

PROBLEMS WITH AN ASTERISK REQUIRE ADDITIONAL RESEARCH.

Problem 8-14.* Mary Lane purchased a ticket to the state lottery, a legal operation, prior to leaving for Japan on a three-month business trip. One week after arriving in Japan, she received notice that she had won but that it was necessary for her to collect the winnings personally within thirty days of the notice or the amount would be forfeited. Since she had won $25,000, she flew home immediately. She purchased the ticket on December 20, left for Japan on December 27, was notified of her winnings on December 30, left for the return trip on January 2, and collected her proceeds on January 4.

(a) If Mary is on the cash method, for which year will she report the gross income?

(b) What if Mary were on the accrual method?

Problem 8-15.* Dan Cole, who is an accrual-basis taxpayer, has been sued for a trade-name infringement. His attorney advised him that the case would probably not come to trial for two years because of a backlog in the courts but that Dan would probably have to pay $25,000 in damages. Dan wants to set up a "reserve" of $10,000 which he will "fund" by purchasing a bank certificate of deposit this year, although he plans to contest the suit to the highest court possible.

(a) Can Dan take a deduction for tax purposes for funding his reserve?

(b) What if Dan were on the cash method?

(c) Is there a smaller amount that Dan could deduct if he made a contribution to a "reserve" fund?

(d) What if Dan were to put $10,000 in escrow to be paid to the claimant *if* Dan loses the suit?
  (1) With the knowledge of the claimant?
  (2) Without the claimant's knowledge?

Problem 8-16.* Ken Estein sold a famous oil painting for $120,000 on March 1, 1990. He acquired the painting by inheritance five years earlier and his basis was $70,000. The sale contract provided for a down payment of $20,000 and the balance in three equal annual payments beginning on March 1, 1991, without interest.

(a) Explain the tax treatment to Ken for the year of sale. Does Ken have any available elections?

(b) Explain the tax treatment of the March 1, 1991 payment.

Problem 8-17.* Mort Brandon, an accrual-basis taxpayer, sold 400 shares of Jimmers Corp. stock for $25,000. Mort had purchased the stock for $10,500 in 1980. Mort's broker completed the sale on the stock exchange on December 30, 1990, but the certificates were not delivered and payment was not received until January 5, 1991.

(a) In which year is Mort required to report his gain?

(b) Would the conclusion be different if Mort were on the cash basis?

(c) What if Mort were on the accrual basis but sold the stock for a loss?

(d) Would there be a difference if the property had been sold for a gain but had been land rather than stock? (Assume that title to the land passed to the buyer on December 30 but that Mort did not get paid until January 5.)

9

asset acquisition, use, and disposition

Chapter 5 briefly discussed property transactions, focusing attention on the tax consequences of disposing of investment property. Chapter 6 was concerned with transactions that are nontaxable and the planning opportunities that nontaxable transactions offer for taxpayers. Chapters 7 and 8 were aimed at the operations of a business—the more or less routine matters. Because acquisition, use, and disposition of assets used in business require some special attention, the present chapter is devoted to that topic. There are two concerns: (1) the owning and using of business assets, which involve some special tax rules, and (2) the extraordinary tax treatment sometimes available when such assets are either acquired or sold.

At the outset, we should make it clear that the rules which are discussed in this chapter are equally applicable to a noncorporate business (proprietorship), which was discussed in Chapter 7, to a partnership, which will be discussed in Chapter 10, and to a corporate business, which will be discussed in Chapter 12.

The assets to be discussed in this chapter can be classified into four groups:

1. *Personal property.* This includes tangible property, such as machinery, equipment, and office furniture, and everything else that a business owns which is not real estate, leasehold improvement, or a natural resource deposit.[1]
2. *Real estate.* This includes land, buildings (because they are attached to the land), the improvements made to buildings, and anything else that cannot easily be separated from the land or buildings, such as fences, sidewalks, and parking lot surfaces.
3. *Leasehold improvements.* These are the improvements made by a tenant to leased real estate. Generally, improvements will be useless to the tenant at the end of the lease because they will then belong to the landlord. However, the useful life of such improvements may extend beyond the end of the lease.
4. *Natural resources.* This includes oil and gas, copper, coal, geothermal deposits, and all other mineral deposits in the land or on the surface of the land.

One attribute that all of these assets have in common is that a business makes an investment to acquire them.[2] They are used in a business and held for the purpose of producing business income either currently or for some future period. All assets except land are consumed. A major tax question is: When can the cost of the investment be deducted for tax purposes?

Except for assets that do not lose their utility with use or the passage of time (such as land or art objects), tax deductions are usually available while the asset is being used.[3] These capital recovery allowances are called depreciation[4] when applied to tangible assets (equipment, buildings, etc.),

[1]Beginning students often have difficulty with the concept of "personal property." Apparently, the problem is that "personal" property can be thought of as that belonging to a person, such as the property that "I" own, or all that "you" own. The authors prefer "personal use" property for that purpose.

[2]Obviously, an individual can purchase such assets, also, and may do so for investment purposes or for other reasons.

[3]For land, see *Leroy B. Williams*, TC Memo 1955-325. For art work, see *D. Joseph Judge*, TC Memo 1976-283.

[4]IRC Secs. 167 and 168.

amortization[5] when applied to intangibles (such as trademarks, leasehold improvements, etc.), and depletion[6] when applied to natural resources.

Any remaining cost not deducted during the time the asset is in use is written off when the asset is sold, scrapped, or determined to be worthless.[7]

Some portion of some assets can even be "recovered" or deducted in whole or in part at the time they are acquired.

9.1 Capital Recovery Allowances in Tax Accounting

Capital recovery allowances mean different things to different people. To a business person, they may mean cash accumulation for replacement. To the person in the street, they may mean "decline in value." For tax purposes, capital recovery means an allocation of part of the original cost (or other tax basis) of an asset to a particular year.[8] In other words, the cost of an asset becomes an expense deduction over time as the asset is consumed.

The basic idea of capital recovery allowances stems from the nature of accounting "income." If a bank loans a customer $10,000 without interest, the bank realizes no income when the customer repays all or any part of the $10,000. That is a recovery of its investment. If the customer pays $10,000 plus $600 of interest, the bank has $600 of income. If, at the end of the first year of the loan, the customer pays only $5,000 on the principal of the note, plus $600 interest, the bank still has income of $600.

If a business pays $10,000 for a piece of equipment that will be used in producing income during the current and following year, income for this two-year period can be fairly determined only if the business is allowed to recoup (deduct) the $10,000 investment. The same principle applies whether the investment is made in something with a useful life of two years or of twenty years or longer. Depletion has some peculiarities all its own.[9]

Two basic rules are immediately apparent:

1. No matter what method of capital recovery allowance is used, the total amount of cost that will be written off will be the same.
2. A capital recovery allowance can be taken only on an asset that can be thought of as having its utility consumed over the passage of time as the asset is used to produce income. Thus, even though the value of a personal residence may decline with the passage of time, depreciation deductions cannot be taken for that residence because it does not produce any income.[10] The same house held for production of rental income will depreciate for tax purposes. The land on which the house stands, however, is presumed not to decrease in value. Even if it does, there will still be no depreciation deductions, regardless of the use of the house.

The second of these two rules—that the property must be used to produce income—probably requires no elaboration. But the first rule immediately raises the question: If the total amount written off will always be the same, how can depreciation or amortization be of any importance in making decisions?

If it could be assumed that tax rates remain constant and that a dollar today means no more or no less than a dollar ten years from now, then the ways in which depreciation is allocated to different tax years would be of interest only to technicians. Consider the question: Is there a difference between a dollar in hand today and the promise of a dollar ten years from now? The answer to that is always "yes."[11]

Although businesses, as such, never consume anything, the dollar can be invested or distributed to owners who can consume it. A business might be able to invest the dollar in something that would produce an after-tax rate of return of 20%, for example. If the 20 cents earned on a dollar in the first year could in turn be invested at 20%, and similarly with the 24 cents earned in the second year, and so forth, at the end of ten years that one dollar will have grown to $6.19!

The concept of present value merely turns this analysis around to ask the question: How much would have to be invested today at an after-tax rate of return of 20% in order to have $6.19 ten years from now? The answer: $1. Assuming that it is only dollars that will be invested, and that there is a known after-tax rate of return, the present value of a dollar to be received at some point in the future can be computed. Using the 20% after-tax rate of return again as an illustration, the present value of the prospect of receiving a dollar ten years from now is the amount that would have to be invested today in order to have a dollar ten years from now.

[5] Various sections of the IRC allow amortization, depending upon the specific asset. For example, leasehold improvements are covered by IRC Sec. 178, organizational expenditures by IRC Sec. 248, research expenditures by IRC Sec. 174(b), and trademark and trade-name expenditures by IRC Sec. 177.

[6] IRC Secs. 611–614.

[7] In case of a sale, the "write-off" is accomplished by comparing the adjusted basis with the selling price in determination of a gain or loss.

[8] One of the major differences between financial accounting and tax accounting is that the method of cost allocation may not be the same for both purposes.

[9] The discussion of capital recovery allowances does not apply to *percentage depletion*, which will be covered later in this chapter.

[10] A personal residence is one that is owned by a taxpayer and used as his or her abode.

[11] Tax rates do change from time to time, sometimes increasing, sometimes decreasing. It may be difficult to predict, particularly in the long run, which way they will move. The second concept, the time value of money, is always valid.

If 16 cents were invested today at 20% after-tax return per year (with the earnings all being received as of the end of the year and reinvested immediately), the following would result:

End of Year	*Amount (1.2 × Previous Amount) R*
1	$0.19
2	0.23
3	0.28
4	0.33
5	0.40
6	0.48
7	0.58
8	0.69
9	0.83
10	1.00

The 16 cents will have grown to a dollar! Of course, if the investment opportunities are such that a return of only 7% after taxes can be earned, the investor would have to invest 51 cents today in order for it to grow to a dollar ten years from now. If the best that can be realized is 4% after taxes on investments, then $0.68 must be invested to have a dollar ten years from now.

9.2 Depreciation

What does all this have to do with depreciation? If a taxpayer in a 40% tax bracket can take one dollar of depreciation now rather than ten years from now, the result is the use of 40 cents for ten years.[12] If 40 cents can earn 20%, it will have grown to $2.48 by the end of ten years.[13] Keep in mind that the 40 cents could be invested in the business itself as well as in some "outside" opportunity. As long as the depreciation deduction reduces the tax bill, that tax saving can be invested. If tax rates remain relatively constant, a dollar of deduction will always be more valuable now than at some future date.

For tax purposes, as mentioned before, the function of depreciation is merely to allocate the original cost of an asset over the period of its useful life. The major techniques for doing this are the straight-line and the accelerated-depreciation methods.[14] The statutory form of accelerated depreciation is the declining-balance. Other methods, not expressed in terms of years, such as the units-of-production method, are also permitted, if they can be shown to be reasonable.[15] But the basic reference points on which to focus as you read the next few sections are: (1) What is the useful life? (2) Is the pattern of depreciation straight-line over that useful life or does it result in more depreciation in the earlier years at the cost of less depreciation in the later years?

COMPUTER FORMULAS: The straight-line calculation in Table 9-1 is fairly simple. The double-declining balance (DDB) is more difficult since, for tax purposes, we switch to straight-line (SL) when it becomes more advantageous. That SL calculation is based on the undepreciated balance taken over the remaining life. DDB can be calculated this way, with B1 being the cost of the asset:

```
        A                      B
15  Year
16     1   0.5*0.2*2*(B$1-@SUM(B$15. .B15))
17     2   0.2*2*(B$1-@SUM(B$15. .B16))
18     3   0.2*2*(B$1-@SUM(B$15. .B17))
19     4   0.2*2*(B$1-@SUM(B$15. .B18))
20     5   0.2*2*(B$1-@SUM(B$15. .B19))
21     6   0.2*2*(B$1-@SUM(B$15. .B20))
```

The alternative SL is calculated only over the remaining life:

```
22
23  Year
24     1   (B$1-@SUM(E$4. .E4))/5*0.5
25     2   (B$1-@SUM(E$4. .E5))/4.5
26     3   (B$1-@SUM(E$4. .E6))/3.5
27     4   (B$1-@SUM(E$4. .E7))/2.5
28     5   (B$1-@SUM(E$4. .E8))/1.5
29     6   (B$1-@SUM(E$4. .E9))
```

The calculations in column E are the actual depreciation taken, and will be the greater of DDB or SL.

```
       D                E
 4   Year
 5          1 @IF(B16>B24,B16,B24)
 6          2 @IF(B17>B25,B17,B25)
 7          3 @IF(B18>B26,B18,B26)
 8          4 @IF(B19>B27,B19,B27)
 9          5 @IF(B20>B28,B20,B28)
10          6 @IF(B21>B29,B21,B29)
```

Some spreadsheet programs have special commands to compute DDB and other depreciation methods. These commands can shorten and simplify the above calculations.

The most customary form of declining-balance depreciation is the 200% declining-balance method, frequently referred to as double-declining-balance depreciation. This method can

[12]For example, corporations paid tax at 39% on taxable income between $100,000 and $335,000, for calendar year 1988.

[13]Even if the rate of return is substantially less than 20%, there will always be a positive effect.

[14]IRC Sec. 167(b), IRC Sec. 168(b).

[15]IRC Sec. 167(b)(4). Treas. Reg. 1.167(b)-4.

TABLE 9-1

	Straight Line		*200% Declining Balance*	
Year	*Annual Charge*	*Cumulative Charges*	*Annual Charge*	*Cumulative Charges*
1	$1,000	$ 1,000	$2,000	$ 2,000
2	2,000	3,000	3,200	5,200
3	2,000	5,000	1,920	7,120
4	2,000	7,000	1,152	8,272
5	2,000	9,000	1,152	9,424
6	1,000	10,000	576	10,000

best be described by an example. Assume that a taxpayer purchased mid-way through year one a $10,000 machine with a useful life of five years. Straight-line depreciation would, therefore, result in annual depreciation deductions of $1,000 each in the first and sixth years, and $2,000 each in the second, third, fourth, and fifth years.[16] The 200% double-declining-balance depreciation method, in contrast, permits a deduction of $2,000 in the first year. The straight-line rate of 20% is doubled. The deduction is based upon 40% of the *undepreciated cost.*[17] Thus, while for the first year the deduction is $2,000, for the second year it is $3,200 (40% of $8,000), and for the third year it is $1,920 (40% of $4,800), and so on. It will eventually be necessary to switch to the straight-line method, because a declining-balance method will never result in the deduction of the full amount of the original cost. In the illustration, the switch would take place in the fifth year, and the undepreciated balance would be written off over the one and one-half remaining years at $1,152 per year (see Table 9-1).

Depending on the nature of the asset and the date of acquisition, the fastest permitted rate of declining-balance depreciation may be the 200% method just illustrated. The 150% method is available for certain longer-life assets.

The remaining discussion of depreciation in this chapter deals with assets placed in service during 1987 or later. The post-1986 rules comprise a modified version of the "accelerated cost recovery system" (ACRS) in effect since 1981. These are often referred to as the "MACRS" rules (i.e., modified ACRS). We will not follow that usage here, however. The modified ACRS rules are mandatory for assets placed in service after 1986, except for those assets which are depreciated under a method which does not use time as a measure of life expectancy. For example, where machinery is depreciated under a "units of production" method, that method and not the modified ACRS rules would be used. From here on, "ACRS" will refer to post-1986 assets unless otherwise indicated. Those are the rules that affect business decisions.

Under ACRS, depreciable property is divided into two classes: (1) depreciable real estate and (2) all other depreciable property.[18] Each class, in turn, is divided into useful-life categories.

9.2.1. Depreciation on Real Estate Placed in Service after 1986

Depreciable real estate placed in service after December 31, 1986 has been assigned a recovery period (life expectancy) dependent upon whether it is residential rental, or non-residential property. Residential rental property is depreciated over 27.5 years while non-residential property has a life of 31.5 years. The method of cost recovery (depreciation) is straight-line for both types of real property. The following summarizes the rules for depreciable real estate:

1. Recovery period for residential property is 27.5 years. For non-residential real property it is 31.5 years.
2. The method of depreciation is straight-line.
3. No salvage value is taken into consideration in calculating cost recovery.
4. Depreciation will be prorated for property which is placed in service during a year, so that depreciation deductions are allowed only for that part of the year during which the property is used. Similarly, where property is disposed of during the year, depreciation will be allowed for that part of the year prior to the disposition. A mid-month convention is used, so property will be assumed to be placed in service in the middle of the month no matter what the actual date of purchase.

[16]A "half-year" convention is commonly used so that a five-year life involves one-half year of depreciation in the first and the "*n* + 1" years.

[17]In financial accounting, the "undepreciated cost" is often called "book value." In tax law, it is called "adjusted basis." See IRC Secs. 167(g) and 1011.

[18]IRC Sec. 168.

TABLE 9-2*

Approximate Depreciation as Percentage of Cost of Depreciable Real Estate Acquired after December 31, 1986, Based on Straight-Line Method, and Prorated for Month of Year Property Was Acquired Based on One-Half Month Convention

Residential Rental—27.5 Year Life *Month of the First Year the Property Was Placed in Service*											
1	*2*	*3*	*4*	*5*	*6*	*7*	*8*	*9*	*10*	*11*	*12*
3.5%	3.2%	2.9%	2.6%	2.3%	2.0%	1.7%	1.4%	1.2%	0.8%	0.5%	0.2%
Later Years—3.6% (Last Year Prorated)											
Non-Residential Property—31.5 Year Life *Month of the First Year the Property Was Placed in Service*											
1	*2*	*3*	*4*	*5*	*6*	*7*	*8*	*9*	*10*	*11*	*12*
3.0%	2.8%	2.5%	2.2%	2.0%	1.7%	1.5%	1.2%	0.9%	0.7%	0.4%	0.1%
Later Years—3.17% (Last Year Prorated)											

* Percentage tables are not required for depreciation of property placed in service after 1986. The above percentages are rounded, and may be slightly more or less than the actual depreciation.

5. There is no distinction between new or used property acquired by the taxpayer. All are subject to the same method. However, where property is acquired from a related party, the ACRS rules may not apply. These "antichurning" rules are explained later.

An example will illustrate the use of these rules. Assume that Billy Barnes purchased an office building in June, 1990. The cost of the property, not including the cost of the land, was $100,000. Billy uses a calendar year for tax purposes. The depreciation for 1990 will consist of one-half month for June, and six months from July to December. Since a full year's depreciation will be $3,175 (1/31.5, rounded), six and one-half months depreciation will be $1,720 ($3,175 × 6.5/12). See Table 9-2. For 1991 the depreciation will be $3,175. Since the straight-line method is used, this will be the depreciation for each year until the final year. Since the property was deemed placed in service June 15, 1990, it will be considered fully depreciated December 15, 2021, 31.5 years later. The depreciation for 2018 will be 11.5 months, or $3,030.

Table 9-2 presents the percentages of the building cost which can be depreciated, based upon the month of the year the property was placed in service. Use of these percentages would simplify the arithmetic.

A fiscal year taxpayer will compute the number of months based on the approximate fiscal year. For example, if Billy were on a fiscal year ending June 30, purchase of real estate in June would result in one-half month of depreciation being taken for that fiscal year.

Between 1980 and 1987 real property was depreciated using an ACRS accelerated method with recovery periods being fifteen, eighteen, and nineteen years depending upon when the property was placed in service. Before January 1, 1987, there was generally no difference for depreciation purposes between residential rental and commercial real property.

Note: Property placed in service between 1980 and March 16, 1984, has a recovery period of fifteen years. See Appendix 9-B. Property placed in service after March 15, 1984 and before May 9, 1985, has a recovery period of eighteen years. Property placed in service after May 8, 1985, and before January 1, 1987, is depreciated over nineteen years. Special rules applied to allow certain low-income housing to use fifteen years for acquisition through 1986.

9.2.2. Depreciation on Non-Real-Estate Properties Placed in Service After 1986

All depreciable property other than depreciable real estate has been assigned a recovery period (life expectancy) of three, five, seven, ten, fifteen, or twenty years. The following list summarizes the accelerated cost recovery system (ACRS) for these assets:

1. The definition of what constitutes three-year property, five-year property, ten-year property, fifteen-year property, and twenty-year property is fairly tight, so that a taxpayer has little opportunity to argue for a different life. This was one of the congressional purposes in creating the ACRS rules.
2. All property of each class (i.e., three-year, five-year, etc.) is depreciated together. That is, there is no need to keep separate tax records concerning the depreciation on each individual asset. Only the year of acquisition is important.
3. The cost recovery arithmetic uses the 200% declining-balance method for three, five, seven,

and ten year property. The 150% declining balance method is used for fifteen and twenty year property.

4. Table 9-3 is used to determine the portion of the cost of assets which will be deducted each year. This eliminates the need to do any further calculation.
5. New property and used property are to be depreciated under the same method, without distinction.
6. Salvage value is not taken into consideration.
7. The depreciation calculation, which is built into the tables, assumes a "half-year convention." This means that one-half of a full year's depreciation is allowed for the first year an asset is placed in service regardless of whether it was purchased near the beginning or end of the year. Note the difference between this and the treatment of real estate.
8. A taxpayer can elect to use straight-line depreciation, but if this is done, it must be done for all assets of the same class (i.e., three-year, five-year, etc.) which were acquired during the same year. When straight-line depreciation is elected, one-half year's depreciation applies for the year of acquisition.
9. A taxpayer can elect to use a longer period for cost recovery, if for some reason the results of the use of the prescribed recovery are unacceptable. This recovery period will be the class life for the asset which is prescribed from time to time by the Internal Revenue Service.[19] When a longer life is used, straight-line must also be used.
10. No deduction is available for the year of disposal of an asset.
11. A taxpayer can elect each year to expense part of the cost of assets which would otherwise have to be capitalized and subject to cost recovery.[20] Up to $10,000 can be expensed. Only property purchased for use in the active conduct of a trade or business can be expensed. Where the cost of qualified property placed in service during the year exceeds $200,000, the $10,000 ceiling is reduced by the amount of the excess. The extra depreciation deduction does not apply to real estate, or to luxury automobiles.
12. The amount of depreciation deductions available on certain luxury automobiles and other "listed property" is limited.
13. If an asset is used for both business and nonbusiness purposes, the depreciation deduction is based on the same percentage of the cost as the business use percentage. There is an exception. If the asset is used 50% or less for business, then (a) the depreciation *must* be calculated under the straight-line method and (b) the life expectancy will be greater. The asset will be depreciated over the class life of that type of asset, rather than the prescribed ACRS period. For automobiles, a five-year life is used.

[19]Most recently in Rev. Proc. 83-35, 1983-1 CB 745. These class lives are especially important because they are used to determine into which ACRS category an asset falls.
[20]IRC Sec. 179.

TABLE 9-3

*Approximate Percentage of Cost of Depreciable Tangible Personal Property to Be Deducted Each Year, Based on 200% and 150% Declining-Balance Methods, and Half-Year Convention, for Property Placed in Service after 1986**

If the Recovery Year Is:	*Approximate Percentage for the Class of Property Is:* 3-Year	5-Year	7-Year	10-Year	15-Year	20-Year
1	33	20	14	10	5	4
2	33	32	25	18	9	7
3	33	19	18	14	9	7
4		12	12	11	8	6
5		12	9	9	7	6
6		5	9	7	6	5
7			9	7	6	5
8			4	7	6	4
9				7	6	4
10				7	6	4
11				3	6	4
12					6	4
13					6	4
14					6	4
15					6	4
16					2	4
17–20						4
21						2

*The percentages are only approximate. Actual depreciation must be calculated using the prescribed method over the prescribed life.

What kinds of property are in each of the four classes of three-year, five-year, and so on?

Three-year property consists of machinery with an "asset depreciation range" (ADR—which is explained later) midpoint life of four years or less. Some horses are in this category.

Five-year property includes all property with an ADR class life of more than four years and less than ten years. This includes many pieces of manufacturing equipment, as well as cars, light, general purpose trucks, qualified technological equipment, semiconductor manufacturing equipment, research and experimentation property, and computer based telephone central office switching equipment.

Seven-year property includes property with an ADR class life of ten years or more but less than sixteen years. This includes most office furniture and equipment, railroad cars, agricultural and mining equipment, and most other manufacturing equipment. The statute specifically adds any railroad track, single purpose agricultural or horticultural structures, and property that does not have a class life and is not otherwise classified.

Ten-year property includes property which has an ADR midpoint life of 16 to 20 years. Only relatively few taxpayers have ten-year property.

Fifteen-year property includes property with an ADR class life of twenty years or more but less than twenty-five years, and includes electrical generation and distribution systems, municipal wastewater treatment plants, and telephone distribution plant and comparable equipment used for the two-way exchange of voice and data communications.

Twenty-year property includes property with an ADR class life of twenty-five years or more, other than real property improvements with an ADR midpoint of 27.5 years or more. Such real property improvements will be depreciated as real property. Twenty-year property specifically includes municipal sewers.

For example, assume that Billy Barnes purchased an automobile for exclusive use in a trade or business in 1990. The cost of the automobile was $9,000. The 1990 depreciation deduction would be 20% of $9,000, or $1,800, because it is five-year property and the 200% declining balance and half-year conventions are used.

Note that the fact that the property may have been acquired early or late during the year does not normally make any difference. For property, other than real property, placed in service after 1986, a special mid-quarter convention may apply. If more than 40% of the aggregate basis of the property purchased by a taxpayer during a year is placed in service during the last three months of the tax year, all property placed in service during any quarter is treated as placed in service at the midpoint of such quarter. This rule removes much of the abuse potential of the half-year convention.

TAX PLANNING TIP: If a taxpayer is planning to purchase an asset next year, acceleration of that acquisition into the current year will accelerate a depreciation deduction. In the case of five-year property, for example, 20% of the cost of the asset can usually be deducted even if the asset is purchased during the last month of the year. But watch out for the mid-quarter convention.

9.2.3 Autos and Computers

There are some special rules which apply to automobiles and other "listed property" mainly computers.[21] The purpose of these rules is to reduce the tax benefits from luxury automobiles and to tighten the rules relative to property which is used in part for business and in part for nonbusiness purposes.

Where such property is used 50% or less for business purposes the depreciation deduction will be based on the straight-line alternative ACRS method (rather than the regular percentages). Note that it is only the business portion which is subject to the depreciation deduction. For example, if a $12,000 computer were purchased, to be used 40% of the time for business, the $4,800 which can be deducted will be deducted under the alternative method over a period of seven years. (The reason it takes seven years to deduct all of the depreciation is that the "half-year convention" permits a deduction for only one-half of one year's depreciation for the first year of the six year class life. The deduction would be $400 for the first year, $800 for each of years two through six, and $400 in year seven.)

In addition, even if an automobile is to be used 100% for business, there are other limitations. For 1989, the depreciation deduction is limited to $2,660 for the first year, $4,200 for the second year, $2,550 for the third year, and $1,475 for each year thereafter. These amounts are adjusted annually for inflation. For example, assume that a $20,000 automobile was placed in service in May, 1989, and is to be used 100% for business. The depreciation for the first year (normally 20% of $20,000, or $4,000) would be limited to $2,660. For the second year, the depreciation (normally 32% of $20,000, or $6,400) would be limited to $4,200. There is some good news, however. The entire $20,000 can be claimed as depreciation. The deduction will be as follows:

1989 (the first year)	$2,660
1990 (the second year)	$4,200
1991 (the third year)	$2,550
1992 (the fourth year)	$1,475
1993–1998 (the fifth to tenth years)	$1,475
1999 (the eleventh year)	$ 265

It is easy to see that if a very expensive car were purchased, it would take many more years to get the entire depreciation deduction with the above limits.

If an automobile is used less than 100% of the time for business, but more than 50%, the maximum amounts are reduced to the business percent. For example, assume that an automobile is to be used 80% for business and 20% for nonbusiness. The maximum $2,660 depreciation deduction for the first year becomes $2,128, 80% of $2,660, and the maximum $4,200 for the second year becomes $3,360.

[21] IRC Sec. 280F. "Listed property" consists of passenger automobiles, other transportation assets (e.g. airplanes), property used for entertainment, recreation, or amusement purposes, computers and cellular telephones. However, computers used at a regular business establishment are not "listed property."

TABLE 9-4
Asset Depreciation Range System
(Example)

Asset Guideline Class	*Description of Assets Included*	*Asset Depreciation Range (in years)*			*Annual Asset Guideline*
		Lower Limit	*Asset Guideline Period*	*Upper Limit*	*Repair Allowance Percentage*
13.3	Petroleum Refining: Includes assets used for the distillation, fractionation, and catalytic cracking of crude petroleum into gasoline and its other components	13	16	19	7
13.4	Marketing of Petroleum and Petroleum Products: Includes assets used in marketing petroleum and petroleum products, such as related storage facilities and complete service stations, but not including any of these facilities related to petroleum and natural gas trunk pipelines	13	16	19	4
15.1	Contract Construction Other than Marine: Includes assets used by general building, special trade, and heavy construction contractors. Does not include assets used by companies in performing construction services for their own account	4	5	6	12.5

9.2.4. ADR Depreciation

For property placed in service prior to 1981, one of the continuing problems was the determination of life expectancy for depreciation purposes. The life expectancy of a depreciable asset varied from taxpayer to taxpayer. Useful life, for tax purposes, meant useful life to the particular taxpayer involved.[24] It was sometimes shorter than the physical life of the asset involved. Therefore, useful life for tax purposes could not be determined by an engineering study. It was a function of taxpayer intent and use. Of course, when the taxpayer's past experience furnished no clue as to probable useful life and it was impossible to determine useful life to the taxpayer in any other way, the physical life of the asset could be relevant for purposes of computing depreciation.

TAX PLANNING TIP: A taxpayer who uses an asset such as an automobile less than 50% for business purposes and more than 50% for nonbusiness purposes should attempt to reduce the nonbusiness usage or increase the business usage so as to be able to document that the asset is used more than 50% for business purposes. By so doing, the accelerated recovery can be used rather than straight-line. For other listed property such as a computer, less than 50% business use also requires a longer recovery period than the ACRS period. Also, in order to avoid "recapture," the business usage should be maintained at an above-50% level in subsequent years.

As an alternative to establishing the asset's actual useful life, taxpayers had the right to utilize the asset depreciation range (ADR) system.[25] Under this approach, the taxpayer elected to keep asset records and compute depreciation either on an item-by-item basis or by "vintage" accounts. The latter grouped similar assets acquired in a given year together in one account. The life expectancy for the assets in an account was selected from a range prescribed by the Treasury. This range was based upon a "guideline" life, which was a sort of average life expectancy. The range ran from 20% less than the guideline life for the asset involved to 20% more than the guideline life.[26] The taxpayer was free to choose any life within that range. Once adopted for the acquisitions of a given year, the life could be changed for those acquisitions only if the taxpayer requested a change and the IRS agreed to it. A sample page from ADR is shown in Table 9-4.

Earlier, it was indicated that whether ACRS

[24]Treas. Reg. 1.167(a)–1(b).

[25]Treas. Reg. 1.167(a)–11.

[26]ADR guidelines were issued in Rev. Proc. 77-10, 1977-1 CB 548, but have been supplemented and amended several times since. See, for example, Rev. Proc. 83-35, 1983-1 CB 745.

property is three-year, five-year, and so on, depends in part upon the ADR guideline life. Thus, despite the fact that property acquired since 1980 generally will be ACRS property, it is continually necessary to refer to the ADR guidelines to determine which ACRS class is applicable.

9.3 Recapture—Personal Property

The sale of property used in a trade or business and held for over one year can sometimes produce gain that is treated as long-term capital gain.[27] For that to happen with personal property, however, the selling price must be more than the original cost. In effect, any gain on sale, up to the amount of depreciation taken will not qualify for Sec. 1231 treatment.[28]

The rules can be illustrated as follows. Assume that an asset (tangible personal property) which originally cost $50,000 has been depreciated by $35,000, so that its adjusted basis is $15,000. The asset is sold for $20,000. The gain is $5,000, measured by the difference between the selling price and the adjusted basis. The "depreciation recapture" rules provide that the $5,000 gain will be taxed as ordinary income. If the asset were sold for more than the original cost, part of the gain would be taxed as long-term capital gain, even though the asset is technically not a capital asset.[29] If the asset in our example were sold for $52,000, the gain would be $37,000. Of that amount, $35,000 would be taxed as ordinary income. This is because the total depreciation deductions since 1961 were $35,000. *It makes no difference which method of depreciation was used.* The remaining $2,000 may be treated as long-term capital gain even though the asset is not a capital asset.[30] We say *may* be treated as a long-term capital gain because of a "lookback" rule which was discussed in Chapter 5. Sec. 1231 gain will still be ordinary income to the extent of any Sec. 1231 losses which were recognized within the past five years.

Obviously, if the asset in this example were sold for anything less than $15,000, there would be a loss. This loss would be fully deductible as an ordinary loss.[31]

[27]IRC Sec. 1231.
[28]IRC Sec. 1245. The ordinary gain resulting from such a sale is known as "depreciation recapture," or "Sec. 1245 recapture." Long-term capital gain classification is beneficial when the gain can be offset by capital losses.
[29]Capital assets do not include depreciable property used in a trade or business. See IRC Sec. 1221 and this book, Chapter 5.
[30]IRC Sec. 1231. If an asset has been held for less than one year, it will not be a Sec. 1231 asset. Thus, any gain would be ordinary gain.
[31]IRC Sec. 165 allows a deduction for a loss.

TAX PLANNING TIP: Timing of a sale of depreciable property can be critical. If a taxpayer is in a 33% bracket in 1990, but expects to be in a 28% bracket in 1991, postponement of the sale until 1991 can result in lower rates of tax being applied to the gain.

There is another kind of recapture for property, such as an automobile,[32] which is used partly for business and partly for nonbusiness. Earlier we discussed the rule which provides for limited depreciation and straight-line calculation where such property is used 50% or less for business. If business use falls below 50% on split-use property which was used over 50% for business in the first year, there will be recapture of the difference. This can be illustrated as follows.

Assume that Billy Barnes in 1990 purchased a $12,000 automobile to be used 80% for business. For the first year, the ACRS deduction would be $1920 (20% of 80% of the cost). The car is used 80% of the time for business during the first year, and 80% for business during the second year. The deduction for the second year will be $3,072, ($12,000 × 32% × 80%). Assume that in the third year the business use drops to 40%. The rules for depreciation where such property is used 50% or less for business were discussed earlier. Recalculating the deduction for years 1 and 2 results in the following:

Deduction for year 1 (straight-line method, five-year life, and half-year convention):	
½ × 20% × $12,000 × 80%	$960
Deduction for year 2:	
20% × $12,000 × 80%	1,920
Total for two years	$2,880
Deductions previously claimed	
($1,920 + $3,072)	4,922
Difference	($2,112)

This $2,112 difference (recapture) must be included in gross income for the third year. In addition, the depreciation deduction for year 3 will be:

20% × $12,000 × 40% = $960

Even if business use should go above 50% in year 4, or later, the cost recovery calculation must

[32]IRC Sec. 280F(b)(3).

continue to be based on the same method as for the year when business usage was less than 50% i.e. straight–time.

The same concept applies for property other than an automobile, if it is used only in part for business. For example, a computer (which is five-year ACRS property) might be used less than 100% for business. If the nonbusiness use should become 50% or more of the total use, then recapture will occur. The straight-line method will be used on the recalculation, but a twelve-year life will be used rather than a five-year life.

TAX PLANNING TIP: Taxpayers who have property used for both business and nonbusiness should be careful that business use remains above 50% in order to assure use of the shorter recovery period and to avoid the "recapture" which results when business use falls to 50% or less. Careful contemporaneous record-keeping is required.

9.3.1 Election for Certain ACRS Property

Tangible personal property which is subject to depreciation and which was acquired after 1980 (ACRS property) may be treated differently at the option of the taxpayer. Instead of calculating the amount of the gain, or loss, from the sale of the specific asset, where assets are in a "mass account" (i.e., all assets of the same class which were purchased during the same year are in one account) the entire amount of the selling price can be treated as income. The original cost of the asset stays on the books and is subject to future write-offs as if the asset had not been sold.[33]

9.4 Recapture—Real Property

On post-1986 residential rental property and nonresidential real property which are depreciated using the straight-line method, there will be no depreciation recapture. For real property placed in service before 1987, accelerated depreciation may have been used and there may be ordinary income for part or all of the gain. The recapture rules are complicated. The following general statements (applicable to property acquired prior to 1981) have some exceptions which are omitted:

1. To the extent the gain is attributable to recovery of straight-line depreciation, it will be treated as long-term capital gain.[34] Thus, if straight-line depreciation has been used and the property has been held over one year, the entire gain will be treated as long-term capital gain.
2. Except for low-income housing, all post-1975 depreciation in excess of what straight-line depreciation would have been is recaptured as ordinary income. This means that any gain on a sale is ordinary income up to the amount of that "excess" depreciation.[35] A percentage of gain attributable to the pre-1976 "excess" of accelerated over straight-line depreciation will also be treated as ordinary income.[36] The ordinary income potential declines with each passing month, for two reasons:
   a. Accelerated depreciation and straight-line depreciation will accumulate to the same total over the period of useful life, but accelerated depreciation exceeds straight-line in the early years of the asset's life, and straight-line exceeds accelerated in the later years. Thus, the ordinary income potential ("excess depreciation") declines in the later years of the asset's life and reaches zero at the end of the useful life used for calculating the depreciation.
   b. The Code provides that a reducing percentage of the pre-1976 excess of accelerated over straight-line will produce ordinary income. The result is that after 120 months in some instances and 200 months in others, there is no ordinary income recapture as to that depreciation, even though the useful life may be considerably greater than ten years or 16⅔ years.[37]
   c. Low-income housing's ordinary income potential drops by one percentage point for each month the housing is held in excess of 100 months (8⅓ years).[38] If the housing has been held for ten years (120 months), for instance, then only 80% of what would otherwise be ordinary income will be treated as such. Thus, if low-income housing is held for at least 200 months (16⅔ years), there is no ordinary income on its disposition.

Depreciation recapture on a piece of real estate purchased before 1981 can be illustrated as follows. Assume that a building was purchased for $100,000 in 1979. Depreciation has been calculated under the straight-line method, and at the time of sale of the building totals $15,000. Thus, the adjusted basis of the building is $85,000. If the building is sold for $110,000, the gain will be

[33] IRC Sec. 168(d)(2).

[34] IRC Sec. 1231.
[35] IRC Sec. 1250.
[36] IRC Sec. 1250(a).
[37] IRC Sec. 1250(a)(2)(B).
[38] IRC Sec. 1250(g).

$25,000. Section 1231 provides that (subject to the five-year "lookback" rules discussed earlier) all of the gain will be treated as long-term capital gain. It makes no difference that the building is sold for more, or for less, than its original cost. The critical factor is that straight-line depreciation was used. Note the difference between this treatment and that of tangible personal property.[39] Note also that capital gain classification will affect tax calculation for years after 1987 only when capital loss offsets are available or where there has been a charitable contribution rather than a sale of the property.

Assume that instead of straight-line depreciation, some accelerated method has been used, resulting in depreciation deductions of $22,000. Since straight-line *would have been* $15,000, the "excess" depreciation is $7,000. Any gain up to $7,000 from the sale of the building will be taxed as ordinary income. This is called "Sec. 1250 recapture." Any gain greater than $7,000 will be treated as long-term capital gain, (again, subject to the five-year "lookback" rule) called "Sec. 1231 gain." Thus, if the building is sold for $89,000, the gain will be $11,000 ($89,000 less adjusted basis of $78,000). Again, it makes no difference whether the building is sold for more or less than its original cost. The $11,000 will be divided into two parts. The amount equal to "excess" depreciation, $7,000, is ordinary income. The balance, $4,000, is *treated* as long-term capital gain, called "Sec. 1231 gain."

Certain depreciable real estate which is subject to the ACRS write-offs (post-1980 and pre-1987 property) is also subject to some different recapture provisions. Under pre-1987 ACRS, a taxpayer had the option to use rapid deductions or the straight-line method. If the accelerated method was used for nonresidential property (the table had the 175% declining-balance method built in), then a disposition which resulted in gain would cause ordinary income up to the amount of the previous deductions. But if straight-line depreciation was elected, there would be no depreciation recapture. For residential rental property, the amount of ordinary income would be that part of the gain equal to the difference between ACRS cost recovery deductions and what the deductions would have been under straight-line depreciation.

These rules can be illustrated as follows. Assume that Billy Barnes purchased a new office building in January, 1986, for a cost of $100,000, not including the land. Assume further that the building was sold on January 1, 1990, for $140,000. The cost recovery deductions, gain, and treatment of gain under the two options are as follows:

	ACRS Cost Recovery Method	
	"Regular"	*Optional S.L.*
1986 (8.8% × $100,000)	$ 8,800	$ 6,667
1987 (8.4% × $100,000)	8,400	6,667
1988 (7.6% × $100,000)	7,600	6,667
1989 (6.9% × $100,000)	6,900	6,667
Total	$31,700	$26,668
Adjusted basis (cost less deductions)	68,300	73,332
Gain (selling price less adjusted basis)	71,700	66,668
Type of gain: Ordinary (recapture)	31,700	–0–
Section 1231 gain (treated as LTCG)	40,000	66,668

If the property had been residential rental property, the cost recovery deductions would have been the same under either option. Gain on disposition, however, would be taxed differently. If the rapid write-off option were used, the difference between the total deductions ($31,700) and what straight-line depreciation would have been ($26,668) would be ordinary income. The balance would receive capital gains classification.

Thus, a taxpayer acquiring depreciable real property between 1980 and 1987 had to make a choice between accelerated and straight-line depreciation not only taking into consideration the present value of the depreciation deductions but also the difference in the expected tax impact if and when the property was disposed of for a gain. A taxpayer expecting to dispose of the property after only five years, for example, might have made a different choice (between straight-line or accelerated depreciation) than a taxpayer expecting to hold on to the property for fifteen or more years.

In Chapter 6, nontaxable exchanges were discussed. Where there is "depreciation recapture potential" in the property that is transferred in a nontaxable exchange, the property that is acquired will keep that potential for ordinary income. Thus, when the second piece of property is sold, it is necessary to go back to the financial data relative to the first piece of property to determine the appropriate tax treatment for gain on the sale. The same result occurs when property is given away. The donee will take the property subject to the same potential for depreciation recapture as existed in the hands of the donor. A subsequent sale by the donee will result in ordinary income to the extent of the ordinary income that would have been recognized by the donor.[40]

Form 4797 is used to report sales of property

[39] If the property were tangible personal property, the $25,000 gain would be $15,000 ordinary and $10,000 Sec. 1231 gain (treated as long-term capital gain).

[40] IRC Secs. 1245(b) and 1250(d). For an exception, see below.

where depreciation recapture or Section 1231 gain results.

9.5 Investment Credit

Prior to 1986, a 10% investment tax credit was allowed on the purchase of tangible business personal property (machinery and equipment).[41] If the property was classified as 3-year ACRS property (under pre-1987 rules), the credit was only 6%. The maximum credit allowed in any one year could offset the first $25,000 of tax liability plus 85% of the tax liability in excess of $25,000.[42]

Except for certain transition property, the Tax Reform Act of 1986 repealed the regular investment tax credit for property placed in service after December 31, 1985.[43] Although the credit generally is no longer available, investment tax credit recapture is possible for transition property and for 1985 purchases which are disposed of before 1991.

9.5.1. Investment Tax Credit Recapture

"Recapture" as it was used in the discussion of depreciation referred to the type of gain recognized on disposition of an asset. That part of gain which is "depreciation recapture" is taxed as ordinary income. "Recapture" as it is used in reference to the investment tax credit means something entirely different. It means an *increase* in the amount of tax liability for the year the recapture occurs.

To "earn" the full amount of investment tax credit, the property has to be held five full years (three full years if the property qualified for the 6% credit). In essence, 2% of the credit is earned for each year that the property is held. In the event that the property is disposed of prior to earning the full amount of credit, a portion of the credit has to be paid back. Because five full years will have passed at the end of 1990 since the repeal of the credit, 1990 is the last year for any potential investment tax credit recapture other than for credits claimed on transition property.

As an example, assume that Billy Barnes purchased five-year recovery property on December 1, 1985, for $50,000 and that $5,000 of investment tax credit was taken on Billy's 1985 tax return. On February 12, 1990, Billy sells the property. As a result, the property has been held only four full years and Billy will incur $1,000 (2% × $50,000) of investment tax credit recapture. This will be reported on Billy's 1990 tax return as an extra tax (see line 50 on Form 1040 at Appendix 1-D).

It is not just a sale of property which will result in investment tax credit recapture. Other dispositions which will result in recapture are (1) sale of a partner's interest in a partnership where the partner has taken his or her share of the partnership credit, (2) sale by a shareholder of stock in an S corporation where the corporation has passed the credit through to the shareholder, (3) conversion of property which has been subject to the credit to personal use, and (4) conversion of a taxable corporation to a tax-exempt corporation.[44]

9.5.2. Building Rehabilitation Credit

There is a type of investment credit for rehabilitation expenditures of buildings.[45] The credit is 10% of the qualified cost of rehabilitation of buildings which were originally placed in service before 1936 and 20% for the rehabilitation of certified historic structures. The 10% credit is available only for nonresidential buildings, but the 20% credit is available for both residential and nonresidential structures. In order to get the credit, the taxpayer must use straight-line depreciation on the structure. Eligible costs are those incurred to rehabilitate or remodel a structure, provided that (1) 50% or more of the external walls continue as external walls, (2) 75% of the external walls are retained as internal or external walls, and (3) 75% of the internal structural framework (load bearing walls, columns, etc.) are retained in place. The basis of the building is reduced by the full amount of the credit.

It is the use of the building *after* the rehabilitation which results in the qualification for the credit rather than the use before the rehabilitation. For example, if Billy Barnes purchased an old residence which had been used as rental property, and converted it to office space or a store, the latter usage would result in the rehabilitation costs qualifying for the credit.[46]

[41]IRC Sec. 38 allows the credit as part of the "general business" credit. IRC Secs. 46–48 provide the details of its application.
[42]IRC Sec. 38(c).
[43]Transition property mainly consists of property contracted for or completed to set levels by December 31, 1985. See IRC Sec. 49.
[44]Where a recapture transaction occurs during the year, it is treated as having occurred on the first day of the year. Treas. Regs. 1.47-1(c) and 1.47-2(e).
[45]IRC Sec. 48(g).
[46]This assumes that the age of the building would permit it to qualify.

TAX PLANNING TIP: Congress has enticed taxpayers to rehabilitate older structures in lieu of constructing new buildings. The 10% or 20% credit for the costs of refurbishing an older building should be taken into consideration by any taxpayer who is thinking about constructing a new building where remodeling of an eligible older building would be an acceptable alternative. It is not necessary for the taxpayer to own the older building for any required period of time before the rehabilitation begins. Therefore, the purchase of an older building, coupled with rehabilitation, might be considerably cheaper, after tax, than the construction of a new building.

9.6 Amortization

Amortization deals with intangibles. A patent right is an intangible. So is the cost of acquiring a business lease.[47]

If a store, office, factory, warehouse, or any other real estate is leased for a long term, many of the improvements that would normally be made to the premises by the lessee will become the property of the landlord at the end of the lease, unless the landlord and tenant agree otherwise. The landlord can, in fact, use the improvements made by the lessee to the property as part of the rationale for charging a higher rent. Thus, although the improvements themselves are tangible enough, they really do not "belong" to the tenant. The tenant cannot use them for the rest of their useful lives, or dispose of them, if they are fastened to the land or building. The only right to the improvements is to their use, so that they constitute a type of prepaid occupancy expense.

Based upon this rationale, the cost of leasehold improvements prior to 1987 was written off over their useful life or the term of the lease, whichever was shorter.[48] Some leases have renewal provisions, so that the term of the lease was not an easily determined period of time. There were special rules covering situations where, under the circumstances, it would seem likely that the lease would be renewed and thus the improvements would be used for a longer period.[49] In such situations, the cost of leasehold improvements would be written off, using as the lease term the renewal period as well as the original lease.[50]

Those rules do not apply to the costs of post-1986 property improvements. The improvement (e.g., a building, a new ceiling, etc.) is depreciated by the tenant just as though the tenant owned the property. If an undepreciated balance remains when the tenant surrenders the property to the landlord, the tenant takes a loss deduction.

However, the costs of acquiring a lease are still amortized as an intangible. For example, assume that a tenant signs a lease for a period of ten years with no renewal option. A bonus payment of $50,000 is made to the landlord. The amortization will be at the rate of $5,000 per year for the ten years. If the lease agreement contains a renewal clause for a second ten years, the amortization period will be twenty years if the taxpayer cannot establish it to be probable that the lease will not be renewed. Amortization is always calculated under the straight-line method.

Goodwill is another intangible. Purchased goodwill must be amortized for financial accounting purposes, but amortization of goodwill is *not* allowed for tax purposes.[51]

Other intangibles, such as patents and trademarks, are amortized over their useful life or legal life, whichever is shorter. Corporations and partnerships can amortize organization costs over a period of sixty months or more. Business start-up costs can be amortized over sixty months.

9.7 Depletion and the Costs of Exploration and Development

A basic accounting objective is to match revenue earned for a time period with the costs of earning that revenue. If $1,000,000 is paid for 1,000,000 units of X, then the cost of each unit of X sold is $1. This basic idea is applied, with variations, to determine the cost of merchandise sold. It is also applied to the determination of depreciation. For example, if a machine costs $100,000 and it is expected to produce 1,000,000 units of product, depreciation can be estimated at 10 cents per unit produced.

9.7.1. Cost Depletion

The same basic concept is applied when dealing with natural resources. If $1,000,000 is spent

[47]The IRC does not provide a definition for amortization. However, it means an equal, or straight-line, allocation of cost over the life expectancy. However, where the term of the lease is more than the ACRS life (usually 15 years), then ACRS would apply as with any building component put in service after 1980.
[48]Treas. Reg. 1.167(a)-4.
[49]IRC Sec. 178.
[50]IRC Sec. 178(c).
[51]The rationale for no deduction is that goodwill cannot be assigned a life expectancy. Treas. Reg. 1.167(a)-3.

for a tract of land that contains an estimated 1,000,000 units of natural resource, the natural resource has cost $1 per unit, which becomes a deduction when units are extracted and sold. This is called "cost depletion."

Each year, a new computation of cost depletion is made. The approach is to divide the unrecovered cost (adjusted basis) of the natural resource by the sum of the units sold during the year plus the estimated number of mineral units remaining as of the end of the year. This gives a cost per unit. This cost is multiplied by the number of units *sold* to get the total depletion deduction by the cost method.[52]

9.7.2. Percentage Depletion

Another way of computing depletion is the "percentage-depletion" technique.[53] This allows a deduction that is a given percentage of *gross income* derived from the sale. Neither cost nor adjusted basis is part of the determination of the deduction. The percentage that is used is a number given taxpayers by Congress and varies from 5% to 22%, depending upon the kind of natural resource.[54] Political and economic factors enter into the determination of the percentages. See Appendix 9A to this chapter.

For example, assume that a taxpayer paid $1,000,000 for an estimated 1,000,000 units of natural resource. During the year 200,000 units were extracted and sold at $10 per unit. Cost depletion would be $1 per unit or $200,000. If the percentage-depletion rate applicable were 22%, the percentage-depletion deduction would be 22% of the $2,000,000 of sales, or $440,000.[55]

Percentage depletion is limited to 50% of *taxable income* from the particular property. Thus, in the example above, if the expenses associated with the sale of the property had been $800,000, taxable income would have been $1,200,000 (before depletion deduction). The depletion deduction would still have been $440,000, because 50% of $1,200,000 is larger. On the other hand, if expenses (not counting depletion) had been $1,300,000, taxable income would have been $700,000 (before depletion). That would result in a limitation upon the depletion deduction of 50% of $700,000, or $350,000. Thus, percentage depletion would have been $350,000 instead of $440,000. There would be no carryover for the amount not deductible. The 50% of taxable income limitation on depletion does not apply to cost depletion.

The taxpayer uses cost depletion or percentage depletion (as limited), *whichever is larger*. Whichever method is used, the amount of the depletion deduction must be subtracted from the unrecovered cost (adjusted basis) of the asset.[56] This might reduce the per unit cost depletion number, which is calculated as of the end of the year, as explained. At some point, cost depletion may turn out to be zero per unit.[57] However, a taxpayer can continue taking percentage depletion even after all of the cost has been recovered and the adjusted basis of the property is zero.[58]

Percentage depletion in excess of the adjusted basis of the property is a "tax preference item," however, and can result in some "minimum tax." See Chapter 16.

Going back to the example with 22% depletion and $1 per unit cost depletion, cost depletion for the year would be $200,000, and percentage depletion would be $440,000. The tax basis for the next year would be $560,000 ($1,000,000 cost less $440,000 depletion). The remaining units that had not been extracted and sold would be 800,000 (assuming that the estimate had not changed). Cost depletion per unit would be reduced to 70 cents ($560,000/800,000) per unit. If during each of the next two years 200,000 units were sold at $10 per unit, percentage depletion could still be deducted at the same 22% of the $2,000,000 gross per year (assuming that the deduction would not be limited by 50% of taxable income). At the end of three years, percentage depletion deductions would total $1,320,000, even though the property cost only $1,000,000. The tax basis in the property, and hence cost depletion, would be reduced to zero.

Percentage depletion is thus unique in the U.S. tax law, in that taxpayers are allowed to deduct amounts in excess of their investment expenditure.

Oil and gas depletion has been the subject of much tax controversy. Percentage depletion is generally allowed for oil and gas in only two situations.[59] The one of most interest here is the allowance for small producers. Percentage depletion at a 15% rate is allowed to small producers for an average of 1,000 barrels per day (or its equiva-

[52]See Treas. Reg. 1.611-2. IRC Sec. 611 allows the deduction for depletion. Section 612 deals with the basis for cost depletion.

[53]IRC Sec. 613.

[54]See IRC Sec. 613(b).

[55]Percentage depletion is at the rate provided by Congress for that particular mineral.

[56]IRC Sec. 1016(a).

[57]Since percentage depletion is a percentage of gross income from the sale of the property, the adjusted basis could be reduced to zero, although the number of units estimated to exist may be the same as originally estimated. If adjusted basis of the property is zero, the cost depletion per unit must be zero.

[58]IRC Sec. 613(a).

[59]IRC Sec. 613A.

lent in cubic feet of gas). In addition, the percentage depletion attributable to the small producer exemption cannot exceed 65% of the taxpayer's taxable income.[60] Generally, the taxpayer is not entitled to the small producer depletion if an interest in an oil or gas property was acquired after 1974 and the property was "proven" at the time. The purpose of this percentage depletion is to encourage the development of new wells and not merely the acquisition of established properties.

9.7.3. Exploration and Development

The intangible drilling and development costs of oil or gas wells may be deducted in the year incurred rather than being treated as part of the cost of acquiring a producing well.[61] If these expenses were capitalized, they would be of relatively little advantage in any situation where percentage depletion exceeded cost depletion, because they would be recovered as a part of the percentage depletion. By having a deduction available for the drilling and development cost, these *and* the percentage depletion can both be taken.

These intangible drilling and development costs include wages, fuel, repairs, hauling, supplies, and related drilling costs. They do not include items essentially related to the production of the oil, such as pumping equipment, flow lines, storage tanks, or even the well casing. Intangible drilling and development costs that have been deducted may be "recaptured," in a manner similar to depreciation, and thus convert into ordinary income part of what would otherwise be a capital gain on sale of an oil or gas property.[62]

Exploration costs of other natural resources may be deducted when incurred.[63] Corporations can deduct only 70% of these costs, with the balance amortized over 60 months. If the project proves successful, the amount deducted will be recaptured.[64] The taxpayer can either report the amount previously deducted as income in the year in which the mine reaches the producing stage, or offset it against the depletion deduction that would otherwise be available. To the extent not deducted, exploration costs become part of the cost of the property and are thus subject to cost depletion. If the exploration project proves unsuccessful, such capitalized costs are, of course, deductible as a part of the loss on the property.

Development expenses are expenses incurred after it has been established that a mine contains commercially marketable quantities of an ore or mineral. These expenses are deductible when incurred and need not be capitalized.[65] A taxpayer may elect to capitalize them and defer the time of deduction until the ore or mineral is sold. This would be done, for example, if the marginal tax rate were expected to be higher in future years. Development expenses include the depreciation on equipment and other depreciable assets used in the development.

9.8 Business versus Personal

It is sometimes hard to distinguish a resort home that is held as an investment (for rental income) from that which is used primarily for personal and family gratification. If a dwelling is used for more than fourteen days during a year (or 10% of the number of days the home is rented, if that 10% would be more than fourteen), deductions for such expenses as depreciation are prorated based upon days rented compared with days of personal use.[66] The expenses are also limited in total to rental income, so that a net loss cannot be derived from depreciation.

Assume that Billy Barnes decides to purchase and rent a house. Billy will live in the house as a vacation residence for three months and rent it out for nine months. Expenses are as follows:

	For Nine Months	*For Three Months*	*Total*
Interest on mortgage	$3,150	$1,050	$4,200
Property taxes	675	225	900
Insurance	180	60	240
Utilities	720	240	960
Depreciation	1,530	510	2,040
Total	$6,255	$2,085	$8,340

Since mortgage interest and property taxes for the entire year are deductible anyway, a recognized loss could result if the rental income is under

[60] IRC Sec. 613A(d).

[61] IRC Sec. 263(c). Treas. Reg. 1.612-4. Geothermal property is also included. Only a percentage of the IDC of "integrated producers" can be currently expensed, with the balance amortized over 60 months.

[62] IRC Sec. 1254. Intangible drilling costs can also result in a tax preference, which can result in a "minimum tax" liability. Tax preferences and the minimum tax are discussed in Chapter 16.

[63] IRC Sec. 617. The deduction is an election available to the taxpayer. There is a lifetime ceiling of $400,000 on the total that a taxpayer can deduct.

[64] IRC Sec. 617(b). The "recapture" here does not come at the time of sale of the property as in the case of Secs. 1245 and 1250 recapture, but at the time the mine reaches production stage.

[65] IRC Sec. 616. Intangible drilling and development costs for oil and gas wells and geothermal wells are covered by some special rules in Sec. 263(c).

Note: Different rules apply to foreign oil, gas, and other mineral operations outside the U.S. These are not discussed here.

[66] IRC Sec. 280A.

$3,825 (the sum of interest and property taxes attributable to the rental period).[67] Expenses that would be allowed as a deduction are subtracted from rental income first. Deductions for other rental-related expenses (insurance and utilities in this example) cannot result in a loss. If rental income is large enough to allow all such expenses to be deducted, then depreciation can be deducted. The tax effect is summarized as follows:

Amount of Rental Income	*Allowable Deductions*	*Gain (Loss)*
$7,000	$6,255	$745
6,000	6,000	0
5,000	5,000	0
4,000	4,000	0
3,000	3,825	(825)

Insurance, utilities, and depreciation applicable to that time during which the property is used as a personal residence are never deductible.[68]

One other rule relative to the rental of vacation homes: If the property is rented for less than fifteen days, the rental income can be excluded from gross income and there will be no expenses deducted relative to the rental income.[69] This is a unique provision in the tax law.

TAX PLANNING TIP: A vacation property can produce untaxed income! If it is rented for less than fifteen days in the year, the rental income need not be reported. But if it is rented for a greater portion of the year, there is still a range where greater rental income does not affect the net gain or loss from the rental property. In the example above, no gain is reported if rental income is $4,000—but neither is there any gain to report if rental income is $6,000. Thus, an extra $2,000 of income can be derived without paying any income tax on it.

[67]IRC Sec. 163 provides for a deduction for interest. Personal interest is not deductible, with the exception of qualified residence interest paid on the principal residence and one other residence of the taxpayer. IRC Sec. 163(h). It does not have to be related to business. Of course, business interest is deductible *for* AGI, whereas personal interest is deductible *from* AGI. IRC Sec. 164 provides the deduction for taxes. As with interest, business taxes are deductible for AGI and nonbusiness taxes are "itemized."

[68]IRC Sec. 262. For the Tax Court's interpretation of the allocation procedures under Sec. 280A, see *Dorance D. Bolton* (CA9 1982), 82-2 USTC 9699, 51 AFTR2d 83-303. The IRS would relate total interest and taxes to only the days the property is in use, thus reducing the amount available for depreciation. The Tax Court, in *Bolton*, characterized that as "bizarre" and allocated interest and taxes to rental income on the ratio of rent use to total days in the year. The Ninth Circuit Court of Appeals agreed.

[69]IRC Sec. 280A(g).

9.9 Obsolescence

Not all depreciable assets are used for their full estimated useful lives. Machinery and equipment may be demolished, abandoned, or scrapped. The remaining unrecovered investment at that point is then written off over the remaining life. Abandonment, demolition, or scrapping will usually justify writing off the entire remaining investment.[70] An exception applies where a building is demolished.[71] Both the cost of the demolition and any remaining adjusted basis for the building must be added to the basis of the land on which the building was located.

9.10 Special Amortization

Various special tax law provisions allow write-off of costs over arbitrary time periods—most commonly over sixty months. These include

Pollution-control facilities;[72]

Rehabilitation expenditures on low-income rental housing.[73]

9.11 Conclusion

With the exceptions of investment credit recapture and percentage depletion, the main focus of this chapter has been on how asset costs are written off for tax purposes. The total amount written off will be the same regardless of "when," but "when" the deduction is allowed makes a big difference to the taxpayer contemplating an investment.

If gain is realized on a later disposition of such an asset, some part of that gain may be classified as ordinary income on the rationale that it is really a "recapture" of a tax deduction previously taken. The balance of the gain will normally be treated as long-term capital gain. This allows it to be offset by capital losses. Buildings get much more favorable tax treatment in this regard than personal property. In the case of nonresidential pre-1987 ACRS buildings, favorable tax treatment applies only if straight-line depreciation was elected.

Percentage depletion interacts with tax basis for other purposes, and thus results in possible lower deductions for cost depletion or greater gain on disposition. Even though percentage depletion reduces tax basis, that reduction cannot create a negative tax basis. Thus, once the investment has been fully recovered, percentage depletion is a type of tax "freebie" as compared with other analogous capital recovery provisions.

[70]IRC Sec. 165.

[71]IRC Sec. 280B.

[72]IRC Sec. 169.

[73]IRC Sec. 167(k).

TRUE-FALSE QUESTIONS

State whether each of the following statements is true or false. For each *false* answer, reword the statement to make it *true*.

T F 1. An automobile placed in service in 1990 and used 100% of the time in business is five-year ACRS property.

T F 2. ACRS property which is tangible personal property will result in depreciation for the first year under a one-half-year convention.

T F 3. A taxpayer can elect to use a longer period for cost recovery of a capitalized business asset. However, such an election will result in depreciation being calculated under the straight-line method.

T F 4. A fee paid to a broker to acquire stocks or bonds is deductible as an expense for the production of income.

T F 5. Even if an automobile is to be used 100% of the time for business purposes, the maximum amount of the depreciation (ACRS) deduction for 1989 is $4,200 regardless of the cost of the car.

T F 6. A taxpayer acquired a used warehouse building on April 15, 1990. The building has a remaining useful life of twenty years. The building can be depreciated over twenty years.

T F 7. If a residential building is sold for a gain, and that building has been subject to straight-line depreciation, there will be no depreciation recapture under IRC Sec. 1250 whether the property was ACRS recovery property or not.

T F 8. If a personal residence is sold and the selling price is less than the basis, the taxpayer can deduct the loss.

T F 9. If a taxpayer purchases tangible personal property which will be used in a business for $5,000, an election can be made to expense that cost the first year rather than capitalize it and take future depreciation deductions.

T F 10. If investment tax credit (ITC) was claimed in 1985 for 3-year property and that property is sold in 1990, the entire amount of the ITC will have to be repaid.

T F 11. If a computer (which was 5-year ACRS property under the pre-1987 rules) was purchased and placed in service in August, 1985, and the maximum investment tax credit (ITC) was claimed because the computer was to be used 100% of the time for business, but it is sold in May, 1990, none of the 1985 ITC will have to be repaid.

T F 12. If a taxpayer purchases and restores a business building which is a "certified historic structure" there will be a tax credit for 20% of the cost of the rehabilitation.

T F 13. For a depreciable business building, such as an office complex, which is acquired in 1990, the tax rules assign a cost recovery period of 31.5 years to the property, whereas a rental building, such as an apartment for human occupancy, has been assigned a cost recovery period of 27.5 years.

T F 14. Depletion will reduce the basis of property that is being depleted, similar to the reduction in basis where depreciation deductions are claimed.

T F 15. Depletion deductions, like depreciation, can never be taken in total for more than the original basis of the property in the hands of the taxpayer.

T F 16. Where a piece of tangible personal property purchased since 1961 is sold for a gain, any gain that is equal to or less than the total depreciation deductions on that property will be classified as ordinary income.

T F 17. There cannot be depreciation recapture on a depreciable building placed in service in 1987 or later because the only method of depreciation which can be used for federal income tax purposes is the straight-line method.

T F 18. A taxpayer is required to calculate depletion under both the cost and the percentage methods and to take a deduction for the larger amount.

T F 19. "Depreciation recapture" is the term used to refer to that part of the gain from the sale of depreciable property which will be taxed as ordinary income.

T F 20. Intangible assets such as patents, goodwill, and trademarks can be depreciated under an allowable accelerated method.

PROBLEMS

Problem 9-1. Washington White purchased an automobile to be used 100% of the time in his business. The car cost $40,000, and he purchased it on June 1, 1990. Prepare a schedule which will show the maximum amount of depreciation deductions over the life of the car.

Problem 9-2. Tom and Toni own a beach condominium that they rent out during the year and use on occasion for personal use. Assume that Tom and Toni's other income is about $60,000 and their itemized deductions, irrespective of the condominium expenses, are greater than the allowed standard deduction. During 1990, rental income was $5,000, and the following expenditures were incurred in connection with the beach condominium:

Mortgage Interest	$3,000
Real Estate Taxes	1,000
Insurance	1,000
Utilities	2,000
Depreciation	2,000

(a) Is the beach condominium considered a vacation home under the following circumstances:
  (1) Personal Use Days 20, Rental Days 220
  (2) Personal Use Days 12, Rental Days 100
  (3) Personal Use Days 16, Rental Days 150

(b) Assume that personal use was 73 days (20%) and the rental use was 292 days (80%). Compute the total amount of deductible expenses. Indicate how much of the allowable deduction is treated as a personal itemized deduction and how much is treated as a deductible rental expense.

Problem 9-3. The Sonny Corporation had a tax liability, before credits, of $170,000 for 1990. During the year, the corporation purchased an office building which had been constructed in 1934. The cost was $100,000, not including the cost of the land. The rehabilitation costs will be $200,000 and the building will be placed in service as an office building at the beginning of 1990.

(a) Determine the amount of the rehabilitation credit for 1990.

(b) What is the depreciation deduction?

Problem 9-4. Mark Gratz owns and operates a foundry and machine shop. Ten years ago he purchased an automated turret lathe for $50,000. Now there is a new computer-controlled lathe on the market. Mark feels that the competition for quality work will force him to purchase the new machine, which is priced at $150,000. The adjusted basis of the old machine is $10,000. He thinks he can sell it for $18,000. The supplier of the new lathe has offered to give him a $22,000 "trade-in" on the purchase of the new model. Mark expects to be in the 33% tax bracket this year.

(a) If Mark sells the old machine, what immediate tax effect, if any, will there be?

(b) If Mark trades the old machine for the new one, what tax effect will there be? What is the difference in immediate cash flow?

(c) Can Mark avoid the depreciation recapture on the old machine by trading it in on a new one? Explain.

Problem 9-5. Mary Garcia owns the Garcia Corporation. During 1990, the corporation purchased a new office building for its administrative headquarters. The cost, not including the land, was $1,200,000. The corporation uses a calendar tax year. Assuming that the building was first open for use on April 10, 1990, answer the following questions. (The depreciation rules for corporations are the same as those for individuals.)

(a) What is the maximum ACRS depreciation for 1990? For 1991? For 1992?

(b) Does the corporation have a choice with regard to the method of depreciation which it will use? Explain.

(c) Assume that the opening of the building got delayed from April until July of 1990. What impact would such a delay have upon the amount of depreciation for 1990 and the next two years? Explain.

Problem 9-6. On January 2, 1988, Jim Robinson purchased a new warehouse for storage of inventory in his business. The total cost was $20,000 for land and $100,000 for building. The estimated useful life of the warehouse was twenty years. Jim is considering the sale of the land and building. It is now December 1990.

Assume that the federal income tax rates for married persons filing a joint return will apply.

(a) Calculate the total depreciation deductions that have been taken to date, including a full year's depreciation for 1990. Use Table 9-2.

(b) If the land is sold for $25,000 and the building for $90,000, what will be the *extra* tax resulting from the sale. Assume that Jim will have $48,000 in taxable income on a joint return before the sale and no other transactions involving capital assets or business assets.

Problem 9-7. Bart Beatty's furniture store and inventory were totally destroyed by fire last July 12. The adjusted basis of the property was as follows:

Inventory	$220,000
Building	175,000
Building fixtures	20,000

The building and fixtures were originally acquired in 1981. Straight-line depreciation had been used on all depreciable property. Insurance proceeds were for replacement cost as follows:

Inventory	$265,000
Building	260,000
Building fixtures	0

(a) If Bart decides to retire rather than continue in business, what tax effect will the loss and insurance recovery have on him? Assume that without any of the foregoing events, Bart would have had $50,000 of taxable income on a joint return. (Use 1990 rates.)

(b) What difference, if any, would there be if Bart had used accelerated depreciation on the building?

(c) Explain how Bart may avoid paying tax on the gain from the insurance proceeds.

Problem 9-8. Max Bowman purchased a warehouse last March. Within the next six months, he spent $14,000 to resurface the floors and to replace the garage doors. Neither of these items prolonged the life of the building or made the building more suitable for a different use than that for which Max originally purchased the property. Also, neither expenditure was a part of an overall plan to improve the property.

(a) Under what theory might Max be required to capitalize the $14,000 rather than take a current deduction?

(b) Under what theory might Max be entitled to an expense deduction for the $14,000?

(c) In arriving at an answer for how Max should treat the $14,000 expenditure, would the original cost of the warehouse to Max be relevant information?

(d) What are the tax planning implications for repairs and improvements to property?

Problem 9-9. Bruce Smith will drive his car a total of 20,000 miles during the current year. Of that amount 17,000 will pertain to business. Bruce has felt that it is just too much trouble to keep records of the costs of operating his car. (He does, however, have all of the necessary records to establish the mileage figures given above.) Consequently, he will use the standard mileage allowance to calculate the deduction for federal income tax purposes (i.e., 26 cents per mile). For purposes of this problem, assume (1) that Bruce is in the 33% tax bracket and (2) that the actual costs of operating the car for the entire 20,000 miles were $5,000 (including depreciation).

How much additional federal income tax will Bruce pay as the result of not keeping adequate records?

Problem 9-10. McDonald Corporation sold a machine for $50,000 on December 27. It had been purchased three years previously at a cost of $40,000. On the date of sale, the machine had an adjusted basis to the corporation of $32,000. (The depreciation recapture rules apply to corporations just as they do to individuals.)

(a) What is the amount and kind of gain or loss recognizable by the corporation?

(b) Does it matter whether straight-line or some accelerated method of depreciation had been used?

(c) What might McDonald Corporation have done to avoid the tax?

(d) What other tax implications are possible? Explain.

Problem 9-11. Indicate which of the following assets, all used in business and held more than twelve months, are Sec. 1231, Sec. 1245, and/or Sec. 1250 assets.

	Section 1231	*Section 1245*	*Section 1250*	*Neither*
Warehouse	______	______	______	______
Accounts receivable	______	______	______	______
Inventory	______	______	______	______
Machinery	______	______	______	______
Office building	______	______	______	______

Patent	______	______	______	______
Delivery truck	______	______	______	______
Timber	______	______	______	______
Copyright	______	______	______	______
Government bonds	______	______	______	______

Problem 9-12. On January 2 of this year, the Ross Manufacturing Co. purchased new factory equipment (seven-year ACRS property) for $100,000. Ross elected to expense $10,000 of the cost under Sec. 179.

(a) What is the maximum amount Ross can deduct as depreciation plus the expense write-off?

(b) What amount can Ross deduct as depreciation if the straight-line method is elected?

(c) If the Ross Company pays tax at a marginal rate of 34% and can earn 8% rate of return *after tax*, what is the advantage of ACRS cost recovery versus straight-line depreciation for the first year? Will Ross Company ever have to repay this advantage? Explain.

Problem 9-13. Carlos McMann purchased an automobile in September 1990 for $10,000. For the balance of 1990, he used the car 90% of the time for business and 10% for nonbusiness. For 1991, he planned to use the car over 50% of the time for business, but due to an unexpected nonbusiness trip late in the year, the business usage fell to 45% of the total.

(a) What was the proper depreciation (ACRS) deduction claimed by Carlos for 1990?

(b) Explain the tax effect of having the business use drop to less than 50%.

Problem 9-14. The Motherload Mining Corporation mines some property that it acquired in 1972 at a cost of $1,600,000. For last year, the corporation had $1,000,000 of gross income and $380,000 of taxable income from this property, before claiming any deduction for depletion. The applicable percentage depletion rate is 15%. In prior years, percentage depletion deductions totaling $1,400,000 have been claimed and allowed.

(a) What will be the depletion deduction for last year?

(b) Does the corporation have a choice between cost and percentage depletion? Explain.

(c) What if the mining operations were closed before the end of the year because the mineral deposits were exhausted? (All mined deposits were also sold. All other facts remain the same.)

Problem 9-15. Lynn Acorn operates a business from a building which is located in the downtown area of the city. The building originally cost $50,000 in 1935 and has since been fully depreciated. The building is no longer suitable for its current use, but could be rehabilitated to serve adequately at a total cost of $200,000. The size of the building would not be increased and no exterior walls would be removed or replaced. As an alternative, Lynn has architects' estimates on the cost of a new building, which would be $250,000. In either case, the building will be residential when it is completed. Prepare an analysis which will indicate the related depreciation deductions for the next three years, under the two alternatives. (Assume that in either event, the depreciation deductions will be available beginning January 1, next year.)

Problem 9-16. Prepare a schedule showing the first five years' annual depreciation deductions for a $600,000 building under the following four different assumptions concerning the recovery period (assuming in all cases that the building was placed in service during the seventh month of the year): See Appendix 9-B(a)-(c).

(a) fifteen years
(b) eighteen years
(c) nineteen years
(d) thirty-one and a half years

PROBLEMS WITH AN ASTERISK REQUIRE ADDITIONAL RESEARCH.

Problem 9-17.* Blake Corporation has been in business for twenty years. On January 2, 1979, it purchased a new machine for $80,000. At that time it was expected that the machine would have a useful life of fifteen years and no salvage value. On January 2, 1982, the corporation spent $7,000 for an addition that increased the output of the machine but did not add to its life expectancy. Straight-line depreciation was used on the original machine and the improvement. On January 2, 1990, the machine was traded in on a new one that had the same function. Blake paid $68,000 boot plus the old machine to acquire the new one.

(a) Was the exchange taxable or nontaxable? Is there an available election?
(b) What is the basis of the new machine?
(c) Can Blake use the 200% declining balance MACRS recovery for the new machine?
(d) If rapid cost recovery can be used, will it affect the tax treatment of the gain or loss on the new machine in the event that it is later sold?

Problem 9-18.* The Afta Corporation operates a factory which includes a substantial amount of heavy machinery. To ensure a minimum delay in production if any of the machines should break down, the corporation has purchased extra "standby replacement parts." These parts are stored in a warehouse until needed. As the tax adviser for Afta, you have been asked how to treat the cost of those replacement parts. The alternatives are (1) capitalize the replacement parts cost and expense each part as used for replacement; (2) capitalize the replacement parts cost and depreciate the cost as ACRS property; (3) expense the replacement parts cost as the parts are purchased. Which would you recommend, and why?

APPENDIX 9A

Percentage Depletion for Various Natural Resources

(1) Sulfur and uranium; and if from deposits in the United States, anorthosite, clay, laterite, and nephelite syenite (to the extent that alumina and aluminum compounds are extracted from it), asbestos, bauxite, celestite, chromite, corundum, fluorspar, graphite, ilmenite, kyanite, mica, olvine, quartz crystals (radio grade), rutile, block steatite talc, zircon, and ores of the following metals: antimony, beryllium, bismuth, cadmium, cobalt, columbium, lead, lithium, manganese, mercury, molybdenum, nickel, platinum and platinum group metals, tantalum, thorium, tin, titanium, tungsten, vanadium and zinc . . 22%

(2) Domestic gold, silver, oil shale (except shale to which (5) applies), copper and iron ore 15%

(3) (a) Ball clay, bentonite, china clay, sagger clay, metal mines (if not allowed in 22% group above), rock asphalt, vermiculite; and

(b) All other minerals [including, but not limited to, aplite, barite, borax, calcium carbonate, clay (refractory and fire) diatomaceous earth, dolomite, feldspar, fullers earth, garnet, gilsonite, granite, limestone, magnesite, magnesium carbonates, marble, mollusk shells (including clam and oyster shells), phosphate rock, potash, quartzite, slate, soapstone, stone (used or sold for use by the mine owner or operator as dimension stone or ornamental stone) thenardite, tripoli, trona and (if not allowed in the 22% group above) bauxite, flake graphite, fluorspar, lepidolite, mica, spodumene, and talc, including pyrophyllite] except as specified in (A) and (B) below 14%

(A) When minerals in group 3(b) are used or sold for use by the mine owner or operator as rip rap, ballast, road material, rubble, concrete aggregates, or for similar purposes the percentage is 5% (unless sold on bid in direct competition with a bona fide bid to sell a mineral listed in 3(a)).

(B) Group 3(b) does not include soil, sod, dirt, turf, water or mosses; or minerals from sea water, the air or similar inexhaustible sources, or oil and gas wells.

(4) Asbestos (if from deposits outside U.S.), brucite, coal, lignite, perlite, sodium chloride, and wollastonite 10%

(5) Clay and shale used or sold for use in the manufacture of sewer pipe or brick, and clay, shale, and slate used or sold for use as sintered or burned lightweight aggregates 7½%

(6) Gravel, peat, peat moss, pumice, sand, scorta, shale (except shale to which 15% or 7½% rate applies), and stone, except stone described in the 14% group; and, if from brine wells—bromine, calcium chloride, and magnesium chloride 5%

SOURCE: Treas. Reg. 1.613-2.

APPENDIX 9–B(a)

15-Year Real Property Acquired After 1980 and Before March 16, 1984 to Be Deducted, Based on 175% Declining-Balance Method, and Prorated for Month of Year Property Was Acquired
For all depreciable real estate other than low-income housing:

	Month of the year the property was placed in service											
Year	*1*	*2*	*3*	*4*	*5*	*6*	*7*	*8*	*9*	*10*	*11*	*12*
1	12%	11%	10%	9%	8%	7%	6%	5%	4%	3%	2%	1%
2	10%	10%	11%	11%	11%	11%	11%	11%	11%	11%	11%	12%
3	9%	9%	9%	9%	10%	10%	10%	10%	10%	10%	10%	10%
4	8%	8%	8%	8%	8%	8%	9%	9%	9%	9%	9%	9%
5	7%	7%	7%	7%	7%	7%	8%	8%	8%	8%	8%	8%
6	6%	6%	6%	6%	7%	7%	7%	7%	7%	7%	7%	7%
7	6%	6%	6%	6%	6%	6%	6%	6%	6%	6%	6%	6%

APPENDIX 9–B(b)

18-Year Real Property (18-Year 175% Declining Balance)
(Assuming No Mid-month Convention)
(Property Placed in Service After March 15, 1984, and Before June 23, 1984)[74]

	Month in th First Recovery Year the Property Was Placed in Service										
Year	*1*	*2*	*3*	*4*	*5*	*6*	*7*	*8*	*9*	*10–11*	*12*
	The applicable percentage is:										
1	10	9	8	7	6	6	5	4	3	2	1
2	9	9	9	9	9	9	9	9	9	10	10
3	8	8	8	8	8	8	8	8	9	9	9
4	7	7	7	7	7	7	8	8	8	8	8
5	6	7	7	7	7	7	7	7	7	7	7
6	6	6	6	6	6	6	6	6	6	6	6
7	5	5	5	5	6	6	6	6	6	6	6
8	5	5	5	5	5	5	5	5	5	5	5
9	5	5	5	5	5	5	5	5	5	5	5
10	5	5	5	5	5	5	5	5	5	5	5
11	5	5	5	5	5	5	5	5	5	5	5
12	5	5	5	5	5	5	5	5	5	5	5
13	4	4	4	5	5	4	4	5	4	4	4
14	4	4	4	4	4	4	4	4	4	4	4
15	4	4	4	4	4	4	4	4	4	4	4
16	4	4	4	4	4	4	4	4	4	4	4
17	4	4	4	4	4	4	4	4	4	4	4
18	4	4	4	4	4	4	4	4	4	4	4
19			1	1	1	2	2	2	3	3	4

APPENDIX 9–B(c)

19-Year Real Property (19-Year 175% Declining-Balance)
(Assuming Mid-Month Convention)
(Property Placed in Service After May 8, 1985, and Before January 1, 1987)

	Month of the Year the Property Was Placed in Service											
Year	*1*	*2*	*3*	*4*	*5*	*6*	*7*	*8*	*9*	*10*	*11*	*12*
1	8.8%	8.1%	7.3%	6.5%	5.8%	5.0%	4.2%	3.5%	2.7%	1.9%	1.1%	0.4%
2	8.4%	8.5%	8.5%	8.6%	8.7%	8.8%	8.8%	8.9%	9.0%	9.0%	9.1%	9.2%
3	7.6%	7.7%	7.7%	7.8%	7.9%	7.9%	8.0%	8.1%	8.1%	8.2%	8.3%	8.3%
4	6.9%	7.0%	7.0%	7.1%	7.1%	7.2%	7.3%	7.3%	7.4%	7.4%	7.5%	7.6%
5	6.3%	6.3%	6.4%	6.4%	6.5%	6.5%	6.6%	6.6%	6.7%	6.8%	6.8%	6.9%
6	5.7%	5.7%	5.8%	5.9%	5.9%	5.9%	6.0%	6.0%	6.1%	6.1%	6.2%	6.2%
7	5.2%	5.2%	5.3%	5.3%	5.3%	5.4%	5.4%	5.5%	5.5%	5.6%	5.6%	5.6%

[74]Note: Property placed in service after June 22, 1984, and before May 9, 1985, used the mid-month convention. The percents in the earlier years were slightly less than Appendix 9-B(b).

10

partnerships and partners

This chapter will first review the tax concept of a partnership and examine the interaction of the partnership tax return with the tax returns of the individual partners.

Having laid this general groundwork, the tax aspects of forming and liquidating a partnership will be discussed. Finally, some special partnership problem areas will be examined, such as sale of a partnership interest, partnership fiscal years, and retirement of a partner. Family partnerships are discussed in Chapter 15.

10.1 What Is a Partnership?

Generally, a partnership is a contractual relationship between two or more persons for the purpose of engaging in business, with mutual ownership and responsibility. The name given an organization does not entirely control its treatment for federal income tax purposes. Thus, the IRS will treat as a corporation both a corporation created as such under state laws and also any other organization that resembles a corporation more than it does a partnership or trust.[1]

Partnerships, in turn, are broadly defined to include syndicates, groups, pools, joint ventures, and other organizations not classifiable as corporations, in addition to organizations that would be labeled partnerships under state law.[2]

Characteristics of a typical general partnership under state law would include the ability of each partner to act as an agent of the partnership (e.g., to enter into contracts); the unlimited personal liability of each partner for partnership debts; the fact that the death, insanity, bankruptcy, or withdrawal of any partner acts to terminate the partnership; and the fact that the partners share profits (and/or losses) equally or in some other agreed-upon manner. These are characteristics that are probably already relatively familiar to you. Less familiar may be such terms as *syndicates, pools,* and *joint ventures.*

Syndicate usually refers to an undertaking for a specific purpose that requires a relatively large aggregate of capital. For example, in order to distribute corporate securities, an underwriting syndicate is often formed. Such a syndicate is a group of security houses, each of which agrees to buy a stipulated portion of the security issue involved. Management of the syndicate is usually the responsibility of one or a few members of the group. Once the underwriting terminates, that particular syndicate is concluded. Syndicates are also found in the real estate business and in oil, gas, and other mineral undertakings that require large amounts of capital.

Pools, on the other hand, tend to be associated with specific trading activities. Thus, several persons or organizations might "pool" their funds to trade actively in a certain stock, with the hope of driving the price upward and then liquidating their position at a profit. The term "pools" is also sometimes applied to simple poolings of funds for general investment purposes, without any specific trading objective.

Because of their nature, which tends to re-

[1]IRC Sec. 7701(a)(3) defines a corporation. It includes "associations," which are organizations that have many of the characteristics of a corporation although not actually organized as corporations under any state law.

[2]IRC Sec. 761(a).

quire centralization of management and often allows free transferability of interests, both syndicates and pools are frequently treated as corporations for federal tax purposes. When not so treated, however, they are partnerships.

Joint ventures may also be classified as partnerships or corporations. A joint venture simply requires the joining together of parties (who may be individuals, partnerships, or corporations) in a venture for their common benefit, with each contributing something (either property or services) and each having an interest in the profits. The term is most commonly employed in construction undertakings, but the joint venture can be used in almost any field of activity, including the operation of a business, the production of a play, the development of mineral properties, or strictly investment activities. The major distinction between the syndicate and the joint venture lies in the number of participants—the syndicate having a relatively large number and the joint venture normally a few.

It is of major importance to note that these are all treated as partnerships for tax purposes when their characteristics are more similar to the typical partnership than to the typical corporation.

As a general rule, starting in 1988, publicly traded partnerships (also known as master limited partnerships) have been treated as corporations. The basic reason for such treatment is that such partnerships generally have continuity of life and have limited liability, so that they function more as a corporate entity than as a partnership. There is an exception (beyond the scope of this discussion) for partnerships that have substantial amounts of passive-type income and for partnerships that were in existence on December 17, 1987. The taxation of corporations and entities that are treated as corporations for federal income tax is discussed in Chapter 12.

10.2 The Aggregate Concept of the Partnership

The characteristics of a non-publicly-traded partnership (mutual agency, unlimited personal liability, termination upon any change in membership, and profit sharing) flow from a basic view of the nature of a partnership. In this view, the partnership is not a separate legal person or entity. It is simply an aggregation of the activities of the individual partners.

An individual engaged in a business would obviously be an agent of that business, capable of making all business decisions without the approval of anyone else. Since the business is not a legal entity separate and apart from the owner, any business creditor would be able to proceed against nonbusiness assets if necessary to satisfy a business debt. Death of the owner terminates his or her legal existence and hence that of the business, even though the business might be carried on by another person (such as a surviving member of the family). And, of course, all profits would belong to the owner, who would also bear all losses.

The aggregate approach essentially views the partnership as a multiple proprietorship. In accounting for a partnership, the owner's equity section of the partnership balance sheet illustrates this treatment, as may be recalled from an accounting course. This can also be seen by a look at Schedule M of a partnership tax return (Fig. 10-1(b)).

10.3 The Conduit Nature of the Partnership Return

A partnership as such does not pay income tax.[3] The basic concept in partnership taxation, like the basic approach to S corporations and their shareholders that will be discussed in chapter 11, is that each partner pays a tax on his or her share of partnership net income, whether distributed by the partnership or not.[4] Also, each partner can deduct his or her share of any partnership loss. This deduction is subject to some limitations, discussed later. Thus, a partnership is viewed as simply a multiple proprietorship. The difference is that in the case of a proprietorship there is no legal distinction between the business and the owner. Business assets belong to the owner, and business debts are debts of the owner. In the case of a partnership, there is a legal distinction. The partners and the partnership are separate "persons." Business assets are owned by the partnership. Each partner owns only an interest in the partnership. Likewise, partnership debts are debts of the partnership and not directly debts of each individual partner. Of course, if the partnership is unable to pay the debts, creditors can proceed to collect from the partners individually.

The ordinary income on the partnership income tax return is comparable in concept to the net profit of a proprietorship. You may want to review Schedule C of Form 1040.[5] In Chapter 9 we discussed the available election under Sec. 179 to expense up to $10,000 of costs for certain asset purchases which would otherwise require capitalization and depreciation. This $10,000 limitation applies to both the partnership and to each partner.[6] If a partnership elects to expense this

[3] IRC Sec. 701.
[4] IRC Sec. 702.
[5] See Appendix 1-C.
[6] IRC Sec. 179(d)(8).

FIGURE 10-1 (a)

Form **1065** Department of the Treasury Internal Revenue Service

U.S. Partnership Return of Income

▶ See separate instructions.

For calendar year 1989, or fiscal year beginning ________, 1989, and ending ________, 19__

OMB No. 1545-0099

1989

A Principal business activity: SERVICES

B Principal product or service: ACCOUNTING

C Business code number: 8933

Use IRS label. Otherwise, please print or type.

Name: BARNES, LARSEN AND HESS

Number and street (or P.O. box number if mail is not delivered to street address): 1600 MAIN ST.

City or town, state, and ZIP code: LOS ALTOS, ARIZONA 85289

D Employer identification number: 86-1234567

E Date business started: 1-2-84

F Total assets (see Specific Instructions): $ 148,680

G Check applicable boxes: (1) ☐ Initial return (2) ☐ Final return (3) ☐ Change in address (4) ☐ Amended return

H Enter number of partners in this partnership ▶ 3

I Check this box if this is a limited partnership ▶ ☐

J Check this box if any partners in the partnership are also partnerships ▶ ☐

K Check this box if this partnership is a partner in another partnership ▶ ☐

See page 4, items L through T, for Additional Information Required.

Designation of Tax Matters Partner (See instructions.)

Enter below the general partner designated as the tax matters partner (TMP) for the tax year of this return:

Name of designated TMP ▶ BILLY BARNES

Identifying number of TMP ▶ 332 00 0001

Address of designated TMP ▶ 1219 E. LOYOLA DR. HAMPTON, ARIZONA 85235

Caution: *Include **only** trade or business income and expenses on lines 1a–21 below. See the instructions for more information.*

Income	1a Gross receipts or sales	1a	211,889 –		
	b Less returns and allowances	1b		1c	211,889 –
	2 Cost of goods sold and/or operations (Schedule A, line 7)			2	
	3 Gross profit (subtract line 2 from line 1c)			3	211,889 –
	4 Ordinary income (loss) from other partnerships and fiduciaries (attach schedule)			4	
	5 Net farm profit (loss) (attach Schedule F (Form 1040))			5	
	6 Net gain (loss) (Form 4797, Part II, line 18)			6	
	7 Other income (loss)			7	400 –
	8 **Total** income (loss) (combine lines 3 through 7)			8	212,289 –
Deductions (see instructions for limitations)	9a Salaries and wages (other than to partners)	9a	14500 –		
	b Less jobs credit	9b		9c	14,500 –
	10 Guaranteed payments to partners			10	
	11 Rent			11	12,600 –
	12 Interest (see instructions)			12	600 –
	13 Taxes			13	1,720 –
	14 Bad debts			14	
	15 Repairs			15	350 –
	16a Depreciation (attach Form 4562) (see instructions)	16a	14,344 –		
	b Less depreciation reported on Schedule A and elsewhere on return	16b		16c	14,344 –
	17 Depletion (***Do not deduct oil and gas depletion.***)			17	
	18a Retirement plans, etc.			18a	2,175 –
	b Employee benefit programs			18b	
	19 Other deductions (~~attach schedule~~) UTILITIES 4,800; SUPPLIES 1,200			19	6,000 –
	20 **Total** deductions (add lines 9c through 19)			20	52289 –
	21 Ordinary income (loss) from trade or business activities (subtract line 20 from line 8)			21	160,000 –

Please Sign Here

Under penalties of perjury, I declare that I have examined this return, including accompanying schedules and statements, and to the best of my knowledge and belief, it is true, correct, and complete. Declaration of preparer (other than general partner) is based on all information of which preparer has any knowledge.

▶ Billy B. Barnes — Signature of general partner ▶ 3-10-90 — Date

Paid Preparer's Use Only

Preparer's signature ▶ | Date | Check if self-employed ▶ ☐ | Preparer's social security no.

Firm's name (or yours if self-employed) and address ▶ | E.I. No. ▶ | ZIP code ▶

For Paperwork Reduction Act Notice, see page 1 of separate instructions.

H732

Form **1065** (1989)

FIGURE 10-1 (b)

Schedule L **Balance Sheets**

(See the instructions for Question N on page 8 of the Instructions before completing Schedules L and M.)

Assets	Beginning of tax year (a)	Beginning of tax year (b)	End of tax year (c)	End of tax year (d)
1 Cash		9,260		13,315
2 Trade notes and accounts receivable				
a Less allowance for bad debts				
3 Inventories				
4a U.S. government obligations				10,000
b Tax-exempt securities				
5 Other current assets (attach schedule)				
6 Mortgage and real estate loans				
7 Other investments (attach schedule)		45000		-0-
8a Buildings and other depreciable assets	65,200		65,200	
b Less accumulated depreciation	9,780	55420	24,124	41,076
9a Depletable assets				
b Less accumulated depletion				
10 Land (net of any amortization)				84,289
11a Intangible assets (amortizable only)				
b Less accumulated amortization				
12 Other assets (attach schedule)				
13 **Total** assets		109,680		148,680
Liabilities and Capital				
14 Accounts payable				
15 Mortgages, notes, bonds payable in less than 1 year		7,000		6,000
16 Other current liabilities (attach schedule)				
17 All nonrecourse loans				
18 Mortgages, notes, bonds payable in 1 year or more		30,000		28,000
19 Other liabilities (attach schedule)				
20 Partners' capital accounts		72,680		114680
21 **Total** liabilities and capital		109,680		148,680

Schedule M **Reconciliation of Partners' Capital Accounts**

(Show reconciliation of each partner's capital account on Schedule K-1 (Form 1065), Item K.)

(a) Partners' capital accounts at beginning of year	(b) Capital contributed during year	(c) Income (loss) from lines 1, 2, 3c, and 4 of Sch. K	(d) Income not included in column (c), plus nontaxable income	(e) Losses not included in column (c), plus unallowable deductions	(f) Withdrawals and distributions	(g) Partners' capital accounts at end of year (combine columns (a) through (f))
72,680		160,000	15,000	( )	(133,000)	114,680

Additional Information Required (continued from page 1)

	Yes	No
L Check accounting method: (1) ☒ Cash (2) ☐ Accrual (3) ☐ Other		
M Check this box if this is a partnership subject to the consolidated partnership audit procedures of sections 6221 through 6233 (see instructions) ▶ ☐		
N Does the partnership meet **all** the requirements shown in the Instructions for **Question N**?		X
O Was there a distribution of property or a transfer (for example, by sale or death) of a partnership interest during the tax year?		X
If "Yes," see the instructions concerning an election to adjust the basis of the partnership's assets under section 754.		
P Does the partnership have any foreign partners?		X
Q At any time during the tax year, did the partnership have an interest in or a signature or other authority over a financial account in a foreign country (such as a bank account, securities account, or other financial account)? (See the instructions for exceptions and filing requirements for form TD F 90-22.1.)		X
If "Yes," write the name of the foreign country. ▶		
R Was the partnership the grantor of, or transferor to, a foreign trust which existed during the current tax year, whether or not the partnership or any partner has any beneficial interest in it? If "Yes," you may have to file Forms 3520, 3520-A, or 926		X
S Check this box if the partnership has filed or is required to file **Form 8264**, Application for Registration of a Tax Shelter ▶ ☐		
T Check this box if the partnership is a publicly traded partnership as defined in section 469(k)(2) ▶ ☐		

FIGURE 10-1 (c)

Schedule K **Partners' Shares of Income, Credits, Deductions, Etc.**

	(a) Distributive share items		(b) Total amount	
Income (Loss)	1 Ordinary income (loss) from trade or business activities (page 1, line 21)	1	160,000	—
	2 Net income (loss) from rental real estate activities (Schedule H, line 17)	2		
	3a Gross income from other rental activities [3a]			
	b Less expenses (attach schedule) [3b]			
	c Net income (loss) from other rental activities	3c		
	4 Portfolio income (loss) (see instructions):			
	a Interest income	4a		
	b Dividend income	4b		
	c Royalty income	4c		
	d Net short-term capital gain (loss) (Schedule D, line 4)	4d		
	e Net long-term capital gain (loss) (Schedule D, line 9)	4e	15,000	—
	f Other portfolio income (loss) (attach schedule)	4f		
	5 Guaranteed payments to partners	5		
	6 Net gain (loss) under section 1231 (other than due to casualty or theft) (see instructions)	6		
	7 Other income (loss) (attach schedule)	7		
Deductions	8 Charitable contributions (attach list)	8		
	9 Section 179 expense deduction (attach Form 4562)	9		
	10 Deductions related to portfolio income (do not include investment interest expense)	10		
	11 Other deductions (attach schedule)	11		
Credits	12a Credit for income tax withheld	12a		
	b Low-income housing credit: (1) Partnerships to which section 42(j)(5) applies	12b(1)		
	(2) Other than on line 12b(1)	12b(2)		
	c Qualified rehabilitation expenditures related to rental real estate activities (attach schedule)	12c		
	d Credits (other than credits shown on lines 12b and 12c) related to rental real estate activities (attach schedule)	12d		
	e Credits related to other rental activities (see instructions) (attach schedule)	12e		
	13 Other credits and expenditures (attach schedule)	13		
Self-Employment	14a Net earnings (loss) from self-employment	14a		
	b Gross farming or fishing income	14b		
	c Gross nonfarm income	14c		
Adjustments and Tax Preference Items	15a Accelerated depreciation of real property placed in service before 1987	15a		
	b Accelerated depreciation of leased personal property placed in service before 1987	15b		
	c Depreciation adjustment on property placed in service after 1986	15c		
	d Depletion (other than oil and gas)	15d		
	e (1) Gross income from oil, gas, and geothermal properties	15e(1)		
	(2) Deductions allocable to oil, gas, and geothermal properties	15e(2)		
	f Other adjustments and tax preference items (attach schedule)	15f		
Investment Interest	16a Interest expense on investment debts	16a		
	b (1) Investment income included on lines 4a through 4f above	16b(1)		
	(2) Investment expenses included on line 10 above	16b(2)		
Foreign Taxes	17a Type of income ________			
	b Foreign country or U.S. possession ________			
	c Total gross income from sources outside the U.S. (attach schedule)	17c		
	d Total applicable deductions and losses (attach schedule)	17d		
	e Total foreign taxes (check one): ▶ ☐ Paid ☐ Accrued	17e		
	f Reduction in taxes available for credit (attach schedule)	17f		
	g Other foreign tax information (attach schedule)	17g		
Other	18a Total expenditures to which a section 59(e) election may apply (attach schedule)	18a		
	b Attach schedule for other items and amounts not reported above (see instructions)			
Analysis	19a Total distributive income/payment items (combine lines 1 through 7 above)	19a		
	b Analysis by type of partner:			

	(a) Corporate	(b) Individual		(c) Partnership	(d) Exempt organization	(e) Nominee/Other
		i. Active	ii. Passive			
1. General partners						
2. Limited partners						

H732

FIGURE 10-2 Any special "source characteristic" of income or deduction that will require special income tax treatment will be retained and passed on to individual partners

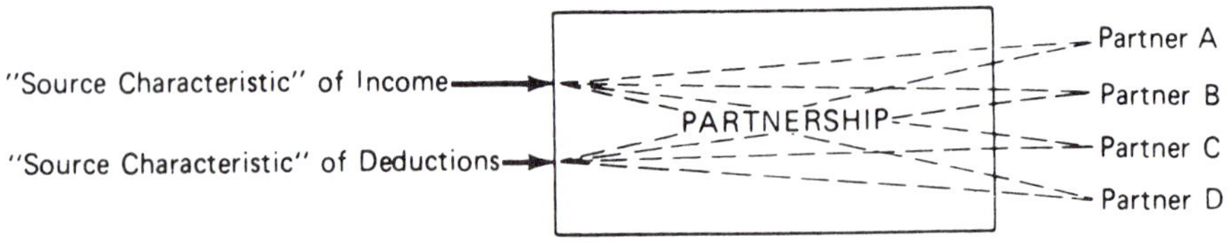

$10,000, each partner must count his or her pro-rata share of that $10,000, and limit other such expense to the remaining amount, if any. For example, if Billy Barnes is a one-fourth partner, and the partnership elects to expense $10,000, Billy's share is $2,500. Billy will be limited to $7,500 of Sec. 179 expense from other business proprietorships or partnerships.

Any item of income that is nontaxable, or that is treated in a special way (e.g., capital gain) will not be reflected in the computation of *ordinary income* of the partnership.[7] Similarly, any deduction that is limited in some manner, such as the charitable contribution deduction, will not be reflected in computing ordinary income. All of these items will appear on a partnership return.[8] The function of the partnership is to act as a conduit. The function of the partnership tax return is to act as an information return regarding that conduit (see Fig. 10-2). The transactions of the partnership are summarized on it and passed through, with their essential tax characteristics unaltered, to be reported on the individual tax returns of the partners. Thus, the partners pay tax on their share of partnership income and *not* on the cash they draw from the partnership. This can be seen on Schedule K of the partnership tax return [see Fig. 10-1(c)].

For example, assume a three-person partnership that has ordinary income (from business operations) of $60,000 for the year plus $15,000 of interest on bank deposits. The taxable income of the partnership is not $60,000 + $15,000, or $75,000. "Taxable income" has no meaning in a partnership. If each partner were simply to include $25,000 in gross income, the principle of retention of "source characteristic" would not be applied (see Fig. 10-2). Instead, each will recognize $20,000 as his or her one-third of ordinary income plus $5,000 of portfolio interest income. On the partner tax returns, that interest income may be a factor in determining how much interest may be deducted under the rules limiting the deductibility of investment interest expense, as discussed in Chapter 17.

This leaves the question of timing. When do the partners pay tax on their share of partnership income or deduct their share of partnership loss? The answer is that partnership items are included on each partner's individual tax return for the taxable year that ends with the partnership year. If the partnership and a partner do not use the same accounting period, a partner will include his or her share for the year *during which* the partnership year ends.

10.4 The Reconciliation Schedule

The distribution schedule [Schedule K, Fig. 10-1(c)] on the partnership return is merely a facilitating device for reporting the aggregate or total of pass-through items to the partners. The reconciliation schedule [Schedule M, Fig. 10-1(b)] functions to provide a net worth type of reconciliation between the transactions reported on the return and their balance sheet effect.

The owner's equity accounts in a partnership normally do not separate the original capital from the changes that take place. Partners can and do contribute additional equity capital to the firm and withdraw capital, with no tax consequences resulting from these transactions.[9] Capital is increased by profits and decreased by losses. The significant factor in the partnership is the capital account balance of each partner.

TAX PLANNING TIP: Generally, each partner's share of each item of income or deduction is the same percentage in which profits are allocated. However, a special allocation of specific items of partnership income or deductions will be recognized if there is a substantial economic effect on the partners' capital account balances.

Thus, on line K of each Schedule K-1 (Fig. 10-3), the beginning-of-the-year and end-of-the-year capital account balances are reconciled for each

[7]IRC Sec. 703. See line 21, Form 1065, Fig. 10-1(a).
[8]See Schedule K-1, Fig. 10-3.

[9]IRC Secs. 721 and 731.

FIGURE 10-3 (a)

SCHEDULE K-1 (Form 1065)
Department of the Treasury
Internal Revenue Service

Partner's Share of Income, Credits, Deductions, Etc.

▶ **See separate instructions.**
For calendar year 1989 or fiscal year beginning ______, 1989, and ending ______, 19__

OMB No. 1545-0099

1989

Partner's identifying number ▶ 332-00-0001 | **Partnership's identifying number** ▶ 86-1234567

Partner's name, address, and ZIP code
BILLY B. BARNES
1219 E. LOYOLA DRIVE
HAMPTON, ARIZONA 85235

Partnership's name, address, and ZIP code
BARNES, LARSEN AND HESS
1600 MAIN ST.
LOS ALTOS, ARIZONA 85289

A Is this partner a general partner? . . . [X] Yes [ ] No

B Partner's share of liabilities:
Nonrecourse. . . . . $ ______
Other . . . . $ 11,333

C What type of entity is this partner? ▶ INDIVIDUAL

D Is this partner a [X] domestic or a [ ] foreign partner?

E Enter partner's percentage of:

	(i) Before decrease or termination	(ii) End of year
Profit sharing	%	33 1/3 %
Loss sharing	%	33 1/3 %
Ownership of capital	%	33 1/3 %

F IRS Center where partnership filed return ▶ OGDEN, UTAH

G(1) Tax shelter registration number ▶ ______

(2) Type of tax shelter ▶ ______

H(1) Did the partner's ownership interest in the partnership change after Oct. 22, 1986? . . . . [ ] Yes [X] No
If "Yes," attach statement. (See Form 1065 Instructions.)

(2) Did the partnership start or acquire a new activity after Oct. 22, 1986? . . . . [ ] Yes [X] No
If "Yes," attach statement. (See Form 1065 Instructions.)

I Check here if this partnership is a publicly traded partnership as defined in section 469(k)(2) . . . . [ ]

J Check here if this is an amended Schedule K-1 . . . . . [ ]

K Reconciliation of partner's capital account:

(a) Capital account at beginning of year	(b) Capital contributed during year	(c) Income (loss) from lines 1, 2, 3, and 4 below	(d) Income not included in column (c), plus nontaxable income	(e) Losses not included in column (c), plus unallowable deductions	(f) Withdrawals and distributions	(g) Capital account at end of year (combine columns (a) through (f))
24,227	53,333	5,000		( )	(44,333)	38,227

Reminder: *If you received a 1987 Schedule K-1 that was for a short year and you chose to report the 1987 amounts over a 4-year period, be sure to include one-fourth of the short year amounts, in addition to the items reported on this Schedule K-1, on the appropriate lines of your 1989 Form 1040 and related schedules.*

Caution: *Refer to Partner's Instructions for Schedule K-1 (Form 1065) before entering information from this schedule on your tax return.*

	(a) Distributive share item		(b) Amount	(c) 1040 filers enter the amount in column (b) on:
Income (Loss)	1 Ordinary income (loss) from trade or business activities	1	53 333	(See Partner's Instructions for Schedule K-1 (Form 1065))
	2 Net income (loss) from rental real estate activities	2		
	3 Net income (loss) from other rental activities	3		
	4 Portfolio income (loss):			
	a Interest	4a		Sch. B, Part I, line 2
	b Dividends	4b		Sch. B, Part II, line 4
	c Royalties	4c		Sch. E, Part I, line 5
	d Net short-term capital gain (loss)	4d		Sch. D, line 5, col. (f) or (g)
	e Net long-term capital gain (loss)	4e	5,000	Sch. D, line 12, col. (f) or (g)
	f Other portfolio income (loss) (attach schedule)	4f		(Enter on applicable lines of your return)
	5 Guaranteed payments to partner	5		(See Partner's Instructions for Schedule K-1 (Form 1065))
	6 Net gain (loss) under section 1231 (other than due to casualty or theft)	6		
	7 Other income (loss) (attach schedule)	7		(Enter on applicable lines of your return)
Deductions	8 Charitable contributions	8		Sch. A, line 14 or 15
	9 Expense deduction for recovery property (section 179) (attach schedule)	9		(See Partner's Instructions for Schedule K-1 (Form 1065))
	10 Deductions related to portfolio income	10		
	11 Other deductions (attach schedule)	11		
Credits	12a Credit for income tax withheld	12a		See Partner's Instructions for Schedule K-1 (Form 1065)
	b Low-income housing credit: (1) Partnerships to which section 42(j)(5) applies	b(1)		Form 8586, line 5
	(2) Other than on line 12b(1)	b(2)		
	c Qualified rehabilitation expenditures related to rental real estate activities (attach schedule)	12c		(See Partner's Instructions for Schedule K-1 (Form 1065))
	d Credits (other than credits shown on lines 12b and 12c) related to rental real estate activities (attach schedule)	12d		
	e Credits related to rental activities other than rental real estate (see instructions) (attach schedule)	12e		
	13 Other credits and expenditures (attach schedule)	13		

For Paperwork Reduction Act Notice, see Form 1065 Instructions. **Schedule K-1 (Form 1065) 1989**

H732

FIGURE 10-3 (b)

		(a) Distributive share item		(b) Amount	(c) 1040 filers enter the amount in column (b) on:
Self-employment	14a	Net earnings (loss) from self-employment	14a		Sch. SE, Section A or B
	b	Gross farming or fishing income	14b		(See Partner's Instructions for Schedule K-1 (Form 1065))
	c	Gross nonfarm income	14c		
Adjustments and Tax Preference Items	15a	Accelerated depreciation of real property placed in service before 1987	15a		(See Form 6251 Instructions and Partner's Instructions for Schedule K-1 (Form 1065))
	b	Accelerated depreciation of leased personal property placed in service before 1987	15b		
	c	Depreciation adjustment on property placed in service after 1986	15c		
	d	Depletion (other than oil and gas)	15d		
	e	(1) Gross income from oil, gas, and geothermal properties	e(1)		
		(2) Deductions allocable to oil, gas, and geothermal properties	e(2)		
	f	Other adjustments and tax preference items (attach schedule)	15f		
Investment Interest	16a	Interest expense on investment debts	16a		Form 4952, line 1
	b	(1) Investment income included on Schedule K-1, lines 4a through 4f	b(1)		(See Partner's Instructions for Schedule K-1 (Form 1065))
		(2) Investment expenses included on Schedule K-1, line 10	b(2)		
Foreign Taxes	17a	Type of income ____________			Form 1116, Check boxes
	b	Name of foreign country or U.S. possession ____________			Form 1116, Part I
	c	Total gross income from sources outside the U.S. (attach schedule)	17c		Form 1116, Part I
	d	Total applicable deductions and losses (attach schedule)	17d		Form 1116, Part I
	e	Total foreign taxes (check one): ▶ ☐ Paid ☐ Accrued	17e		Form 1116, Part II
	f	Reduction in taxes available for credit (attach schedule)	17f		Form 1116, Part III
	g	Other foreign tax information (attach schedule)	17g		See Form 1116 Instructions
Other	18a	Total expenditures to which a section 59(e) election (relating to the optional 10-year writeoff of certain tax preference items) may apply (attach schedule)			(See Partner's Instructions for Schedule K-1 (Form 1065))
	b	Other items and amounts not reported on lines 1 through 17g, 19, and 20 that are required to be reported separately to you			
Recapture of Tax Credits	19a	Low-income housing credit: Partnerships to which section 42(j)(5) applies	19a		Form 8611, line 8
	b	Low-income housing credit recapture other than on line 19a	19b		

20 Investment Tax Credit Property:	A	B	C	
a Description of property (State whether recovery or nonrecovery property. If recovery property, state whether regular percentage method or section 48(q) election used.)				Form 4255, top
b Date placed in service				Form 4255, line 2
c Cost or other basis				Form 4255, line 3
d Class of recovery property or original estimated useful life				Form 4255, line 4
e Date item ceased to be investment credit property				Form 4255, line 8

Other Information Provided by Partnership:

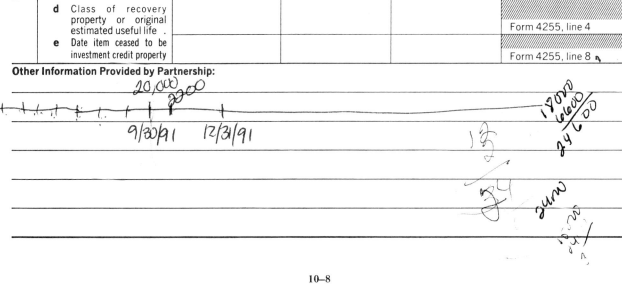

20,000 2000

9/30/91 12/31/91

17000
6600
24600

24000

partner for whom a K-1 is prepared. The reconciling items for each partner can be tied in to the income and expense, which is "passed through" from the partnership to the individual partner. Additional capital contributed by each partner, withdrawals, and any tax-exempt income or nondeductible expenses are also shown. A Schedule K-1 is prepared for each partner. Note that Schedule M of the Form 1065 [Fig. 10-1(b)] reports and reconciles the total of the capital accounts for all partners.

10.5 Partners' Salaries and Interest Payments

One of the confusing aspects of the partnership return is the treatment of partners' salaries. They are recorded on the partnership's books as deductions. This may seem strange, because financial accounting normally treats such items as distributions of income rather than as deductions. There is no real difference for tax purposes. If there were, a partnership's profits could be manipulated so as always to be zero. This will be of no tax help to the partners. Each partner must include in gross income both salary and share of partnership taxable income, after *all deductions,* including salaries. Thus, if one variable goes up, the other goes down by an equal amount, at least in the aggregate.

The difference in the timing of the recognition of gross income can be explained with the following example. Assume that Billy Barnes is a 50% partner in a partnership with a September 30 year end. Billy also draws a salary. For all months prior to 9/30/X1 Billy's salary was $2,000 per month. On 10/1/X1, the salary was increased to $2,200 per month. The partnership's taxable income for the year ending 9/30/X1 was $30,000, after deducting the salary. How much should Billy report for calendar 19X1? The answer is $39,000, which is $2,000 for each of the twelve months ending Sept. 30, 19X1 plus Billy's one-half of the remaining $30,000. The $2,200 monthly salary for October through December 19X1 will be taken into consideration when determining Billy's gross income for 19X2, since those were the first three months of the partnership Sept. 30, 19X2 year, the results of which are taxable to the partners for their calendar year during which the partnership year ends. In Fig. 10-1 we did not include partners' salaries (see line 9). Partners' drawing accounts are reported on Schedule M (Figure 10-1(b)) in the aggregate and on line K(f) of Schedule K-1 (Figure 10-3(a)) for each partner individually.

10.6 Self-employment Income

"Salaries" to partners are not subject to payroll taxes. Does this mean that partners pay no social security tax and get no social security benefits when they reach retirement age or become disabled? Not at all. Partnerships calculate the amount of the partnership's business income attributable to each partner whether labeled as salary or not. On the individual income tax return, each partner reports his or her share of the partnership business income and pays the social security tax.[10] Figure 10-4 shows a Schedule SE, which is used to report self-employment tax. Note line 2, where partnership income is reported, except for farm partnerships.

The preceding paragraph referred to the "business income" of a partnership. Partnerships have many types of income, some of which are essentially passive, such as dividends, interest, and capital gain. These types of income are not subject to social security tax. "Net profit" from a partnership must be calculated by adding a partner's salary to that portion of the partnership taxable income which is not from investments.

Rental income may or may not be passive investment income for this purpose.[11] Operation of a motel produces rental income, but it is usually not passive and is subject to social security tax. Operation of an apartment house normally produces passive rental income that is not subject to self-employment tax.[12]

COMPUTER FORMULAS: Self-employment tax is only imposed on earned income, for example, up to $51,300 (for 1990). The computer can calculate this using an @ IF formula.

	A	*B*	*C*	*D*
1	SE Income	*x*		
2	SE Tax	@IF (*x* > 51,300, 7848.90, *x* * .153)		
3				

The formula tells the computer that if self-employment income is greater than $51,300, the tax will be the maximum, $7,848.90. If self-employment income is not greater than $51,300, i.e., is equal to or less than $51,300, the tax will be 15.3% (.153%).

10.7 The Entity Concept of the Partnership

Although the aggregate concept of the partnership dominates its income tax status, traces of

[10]IRC Secs. 1401 and 1402.
[11]IRC Sec. 1402(a)(1).
[12]The distinction is based upon the participation of the partners in the business operations. Rent can be derived from active participation or it can be passive income, similar to interest or dividends in terms of the taxpayer's efforts expended.

FIGURE 10-4

SCHEDULE SE (Form 1040)
Department of the Treasury
Internal Revenue Service

Social Security Self-Employment Tax

▶ See Instructions for Schedule SE (Form 1040).
▶ Attach to Form 1040.

OMB No. 1545-0074
1989
Attachment Sequence No. **18**

Name of person with **self-employment** income (as shown on social security card)	Social security number of person with **self-employment** income ▶
BILLY B. BARNES	332 : 00 : 0001

Who Must File Schedule SE

You must file Schedule SE if:

- Your net earnings from self-employment were $400 or more (or you had wages of $100 or more from an electing church or church-controlled organization); AND
- Your wages (subject to social security or railroad retirement tax) were less than $48,000.

Exception. If your only self-employment income was from earnings as a minister, member of a religious order, or Christian Science practitioner, AND you filed **Form 4361** and received IRS approval not to be taxed on those earnings, DO NOT file Schedule SE. Instead, write "Exempt–Form 4361" on Form 1040, line 48.

For more information about Schedule SE, see the Instructions.

Note: *Most people can use the short Schedule SE on this page. But, you may have to use the longer Schedule SE that is on the back.*

Who MUST Use the Long Schedule SE (Section B)

You must use Section B if ANY of the following applies:

- You choose the "optional method" to figure your self-employment tax (see Section B, Part II);
- You are a minister, member of a religious order, or Christian Science practitioner and you received IRS approval (from **Form 4361**) not to be taxed on your earnings from these sources, but you owe self-employment tax on other earnings;
- You were an employee of a church or church-controlled organization that chose by law not to pay employer social security taxes;
- You had tip income that is subject to social security tax, but you did not report those tips to your employer; OR
- You were a government employee with wages subject ONLY to the 1.45% Medicare part of the social security tax.

Section A—Short Schedule SE
(Read above to see if you must use the long Schedule SE on the back (Section B).)

1	Net farm profit or (loss) from Schedule F (Form 1040), line 36, and farm partnerships, Schedule K-1 (Form 1065), line 14a	1		
2	Net profit or (loss) from Schedule C (Form 1040), line 30, and Schedule K-1 (Form 1065), line 14a (other than farming). See the Instructions for other income to report	2	53,333	–
3	Add lines 1 and 2. Enter the total. If the total is less than $400, **do not** file this schedule; you **do not** owe self-employment tax ▶	3	53,333	–
4	The largest amount of combined wages and self-employment earnings subject to social security or railroad retirement tax (tier 1) for 1989 is	4	$48,000	00
5	Total social security wages and tips (from Form(s) W-2) and railroad retirement compensation (tier 1)	5		
6	Subtract line 5 from line 4. Enter the result. If the result is zero or less, stop here; you **do not** owe self-employment tax ▶	6	48,000	–
7	Enter the **smaller** of line 3 or line 6	7	48,000	–
8	Rate of tax	8	×.1302	
9	**Self-employment tax.** If line 7 is $48,000, enter $6,249.60. Otherwise, multiply the amount on line 7 by the decimal amount on line 8 and enter the result. Also enter this amount on Form 1040, line 48	9	6,250	–

For Paperwork Reduction Act Notice, see Form 1040 Instructions. **Schedule SE (Form 1040) 1989**

H732

the entity approach are still visible. These relate mainly to elections made in connection with the tax return, to transactions between the partners and the partnership, and to changes in the composition of the partnership.

Thus, the decision as to accounting methods must be made by the partnership, not by the partners individually. It is not difficult to visualize the impossible accounting situation that might result if each of five partners in a partnership could make a different choice of accounting methods (cash versus accrual, nonaccrual-experience method versus full accrual and others).

A partner may sell an asset to the partnership and have a gain or loss on the transaction. The reverse is also true.[13]

In spite of changes in the composition of the partnership, the partnership will not be deemed to have terminated for federal tax purposes unless there is a change within a twelve-month period of 50% or more of the total interest in partnership capital and profits.[14]

10.8 Credits

Since a partnership as such does not have an income tax liability, it cannot use any credits to reduce that tax. Consequently, credits, like income and deductions, are passed through the partnership and treated by the partners as if each partner had realized the credit individually. The most common credits applicable to partners are the targeted jobs credit, low income housing credit, and the credit for research and experimental costs. These credits were discussed in Chapter 7. On the partnership tax return, the information relative to credits appears on line 12. See Figure 10-1(c). Each individual partner is notified of his or her share of the credit on the K-1 at line 12. See Figure 10-3(a). If a credit is taken in one year and some event occurs in a later year that causes the credit to have to be repaid, each partner is required to repay his or her share rather than for the partnership to repay the credit. This is called "recapture." See line 20 of the K-1, Figure 10-3(b).

TAX PLANNING TIP: A partner may sell property to a partnership of which he or she is a member and realize a gain or loss. The basis of the property to the partnership will be its cost. If a partner contributes property to a partnership, the partnership's basis will be the basis of that property to the partner. This gives partners and partnerships considerable flexibility with respect to recognition of gain or loss and basis of property which will affect future depreciation deductions.

10.9 Becoming a Partner

When a person transfers assets (cash or other property) to a partnership in exchange for a partnership interest, no gain or loss is recognized to either the partner or the partnership.[15] This is true whether the partnership is new or is an existing partnership.

As with other tax-free transactions, the quid pro quo is that the transferee (the partnership) takes the property with the same adjusted basis as the transferor (the partner).[16] The partner then has an adjusted basis for the partnership interest that is the same as for the property transferred to the partnership.[17]

TAX PLANNING TIP: Family partnerships can result in multiple advantages:

1. ***Income tax.*** *By spreading income among more persons, total tax sometimes can be kept lower. With less money paid in taxes, family wealth can increase more rapidly (see Chapter 15).*
2. ***Gift tax.*** *The gift tax is imposed on the value of property at the time of gift (see Chapter 15). By transferring an interest in a family business before it has become too valuable, the transfer tax can be reduced. Also, advantage can be gained from full utilization of the $10,000 annual exclusion per donee.*
3. ***Estate tax.*** *The estate tax is imposed on the value of property owned at death (see Chapter 15). By removing property, such as an interest in a partnership, from the estate of older family members (presumably those who will die first), the future increases in value will accrue to family members who are expected to live longer, thus postponing payment of estate tax. Careful structuring of the rights and interests of the various family partners can often be done with little or no gift tax consequence.*

For example, assume that three persons, A, B, and C, decide to form a partnership and start a

[13]IRC Sec. 707. Generally, a partner may engage in "arm's-length" business with a partnership of which he or she is a member.

[14]IRC Sec. 708(b). Not all changes count for this purpose.

[15]IRC Sec. 721. The one exception to this rule, which is relatively uncommon, is where the partnership would be treated as an investment company if it were a corporation.

[16]IRC Sec. 723.

[17]IRC Sec. 722.

new business. A contributes cash of $25,000. B has a building that will be transferred to the partnership. The fair market value of the building is $50,000, but B's tax basis in the asset is $25,000. C, on the other hand, will contribute machinery worth $18,000, but which has an adjusted basis of $25,000. Their respective basis for their new asset, an interest in the BAC partnership, is as follows:

A	$25,000
B	25,000
C	25,000

None of the three will have a recognized gain or loss resulting from the transfer of assets to the partnership. By the same token, the partnership will recognize no gain or loss. The partnership's basis in the three assets will be as follows:

Cash	$25,000
Building	25,000
Machinery	25,000

This can create some tax inequities, and the tax law requires the partnership to make adjustments as between the partners so that they can be treated equitably.[18] Since the partnership must use $25,000 as the basis for the building, the tax return depreciation deductions will be based upon $25,000. However, if the building is indeed worth $50,000, it seems that $50,000 of depreciation should be charged in calculating partnership financial income (assuming that the partnership continues to own the property for its remaining life expectancy). If B had contributed $50,000 in cash and the partnership had purchased the building for $50,000, the depreciation deductions would be larger and all partners would benefit (taxwise) from the lower partnership taxable income. If the $25,000 cash contributed by A is used to buy depreciable assets, then $25,000 of depreciation deductions will be taken, not some larger amount.

The effect is that B has contributed more to the partnership than A has contributed. The partners are thus required by the tax law to allocate deductions or allocate gain or loss in such a way that B bears the tax brunt of the difference between the $50,000 agreed-upon value of the property and the $25,000 tax basis.

C creates the opposite problem. The depreciation deductions that C could have obtained (assuming that the machinery would have been depreciable property in C's hands if it had not been contributed to the partnership) are now available to the partnership and thus spread among all the partners. But C should get a disproportionately larger allocation of the depreciation to reflect the excess of tax basis over partnership value. While the partners are required to take the variation between tax basis and fair market value into consideration so as to prevent unjustified shifting of gain to the other partners, just how this will be done is rather complex and beyond the scope of this discussion. Prior to 1984, the law permitted the partners to elect to make such an allocation, but did not require that they do so. Now it is required.

TAX PLANNING TIP: A family trust can be a partner in a business. There should be an independent trustee. Tax savings can be realized by spreading income among more taxpayers and reducing the marginal tax rate. Requirements are:

1. *The donors of the trust property must divest themselves of trust property so that they are not treated as owners of the trust income.*
2. *The family members who are active in the management of the business must draw reasonable compensation for their services before profits are divided among the partners, including the trust.*
3. *The trustee must have sufficient control over the trust investment in the business so that the trust has the usual attributes of ownership.*

Some partners contribute services rather than assets, in whole or in part, for their partnership interests. If a partner receives a capital interest (as opposed to a mere income interest) in a partnership in exchange for services, that partner may realize income.[19] The income would be compensation income, and the partnership would get a corresponding deduction. The partner's tax basis in the partnership interest thus acquired would be increased by the income required to be reported, as though the partnership had paid the compensation in cash and the partner had then used that cash to buy the partnership interest. An income interest (as opposed to an interest in capital) in a partnership *can* also result in taxable income if received for services. But this will usually not result, because such an interest is usually dependent upon continuing services, thus impossible to value, and therefore not realized as income upon receipt.

10.10 Tax Basis

A partner's tax basis in the partnership interest goes up and down. It starts with the tax basis

[18] IRC Sec. 704(c).

[19] Treas. Reg. 1.721-1(b).

of assets transferred into the partnership. It is increased by the share of partnership income required to be included in gross income and by subsequent capital additions.[20] It is reduced by his or her share of the partnership losses and by amounts that are withdrawn from the partnership.[21]

For example, assume the A,B,C partnership is formed as before, with A having a basis in the partnership of $25,000. Also assume that during th first year of operation there are no special items of income or deduction that have some special characteristic requiring special allocation. At the end of the first year, the partnership net income (all from ordinary business operations) is $15,000, of which $5,000 is A's share. During the year, A withdrew $1,000 of cash. At the end of the year, A's basis in the partnership is $25,000 + $5,000 − $1,000, or $29,000.

Remember the concept that the partnership is really no more than the aggregate of the individual partners. Part of this aggregate approach results in debts of the partnership being treated for tax purposes as debts of the individual partners. The result is that a partner's share of the partnership's debt is treated for tax basis purposes as if cash had been personally borrowed and transferred into the partnership. Any reduction in a partner's share of the partnership debt is treated like cash that was withdrawn from the partnership.[22]

TAX PLANNING TIP: Partners have a great deal of flexibility in arranging financial transactions between themselves and the partnership. The partnership agreement will govern the tax impact of these transactions unless the principal purpose is the avoidance or evasion of tax or the tax rules provide otherwise. Therefore, extreme care should be taken to write the partnership agreement clearly and to establish business reasons for the transactions. This is especially important with respect to (1) retirement of a partner, (2) payments to be made to the estate of a deceased partner, and (3) situations where the fair market value of property contributed to a partnership by a partner differs significantly from the contributing partner's tax basis.

Remember the earlier example of A, B, and C. A contributed $25,000 cash to the partnership while B contributed a building. Assume that A, B, and C became equal partners. Now assume that B had a mortgage on the building for $30,000, the partnership became liable on the mortgage, and B does not continue to remain *exclusively* personally liable on the debt. A's tax basis in the partnership is now the $25,000 cash plus one-third of the $30,000 mortgage, or a total of $35,000. Similarly, C's tax basis is $25,000 plus one-third of the $30,000 mortgage, or a total of $35,000.

What about B, who contributed property with a tax basis of $25,000 subject to a $30,000 mortgage? Since A and C together "assumed" two-thirds of the $30,000 mortgage, that $20,000 is treated like a cash distribution to B. B's tax basis in the partnership interest is thus $5,000, which is the $25,000 basis in the property, less the $20,000 of cash that is deemed to have been withdrawn by B.

10.11 Liquidation

The tax consequences of liquidating a partnership flow from the same aggregate approach already discussed. If the partnership first sells the assets, the partners recognize gain or loss through the partnership. This gain or loss results in the partners' tax basis being adjusted upward or downward, respectively. If the sales proceeds (cash) are distributed, each partner will have taxable gain or loss only to the extent that the amount received is greater or less than his or her adjusted basis in the partnership.[23] It is generally a capital gain or loss.[24]

Assume that Smith and Jones have been operating as a partnership. Smith's basis is $50,000 and Jones's is $30,000. The only asset is a building that has an adjusted basis to the partnership of $70,000. The building is sold for $100,000, resulting in a $30,000 gain to the partnership. Since partnerships pay no income tax, Smith and Jones must report the $30,000 as additional gross income. Assuming that they share profits equally, Smith and Jones will each report $15,000 of gross income.[25] Because of this recognized gross income, each partner's adjusted basis in the partnership will be increased by $15,000. If the $100,000 cash is distributed equally to the partners, Smith will have a $15,000 capital loss and Jones will have a $5,000 capital gain from the liquidation. (The gain or loss is

[20]IRC Sec. 705. Remember that a partner is taxed on his or her share of partnership profits whether withdrawn or not. If a partnership receives nontaxable income, such as interest from state and local bonds, a partner's basis is also increased by his or her share of such nontaxable income.

[21]IRC Sec. 733. But note that Sec. 704(d) limits the allowance of losses to the adjusted basis of the partner's partnership interest. This provision is mainly of interest to investors in limited partnership tax shelters although it can apply where losses are shared in a ratio that differs from the capital ratio.

[22]Treas. Reg. 1.722-1.

[23]IRC Sec. 731.

[24]IRC Sec. 741. But the gain can be wholly or partially ordinary.

[25]This example ignores the "character" of the gain because that is relevant only as to the amount of tax that will be paid on the $15,000.

"capital" because an interest in a partnership is a capital asset. See Chapter 5.) The result is summarized as follows:

	Smith	*Jones*
Basis before sale of building	$50,000	$30,000
Gain, taxed to partners	15,000	15,000
Basis after sale of building	$65,000	$45,000
Cash to each partner	$50,000	$50,000
Gain (loss)	($15,000)	$ 5,000

The liquidation may not be complete—in fact, may only involve one partner leaving. Or some partners may take certain operating or investment assets, while others take different assets. In such a situation, the partners will not recognize gain except to the extent that the cash they receive (which, remember, includes any debt of which they are relieved) exceeds the tax basis of their partnership interests.[26] The partnership's tax basis of any noncash assets received by a partner from the partnership is normally treated as if it were cash. The property will have a basis to the partner which is the same as the basis to the partnership before the distribution.[27] In addition, the partner's basis in the partnership interest is reduced by the basis in the property distributed. However, when the partner's interest in the partnership is being liquidated, such treatment would result in gain or loss to the extent that the basis in the partnership interest differed from the basis of the assets received in liquidation. Instead of gain or loss recognition, the assets received by a partner in complete liquidation of his or her partnership interest take as their tax basis the basis that the partner had in the partnership interest.[28] This is just the opposite of the situation when the partnership was formed. In other words, neither the formation of a partnership nor the liquidation of a partnership generally result in the recognition of gain or loss.[29]

Some partnership assets produce ordinary income upon disposition, while others produce capital gain in the same manner as for other taxpayers. There are special rules which have the effect of categorizing as ordinary income the gain realized on those assets which represent the former partner's share of the partnership's ordinary income assets.[30]

For example, assume that a partnership is liquidated and one of the partners receives property that was inventory to the partnership. Even though that property may not be inventory to the partner and thus could receive capital gain treatment, the former partner will still have ordinary income from the sale of the property because it would have produced ordinary income if sold by the partnership.[31]

Similarly, special rules may result in ordinary income for a portion of the gain on sale of a partnership interest if cash distributions exceed the withdrawing partner's tax basis.[32]

In some situations, a partnership may pay a withdrawing partner more than his or her pro-rata portion of the tax basis of the partnership assets. If so, the partnership may make an election to adjust the tax basis of those assets to reflect that excess.[33] It has, in a sense, bought back the interest from the withdrawing partner, and thus has a type of added cost for those assets. (Once made, the election applies to a number of similar transactions, and applies whether it results in increasing or in reducing the partnership's tax basis. Note that it does not affect the partner's basis in the partnership interest.)

10.12 Fiscal Year Partnerships

While it is possible for a partnership and a partner to have different taxable years, as illustrated earlier, partnerships generally use a calendar year. This is because of a rule which provides that a partnership cannot adopt or change to a taxable year which is different from that of its partners who together own more than 50% of the partnership, or of its "principal" partners (unless a satisfactory business purpose can be demonstrated to the IRS). A "principal" partner is defined as one with a 5% or more ownership interest.[34] Where the partners are individuals—and almost all individuals use a calendar year—the partnership will also have to use a calendar year. However, it must be noted that corporations and some fiduciaries can also be partners. Many corporations and some fiduciaries use a fiscal year rather than a calendar year for tax purposes.[35]

[26] IRC Sec. 731.
[27] IRC Sec. 732(a).
[28] IRC Sec. 732(b).
[29] There is an exception where cash and "unrealized receivables" are distributed to a partner in liquidation. This will be discussed later.
[30] If a partnership is on the cash method of accounting, it may have unrealized receivables, meaning accounts receivable that have never been recognized as gross income. These will produce ordinary income when collected and not capital gain.

[31] IRC Sec. 751. But if the partner holds the property for at least five years before selling, capital gain is possible. IRC Sec. 735(a)(2).
[32] IRC Sec. 736(b).
[33] IRC Sec. 743.
[34] IRC Sec. 706.
[35] Where the partners have different fiscal years, the partnership will use a calendar year. Note that some partnerships may elect a fiscal year pursuant to IRC Sec. 444. Discussion of the section 444 election is beyond the scope of this text. The IRS usually will grant permission for a partnership to use a different fiscal

Partners include partnership items on their tax returns for their years during which the partnership year ends.[36] Thus, if a partnership is on a September 30 fiscal year, partners on a calendar year will include on their 1990 tax returns the share of partnership items reported on the partnership return for the partnership year ending September 30, 1990.

Notice the tax consequences to the partner. Assume that an employee is promoted to partner on October 1, 1990. The employee's 1990 income tax return will include nine months of salary as an employee. The share of partnership income for the last three months of 1990 will not be taxed to the new partner until 1991. The taxpayer thus obtains a deferral of the tax on three months of income—with the deferral ending when the person ceases to be a partner. Assume that the taxpayer leaves the partnership on September 30, 1999, and becomes a corporate employee. In 1999, fifteen months of income will be reported—the partnership income for the twelve months ended September 30, 1999, plus corporate salary for the final three months of 1999.

10.13 Sale of Partnership Interest

It is possible for a partnership to pay a withdrawing partner more or less than his or her share of the partnership assets. Similarly, a partner may sell the interest in the partnership to an existing partner or a new incoming partner.

The purchasing partner starts with cost as the tax basis. The partnership can elect to adjust the tax basis of its assets, as to the new partner's pro-rata share, so that the initial difference between the partner's cost for the partnership interest and the tax basis of the partnership assets is eliminated. This is the same election previously discussed as a possibility in the context of distributions to a withdrawing partner which differed from his or her share of the partnership assets' tax basis.[37]

For example, assume that D and E form an equal partnership. D contributes cash of $10,000. E contributes property valued at $10,000 but with a basis of $4,000. Recall from Section 10.9 that E is responsible for reporting the $6,000 pre-contribution gain when the property is sold. Assume that during the life of the DE partnership, the property appreciates in value to $14,000 and E sells the 50% interest in the partnership to F for $12,000 (50% of $10,000 + $14,000). If the partnership makes the election described above, the adjusted basis of the partnership property to F will be increased by the excess of (1) F's basis in the partnership interest, which is $12,000, less (2) E's proportionate share of the basis of the partnership assets which is $4,000 or a total adjustment of $8,000. This $8,000 will be added to the basis of the partnership property, but only as to F's interest. If the partnership were to sell the property for $16,000, the partnership will have a gain of $12,000 ($16,000 – $4,000) but only $4,000 of gain will be reported by D and F because of the $8,000 basis adjustment. Note that the appreciation after the contribution is only $6,000. Accordingly, D reports one-half of $6,000 or $3,000 of gain. After F's admittance, the property has appreciated by only $2,000 so F reports one-half of $1,000 of gain.

You may be wondering what happened to E's $6,000 pre-contribution gain. Because E's basis in partnership interest was only $4,000, the gain realized by E upon the sale of the partnership interest was $8,000 ($12,000 – $4,000). This gain can be attributed solely to the appreciated property contributed by E. As described above, $6,000 of this gain had accrued before the contribution of the property to the partnership and $2,000 had accrued after the contribution. Notice that all $12,000 of the gain realized from the sale of the property has been accounted for ($3,000 by D, $8,000 by E and $1,000 by F).

What is the nature of a partner's gain when a partnership interest is sold? Essentially, it is capital gain.[38] However, to the extent the gain is attributable to a pro-rata interest in certain ordinary income assets of the partnership (e.g., "unrealized receivables"), the gain will be ordinary income.[39]

For example, a retiring partner receives $100,000 cash for an interest in a partnership. If the basis of that interest is $60,000, the partner has a $40,000 gain. Under the general rule, this $40,000 gain would be capital gain. However, if the partnership has "unrealized receivables" of $50,000 and the retiring partner's share of those receivables is $10,000, then $10,000 of the gain will be taxed as ordinary income. The remaining $30,000 will be treated as capital gain. Notice that the recognition of ordinary income comes first, with the remainder being treated as capital gain.

year without electing under Sec. 444 only when there are substantial business reasons for the year being sought.

[36]IRC Sec. 706(a).

[37]IRC Sec. 743.

[38]IRC Sec. 741.

[39]Although the term "unrealized receivables" is used, the ordinary income portion is not restricted to the sale of accounts receivable. The term also includes substantially appreciated inventory items and depreciation recapture.

10.14 Retiring Partners

When a partner dies or retires, the payments made by the partnership must be allocated between those for the partner's interest in the partnership assets and all "other" payments.[40] Payments for the partner's interest in the partnership assets will result in gain or loss, as discussed before on withdrawal of a partner or sale of a partnership interest. It is worth emphasizing that none of the payments to a partner will be treated as being for partnership goodwill unless the partnership agreement specifically provides for payments for goodwill.[41]

The "other" payments will be treated as distributions of current income to a partner, thus reducing the partnership's income taxable to the continuing partners. The partnership is thus able to finance much of its buy out of a deceased or withdrawing partner with what are, in effect, deductible payments.

TAX PLANNING TIP: When a partner withdraws from a partnership, there are alternative ways of disposing of the partnership interest.

1. *By selling the partnership interest to another existing partner or to an "outside" party, capital gain can be realized if the selling price is greater than the adjusted basis. However, no one gets an immediate tax deduction for the amount paid.*
2. *By having the partnership liquidate the partner's interest with funds from partnership operations, the partnership can get a deduction and the retiring partner may have ordinary income.*

Partners have a great deal of flexibility in structuring the transactions for maximum after-tax advantage to the retiring partner and the remaining partners.

Assume that Billy Barnes has been a partner in a CPA firm. The firm has five other partners and it earns $600,000 in taxable income each year. Each partner pays tax on $100,000 of partnership taxable income. If Billy resigns from the partnership and receives "other" payments of $100,000 a year for five years, the partnership can deduct the $100,000 each year. This leaves $500,000 of taxable income per year divided equally among the five remaining partners (i.e., $100,000 each). If Billy had been bought out with before-tax money rather than with after-tax money, the other five partners would have had to pay tax on $120,000 per year each during the buy-back period.

[40]IRC Sec. 736.
[41]IRC Sec. 736(b).

10.15 Limited Partnerships

The partnership is an ideal vehicle, from an income tax viewpoint, for pooling funds in order to make investments. The tax attributes of the investment (e.g., capital gain) pass through to the partners as a "source characteristic." See Figure 10-2. In fact, the typical investment club is a partnership and files a partnership tax return.

Through making an investment via a partnership, a small investor can participate in big transactions. For $5,000, a person may own an interest in a multimillion-dollar oil exploration and development project; or for $10,000 a person may have a portion of a $50 million office building. Such an investor would, however, probably be apprehensive about the unlimited liability for the building's $40 million mortgage that might be attached to being a partner.

To meet that type of concern, state laws have evolved a modified form of partnership organization called the limited partnership. The *general* partner(s) of the limited partnership have the same relationship to the partnership as any partner, including unlimited liability for debts. The *limited* partners, who must not be held out to the public as general partners and must not be active in the day-to-day management of the business, are not liable for the debts of the partnership except to the extent that they have specifically agreed to be.

Earlier, this chapter included a discussion of the characteristics that distinguish a partnership from a corporation. Each partner is an agent for the partnership, has unlimited liability for its debts, and shares in profits or losses. The partnership ends upon the death, withdrawal, bankruptcy, or insanity of any partner. Other than sharing in profits or losses, none of these characteristics applies to the limited partner.

Is the limited partnership a partnership or a corporation for tax purposes? The question is being reexamined, especially as to limited partnerships with large numbers of partners even though not publicly traded. At the moment the rule is that a limited partnership will be treated as a partnership for tax purposes if the general partners have a substantial enough interest in the partnership and are themselves sufficiently well-off financially that their liability exposure as general partners is significant.[42]

Thus, if a person wants to make an investment in oil in order to take advantage of the immediate deductibility of the intangible drilling and development costs, plus the sheltering of income afforded by percentage depletion, such a

[42]Reg. Sec. 301.7701-2(d). However, publicly-traded limited partnerships are taxed as corporations.

person need not become an expert on oil and gas (although that certainly would not hurt). An investment of almost any size can be made (but usually not for less than several thousand dollars). Limited partnerships raise equity capital for natural resource development, real estate, and a wide range of projects—some of which are quite gimmicky. Interests in limited partnerships sometimes seem like corporate stock but, unlike many stock investments, most limited partnership investments are relatively illiquid. They may be easy to buy, but they are usually hard to sell. Initial investors buy them for the immediate tax deductions. Once the initial tax benefits have been obtained, the partnership interests look much less attractive to a potential investor.

A good rule to remember about so-called tax shelters is that they should really be called "tax shelter investments" or "tax-sheltered investments." Tax benefits will not convert a bad investment into a good one, although they may make a good investment even more attractive. A prudent rule is "investigate before investing." The tax effects in years after the initial year should be considered very carefully. It is not uncommon for a tax shelter to produce deductions that offset current income subject to tax of, say, 28%, and thus are worth 28 cents on the dollar, with offsetting taxable income being realized in a few years that may be taxed at, say, 33 cents on the dollar. That being the case, there is only an advantage if the time value of the tax deferral exceeds the 5-point tax rate difference.

Assume that an investment of $50,000 is made in a limited partnership. Within the first two years, the investor's share of partnership losses amounts to $50,000.[43] These deductions reduce income which would otherwise be subject to tax of 28%. Thus, the tax savings will be $14,000. At this point the investor has spent $50,000 and has received $14,000 of tax reduction. Later, if the partnership is a financial success, assume that the investor's taxable income from the partnership is subject to tax at a 33% marginal rate. If the before-tax return on original investment is 20% per year, the investor will receive $10,000, which is $6,667 after tax. This return on the original investment is hardly spectacular considering the usual risks involved.

The discussion and examples here have not included consideration of the limitations on the deductibility of passive losses. This and other tax shelters are discussed further in Chapter 17.

[43]As mentioned in footnote 21, the pass-through of partnership losses to partners, particularly to limited partners, has limitations. The basic limitation prevents deductions of cumulative losses in excess of the partner's investment in the partnership interest. These are called the "at risk rules." The limitations on passive losses discussed in Chapter 16 will also be important since limited partnership interests will produce passive income and losses. Special limits apply to the losses of publicly traded limited partnerships.

10.16 Conclusion

For most tax purposes, a partnership is viewed much as a multiple proprietorship. The partnership return, in this view, is merely a convenient place for assembling information that will be reported on the tax returns of the partners. However, many tax elections, especially those dealing with accounting periods and methods, are made by the partnership.

A partnership, for tax purposes, arises in many business and investment relationships that would not be partnerships under state law. Partnerships are easy and inexpensive to form. They usually involve fewer unmanageable tax problems than do corporations—especially when a partner wants to withdraw, the partners decide to take assets out of the business, or the decision is made to liquidate. (Partnerships can also be quite expensive in a nontax sense, however, owing to the unlimited liability of general partners for partnership debts.)

Partnerships can prove useful in deferring taxes, as compared with other ways of structuring a relationship. Take, for instance, B in the example earlier in this chapter, involving the BAC partnership. B could have sold A a 50% interest in the building rather than entering into a partnership with A.

The sale of a 50% interest in the building would have had the following tax effect:

Selling price (½ of FMV)	$25,000
Basis to B (½ of $25,000)	12,500
Gain	$12,500

Thus, B would have realized a taxable gain of $12,500. The partnership produces a similar economic effect, but the tax effect will occur in the future.

Because of its "tax transparency" (its ability to pass its gains or losses through to its partners), the partnership, especially the limited partnership, has been widely used for certain types of tax-sheltered investments.

This chapter has only touched on the very basic rules of partnerships. Entire graduate-level tax courses deal just with partnership taxation. With a grasp of the basics, however, you are in a position to consider partnerships in your tax planning thinking and to understand the complexities sometimes encountered in specific transactions as you either research a problem for yourself or work with an adviser.

TRUE-FALSE QUESTIONS

State whether each of the following statements is true or false. For each *false* answer, reword the statement to make it *true*.

T F 1. A partnership, for tax purposes, can include organizations known as syndicates, groups, pools, and joint ventures.

T F 2. In all partnerships, each partner will bear the risk of unlimited liability for debts of the partnership.

T F 3. An important feature of a partnership is that it does not pay federal income tax.

T F 4. Certain partnerships may be taxed as corporations if they have the characteristics of a corporation, such as centralized management, transferability of ownership interests, and limited liability.

T F 5. A basic concept of a partnership as far as the federal income tax law is concerned is that it serves as a conduit for special characteristics of income, deductions, and credits to the partners.

T F 6. If a partnership is formed and Ms. A contributes property in exchange for an interest in the partnership, she will recognize gain if the fair market value of her partnership interest is greater than the adjusted basis of the property she contributed.

T F 7. If a partnership is formed and Mr. B contributes property in exchange for an interest in the partnership, the partnership's basis in that property will be the same as Mr. B's basis before he transferred it to the partnership.

T F 8. Because of the relationship, a partner cannot sell property to a partnership of which he is a partner and recognize a gain for federal income tax purposes.

T F 9. Since a partnership does not have a tax liability that can be reduced by credits, a partnership should not purchase and rehabilitate an old building which will result in a credit for the rehabilitation costs.

T F 10. A partner's adjusted basis in a partnership is $80,000. In complete liquidation of his interest he receives the following:

Cash	$30,000
Inventory (basis to partnership)	44,000
Fixed asset (adjusted basis to partnership)	12,000

The fixed asset will have a basis of $12,000 to the partner after the liquidation of his interest.

T F 11. The amount shown on a partnership's books as a partner's capital account is the same as the basis of that partner's interest in the partnership.

T F 12. A calendar-year partner is entitled to a $1,000 distributive share of partnership income from a partnership, which uses a fiscal year ending March 31 of the current year. The partner must include $250 of this on his income tax return for the year.

T F 13. Mr. Rush, a calendar-year taxpayer, is a partner in the Stop & Go partnership, which uses a fiscal year ending August 31. He received guaranteed payments of $400 on November 30 last year and May 31 of the current year. The entire $800 should be included in Mr. Rush's gross income for the current year.

T F 14. Ima Lawler received a 10% interest in a new partnership (Land Associates) in exchange for having provided legal services to the partnership and to the other partners. She will not have taxable income and her basis in the partnership will be zero.

T F 15. Mr. Red and Mr. Black are both certified public accountants and each maintains a separate practice. They share the same office, dividing expenses, such as rent and utilities, equally. This arrangement is a partnership for federal income tax purposes.

T F 16. A sale of partnership interest always results in the recognition of capital gain or loss.

T F 17. A partner must include his or her distributive share of partnership income or loss in computing net earnings from self-employment.

T F 18. Mr. Wyndelts is a partner in the E-R partnership. His adjusted basis for the partnership interest was $10,000 at the beginning of the year. He received a distribution of $8,000 cash, plus land with a value of $3,000, during the year. Neither partnership transfer to him was a liquidating distribution. There was no sale of an interest in the partnership. He must report a $1,000 gain on his individual tax return for the year.

T F 19. If a partnership year ends on September 30, 1990, and a partner's share of the partnership income is $20,000, and the partner's year ends December 31, that partner must include $20,000 in income for 1990, even if no assets were received from the partnership during the year.

T F 20. Sam Bird's distributive share of income from the Feather partnership was $22,000 for the last calendar year. Sam received a distribution of $15,000 of the partnership's last year's earnings on December 12. Feather is a calendar-year partnership. Sam should report $15,000 as ordinary income from the partnership on his Form 1040 for last year.

PROBLEMS

Problem 10-1. Barry Lett is a member of the partnership of Lett and Austin. Barry files his tax return on a calendar-year basis but the partnership uses a fiscal year ending March 31. Barry received a guaranteed salary of $1,000 each month during calendar year 1989 and 1990. For calendar year 1991, that payment was increased to $1,500 per month. The partnership deducted this "salary" as an operating expense. After this deduction, the partnership realized ordinary income of $80,000 for the year ended March 31, 1991 and $90,000 for the year ended March 31, 1992. The partnership agreement provides that Barry's share of the partnership profits will be this salary plus 40% of the ordinary income after the salary deduction.

(a) For calendar 1991, calculate Barry's taxable income from the partnership.

(b) What difference would it have made, assuming all of the same facts except that the partnership's fiscal year ended February 28?

(c) If Barry expected to be in a lower tax bracket for the year 1990 than for 1991, could he have arranged for a "bonus" payment during December 1990 with the result of "accelerating" the recognition of income to 1990 rather than 1991? Explain.

Problem 10-2. The partnership of Yee and Yuan uses a calendar tax year. For the year ended December 31, 1990, the partnership reported ordinary income of $260,000, which was *after* deductions for the following items:

Real estate taxes	$ 8,000
Charitable contributions	2,000
Repairs to partnership machinery	1,000
Foreign income taxes	5,000
Interest	4,000
Salaries	70,000
Loss from sale of delivery truck	12,000

The interest and salaries were paid to persons other than partners. The delivery truck had been owned for eight years before sale.

(a) Which of the items should not be reported as operating expenses by the partnership, but passed on separately to the partners? Explain.

(b) Would it have made any difference if the partnership had operated at a loss for the year?

(c) Would it have made any difference if the partnership had been on a fiscal year?

Problem 10-3. The Butler and Bradshaw partnership had $75,000 of net income for the year ended December 31, 1990. This number *included* the following:

Interest & Income	$1,000
Dividends from taxable U.S. corporations	200
Section 1245 recapture (ordinary income)	600
Section 1231 gain (from sale of building)	1,500
Long-term capital gain (from sale of stock)	4,300
Short-term capital loss (from sale of stock)	(3,100)

The building that was sold had been held for several years and depreciated under the straight-line method. Butler and Bradshaw share profits and losses equally.

(a) Calculate the partnership taxable income, *excluding* all items that will be accounted for separately by the partners.

(b) Which items will be reported separately by each partner? Explain why it is necessary for each partner to report these items separately.

(c) Would it make any difference if the partnership were on a fiscal year ending January 31 rather than a calendar year? Explain.

Problem 10-4. The partnership of Stern and Wheeler purchased a new "MACRS five-year" asset for $80,000 on July 1, 1990. The partnership elects to expense $10,000 of the cost of this machine in addition to the normal depreciation deduction. The partnership is on a fiscal year ending June 30. Both partners are on a calendar tax year. Stern is single. Wheeler is married and will file a joint income tax return with her husband. Stern and Wheeler divide all profits and losses 60:40. Neither of them has any other business interests.

(a) Explain the impact of the $10,000 expense election upon the partnership and upon the partners.

(b) What difference would it have made if the asset had been purchased by the partnership on January 2, 1990?

(c) What difference would it have made if the asset had been purchased by the partnership on July 1, 1990, but the partnership was on a calendar year, the same as the partners?

Problem 10-5. In February 1991 Marshall contributed the following assets to the MNOP partnership:

Cash	$10,000
Machinery (adjusted basis)	6,000

Marshall had acquired the machinery two years earlier and used it in his proprietorship. The original cost to him was $12,000. Marshall's partnership account was credited for $20,000; total capital of all partners, including Marshall's, is $80,000. The machinery is valued at $10,000 on the partnership books.

(a) What is the tax effect to the partnership from Marshall's joining the firm as was done?

(b) What is the tax effect to Marshall from joining the partnership as was done?

(c) If the machinery had an adjusted basis of $10,000 and a fair market value of $7,000 at the time of the transfer to the partnership, would Marshall have a recognized loss?

Problem 10-6. Mr. Flate and Mr. Tire are thinking of organizing the Flate-Tire Company as a partnership. Mr. Flate has been operating a similar business as a proprietorship for several years. He wants to expand but does not have the capital to do so. Mr. Tire has $100,000 in cash that he is willing to invest in new plant and equipment. They agree that Mr. Flate's assets are worth $100,000, thus providing each with a one-half interest, but the adjusted basis of Mr. Flate's depreciable assets is only $55,000 because he has been taking accelerated (MACRS) depreciation. The assets purchased with the $100,000 cash which Mr. Tire will contribute to the partnership will have an initial tax basis of $100,000. Will Mr. Flate and Mr. Tire have to structure their arrangement so that the apparent inequities of depreciation deductions division on a 50–50 ratio will be overcome? Explain.

Problem 10-7. Bison and Buffalo operate a two-person partnership in which they share profits and losses equally. During the most recent year, the partnership incurred expenses and losses as follows:

Salaries (paid to employees of the partnership)	$140,000
Interest (paid to third-party lenders)	8,000
Real estate taxes	16,000
Charitable contributions	4,000
Repairs to machinery	2,000
Foreign income taxes	10,000
Loss on sale of a machine held for six years	24,000

Including these items, the partnership reported ordinary income of $520,000 for the year. There were no capital gains or losses incurred during the year.

(a) Which of the items must be reported separately by the partnership rather than as a part of the $520,000 ordinary income? Why?

(b) How much, and where, would Bison report on Form 1040 his interest in this partnership?

Problem 10-8. Charles has operated a business as a proprietorship for a number of years. Recently, Charles and Dobson have agreed to join together and operate a business as a partnership. They plan to form the C&D Company and to transfer assets to it as follows:

Investor	*Property*	*Tax Basis of Property*	*Fair Market Value*	*Value of Interests to Be Received*
Charles	Real estate	$140,000	$200,000	$200,000
Dobson	Cash		200,000	200,000

(a) What is the tax effect of the formation of the partnership to Charles?

(b) What is the tax effect of the formation of the partnership to Dobson?

(c) In the negotiations for forming the partnership, they also discussed the possibility that Everett might join with them. Everett has property that has a tax basis of $240,000 and a fair market value of $200,000. Everett decided not to join the partnership at its initial formation but to transfer property to the partnership a few months later in exchange for a $200,000 partnership interest. Charles and Dobson agreed to this. What would be the tax effect on the partnership and on Everett if this transfer took place? Can Everett elect to recognize the loss?

Problem 10-9. Indicate whether the following items are examples of the aggregate concept or the entity concept of partnership taxation.

(a) The partnership pays no income tax.

(b) The character of an item (for example capital gain) is retained and passed on to the individual partner as if the partner had earned or incurred the item directly.

(c) Depreciation method is elected by the partnership.

(d) The sale of a partnership interest my result in the recognition of both capital gain and ordinary income.

Problem 10-10. Partner A has a $20,000 basis in the ABC partnership. As part of a nonliquidating distribution, Partner A receives common stock worth $25,000 with a basis of $18,000.

(a) Compute the gain or loss (if any) as a result of the distribution.

(b) Compute the basis of the common stock in the hands of the partner.

(c) Compute the basis of Partner A's interest in the partnership immediately after the distribution.

(d) Answer questions (a) and (b) assuming that the distribution was in complete liquidation of Partner A's partnership.

Problem 10-11. Jason Most sells his 40% partnership interest for $35,000 Cash plus assumption of partnership liabilities. His share of partnership unrealized receivables and partnership liabilities is $15,000 and $10,000 respectively. The basis of his partnership interest is $20,000.

(a) What is the total gain recognized on the sale of Jason's partnership interest?

(b) Break down the gain into capital gain and ordinary income.

PROBLEMS WITH AN ASTERISK REQUIRE ADDITIONAL RESEARCH.

Problem 10-12.* Wilson and Monroe formed a partnership on April 1 of last year with each contributing cash as follows:

Wilson	$30,000
Monroe	6,000

They agreed to share profits and losses equally, although Monroe will do most of the work. They will use a calendar year for the partnership's tax year. For the nine months ending December 31 last year, the partnership operated at an $8,000 loss. During that same period each withdrew $3,000. As of the end of December, the partnership had no liabilities.

(a) What amount may Monroe deduct on his personal tax return for last year as the result of the Wilson and Monroe partnership? (Assume that Monroe has another job which pays a salary of $50,000, that he has $10,000 of passive income, and that he has only a small amount of other deductions.) Explain.

(b) What amount may Wilson deduct under the same assumption?

(c) What effect would there be on Monroe if the partnership had borrowed $5,000 from a bank on December 31?

Problem 10-13.* Pitt and Reneau formed a partnership. Pitt contributed land that had a basis to him of $18,000 and a fair market value of $64,000. The partnership intended to erect a building on the land and, accordingly, the partnership agreement provided that the new business would obtain a construction loan of $250,000 for that purpose. Pitt and Reneau were each to sign the loan agreement and be personally liable for the entire loan in the event that the partnership defaulted. When the partnership obtained the loan, Pitt withdrew $64,000 from the partnership.

(a) Will Pitt have to recognize the $64,000 gain on the transaction?

(b) What if Pitt had been guaranteed $64,000 in all events, whether the partnership failed or succeeded?

(c) What if Pitt's property had depreciated in value and he wanted to sell it to the partnership and recognize the loss? Could he do this? Explain.

11

the S corporation

In Chapter 10, the partnership was discussed as an economic middleman, not subject to federal income tax. From this point of view, it is logical to conclude that the income of the corporation is also the income of its shareholders. It should not be too surprising, therefore, to discover that some corporations can elect to have their income taxed directly to the shareholders and not pay the corporate income tax.[1] With the exceptions pointed out in this chapter, such a corporation and its shareholders will be treated tax-wise very much as if it were a partnership.

These corporations are labeled "Subchapter S" or "S" corporations after the Internal Revenue Code subchapter that gave them birth.[2] We will refer to non-S corporations as "C" corporations.

There are over 1,250,000 S corporations.[3] This is about 30% of the corporations presently filing income tax returns. The law restricts this optional treatment on the basis of number and kind of shareholders rather than on total income or total assets. Nevertheless, these *are* relatively small businesses compared with regular corporations. The authors estimate that less than 11,000 S corporations had assets of $10 million or more, whereas over 47,000 regular corporations have assets in that bracket.[4]

[1]IRC Sec. 1362(a) and 1363.

[2]Previously, electing corporations were called "small business corporations."

[3]Internal Revenue Service. *Statistics of Income Bulletin*, Vol. 9, No. 2. U.S. Department of Treasury Publ. 1136. Table 19, p. 96. U.S. Government Printing Office, Washington, D.C. (Fall 1989).

[4]Internal Revenue Service, *Statistics of Income Bulletin*, Vol. 9, No. 2, Table 12, p. 88. U.S. Government Printing Office, Washington, D.C. (Fall 1989).

11.1 Making and Keeping the Election

To elect the optional tax treatment, the corporation must be a U.S. corporation with only one class of stock outstanding and with no more than thirty-five shareholders.[5] The shareholders can be only individuals, estates, and "qualified" trusts.[6] If a corporation does not meet *all* of the requirements, the S election cannot be made. In addition, an electing corporation must continue to meet all of the requirements or the election will terminate.[7]

The election is made by the corporation (on Form 2553), and all shareholders must file a signed consent to the election.[8] Once the election is made, it will continue for future years as long as the corporation continues to qualify and there is no election to terminate the S status. The election to be an S corporation can be made at any time during the year and will be applicable for the following year. To be effective for the same year, the election must be made during the first two and

[5]IRC Sec. 1361(b). Differences in voting rights of outstanding stock are permissible. Certain corporations are ineligible, such as members of an affiliated group (a corporation with an 80% or more subsidiary), financial institutions, and insurance companies.

[6]Nonresident aliens are not qualified shareholders. Generally, a trust can qualify if there is only one beneficiary, that beneficiary elects the S treatment, and all of the trust income is distributable to the beneficiary each year. A trust not meeting these requirements can also be an S shareholder (but only for a limited time) if it is a testamentary trust. For a discussion of trusts, see Chapter 14.

[7]See Section 11.8 for a discussion of the effects of termination of the election.

[8]IRC Sec. 1362(a)(2).

one-half months of the year.[9] Where a qualified owner becomes a shareholder after the election is in effect, that owner will be treated as if he or she had previously consented to the election.

For example, assume that Barnes corporation, already operating as a C corporation, wanted to make the Subchapter S election to be effective for calendar 1990. The election would have to have been made at any time during 1989, or prior to March 16, 1990.

There is no requirement that an S corporation be a new business. In other words, a corporation that has been in business as a nonelecting corporation can elect the S status if it qualifies. If a corporation has always been an S corporation, there is no problem with "passive income" that it may receive. ("Passive income" is income from interest, dividends, royalties, annuities, gross rents, and gains from sale of capital assets.) The same is true for a corporation that is an S corporation but was at sometime in the past a C corporation *if* it does not have any earnings and profits left over from its C years. Too much "passive income" can result in a special tax or ultimately in the loss of the S election for corporations that were previously C corporations and have earnings and profits from the pre-S years.[10]

If a corporation has C earnings and profits, *and* more than 25% of its gross receipts for *each* of three consecutive taxable years is from passive income, the S status will terminate.[11] Where termination occurs because of failing this passive income test, the effective date of the termination will be the first day of the taxable year after such third year. For example, assume that the Barnes Corporation elected S status for 1989, after having been a C corporation with earnings and profits for each of the previous three years. In 1989, 1990, and 1991 more than 25% of its gross receipts are from passive sources. The Barnes Corporation will lose its S status as of January 1, 1992.

An S election will also be lost, for example, at any time the corporation has thirty-six shareholders, has a nonqualified shareholder (such as another corporation or a nonresident alien), or has a second class of stock outstanding. The tax results from loss of the S election are discussed later in this chapter.

TAX PLANNING TIP: If a corporation with C earnings and profits has had more than 25% of its gross receipts from passive sources in two years, it can often manage to avoid losing the S status by arranging to have less than 25% of its gross receipts from passive sources for the third year. Transactions in commodities (e.g., feeder cattle) might accomplish this by substantially increasing gross receipts (although having little impact on net income). Note, however, that this will not result in alleviation of the tax that will have to be paid on net passive income (discussed later) in those years when passive income exceeds 25%.

11.1.1. Taxable Year and Elections

If an S corporation and a shareholder could have different year ends, there would be the possibility of a deferral of income by the shareholder. For example, if the corporation's year ended on September 30, the income for its year ending September 30, 1990 would be included in the 1990 income of shareholders. The income earned by the corporation after September 30, 1990 would not be included in the income of the shareholders until 1991.

In order to prevent stockholders from delaying the year in which they report income from an S corporation, there is a general requirement that an S corporation use a calendar year.[12] Since most individuals use a calendar year, this means that the S corporation and the individual shareholders will be on the same year. There is an exception which allows a fiscal year if the corporation can satisfy the IRS that there is an acceptable business purpose for such a different accounting period.

As with the partnership, there is also an election available under Sec. 444 (see Chapter 10) to use a fiscal year of September 30, October 31, or November 30. However, the election requires a deposit be made with the U.S. Treasury in an amount approximating the tax deferred by the fiscal year election.

As discussed elsewhere in the text, there are numerous opportunities for a taxpayer to make elections that impact tax treatment. As a general rule, any election will be made by the S corporation rather than by the shareholders—for example, elections as to accounting methods, depreciation, expensing the first $10,000 of capital expenditures, and treatment of research and development expenses. Some specific elections are reserved for the shareholders in their individual capacities:

1. Election to apply discharge of indebtedness as a reduction to basis of property.[13]

[9] IRC Sec. 1362(b). If the first taxable year is 2½ months or less in length, the election can be made within 2½ months of the first day of the first taxable year.

[10] IRC Sec. 1362(d)(3).

[11] Only taxable years beginning after 12-31-81, and for which the corporation has been an S corporation for the year, will be taken into account.

[12] IRC Sec. 1378.

[13] IRC Sec. 108(b)(5). Note that such discharge of indebtedness must have occurred in connection with a title 11 (bankruptcy)

2. Election to deduct certain mining exploration expenditures.[14]
3. Election to use taxes paid to foreign countries and U.S. possessions as credits.[15]

All other elections will be made by the corporation. There is no requirement that shareholders consent to these corporate elections, but there must be consistency between the manner in which an S corporation treats an item and what the shareholders do on their personal tax returns.[16]

11.2 Taxable Income or Loss and Its Allocation

The tax return used by an S corporation is Form 1120S. The 1120S reflects the general concept of the S corporation's taxation. Like the partnership, which was discussed in Chapter 10, the S corporation functions for the most part as a conduit, passing through to its shareholders the ultimate tax incidence of transactions as the partnership does to its partners. There are four major differences between the treatment of partnerships and that of S corporations:

1. In some circumstances, an S corporation may have tax to pay on its built-in gains. The partnership *never* pays any federal income tax itself.
2. An S corporation may have tax to pay on its excessive passive income.
3. The S corporation itself will realize income when distributing appreciated property to a shareholder. A partnership does not normally realize income from distributing property to a partner. (Exceptions in the partnership situation occur when appreciated property is involved in a disproportionate liquidation of a partner's interest.[17])
4. The S corporation may have to pay tax because of a recapture of investment credits relating back to corporate acquisitions of property that predate the S corporation election.

All four of these points will be discussed further in this chapter.

Assume that the Barnes Corporation has only ordinary income from the sale of services or merchandise, and ordinary business expenses. If Billy is the only shareholder and has been the only shareholder for the entire corporate year, Billy will include in gross income the amount of the corporation's taxable income, or deduct the corporation's loss. If Billy and the corporation are both on a calendar year (1990, for example), then Billy's gross income for 1990 will be increased by the full amount of the corporation's taxable income for 1990.

As in a partnership, Billy's basis for the stock in the corporation will be increased by the amount of corporate taxable income required to be included in gross income. Likewise, should the corporation have a loss which is deductible on Billy's tax return, Billy's basis in the stock of the corporation will be decreased by that amount.

The Barnes Corporation may be on a fiscal year. This is possible if it has been able to establish a business purpose for a noncalendar fiscal year.[18] The taxable income of a fiscal-year S corporation is includable (or a loss is deductible) in the shareholder's year during which the corporation's year ends. Thus, if the corporation's year ends on September 30, 1990, Billy will include in 1990 income the taxable income of the corporation for its fiscal year October 1, 1989 to September 30, 1990.

Where there has been any change in stock ownership during a corporate year, an allocation is required to all persons who were shareholders during the year. Assume that Lynn Larsen was an owner, along with Billy Barnes, at some time during the corporate year. It is necessary to allocate the taxable income (or loss) on a per-share, per-day basis. For example, assume that corporate taxable income is $30,000, that Lynn was a 25% shareholder for 190 days, and that Billy was a 75% shareholder for 190 days and a 100% shareholder for 175 days. The taxable income per day is $30,000 divided by 365, or $82.19. Billy is required to include the entire $82.19 for 175 days *plus* 75% of $82.19 for 190 days. That equals $26,095. Lynn must include 25% of the $82.19 for 190 days, or $3,904.

In the example above, it was assumed that stock was bought and sold between Billy and Lynn. The allocation procedure would also be used if the corporation issued some new stock. Billy might have been the sole owner for 210 days, at which time the corporation issued new shares to Lynn. Billy's number of shares remained constant, but the percentage decreased when Lynn became an owner. Thus, if Billy owned 1,000 shares and 200 shares were issued to Lynn, the ratio would be 100% for Billy for 210 days plus 83.3% for 155 days. For Lynn, the ratio would be 16.7% for 155 days. As with the previous example, it is the percentage of ownership that is used to allocate the corporate results to the shareholders for the year.

If the corporation's taxable income was $30,000 as before, Billy's share of the $30,000 would be:

case, a situation when the taxpayer is insolvent, or a discharge of a qualified farm indebtedness.

[14]IRC Sec. 617.

[15]IRC Sec. 901.

[16]IRC Sec. 6242.

[17]IRC Sec. 751.

[18]IRC Sec. 1378(b)(2) or if it has made an election under IRC Sec. 444.

$82.19 × 210 days =	$17,261
+83.3% ($82.19) × 155 days =	10,612
	$27,873
Lynn's share of the $30,000 would be:	
16.7% ($82.19) × 155 days =	2,127
Total	$30,000

Note that in the allocation of taxable income among shareholders, the timing of actual income is generally not relevant. Income is assumed to have been earned uniformly during the year. It makes no difference if the shareholders can show that the income was earned in a different ratio or can be attributed to a time when someone was or was not a shareholder. Thus, in the above example of Billy and Lynn, it normally makes no difference that the accounting records may "prove" that all of the income was earned during the time when Lynn was a shareholder and that the corporation merely broke even during the 210 days when Billy was the sole shareholder, or vice versa.

Careful planning is called for when a person is thinking of acquiring or disposing of S stock during the corporate year. It may not be possible to foresee the tax impact because of the inability to foresee the results of the corporate operations for the remaining portion of the year. Where the timing of the transaction is not crucial, it may be advantageous to wait until the beginning of the corporate year to change stock ownership or to issue stock to a new shareholder. Note that there is an election available to mitigate this problem when *all* of a shareholder's stock is disposed of. See Section 11.2.2.[19]

TAX PLANNING TIP: It may be wise, where a person is acquiring or disposing of S stock during the year, to negotiate for a "contingent" price or for a retroactive price adjustment based upon subsequent events. Then, if the corporate operating results (profit or loss) should be different from what was expected, the fact that the part-year shareholder has to pay tax (or gets to take a deduction) for an amount different from what was expected can be adjusted retroactively by an alteration in the selling price or by a "refund" from the other party.

Where an S corporation shareholder dies during the year, there is a similar allocation. As we saw in Chapter 8, a person's taxable year ends on the date of death. The new owner of stock will be either the decedent's estate or an heir. The allocation arithmetic is no different from what would be required if the decedent had sold all of the stock on the date of death. In other words, the percentage of ownership and the number of days for which the stock was owned during the year will be used to determine the amount of income taxable to the decedent. The estate or heir will be the new shareholder, and an allocation based upon the percentage of ownership and the number of days will be used to determine how much income (or loss) shall be allocated to the estate or heir. Of course, it is also possible that the estate would be the owner for a few months and would then transfer the stock to an heir or heirs, all within the same taxable year of the corporation. In that case, the arithmetic gets more complicated, but the concept remains the same.

Where an S corporation has a loss, the shareholders may include their share of the loss as a deduction on their individual tax returns.[20] The shareholders will reduce the basis of their S stock (discussed later) by the prorated loss. Should a shareholder's pro-rata share of the loss exceed the sum of his or her basis in the stock, the balance will reduce the basis of any debt owed to that shareholder by the corporation. If a shareholder's pro-rata share of the corporate loss is larger than the sum of his or her basis in stock and debt, the amount of the current deduction is limited to the sum of those bases. The amount of the allocated loss not deductible for the current year because of lack of basis can be carried forward to subsequent years and deducted when there is basis, without any limit on the number of carryover years.[21]

For example, assume that Billy Barnes is the 100% owner of Barnes Corporation. Billy's basis in the stock is $30,000. The corporation also owes Billy $5,000 on a note. The corporation's loss for the year is $38,000. Billy may only deduct $35,000 currently, with a $3,000 carryover to the following year. If for any reason Billy's basis in stock or debt should increase in a future year, the $3,000 (or part thereof) will be deductible at that time.

TAX PLANNING TIP: A taxpayer can control the year in which S corporation losses get utilized by buying stock or making a loan to the S corporation. If a loss could be better utilized in the individual's 1991 rather than 1990 return, a loan in 1991 will provide basis to use the loss unused in 1990 because of lack of basis.

[19] Under the election, there is a cut-off calculation when the shareholder disposes of all stock and the other shareholders agree.

[20] IRC Sec. 1366.

[21] IRC Sec. 1366(d).

Where there is a change in ownership during a loss year, the loss is allocated to the shareholders exactly the same way in which a profit would be allocated. The percentage of ownership and the number of days are used to determine the amount of the loss allocable to each person who was a shareholder at any time during the corporation's year. After each shareholder's pro-rata share of the loss is determined, that shareholder's basis in stock and debt must then be reviewed to determine if the shareholder will be permitted to deduct all of the allocated loss.

11.2.1. Adjustment of Basis in S Stock and Debt

You will recall from Chapter 10 that a partner adjusts his or her basis in the partnership interest as the result of reporting partnership income. Shareholders of S corporations do likewise.[22] For example, assume that Billy Barnes has owned for the entire year 30% of the stock of Barnes Corporation, which has an effective S election for 1990. The corporation has taxable income (all ordinary income and deductions) of $50,000. As a result, Billy is required to include $15,000 in gross income *and* will increase the basis of the corporate stock by $15,000. If the corporation had incurred a loss of $20,000 instead, Billy could deduct $6,000 and would *reduce* stock basis by $6,000.[23]

Where an S corporation has some special items of income, the source characteristic of which is passed through to the shareholders (discussed later), basis is also adjusted for the pro-rata share of such special items. For example, if the corporation had $50,000 of ordinary taxable income *plus* a long-term capital gain of $10,000, Billy (30% owner) would include on a Form 1040 $15,000 of ordinary income and $3,000 of long-term capital gain. Billy's stock basis would increase by $18,000. Basis adjustments will be made as the result of *any* special item of income, loss, or deduction that is "passed through" to the shareholders.

An S corporation will pass charitable contributions through to shareholders. The reason is that there is a limit on the amount an individual can deduct for charitable contributions (see Chapter 3). If the Barnes Corporation contributed $1,000 to charity, Billy (still a 30% owner) would be allocated $300 which would be a part of Billy's itemized deductions. Billy would also *decrease* stock basis by $300.

If an S corporation owns tax-exempt municipal bonds and receives the resulting tax-free interest, each shareholder will be allocated a pro-rata portion of the interest. The interest is not included in gross income of the shareholder because the "source characteristic" (see Figure 10-2) remains intact. However, the shareholder will increase stock basis by the amount of the allocated interest. It is as if the shareholder received the interest directly and then contributed it to the capital of the corporation.

As we saw in Chapter 9, percentage depletion deductions may exceed the basis of the asset being depleted. Where this occurs to an S corporation, the effect of passing through the excess deductions to the shareholders is to reduce their basis in their S stock. To restore that basis, the shareholders will increase stock basis by the amount of the excess. For example, if Barnes Corporation owns a gold mine with a basis of $100,000 and the percentage depletion for the year is $130,000, the basis of the mine will be reduced to zero at the end of the year. For that year, the excess is $30,000. Billy, a 30% owner, will have been allocated $9,000 of the excess which will have reduced basis. Billy will get to increase stock basis by $9,000. For each following year, the full amount of the percentage depletion will be "excess" and the shareholders will get an offsetting increase in basis by the appropriate pro-rata share.[24]

If an S corporation has an expense that is not deductible in computing taxable income, and not properly chargeable to capital, each shareholder's pro-rata share of that expense will reduce stock basis. For example, assume that Barnes Corporation paid a fine because of an overloaded truck on the highway. The fine was $1,000 and is not deductible. Billy's share, $300, will result in a *decrease* in basis of Billy's stock. This treatment is *as if* the corporation had distributed $300 to Billy. As we will see later in this chapter, distributions to shareholders do not result in a deduction to the corporation nor in income to the shareholder. Also, Billy would get no deduction as the result of the portion of the fine deemed to have been paid. (See Chapter 3).

Later we will see that S corporation shareholders, having paid tax on corporate profits that they did not receive, can receive distributions tax-free from the corporation. When this is done, the stockholder's stock basis is reduced, similar to what happens to a partner.

[22]IRC Sec. 1367(a)(1).

[23]IRC Sec. 1367(a)(2). This example assumes that the basis was at least $6,000 before year end.

[24]A special rule applies for S corporations that are eligible for depletion of oil and gas wells, whether under the cost or percentage method. The full amount of each shareholder's pro-rata share of the depletion will result in a decrease in basis of that person's stock. However, once the basis of the well has been reduced to zero, no further reduction is made to the basis of the stock. IRC Sec. 1367(a)(2)(E).

There is (theoretically, at least) no upward limit as to how large a shareholder's basis in his or her S corporation stock may become. On the reverse side, there is a limit. The downward basis adjustments to stock can never reduce the basis of the stock to less than zero. If a shareholder's downward basis adjustments (not including actual distributions) do exceed the preadjustment stock basis, the excess will reduce the basis of any debt owed to the shareholder by the corporation.[25] Where a reduction in the basis of debt occurs as the result of loss pass-through, pass-through of gain in a later year will restore the basis of the debt before being applied to increase the basis of stock.[26] For example, assume that Billy Barnes had a basis of $30,000 in stock and $5,000 in a note before allocation of a $33,000 loss. Billy would deduct the $33,000. The basis in stock would be reduced to zero, and the basis of the note would be reduced to $2,000. The $3,000 write-down in the basis of the note will be restored prior to any subsequent increase in basis of the stock. If Billy's pro-rata share of corporate taxable income for the following year were $10,000, for example, the basis of the debt would be restored to $5,000 and the basis of the stock would become $7,000.

11.2.2. Transfers of Entire Ownership

If a person disposes of his or her entire interest in an S corporation during the year, the allocation of a portion of that year's gain or loss, and the related basis adjustments, can cause a problem. For example, assume that three months into a year Billy Barnes sells all the shares of Barnes Corporation. A gain or loss would be determined by deducting the adjusted basis of the stock from the selling price. At the end of the corporate year, part of the corporation's taxable income (or loss) will be allocated to all persons who were shareholders *at any time* during the year, including Billy. The resulting basis adjustment for the stock will make Billy's gain or loss different from what was calculated at the time of the sale. This problem can be avoided by use of an election.

If a shareholder disposes of *all* shares of an S corporation and if all persons who were shareholders at any time during the year elect to do so, the corporate year can be divided into two short years: (1) from the beginning of the year to the date of the shareholder's total disposition of the S stock and (2) the remaining portion of what would have been the full taxable year. Only one tax return is filed, with the cut-off affecting calculation of the income or loss of the selling shareholder. This election can be an advantage to a shareholder who is "getting out" because he or she will not then be impacted by the results of corporate operations (good or bad) after that point. It can also be advantageous for the remaining shareholders because they will not have to "share" with the former stockholder the tax consequences of corporate operations after the disposition of stock. In the absence of this election, the corporate taxable income or loss for the year will be treated as if it had occurred uniformly during the year, as mentioned before. Those readers familiar with accounting terminology will recognize that the result of this election is *as if* the corporation "closed its books" as of the date of the change in ownership, and calculated net income for each of two "short fiscal periods."

11.3 Pass-through of "Source Characteristics" of Income, Deductions, and Credits

In Chapter 10 we saw that where a partnership recognizes income that has some special tax treatment there is an allocation of that income to each partner in accordance with the provisions of the partnership agreement. The partnership prepares a Form K-1, which is used to report to each partner (and to the IRS) the amount of each item that potentially may have some special tax treatment. The same procedure is used for any deductions that may have some special applicable rules (capital losses, for example). Also, where the partnership entered into a transaction that would have resulted in a credit (such as hiring employees which would result in the "targeted jobs" credit), there is an allocation to each partner so that he or she can claim the credit on the individual income tax return.

The same approach is used by S corporations. The difference is that there is no partnership agreement to determine the method of allocation. Instead, the allocations are made on the same basis as ordinary corporate taxable income is allocated, as explained earlier. For any item of corporate income, deduction, or credit that could affect the tax of any shareholder if reported separately rather than as a part of the corporate activities, there is to be a separate reporting *as if* the shareholder had realized such item directly from the source from which it was realized by the corporation.[27] The corporation will prepare a Form K-1 for each share-

[25] IRC Sec. 1367(b)(2)(A).

[26] IRC Sec. 1367(b)(2)(B). The restoration of basis of debt will apply only to the extent that the basis of debt was reduced by loss pass-through *after* 1982.

[27] IRC Sec. 1366(b).

holder, and each shareholder will include each special item on his or her tax return.

For example, assume that the Barnes Corporation has 1990 taxable income, not including any special characteristic items, of $25,000. In addition, the corporation has the following items during the year:

Charitable contributions (deduction)	$1,000
Long-term capital gain (income)	4,000
Dividend income (income)	600

Billy has been a 30% shareholder of Barnes Corporation for the entire year. Billy's individual income tax return will reflect the following items:

30% of corporate ordinary taxable income	$7,500
30% of corporate charitable contributions	300
30% of corporate long-term capital gain	1,200
30% of corporate dividend income	180

11.4 Why Elect S Corporation Treatment?

By allowing corporations to avoid paying tax if their shareholders will elect to report all of the corporate income as their own, Congress intended merely to remove tax considerations as a factor in the choice of the legal form that a particular enterprise might adopt. But even a simple provision added to the law fits into a framework that is already complex. The imagination and ingenuity of taxpayers, their advisers, and the IRS are almost infinite. Hence, even a simple provision can have unexpected consequences. The S corporation provisions, not being entirely simple in themselves, have thus spawned a certain degree of complexity.

It is true, however, that a major reason for choosing S treatment fits naturally into the congressional intention. There are certain business reasons why a business enterprise might be organized as a corporation. These are, in part:

1. Limited liability of the owners for the enterprise's debts.
2. Employee incentive through stock ownership.
3. Relatively greater ease of handling corporate stock rather than diverse business assets in estate planning.
4. Raising capital funds through stock sale to friends and relatives who might not wish the risks of partnership.
5. Avoid a corporate level tax on the appreciation in value of corporate assets.

Thus, it may be desirable to form a business as a corporation. Yet, a regular corporation would find the corporate earnings subject to a tax of at least 15%. Any dividends paid would be subject to at least a 15% tax. Thus, a combined total tax of 27.75% or more would result. [How can 15 plus 15 total 27.75? The corporation can distribute only its after-tax income. Therefore, the 15% applies to 85% (100% × 15%) of the corporate income. Thus, the 15% paid by the shareholders is 12.75% of what the corporation earned.] As an S corporation, the same earnings might be subject to a tax of only 15% (i.e., the lowest stockholders' rate).

Also, a C corporation may become faced with a penalty surtax for unreasonable accumulation of earnings. As will be discussed in Chapter 12, this penalty is an *additional* 28% on the corporate income after taxes.[28] That is a combined total tax of 38.8%.[29] If the shareholders are in a lower tax bracket than this—and all stockholders currently are—then the S corporation election may appear prudent. This election might also be advisable when the corporation is formed for a project that will last only a relatively short time. Thus, if the corporation were formed to subdivide a tract of land and it was estimated that the entire operation would be liquidated within five years of its beginning, the double corporate taxation might appear too burdensome. Again, the minimum regular corporate tax would be at least 15%. There would be an additional tax on the shareholders upon liquidation of the corporation. This could be as high as 33% of the after-tax profits that had accumulated.[30]

TAX PLANNING TIP: The S election can be used as a means of avoiding the accumulated earnings tax without incurring a double tax on corporate earnings. Although the tax rate of the shareholders may be higher than the tax rate for a regular corporation, the accumulated earnings penalty is avoided when an S corporation is used.

Also, there are some business operations that are expected to produce a loss in the early years. With a regular corporation, such a loss is of no immediate tax benefit. Stockholders of an S corporation get to deduct such losses on their personal tax returns, especially if active in the business. Thus, to the extent of their personal tax rate, they can put the government in the position of sharing in their losses. Through a tax reduction, the government helps to finance them.

[28]The 28% penalty tax generally can be imposed only after a corporation has accumulated $250,000 in after-tax earnings.
[29]Actually, the rate might be more than 38.8% because the 15% regular tax rate only applies to the first $50,000 of corporate taxable income.
[30]Here, the 33% comes from the highest individual tax rate.

TAX PLANNING TIP: Whenever substantial appreciation of corporate assets is anticipated, an S election should be considered. Prior to the Tax Reform Act of 1986, a corporation could liquidate and any increase in the value of its assets would be subject to tax only at the shareholder level. Now the increase will incur two levels of taxation—to the corporation, and to the shareholder. An S election made at the time of incorporation will result in no corporate tax upon liquidation.

There are other uses of the S corporation that may not fit the congressional intention quite so neatly. Two examples may be indicative of the type of tax savings that are possible:

1. The S corporation's stock can be given to various members of the primary stockholder's family. The advantage is that the income will be taxed to those persons *at their tax rate,* which may be substantially lower. (Assuming the children are over 14. See the discussion of income transfers in Chapter 15.) For example, a father may give 10% of the family corporation's stock to each of his three school-age children. This might remove income from his 28% tax bracket and result in no tax, or a much lower tax, for the children. Recognizing this possibility, the law provides that where this is done, the family member active in the business must be paid reasonable compensation for services and for capital furnished to the corporation.[31] To the extent that the shareholder is underpaid for services or capital, income would be reallocated to that person for tax purposes. For example, without such a provision in the law, if corporate earnings were $50,000, and the father paid no salary to himself, he could shift $5,000 (10% of the $50,000) to each of the three children. He would be taxed on $35,000 rather than on $50,000. Assuming, however, that a reasonable salary for his services was $20,000, then the most income that he could shift (with a 30% shift in stock ownership) to each child would be $3,000 [10% of ($50,000 − $20,000)]. He would pay tax on the salary plus $21,000, or $41,000. The same result would occur if the primary shareholder let the corporation use an income-producing asset without charging the corporation any rent, or charging an unreasonably low rent. For example, assume the father owned an office building and the reasonable rent was $20,000 per year. If he charged the corporation no rent, the corporation's taxable income would be $20,000 higher, and part of that would be taxed to the children. Again, it won't work. The IRS can increase his income by $20,000 (and reduce the corporation's by $20,000) to arrive at the proper amount to be taxed to the children as the result of their stock ownership.

2. A taxpayer who conducts an unincorporated business as a proprietorship may have trouble drawing full social security benefits as long as there is substantial self-employment income—that is, profit from his business—even though few or no services are rendered to the business.[32] If the business is incorporated, however, the person is no longer self-employed. If few services are rendered and the corporation pays only a nominal salary, the person has little earned income. The net income of the corporation, on which income tax will be paid, normally is deemed to be dividend income. Investment income (including dividend income) does not result in a decrease in social security benefits. Thus, a social security recipient may find that the S corporation reduces the risk that the Social Security Administration will challenge the right to draw social security benefits, while complete use and enjoyment of the profits of the business can be obtained.

TAX PLANNING TIP: Some taxpayers may be reluctant to organize a family business as a corporation even though corporate stock may be more easily transferred (spread) among family members than may the assets of a noncorporate business. This reluctance stems from the fact that a regular corporation will incur the regular corporate income tax on its profits. Use of an S corporation solves that problem by eliminating the corporate income tax.

11.4.1. Net Operating Losses

As mentioned earlier, net operating losses of an S corporation are deductible by the shareholders, subject to certain limitations.[33] One of the tax planning devices frequently used for new corporations utilizes this treatment of losses. Many new business endeavors are not expected to be profitable at first. It may take a few years to produce profitable operations, at least for tax purposes, such as where

[31]IRC Sec. 1366(e).

[32]One of the controversial provisions of the social security benefit structure is that benefits will be reduced if earned income (including wages or profits from a proprietorship) is above a certain level, but will not be reduced because of investment income, no matter how large. For 1990, persons under age sixty-five will have social security benefits reduced if their earned income exceeds $6,840. That income level is increased to $9,360 for persons age sixty-five to sixty-nine. The effect is the same as an additional income tax on the "excess" income. Social security recipients age seventy or older will not have their benefits reduced because of "too much" earned income.

[33]IRC Sec. 1366(d).

large depreciation deductions are available. If the business were organized as a regular (C) corporation, any net operating loss would not produce an immediate tax benefit to the shareholders. Net operating losses (NOL) can be carried back three years to recalculate tax for a prior year, but if the business is new, there are no prior years.[34] The NOL can then only be carried forward.

Where losses are anticipated, the shareholders may find it advantageous to adopt the S corporation option, thereby obtaining the deduction on their personal tax returns. If the corporation becomes profitable, the election can be retained or abandoned as the shareholders see fit.

The limitations upon the deductibility of losses, and the carryover where losses are greater than the allowable deduction, were discussed earlier. Passive loss rules, discussed in Chapter 17, can postpone the time when S corporation losses can be deducted.

TAX PLANNING TIP: The S corporation election can be advantageous to the shareholders of a new corporation which expects to operate at a loss for the first year or so of the corporation. Such corporations should carefully evaluate the S corporation election as a means of allowing the shareholders to deduct the corporate net operating loss.

11.5 Tax on S Corporations

As a general rule, S corporations do not pay federal income tax, and that is the biggest advantage of making the election. Some situations, however, will result in an S corporation being liable for income tax. The most important of these is the possibility of a tax on built-in gain. Also, under certain circumstances an S corporation may have to pay tax on "excess net passive income." Finally, an S corporation will be liable for investment tax credit recapture (see Chapter 9) where the credit was claimed when it was a C corporation and the early disposition takes place in a year when the S election is in effect. Each of these situations will be discussed here.

11.5.1. Built-In Gains and Capital Gains

There are two different ways of taxing the appreciation in assets sold by S corporations. Both of these methods are intended to discourage a C corporation from electing S status in order to avoid the corporate level tax on the sale of assets or the liquidation of the company. The first method applies to former C corporations that made an S election before 1987 (or to certain small closely-held corporations that made the election before 1989), and consists of the special capital gains tax on S corporations in effect before the Tax Reform Act of 1986. The second method taxes the "built-in gains" when recognized by a former C corporation making an S election after 1986.[35]

The capital gains tax will only apply if the corporation has not been an S corporation for one or more of the three years preceding the sale that resulted in the capital gain. The tax won't apply if the corporation has been an S corporation since it began, even though that may have been less than three years ago. In addition, for the corporate capital gains tax to apply, the net long-term capital gain (that is, long-term capital gain reduced by short-term capital loss) must be greater than $25,000 *and* also greater than 50% of the corporation's taxable income. If the corporation has an ordinary loss for the year, the tax will not apply unless the net long-term capital gain minus the ordinary loss is greater than $25,000.

In each of the following examples, it is assumed that neither the three-year exception nor the S-corporation-since-beginning exception is applicable:

Example 1

NLTCG − NSTCL = $60,000
Ordinary income = $20,000
Taxable income = $80,000
Capital gain exceeds $25,000 and also exceeds 50% of taxable income. Therefore, the capital gains tax will apply to the corporation.

Example 2

NLTCG − NSTCL = $60,000
Ordinary income = $70,000
Taxable income = $130,000
Capital gain exceeds $25,000 but does not exceed 50% of taxable income. Therefore, the capital gains tax will not apply.

Example 3

NLTCG − NSTCL = $60,000
Ordinary loss = $10,000
Taxable income = $50,000
Capital gain exceeds both $25,000 and 50% of taxable income. Therefore, the capital gains tax will apply.

Example 4

NLTCG − NSTCL = $60,000

[34] IRC Sec. 172.

[35] IRC Sec. 1374. The capital gains tax is imposed by Sec. 1374, as in effect before the Tax Reform Act of 1986. The last returns to which it should apply will be certain fiscal year returns ending in 1990.

Ordinary loss = $45,000
Taxable income = $15,000
Capital gain reduced by the ordinary loss is under $25,000. Therefore, the capital gains tax will not apply.

If the S corporation is liable for the capital gains tax, the amount of tax is computed in a special way. There are two calculations of tax. The amount that the corporation must pay is the *lesser* of the two. The first calculation ignores the first $25,000 of long-term capital gain and applies a rate of 34% to the balance. The second calculation results in application of the regular corporate rates to the entire amount of taxable income, including the capital gain. The regular corporate income tax rates for 1989 and 1990 are 15% on the first $50,000 of taxable income, 25% on the next $25,000 of taxable income, and 34% on the taxable income in excess of $75,000. If taxable income exceeds $100,000, there is an extra 5% surtax on the amount in excess of $100,000, but the surtax is limited to $11,750.

The tax on built-in gains applies only to former C corporations making an S election after 1986, and is imposed during any taxable year within the ten-year period beginning with the first day of the first taxable year for which the S election was effective, if the corporation has a recognized built-in gain. Generally, built-in gain is the amount of gain that would have been recognized on an asset if that asset had been disposed of at the time the S election became effective. The tax will not apply if the corporation has been an S corporation since it began.

The result of this rule is that the built-in gains tax will be imposed at the corporate level with regard to any appreciation in the value of its assets prior to the effective date of the S election. Any appreciation after that date will be taxed only to the shareholders. The built-in gains tax will apply not only to the sale of assets, but to the liquidation of the corporation. It therefore limits any possible abuse of the S corporation's freedom from corporate level tax upon liquidation. The amount which would have been taxed if the corporation had liquidated while still a C corporation will still be taxed if liquidation occurs within ten years of the S election.

In each of the following examples, it is assumed that a corporation made an election after 1986, and the ten-year exception does not apply:

Example 5

Built-in gain = $60,000
Total gain on sale (or liquidation) = $100,000
The $60,000 of built-in gain will be taxable at the corporate level at a rate of 34%.

Example 6

FMV at date of election = $100,000
Basis = $50,000
Sales price = $200,000
The built-in gain is not taxed until the asset is sold. At that time the corporation pays tax on $50,000 of built-in gain. The $50,000, less any tax paid, plus the $100,000 gain not taxable at the corporate level, will pass through to the shareholders.

Just as the capital gains tax is imposed a special way, the built-in gains tax will be the lesser of the highest corporate tax rate times the recognized gain, or the highest corporate rate imposed on the entire taxable income of the S corporation. To the extent that the second limitation limits the amount subject to tax, corporations which made S elections after March 22, 1988, will carryover the untaxed built-in gain and treat it as realized in the next year.

Three other points merit mention relative to the capital gains and built-in gains tax on an S corporation. First, where the tax is imposed, it cannot be reduced by any credits that might otherwise apply to a corporation.[36] Second, where an S corporation pays a tax, the amount of "pass-through" of gain to the shareholders will be reduced by the amount of the tax.[37] The third point applies only to the built-in gains tax, and it is that any net operating loss carryforward arising in a taxable year in which the corporation was a C corporation is allowed as a deduction against the built-in gain later imposed in the alternative calculation.

If, as a regular corporation, the corporation would realize the built-in gain, pay tax on *all* the gain, and then distribute the proceeds to the stockholders, who in turn will be taxed, the potential tax cost exceeds 50%. The following example illustrates the saving resulting from being an S corporation all along. It assumes that the corporation has $100,000 of built-in gain and other income in excess of $335,000.

	S Corporation	*C Corporation*
Taxable built-in gain	$100,000	$100,000
Corporate tax (34%)	—0—	(34,000)
Distributable to stockholders (sales price less tax)	$100,000	$ 66,000
Tax to stockholders on gain (28%)	(28,000)	
Tax to stockholders on corporate dividend (28%)		(18,480)
After-tax cash	$ 72,000	$ 47,520

[36]IRC Sec. 1374(b)(2). There is an exception. If the corporation is eligible for any credit due to the purchase of gasoline, special fuels, or lubricating oil, such as for farming or other "off highway" usage, the credit under IRC Sec. 39 can be applied.
[37]IRC Sec. 1366(f)(2).

COMPUTER FORMULAS: A simple formula can show the net income available to the shareholder of a C corporation after two levels of tax.

	A	*B*	*C*
1	Taxable income		*x*
2			
3	Corp. tax	.34**x*	
4	Dividend	+C1 − B3	
5	Indiv. tax	.28*B4	
6	Net distrib.	+B4 − B5	
7			

The maximum tax rates for both corporations and individuals are assumed.

11.5.2. Alternative Minimum Tax

In Chapter 16 we will discuss the alternative minimum tax which is imposed on corporations that have "tax preference" items and adjustments in excess of certain limits. The S corporation will not pay any alternative minimum tax itself, but it will act as a conduit. Any tax preferences will be passed through to the shareholders, and any adjustments to S corporation items will have to be made at the shareholder level.

11.5.3. Tax on Excess Net Passive Income

At the beginning of this chapter we discussed the rules whereby an S election will be lost because of too much passive income for each year of a three-year period if the corporation also has earnings and profits from pre-S years. Even though the S status may not be lost, such as where the three-consecutive-year rule has not been violated, a corporation may have to pay a tax because of passive income. If an S corporation with C corporation earnings and profits has "excess net passive income," a tax of 34% will apply to that amount.[38] Passive income was identified earlier. "Net passive income" is passive income reduced by allowable deductions directly connected with it. "Excess net passive income" is "net passive income" multiplied by the following fraction:

$$\frac{\text{Passive income} - 25\% \text{ of gross receipts}}{\text{Passive income}}$$

For example, assume that the Barnes Corporation, which has elected to be an S corporation, has pre-S earnings and profits. Passive income for the year 1990 exceeds 25% of gross receipts. The corporation will not lose its S election because, we assume, it has not violated the gross receipts rule for each of three consecutive years. The following are the results of 1990 operations:

Gross receipts = \$100,000
Passive (investment) income = \$45,000
Expenses directly allocable to passive income = \$10,000
Taxable income = \$20,000
"Net passive income" = \$35,000
"Excess net passive income"

$$= \$35,000 \times \frac{\$45,000 - 25\%(\$100,000)}{\$45,000}$$

$$= \$15,556$$

Tax = 34% (\$15,556) = \$5,289

TAX PLANNING TIP: The possible loss of the S election from too much passive income, and the possibility of an extra tax on net excess passive income, can result only *if the S corporation has pre-S-years earnings and profits. A corporation that has always been an S corporation, as well as one that has been a C corporation but has no earnings and profits from pre-S years, need not be concerned about either the loss of the election or the extra tax. C corporations that have earnings and profits and are anticipating an S election should consider the impact of passive income. If passive income will always be less than 25% of gross receipts, neither the loss of the election for that reason nor the extra tax will be a problem.*

Note that the tax is a flat 34%. In the above example, the tax of \$5,289 is 15.1% of the net passive income. Such a levy can substantially reduce the return on investment (perhaps convert it into a loss) from passive sources. Consider one further illustration:

Gross receipts = \$100,000
Passive income = \$26,100
Expenses directly allocable to passive income = \$1,000
"Net passive income" = \$25,100
"Excess net passive income"

$$= \$25,100 \times \frac{\$26,100 - \$25,000}{\$26,100} = \$1,058$$

Tax on \$1,058 at 34% is \$360. But note the effect of incurring \$200 more in expenses:

"Net passive income" = \$24,900
"Excess net passive income"

$$= \$24,900 \times \frac{\$26,100 - \$25,000}{\$26,100} = \$1,049$$

Tax on \$1,049 at 34% is \$357. The \$200 of additional expenses only reduced the tax by \$3.

[38]IRC Sec. 1375(a).

In the example above, if it had been possible to defer $1,100 of the passive investment income to the following year, thereby keeping it at 25% or less of gross receipts, there would be no tax. A tax savings of $360 for waiting one year, or less, to receive $1,100 is a substantial payoff.

The tax on excess net passive income cannot be reduced by credits.[39]

Note that the "excess net passive income" (ENPI) is what is taxed. A special rule provides that the ENPI that is taxed will not be greater than the taxable income for the year.[40] Thus, in the first example of the Barnes Corporation above, if taxable income had been $11,000 for the year (instead of $20,000) the amount of tax would be 34% of $11,000 ($3,740) rather than 34% of $15,556 ($5,289). Additional expenses of $9,000 would have saved $1,549 in taxes.

Where the taxable income will be subject to the 34% tax because taxable income will be less than "excess net passive income," additional expenses (whether directly related to passive income or not) will reduce that tax by 34% on the $1. This presents the same decision rule for the marginal tax rate as that used by C corporations that are consistently above the $335,000 taxable income level.

TAX PLANNING TIP: Presumably even a few dollars of C corporation earnings and profits will make an S corporation eligible for the 25%-of-gross-receipts-passive-income test for purposes of either (1) loss of the S election or (2) the 34% tax on "excess net passive income." Where a corporation could do so without serious detrimental impact, getting rid of the C earnings and profits could save some future troubles or taxes. For example, payment of dividends in an amount equal to the C earnings and profits prior to an S election or even prior to the third year might be feasible.

11.5.4. *Investment Tax Credit Recapture from Pre-S Years*

The investment tax credit recapture provisions were discussed in Chapter 9. Basically, where there is an early disposition of property upon which the ITC was claimed, all or part of the credit must be repaid by an addition to tax for the year in which the early disposition took place.

If a C corporation has purchased investment tax credit property and has taken the credit, no recapture will result just because the corporation makes an S election.[41] However, if the S corporation makes an early disposition of the property, the corporation will be liable for the recapture tax.[42] The tax impact to the corporation will be the same as if the S election had not been made.

TAX PLANNING TIP: A C corporation that has unused investment tax credit to carry forward may wish to defer an S election until the ITC has been used. The reason is that ITC from pre-S years cannot be used during S years. However, where there is ITC carryover and the S election is very important and will be of somewhat short duration, the ITC may be available in future years when the corporation is again a C corporation. This is because of the fifteen-year carryforward for unused ITC. But remember that the fifteen years continues to run even during those years when the S election is in effect.

11.6 Disadvantages of the Election

The double taxation of corporate earnings arouses many persons to a level of passionate excitement. It is sometimes disconcerting to a theoretician, sincerely upset by the inequity of double taxation, to be told that most corporations that could eliminate it have not chosen to do so. Since the passage of the Tax Reform Act of 1986 many additional corporations have made an S election to avoid corporate level tax, but many have not. We estimate that perhaps 2.4 million corporations are eligible to elect S corporation treatment. With minor changes in capital structure, such as elimination of stock held by trusts or elimination of a second class of stock, several hundred thousand more could make themselves eligible. Yet less than half of these 2.4 million have done so. Why?

Certainly, the complexity of the S corporation provisions is a partial answer. Small corporations, all other things being equal, tend to have limited access to tax advice and many of them simply shy away from anything they do not fully understand. For existing corporations, the built-in gains tax on the passive income tax may represent a toll charge for the S election that is unacceptably high. But there are other reasons, too.

[39]IRC Sec. 1375(c). There is one exception. See footnote 36.

[40]IRC Sec. 1375(b)(1)(B). Taxable income must be computed for this purpose without any deduction for a net operating loss or the amortization of organization expenses.

[41]IRC Sec. 1371(d)(1). Under pre-1983 rules, the shareholders of the S corporation were required to file a statement that they would be personally liable for any recapture resulting from early disposition of ITC property by the corporation where the corporation had claimed the ITC for a pre-S year.

[42]IRC Sec. 1371(d)(2).

Some small corporations hope to become big corporations. They can justify accumulating their earnings and so have no worry about paying a penalty surtax for unreasonable accumulations.[43] They do not plan to liquidate in the foreseeable future. If the corporate income can be kept below $75,000 by payment of substantial salaries to the stockholders who also serve as officers, the income tax will be at 15% and 25% rates. If S corporation treatment were elected, the effective tax rate on the same income might be as high as 33%.[44]

In some corporations, there are stockholder conflicts that make the unanimous consent of the stockholders difficult to obtain or that make it possible for one stockholder to dominate the others if the election is made. By simply transferring some of the stock to a trust (other than a grantor or voting trust) or to another corporation, any stockholder can invalidate the election for the year in which such a transfer takes place. Thus, when there is stockholder conflict, the election may prove so potentially unstable that it is not worth making.[45]

The conflict between state and federal tax concepts may be a minor cause of some corporations avoiding S corporation treatment. Many state income tax laws do not recognize the S corporation. As a regular corporation, the corporation may be able to obtain a deduction, for state income tax purposes, for the federal income tax paid. Under the election, it pays no federal tax and gets no deduction for state purposes. On the other hand, the increased federal income tax paid by the stockholders may not be of state income tax benefit to them because it is imposed on income which is not "their" income under the state's tax law.

Finally, an S corporation election is sometimes touted as a means of avoiding corporate income tax where there are compelling reasons for the business to be organized as a corporation. It may be that the corporation does not pay any income tax anyway. If the corporate owners can draw enough salary, enough interest, and enough rent from the corporation, and arrange for such expenses to be deductible by the corporation, the corporation may have no taxable income even though the corporate operations are increasing the wealth of those who own it.[46]

[43]IRC Sec. 531. See the discussion in Chapter 12.

[44]Chapter 12 discusses the creation of a corporation as another taxable entity for the purpose of spreading income among more taxpayers and reducing the marginal tax rates. In effect, the S election does just the opposite because the corporation is removed from the status of taxpayer.

[45]Some commentators have suggested that a dissident shareholder could, in effect, blackmail the other shareholders by threatening to cause the election to terminate.

[46]Deductions are limited to "reasonable amounts." Thus, there are some limitations, although flexible ones, upon the amount of salary that a corporation can pay to an employee who is also a majority stockholder. The same is true for interest and rental payments.

11.7 Payment of Dividends by S Corporations

Earlier in this text we discussed the definition of a corporate dividend as a distribution (cash or property) from the corporation's earnings and profits. For C corporations and for S corporations, if the distributing corporation does not have current or accumulated earnings and profits, the shareholder(s) will have a tax-free receipt which will reduce the basis of stock.[47] If the distribution is larger than the basis of a shareholder's stock, the excess will be capital gain to that shareholder. If an S corporation has been profitable, a distribution will *not* be treated as a distribution of earnings and profits but will be considered to be from an "accumulated adjustments account."[48] This allows the shareholders to receive tax-free amounts upon which they have already paid tax. Cash distributions count at face value. Noncash distributions are counted at fair market value. The most simple example is that of a corporation that began business in 1990 and elected S corporation treatment from the beginning. If taxable income for 1990 were $40,000, the shareholders would include $40,000 in their 1990 gross income. If there were only one shareholder, his or her "accumulated adjustments account" would be $40,000. During 1991, or any later year, the corporation can make a distribution of up to $40,000 to the shareholder and it will be tax-free because tax was paid for 1990.

Where a corporation was an electing S corporation prior to 1983, some special rules must be followed in order for the shareholders to receive tax-free the amounts upon which they have already paid a tax. Because these rules are somewhat complex, and require an understanding of the pre-1983 rules and terminology, they are more properly covered in an advanced tax course. However, even for a post-1982 S corporation, there is a problem if there has been a break in its S status (i.e., it has had some intervening C years). The "accumulated adjustments account" applies only to the most recent continuous S period.

TAX PLANNING TIP: Corporations using the S election should be careful about distributions of noncash property to shareholders. If the fair market value of the property is greater than the adjusted basis, the corporation will recognize gain just as if the property had been sold.

[47]IRC Sec. 1368(b).

[48]IRC Sec. 1368(c).

This gain will increase the amount that will be taxable (or decrease the amount of loss which would be deductible) to the shareholders. Also, it can sometimes result in a tax to the corporation on capital gain or built-in gain.

Corporations that lose the S election can continue to distribute amounts tax-free to shareholders for a limited time to the extent of each shareholder's "accumulated adjustments account" which, generally, is the amount the shareholder has paid tax on but has not received.

For example, assume that Barnes Corporation has been an S corporation for several years and that Billy has accumulated $35,000 upon which tax has been paid but which Billy has not received from the corporation. The corporation loses or revokes its S election. During the next year, the corporation can still distribute tax-free up to $35,000 to Billy despite the fact that it is now a C corporation.

11.7.1. Distributions of Noncash Property

As mentioned above, where an S corporation distributes noncash property (other than its own bonds or notes) to a shareholder, the distribution will be measured by its fair market value. Where the fair market value is greater than the basis of the property to the corporation, the distribution will result in recognized gain to the corporation just the same as if a sale had been made.[49] The kind of gain will depend upon the kind of gain that would have been recognized if the property had been sold to an unrelated person.

For example, assume that the Barnes Corporation distributes a piece of property to its sole shareholder, Billy. The fair market value of the property is $40,000 and it has a basis to the corporation of $25,000. The corporation will recognize $15,000 of gain. If the asset was a long-term capital asset to the corporation, the gain will be long-term capital gain. If the asset was a Sec. 1245 asset, then gain will be calculated under the Sec. 1245 recapture provisions as discussed in Chapter 9.

Note that the shareholder in the example above will have increased income as the result of any gain recognized by the corporation.

11.8 Termination of S Status

As pointed out in the discussion of qualifications for making the S election, each shareholder must consent. However, if an election is already in effect, any new shareholder is treated as having agreed, despite the fact that no statement from that shareholder is required to be filed.[50] Termination of an S election can result from a revocation or from some disqualifying event.

11.8.1. Revocations

A revocation can only be made by a shareholder who owns more than 50% of the stock, or by a group of shareholders who together own more than 50% of the stock.[51] If a revocation is made during the first two and a half months of a year, it can be made retroactive to the beginning of that year. A revocation made at any time during the year can be effective for any date after the revocation. If no date is chosen by the revoking shareholders, the termination will be effective as of the first day of the following year.[52]

11.8.2. Other Terminations of the S Election

At the beginning of this chapter we discussed the requirements a corporation must satisfy to be eligible to make the S election. Those requirements must continue to be satisfied every day, or the election will terminate. In other words, if a thirty-sixth person becomes a shareholder,[53] if a second class of stock is issued, if a corporation, partnership, or nonqualified trust becomes a shareholder, or if a nonresident alien becomes a shareholder the election will end. Such terminations have been called "involuntary" terminations despite the fact that a transfer to a nonqualified shareholder could be an intentional act on the part of the corporation or one of the shareholders. Where an S corporation ceases to qualify and, thus, loses the election, the effective date is the date of the event that caused the termination.[54]

TAX PLANNING TIP: It takes a majority of voting stock to terminate an S election by revocation. Therefore, where no one shareholder owns more than 50% of the stock, two or more shareholders will have to agree that the election should be terminated. Just one shareholder, however, could transfer stock to a nonqualified holder and cause the election to terminate as of the date of the transfer.

[49] IRC Sec. 1363(d).

[50] Prior to 1983, a new shareholder, regardless of the number of shares held, who did not agree to the election, could file an affirmative dissent within 60 days of becoming a shareholder and the election would end.

[51] IRC Sec. 1362(d).

[52] IRC Sec. 1362(d)(1)(C).

[53] A married couple owning stock will be counted as only one shareholder.

[54] IRC Sec. 1362(d), (e).

11.8.3. Effect of Termination

A termination of an S election sometime during what would otherwise have been a full S year means the creation of two short taxable years.[55] The first short year will be from the beginning of the "normal" taxable year to the day before the date of the termination. That short year will be an S year. The second short year will be from the date of termination to the end of the year. That short year will be a C year. For example, assume that Barnes Corporation was using an S election and a calendar year. On May 20, an ineligible shareholder acquired stock. The S election terminates on May 20. It will be necessary to file a tax return for the short year January 1 to May 19, which will be an S year. A tax return will also have to be filed for the period May 20 to December 31. That will be a C year.

Where there are two short taxable years as the result of a termination of an S election, there are two possible methods by which the income and deductions for the full year can be allocated to the two short years. Unless the alternative election, discussed below, is made, the allocation of ordinary income or loss and of each of the special-characteristic items shall be made on a daily basis between the two short taxable years.[56] For example, assume that the Barnes Corporation lost its S election on the 140th day of its normal taxable year. The result will be two short years, the first (as an S corporation) being 139 days long and the second (as a C corporation) being 226 days long. If the corporation had $46,000 of ordinary taxable income *for what would have been* its full taxable year if the election had not been lost, plus a $4,000 long-term capital loss and a $2,000 Sec. 1245 recapture, the allocation would be as follows:

	To the First (S) Year	*To the Second (C) Year*
Ordinary income	$17,518	$28,482
Long-term capital loss	1,523	2,477
Section 1245 recapture	762	1,238

The allocation is 139/365 of each item to the S year and 226/365 to the C year. Each shareholder of the S corporation during the S year will include in gross income (or deduct) his or her share according to the allocation procedure explained earlier as if the election had not terminated. The C corporation will report income and pay tax for its short year using the annualizing procedures explained in Chapter 8.[57] Thus, in the above example, there is $28,482 of ordinary income plus $1,238 of Sec. 1245 recapture. Since there are no offsetting items, these are added together to get $29,720 of "ordinary income" for the short period. Since a C corporation gets no deduction for a capital loss, the $2,477 will be a carryover to the second C year. The $29,720 becomes $47,999 when annualized ($29,720 × 365/226). Tax on $47,999 is $7,200 before reversing the annualizing procedure. The tax due will be $4,458 ($7,200 × 226/365).

TAX PLANNING TIP: If an S election terminates, the C corporation should begin immediately to get a "fix" on what its tax liability will be for the first (short) year regardless of the election to prorate income and deductions uniformly between the S and C years or to treat each of the S and C years under the normal accounting methods that are used. The reason is that if the corporation will be liable for some tax, it should begin to make estimated tax payments in order to avoid penalties that will be imposed for failure to do so.

As you can see, the above option relative to the allocation of income (or loss) and special-characteristic items between the two short years is based upon an assumption that the income (or loss) and all special-characteristic items were incurred uniformly throughout the twelve-month year which includes the two short taxable years. This may or may not be the case. For example, the capital loss in the above example might have been incurred before the termination date. At any rate, there is an available alternative, if the corporation elects *and* each S corporation shareholder consents to the election.[58] Under this election, each item will not be allocated but will be determined under normal tax accounting rules. What this means is that the books will be closed for the short (S) year and the income and deductions incurred during that period will be "booked." A new taxable year will begin on the following day (the first day of the C year) and income and deductions will be accounted for under the normal accounting procedures used by the corporation.

Use of the alternative can be advantageous. In the above example, if the capital loss occurred prior to termination of the S election, it could flow through in its entirety to the shareholders. Marginal tax rates and other considerations will impact the choice.

[55]IRC Sec. 1362(e)(1).
[56]IRC Sec. 1362(e)(2).
[57]IRC Sec. 1362(e)(5).

[58]IRC Sec. 1362(e)(3). All shareholders at any time during the short S corporation year must consent as must all who are shareholders on the first day of the short C corporation year. Usually all the former will encompass the latter.

Once an S election is terminated, unless beyond the control of the corporation, the corporation will have to wait five years before it will again be eligible to make an S election.[59] Certain "inadvertent" terminations can result in a waiver of the five-year waiting period, or can result in a continuation of the S election (i.e., no S termination). If the IRS agrees, if steps are taken by the corporation to correct the error within a reasonable time, and if the corporation and all shareholders agree to certain adjustments that may be made by the IRS, an "inadvertent" (accidental) termination of the S election will be ignored.[60]

TAX PLANNING TIP: In a seasonal or growing business, plan the termination of an S corporation election so as to maximize the loss that can be passed through to the shareholders by electing to "close the books" as of the date of termination.

11.9 Fringe Benefits

Fringe benefits, particularly pension and retirement plans, are discussed in Chapter 18. There is a fundamental difference in the treatment of self-employed persons as compared with that of employees. Generally, partners (see Chapter 10) are treated as self-employed persons. Shareholders owning more than 2% of an electing S corporation will be treated the same as if they were partners in a partnership.[61]

In small incorporated businesses it is common practice for the majority owners to transfer some stock to valued employees. The reasons probably vary from one situation to another, but in general it may be thought that a valued employee will be more conscientious, or less mobile, with some proprietary interest in the business. One disadvantage of issuing S stock to such a person is that if he or she obtains more than a 2% interest in the corporation, the result will be tax treatment of fringe benefits under the "partner" rules rather than as an employee. Partners get less advantageous tax treatment on fringe benefits than do employees.

11.10 Conclusion

The S corporation is a tremendously flexible tool for planning. It is also full of pitfalls and complexities, and thus should be utilized only with great care. Because it can be elected, terminated, and then elected again (albeit after the expiration of five years), it adapts itself to the changing needs of a changing business in a changing environment. Useful as a device for passing losses through to shareholders in its early years, the election may be terminated during a period of profit and expansion. Later, during a period of profit without expansion, the election may again be made to allow earnings to pass through to the shareholders without double taxation. For hundreds of thousands of corporations, it does, indeed, fulfill the congressional objective of allowing smaller businesses to choose their legal form (i.e., the corporate form) without major concern over adverse tax consequences.

[59]IRC Sec. 1362(g). This does not apply if the termination was prior to 10/22/86 and the new election is after that date.
[60]IRC Sec. 1362(f).
[61]IRC Sec. 1372.

TRUE-FALSE QUESTIONS

State whether each of the following statements is true or false. For each *false* answer, reword the statement to make it *true*.

T F 1. If a person was a shareholder of an electing S corporation at any time during its taxable year, that person will be required to report on his or her personal income tax return the pro-rata share of any corporate gain or loss for the year.

T F 2. If a taxpayer is a shareholder in an S corporation, the basis of stock in that corporation is increased by the share of the corporation's taxable income that is required to be included in the taxpayer's gross income.

T F 3. An electing S corporation is entitled to a deduction for charitable contributions.

T F 4. If a corporation which has an "S" election in effect receives interest from state or local government bonds, that interest will increase its taxable income and hence increase the amount which will be taxable to the shareholders.

T F 5. If an S corporation's shareholder has a pro-rata share of the corporation's loss for the taxable year which is larger than that shareholder's basis for the stock, the basis of the stock will be reduced to zero, and any balance will reduce the basis of debt which the corporation owes to that shareholder.

T F 6. Better Trucking Co., Inc. is chartered in Arizona. It has 1,000 shares of common stock and 500 shares of preferred stock outstanding which are held by four individuals who also live in Arizona. These are the only shareholders. The corporation owns no subsidiaries and obtains all of its revenue from trucking fees. It will qualify as an S corporation.

T F 7. If an "S" corporation has taxable income of $20,000 for the year and also has a long-term capital loss of $4,000, only $3,000 of that loss will be passed through and deducted pro rata by the shareholders.

T F 8. If an S corporation has a net operating loss for the year, the general rule is that the loss is deducted pro rata by the persons who are shareholders on the last day of the corporate year.

T F 9. An S corporation may not have any stockholders other than individuals or an estate.

T F 10. If a corporation has a valid S corporation election in effect and a person who is a shareholder sells stock to another person, the buyer will be considered to have consented to the election.

T F 11. An S corporation will lose its election if it has gross income from a foreign source.

T F 12. The total number of shareholders of a Subchapter S corporation is limited to thirty-five.

T F 13. If a corporation becomes a shareholder of an S corporation, the S election will be voided for the following taxable year.

T F 14. The amount that an S shareholder may deduct on his or her personal income tax return as the result of a loss by the corporation is limited to that stockholder's basis in the stock of the corporation.

T F 15. Except for the deduction for net operating loss, an S corporation will compute taxable income the same as a regular corporation.

T F 16. An S corporation must have the same method of accounting as its shareholders.

T F 17. As a general rule an S corporation must have a taxable year that is a calendar year.

T F 18. Generally, an S corporation's taxable income will be determined as if it were a partnership.

T F 19. A minor child can be a shareholder of an S corporation.

T F 20. Where an S corporation hires persons for whom the targeted jobs credit would be available, those persons who were shareholders during the corporate year will be able to claim a pro-rata share of the credit on their individual income tax returns.

PROBLEMS

Problem 11-1. The Chris Corporation is an S corporation. There are three stockholders who own shares as follows:

Ms. Chris	1,000
Ms. Dalie	400
Ms. Eck	600

There was no change in stock ownership during this past year. The corporation's gross receipts last year consisted solely of sales of merchandise within the United States. The corporation uses the accrual basis and a calendar year for tax purposes. All shareholders are on the cash basis and a calendar year. The corporation paid $1 per share cash dividends on the first day of April, July, and October 1990. No other distributions were made to shareholders. All three stockholders are employees of the corporation. The salaries, listed here, were deducted in arriving at last year's taxable income of $70,800:

Ms. Chris	$31,000
Ms. Dalie	35,000
Ms. Eck	19,000

(a) What is the corporation's tax liability for 1990?

(b) Assuming that Ms. Chris has no other source of income, what is her adjusted gross income for 1990?

(c) What difference would it make if Ms. Chris had given 200 shares of Chris stock to her father on December 25, 1990? (Her father has no other taxable income.) Explain.

(d) Ignoring part (c), what difference would it make if the corporation had paid a $1-per-share cash dividend on February 1, 1991?

Problem 11-2. Assume the same facts as in Problem 11-1 except that the corporation did not pay any cash dividends during the year and incurred a net operating loss of $40,000 for the year. As of the beginning of last year, the three stockholders had basis for their shares as follows:

Ms. Chris	$40,000
Ms. Dalie	17,000
Ms. Eck	25,000

None of them had loaned any money to the corporation.

(a) How would the corporation and the shareholders treat the loss? Explain.

(b) Explain the tax effect if a shareholder's pro-rata loss is greater than the amount that can be claimed as a current deduction.

Problem 11-3. Simpson, Inc. is an S corporation which uses a calendar tax year and the cash basis of accounting. At the beginning of last year, there were two shareholders, Jim Simpson and Bob Newburg. Jim owned 5,000 shares of stock and Bob owned 4,000 shares. Jim's basis was $100,000 and Bob's basis was $64,000. On June 1 of last year, the corporation issued another 1,000 shares to Jerry Bassford for $18,000 cash. For the corporate year ended last December 31, the corporation had a taxable income of $65,700 and had paid no cash dividends during the year.

(a) What amount must each shareholder include in taxable income for the calendar year as the result of corporate stock ownership?

(b) What difference would it have made to each of the three if Jerry had purchased 1,000 shares from Jim for $18,000 rather than 1,000 newly issued shares from the corporation?

Problem 11-4. Beta Alpha Corporation is an S corporation which uses the cash basis and a calendar year. There are four shareholders who own shares and had taxable income as follows:

	Number of Shares	*Taxable Income*
Sue Redman	2,600	$42,000
Mary Heartman	2,400	38,000
Linda Searman	1,700	20,000
Becky Steadman	2,300	63,000

All are single.

The corporation has operated with the S election and no change in stock ownership for four years. The corporation has never paid any cash dividends. Instead, the salaries of the four shareholders have been adjusted each year so that the corporation would have about $20,000 of taxable income which was kept in the corporation for growth purposes.

Assuming that the four shareholders could justify their salaries as reasonable in amount, does the S corporation appear to be to their advantage? Explain.

Problem 11-5. The Daly Corporation began operations on January 1 of last year. It elected to be an S corporation. Net income for the first year was $84,000. In determining this amount, there was dividend income of $5,000 from taxable domestic corporations and there were charitable contributions of $8,000. During the year, the corporation made cash distributions of $20,000 to the shareholders. There are eight equal shareholders.

(a) What is Daly's taxable income for the year?

(b) What difference would it make if the $20,000 distributed to the shareholders had been noncash property?

(c) What effect does the corporate action have on the shareholders? [Consider both parts (a) and (b).]

Problem 11-6. Padd, Inc. is a corporation which has been operating for six years with ten shareholders. On January 1 of last year, the corporation elected to be an S corporation. On January 12, twenty-five other persons became shareholders, making a total of thirty-five. On March 31, the corporation paid cash dividends of $1 per share to all shareholders. On April 15, Mr. Acorn, one of the thirty-five shareholders, sold all of his stock in Padd to Mr. Elm. On June 30, the corporation paid $1 per share in cash dividends to all shareholders.

(a) Will Padd lose its S election as the result of paying dividends to more than thirty-five shareholders during the same year?

(b) What if Padd ends its year with a loss? Will Acorn and Elm each get a deduction as the result of Padd's loss? Explain.

Problem 11-7. The Botanical Corp. was formed on July 1, 1990. The five equal shareholders contributed property or cash to the corporation so that their basis in the stock was as follows:

Shareholder	*Number of Shares*	*Basis for Shares*
A	100	$40,000
B	100	15,000
C	100	20,000
D	100	27,000
E	100	18,000

At the end of the corporation's first year, December 31, 1990, the taxable income was determined to be $22,000. No dividends were paid during the first year.

(a) How much income must A report for this year as the result of his ownership of Botanical Corp. stock?

(b) Assume that B made a valid gift of 50 shares of stock to his son, age 16, on November 15, 1990. His son has had no income from any source for the year. What federal income tax results will this have?

Problem 11-8. Belle's, Inc. is an S corporation with a fiscal year ending April 30. For the year ended April 30, 1991, it had taxable income of $60,000. Cash dividends of $20,000 and $30,000 were paid on October 15, 1990 and March 15, 1991, respectively. Cash dividends of $5,000 were also paid on May 30, 1991.

Bill Zane owns 25% of the Belle's stock and received 25% of the corporate dividends. As of the beginning of the last fiscal year, Bill's basis in the Belle stock was $35,000. Bill is a cash-basis calendar-year taxpayer.

(a) What was Bill's gross income for the year ended December 31, 1991?

(b) Assuming that the corporation makes no further cash dividends during the year 1991, will Bill be required to pay a tax on money that he has not received from the corporation? Explain.

(c) What if the corporation had paid $30,000 in dividends on both October 15, 1990 and March 15, 1991, and no dividends during the remainder of 1991? Explain.

Problem 11-9. The Daily Corporation was incorporated at the beginning of last year and elected to be an S corporation. For its first year of operations, it reported $94,000 net income, including gross receipts of $4,000 from dividends from other U.S. corporations and a deduction of $6,000 for contributions to qualified charitable organizations. In addition, the corporation made cash distributions to its shareholders during the year in the amount of $20,000. The corporation has had ten shareholders throughout the year, each owning the same number of shares.

(a) What is the corporation's taxable income for the year?

(b) Assuming that the corporation and each of the shareholders are on a calendar-year basis, what amount must the shareholders report as income from the corporation for the year?

(c) What effect, if any, will the corporation's operations have on the basis that each shareholder has in the stock of the corporation?

Problem 11-10. Black and White Corporation, a closely-held corporation, has been operating as a C corporation using a calendar tax year for several years. In January, 1988, the corporation elected S status and the two equal shareholders filed timely consents to that election. Ordinary taxable income will be $300,000 for 1990. In addition, the corporation will have a $400,000 long-term capital gain.

(a) What will be the amount of tax which the corporation will have to pay?

(b) Explain how the capital gain will be taxed to Black and White, and the two shareholders, as the result of the payment of the tax by the corporation.

Problem 11-11. On January 15, 1990 the Too Late Corporation elected S Corporation after operating as a C Corporation for several years. In 1991, it sold a capital asset which had been acquired before the S election. It had a basis of $60,000 and was sold for $100,000. At the date of the S Election, the fair market value of the asset was $90,000. Assume that the *S* Corporation's taxable income for 1991 was $80,000. In addition, the corporation has a $10,000 NOL carryforward which was generated when the corporation was a regular C Corporation.

Compute the amount of tax which the corporation will have to pay as a result of the sale of the capital asset.

Problem 11-12. Shareholder A has a $20,000 basis in the ABC corporation. As part of a nonliquidating distribution, Shareholder A receives land worth $25,000 with a basis of $18,000.

(a) Compute the gain or loss (if any) as a result of the distribution.
(b) Compute the basis of the land in the hands of the shareholder.
(c) Compute the basis of Shareholder A's stock immediately after the distribution.
(d) Would your answer differ for parts (a) and (b) if the distribution were in complete liquidation of the shareholder's interest.
(e) Compare the above results with Problem 10-10.

Problem 11-13. The Harcourt Corporation is an S corporation. All of the stock is owned by Janice Harcourt. She uses a calendar year for federal income tax purposes, as does the corporation. The corporation is on the accrual method of accounting and Janice is on the cash method. She would like to have the corporation deduct an accrued salary to her for the year just ended, and have the corporation make the salary payment during January. This procedure, she reasons, will permit the corporation to take a deduction for the salary, while at the same time postpone for one year the tax liability which will result to her from receipt of the salary. Can this procedure be used? Explain.

Problem 11-14. Answer Problem 10-2 under the assumption that the Yee-Yuan business is a corporation with an S election and that each person owns 50% of the stock.

Problem 11-15. Answer Problem 10-3 under the assumption that the Butler-Bradshaw business is a corporation with an S election and that each person owns 50% of the stock.

Problem 11-16. Answer Problem 10-4 under the assumption that the Stern-Wheeler business is a corporation with an S election and that each person owns 50% of the stock.

PROBLEMS WITH AN ASTERISK REQUIRE ADDITIONAL RESEARCH.

Problem 11-17.* Joe Barry owns all of the stock in an S corporation which has been operating profitably for several years. Joe has three minor children. He has mentioned that he would like to transfer some of his corporate stock into a trust, if possible, for the benefit of his children.

(a) Explain to Joe what kinds of trusts are qualified stockholders in an S corporation. (Assume that the children are all over age 14.)
(b) Can Joe create one trust and have the three children as equal beneficiaries of that trust? Explain. Are there any alternatives? Explain.
(c) What difference would it make if all of the children were under age 14? Explain.

12

corporations: a first look

The tax relationship between a partnership and its owners minimizes the impact of the partnership itself on their personal tax liabilities. There are exceptions. Different tax years of partnership and partners is one. Nevertheless, the general thrust of the partnership rules is to pass tax consequences through to the partners intact—neither enhanced nor diluted, and certainly not altered. Tax-free income remains tax-free income, and ordinary income does not become capital gain.

The impact of a corporation is different. It is a separate tax person.[1] It reports and is taxed on its transactions; its owners (stockholders) have tax consequences resulting from their transactions with the corporation. Because it is a separate legal person, the tax problems of the corporation multiply if it operates in states other than its state of incorporation. Forty-five states plus the District of Columbia impose a corporate tax based on or measured by net income. This discussion will deal with federal taxes only, but the impact of applicable state income taxes should not be overlooked in real-world decision making.[2]

12.1 Forming the Corporation

Nontaxable exchanges were discussed in Chapter 6. Generally, the transfer of property to a new corporation for its stock also will be tax-free.[3] In order to qualify for tax-free exchange treatment, all persons who are acquiring stock at the same time must in the aggregate own at least 80% of the stock immediately after their transfers. Some may transfer cash and some may transfer other property to the corporation in exchange for its stock.

Assume that Billy Barnes decides to form a corporation with two friends. Each person may transfer different kinds of property, such as cash, buildings, equipment, and inventory. As long as the three, as a group, own at least 80% of the stock after the transfer, the transfer will be tax-free for each of them.[4] If they should transfer their property to an existing corporation in exchange for its stock, the same result would occur so long as the three ended up with at least 80% of the outstanding stock. The percentage of ownerships before the transfer is irrelevant. If they should own less than 80% of the stock after the transfer, each person would recognize gain measured by the difference between the fair market value of the stock received and the adjusted basis of property transferred.

Two problems can arise. The first is where a person receives stock for services, management skills, contacts, or similar "nonproperty" considerations.[5] Services do not qualify for tax-free treatment.[6] Thus, if Billy performed services

[1] IRC Sec. 11(a).

[2] State taxes impact others who derive income from more than one state, too, of course. Nevada, South Dakota, Texas, Washington, and Wyoming impose no state income tax on corporations.

[3] IRC Sec. 351(a).

[4] The 80% control requirement is in IRC Sec. 368(c).

[5] The major exception to the tax-free transfer rule results in taxation if the corporation is essentially an investment company. See IRC Sec. 351(e).

[6] IRC Sec. 351(d).

for 30% of the stock and put in property (including cash) for the other 70%, there is not a transfer of property in exchange for 80% of the stock. The result is that Billy is taxable on the value of the stock received for services despite the fact that more than 80% of the corporation is owned. The transfer of property is not taxable because Billy owned 80% or more of the corporation immediately after the transfer.[7]

The person receiving stock for services has taxable income regardless of how persons who transfer property are treated.

The second major problem arises when property which is subject to a debt is transferred, the corporation assumes the debt, and the debt exceeds the adjusted basis of the property. The excess of debt over basis then becomes taxable, in the same fashion as "boot" in an otherwise tax-free real estate exchange.[8] The tax-free nature of the exchange is not otherwise destroyed, however.

Assume that Billy Barnes owns a piece of real estate which has an adjusted basis of $50,000 and is subject to a mortgage of $60,000. If Billy transfers the property to a corporation and the corporation takes it subject to the mortgage, Billy must recognize gain in spite of owning 80% or more of the stock after the transfer. The recognized gain would not be greater than $10,000, the amount of mortgage in excess of the adjusted basis. Note that the recognized gain will be less than $10,000 if the realized gain is less. Thus, if the fair market value of the property at the time of Billy's transfer was only $58,000, then Billy's realized gain is $8,000 and the recognized gain is also $8,000.

From the corporation's perspective, no gain or loss occurs when it issues its own stock.[9] However, its tax basis for the assets received for that stock is affected by the tax-free or taxable nature of the transaction. In a tax-free transfer, the corporation takes as its tax basis for property received the tax basis of the stockholder/transferor.[10] That basis is increased by any gain recognized to the shareholder in the transfer. Such gain can arise if liabilities transferred exceed tax basis of the property transferred, or if the shareholder receives anything in addition to stock. Thus, in the example in the preceding paragraph, Billy's property transferred to the corporation had a tax basis of $50,000 but was subject to a mortgage of $60,000 when transferred. Assuming that the fair market value of the property was at least $60,000, gain of $10,000 was recognized to Billy because that was the amount by which the mortgage exceeded Billy's tax basis. Result: The corporation's tax basis is $60,000, based on Billy's tax basis of $50,000 increased by the $10,000 gain recognized in the transfer. The shareholder takes as tax basis for the stock received the tax basis of the property transferred, increased by any gain recognized on the transfer, and decreased by the value of property (other than stock) received in the transfer.[11] Thus, Billy's basis in the stock will be zero—tax basis of $50,000 increased by $10,000 gain and then reduced by $60,000 of released debt.

Both the services and the excess debt problems can often be solved with advance planning. For example, if Billy is going to organize a corporation and receive stock for services, then doing so before receipt of commitments from the people who will transfer cash and other property for stock may reduce or eliminate the tax impact.[12] If $500 were paid to a new corporation for 100% of its then-issued stock, no tax results. If that corporation later sells additional stock for cash or other property, no income is recognized by either the stockholder or the corporation, even if the willingness of others to invest is based, for instance, upon an agreement by the original shareholder to work full time for the corporation.

If property mortgaged in excess of its tax basis poses a tax problem to one of the potential stockholders, there is a way to eliminate the problem. Determination of whether liabilities exceed tax basis is not made on an asset-by-asset basis. Rather, it is made on a transferor-by-transferor basis. Thus, the receipt of "boot" because of liabilities can be avoided by putting in additional property with sufficient tax basis (in excess of any related debt) to offset the excess of debt over basis in the aggregate.

Assume from the previous example that Billy Barnes transferred another piece of property, without mortgage, to the corporation along with the real estate. The second property had an adjusted basis to Billy of $10,000. The two properties are counted together. The combined adjusted basis is $60,000 and the mortgage is $60,000. Billy will not recognize any gain, so long as there is at least 80% ownership of the corporation immediately after the transfer. Again, however, Billy's tax basis in the corporate stock will be zero—$60,000 of asset basis less relief from $60,000 of debt.

[7]Treas. Reg. 1.351-1(a)(2), Example 3.
[8]IRC Sec. 357(c). See Chapter 6.
[9]IRC Sec. 1032.
[10]IRC Sec. 362.
[11]IRC Sec. 1031(d).
[12]This conclusion is based on the fact that the stock issued for the services may have a value of zero or a value that is not determinable and is therefore treated as zero.

12.2 The Corporation as a Taxpayer

A corporation is a legal entity; it is also a tax-paying entity. Since the essential concepts of income determination for tax purposes are accounting concepts, it should not surprise us that the corporation income tax return is built around an income statement similar to those encountered in any introductory accounting text. Some of the items have been rearranged; that is all.

In Chapter 1, there is an outline of the steps involved in the determination of tax liability for an individual. The outline is much simpler for a corporation because there is no distinction between deductions *for* adjusted gross income and deductions *from* adjusted gross income. In fact, there is no adjusted gross income for a corporation. Also, there is no exemption amount deduction and no deduction comparable to the standard deduction. Corporate tax liability is determined as follows:

Gross income
less
Deductions
equals
Taxable income

Appendix 12-A(a), which is page 1 of the corporate tax return, shows the equivalent of an income statement. Pages 2 through 4 [Appendix 12-A(b) to 12-A(d)] are also shown and will be discussed later.

Approximately 4.3 million corporation income tax returns (including S corporations) are filed annually.[13] But only about 56% of these returns generally show net income.[14] It is probable that nine out of ten of the corporations with net income under $100,000 keep their accounting records on the same basis as they file their tax returns. For this majority (in number) of corporate taxpayers, the computation of the corporate income tax is quite straightforward.

The current corporate income tax rate structure itself is fairly simple:[15]

15% on the first $50,000 of taxable income;

25% on the next $25,000 of taxable income; and

34% on all taxable income in excess of $75,000.

An added 5% tax is imposed on corporate income between $100,000 and $335,000 of taxable income.

[13]Data are estimated for 1990. Internal Revenue Service, *Statistics of Income Bulletin*, U.S. Department of Treasury Publ. 1136, Vol. 9, No. 2, p. 96, U.S. Government Printing Office, Washington, D.C. (Fall, 1989).
[14]Ibid. Table 13. Data are for 1986.
[15]IRC Sec. 11(b).

The $11,750 maximum that this 5% surtax can produce is the difference between the tax actually paid on the first $75,000 of corporate income and what it would be at 34%.

The amount of tax, before credits, is reported on line 3 of Schedule J [Appendix 12-A(c)] of the corporate tax return. Credits are reported on line 4. Additional taxes, discussed elsewhere, are added on lines 7, 8, and 9, and the final tax liability is on line 10, and on line 31 of page 1 (Appendix 12-A(a)). Prepayments are on line 32 of page 1.

For example, if a corporation had taxable income of $60,000, the tax would be:

15% × $50,000	=	$ 7,500
+ 25% × $10,000	=	2,500
Total		$10,000

Another corporation with taxable income of $200,000 would have a tax liability of:

15% × $50,000	=	$ 7,500
+ 25% × $25,000	=	6,250
+ 34% × $125,000	=	42,500
+ 5% × $100,000	=	5,000
Total		$61,250

Certain personal service corporations (e.g., law firms, medical practices, and CPA firms) do not have the graduated tax rate but pay a flat 34% tax rate on their entire taxable income. Where this occurs, there is no additional 5% surtax. Thus, a personal service corporation with taxable income of $70,000 will pay tax of $23,800.

Also, there is a special tax that certain corporations are required to pay, officially known as the "environmental tax," but sometimes called the "superfund tax." This tax has been specifically earmarked by Congress for use in various environmental cleanup activities. The rate of tax is 0.12%. That rate is applied to "modified alternative minimum taxable income" in excess of $2,000,000. The alternative minimum tax is discussed more fully in Chapter 16.

In Chapter 7 we discussed the requirement that business expenses need to be "ordinary and necessary" in order for the taxpayer to get a deduction. The same requirement applies to corporations. Sometimes the owners of closely held corporations may attempt to have the corporation pay for expenses that are really personal expenses of the owners. Travel and entertainment expenses are examples. Thus, when a corporate tax return is audited by the IRS, such items frequently draw the auditor's attention. This is discussed further in Chapter 13.

12.3 The Balance Sheet

Of course, the tax calculation is not all there is to a corporation tax return—even a simple one. Supporting schedules have to be provided, explaining details on certain items of income or deduction. Furthermore, a balance sheet, a reconciliation of income per books with income per tax return, and a reconciliation of retained earnings must be completed.[16] These are contained in Schedule L and Schedule M, respectively, Appendix 12-A(d).[17]

12.4 Everything Comes from Somewhere

The tax-return balance sheet is basically the same as an accounting balance sheet, with some slight rearrangement to emphasize data important for tax administration. The balance sheet shows the assets of the corporation valued basically at their unexpired cost, the same as for financial statement purposes.

The liabilities are *sources* of assets in the sense that the corporation has been able to retain assets because of the willingness of creditors (including the tax collector) and owners to defer receipt of payment.

The changes in retained earnings are traced through a separate schedule (M-2). If the only changes result from the taxable income reported on the tax return and the tax liability also reported on the tax return, the income statement and balance sheet need no reconciliation. Unless some of the figures are falsified, it appears that everything has been accounted for. The balance sheet and surplus reconciliation provide a type of net worth cross-check.

12.4.1. Tax v. Financial Accounting

There are several reasons why the net income, which affects the balance sheet for financial statement purposes and which is frequently determined in accordance with financial accounting principles, may be different from the taxable income, which is determined in accordance with tax accounting rules. For example, if a corporation receives interest from state government bonds, or proceeds from a life insurance policy,[18] the balance sheet will show an increase in assets. Neither of these items represents taxable income and would be excluded from income on the tax return.[19] On the expense side, for example, the balance sheet may reflect a liability for product warranty or self-insurance, but the income, as measured for tax purposes, will not reflect similar expenses.[20] Also, a method of depreciation may be used for accounting purposes that is different from that used for tax purposes. It is fairly common that taxpayers who use accelerated depreciation (ACRS) for tax purposes use straight-line (with longer asset lives) for financial statement purposes.[21] These differences between tax and financial accounting thus fall into two distinct categories:

1. Permanent differences, such as tax-exempt bond interest; and
2. Timing differences, such as depreciation, where the same total amount will affect taxable and financial income but at different times.

Financial accounting is concerned with allocating income tax expense to the same year in which financial accounting reports the related expense item. You will see a balance-sheet item labeled "Deferred taxes" in many financial statements. Deferred taxes reflects the tax impact of the timing differences between financial and tax accounting.

Example 1. A corporation reports $1,000,000 of ACRS (depreciation) expense on its income tax return but only $300,000 of depreciation expense on its financial statements for the same assets. Its combined federal and state income tax rate is 40%. It will calculate income tax expense on its income statement reflecting $700,000 more profit than shown on the tax return. This means that it will show 40% of the $700,000, or $280,000, as a current expense even though it will not be paying this in current income taxes. That $280,000 will be added to the "Deferred Taxes" liability account on the corporation's balance sheet. In future years, when the financial statement depreciation exceeds the amount allowed for tax purposes on those assets, the process will be reversed. The amount of income tax expense reported on the financial

[16]The reconciliation of retained earnings merely explains why "net income" (for financial statement purposes) and "taxable income" (for tax purposes) are not the same.

[17]Appendix 12-B reproduces Form 1120-A, a simplified corporate return form which can be filed by small corporations with simple tax situations. Approximately 300,000 corporations use this simplified form.

[18]In order for life insurance proceeds to be excluded from gross income, the payment must have been made because the person whose life was insured died.

[19]In Chapter 2, items of gross income were discussed. With only minor exceptions, gross income items are the same for corporations as for individuals.

[20]Neither corporate businesses nor noncorporate businesses are permitted a deduction for tax purposes for the estimated future costs that may arise from product warranty or self-insurance.

[21]The tax law does not require that the same method of estimating depreciation be used for tax purposes and financial statement purposes.

statements will be less than the amount of tax actually payable, and the excess will reduce the Deferred Taxes liability account.

12.5 Some Exceptions to the Simple Situation

In a really simple situation, revenue and expense for tax purposes would be defined in the same manner as for financial accounting. But complete conformity is seldom encountered. Tax accounting has some special exceptions, some of which have been inserted to achieve equity among different types of taxpayers, some of which are designed to further social policies believed desirable, some of which are to stimulate certain types of economic behavior, and some of which reflect political expediency. The following are three such exceptions:

1. To reduce the double taxation of corporate earnings somewhat, a special deduction is allowed a corporation that receives dividends from other corporations which pay United States income tax. The deduction is 80% of the dividends received from a corporation in which at least 20% of the stock is owned, and is 70% otherwise.[22] The rationale is simple. A corporation pays an income tax. If it pays a dividend to another corporation, that dividend will be taxed to the recipient. Its earnings, in turn, presumably will be distributed to a stockholder on whom another layer of tax will be imposed. To alleviate a double or triple tax, at least partially, the deduction is allowed.
2. Limits have been put on certain types of corporate deductions. The deduction for charitable contributions made by a corporation is not allowed to exceed 10% of net income before deducting contributions (and before taking the dividends-received deduction).[23] Certain other corporate deductions are reduced by 20%. This is discussed in Chapter 17. IRC Sec. 291.
3. Because of the separation of powers between the federal and state governments, it was long believed that the federal government did not have the power to tax interest from the bonds or notes of states or their subdivisions. This opinion was prevalent at the time the income tax amendment to the Constitution was ratified in 1913, and it still has staunch supporters. As a result, the law has always contained an express exemption of such interest from federal income tax.[24] Even though it may be constitutional to tax such interest today, to change a tax rule of such long standing would be difficult and perhaps not politically expedient.

Example 2 (Dividends-Received Deduction). Assume that Billy Barnes owns 100% of the stock of the ABC Corporation, which in turn owns 30% of the DEF Corporation. The balance of DEF stock is widely held and publicly traded. Assume that ABC is in the 34% marginal tax bracket. If DEF paid $1,000 to ABC and there were no dividends received deduction, ABC's tax would increase by $340. This would leave only $660 to be paid to Billy. Remember, also, that the $1,000 paid by DEF was *after tax* paid by DEF. Assuming that ABC paid the remaining $660 to Billy, who is in the 28% bracket, there would be only $475 left over for Billy. But that is not the effect. The dividends-received deduction will be taken by ABC, resulting in tax of 34% ($1,000 − $800), or $68. Thus, ABC can pass $932 on to Billy, who would pay $261 tax, leaving $671. Since, for accounting purposes, there would be no deduction for 80% of dividends received, a reconciliation of taxable income with book income would appear to be needed. Schedule M-1 finesses this situation by focusing on reconciliation of taxable income *before* special deductions (including this deduction) with book income. See line 10, Schedule M-1, Appendix 12-A(d), and line 28, page 1, Appendix 12-A(a).

Example 3 (Charitable Contribution Deduction). Assume that Billy Barnes has ABC contribute $9,000 to charity. The taxable income of ABC, without any deduction for the contribution or for any net operating loss, is $80,000. This means that the deduction is limited to 10% of $80,000, or $8,000. The $1,000 that cannot be deducted for the current year is carried forward to the following year.[25] Because the entire $9,000 would be deducted for book purposes, the $1,000 not currently deductible will be an element in reconciling book income to taxable income. See line 5b, Schedule M-1, Appendix 12-A(d).

As a general rule, where a corporation makes a charitable contribution of property which was inventory to the corporation, the amount of the deduction cannot be greater than the corporation's cost for that property, regardless of its fair market value. There is an exception for certain types of ordinary income property, such as medical equipment, if given for the benefit of the needy, ill, or infants. Also, there is an exception if a corporation donates scientific equipment to colleges and universities for use in research activities. Where a set of rather involved conditions are met, the deduction can be the corporation's basis for the asset plus one-half of the unrealized appreciation. The limitation of 10% of taxable income

[22]IRC Sec. 243. In the case of dividends paid to a parent corporation by a subsidiary, 100% of the dividends received usually can be deducted by the parent. See line 29b of Appendix 12-A(a), and Schedule C of Appendix 12-A(b).

[23]IRC Sec. 170(b)(2).

[24]IRC Sec. 103. See Chapter 2 for further discussion.

[25]IRC Sec. 170(d)(2). If a corporation contributes to charity more than can be deducted currently, a five-year carryover is allowed.

would still apply, however, with a carryover if the latter limit is exceeded for any one year.

Example 4 (State and Local Government Bond Interest). Assume that the ABC Corporation purchases some state bonds which pay interest to ABC of $6,000 during the year. ABC Corporation will report this interest on its financial statements but will not report this interest as income on its tax return. It will, however, need to report the $6,000 as part of its assets on the corporate balance sheet. This $6,000 will be part of a reconciliation of taxable income to book income. See line 7a, Schedule M-1, Appendix 12-A(d).

All of the above are permanent rather than timing differences (see Section 12.4.1).

TAX PLANNING TIP: The owner of a corporation may not be able to use a charitable contribution deduction because total itemized deductions will be less than the standard deduction. Therefore, the corporation may contribute to charity, since a deduction is allowed the corporation. On the other hand, if the owner is in a higher marginal tax bracket than the corporation and will itemize deductions, a personal charitable contribution rather than one through the corporation may save more taxes.

In fact, any transaction or entry that affects a balance sheet account without having its effect fully offset against some other balance sheet account (other than retained earnings) will have to appear either on Schedule M or in the computation of taxable income.

If cash is borrowed from a bank, the increase in the asset account "Cash" is fully offset by the increase in the liability account "Notes Payable." Schedule M is not involved, therefore. If $200,000 of "Bonds Payable" are outstanding but are retired for $160,000, the $40,000 gain on retirement will either show up in the gross income (where it belongs), or the tax basis of some of the assets will have to be reduced (which is a possible result under certain circumstances), or the $40,000 will have to be shown on Schedule M, if the balance sheet is to balance.

Of course, the $40,000 could merely be carried as a balance in the "Bonds Payable" account and everything would still balance. In the auditing of the corporate return, such an error (or attempt at tax evasion, if it were intentional) would be easily spotted. With the exception of the figure for "Inventory," most of the balance sheet account balances can be readily verified with an audit. Thus, individual transactions do not have to be painstakingly investigated. Instead, the balance sheet accounts can be reviewed against supporting data, the Schedule M items can be reviewed, and those areas of income and deductions where experience indicates tax problems tend to lie can be examined more thoroughly.

12.6 Unreasonable Accumulation of Earnings

One question that arises from a review of tax returns of some corporations is whether the accumulation of assets is in excess of business needs. Because a corporation might refrain from paying dividends to keep its stockholders' taxes reduced, the law imposes a penalty tax of 28% on what are described as unreasonable accumulations of earnings.[26] The tax is imposed only on the after-tax earnings for the current year, to the extent deemed *excessive*, and not on the balance of the retained earnings account.[27]

Although the law is not limited by its terms to corporations with only a few shareholders, the practical application of it is such that it will normally apply in situations where there are only a few shareholders in a position to control corporate dividend policy (even though there may also be a large number of small shareholders).

Corporations, other than personal service corporations, are allowed to accumulate up to $250,000 of retained earnings without any need to show a business purpose.[28] When the retained earnings pass the $250,000 mark, it may have to establish the fact that failure to pay substantial current dividends is for good business reasons if it hopes to avoid the penalty tax.

For example, assume that a corporation has retained earnings of $500,000. Taxable income for the current year is $200,000, but only $20,000 of that amount can be justified as retained for business purposes. No dividends have been paid. The accumulated earnings tax might be determined as follows:

[26] IRC Sec. 531.

[27] Whether the corporation has *excessive* retained earnings or not is usually determined by the nature of the *assets*. If the corporation has grown and expanded by "plowing back" its earnings in operating assets, there is little chance that the penalty tax will be imposed. However, if the corporation has accumulated highly "liquid" assets, not needed for ongoing business operations or future needs, the purpose of the accumulation may well be deemed to be to avoid the tax the shareholders would have to pay if dividends were paid.

[28] IRC Sec. 535(c). The $250,000 is referred to as a "credit." Certain service corporations are only allowed a credit of $150,000.

Taxable income	$200,000
Regular corporate income tax (including surtax)	61,250
Balance	$138,750
Amount needed for business purposes	20,000
Unreasonable accumulation	$118,750
Penalty tax: (28%)	$ 33,250

One criticism levied against the accumulated earnings tax is its ambiguity and the subjective nature of what constitutes accumulation of earnings for reasonable business needs.

Acceptable business reasons for accumulating earnings may include expected debt retirement, expected plant expansion, expected increases in the costs of doing business, expected expansion into new products or into new geographic areas, or expected labor difficulties or law suits. Naturally, most of these "expectations" are subjective in nature. Escaping this penalty tax is sometimes a matter of being able to shift the burden of proof from the taxpayer (to prove that earnings were not unreasonably accumulated) to the IRS (to prove that earnings were unreasonably accumulated).

Other detailed rules associated with the accumulated earnings tax are beyond the scope of this book.[29]

12.7 The Role of the Corporation in the U.S. Income Tax

Which corporations pay the most tax under U.S. income tax rules? Out of $111 billion of total corporation tax (before credits) in one recent year, less than 9,300 corporations accounted for over $78 billion. The 4,471 corporations with net assets of over $250 million had $197.5 billion of aggregate net income and incurred total income tax of $71.7 billion. At the other end of the scale, some 1,946,000 corporations that had total assets of less than $100,000 each incurred only a little over $3.4 billion in aggregate income taxes.[30]

Thus, the corporate income tax collected by the government comes mostly from large corporations, whether size is measured by assets or income. Almost 92% of corporate tax collections come from corporations that have assets of over $1 million each, which is 8.9% of the total. This is the reverse of the situation we encounter in the case of individual income taxes.

[29]The rules are contained in IRC Secs. 531–537.
[30]Internal Revenue Service, *Statistics of Income Bulletin*, Vol. 9, No. 1 (Summer, 1989) U.S. Government Printing Office, Washington, D.C., 1987, p. 25.

12.8 Double Taxation of Corporate Income and Internal Investment

Corporations, as mentioned earlier, cannot consume. They are merely economic middlemen. But they are peculiar middlemen—especially the bigger and older corporations. They come to have a life of their own, in the sense that any big organization tends to develop a life of its own.

Managers do what they think is best for the organization (with appropriate attention to their own careers, of course). To top managers of large corporations, stockholders are just another claimant for corporate assets. Dividends decrease the wealth controlled by the corporation. Consequently, dividend policies are calculated in terms of their effect on stock market values, on stockholder and financial press criticism of the corporation, and on the possibilities of obtaining new financing on favorable terms, if future financing is contemplated. Although corporate earnings may "belong" to the shareholders, it is a rare publicly owned corporation that can justify paying out all those earnings in dividends. It is better for the organization to reinvest earnings in excess of a reasonable dividend rate. What is beneficial for the organization is also defensible as being for the good of the shareholders in the long run.

Assume that the managers of a corporation could pay out all earnings in dividends. They have analyzed the shareholders and found that the average shareholder pays an effective tax of 30% on each dollar of dividend income received. The corporation can invest that dollar internally. If that is done, the managers believe that the market value of the stock will increase by approximately $1 (not immediately, but in the long run).

The internal investment can be made at a return of 5% after taxes. The average stockholder could take the dividend and invest it at 5% after taxes. The corporation would have $1 to invest, whereas the stockholder would have only 70 cents, after paying 30 cents in tax.

If the corporation, year after year, retains and reinvests the dollar, the difference between what it will accumulate and what the stockholder could accumulate may be quite impressive:

	Corporation— *$1 per Year*	*Stockholder—* *$0.70 per Year*
After 5 years	$ 5.526	$ 3.868
After 10 years	12.570	8.799
After 20 years	33.066	23.146

This assumes that the corporation and the stockholder each have available to them investments offering the same 5% after-tax return. If,

TABLE 12-1

Summary of Capital Gain and Capital Loss Treatment of Individuals and Corporations, Assuming One Capital Asset Transaction for the Year

	Individuals	*Corporations*
Short-term capital gain and Long-term capital gain	Taxed at ordinary rates	Taxed at ordinary rates
Short-term capital loss and	Deducted $1 for $1 with $3,000 limitation	No deduction against ordinary income
Long-term capital loss	Deducted $1 for $1 with $3,000 limitation	No deduction against ordinary income
Capital loss carryover		
Character	Retains character of short term or long term	All carryovers or carrybacks are treated as short term
Time limit	None	Five years
Capital loss carryback	None	Three years
Tax preference (alternative minimum tax)	No	No

more realistically, we assume that the corporation can earn the greater return, the gap becomes greater. If the corporation can earn 10% after taxes and the stockholder 5%, these are the dramatic results:

	Corporation— $1 per Year	*Stockholder— $0.70 per Year*
After 5 years	$ 6.105	$ 3.868
After 10 years	15.937	8.799
After 20 years	57.275	23.146

TAX PLANNING TIP: Many small corporations can keep the marginal tax rate at a lower level than the owner would have on a personal tax return. Where profits are to be reinvested in the business, there will be more after-tax dollars to reinvest if the corporate income tax is paid rather than the individual tax.

Managers of the corporation can thus conclude that the average stockholder benefits more by having the corporation retain the dollar and invest it than by paying dividends to shareholders for investment. Thus, this double-taxation aspect of the tax structure tends to encourage the expansion of existing successful corporations and to intensify their search for profitable investment opportunities.

Of course, the closely held corporation's shareholder may have more difficulty using the corporation as a tax shelter. Why? The penalty surtax on unreasonably accumulating earnings exerts pressure toward dividend payments. However, expansion into new operating ventures is a justifiable business reason for accumulations. Many closely held corporations proceed to grow aggressively with only minor concern that a policy of no dividends or low dividends will result in imposition of the accumulated earnings tax.[31]

12.9 Corporate Capital Gains and Losses

Corporate regular tax rates were shown earlier. Capital gains are includable in taxable income and taxed at the regular rates. However, the tax computation puts a 34% ceiling[32] on corporate long-term capital gains just as it does for short-term capital gain and ordinary income.[33]

Individual capital losses can be partially offset against other income, as was discussed in Chapter 5. The maximum is $3,000 per year. Corporate capital losses are not deductible from ordinary income. They can only be used to offset corporate capital gains. Individual capital losses can be carried forward indefinitely (i.e., until death, if necessary) until fully used as a deduction or offset against capital gains; corporate capital losses expire if not offset by capital gains by the end of the fifth year following the year of the loss. However, while individuals cannot carry back a capital loss, corporations can—to the third prior year. Table 12-1 summarizes the capital gain and loss treatment by individuals and corporations, assuming just one transaction for the year.

[31]The burden of proof for the imposition of the accumulated earnings tax can be shifted, to a limited extent, to the government. Moreover, where assets are used for reinvestment in operating assets, the IRS normally does not assert that the penalty tax should be paid.

[32]Or 39% in the $100–335,000 range.

[33]IRC Sec. 1201(a). But 20% of what would otherwise be long-term capital gain on the sale of Sec. 1250 real estate is treated as ordinary income under IRC Sec. 291. See Chapter 16.

Assume that the Barnes Corporation has ordinary taxable income of $30,000 plus a capital loss of $10,000. No part of the capital loss is deductible for the current year.[34] It can be carried back for a recalculation of tax liability of the third preceding year *if* there was capital gain in that third prior year.[35] For example, if the corporation had a $12,000 capital gain three years ago, the recalculation results in a $2,000 gain. The corporation will receive a refund of the tax paid on $10,000 of capital gain three years previously.

Another difference between capital loss treatment for corporations and for individuals is that a corporate capital loss carryback (or carryforward) becomes a short-term capital loss regardless of whether it was long term or short term when incurred.[36] In the preceding paragraph, the $10,000 capital loss of the Barnes Corporation could have been long term or short term. When it is used in the recalculation of tax for the third preceding year, it is treated *as if* it were a short-term capital loss *incurred in that year.*

12.10 Transactions Between Corporation and Shareholders

Some types of losses that would otherwise be recognized may not be if incurred between related corporations, or between shareholders and corporations which they control.[37] The tax effect is usually to defer recognition of the loss until there is a transaction with an unrelated party rather than allowing a loss on a sale which could be viewed as a transfer from one pocket to another. Note that where a loss is disallowed as a deduction for this reason, there is *no* adjustment in basis for the buyer but there may be an adjustment in calculating the gain (but not loss) on a subsequent sale by the buyer.

For example, assume that the Barnes Corporation has one stockholder, Billy, who sells an asset to the corporation for a $5,000 loss (selling price of $20,000 and adjusted basis of $25,000). Billy will not be able to recognize the loss for tax purposes.[38] The corporation has a basis of $20,000 for the asset, but if the corporation later sells that asset to an unrelated party for a gain of $5,000, the corporation will not recognize the gain. If that asset is sold for a $6,000 gain, only $1,000 of gain will be recognized for tax purposes.

Sales of depreciable assets by an individual to a controlled corporation, by a controlled corporation to the individual, or between two corporations controlled by the same individual will not produce capital gain.[39] The idea is to prevent "stepping up" the tax basis, which will result in greater depreciation deductions, at the cost of paying a capital gain tax, which may be less than the tax benefit obtained from the increased depreciation.

Assume that Billy Barnes sold a building to the 100%-owned Barnes Corporation for $50,000. If Billy had previously used the building as a business asset and had calculated depreciation under the straight-line method, any gain on a sale to an unrelated party would be treated as capital gain.[40] However, since Billy controls the Barnes Corporation, any gain to Billy will be ordinary income. If Billy owned only 79% of Barnes Corporation, the capital gain treatment would be allowed.[41]

12.11 Related Corporation

Normally, a loss on worthless stock is treated as though the stock were sold as of the last day of the year it became worthless. Thus, it is a capital loss.[42] However, if a corporation owns 80% or more of an operating subsidiary, it is able to treat its loss on worthlessness of the stock of that subsidiary as an ordinary loss rather than a capital loss.[43]

Corporations can face special problems if they are related, meaning owned by the same interests (see Fig. 12-1); they may also have some tax savings opportunities. The ownership involved can be direct, such as where a corporation owns 80% or more of another corporation.[44] Also, corporations are related if each of an entire group of corporations is owned 80% or more within the group and one of the corporations (the common parent) directly owns at least 80% of the stock of one of the other corporations. Ownership can also be indirect—such as where five or fewer individuals own 80% or more of two or more corporations.[45]

[34] It does not matter whether the capital loss was short term or long term.
[35] IRC Sec. 1212(a)(1).
[36] IRC Sec. 1212(a)(1)(c). Academic under Jan. 1990 law, but potentially relevant in the event capital gains (long-term) are again subject to special treatment.
[37] IRC Sec. 267. See discussion of this topic at Section 5.23.2.
[38] IRC Sec. 267. For this purpose the loss would be disallowed if the shareholder owns *more* than 50% of the stock. Constructive ownership rules apply for purposes of determining the 50% ownership. See Section 5.23.
[39] IRC Sec. 1239. Unlike the denial of loss deduction, which requires more than 50% ownership, this rule requires ownership of 50% or more of the value of the stock before capital gain treatment will not be allowed on the sale.
[40] IRC Sec. 1231. See Chapters 5 and 9.
[41] As with Sec. 267, the constructive ownership rules apply for purposes of determining percentage of ownership.
[42] It is possible, but unlikely, that stock would become worthless by the end of the year during which it was purchased. If so, it would be a short-term capital loss.
[43] IRC Sec. 165(g)(3).
[44] IRC Sec. 1504(a).
[45] IRC Secs. 1561(a) and 1563(a).

FIGURE 12-1 Types of corporate relationships

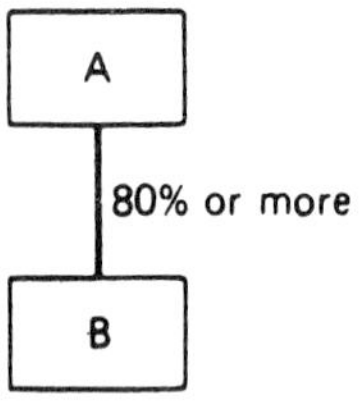

Corporations A and B are related because A is the parent of B.

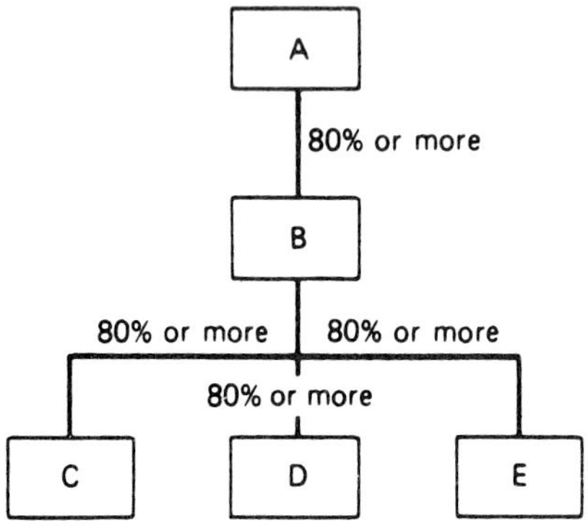

Corporations A, B, C, D, and E are related, with A as the common parent.

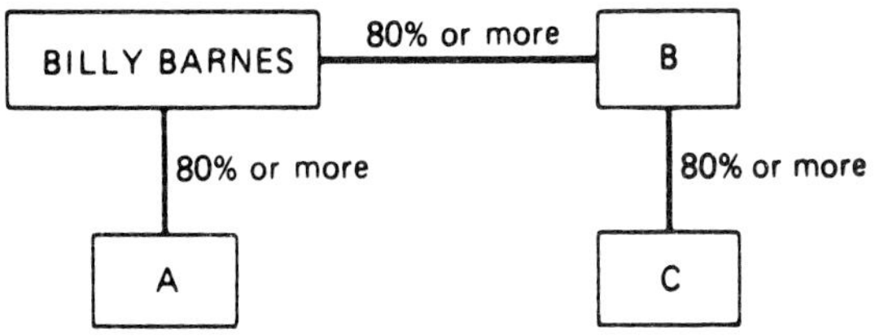

Corporations A, B, and C are related. This would also be true if Billy and four or fewer other persons together owned 80% or more of A and B.

Ownership can also be a combination of direct and indirect.

The major "problems" considered here relate to the way in which the related corporations calculate their income tax and the treatment of the $250,000 accumulated earnings credit for purposes of the accumulated earnings penalty.[46] Because the corporate tax is "graduated" (the first $50,000 of income being taxed at 15%, the next $25,000 at 25%, with income above $75,000 being taxed at 34% or 39%), a large number of corporations with small profits would pay less tax than one corporation receiving the same amount of income. However, where corporations are under common control, they must allocate the bracket amounts among all of the corporations in the group.[47] The effect is the same as if the group were really one corporation. The allocation is equal if they do not choose any other method, or it can be in any other fashion they elect. Similarly, the $250,000 credit for accumulated earnings tax purposes must be allocated among the corporations in the group.

Assume that Billy Barnes owns Corporation A and that it has a profit of $50,000, paying the 15% tax. As the corporation becomes more profitable, Billy decides to form a second corporation, B, to handle some of the business. Because A and B are "related" (sometimes called "brother-sister" corporations), the 15% rate can be applied only to the *combined* taxable income of two corporations. Taxable income in excess of $50,000 will bear a tax at the next highest rate, which is 25%. Similarly, if profits exceed $75,000 for the related group as a whole, the next highest tax rate, 34% or 39%, will apply. It really does not matter to the government which corporation pays the higher rate.

TAX PLANNING TIP: Corporations in a "controlled group" must pay income tax under the corporate rate structure as if *they were one corporation. If corporate stock ownership can be spread so that the definition of "controlled group" is not satisfied, each corporation can pay tax on its own income at the lower rates.*

Where the related corporations are not just under common ownership, but are an "affiliated group" (i.e., where a parent corporation owns directly at least 80% of one other member of the group and at least 80% of the stock of all members of the group except the parent is owned within the group), tax consequences of transactions within the group can sometimes be eliminated. This may be done in one of two ways:

1. Dividends within the group can qualify for a 100% (instead of an 80%) dividends received deduction if the group so elects;[48] or
2. The group can file one tax return covering all the corporations within the group (a "consolidated" return).[49] The tax complexities of consolidated returns can be staggering—however, the basic idea is straightforward: Gains or losses from transactions within the group are not reflected in taxable income of the group, but transactions of the group with the outside world are all reflected. A consolidated return is especially useful if some members of the group have losses or credits which they would not be able to use on separate tax returns but which can be utilized on a consolidated return.

[46]Some special rules covering employee benefit plans of related corporations will be discussed in Chapter 17.
[47]IRC Sec. 1551.
[48]IRC Sec. 243.
[49]IRC Secs. 1501–1504.

Assume that corporations A, B, and C are affiliated. Corporation C has deductible expenses of $100,000, but Corporation C has no taxable income to be offset by the deduction. The consolidated tax return permits A or B to use C's deduction, and this could be more advantageous than for C to wait for the use of the net operating loss carryover.

Assume that corporations D, E, and F are affiliated. D has a net operating loss which can be carried back to the third prior year. But if D paid tax at 15% in the third previous year, the carryback will result in a refund of tax at the 15% rate. If E and F are currently in the 39% bracket, D's net operating loss may result in tax savings at the 39% rate if a consolidated return is filed.

It should be noted that "brother-sister" corporations cannot file a consolidated return.

12.12 Alternative Minimum Tax

Chapter 16 includes a discussion of the corporate "alternative minimum tax." The tax is a flat rate of 20% applied to the alternative minimum taxable income (AMTI), reduced by a $40,000 exemption for some corporations. AMTI is regular taxable income increased by tax preferences and adjusted for items requiring recomputation. If the resulting tax is higher than the regular tax, the alternative minimum tax will be the actual tax liability.

These provisions deserve special study. The alternative minimum tax will affect many corporations, not just the large, wealthy ones, and any tax planning must consider its implications. For a more complete discussion, see Chapter 16.

12.13 Conclusion

A corporation is a tax person separate and apart from its owners. From this flows much of its complexity. The corporation is an essential vehicle for the conduct of business. For example, it has the ability to raise equity capital without subjecting investors to risk of personal loss beyond their investment. It also offers tax opportunities as well as posing tax pitfalls.

For instance, the 80% deduction for dividends received results in $1 of dividend income being taxed at a maximum of 7.8% to a corporation,[50] whereas a dollar of dividend income might be taxed at 28% or 33% to an individual. Chapter 13 contains a discussion of some of the tax provisions aimed at preventing abuse of the corporate tax shelter. As discussed there, too much investment income can subject closely held corporations (personal holding companies) to tax penalties.

Similarly, the maximum corporate tax rate of 34% or 39% contrasts to the 28% or 33% that could be charged an individual on business income. The graduated corporate tax structure makes possible tax savings for small businesses as compared with a proprietorship or a partnership as a means of conducting business.

Assume that Billy Barnes has a salary such that the marginal tax rate is 28%. In addition to salary income, Billy operates a small independent business. To conduct that business as a proprietorship would result in tax at 28%, or $11,200 if the business nets $40,000. If the profits would be reinvested in the business anyway, Billy can incorporate and pay $6,000 in tax (15% of $40,000), for a savings of $5,200.

In Chapter 13 some of the additional complexities of corporate taxation will be considered.

[50] 39% ($1 − $0.80) = $0.078.

TRUE-FALSE QUESTIONS

State whether each of the following statements is true or false. For each *false* answer, reword the statement to make it *true*.

T F 1. If a corporation has a net capital loss for the year, there is no deduction, but the loss can be carried forward indefinitely.

T F 2. If a corporation has a net operating loss of $10,000 for the current year and had taxable income of $15,000 three years ago, the net operating loss can be carried back so that the corporation will receive a refund of part of the tax paid on the $15,000 for three years ago.

T F 3. If a corporation has a net operating loss of $10,000 for the current year and had taxable income of $8,000 three years ago, and taxable income of $4,000 two years ago, the net operating loss can be carried back so that the corporation will receive a refund of all of the tax paid on the $8,000 and half of the tax paid on the $4,000.

T F 4. If a person transfers property to a corporation and receives shares of that corporation's stock for the property and owns 70% of the stock of the corporation after the transaction, the individual will have recognized gain or loss equal to the difference between the fair market value of the stock received and the adjusted basis of the property which was transferred.

T F 5. The marginal tax rate for a corporation with $60,000 of taxable income is 25%.

T F 6. If a corporation has a net long-term capital loss that it carries to a different year, the loss carryover will be treated as a long-term capital loss.

T F 7. A group of corporations that is controlled by one individual must file a consolidated income tax return.

T F 8. Where one corporation (a parent) owns at least 80% of another corporation (a subsidiary), the federal income tax rate that applies to the two corporations will be determined as if the two were one corporation.

T F 9. Where one U.S. corporation receives dividends from a 20% or more interest in another U.S. corporation, there is a deduction available to the receiving corporation for 80% of the dividends received.

T F 10. A corporation may claim a deduction for a contribution to a charitable organization, but that deduction is limited to 50% of the corporation's taxable income.

T F 11. A corporation which pays a salary to an employee who is also a shareholder will only be permitted to deduct that salary to the extent that it is "reasonable" in amount.

T F 12. The transfer of property to a corporation in exchange for its stock will be a tax-free exchange to the persons transferring the property if they control the corporation (at least 80% ownership) immediately after the transfer.

T F 13. Where property is transferred to a corporation by a person who already owns 100% of the stock, and the property transferred has a mortgage on it which is greater than the adjusted basis of the property, it is still a tax-free exchange, even if the corporation assumes the mortgage.

T F 14. Where a corporation receives property in exchange for its stock in a transfer that is not taxable to the stockholders, the corporation's basis in the property received will be the same as that of the stockholders before the transfer.

T F 15. A corporation's tax return is filed on Form 1120, which includes a balance sheet.

T F 16. There is a 28% tax imposed upon the taxable income of a corporation that has an unreasonable accumulation of earnings.

T F 17. In determining the amount which is subject to the unreasonable accumulated earnings tax, a corporation may deduct the amount of its regular tax.

T F 18. There is a 100% dividends received deduction for dividends paid between the corporations in an "affiliated group."

T F 19. If a corporation's tax, computed on its alternative minimum taxable income, is higher than its regular tax, then alternative minimum tax will have to be paid in addition to the regular income tax.

T F 20. The purpose of the Schedule M on a corporate income tax return is to explain why the net income as computed for financial statement purposes and the taxable income as computed for federal income tax purposes are different.

PROBLEMS

Problem 12-1. The Dromidary Corporation reported financial statement after-tax net income of $300,000. Included on the income statement were the following items:

Interest income on City of Newport bonds	$ 10,000
Gain from collection of life insurance on deceased officer's life	50,000
Interest expense paid to borrow money to buy City of Newport bonds	2,000
Estimated federal income tax expense	131,000

(a) Calculate the taxable income for Dromidary Corporation.

(b) Which items will be reported on the corporation's Schedule M and why?

Problem 12-2. The Nogales Corporation had long-term capital gains in each of the past three years as follows:

1988	$4,000
1989	8,000
1990	2,000

In 1991, the corporation suffered a net long-term capital loss of $20,000.

(a) What amount may the corporation deduct in 1991 as the result of the loss, assuming that other net income is $50,000?

(b) How will years 1988, 1989, and 1990 be affected by the 1991 loss? Will 1992 be affected by the loss? Explain.

Problem 12-3. Marvin Ace is an accounting major at a major university. He consistently has made A's in all of his college courses, has participated in extracurricular activities, and has all the attributes that recruiters look for in hiring college graduates. He recently has interviewed with a major industrial firm, which has made him an offer of $35,000 annual starting salary. Marvin was somewhat amazed at the size of the offer, particularly since he expects to spend the first year in the firm's training program and not contribute to the firm's profits during that time. The firm always has profits of several million dollars.

(a) What is the after-tax cost to the company of hiring Marvin?

(b) What would be the difference if the firm that made Marvin the offer were a large, profitable, accounting partnership?

Problem 12-4.

(a) The ABC Corporation has taxable income of $40,000 for 1990. Compute its regular federal income tax.

(b) Compute the regular federal income tax if the taxable income had been $60,000.

(c) If taxable income were $110,000, what would be the regular federal income tax?

Problem 12-5. The PPP Corporation had capital asset transactions which resulted in the following net capital gains and losses for the years indicated:

1986	$10,000 net short-term capital loss
1987	$6,000 net long-term capital gain
1988	0
1989	$12,000 net long-term capital gain

(The numbers given *do not* reflect any carrybacks or carryforwards.)

In 1990 the corporation has a net long-term capital loss of $20,000. Assume that PPP pays tax at the highest rates but is not subject to the corporate alternative minimum tax.

(a) What is its capital loss deduction for the year 1990?

(b) What is its capital loss carryover, if any, to 1991?

(c) Assuming that PPP could have arranged for the 1990 capital loss to be short term rather than long term, would there have been any advantage in doing so?

Problem 12-6. The Owl Corporation had the following cash receipts and disbursements for 1990:

Sales	$200,000
Operating expenses	117,000
Dividends received from unaffiliated (but more than 20%-owned) corporations	20,000
Charitable contributions paid	12,000

The corporation is on the cash method of accounting.

(a) What amount may the corporation deduct for charitable contributions?

(b) What is the corporation's tax liability for the year?

Problem 12-7. Phil Mulvihill and Andy Barnett formed a corporation last year. Phil transferred $100,000 cash to the corporation in exchange for 500 shares of stock. Andy transferred a building to the corporation in exchange for 500 shares of stock. The building had a fair market value of $120,000 and a basis of $80,000 to Andy. At the time of transfer, the building was subject to a $20,000 mortgage, which the corporation assumed. Prior to this corporate formation, Phil and Andy were not related to each other by family or business association.

(a) Do either Phil or Andy have recognized gain as the result of the transfer of property to the corporation in exchange for its stock?

(b) What if Phil and Andy incurred $1,000 of legal expenses in connection with the corporate organization, and the attorney, Art McCall, agreed to accept five shares of the corporate stock as payment of his fee?

(c) Would there be any change in the tax consequences if the building that Andy transferred had a mortgage of $100,000 which the corporation assumed? Explain.

Problem 12-8. Tom Sewell and Jerry Jackson have operated the S-J partnership for several years. They are in the retail clothing business. They have decided to incorporate, and each will become a 50% owner of the new corporation. The partnership assets have a total adjusted basis of $84,000 and an estimated value of $126,000. The partnership has a bank loan of $25,000 with the store building pledged as collateral for the loan. The bank has agreed to continue the loan under the same terms but with the corporation as the borrower rather than the partnership. Tom's basis in the partnership is $40,000 and Jerry's is $32,000.

(a) Will either partner recognize gain, and if so, how much, on the formation of the corporation and transfer of partnership assets and liabilities to the corporation?

(b) What will be the basis of their respective interests in the corporate stock?

(c) Assume that a year later Marvin Solomon wishes to join their business. He will transfer all of the assets of his ladies' ready-to-wear business in exchange for 1,000 shares of the corporate stock. After this transfer, the corporation will have 6,000 shares outstanding. Marvin's basis in the proprietorship is $23,000 and the assets are valued at $31,000. Will Marvin have recognized gain, and if so, how much?

(d) Would it have made any difference in the tax result if Tom, Jerry, and Marvin had joined together at the time the S-J partnership was incorporated?

Problem 12-9. Charles has operated a business as a proprietorship for a number of years. Recently, Charles and Dobson have agreed to join together and operate a business as a corporation. They plan to form the C&D Corporation and to transfer assets to it as follows:

Investor	*Property*	*Tax Basis of Property*	*Fair Market Value*	*Par Value of Stock to Be Received*
Charles	Real estate	$140,000	$200,000	$200,000
Dobson	Cash		200,000	200,000

(a) What is the tax effect of the formation of the corporation to Charles?

(b) What is the tax effect of the formation of the corporation to Dobson?

(c) In the negotiations for forming the corporation, they also discussed the possibility that Everett might join with them. Everett has property that has a tax basis of $240,000 and a fair market value of $200,000. Everett decided not to join the corporation at its initial formation but would transfer property to the corporation a few months later in exchange for stock with a par value of $175,000. Charles and Dobson agreed to this. Discuss the possible tax motive that Everett had.

(d) Compare your answers to parts (a) to (c) with the answers to Problem 8 of Chapter 10, where the same facts were set in a partnership context. What are the differences in tax treatment?

Problem 12-10. Cactus Corporation will have ordinary operating taxable income of $40,000 for its taxable year, which ends next month. The corporation will sell assets before the end of the year for a profit of $30,000. These assets are not capital assets. The corporation can arrange to receive all of the selling price before the end of the fiscal year, or it can arrange to receive 50% of the selling price before the end of the year and the balance early in the new year. If the latter arrangement is used, the installment sales method will be used to report the profit for federal income tax purposes. Next year's taxable income is expected to be only $20,000 without the results of this specific transaction.

What will be the difference in current year's tax between the two alternatives? (Ignore any interest income because the installment receivable will be outstanding only for a few days.)

Problem 12-11. For the fiscal year ending 9/30/90, the XYZ Corporation has $250,000 of sales revenue, $200,000 of operating expenses, $15,000 of charitable contributions, It also received $30,000 of dividend income from domestic corporations which XYZ had less than a 20% interest and $20,000 of dividends from domestic corporations in which XYZ had between a 20% and 80% interest. Compute the corporation's taxable income for the year.

PROBLEMS WITH AN ASTERISK REQUIRE ADDITIONAL RESEARCH.

Problem 12-12.* Valley Corporation has a 100%-owned subsidiary, Maul Corporation. A consolidated income tax return is filed on a calendar-year basis. In November of last year, the parent corporation sold a tract of land to its subsidiary for $60,000. The land had been used in the business of the parent corporation for ten years prior to the sale. The basis to Valley at the time of the sale was $40,000. Maul Corporation then held the land as a capital asset until February of the current year and sold it to an unrelated party for $75,000.

(a) In filing the consolidated income tax return for last year, what amount should Valley have reported as income from the sale?
(b) What was Maul's basis in the land?
(c) What is the amount and kind of gain to be reported on the consolidated income tax return for the current year?
(d) What tax-saving steps might they have taken with more foresight?

Problem 12-13.* Tom Arbor owns all of the outstanding stock of Arbor, Incorporated, which has been a highly successful advertising agency. The corporation had abundant cash and Tom would like to get $100,000 out of the corporation for an alternative investment opportunity that has arisen. One problem is that Tom will have taxable income of approximately $300,000 on a single return even without additional dividend income from the corporation.

(a) How much dividend would the corporation have to pay to Tom in order for him to have an additional $100,000 after taxes?
(b) Would there be any tax advantage if Tom were to sell some of his stock back to the corporation?
(c) If Tom donates some of the stock to charity, could he get a deduction? What limitations exist on such a deduction? How would Tom establish a value for the stock?
(d) Ignoring any percentage limitations, how much stock would Tom have to donate to charity to reduce his taxes by $100,000?
(e) Could the corporation redeem the stock from the charitable organization after Tom's gift? Are there any restrictions on such a redemption?
(f) If Tom donates the stock and it is subsequently redeemed so that Tom saves $100,000 in taxes, how much must the corporation pay to redeem the stock?

Problem 12-14.* The Austin Corporation, not a Subchapter S corporation, donated $14,000 to recognized charitable organizations last year. Taxable income, not including any deduction for contributions, was $86,000. This figure includes dividends of $25,000 received from other taxable domestic corporations in which Austin owns more than 20% of the stock. No capital gain or loss was recognized during the year.

(a) What amount may Austin deduct for charitable contributions?
(b) Does the corporation lose any portion of the contribution as a deduction?
(c) Would it make any difference if the corporation had donated property other than cash?
(d) Discuss the planning strategy of donating scientific equipment to a university.

Problem 12-15.* Hill Corporation has a 100%-owned subsidiary, Mound Corporation. On December 12, Mound sold land, which it had held as an investment for eight years, to Hill for $120,000. Mound's basis in the land was $80,000. Mound had a capital loss carryover from five years earlier. Hill and Mound do not file a consolidated tax return.

(a) Will Mound Corporation recognize the $40,000 of long-term capital gain?

(b) What would be the tax effect if Mound had sold the property to an unrelated taxpayer?

(c) What problems exist with this alternative?

Problem 12-16.* Robert Tully has some publicly traded stock which he has held for several years and which has increased in value by $50,000. Robert is consistently in the highest marginal tax bracket. Robert also owns 80% of the stock of his construction business. The corporation also consistently has an operating profit, which results in paying tax at the highest marginal rates.

(a) If Robert sells the stock, how much additional tax will he be required to pay?

(b) Since Robert owns 80% of his corporation, he can transfer the stock to the construction corporation in exchange for more construction corporation stock and not incur any tax on that transaction. If that is done, and the construction corporation then sells the stock, how much tax will the construction corporation incur on the sale?

(c) Is there any advantage or disadvantage to Robert from selling the stock himself?

Form **1120** Department of the Treasury Internal Revenue Service

U.S. Corporation Income Tax Return

For calendar year 1989 or tax year beginning ______________, 1989, ending ______________, 19 ____

▶ Instructions are separate. See page 1 for Paperwork Reduction Act Notice.

OMB No. 1545-0123

1989

Check if a—	Use IRS label. Otherwise, please print or type.		
A Consolidated return ☐		Name	D Employer identification number
B Personal holding co. ☐		Number and street (or P.O. box number if mail is not delivered to street address)	E Date incorporated
C Personal service corp.(as defined in Temp. Regs. sec. 1.441-4T—see instructions) ☐		City or town, state, and ZIP code	F Total assets (see Specific Instructions)

G Check applicable boxes: (1) ☐ Initial return (2) ☐ Final return (3) ☐ Change in address $

Income	1a	Gross receipts or sales ____ b Less returns and allowances ____ c Bal ▶	1c	
	2	Cost of goods sold and/or operations (Schedule A, line 7)	2	
	3	Gross profit (line 1c less line 2)	3	
	4	Dividends (Schedule C, line 19)	4	
	5	Interest	5	
	6	Gross rents	6	
	7	Gross royalties	7	50000
	8	Capital gain net income (attach Schedule D (Form 1120))	8	
	9	Net gain or (loss) from Form 4797, Part II, line 18 (attach Form 4797)	9	
	10	Other income (see instructions—attach schedule)	10	
	11	**Total** income—Add lines 3 through 10 ▶	11	
Deductions (See instructions for limitations on deductions.)	12	Compensation of officers (Schedule E, line 4)	12	
	13a	Salaries and wages ____ b Less jobs credit ____ c Balance ▶	13c	
	14	Repairs	14	
	15	Bad debts	15	
	16	Rents	16	
	17	Taxes	17	
	18	Interest	18	500
	19	Contributions (**see instructions for 10% limitation**)	19	
	20	Depreciation (attach Form 4562) 20 ____		
	21	Less depreciation claimed on Schedule A and elsewhere on return 21a ____	21b	
	22	Depletion	22	
	23	Advertising	23	
	24	Pension, profit-sharing, etc., plans	24	
	25	Employee benefit programs	25	
	26	Other deductions (attach schedule)	26	
	27	**Total** deductions—Add lines 12 through 26 ▶	27	
	28	Taxable income before net operating loss deduction and special deductions (line 11 less line 27)	28	
	29	**Less: a** Net operating loss deduction (see instructions) 29a ____		
		b Special deductions (Schedule C, line 20) 29b ____	29c	
Tax and Payments	30	Taxable income—Line 28 less line 29c	30	131000
	31	**Total tax** (Schedule J, line 10)	31	300,000
	32	**Payments: a** 1988 overpayment credited to 1989 32a ____		
		b 1989 estimated tax payments 32b ____		
		c Less 1989 refund applied for on Form 4466 32c ( ) d Bal ▶ 32d ____		
		e Tax deposited with Form 7004 32e ____		
		f Credit from regulated investment companies (attach Form 2439) 32f ____		
		g Credit for Federal tax on fuels (attach Form 4136) 32g ____	32h	
	33	Enter any **penalty** for underpayment of estimated tax—Check ▶ ☐ if Form 2220 is attached	33	
	34	**Tax due**—If the total of lines 31 and 33 is larger than line 32h, enter amount owed	34	
	35	**Overpayment**—If line 32h is larger than the total of lines 31 and 33, enter amount overpaid	35	
	36	Enter amount of line 35 you want: **Credited to 1990 estimated tax ▶** ____ **Refunded ▶**	36	

Please Sign Here

Under penalties of perjury, I declare that I have examined this return, including accompanying schedules and statements, and to the best of my knowledge and belief, it is true, correct, and complete. Declaration of preparer (other than taxpayer) is based on all information of which preparer has any knowledge.

▶ Signature of officer ____ Date ____ ▶ Title ____

Paid Preparer's Use Only

Preparer's signature ▶ ____ Date ____ Check if self-employed ☐ Preparer's social security number

Firm's name (or yours if self-employed) and address ▶ ____ E.I. No. ▶ ____ ZIP code ▶ ____

H732

Form 1120 (1989) Page 2

Schedule A **Cost of Goods Sold and/or Operations** (See instructions for line 2, page 1.)

1	Inventory at beginning of year	1	
2	Purchases	2	
3	Cost of labor	3	
4a	Additional section 263A costs (see instructions—attach schedule)	4a	
b	Other costs (attach schedule)	4b	
5	Total—Add lines 1 through 4b	5	
6	Inventory at end of year	6	
7	Cost of goods sold and/or operations—Line 5 less line 6. Enter here and on line 2, page 1	7	

8a Check all methods used for valuing closing inventory:

(i) ☐ Cost (ii) ☐ Lower of cost or market as described in Regulations section 1.471-4 (see instructions)

(iii) ☐ Writedown of "subnormal" goods as described in Regulations section 1.471-2(c) (see instructions)

(iv) ☐ Other (Specify method used and attach explanation.) ▶ ____________

b Check if the LIFO inventory method was adopted this tax year for any goods (if checked, attach Form 970) ☐

c If the LIFO inventory method was used for this tax year, enter percentage (or amounts) of closing inventory computed under LIFO . . . **8c** ______

d Do the rules of section 263A (with respect to property produced or acquired for resale) apply to the corporation? ☐ Yes ☐ No

e Was there any change in determining quantities, cost, or valuations between opening and closing inventory? If "Yes," attach explanation ☐ Yes ☐ No

Schedule C **Dividends and Special Deductions** (See instructions.)

		(a) Dividends received	(b) %	(c) Special deductions: (a) × (b)
1	Dividends from less-than-20%-owned domestic corporations that are subject to the 70% deduction (other than debt-financed stock)		70	
2	Dividends from 20%-or-more-owned domestic corporations that are subject to the 80% deduction (other than debt-financed stock)		80	
3	Dividends on debt-financed stock of domestic and foreign corporations (section 246A)		see instructions	
4	Dividends on certain preferred stock of less-than-20%-owned public utilities		41.176	
5	Dividends on certain preferred stock of 20%-or-more-owned public utilities		47.059	
6	Dividends from less-than-20%-owned foreign corporations and certain FSCs that are subject to the 70% deduction		70	
7	Dividends from 20%-or-more-owned foreign corporations and certain FSCs that are subject to the 80% deduction		80	
8	Dividends from wholly owned foreign subsidiaries subject to the 100% deduction (section 245(b))		100	
9	**Total**—Add lines 1 through 8. See instructions for limitation			
10	Dividends from domestic corporations received by a small business investment company operating under the Small Business Investment Act of 1958		100	
11	Dividends from certain FSCs that are subject to the 100% deduction (section 245(c)(1))		100	
12	Dividends from affiliated group members subject to the 100% deduction (section 243(a)(3))		100	
13	Other dividends from foreign corporations not included on lines 3, 6, 7, 8, or 11			
14	Income from controlled foreign corporations under subpart F (attach Forms 5471)			
15	Foreign dividend gross-up (section 78)			
16	IC-DISC and former DISC dividends not included on lines 1, 2, or 3 (section 246(d))			
17	Other dividends			
18	Deduction for dividends paid on certain preferred stock of public utilities (see instructions)			
19	Total dividends—Add lines 1 through 17. Enter here and on line 4, page 1. ▶			
20	Total deductions—Add lines 9, 10, 11, 12, and 18. Enter here and on line 29b, page 1 ▶			

Schedule E **Compensation of Officers** (See instructions for line 12, page 1.)

Complete Schedule E only if total receipts (line 1a, plus lines 4 through 10, of page 1, Form 1120) are $500,000 or more.

	(a) Name of officer	(b) Social security number	(c) Percent of time devoted to business	Percent of corporation stock owned (d) Common	(e) Preferred	(f) Amount of compensation
1			%	%	%	
			%	%	%	
			%	%	%	
			%	%	%	
			%	%	%	

2	Total compensation of officers	
3	Less: Compensation of officers claimed on Schedule A and elsewhere on return	( )
4	Compensation of officers deducted on line 12, page 1	

Schedule J Tax Computation

1 Check if you are a member of a controlled group (see sections 1561 and 1563) . . . . . . ▶ ☐

2 If the box on line 1 is checked:

a Enter your share of the $50,000 and $25,000 taxable income bracket amounts (in that order): (i) $ ____ (ii) $ ____

b Enter your share of the additional 5% tax (not to exceed $11,750) ▶ $ ____

3 Income tax (see instructions to figure the tax). Check this box if the corporation is a qualified personal service corporation (see instructions). ▶ ☐ **3**

4a Foreign tax credit (attach Form 1118) **4a**

b Possessions tax credit (attach Form 5735) **4b**

c Orphan drug credit (attach Form 6765) **4c**

d Credit for fuel produced from a nonconventional source (see instructions) **4d**

e General business credit. Enter here and check which forms are attached:
☐ Form 3800 ☐ Form 3468 ☐ Form 5884
☐ Form 6478 ☐ Form 6765 ☐ Form 8586 . . . . . **4e**

f Credit for prior year minimum tax (attach Form 8801) **4f**

5 Total—Add lines 4a through 4f **5**

6 Line 3 less line 5 . . . . . **6**

7 Personal holding company tax (attach Schedule PH (Form 1120)) **7**

8 Recapture taxes. Check if from: ☐ Form 4255 ☐ Form 8611 . . . . . **8**

9a Alternative minimum tax (attach Form 4626) **9a**

b Environmental tax (attach Form 4626) **9b**

10 Total tax—Add lines 6 through 9b. Enter here and on line 31, page 1 . . . . . **10**

Additional Information (See instruction F.) — Yes | No

H Refer to the list in the instructions and state the principal:

(1) Business activity code no. ▶ ____

(2) Business activity ▶ ____

(3) Product or service ▶ ____

I (1) Did the corporation at the end of the tax year own, directly or indirectly, 50% or more of the voting stock of a domestic corporation? (For rules of attribution, see section 267(c).) . .

If "Yes," attach a schedule showing: (a) name, address, and identifying number; (b) percentage owned; and (c) taxable income or (loss) before NOL and special deductions of such corporation for the tax year ending with or within your tax year.

(2) Did any individual, partnership, corporation, estate, or trust at the end of the tax year own, directly or indirectly, 50% or more of the corporation's voting stock? (For rules of attribution, see section 267(c).) If "Yes," complete (a) through (c) . . . .

(a) Attach a schedule showing name, address, and identifying number.

(b) Enter percentage owned ▶ ____

(c) Was the owner of such voting stock a person other than a U.S. person? (See instructions.) **Note:** *If "Yes," the corporation may have to file Form 5472.* . . . . .

If "Yes," enter owner's country ▶ ____

J Was the corporation a U.S. shareholder of any controlled foreign corporation? (See sections 951 and 957.) . . . .

If "Yes," attach Form 5471 for each such corporation.

K At any time during the tax year, did the corporation have an interest in or a signature or other authority over a financial account in a foreign country (such as a bank account, securities account, or other financial account)? . . . . . .

(See instruction F and filing requirements for form TD F 90-22.1.)

If "Yes," enter name of foreign country ▶ ____

L Was the corporation the grantor of, or transferor to, a foreign trust that existed during the current tax year, whether or not the corporation has any beneficial interest in it? . . . . . .

If "Yes," the corporation may have to file Forms 3520, 3520-A, or 926.

M During this tax year, did the corporation pay dividends (other than stock dividends and distributions in exchange for stock) in excess of the corporation's current and accumulated earnings and profits? (See sections 301 and 316.) . . . . . .

If "Yes," file Form 5452. If this is a consolidated return, answer here for parent corporation and on **Form 851**, Affiliations Schedule, for each subsidiary.

N During this tax year, did the corporation maintain any part of its accounting/tax records on a computerized system? . . . . .

O Check method of accounting:

(1) ☐ Cash

(2) ☐ Accrual

(3) ☐ Other (specify) ▶ ____

P Check this box if the corporation issued publicly offered debt instruments with original issue discount . . . . . . ☐

If so, the corporation may have to file Form 8281.

Q Enter the amount of tax-exempt interest received or accrued during the tax year ▶ $ ____

R Enter the number of shareholders at the end of the tax year if there were 35 or fewer shareholders ▶

H732

Form 1120 (1989) Page 4

Schedule L Balance Sheets

Assets	Beginning of tax year (a)	(b)	End of tax year (c)	(d)
1 Cash				
2a Trade notes and accounts receivable				
b Less allowance for bad debts				
3 Inventories				
4 U.S. government obligations				
5 Tax-exempt securities (see instructions)				
6 Other current assets (attach schedule)				
7 Loans to stockholders				
8 Mortgage and real estate loans				
9 Other investments (attach schedule)				
10a Buildings and other depreciable assets				
b Less accumulated depreciation				
11a Depletable assets				
b Less accumulated depletion				
12 Land (net of any amortization)				
13a Intangible assets (amortizable only)				
b Less accumulated amortization				
14 Other assets (attach schedule)				
15 Total assets				
Liabilities and Stockholders' Equity				
16 Accounts payable				
17 Mortgages, notes, bonds payable in less than 1 year				
18 Other current liabilities (attach schedule)				
19 Loans from stockholders				
20 Mortgages, notes, bonds payable in 1 year or more				
21 Other liabilities (attach schedule)				
22 Capital stock: a Preferred stock				
b Common stock				
23 Paid-in or capital surplus				
24 Retained earnings—Appropriated (attach schedule)				
25 Retained earnings—Unappropriated				
26 Less cost of treasury stock		( )		( )
27 Total liabilities and stockholders' equity				

Schedule M-1 Reconciliation of Income per Books With Income per Return (You are not required to complete this schedule if the total assets on line 15, column (d), of Schedule L are less than $25,000.)

1 Net income per books		7 Income recorded on books this year not included on this return (itemize):	
2 Federal income tax		a Tax-exempt interest $	
3 Excess of capital losses over capital gains			
4 Income subject to tax not recorded on books this year (itemize):		8 Deductions on this return not charged against book income this year (itemize):	
5 Expenses recorded on books this year not deducted on this return (itemize):		a Depreciation $	
a Depreciation $		b Contributions carryover $	
b Contributions carryover $			
c Travel and entertainment $			
		9 Total of lines 7 and 8	
6 Total of lines 1 through 5		10 Income (line 28, page 1)—line 6 less line 9	

Schedule M-2 Analysis of Unappropriated Retained Earnings per Books (line 25, Schedule L) (You are not required to complete this schedule if the total assets on line 15, column (d), of Schedule L are less than $25,000.)

1 Balance at beginning of year		5 Distributions: a Cash	
2 Net income per books		b Stock	
3 Other increases (itemize):		c Property	
		6 Other decreases (itemize):	
		7 Total of lines 5 and 6	
4 Total of lines 1, 2, and 3		8 Balance at end of year (line 4 less line 7)	

APPENDIX 12-B (a)

Form 1120-A may be filed by a corporation if it meets all of the following requirements:

- Its gross receipts (line 1(a) on page 1) must be under $500,000;
- Its total income (line 11 on page 1) must be under $500,000;
- Its total assets (line 11, Column (B), Part II on page 2) must be under $500,000;
- It does not have any ownership in a foreign corporation;
- It does not have foreign shareholders who own, directly or indirectly, 50% or more of its stock;
- It is not a member of a controlled group of corporations (sections 1561 and 1563);
- It is not a personal holding company (sections 541 through 547);
- It is not a consolidated corporate return filer;
- It is not a corporation undergoing a dissolution or liquidation;
- It is not filing its final tax return;
- Its only dividend income is from domestic corporations (none of which represents debt-financed securities), and those dividends qualify for the 70% deduction;
- It has no nonrefundable tax credits other than the general business credit and the credit for the prior year minimum tax.
- It is not subject to environmental tax under Section 59A.
- It is not required to file a special tax return as stated below under Special Returns for Certain Organizations.
- It has no liability for interest under section 453(1)(3) or 453A(c) (relating to certain installment sales) or installment payments of tax under section 453C or 1363(d).

Appendix 12-B illustrates the Short Form 1120-A, which eligible corporations may file. Other corporations must file on Form 1120, which is reproduced in Appendix 12-A. The Schedule D, for reporting capital gains, has been omitted.

Form **1120-A** Department of the Treasury Internal Revenue Service

U.S. Corporation Short-Form Income Tax Return

Instructions are separate. See them to make sure you qualify to file Form 1120-A.

For calendar year 1989 or tax year beginning ______________, 1989, ending ______________, 19 ____

OMB No. 1545-0890

1989

A Check this box if corp. is a personal service corp. (as defined in Temp. Regs. sec. 1.441-4T—see instructions) ▶ ☐

Use IRS label. Otherwise, please print or type.

Name	B Employer identification number
Number and street (or P.O. box number if mail is not delivered to street address)	C Date incorporated
City or town, state, and ZIP code	D Total assets (see Specific Instructions) $

E Check applicable boxes: (1) ☐ Initial return (2) ☐ Change in address

F Check method of accounting: (1) ☐ Cash (2) ☐ Accrual (3) ☐ Other (specify) . . ▶

Income	1a	Gross receipts or sales ______ b Less returns and allowances ______ c Balance ▶	1c	
	2	Cost of goods sold and/or operations (see instructions)	2	
	3	Gross profit (line 1c less line 2)	3	
	4	Domestic corporation dividends subject to the 70% deduction	4	
	5	Interest	5	
	6	Gross rents	6	
	7	Gross royalties	7	
	8	Capital gain net income (attach Schedule D (Form 1120))	8	
	9	Net gain or (loss) from Form 4797, Part II, line 18 (attach Form 4797)	9	
	10	Other income (see instructions)	10	
	11	**Total** income—Add lines 3 through 10 ▶	11	
Deductions (See Instructions for limitations on deductions.)	12	Compensation of officers (see instructions)	12	
	13a	Salaries and wages ______ b Less jobs credit ______ c Balance ▶	13c	
	14	Repairs	14	
	15	Bad debts	15	
	16	Rents	16	
	17	Taxes	17	
	18	Interest	18	
	19	Contributions **(see instructions for 10% limitation)**	19	
	20	Depreciation (attach Form 4562) . . . 20 ______		
	21	Less depreciation claimed elsewhere on return . . . 21a ______	21b	
	22	Other deductions (attach schedule)	22	
	23	**Total** deductions—Add lines 12 through 22 ▶	23	
	24	Taxable income before net operating loss deduction and special deductions (line 11 less line 23)	24	
	25	**Less: a** Net operating loss deduction (see instructions) . . . 25a ______ **b** Special deductions (see instructions) . . . 25b ______	25c	
Tax and Payments	26	Taxable income—Line 24 less line 25c	26	
	27	**Total tax** (Part I, line 7)	27	
	28	**Payments:**		
	a	1988 overpayment credited to 1989 . 28a ______		
	b	1989 estimated tax payments . . 28b ______		
	c	Less 1989 refund applied for on Form 4466 28c (______) Bal ▶ 28d ______		
	e	Tax deposited with Form 7004 . . . 28e ______		
	f	Credit from regulated investment companies (attach Form 2439) . . 28f ______		
	g	Credit for Federal tax on fuels (attach Form 4136) . . . 28g ______		
	h	Total payments—Add lines 28d through 28g	28h	
	29	Enter any **penalty** for underpayment of estimated tax—Check ▶ ☐ if Form 2220 is attached	29	
	30	**Tax due**—If the total of lines 27 and 29 is larger than line 28h, enter amount owed	30	
	31	**Overpayment**—If line 28h is larger than the total of lines 27 and 29, enter amount overpaid	31	
	32	Enter amount of line 31 you want: **Credited to 1990 estimated tax ▶** ______ **Refunded ▶**	32	

Please Sign Here

Under penalties of perjury, I declare that I have examined this return, including accompanying schedules and statements, and to the best of my knowledge and belief, it is true, correct, and complete. Declaration of preparer (other than taxpayer) is based on all information of which preparer has any knowledge.

▶ Signature of officer | Date | ▶ Title

Paid Preparer's Use Only

Preparer's signature ▶	Date	Check if self-employed ▶ ☐	Preparer's social security number
Firm's name (or yours if self-employed) and address ▶		E.I. No. ▶	
		ZIP code ▶	

For Paperwork Reduction Act Notice, see page 1 of the instructions. Form **1120-A** (1989)

Part I Tax Computation

1 Income tax (see instructions to figure the tax). Check this box if the corp. is a qualified personal service corp. (see instructions). ▶ ☐		1	
2a General business credit. Check if from: ☐ Form 3800 ☐ Form 3468 ☐ Form 5884 ☐ Form 6478 ☐ Form 6765 ☐ Form 8586	2a		
b Credit for prior year minimum tax (attach Form 8801)	2b		
3 Total credits—Add lines 2a and 2b		3	
4 Line 1 less line 3		4	
5 Recapture taxes. Check if from: ☐ Form 4255 ☐ Form 8611		5	
6 Alternative minimum tax (attach Form 4626)		6	
7 Total tax—Add lines 4 through 6. Enter here and on line 27, page 1		7	

Additional Information (See instruction F.)

G Refer to the list in the instructions and state the principal:

(1) Business activity code no. ▶ ________________

(2) Business activity ▶ ________________

(3) Product or service ▶ ________________

H Did any individual, partnership, estate, or trust at the end of the tax year own, directly or indirectly, 50% or more of the corporation's voting stock? (For rules of attribution, see section 267(c).) Yes ☐ No ☐

If "Yes," attach schedule showing name, address, and identifying number.

I Enter the amount of tax-exempt interest received or accrued during the tax year ▶ $

J (1) If an amount for cost of goods sold and/or operations is entered on line 2, page 1, complete (a) through (c):

(a) Purchases (see instructions)

(b) Additional sec. 263A costs (see instructions —attach schedule)

(c) Other costs (attach schedule)

(2) Do the rules of section 263A (with respect to property produced or acquired for resale) apply to the corporation? Yes ☐ No ☐

K At any time during the tax year, did you have an interest in or a signature or other authority over a financial account in a foreign country (such as a bank account, securities account, or other financial account)? (See instruction F for filing requirements for form TD F 90-22.1.) Yes ☐ No ☐

If "Yes," enter the name of the foreign country ▶ ________________

L Enter amount of cash distributions and the book value of property (other than cash) distributions made in this tax year ▶ $

Part II Balance Sheets

		(a) Beginning of tax year	(b) End of tax year
Assets	1 Cash		
	2a Trade notes and accounts receivable		
	b Less allowance for bad debts	( )	( )
	3 Inventories		
	4 U.S. government obligations		
	5 Tax-exempt securities (see instructions)		
	6 Other current assets (attach schedule)		
	7 Loans to stockholders		
	8 Mortgage and real estate loans		
	9a Depreciable, depletable, and intangible assets		
	b Less accumulated depreciation, depletion, and amortization	( )	( )
	10 Land (net of any amortization)		
	11 Other assets (attach schedule)		
	12 Total assets		
Liabilities and Stockholders' Equity	13 Accounts payable		
	14 Other current liabilities (attach schedule)		
	15 Loans from stockholders		
	16 Mortgages, notes, bonds payable		
	17 Other liabilities (attach schedule)		
	18 Capital stock (preferred and common stock)		
	19 Paid-in or capital surplus		
	20 Retained earnings		
	21 Less cost of treasury stock	( )	( )
	22 Total liabilities and stockholders' equity		

Part III Reconciliation of Income per Books With Income per Return (Must be completed by all filers)

1 Net income per books		5 Income recorded on books this year not included on this return (itemize) ________	
2 Federal income tax		6 Deductions on this return not charged against book income this year (itemize) ________	
3 Income subject to tax not recorded on books this year (itemize) ________		7 Income (line 24, page 1). Enter the sum of lines 1 through 4 less the sum of lines 5 and 6	
4 Expenses recorded on books this year not deducted on this return (itemize)			

13

advanced corporate tax topics

Formation of corporations was discussed in Chapter 12, and many tax aspects of the operations of both "regular" and S corporations were discussed in Chapters 11 and 12. This chapter expands that discussion to include the following: (1) corporate reorganizations, (2) corporate liquidations, (3) collapsible corporations, (4) the difficult distinction between compensation and dividend distributions when employees are both officers and stockholders of closely held corporations, (5) personal holding companies, (6) foreign sales corporations (FSCs), and (7) foreign operations of U.S. corporations. Most of the discussion will be as applicable to S corporations as to other corporations, since they are the same as other corporations for most tax purposes.

The topics involved are generally quite complex. The intent here is not to deal with them in such a way as to answer all the nitty-gritty questions encountered in practice. Rather, as throughout the book (but perhaps a little more so here), a broad picture of problems and opportunities is provided. With that broad picture, you will be prepared for advanced study or will know when to use tax consultants or do research in reference books (see Chapter 20) in formulating tax plans and the solutions to business and tax problems.

13.1 Reorganizations

The act of forming a corporation in itself usually results in no income tax, as explained in Chapter 12. The transfer of property to a noncontrolled corporation (less than 80% ownership) is normally a taxable transaction. Realized gain or loss is measured by the difference between the fair market value of property (including the value of the corporate stock) received from the corporation and the tax basis of the property transferred to the corporation. However, as discussed in Chapter 12, if property is transferred to a corporation solely in exchange for stock,[1] no gain or loss will be recognized to the transferors if immediately after the transfer 80% or more of all stock of the corporation is owned by them.[2]

The theory behind this tax-free transfer of property to a corporation is that a change in *form* only, not a change in *substance*, has taken place. There is a continuity of ownership. It is important to keep in mind that the tax-free nature of the transaction means tax-free as far as both the corporation *and* the shareholders are concerned.

This same rationale tends to be followed in the area of corporate reorganizations. Usually, a reorganization involves shareholders' exchanging some securities for other securities.[3] Unless such an exchange of securities is rendered tax-free by the reorganization provisions of the tax law, it will normally be taxable.[4] A reorganization, to be tax-free, must have a legitimate business purpose.[5]

The most common type of tax-free reorgani-

[1]Or as a contribution to capital.

[2]IRC Sec. 351.

[3]It is important to keep in mind that a "shareholder" can be another corporation as well as a person.

[4]Earlier we said that deductions are "by the grace of Congress." The same concept applies here. Unless there is a specific statutory rule that allows an exchange to be nontaxable, it is taxable.

[5]The general rule for nontaxable corporate reorganizations is found in IRC Sec. 361.

FIGURE 13-1 Sample "B" reorganization

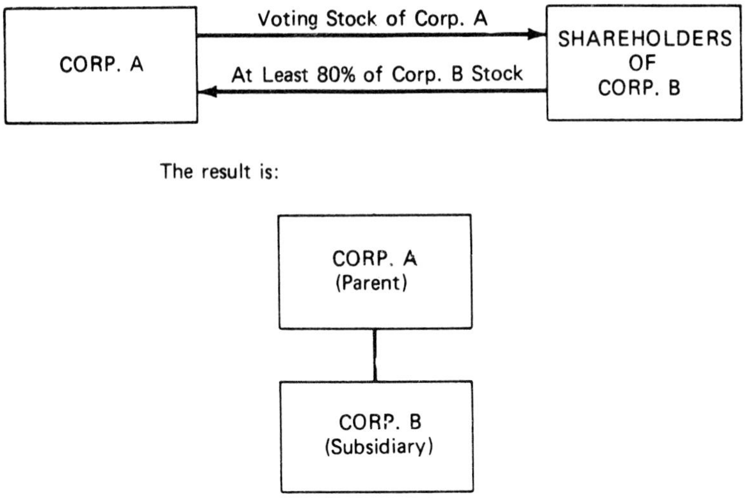

zation is the acquisition by one corporation (the *acquiring* corporation) of stock of another corporation (the *acquired* corporation) in exchange for its own stock.[6] For such an acquisition to be tax-free, the acquiring corporation must own at least 80% of the acquired corporation's stock immediately after the transaction. A variation is the acquisition of the acquired corporation's assets, or substantially all of them, for just the voting stock of the acquiring corporation.[7] With some minor exceptions, if there is "boot" (i.e., nonvoting stock or other consideration) given in these types of reorganizations, the entire transaction will be taxable.[8] The stock for stock transaction is often referred to as a "B" reorganization, while stock for assets is called a "C" reorganization. These letters come from the last letter in the citation (see the footnotes).

Corporate reorganizations are sometimes better visualized with a diagram. A "B" (stock for stock) reorganization might look like that in Fig. 13-1.

So called "hostile" corporate takeovers are sometimes "B" reorganizations because the "acquiring" corporation deals directly with the stockholders of the corporation to be acquired (sometimes called the "target" corporation) by enticing them to exchange their stock in the target corporation for (presumably) more valuable stock of the acquiring corporation or one of its subsidiaries.

A variation on this theme, but still a "B" reorganization, is where a parent-subsidiary group already exists and stock of the parent or subsidiary is used to acquire the stock of another corporation. This is shown in Fig. 13-2.

A "C" reorganization (stock for assets) is essentially the same thing, except that the acquiring corporation "buys" the assets rather than the stock. As Fig. 13-3 shows, Corporation B will end up owning virtually no assets except voting stock of Corporation A, and that stock generally must be distributed to the Corporation B shareholders. In general, Corporation B is required to liquidate, but this may be waived by the IRS.

A variation of the "C" reorganization is shown in Fig. 13-4. Here, Corporation B ends up owning the assets of Corporation C, with Corporation C distributing voting stock of Corporation A or B.

Another type of reorganization (called "A") is the statutory merger of one corporation into another.[9] In such a reorganization, the acquired corporation disappears and its stock is converted into stock of the surviving corporation. In a statutory merger, if there is boot, gain will be recognized, but only to the extent of such boot. Unlike the situation with a "B" or a "C," the presence of boot does not, in other words, "poison" the whole transaction (i.e., make the whole transaction taxable).

TAX PLANNING TIP: Where there is a good business reason why two or more corporations should get together, care should be taken to fit into one of the provisions of the Internal Revenue Code which permits a tax-free transaction. Otherwise, the corporation or the stockholders, or both, may end up paying tax.

As explained above, there are some very specific tax requirements in order for a reorganization to satisfy the "B" or "C" provisions. The "A"

[6]IRC Sec. 368(a)(1)(B). Definitions relative to corporate reorganizations are in IRC Sec. 368.

[7]IRC Sec. 368(a)(1)(C).

[8]One such exception would be in the case of a shareholder of the acquired corporation who would receive a small amount of cash to equalize a fractional share.

[9]IRC Sec. 368(a)(1)(A).

FIGURE 13-2 Variation of sample "B" reorganization

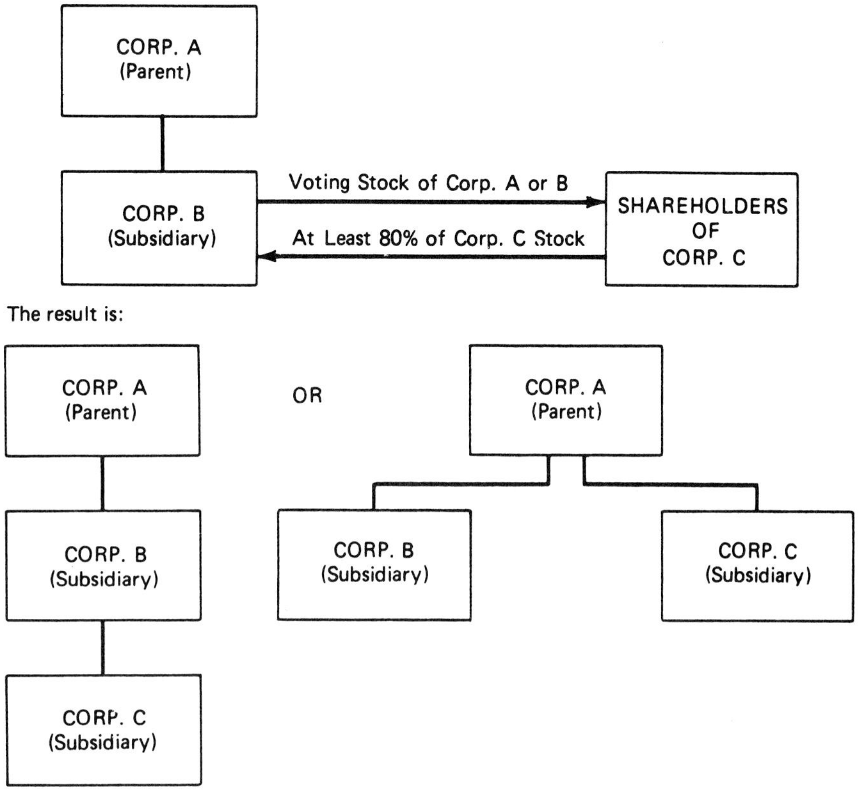

FIGURE 13-3 Sample "C" reorganization

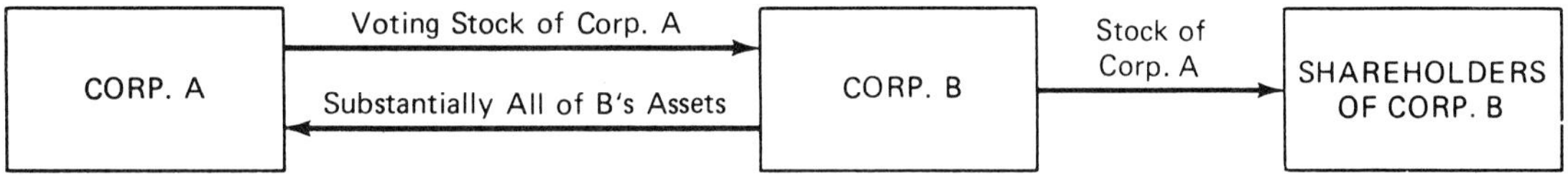

FIGURE 13-4 Variation of sample "C" reorganization

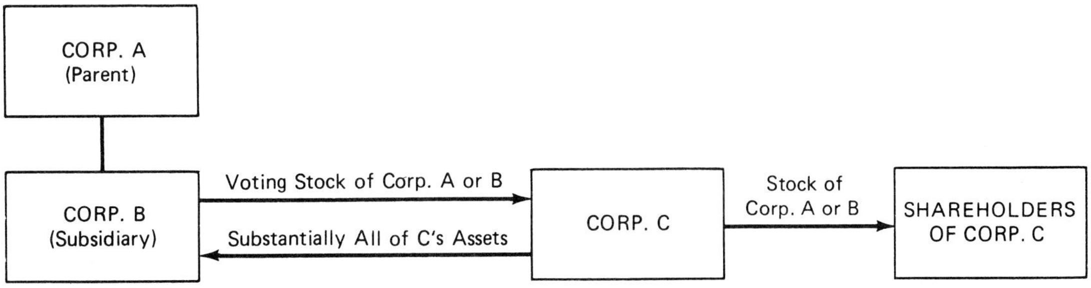

FIGURE 13-5 Sample "A" reorganization

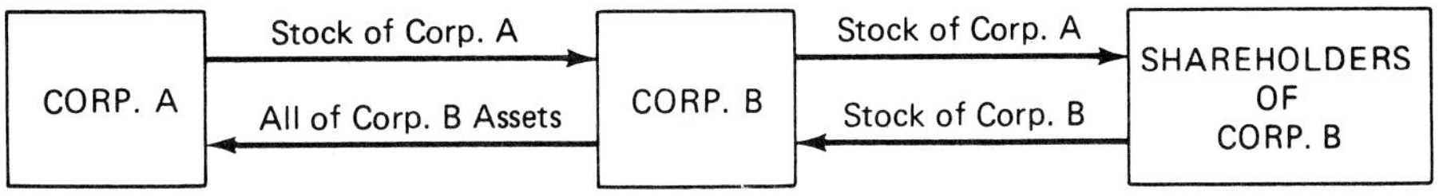

FIGURE 13-6 Variation of sample "A" reorganization

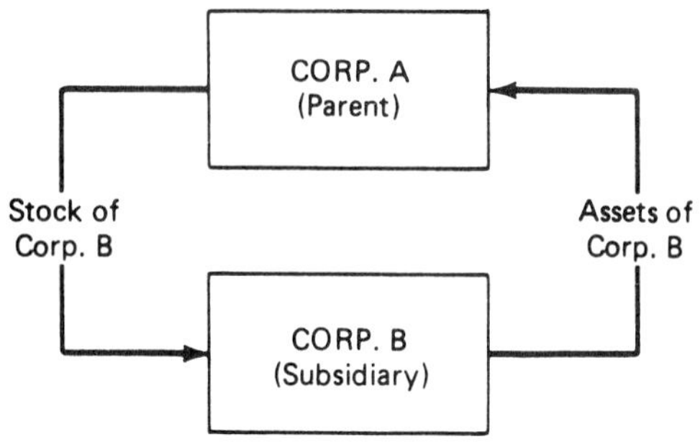

TAX PLANNING TIP: If there is a good business reason why some party to a reorganization should receive boot, then an "A" reorganization should be the goal. In that event, the boot will not cause the entire transaction to be taxable but will result only in recognized gain (to the extent of boot received) by the party receiving the boot.

rules, on the other hand, are less definitive. The most fundamental requirement is that the "A" transfer must satisfy the corporate laws of the United States or one of the states. Since each state as well as the District of Columbia has a different set of rules, space here does not permit a discussion. One version of an "A" reorganization is shown in Fig. 13-5. Corporation B goes out of existence and the individuals who were shareholders of B become shareholders of A.

A variation of this is shown in Fig. 13-6. Sometimes called an "upstream merger," the subsidiary corporation disappears and the parent continues to operate. Another possibility is the "downstream merger," where the surviving corporation is B, the one that was previously a subsidiary.

Still another possibility for an "A" merger is where a new corporation is formed and two previously operating corporations each disappear after the new corporation has acquired them. Figure 13-7 depicts such a situation. Corporation C is new. Using its own stock, C acquires the assets of Corporation A and Corporation B. Corporations A and B disappear and their former stockholders become stockholders of C.

13.2 Carryovers

In "A" or "C" reorganizations (as well as in "D" and "F" reorganizations, which are not discussed here), the continuing corporation "inherits" some part of the predecessor's tax history. These include the retained earnings balance, carryovers of excess charitable contributions, and some accounting methods (e.g., depreciation, installment sales, and inventory).[10] Tax credits, net operating losses of the disappearing corporation (or even of the continuing corporation), and capital losses may or may not be available to the "surviving" corporation.[11] It depends on the continuing ownership interest of the disappearing (or "loss") corporation's shareholders.

For taxable years after 1986, the law does not distinguish between tax-free and taxable changes in ownership. If the ownership of more than 50% in value of a corporation's stock changes during a prescribed period, the corporation becomes a *new loss corporation.* The amount of loss carryovers which may be used to offset later income is then limited. (If

[10]Chapter 8 covered accounting methods. As mentioned there, a general rule is that an accounting method may not be changed without permission of the IRS. This is significant to the *acquiring* corporation in a reorganization.

[11]The rules are in IRC Secs. 381–383.

FIGURE 13-7 Another variation of sample "A" reorganization

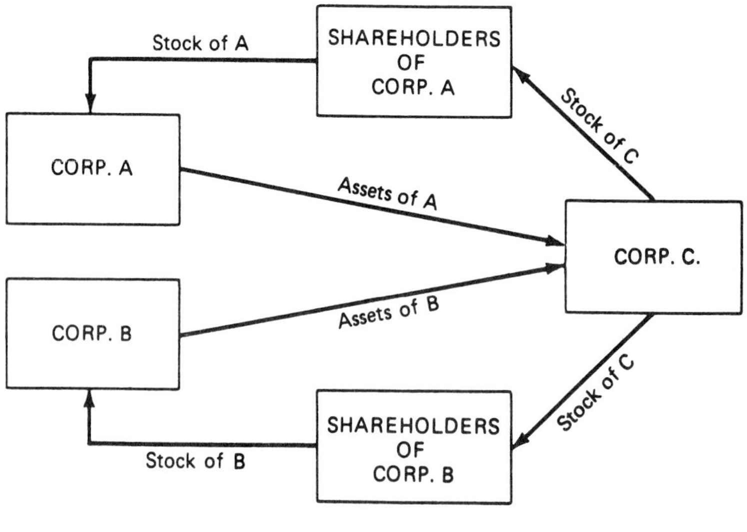

the corporation fails to meet business continuity requirements, the losses will be eliminated completely.) For any taxable year after the change in ownership, the amount of a new loss corporation's taxable income which may be offset by loss carryovers is limited to the value of the corporation immediately before the change multiplied by the Federal long-term tax-exempt interest rate. This limitation is increased by any gain recognized within five years of the change attributable to unrealized built-in gain at the time of the change. This gain is the amount by which the value of the corporation's assets exceeds their cost basis. This rule recognizes that the income attributable to the built-in gain was earned before the change and should be matched with the losses from those periods.[12]

For example, assume that the Barnes Corporation has an unused net operating loss of $1,000,000 on December 31, 1989, when 100% of the stock is purchased by unrelated parties. The corporation uses a calendar year and is worth $500,000 at that time. During 1990, the Barnes Corporation has taxable income of $100,000. Assume the long-term tax-exempt rate was 10% on December 31, 1989, so the corporation can only use $50,000 of the NOL to offset income ($500,000 × 10%). An additional $50,000 may be used in each later year. If the limitation is not exceeded, any excess may be carried over to the next year.

These rules not only severely limit when a loss may be used, they may result in losing the loss entirely. The fifteen-year limit on carryovers still applies, so if the loss is not used within that time, it will be lost. Using our example above, full use of the $50,000 limitation over fifteen years will only use $750,000 of the loss. The remaining $250,000 will be useless. These are important considerations when planning for the purchase of corporations. The tax cost of losing net operating losses will have a significant effect on the overall cost of the transaction.

TAX SAVING TIP: Corporations with net operating loss carryovers can usually best utilize them by injecting profitable businesses or transactions into them without a more than 50% change in stock ownership.

Similar rules on carryovers apply to taxable reorganizations and to changes in corporate ownership that are not reorganizations.

[12]IRC Secs. 381, 382.

13.3 Divisive Reorganizations

The reorganizations just discussed involve joining more than one corporation. There is also a type of reorganization that involves splitting up a corporation or affiliated group of corporations. This is called a divisive reorganization.[13]

Thus, if Ex and Why are both stockholders of a small corporation and find themselves at a point where *each* would like to take a part of the business and have a separate, 100%-owned corporation, they may be able to do so tax-free through a divisive reorganization.

The main requirements are (1) a business purpose, (2) that the business or businesses must have been operated for at least five years and (3) that the divisive reorganization not be used as a way of distributing accumulated earnings of the corporation.[14] Note that neither Ex nor Why needs to have been a stockholder for the full five years—it is the business of the corporation to which the five-year rule relates.

Ex and Why might have Old Corporation transfer the part of the business that is to go to Why to New Corporation, which would then be a 100%-owned subsidiary of Old Corporation. Such a transfer would be tax-free.[15] Why would then exchange the stock in Old Corporation for all of the stock of New Corporation. This would leave Ex with 100% of the stock of Old Corporation and Why with 100% of the stock of New Corporation. This second step in the process is also tax-free.

13.4 Distributions and Liquidations

Cash dividends are fully taxable to a shareholder as long as they are from either current or accumulated earnings.[16] Otherwise, they are considered a tax-free recovery of investment until the shareholder's tax basis has been returned. After that, they are capital gains.[17] For example, assume that Barnes Corporation had total earnings and profits of $10,000. Billy is the sole shareholder and has a basis in stock of $3,000. If the corporation distributes $10,000 to Billy, the entire amount will be a dividend. If Billy receives $13,000, the first $10,000 will be dividend income, but the remaining $3,000 will be tax-free as a return of basis. Any amount in excess of $13,000 would result in capital gain.

[13]IRC Sec. 355.
[14]IRC Sec. 355(a)(3).
[15]These divisive reorganizations are sometimes called "split-ups," "split-offs," or "spin-offs," depending upon the details of how the separation is accomplished.
[16]IRC Sec. 316.
[17]IRC Sec. 301(c).

Property dividends paid to an individual shareholder are taxable to the shareholder at fair market value.[18] The paying corporation will recognize gain as the result of distributing appreciated property as a dividend.

Shareholders, especially of closely held corporations, frequently seek to get earnings out of a corporation as stock redemption, which allows tax-free recovery of the tax basis of the shares redeemed, rather than as fully taxable ordinary dividend income. If some of a shareholder's stock is redeemed so that his or her *proportionate interest* in the corporation is *substantially* reduced, redemption treatment can often be obtained.[19] This is called a partial redemption. A *complete* redemption, of course, will have such an effect.[20] A liquidation can be thought of as a complete redemption of all the outstanding stock of a corporation.

Corporations, unlike individuals, can have perpetual life; but in spite of this legal potential, many are liquidated each year. If a corporation adopts a plan of liquidation and then sells its assets at a profit and liquidates, it cannot avoid corporate tax on those profits.[21] The shareholders will usually recognize capital gain or loss on the amount received in liquidation of the corporation, just as though it were any other sale of stock.

There are several major exceptions to this description of what happens in a corporate liquidation. A parent corporation which liquidates an 80%-or-more subsidiary generally realizes no gain.[22] The parent's tax basis for the subsidiary's assets will be a carryover of the subsidiary's tax basis.[23]

For example, assume that ABC Corporation owns DEF Corporation as a 100% subsidiary. DEF owns one asset, a building that has a value of $100,000 but an adjusted basis of $60,000. If DEF is liquidated, the building is passed to ABC with a basis of $60,000. It does not matter what the basis of DEF stock was in the hands of ABC. On the other hand, if DEF had been owned by Billy Barnes, the corporation would have to pay tax on the difference between the building's value and its basis, $40,000. Billy would pay tax on the difference between the basis in DEF stock and the value of the building. Since the corporation's only asset is the building, it would have to get the cash to pay the tax either from Billy or by borrowing with the building as security, thereby reducing its value upon distribution. This can be illustrated as follows assuming the corporation has no other taxable income and therefore has a marginal tax rate of 15%:

Corporation	
Value of building	$100,000
Basis	60,000
Income to DEF upon liquidation	$ 40,000
Corporate tax (15% for 1990)	6,000
Net value to distribute ($100,000–$6,000)	$ 94,000
Shareholder	
Distribution	$ 94,000
Tax, assuming 0 basis (28%)	26,320

The combined tax cost of distributing the building is around 32% of its value, and could rise to more than 44% if the corporation had little or no basis in the building ($100,000 less $22,250 of tax on $100,000 of taxable income = $77,750 distribution, less 28% tax = $55,980 net distribution).[24]

There are some special rules that apply when a corporation acquires the stock of another corporation in order to get the assets. In order to obtain a basis for the assets which is equal to the purchase price of the stock, the acquiring corporation must (1) purchase 80% or more of the "target" corporation within a twelve-month period and (2) elect within seventy-five days after a qualified stock purchase to have the target corporation treat its assets as if sold under the liquidation rules.[25]

13.5 Collapsible Corporations

One exception to the general rule of capital gains on stock sales or in liquidation is in the area of what are known as "collapsible corporations."[26] These are corporations that are used to attempt to convert what would otherwise be ordinary income into capital gains and yet avoid the corporate tax on the gain. For example, assume that a builder transferred raw land to a corporation in 1984. The

[18]IRC Sec. 301(b)(1). This is the rule if the shareholder is an individual. If the shareholder is another corporation, the dividend is the lesser of (a) the fair market value of the property distributed, or (b) the adjusted basis of the property distributed. Special rules apply if the corporation is a party to a reorganization.

[19]IRC Sec. 302 contains some detailed rules which govern whether the redemption of part of a shareholder's stock resulted in a "substantially disproportionate" change in ownership.

[20]If all of a shareholder's stock is redeemed, the gain or loss would be calculated just as if the shareholder had sold all of his or her stock for an amount equal to the redemption price.

[21]This was not so before 1987 under IRC Sec. 337. The theory was to avoid the double tax that will result if the corporation recognized gain or loss on the disposition of its assets and the shareholders recognized gain or loss on the redemption of their stock. Also, a corporation would not recognize gain on a liquidation. IRC Sec. 336 (before 1987).

[22]IRC Sec. 332.

[23]IRC Sec. 334(b).

[24]These tax results are in sharp contrast to the results under pre-1987 law. No corporate level tax was imposed and the top individual capital gains rate was 20%. In the example above, the highest federal tax for pre-1987 years would have been $20,000 versus $44,020.

[25]IRC Sec. 338.

[26]IRC Sec. 341. This may be largely irrelevant in any year in which capital gains are taxed the same as ordinary income.

corporation subdivided the land, installed streets, sewers, water, and gutters, and graded the property. The market value of the property was considerably enhanced. Then, in 1990, before the corporation has sold any of the lots, the builder sells the stock at a price that reflects the increased value of the corporate assets. Under the general rule, the stockholder would have a capital gain based upon the difference between the amount he received for the stock and the amount originally invested in the corporation. This excess, as you can see, is essentially the *unrealized* increase in value of the improved land. If this scheme would work, income that would have been ordinary income if the corporation had sold the lots, then ordinary dividend income when distributed by the corporation, is converted to capital gain. It won't work.[27] Not only will the shareholder have ordinary income, but the corporation will ultimately have tax to pay on the unrealized appreciation. That tax will be incurred by the corporation whether it ultimately sells the property or distributes it in liquidation, and will be reflected in the price at which the stock is sold.

The collapsible corporation rules provide that, in a situation of this sort, the shareholder's gain on liquidation shall be ordinary income.

TAX PLANNING TIP: There are ways around the collapsible corporation problem. For example, if the builder can delay sale of the stock until after realizing a substantial (e.g., 2/3 or more) part of the potential gain, the capital gain will apply to his gain.

13.6 Mergers

In many specific situations, some sort of merger is a logical solution to a tax problem. The word *merger* is used here in a loose sense to mean acquisition of control of one corporation by another, even though neither a statutory merger nor a consolidation may be involved.[28] For example, a corporation with capital loss carryovers that might otherwise be of no use (because the carryover period is running out) may find itself eager to acquire profitable subsidiaries with unrealized capital gains. This would permit the loss carryover to be used to offset profits of the subsidiaries. Another possibility would be to allow itself to be acquired by a profitable company. In the former situation, where the loss corporation seeks acquisitions, it can afford to pay somewhat more for a profitable business than could a corporation not having the contingent asset of tax-loss carryovers. A similar situation can result from a net operating loss carryover. However, now that the NOL loss carryover period is fifteen years, expiration may be less likely to occur than previously, when the loss carryover period was limited to seven years.

A corporation with operating loss carryovers of $1 million, which it can utilize only if it acquires a company with the ability to earn a profit, has a *contingent* asset of $340,000 *if* the corporate tax rate is a flat 34%.[29] This contingent asset can be made actual only by earning a profit. Theoretically, the loss corporation could afford to pay up to $340,000 more to acquire a company that could allow it to use this loss than could a corporation not so situated. As noted earlier, the availability of the full amount of the net operating loss of an acquiring company may depend upon the value of the loss corporation and the federal interest rate.

Another situation in which a merger has tax advantages is the collapsible corporation. For example, assume that a taxpayer is the sole stockholder of a corporation that has just completed construction of a shopping center. Long-term leases from responsible tenants have been obtained, and the value of the shopping center is considerably more than its cost.[30] The stockholder would like to sell the stock and go on to more remunerative pastures. Having built shopping centers before, the stockholder is considered a dealer for tax purposes. Therefore, if the stock is sold, gain will be ordinary rather than capital gain under the collapsible corporation rules discussed in the preceding section. By merging the corporation into a corporation whose stock is marketable, the stockholder incurs no tax. The securities thus acquired are no longer securities in a collapsible corporation. After a waiting period and with due regard for applicable SEC rules, the stockholder can dispose of the stock and the gain will be capital gain. Because the specific securities issued by the *buying* corporation in such a reorganization frequently are not registered with the SEC, a letter from the *selling* stockholder (who is receiving the securities of the *buying* corporation) will normally be required, affirming that the securities are being

[27]Another example would be that in which the corporation produced a movie. Just prior to selling the stock the movie's value was substantially greater than its cost.

[28]A statutory merger or consolidation, as explained earlier, can often be accomplished without a resulting tax liability.

[29]If the *acquired* company had annual profits over $75,000, the rate would be 34% and the contingent asset would be worth $340,000. Of course, where the contingent asset will not result in actual tax savings until sometime in the future, a present-value calculation should be used to refine the "value" of the asset.

[30]One way of valuing a business is to capitalize future earnings. Here, future earnings are the anticipated rental income.

acquired as an investment and not for resale. Subsequent sale of these securities is subject to limitations based on SEC rules, but when the sale does take place the gain is capital gain rather than ordinary income. In the meantime, the selling stockholder will have stock that may pay cash dividends.

Perhaps the most frequent tax influence on mergers is the estate tax. Although the estate tax itself will be discussed in Chapter 15, it should be noted here that the owner of stock in a closely held corporation faces a dual estate tax problem. The estate tax begins with the *value* of property owned by the decedent. Therefore, the first problem is the uncertainty as to the value of the stock for estate tax purposes. The fair market value of something for which there is no market is a highly subjective matter. Yet the optimum tactics in estate planning will differ substantially depending on whether the taxpayer's stock in the corporation will be valued at, for example, $600,000 or $1,600,000.

Added to this is the difficulty of obtaining the money to pay the estate tax. The corporate stock may have value, but when there is no market, just how is that value to be turned into cash? The Internal Revenue Service does not accept stock certificates in payment of taxes.

By merging a corporation with a corporation whose stock is actively traded, the stockholder solves both problems. There is an ascertainable market price for the new stock. The executor may argue (even successfully) that it is worth less than the market indicated, but at least the valuation will not be more.[31] Furthermore, since there is a market, enough stock can usually be sold to obtain the cash necessary to pay the taxes. Another way to solve this problem is through use of an ESOP (employee stock ownership plan), as discussed in Chapter 18.

13.7 Unreasonable Compensation

If a closely held corporation unreasonably accumulates its earnings in order that its shareholders will not have to pay tax on dividends, a penalty surtax can be imposed, as discussed in Chapter 12.[32] The penalty can be avoided by establishing bona fide business reasons for having not paid larger (or any) dividends. To the extent that what otherwise would be corporate profit can be paid to the stockholders as deductible salaries (or deductible rent, consulting fees, or interest), the corporate tax is reduced and the potential penalty for accumulating earnings is also reduced.

Thus is set the stage for one of the perennial tax controversy issues. A successful closely held corporation attempts to raise its stockholder-officer salaries to the highest level possible.[33] The IRS argues that the salaries are, in part, disguised dividends.[34] At stake can be substantial dollars. Thus, if $300,000 of the salaries paid by a 34% bracket corporation to its three shareholders is disallowed, the corporation faces a direct tax levy of $102,000.

Note that paying the $300,000 of "excessive" salaries, if they are disallowed as a deduction to the corporation, may be more expensive than retaining the $300,000 in the corporation and paying the regular tax plus the full penalty surtax on an unreasonable accumulation of earnings. The cost of having the $300,000 in salaries disallowed as a deduction to the corporation would be:

Additional tax to corporation:	
$300,000 × 34%	$102,000

To this the regular tax to the shareholders must be added:

Tax paid on $300,000 of salaries that would not have been paid if the salaries were not paid	$ 84,000[35]
Total tax from paying salaries and having them disallowed as a deduction to the corporation	$186,000

If $300,000 of salaries had never been paid in the first place, the additional tax (under the worst conditions) would have been:[36]

[31]As discussed in Chapter 15, one problem is that called "blockage." A sizable number of shares of stock, if put on the market at one time, could drive the price (value) down.

[32]The penalty is not imposed until accumulated earnings are over $250,000 (or $150,000 for certain professional service corporations). After that, the tax may be imposed at the rate of 28%.

[33]It should be recognized that not all successful corporations do this. If the shareholders have a higher marginal tax rate than the corporation, the corporation may retain its profits. The problem being described here arises when the attempt is to have the corporate taxable income reduced to a minimum so that there is less corporate tax.

[34]The IRS's authority for disallowing a deduction to the corporation is based on the statutory language of IRC Sec. 162. "There shall be allowed as a deduction all the ordinary and necessary expenses . . . including a *reasonable* allowance for salaries. . . ." [Italic added.] The argument is over what is a reasonable salary. Of course, there is not much basis for argument if the officers are not also shareholders. It is where the stockholders have "control" over their salaries as officers or employees that the problem arises. However, unlike other areas of the tax law, there is no specific percentage of stock ownership which results in a presumption that a person has "control."

[35]This assumes that the shareholders had other income which resulted in their being in the 28% tax bracket with or without this $300,000.

[36]The worst conditions are (a) the corporation pays 34% tax on all additional taxable income and (b) the corporation pays the full accumulated earnings tax penalty on all additional taxable income, net of the regular tax.

Additional regular tax to corporation: $300,000 × 34%		$102,000
Additional after-tax corporate accumulated earnings:		
Additional taxable income	$300,000	
Less regular tax (as above)	102,000	
Amount subject to penalty tax	$198,000	
Penalty tax:		
$198,000 × 28%		$ 55,440
Total additional tax if salaries had not been paid		$157,440

The latter strategy saves $28,560.

A key to minimizing the probability of IRS raising the compensation issue is to have supporting documentation for the salaries that are paid. For example, if it is customary in a particular type of business to pay a general manager a base salary plus 25% of the pretax profit, it should be possible to obtain written support for that practice and use that as a basis for the salary. Descriptions of the jobs performed by the various stockholder-officers can be put together by job analysts. Opinions can be obtained from outside experts (e.g., executive search people, employment agencies, industry experts) as to the amount of compensation that would have to be paid to obtain someone able to perform the job. Sometimes it turns out that the officer is so uniquely qualified and so hard-working that it would be unlikely that any one person could fill the job—that two or three might instead be needed (e.g., an entomologist with a private pilot's license, substantial experience in negotiating short-term and intermediate-term loan arrangements, fluency in Spanish, and willing to work eighty hours a week and be in travel status 70% of the time). Some CPA firms will do studies providing a basis for setting "reasonable" compensation.

TAX PLANNING TIP: The "reasonable salary" issue can be best handled by contemporary data gathering and record keeping aimed at being able to "prove" that a corporate officer, even one who is also a shareholder, is really worth the amount of salary being paid.

There also are some ways *not* to handle stockholder compensation:

1. Bonuses set at or after the end of the year, especially when proportionate to stock ownership.
2. Agreements with stockholders that if their compensation is deemed unreasonable by IRS, they will repay the "excessive" portion.
3. Payments to spouses (or children) of substantial salaries when they lack meaningful qualifications and are doing routine work (or little or no work).
4. Salary and bonus arrangements which, when taken in their entirety, siphon off substantially all of the profits of the corporation.

Compensation arrangements that result in little or no profit being left for the corporation pose less tax risk in service businesses (such as a professional corporation of physicians). There it is easier to support the position that all of the corporate earnings are produced directly by the services of the stockholders than it is in businesses where capital is a material factor in producing income, or where much of the profit can be attributed to efforts of nonstockholder employees.

13.8 Personal Holding Companies

Historically, corporate tax rates at higher income levels have usually been less than the rates for individuals. With 15% to 34% tax rates for years beginning after 6/30/87 and the 70% dividends received deduction, a corporation still may be used to earn investment income that would be taxed at higher rates to individuals, but to a much more limited extent than pre-1987. The tax law discourages closely held corporations from being primarily investors by imposing a 28% tax on the *undistributed income* of personal holding companies.[37] A PHC is one that satisfies two tests: (1) a stock ownership test and (2) a passive income test.

In order to be a PHC, a corporation must be closely held. This means that half or more of the stock must be owned by five or fewer individuals.[38] For purposes of counting the number of shareholders, a person is considered to be the owner of stock that is owned directly and also the owner of stock that is owned by other persons to whom he or she is related. These are known as the constructive ownership rules.[39] Thus, if a person owned only 10% of the stock of a corporation but a brother owned another 10% and a sister owned 11%, the first person would be considered as the owner of 31%. If any four other persons owned at least 19% of the stock, the 50% stock ownership requirement would be satisfied.

The second requirement relates to income. A PHC is onc that derives more than 60% of its *adjusted ordinary gross income* (AOGI) from invest-

[37] IRC Sec. 541. For years prior to 1982, the penalty tax rate was 70%. From 1982 to 1986 the penalty tax rate was 50%.
[38] IRC Sec. 542(a)(2).
[39] The constructive ownership rules are very detailed. They are in IRC Sec. 544.

ment sources.[40] Basically, this means dividends, interest, royalties, and in some cases personal service contracts. AOGI is most commonly gross income, less capital gains and less rent and royalty income up to the amount of the respective deductions connected with that income. Also, the dividends received deduction is added back, and certain other adjustments are made, to determine undistributed income.[41]

Before proceeding, consider an example. A corporation has income from dividends, interest, and royalties as follows:

Dividends	$10,000
Interest	20,000
Royalties	40,000
Total	$70,000

Assume that the corporation has $5,000 of deductible expenses. Therefore, taxable income is $58,000 ($70,000 − $7,000 dividends received deduction − $5,000 expenses). Regular corporate tax would be $9,500, or ($50,000 × 15%) + ($8,000 × 25%). Assume that the corporation paid $3,000 in dividends during the year. Its undistributed income would be as follows:

Taxable income		$58,000
Less: Regular tax	$9,500	
Dividends	3,000	12,500
Balance		$45,500
Add: Dividends received deduction		7,000
Undistributed income		$52,500

If the corporation did none of the things explained later to alleviate the penalty tax, it would have to pay an additional $14,700 ($52,500 × 28%).

Rent is included in PHC income only if the net rent is not more than 50% of AOGI.[42] Rental income poses some conceptual difficulties with personal holding companies. The concept of the PHC is that it is a corporation used to "pocket" income derived basically from passive sources and thus to avoid the possible higher tax rates that would result if that income were received by the individuals who are shareholders. Rent is a problem because it can be passive *or* active, depending upon the nature of the rental property and the extent to which the owner gets involved in managing it. Rather than look at these variables, Congress has written some arbitrary rules that make rental income subject to the PHC penalty tax if certain tests are satisfied.[43] At one extreme, for example, if a corporation's only source of income is rent, then rent is not PHC income and the corporation is not subject to the penalty tax. At the other extreme, if 99% of a corporation's income is from dividends and interest, for example, and 1% is from rent, the rent is also PHC income. What about other situations? If rent exceeds 50% of PHC income, it can only be excluded from PHC income in making the 60% test if any other PHC income (e.g., interest, dividends, royalties, etc.) that exceeds 10% of ordinary gross income (i.e., gross income less capital gains) is paid out in dividends.

For example, assume that the Barnes Corporation has $100,000 of AOGI from the following sources:

Interest	$ 70,000
Royalties	20,000
Rent	10,000
Total	$100,000

The rent is PHC income because it is not more than 50% of AOGI.

Suppose that the income has been derived as follows:

Rent	$ 60,000
Interest	25,000
Royalties	15,000
Total	$100,000

Is the rent included as PHC income? It can be excluded only if the other income ($40,000 in this example) in excess of $10,000 (10% of ordinary gross income) is paid out in dividends. If $30,000 or more has been paid in dividends, the rent will not be PHC income. Suppose that $28,000 has already been paid in dividends. An additional dividend of $2,000 will result in the rent's being excluded as PHC income. If rent is not PHC income, then less than 60% of AOGI is PHC income and the penalty tax will not apply.

Generally, corporations that are known to be PHCs do not, in fact, pay the tax on their undistributed income. Instead, they pay dividends — and the law encourages them to avoid paying tax at the corporate level by allowing certain special dividends. *Consent dividends*, for example, allow a corporation to take a dividends-paid deduction in calculating the PHC tax without actually paying a dividend.[44] The shareholders *consent* to report the

[40]IRC Sec. 542(a)(1).
[41]IRC Sec. 545(b).
[42]IRC Sec. 543(a)(2).

[43]IRC Sec. 543 also contains some special rules for rent from produced films and rent received from the same persons who are shareholders.
[44]IRC Sec. 565.

amount as dividend income (and increase their tax basis in their stock). The effect is the same *as if* the corporation had paid a cash dividend and the shareholders had immediately reinvested the amount received back with the corporation.

If a PHC is not initially recognized as such, or if IRS increases the PHC's undistributed income as the result of an audit, the PHC can pay a *deficiency dividend* in a later year and reduce its undistributed income of the earlier year.[45] The stockholders who receive the deficiency dividend in the later year pay tax on it in that year. Taxpayers have been known to transfer PHC stock to their children, for example, just prior to the deficiency dividend—thus moving the dividend income that would otherwise be subject to their own high income tax brackets into the lower income tax brackets of the children.

TAX PLANNING TIP: Substantial investment income can be accumulated at lower corporate income tax rates by having a closely held corporation invest in securities that will generate dividends and interest. The trick is to avoid the personal holding company status and to avoid the top 34% corporate tax rate. If a corporation has less than 60% of its adjusted ordinary gross income from investment sources, it will not be a personal holding company and if it keeps its taxable income below $75,000, it will stay below the 34% rate.

13.9 Foreign Operations of U.S. Corporations and Subsidiaries

The United States taxes its citizens (and aliens with U.S. resident status) on their worldwide income. The same is true for the taxation of U.S. corporations. The result is that a U.S. corporation operating in a foreign country must not only pay the taxes of that foreign country but must also pay U.S. income taxes.

U.S. corporations thus frequently find it convenient to operate through foreign subsidiaries, since a U.S. corporation with a heavier tax burden may not be competitive. U.S. oil companies are an exception to this rule; through a combination of special tax benefits granted by the United States to oil companies (intangible drilling expense deduction, percentage depletion allowances, foreign tax credit), these companies have found it advantageous to operate abroad as U.S. corporations, even though their special benefits have been sharply curtailed by recent tax law changes. As a consequence, virtually all U.S. oil companies operate abroad through U.S. subsidiaries, but most other U.S. corporations prefer to use foreign subsidiaries for their foreign operations. These foreign subsidiaries are subject to no U.S. tax unless they do business in the United States.[46]

Situations inevitably developed in which foreign corporations were used principally for tax avoidance. One of these situations was eliminated through the introduction of a provision for foreign personal holding companies that taxes the U.S. shareholders on the foreign PHC's undistributed income.[47] Even so, the rules for foreign personal holding companies failed to reach many situations that were felt to involve tax avoidance. To deal with this problem, the Congress created what is known as Subpart F of the Internal Revenue Code.[48]

The law provides that U.S. persons who own 10% or more of a "controlled foreign corporation" have to include in their taxable income their ratable share of the corporation's "Subpart F Income."[49]

"Subpart F income" includes:

1. Foreign-personal-holding-company income (e.g., interest, dividends, capital gains).
2. "Foreign-base-company sales income," that is, the income from sales that either are made *to* a related person or entity or involve a product originally purchased *from* such a related person or entity, but only if the property is produced outside the country in which the controlled foreign corporation is organized and is sold for use, consumption, or disposition outside such foreign country.
3. "Foreign-base-company services income," that is, income from the performance of services for or on behalf of any related person, performed outside the country under the laws of which the controlled foreign corporation is created or organized.
4. "Insurance income" from the insurance of risks outside the country in which the controlled foreign corporation is organized.

These items are grouped under the common name of "foreign-base-company income."[50] If foreign-base-company income plus gross insurance income is less than 5% of gross income or $1,000,000, it is disregarded; if it exceeds 70% of gross income, the entire gross income is treated as foreign-base-company income.[51]

[45]IRC Sec. 547.

[46]See IRC Secs. 881 and 882.

[47]IRC Secs. 551–558.

[48]IRC Secs. 951–964.

[49]IRC Sec. 951(a)(1)(A).

[50]IRC Sec. 954.

[51]IRC Sec. 954(b)(3).

A "controlled foreign corporation" is defined as one in which more than 50% of the voting power or value is owned by U.S. persons, each of whom owns more than 10% of its stock.

If a controlled foreign corporation invests any of its earnings in U.S. property, the U.S. shareholders realize a constructive dividend to the extent of their ratable share of the net increase in U.S. properties during the taxable year. What constitutes U.S. property is determined under special rules.[52] Bank deposits in the United States are not "U.S. property" if they do not exceed the amount that is ordinary and necessary to carry on the trade or business. Stock of a U.S. corporation is not "U.S. property" unless the investee either owns 10% or more of the controlled foreign corporation or is 25% or more owned by the shareholders of the controlled foreign corporation. However, there is no prohibition against investment in stocks of Puerto Rican corporations, since these corporations are considered to be "foreign" under the Internal Revenue Code.

It should be realized that while Subpart F has a much broader scope than the foreign-personal-holding-company legislation, it reaches a fairly limited number of special situations that were considered by the legislators to be especially conceived for tax avoidance purposes. The Internal Revenue Service, in addition, has a powerful all-purpose tool in Sec. 482 of the Internal Revenue Code, which can reach situations not reached by Subpart F. Section 482 authorizes the Internal Revenue Service to distribute, apportion, or allocate income, deductions, credits, or allowances among related businesses if such allocation is necessary to prevent evasion of taxes or to reflect clearly the income of any such entity. Although this weapon is widely used within the United States, its principal use is in situations involving a foreign entity.

Typically, the situation that justifies a Sec. 482 attack involves an intercompany transaction that is not an arm's-length deal. For example, a foreign subsidiary is located in a low-tax country. It sells merchandise to its parent in the United States. It charges high prices for the merchandise in order to siphon off a large part of what would otherwise be a profit for the affiliated group into a country where it is subject to low taxes. Under the authority of Sec. 482, the Internal Revenue Service can modify this transaction, treating it for tax purposes as if the subsidiary had charged the parent the prevailing arm's-length price for the merchandise.

With the exception of pre-1976 accumulated earnings of stock held for over ten years in less-developed-country corporations, U.S. persons owning 10% or more of the stock of a foreign corporation will realize ordinary income upon sale of the stock or liquidation of the corporation, based upon the amount of the earnings and profits of the corporation accumulated during their ownership. So, in reality, the ability to tax shelter the income of a foreign corporation is often merely an ability to defer the time when the tax will have to be paid.[53]

The appropriateness of allowing U.S. individuals and corporations to defer taxation of their foreign income by using foreign corporations depends on your point of view. Proponents of tax deferral emphasize that it creates an equitable (and competitively neutral) situation vis-à-vis foreign persons. Opponents contend that it is unfair to allow some U.S. taxpayers to avoid current taxation of current income when other U.S. taxpayers are denied that privilege. Proponents of deferral argue that its elimination would make U.S. business uncompetitive with foreign business in every country of the world that has lower income tax rates than does the United States. They point out that removing the U.S. business presence from these lower income tax countries, which are mainly underdeveloped or emerging economies, in effect abandons them to foreign businesses and may have substantial long-run detrimental effects on the global balance of power. Opponents of deferral respond that multinational corporations operate in many countries and that their *effective* worldwide tax rates are not so much below U.S. rates as to render ineffective the erasure of double taxation that is performed by the foreign tax credit.

13.9.1. Foreign Tax Credit

With some exceptions (notably S corporations and certain nonresident aliens), taxpayers are allowed to claim foreign income taxes paid or accrued as a credit against U.S. income tax rather than as a deduction in computing taxable income.[54] Claiming the foreign taxes as a credit is optional, and the election may be made either on the original return or at any time later, as long as the statute of limitations has not run on filing a refund claim.

Three kinds of taxes qualify for the foreign tax credit treatment:

1. income taxes;
2. excess profit taxes; and
3. "in lieu" taxes.

An "in lieu" tax is a tax that is an integral part of a foreign income tax system and, for purposes of

[52]IRC Sec. 956.

[53]IRC Sec. 1248.

[54]IRC Sec. 901.

administrative convenience, is imposed upon the taxpayer *in lieu* (in place) of the income taxes imposed by the same law.[55] For example, if a foreign country imposes an income tax and provides that in lieu of computing their net taxable income, farmers may pay an income tax based on 5% of their gross product, this tax will qualify as an in lieu tax.

In determining what constitutes an income tax, the language of the foreign law is frequently disregarded to obtain some uniformity of criteria. If the tax is imposed on an item that is income under U.S. standards, the tax will be considered an income tax. Accordingly, the social security taxes of several countries do qualify, even though the foreign law does not give them the classification of "tax." However, a tax imposed on the fair rental value of an owner-occupied residence would not be an income tax because the fair rental value of an owner-occupied residence does not constitute income under U.S. standards, even though several European tax systems consider it the equivalent of income received.

Accrual-basis taxpayers have to claim foreign tax credit on an accrual basis. Cash-basis taxpayers have a choice of claiming the foreign tax credit on a cash or on an accrual basis.[56] If they convert to the accrual basis, in the year of conversion they may deduct both taxes paid and those accrued, but they may not change their method back to cash thereafter without permission of the IRS.

The purpose of the foreign tax credit is to avoid double taxation of income. If the same income is taxed by both the United States and another country, and the U.S. tax rate is higher, the taxpayer pays the foreign tax and claims credit for it on the U.S. tax return. The actual U.S. tax is limited to the difference between the U.S. tax rate and the foreign tax actually paid. If the two tax rates are equal, the foreign tax exactly offsets the U.S. tax, and the taxpayer pays tax to the foreign country but none to the United States. If the foreign tax rate is higher than the U.S. tax, the taxpayer pays the foreign tax and no U.S. tax; in this case, although the total tax burden is heavier than that of a taxpayer operating exclusively in the United States, this occurs not because of the operation of the U.S. tax law, but because of the decision to do business in a high-tax foreign country.

13.9.2. Foreign Tax Credits of Corporations

Corporations are entitled to foreign tax credits under the same rules applicable to noncorporate taxpayers. In addition to this, a domestic corporation that owns at least 10% of the voting stock of a foreign corporation from which it receives dividends is entitled to a foreign tax credit for its ratable share of the foreign taxes paid by the foreign corporation if all the earnings of the foreign corporation are distributed as a dividend.[57] If the foreign corporation distributes only part of its earnings as a dividend, the credit available to the parent is reduced according to the percentage of earnings retained by the foreign corporation. If the foreign corporation owns 10% or more of another foreign corporation, a ratable share of the taxes paid by this second-tier foreign corporation is attributed to the first-tier foreign corporation and then to the U.S. parent. If a second-tier foreign subsidiary owns at least 10% of a third-tier foreign subsidiary, the U.S. corporation may also be entitled to a credit.

It should be noted that the U.S. corporation realizes a constructive dividend in the amount of the foreign tax credit made available by the foreign corporation.

13.9.3 Excess Foreign Tax Credits

A major tax management problem of U. S. corporations today is that they have foreign tax credits they cannot use. This raises their effective rate of tax on their worldwide income. The increased inability to reduce U.S. income tax by foreign taxes paid is the result of several factors:

1. Reduction of the top U.S. tax rate on corporations to 34%, making the U.S. corporate tax rate lower than most of the developed countries in which U.S. corporations operate.
2. Fragmentization of the foreign tax credit calculation. Income from different foreign sources is put into different "baskets" for purposes of calculating the foreign tax credit. There are nine such baskets in total, and there are also subbaskets. Example:
   Global pays U.S. tax at 34%. It has $100 foreign source income from a wholly-owned subsidiary on which the foreign tax paid was $50. It has $100 from a 50-50 joint venture on which the foreign tax paid was $18. Aggregated, it has $200 of foreign source income on which it paid $68 in foreign tax. The $200 of foreign source income will cost $68 in U.S. tax. Controlled foreign corporations and entities in which the U.S. taxpayer owns 50% or less are in separate "baskets" for calculating limitations on use of the foreign tax credit. Thus, the $68 cannot be offset in full by the $68 of foreign tax paid. Only $34 of the $50 can be used, along with the full $18, or $52 of the $68. Global has an excess foreign tax credit of $16.

[55]IRC Sec. 903.
[56]IRC Sec. 905.
[57]IRC Sec. 960.

3. Reallocations of income under section 482. The IRS now has the authority to reallocate income on intangibles (such as patents, trade secrets, goodwill, know-how) so that the amount received by the U.S. taxpayer is commensurate with the actual return being realized from exploiting the intangible. Foreign countries often decline to allow these revalued transfer prices as deductions in calculating their income tax. The result is that the foreign source income of the U.S. parent is reduced even though the foreign tax paid is not, thus reducing the ability to fully utilize the foreign tax paid as a credit against the U.S. tax.

13.9.4. Foreign Sales Corporations

Businesses that make, sell, or service products sold in foreign countries can reduce their overall tax burden by using a separate Foreign Sales Corporation (FSC). The FSC replaced something called a DISC as of January 1, 1985. Domestic International Sales Corporations (DISCs) had allowed federal income tax *deferral* of as much as 50% of the taxable income from export transactions. They were relatively easy and inexpensive to utilize, sometimes consisting of little more than some corporate papers and accounting entries. Whereas the DISC was a U.S. corporation, the FSC is required to be a foreign corporation; and whereas the DISC deferred taxation, the FSC confers a *permanent* tax benefit equal to an estimated 16% of the profit from export business.[58]

The FSC, moreover, must perform "foreign economic processes," and cannot be passive as could the DISC. The FSC must, either itself or through agents, both participate in the sales process and incur foreign direct costs. FSCs with gross receipts not in excess of $5 million for a year can elect "small FSC" treatment, which excuses them from the foreign economic process requirement and from the foreign management rule discussed below.

An FSC can have no more than 25 shareholders, but those shareholders, unlike the S corporation discussed in the prior chapter, can include corporations. Like the S corporation, only common stock can be used.

TAX PLANNING TIP: More than one class of common stock can be used in an FSC which handles export business for a number of smaller companies. This would enable small companies to cut the overall cost of having an FSC by having one FSC owned by a number of companies, with profits allocated to the class of common owned by a particular shareholder based on the volume of business done through the FSC by that shareholder and affiliates.

The FSC must be incorporated in a U.S. possession other than Puerto Rico (e.g., Guam or the U.S. Virgin Islands) or in a foreign country that meets certain requirements as to exchanging information with the United States. The list of qualifying countries changes from time to time, but has included Jamaica, Ireland, Barbados, and the Netherlands, along with twenty or so others.[59] The FSC must always have at least one director who is not a U.S. resident.

The foreign management rule has three parts: Shareholders' and directors' meetings of the FSC must all be held outside the United States, although not necessarily in the country of incorporation; the FSC's principal bank account must be maintained abroad; and dividends, professional fees, officers' salaries, and directors' fees must be paid out of foreign bank accounts.

TAX PLANNING TIP: Locating an FSC in, for instance, Barbados can provide a legitimate reason for business trips (e.g., the annual directors' meeting) to that Caribbean resort, resulting in a tax-deductible minivacation.

What, then, is exempt from U.S. income tax? The starting point is "foreign trading gross receipts," a term defined in the tax law.[60] It includes gross receipts of the FSC from:

1. sale of export property;
2. lease or rental of export property for use outside the United States;
3. any services related to (1) or (2) above;
4. engineering or architectural services for construc-

[58]IRC Secs. 921–927 set forth the FSC rules. Note that while the DISC only *deferred* income, the 1984 legislation that terminated DISCs also permanently forgave the tax on pre-1984 deferred income. Note also that existing DISCs are allowed to continue under the pre-1985 DISC rules as to annual receipts not in excess of $10 million. Those rules are modified to provide for a larger deferral as well as payment of an interest charge on the tax deferred by using the DISC.

[59]As of August, 1987, the countries in which an FSC could be incorporated included: Australia, Austria, Barbados, Belgium, Canada, Cyprus, Denmark, Egypt, Finland, France, Germany, Iceland, Ireland, Jamaica, Korea, Malta, Morocco, the Netherlands, New Zealand, Norway, Pakistan, Philippines, Sweden, and Trinidad and Tobago. IRS Notice 87-52 and 87-53, 1987-2 C.B. 362 and 363.

[60]IRC Sec. 924.

tion projects located or to be located outside the United States; or

5. managerial services for an unrelated FSC or for one of the interest charge DISCs still remaining, but only if sale, lease, or rental of export property, and related services [(3) above], are at least 50% of gross receipts.

These receipts can include profits on the FSC's own sales as well as commissions on the sales of others. If the transactions involve unrelated parties or arms-length pricing, then 30% of the gross income attributable to the foreign trading gross receipts is exempt from federal income tax. As one of two additional alternatives for dealing with purchases from related parties, the FSC is permitted to earn up to 23% of the combined taxable income of itself and a related supplier. Under the other alternative to arms-length pricing, the FSC taxable income would not exceed 1.83% of the foreign trade gross receipts. The FSC would use whichever of these alternatives produced the best tax result, with the limitation that the 1.83% alternative amount cannot exceed twice the amount determined under the 23% rule. Under either of these alternative approaches, $^{15}/_{23}$ to $^{16}/_{23}$ of the gross income attributable to the foreign trading gross receipts is then exempt from U.S. income tax.

How does a business decide whether to use an FSC? There is a cost to setting up and operating an FSC that can be quantified. Assume that it is estimated to cost $4,000 to create a small FSC and $3,000 per year to maintain it. The possible savings from the FSC can also be quantified. Assume that foreign trade gross receipts are estimated to be $5 million annually. Therefore, using the 1.83% alternative, the maximum possible exclusion from gross income would be $^{15}/_{23}$ of 1.83% of $5 million, or just over $59,600. It is clearly worthwhile to spend $4,000 initially, and $3,000 per year, to save 34% (i.e., the assumed incremental corporate income tax return rate) of $59,600, or $20,264 per year. This is especially so since the portion of the $3,000 per year of expenses attributable to the income taxed by the United States will be deductible, thus reducing the after-tax cost.

Assume now that the U.S. corporate stockholder of an FSC has saved some income tax dollars, which are now lodged in the FSC. What can be done with those dollars? They can be taken out of the FSC as dividends by the U.S. stockholder without incurring any additional U.S. income tax. This is done by allowing a 100% dividends received deduction to a U.S. corporation receiving a dividend from an FSC if that dividend is being paid out of the FSC's retained earnings attributable to foreign trade income.

TAX PLANNING TIP: Foreign sales, services, construction, and so on, operations which do not involve purchases from or sales to related taxpayers, can defer U.S. tax on 100% of their income by utilizing a foreign corporation as the operating vehicle. Tax will ultimately be payable to the United States when, and if, these earnings are repatriated to the United States. If earnings are not expected to be returned to the United States in the foreseeable future, profit will generally be maximized by using a foreign corporation that is not an FSC rather than electing FSC treatment.

FSC elections must be made within the first ninety days of a tax year in order to be effective for that year. Operating an FSC requires care in segregating costs between export and other activities as well as an accounting system capable of providing meaningful managerial reports in spite of insertion of what is usually an organizationally irrelevant entity, the FSC itself, while still providing that data required of the FSC by law if its contribution to tax reduction is to be maximized. At the same time, management controls over the FSC assets, including its foreign bank account(s), are essential if they are to be properly safeguarded.

If all the requirements are met and obstacles conquered, the FSC will provide a corporate shareholder with an exemption from U.S. tax on a portion of the FSC's foreign trade income at both the FSC and the shareholder levels, taxation on the balance of the foreign trade income at only one level, that of the FSC itself, and double taxation of any investment income. An individual owning stock in an FSC will pay taxes on dividends from it as ordinary income, so that the primary tax benefit in such a situation lies in the FSC's tax saving at its level.

13.9.5 Section 936 Possession Corporations

Puerto Rico is part of the U.S. for purposes of citizenship, but it (and certain other possessions, such as the Virgin Islands and Guam) is treated in a manner similar to a foreign country for some tax purposes. Our discussion here will be limited to Puerto Rico because it is the most significant for business purposes and the most politically controversial.

A corporation organized under U.S. law and doing business in Puerto Rico is generally subject to U.S. tax on its Puerto Rican income. In addition, it would be subject to income tax as a "foreign" corporation in Puerto Rico. However, a U.S. corporation which meets certain requirements can eliminate all U.S. income tax on its Puerto Rican income, and may be able to negotiate a "tax holiday" from Puerto Rico. Those requirements are:

1. Derive at least 75% of its gross income from the active conduct of a trade or business within Puerto Rico during the preceding three years;
2. At least 80% of the gross income of the corporation must be derived from sources within a U.S. possession during the preceding three years; and
3. Makes an election under IRC Section 936.

Thus, a U.S. corporation can form a U.S. subsidiary to manufacture its products in Puerto Rico. With a tax holiday from Puerto Rico, and a Section 936 election, it can avoid paying any tax on its operating income. By investing its accumulated earnings in Puerto Rico (or, indirectly through Puerto Rico connected financial institutions, in certain foreign countries), it can also avoid tax on its investment income. Finally, since the corporation is a U.S. corporation, its dividends to its U.S. parent will normally be eligible for a 100% dividend-received deduction.

The Section 936 corporation's earnings can literally escape income tax entirely. This makes Section 936 quite controversial. The tax treatment, in turn, gets entangled in the highly-political question of possible Puerto Rico statehood, independence, or continuation of the present commonwealth status. One problem of either statehood or independence would be the need to terminate the Section 936 subsidy that Puerto Rico uses to help attract U.S. manufacturers to set up operations. It is estimated by the Joint Committee on Taxation of the U.S. Congress that Section 936 corporations may account directly for about half of total manufacturing employment in Puerto Rico (but only for about one-tenth of total employment). While existing operations would not necessarily terminate, those companies that had located in Puerto Rico primarily for the tax advantages might ultimately leave, and other companies similarly motivated would no longer be inclined to establish Puerto Rican operations.

13.9.6. Tax Treaties

Tax treaties with foreign countries may supersede any provisions of the Internal Revenue Code. This right to modify tax law through international treaties has been used widely by the U.S. government. As applicable to the residents of treaty countries, tax treaties concluded with those countries modify the provisions of the Internal Revenue Code as to what is includable in taxable income, what deductions and personal exemptions are allowable, and what tax rate applies to the taxpayers. In any foreign tax matter, it should therefore be ascertained whether the United States has a tax treaty with the country involved. If such a treaty exists, its provisions should be carefully reviewed to determine the extent to which they affect the taxpayer. One of the disadvantages of an FSC is that it waives its rights to claim any treaty benefit that it might otherwise invoke by being a foreign corporation (e.g., even though a Canadian corporation, an FSC could not take advantage of the U.S.–Canada tax treaty to reduce its U.S. income tax).

TRUE-FALSE QUESTIONS

State whether each of the following statements is true or false. For each *false* answer, reword the statement to make it *true*.

T F 1. A type "B" statutory reorganization is otherwise known as a "stock for stock" exchange, and a type "C" statutory reorganization is otherwise known as a "stock for assets" exchange.

T F 2. If a person owns 100% of the stock of Corporation A and transfers all of that stock for voting stock in Corporation B, after which he owns 5% of the stock of B, the result is a nontaxable corporate reorganization.

T F 3. If a person who owns 100% of the stock of Corporation A causes Corporation A to transfer all of its assets to Corporation B in exchange for which she receives shares of Corporation B's voting stock, the exchange will be tax free only if she ends up with at least 80% of B's voting stock.

T F 4. In a reorganization, the corporation and the shareholders both receive the tax-free benefits under the theory that the economic substance of the situation is the same before and after the reorganization.

T F 5. In a statutory merger ("A") reorganization, if boot is paid, gain will be recognized, but only to the extent of the boot.

T F 6. An example of a "B" reorganization is one in which the *acquiring* corporation uses only its own voting stock to "buy" at least 80% of the stock of the *acquired* corporation from the shareholders of the acquired corporation.

T F 7. An example of a "C" reorganization is one in which the *acquiring* corporation uses only its own voting stock to "buy" at least 80% of the stock of the *acquired* corporation from the shareholders of the acquired corporation.

T F 8. In a "C" reorganization, the acquiring corporation must continue to use the same depreciation method for the acquired assets as was used by the acquired corporation.

T F 9. If Corporation A acquires all of the assets of Corporation B, in a type "C" reorganization, and Corporation B had a capital loss carryover, Corporation A will not be able to use that capital loss carryover to reduce its own capital gains.

T F 10. In one type of divisive reorganization, a corporation becomes two corporations, with shareholders of the former corporation becoming shareholders of both corporations.

T F 11. A corporate liquidation always involves the selling of all the corporate assets and the distribution of the cash to the corporate shareholders.

T F 12. Where a corporation liquidates a 100% subsidiary corporation by absorbing all of the subsidiary's assets, the parent's basis in the assets will generally be the same as the subsidiary's basis.

T F 13. Where an individual liquidates a 100%-owned corporation by having the corporation distribute all its assets to him, his basis in the assets will be the same as the corporation's basis in the assets.

T F 14. If a "collapsible corporation" is involved, the sale of the corporate assets in liquidation will result in the recognition of gain to the corporation.

T F 15. If a corporation which has accumulated net operating losses for several years is acquired by another corporation which has substantial accumulated profits, and the acquisition is a nontaxable exchange, the acquiring corporation will be able to deduct the acquired corporation's entire loss.

T F 16. One advantage of merging a closely held corporation into a publicly held corporation is that the shareholders of the publicly held business can objectively determine the value of the shares for estate tax purposes.

T F 17. If a closely held corporation accumulates its earnings beyond the reasonable needs of the business and the purpose is to avoid the tax that would otherwise have to be paid by the shareholders on dividend income, the corporation is a collapsible corporation.

T F 18. One way in which a closely held corporation can avoid the accumulated earnings tax is to pay salaries to its shareholder-employees at such a rate that the corporation has no profit.

T F 19. A personal holding company is one that has more than one-half in value of its outstanding stock owned by five or fewer individuals and has more than 60% of its adjusted ordinary gross income from investment sources.

T F 20. If a U.S. corporation has a 100%-owned foreign subsidiary which operates exclusively in a foreign country, the two corporations, one way or another, will always pay income tax twice on the foreign income—once to the foreign country as the income is earned and again to the U.S. parent as, if, and when the income is distributed in the form of dividends from the subsidiary to the parent.

PROBLEMS

Problem 13-1. The Zuba Corporation is owned by the following five persons:

	Number of Shares
Frank Zuba	1,500
Marsha Zuba (Frank's wife)	1,500
Bill Crane (Marsha's brother)	800
Linda Crane (Bill's wife)	800
Susan Ryan (Marsha's sister)	500
Total	5,100

Zuba is in the construction business and uses the completed-contract method. During 1990, a contract that was expected to be completed was delayed due to weather, and as a result the net income from construction activities was only $50,000. If the other contract had been completed, the construction operation income would have been $400,000. Zuba also had interest income from investments of $95,000.

The corporation did not pay any dividends during the year. The $50,000 net construction income was the result of $90,000 of gross income less $40,000 of business expenses.

(a) What is the Zuba Corporation's taxable income for 1990?

(b) Is the Zuba Corporation a personal holding company? Explain.

(c) What difference, if any, would it make if another contract had not been completed and the gross construction income had been $60,000 with business expenses of $40,000 for a net construction profit of $20,000?

Problem 13-2. Bellmont Corporation owns all of the stock of Bellmate Corporation. On March 15 of the current year, Bellmate, which also owned 100 shares of Bellmont voting stock, transferred those 100 shares and $5,000 cash to Elaine Cookie Corporation in exchange for all of Elaine's assets. Elaine was then dissolved, its shareholders taking the Bellmont stock and cash. At the time Bellmate acquired Elaine's assets, the assets had a fair market value of $40,000 and an adjusted basis of $28,000. The fair market value of Bellmont Corporation stock was $350 per share, although Bellmate's basis in the stock was $250 per share.

(a) Is the acquisition of Elaine's assets by Bellmate a tax-free reorganization? Explain.

(b) Assume that part of Elaine's assets acquired by Bellmate was $10,000 of accounts receivable. Assume that Elaine distributed $5,000 of the receivables to its shareholders and then sold the balance of its assets to Bellmate for the Bellmont stock *without* any cash being paid by Bellmate. Would this have made any difference in the tax effect? Explain.

(c) Does it matter that the "payment medium" used by Bellmate is voting stock? Explain.

Problem 13-3. Thompson Corporation is not related to any other corporation. Thompson has been very successful, but its owner and founder is considering retirement. He has been negotiating with Delta Alpha Corporation for the sale of Thompson Corporation to Delta Alpha. Delta Alpha is a 100%-owned subsidiary of Zeta Beta Corporation, a publicly held conglomerate. Mr. Thompson would like to sell Thompson Corporation without having any immediate tax liability. Because his basis in the Thompson stock is very low, he will have a substantial realized gain no matter what final arrangements are agreed upon.

(a) Describe how Mr. Thompson could arrange for a "B" reorganization.

(b) Describe how Mr. Thompson could arrange for a "C" reorganization.

(c) Does it make any difference to Mr. Thompson whether a "B" or a "C" reorganization is used for him to retire? Explain.

Problem 13-4. Henry Corporation exchanges 15% of its voting stock for substantially all of the assets of Jackson Corporation.

(a) Is this a nontaxable exchange, and if so, what type? What is the tax effect to all the parties?

(b) Would it make any difference if Henry Corporation transferred some nonvoting stock along with its voting stock in "payment" for the assets of Jackson? Explain.

(c) Would it make any difference if Jackson Corporation had a mortgage liability on one of the assets acquired by Henry and Henry agreed to assume the liability?

Problem 13-5. On February 1 of last year, the Kindrid Corporation bought all of the outstanding common stock of the Curry Corporation for $400,000 cash. Curry had no other stock outstanding. In March of this year, Kindrid decided to liquidate Curry. There were good business reasons for Curry to go out of business. The Curry stock that was owned by Kindrid had a fair market value of $450,000. Kindrid had never received any dividends from Curry. Curry's basis for all of its assets was $360,000. Curry had no liabilities.

(a) Can Kindrid dissolve the Curry Corporation without recognizing a tax liability? Explain.

(b) Assume that Kindrid and Curry merge. Can Kindrid then sell the assets of Curry without recognizing a gain? Explain.

(c) What steps can Kindrid take to sell the Curry assets and minimize the tax effect?

Problem 13-6. Comtrade Corporation owns all of the stock of Teletrade Corporation. Teletrade Corporation owned 800 shares of the 40,000 outstanding shares of Comtrade common stock. Teletrade's basis in those 800 shares was $75 per share. Comtrade had no other stock outstanding. On March 15 of this year, Teletrade transferred its 800 shares of Comtrade and $6,000 cash to the Gerard Manufacturing Corporation in exchange for substantially all of the assets of Gerard. The transfer qualified as a "C" reorganization. Gerard had purchased its assets several years ago. They had an adjusted basis of $63,000 on March 15, but a fair market value of $71,000. On the date of the exchange, the Comtrade stock had a fair market value of $81 per share. On April 30 of this year, Gerard sold 200 shares of Comtrade Corporation stock for $74 a share.

(a) What is Gerard's gain or loss on the sale?

(b) Did the payment of $6,000 cash by Teletrade to Gerard have any detrimental tax effect? Explain.

Problem 13-7. Dale Bowman owns 100% of the stock of Flame Corporation, which had the following income:

Dividends from other U.S. corporations	$110,000
Rent income	330,000
Long-term capital gain	70,000

Operating expenses, all attributable to the rental income, amounted to $190,000. Assume that all operating expenses were for depreciation, property taxes, and interest. During the year, the corporation paid $50,000 in dividends to Dale.

(a) What is the adjusted ordinary gross income?

(b) What is the adjusted rental income?

(c) Is the rental income considered to be personal holding company income? Explain.

(d) Suggest two ways in which Dale might have avoided the PHC penalty tax.

Problem 13-8. The Orange Corporation and the Tangarine Corporation are consolidated under state law as a new corporation, Mixed Fruit, Inc. Mr. Pitts, an owner of Orange stock, surrenders his Orange stock and receives Mixed Fruit stock in exchange. His basis in the Orange stock was $4,000. The market value of the Mixed Fruit stock that he received was $7,200.

(a) Will Mr. Pitts have any gain from the exchange? Explain.

(b) What will be his basis in the Mixed Fruit stock?

(c) Assume that Mr. Pitts has a long-term capital loss carryover that he could offset in part by recognizing gain on this exchange. Will he be permitted to make an election to recognize gain from the exchange of Orange stock for Mixed Fruit stock? Explain.

Problem 13-9. The Holiday Corporation transfers 25% of its voting stock to the Flagstaff Corporation for one-half of Flagstaff's properties. Neither Flagstaff nor Flagstaff's shareholders were in control of Holiday after the transfer. Flagstaff distributed the Holiday stock to its (Flagstaff's) shareholders, but did not liquidate.

(a) Will Flagstaff Corporation recognize a gain on this transaction, assuming that the fair market value of the Holiday stock it received is more than the adjusted basis of the property it transferred? Explain.

(b) Will the shareholders of Flagstaff recognize gain, or dividend income, from the distribution of Holiday stock? Explain.

(c) Does it make any difference if Flagstaff has no accumulated earnings and profits?

Problem 13-10. The Tile Corporation transfers all of its assets to the Brick Corporation, in exchange for which Brick issues an additional 20,000 shares of its common stock. Brick has 200,000 shares outstanding after this exchange. Tile Corporation liquidates by transferring the Brick stock to its shareholders. There are no persons who, prior to the transfer, were both shareholders of Tile and of Brick.

(a) Is Tile Corporation taxable on the exchange? Explain.

(b) Are the Tile shareholders taxable on the receipt of Brick stock? Explain.

(c) What is the basis of the Brick Corporation stock to the shareholders of Tile?

(d) Does it matter that there were no persons who owned both Tile and Brick stock before the transfer?

Problem 13-11. On November 1, 1990 the stockholders, all individuals, of Schaffer Corporation have voted to liquidate the business. Cash was sufficient to pay all known liabilities, which was done. The balance sheet following was then prepared.

	Adjusted Basis
Cash	$ 50,000
Inventory	150,000
Buildings and equipment	600,000
Land	100,000
Total	$900,000
Common stock outstanding	$200,000
Retained earnings	700,000
Total	$900,000

The earnings and profits for tax purposes is $700,000. The fair market value, determined by an appraisal, of inventory, buildings and equipment, and land is $200,000, $600,000, and $400,000, respectively. A plan of liquidation was adopted.

(a) Compute the gain recognized and tax liability incurred by the Schaffer Corporation as a result of the liquidation. Assume the corporation had no other income or expenses for the year.

(b) Assuming that the stockholders have an adjusted basis of $200,000 for their stock, all of which has been held for five years, how much gain or loss will be recognized if the corporation is liquidated? Assume that the shareholders assume any tax liability resulting from part (a).

(c) What will be the basis in the assets received?

(d) What difference would it make if Schaffer were being liquidated as earlier except that the only stockholder of Schaffer was Butler, Inc.?

Problem 13-12. Bart Jamison owns 100% of the outstanding stock of a manufacturing corporation, Jamison, Inc., which has been operating for fifteen years. The corporation has been successful, but Bart is thinking of retirement. Several publicly held corporations are interested in acquiring the business. Bart has received one recent offer for $2,000,000 cash. His basis for the stock is $200,000. The balance sheet date as of December 31, 1990 was as follows:

	Adjusted Basis	*Fair Market Value*
Cash	$ 100,000	$ 100,000
Accounts receivable (net)	400,000	400,000
Inventory	200,000	250,000
Buildings and equipment	900,000	1,100,000
Goodwill	0	750,000
Total	$1,600,000	$2,600,000
Accounts payable	$ 200,000	$ 200,000
Long-term debt (bank notes)	400,000	400,000
Total	$ 600,000	$ 600,000
Shareholders' equity	1,000,000	2,000,000
Total	$1,600,000	$2,600,000

(a) What would be the tax effect of selling his stock for $2,000,000 cash? Explain.

(b) Assume that Bart receives an offer to purchase the corporate assets for $2,600,000 with Jamison, Inc. to pay its own liabilities and then liquidate. Explain the tax effect to Jamison, Inc. and to Bart.

(c) Could Bart accomplish the same objective as in part (b) by first liquidating the corporation and then selling the assets to the buyer? Would the tax effects be the same?

Problem 13-13. Bumbullis Manufacturing Corp. is in need of capital to finance the marketing of a new product which it has developed. It has $20,000 in cash, although total assets are worth $1,000,000. Liabilities total $600,000. Bumbullis is owned by three stockholders. Ms. Angel owns 45%, Ms. Baker owns 45%, and Ms. Charoil owns 10%. Ms. Charoil wants to sell her stock and retire. She insists upon a minimum of $40,000, the book value. Angel and Baker have negotiated a merger possibility with a larger well-financed corporation which will provide the necessary capital. It is proposed that Bumbullis will receive $60,000 in cash plus 32,000 shares of voting common stock (fair market value $10 per share) of Overall Good Corp. In exchange, Bumbullis will transfer all of its assets (except cash) and all of its liabilities to Overall Good. Bumbullis could then liquidate by distributing the Overall Good stock to Angel and Baker and $40,000 cash to Charoil. The remaining $40,000 of cash would be used by Bumbullis to pay the expenses of liquidation.

(a) Will the transaction satisfy the IRC provisions for a nontaxable reorganization? Explain.

(b) Suggest a rearrangement of the transaction that would accomplish the same economic result and satisfy the requirements of a "B" reorganization.

Problem 13-14. Pursuant to a plan of reorganization, Mr. Baron exchanged 1,000 shares of Drape Corporation common stock, which he had purchased five years earlier for $50,000, for 1,700 shares of Del Ripe Corporation common stock, which had a fair market value of $62,000.

(a) What is Mr. Baron's realized gain on this exchange?

(b) What is his recognized gain?

(c) What is his basis in the Del Ripe stock?

(d) What difference, if any, would it make if the exchange were not made pursuant to a plan of reorganization?

(e) Assume that instead of a fair market value of $62,000, the Del Ripe stock that he received had a fair market value of $48,000. The exchange was made pursuant to a plan of reorganization. What is the tax effect to Mr. Baron?

(f) Would your answer to part (b) be changed if Mr. Baron were a majority stockholder in either Drape Corporation or Del Ripe Corporation rather than a minority stockholder in both?

Problem 13-15. Jim Wheeler operates his business as a corporation because he wants to protect his personal assets from claims by creditors. However, Jim is not happy with the fact that by doing so the corporation will pay federal income tax on any profits it may have. In order to reduce the corporate profit (taxable income) to zero, Jim has set his salary, which will be a deduction to the corporation, at $200,000 per year. As a result the corporation's taxable income for the year was only $3,000. The corporation paid the resulting $450 in federal income tax. If the IRS were to audit the corporate income tax return and determine that a reasonable salary for Jim should not be more than $125,000, and Jim could not demonstrate that the IRS was incorrect, how much additional tax would have to be paid by (a) Jim and (b) the corporation?

PROBLEMS WITH AN ASTERISK REQUIRE ADDITIONAL RESEARCH.

Problem 13-16.* Miller Corporation, the parent, and Baker Corporation, its wholly owned subsidiary, file a consolidated tax return on a calendar-year basis. In January of last year, Miller sold land to Baker for $70,000, its original cost. Miller had held the land as an investment for five years. Its fair market value at the time of the sale was $100,000. Baker, a housing subdeveloper, then held the land for sale to its customers in the ordinary course of its business. In August of this year, Baker sold the land to a customer for $130,000.

(a) Last year, when Miller sold the land to Baker, would there be a recognized gain to either corporation? If so, how much and what kind? Explain.

(b) This year, when Baker sold the land, would there be a recognized gain to either corporation? If so, how much and what kind? Explain.

(c) Would it have made any difference if Miller had just kept the land while Baker looked for a buyer, with Miller selling the land to the buyer upon Miller's "recommendation"?

(d) Suppose that Miller and Baker did not file a consolidated return but filed separate returns. How would that affect your answer to part (a)?

Problem 13-17.* Hal McKenzie owned all of the stock of the Freelance Corporation, which has been determined to be collapsible. Hal's basis in the stock was $50,000 and the corporation had accumulated earnings and profits of $2,000. He sold half of his stock for $40,000.

(a) What is the tax effect of the sale to Hal? Explain.

(b) What is the significance of the fact that the corporation was collapsible? Explain.

(c) Is there some action that Hal might have taken which would cause the corporation not to be collapsible? Explain.

PART THREE

OTHER OPPORTUNITIES

"I wish for happiness, long life, and a tax-free way to get the profits out of my closely held corporation." *"Try an ESOP!"*

14

fiduciaries

This book began with a discussion of individuals as taxpayers. In Chapter 10, the tax treatment of partnerships and partners was discussed. As we saw, a partnership normally is referred to as a "taxpayer" even though it does not pay federal income tax. Chapters 11 to 13 were concerned with various aspects of corporations as taxpayers. Many corporations pay federal income tax, but some do not, such as those that elect Subchapter S of the Internal Revenue Code.[1] This chapter deals with yet another entity, a fiduciary. In some cases a fiduciary must pay federal income tax, and under other factual circumstances will only report certain events to the government without paying tax. Some of the rules that apply to fiduciaries are different from those for other taxpayers. As a result, there are many unique tax planning opportunities for a fiduciary.

A fiduciary can be defined as a "person" (meaning an individual or a corporation) that holds property in trust for someone else. Also, the term "fiduciary" includes executors, administrators, guardians, receivers for individuals, and conservators, as well as trustees.[2] It also includes estates. Later we will examine the differences between the tax treatment of a trust and that of an estate. First, however, consider that a fiduciary holds *legal* title to property for the benefit of one or more others. The latter, in turn, are referred to as beneficiaries.

A trust can be created by a living person. Such a trust is called an *inter vivos* trust. Normally, the person creating the trust has some other person or persons in mind as beneficiary or beneficiaries. For example, assume that Billy Barnes transfers $200,000 cash into a trust. The terms of the trust require the trustee to invest in corporate stocks and to pay the resulting dividend income to Billy's mother, as beneficiary, for the remainder of her life. Upon his mother's death, the trust property is to be paid to Bigtime University, Billy's alma mater.

A different way to create a trust is to do so by operation of a will. This is called a *testamentary* trust. The terms of the legal document are set forth in the creator's will, but the trust does not come into existence, and hence is not operational until the creator dies.

An estate is the entity which acquires property upon a person's death, and manages and conserves that property until such time as it can be disbursed among the various heirs. An estate is also a fiduciary.

If a person dies without a will, he or she is said to have died "intestate." In such event, property owned by the decedent at the time of death will be distributed among the heirs according to the laws of the state, usually the state of residence of the decedent. The state "intestate" laws will also define who is entitled to be an heir of such a decedent. Where a decedent had a will, the estate will hold the property until such time as the terms of the will can be carried out (the process is called "probate") and the property distributed in accordance with the wishes of the decedent, as expressed in the will. Until the estate is terminated, it is a taxpayer, subject to certain requirements for filing a tax return and paying federal income tax.

Another operational difference between a

[1]See Chapter 11.

[2]The distinction between these functions is not important for purposes of this introductory discussion. Those who are interested in the technical differences in the definitions should consult a law dictionary, such as *Black's Law Dictionary*, published by West Publishing Co.

trust and an estate is the period of time each will exist. An estate will terminate when its purpose is completed, perhaps after having been in existence only a few months. Normally, it is a relatively temporary mechanism for handling the transition between the decedent's ownership and the final distribution of assets to pay all debts, taxes, legacies, and bequests.[3] There have been special situations, however, where an estate remained "open" for several years because of some special problem. A trust, on the other hand, will terminate only when the trust document provides for it to end.[4] Thus, if a trust were created for the life-time of a child, currently age 2, we could expect that trust to exist for a long-time, but not for an indefinite time.

The fiduciary is responsible for paying the federal income tax,[5] although the funds used for such payment will be the funds of the estate or trust and not the personal funds of the fiduciary.

There are some fundamental terms which should be understood in connection with fiduciaries:

Grantor: The person who creates a trust by transferring property (which may include cash) to it. Other terms for "grantor" are: "maker," "creator," and "settlor."

Testator: The grantor of a testamentary trust.

Trustee: The entity which acts on behalf of a trust or estate for the decisions, management, record keeping, and other duties and obligations of the trust. Remember, a trustee can be a corporation and many commercial banks, for example, have trust departments which perform this function. The trustee's relationship to the trust is somewhat analogous to that of the relationship of corporate officers to the corporation. That is to say, the trustee acts on behalf of the fiduciary rather than on his/her own behalf.

Beneficiary: The person or organization that will receive some benefits from the trust or the estate. The benefits usually consist of the receipt of money or other property. Where a beneficiary will receive, for example, payments of money from a trust for a fixed period of time, the beneficiary is said to have a "term" interest in the trust. For example, you might be the beneficiary of a trust under the terms of which you will receive $300 per month until such time as you reach age 30. Where the beneficiary will receive payments from a trust for life, the beneficiary is said to have a "life estate" or "life interest" in the trust. For example, you may be the beneficiary of a trust under the terms of which you will receive 10% of all of the trust income each year until you die, but you have no right to determine the disposition of the trust income or property after your death.

Remainderman: A type of beneficiary (person or other entity) that will receive the property at the time the trust ends. For example, you might be the remainderman of a trust under the terms of which your mother will receive all of the trust income for as long as she lives, and upon her death the trust will terminate with the trust property being distributed to you. You are the remainderman. You are also said to have a "remainder interest" in the trust. Where a charitable organization is the remainderman, the trust is called a charitable-remainder trust.[6] It is possible for a person to have both a term interest in the income of a trust and to be the remainderman. For example, it is not uncommon for a parent or grandparent to create a trust for a child, with the trust income to be paid to the child monthly until such time as the child reaches a certain age (e.g. 30) at which time the trust will terminate and the corpus will be transferred to the child. There is no limit on the number of beneficiaries or remaindermen. Thus, a grandparent could create a trust for the benefit of a large number of grandchildren, with each of them also sharing in the property as remaindermen upon termination. There is no requirement that all beneficiaries or remainder be treated equally. Normally, the term remainderman is not used to describe the person who receives property from an estate. Such a person is an heir, and is sometimes said to have received a bequest or devise.[7]

Corpus: The property which is held in a trust or in an estate. Sometimes "corpus" also is called "principal," "capital," or "body."

14.1 Grantor Trusts

Where a "grantor trust" is created, the grantor will be taxed upon the income from the trust property just as if the trust did not exist.[8] Also, the grantor will be entitled to deduct those expenditures made by the trust that would be deductible by him if he had paid them instead of the trust having paid them. When the trust terms include conditions that make it a "grantor trust," it is sometimes said that there was "prohibited re-

[3]See Treas. Reg. 1.641(b)-3.

[4]Unlike a corporation, which will exist for as long as there is a business purpose, a trust cannot be created so that it will exist for an indefinite future period. Known as the "anti-perpetuity rule," there is a requirement that a trust be terminated at some point. Generally, a trust may last for as long as 21 years after the death of a person who is named in the trust instrument. This is not a matter of tax law, but a matter of state statute, so the rules may be different in different states.

[5]IRC Sec. 641(b).

[6]IRC Sec. 664.

[7]Bequest and devise are used synonymously, but technically a bequest is a testamentary receipt of personal property, whereas a devise is a testamentary receipt of real property.

[8]IRC Sec. 671. This not only means that the gross income of the trust will be included in the grantor's personal gross income, but that the grantor will be entitled to the deductions and credits which would otherwise have been claimed by the fiduciary.

tained control" by the grantor. After reviewing the following requirements, it will be clear that only *inter vivos* trusts can be grantor trusts. The situation can be viewed in either of two ways:

a. There are certain requirements that must be satisfied in order for the grantor to obtain the tax advantage of not being required to include trust income in his/her personal gross income, or

b. There are certain limitations upon the creation of a trust, and, if these limitations are not met, the trust income will be taxed to the grantor as if the trust did not exist.

An exhaustive discussion of the various conditions that will result in a grantor trust is beyond the scope of this book. We will provide a few examples.

Revocable Trusts. Sometimes a grantor will create a trust but keep the right to revoke it. This is called a revocable trust.[9] For example, assume that Billy decides to create a trust for the benefit of a nephew. However, Billy is concerned that the nephew may "go astray" in his personal life. Therefore, Billy reserves the right to revoke (terminate) the trust at any time. The trust will be a grantor trust because of the revocable provision.

Reversionary Trusts. A grantor may create a trust with a provision that the property will revert to the grantor at some specified future time or in the event certain conditions exist. Such an arrangement is called a "reversionary trust," and the grantor is said to have retained a reversionary interest.[10] For example, Billy might create a trust under which the trust income will be paid to a niece for 12 years after which the trust will terminate and the corpus will be paid back to Billy. The trust will be a grantor trust.

There is an exception. If the value of the reversionary interest is less than 5% of the value of the trust corpus, such a reversionary interest will not cause the trust to be a grantor trust.

Retained Control. Another possibility is that a grantor will create a trust such that he can continue to control (change) who shall benefit from it, or change the extent of the beneficial interest.[11] For example, assume that a grantor created a trust with income to be paid equally to her two children. However, the grantor retained the right to change the division from 50-50 to some other ratio, or the right to add a third beneficiary. The trust will be a grantor trust.

The prohibited retained control does not mean that the trust agreement must "set in concrete" all of the provisions relative to the beneficiaries. If the trust agreement allows the trustee to make decisions relative to who shall be a beneficiary (within a defined set of persons, for example) and to what extent, then it is the trustee who has control and not the grantor. For example, a common trust arrangement is that a beneficiary shall receive as much as is required for normal living expenses, and the trustee shall determine that amount. Any trust income not distributed to the beneficiary shall be retained by the trust or distributed to a different beneficiary. Such an arrangement is frequently referred to as a "discretionary trust," meaning that the trustee has the power to decide those matters.

Retained Benefit. If the grantor will continue to benefit from the trust income, the trust will be a grantor trust.[12] For example, if you created a trust and the income from the trust property were to be used to support your minor child for whom you have an obligation for support, you would continue to benefit from the trust property. The trust will be a grantor trust.

Retained Administrative Powers. Yet another possibility is that a trust will be created and the grantor will retain certain administrative powers.[13] A common arrangement is where the grantor names himself as trustee. Another is where the grantor reserves the right to appoint a different trustee at any time. Such trusts will be grantor trusts for purposes of federal income tax.

As can be seen from the examples given above, trusts may be created for a variety of valid reasons that have nothing to do with income taxes. The remainder of the discussion in this chapter, however, will be concerned with trusts which have a primary objective, if not a sole objective, of saving income taxes. Thus, unless otherwise stated, all trusts discussed in this chapter have the following minimum characteristics which will assure that they are not "grantor trusts:"

a. Irrevocable.

b. No reversionary interest by the grantor, or if there is a reversionary interest its value is less than 5% of the value of the trust property.[14]

c. No prohibited beneficial interest, enjoyment, control, or administrative power has been retained by the grantor.

[9]IRC Sec. 676.

[10]IRC Sec. 673. If a reversionary trust was created prior to March 2, 1986, but with a provision that there would be no reversion within the first ten years following its creation (unless the reversion was to be caused only by the death of the income beneficiary), then the income will not be taxed to the grantor. Generally, such trusts are called "Clifford trusts" or "short-term trusts." Also, see note #14 below.

[11]IRC Sec. 674.

[12]IRC Sec. 677.

[13]IRC Sec. 675.

[14]IRC Sec. 673(a). Another exception exists if the beneficiary of the trust is the grantor's child, grandchild, or great-grandchild who is less than 21 years old when the trust is created, and the reversion will occur only upon the death of the beneficiary. Such a reversionary interest will not result in the trust income being taxed to the grantor. IRC Sec. 673(b).

A brief additional explanation of item "b" above may be helpful. As explained earlier, a reversionary interest in a trust is a provision in the trust agreement which will permit or require that the corpus be paid back to the grantor at some time or under some circumstances. For example, assume that Billy Barnes is the creator of a trust. Trust income will be paid to Billy's mother as long as she is alive and Billy retains a reversionary interest that requires the corpus to be returned to Billy upon her death. The value of that reversionary interest depends upon, among other things, the expected time that will elapse between the creation of the trust and the event that will result in the reversion to Billy. The arithmetic calculations may become very complex, but the concept is rather simple. If Billy's mother is elderly at the time the trust is created, so that the reversion can be expected to occur within a relatively few years, then the value of Billy's interest is high relative to the value of the trust property. For example, if mother's life expectancy is only seven years, then Billy's interest might be 50% or more of the total. (The exact answer, of course, depends upon the discount rate which is used to calculate the present value.) If Billy's mother has a life expectancy of 40 years, then Billy is not expected to receive the property for 40 years and the present value of Billy's interest is substantially less. If the reversionary interest is calculated to be more than 5% of the value of the trust property, then the trust is a grantor trust. If it is 5% or less, then the trust is not a grantor trust.

A grantor trust may be required to file an income tax return (Form 1041) despite the fact that the grantor will pay tax on all of the trust income and the trust will not pay tax. Note Figure 14-1 (see p. 14-8) in the upper left hand corner. The appropriate box would have to be checked for grantor trust.

14.2 Nongrantor Trusts

A nongrantor trust is one which contains none of the conditions that will cause the trust income automatically to be taxed to the grantor as described in the previous section. In the remainder of this chapter, we will discuss nongrantor trusts and estates.

Consider an example. Assume that a wealthy individual (the grantor) wants to put some corporate bonds into a trust instead of making a direct gift to her father. The grantor has several purposes in mind other than tax savings. She wants assurance that her father will not mismanage the property, or she wants to alleviate him from the responsibility of managing the property. She also wants to provide financially for her sister and children for a specific period of time. After her father's death, and the other family members have been cared for, the trust will terminate and the property will be transferred to a charity.

The trust instrument (contract) is prepared. It provides that the trust department of the Mountain National Bank will be the trustee, and sets forth the exact terms under which the trustee is to operate and manage the trust. The trust agreement, once executed, cannot be revoked by the grantor, and there are no other terms in the trust that will cause it to be a grantor trust. The bonds are transferred to the bank.

The bank has legal title to, and possession of, assets which it owns for somebody else (the beneficiaries). As a fiduciary, the bank collects the income (interest, in this example) and pays the income to the beneficiaries in accordance with the instructions in the trust agreement. Throughout the term of the trust, the trustee, as directed by the trust instrument, will have responsibility to monitor the investment and to perform whatever duties are required. For example, the trust may permit the trustee to sell the bonds and buy different bonds, or even stock, under certain stated conditions. Also, the trust contract may permit the trustee to decide if and when the bonds should be sold and other securities purchased. Upon termination of the trust, the trustee will have the responsibility to see that the trust corpus is distributed to the remainderman in accordance with the terms of the trust instrument. Since an income tax return will be required for the trust each year, the trustee will be responsible for that also.[15]

The income tax rules that determine what is and is not gross income, and what can and cannot be deducted, are substantially the same for a fiduciary as they are for individuals.[16] The important differences will be discussed in this chapter.

A fiduciary is permitted to deduct reasonable trustees' fees and other expenses, including interest expense, incurred in administering the trust property. There is no standard deduction for fiduciaries as there is for individuals.[17] Instead of the personal exemption deduction that is available for individuals,[18] fiduciaries can deduct what is called a "personal exemption" as follows:[19]

Simple trust	$300
Complex trust	100
Estate	600

[15]IRC Sec. 6012(b).
[16]IRC Sec. 641(b).
[17]See Chapter 1, particularly Figure 1-2, and Chapter 4.
[18]See Chapter 4. The personal exemption deduction for 1990 is $2,050 for individuals with price level adjustments each year.
[19]IRC Sec. 642(b).

The terms "simple" and "complex" are defined and discussed in the sections that follow.

Fiduciaries are also subject to a different tax rate schedule.[20] There is no tax table such as that for individuals which is reproduced in Appendix 1-A. The tax rates for fiduciaries will be adjusted each year for a price level factor in the same manner as for individuals, as explained in Chapter 1.

TAX PLANNING TIP: Although there may be no tax advantages in doing so, trusts are sometimes used for other purposes, such as (1) passing the management of trust assets to another party, (2) avoiding probate costs upon death, or (3) ensuring that a beneficiary who might not use property wisely will not be able to obtain control of the whole corpus. Tax savings goals and nontax goals must both be considered when plans are being made.

An example will be helpful. Assume that a trust or an estate had 1990 taxable income of $20,000. (See the rate schedule at Appendix 14-A.) Keep in mind that this means that the eligible deductions have already been taken into account. The tax rate schedule provides that the tax is:

$3,253.50 + 33% ($20,000 − $14,150) = $5,184

Note that the marginal rate in this example is 33%, but that it drops to 28% for taxable income in excess of $28,320. The reason for the extra 5% rate is the same as it was for individuals,[21] i.e., the phase-out of the 15% rate bracket.[22] Thus, where 1990 taxable income for a fiduciary is in excess of $28,320, the effect is a "flat tax" of 28% on all taxable income. Where taxable income is below $28,320, part of it will be taxed at the 15% rate.

14.3 Simple Trusts

A "simple" trust is one that is required to distribute all of its income currently, has no charitable beneficiary, and does not make a distribution of corpus during the year.[23] Figure 14-1 illustrates a fiduciary tax return for a simple trust (Form 1041). A 1989 tax form is used because the 1990 form is not available as this book goes to press. In this illustration, the only source of trust income is interest. The deductions include the fiduciary's fee and the fee for attorney, accountant, or tax return preparation.

[20]IRC Sec. 1(e). The rates are reproduced in Appendix 14-A.
[21]See Chapter, section 1.3.4.
[22]There is no phase-out of the exemption deduction.
[23]IRC Sec. 651.

Note that the expenses mentioned above, if incurred by an individual, might not result in a deduction because of the 2% of adjusted gross income "floor" that applies to miscellaneous itemized deductions.[24] The same rule may be applied to a grantor-trust because it is defined as a "pass through" entity, just as partnerships and Subchapter S corporations are "pass through" entities.[25] Hence, on Form 1041 (Figure 14-1(a)) at line 15 (b), there is provision for reduction of certain expenses by 2% of AGI. [26] Estates and nongrantor trusts are not "pass through" entities and, hence, neither the fiduciary nor the beneficiary is subject to the 2% "floor" reduction for certain expenses. Fiduciaries which are not "pass through" entities will deduct all ordinary and necessary business expenses.[27]

The other deduction illustrated in our example is for distributions made by the fiduciary to beneficiaries.[28] In our example, all of the trust's income was distributed, leaving no taxable income.

If less than all of the income had been distributed, then there would be a deduction only for the amount distributed. The trust would not be a simple trust. There would have been taxable income and some tax liability. For example, assume 1989 gross income was $34,000, and that the distribution was $10,000 and expenses were $1,400:

Gross income		$34,000
Deductions:		
Expenses	$ 1,400	
Distributions	10,000	
Exemption	100[29]	11,500
Taxable income		$22,500

Tax = $3,104 + 33% ($22,500 − $13,500) = $6,074

For a trust to receive a deduction for a "distribution" to a beneficiary, it is not necessary for an actual cash or property transfer to have taken place. If an amount is permanently set aside by the trust and held for the benefiary rather than paid to the beneficiary, the deduction is allowed.[30]

[24]IRC Sec. 67. See Chapter 3 at Section 3.8.10.
[25]Temp. Reg. 1.67-2T(g).
[26]The IRS has the authority to issue Regulations which will result in application of the 2% "floor" to a beneficiary of a simple trust. See IRC Sec. 67(c). As of the time this is being written, such Regulations have not been issued. Where the reduction will apply, it will be the beneficiary and not the fiduciary who will be required to make the reduction.
[27]IRC Secs. 161 and 162. See Chapter 7.
[28]IRC Secs. 651, and 661.
[29]Note that the trust would be a complex trust. A complex trust is one which is not a simple trust. If a trust is not required to distribute all of its income for a year, it will not be a simple trust for that year.
[30]IRC Sec. 651.

FIGURE 14-1(a)

Form **1041** Department of the Treasury—Internal Revenue Service
U.S. Fiduciary Income Tax Return **1989** IRS Use Only

For the calendar year 1989 or fiscal year beginning , 1989, and ending , 19 OMB No. 1545-0092

Check applicable boxes:	Name of estate or trust (grantor type trust, see instructions)	Employer identification number
☐ Decedent's estate	BILLY BARNES TRUST	86-0001034
☒ Simple trust	Name and title of fiduciary	Date entity created
☐ Complex trust	MOUNTAIN BANK TRUST CO.	1-2-87
☐ Grantor type trust	Address of fiduciary (number and street or P.O. Box)	Nonexempt charitable and split-interest trusts, check applicable boxes (see instructions):
☐ Bankruptcy estate	ONE NEW YORK PLAZA	
☐ Family estate trust	City, state, and ZIP code	
☐ Pooled income fund	PHOENIX, ARINONA 85012	☐ Described in section 4947(a)(1)
☐ Initial return		☐ Not a private foundation
☐ Amended return		
☐ Final return	Number of Schedules K-1 attached (see instructions) ▶ 1	☐ Described in section 4947(a)(2)

Income

Line	Description			No.	Amount
1	Dividends			1	
2	Interest income			2	34,000 —
3	Income (or losses) from partnerships, other estates, or other trusts (see instructions)			3	
4	Net rental and royalty income (or loss) (attach Schedule E (Form 1040))			4	
5	Net business and farm income (or loss) (attach Schedules C and F (Form 1040))			5	
6	Capital gain (or loss) (attach Schedule D (Form 1041))			6	
7	Ordinary gain (or loss) (attach Form 4797)			7	
8	Other income (state nature of income)			8	
9	**Total** income (add lines 1 through 8) ▶			9	34,000 —

Deductions

Line	Description	No.	Amount	No.	Amount
10	Interest	10			
11	Taxes	11			
12	Fiduciary fees	12	1,000 —		
13	Charitable deduction (from Schedule A, line 6)	13			
14	Attorney, accountant, and return preparer fees	14	400 —		
15a	Other deductions NOT subject to the 2% floor (attach schedule)	15a			
b	Allowable miscellaneous itemized deductions subject to the 2% floor	15b			
c	Add lines 15a and 15b	15c			
16	**Total** (add lines 10 through 15c)			16	1,400 —
17	Adjusted total income (or loss) (subtract line 16 from line 9). Enter here and on Schedule B, line 1 ▶			17	32,600 —
18	Income distribution deduction (from Schedule B, line 17) (see instructions) (attach Schedules K-1 (Form 1041))			18	32,600 —
19	Estate tax deduction (including certain generation-skipping transfer taxes) (attach computation)			19	
20	Exemption			20	300 —
21	**Total** deductions (add lines 18 through 20) ▶			21	32,900 —

Tax and Payments — Please attach check or money order here

Line	Description	No.	Amount
22	Taxable income of fiduciary (subtract line 21 from line 17)	22	-0-
23	**Total** tax (from Schedule G, line 7) ▶	23	-0-
24a	Payments: 1989 estimated tax payments and amount applied from 1988 return	24a	
b	Treated as credited to beneficiaries	24b	
c	Subtract line 24b from line 24a	24c	
d	Tax paid with extension of time to file: ☐ Form 2758 ☐ Form 8736 ☐ Form 8800	24d	
e	Federal income tax withheld	24e	
	Credits: f Form 2439 ....; g Form 4136 ....; h Other ....; Total ▶	24i	
25	**Total** payments (add lines 24c through 24e, and 24i) ▶	25	
26	If line 23 is larger than line 25, enter **TAX DUE**	26	
27	If line 25 is larger than line 23, enter **OVERPAYMENT**	27	
28	Amount of line 27 to be: a **Credited to 1990 estimated tax** ▶ ....; b **Refunded** ▶	28	
29	**Penalty** for underpayment of estimated tax (see instructions)	29	

Please Sign Here

Under penalties of perjury, I declare that I have examined this return, including accompanying schedules and statements, and to the best of my knowledge and belief, it is true, correct, and complete. Declaration of preparer (other than fiduciary) is based on all information of which preparer has any knowledge.

▶ Charles C. Smith, V.P.	3-3-90	▶ 86 0000001
Signature of fiduciary or officer representing fiduciary	Date	EIN of fiduciary (see instructions)

Paid Preparer's Use Only

Preparer's signature ▶	Date	Check if self-employed ▶ ☐	Preparer's social security no.
Firm's name (or yours if self-employed) and address ▶		E.I. No. ▶	
		ZIP code ▶	

For Paperwork Reduction Act Notice, see page 1 of the separate Instructions. Form **1041** (1989)

FIGURE 14-1(b)

Schedule A **Charitable Deduction—Do not complete for a simple trust or a pooled income fund.**
(Write the name and address of each charitable organization to whom your contributions total $3,000 or more on an attached sheet.)

1	Amounts paid or permanently set aside for charitable purposes from current year's gross income	1	
2	Tax-exempt interest allocable to charitable distribution (see instructions)	2	
3	Subtract line 2 from line 1	3	
4	Enter the net short-term capital gain and the net long-term capital gain of the current tax year allocable to corpus paid or permanently set aside for charitable purposes (see instructions)	4	
5	Amounts paid or permanently set aside for charitable purposes from gross income of a prior year (see instructions)	5	
6	Total (add lines 3 through 5). Enter here and on page 1, line 13	6	

Schedule B **Income Distribution Deduction (see instructions)**

1	Adjusted total income (from page 1, line 17) (see instructions)	1	32,600 —
2	Adjusted tax-exempt interest (see instructions)	2	
3	Net gain shown on Schedule D (Form 1041), line 17, column (a). (If net loss, enter zero.)	3	
4	Enter amount from Schedule A, line 4	4	
5	Long-term capital gain included on Schedule A, line 1	5	
6	Short-term capital gain included on Schedule A, line 1	6	
7	If the amount on page 1, line 6, is a capital loss, enter here as a positive figure	7	
8	If the amount on page 1, line 6, is a capital gain, enter here as a negative figure	8	
9	Distributable net income (combine lines 1 through 8)	9	32,600 —
10	Amount of income for the tax year determined under the governing instrument (accounting income) 10		
11	Amount of income required to be distributed currently (see instructions)	11	32,600 —
12	Other amounts paid, credited, or otherwise required to be distributed (see instructions)	12	
13	Total distributions (add lines 11 and 12). (If greater than line 10, see instructions.)	13	32,600 —
14	Enter the total amount of tax-exempt income included on line 13	14	— 0 —
15	Tentative income distribution deduction (subtract line 14 from line 13)	15	32,600 —
16	Tentative income distribution deduction (subtract line 2 from line 9)	16	32,600 —
17	Income distribution deduction. Enter the smaller of line 15 or line 16 here and on page 1, line 18	17	32,600 —

Schedule G **Tax Computation (see instructions)**

1	Tax: a Tax rate schedule ....; b Other taxes .... Total ▶			1c	
2a	Foreign tax credit (attach Form 1116)	2a			
b	Credit for fuel produced from a nonconventional source	2b			
c	General business credit. Check if from: ☐ Form 3800 or ☐ Form (specify) ▶	2c			
d	Credit for prior year minimum tax (attach Form 8801)	2d			
3	**Total** credits (add lines 2a through 2d) ▶			3	
4	Subtract line 3 from line 1c			4	
5	Recapture taxes. Check if from: ☐ Form 4255 ☐ Form 8611			5	
6	Alternative minimum tax (attach Form 8656)			6	
7	**Total** tax (add lines 4 through 6). Enter here and on page 1, line 23 ▶			7	

Other Information (see instructions)

		Yes	No
1	If the fiduciary's name or address has changed, enter the old information ▶		
2	Did the estate or trust receive tax-exempt income? (If "Yes," attach a computation of the allocation of expenses.) Enter the amount of tax-exempt interest income and exempt-interest dividends ▶ $		X
3	Did the estate or trust have any passive activity losses? (If "Yes," enter these losses on **Form 8582**, Passive Activity Loss Limitations, to figure the allowable loss.)		X
4	Did the estate or trust receive all or any part of the earnings (salary, wages, and other compensation) of any individual by reason of a contract assignment or similar arrangement?		X
5	At any time during the tax year, did the estate or trust have an interest in or a signature or other authority over a financial account in a foreign country (such as a bank account, securities account, or other financial account)? (See the instructions for exceptions and filing requirements for Form TD F 90-22.1.) If "Yes," enter the name of the foreign country ▶		X
6	Was the estate or trust the grantor of, or transferor to, a foreign trust which existed during the current tax year, whether or not the estate or trust has any beneficial interest in it? (If "Yes," you may have to file Form 3520, 3520-A, or 926.)		X
7	Check this box if this entity has filed or is required to file **Form 8264**, Application for Registration of a Tax Shelter ▶ ☐		
8	Check this box if this entity is a complex trust making the section 663(b) election ▶ ☐		
9	Check this box to make a section 643(e)(3) election (attach Schedule D (Form 1041)) ▶ ☐		
10	Check this box if the decedent's estate has been open for more than 2 years ▶ ☐		
11	Check this box if the trust is a participant in a Common Trust Fund that was required to adopt a calendar year ▶ ☐		

FIGURE 14-2

SCHEDULE K-1 (Form 1041)

Department of the Treasury
Internal Revenue Service

Beneficiary's Share of Income, Deductions, Credits, Etc.—1989

for the calendar year 1989, or fiscal year

beginning ...., 1989, ending ...., 19 .....

Complete a separate Schedule K-1 for each beneficiary.

OMB No. 1545-0092

1989

Name of estate or trust: BILLY BARNES TRUST

Beneficiary's identifying number ▶ 777-55-3333

Estate's or trust's employer identification number ▶ 86-000000 1

Beneficiary's name, address, and ZIP code:
VICTOR H. PASSETTI
1712 YORK ST.
PASADENA, IOWA 52241

Fiduciary's name, address, and ZIP code:
MOUNTAIN BANK TRUST CO.
ONE NEW YORK PLAZA
PHOENIX, ARIZONA 85012

Reminder: *If you received a short year 1987 Schedule K-1 that was from a trust required to adopt a calendar year, be sure to include one-fourth of those amounts reported as income, in addition to the items reported on this Schedule K-1, on the appropriate lines of your 1989 Form 1040 and related schedules.*

(a) Allocable share item	(b) Amount	(c) Calendar year 1989 Form 1040 filers enter the amounts in column (b) on:
1 Interest	32,600	Schedule B, Part I, line 2
2 Dividends		Schedule B, Part II, line 4
3a Net short-term capital gain		Schedule D, line 5, column (g)
b Net long-term capital gain		Schedule D, line 12, column (g)
4a Other taxable income: (itemize)		Schedule E, Part III
(1) Rental, rental real estate, and business income from activities acquired before 10/23/86		
(2) Rental, rental real estate, and business income from activities acquired after 10/22/86		
(3) Other income		
b Depreciation, including cost recovery (itemize):		
(1) Attributable to line 4a(1)		
(2) Attributable to line 4a(2)		
(3) Attributable to line 4a(3)		
c Depletion (itemize):		
(1) Attributable to line 4a(1)		
(2) Attributable to line 4a(2)		
(3) Attributable to line 4a(3)		
d Amortization (itemize):		
(1) Attributable to line 4a(1)		
(2) Attributable to line 4a(2)		
(3) Attributable to line 4a(3)		
5 Income for minimum tax purposes		
6 Income for regular tax purposes (add lines 1 through 4a)		
7 Adjustment for minimum tax purposes (subtract line 6 from line 5)		Form 6251, line 4t
8 Estate tax deduction (including certain generation-skipping transfer taxes) (attach computation)		Schedule A, line 25
9 Excess deductions on termination (attach computation)		Schedule A, line 21
10 Foreign taxes (list on a separate sheet)		Form 1116 or Schedule A (Form 1040), line 7
11 Tax preference items (itemize):		
a Accelerated depreciation		(Include on the applicable line of Form 6251)
b Depletion		
c Amortization		
12 Other (itemize):		
a Trust payments of estimated taxes credited to you		Form 1040, line 57
b Tax-exempt interest		Form 1040, line 8b
c Short-term capital loss carryover		Schedule D, line 6, column (f)
d Long-term capital loss carryover		Schedule D, line 15, column (f)
e		(Include on the applicable line of appropriate tax form)
f		
g		

For Paperwork Reduction Act Notice, see page 1 of the Instructions for Form 1041. **Schedule K-1 (Form 1041) 1989**

The beneficiary is required to include in gross income the amount that is deducted by the fiduciary.[31] This eliminates the double taxation of fiduciary income. The income will be taxed either to the beneficiary or to the fiduciary, but not to both. A beneficiary will receive a Schedule K-1 indicating the amount of income from the trust or estate. (See Fig. 14-2.) This schedule is similar to the K-1 used by partnerships to report the amount, and kind, of income taxable to the partners. Note the instructions on the K-1 concerning which form or schedule the beneficiary is to use to report the income. In our example, the trust income was interest.

A common trust provision, where the trust assets include property subject to depreciation deductions, is for the trust instrument to require that the trust add to corpus each year an amount equal to the depreciation deduction so that such amount will not be distributed. "Income" will not include an amount equal to the depreciation deduction if the trust agreement so provides. Thus, where there is a remainderman who is a different person from the income beneficiary, an amount equal to the original corpus is retained for ultimate transfer to that remainderman.

Before moving on to a discussion of complex trusts, we should note three other important points. First, a simple trust is one which *by its terms* requires that all income be distributed.[32] Thus, even if all income is distributed by a trust, it will not be a simple trust unless the trust agreement required such action. For example, a trust agreement might grant the power to the trustee to determine each year how much to distribute to a beneficiary, based on certain criteria, such as need. If the trustee determined that it was prudent to distribute all income, but the trust agreement did not *require* such a distribution, then the trust would not be a simple trust.[33]

Second, the determination of simple vs. complex is made each year, independent of other years. Therefore, a trust could be simple one year and complex another year. For example, a trust might be required to distribute all of its income in a year if certain conditions exist. If those conditions do not exist, the trust is not required to distribute all income.

Third, where a distribution is made, whether required or not, the fiduciary must treat any distribution as having been made from the current year's income (to the extent thereof). Only after all of the current income has been distributed, can a fiduciary make a further distribution to a beneficiary and treat that distribution as having been made from corpus.[34]

[31]IRC Sec. 552 and Sec. 662.

[32]This assumes that the other requirement, no charitable distributions, is satisfied as well.

[33]At this point, you should understand that there are at least three possible definitions of "income." One is the result of the tax rules and another can be the result of the trust instrument's specific definition. The third, of course, is the definition resulting from the application of "generally accepted accounting principles." In any given situation, each can be different from the other.

TAX PLANNING TIP: A trust can be used as a way of removing income from the grantor's gross income and having it included in the gross income of a beneficiary or of the trust itself. The essential requirement is that the grantor must be willing to part with ownership and control of the property. There can be no revocable provision, and no reversion, (unless its value is less than 5% of the value of the property).

14.4 Complex Trusts

A complex trust is defined as any trust which is not a simple trust. Thus, a trust will be complex if it is not required to distribute all of its income, or if it has a beneficiary that is a charity. For example, assume that a trust agreement provides that only half of the trust's gross income is to be distributed currently to a beneficiary, with the other half being accumulated for a later distribution to a different beneficiary. The later distribution need not coincide with the termination of the trust.

The trust income tax return would be different from that shown in Figure 14-1 in the following ways:

1. In the upper left hand corner, the box for complex trust would be checked.
2. The deduction for exemption would be $100 instead of $300.
3. The deduction for distributions to beneficiaries would reflect the fact that only one-half of the income had been distributed.

Although not in the format of the Form 1041, the following example reflects the numbers:

Gross income		$40,000
Deductions:		
Distributions	$20,000	
Exemption	100	
Expenses	1,000	21,100
Taxable income		$18,900

1990 tax on $18,900 = $3,253.50 + 33% ($18,900 − $14,150) = $4,821

[34]IRC Sec. 662.

The trust tax return is unique. It follows the *conduit theory*[35] to the extent of the amount distributed to the current income beneficiary. As noted before, the trust deducts the amount distributed to the beneficiary and the beneficiary includes in gross income that same amount. The trust is also treated as a taxable entity, paying tax on income *not* distributed.

Generally, if a beneficiary of a trust or estate receives a distribution from corpus, that amount is not taxable to the beneficiary. Assume that a trustee wanted to distribute corpus to the beneficiary instead of income. The desired result might be to cause the trust to be taxable on the entire income (since it was not distributed) and cause the beneficiary to have a receipt which would not be included in gross income because it would be a receipt of principal rather than income. The tax rules prohibit this kind of potential manipulation on the part of the fiduciary. The rule is that *any* distribution will be treated as a distribution of income, to the extent of income.[36] Thus, a fiduciary can make a distribution to a beneficiary which will be treated as having been paid from corpus only after all of the income for the current year has been distributed. This is the tax result even if the trust instrument, for example, provides that the trustee can, or should, distribute principal to cover an emergency such as medical expenses.

If a fiduciary does not distribute income, which means that the fiduciary will pay tax on it, that income will then be *treated as* corpus so that when a beneficiary does receive it, it will not be taxed again. The concept is similar to that in a partnership. In that case, a partner, once having paid tax on his/her share of partnership taxable income, may later receive the amount free of tax. In this case, the previously taxed amount can also be distributed tax-free, although it was the fiduciary that paid the tax. We will illustrate a modification later in connection with an "accumulation distribution."

Tax savings can result from the shifting of income from the higher tax brackets of a grantor to lower tax brackets of a trust or a beneficiary. The optimum shift in income yielding the largest possible tax savings will result when all three taxpayers have the same marginal bracket after the income allocation.

Assume that Billy Barnes is in the 33% tax bracket and wants part of the interest income received from corporate bonds to be taxed to a brother and a niece each of whom will be in the 15% bracket. Billy creates an irrevocable trust and transfers bonds with a face value of $100,000 to the trust.[37] The bonds are expected to generate $9,000 of interest income each year. By removing this income from tax at 33%, Billy saves $2,970 in federal tax. If the trust does not distribute any of the income, then it will pay tax on taxable income of $8,900 ($9,000 gross income less the exemption of $100 for a complex trust). The tax (at 1990 rates) will be $1,784. Thus, the net tax savings will be:

Tax savings to Billy	$2,970
Tax to trust	1,784
Net savings	$1,186

This example assumes that the trustee will not charge a fee for managing the trust, which might be the case if another family member or a friend were the trustee. If Billy obtained the services of a commercial trust company or bank there would be a fee, but the fee would be deductible in determining the trust's taxable income. Assume that the trustee's fee is 2% of trust income:

Gross income		$9,000
Fee	$180	
Exemption	100	280
Taxable income		$8,720

Tax (1990 rates) on $8,720 would be $1,733. The net savings have been reduced to $1,057. Note that the *after tax* cost of the trustee's fee is not $180, but $130 because the trust's tax liability was reduced by $50 as the result of the $180 deduction.

Let's change the example. Assume now that the trust were to distribute $4,000 to a beneficiary and retain the balance, after expenses. The tax result would be:

	Trust	*Beneficiary*
Gross income	$9,000	$4,000
Deductions:		
Distributions	(4,000)	
Exemption	(100)	
Expenses	(180)	
Taxable income	$4,720	$4,000

(We assume that the additional $4,000 of gross income to the beneficiary would not result in a change in any deductions, and that the beneficiary will be taxed at 15% on this additional income.)

Tax savings to Billy (same as before)	$2,970
Tax on $4,720 to trust at 15%	(708)
Tax on $4,000 to beneficiary at 15%	(600)
Total tax savings	1,662
Trustee fee	(180)
Net savings from trust arrangement	$1,482

[35]See Section 10.3 in Chapter 10.
[36]IRC Sec. 662.

[37]This transfer could result in Billy being liable for some federal gift tax. See Chapter 15, starting at Section 15.12.

TAX PLANNING TIP: It is a mistake to think that trusts are only useful as a tax benefit for wealthy persons. The $500 standard deduction that each child could *use if he or she had income can be used to shelter investment income diverted to a trust that would otherwise be taxed to the parents, for example. This remains true even for children under 14 whose income in excess of $1,000 will ordinarily be taxed at their parents' rates. Even a moderate tax savings* per year *can mean a substantial accumulation over a period of ten years or more.*

14.5 "Source Characteristic" of Fiduciary Items

In earlier chapters, we saw the "source characteristic" of income, deductions, and credits is retained for partnerships and Subchapter S corporations. This means, for example, that if a partnership recognizes long-term capital gain, the pro rata share of that long-term capital gain will be reported by each partner as if he/she recognized it personally rather than through the partnership. In the case of partnerships and Subchapter S corporations, it is not necessary for the partner or shareholder to have received a distribution in order to have the income retain some special source characteristic. Earlier in this chapter we said that some fiduciaries are not "pass through" entities for purposes of the 2% "floor" on the deduction for miscellaneous items. However, the concept of retention of "source characteristic" does apply to fiduciaries and the beneficiaries, but with a slight difference. Only the income which is *distributed* retains the source characteristic to the beneficiary. For example, if a trust were to recognize long-term capital gain,[38] which was distributed to a beneficiary, the beneficiary would treat the income as long-term capital gain on his/her personal tax return. If the trust did not distribute the gain, then the trust would report the long-term capital gain, with whatever special tax treatment might be afforded that kind of income. The same concept applies to deductions and credits.

Other examples are interest and dividend income which the trust distributes to a beneficiary. This is important because these "passive" sources of income could change the amount which the beneficiary could deduct for investment interest expense, for example.[39] Nontaxable income also retains its characteristic as such. Thus, if a trust earns interest from state or local government bonds, and makes a distribution to a beneficiary, the beneficiary will be treated as if he/she received the interest directly rather than through the trust. Such interest will not become part of the beneficiary's gross income, but it could result in a change, for example, in the amount of social security benefits that are taxed to the beneficiary.[40] The importance of the retention of the "source characteristic" of certain deductions is that the beneficiary *might* be impacted by a limitation on the amount of a deduction.[41] For example, where a trust owns depreciable property, the depreciation deduction may be allocated between the fiduciary and the beneficiary.[42] The same is true for depletion. In Chapter 16, we will see that there is something called "tax preference items" that must be taken into consideration for purposes of the "alternative minimum tax."[43] Where the fiduciary has any tax preference item related to a distribution, that characteristic will pass through and be a tax preference item to the beneficiary.

Credits might be retained by a fiduciary if there is no distribution to beneficiaries. Since the fiduciary may have a tax liability (before credits), that tax could be reduced by any applicable credit. On the other hand, if the fiduciary distributes all income (which is a deduction) then there will be no tax and the fiduciary would have no need for a credit. The credit is passed through to the beneficiary.

The mechanism for reporting the pass through to the beneficiary is a Form K-1, such as is illustrated in Figure 14-2.

14.6 Distributable Net Income

Our discussion of fiduciaries would not be complete without a brief consideration of distributable net income (DNI). DNI has two purposes. First, DNI represents the maximum amount beneficiaries are required to include in gross income. Remember, a beneficiary who receives a distribution is treated as having received fiduciary *income*, to the extent thereof. If a beneficiary receives distributions which are more than *income*, the excess is treated as a distribution of corpus

[38]See Chapter 6.
[39]See Chapter 4 for discussion of limitation on deduction for investment interest expense. See also, Chapter 17.

[40]See Chapter 2 for discussion of the amount of social security benefits which must be included in gross income.
[41]See, for example, Chapter 17 concerning the deductibility of certain "passive losses."
[42]Whether this is done or not will depend upon the terms of the trust agreement. Clearly, that is something which the grantor should consider at the time the trust document is created.
[43]One example of a tax preference item is where a depletion deduction exists even though the basis of the property is zero. See Chapter 9.

and is not included in the beneficiary's gross income. Secondly, DNI represents the maximum amount which the fiduciary can deduct as the result of distributions to beneficiaries. Remember, a fiduciary gets to take a deduction for distributions to a beneficiary, to the extent that the distribution is from *income*. But, what is income? "Income" can be defined by the trust agreement, but "distributable net income" is defined by the tax rules.

Earlier we mentioned that there may be a distinction between "income" and capital gains, as in the example where all "income" is required to be distributed to a beneficiary but capital gains are retained by the fiduciary for ultimate distribution to the remainderman. Such a trust would be a "simple" trust because all *income* is required to be distributed each year. Income may not include capital gains. Again, what is *income*?

Income is what the grantor has defined it to be in the trust instrument. Not only does this mean that the trust document can define "income" in the sense of the *sources*, i.e. interest, dividend, capital gain, but it can also define which expenses, if any, are to be allocated to *income* and which expenses are to be allocated to corpus. Hence, the term "net income" is used. In the absence of a definition in the trust document, state law will govern. A grantor is not required to define "income" the same way as "income" is defined by the tax rules.[44] Although the trustee might be required, for example, to distribute all "income" as defined by the trust instrument, what the trust might retain could include income as defined by the tax rules. Consequently, the trust could have taxable income and pay income tax because not all "taxable income" was distributed.

The following example will illustrate the use of DNI. (For a more detailed statement of the DNI computation, see Appendix 14-B).

The Hard Rock Trust provides that the trustee can determine the amount to be distributed to the two beneficiaries, Billy Barnes and Lynn Larson, each year. The trust is not *required* to distribute all of its income, so it is not a simple trust even if all income is distributed. The results for the year were as follows:

Income from corporate bond interest		$18,000
Income from short-term capital gain		8,000
Operating expenses:		
Allocable to income	$ 800	
Allocable to corpus	3,000	3,800

[44]Again, see Figure 14-1(b), Form 1041, Schedule B, line 10.

Assume that the trust instrument defines "income" as not including short-term capital gains. Thus, what was distributed was $17,200 which was the corporate bond interest of $18,000 less the expenses allocable to income of $800. The trustee distributed $10,320 to Billy and $6,880 to Lynn. The distribution was from "income" and "income" was $17,200, corporate bond interest of $18,000 less $800 of expenses allocable to income. Assume that Billy received 60% and Lynn received 40%.

The Hard Rock Trust has DNI of $14,200 which is the $18,000 of corporate bond interest less the *entire* amount of operating expenses of $3,800. Billy is treated as having received 60% of the DNI, or $8,520, and Lynn is treated as having received 40% of the DNI, or $5,680. Billy has gross income of $8,520 and Lynn has gross income of $5,680. Note that Billy and Lynn each have some tax-free amount that was either a distribution of corpus or a distribution of income previously taxed to the trust.

The trust's taxable income was:

Bond interest	$18,000
Short-term capital gain	8,000
Expenses	(3,800)
Distributions (Max. = DNI)	(14,200)
Exemption	(100)
Taxable income	$ 7,900

The tax, using 1990 rates, would be $1,504. (In Fig. 14-3 we used the 1989 rates, hence, the tax there is $1,536.) Note that taxable income in this example is short-term capital gain less the exemption of $100 because all of the "income" was distributed. "Income" was interest less expenses.

Further consideration of this topic, or of the allocation of expenses, such as depreciation and depletion, between the fiduciary and the beneficiaries is beyond the scope of this introductory text.

14.7 Some Special Rules

Charitable Contributions. A fiduciary can make charitable contributions (providing the underlying instrument requires or permits such payments) and can deduct such payments.[45] Unlike the rules applicable to individuals, as explained in Chapter 3, there is no limit on the amount of the deduction. Generally, the deduction is the amount of cash and the fair market value of any non-cash property transferred to a qualified charity. As we saw in Chapter 3, an individual on the cash method can only take a charitable contribution deduction for

[45]IRC Sec. 642(c). See line 13 of Form 1041, Fig. 14-1.

FIGURE 14-3 (a)

Form **1041** Department of the Treasury—Internal Revenue Service

U.S. Fiduciary Income Tax Return **1989** IRS Use Only

For the calendar year 1989 or fiscal year beginning , 1989, and ending , 19 OMB No 1545-0092

Check applicable boxes:	Name of estate or trust (grantor type trust, see instructions)	Employer identification number
☐ Decedent's estate	HARD ROCK TRUST	86-1001001
☐ Simple trust	Name and title of fiduciary	Date entity created
☒ Complex trust	MOUNTAIN BANK TRUST CO.	7-1-87
☐ Grantor type trust	Address of fiduciary (number and street or P.O. Box)	Nonexempt charitable and split-interest trusts, check applicable boxes (see instructions):
☐ Bankruptcy estate	ONE NEW YORK PLAZA	
☐ Family estate trust	City, state, and ZIP code	
☐ Pooled income fund	PHOENIX, ARIZONA 85012	☐ Described in section 4947(a)(1)
☐ Initial return		☐ Not a private foundation
☐ Amended return		
☐ Final return	Number of Schedules K-1 attached (see instructions) ▶ 2	☐ Described in section 4947(a)(2)

Income

Line	Description			Line	Amount
1	Dividends			1	
2	Interest income			2	18,000 —
3	Income (or losses) from partnerships, other estates, or other trusts (see instructions)			3	
4	Net rental and royalty income (or loss) (attach Schedule E (Form 1040))			4	
5	Net business and farm income (or loss) (attach Schedules C and F (Form 1040))			5	
6	Capital gain (or loss) (attach Schedule D (Form 1041))			6	8,000 —
7	Ordinary gain (or loss) (attach Form 4797)			7	
8	Other income (state nature of income)			8	
9	**Total** income (add lines 1 through 8) ▶			9	26,000 —

Deductions

Line	Description	Line	Amount	Line	Amount
10	Interest	10			
11	Taxes	11			
12	Fiduciary fees	12	3,800 —		
13	Charitable deduction (from Schedule A, line 6)	13			
14	Attorney, accountant, and return preparer fees	14			
15a	Other deductions NOT subject to the 2% floor (attach schedule) — 15a				
b	Allowable miscellaneous itemized deductions subject to the 2% floor — 15b				
c	Add lines 15a and 15b	15c			
16	**Total** (add lines 10 through 15c)			16	3,800 —
17	Adjusted total income (or loss) (subtract line 16 from line 9). Enter here and on Schedule B, line 1 ▶			17	22,200 —
18	Income distribution deduction (from Schedule B, line 17) (see instructions) (attach Schedules K-1 (Form 1041))			18	14,200 —
19	Estate tax deduction (including certain generation-skipping transfer taxes) (attach computation)			19	
20	Exemption			20	100 —
21	**Total** deductions (add lines 18 through 20) ▶			21	14,300 —

Tax and Payments (Please attach check or money order here)

Line	Description	Line	Amount
22	Taxable income of fiduciary (subtract line 21 from line 17)	22	7,900 —
23	**Total** tax (from Schedule G, line 7) ▶	23	1,536 —
24a	Payments: 1989 estimated tax payments and amount applied from 1988 return	24a	
b	Treated as credited to beneficiaries	24b	
c	Subtract line 24b from line 24a	24c	
d	Tax paid with extension of time to file: ☐ Form 2758 ☐ Form 8736 ☐ Form 8800	24d	
e	Federal income tax withheld	24e	
	Credits: **f** Form 2439 ....; **g** Form 4136 ....; **h** Other ....; Total ▶	24i	
25	**Total** payments (add lines 24c through 24e, and 24i) ▶	25	
26	If line 23 is larger than line 25, enter **TAX DUE**	26	
27	If line 25 is larger than line 23, enter **OVERPAYMENT**	27	
28	Amount of line 27 to be: **a Credited to 1990 estimated tax** ▶ ....; **b Refunded** ▶	28	
29	**Penalty** for underpayment of estimated tax (see instructions)	29	

Please Sign Here

Under penalties of perjury, I declare that I have examined this return, including accompanying schedules and statements, and to the best of my knowledge and belief, it is true, correct, and complete. Declaration of preparer (other than fiduciary) is based on all information of which preparer has any knowledge.

▶ Signature of fiduciary or officer representing fiduciary — Date — ▶ EIN of fiduciary (see instructions)

Paid Preparer's Use Only

Preparer's signature ▶ — Date — Check if self-employed ▶ ☐ — **Preparer's social security no.**

Firm's name (or yours if self-employed) and address ▶ — E.I. No. ▶ — ZIP code ▶

For Paperwork Reduction Act Notice, see page 1 of the separate Instructions. Form **1041** (1989)

FIGURE 14-3 (b)

Schedule A Charitable Deduction—Do not complete for a simple trust or a pooled income fund.

(Write the name and address of each charitable organization to whom your contributions total $3,000 or more on an attached sheet.)

1	Amounts paid or permanently set aside for charitable purposes from current year's gross income	1		
2	Tax-exempt interest allocable to charitable distribution (see instructions)	2		
3	Subtract line 2 from line 1	3		
4	Enter the net short-term capital gain and the net long-term capital gain of the current tax year allocable to corpus paid or permanently set aside for charitable purposes (see instructions)	4		
5	Amounts paid or permanently set aside for charitable purposes from gross income of a prior year (see instructions)	5		
6	Total (add lines 3 through 5). Enter here and on page 1, line 13	6		

Schedule B Income Distribution Deduction (see instructions)

1	Adjusted total income (from page 1, line 17) (see instructions)	1	22,200	—
2	Adjusted tax-exempt interest (see instructions)	2		
3	Net gain shown on Schedule D (Form 1041), line 17, column (a). (If net loss, enter zero.)	3		
4	Enter amount from Schedule A, line 4	4		
5	Long-term capital gain included on Schedule A, line 1	5		
6	Short-term capital gain included on Schedule A, line 1	6		
7	If the amount on page 1, line 6, is a capital loss, enter here as a positive figure	7		
8	If the amount on page 1, line 6, is a capital gain, enter here as a negative figure	8	(8,000	—)
9	Distributable net income (combine lines 1 through 8)	9	14,200	—
10	Amount of income for the tax year determined under the governing instrument (accounting income) 10 17,200 —			
11	Amount of income required to be distributed currently (see instructions)	11		
12	Other amounts paid, credited, or otherwise required to be distributed (see instructions)	12	14,200	—
13	Total distributions (add lines 11 and 12). (If greater than line 10, see instructions.)	13	14,200	—
14	Enter the total amount of tax-exempt income included on line 13	14		
15	Tentative income distribution deduction (subtract line 14 from line 13)	15	17,200	—
16	Tentative income distribution deduction (subtract line 2 from line 9)	16	14,200	—
17	Income distribution deduction. Enter the smaller of line 15 or line 16 here and on page 1, line 18	17	14,200	—

Schedule G Tax Computation (see instructions)

1	Tax: a Tax rate schedule ......; b Other taxes ...... ; Total ▶			1c	1,536	—
2a	Foreign tax credit (attach Form 1116)	2a				
b	Credit for fuel produced from a nonconventional source	2b				
c	General business credit. Check if from: ☐ Form 3800 or ☐ Form (specify) ▶	2c				
d	Credit for prior year minimum tax (attach Form 8801)	2d				
3	**Total** credits (add lines 2a through 2d) ▶			3		
4	Subtract line 3 from line 1c			4	1,536	—
5	Recapture taxes. Check if from: ☐ Form 4255 ☐ Form 8611			5		
6	Alternative minimum tax (attach Form 8656)			6		
7	**Total** tax (add lines 4 through 6). Enter here and on page 1, line 23 ▶			7	1,536	—

Other Information (see instructions)

		Yes	No
1	If the fiduciary's name or address has changed, enter the old information ▶		
2	Did the estate or trust receive tax-exempt income? (If "Yes," attach a computation of the allocation of expenses.) Enter the amount of tax-exempt interest income and exempt-interest dividends ▶ $		X
3	Did the estate or trust have any passive activity losses? (If "Yes," enter these losses on **Form 8582**, Passive Activity Loss Limitations, to figure the allowable loss.)		X
4	Did the estate or trust receive all or any part of the earnings (salary, wages, and other compensation) of any individual by reason of a contract assignment or similar arrangement?		X
5	At any time during the tax year, did the estate or trust have an interest in or a signature or other authority over a financial account in a foreign country (such as a bank account, securities account, or other financial account)? (See the instructions for exceptions and filing requirements for Form TD F 90-22.1.) If "Yes," enter the name of the foreign country ▶		X
6	Was the estate or trust the grantor of, or transferor to, a foreign trust which existed during the current tax year, whether or not the estate or trust has any beneficial interest in it? (If "Yes," you may have to file Form 3520, 3520-A, or 926.)		X
7	Check this box if this entity has filed or is required to file **Form 8264**, Application for Registration of a Tax Shelter ▶ ☐		
8	Check this box if this entity is a complex trust making the section 663(b) election ▶ ☐		
9	Check this box to make a section 643(e)(3) election (attach Schedule D (Form 1041)) ▶ ☐		
10	Check this box if the decedent's estate has been open for more than 2 years ▶ ☐		
11	Check this box if the trust is a participant in a Common Trust Fund that was required to adopt a calendar year ▶ ☐		

the year in which payment is actually made.[46] Fiduciaries, on the other hand, can elect to treat a charitable contribution made in one year as having been made during the previous year.[47]

For example, assume that Big Money Trust, which uses a calendar taxable year, transfers $20,000 to a qualified charity on March 1, 1991. The trust can treat that amount as a deduction for taxable year 1991 or as a deduction for taxable year 1990.

Losses. Unlike the rules for partnership and Subchapter S corporations, under which the partners or shareholders can deduct a pro rata share of the entity's loss, losses do not pass through as a deduction to beneficiaries. Fiduciaries can deduct casualty and theft losses the same as individuals, which means the amount of the deduction is the amount of the loss in excess of the sum of $100 plus 10% of adjusted gross income.[48] Fiduciaries normally do not calculate an "adjusted gross income" number, but must do so for purposes of such a loss deduction.

If a fiduciary incurs a net operating loss, it is treated in the same manner as for individuals, i.e. a three year carryback and a fifteen year carryforward.[49]

A fiduciary that recognizes a net capital loss has the same $3,000 limitation on the deduction as that for individuals, subject to a carryover to future years for any nondeductible amount.[50]

Two Year Waiting Period for Appreciated Property. A person owning property that has appreciated in value may be tempted to transfer that property to a trust with the idea that the trustee will sell or exchange the property shortly thereafter. The goal might be to have the trust, or a beneficiary—either or both of whom are in a lower tax bracket—pay tax instead of the grantor.

Congress has discouraged this sort of short-term game plan by providing a special tax computation for a trust where appreciated property is transferred to the trust *and* the trust sells or exchanges the asset within two years of the transfer.[51] Where such a transfer and subsequent sale or exchange occurs, the appreciation at the time of the transfer will bear a tax determined by what the tax would have been if the grantor had sold it. Any post-transfer appreciation will be taxed at the trust's rates.

[46]An exception applies, of course, where there is a carryover from a prior year because the amount contributed in a prior year exceeded the deduction limitation.
[47]IRC Sec. 642(c). The election must be made by the due date of the tax return. Treas. Reg. 1.642(c)-1(b) contains instructions for making the election.
[48]See Chapter 4 for discussion of casualty and theft losses by individuals.
[49]See Chapter 7.
[50]See Chapter 5.
[51]IRC Sec. 644.

For example, assume that Billy Barnes transfers property with a basis of $15,000 and a fair market value of $25,000 to Good Times Trust. Eighteen months later Good Times Trust sells the property for $28,000. The trust will have taxable gain of $13,000. However, the amount of tax on that $13,000 will be the sum of:

1. An amount equal to what Billy's tax would have been on $10,000 gain, plus
2. the amount of the trust's tax on $3,000 of gain.

TAX PLANNING TIP: A trustee planning to sell trust assets should remain aware of the two-year holding period requirement in order to avoid paying tax at the grantor's rate on appreciation in the property at the time it was transferred to the trust. It may be possible that a proposed sale would only have to be delayed a short time in order to meet the two-year holding period requirement. Even if the value of an asset dropped between the time of a proposed sale and expiration of the two-year period, the tax savings from waiting may be more than offset by the difference in sales price.

14.8 Throwback Rules

A previous illustration showed how a grantor could save income tax by creating a trust, thus shifting certain investment income to the trust, to a beneficiary, or a combination of both. If a trust agreement were to grant the trustee the authority to decide how much to distribute and when to make distributions, there is the possibility that the trust would distribute income to a beneficiary during years when he/she was in a low tax bracket and refrain from making distributions when the beneficiary was in a high bracket year. The tax rules place some limitations upon the tax savings resulting where a trust accumulates its income over several years and then distributes it to a beneficiary in a lump sum. These rules are referred to as "throwback rules."[52] The procedure is a bit complex, but an example will show how it works. The end result is to tax the beneficiary "somewhat" as if he/she had received distributions over the number of years that the trust earned the income and did not make distributions. We say " 'somewhat' as if," because there is not an actual recalculation of what

[52]IRC Secs. 665-668.

the beneficiary's tax would have been if the trust had made distributions during those years. Instead, there is a recalculation of the *average* amount by which the beneficiary's income tax would have increased each year over a three-year period *if* the trust actually had made distributions.

Assume that Billy Barnes is the beneficiary of the Goodluck Trust. The trust has accumulated income each year for a number of years, paying the federal income tax as required. This year, the trust distributes its accumulated after-tax income to Billy. The purpose for not making distributions to Billy during those years may or may not have been to avoid the extra tax which Billy would have had to pay on the distributions. Imposition of the "throwback rules" is not dependent upon the reason why the trustee did not make distributions.

In the absence of the "throwback rules," Billy would include the full amount of the trust's current distributable net income in gross income and would exclude from gross income the amount received which represents prior years' trust earnings upon which the trust paid income tax. The "throwback rules" provide that Billy must make a special calculation based upon:

1. The number of years during which the amount distributed by the trust was accumulated, and
2. Billy's own taxable income during the five years immediately prior to the distribution year.

The trust must calculate an amount known as the "accumulation distribution." This is the amount distributed in the current year that has been accumulated over prior years, *plus* the amount which the trust has already paid in federal income taxes for those prior years. In other words, the arithmetic is as if the trust had distributed its entire income to the beneficiary in prior years, but because some of that income went to the government in taxes, the beneficiary is treated as if he or she also had received the money that went to pay the taxes. The beneficiary is given a credit for the amount of tax that has already been paid.

The amount of the "accumulation distribution" is divided by the number of years during which it was accumulated by the trust. This results in an "*average* annual accumulation." The tax on the average annual accumulation is computed in the following manner:

1. Determine the beneficiary's taxable income for the five years prior to the distribution. Remove the highest and lowest taxable income numbers.
2. Add to each of the remaining three taxable income numbers the "average annual accumulation" of the trust.
3. Calculate the *additional* tax that would have resulted if the beneficiary had received the "average annual accumulation" in each of those three years.
4. Add the *additional* tax for each of those three years and divide by three. The result is the average annual increase in tax to the beneficiary.
5. Multiply the average annual increase in tax by the number of years during which the trust accumulated the income. The result is the additional tax (before credit) that the beneficiary must pay because of the accumulation distribution.
6. Reduce the beneficiary's total tax for the year by the income tax already paid by the trust during the years when it accumulated the income. This credit avoids a double tax on the trust income.

An accumulation distribution will not include an amount earned by the trust before the beneficiary reached the age of twenty-one.[53] For example, a family can use a trust to accumulate funds for the college education of a child up to that child's twenty-first birthday and not be subject to the "throwback rules."

All other things being equal, the longer the period over which a trust accumulates income, the lower the beneficiary's tax, because the *average* increment is reduced. Also, the lower the income of the beneficiary during the five years preceding the distribution, the lower the tax because of the lower marginal tax rate.

TAX PLANNING TIP: The year of an accumulation distribution can be critical. The reason is that under the "throwback rules," the taxable income of the beneficiary for the previous five years is considered. If a trust is going to make an accumulation distribution in December, the previous five years of the beneficiary will not be the same as if the accumulation distribution is made in January. By waiting, the earliest year will be disregarded and the latest year will be substituted. This can be advantageous or disadvantageous. In most cases it will make a differene and is something that the trustee should consider when making a decision about an accumulation distribution.

Let's continue with Billy and the Goodluck Trust by using some numbers to show the calculation of tax where the trust makes an "accumulation distribution." Assume that, in 1990, Goodluck Trust distributed all of its current income ($2,000) to Billy. In addition, Goodluck Trust distributed

[53] IRC Sec. 665(b). This includes distributions of income which was earned by the trust prior to the birth of the beneficiary.

$8,000 which was previously accumulated. All of that amount was accumulated after Billy's twenty-first birthday. The trust records show that it had paid a total tax of $2,000 on its taxable income during those years. Thus, the accumulation distribution is $10,000 because Billy is treated *as if* the total earnings (including tax) were distributed. Billy's tax returns for the five prior years show taxable income as follows:

1989	$ 9,000
1988	28,000
1987	18,000
1986	36,000
1985	11,600

The highest year (1986) and the lowest year (1989) are disregarded. The accounting records of the trust reveal that the $10,000 accumulated by the trust was earned over a period of four years. Thus, the average is $2,500 per year. This $2,500 is added to Billy's actual taxable income for each of the following years to arrive at a "new" taxable income:

1988	$28,000 + $2,500 = $30,500
1987	$18,000 + $2,500 = $20,500
1985	$11,600 + $2,500 = $14,100

The *additional* tax resulting from the change in taxable income is calculated using the beneficiary's filing status. (Since Billy was single for all applicable years, the revised tax is as follows:

Tax Year	*Tax on[54] "New" Taxable Income*	*Tax on "Old" Taxable Income*	*Difference*
1988	$6,220	$5,520	$ 700
1987	3,484	2,784	700
1985	1,781	1,317	464
Total			$1,864

Average difference for the three years: $621

Billy's *additional* tax (before consideration of any credit) on the $10,000 treated as having been received from the trust during 1990, is $621 multiplied by 4. The multiple of 4 is used because that is the number of years during which the trust accumulated the amount that was deemed to be distributed in 1990. Thus, Billy's total tax for 1990 is $2,484, plus whatever it would have been if the trust had made no "accumulation distribution." (Remember, Billy must also include in 1990 gross income the amount of 1990 trust income that was distributed.) That is not the end of the story, however. Billy gets a credit of $2,000 which is the amount of tax paid by the trust during those four years. Therefore, Billy's tax is $484 more than it would have been if Goodluck Trust had made no accumulation distribution in 1990. The *theory* is that this is approximately what Billy's additional tax would have been if the trust had made distributions throughout the four year period, rather than accumulate the earnings.

[54] This text does not contain the rate schedules for the years which are shown in the illustration.

A trustee may desire to have the trust distribute all "distributable net income" (DNI) each year in order to avoid any future application of the throwback rules, or for other reasons. Yet it may be the end of the fiscal year, or later, before data can be gathered to calculate the amount of DNI. There is a special rule applicable to alleviate this problem.[55] The trustee is permitted to elect to treat any distribution made within the first sixty-five days of a taxable year as if it had been made on the last day of the previous year.

For example, assume that the trustee of Big Money Trust, which uses a calendar taxable year, distributed $10,000 to a beneficiary on March 1, 1991. The trustee can treat that amount as a distribution of 1991, or as a distribution of 1990 income made on December 31, 1990.[56]

14.9 Taxable Years of Fiduciaries

A few years ago, it was possible to obtain some substantial deferral of payment of federal tax by having a trust elect a fiscal year which overlapped that of the beneficiary. Thus, for example, if a beneficiary were using a calendar taxable year, a trust could select a taxable year ending January 31. Distributions by the trust in January could be deductible for its year ending January 31. Since the beneficiary would receive the income during the first month of his/her taxable year, payment of the tax on that amount would be postponed until April 15 of the following year.[57] That is no longer possible. Trusts are required to use a calendar taxable year.[58] Estates, however, are permitted to elect a fiscal year. Thus, it is possible to arrange for some short-term tax deferral by an appropriate selection of an estate's fiscal year.

14.10 Income Tax For Decedents

The rules for taxation of trusts offer some interesting opportunities for tax planning. We

[55] IRC Sec. 663(b).

[56] Treas. Reg. 1.663(b)-2 contains detailed rules concerning how and when to make the election. The election must be made each year if the retroactive effect is desired.

[57] See Chapter 19 for discussion of due dates for tax returns.

[58] IRC Sec. 645. It is beyond the scope of this introductory text to discuss the circumstances under which a trust can use a fiscal year.

shall return to that topic shortly. First, let's consider some matters related to estates. As mentioned earlier, an estate usually is a relatively short-lived fiduciary, existing only for the time required to carry out the wishes of the decedent as reflected in a will, or to dispose of the assets in accordance with state intestate laws. This orderly process is called "probate" and is managed by a fiduciary called an "executor" (if appointed by the will) or an "administrator" (if appointed by a court).[59] During probate, the fiduciary will manage and conserve the property, and will do so under the direct supervision of, and deriving authority from, the state court responsible for probate matters.

An income tax return for the decedent—normally a Form 1040—must be filed for his/her last taxable year, the year that ended with the date of death. This return will include all income received, the allowable deductions, exemption, and credits.[60] The return will be prepared using the same method of accounting that the decedent would have used if he had not died.[61]

Where a decedent is married at the time of death, and could have filed a joint income tax return with his/her spouse if death had not occurred, a joint tax return can be filed by the surviving spouse. Income and deductions for the decedent will be reported for the period from the beginning of the year to the date of death. Income and deductions for the survivor will be reported for the entire year. It is not necessary to file a separate tax return for the decedent and another separate tax return for the survivor, although that can be done.[62]

Since everything belongs to someone at all times, title to a decedent's assets will pass immediately upon death. Married couples often own property as "joint tenants with right of survivorship."[63] This means that the survivor immediately acquires title to the property upon the death of the other joint tenant. Normally, when that happens, the estate of the decedent never acquires title to the property because the survivor acquires title. Otherwise, the estate acquires title to the property and the final determination of who is entitled to acquire title—including creditors as well as heirs—and the actual transfer of title may take a long time or only a short time. It is possible, of course, that one of the heirs to an estate may be a testamentary trust. Until the fiduciary has completed all of the necessary acts, the estate is said to remain "open."

If there is income generated by the estate assets while it is "open," it is necessary for the estate to file an income tax return. This will be done on a Form 1041, the same form as used by a trust. (Note the upper left corner of Form 1041 in Figure 14-1 where the type of fiduciary is indicated. The exemption deduction is $600 for an estate.[64]) Income will include all items earned by the decedent prior to death, but which were not included on the decedent's final tax return. These items are called "income in respect of a decedent."[65] For example, a salary check received two weeks after death will not be part of a cash-basis decedent's final income tax return but will be reported on the first income tax return for the estate.

A corresponding rule, called a "deduction in respect of a decedent," applies to any item the decedent could have deducted had he lived to pay the amount.[66] Such amounts are deductible on the fiduciary income tax return. For example, assume that prior to death, a decedent had made a pledge to contribute to a charity. As explained in Chapter 3, such a pledge results in no deduction for income tax purposes until the pledge is paid. Since the decedent's taxable year ends at death, no deduction is available on the final income tax return. The estate would, however, be able to take the deduction on its income tax return upon payment of the pledge. Note the difference between the facts of this example and the situation where a decedent provides in his will that a charity shall receive some of the estate assets.[67]

It is important not to confuse the estate's income tax liability with the estate tax, which is an excise tax on the transfer of property which occurs at death. The *estate tax* calculation begins with the value of all assets owned by the decedent at the time of death. Since "income in respect of a decedent" is really a receivable at the date of death, the taxable estate, and the amount of the estate tax, will be larger because of this asset. When these amounts are also included in gross income for the income tax of the estate, a form of double taxation

[59] The practice has been to use the word "executrix" for a female who has this responsibility.

[60] The full amount of the exemption deduction (see Chapters 1 and 4) is available, although the last taxable year may not have consisted of the entire 365 days.

[61] For most decedents this will mean the cash receipts and disbursements method. For those rare situations where the decedent used the accrual method, that would continue for the final year's return. See Chapter 7 for discussion of accounting methods.

[62] See discussion of married filing jointly versus married filing separately in Chapter 4.

[63] The manner in which title to property is held is not a matter of federal tax law, but a matter of state law which may vary from state to state. It may be possible for two persons who are not married to own property as "joint tenants with right of survivorship" (JTROS). Also, there are some states, known as "community property" states, which have some specific rules related to certain property owned by a married couple. We use JTROS only as an example.

[64] IRC Sec. 642(b).

[65] IRC Sec. 691(a).

[66] IRC Sec. 691(b).

[67] For the estate tax consequences of that latter fact situation, see the discussion of the estate transfer tax in Chapter 15.

results.[68] As a partial relief from this double tax, there is a deduction allowed in the calculation of the income tax for the estate. The amount of the deduction is the *additional* amount of estate tax that resulted from including "income in respect of a decedent" in the estate tax calculation.[69] See line 19 on Form 1041 in Fig. 14-1(a).

For example, assume that the salary check which we mentioned was $2,000. This would be included in the income tax return (Form 1041) as gross income for the first taxable year of the estate. We assumed that the salary was earned prior to death, and as a result was a receivable included among the assets of the estate. If the estate tax increased by $820 as the result of this $2,000 asset, then the deduction on the estate's income tax return would be $820.[70] Assuming that the marginal tax rate for the estate's income tax is 28%, the income tax savings from this deduction would be $230. Note that the deduction does not relieve the entire tax burden from the "double tax," but reduces it somewhat.

14.11 Estimated Tax Payments

Generally, trusts are required to make quarterly estimated income tax payments, the same as individuals.[71] Estates, also, are required to make these payments but are exempt from the requirement until taxable years which end two or more years after the date of the decedent's death.[72]

If a trust makes an estimated tax payment to the IRS, it can elect to treat all or part of the payment as if it were a distribution to a beneficiary.[73] The beneficiary would include the amount in gross income, but would also treat the amount as if he/she had made an estimated tax payment to the IRS.

14.12 Summary of Rules

Some of the points made in the chapter thus far are summarized here:

1. The term "fiduciary" includes executors, administrators, guardians, receivers for individuals, and conservators, as well as trustees. Where a trust is created by a will, it is called a testamentary trust. Trusts created by living persons are called *inter vivos* trusts.
2. Some trusts, called "grantor trusts," will be ignored for tax purposes, with the trust income being taxed directly to the grantor. These include trusts which are revocable, trusts where the grantor has a reversionary interest—the value of which exceeds 5% of the trust corpus, trusts in which the grantor has a right to change the trustee or to exercise other control, and trusts which permit the grantor to receive or enjoy the trust income or property, or, to have the trust income or corpus used for his benefit.
3. The income of a fiduciary may be taxed entirely to the fiduciary, entirely to the beneficiaries, or partly to each, depending upon distributions. This is accomplished by a deduction for the fiduciary for amounts distributed to beneficiaries. Where a fiduciary makes a distribution to a beneficiary, it is treated as having been made from the fiduciary's income for the year, to the extent of such income, regardless of its actual source.
4. A simple trust is one that is required to distribute all of its income currently to beneficiaries, has no charitable beneficiary, and distributes no corpus to a beneficiary. "Income" for this purpose is defined by the trust instrument. A complex trust is any trust which is not a simple trust.
5. Income concepts for tax purposes are basically the same for a fiduciary as for an individual.
6. Deductions for a fiduciary are generally the same as for an individual except for the exemption amount and the standard deduction. Another difference is the deduction which a fiduciary gets for distributions to beneficiaries, with that deduction being limited to the amount of "distributable net income" (DNI). Deductible expenses include those for preservation and management of the trust or estate, including fiduciary fees.
7. Beneficiaries include in gross income the amount received from the fiduciary, with that gross income being limited to DNI. Where a beneficiary receives a distribution from a trust which is an "accumulation distribution," the amount of income tax to the beneficiary may have to be determined under the "throwback rules."
8. Trusts and estates use a separate tax rate schedule.
9. When a person dies, a personal income tax return is filed, including income and deductions for the period prior to death. Income received and deductions paid by an executor after the decedent's death must be reported on a fiduciary income tax return.

Trusts are usually created by people in order to accomplish some family objective other than tax

[68]It is important to note that the income tax and the excise tax are two completely different "kinds" of tax. The former is a tax on income, and the latter is a tax upon the transfer of property. It is interesting to note that if a decedent actually received a salary check before death, for example, and did not spend the money, his final income tax return would include the income, and the estate tax would be increased as the result of the money being in the estate. There is no tax relief from this situation, however.

[69]IRC Sec. 691(c).

[70]Note that the marginal tax rates which might apply to a taxable estate can be substantially higher than those which apply to tax on income. See Fig. 15-2. Here, we assumed a marginal tax rate of 41%, which means that the taxable estate was between $1,000,000 and $1,250,000.

[71]See Chapter 19 for details of due dates and penalties for not paying on time.

[72]IRC Sec. 6654(l).

[73]IRC Sec. 643(g).

savings. For example, a trust might be created in order to permit a young adult to receive the income each year with postponement of transfer of the corpus until the grantor feels that the beneficiary will be more mature and financially responsible. Through the trust device, personal goals can often be achieved while at the same time the tax impact on earnings can be reduced.

With these basic provisions in mind, consider a few uses of trusts in tax planning.

14.13 Trusts in Tax Planning

Earlier we provided an example of a trust created to shift income to a lower-tax-bracket individual. In order to avoid the "grantor trust" provisions, the grantor must forfeit control over the property, and the income from the trust must not be used to discharge the grantor's legal obligations to support a spouse or dependent. For example, a parent would obtain no tax benefit from creating a trust for the benefit of a minor child, where the only purpose of the arrangement would be to shift income to the child for payment of those routine items (food, clothing, basic education, medical needs, etc.) which the parent has a legal obligation to provide anyway. However, a family can realize a substantial tax savings by use of a trust to accumulate income to be used by a child for college education expenses, since such educational support usually is not a legal obligation for a parent.

If a person dies and leaves property to another person, that property could be subject to a second estate tax upon the death of the second person.[74] Reducing the harsh impact of successive estate taxes is a major estate planning role performed by trusts. A testamentary trust, as will be discussed in Chapter 15, can be designed in such a way that at the death of the second person, the value of the trust property will not again be subject to estate taxes. Nevertheless, the second decedent (who was the beneficiary of the first estate) will have received during life, virtually all of the economic benefit of the property held in trust because he/she received the income from the property.

For example, assume two taxpayers, Mary and John. Mary dies first leaving a testamentary trust under the terms of which John will receive the trust income for life. John, however, cannot acquire the corpus and cannot determine where the corpus will be distributed upon his death. That decision was made by Mary and was part of her will. Mary provided that the remaindermen of the trust will be Jane and Henry. Clearly, John has almost all of the same economic benefits as if he owned the property directly. There is a large tax difference, however. When John dies, his estate will not include any of the trust property because his rights were limited to the receipt of trust income, and those rights ceased upon his death.[75]

A *charitable remainder* trust offers both income tax and estate tax benefits. Such a trust can be created while the grantor is alive (*inter vivos*) or can be a testamentary trust. The trust will pay its income to one or more beneficiaries during their life. Upon the death of the last income beneficiary, the trust assets will be distributed to a charitable organization (such as a college or university). As explained above, the estates of the income beneficiaries will not include any of the trust property. A charitable contribution deduction will be available to reduce the income tax of the grantor if the grantor creates an *inter vivos* trust.[76] Also, having given up title to the property prior to death, the grantor's estate will not include the property, thus reducing estate tax. If the grantor creates a testamentary trust, the estate will take a deduction for the present value of the charitable bequest. In either case, the income from the trust property is diverted to the tax brackets of the beneficiaries during the term of the trust.

TAX PLANNING TIP: A trust can be used as a way of having investment income flow to a person during his/her lifetime while removing the value of the property from his/her estate at death. This is often done between spouses where the first spouse to die creates a testamentary trust with the trust income to be paid to the surviving spouse for lifetime (known as a "life income interest") and remainder to be paid to other beneficiaries, such as their children. When the second spouse dies, his/her estate is not taxed on the value of the trust property.

A *charitable lead trust* is the exact opposite of a charitable remainder trust. The income from the trust property is distributed to a designated charity for a specified number of years or until the occur-

[74]As we will see in Chapter 15, there is some relief from the successive estates tax problem if the second estate follows the first within ten years. This relief, however, may be only partial.

[75]Technically, John's rights are those of an "income beneficiary" without a right to "invade" corpus or to exercise a "general power of appointment."

[76]See Chapter 3. The amount of the deduction is not the total current value of the property transferred into the trust. Rather it is the *present value* of the expected future transfer. The period of time which is expected to lapse before the charity will receive the property depends upon the life expectancies of the income beneficiaries.

rence of a specified event, at which time the remainder is distributed to a remainderman.[77]

An estate can only be kept "open" for tax purposes for that length of time that is reasonably necessary to settle all estate matters. A combination of the estate and a testamentary trust can result in substantial tax savings. Despite the limitation that a trust cannot be created to last forever, its term can still be a very long time. The goal can be to keep the distributions from the fiduciaries balanced so that the taxable incomes of all parties are in the same marginal tax bracket. This can be accomplished in part by allowing the trustee to have certain discretionary powers relative to the amount and timing of distributions. The result can be somewhat the same income tax benefit, perhaps more so, as that obtained by filing a joint income tax return.

For example, assume that a married couple with no dependents has annual taxable income of $100,000, all from interest and dividends. The 1989 tax on $100,000 on a joint return was $25,234 with a marginal tax rate of 33%. Assume that one of the spouses dies, and that the survivor will continue to have taxable income of $100,000 per year.[78] The survivor, now a single person, would incur a tax of $28,344 (using 1989 rates) on $100,000 of taxable income, with a marginal tax rate of 33%. If the decedent were to transfer the property into a trust, with the trust income payable in part to the survivor, the tax could be reduced as shown in the following example (again, using 1989 rates for comparison):

	Trust	*Survivor*	*Total*
Taxable income	$50,000	$50,000	$100,000[79]
Tax	14,000	11,844	25,844
Marginal tax rate	28%	33%	

This arrangement results in tax savings of $2,500. There is a possible disadvantage, however, in that the survivor will not have the $50,000 of trust income at his/her immediate disposal for living expenses.

[77]Such a trust can be used to transfer income to a charity where a current payment each year would not be deductible, either because of the limitation on charitable contributions deductions or because the grantor does not itemize deductions. See Chapter 3.

[78] The total assets available to produce investment income will not be reduced by any estate tax if the decedent spouse's will provides for all property to pass to the surviving spouse. This is the result of the "marital deduction" for estate tax purposes. See Chapter 15. Note that the example assumes a continuation of $100,000 of *taxable income* even though there would probably be a change in deductions, such as the deduction for personal exemption.

[79] The difference in combined taxable income resulting from change in deductions, such as the exemption deduction for the trust, has been ignored in this example.

A trust can be used effectively to save taxes while providing for the expected future expense of a child's college education. For example, assume that $2,000 of interest or dividends would be taxed to parents at the 28% rate, a tax of $560. If a child had no other income, that $2,000 would be taxed to the child under age 14 as follows:

Tax on first $500 (because of standard deduction)	0
Tax on next $500 at child's rate (15%)	$75
Tax on next $1,000 at parent's rate (28%)	$280
Total tax to child	$355
Savings per year	$205
Savings over period of 14 years	$2,870

After the child reaches age 14, the tax on $2,000 will be:

Tax on first $500	0
Tax on next $1,500 at child's rate (15%)	$225
Savings per year	$335
Savings over six years (to child's age 20)	$2,010
Total tax savings for child to age 20	$4,880

Note that these numbers do not reflect any additional interest that could be earned on those savings by investing them. Is there a parent who would not like to give his/her child an additional $4,880 at age 20 which is money that otherwise would have gone to pay taxes?

Trusts can be used to provide financial support for a person who would be supported anyway (except for children under age 14). Without a trust arrangement, the only tax advantage to supporting one more person would be the exemption amount deduction, and then only if *all* of the tests are satisfied.[80] By using a trust, the support provided can be with income which is removed from the grantor's gross income at the highest marginal rates and taxed at either the trust's or the beneficiary's lower rate (which might be zero). The result to the grantor is the same as if a deduction were allowed for the amount spent. Of course, that is offset, in part, by any tax paid by the trust, the beneficiary, or both combined.

For example, assume that a woman wants to provide $3,000 per year additional income to her mother who is elderly and retired. Assume that her mother receives only social security, none of which is included in gross income. In effect, her mother has potential deductions each year of the standard deduction (basic plus additional amount—assuming over age 65) plus the exemption amount, a total of $6,100 (using 1990 amounts). With no income, these potential deductions are wasted. If

[80] The five tests which must be satisfied in order to claim someone as a dependent are listed and discussed in Chapter 4.

the daughter is in the 28% tax bracket, she must earn $4,167, which will result in tax of $1,167, in order to have $3,000 left to give to her mother. With those facts, it is doubtful that the daughter would be able to claim her mother as a dependent because the $3,000 would be less than one-half of her mother's total support for the year. If enough investments are transferred into trust so that the trust income will be $3,000 per year, the result is as follows:

1. The grantor reduces her gross income by $3,000 and her tax by $840.
2. The trust will pay no tax because it will distribute the entire $3,000 each year to the beneficiary and deduct that amount.
3. The mother will pay no tax because her standard deduction and personal exemption deduction result in taxable income of zero.

There is one possible disadvantage to the above arrangement. Since the trust agreement must provide that the property which is transferred into trust cannot revert to the grantor, the grantor must be willing to give up any future ownership or control over the property when the trust is created. There is no requirement, however, that the grantor provide that the corpus of the trust be distributed to a different party upon the beneficiary's death. There is only a requirement that the corpus cannot revert to the grantor. The terms of the trust may provide that the principal will be distributed to the estate of the income beneficiary upon the latter's death. The original grantor might then be an heir to the estate and thereby reacquire the property. So long as the reacquisition is not a condition set forth by the grantor, there is nothing that prohibits the income beneficiary from bequeathing the property (back to) the grantor. Thus, it is possible that the grantor will reacquire the property after the death of the income beneficiary.

14.14 Bankruptcy

When a corporation or partnership goes into bankruptcy, control of the entity shifts to trustees as appointed by the bankruptcy judge or magistrate. However, the corporation or partnership as a legal entity continues to own the assets, engage in transactions, and file income tax returns.[81]

Individual debtors in bankruptcy also have a trustee appointed to control their assets and liabilities. For wage earners supporting a family and having unsecured debts of less than $100,000 and secured debts of less than $350,000, the bankruptcy case is under Chapter 13 of Title XI. In such a bankruptcy case, there is no separate taxable entity. However, there is a separate taxable entity for individuals filing bankruptcy under Chapter 7 (relating to liquidation for benefit of creditors) or Chapter 11 (relating to reorganization of a business interest such as a sole proprietorship).[82] The trustee for such a bankruptcy estate must file a fiduciary income tax return if the estate in bankruptcy has income equal to or more than the sum of the exemption amount plus the basic standard deduction.[83]

Gross income of a bankruptcy estate includes any gross income of the individual debtor not received or accrued prior to commencement of bankruptcy.[84] A bankruptcy estate can deduct expenses it pays or incurs to the same extent that the debtor would have been allowed a deduction.[85] The Act does not clarify which entity can deduct expenses incurred by the debtor before bankruptcy but paid after bankruptcy. If the debtor is on the cash basis, the estate would be entitled to the deduction for expenses it pays.

Tax claims against the bankrupt and the trustee do not necessarily get handled in the same fashion as do normal tax claims (see Chapter 18). The court that has bankruptcy jurisdiction has the authority to deal with IRS as well as all other claimants to a share of the assets. The Bankruptcy Court also has the authority to decide whether a tax liability shall be decided in the Bankruptcy Court or in the Tax Court.

14.15 Conclusion

Trusts were conceived by the English common law in the thirteenth century. They have proven to be useful for nontax as well as for tax purposes to this day. We will take a continued look at them in Chapter 15 because they are common planning tools. In this chapter, we have demonstrated some of the tax savings potential from their use. Estates, of course, are even more frequent—since everyone ultimately dies. Even relatively small estates can have complicated income tax problems in spite of the fact that they may not owe any estate tax.

[81] IRC Sec. 1399.

[82] IRC Sec. 1398(a).
[83] IRC Sec. 6012(a)(9).
[84] IRC Sec. 1398(e)(1).
[85] IRC Sec. 1398(e)(3).

TRUE-FALSE QUESTIONS

State whether each of the following statements is true or false. For each *false* answer, reword the statement to make it *true.*

T F 1. Fiduciaries file an income tax return on Form 1040.

T F 2. Administrative expenses and debts of a decedent are deductible on the estate's income tax return.

T F 3. The final income tax return for a cash-basis, single decedent who died on July 10, 1990, should include rental income received on August 12, 1990.

T F 4. Distributable net income (DNI) is equivalent to taxable income of a fiduciary tax return.

T F 5. A remainderman is a type of beneficiary that will receive the property at the time the trust ends.

T F 6. Distributable net income (DNI) of a trust represents the maximum amount that the trust can take as a deduction because of distributions to beneficiaries and the maximum amount that the beneficiaries will be required to include in gross income.

T F 7. An estate income tax return may claim only one $600 exemption amount for any one year.

T F 8. If a trust distributes to a beneficiary an amount upon which the trust has already paid tax in prior years, the amount is called an accumulation distribution.

T F 9. A trust created by a person's will upon his or her death is called an *inter vivos* trust.

T F 10. An effective way to reduce income taxes is to transfer appreciated property to a trust and have the trust sell the property immediately after the transfer.

T F 11. A trustee is a person who will receive the trust property when the trust is terminated.

T F 12. Income from an *inter vivos* trust, which is revocable, will be taxed to the grantor of the trust as if the trust did not exist.

T F 13. A complex trust would include a trust that did not distribute all of its income for a year as well as one that distributed part of its corpus during the year.

T F 14. A charitable remainder trust is one that is created for the purpose of providing current income to a charity, but with the remainder of trust property to be paid to an individual upon termination of the trust.

T F 15. In order to produce any income tax savings to a grantor, a trust must be irrevocable, must not generate any income for the benefit of the grantor, and must not revert to the grantor when the trust is terminated.

T F 16. A trustee is a person who acts on behalf of a trust for the decisions, management, record keeping, and other duties and obligations of the trust.

T F 17. When a trust is required to pay income tax, the rates that apply are the same as those which apply to a single individual.

T F 18. A simple trust is one that has only one kind of property, such as bonds, and is therefore easy to manage.

T F 19. A trust is entitled to a deduction for either $300 or $100, depending upon whether it is a simple trust or a complex trust.

T F 20. The basic purpose of the "throwback" rules is to prevent undue tax savings from having a trust accumulate income when a beneficiary is in a high-tax-bracket year and distribute income when a beneficiary is in a low-tax-bracket year.

PROBLEMS

Problem 14-1. Wendell Jamison died in 1990. His estate was so small that there will be no estate tax. However, the estate did receive $6,000 as "income in respect of a decedent," which was the previously unreported short-term capital gain which Mr. Jamison realized from the installment sale of an asset two years prior to his death. The only other income of the estate was $600 of interest. The only deduction which the estate will have will be the $600 exemption. Calculate the federal income tax liability of the estate.

Problem 14-2. Bob Balloon created the Balloon Trust and transferred $100,000 of corporate bonds, paying interest at 8% per year. The trust was irrevocable. The trust is to accumulate the income until Bob's daughter Betty starts college. At that time, the trust is to pay Betty enough to meet college expenses each year. Upon completion of her college education, or upon her reaching the age of twenty-five, whichever comes first, Betty is to receive all of the trust property plus any accumulated trust income. At the time the trust was created, Betty was age fourteen. The trustee will be paid $500 per year.

(a) Assuming that the first taxable year of the trust is a full year, what is the trust's income tax liability? (Use 1990 rates.)

(b) Assume that the trust paid all of its first year's income after expenses to Betty. Would the trust have any federal income tax liability? Would Betty have any tax liability? If so, how much? What problems arise with this arrangement? Discuss.

(c) Assume that it is the fifth year of the trust. Gross income is $8,000 for the year. The trust pays $5,000 to Betty. What is the trust's tax liability? What is Betty's tax liability? (Assume that Betty has no other income and is not Bob's dependent. Use 1990 rates.)

(d) If, in part (c), $6,000 were paid to Betty, would the total tax be more or less than if $5,000 were paid?

Problem 14-3. Mable Burns established a trust for the benefit of her dependent mother. Mable transferred bonds to the trust. These bonds normally generate $20,000 of interest income per year. The trust is irrevocable. When Mable's mother dies, the trust property will pass to Mable's daughter, who is now age 35. All trust income is to be paid to the beneficiary each year, with the exception of long-term capital gains, which will remain in the trust. As the result of this arrangement, Mable will no longer be able to claim her mother as a dependent. Last year, Mable's taxable income on a single return was $90,000, including the $20,000 of interest from the stock that is now in the trust. Mable's mother has no income and relies entirely upon Mable. Mable spent $15,000 last year for her mother's support. None of this $15,000 resulted in any additional deductions to Mable. At the time the trust was created, Mable's mother had a life expectancy of eight years. Mable's sister will be the trustee and there will be no trustee fees. Mable's mother is eighty-three years old. (Use 1990 rates for "last year" and "this year" and assume Mable's filing status in each year is single.)

(a) Does the fact that the trust is not expected to last for more than ten years mean that Mable will receive no tax benefit from this arrangement? Explain.

(b) How much less will Mable's tax be this year compared with last year? (Assume that gross income, deductions, and rates will be the same for both years.)

(c) What will be the tax liability for Mable's mother?

(d) How much total tax is saved each year (assuming that gross income will be the same each year) as the result of the trust created by Mable for her mother's support?

Problem 14-4. Mike Lane died on August 15 of last year. He was a cash-basis taxpayer and single. The executor filed an income tax return for Mr. Lane for the tax year beginning January 1 and ending August 15. Between August 15 and December 31, the estate received the following items of income which were not included on the income tax return for the year of Mr. Lane's death:

U.S. government bond interest	$ 6,000
Corporate bond interest	11,200
Sales commissions	3,000

The executor's fee related to this income was $300.

(a) Calculate the income tax that will be due by the estate for the period August 15 to December 31, assuming that the executor did not distribute to beneficiaries any of the items listed above. (Use 1990 tax rates.)

(b) What difference would it have made if the executor paid $4,000 of funeral expenses from the sources of income listed? Explain.

(c) What difference would there be in the total amount of tax if the executor had distributed $4,000 on December 28 to a beneficiary who was married filing a joint tax return and who had $18,200 of other taxable income?

Problem 14-5. The Harry Wendell trust was created upon Mr. Wendell's death. It consists of bonds that produce annual interest income. The trust instrument provides that all of the income each year except capital gain is to be paid to Mr. Wendell's widow until her death. At that time, the trust corpus is to be transferred to a specified church. The trustee is given discretion to sell certain bonds and buy others if market prices and certain other conditions are satisfied. For the year just passed, the trust generated $41,000 of interest income and $6,000 of long-term capital gain. Mrs. Wendell received $40,000 because the trustee's fees of $1,000 were charged to income.

(a) Calculate the federal income tax liability for the trust. (Use 1990 rates.)

(b) How much tax was paid as the result of the $6,000 long-term capital gain?

Problem 14-6. The Blaine Truman Trust has accumulated its after-tax income for ten years. All of its $10,000 annual income is from U.S. government bonds. The trustee's fee is $200 per year. On the first day of the eleventh year, the trust was dissolved and the beneficiary was given the entire accumulated income, in cash. (Assume that the bonds were redeemed for no gain or loss. Use 1990 rates throughout.)

(a) How much cash did the beneficiary receive?

(b) What is the average annual accumulation?

(c) Assume that the beneficiary's taxable income for the last five years is as follows: $22,000, $14,000, $31,000, $19,000, and $27,000. The beneficiary has filed a single tax return for all relevant years. Calculate the *additional* tax that the beneficiary will have to pay.

(d) What difference would it make if the taxable income for the beneficiary's last five years had been $22,000, $14,000, $31,000, $5,000, and $9,000? Explain.

Problem 14-7. Max Jennings has a twenty-one-year-old son, Bert, who Max thinks is a playboy who would probably squander Max's wealth if it were available. Max has decided to create a trust that will permit Bert to have the income from certain rental properties each year, but Bert will not be able to sell the properties. Bert will receive the trust corpus when he is age 35. Max transfers office buildings worth $600,000 into the trust. These properties produce a cash flow of $60,000 per year, although depreciation will result in only $40,000 of taxable income.

(a) Will Bert have to include in his gross income the $60,000 that he receives each year from the trust? Explain.

(b) If Bert receives the trust property upon reaching age thirty-five, what will be the income tax effect for him? Explain.

(c) What difference would it have made in income tax effect, if any, if Max had not created the trust but instead just gave Bert the cash flow from the property each year? Explain.

Problem 14-8. The Hill National Bank is trustee of the Hercules Trust, which owns a piece of rental property. The trust was created by the will of Bart Hercules upon his death and provides that Sue Hercules, his widow, is to receive all of the trust's net income for the remainder of her life, after which the trust corpus will go to Helen James, their daughter.

(a) Explain the income tax effect to
  (i) the Hill National Bank
  (ii) the estate of Bart Hercules
  (iii) Sue Hercules
  (iv) Helen James

(b) What difference would result if a charity had been named as the remainderman instead of Helen James?

Problem 14-9. The Malcolm Henning estate is required, under the terms of Mr. Henning's will, to proceed with an orderly liquidation of the estate assets and distribute the cash to various named beneficiaries. For the first year of the estate, the gross income was as follows:

Dividends from taxable U.S. corporations	$ 7,400
Interest from U.S. government bonds	14,600
Interest from State of Illinois bonds	8,000
Long-term capital gains	10,000
Commissions earned but not paid prior to Mr. Henning's death	5,000

Distributions of cash included the following:

Executor's fees	$ 2,600
Funeral expenses	6,000
Transfers to beneficiaries	12,000
Interest on debts not yet liquidated	600

It was determined that for the final taxable year of Mr. Henning there was an unused short-term capital loss carryover of $4,000. (This is not available as a deduction to the estate.)

(a) Calculate the federal income tax liability for the estate. Use 1990 rates.

(b) Comment on the wisdom of a charitable transfer as a deduction on the income tax return as contrasted with a deduction for estate tax purposes if the estate was large enough to be in the 22% marginal tax bracket.

Problem 14-10.

(a) What is meant by the term "income in respect of a decedent"?

(b) Why is "income in respect of a decedent" subject to both the federal estate tax and the federal income tax on estates?

(c) How is the "double tax" from the estate and income tax alleviated?

(d) Give five examples of "income in respect of a decedent."

(e) Would you say that there are many tax planning opportunities related to "income in respect of a decedent"? Explain.

Problem 14-11. The Clair Boone Trust received income and incurred expenses for the calendar year 1990 as shown below. The trustee is granted complete discretion by the terms of the trust instrument to distribute or accumulate income during the life of the beneficiary. The trust will terminate and all accumulated income and corpus will be distributed to the beneficiary at the end of 1993. Under both the state law and the terms of the trust, the capital gains are to be treated as additions to corpus and not as income. The trustee does not make any specific allocation of expenses as between "income" and capital gain. The trust requires that the trustee retain cash each year in an amount equal to the depreciation deduction for federal income tax purposes.

Trust income for 1990:	
Interest from corporate bonds	$16,000
Interest on City of Cleveland bonds	2,400
Rent from office building	7,200
Gain (long-term) from common stock	9,000
Expenses for 1990:	
Trustee's fees	4,000
Maintenance on office building	1,200
Depreciation on office building	1,800
Property taxes on office building	1,600

In addition, the trustee paid $10,000 to the beneficiary.

(a) Is the trust "simple" or "complex"? Explain.

(b) What is the trust's tax liability for 1990? (*Note:* Only $3,625 of the trustee's fees will be deductible because $375 is allocated to the tax-exempt income. Use 1990 rates.)

(c) How much gross income will the beneficiary have as the result of the $10,000 distribution?

(d) Has anything been lost as the result of having the trust be the recipient of tax-exempt income? If so, suggest an alternative.

Problem 14-12. The Stanley Trust was created by Mr. K. L. Stanley. In preparing the trust agreement, Mr. Stanley included a provision that 10% of the trust income each year was to be paid to his favorite charity. The balance of the trust income was to be distributed equally to his father and his sister, both of whom had no other income and relied entirely upon Mr. Stanley for support. The trust property consists of bonds that generate $25,000 of interest income per year. Mr. Stanley's income each year places him in the highest marginal tax bracket.

(a) Approximately how much tax did Mr. Stanley save by creating this trust, considering that his only deductions for his father and sister had been the exemption deductions and that he will now not even get those two deductions? (Use 1990 rates.)

(b) What would the effect have been if he had transferred enough property into the trust to generate $22,500 of annual interest and then made an annual gift to charity of $2,500?

(c) Would your answer be any different if Mr. Stanley made it a practice each year of donating to charity an amount equal to one-half of his adjusted gross income?

APPENDIX 14-A

Tax Rate Schedule for Fiduciaries—1989

IF TAXABLE INCOME IS:	TAX IS:
Not over $5,200	15% of taxable income
Over $5,200	$780, plus 28% of the excess over $5,200
Over $13,500	$3,104 plus 33% of the excess over $13,500
Over $27,020	28% of taxable income

Tax Rate Schedule for Fiduciaries—1990

IF TAXABLE INCOME IS:	TAX IS:
Not over $5,450	15% of taxable income
Over $5,450	$817.50 plus 28% of the excess over $5,450
Over $14,150	$3,253.50 plus 33% of the excess over $14,150
Over $28,320	28% of taxable income

Note that the fiduciary tax rate schedule provides for an additional 5% tax (i.e., the difference between 33% and 28%) as does the tax rate schedule for individuals, the purpose of which is to phase out the benefit of the 15% tax rate. Unlike the tax for individuals, however, the rate structure for fiduciaries does not phase out the tax reduction for the exemption deduction.

APPENDIX 14-B

Computation of Distributable Net Income

The determination of a fiduciary's distributable net income (DNI) can be made by starting with taxable income (gross income less all deductions) and making the following adjustments:

Add:

(a) the exemption, which is either $100, $300, or $600

(b) the deduction for distributions

(c) the net capital loss deduction

(d) the net capital gains deduction (pre-1987 only)

(e) the *net* tax-exempt interest
(net tax-exempt interest is tax exempt interest reduced by (1) any portion of such interest which is either paid or set aside for charitable purposes and (2) nondeductible expenses related to the tax-exempt interest)

Deduct:

(a) net capital gains taxable to the fiduciary

15

family tax planning, including estate tax and gift tax

Previous chapters have dealt with some of the rules applicable to the federal income tax and how they can be used to keep taxes at a minimum. This chapter focuses attention on the family as a unit for which tax planning is frequently done. Beginning with section 15.11 the rules concerning federal estate and gift taxation will be discussed. The rules and opportunities previously discussed are reviewed and summarized in the context of tax savings opportunities available to a family.

Substantially greater tax planning and saving opportunities exist for a family group than for an individual required to function entirely alone. A family group can often arrange financial affairs so as to reduce taxes and enhance the net worth of the group. Some of these basic planning techniques have already been mentioned.

There is sometimes a difference in what people are willing to do in transactions with family members and what they might be willing to do in transactions with complete strangers. To counter this, many tax rules are designed to curb abuses and excesses in transactions between family members.[1]

Although the possibilities for tax planning are as varied as the circumstances of taxpayers, this chapter focuses on a few common variations that have income tax implications. Many of them also have gift and estate tax implications, so that some grasp of Section 15.12 on will ultimately be needed to fully comprehend family tax planning. However, far more people have income tax problems than have estate and gift tax problems; for a majority of taxpayers, the techniques discussed through Section 15.10 can stand alone.

15.1 Clifford Trusts

The Clifford trust is a good example of a device that had income tax objectives. "Clifford trust" is the term applied to a trust arrangement whereby the grantor would transfer income producing property into a trust with the income to be paid to a beneficiary for a term of more than ten years (e.g., ten years and one month) after which time the corpus of the trust will revert to the grantor. Except for such trusts created before March 1, 1986, such arrangements are now "grantor trusts" as discussed in Chapter 14. The Tax Reform Act of 1986 has eliminated the use of Clifford trusts for transfers in trust after that date. Transfers before that date continue to generate income not taxable to the grantor.[2] The following illustration shows how it would work even for a moderate-income family. A married couple with two young children planned for those children to attend college. They had no substantial net worth except a home, but did have a reasonably good level of income and the potential to acquire some cash (for example, \$30,000) by placing a second mortgage on their residence. The loan was made. A short-term trust was created to exist for more than ten years. The trust was funded with the \$30,000. Income is not taxed to the trust if it is permanently held (set aside) for the beneficiaries. Except for

[1]For example, the Sec. 267 rules provide that a loss on a sale to a relative (as defined) cannot be recognized.

[2]Since no new Clifford trusts can be created, the rules in this section will only apply to trusts already in existence.

distributions to the children to permit payment of their income tax, income from the trust is to be distributable currently to the children only if they demand it, and is otherwise to accumulate until they reach postsecondary schools or the trust terminates, whichever occurs first. At termination, the original $30,000 put into the trust is to be returned to the parents.

The Clifford trust could be used for children (as long as not used to discharge the grantor's obligation to support them) and to handle the moral (if not legal) obligation to support parents or anyone else. (But see Sec. 15.2.) Thus, two people living together, such as a mother and daughter, were unable to get the income-splitting benefits of a joint return, although financially their situation might not differ from that of a married couple. If the daughter alone had income, a Clifford trust might have been a way of getting some of the split income benefits while still protecting the ownership rights of the individuals. If the person earning the income had no investment assets, but could borrow the necessary cash, the loan proceeds could be used to create a Clifford trust *with an independent trustee*. It is possible that the money could later even be borrowed from the trust to pay back the original loan so long as such a loan would be enforceable under state law. Subject to certain limitations, discussed in Chapter 3, interest paid on the loan whether to a third party or to the trust would be deductible; and there would be income to the trust.[3] The trust would then distribute the income to the trust beneficiary who would pay the tax. The effect would be a type of income splitting.

One of the rules was that the Clifford trust must be irrevocable for a period of more than ten years. The exception to this rule was especially important when dealing with older people as beneficiaries. The trust instrument can provide that the trust will terminate upon the beneficiary's death, even if that turns out to be less than ten years after creation of the trust.[4] Also, the life expectancy of the beneficiary at the time the trust was created need not have been ten years.

The income splitting benefits described here can still be obtained with the use of a trust. The difference now is that when the trust is created, there must be no reversionary provision for the corpus. Thus, the income producing property cannot be reacquired by the grantor except under those circumstances where the remainderman of the trust voluntarily transfers the corpus to the individual from whom it originated.

15.2 Unearned Income of a Minor Child

Recognizing the widespread attempts to transfer income-producing property to children who are taxed at lower rates, the law imposes special rules on unearned income of children under 14 years of age. As discussed in Chapter 4, all net unearned income in excess of $1,000 of such a child will be taxed at the parents' marginal tax rate. Earned income will be taxed at the child's marginal rate. Net unearned income is calculated by taking the child's total unearned income from interest, dividends, rents, etc., and subtracting the sum of the standard deduction of $500 plus the greater of $500 or the amount of deductions connected with the production of the unearned income.[5]

This calculation allows each child to have at least $1,000 of unearned income, $500 of which will not be taxed and $500 taxed at 15%. The excess will be added to the parents' taxable income. The tax on that amount minus the tax on the parents' regular income will be the tax due on the child's unearned income. Any tax on earned income and unearned income not included in net unearned income will be computed separately and added to the unearned income tax. Where the parents are divorced, it will be the income of the custodial parent which is taken into account.

For example, if a dependent child has $2,000 of unearned income and no earned income, the net unearned income will be $2,000 minus $500 (standard deduction). The excess of the difference ($1,500) over $500 is the net unearned income ($1,000) and will be taxed at the parents' rate.

This tax provision is effective for all years after 1986. Even income taxed to a child through a Clifford trust will be included, even though the property was transferred before March 1, 1986, and is not taxable to the grantor. The effect is to eliminate the value of any Clifford trust for children under 14, no matter when the trust was created. Since those trusts were irrevocable, at least for ten years, many people will find they have given up control of their money or property without having the benefit of tax savings they had counted on. This effect can sometimes be avoided by shifting the investments of the Clifford trust into assets that defer income, such as growth stocks

[3] *W.P.T. Preston* (CA2) 30 AFTR 680, 43-1 USTC 9215, 132 F.2d 763; Avery L. Cook (DC La.), 40 AFTR2d, 77–5486. But the issue is not free from doubt, and there are some cases in which such a transaction has been viewed as a sham and the interest paid disallowed—e.g., *Sall* v. *Smith* (DC Pa.), 45 AFTR 1018, 53–1 USTC 9123; and *Robert W. Wilken*, T. C. Memo 1987–272.

[4] IRC Sec. 673(c). Note that a way of eliminating the applicability of the ten-year rule was to have the property revert to the donor's spouse at the end of the trust term. The donor then had no reversionary interest, and Sec. 673 would not apply. But see Sec. 672(e)

[5] IRC Sec. 1(i).

or market discount bonds issued before July 18, 1984 and not maturing until the child reaches 14.

One additional part of the special rule on unearned income of a minor child is that the rules apply to any income, no matter what the source of the property. Net unearned income from property given to a child by a grandparent or a friend of the family will be taxed at the parents' tax rate just as net unearned income from a trust founded by a parent.

15.3 Family Partnerships

As noted before, a major objective of family tax planning is to shift income from higher-tax-bracket persons to those in lower tax brackets. A partnership allows this to be done with a great deal of flexibility and efficiency, since a number of assets can be brought together into one conduit—and the income of that conduit can be allocated to the family members in predetermined ways. Partnership allocations are generally accepted for tax purposes.[6]

Not every organization that is called a partnership will accomplish its tax objectives. For family planning purposes, partnerships can be divided into those in which capital is a material factor in producing income and those in which it is not.

Capital is material if a substantial part of business gross income is due to the use of capital. Thus, a business that has a large investment in equipment or carries substantial inventories will usually be considered one in which capital is a material factor in producing income. A personal service business such as a CPA firm or a law firm will not. A family member who actually owns a capital interest in a partnership in which capital is a material income-producing factor will be accepted as a partner for tax purposes. It does not matter if the partner acquired the partnership interest by contributing assets or received the partnership interest as a gift or inheritance. *Intent* to create a partnership is the primary variable. The way the partnership agreement divides earnings will then usually be accepted for tax purposes if it makes economic sense.

If capital is not material, a partnership interest acquired by gift may be more critically scrutinized.[7] Does the purported partner share in management or control? Does he or she perform vital services? Even if the partner passes those tests, income may be reallocated among the family members where the partnership interest was acquired from a family member. Such reallocation usually involves attributing a salary allowance to the partner(s) who is (are) active in the business.

The rules concerning unearned income of a minor child have a major impact on this area. The benefit of shifting income is drastically reduced since most of the under-14 child's unearned income will be taxed at the parents' rates. However, for children 14 or over, the concepts still apply. In the following examples, it will be assumed that both children are at least 14.

Assume, for example, that a husband and wife have been operating a business as proprietors. It may be a moot point whether the business is a partnership between the two of them because they get the benefit of income splitting on a joint tax return anyway. Later, when the couple has two children, they decide to form a family partnership, with all four members of the family as equal partners. We will ignore, for now, any gift tax on the transfer. The parents decide that more income can be diverted to the children if they, the active members of the business, do not draw a salary for their efforts. Without their salaries as business expenses, the partnership has taxable income of $68,000, divided equally among them, with the following result (using 1990 numbers):

	Parents	*First Child*	*Second Child*
Gross income	$34,000	$17,000	$17,000
Standard deduction	– 5,450	– 500	– 500
Exemption(s)	– 8,200	-0-	-0-
Taxable income	$20,350	$16,500	$16,500
Tax (for 1990)	$ 3,053	$ 2,475	$ 2,475

The total tax will be $8,003.

If the parents perform services that are valued at $44,000 with the balance of the income equally divided among the four partners, the income and the tax effect will be as follows:

	Parents	*First Child*	*Second Child*
Gross income	$56,000	$6,000	$6,000
Standard deduction	– 5,450	– 500	– 500
Exemption(s)	– 8,200		
Taxable income	$42,350	$5,500	$5,500
Tax (for 1990)	$ 7,640	$ 825	$ 825

The total tax will be $9,290 an increase of $1,287.[8]

By reallocating the partnership income (i.e., the provision for fair salary for those persons who

[6]IRC Sec. 704(a). See the discussion in Chapter 10. Care must be taken to document the allocations properly so the IRS cannot assert a tax avoidance motive.

[7]A leading case in this area is *Comm. v. Culbertson* (S. Ct. 1949), 337 U.S. 733, 93 L. Ed. 1659, 69 S. Ct. 1210, 37 AFTR 1391, 49-1 USTC 9323.

[8]The tax savings would decrease if the children were under 14, since most of the children's income would be taxed at their parents' rate of 28% rather than their current 15% rate.

provide valuable services), there is more tax collected. Congress has given the IRS the authority to make such reallocations in order to prevent or discourage abuses that might otherwise result.

Reallocation may also be based upon equalizing the return on the partners' capital accounts (e.g., so that the partner receiving an interest as a gift is not allocated proportionately more income than the partner who made the gift).

Assume that a partnership consists of four members of a family, each with a capital account balance of $30,000. A fifth member of the family becomes a member of the partnership as the result of each of the original four making a gift of $6,000 of partnership interest to the newcomer. The result is that each of the five partners has a capital account of $24,000. The partnership agreement allocates one-half of partnership profits to the new partner, after payment is made to each partner for services rendered. Unless there is some good business reason for the new partner to receive such a disproportionate share of the profits, the IRS is empowered to reallocate the partnership income, after payment for services rendered by partners, to reflect the return on capital.[9] Such a reallocation would result in the new partner being taxed on one-fifth of the balance rather than one-half.

An added advantage of a family partnership is the ability to structure the interests of the different partners to achieve family objectives and estate planning benefits. A partnership agreement can provide that partnership interests cannot be transferred during lifetime except to another partner (i.e., family member), and then only after first being offered to the partnership at book value. Further, upon death, the deceased partner's estate is required to sell the partnership interest back to the partnership at current value. This may help keep the value of the partnership interest closer to book value for any gift or estate tax purposes. This provision facilitates the transfer of assets from one generation to another.

15.4 Family Corporations

A family corporation with an S corporation election will also allow a family to minimize taxation by shifting income from high-bracket family members to lower-bracket ones, as well as to minimize the tax costs of transferring assets from one generation to another.

In Chapter 11 it was pointed out that, in a family S corporation, income may be paid to family members active in the business to provide a reasonable allowance for their services. Thus, the family S corporation is similar to the family partnership on this point. The corporation sometimes lacks the flexibility of the family partnership, however. For example, since it can have only one class of stock, it cannot divide the income among family members in a manner similar to where participating preferred stock is used. But especially where a family already has a corporation with substantial assets, electing S status, accompanied by gifts of stock, is a useful device.

For example, assume that a family business is organized as a corporation for nontax reasons. Two members of the family own all of the stock. The shareholders (married, but not to each other) draw a salary of $50,000 each, after which the corporation has taxable income of $40,000, which is retained by the corporation. The total tax paid, assuming that the shareholders file joint tax returns, is as follows. (For illustration purposes we assume use of only the exemption amount as a deduction from AGI.)

	Shareholder 1	*Shareholder 2*	*Corporation*
Gross income	$ 50,000	$ 50,000	
Exemptions	(4,100)	(4,100)	
Taxable income	$ 45,900	$ 45,900	$40,000
Tax (for 1990)	$ 8,634	$ 8,634	$ 6,000

The total tax is $23,268.

Use of the S election, without any change in stock ownership, will result in the following:

	Shareholder 1	*Shareholder 2*
Salary	$ 50,000	$ 50,000
Undistributed taxable income	20,000	20,000
Exemptions	(4,100)	(4,100)
Taxable income	$ 65,900	$ 65,900
Tax (for 1990)	$ 14,234	$ 14,234

The total tax is $28,468. The increase of $5,200 is due to the shifting of income from the corporate rate of 15% to the individual marginal rate of 28%.

If the S stock were transferred among other family members, who would pay no tax on the corporation's undistributed taxable income, the result would be a savings of all of the tax on $40,000 of corporate profits. The only tax would be that which the shareholders would pay on the salaries. Of course, it may not be possible to escape tax on the entire $40,000 of corporate undistributed taxable income. Some family members might have to pay tax at low rates. The higher the corporate marginal tax rate (34% or 39% if taxable income is over $75,000 and the S election is not used), the greater the possible savings by using the

[9]See Treas. Reg. 1.704-1(b)(2).

combination of the S corporation election with stock spread among various family members.

A corporation that is subject to tax introduces an element missing from the partnership. The family has a new tax entity, paying a 15% tax on its first $50,000 of taxable income, and so on. If that corporation can avoid personal holding company problems (Chapter 13) and unreasonable accumulation of earnings problems (Chapter 12), it can save substantial money for the family group.

Assume that members of a family want to invest in rental property. If the rental operation is expected to result in a net gain for tax purposes, it may not be desirable to have that gain taxed at the marginal tax rates of the family members. Consequently, a corporate entity is used for the rental operation. If the family members are independently successful, the corporation will probably pay tax at lower rates, at least until profits exceed $75,000 per year, than would the individuals.

15.4.1. Multiple Corporations

As explained earlier, the present corporate tax rates are 15% on the first $50,000 of taxable income, 25% on the next $25,000, and so forth. A logical tax reduction strategy for a family would be to have several corporations so that the higher rates of 34% would not have to be paid. Such a plan could also reduce the risk of the accumulated earnings tax penalty being assessed, since each corporation could accumulate up to $250,000 without any danger of incurring that penalty.

That scheme will work, but only to a limited extent. For example, if one person owns all of the stock of two corporations, the taxable income of both must be considered together for purposes of determining the tax rates that will apply. If one corporation has $30,000 of taxable income and the other has $40,000 of taxable income, the tax would be $10,500 *if* they could be treated separately.[10] Since they cannot be treated separately, the tax is $12,500.

For determining whether two or more corporations must add their taxable incomes together to determine the applicable tax rates, the IRC defines a "controlled group" of corporations.[11] If corporations are part of a controlled group, their taxable incomes must be combined. If they are not part of a controlled group, their taxable incomes are treated separately for purposes of the tax rates.

There are two kinds of controlled groups. One is a parent-subsidiary relationship, where one corporation owns 80% or more of the stock of another corporation. The second kind is called a "brother-sister" group and exists if (1) five or fewer persons own at least 80% of the stock of the corporations and (2) these persons own more than 50% of the stock of each corporation. For this purpose a stockholder is not only considered to be the owner of stock owned directly but is also considered to be the owner of stock that is owned by other persons to whom he or she is related (called "constructive ownership").

Certain family relationships and ownership structures can be used to reduce the overall tax effect. A husband and a wife can each have a separate corporation, as long as not more than half of corporate gross income comes from royalties, rents, dividends, interest, or annuities, and:

1. Neither spouse owns stock in the other corporation.
2. Neither spouse is involved in the affairs of the other corporation as a director, employee, or in any other management role.
3. Neither spouse's stock has any restrictions on its disposition running to the other spouse or the other spouse's children under age twenty-one.

Thus, a husband who sells real estate can have one corporation for his real estate business while his wife, an art dealer, can have another for her art gallery. If the conditions listed above are satisfied, each corporation will be treated separately for purposes of the tax rates that will apply.

Further, stock owned by a brother or a sister is not attributed to other brothers or sisters. As Fig. 15-1 shows, each of three sisters can own her own incorporated retail store, plus owning one-third of the stock of a fourth business. If the taxable income happened to come out even for all four, the 15% federal income tax rate would apply to $200,000 of taxable income for the combined businesses.

Assume that each corporation has taxable income of $50,000. If the four corporations were members of a controlled group, the tax would be as follows:

Taxable Income	*Rate*	*Tax*
$ 50,000	15%	$ 7,500
25,000	25%	6,250
25,000	34%	8,500
100,000	39%	39,000
Total tax		$ 61,250

But it does not work that way because the four corporations are not a controlled group. Therefore, each will pay tax of $7,500, for a total of $30,000. Thus, the use of four corporations instead of one will save this family group $31,250 per year of tax.

[10] 0.15($40,000) + 0.15($30,000) = $10,500.
[11] See the discussion in Chapter 12.

FIGURE 15-1 Attribution of stock among family members

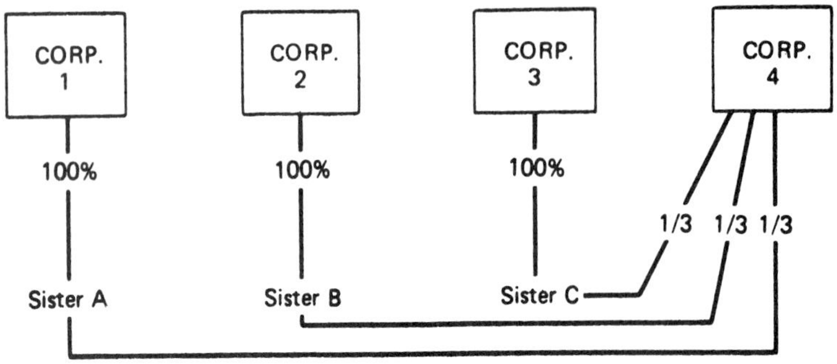

It should be clear from the example that careful placement of stock among members of a family, friends, and other close associates can be arranged in such a way as to save current tax dollars.[12]

If separate key employees (unrelated to the principal shareholders or to each other) were to each own 21% of the stock of each separate corporation, with the other 79% owned by the family members, the family business could be operated as several corporations, each with its own tax computation, because the 80% or more ownership test would not be satisfied. Such stock ownership not only has income tax implications but may also serve the purpose of keeping the key employees (a) more happy, (b) less likely to leave their employment, and (c) more productive.

Let us take one more example. A father owns 50% of the stock of a corporation. Each of five children, all adults, owns 10% of the same corporation. Each child also owns 50% of the stock of his or her own corporation, with Father and the other four siblings owning 10% each. There are six corporations, none of which is a member of a controlled group. Therefore, each can file a tax return and get the advantages of the basic corporate rate structure. Remember "constructive ownership" of stock for this purpose does not include stock owned by a sibling.

The IRS is not completely helpless in dealing with family corporate groups, of course. Where income or expense is artificially pushed around among the various corporate taxpayers, the IRS has the legal right to reallocate in such a fashion as clearly to reflect the income of each unit. It can also attack the various corporations as shams, or argue that they were created primarily for tax purposes and should be ignored. It thus becomes important that multiple corporate groups, of the sort discussed here, be able to document the valid nontax business purposes for their existence. Both the family members and the corporations should meticulously document that they dealt with each other at arm's length just as they would have dealt with nonfamily persons.

A variety of nontax business reasons can help justify a separate corporation for each family member. One common one is the real desire to have an operation where that family member is the boss. This may be particularly convincing if the corporations engage in different businesses. Another is the desire to follow separate investment policies, including the creation of different types of retirement programs.

Of course, in family situations where relationships are fragile, having separate corporations may be both a plus and a minus. When family members quarrel, a person with a separate corporation does not have the risk of being a minority stockholder in just one entity that contains all or most of the family wealth. Each has control over his or her own business affairs. If arguments and disagreements happen often enough, and turn into permanent estrangements, the family's wealth may become splintered and its ability to function as a major economic unit may be destroyed.

In fact, a generalization can be made. Much, or most, family tax planning requires faith in the ultimate family loyalty of at least a majority of the family members. When that faith is lacking, some of the protective devices (such as older members of the family holding options to buy out the stock of younger family members or in-laws) may frustrate the ability to achieve optimum tax results. (A family member who has an option to acquire stock is deemed to own that stock for most tax purposes.) So there is a trade-off between gambling on family solidarity and achieving tax benefits. Will the children be willing to continue my corporate salary as I get older if I gift the stock to them now? Will my sister-in-law operate the corporation as my brother would, in the event my brother were to die prematurely? The questions and doubts can be endless!

15.5 Family Members as Employees

When an individual employs a spouse or children in a trade or business, a deduction is allowed

[12]The quid pro quo is that a second tax will be incurred in the future if the corporation, e.g., liquidates.

for the *reasonable* amounts paid to them. Of course, they report salary or wages as gross income. If a joint return is to be filed, there will normally be no tax advantage to employing one's spouse. However, even in such a situation, the ability to justify a deduction for payments to a retirement plan may make employee status worthwhile.[13] No social security tax is imposed on wages paid one's children under the age of eighteen.[14] By having them as employees, not only can they obtain the tax shelter of a qualified retirement plan, but they can also help the family participate in many other tax-favored employee fringe benefits. For nondependent children, the combined exemption amount and standard deduction mean that $5,300 of earned income (for 1990) can result in no tax.

The owner of an unincorporated business cannot obtain those tax benefits that come solely by reason of employee status (except for retirement plan benefits, which, however, have some limitations). But a person can be an employee of a corporation, even if he or she owns all of the stock. It may be more desirable to have family members employed by one or more corporations. One corporate advantage lies in the area of retirement plans, although the Tax Equity and Fiscal Responsibility Act of 1982 went a long way toward equalizing the retirement benefits between self-employed persons and those who are employees—even of their own corporation. In addition, employee fringe benefits, such as tax-sheltered group term life insurance, tax-free medical insurance, and the deductibility of disability insurance premiums, or some of the other fringe benefits discussed in Chapter 2, are available to the stockholder-employee but not to an unincorporated owner.[15]

Those parents who are willing to make long-term financial commitments to their children can hire them in the business with the view that the child will take up to $2,000 of earnings and contribute it to an Individual Retirement Account.[16] The resulting deduction for adjusted gross income ensures no current tax on that amount, but the child will have to wait until age 59½ before the money will be available, unless penalties are to be incurred. (See Chapter 17.) Thus, a dependent child could have $5,250 of earned income for 1990 (basic standard deduction plus IRA) without paying any income tax. A nondependent child could have 1990 gross income of $7,300 (basic standard deduction plus IRA plus exemption deduction).

[13]Retirement plans are discussed in Chapter 17.
[14]IRC Sec. 3121(b)(3).
[15]Until September 30, 1990, the unincorporated owner can deduct 25% of amounts paid for health insurance in arriving at adjusted gross income. IRC Sec. 162(l).
[16]See discussion of individual retirement accounts in Chapter 17.

15.6 Equipment Leasing

A common family tax planning device is equipment leasing, which may be carried on through a partnership or through a trust. The basic idea is that equipment (or a building) is owned by or for the children, who are in low tax brackets, and is leased by the parents (or their partnership or corporation) for use in the business. The objective is to build up a fund of assets for the children out of tax-deductible rental payments.

This plan can be demonstrated with the following situation. A medical doctor decides to go into practice for herself. She needs a building and equipment for the office. A trust is created for the benefit of the doctor's children. The trust borrows the money to build the building and buy the equipment, which in turn is leased to the doctor. The trust uses the rental income to pay off the debt. Any taxable trust income is taxed to the trust or to the children.[17] The doctor gets a deduction, at her highest tax rates, for the rental expense, the only restriction being that the rental payments must be "reasonable" under the circumstances. The trust or children pay tax at lower rates. The trust income is ultimately used by the children for a college education as explained in Chapter 14.

A related estate tax advantage can come about from this arrangement. There is a good chance that the building will appreciate in value. If the doctor owned the building, her estate would include that asset at its current value. If the trust owned the building, the doctor's estate would not be taxed upon the value of the building. This latter estate tax matter may not be a major consideration for people with high current income but low net worth, such as many young professionals and new small business owners.

The variations are endless. Sometimes the property is in a Clifford trust set up before March, 1986, and thus reverts to the parents. This may jeopardize deductibility of the rent. Further, it fails to remove appreciation in value of the assets from the taxable estates of the parents.

15.7 Interest-Free Loans

Although interest-free demand loans were once an excellent family tax planning tool, a 1984 Supreme Court decision and 1984 legislation have dramatically altered the tax treatment accorded such loans.[18] The Court held that intrafamily

[17]As explained in Chapter 14, the trust income will be taxed to the children if distributed to them or if permanently set aside for them.
[18]*Est. of Dickman*, 104 S. Ct. 1088, 84-1 USTC ¶ 9240 (Sup. Ct. 1984); IRC Sec. 7872.

interest-free demand loans give rise to a taxable gift. The tax is imposed not on the funds loaned, but instead on the value of the forgone interest. However, such "gifts" of forgone interest are eligible for the $10,000 annual gift tax exclusion discussed later in this chapter. Secondly, the 1984 tax law has the effect of imputing taxable *income* to the lender in an amount equal to the forgone interest, at a rate set by the Treasury Department. The borrower is allowed a corresponding deduction for the interest expense, which can partially offset any income actually earned with the loaned funds.

Interest-free loans of small amounts can still achieve tax benefits. The imputed income rule does not apply to a family loan of $10,000 or less, regardless of what the borrower does with the money; nor does it apply to family loans of up to $100,000 per borrower where the borrower has not over $1,000 of net investment income and tax avoidance is not a principal purpose of the loan. Thus, loans to provide a down payment on a house, finance college, and so on, can still be interest free without creating income to the lender, even though the lender may, for example, be paying interest on a home equity loan to carry the loan amount.

15.8 Sale to Family Trust or Family Member

A deferral of tax can sometimes be arranged by making a sale of property under the installment method to a family trust (or to another member of the family) prior to a sale for cash outside the family. The property cannot be a marketable security, however, and the second sale cannot take place until at least two years after the first. But if the property is not a marketable security and the two-year test is met, then:

1. The first seller will pay tax only as payments are received from the trust, while
2. The trust, which sells the property for cash, will have little taxable gain because it only held the property for two years, will thus have little tax to pay and can invest the sales proceeds profitably until it must use them to make its installment payments to the first seller.

Installment sales were discussed in Chapter 8. Court decisions have upheld the validity of such arrangements when the installment sales to the trusts (or family members) were bona fide.[19]

For example, assume that Billy Barnes, who owes no debts, owns a piece of unimproved real estate that would produce a gain of $100,000 if sold. Billy forms a trust with a child as the beneficiary and sells the property to the trust under an installment sale, thus spreading the recognized gain over ten years. The trust sells the property two years later, recognizing little or no gain. The trust then has the use of cash equal to the difference between the sales price it receives and the installment payment to Billy. The trust is required to pay interest to Billy, which will be ordinary income. This may be a small price to pay for the family group advantages of the deferral of taxable gain and may not even be a tax disadvantage.

15.9 Private Annuities

An annuity is a contract whereby one party is obligated to make periodic payments of some amount to the other party or parties, usually for life. Thus, a person might buy a commercial annuity from an insurance company. The buyer would receive a fixed monthly payment for life, starting at some predetermined age. In a joint and survivor annuity, the insurance company agrees to pay the monthly amount to both husband and wife, and to the survivor until his or her death. These concepts, and the tax treatment accorded annuity payments (the use of an exclusion allowance to spread the cost of the annuity over the expected return), were discussed in Chapter 2.

The private annuity differs from the commercial annuity in both its economic substance and its tax treatment. Assume that the major family asset is an S corporation that owns a department store. The parents own 60% and each of four children owns 10% of the stock. The parents want to pass the 60% of the corporation to their four children. However, they also want to have an independent source of income for as long as they live. A gift will not achieve their goals. A sale of the stock at a fixed price won't either—because they do not know how long they will live and could outlive the proceeds of the sale. Sale of the stock to either the corporation or the children may solve the problem, with the sale proceeds taking the form of an annuity.

The price should be based upon Treasury Department tables used in valuing annuities generally.[20] The exclusion ratio should be based upon the tax basis of the stock.[21] For example, assume that the stock the parents own has a basis to them of $100,000, but a current value of $900,000. Also assume that the annuity the parents are to receive is valued at $900,000 and would produce payments of $1.2 million if they lived for exactly as long as the life expectancy set out in Treasury Department tables. The exclusion ratio, based upon the $100,000 basis

[19]See, for example, *William D. Pityo*, 70 TC 125 (No. 21); *James H. Weaver, Jr.* (CA6 1981), 47 AFTR2d 81-1404; and *Charles L. Vaughan*, 81 TC No. 55, in conjunction with IRC Sec. 453(e).

[20]Treas. Reg. 20.2031-10.
[21]Rev. Rul. 69-74, 1969-1 CB 43.

of the stock, would be 8½%.[22] As the parents received annuity payments, 8½% would be excluded from gross income. The balance would be ordinary income. This 8½% exclusion would apply until they had recovered the $100,000 tax basis.[23]

In our example, the parents bought the annuity. Who sold it? The answer could be either the corporation or the children. Neither alternative produces any tax benefits to the seller of the annuity if the transaction is viewed as an annuity. If the corporation is the seller, it has redeemed some of its outstanding stock. As was discussed earlier, a corporation has no gain or loss from redemption of its stock. If the children sell the annuity, they are treated as having purchased stock from their parents and their cost (basis) will ultimately be the total of the annuity payments made. No portion of the annuity payments made to the obligor is deductible as interest expense.[24]

The parents will get what they want: a steady income for life. The children probably will get what they want, all of the stock of the business. Upon the death of the parents, there may be nothing to be included in their gross estates because the annuity payments are not to continue beyond death.[24a]

15.10 Gifts—Built-in Gains

A person receiving a gift of property is treated in some ways the same as the donor of the property as far as a later sale. The holding period of the property and its tax basis (subject to some adjustments on occasion) are the same as before the gift. Assume that a high-tax-bracket parent owns property currently worth a great deal more than its tax basis. A gift of the property to a low-bracket child prior to its sale can result in tax savings.

For example, a parent has a piece of property that is to be sold for a gain of $15,000. If the taxpayer is in the 28% tax bracket, the result will be a tax of $4,200. If a bona fide gift is made to a dependent child (14 or over) with no other income, the same $15,000 of adjusted gross income will bear a (1990) tax of $2,175. The donor *might* incur a gift tax on the transfer, but in exchange for $2,025 savings in income tax each year, the gift tax may be nominal.[25] This strategy should only be used after careful planning. Since the highest tax rates start at fairly low levels, the actual tax savings may be small, and the rules concerning unearned income of children under 14 make it even more difficult to shift large amounts of income.

The example is of a direct gift. A gift to a trust may also seem desirable, since it allows the giver to retain some degree of control over the property. However, if a trust that acquires property by gift sells the property within two years of the gift, it must pay tax on its gain at the donor's tax bracket and not its own.[26] If the sale is an installment sale, this rule applies to all the payments received as long as the sale took place within the two-year period.[27]

15.11 Sale of Loss Assets

Sometimes family members in relatively low tax brackets have assets which have declined substantially in value (i.e., the tax basis is much higher than the current value of the asset). They may feel that the asset has great long-range value and so want to keep it. But there is a current need for cash.

A sale within the family group may provide a taxwise answer. A sale to an outsider would raise the desired cash, but also would generate a tax loss that may be of little benefit because the seller's tax bracket is low or the capital loss limitations might apply. (See Chapter 5.) A sale to a family member (ancestor, descendant, spouse, brother, or sister) will not produce a tax loss. Losses on sales of property to certain relatives are not recognizable for tax purposes.[28] The buyer, however, in calculating any gain from a subsequent sale, can have unrecognized gain to the extent of the disallowed loss on the first sale. There is no limit on the number of years between the two transactions. Thus, if the value of the property does bounce back, the benefit of the loss will inure to a family member through a reduction of gain that would otherwise be taxed at higher rates.

For example, assume that a taxpayer has a piece of property which, if sold, would generate a loss of $10,000. This loss would produce only a small tax savings because taxable income is only expected to be $15,000 without the loss. In 1990, the property is sold to a brother for its fair market value. The loss is not recognized to the seller, but the seller has the benefit of the cash flow from the sale. In 1992, when the property has regained its value, the brother sells

[22]$100,000 ÷ $1,200,000 = 8½%.

[23]See *Simon M. Lazarus* (CA9 1975), 513 F.2d 824, 35 AFTR2d 75-1191, 75-1 USTC 9387. In this approach, the transaction is treated as a combination of an installment sale and an annuity purchase. It could also be argued that the private annuity should be treated as an installment sale for an indefinite price under Temp. Reg. 15a.453–1(c)(4). The $100,000 of basis would be recovered pro rata over a fifteen-year period (i.e., $6,666.67 per year).

[24]See *Rebecca Bell* (CA8), 49 AFTR2d 82-538, 82-1 USTC 9148. But if the transaction is treated as an installment sale for an indefinite amount, as in footnote 30, then there will be interest imputed into the transaction under IRC Sec. 483.

[24a]It is possible, however, that IRS will interpret IRC Sec. 2036(c) to require inclusion of some amount in their estates.

[25]There is a good chance that no gift tax will result, particularly if the parent has not made substantial gifts before. See discussion later in this chapter.

[26]IRC Sec. 644(a). This rule does not apply if the transferor dies within the two-year period.

[27]IRC Sec. 644(f).

[28]IRC Sec. 267. (See Sec. 5.23 of this text.)

it for a gain of $12,000, measured just the same as any gain, by the difference between selling price and original cost. Because the first seller could not recognize $10,000 of loss, the second seller does not have to recognize $10,000 of the gain. The higher the tax bracket of the second seller, the greater the savings that can result from not having to pay tax on $10,000 of the $12,000 gain.

15.12 Federal Estate and Gift Taxes—An Introduction

Since the income tax applies to almost everyone and applies each year, it has occupied most of our attention in this book. But tax planning, whether for the individual or the family, should also involve at least a look at transfer taxes (federal estate and gift taxes).

Few families today have severe transfer tax problems. With reasonable planning, a family can have a net worth of $1.2 million or more and still avoid paying any transfer taxes as property descends from one generation to the next. But note that planning is necessary to achieve this result. Life insurance proceeds, escalating residential property values, and retirement benefits payable to surviving spouses result in a substantially greater number of business executives and professional people having the potential for transfer tax problems than is generally realized.

More significant is the potential for future problems. The transfer tax rates and exemptions remained substantially unchanged for over forty years before 1976. Then, and again in 1981, the tax rules were changed substantially. If the current rates and exemptions endure, inflation will create transfer tax problems for more and more people. A family with a net worth of $500,000 has no transfer tax problems today. But assume that inflation proceeds at an average of 8% per year, and that the family net worth increases at the same rate. Then twenty years from now, the net worth of today's $500,000 family will be $2.3 million, in thirty years it will be $5.0 million, and in forty years it will be $10.86 million. The estate tax on a $10.86 million estate can be over $5.0 million.

Within that forty-year time, therefore, transfer taxes may well become critical to the tax planning of most readers of this book.

15.13 Transfer Tax

Prior to 1976, there were two separate transfer taxes, the gift tax and the estate tax.[29] The rules were somewhat different, and the rate structures were different, with the gift tax being slightly less than the estate tax.[30] Today, the U.S. tax law integrates the estate tax and the gift tax through the use of one tax table, which is shown in Table A, Fig. 15-2.[31]

Until 1993, the highest rate will be 55% and will apply to taxable transfers over $3,000,000. For 1993 and thereafter, the highest rate will be 50%, which will apply to taxable transfers in excess of $2,500,000. Taxable transfers in excess of $10 million are subject to an additional 5% surtax as explained in the footnote to Fig. 15-2.

Like the income tax, the transfer tax is progressive, meaning that the larger the amount being taxed, the higher the rate of tax. Unlike the income tax, a taxpayer does not start over each year with a new taxable base. The law treats lifetime gifts and transfers at death as part of one unified computation.[32] The effect is that a person moves up on the progressive rate scale as taxable gifts are made during life, so that the tax rate at death generally starts at the last tax rate that applied to gifts made prior to death.[33](An exception applies to a taxpayer who had made substantial pre-1977 gifts.) The purpose of this system is to prevent wealthy persons from obtaining a significant tax benefit through lifetime transfers. This goal has not been fully achieved by Congress. Significant tax reductions can still be obtained by making gifts during one's lifetime. This will be illustrated later.

The transfer tax does not fall upon the recipient of property. It was mentioned in Chapter 2 that gross *income* for purposes of the income tax does not include either gifts or inheritances. Neither is subject to income tax. Similarly, the recipient of a gift or an inheritance is not subject to the transfer tax. It is the donor, in the case of lifetime gifts, and the estate of the decedent, in the case of transfers at death, that must pay the tax.[34]

The footnote to Figure 15-2 indicates that there is a surtax of 5% applied to the taxable transfers between $10,000,000 and $21,040,000. A reader might ask, "What is the purpose of that

[29]The gift and estate taxes were unified by the Revenue Act of 1976, P.L. 94-455. Prior to that time, the estate tax rates were contained in IRC Sec. 2001 and the gift tax rates were contained in IRC Sec. 2502(a).

[30]The gift tax rates were progressive from 2¼% (on taxable gifts of $5,000 or less) to 57¾% (on taxable gifts over $10,000,000). The estate tax rates were progressive from 3% (on taxable estates of $5,000 or less) to 77% (on taxable estates over $10,000,000).

[31]IRC Sec. 2001(c) contains the rates.

[32]The gift tax is imposed by IRC Sec. 2501(a). The estate tax is imposed by IRC Sec. 2001(a).

[33]This is done by defining taxable estate to include taxable gifts made by the taxpayer during his or her lifetime. Taxable estate is defined by IRC Sec. 2051.

[34]The gift tax liability is imposed primarily upon the donor (Treas. Reg. 25.2502-2). The estate tax liability is imposed upon the estate [IRC Sec. 2001(a)], but the executor is liable for payment (IRC Sec. 2002). However, if the donor (or the estate) is unable to pay, the IRS may be able to collect from the donee (or the heir) as a transferee.

FIGURE 15-2
TABLE A
Unified Gift and Estate Tax Rate Table until 1993

Column A	Column B	Column C	Column D
Taxable Amount Over—	Taxable Amount Not Over—	Tax on Amount in Column A	Rate of Tax on Excess Over Amount in Column A
....	$10,000	....	18%
$10,000	20,000	$1,800	20%
20,000	40,000	3,800	22%
40,000	60,000	8,200	24%
60,000	80,000	13,000	26%
80,000	100,000	18,200	28%
100,000	150,000	23,800	30%
150,000	250,000	38,800	32%
250,000	500,000	70,800	34%
500,000	750,000	155,800	37%
750,000	1,000,000	248,300	39%
1,000,000	1,250,000	345,800	41%
1,250,000	1,500,000	448,300	43%
1,500,000	2,000,000	555,800	45%
2,000,000	2,500,000	780,800	49%
2,500,000	3,000,000	1,025,800	53% } will change after 1992
3,000,000	....	1,290,800	55% }

Estates between $10 million and $21,040,000 pay an additional 5% (i.e., 60%) on the taxable amount over $10 million. After 1992, the additional 5% rate will apply to transfers between $10,000,000 and $18,340,000.

TABLE B
Table for Unified Credit Against Gift and Estate Tax
United States Citizen or Resident Donor

For gifts made, or estates occurring:	*The credit is—*
After December 31, 1982, and before January 1, 1984	79,300
After December 31, 1983, and before January 1, 1985	96,300
After December 31, 1984, and before January 1, 1986	121,800
After December 31, 1985, and before January 1, 1987	155,800
After December 31, 1986	192,800

additional tax?" In response to that question, note that the maximum amount of the surtax will be 5% ($11,040,000), which is $552,000. Why collect an additional $552,000 when taxable transfers are equal to or greater than $21,040,000? The purpose is twofold, first to remove the tax reduction from rates which are lower than the 55%, and second, to remove the tax reduction from the $192,800 credit. Let's consider the removal of the tax benefit of the lower rates. The tax reduction resulting from rates less than 55% is $359,200 as can be seen from the following example:

Assume taxable transfers of $4,000,000. *If* the tax rate were a flat 55% on taxable transfer of $4,000,000 (note that it is not) the tax on $4,000,000 would be $2,200,000. Actually, the tax on $4,000,000 (using the Table A rates) is $1,290,800 + 55% ($1,000,000), which is $1,840,800. Thus, the amount of tax reduction as the result of tax rates below the 55% level is $2,200,000 − $1,840,800, which is $359,200.

The second purpose of the surtax is to remove the tax reduction of the unified credit, which is $192,800.

Tax reduction from rates of tax that are under 55%	$359,200
Tax reduction from unified credit	192,800
Total	$552,000

The effect of the surtax on taxable transfers in excess of $21,040,000 is to apply a tax rate at a flat 55% without any unified credit.

To illustrate the basic computation, assume that Billy Barnes dies in 1995, having never made any taxable gifts.[35] Assume that the "taxable estate" will be $820,000. The rate table in Fig. 15-1 shows a tax of $248,300 plus 39% of the taxable estate in excess of $750,000. Thus, the total tax, *before credits,* would be $275,600. From this, a credit of $192,800 would be deducted (see Table B, Fig. 15-2), leaving a total tax due to the federal government of $82,800.[36]

[35]Some say Billy died of an overtaxing life. It was certainly true that the collapsible corporation had collapsed and Billy was finding it harder to hold on to the personal holding company. Billy no longer even trusted the *inter vivos* trust! And filling out a Form 1040 had lost its zest. *Requiem in taxem.*

[36]The credit is allowed by IRC Sec. 2010. It is possible that some other credits would be available, as discussed later. If so, the amount payable to the federal government would be reduced.

"Taxable estate," "taxable gifts," and other technical terms will be discussed later, but for now consider how the gift and estate taxes are "unified."

Assume that Billy Barnes in the example given did not die. Instead, assume that a *taxable* gift of $100,000 had been made by Billy in 1984.[37] Since no pre-1984 taxable gifts were made, the gift tax would have been imposed as follows:

Tax on $100,000 (from the rate table)[38]	$23,800
Less: Credit (for 1984—Table B)	96,300
Tax due	$ 0

COMPUTER FORMULAS: The estate tax rate table could be put on the computer either as a LOOKUP or a series of @IF statements. The @IF would consist of a different formula for each bracket. For example, @IF (TA < 20,000, 1800 + .20 (TA − 10,000), *x*), where *x* is the cell locator for the next bracket tax formula, and TA is the taxable amount. The process could be simplified by using cell locations for the percentages and brackets, rather than numbers. Below is a table showing the first four brackets.

	A	*B*	*C*
1	Taxable amount		*x*
2	Tax		+D4
3			
4	10,000	0	18%
5	20,000	1800	20%
6	40,000	3800	22
7	60,000	8200	24

In cell D4 would be the formula @IF (C$1 < A4, B4 + C4 * (C$1 − A3)), D5). This formula is useful because it can be copied and the computer will automatically change its locators relative to where it is copied. The only number which will remain constant is C1, which on Lotus is done by inserting the $ sign within the locator. By copying this one formula you will not have to rewrite the formula for every bracket.

The unified credit is available only once. You use it like writing checks against a bank account balance. It is not a credit of $192,800 per year and it is not a credit of $192,800 for lifetime gifts plus another $192,800 for transfers at death. Prior to 1987, there was a transition period during which the credit increased each year. This is reflected in Table B.

Gifts are *cumulative,* meaning that current gifts are added to prior gifts for purposes of the progressive rate application. Taking the example a step further, assume that Billy made another *taxable* gift in 1985, this time of $330,000. The 1985 tax was computed as follows:

Current year's (1985) taxable gifts	$330,000
Prior years' taxable gifts	100,000
Total taxable gifts	$430,000
Tax (from rate table)[39]	$132,000
Less credit (for 1985—Table B)	121,800
Tax due	$ 10,200

Note that the credit was not an *additional* $121,800 for the year 1985. Because of the transitional period, there was an increase in the credit of $25,500 from 1984 to 1985. But because the computation requires that prior gifts be added to current taxable gifts before going into the table, the full $121,800 is used in the calculation. For 1986, the credit was $155,800. For 1987 and thereafter, the credit is $192,800.

Notice that the first gift of $100,000 put Billy in the 30% tax bracket for future transfers despite the fact that no tax was payable because of the credit. The next gift of $330,000 resulted in a marginal tax rate of 34%. Notice also that the credit has not been subtracted twice, only once. See Fig. 15-3.

Assume that Billy dies in 1991 without making further gifts and with a *taxable estate* of $400,000. *Taxable estate* means the estate *after* deductions. (See Figure 15-5.) The tax is calculated as follows:

Taxable estate		$400,000
Taxable gifts during life		430,000
Total		$830,000
Tax on $830,000[40]		$279,500
Less: Tax previously paid	$ 10,200	
Credit (1991)	192,800	203,000
Tax due		$ 76,500

The $192,800 credit means that no transfer tax is due until total taxable transfers exceed $600,000.[41] This, in turn, means that fewer than 2% of the estates of people dying in any given year will currently need to file a federal estate tax return.[42] For 1988, only 52,449 decedents had estates large enough to require that tax returns be filed.[43] The 15% of filed returns showing estates of

[37]Note that the *taxable* gift is $100,000. Not all gifts are taxable. As will be explained in more detail later, the donor can exclude gifts of $10,000 *each year* to *each donee.*
[38]This does not require any computation, since the $100,000 is where a new marginal rate begins.

[39]$70,800 + 34% ($430,000 − $250,000) = $132,000.
[40]$248,300 + 39% ($830,000 − $750,000) = $279,500.
[41]If taxable estate is $600,000, the tax is $155,800 + 37% ($600,000 − $500,000) = $192,800. The credit will reduce the tax to zero.
[42]For decedents dying after 1986, an estate tax return must be filed if the gross estate is $600,000 or more. This is true even though the deductions may be large enough to reduce the taxable estate to zero.
[43]*Statistics of Income Bulletin,* Vol. 9, No. 2 (U.S. Treasury Department, Fall, 1989), p. 96. Preliminary data for 1989 indicates that the number will be 55,000.

FIGURE 15-3

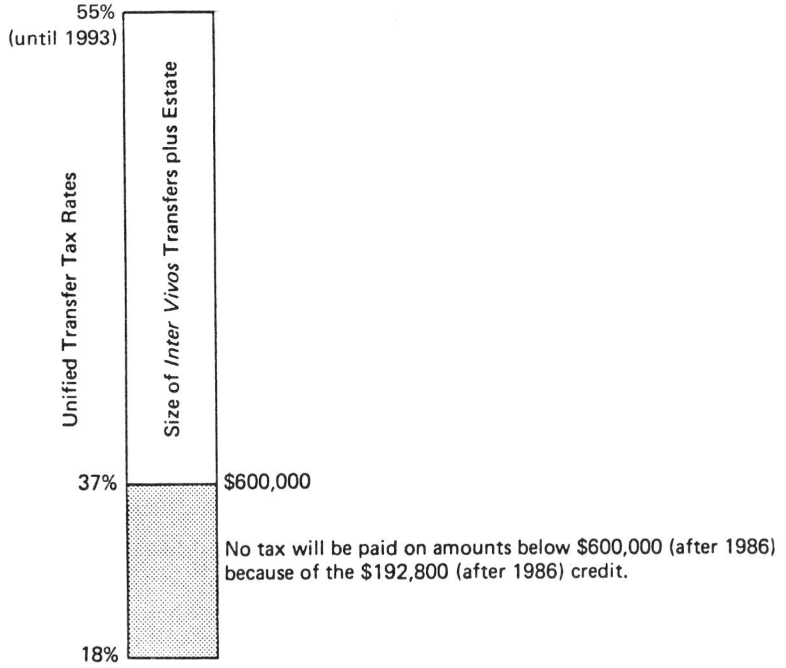

Although the Unified Transfer Tax Rates are from 18% to 55%, In Fact, No One Will Pay Tax At Rates of 18% to 34% Because the Credit Will Eliminate Tax at Those Rates. The Lowest Marginal Tax Rate at Which Tax Will Actually Be Paid Will Be 37%.

over $1 million paid 65% of the total $5 billion of estate tax for 1983.[44] Thus the estate tax is clearly one that falls upon the rich and not the poor.

For that minority of persons with sufficient assets to have a possible estate tax liability at current price levels, planning for the minimization of the estate tax, and for other expenses associated with transfer of an estate, is often a major undertaking. The costs of administering an estate, getting it through probate, and so forth, are often more substantial than the estate tax, running about 8% of the total estate.[45]

Planning for minimum transfer tax usually involves:

1. Disposing of property during life (*inter vivos* gifts).
2. Taking maximum advantage of the marital deduction.
3. Imaginative use of charitable beneficiaries.
4. Using trust devices to prevent transfer taxes from depleting capital in each generation.

Each of these will be considered in order.

15.14 Taxable Transfers

Inter vivos gift merely means a lifetime gift ("during life"). It may be contrasted with the term *testamentary gift* or *testamentary transfer*, which is a transfer of property at death.

Inter vivos gifts generally are subject to the gift tax, although, as we have seen, the application of the credit means that there is no tax due until a substantial cumulative sum has been transferred.[46] But there are other important exceptions that can have significant tax savings implications.

There is a $10,000 *annual* exclusion for each person *to whom* gifts are made.[47] This $10,000 is not cumulative. In other words, if a donor does not make a gift to a donee in one year, there cannot be a $20,000 tax-free transfer in the following year as a "catchup." On the other hand, there is *no limit* on the number of donees in any one year or during the donor's lifetime. Thus, substantial amounts can be given away tax-free at the rate of $10,000 per year per donee. The donor and the donee do not have to be related. Figure 15-4 demonstrates the tax savings potential. Note that the nontaxable gifts are removed from the highest potential marginal tax rates. Only gifts in excess of this $10,000 exclusion are included as "taxable gifts," subject to the rates shown in Table A, Fig. 15-2.

[44]*Statistics of Income Bulletin*, Vol. 4, No. 2 (U.S. Treasury Department, Fall, 1984), p. 12.
[45]Authors' estimate.

[46]Throughout this chapter, the $192,800 credit is used as an example. For years prior to 1987, a lower credit applied. See Table B, Fig. 15-2.
[47]IRC Sec. 2503(b). Prior to 1982, the annual exclusion per donee was $3,000.

FIGURE 15-4 Annual gifts of up to $10,000 per donee can be made without a gift tax, at the same time reducing the ultimate taxable estate of the donor

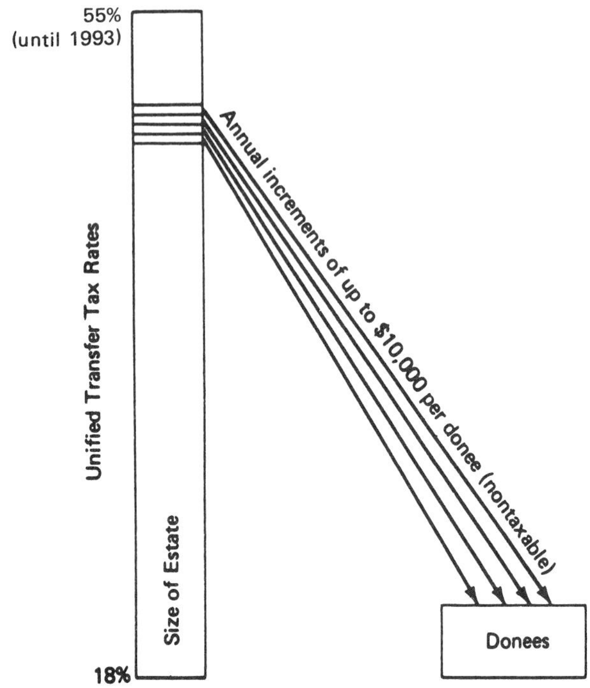

TAX PLANNING TIP: A person who might otherwise have enough assets to result in an estate tax upon death may consider beginning a gift program, thereby using the $10,000 annual exclusion for each donee per year. If there are several donees and the gifts continue over several years, a substantial amount of property can be given away tax-free. The estate tax savings can be large.

To illustrate, assume that a married couple, both age forty-five, have two married children. Each parent can be a donor. Each child and each child's spouse can be a donee. There could be even more donees, for example, if there were grandchildren. The parents can give away $80,000 per year (2 donors × 4 donees × $10,000) without filing a gift tax return or paying any gift tax. Thus, if gifts continue for twenty years, a total of $1.6 million can be transferred. Assuming that these gifts were invested by the donees and compounded at an after-tax return of 5%, about $2,777,000 would be accumulated by the children. Had the parents retained that property, and accumulated the income from it, that $2,777,000 could have cost $1,388,000 in estate taxes.[48] *Where noncash property is given away, it is the value on the date of the gift* that measures the gift for tax purposes.[49]

There is no requirement that a donee be related to the donor. Thus, the $10,000 annual exclusion can be used for nonrelatives as well.

In the previous example, the parents each made gifts of $10,000 to each child per year. In some situations, only one of the spouses may own the property to be gifted. The tax law permits a married couple to *elect* to treat a gift made by them, or either of them, as if made one-half by each. This is called "gift splitting." Thus, if a wife gives her son $23,000 in one year, she and her husband can agree to treat one-half of the gift as coming from him. If there are no other gifts to the donee for that year, *each* has made a taxable gift of $1,500 ($11,500 from each less the $10,000 exclusion for each).

Unlike the income tax, there is no opportunity for a joint tax return. Each donee must file a tax return if his or her gifts exceed the $10,000 amount to any one donee. This includes taxable gifts which are deemed to have been made by the donor as the result of a gift splitting election.

Three other types of transfers that are not "gifts" for purposes of the transfer tax are worthy of mention. First, if a donor pays for the education expenses of a donee, and makes the payment directly to the provider of that service, the amount is not considered a gift. Thus, a grandparent, for example, could give $10,000 in cash to a grandchild *and in addition* pay all of the grandchild's tuition, and there would be no taxable gift, no requirement to file a gift tax return. Second, payment of medical expenses, if made directly to the provider of such services, will not be a gift subject to tax. There is no dollar limit on such an exclusion. Finally, gifts made to qualified charitable organizations are not subject to the federal gift tax. In fact, as we saw in Chapter 4, they generally will result in a deduction for federal income tax purposes for the donor.

The following example illustrates how making gifts during one's lifetime can save tax dollars even though the tax rate table and the credit remain the same and a tax is paid on the gift. The reduction comes as the result of a smaller estate if substantial gift taxes are paid.

In the prior example of Billy Barnes's 1985 gift, the federal gift tax was $10,200. Having made that payment, the 1991 taxable estate of the decedent was lower by $10,200.[50] (We assume that if this

[48]The accumulation would depend, in part, upon the income tax rate of the parent as compared with that of the child. One of the additional motivations for giving away income-producing property sometimes is that the donee may have to pay less income tax than if the donor had retained the property.

[49]IRC Sec. 2512; Treas. Reg. 25.2512-1. If property is transferred for less than its full value, the difference between its value and the consideration paid will be a gift.

[50]Actually the estate is likely to be reduced more than the amount of the gift tax because of accumulated earnings which would have resulted on that money. This is discussed shortly.

$10,200 had not been paid to the IRS, it would still remain in the estate several years later.) In that example the marginal tax rate was 39%. Thus, the estate tax was lower by $3,978 (39% of $10,200) than if the gift tax had not been incurred. Obviously, the saving is larger for larger gifts, which result in a larger gift tax, and in larger estates, which are in a higher tax bracket. The resulting tax savings will depend upon the marginal tax rate. If a taxable gift of $1 million would result in a tax of 50%, or $500,000, the subsequent estate would be $500,000 smaller. At 50%, the estate tax would be $250,000 less than if the gift had not been made and the gift tax paid. As we will see later, it is necessary for the donor to live at least three years after the date of the gift in order to obtain this tax savings.

A second way in which gifts prior to death result in tax savings has to do with income-producing property. Assume that $1 million of bonds generates a 10% rate of return, or $100,000 per year. If the bonds are given away, the income generated between the date of gift and the date of death will be excluded from the transfer tax on the decedent's estate, assuming that the decedent would not have consumed that amount.

As with interest in the foregoing example, nonrecognized gain in the value of property will be removed from the taxable estate if property is given away during lifetime. For example, assume that a person owns stock worth $1 million. The stock does not pay any dividends, but the value of the stock increases year by year. If the stock is given away, the gift tax calculation will be based on $1 million (actually, $990,000, if there is only one donee). If the stock is retained and the owner dies when the stock is worth $1.3 million, the larger number will be included in the gross estate. Also, the $10,000 exclusion does not apply to transfers at death.

One income tax advantage of lifetime gifts is that the donee may be in a lower income tax bracket than the donor. Hence, the donee may have less income tax to pay on the income from the property or on gain from the sale of the property. Of course, the opposite could also occur.

Many people also find nontax satisfactions in transferring their wealth to the persons for whom it is ultimately intended anyway. The donor may enjoy seeing the donee own and use the property.

One other type of gift needs to be mentioned, and that is the gift which can result from making a non-interest- or low-interest-bearing loan to another person.[51] Non-interest-bearing loans, or below-market-rate interest-bearing loans which are $10,000 or less will not result in a taxable gift for the imputed interest. Where the amount of the loan is over $10,000, however, there will be a taxable gift by the lender to the borrower equal to the imputed interest. The rule can be illustrated as follows. Assume that Billy Barnes made a non-interest-bearing loan of $120,000 to Lynn Larsen for one year. If the imputed rate is 12%, the imputed interest on the loan is $14,400, and Billy is treated as having made a taxable gift of $14,400 to Lynn. Such loans are more likely to occur between family members, but the same rules apply whether the parties are related or not. Where the total amount loaned is $100,000 or less, the maximum amount of imputed interest is limited to the total net investment income of the borrower. Thus, if the loan above had been $90,000, and Lynn's net investment income for the year had been $6,000, the imputed interest would have been $6,000 even if the rate was such that the interest calculation would have resulted in a larger amount.

If the lender charges less than the *applicable* rate (and the loan amount is over $100,000), the imputed interest is the difference between the interest charged and the *applicable* rate. What is the *applicable* rate? Generally, it is the average market yield of outstanding marketable U.S. government bonds and notes during the one month period ending on the 14th day of the preceding month.[52] Thus, the applicable rate for a loan made on August 10, for example, would be the average U.S. government bond yield for the period June 14 to July 14. The income tax treatment of non-interest-bearing and below-market-rate interest-bearing loans was discussed in Chapter 2.

We mentioned earlier that it is the *taxable estate* that is added to the total of *taxable* inter vivos gifts in order to determine the total amount subject to the estate tax, before credit. Fig. 15-5 is a summary of the calculation of a taxable estate.

FIGURE 15-5 Summary of the computation of the taxable estate

Gross Estate (fair market value of all property owned by decedent at date of death or six months later)
Less: **Debts of the decedent**
Funeral and administrative expenses
Losses incurred by the estate
Marital deduction
Charitable bequests
Equals: **Taxable estate**
Plus: ***Inter vivos* gifts**
Equals: **Total amount subject to transfer tax**

15.15 Marital Deduction

Gifts to one's spouse offer a unique transfer tax saving potential, because of the gift tax marital

[51] IRC Sec. 7872.

[52] Temporary Regs. IRC Sec. 1276(d).

deduction.[53] With some exceptions which will be explained later, gifts made by a spouse to the other spouse are not subject to the gift tax. This is accomplished by a marital deduction equal to 100% of the transfer. In other words, the transfer is included in gross gifts, but a deduction for that amount is also taken, so there is no tax.

A marital deduction is *also* available to the estate of a decedent who leaves property to a surviving spouse.[54] There is no distinction between community property states and noncommunity property states.

One situation exists where the 100% marital deduction will apply only if an election is made. This is where the transfer to a spouse is a terminable interest.[55] Even with the election, some terminable interests will not qualify for the marital deduction. To understand this provision, it is first necessary to understand a terminable interest transfer.

A terminable interest in property is an ownership interest that will cease after a period of time, or after the occurrence of some event. Most transfers are probably not of this type. In other words, if Billy Barnes transfers $20,000 in cash to Lynn Larsen, the transfer is complete and there are no future contingencies. Thus, there is no terminable interest. On the other hand, assume that Billy transfers $20,000 of Supercorp. stock in trust for the benefit of Lynn, with the provision that enjoyment of the benefits (receipt of the dividend income from the stock) will be available to Lynn only for as long as Lynn remains unmarried. That is a transfer of a terminable interest, because Lynn's interest in the property may terminate. This is only one example. There are countless alternative possible conditions that a donor could impose on the transfer.

As a general rule, if a person dies owning only a terminable interest in property, his or her gross estate does *not* include any amount as the result of the rights in that property. (See Fig. 15-5.) Also, as a general rule, the transferor of such an interest in property to his or her spouse is not allowed a marital deduction for the transfer. On the other hand, if the owner of a terminable interest in property is the spouse of the transferor, and the transferor qualified to make the election to take the marital deduction, and did make that election, the holder of the terminable interest is required to include the value of the property in his or her estate.

[53]IRC Sec. 2523. No marital deduction is available for a non-citizen spouse, however.

[54]IRC Sec. 2056. There are restrictions on use of the marital deduction for a non-citizen spouse.

[55]IRC Sec. 2523(f). It should be noted that this is not the only way to avoid the estate tax. More sophisticated techniques are beyond the scope of this discussion.

If a married person transfers a terminable interest to the other spouse, there are some conditions which must be satisfied in order for the 100% marital deduction to apply. First, the spouse receiving the interest in the property must be entitled to all the income from the property for life, and the income must be paid to that spouse at least annually. In other words, an income interest that will last for only a term of years, or an income interest which will terminate upon the occurrence of some event (such as death), will not qualify for the marital deduction. Also, no one can have the power to appoint any part of the property to anyone other than the receiving spouse during that receiving spouse's life. If those conditions are satisfied, the 100% marital deduction can be elected.

For example, assume that Mr. Smith dies and leaves income-producing property in trust to Mrs. Smith, with provisions that meet all of the foregoing requirements. Mr. Smith's estate can elect to use the marital deduction. Why would the estate choose not to make the election since the result of not electing might well be to cause Mr. Smith's estate to have to pay some estate tax? The answer is that there will be a corresponding impact upon the estate of Mrs. Smith. If the election is made by Mr. Smith's estate, Mrs. Smith's estate will include the value of the property. (Note that this result is an exception to the general rule which provides that Mrs. Smith's estate would not be required to include the value of the property because it is a terminable interest.) If the election is not made by Mr. Smith's estate, Mrs. Smith's estate will not include the value of the property.[56] Thus, if it is expected that Mrs. Smith's estate will be larger than Mr. Smith's, and the result will be that more tax will be paid by having the property included in her estate, the election should not be made. However, a refinement of the analysis which should be made prior to reaching such a conclusion is to convert the expected tax liability of the two estates into a present value number. This would involve some forecast of how long it will be before Mrs. Smith will die and her estate tax will be due. Another reason for electing to have property included in Mr. Smith's estate might be that his estate will not pay any tax anyway. If the total *taxable* estate of Mr. Smith will be small enough that there will be no tax because of the application of the unified credit, there is no tax payment resulting from including the property in his estate. Then, upon the death of Mrs. Smith, the property will be excluded from her estate as well, because she only owned a terminable interest.

[56]IRC Sec. 2031 defines gross estate.

Leaving a surviving spouse all of the property in order to get the maximum marital deduction may not always be good planning. This is due to the potential credit which is wasted if the before-credit tax is not at least equal to the available credit. Assume that a taxpayer will have an estate of $800,000. The will leaves everything outright to the surviving spouse (all eligible for the marital deduction). If the survivor's taxable estate is $800,000 that second estate will owe a tax of $75,000, although the original estate avoided all tax.[57]

The $75,000 can be saved. Assume that the original decedent made a $550,000 transfer to the surviving spouse which was subject to the marital deduction. The remaining $250,000 was transferred into a bypass trust for the benefit of the surviving spouse.[58] The $250,000 was included in the estate of the first decedent. There would be no estate tax to the first estate:

Gross estate	$800,000	
Marital deduction	550,000	
Taxable estate	$250,000	
Tax (before credit)		$ 70,800
Credit		192,800
Tax		$ 0

The survivor has full benefit of income generated by these assets during lifetime. The second estate, again assuming that all property from the deceased spouse is still owned at death, will be $550,000, even without deductions. No tax will result to the second decedent's estate because of the $192,800 credit.

Even if the surviving spouse will have other assets that might create an estate tax liability, certain things can be done to reduce the amount. Gifts using the annual $10,000 per donee exclusion are often utilized. Purchase of an annuity can provide an assured income and yet leave nothing to be subject to estate tax.[59] Remarriage may either dissipate the inheritance or provide another marital deduction with the new spouse.

In planning for disposition of an estate, it is common to take maximum advantage of the marital deduction.[60] This does not mean, however, leaving all property to the surviving spouse, although that would reduce the tax to zero. There may be other beneficiaries to whom a person would like to transfer some of the property. It should be clear at this point that if a person did not use any of his or her unified credit to reduce the tax on *inter vivos* gifts, a taxable estate of $600,000 or less will result in no transfer tax to be paid. The credit will reduce the tax on $600,000 to zero. We therefore say that any part of the credit that is not used to reduce tax is "wasted." Part of the planning strategy for the transfer tax is to avoid any "wasted" credit. Where the planning is done for a married couple (two potential credits of $192,800 each), there is the opportunity to have $1,200,000 of taxable transfers that will result in no tax. The following example illustrates the use of the marital deduction.

A married person has a net worth of $1,000,000. There is a spouse, but also children by a previous marriage. The taxpayer is expecting to die before the spouse, so drafts a will with provisions that the children by the previous marriage are to receive $600,000 and that the surviving spouse will receive the balance. Upon death, the spouse receives $400,000, which is a deduction to the estate, leaving $600,000 which is subject to tax (before the unified credit).[61] The tax, before credit, is $192,800, but the credit reduces tax liability to zero. Upon the death of the second spouse, there will be no estate tax if that estate is $600,000 or less. Of course, if the person making the plans would like to leave more than $400,000 to the surviving spouse, this could be done and there would still be no tax upon the first death, and perhaps none upon the second death. We used the $600,000 transfer to children as an example only to illustrate the amount of taxable estate which can be left without any tax because of the credit.

In an estate which is larger and where there may be a tax because it is desirable to leave more than $600,000 to persons other than the surviving spouse, the plan might call for making gifts prior to death. Since husband and wife can be treated as two donors, up to $20,000 per year can be given to each donee without any gift tax, and without the requirement of having to include the gift in the estate.[62] The $10,000 annual exclusion also applies to transfers made by one spouse to the other.[63]

[57]Note that the marital deduction was $800,000 which is more than necessary to reduce the tax to zero if the entire $192,800 credit is available.

[58]Note that this does not utilize all of the potential marital deduction, but by leaving more assets in the "bypass trust," the tax to the second decedent is reduced.

[59]The income tax treatment of annuities is discussed in Chapter 2.

[60]Under the rules in effect prior to 1982 there was a substantially different result. Many persons had written wills providing for disposition according to old rules. Therefore, it is extremely important for persons who had wills prepared prior to the Economic Recovery Tax Act of 1981 to have such wills rewritten under the provisions of current law.

[61]Actually, the property not passing to the surviving spouse could be larger than $600,000 because there undoubtedly will be other deductions such as funeral and administrative expenses.

[62]For transfers by husband and wife to third parties, see IRC Sec. 2513.

[63]This exclusion is of some benefit even though there is now an unlimited marital deduction because under the marital deduction, property can be transferred to a qualified terminable interest and will be included in the spouse's estate, whereas property transferred outright may not be included in the spouse's estate.

Therefore, where it is expected that one spouse will die sooner, that spouse can make up to $10,000 of gifts each year to the expected survivor and thereby reduce the estate.[64]

Even with the unlimited marital deduction, there is still a problem. What about the death of the surviving spouse at some later time? Assuming that there is not a remarriage and that the survivor does not consume the property (or all but $600,000 of it) during life, the survivor will face a substantial estate tax problem. As pointed out in Figure 15-3, if there is estate tax to be paid, the marginal rate will be 37% and could go as high as 55% (50% after 1992).

This result may lead to the generalization that some of the planning that can be done to save taxes in the estate of the first of a married couple to die can lead to estate tax problems when the survivor dies. Nevertheless, the postponement can be well worth the effort. It is often many years between the death of the first spouse and the death of the second. Also, the estate of the second may be reduced by consumption and by nontaxable gifts, or the second spouse may remarry and thus be able to take advantage of the marital deduction upon his or her death, so that the "day of reckoning" may never come, at least taxwise. The welfare of the surviving spouse is often of primary concern in families with net worth of about $1 million or less.[65] But tax planning often focuses on achieving the minimum transfer taxes for an entire family group and not just on the assets available for one person, as will now be discussed.

TAX PLANNING TIP: When using life insurance to provide estate tax dollars, a married couple should consider one policy which will pay its proceeds upon the death of the survivor of the two. If the unlimited marital deduction is used to reduce the estate tax to zero upon the death of the first to die, there is no need for life insurance for this purpose. A survivor policy will cost less than policies of equal coverage on each of the two separately.

15.16 Bypassing an Estate

In moderately sized estates of married persons, the primary interest of a spouse is often that all property go to the survivor. The desired result can be obtained with the marital deduction and the credit. However, for single persons, the former deduction will not be available. Very often, of course, the planner does not know if the expected decedent will be married or single upon death. One possibility is to assume that a decedent will be single. Therefore, where the gross estate will be in excess of $600,000, some estate tax can be expected.

The solution is often the use of a trust. If a person is the beneficiary of a trust, receiving the trust income but not having the power to dispose of trust property, his or her gross estate will *not* include the trust property upon death.[66] This is the "terminable interest" provision discussed earlier. Such a trust can be used to provide a beneficiary with income from property for life and at the same time ensure that upon death no (or very little) estate tax will be paid. For example, a decedent can leave property in a testamentary trust for the benefit of the survivor. Such a trust might provide, for example, that all of the trust income will be paid to the survivor each year and that the survivor will be able to obtain any amount of principal needed to maintain his or her standard of living in the event other resources are insufficient. The assets not used, and therefore remaining in the trust upon the death of the survivor, will pass to the remainderman (those persons chosen by the survivor), with the limitation that the survivor cannot direct that any amounts be paid to his or her estate or creditors.[67] Thus, the survivor can have the benefit of the income and can decide the ultimate disposition of the trust property, while at the same time excluding the property from his or her own estate.

TAX PLANNING TIP: A person who is concerned with the economic welfare of a survivor should consider having his or her estate pass to a trust, with the survivor having the income from the trust. Properly handled, the estate of the second person to die will then not include the value of the property received from the first decedent.

The bypass trust concept can be applied to beneficiaries other than a surviving spouse. For example, a widow or widower whose children have become financially successful might hesitate to

[64]Prior to 1982, gifts made to a spouse or to other parties within three years of death had to be included in the gross estate of the decedent.

[65]There is nothing technical about this $1 million number. It just seems to be a convenient benchmark.

[66]An interest in a trust, where the interest terminates upon the death of the beneficiary, is excluded from gross estate unless an election has been made to treat it as qualified terminable interest property for marital deduction purposes.

[67]Such a power held by the survivor is known as a "limited power of appointment." A "general power of appointment" is one in which the beneficiary can direct, without restriction, the disposition of the trust property. Powers of appointment are the subject of IRC Sec. 2041.

leave property outright to them because it would aggravate their own tax problems. The property can be left in trust upon death, with the children having the right to obtain trust assets if needed. Otherwise, the property is to pass to their children, the grantor's grandchildren.[68] This can be done, but will be tax-free only to the extent of $1,000,000 per grantor.[69] Thus, a married couple could bypass the estate tax for their children on as much as $2,000,000 of trust assets by creating a trust or trusts for the grandchildren.

An *inter vivos* transfer of property into trust will not result in escaping transfer tax altogether. Where an *inter vivos* trust is created, a gift tax will result, but with one difference. Instead of measuring the gift by the fair market value of the property, a discounted present value (of the future stream of earnings) is used. For example, assume that Billy Barnes has $1,000,000 that is to be transferred to a loved one. Assume that if that property were to remain in Billy's estate the additional estate tax would be $500,000, even if there is no change in the value of the property between now and the time of Billy's death. Instead, Billy decides to make an *inter vivos* transfer of the property into a trust with the income from the property flowing to the loved one for life and upon that person's death the trust corpus is to be paid to charity. (Charitable remainder trusts were mentioned in Chapter 14.) If the discounted present value of the gift is $400,000, Billy's taxable gift is $400,000 instead of $1,000,000. If Billy's marginal tax rate on the $400,000 transfer is 50%, the tax will be $200,000. In addition, Billy will be able to claim a deduction for income tax purposes equal to the present value of the remainder interest that will go to the charity. It is beyond the scope of this text to go into more detail.

15.17 Charitable Transfers

The estate and gift tax is imposed on the transfer of property. With two exceptions, it does not matter who the beneficiary may be. One exception is the allowance of the marital deduction for transfers to a spouse, already discussed. The other exception allows a deduction for transfers to religious, charitable, scientific, literary, or educational organizations.[70]

[68]This arrangement is called a "generation-skipping trust" because the children's estate will not include the property.

[69]Generation-skipping transfers, and the tax thereon, are covered by IRC Secs. 2601–2603 and 2611–2614. It is beyond the scope of this book to cover this topic in any more detail.

[70]In the case of *inter vivos* transfers, IRC Sec. 2522 defines taxable gifts to exclude gifts to charities. In the case of charitable bequests, IRC Sec. 2055 permits a deduction. Although political parties are not charitable organizations, the transfer of property to a political party is not a gift. *Stern* v. *U.S.* (CA5 1971) 71-1 USTC 12, 737, 27 AFTR2d 71-1647, 436 F.2d 1327.

The following is an extreme example, but will illustrate how charitable transfers are treated. Tracy owns 70% of the stock of the Tracy Manufacturing Company. Other members of the family own the remaining 30%. The fair market value of Tracy's stock is approximately $20 million. The corporation is engaged in a vigorous expansion, and Tracy hopes that this can be carried through without diluting the family's control. Borrowing power is already strained to the limit.

Tracy's tax advisers suggest that the stock be left to the Arizona State University Foundation, which is organized and operated exclusively for scientific and educational purposes. Because Tracy's spouse is already dead, and the 30% of the stock not owned by Tracy is distributed in the proportions in which Tracy desires to see control maintained, the suggestion is made that the corporate charter be amended to authorize a class of 10% cumulative nonvoting preferred stock. The will is amended to provide that the voting stock that the estate will acquire will be exchanged for the preferred stock. Then all the preferred stock will be distributed to the foundation. This effectively eliminates all estate tax because all of Tracy's preferred stock goes to charity and the estate gets a deduction for the entire amount of such a charitable bequest. Since the university will receive only nonvoting stock, control will remain within the family. In the absence of such a program, or some alternative, the estate tax on Tracy's $20 million estate could have been over $10 million. To raise this sum, family control of the corporation would almost certainly have had to be relinquished—or, at best, seriously weakened. The basic plan can be made more attractive by having Tracy start donating stock to the foundation during lifetime, thus gaining the income tax benefit of a charitable contribution and also participating in setting up the foundation's *modus operandi* relative to the corporation.

15.18 The Transfer Tax Credit

How should the transfer tax credit of $192,800 be reflected in an analysis of the costs of making gifts? One approach is to look at cash flows. Using all or part of the credit involves no present cash flow. Thus, the appropriate measure for the cost of the gift is only the tax payment that has to be made because of the gift.

The opposite approach would be to ignore differences in timing. If it appeared almost certain that a credit not used now would be used in full at some later date (either against gifts or upon the taxpayer's death), the gift tax *before the credit* would be considered the appropriate measure of cost.

The most precise approach would be to look at the probable life expectancy of the taxpayer. To the extent that gift tax is not currently paid because of the credit, more estate tax will ultimately be due, *but it will be due later.* The amount of credit being utilized, discounted at an appropriate rate for the taxpayer's life expectancy, would then be the amount to be added to the gift tax actually being paid.

For example, assume that a person has a life expectancy of twenty-two years. Because of expectations as to inflation, it is believed that 10% is an appropriate discount rate to use. The present value of $192,800 due in twenty-two years, discounted at 10%, is $23,685—and this would then be the amount to be used in an analysis for that person.

The examples in this chapter use the cash flow method, however, because it makes them easier to follow.

15.19 Gifts, Death, and Tax Basis

Gifts can be used to shift gains, but not losses, within a family group. Assume that Dad, who is widowed, owns a piece of property that cost him only $10,000, but for which he has had an offer of $70,000 cash. He wants to sell, and yet the income tax will be so large on the $60,000 gain that he feels better off not selling. A gift of the property to his three children (all over age 14), followed by a sale of the property by them, may prove much less expensive.

Assume that Dad is in the 33% income tax bracket so that a gain of $60,000 would result in income tax of $19,800. He has made prior taxable gifts, but still has some unused credit so that additional taxable gifts of $40,000[71] will not result in any transfer tax. With no transfer tax paid by the donor, the combined donees' basis will also be $10,000. A sale will result in a taxable gain of $60,000 to them, but (a) they are in a lower tax bracket and (b) the gain will be divided equally among them.[72] Their income tax would be approximately $8,796.[73] That is a considerable savings from the $19,800 which Dad would have paid on the sale, and the proceeds are now out of his estate and in the hands of the next generation.

The following is a brief review of the basis rules for gift property and inherited property which were discussed in Chapter 5.

[71]There would be a $30,000 exclusion with three donees.

[72]The basis of gift property was discussed in Chapter 5. See also IRC Sec. 1015.

[73]This is an estimation based on dividing the income equally among the three children and using 1990 rates and assuming a standard deduction of $500. This could be accomplished by gifting the property to them as joint tenants, each owning an undivided one-third interest.

The general rule for the basis of gift property is that it is the donor's basis (if less than fair market value) increased by a part of any gift tax paid on the transfer. What if the fair market value of the property on the date of the gift is less than the donor's tax basis? Here the rule becomes more complex. The objective is to prevent taxpayers from shifting losses around within a family group. If the fair market value is less than the donor's basis and the property is subsequently sold for less than the fair market value at the time of the gift, the amount of income tax loss is measured by the difference between the fair market value on the date of gift and the selling price. If the property is sold for more than the donor's basis, gain is measured by the difference between the donor's basis and the selling price. If the property is sold for more than fair market value but less than the donor's basis, there is neither gain nor loss.

Assume that a parent gives a child property with a tax basis of $50,000 but a fair market value of $40,000. The gift tax paid obviously does not increase the basis, since fair market value is the upper limit of such an increase, and the basis is already higher. If the child subsequently sells the property for $35,000, there will be a $5,000 tax loss ($40,000 − $35,000). If the property is sold for $55,000, there will be a gain of $5,000 ($55,000 − $50,000). If the property is sold for any amount between $40,000 and $50,000, there will be neither gain nor loss.

In selecting property for gifts, therefore, it is important to bear in mind the tax basis and fair market value of the property. Giving away property that has declined in value may result in no one ever getting any tax benefit from the unrealized loss. Giving away property that has appreciated in value may result in tax when the donee sells it, as explained earlier. If the purpose of the gift is to reduce the taxable estate, the ideal gift property is property that is worth approximately its tax basis. If the property has depreciated in value, it is usually advantageous to sell it, get the income tax benefit, if any, of the loss and give away the proceeds. In a large estate, there is usually enough variety in the types of assets held to allow for reasonable choice in constructing a gift program.

Note that the alternative minimum tax (discussed in Chapter 16) may add attractiveness to a plan to make gifts within a family.[74] Each single taxpayer can have up to $30,000 of AMT income without incurring any alternative minimum tax at the 21% rate.[75] When parents have different properties

[74]The alternative minimum tax is imposed by IRC Sec. 55.

[75]The $30,000 is phased down as taxable income increases above $112,500. See Chapter 16.

that will result in the AMT exceeding the regular tax, shifting of those properties among the family members might eliminate the AMT problem for the parents, while not creating any AMT problem for the donee family members, because of the $30,000 ($40,000 on a joint return) AMT exclusion.[76]

As noted in Chapter 5, the general rule is that the tax basis of inherited property is its fair market value at the date of death (or at an alternative valuation date, as will be discussed shortly).[77] Each person inheriting property takes as tax basis its value as of the same date as all the decedent's other heirs, regardless of whether the property is acquired immediately upon death (e.g., by action of law, such as joint tenancy property) or is received some time later when the estate makes a distribution.

A major exception to this general rule is property that represents "income in respect of a decedent." This includes the accrued income of a cash-basis taxpayer (e.g., interest or salaries earned but not collected) and receivables resulting from sales of property where the decedent was reporting income on the installment method.[78] It can also include any income to which the decedent had a contingent claim at the time of his death, such as the proceeds of a sale of property which the decedent had contracted to sell, even though the sale had not been finalized before death.[79]

Since the income in respect of a decedent will be subject both to estate tax and to income tax when collected, a portion of the estate tax attributable to the item is allowed as a tax deduction in figuring the income tax.[80]

For example, assume that Billy Barnes died without having received the last salary check of $30,000. Billy's income tax year ends with the date of death. Therefore, the $30,000 is not included in Billy's cash basis income tax return. The $30,000 does increase the estate (it is a receivable as of the date of death) *and* will also be included in the gross income of the estate (see Chapter 14). If Billy's taxable estate were large enough to be in the 41% marginal tax bracket, the estate tax would be $12,300 larger because of the $30,000 asset. Assuming that the estate (rather than an heir) receives the $30,000 and thus includes it in gross income, the estate will be entitled to an income tax deduction as the result of the $12,300 extra estate tax which was paid. Note that this does not eliminate the double tax effect completely because the $12,300 is a deduction and not a credit. However, it does provide some relief.

[76]Also, corporations and family trusts can be used for this purpose.

[77]IRC Sec. 1014(b).

[78]IRC Sec. 1014(c).

[79]*Trust Company of Georgia et al.* v. *Ross* (CA5 1967), 21 AFTR2d 311, 68-1 USTC 9133.

[80]IRC Sec. 691(c). Note that the rule as to the survivor portion of a joint and survivor annuity under IRC Sec. 72 is similar.

15.20 Some Modifications

So far we have discussed some general rules. There are also some special rules to take care of special problems. The first is with respect to gifts "immediately" before death. The second deals with modification of the "step-up" basis rule. The third is the requirement that an estate must include the value of some property even though the decedent did not own the property at the date of death. The fourth deals with a second decedent, who acquires property by inheritance and dies shortly thereafter, creating a second estate tax.

15.20.1 "Gross up" of Gift Tax

Prior to 1976, the estate and gift tax rates were not unified, with the gift tax rates being somewhat less. This led to some attempts at "deathbed" transfers and arguments between the IRS and taxpayers as to whether a transfer was a bona fide gift or just an attempt to reduce the estate tax.[81] In an attempt to create a simple rule that would eliminate the argument, Congress amended the statute to provide that *any* transfer by a person within three years prior to his or her death would automatically be treated as part of the gross estate. The rule has since been changed again.[82] The present rule is that deathbed transfers up to $10,000 per donee can be made without incurring any gift or estate tax.[83]

For example, assume that a taxpayer expects the estate to be in the 37% marginal tax bracket. Transfers of $10,000 each to twelve children and grandchildren will reduce the estate by $120,000 and the estate tax by $44,400, and cost no gift tax.[84]

[81]There were two reasons why a gift might be taxed less than if the property stayed in the estate. First, the gift tax rates were a little less. Second, because they were two separate tax computations, both progressive, the total tax could be reduced by removing property from higher marginal rates applicable to the estate and taxing them at lower marginal rates applicable to gifts. The advantage was most significant if the decedent had a large estate and had not made many taxable gifts during his or her lifetime.

[82]The "new" rules have applied since 1981.

[83]The estate tax savings by making a gift, paying the gift tax, and having more than three years elapse before death can be significant. For example, assume that a gift of $250,000 is subject to gift tax rates of 39%. The gift tax will be $97,500. If at least three years expires, the estate will not include this $97,500. If the estate is also in the 39% tax bracket, the resulting savings will be $38,025.

[84]Obviously, the potential tax savings increase as the tax rate and the number of donees increases.

Any gift tax paid on a gift made within three years of the date of death must, however, be included in the gross estate.[85] For example, assume that Lynn Larsen made a gift to Billy Barnes and incurred a $12,000 gift tax. Two years later Lynn died. Lynn's estate will not include the value of the property given to Billy, but will include the $12,000 gift tax paid to IRS. This concept is called "gross up" of the gift tax. If more than three years elapse between the time of the gift and the date of death, the gift tax will be excluded from the gross estate of the donor. See Fig. 15-6.

FIGURE 15-6

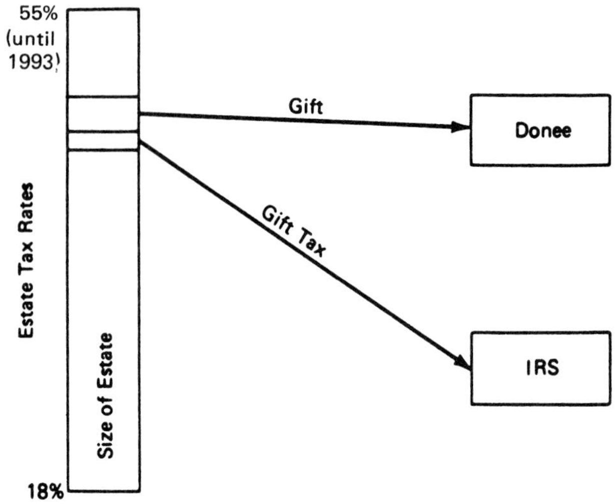

Under present law, an inter vivos gift will reduce the estate by the amount of the gift and by the amount of the gift tax if the gift is more than three years before death.

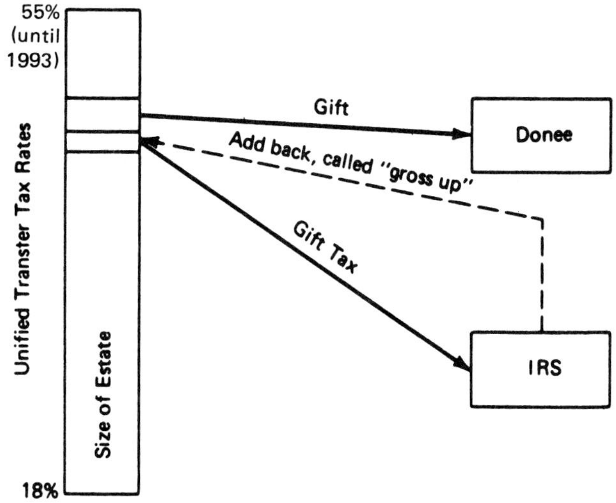

Under present law, an inter vivos gift made within three years of death will require that the gift tax paid on the gift be added to the estate. This is called "grossing up" the gift tax.

15.20.2 *Exception To the "Step-Up" Basis Rule*

There is a "one-year contemplation of death" rule that will apply in the event that a decedent leaves property to a person from whom that same property was received as a gift within one year of the date of death.[86] The rule prohibits an heir from getting a step-up in basis under certain circumstances. The result of the rule can be illustrated with the following example. Assume that Billy Barnes has a piece of property that has appreciated substantially in value. Sale of the property would result in a substantial taxable gain for income tax purposes. Billy gives the property away to an elderly relative who is expected to die shortly. Within one year the relative dies, leaving the property to Billy. Under the basis rules, discussed earlier, Billy's basis would be the fair market value as of the date of the relative's death and the property could then be sold with no resulting taxable gain. The price which would have been paid for this step up in basis would be the gift tax, if any, paid by Billy, and the estate tax, if any, paid by Billy's relative's estate. This plan will not work *unless* Billy's relative lives for more than one year following the date of the gift by Billy. Unless more than one year passes between the time of Billy's gift and the date of the relative's death, Billy's basis for the property will be the same as the relative's basis before death, which means Billy's original basis, increased by a portion of the gift tax, if any.

15.20.3 *Property Included in Gross Estate Although Not Owned*

In Chapter 14, we discussed "grantor trust" provisions relative to the income tax. Where a grantor creates a "grantor trust" (which means, in general, that the grantor retained certain "prohibited powers") the income tax rules in effect result in ignoring the trust and requiring that the grantor's gross income include any income earned by the trust. There is a similar provision in the estate tax rules, but these provisions contain a three-year clause as described here. Even if a person does not "own" certain property, his gross estate will include the value of the property if the transfer was made within the three year period prior to his death. For example, assume that Billy Barnes transferred property into a trust with a provision that the trust could be revoked. Even if Billy does not revoke the trust, but dies within three years of having created the trust, Billy's estate will include the value of the trust property. Obviously, if Billy should revoke the trust, then the property is included in the estate because the trust no longer owns it after revocation. If Billy does not revoke the trust and lives more than

[85] IRC Sec. 2035(c).
[86] IRC Sec. 1014(e).

three years after its creation, the estate will not include the value of the trust property.

Similar provisions require that an estate include the following *if* the transfer took place within three years prior to the decedent's death:

1. Transfers with a retained life interest;
2. Transfers that take effect at death;
3. Transfers of powers of appointment; and
4. Transfers of the proceeds of life insurance.

Further consideration of these provisions is beyond the scope of an introductory text.

15.20.4 Credit for Estate Tax Paid by a Previous Estate

Another modification is necessary as a relief provision where an estate includes property taxed to a previous estate a few years earlier.[87] Assume that taxpayer A dies and leaves some property to taxpayer B. A's estate paid estate tax. Shortly thereafter, B dies, still owning the property inherited from A. The same property could get taxed twice within a short period because of the successive deaths. The relief comes in the form of a credit. If B's death occurs within two years of A's death, B's estate will get a tax credit for *that part of* A's estate tax that resulted from the property inherited by B from A. The concept is fairly simple. The arithmetic required to determine how much tax was paid by A's estate as the result of the property that was inherited by B can be troublesome. The credit is further complicated by a limitation. The credit available to B's estate cannot be larger than the amount of additional tax that B's estate would have to pay as the result of including in the estate the property inherited from A. Such would be the case if the marginal tax rate of A's estate were higher than the marginal tax rate of B's estate.

Where the second estate follows the first by more than two years, there is a reduction in credit. After ten years, the second estate will get no credit for estate taxes paid by the first estate. The following table shows the credit available to the second estate:

Years Between Estates	*Percentage of First Estate's Tax Available as Credit to Second Estate*
0–2	100%
2–4	80%
4–6	60%
6–8	40%
8–10	20%
Over 10	0

[87]IRC Sec. 2013.

15.21 Extension of Time for Payment of Estate Tax

Normally, an estate tax return is due nine months after the death of the decedent, and payment is due when the return is filed.[88] Extensions of time are available when there is reasonable cause.[89] There are some special circumstances under which an executor can elect to pay over a fifteen-year period a portion of the estate tax.[90] The tax which may be deferred is that which resulted from the inclusion in the gross estate of an interest in a closely held business.[91] To be eligible for the deferral, the value of the business interest must have exceeded 35% of the value of the adjusted gross estate.

If the election is made to postpone payment of the estate tax because it contained an interest in a closely held business, there are some special rules that apply to ensure that most of the business stays in the family during that period of time, or the balance of the estate tax will be payable upon disposition.[92]

A special 4% interest rate is charged on approximately the first $153,000 ($345,800 − $192,800) of tax attributable to the closely held business interest. Interest at the current rate is charged on the balance.[93]

Any estate is eligible for a discretionary extension of up to ten years to pay the estate tax upon a showing of "reasonable cause."[94]

15.22 State Law Caution

Most of the states impose some sort of death taxes, and some of them also impose gift taxes. The variations among the states are so great that any attempt to generalize would be meaningless, and any attempt to be specific would require too much space. Adequate tax planning requires that state law and its effect be considered carefully. Taxpayers have been known to change their state of legal residence because tax laws in one state were more favorable than in another, especially if some time was spent in both states.

[88]IRC Sec. 6075.
[89]IRC Sec. 6081 provides for extensions of time to file returns. IRC Sec. 6161 provides for extensions of time to pay tax. Where an extension is obtained, and the tax not paid on the normal due date, an interest charge will apply. IRC Sec. 6601.
[90]IRC Sec. 6166. Only interest is paid for the first five years, and the installments on the tax, plus interest, are paid over the following ten years.
[91]Closely held business for this purpose is defined by IRC Sec. 6166(b).
[92]IRC Sec. 6166(g).
[93]The current rate can fluctuate, depending upon the prime rate charged by banks. See IRC Secs. 6621, and 6601(j). See Chapter 19.
[94]IRC Sec. 6161(a)(2).

Consider this one situation, not unlikely for a retired person. The state of A is where working years were spent and where legal residency has been maintained. Investment real estate is owned in the state of B. The state of C includes a retirement community where the taxpayer spends the winter months. The taxpayer dies and the state of A wants to impose an estate tax because it is the state of legal residency. The state of B wants some estate tax because of the property located within its borders. The state of C imposes a tax because the taxpayer also owned a residence there, maintained a mailing address, and was in the state of C at the time of death. The lawyers may do better financially than the heirs before which state gets what is sorted out. Planning can minimize such problems.

The federal estate tax may get reduced by a part of estate tax paid to a state. This is accomplished by a credit to the federal tax for part of the state tax.

15.23 Gift Tax Annual Exclusion

The $10,000-per-donor-per-donee annual exclusion referred to several times earlier is not quite as simple as it first appears. It is only for gifts of "present interests."[95] Thus, it is not normally available for gifts in trust, since the purpose of the trust is usually to postpone possession or enjoyment of the property for a time or forever.[96] However, gifts to minors (under age twenty-one) in trust are considered "present interests" which qualify for the $10,000 exclusion if the property or the income may be used for the minor's benefit, and the unused property and accumulated income pass to the donee at age twenty-one or to the donee's estate in case of earlier death.[97]

15.24 Valuation of Estates

The term "fair market value" has been used frequently in this and in previous chapters. There are times when it may not be easy to determine the fair market value of a piece of property. The term can be defined as the price at which property would be transferred between a willing seller and a willing buyer, both with complete knowledge, and neither under any compulsion to act.

If an estate actually sells the property at a date close to the date of death, that sale is excellent evidence of its value. Many estate assets are not sold, however, and, like stock in a closely held corporation, are not directly comparable to property that is bought and sold with frequency. The valuation process attempts to ascertain what a buyer would be willing to pay and the seller would be willing to accept. Thus, stock of a closely held corporation might be valued by reference to stocks of publicly traded corporations deemed to be similar. Appropriate discounts would have to be estimated for lack of marketability or other relevant factors.[98] What factors? If the stock represented a minority interest in a closely held corporation, it might be worth considerably less per share than if it represented the controlling interest. The most frequent issue involved in tax litigation over estate and gift tax questions is the valuation of property.

TAX PLANNING TIP: Fair market value can be changed as to some types of property by rearranging ownership. A fractional piece of something is usually worth less than the pro-rata portion of the total value of that something. Thus, the owner of 100% of the stock of a corporation could reduce the value of all the corporate stock by giving 10%, say, to his or her spouse, and 24% to each of their two children. At death, only 42% of the stock would be owned—and the estate might well be able to value this minority interest at as much as a 50% discount from the per share value that would apply to a controlling interest.

The following factors are important, and have been considered in the valuation of closely held corporate stock:

1. The nature of the business and the history of the enterprise from its beginning;
2. The economic outlook in general, and the condition and outlook of the specific industry in particular;
3. The book value of the stock and the financial condition of the business;
4. The earning capacity of the business;
5. The dividend-paying capacity of the business;
6. Evidence of the existence of goodwill and other intangibles of value;
7. Sales of stock and the size of the block of stock to be valued; and
8. The market value of other businesses in the same industry.

[95] IRC Sec. 2503(b).

[96] Such transfers are called gifts of a "future interest."

[97] IRC Sec. 2503(c). Students interested in this point may wish to read *D. C. Crummey* (CA9 1968), 68-2 USTC 12,541, 397 F2d 82, 22 AFTR2d 6023.

[98] IRC Sec. 2031(b). The IRS has listed those factors which it believes should be considered in Rev. Rul. 59-60, 1959-1 CB 237, and Rev. Rul. 65-193, 1965-2 CB 370.

The date as of which the valuation is made can also make a difference. The estate may elect to value all of the property at either the date of death or at an alternative valuation date six months after the date of death.[99] In order for the alternative valuation date to be used, however, the value of the entire estate on the alternative valuation date must result in both a reduction in the gross estate *and* a reduction in the amount of estate tax.[100] The reason for this rule is to prohibit the use of the alternative valuation where there would be no estate tax anyway (primarily because of the "unified" credit) and the alternative valuation would be higher, thus resulting in a higher income tax basis for the property to an heir.

There are a variety of reasons why the property in an estate might be valued at an artificially high amount on the date of death. The "alternative valuation date" provides an "escape valve" for the estate. If the value of the property does decline within that six-month period, the alternative date can be used by the executor. If the alternative date is used, however, it must be used for all property in the estate and not merely for selected items.

What if the executor sells some of the property or distributes some of it to the heirs before the six months have passed? How will such property fit into the alternative valuation six months after death? The answer is that the value of that property as of the date of sale or distribution will be used if the alternative valuation date is elected.

TAX PLANNING TIP: When actually valuing assets in a decedent's estate, pay special attention to the interaction between estate tax and income tax. In a "small" estate, property bequeathed to a person in a relatively high income tax bracket should probably be valued on the high side. Why? For little or no increase in estate tax, the heir will realize meaningful income tax benefits through having a higher tax basis. On the other hand, property (e.g., installment obligations) which will be taxed to the heir without regard to the estate tax valuation should be valued at as low an amount as is supportable.

15.25 Expenses, Debt, and Taxes

The estate tax is not imposed on a gross estate, but rather on a net amount after taking a number of possible deductions.[101] The most important deductions, from a tax planning standpoint, have already been discussed—the marital deduction and the charitable deduction. In addition, the following may be deducted:

1. Funeral expenses;
2. Administration expenses, which include amounts paid to the executor and to the attorney;
3. Claims enforceable against the estate, such as for money the decedent owed to a bank;
4. Taxes accrued but unpaid at death, including income taxes due on the decedent's final return, as previously discussed in Chapter 14; and
5. Casualty losses (fire, storm, theft, etc.) incurred during settlement of the estate.[102]

The administration expenses and casualty losses are items that could be deducted on the estate's income tax return as well, but no such deduction can be taken if they are deducted on the estate tax return. Some of the taxes may constitute "expenses in respect of a decedent" for income tax purposes, as discussed in Chapter 14.

15.26 Credits

Credit may be taken against the estate tax for certain inherited property that was previously and recently included in someone else's taxable estate,[103] for state death taxes (but only up to a maximum set forth in the estate tax law),[104] and for certain foreign death taxes (but also subject to a maximum).[105]

Since the estate tax is a transfer tax that is calculated on the total of the estate at time of death plus all taxable gifts made after 1976, the gift taxes previously paid can also be claimed as a credit against the transfer tax.[106] See the example earlier in this chapter for Billy Barnes, who died in 1991.

15.27 Conclusion

The tax law has only a hazy concept of family. It deals with individual taxpayers. Where an individual identifies economic well-being in terms of a larger group, careful management of transactions can frequently minimize the aggregate taxes paid over time by the members of that family group. A

[99]IRC Sec. 2032(a). Note that real property used in farming, or even in a trade or business other than farming, may have the value includable in the estate reduced by as much as $750,000 under IRC Sec. 2032(a).
[100]IRC Sec. 2032(c).

[101]IRC Sec. 2053. See Fig. 15-4.
[102]IRC Sec. 2054.
[103]IRC Sec. 2013.
[104]IRC Sec. 2011.
[105]IRC Sec. 2014.
[106]IRC Sec. 2012.

number of approaches and situations have been discussed in this chapter. Most of them involve shifting income either to other family members or to corporations or trusts that will be in lower tax brackets or through which the imposition of tax can be deferred.

Estate and gift taxes are a much more complex field of taxes and law than this oversimplified presentation may suggest. Effective estate planning requires intimate knowledge of the taxpayer's affairs, objectives, and value system; detailed understanding of the property and probate laws of the various jurisdictions that may be involved; a firm grasp of the intricacies of life insurance, annuities, and trusts; and a mastery of applicable federal and state tax provisions. It is seldom that all of this knowledge can be found in one person. Even someone who has had the formal training to have mastered all of these disparate disciplines is unlikely to have been able to keep current on them all. Thus, estate planning is almost always a team effort—with the CPA and the attorney being key advisers to the taxpayer and family, but with the insurance specialist, and frequently a bank trust officer, as valuable and necessary participants.

TRUE-FALSE QUESTIONS

State whether each of the following statements is true or false. For each *false* answer, reword the statement to make it *true*.

T F 1. A trust will pay tax on its income which is not distributed to beneficiaries even though the trust is required to "set aside" the income for beneficiaries.

T F 2. The only advantage which a trust has is that of paying a lower rate of income tax than the grantor.

T F 3. If a trust is irrevocable for the life expectancy of the beneficiary, the grantor will not be taxed on the trust income, even though the life expectancy of the beneficiary is less than ten years at the time the trust is created.

T F 4. Members of a family, all of whom are partners in a partnership, can divide partnership profits among the family members in any manner they wish without fear that the IRS will disallow the allocation.

T F 5. If one person owns all of the stock of two corporations, each of those corporations will calculate its federal income tax independent of the other corporation.

T F 6. A corporation and its 100%-owned subsidiary must combine their taxable incomes for purposes of applying the federal corporate income tax rates.

T F 7. If two sisters each own their own corporation, the stock owned by each will be attributable to the other and each corporation will be considered part of a "controlled group."

T F 8. In order for a parent-subsidiary relationship to exist for purposes of the "controlled group" test, the "parent" must own at least 80% of the "subsidiary."

T F 9. Where income is artificially allocated to corporations that are owned by members of a family although not part of a controlled group, the IRS can reallocate the income in a manner to reflect more clearly the "correct" income of each unit.

T F 10. One disadvantage that a parent faces in hiring his or her own child as an employee in a family business is that the social security tax must be paid even though the child is under age twenty-one.

T F 11. A person who operates a noncorporate business cannot adopt a group term life insurance plan covering just himself, spouse, and dependents, if there are other full-time employees of the business.

T F 12. If a parent makes an interest-free loan of more than $10,000 to his or her own child, the tax law generally requires that the parent include in gross income an "imputed" interest amount.

T F 13. The unified transfer tax imposes a graduated or progressive tax rate structure on transfers of property whether made during lifetime or upon death.

T F 14. If a gift of property other than cash occurs, the measurement of the value for purposes of the gift tax is the donor's basis.

T F 15. The federal gift tax rules allow a donor to give away $10,000 per year to as many donees as he or she wishes without any obligation to pay a transfer tax or even to file a tax return.

T F 16. Since the gift and estate taxes have a unified rate, there is no tax advantage to giving away property prior to death.

T F 17. The gift tax marital deduction allows a spouse to give any amount to the other spouse tax-free without using any of the "unified" credit.

T F 18. The estate tax marital deduction allows a decedent spouse to transfer all of his or her property to the surviving spouse without any estate tax.

T F 19. The gift tax marital deduction can only be used once in a donor's lifetime.

T F 20. The estate tax marital deduction can only be used once by each transferor.

T F 21. An *inter vivos* transfer is one that takes place when a person dies and leaves property without a will to specify where that property shall go.

T F 22. One way to avoid paying the gift tax is to transfer property into trust for the benefit of another person rather than transferring the property directly to that person.

T F 23. If a person is an income beneficiary of a trust at the time of death and did not have the power to obtain the trust property for himself, the value of the trust property must be included in his estate.

T F 24. For purposes of the unified rate structure, taxable *inter vivos* gifts made by the decedent after 1976 are added to the value of property owned at death to determine the marginal tax rate.

T F 25. If a decedent bequeaths property to a charitable organization, the maximum amount that the estate can deduct as the result of that transfer is 50% of the gross estate.

T F 26. The general rule for the determination of basis of property inherited from a decedent dying after 1976 is that it is the fair market value of the property at death.

T F 27. If a donor's basis in property is $100,000, the donor paid a gift tax of $34,000 as the result of the gift and the fair market value of the property on the date of the gift was $95,000, the donee would not be allowed to increase basis by any portion of gift tax paid by the donor.

T F 28. If a decedent purchased property in 1977 and transferred it upon death, in 1990, the beneficiary's basis will be the fair market value of the property on the date of death, unless the alternative valuation date was used.

T F 29. If a decedent's taxable estate includes property which was also included in a prior decedent's taxable estate within the past ten years, the second estate will receive a tax reduction (credit) for all or part of the tax paid by the first estate.

T F 30. A decedent's estate will include any gift tax paid on a gift made within three years prior to death.

PROBLEMS

Problem 15-1. Although not legally obligated to do so, Mr. Hart (who is single) desires to support his aged aunt. Hart's total income puts him in a marginal tax bracket of 33%. His aunt has no income for tax purposes, although she does receive $250 per month in social security benefits. If Hart makes any gifts in addition to those which he has made in prior years, he will have to pay a gift tax of 40% of the amount in excess of $10,000 each year. Assume that Hart's aunt has a life expectancy of ten years. Ignore the time value of money involved.

(a) What will be the income tax effect if Hart provides his aunt with $12,000 per year which she will use for living expenses? The gift tax effect?

(b) What will be the income tax effect if Hart notifies his employer to pay $1,000 per month of his (Hart's) salary directly to his aunt? The gift tax effect?

(c) What will be the income tax effect if Hart creates a trust and transfers enough securities to the trust to pay his aunt $12,000 per year? The provisions of the trust are that Hart can at any time direct the trustee to return the securities to him. Discuss the gift tax effect.

(d) What will be the income tax effect if Hart creates a trust and transfers securities valued at $100,000 to the trust? The securities will generate enough income to pay his aunt $12,000 per year plus the $200 per year trustee's fee. The provisions of the trust are that the trust will terminate when his aunt dies and the securities will then be transferred to Hart's brother Harry. Hart will not be able to terminate the trust prior to his aunt's death. What will be the gift tax effect? Assume that the value of the gift is 45% of $100,000.

(e) Evaluate the four alternatives given.

Problem 15-2. Martha Silverton is expecting taxable income of $20,000 for the current year. She owns a piece of property that is a long-term capital asset. The property was acquired three years ago at a cost of $50,000. The property is estimated to have a value of $30,000. Martha needs some cash and proposes to sell the property.

(a) If Martha sells the property to an unrelated person, what tax benefit will she recognize? (Assume that she has no other capital asset transactions for the year and is married and filing jointly.)

(b) If Martha sells the property to her father, what tax benefit will she recognize?

(c) Assume that Martha sells the property to her father for $30,000. Three years later, her father, who has taxable income of $90,000 on a joint return, sells the property for $50,000. Explain the tax effect to her father.

(d) How much tax would Martha's father have had to pay if the gain were all recognized by him? (Assume that the asset is a capital asset to father as well as to Martha.)

(e) Can it be said that Martha's father saved tax to the extent of the answer to part (d)? What about the tax savings to the family?

Problem 15-3. Jeff Heath is permanently disabled. His only income is $200 per month from social security plus $400 per month that is provided as a gift by his sister Jane. Jane has taxable income of $40,000 per year after deducting an exemption amount for Jeff. Because Jeff lives in her house, Jane is able to claim head-of-household status.

(a) What is Jane's 1990 federal income tax liability?

(b) Jane makes arrangements to borrow $30,000 from the bank on a home equity loan at 10%. She creates a trust, for the benefit of Jeff, and transfers the $30,000 to it. The trust will pay income to Jeff until he dies, then transfer the corpus to State College. The trustee is independent. What are the tax consequences?

(c) Will Jeff incur any tax liability from this arrangement? Explain.

(d) How much income would the trust have to earn in order for Jeff to have the same amount of income as he had when Jane was supporting him without the trust arrangement?

Problem 15-4. The Longs have operated a family retail department store for several years as a proprietorship. Mr. and Mrs. Long both work in the business, which produces a steady profit of $70,000 before any deductions for taxes or for salaries to themselves. They withdraw $30,000 for personal and living expenses, including the payment of income tax and social security taxes. The balance is left in the business for growth and expansion. Assume the self employment tax for a proprietorship is 15.30% and applies to the first $51,300 of income and must be paid for only one of the spouses even though both work in the business. Their itemized deductions are $8,000. They have no deductions for adjusted gross income. The Longs have two children, ages 15 and 16.

(a) What is their federal income tax liability?

(b) The Longs are thinking of incorporating the business. If they do, they will both be employees. The social security tax will be 7.65% of the first $51,300 of salary or wages and will apply to both the employer and employee. Mr. and Mrs. Long will each draw a salary of $15,000 from the corporation. (Note that the corporation can deduct both the salary payment and its share of social security tax.) What will be the combined federal income tax of the corporation and the Longs under this arrangement?

(c) Considering both the income tax and the social security taxes paid by all parties, what is the tax advantage or disadvantage of incorporating under the terms set forth in part (b)?

(d) Another possibility that the Longs are considering is incorporating the business and electing the Subchapter S provisions of the IRC. They would continue to draw salaries as before. Both Mr. and Mrs. Long would own 25% of the corporate stock and 25% would be owned by each of their two children. The children have no other income. What would be the total income tax paid by the family? (Assume that the corporation does not pay any cash dividends during the year.)

(e) Considering both the income tax and social security taxes paid by all parties, what is the tax advantage of incorporating and electing Subchapter S under the terms set forth in part (d) as compared with not incorporating? (There is no social security tax on the undistributed taxable income of an S corporation.)

(f) Discuss possible plans whereby the tax savings could be increased.

Problem 15-5. The Furr Hardware is owned and operated by Raymond Furr as a proprietorship. It makes a profit of about $45,000 each year. Mr. Furr is the only member of the family who works in the store. He hires employees for most of the work except general management. The Furrs have three children, ages seventeen, fifteen, and twelve. Mr. Furr wants to send each of his children to college and has been saving money over the years to do that. In addition to the profit from the business, the Furrs have some investment income, in part resulting from a small inheritance received by Mrs. Furr about four years ago. The oldest child will start college next year. They estimate that it will require $6,000 for all expenses. The Furrs' personal budget requires that they have $18,000 (before taxes) for their living expenses. Other income is either reinvested in the hardware business or is invested in various securities. Other income consists of the following:

Dividends from U.S. corporations	$4,000
Interest from U.S. government notes	2,500
Interest from state and local bonds	1,800
Interest from savings account	900

The Furrs have itemized deductions of $6,000 each year. The children are not employed. Their only deduction for adjusted gross income is $2,000, which Mr. Furr contributes to an individual retirement account each year.

(a) What is their current federal income tax per year? (Use 1990 rates.)

(b) If Mr. and Mrs. Furr were to transfer all of their investments to a trust, with the income to be divided equally among the three children for use in paying education expenses, what would be the tax effect? (Assume that all income will be distributed to the children so that the trust will have no undistributed income. The trust corpus will be paid to the children equally when the youngest becomes age 21. Note that the income to be received by each child will still mean that Mr. and Mrs. Furr provide over one-half of their support.)

(c) If Mr. Furr creates a family partnership and transfers 15% of the business to each child, the business profits can be divided among the family. Assume, however, that before dividing profits, a reasonable "salary" for Mr. Furr would be $20,000. The investments would be transferred to the partnership so that business profits would include the hardware operations plus interest and dividends. What would be the tax effect of this arrangement?

Problem 15-6. Jane Franklin owns two corporations. One is in the apartment management business, and the other is a food-catering service. The two businesses never have any contact with each other except for the fact that Jane owns all of the stock of each. The businesses are operated from two separate locations, in two different cities. None of the employees of either corporation ever do any work for the other corporation. The two corporations maintain two completely different sets of financial records. In fact, Jane has retained two different CPAs to perform audits on the two companies. Last year, the apartment management corporation had taxable income of $60,000. The catering service business had taxable income of $25,000.

(a) How much federal income tax did the two businesses have to pay?

(b) Would there be any tax reduction by arranging for one of Jane's corporations to be a 100%-owned subsidiary of the other? Explain.

(c) What would be the result if Jane transferred all of the stock of one of the corporations to her husband so that he owned 100% of one corporation and she owned 100% of the other, but Jane continued to manage both?

(d) Assume that Mr. Franklin acquires 100% of the food-catering business and becomes completely and independently responsible for all of its operations. Will there be any tax savings? Explain.

Problem 15-7. Robert, Henry, and Patrick McClintock own one-third each of the stock of McClintock Homes, a housing developer. Robert specializes in land acquisition and preparation for housing construction. Henry specializes in the construction process from start to finish. Patrick is the sales and financial whiz of the group, handling all such matters. For 1990, after drawing as much salary for themselves as they felt could possibly be justified as reasonable, the corporation will still make a profit of $210,000.

(a) How much federal income tax will the corporation have to pay?

(b) The McClintock brothers are upset about the amount of corporate federal income tax. They feel that the business will continue to be at least as profitable in the future and would like to arrange to reduce the taxes. Their CPA has suggested that they form two more corporations, with each owning 100% of his own separate corporation. With careful pricing, they could arrange for each of three corporations to make approximately an equal profit. To accomplish this plan would result in extra costs of approximately $20,000 each for the two new corporations because of additional accounting, record keeping, and personnel expenses. Would this plan result in tax savings? If so, how much?

(c) Assume that they could form a fourth corporation. Each brother would own 100% of the stock of his own corporation and one-third of the stock of the fourth corporation. Assume that profits would be as follows:

Corp. A	$ 45,000
Corp. B	45,000
Corp. C	45,000
Corp. D	35,000
Total	$170,000

What would be the federal income tax liability for all corporations combined?

Problem 15-8. Edward Owens is age forty-five. He contributes toward the support of his sister and her daughter, but does not provide over one-half of their support. Consequently, he does not claim either of them as a dependent. Edward's income consists of the following:

Dividends	$ 3,000
Taxable interest	1,080
Gross rent	12,000
Salary	47,000

His annual expenses in connection with the rental property are:

Taxes	$2,700
Mortgage interest	4,100
Depreciation	3,600

Edward has itemized deductions of $4,500. He files a tax return as a single person.

(a) What is Edward's federal income tax liability?

(b) Assuming that he contributes $450 per month to his sister and niece, what tax benefit does he obtain for that support? Explain.

(c) Edward has decided to create a trust. His sister will be the beneficiary, receiving all trust income for as long as she lives. After his sister's death, his niece will receive the income until she reaches age thirty, at which time the trust corpus will also go to her. If his niece does not survive him, the trust corpus will be paid to charity. The trust corpus will consist of the rental property. The trust will distribute to the beneficiary each year an amount equal to its net cash flow from the rental property. How much will the beneficiary receive per year?

(d) How much tax will Edward save as the result of the creation of the trust?

(e) What would Edward save in tax if he were to transfer the investment assets to the trust rather than the rental property?

(f) Could Edward transfer part of his salary to the trust and reduce his taxes? Explain.

Problem 15-9. Ranbow Corporation owns all of the stock of Colorful Corporation, although the two are engaged in totally separate businesses. The reason for this arrangement is that Ms. Ranbow, who owns all of the stock of Ranbow Corporation, is in the highest tax bracket and wants Colorful to use all of its profits for expansion, without a salary payment to her. Ranbow has a taxable income of $120,000 for the year. Colorful has a taxable income of $70,000.

(a) Explain the tax treatment afforded the two corporations. How much tax will be paid by Colorful?

(b) Ms. Ranbow has been very satisfied with the performance of the general manager of Colorful and is considering transferring some of the Colorful stock to him in appreciation for a good job. If 21% of the Colorful stock is transferred to the manager, who is not a relative of Ms. Ranbow, what tax effect will this have, if any, on Ranbow and Colorful?

Problem 15-10. Dr. Hugh Englewood, a dentist, owns all the equipment in his office, although he had to borrow the money to pay for it. The equipment cost $100,000 and is being depreciated over ten years under the straight-line method. His interest expense deduction is $6,000 per year. Not counting any deduction for depreciation or interest, his taxable income on a joint return is $74,000.

(a) What is the 1990 federal income tax liability?

(b) The Englewoods have three dependent children all older than age 14. Dr. Englewood is thinking of creating an equipment-leasing trust. He would transfer all of the equipment to the trust. Since there is no mortgage on the bank loan, he would continue to pay the interest expense as before. (Assume he creates a home equity loan so the interest is fully deductible.) The trust would be for the benefit of the three children, share and share alike. Dr. Englewood would lease the equipment from the trust for $18,000 per year. The trust would distribute all cash to the children, who would buy state and local government bonds and have nontaxable interest income. The trust corpus would be distributed to the children when the youngest reaches age 25. What will be the tax liability, and the tax savings, to the Englewoods with this arrangement?

(c) Will the trust have to pay any tax? Explain.

(d) How much will the Englewood family save per year with this arrangement, assuming that a trustee will cost $200 per year?

Problem 15-11. Janice Jones died in 1990 leaving a gross estate of $800,000. The deductions for the estate consisted of the following:

Debts	40,000
Funeral expenses	10,000
Administrative expenses	20,000

There were no charitable bequests.

Janice's husband died twelve years earlier.

(a) What is the estate tax liability?

(b) What would the estate tax liability have been if her estate had been $90,000 smaller due to the fact that she gave $10,000 to each of nine grandchildren prior to her death?

(c) How much would Janice have to have given away in order to have her estate small enough so that no estate tax would result?

(d) Assume that Janice did not make any gifts to her grandchildren, but bequeathed $55,000 of her property to charity. How much less would the heirs receive as compared with no charitable bequest?

Problem 15-12. Barry Marlowe has never made any gifts of more than $10,000 to anyone in his entire life. In 1990, Barry gave his mother $50,000 in cash and his brother $40,000 worth of stock. No other gifts were made in 1990.

(a) How would this be reported on Barry's gift tax return? Explain.

(b) Since no tax is due, why must Barry file a tax return? Explain.

(c) What if, in addition to the transfers noted, Barry gave his sister an apartment building worth $100,000? Calculate the tax before and after credits.

Problem 15-13. Marshall Daly has been widowed for seven years. He has eleven grandchildren and four great-grandchildren. All of his six children are alive and married. Two of his grandchildren are married. Marshall is very wealthy and has decided that he will begin a plan of disposing of his assets prior to his eventual death. The year is 1990.

(a) Considering just the children, grandchildren, and great-grandchildren (no spouses), how much could Marshall give away this year without incurring a tax liability or being required to file a gift tax return?

(b) Assuming that Marshall decided to give the maximum to each of the persons listed above *and* to each of their respective spouses, how much could be transferred each year without a gift tax return being filed?

(c) If Mrs. Daly had not died before the gift program began, how much could have been transferred in both parts (a) and (b)? (Ignore possible gifts from Marshall to his wife, and vice versa. Assume that Mrs. Daly is also independently wealthy.)

Problem 15-14. Maude Baker has never made any taxable gifts to anyone in her entire life. She is fifty years of age. She has three grandchildren and would like to transfer some cash into savings accounts for each of them.

(a) What will be the gift tax effect *to her children and grandchildren* if she opens a bank savings account for each grandchild and deposits $15,000 into each account? What about the income tax effect?

(b) What will be the gift tax effect for her?

(c) What difference would it make if she were to give $10,000 to each grandchild this year and another $5,000 next year?

(d) Which course of action would you recommend, and why?

Problem 15-15. Jim and Ida Tooke have total assets valued at $1,000,000. For purposes of this exercise, disregard any possible deductions for the estate tax computation other than the marital deduction. Neither Jim nor Ida has ever made any taxable gifts before. In planning for the transfer taxes, it is assumed that Ida will survive Jim. It is 1990.

(a) If Jim makes a gift of $200,000 to Ida, what amount of gift tax will be incurred?

(b) Assuming that Jim dies later with an estate of $800,000, all of which passes to Ida, how much estate tax will result?

(c) Assume that Jim wrote his will so as to leave $150,000 outright to Ida and $650,000 in trust for her benefit. Under the trust agreement, she would receive the income from the trust, but not the corpus. How much estate tax would be payable by Jim's estate? (Assume a 1990 estate.)

(d) Assume that Ida dies after Jim. Disregard the time value of money and any possible credit that her estate might receive as the result of taxes paid by Jim's estate. Further assume that Ida's estate would include both the gift of $200,000 received from him and the estate property from part (b) above (net of the estate tax). How much tax would her estate have to pay?

(e) Explain an alternative that would result in less estate tax upon both estates.

Problem 15-16. Ron Ownbey's net assets, after all deductions for debts, funeral expenses, and charitable bequests, but before taxes, were $427,000 after his death in 1990. Linda Raymond, his sister, is Ron's only heir. Ron's executor has informed Linda that the estate taxes total $50,400 and that she will receive the balance of $376,600. Linda has looked at the estate tax rate table and does not understand how an estate of only $427,000 could result in taxes of $50,400 after the $192,800 credit. She has asked you for a possible explanation before she approaches the executor about the matter.

(a) Explain how the computation might have been correct.

(b) Support the explanation with calculations based upon the assumptions you made.

(c) Explain how Linda might confirm your explanation of the situation.

Problem 15-17. Marshall Reading died in 1990 leaving a taxable estate of $6,000,000, upon which the estate tax was $2,940,800 (before credit). Some shares of stock valued at $60,000 were willed to his cousin, Clarence. Six months later, Clarence died, leaving a taxable estate of $2,000,000, including the stock inherited from Marshall. The value of the stock did not change from the time of Marshall's death until the time of Clarence's death. Clarence's executor has determined that since the stock was 1% of Marshall's estate, 1% of the tax paid by Marshall's estate was attributable to that stock. Assume that the full general credit applied to both estates ($192,800 to Marshall's and $192,800 to Clarence's).

(a) Calculate the amount of Clarence's estate tax before any credits.

(b) Will Clarence's estate get a credit for the entire additional estate tax paid by Marshall's estate because of the stock? Explain.

(c) Explain the application of the credit if Clarence had died three years after Marshall.

(d) What if Clarence had lived eleven years after Marshall's death?

Problem 15-18. Sharon Bihlmire is thinking about giving some shares of stock to her son (age 17). She has the following portfolio, all of which were purchased after 1976:

Stock	*Basis*	*Current Fair Market Value*
A	$163,000	$185,000
B	217,000	232,000
C	252,000	237,000
D	277,000	320,000

Sharon has already made taxable gifts since 1976, but before the current year, which is 1990, of $450,000. She has previously paid $42,500 in gift tax. If she makes a gift, it will be the entire block of one of the stocks in the portfolio.

(a) Explain how Sharon could have been required to pay transfer tax of $42,500 when her taxable gifts totaled less than $600,000.

(b) For each stock, indicate the amount of gift tax she will incur upon the transfer.

Problem 15-19. Mike Manhart is considering making a gift of property to his daughter. There are four pieces of property which are under consideration. The amount of Mike's basis, the current fair market value, and the amount of gift tax which Mike would incur if he makes the gift are as follows:

Property	*A*	*B*	*C*	*D*
Mike's basis	$20,000	$30,000	$44,000	$50,000
Fair market value	$40,000	$50,000	$45,000	$40,000
Amount of gift tax	-0-	$16,400	$13,650	$15,000

For each of the four properties, calculate and explain the amount of the basis which his daughter will have if the gift is made. (*Note:* Solution to problem 15-19 may require a review of Chapter 5.)

Problem 15-20. Lewis Welch has taken an inventory of his property and debts, has estimated his funeral and administrative expenses and has concluded that if he were to die at the moment (1990), his taxable estate would be $730,000, all of which is income-producing property. He is single. He does not expect to die for at least ten years. Regardless of the timing of his death, however, he thinks his estate will remain at about $730,000, because he consumes all of the income generated by these assets. The only person Lewis has in mind to receive his assets during his lifetime or upon death is his sister. Having made taxable *inter vivos* gifts in the past of $700,000 (on which he paid gift tax of $74,000) he is aware that any future gifts will result in some transfer tax. He has not made any gifts so far this year.

(a) Is there any positive or negative tax effect to giving away property now rather than waiting until he dies? (Ignore the nontax considerations, such as his need for the income from the assets to support himself.) Consider both the transfer tax and the income tax.

(b) Assume that he gives her property valued at $110,000 in 1990. What will be the transfer tax effect?

(c) Calculate the difference in tax, assuming that (1) the gift is not made, and (2) the gift is made and he lives until 1993. (Ignore the discounted value of the difference in timing, but consider that the estate will be smaller by the sum of the gift and the gift tax.)

(d) Explain why there is a difference.

Problem 15-21. Max Wentworth's estate was settled under the terms of his will. Property valued at $500,000 was transferred to trust with Max's wife, Martha, as the beneficiary. Under the terms of the testamentary trust, Martha was to receive all of the income generated by the trust each year. In addition, the trust agreement required the trustee to pay any amount of the trust principal to Martha, or to any of her creditors, upon her written request. In addition, the trust agreement provided that the trust property was to pass to their only child, Henry, upon Martha's death, unless Martha left a will in which she directed the disposition of the trust property to someone else.

(a) Assuming that the trust property is worth $600,000 upon Martha's death, will her estate be taxed on the $600,000? Explain.

(b) What would the result have been if thc trust created by Max's will had provided that Martha could have the trust income each year *and* payments from corpus if necessary to maintain her standard of living, but Martha could not change the fact that Henry would receive the remainder of the trust property upon her death? Explain.

Problem 15-22. Lawrence O'Ryan died in 1990. He left an estate that included shares of stock valued for estate tax purposes at $200,000. He had acquired these shares in 1971 at a cost of $40,000. The executor also determined that the total taxable estate was $2,000,000, on which the estate paid $588,000 in taxes. Mr. O'Ryan's nephew has inherited this stock and has retained you for tax advice. He is thinking of selling the stock and wants to know his tax basis. Advise the nephew.

Problem 15-23. Prior to 1983, Faye Duncan never made any *taxable* gifts. During 1983, she made *taxable* gifts of $305,000. During 1984, she made additional *taxable* gifts of $290,000. She made no taxable gifts during the years 1985–1989. She is considering making *taxable* gifts of $175,000 during 1990.

(a) What was the gift tax in 1984?

(b) What was the gift tax in 1985?

(c) What would be the gift tax in 1990 if the proposed gifts are made? Explain.

PROBLEMS WITH AN ASTERISK REQUIRE ADDITIONAL RESEARCH.

Problem 15-24.* Clara Miles is a recent graduate of Slippery Stone Medical School, where she received an M.D. degree. She has moved to Smalltown, Largestate to establish a medical practice. Smalltown has no available apartments, and Dr. Miles found it necessary to build a new house. She borrowed the money from the bank, but being financially strapped with the purchase of office equipment, furniture, and so on, is unable to meet the interest payments on the house loan. Her father, a wealthy industrialist, has agreed to pay the interest for her. The interest is $900 per month.

(a) Does the payment of the interest by Mr. Miles constitute a taxable gift to Dr. Miles? Does it make any difference if he is married? Explain.

(b) Will Mr. Miles be able to take a deduction on his personal income tax return for the interest he is paying? Explain.

(c) Assume that Mr. Miles purchased the house and made the payments to the lender, then leased the residence to Dr. Miles. Would there be a gift from him to her if the rent were less than the fair value for a similar residence? Explain. Is there an advantage in this arrangement?

(d) What if Mr. Miles made an interest-free demand loan to Dr. Miles? What would be the income and gift tax consequences?

COMPUTER PROBLEM

Problem 15-25. To begin this problem, create a worksheet with a "lookup file" which will be the tax schedule from Table A at Figure 15-2.

Create a worksheet which will calculate the transfer tax for a basic estate. Identify as many different types of assets as you wish for the gross estate. You might, for example, wish to add a gross estate line for "gross up" of gifts which had been made within three years of the date of death. We suggest, just to get you started, the following:

Line 1: Cash
Line 2: Insurance policies (at face amount)
Line 3: Real estate, including personal residence
Line 4: Investments in stocks
Line 5: Investments in bonds
Line 6: Automobiles
Line 7: Personal effects (jewelry, clothing etc.)
Line 8: Total gross estate (sum of previous lines)
Line 9: Debts (You can create more lines and identify different types of debts as you wish.)
Line 10: Funeral expenses
Line 11: Administrative expenses
Line 12: Losses incurred by the estate
Line 13: Marital deduction
Line 14: Charitable bequests
Line 15: Total deductions (sum of above lines)
Line 16: Taxable inter vivos gifts
Line 17: Taxable estate (line 8 minus line 15 plus line 16)
Line 18: Tax before credits (Look up line 17 in the rate schedule which was prepared earlier.)
Line 19: Credit for gift tax previously paid
Line 20: Credit for tax on previous estates
Line 21: Credit for state estate taxes
Line 22: Unified transfer credit
Line 23: Total credits (sum of above lines)
Line 24: Amount of tax due (line 18 minus line 23)

Required:

(a) Create a hypothetical estate which will include all of the items for which you have provided in the worksheet, enter the data and print the results.

(b) Do some estate planning and enter the data followed by a printout of the results. For example, assume a change in the amount of charitable bequests. Put the revised numbers in the worksheet and determine the change in the estate tax. Also, assume that the estate is somewhat smaller as the result of gifts of $10,000 each to various family members before death. How much tax will be saved?

16

alternative minimum tax

INTRODUCTION

Pity the poor legislators! It is their job to take the tax law as it exists at any given moment and attempt to simultaneously achieve fairness and simplicity while still raising revenue. All this must be accomplished without offending too many major constituencies.

Thus, changes are made slowly and in small chunks. It is like a parent doling out an allowance. You want $20? You get $5. There is apt to be something for everyone, but there is always concern that there not be too much for anyone. The concern is not just that of those in Congress. Many people and groups seem to feel it is almost more important that someone else not get away with something than that they themselves get a special break. If there is to be a tax increase, most people seem to hope that it will apply to someone else.

The regular income tax, as we have discussed in prior chapters, provides exclusions from income, such as old age benefits under social security; deductions, such as those for casualty losses; and credits, such as those for child care. Some of these, such as casualty losses, have floors. Others, such as child care, have ceilings. The social security income exclusion is sliced in half if the taxpayer has too much income from other sources, including even tax exempt bond interest as a source. All of these ceilings, floors, and special limitations are ways of limiting benefits to make them more acceptable—and less expensive.

But, in recent years, Congress has concluded that ceilings and floors are not enough. They need to put a lock on the front door of the income tax house, so to speak.

That lock is the ALTERNATIVE MINIMUM TAX (AMT).

As you will see, there are in reality two separate AMTs, one at 21% for individuals and one at 20% for corporations. They are conceptually almost identical. Each is a more inclusive tax than the regular income tax in that it reduces the available deductions and credits and eliminates some of the special options available in calculating income. To this broader base of taxable income, it then applies a flat rate of 21% or 20%. If the resulting tax is greater than the regular income tax, then that greater amount is the tax that will actually be due.

A look at the tax forms, which are included in the Appendix to this chapter, will reveal that the AMT, technically, is a tax that is paid in addition to the regular tax, with the amount of the additional tax being the difference between the regular tax and the AMT. The effect is the same as saying that either the regular tax or the AMT, whichever is larger, must be paid.

If individual tax rates were 50% and corporate 46%, such a broad-based flat tax at rates like 21% and 20% would probably not impact many taxpayers. In fact, the individual AMT did not affect many people in the years prior to 1987—and there was no corporate AMT in its present form. But when tax rates at higher income levels are only 28% for individuals and 34% for corporations, it does not take nearly as much in the way of differences between the regular tax base and the AMT tax base for the AMT to produce a larger tax liability than the regular tax. Many millions of individuals and hundreds of thousands of corporations thus need to be concerned about paying the AMT.

Unfortunately, while the AMT concept is relatively simple, the details of its calculation are nauseatingly complex. It starts with the income calculated for the regular tax, and then makes adjustments to that income figure. The adjustments are to remove what can be perceived as either special tax benefits that should not be unduly abused or to correct what some elements of the public perceive as problems. For example, medical expenses for AMT purposes must exceed 10% of AGI, instead of the regular 7½% of AGI, before being deductible. Interest on certain home equity loans is deductible for the regular tax, but only the amount borrowed to buy, build, or substantially rehabilitate is deductible for AMT. And corporations have to include in AMT income 75% of the excess of adjusted current earnings (ACE) over their alternative minimum taxable income.

While the rest of this chapter details the computation of AMT, it is not important that you memorize the elements that enter into the final number; rather, it is important that you get a sense of the types of adjustments that are being made to the regular tax concepts.

16.1 Individual Alternative Minimum Tax

The individual "alternative minimum tax" (hereafter referred to as AMT) is applicable to noncorporate taxpayers, including estates and trusts. It must be paid if it is larger than the regular tax.[1] It is a "flat tax" in the sense that the tax is 21% of the amount by which alternative minimum taxable income (AMTI) exceeds $30,000 ($40,000 on a joint return and $20,000 for a married person filing separately or for an estate or trust).

The calculation of AMTI starts with taxable income. From the taxable income starting point certain adjustments are made and preferences added.[2] Adjustments require the recomputation of regular tax deductions and may either increase or decrease taxable income. Tax preferences will always be an increase.

For example, assume a married couple filing a joint return had 1990 taxable income of $90,000. The regular tax is $21,562. If their adjustments and preferences for AMT purposes total $60,000, then the calculation of AMT is as follows:

Regular tax taxable income	$ 90,000
Adjustments and preferences	60,000
Alternative minimum taxable income (AMTI)	150,000
Exemption	40,000
Balance	110,000
AMT tax rate	21%
AMT	$ 23,100

The amount to be paid is $23,100, but technically it is the regular tax of $21,562 plus $1,538 which is ($23,100 − $21,562).

Note that there is a bit of strange terminology in the calculation of the AMT. Normally, taxable income is the number to which the tax rate is applied to determine the amount of tax. Not so with the AMT calculation. "Alternative minimum taxable income" is the number *before* the deduction for the exemption. The number *after* the exemption deduction is then multiplied by 21% to determine the amount of the tax.

16.2 Adjustments to Taxable Income

Adjustments for AMT purposes is a fairly new idea in the tax law, having only been added in the Tax Reform Act of 1986.[3] Adjustments can increase or decrease AMTI. (See Appendix 16-A, line 4.) Some of these items involve differences in the timing of deductions. The taxpayer gets higher regular tax benefits in the early years than in the later years. This is taken into account by the AMT adjustments. In an early year when the regular deduction is higher than the AMT deduction, AMTI will be increased. Later, when the regular deduction drops below the AMT deduction, AMTI will be decreased. Over the years, the taxpayer will be able to net the increases and decreases with the only effect being the timing of tax payments (assuming constant tax rates).

16.2.1 Depreciation

Property placed in service after 1986 must be depreciated for AMT purposes using the alternative depreciation system rather than regular ACRS.[4] For real property this will mean straight-line over forty years. For personal property the life will be the period prescribed under the alternative system (generally the class life, which is longer than the ACRS life), and the method will be 150% declining balance switching to straight-line when it

[1]IRC Sec. 55(a).
[2]IRC Sec. 55(b).

[3]IRC Secs. 56 and 58.
[4]IRC Sec. 56(a)(1)(A). Including property placed in service after July 31, 1986 and before 1987, if an election has been made to use post-1986 rules.

becomes more advantageous. The 150% declining balance method will not be used where the regular method is straight-line. If a taxpayer has made an election to use the alternative depreciation method for regular tax purposes, no adjustment will be needed since the regular deduction and the AMT deduction will be the same.

For example, assume an individual has bought an office building with a depreciable cost of $100,000. The ACRS life is 31.5 years, and the annual deduction will be $3,175 (the first year will be prorated). Under the alternative method the life will be 40 years, and the annual deduction for AMT purposes will be $2,500. If this is the taxpayer's only adjustment or preference item, AMTI will exceed taxable income by $675. On the other hand, even after the property is fully depreciated for regular tax purposes, there will still be 8.5 years of AMT depreciation. Then the $2,500 will serve to reduce AMTI below taxable income.

One consequence of different depreciation methods for AMT is that assets will have a different basis for AMT from what they will have for regular tax purposes. If the building mentioned above is sold after $25,000 of regular depreciation, the gain will be computed using an adjusted basis of $75,000. But for AMT purposes if only $20,000 of depreciation has been taken, the AMT adjusted basis is $80,000, and the gain or loss on sale will be $5,000 different for AMT purposes.

16.2.2. Long-Term Contracts

Long-term contracts entered into on or after March 1, 1986, must be accounted for under AMT using the percentage of completion method.[5] The completed contract method or any method which uses it in part will not be allowed. This adjustment should be an increase to AMTI in the early years, and a decrease in later years when more income is recognized for regular tax purposes than for AMT.

16.2.3. Passive Losses

Losses generated by passive activities are generally not deductible, but these rules phased-in over a five-year period that began in 1987 (See Chapter 17).[6] For AMT purposes the phase-in does not apply and the entire loss is disallowed in computing AMTI.[7] If a taxpayer has large passive losses, this adjustment may by itself give rise to AMT.

For example, assume Billy Barnes had a 1989 passive loss of $50,000 of which 10% was deductible for regular tax purposes due to the rules for the phase-in of the disallowance. The result was a $5,000 deduction. However, there is no deduction for AMT purposes, therefore there is a positive adjustment of $5,000.

In figuring allowable passive losses under Code Section 469 for AMT purposes all the other AMT adjustments must be taken into account and all tax preferences must be taken out of the calculation. These adjustments will increase or decrease the income or loss from the passive activity to the extent they relate to that activity. For example, the deductions associated with a passive activity will be increased or decreased by the depreciation adjustment. This will increase or decrease the income or losses from that activity. The effect is to make any adjustments be adjustments to the income or loss of the activity itself. The adjustment for passive losses will apply where losses exist, and they will serve to increase AMTI. Any disallowed passive losses will be carried forward and can be offset against later passive income included in the AMT calculation.

16.2.4. Itemized Deductions

Itemized deductions have been included in the calculation of taxable income. Only some of those deductions are allowable for AMTI, so the ones not allowed must be added back. These include taxes (except estate taxes on income in respect of a decedent), interest, except "qualified interest," medical expenses to the extent they do not exceed 10% of AGI, nonbusiness casualty losses to the extent they do not exceed 10% of AGI, and all other miscellaneous deductions.

Qualified interest includes investment interest to the extent of net investment income, without regard to the phase-in provided by the Tax Reform Act of 1986 (see Chapter 17 for a discussion of limitations on investment interest for regular tax purposes), and qualified housing interest. Investment interest in excess of net investment income may be carried over for AMT purposes. Qualified housing interest is interest on debt incurred to construct, acquire, or substantially rehabilitate either the principal residence or one other residence. Loans for other purposes will not qualify, so interest on a second mortgage or a loan refinanced for a higher amount may not be fully deductible for AMT purposes even though it would be for regular tax calculations.[8]

[5]IRC Sec. 56(a)(3).
[6]IRC Sec. 469(l).
[7]IRC Sec. 58(b).

[8]IRC Sec. 56(b)(1).

For example, assume that Billy Barnes had AGI of $30,000. Itemized deductions included the following:

Medical expenses of $6,000 less 7.5% of AGI ($2,250)	$3,750
Property taxes on personal residence	9,000
State income taxes	4,000
Miscellaneous itemized deductions	1,000

Adjustments necessary for AMT include $14,000 for the last three items above. Also, the adjustment for medical expenses will be $750 which is the difference between 7.5% of AGI and 10% of AGI.

16.2.5. Other Adjustments

The above are only some of the required adjustments. Others include mining exploration and development costs,[9] alternative tax net operating loss deduction,[10] certified pollution control facilities,[11] circulation and research and experimental expenditures, and the individual personal exemption deductions.[12] Each of these adjustments has its own method of being calculated, and must be considered if applicable to a particular taxpayer. The alternative tax net operating loss (NOL) will be the most commonly used, and is calculated by taking regular NOL and recalculating it taking into account all other adjustments as well as items of tax preference.[13] NOLs cannot offset more than 90% of AMTI. Alternative minimum tax NOLs generated before 1987 need not be recalculated, and may be used to reduce post-1986 AMTI.

16.3 Tax Preferences

Tax preferences will increase AMTI. Congress regards these items as benefits that should be curtailed if the taxpayer benefits too much. By adding them into the AMTI calculation, at least some part will be subject to tax.

16.3.1. Depreciation of Pre-1987 Property[14]

Before 1987 only depreciation on certain property was a tax preference. Now adjustments are required for all post-1987 property (see above). Depreciation on pre-1987 property continues to be a tax preference to the extent it was a preference under pre-1987 law. For real property, the amount by which accelerated depreciation exceeds straight-line depreciation will be a tax preference. Such amount is determined on a property-by-property basis. Similarly, for leased personal property, AMTI will be increased by the amount accelerated exceeds straight-line depreciation. These items are important for current AMT purposes since much of this pre-1987 property will continue to be depreciated for many years. A piece of real property placed in service in 1986, with a nineteen year life will be depreciated until 2006. For the later years straight-line will exceed accelerated depreciation. However, since this preference item can only increase AMTI, there will be no corresponding reduction in AMTI at that time. Note the difference between this treatment and the treatment of an "adjustment." If the excess depreciation were an adjustment, there would be a negative adjustment in the years when straight-line depreciation exceeds accelerated depreciation. Also, note that there will be no preference items for real property placed in service currently because there can be no accelerated depreciation on such property. See Chapter 9 where we discussed the requirement that straight line be used to depreciate certain real estate.

16.3.2. Percentage Depletion and Intangible Drilling Costs

On a property-by-property basis, the excess of the percentage depletion deduction for a taxable year over the adjusted basis of the property will be a tax preference.[15] Since percentage depletion is regarded as a special incentive given to oil producers, the benefit will be limited where too little tax is paid.

Intangible drilling costs are also a preference to the extent they exceed the amount allowable during the year if amortized over ten years on a straight-line basis. If the taxpayer has elected to amortize the costs over ten years, there will be no preference treatment. Further, only the amount by which the excess is greater than 65% of the net income of the taxpayer from oil, gas, and geothermal properties will be included.[16]

In Chapter 10 we discussed the concept of the "pass through" of certain source characteristics of income and deductions from a partnership to the partners. That same concept applies to tax

[9]IRC Sec. 56(a)(2).
[10]IRC Sec. 56(a)(4).
[11]IRC Sec. 56(a)(5).
[12]IRC Sec. 56(b)(2).
[13]IRC Sec. 56(d).
[14]Not including property acquired in 1986 which is depreciated under the post-1986 rules.
[15]IRC Sec. 57(a)(1).
[16]IRC Sec. 57(a)(2).

preferences. Thus, if a partnership that is engaged in natural resource (e.g. oil or gas) exploration and development should have percentage depletion in excess of the basis of property or should have a deduction for intangible drilling costs, each partner will be allocated a share of such preferences and will be required to consider that as part of his or her individual AMT calculation. (See Figure 10-3(b), line 15.)

16.3.3. Incentive Stock Options

Incentive stock options (ISOs) enjoy favored tax treatment. (See Chapter 18.) If all requirements are met an employee may receive stock options, exercise them at a bargain price, and hold the stock indefinitely without ever recognizing income on the receipt of the stock. Only when the stock is sold will gain be recognized, and then it will be a capital gain, not ordinary income.[17]

The bargain element at the time of the exercise of an ISO is a tax preference. The bargain element will be the excess of fair market value (FMV) over the amount actually paid for the stock. FMV will be determined without regard to any restriction other than a restriction which, by its terms, will never lapse.[18]

A complicating element is that the amount included as a tax preference upon the exercise of an ISO will serve to increase the basis of the stock acquired by the amount of the preference for AMT purposes only. When the stock is later disposed of, the gain or loss for AMT will be different than that for regular taxes.[19] This difference will be an adjustment in arriving at AMTI.

For example, assume that Billy Barnes held an option to purchase stock under an ISO contract. At the time 1,000 shares of stock had a value of $25,000, Billy purchased them for $10,000. Because the purchase qualified as an ISO, the $15,000 bargain price was not included in Billy's gross income for regular income tax purposes at the time of purchase. However, the $15,000 is a tax preference for Billy's AMT purposes. If Billy sells the stock six years later for $37,000 there is a recognized gain for regular income tax purposes of $27,000, but a recognized gain for AMT purposes of $12,000. Since Billy's AMT calculation begins with regular tax taxable income, it will be necessary to subtract $15,000 to arrive at AMT taxable income, in the year of sale.

[17]IRC Sec. 422A.
[18]IRC Sec. 57(a)(3)(A).
[19]IRC Sec. 57(a)(3)(B).

16.3.4. Tax-Exempt Interest

Tax-exempt interest earned on "private activity bonds" became a preference starting in 1986. What constitutes a private activity bond is beyond the scope of this book, but it generally includes a bond issued after August 7, 1986, which meets certain tests concerning the amount of the proceeds which will benefit private parties rather than the issuing government.[20]

16.3.5. Charitable Contributions of Appreciated Property

If a taxpayer donates capital gain property to a charity, a deduction is generally available equal to the fair market value of the property, regardless of the purchase price (basis). (See Chapter 3.) For AMT purposes, the untaxed appreciation is a preference if it is allowed as a deduction for regular tax purposes.[21] If the taxpayer has elected to limit the charitable deduction to the adjusted basis of thc property (in order to take advantage of a higher charitable contribution limit), there will be no preference.[22] Unrealized gains may be offset by unrealized losses, so the AMT preference will come close to treating the taxpayer as if the property had been sold, gain or loss recognized, and the proceeds contributed to the charity.

For example, assume that Billy contributed 1,000 shares of ABC stock to a favorite charity. The stock had originally cost $5,000 but had a value of $12,000 at the time of contribution. Assume that adjusted gross income was sufficiently large so that there was no limitation on the deduction and Billy deducted the $12,000 as a part of itemized deductions for regular tax purposes. The $7,000 appreciation in the stock is a "preference" for AMT purposes.

16.4 Individual Exemption Amount

Before AMT is calculated, AMTI is reduced by an exemption amount. For a couple filing a joint return (or a surviving spouse) the exemption will be $40,000. The exemption amount is $30,000 for single individuals, and $20,000 for married taxpayers filing separately, or an estate or trust.[23]

These exemptions are eliminated after AMTI reaches certain levels. The exemption is reduced

[20]IRC Sec. 57(a)(5).
[21]IRC Sec. 57(a)(6).
[22]IRC Sec. 57(a)(6)(B).
[23]IRC Sec. 55(d)(1).

(but not below zero) by $0.25 for each dollar AMTI exceeds:

Married	$150,000
Single	$112,500
Married filing separately, trusts and estates	$ 75,000

The exemption is therefore fully eliminated when AMTI is greater than $310,000, $232,500, and $155,000, respectively, for the above types of taxpayers.[24] (See Appendix 16-A, lines 9 to 13 for illustration of the phase-down of the exemption.)

16.5 Credits

16.5.1. Foreign Tax Credit

The foreign tax credit (FTC), as specially computed, will reduce the tentative minimum tax, but not by more than 90%.[25] FTC limitations must take into account all of the differences between regular taxable income and AMTI. Therefore, AMT FTC will differ from regular FTC, and the carryovers available from one year to the next will also differ.

16.5.2. Minimum Tax Credit

Beginning in 1987, a taxpayer may accumulate credits based on all or part of the AMT paid. These credits may be used in later years to reduce regular tax when regular tax exceeds calculated AMT. Minimum tax credits (MTC) cannot reduce regular tax below AMT. No carrybacks of MTCs are allowed, but unlimited carryovers are available.[26]

The purpose of this credit is to recognize the positive or negative effect of many of the adjustments. Where AMT affects primarily the timing of a tax payment, tax increases in an early year should be balanced by later tax decreases. More permanent differences cannot be included in computing MTC. These include adjustments and preferences relating to (1) itemized deductions, (2) depletion, (3) tax-exempt interest, and (4) charitable contributions.[27]

16.5.3 Other Credits Do Not Reduce Alternative Minimum Tax

The only credit that can be used in the current year to reduce the AMT is the foreign tax credit. Thus, the other credits discussed in Chapter 4 and Chapter 7 (e.g. the credit for child or dependent care and the general business credit) will reduce the regular tax but not the AMT. (See Appendix 1-D(b), lines 41 to 47, and note that the AMT is added at line 49, *after* those reductions.) Assume that Billy Barnes has no foreign tax credits. Other credits total $1,000. Regular tax is $20,000 before credits and $19,000 after credits. AMT is $24,000 which does not get reduced by any credits. Thus, Billy's tax for the year is $24,000, not $23,000.

16.6 Corporate Alternative Minimum Tax

For tax years beginning after 1986, corporations are also subject to a 20% AMT. Prior to that a separate corporate minimum tax based on total tax preferences was imposed. With the application of AMT to corporations, the minimum tax imposed on noncorporate and corporate taxpayers became very similar, with some important differences, which are discussed below.

16.7 Corporate Adjustments

The following adjustments apply to corporations just as they do to individuals:

1. Depreciation
2. Mining exploration and development costs
3. Long-term contracts
4. Certified pollution control facilities
5. Alternative tax net operating loss

Adjustments which apply only to individuals are those for itemized deductions, and the adjustment for circulation and research and experimental expenditures.[28] The adjustment that applies only to corporations is that for adjusted current earnings (ACE), discussed below.[29]

16.7.1. ACE Adjustment

Congress has always been disturbed by reports of huge corporations which paid little or no income tax, yet reported large profits to shareholders. The ACE adjustment is part of an attempt to ensure that all taxpayers with substantial economic income will pay some tax.

[24] IRC Sec. 55(d)(3).
[25] IRC Sec. 55(b).
[26] IRC Sec. 53.
[27] IRC Sec. 53(a)(1)(B)(ii).
[28] IRC Sec. 56(a), (b).
[29] The adjustment for merchant marine capital construction funds only applies to corporations, but is not discussed. IRC Sec. 56(c)(2).

Corporations are required to increase AMTI by 75% of the amount the adjusted current earnings of the corporation exceeds AMTI (calculated without this adjustment or the alternative tax net operating loss deduction).[30] For example, assume corporation A has ACE of $200, and taxable income of $100. If there are no other adjustments or tax preferences, AMTI would be the $100 of taxable income, plus 75% of $100 ($200 − $100), or $175.

What, then, is (or are) "adjusted current earnings" (ACE)? The focus in arriving at ACE is on those items which affect the corporation's earnings and profits without being reflected in the calculation of taxable income for either regular tax or alternative minimum tax. "Earnings and profits" is the tax analog to "retained earnings" in financial accounting.

Typical examples of ACE adjustment items would be interest on tax-exempt bonds, proceeds of corporate life insurance, and federal income taxes. The first two are not reported in calculating taxable income, while the federal income tax item is not deducted, but all three affect earnings and profits. The difference between regular tax depreciation and that which is allowed for earnings and profits is almost always present for property acquired after 1989.

If you look back at schedule M-1 in Appendix 12-A(d), you will find where most ACE adjustments will surface. Schedule M-1 reports the items that differ between taxable income and financial statement income. Lines 3 and 6 of schedule M-2, in the same appendix, may on rare occasions contain entries used in reconciling retained earnings, and which represent direct charges or credits to retained earnings that would also affect earnings and profits. Such adjustments as that for ACE depreciation, however, will not usually show up on either Schedule M-1 or M-2. In addition, amounts excludible from taxable income under Section 108 from forgiveness of indebtedness, while they may appear in Schedule M-1, will not be reflected in calculating ACE.

16.8 Corporate Preferences

Tax preferences for corporations are the same as for individuals (see above).[31] An additional preference for corporations is that a reserve for losses for bad debts will be a preference to the extent it exceeds the deduction based on actual experience.[32]

[30] IRC Sec. 56(c)(1). ACE applies to years beginning after 1989. For 1987, 1988, and 1989, book income as determined under generally accepted accounting principles was used.
[31] IRC Sec. 57.
[32] IRC Sec. 57(a)(4).

16.9 Corporate Exemption Amount and Credits

Corporations have an exemption of $40,000 in calculating AMTI. As with married individuals, this exemption will be phased out if the taxpayers AMTI (before the exemption) exceeds $150,000. The amount disallowed is 25% of AMTI over $150,000, so no exemption will be available if AMTI is over $310,000.[33]

Similarly, the foreign tax credit and minimum tax credit will be calculated the same for individuals and corporations. Corporations have an added advantage in that investment tax credits from carryovers or transition property may offset the greater of (1) either the lesser of regular tax liability over 75% of tentative minimum tax for the year (i.e., AMT before reduction by any credits), or (2) 25% of the tentative minimum tax liability. These credits cannot be used to the extent they reduce AMT to below 10% of the amount of tax determined without regard to net operating loss or foreign tax credits.[34] The net result is that the credit will be used to reduce AMT *or* regular tax, depending upon which route will use the most credit.

Appendix 16-B is the form on which a corporation reports its AMT. It is included here for the same reason other forms are included in this text, not for the purpose of teaching how to complete tax forms, but to illustrate the concept and to provide examples. Note the similarity between the adjustments and preference items for individuals and corporations as reflected on the forms in Appendix 16-A and 16-B. Since the form is for 1989, the preference that we have called ACE is called the "book income adjustment" on line 5 of Form 4626. That terminology will change for the 1990 form. Note that the exemption for a corporation is $40,000 (Appendix 16-B, line 9a), and that the exemption gets phased down if alternative minimum taxable income exceeds $150,000 (lines 9b through 9e). Also note that the tax rate is 20% (line 11).

The following simple illustration for the ABC corporation shows AMT greater than the regular tax. Assume the following facts:

Regular tax taxable income	$500,000
Adjustments for depreciation	80,000
Preferences for intangible drilling costs	200,000
ACE adjustment	100,000
AMTI	$880,000

Regular tax will be 34% × $500,000 = $170,000
There will be no exemption because AMTI is larger than $310,000.
AMT = 20% × $880,000 = $176,000

[33] IRC Sec. 55(d).
[34] IRC Sec. 38(c)(3).

16.10 Estimated Tax

Corporations are required to take AMT into account in making estimated tax payments.[35] Individuals are subject to similar requirement.[36] This may be very difficult since AMT will not be simple to calculate. The ACE adjustment will be especially difficult to estimate. Given the high penalties for underpayment of estimated tax and increased enforcement, it will be very important to keep on top of the various payment requirements.

16.11 Planning Considerations

The complexity of the AMT makes planning difficult, at best. Just understanding the rules and their effects on a particular taxpayer will involve detailed analysis. Since AMT requires dual treatment of so many items, tax planning will also have to consider both regular and AMT aspects. What looks like a great tax opportunity may evaporate if the AMT rules put the advantageous deductions back into the taxable pot of AMTI.

One option is to treat items the same for regular tax and AMT purposes. For example, property may be depreciated for regular tax purposes using the alternative depreciation methods, and other costs, such as intangible drilling costs, may be amortized rather than deducted. This would definitely simplify record keeping. However, if the minimum tax credit, AMT net operating loss and AMT foreign tax credit work as they are intended, the tax savings from this option may be minimal. Those provisions are designed to eliminate the effects of timing differences by reducing regular tax in later years as an offset to AMT.

Techniques which have been used for many years in AMT planning are also available. These methods are often the opposite of those used in regular tax planning. For example, if a taxpayer is already subject to AMT, additional deductions may have no impact (i.e., most itemized deductions), or at best will only produce a 21% benefit (20% for corporations). The normal planning technique of accelerating deductions will be replaced by a desire to defer deductions to a year when AMT will not apply and the tax rate is higher. Similarly, it may make sense to accelerate income into a year when the tax will be at the AMT rate, rather than the higher regular tax rate.

Many corporations have considered the ACE adjustment as an important factor in their decisions to become an S corporation. This adjustment does not apply to S corporations. Adjustment and preferences which apply to individuals will be passed-through to the S corporation shareholders, but ACE greater than AMTI will not serve to increase the shareholders AMTI.

16.12 Conclusion

The AMT is very much a second taxing structure. Separate records must be maintained, tracking regular tax and AMT. Depreciable property must be recorded with regular basis and AMT basis. These requirements place great burdens on taxpayers and tax practitioners. Record keeping is more difficult and planning becomes more complex. As regular tax rates have dropped closer to the 20%/21% AMT rates, an increasing percentage of taxpayers have found the AMT rather than the regular tax must be the main tax focus of their planning attention. For most, the added tax it represents may prove to be minor compared to the cost and confusion it creates. If, in fact, upper-income taxpayers mainly pay the AMT, it is possible that the regular tax option (and calculation) might ultimately be eliminated for them "to simplify the law."

[35]IRC Sec. 6154(c).
[36]IRC Sec. 6654(d)(2)(B).

TRUE-FALSE QUESTIONS

State whether each of the following statements is true or false. For each *false* answer, reword the statement to make it *true*.

T F 1. The ordinary federal income tax rates are progressive, meaning that they increase as the amount which is being taxed increases, but the alternative minimum tax rate is flat, meaning that it is always the same rate regardless of the amount which is subject to tax.

T F 2. The alternative minimum tax rate which applies to corporations is 21%.

T F 3. The alternative minimum tax rate which applies to individual taxpayers is 21%.

T F 4. The alternative minimum tax rules which apply to corporations also apply to an estate or trust which is required to file a federal income tax return.

T F 5. Except for the exemption deduction ($40,000, $30,000, or $20,000), the alternative minimum tax is computed in the same manner for individual taxpayers regardless of marital status.

T F 6. For purposes of the alternative minimum tax, an amount equal to the excess of accelerated depreciation on real property over what straight-line depreciation would have been must be added to taxable income.

T F 7. The alternative minimum tax never applies to corporations.

T F 8. If a married couple file a joint federal income tax return, they will be able to deduct $40,000 in the determination of the amount which is subject to the alternative minimum tax regardless of the amount of their total income.

T F 9. Alternative minimum taxable income (AMTI) will always be larger than the regular tax taxable income because the calculation of AMTI starts with regular tax taxable income, to which the tax preference items must be added.

T F 10. For purposes of the AMT, depreciation on real estate which was acquired after 1986 must be based upon the straight-line method and a life expectancy of 40 years rather than the 31.5 year life expectancy which can be used for the regular tax depreciation calculation.

T F 11. For an individual, the amount of medical expense which can be deducted for the AMT is that amount which is greater than 10% of adjusted gross income whereas the amount of medical expense which can be deducted for the regular tax is the amount which is greater than 7.5% of adjusted gross income.

T F 12. Tax preference items are those items which must be added to regular tax taxable income to determine the amount of alternative minimum tax taxable income.

T F 13. If an individual deducts appreciated capital gain property for the regular income tax, then the amount of the appreciation for that property must be subtracted from regular taxable income in the determination of AMT taxable income.

T F 14. For all taxpayers who take percentage depletion deductions in excess of the adjusted basis of the property, such excess is a tax preference for purposes of the alternative minimum tax.

T F 15. Where pre-1987 real property is being depreciated under the ACRS method (which uses a fifteen-, eighteen-, or nineteen-year life and the 175% declining-balance method) the "excess depreciation" (tax preference item) for alternative minimum tax purposes is determined by using straight-line depreciation and a fifteen-, eighteen-, or nineteen-year life for the property.

T F 16. In determining the amount that is subject to the alternative minimum tax for an individual, a deduction can be taken for charitable contributions.

T F 17. In determining the amount that is subject to the alternative minimum tax for an individual, a deduction can be taken for casualty losses.

T F 18. In determining the amount that is subject to the alternative minimum tax, a deduction is allowed for all interest expense incurred.

T F 19. In determining the amount that is subject to the alternative minimum tax, there is no deduction for state and local sales or property taxes.

T F 20. Where a taxpayer is entitled to a deduction for alimony paid, the amount of the deduction will reduce the regular tax as well as the alternative minimum tax.

PROBLEMS

Problem 16-1. Sally Liberman plans to have taxable income of $32,000 for 1990. Her adjusted gross income will be $40,000. She is single. Her adjustments to arrive at the alternative minimum tax income will be + $20,000.

(a) If all goes according to plan, what will be Sally's federal income tax for the year?

(b) Will she be subject to the alternative minimum tax? Explain.

(c) Determine the amount of regular tax and alternative minimum tax if everything remains the same except her adjustments were + $30,000.

Problem 16-2. James and Janet Kofmehl expect to have taxable income of $50,000 for 1990 on a joint income tax return. Adjusted gross income will be $70,000. What would be the necessary amount of adjustments that could be incurred so that the alternative minimum tax would be exactly equal to the regular tax?

Problem 16-3. For 1990 Roberta Cheryle, who is single (one exemption amount), will have $100,000 in salary from Moon, Inc., $225,000 of net long-term capital gains, and $10,000 of taxable interest. Itemized deductions will be $20,000. All of those deductions are allowable for the AMT.

(a) What is the regular federal income tax? The alternative minimum tax?

(b) What would be the difference in the regular tax and in the AMT if Roberta had tax preference items of $80,000.

Problem 16-4. Clarence DeNiro is single. His salary is $97,600. He has interest income of $20,000. Deductions for adjusted gross income are $10,000 for alimony and $2,000 for a contribution to an Individual Retirement Account. Itemized deductions total $80,000. Included in itemized deductions was a charitable contribution of a capital asset which had a fair market value of $30,000 but an original cost to Clarence of $4,000. There is no deduction for medical expenses. He has only himself to claim as a personal exemption. He has no credits. Itemized deductions do not include any medical expenses, excess interest, or local taxes.

(a) What is his 1990 regular tax liability?

(b) Will he be subject to the alternative minimum tax? Explain.

(c) Clarence had an opportunity during the year to purchase some depreciable real property which would have resulted in an ACRS deduction of $50,000 using the 31.5 year cost recovery period and straight-line depreciation. The cost of the property would have been $1,575,000. What would have been the regular tax and the AMT tax resulting from the acquisition of that property? Explain.

Problem 16-5. Bill Singleton is unmarried, but qualifies as a head of household for federal income tax purposes. His income and deductions for 1990 are as follows:

Salary	$ 35,000
Long-term capital gain	250,000
Itemized deductions	25,000
Personal exemptions (4)	8,200

Itemized deductions do not include any medical expenses, excess interest, local taxes, or other items not deductible for the AMT.

(a) What is Bill's regular tax liability?

(b) Will Bill be subject to the alternative minimum tax? Explain. Show your calculations.

(c) What amount of tax preferences could Bill have had without being subject to the AMT?

(d) Would it have made any difference if Bill were eligible to file a joint income tax return, assuming that everything else remained the same? Explain.

(e) Is it possible that the AMT would have to be paid if one were filing as a single person but not paid if one were filing a joint return? Explain.

Problem 16-6. In computing its taxable income for the fiscal year ending August 31, 1990, the following information was obtained from your *corporate* client:

1. Depreciation expense was $100,000. Financial statement depreciation was $60,000. Depreciation under the alternative depreciation system would have been $80,000.
2. The company uses the installment method of accounting for tax purposes for casual sales of real property. This year it recognized income of $40,000 relating to an installment sale in 1989. In 1989, the company had recognized the full profit of $100,000 on the entire sale for financial statement purposes.
3. The company deducted a charitable contribution of $64,000. Its basis was $14,000 and its fair market value was $64,000.
4. The company uses the percentage of completion method for financial accounting purposes and the completed contract method for tax purposes. It recognized profit of $150,000 for financial purposes and $130,000 profit for tax purposes.
5. The company sold a building for $300,000. Its basis for regular tax purposes was $250,000. Had it depreciated the building under the alternative depreciation system, its basis would have been $280,000.
6. In computing its regular tax liability, it had deducted a $60,000 net operating loss from its fiscal year ended 8/31/89. In 1989, its AMT NOL was $20,000.
7. The company uses the LIFO method of inventory. Had it used the FIFO method, its cost of goods sold would have been $40,000 less.

(a) For each of the above items indicate whether the item is an adjustment, preference, or has no effect on the corporation's alternative minimum tax.

(b) For the adjustments identified in part (a), indicate whether the adjustment increases or decreases alternative minimum taxable income.

Problem 16-7. The "normal" income tax planning strategy calls for (1) accelerating deductions into the earlier of two years in order to obtain the tax advantage sooner and (2) deferring income into a later year in order to postpone the payment of tax on that income. That planning strategy could be reversed, however, where the current year will be an "alternative minimum tax" year and the following year is expected to be a "regular tax" year. Explain.

Problem 16-8. Patricia and John Sanchez had the following items of income and deductions for the year 1990.

Salary—John	$28,000
Salary—Patricia	26,000
Gross dividends	1,000
Long-term capital gain	70,000
Net rental income (loss)	(10,000)*
Interest on mortgage on personal residence	7,000
Charitable contributions (all cash)	1,000
State and local property and income taxes	2,000
Exemption amounts	4

* Accelerated depreciation was used and was $12,000 more than straight-line depreciation would have been.

(a) Compute the regular income tax liability.

(b) Compute the alternative minimum tax.

Problem 16-9. Lynn Linds (single) will have the following income and deductions for 1990:

Salary	$70,000
Schedule E loss (from investment in real estate)*	(23,000)
Itemized deductions:	
State and local taxes	7,000
Charitable contributions (all cash)	2,000
Interest on personal loan	40,000
Exemption amount (1)	2,050

* 10% is deductible for regular tax assuming taxpayer is not an active participant. See Chapter 17.

(a) Calculate the regular tax and the alternative minimum tax for the year.

(b) Lynn also owns a corporation which has sufficient funds to pay a dividend before year end. If dividends of $3,100 are paid, what will be the impact on (1) the regular tax and (2) the alternative minimum tax?

Problem 16-10. Big Corporation will have taxable income of $600,000 for 1990.

(a) If it has no tax preference items or adjustments, what will be the amount of the regular tax and the amount of the AMT?

(b) If the corporation has $500,000 of tax preference items, compare the regular tax and the AMT. Which will be paid?

Problem 16-11. Little Corporation will have taxable income of $120,000 for 1990. It will have tax preference items consisting of the following:

a. Depreciation for regular tax purposes exceeds depreciation for AMT purposes by $10,000.

b. Regular taxable income includes $20,000 gain from an installment sale of real estate used in its business. The total gain on the sale was $35,000.

c. A deduction for percentage depletion was $8,000. The basis of the natural resource was zero at the beginning of the year.

(a) What will be the amount of the corporation's regular tax for 1990?

(b) What will be the amount of the corporation's AMT for 1990?

(c) What would have been the result if the entire amount of the gain on the sale of the real estate had been deferred due to the installment sales method?

Problem 16-12. Middle Corporation will have taxable income of $80,000 for 1990.

(a) If it has no tax preference items, what will be the amount of the regular tax and the amount of the AMT?

(b) Compare the regular tax and the AMT if the corporation has tax preference items of $39,000. Which will have to be paid?

Problem 16-13. The ABC Corporation's regular taxable income for 1990 was $100,000. Its adjusted current earnings for the year was $300,000. One of the major reconciling items between the two figures was $100,000 of the tax-free interest income which the company earned as a result of investing in state and local bonds. In computing its alternative minimum tax, the corporation's adjustments and preferences, exclusive of the ACE adjustment, equal $60,000 and $40,000 respectively.

(a) Compute the ACE adjustment.

(b) Compute the alternative minimum tax.

(c) If there were no ACE adjustment, what would have been the allowed exemption and alternative minimum tax?

(d) If the corporation had not earned any of the tax-exempt interest, adjusted current earnings would have been $200,000. What would have been the alternative minimum tax.

(e) As a result of the alternative minimum tax and the ACE adjustment, is the "tax-exempt" interest income really nontaxable.

Problem 16-14. For 1991, LMN Corporation computed its tentative minimum tax to equal $200,000. Since its regular income tax equaled $260,000, the company incurred no alternative minimum tax for the year. In 1990, the company had computed a $100,000 alternative minimum tax credit.

(a) How much of the 1990 alternative minimum tax credit may be used in 1991?

(b) What is the purpose of the alternative minimum tax credit?

Form **6251**

Department of the Treasury
Internal Revenue Service

Alternative Minimum Tax—Individuals

▶ See separate Instructions.

▶ Attach to Form 1040 or Form 1040NR. Estates and trusts, use Form 8656.

OMB No. 1545-0227

1989

Attachment Sequence No. 32

Name(s) shown on Form 1040 | Your social security number

1	Taxable income from Form 1040, line 37 (can be less than zero)			1
2	Net operating loss deduction, if any, from Form 1040, line 22. (Enter as a positive amount.)			2
3	Add lines 1 and 2			3
4	**Adjustments:** (See Instructions before completing.)			
a	Standard deduction, if applicable, from Form 1040, line 34	4a		
b	Personal exemption amount from Form 1040, line 36	4b		
c	Medical and dental expense	4c		
d	Miscellaneous itemized deductions from Schedule A (Form 1040), line 24	4d		
e	Taxes from Schedule A (Form 1040), line 8	4e		
f	Refund of taxes	4f	( )	
g	Personal interest from Schedule A (Form 1040), line 12b	4g		
h	Other interest adjustments	4h		
i	Combine lines 4a through 4h			4i
j	Depreciation of property placed in service after 1986	4j		
k	Circulation and research and experimental expenditures paid or incurred after 1986	4k		
l	Mining exploration and development costs paid or incurred after 1986	4l		
m	Long-term contracts entered into after 2/28/86	4m		
n	Pollution control facilities placed in service after 1986	4n		
o	Installment sales of certain property	4o		
p	Adjusted gain or loss	4p		
q	Certain loss limitations	4q		
r	Tax shelter farm loss	4r		
s	Passive activity loss	4s		
t	Beneficiaries of estates and trusts	4t		
u	Combine lines 4j through 4t			4u
5	**Tax preference items:** (See Instructions before completing.)			
a	Appreciated property charitable deduction	5a		
b	Tax-exempt interest from private activity bonds issued after 8/7/86	5b		
c	Depletion	5c		
d	Add lines 5a through 5c			5d
e	Accelerated depreciation of real property placed in service before 1987	5e		
f	Accelerated depreciation of leased personal property placed in service before 1987	5f		
g	Amortization of certified pollution control facilities placed in service before 1987	5g		
h	Intangible drilling costs	5h		
i	Add lines 5e through 5h			5i
6	Combine lines 3, 4i, 4u, 5d, and 5i			6
7	Alternative tax net operating loss deduction. (Do not enter more than 90% of line 6.) See Instructions			7
8	Alternative minimum taxable income (subtract line 7 from line 6). If married filing a separate return, see Instructions			8
9	Enter: $40,000 ($20,000 if married filing separately; $30,000 if single or head of household)			9
10	Enter: $150,000 ($75,000 if married filing separately; $112,500 if single or head of household)			10
11	Subtract line 10 from line 8. If the result is -0- or less, enter -0- here and on line 12 and go to line 13			11
12	Multiply line 11 by 25% (.25)			12
13	Subtract line 12 from line 9. If the result is -0- or less, enter -0-. If completing this form for a child under age 14, see the Instructions for the amount to enter on this line			13
14	Subtract line 13 from line 8. If the result is -0- or less, enter -0- here and on line 19			14
15	Multiply line 14 by 21% (.21)			15
16	Alternative minimum tax foreign tax credit. See Instructions			16
17	Tentative minimum tax (subtract line 16 from line 15)			17
18	Enter your tax from Form 1040, line 38, minus any foreign tax credit on Form 1040, line 43. If an amount is entered on line 39 of Form 1040, see Instructions			18
19	**Alternative minimum tax** (subtract line 18 from line 17). Enter on Form 1040, line 49. If the result is -0- or less, enter -0-. If completing this form for a child under age 14, see the Instructions for the amount to enter			19

For Paperwork Reduction Act Notice, see separate Instructions. Form **6251** (1989)

H732

Form **4626**

Department of the Treasury
Internal Revenue Service

Alternative Minimum Tax—Corporations
(including environmental tax)

► See separate instructions.
► Attach to your tax return.

OMB No. 1545-0175

1989

Name as shown on tax return | **Employer identification number**

1 Taxable income or (loss) before net operating loss deduction			1
2 Adjustments:			
a Depreciation of tangible property placed in service after 1986	2a		
b Amortization of certified pollution control facilities placed in service after 1986	2b		
c Amortization of mining exploration and development costs paid or incurred after 1986	2c		
d Amortization of circulation expenditures paid or incurred after 1986 (personal holding companies only)	2d		
e Basis adjustments in determining gain or loss from sale or exchange of property	2e		
f Long-term contracts entered into after February 28, 1986	2f		
g Installment sales of certain property	2g		
h Merchant marine capital construction funds	2h		
i Section 833(b) deduction (Blue Cross, Blue Shield, and similar type organizations only)	2i		
j Tax shelter farm activities (personal service corporations only)	2j		
k Passive activities (closely held corporations and personal service corporations only)	2k		
l Certain loss limitations	2l		
m Other	2m		
n Combine lines 2a through 2m			2n
3 Tax preference items:			
a Depletion	3a		
b Tax-exempt interest from private activity bonds issued after August 7, 1986	3b		
c Appreciated property charitable deduction	3c		
d Add lines 3a through 3c			3d
e Intangible drilling costs	3e		
f Reserves for losses on bad debts of financial institutions	3f		
g Accelerated depreciation of real property placed in service before 1987	3g		
h Accelerated depreciation of leased personal property placed in service before 1987 (personal holding companies only)	3h		
i Amortization of certified pollution control facilities placed in service before 1987	3i		
j Add lines 3e through 3i			3j
4 Combine lines 1, 2n, 3d, and 3j			4
5 Excess book income adjustment:			
a Enter your adjusted net book income	5a		
b Subtract line 4 from line 5a (even if one or both of these figures is a negative number). (Enter zero if the result is zero or less)	5b		
c Multiply line 5b by 50%			5c
6 Combine lines 4 and 5c. If zero or less, stop here (you are not subject to the alternative minimum tax)			6
7 Alternative tax net operating loss deduction. (Do not enter more than 90% of line 6.)			7
8 Alternative minimum taxable income (subtract line 7 from line 6)			8
9 Exemption phase-out computation:			
a Tentative exemption amount. Enter $40,000 (members of a controlled group, see instructions)	9a		
b Enter $150,000 (members of a controlled group, see instructions)	9b		
c Subtract line 9b from line 8. If zero or less, enter zero	9c		
d Multiply line 9c by 25%	9d		
e Exemption. Subtract line 9d from line 9a. If zero or less, enter zero			9e
10 Subtract line 9e from line 8. If zero or less, enter zero			10
11 Multiply line 10 by 20%			11
12 Alternative minimum tax foreign tax credit			12
13 Tentative minimum tax (subtract line 12 from line 11)			13
14 General business credit allowed against alternative minimum tax (see instructions)			14
15 Regular tax liability before all credits except the foreign tax credit and possessions tax credit			15
16 Alternative minimum tax—Add lines 14 and 15 and subtract the total from line 13. If the result is greater than zero, enter on line 9a, Schedule J, Form 1120, or on the comparable line of other income tax returns			16
17 Environmental tax—Subtract $2,000,000 from line 6 (computed without regard to your environmental tax deduction), and multiply the result, if any, by 0.12% (.0012). Enter on line 9b, Schedule J, Form 1120, or on the comparable line of other income tax returns (members of a controlled group, see instructions)			17

For Paperwork Reduction Act Notice, see separate instructions.
H732

Form **4626** (1989)

17

tax shelters

Sometimes Congress discovers that it has provided some taxpayers with more incentives, subsidies, loopholes, or special benefits than was intended. Rather than repeal the provisions, the typical congressional reaction has been to create limitations and restrictions upon the extent to which taxpayers can use the rules to their benefit. The previous chapter dealt with one such limiting approach—the alternative minimum tax (AMT). The subjects of this chapter, the passive loss limitations, limitation on the deduction for "excess investment interest," the 20% reduction of certain corporate deductions, and the "at-risk" rules, are all reactions by Congress to what were viewed as overly aggressive approaches to the tax law taken by taxpayers. The above is not a complete listing of all tax shelter actions Congress has taken. Other provisions are, however, integrated into the substance of other areas of the tax law, and are discussed at appropriate points throughout the book.

Before proceeding any further we must try to define "tax shelters." That is a term which most people have heard, and which means different things to different people. There is no precise, generally accepted definition. Unfortunately, it is a term which is both misused and vague. For our purposes, a tax shelter is any financial arrangement, or set of financial arrangements, which has the result of reducing current tax with the expectation of generating tax benefits or future income in an amount greater than the current outlay. Note that it is not just a tax provision which will reduce current taxes. Any legitimate deduction will do that. For example, a casualty loss will result in a current deduction, but we have not heard of any recommendations that casualty losses be incurred intentionally with the sole purpose of obtaining the benefit of a tax deduction. There must be some *quid pro quo.* A tax deferral can be a tax shelter, even if the future tax rate will be the same as the current tax rate. The reason is that money has a time value. Payment of the amount of tax in the future rather than today is an advantage because of the concept of present value.

Congress has not attempted to eliminate all tax shelters. Quite to the contrary, some have been purposefully created. For example, pension and profit-sharing plans continue to be encouraged by the deductibility of contributions and build-up of tax free income (see Chapter 18). The purpose is to encourage employers to provide for employee retirement and individuals to set aside money for the same purpose. Congress does this by allowing certain amounts to be "sheltered" from tax. In this sense, a shelter is merely a plan for the deferral of payment of tax.

17.1 Some Typical Tax Shelters

Commercial and residential rental real estate is probably the shelter in which more people participate than any other, not counting the millions who view their personal residence as a form of tax shelter. (The personal residence actually meets our definition of a tax shelter because the bulk of the house payments of most people consists of deductible interest and real estate taxes, while they believe that the value of the house, at least over a period of years, will increase.) Real property improvements to rental property since 1986 can be depreciated over either 27.5 or 31.5 years, interest paid on the mortgage is deductible (subject to the limitations discussed in Chapter 3), and there are numerous ways for an investor to acquire such a tax shelter—limited partnership interests, joint venture deals with a local developer, and individual purchase of smaller properties. Financing is often already in place, or can be obtained rather easily. Personal liability can often be avoided, even with modest amounts of equity relative to debt. Perhaps of most importance, investors believe that real estate will increase in value and is an inflation hedge.

Oil and gas properties are another popular shelter that is vigorously marketed. The tax attraction is the deductibility of the intangible drilling and development cost and the possible lower effective rate on income realized resulting from percentage depletion on certain oil and gas investments.

Then there is a wide range of more exotic (and often riskier, both in a tax and in an investment sense) tax shelters. Equipment leasing (the investor buys the equipment, such as a large computer, which is or will be leased to a user, seeking the tax benefits of depreciation and interest deductions); computer software (the investor leases the software from the promoter, and the software is then distributed by an independent third party with the investor receiving a royalty on each diskette sold); and research and development (taking advantage of the current deductibility under IRC Sec. 174 of R & D expenditures, while paying for them with long-term notes or borrowed cash).

Many shelters are accrual-basis partnerships which take deductions for items that may not be paid for some time. The bona-fides of the prices paid for the goods or services being received may be questioned by the IRS. At the same time, the accrual rules for tax accounting purposes, as discussed elsewhere, more closely align deductions with the present value of future payments than do the rules of financial accounting.

17.2 Public Policy Questions re: Tax Shelters

Use of tax shelters has risen rapidly in the past fifteen years. The first tax law to attempt consciously to cope with the shelter phenomena was the 1976 Tax Reform Act (although some steps had been taken in the 1969 Tax Reform Act). Spurred on by the IRS, the Congress has evidenced increasing concern over taxpayer use of the law to "evade" rather than to "merely reduce" taxes. It was widely believed that reduction of the top individual income tax rate to 50% in 1981 would eliminate much of the motivation toward "abusive" tax shelters. But tax shelter sales increased, and to taxpayers in lower tax brackets than 50%, rather than decreased. The IRS was "inundated with cases for investigation."[1] In response Congress has continued to enact new provisions intended to discourage abusive tax shelters. These have included higher penalties and interest, and, in the Tax Reform Act of 1986, the passive loss limitations (see Section 17.4).

Your authors believe the increased use of tax shelters was more symptom than cause. The complexity of the tax structure, and the extreme time lags possible between a transaction and the ultimate resolution of its tax consequences, made it possible for promoters to wrap themselves in a mantle of tax law plausibility, supported by respectable law and accounting firms, producing apparent cash flow savings to taxpayers for several years and thus benefiting from repeat business and word-of-mouth advertising from satisfied customers, before the tax issue really hit the fan—if it ever did. It could take six or seven years from the time of a transaction before the tax shelter investor really realized that he got neither the promised tax benefits nor an investment of any value. And, with the limited audit capability of the IRS, the statute of limitations ran out on many tax shelter investments before the IRS ever got to them.

The IRS short-run solution was to throw more resources into dealing with tax shelters, and to use more effectively some of the legal tools at its disposal. This could, at best, deal with the most extreme situations. Decreased availability of special tax law provisions (for example, passive losses, credits, availability of cash basis, special deductions for farmers, for research, and so on) became a major first step in the 1986 income tax reform.

If fundamental changes had not been made, the tax shelter phenomena would have been to the late eighties what prohibition was to this country in the late twenties—a quasi-legitimate form of lawlessness, undercutting the cohesiveness of society, the effectiveness of its institutions, and the moral fiber of its middle class. See also the Epilogue to this book in which we discuss issues of tax reform at greater length.

17.3 Shelter Limitations

In attempting to stem the tax shelter tide, Congress has enacted a number of special rules. Unfortunately, they do not apply merely to tax shelters. Because of the apparent impossibility of distinguishing the "abusive" situation from those situations where taxpayers are doing exactly what Congress provided an incentive for doing, all tax-

[1] Roscoe L. Egger, Jr., "Maintaining the Viability of the U.S. Tax System," *J. of Accountancy* 84 (December 1983). See also the comments of one of your authors on pages 60 and 66 of that same issue.

payers have the potential of being affected by the technical subjects to which the balance of this chapter is devoted. These are the passive loss limitations, the limitation on deduction of excess investment interest, the reduction of certain corporate deductions, and the "at risk" rules.

17.4 Passive Activities

A very popular way to shelter income from taxes has always been to invest in some activity which both produces a tax loss and, it is hoped, an economic gain. This loss is then used to offset income from other sources. Often the losses generated would equal or exceed the amount invested, and the taxpayer's only connection with the activity would be to pay the original investment. The result was that persons with otherwise large taxable income (such as large salaries) reduced their effective tax rate to rates lower than those paid by people with much less income.

Congress perceived this as being unfair to the majority of taxpayers and in the Tax Reform Act of 1986, sought to limit the use of losses to offset unrelated income. New limitations are now placed on the passive losses of individuals, estates, trusts, and many closely held corporations.

A passive activity is defined as (1) any activity which involves the conduct of a trade or business, (2) in which the taxpayer does not materially participate, and (3) includes *any* rental activity. Working interests in oil and gas properties are not included. Nor are items generally thought of as portfolio income sources, such as interest, dividends, annuities, and royalties not derived in the ordinary course of business. Since portfolio income sources generally do not produce losses, the law states that such income cannot be offset by passive losses anymore than can wages or trade or business income.

For any given year, the gains and losses from passive activities are combined. If the net result is a gain from such activities, then there are no special restrictions on the deductibility of the passive losses. If the net result is a loss, however, then that loss (subject to certain transitional rules) is not currently deductible.[2]

For example, assume that Billy Barnes invested in two limited partnerships named, respectively, 1A and 2B. Billy's investment is small relative to the total assets of the partnership and Billy does not participate in the management or daily operations of either business. For 1991, neither partnership had any items of special characteristic. Partnership 1A operated at a profit and Partnership 2B operated at a loss. Billy's share of the 1A taxable income was $3,000 and his share of the 2B loss was $2,000. Billy will net the two items and include the $1,000 net gain in gross income. Assume, on the other hand, that Billy's share of the 2B loss had been $4,500. The net result of combining the two activities is a loss of $1,500. Except for the transition rules, discussed later, the loss is not deductible. All is not gone, however. Billy can carry the nondeductible loss forward to the following year for matching with gains next year. Also, should the partnership go out of business or should Billy sell the interest in 2B, any previously nondeducted losses will be deductible for the year in which that event occurs.

17.4.1. Material Participation

A taxpayer is treated as materially participating in an activity only if there is involvement in the operations of the activity that is regular, continuous, and substantial. Over 500 hours a year devoted to the activity is material; under 100 is not. Between 100 and 500 is material if the activity produces a gain, but is not if it produces a loss. No limited partner will be treated as materially participating.[3] This test is open to many different interpretations. It is quite clear, though, that actual participation in the operations of the activity is required, and a merely formal participation without true exercise of independent discretion and judgment will not constitute material participation.

17.4.2. Rental Real Estate Losses

One exception to the passive loss limitations is that up to $25,000 of passive losses attributable to rental real estate activities can be deducted if the taxpayer actively participates in the rental activity. This is a special exception and assumes that the activity has already been classified as rental and thus as passive. The $25,000 deduction is not available to any taxpayer having adjusted gross income (AGI) greater than $150,000. If AGI is between $100,000 and $150,000 the maximum deduction is decreased by $0.50 for every $1.00 of AGI over $100,000.[4]

For example, assume that Lynn Larsen has 1991 gross income only from a salary of $80,000. In addition, Lynn owns one single-family dwelling unit that is rented to tenants, and Lynn qualifies as an active participant in that rental. The result of the rental activity for last year was a loss of $5,000. Since such an activity is defined by the tax rules as a "passive activity," Lynn would not be able to deduct any of the loss were it not for the special rule. Since Lynn's AGI is under $100,000, and the loss is under

[2]IRC Sec. 469.

[3]IRC Sec. 469(h).
[4]IRC Sec. 469(i).

$25,000 the loss is fully deductible. On the other hand, assume that Lynn's salary were $120,000, (and no other income, so AGI is $120,000 without the rental loss) and the loss was $30,000. Lynn's deduction would be determined as follows:

Maximum deduction	$ 25,000
Reduction in maximum because of AGI > $100,000 ($120,000 − 100,000) (50%)	(10,000)
Lynn's deduction	15,000

The remaining loss of $15,000 ($30,000 − $15,000) can be carried forward indefinitely.

Active participation is a different and lesser standard than material participation. It is not clearly defined by the law, but it seems that regular, continuous, and substantial involvement in operations is not required. Participation in the making of management decisions in a true sense would be required. Active participation does require ownership of at least 10% of the value of the activity.[5]

This $25,000 exception is mainly useful to people owning only a few rental properties, who do not have very large income from other sources, and who closely monitor the properties on their own behalf. The tax benefits of owning those properties will continue, even though by definition they are passive activities subject to limitation. Congress decided that the tax shelter aspects of those activities are small compared to the benefits of encouraging small investors.

17.4.3. Phase-In

To lessen the blow of the passive activity rules on existing interests, the rules are being phased in over a five-year period starting in 1987. The phase-in only applies to passive losses and credits from activities owned before October 22, 1986. The amount of loss which would otherwise be disallowed entirely will be disallowed only to the extent of the following percentages:

Year	*Percentage Disallowed*
1987	35
1988	60
1989	80
1990	90
1991	100

The percentage above which is subject to the passive activity rule may still be carried over to later years, but is not currently deductible.[6]

These percentages do not change the potential $25,000 deduction exception for rental real estate losses.

[5]IRC Sec. 469(i)(6).
[6]IRC Sec. 469(l). Carried-over passive activity losses are offsets against passive income and are ultimately deductible in the year of disposition of the passive activity.

17.4.4. Publicly Traded Partnerships

Losses from a publicly traded partnership (that is not treated as a corporation) can't be used to offset income from a passive activity or to offset income from another publicly traded partnership. Each such partnership, instead, is a separate category of passive activity. Its losses are deferred, to be used only against its own income, until the partnership interest is disposed of; and its income cannot be offset by losses from any other passive activity.

17.5 Excess Investment Interest

As explained in earlier chapters, non-consumer business interest expense is generally deductible. If a taxpayer incurs interest in connection with a trade, business, or activity which has profit as its purpose, the deduction is *for* adjusted gross income. (See Chapter 7.) On the other hand, interest on a residential mortgage is one of the itemized deductions. Interest is not deductible if paid for someone else's debt or if paid in connection with a loan where the proceeds are used to generate tax-exempt interest, such as the purchase of municipal bonds, or for the payment of some premiums on life insurance, or for consumer purposes. (See Chapter 3.)

In the previous discussion of interest deductions, we did not mention (except in passing) the limitations that apply where there is "excess" investment interest.[7] The limitations came about as the result of a congressional view that some taxpayers were taking too much advantage of a good thing. For example, a taxpayer might borrow large amounts of money, incur high interest expense (previously fully deductible), but use the loan proceeds to invest in property which will not produce any current taxable income and is expected to result in long-term capital gain (possibly taxed at a lower rate) in some future year. This type of investment was viewed as a misuse or abuse of the interest deduction allowance. Rather than repeal the deduction for everyone, some special rules were created in an attempt to apply a limitation applicable only to those taxpayers who were going beyond some arbitrary bounds in obtaining a tax advantage.

The limitation on the deduction for interest applies only to "investment interest" of individuals and trusts. It affects interest on indebtedness incurred to purchase or carry property held for investment.[8] It does not include any interest taken into account in computing the income or loss from a passive activity. Such investment interest can only

[7]IRC Sec. 163(d).
[8]IRC Sec. 163(d)(3)(A).

FIGURE 17-1 Individual Interest Deduction

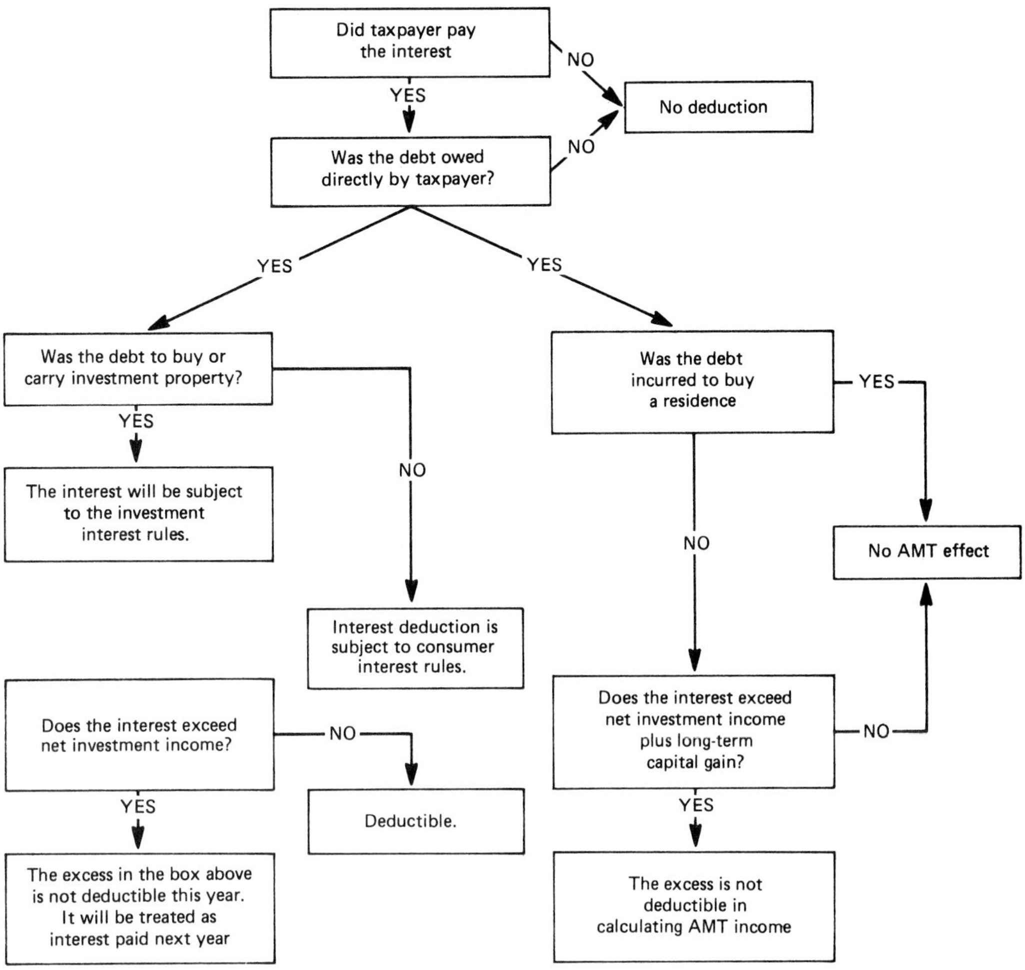

be deducted to the extent of the net investment income of the taxpayer for the taxable year.[9]

Where the limitation applies, and part of the interest expense is not deductible, the nondeductible portion can be carried forward to the following year when it will be deductible, subject to the limitation applying again in that year. Thus, the deduction is not lost, merely deferred.

Net investment income means the excess of investment income over investment expenses. Investment income is the sum of dividends, interest, rents, royalties, and net gain from the disposition of property held for investment, but only to the extent not derived from a trade or business. Investment expenses are any expenses (other than interest) allowable as deductions which are directly connected with the production of income. Investment income and expenses do not include any income or expenses taken into account in computing income or loss from a passive activity.

For example, assume that Billy Barnes borrows $200,000 to be used to purchase investment property. The interest expense for the year is $28,000. If the net investment income is $20,000 for the year, Billy can deduct only $20,000 this year and must carry the remaining $8,000 of interest expense to the following year.

TAX PLANNING TIP: Sometimes, small business owners borrow money to loan to their corporation. Part of the interest expense incurred might not be deductible because of the limitations discussed here. If the corporation were to borrow the money, even if the owner were to be a guarantor of the loan, the corporation could take the interest expense deduction without limit because the excess investment interest rules do not apply to corporations.

It is noteworthy that certain deductible expenses can result in a corresponding reduction in the deduction for interest. Remember that *net*

[9]IRC Sec. 163(d)(1), 163 (d)(4).

FIGURE 17-2 Corporate depreciation recapture on sale of real estate

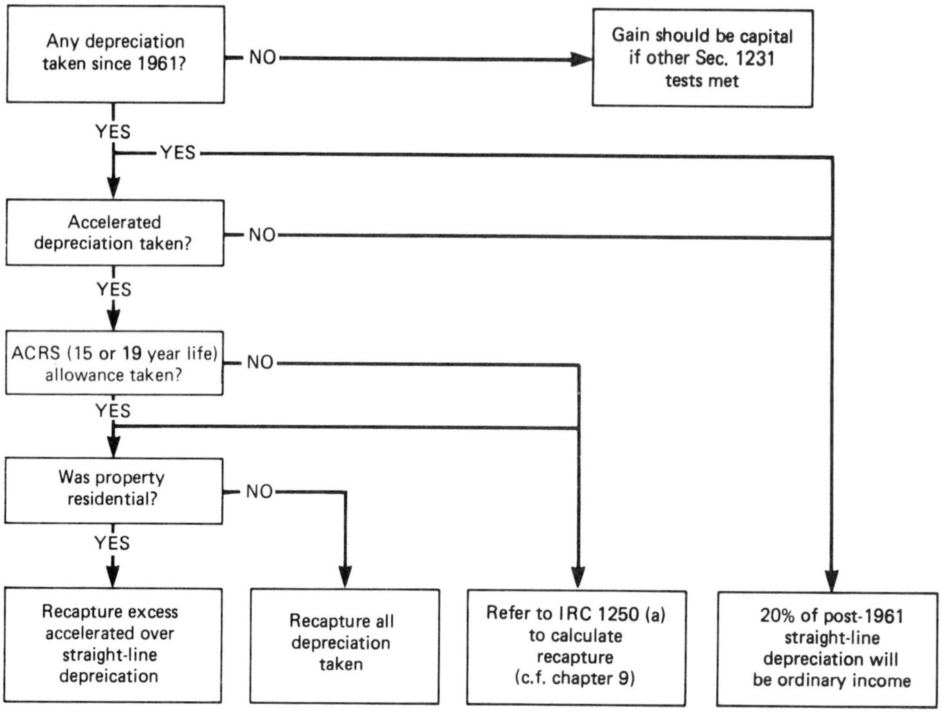

Note: Recapture amount (i.e., ordinary income) cannot in total exceed gain on disposition.

investment income means gross investment income less expenses connected with investments. If investment expenses increase, net investment income will decrease, which will reduce the interest deduction. Consider the following example:

> **Example.** Billy Barnes incurs $30,000 of interest expense on loans made to invest in the stock market. If net investment income is $15,000, Billy can deduct $15,000 of the interest expense. If net investment income were to decrease by $1,000 because Billy paid (and deducted) $1,000 for investment advice, the limitation on the deduction for interest expense would decrease to $14,000 because net investment income would decrease to $14,000.[10]

The investment interest rules are set out in a more graphic way in Fig. 17-1.

The rules outlined above were enacted as part of the Tax Reform Act of 1986, and are being phased in using the same phase-in schedule as the passive activity limitations. The amount which can be deducted without regard to the post-1986 rules is the phase-in percentage times the interest otherwise disallowed, but not to exceed $10,000 ($5,000 for a married individual filing a separate return and zero for a trust).

[10] Any expense deducted under IRC Sec. 212 is treated as investment expense by IRC Sec. 163(d). *Sam E. Wyly* (CA5), 49 AFTR2d 82–314. Tax fees not connected with a trade or business are deductible under IRC Sec. 212(3), subject to the limitations on miscellaneous deductions.

17.6 Reduction in Certain Corporate Preference Items

In Chapter 16, we discussed the 20% alternative minimum tax imposed on corporations. In addition to that tax, Congress has selected certain corporate preference items for special attention. The tax benefit otherwise obtainable from these items is reduced by 20%.[11] To prevent the combination of the alternative minimum tax and this reduction in deductions from reducing the tax benefit from a marginal dollar of a preference item by too much, only $59\frac{5}{6}\%$ of certain specified deduction items will be subject to the alternative minimum tax. The items affected by the reduction include the following:

- —Capital gain on real estate improvements, to the extent that it reflects depreciation previously taken, is 20% treated as ordinary income.
- —Bad-debt reserves of financial institutions, in excess of the amounts that would be allowed based upon prior actual bad-debt experience of the institution, are to be reduced by 20% of the excess.
- —Intangible drilling costs in connection with oil and gas, mineral exploration and development costs, depletion for coal and iron ore, and amortization of pollution control facilities eligible for a five-year write-off all lose 30% of the tax deduction otherwise available under the tax law.

[11] IRC Sec. 291(a).

The impact of the reduction in corporate tax preferences is particularly noteworthy in corporate real estate transactions. Assume that a corporation purchased a building in 1971 for $1 million. It took straight-line depreciation deductions over a forty-year useful life. At a point when the building is approximately 50% depreciated in early 1991, it proposes to sell the building for its original cost of $1 million. It has not taken advantage of accelerated depreciation or short useful lives. Nevertheless, $100,000 of what would have been a $500,000 long-term capital gain will be converted into ordinary income. This may not be of great importance in years when the tax rate is the same for capital gains and ordinary income, but when the capital gains tax is lower (such as has been recently proposed) or the corporation has unused capital loss carryovers, the tax impact will be substantial.

Figure 17-2 integrates the discussion in the preceding paragraph with the general framework for depreciation recapture discussed in Section 9.4. Frequent changes in the underlying law have led to this layering of specific rules, one upon another.

17.7 At-Risk Provisions

In order to understand the "at-risk" provisions, it is first necessary to understand the difference between "recourse" and "nonrecourse" debt, and to understand the basics of "limited" partnerships.

A recourse obligation is one where the lender can proceed to collect personally from the borrower if the borrower does not pay the debt in accordance with the terms. A nonrecourse debt, on the other hand, is one where the lender's rights to receive satisfaction in the event of the borrower's default only extend to repossession of the property upon which a lien exists for the debt. This can be illustrated as follows. Assume that Billy Barnes purchased property for $50,000, with $10,000 down payment and notes for the balance. If Billy defaults and the notes are recourse notes, the lender (who may or may not be the seller) can collect from Billy if the property cannot be sold for as much as the balance due. If the notes are nonrecourse debt, and Billy defaults, the lender can repossess the property, but cannot otherwise force Billy to pay the balance due.

A limited partnership is one in which the terms of the partnership protect a limited partner from further financial commitment beyond that which he or she has already invested in the partnership. In a regular partnership, if the partnership gets into financial difficulty, the creditors of the partnership will proceed first to collect from the partnership, but if satisfaction is not obtained there, the creditors can proceed to collect personally from the individual partners. Again, let us use Billy Barnes as an example. Assume that Billy invests $10,000 in a partnership. The partnership has financial difficulty and loses money. Billy's $10,000 is gone, together with whatever amounts were invested by the other partners. The creditors have not been totally satisfied from partnership assets, which are exhausted. The creditors can legally require that each partner contribute more money to cover the unpaid partnership obligations. Thus, Billy might be required to pay. In addition, if Billy has assets after making such payments, and the other partners do not have resources to pay their proportionate share, Billy can be required to pay that part of the debts which the other partners cannot pay. If the partnership were limited, and if Billy were a limited partner, there would be no risk on Billy's part of losing more than the original $10,000 investment.

17.7.1. Application of At-Risk Provisions in Partnerships

In large investment endeavors, it may be necessary to bring together assets from dozens, perhaps hundreds, of individuals. Naturally, a taxpayer should be concerned about the potential liability should the partnership fail. Frequently, such investment opportunities represent fairly high-risk investments in the first place. Given the potential liability, and the fact that a potential partner may have no personal knowledge of the financial integrity of the other partners, it is no wonder that persons would be hesitant to invest. Therefore, the limited partnership arrangement was invented. Such a partnership offers the opportunity to share in the profits of a high-risk venture, but limits any liability on the part of the limited partners to that amount which each has originally invested, or pledged to invest, in the partnership. For example, assume that Billy Barnes invests $10,000 in a limited partnership which later fails. The general partner will be responsible for those partnership debts which have not been satisfied, but Billy (and the other limited partners) will not lose more than the amount originally invested.

With the background described above, we can discuss the tax rules which limit the amount of certain deductions, and credits, to the at-risk amount. Back in Chapter 10 we discussed partnerships. You will remember that a partnership does not pay tax, but partnership taxable income is divided among the partners who pay income tax on their share whether received or not. We said also that each partner is entitled to deduct his or her share of the partnership loss, limited only by the sum of that partner's capital investment, plus that partner's loans to the partnership, plus that partner's share of any partnership indebtedness. However, if that partner does not have a share of the partnership debt because that debt is nonrecourse, or because the partner is a limited partner, the partner will not be entitled to take a deduction for an amount in excess of the capital investment plus any debt for which he or she is "at risk."[12] Two examples will illustrate the rule.

Assume that Billy Barnes invests $30,000 in a limited partnership. The partnership loses money, and Billy's share of the total loss is $33,000. Billy can only deduct $30,000 because under the provisions of limited partnership law, Billy will not have to contribute the extra $3,000 for satisfaction of the creditor's claims.

In a different situation, assume that Billy Barnes enters into a partnership not as a limited partner, but as a general partner, with a one-third interest. The partnership purchases equipment for $140,000 paying $20,000 down and giving a nonrecourse debt for the balance of $120,000. If the lender cannot be financially satisfied, the property will be repossessed, but since there is no liability on the part of the partnership or on the part of any partner (not even a general partner), there is no at-risk amount for tax purposes, and the partners will be unable to take any loss deduction beyond that which is at risk. In Billy's case, the maximum loss deduction would be one-third of the $20,000, or $6,667.

The at-risk rules apply to individuals, to S corporations, and to "closely held" corporations. For this purpose, a closely held corporation is defined as one where five or fewer individuals own more than 50% of the stock.

There are some notable exceptions to the at-risk provisions. An investment in real estate will be considered at-risk to the extent of any qualified nonrecourse financing secured by the real property. Qualified financing includes loans from any person in the business of lending money, any federal, state, or local government or their instrumentalities, or any loans guaranteed by a government. Convertible debt will not be included. Loans from related persons will be qualified only if the financing is commercially reasonable and on substantially the same terms as loans involving unrelated persons.[13] Also, active leasing of equipment by a closely held corporation, except for S corporations, is an activity which is exempt from the at-risk loss limitation rules.[14]

If a person is unable to take a deduction because of application of the at-risk provisions, and that person later does become at risk with respect to the amount, or part of the amount, a deduction will be allowed for that additional amount. For example, assume that a taxpayer is not able to deduct $10,000 because of the limited partnership provisions, but later that person invests another $8,000 in the partnership. An additional deduction of $8,000 will be allowed for the year in which the additional investment was made. The opposite effect can also occur. There will be a "recapture" of losses previously allowed where the amount at risk has been reduced. This could occur, for example, where the amount of nonrecourse indebtedness is increased and the amount of recourse debt is decreased.

17.8 Summary

The limitations and restrictions discussed in this chapter originated as congressional attempts to discourage overuse or misuse of certain tax advantages (sometimes called tax shelters). The two minimum taxes discussed in Chapter 16, the excess investment interest limitation, the 20% reduction in certain corporate preference items, and the at-risk provisions, attempted to curb some perceived abuses. However, congressional foresight in attempting to limit overuse of certain tax advantages is often no greater than the foresight which was absent when the original provisions were enacted. When these "best laid plans" begin to result in too much reduction in the Treasury's receipts, or when there is perceived inequity created, Congress will again react. The end is not yet to changes in this area.

[12]IRC Sec. 465.

[13]IRC Sec. 465(b)(6).

[14]IRC Sec. 465(c)(4). The corporation must derive at least 50% of its gross receipts from leasing.

TRUE-FALSE QUESTIONS

State whether each of the following statements is true or false. For each *false* answer, reword the statement to make it *true*.

T F 1. Qualified pension and profit sharing retirement plans are "tax shelters" because they (a) provide an opportunity for a person to earn income which is not subject to taxation until later and (b) the earnings from investment of the funds are not subject to current taxation.

T F 2. If a taxpayer has invested in two passive activities, one of which results in a gain and one of which results in a loss for the year, the gain will be included in gross income but there will be no deduction for the loss.

T F 3. The "material participation" test, which is one of the requirements related to investment in a passive activity, means that a taxpayer must be regularly, continuously, and substantially involved in the activity.

T F 4. The general rule is that where a taxpayer has invested in rental property which results in a loss for the year, that loss will not be deductible currently, but if the taxpayer can demonstrate that he has been an active participant in the rental activity, then all of the loss will be deductible currently.

T F 5. If a taxpayer has been an active participant in a rental activity which resulted in a loss for the year, then up to $25,000 of that loss can be deducted for the year regardless of the amount of the taxpayer's adjusted gross income.

T F 6. In order to get a current deduction for a loss from rental property, a taxpayer must show that he has been an active participant, which means, among other things, that he must own at least 10% of the value of the activity.

T F 7. Where a taxpayer has invested in rental property which results in a loss for the current year, and there is no current deduction for that loss, there is a carryover of the loss to later years.

T F 8. A person who is a "limited" partner in a partnership which engages in an active trade or business will be able to take a current deduction for his/her share of partnership loss because the loss limitation rules apply to the partnership and not to the persons owning the partnership.

T F 9. Where a taxpayer is not permitted to deduct all of his or her interest expense because of the limitation on "investment interest," the nondeductible portion can be carried back as a deduction on the tax return of the third prior year.

T F 10. Even though a loss from a passive activity cannot be used to reduce income from salary, such a loss can be used to reduce dividend and interest income.

T F 11. Even though a loss from a passive activity cannot be used to reduce income from salary, such a loss can be used to reduce annuity and royalty income.

T F 12. The special exception which allows a person to deduct a loss from rental of real estate will apply only to those persons who have less than $150,000 of adjusted gross income.

T F 13. If a person incurs $12,000 of interest expense on money borrowed to invest in the stock market, and earns dividend and interest income of $7,000 for the year, then the interest expense cannot be deducted for the current year but can be carried forward to next year.

T F 14. If a person borrows money and signs a "nonrecourse" note, then the money will not have to be repaid.

T F 15. If a partnership borrows money on a "nonrecourse" debt, and the collateral for the loan is tangible personal property, then the partners will still be obligated to repay the loan if the partnership does not do so.

T F 16. The general rule for nonrecourse debt is that the lender can force the borrower to repay the balance of the loan if the proceeds from sale of the mortgage property are not sufficient to pay off the balance of the defaulted debt.

T F 17. If an investor borrows $50,000 from an unrelated medical doctor who is not in the business of loaning money, and the doctor accepts a nonrecourse note for the loan, that loan will not be "qualified" for purposes of the "at risk" rules even if the proceeds of the loan are used to purchase investment real estate.

T F 18. A corporation which has investment interest expense which is $14,000 greater than its investment income will be able to deduct an amount equal to the investment interest income plus $10,000, but will be required to carry the $4,000 balance to the following taxable year.

T F 19. An individual can deduct investment interest expense in an amount which is equal to or less than investment income, and investment income includes capital gain from the sale of securities.

T F 20. A corporation will never have excess investment interest because any loan which a corporation makes will be considered to be business related rather than for investment purposes.

PROBLEMS

Problem 17-1. What is meant by "excess investment interest" and what is its significance for federal income tax purposes?

Problem 17-2. Sonja Kurtzberg is single and age 62. For the current year (1991), she invested in the stock market and earned dividend and interest income of $12,000. The capital to invest was obtained by making a loan from her broker with the stocks and bonds being used as collateral for the loan. Her interest expense incurred for this purpose was $14,000. Her portfolio increased in value by $9,000 during the year although she had no recognized capital gains or losses because she did not sell any securities. She will itemize deductions for the year, but the only deductible items other than interest expense will be state income tax of $3,000 and charitable contributions of $7,000.

(a) How much of her interest expense, if any, can she deduct? Explain the treatment of any nondeductible interest.

(b) Would it have made any difference in her federal income tax for the year if she had borrowed the money to invest in the stock market by obtaining a bank loan and placing a mortgage on her residence? (Assume that the total amount of the loan would have been less than her original cost for the residence plus improvements.) Explain.

(c) Ignoring part (b) above, would there have been any change in Sonja's federal income tax for the year if she had sold some securities during the year and recognized a $2,000 short-term capital gain? A $2,000 long-term capital gain? Explain.

Problem 17-3. Sam and Sally Libermann will file a joint tax return for the current year. Their adjusted gross income (AGI) and taxable income will be $170,000 and $155,000, respectively, *not including* the following item. Last year (1989) they invested in a real estate rental venture with other persons. The venture is a partnership and the Libermanns own a 30% interest which cost them $50,000 cash. Neither Sam nor Sally will qualify as being an active participant in the venture. The partnership resulted in a loss of $20,000 for the year. Sam and Sally have received a K-1 from the partnership which indicates that their pro rata share of the loss is $6,000.

(a) Will Sam and Sally be able to deduct all or part of the $6,000 loss? Explain.

(b) Fred and Freda McCain have *exactly* the same facts as Sam and Sally *except* that their AGI and taxable income (before the partnership loss) are $90,000 and $75,000, respectively. Will Fred and Freda be able to deduct all or part of their $6,000 loss? Explain.

(c) Bob and Betty Gratz have *exactly* the same facts as Sam and Sally *except* that their AGI and taxable income (before the partnership loss) are $140,000 and $120,000, respectively. Will Bob and Betty be able to deduct all or part of their $6,000 loss? Explain.

(d) Answer parts (a), (b), and (c) above under the assumption that each couple could satisfactorily demonstrate that they were active participants in the rental activity.

Problem 17-4. Jack Oaks owns a retail shoe store as a proprietor. Jack, however, hates the shoe business and does not work in the store himself. He spends most of his time on the golf course. Even on rainy days, he plays the 19th hole. He hires employees to handle every phase of the business. Jack had $90,000 of interest and dividend income last year, but the store operated at a $20,000 loss.

(a) Assuming that Jack does not pass the requirements for "material participation" in the shoe store business, can he deduct the loss? Explain.

(b) Assuming that Jack does pass the requirements for "material participation" in the shoe store business, can he deduct the loss? Explain.

(c) Assume that Jack also owns another store, a sporting goods shop, in which he is equally disinterested, but it operated at a $30,000 profit for the year. Explain the tax consequences. Does the "material participation" test apply?

Problem 17-5. Lisa Dollar (single) wanted to invest in stock of the Go-Go Corporation because she was convinced that there would be long-term capital gain within a few years. She borrowed $80,000 from the bank to make the investment, using some raw land which she owns as collateral. The land does not produce any rental income. Go-Go did not pay any dividends during the year. She had no other investment income for the year. The interest on the $80,000 loan was $12,800. Assume the year is 1991.

(a) May she deduct the entire $12,800? Explain.

(b) If Lisa also owned some stock which paid $3,000 in dividends during the year, what impact would that have on her interest deduction? Explain.

Problem 17-6. In 1991, the Big-Lumbar Partnership (BLP) was organized to engage in the business of operating a miniature golf course in suburban Largetown. The land was rented. The only assets which the partnership purchased were the tangible personal property needed for the operation. Mr. Ling invested $10,000 in the business as a limited partner. He paid the $10,000 in cash and has no further obligation to make any payments to BLP. The partnership was able to borrow $500,000 from a local bank on a nonrecourse loan, with only the partnership assets as security for the loan. Because of large start-up costs, Mr. Ling's share of the partnership loss for the first year was $12,000.

(a) Explain the treatment of the partnership loss as a tax item on Mr. Ling's personal federal income tax return.

(b) Explain the difference in tax treatment, if any, if the partnership loan from the bank had been a recourse debt with each of the partners being potentially liable to repay the loan if the partnership did not do so.

(c) Ignoring part (b) above, what would have been the tax impact to Mr. Ling if he had loaned BLP $3,000 in addition to the $10,000 equity investment which he made?

Problem 17-7. Little-Acres Partnership (LAP) was organized for the purpose of purchasing and remodeling an office building in downtown Megaville. The building will house a group of small retail stores with each tenant leasing for a minimum of three and a maximum of ten years. Lester Barr invested in the partnership by purchasing a 2% interest for $30,000 cash. Approximately 80% of the partnership capital requirements will be obtained by a nonrecourse loan from Freelance Savings and Loan, which will hold a first mortgage on the office building. At the end of the first calendar year, the partnership accountant prepared the necessary K-1 tax forms and Mr. Barr's shows that his share of the LAP loss for the year is $4,000. Assume that the year is 1991.

(a) Explain the tax treatment of the $4,000 loss to Mr. Barr.

(b) What difference would there have been in the treatment if Mr. Barr's share of the LAP loss had been $33,000? Explain.

Problem 17-8. Fred White had invested in four businesses. He was considered a material participant in Business 4. For the year ended 1990, Fred's share of profit or (loss) in the four businesses was as follows:

Business 1	$20,000
Business 2	($40,000)
Business 3	($10,000)
Business 4	$10,000

Fred initially invested in Business 1 in 1988, Business 2 in 1983, Business 3 in 1987, and Business 4 in 1988. In addition, Fred had earned wages of $50,000, and interest income of $2,000.

(a) Compute Fred's adjusted gross income.

(b) Assume that Fred was not a material participant in Business 4. Compute Fred's adjusted gross income.

(c) Refer to the original facts. Assume that Business 3 was initially invested in 1983. Compute Fred's adjusted gross income.

18

employee benefit plans and retirement income

18.1 Trusteed Benefit Plans

The key tax feature of the trusteed benefit plans[1] (pension plans, profit-sharing plans, stock bonus plans, H.R. 10 plans, and IRAs) is that the employer, or employee in the case of an IRA, gets a current tax deduction for a contribution to the plan, whereas the employee has no tax to pay until the money is withdrawn from the plan, usually at retirement. An added tax benefit is that the earnings of the plan can accumulate without incurring any income tax because such trusts are exempt from tax.

The latter feature can make more difference than is generally realized. For example, assume that the trust can earn 9% per year on its investments. Over a thirty-year period, $1 invested at 9% will accumulate to $13.27. If the individual were in a 28% tax bracket, the after-tax rate of return would be only 6.5% per year. At that rate, the $1 would accumulate to only $6.61 during the same period.

The fact that the employee has no current tax to pay means that more can be invested than if tax first had to be paid on the same amount of salary, with the after-tax amount being invested.

For example, assume that a person in the 28% tax bracket earned an extra $1,000. There would be $720 to invest if tax had to be paid first. If the $1,000 is not taxed, the full amount can be invested.

Ignoring the time value of money, these benefit plans involve nothing more than a deferral of tax imposition. In most instances, the employer theoretically should be indifferent to whether $1 is paid in wages or as a benefit plan contribution. In either case, the payment is equally deductible.[2] What restrictions or limitations that do exist on deductibility apply to the benefit plan rather than to the wage payment.[3] The employee, on the other hand, should be far from indifferent. Through the benefit plan, there is the dual advantage of a tax deferral on amounts invested and an increase in the effective rate of return through deferral of income tax on the earnings of the trust investment.

18.1.1. Pension Plans

The tax rules do not require any employer to have a pension plan, except for required payments to the social security system. Likewise, the tax rules do not require that an employer who has a retirement plan must arrange for such a plan to be "qualified." Where a plan is "unqualified," either the employer will get no current deduction or the employees will be currently taxable on the contributions which the employer makes to the plan.

[1]A trusteed benefit plan means a benefit plan that includes a trust to which the employer and/or employee makes periodic contributions which will ultimately be used to pay retirement benefits. Unlike the trusts discussed in Chapter 14, these trusts are tax-exempt.

[2]IRC Sec. 162 provides a deduction for reasonable salaries "or other compensation" paid to employees. Thus, some "fringe benefits" paid by employers are deductible. But see Sec. 404, which provides that in the case of retirement plan contributions, the payments must meet certain qualifications or there will be no deduction. A problem may also arise, as explained in Chapter 13, when an employee is also a stockholder and the total amount of the compensation is unreasonably high.

[3]IRC Sec. 404 provides for the deduction for contributions to stock bonus, pension, profit-sharing, or annuity plans. The requirements of Subchapter D must be satisfied in order to get the deduction. It is beyond the scope of this introductory text to deal with all of these requirements, but the basic ones will be mentioned.

Taxability of the employee and allowance of a deduction to the employer will generally occur when payments are made to the employee when an unqualified plan of deferred compensation is involved.

A "qualified" pension plan is one which meets all of a group of requirements set forth in the tax laws. The basic purpose of the requirements is to protect the employees' interests so that there will be money to pay retirement benefits when retirement age arrives. Our purpose here is to sketch some basic ground rules and postpone consideration of any detailed provisions to an advanced tax course. A pension plan may take on one of several forms. In any event, the advantage of having a "qualified" plan is threefold. First, the employer gets a deduction for contributions to the plan trust. Second, the earnings of the plan are not subject to current tax. Third, the employees do not have any recognized income until distributions are made from the plan.

A *defined benefit pension plan* provides for payment after retirement of specific or determinable amounts. For example, a plan might provide that the retiree is to receive $600 per month for the remainder of his or her life. Another example would be payments equal to 60% of the average annual earnings for the five years immediately preceding retirement. In either case, the plan is called a "defined benefit plan" because the amount of retirement benefits can be determined in advance.

A pension plan can be "contributory" or "noncontributory." A contributory plan is one in which both the employer and employee make investments. A noncontributory plan is funded entirely by the employer.

In many plans the employee is required to contribute to the plan.[4] In some, employees may increase the future benefits by making voluntary contributions to the plan. There is normally a limit on the amount of a voluntary contribution, and the employee normally gets no tax deduction for such payments to the trust.[5] Even though there is no tax deduction, the advantage of making voluntary contributions, where permitted, is that the amounts which the trust earns are not subject to current tax. Thus, as explained earlier, the trust can realize a higher rate of return than employees can earn for themselves in comparable investments.

The general limit on the amount that the employer can deduct for contributions to a defined benefit pension plan is the amount necessary to provide the ultimate benefits. This takes into consideration both the contributions and the amount that the trust is expected to be able to earn, as well as the benefits expected to be paid. Another element in estimating *total* benefits to be paid, even where the monthly or annual benefits are known, is the length of time the benefits are to be paid. This is normally the life expectancy of the retiree, but it may also include the life expectancy of the retiree's spouse. Consider a simple illustration. The employer has one employee who is thirty years from retirement. Normal retirement is age sixty-five. The employee is married, and the plan calls for retirement benefits to be paid at $500 per month for as long as the employee or spouse continues to live after the employee retires. By considering the estimated rate of return that the trust will earn on investments, together with estimates of the life expectancies of employee and spouse, it is possible to estimate how much money the employer should contribute each month (or quarter) over the thirty-year period in order for the trust to have the necessary funds to pay the retirement benefits. The problem of adequate funding gets more complex as the number of employees increases, and as consideration is given to the various ages of these employees, the probability that retirement benefits will not be paid because of death or termination of employment, and other factors.[6]

Another problem arises where the employer adopts a retirement plan to include employees who have already been on the payroll for several years. Such employees are usually entitled to retirement benefits based on the total years of service and not just on their employment after the date the plan is adopted. The employer must estimate the additional cost of funding these "past service credits."[7] A deduction is allowed the employer for that cost as well as the cost of present and future service benefits. The same problem arises when the plan is liberalized, if the effect is to increase retirement benefits earned by service prior to the date of plan change. Since 1974, the law has required a minimum funding of past service credits.[8] Past service liabilities in existence on January 1, 1974 have to be "funded" in equal annual amounts over forty years or less. Past service liabilities created after January 1, 1974 have to be funded over thirty years or less.[9] "Funding" refers to the payment of cash by the employer to the retirement trust.

[4]The requirement is not one of the tax rules, but under the terms of the plan itself. Where the employer and employee both help fund the plan, the contributions do not necessarily have to be equal.

[5]There is a 10% cumulative limitation for nondeductible voluntary contributions. See Rev. Rul. 70-658, 1970-2 CB 86; Rev. Rul. 69-217, 1969-1 CB 115; Rev. Rul. 69-627, 1969-2 CB 92; and Rev. Rul. 59-185, 1959-1 CB 86. Note that these may be deductible, up to the IRA limits, in the same fashion as the IRA plans discussed in Section 18.6. Note also that the same result as a deduction can be obtained with a "cash or deferred" program under IRC Sec. 401(k).

[6]Other factors would include the vesting schedule.

[7]IRC Sec. 404(a)(1)(A).

[8]IRC Sec. 412(a).

[9]IRC Sec. 412(b).

Generally, no employee can receive an annual retirement benefit of more than $90,000 adjusted for cost-of-living changes, or the average compensation for the three highest paid years, whichever is less.[10]

Between the minimum that has to be paid to the plan trustee, and the maximum that can be deducted, there is a wide area where individual employers have discretion as to what they will pay in a given year.

In addition to the defined benefit pension plan, there is the *money purchase pension plan,* which is one form of a defined contribution plan. In such a plan, the employer agrees to a fixed or determinable contribution to the plan. For example, the payment might be 12% of the compensation paid to covered employees. When they retire, employees will receive whatever benefits the amounts accumulated for each of them in the trust will provide. Obviously, the computation of the contribution is much easier, but potential recipients of benefits may have more difficulty estimating the amount that will be received.

Such a plan may be more attractive to an employer than a defined benefit plan, since the pension plan costs are known (e.g., 12% of compensation). In a defined benefit plan, costs can fluctuate depending upon inflation, investment performance, abnormal employee turnover, and other factors beyond the employer's control. Further, in a defined benefit plan, the employer becomes a potential guarantor of a minimum level of benefits, *regardless* of plan performance, up to *30%* of the employer's net worth.[11]

An employee may also find a money purchase pension plan more attractive than a defined benefit plan. Exceptional investment performance by the trust will, for instance, increase the amount of benefits flowing to the employee in the future.

The maximum contribution by an employer under a defined contribution pension plan is the lesser of (a) 25% of the compensation paid to the employee covered by the plan or (b) $30,000.[12] The 25% or $30,000 is reduced by a portion of employee voluntary contributions to the plan in excess of 6% of each employee's wages.[13]

[10]IRC Sec. 415(b). The $90,000 changes each year to reflect increases in the cost of living. For 1989 the adjusted number was $98,064.

[11]Sec. 4062(a), Employee Retirement Income Security Act of 1974 (ERISA).

[12]IRC Sec. 415(c)(1).

[13]There is also a reduction in the limitation for any amounts added to the plan as the result of forfeitures. See Sec. 415(c)(2). The $30,000 limitation changes to reflect increases in the cost of living. For 1990, the adjusted amount is still $30,000 and will not increase above $30,000 until the adjusted $90,000 number exceeds $120,000.

18.1.2. Profit-Sharing Plan

A profit-sharing plan's benefits will depend upon the employer's contributions as well as the plan's income from investment.[14] No set benefits are given in the plan, although various optional ways of receiving benefits may be provided. The employer cannot deduct more than 15% of the aggregate compensation of the employees covered under a profit-sharing plan.[15] No one employee can have added to his or her profit-sharing account in any year more than 25% of his or her compensation, or $30,000, whichever is the lesser, just as with a money purchase pension plan.[16] However, the profit-sharing plan differs from the money purchase plan mainly because it is subject to an overall 15% deduction limit, does not require any advance or continuing commitment as to the level of annual contributions, and because amounts forfeited (e.g., because of early termination of employment) will be reallocated among remaining plan participants rather than used to reduce the employer's contributions.

TAX PLANNING TIP: Profit-sharing plans provide several advantages over other types of retirement funding arrangements. With a defined benefit plan, contributions to the plan may be required whether the employer is profitable or not. With a profit-sharing plan, contributions can be made in years of profit, with no contributions required for loss years. In fact, the portion of profit going to the retirement fund can be varied so that it is larger if profits are higher. This can serve as an incentive to employees.

18.1.3. Stock Bonus Plan

A stock bonus plan is similar to a profit-sharing plan.[17] Instead of investing in the securities of other companies, the plan (a trust) invests in the securities of the corporate employer. Distributions to beneficiaries must be in the form of employer corporation stock. The same 15% limit that applies to profit-sharing plans applies to stock bonus plans.

[14]A profit-sharing plan is, of course, a form of defined contribution plan. For example, contributions may equal 10% of the employer's profit. For detailed distinctions among pension, profit-sharing, and stock bonus plans, see Treas. Reg. 1(b).

[15]IRC Sec. 404(a)(3)(A).

[16]IRC Sec. 415(c).

[17]IRC Secs. 401–404.

Relatively little use has been made of the stock bonus plan provisions until recent years.[18] Yet these provisions may, in effect, allow the corporation to print its own money. This results from the fact that in one type of stock bonus plan, the trust acquires the stock directly from the employer. Thus, the employer can reduce its tax liability and generate cash in the amount of the tax rate times the fair market value of the stock transferred to the trust. For example, assume that a corporation is in the 34% marginal tax bracket. Under a stock bonus plan, it transfers new shares of its own stock to the pension trust at year end. If these shares are valued at $100,000, which amount the corporation takes as a deduction, the federal income tax is reduced by $34,000 even though the corporation has spent no money.

However, a price must be paid in order to obtain the income tax deduction. That price is the dilution of the ownership interests of the other stockholders. That dilution will, in turn, vary to the extent that stockholders are also employees, and thus beneficiaries of the stock bonus trust. At the extreme, if all beneficiaries are shareholders, and compensation is proportionate to stock ownership, then no dilution will take place—and any tax deduction is without cost.

18.1.4. Employee Stock Ownership Plans

An employee stock ownership plan (ESOP) is a stock bonus trust that has certain special tax benefits.[19] An ESOP can engage in some transactions barred to a regular stock bonus trust, and is subject to some special restrictions.[20] The special status of ESOPs reflects objectives other than employee compensation or retirement. ESOPs are encouraged because of a belief that employee ownership of U.S. industry, or at least of major interests therein, would be desirable for the American economy.[21] While many employee benefit plans do invest in stocks and bonds of other U.S. companies, ESOPs are a device for specific companies to set up plans whereby the employees acquire stock in the employer-corporation.

Some of the interesting ways in which ESOPs have been used include the following:

1. A corporate division was going to be discontinued, resulting in several thousand people being out of work. Instead, the corporation set up an ESOP for the employees of that division. The ESOP borrowed money at a low interest rate and with a long repayment period. The money was used to buy the division from the corporation. The former division, now a separate corporation owned by the ESOP trust, annually will contribute to the ESOP trust the amount needed to pay off the loan—and will be able to take a tax deduction for the loan payment. The employees, through the ESOP trust, have become the owners of the corporation.
2. The controlling stockholder of a corporation was willing to sell 50% of his stock to the employees. However, the purchase did not seem feasible to the key employees if it had to be made with after-tax income. An ESOP trust was created, and the stock was sold to that trust. To make the purchase, the trust obtained a bank loan at a bargain ESOP rate. The corporation got a tax deduction for the amounts it contributed to the trust. These amounts were used to pay off the amounts due on the bank loan, but the employees will have no taxable income until the stock is distributed to them by the trust. Further, the controlling stockholder was able to avoid any tax on the sale of the corporate stock by reinvesting the proceeds after the sale in a diversified security portfolio.
3. Three shareholder-officers disagreed on company policy. For the company to continue, one of the three had to go. He was willing to sell out—but only for cash. Neither the other two stockholders nor the corporation had the cash. The corporation's projected cash flow indicated that it could pay off a loan of the amount needed if it could take a tax deduction for the principal payments. The corporation's attorney further opined that it would be illegal under state law for the corporation to redeem the shareholder's stock because it lacked sufficient retained earnings. An ESOP was created. The ESOP borrowed the needed cash from a bank (backed by the guarantee of the corporation and the two shareholders), and purchased the third shareholder's stock. The corporation got a tax deduction for the annual payments made to the trust, even though the trust used those same dollars to pay off the debt.

While ESOPs have been in use for many years, recent tax legislation has enhanced their usefulness. Some of them can borrow at bargain rates to purchase employer stock because banks and other lenders can exclude from income half of the inter-

[18]This may be because there were other arrangements for compensating employees by getting stock into their hands. "Restricted stock options" (IRC Sec. 424) were available before 1964. "Qualified stock options" (IRC Sec. 422) were used from 1964 to May 21, 1976. "Employee stock purchase plans" (IRC Sec. 423) are still used, but require that the option price be at least 85% of the value of the stock at the time the option is granted or exercised. Incentive stock options were added to the law in 1981 (see Section 18.12). Under a stock bonus plan, discussed here, the employee is not required to purchase the stock and therefore has no cash outlay.

[19]IRC Sec. 409.

[20]Generally, an ESOP must meet the requirements of IRC Sec. 401(a), be designed to invest primarily in securities of the employer corporation, and meet other requirements, such as nonforfeitability of rights of the participants.

[21]*Conference Committee Report* on 1978 Revenue Act.

est they earn on an ESOP loan.[22] A stockholder selling stock to an ESOP can avoid any current tax on the sale if the ESOP owns 30% or more of the employer's stock after the sale, the stockholder reinvests the proceeds in other corporate securities, and certain other requirements are met.[23] Dividends paid on stock owned by the ESOP are deductible by the employer if the trust, in turn, distributes them to its beneficiaries or uses them to make payments on its debt.[24] A decedent's gross estate could exclude 50% of the proceeds from a qualified sale of employer securities to an ESOP, but this provision was repealed for the estates of decendents dying after Dec. 19, 1989.[25]

TAX PLANNING TIP: The ESOP trust provides for a way to reward employees with very small cost to the employer corporation. One disadvantage of some other types of retirement plans is that the corporation-employer is required to contribute cash to the fund. Many businesses, although profitable, find that the need for cash for expansion of plant and equipment, for example, creates a cash shortage for such things as retirement plans. The contribution to the ESOP can be made with employer stock rather than cash.

18.1.5 401(k) Plans

Also known as CODAs (cash or deferred arrangements), these plans allow employees to elect to put into the employer plan up to a $7,000 per year adjusted for changes in the cost-of-living index ($7,627 for 1989). The employee is not taxed on what goes into the plan until it comes out. Some employers partially match employee contributions to encourage participation, since a 401(k) plan cannot qualify unless there is substantial employee participation. Nonprofit organizations and governments generally cannot use 401(k) plans—although some can use 403(b) plans (see Section 18.7).

18.1.6. Nondiscrimination

Most qualified plans (either defined contribution or defined benefit) can define "employees" somewhat narrowly. Under some circumstances, for example, persons with less than one year of employment, and persons who work less than 1,000 hours per year, can be excluded.[26] In other words, the qualified pension or profit-sharing plans are designed for full-time, regular employees. At the same time, there are nondiscrimination rules that do not permit either the contributions to the plan or the benefits to be received from the plan to favor key employees. Any plan that provides more than 60% of its benefits to key employees is called "top heavy."[27] The rules contain many detailed provisions which must be satisfied in order for a "top heavy" plan to be qualified. The purpose of these rules is to protect the interests of those employees who are not "key."

In order to enhance the restriction that a retirement plan not be discriminatory in favor of key employees, there are some general requirements concerning the percentage of total employees who must be eligible for participation in the plan, and the percentage of the eligible employees who must be active participants in the plan. As a general guideline, 70% of all non-highly compensated full-time employees must be covered by the plan. [28] In addition to the eligibility and participation requirements, a plan must not favor the "key" employees in terms of vesting, funding, or payment of benefits.

18.1.7. Operation of a Benefit Plan

The corporation transfers cash, or other property, to a trust. The covered employees will be the beneficiaries of the trust. The trustees receive the funds, keep an account for each covered employee (if it is a defined contribution plan), and invest and reinvest the trust funds. They may buy stocks, bonds, mortgages, real estate, or even annuities.[29] The trust files an information income tax return, but since it is a tax-exempt organization, it normally pays no income tax.

Upon qualifying for benefits under the terms of the plan, an employee will file a request with the trustees. The trust will then start making disbursements to the employee, according to the provisions of the plan. Generally, since the employee was not

[22]IRC Sec. 133 and especially Secs. 133(b) and (g). Also IRC Sec. 291(e)(1)(B)(iv).
[23]IRC Sec. 1042.
[24]IRC Sec. 404(k).
[25]IRC Sec. 2057. The tax reduction could not exceed $750,000.

[26]IRC Sec. 410(a). The one year becomes three years if 100% vesting occurs.
[27]IRC Sec. 416. Generally, a key employee is one who is an officer, one who owns one of the ten largest interests in the corporation, one who owns a more-than-5% interest in the corporation, or one who owns a more-than-1% interest if earning over $150,000 per year.
[28]A plan actually has to pass any one of three tests, all of which look at the percentage participation.
[29]It is beyond the scope of this book to deal with the details. There are some restrictions on the types of investments that can be made by the trust, called "prohibited transactions."

taxed when the employer made contributions to the plan on behalf of the employee, the benefits are taxable when received.[30]

TAX PLANNING TIP: If a small corporation's controlling stockholder wants to have the corporation contribute substantial amounts toward his or her own retirement, but not be as generous with employees, perhaps the eligible and covered employees can be defined to exclude certain persons. Employees who work less than 1,000 hours per year (normally, that is half-time), and employees with under one year of service, can be excluded.

18.2 Annuities

Instead of using a trust, an employer may buy annuities directly for the employees, usually from an insurance company.[31] Such annuity plans generally must meet the same nondiscrimination tests as trusteed plans. The limit on the amount deductible is the amount needed to provide the benefits to be provided by the annuity contract.

18.3 Tax Treatment of Distributions to Employees

18.3.1. Payment in One Year

If an employee receives the total balance due from the plan all in one taxable year, because of death or termination of employment, some special rules apply. The total gain will be the excess of what is received over any amounts contributed to the plan by the employee. (Remember, the employee already paid tax on the latter.) If the employee receives $20,000, for example, and contributed a nondeductible $5,000, then $15,000 will be gain. In the case of a noncontributory plan, all of the receipt will be gain because the employer paid all of the contributions.

The portion of the employee's gain represented by total benefits accrued during plan years prior to 1974 can be treated as capital gain.[32] That part of the gain which is not capital gain is ordinary income, *but* there are some special income averaging rules which serve to reduce the tax impact when a large amount of ordinary income is received in one year.[33] These special income-averaging rules may make it more advantageous to take a lump-sum distribution rather than an annuity, if the recipient has a choice.[34] Sometimes called "five-year forward averaging," this involves a special calculation. Despite its name, it is not a spreading of the tax over the next five years.[35] It is a device for determining the amount of tax to be paid for the year of the receipt of the lump sum. Basically, the total receipt is divided by 5. The resulting one-fifth of the receipt is taken to the tax rate schedule which applies to single individuals. After the tax on that amount is determined, the result is multiplied by 5 to obtain the total tax. This amount, in turn, is added to the tax which the taxpayer may have on other income for the year in order to arrive at the total tax liability for the year. Five-year averaging may be elected only once. Later lump sum distributions, from the same or a different plan, cannot take advantage of it.

Since a lump-sum distribution in one year offers the employee favored income tax treatment, one of the purposes of the special tax provisions governing pension and profit-sharing plans thereby tends to be frustrated. A major purpose of such plans is to provide the employee with retirement income, but this goal is hardly furthered by encouraging the employee to take a lump-sum settlement rather than a life annuity.

TAX PLANNING TIP: Before 1987, taxpayers could use ten-year forward averaging, taxing the lump sum distribution as if received over ten years. Any plan participant who was age 50 by January 1, 1986, can make one election to use five-year or ten-year averaging for a single lump sum distribution. If such an election is made, five-year averaging will not be available for any later lump sum distribution.

If part of what is received by the employee is securities in the employer corporation, then the employee gain on the distribution will be figured on the amount the trust paid for those securities (the basis) rather than on their current fair market value.[36] Of course, the employee's tax basis for any

[30]IRC Sec. 402(a)(1). Under some plans, a lump-sum distribution is made to the retired employee. This is discussed below. In other situations, the payout is in the form of an annuity, taxed under IRC Sec. 72. See the discussion of annuities in Chapter 2.

[31]IRC Sec. 403.

[32]IRC Sec. 402(a)(2).

[33]IRC Sec. 402(e).

[34]IRC Sec. 402(e)(4)(B).

[35]The income is taxed at the lowest rates for a single person, regardless of how high the taxpayer's marginal bracket might be, and regardless of marital status. Five-year averaging is generally only available for distributions to people who are over 59½ years of age.

[36]IRC Sec. 402(e)(4)(j) and Treas. Reg. 1.402(a)(1)(B).

subsequent gain or loss will also be the amount the trust paid for the securities. This gives the employee some control over recognition of gain, since the timing and amount of sales can be controlled.

18.4 Rollovers

If an employee changes jobs, or the employer terminates its plan and distributes the fund balance to employees, an employee may receive a distribution that he or she really would prefer to have kept accumulating to help fund retirement. A recipient of such funds can avoid paying tax on the distribution to the extent that the amount received is reinvested in a qualified plan of a new employer or in an Individual Retirement Account.[37] The general rule is that the employee who receives such a distribution has sixty days within which to reinvest the amount and qualify for the "rollover." (IRAs are discussed later.) Similarly, death benefit payouts to spouse-beneficiaries can be rolled over tax-free into an individual retirement account.[38]

In some instances a recipient of a lump-sum amount from a qualified retirement plan may be eligible to use either the five-year forward averaging, discussed earlier, or the tax-free "roll over" into an IRA. In the case of the latter, the money will be taxed later as it is withdrawn from the IRA. Evaluation of the tax results of the two alternatives will be extremely important to a person facing that decision.

TAX PLANNING TIP: An employee who receives a lump-sum distribution from a retirement plan because of termination of employment or termination of an employer's plan can continue to defer both the current tax on the distribution and tax on the earnings of the investment by investing the proceeds in an IRA. On the other hand, if over 59½, the amount of tax on the lump-sum receipt should be calculated, because of the special "five-year forward averaging" rules. The recipient might prefer to pay the tax under these rules in order to have the proceeds for other purposes, such as starting a business.

18.5 Plans for the Self-Employed

Self-employed people (i.e., sole proprietors of businesses, individual professional practitioners, and partners in partnerships) are not employees. Nevertheless, they can be treated as if they were employees for purposes of pension or profit-sharing plans, subject to some limitations.[39] These plans are called "self-employed retirement plans," or "Keogh plans" (after a congressman who helped sponsor legislation that created them) or "H.R. 10 plans" (after the House Resolution in 1962 that embodied them).[40]

Tax-qualified Keogh plans for self-employed persons are generally subject to the same contribution and benefit limitations as other qualified plans.[41] The maximum amount that can be contributed and deducted is the lesser of $30,000 or 25% of earned income where there is a defined contribution plan.[42] For a defined benefit plan, the maximum is the amount needed to fund an annual benefit of 100% of earned income or $90,000, as adjusted, whichever is smaller.[43] As with corporate plans discussed earlier, these plans must meet the provisions of "top heavy" rules designed to protect the employees of self-employed persons.[44]

Since a self-employed person is not an employee, how can the employer and employee receive the deduction and the exclusion, respectively, available to employees? The answer is that the self-employed person puts the funds into a trust and takes a deduction *for* adjusted gross income for that amount. (See Appendix 1-D(a), line 27.) For both, there is the dual tax advantage that (1) a deduction is taken for the amount of the contribution, and (2) the earnings of the trust are not subject to tax until withdrawn.

18.6 Individual Retirement Accounts

The following discussion is limited to four types of IRAs.[45]

First, there is the "rollover" IRA, which is funded with the amount distributed from another qualified plan, as explained already. By contribut-

[37] IRC Sec. 402(a)(5). An Individual Retirement Account may be used by anyone eligible to roll over distributions, even if they could not make a regular contribution to an IRA. See Section 17.6.

[38] IRC Sec. 402(a)(7).

[39] IRC Sec. 401(c). A partnership is treated as the employer of the partners. A sole proprietor is treated as both an employer and employee. For purposes of fringe benefit treatment, an S corporation is treated as a partnership, and a person who owns 2% or more of an S corporation is treated as a partner. IRC Sec. 1372.

[40] Generally, such retirement plans must meet the requirements discussed earlier for employee retirement plans (IRC Sec. 401) plus meet some special requirements discussed here.

[41] IRC Sec. 401(c).

[42] IRC Sec. 415(c). The amount of the contribution must be deducted *before* applying the 25% limitation. In effect, this means that the maximum contribution is 20% of the earned income of the proprietor.

[43] IRC Sec. 415(b)(1). The adjusted $90,000 was $98,064 for 1989.

[44] IRC Sec. 416. For example, an employer cannot have such a plan which covers only himself, if he has one or more full-time employees.

[45] IRC Sec. 408.

ing the prior distribution to this IRA, the taxpayer avoids having to pay tax on the lump sum that is being rolled over. Otherwise, there is no immediate tax benefit. The earnings continue to accumulate tax-free until distributed.

Second, there is the employer IRA. The employer contributes up to the lesser of $30,000 or 25% of compensation to individual IRAs set up for the individual employees (including owners).[46] Contributions may not discriminate in favor of persons who are officers, shareholders, self-employed, or highly paid.[47] Advantages of the employer IRA, sometimes called a "Simplified Pension Plan," are ease of creation, simplicity, and economy of operation. Employee advantages are the immediate 100% vesting, and the fact that the IRA is a separate account in the employee's name at all times, subject to the employee's investment direction.

Third, there is the IRA created by a person who has earned income, is not covered by any other qualified plan, or has income below the limitations discussed below. Such a taxpayer can deduct 100% of compensation, up to a maximum of $2,000.[48] (See Appendix 1-D(a), line 24.) Self-employed persons sometimes prefer such a plan instead of an H.R. 10 plan. The reason is that where the self-employed person has full-time employees, the rules require that the employees be included if an H.R. 10 plan is adopted. Adoption of an IRA does not require that employees also be covered. The disadvantage of this alternative is that the lower limit ($2,000) on the amount contributed and deducted exists for each year.

The fourth IRA is merely a variation on the third. If the taxpayer has a nonworking spouse, he or she can also be covered under the plan. The maximum deduction is then raised to $2,250, as long as the contribution on behalf of one spouse does not exceed $2,000.[49] (See Appendix 1-D(a), line 25.)

The third and fourth kinds of IRAs are limited as to who can participate. If an individual is an active participant in an employer maintained retirement plan at any time during the tax year, an IRA contribution can only be made if adjusted gross income is less than $25,000 ($40,000 for a married couple filing a joint return). If AGI is between $25,000 and $30,000 ($40,000 and $50,000 for a married couple) a partial pro rata contribution may be made. If an individual is not a participant in a retirement plan, but has a spouse who is, the spouse's participation will bar both from making a contribution unless their income is below $50,000. If a couple files separate returns only their own participation in a plan will be considered as disqualifying them from making a contribution. However, a person who files a married filing separately return who is an active participant in a retirement plan will only be able to make a contribution if AGI is less than $10,000, and the contribution limit will be reduced to the extent AGI exceeds zero.[50]

Any individual may make a nondeductible contribution to an IRA up to the regular IRA limits.[51] The advantage to this is that income can accumulate tax-free. This may be a valuable benefit, but any contribution will be subject to the same payout limitations as a regular IRA, so this form of investment may not be as attractive as some other tax-free income investment.

TAX PLANNING TIP: Some persons who have a regular full-time job also carry on a part-time business as a "side line." The extra income from such an activity might qualify as self-employment income. Thus, the person could invest 25% of such income up to $30,000 into an H.R. 10 plan and get a deduction for AGI. In addition, the earnings on the investment will go untaxed until the money is withdrawn.

In all of these plans, payouts are taxed as ordinary income in their entirety. Penalties are imposed for "early distribution," generally any withdrawal of funds prior to the taxpayer's reaching age 59½.[52] Payouts must be made by the time the taxpayer reaches age 70½, or payments begun which will extend over a period not to exceed the life of the taxpayer, or the joint lives of the taxpayer and spouse.[53] The special five-year averaging rule is not available for IRAs.

TAX PLANNING TIP: An employee who is not a participant in an employer retirement plan can still set aside money for eventual retirement by creating an individual retirement account. The contribution, and deduction, can be any amount up to $2,000 of earnings.

[46]IRC Secs. 408(j) and 415(c).
[47]IRC Sec. 408(k)(3).
[48]IRC Sec. 408(a).
[49]IRC Sec. 219(c).
[50]IRC Sec. 219.
[51]IRC Sec. 408(a).
[52]IRC Sec. 408(f). As this edition of the text is going to print, President Bush has proposed that first-time homebuyers under age 59½ be allowed to withdraw funds up to $10,000 from an IRA without penalty if the funds are used to make a down payment on a personal residence. The withdrawal would still be subject to regular income tax, but the 10% penalty would not apply.
[53]IRC Sec. 408(b).

An advantage of both H.R. 10 and IRA plans is that the self-employed person has until the due date (April 15 for calendar-year taxpayers) for making the contribution to the plan and still taking the deduction for the prior year. However, an H.R. 10 plan must be *established* within the taxable year, whereas an IRA can be established as late as the due date for filing the return.

TAX PLANNING TIP: Money can't be borrowed from an IRA. However, the IRA can be "rolled over" no more often than once a year—and a sixty-day "loan" thereby obtained.

18.7 Section 403(b) Plans

Employees of churches, hospitals, schools, and certain other tax-exempt organizations are allowed to exclude from their income amounts used to purchase a nonforfeitable annuity or shares of a mutual fund.[54] To qualify, the employee must agree to such an arrangement for a minimum of one year, and agree in advance of earning anything under the employment contract for that year.[55] The employee directs the employer to pay part of the compensation directly to the fund. In the case of an annuity underwritten by an insurance company, payment would be made directly by the employer to the insurance carrier. Such amounts, which may be treated by the employer as a payroll deduction, are excludable from the employee's income.[56]

Unlike pension or profit-sharing plans of corporations engaged in profit-seeking business, there is no requirement for a formal plan or agreement. IRS approval is not required in advance.

TAX PLANNING TIP: An employee of a tax-exempt organization or a public school has a lot more control and flexibility with respect to a tax-free contribution to a retirement annuity than employees of other organizations, or than self-employed persons. Each year the employee can decide how much he or she wants to contribute to the plan. There need be no concern about what the other employees do, as long as the employer will cooperate by entering into the salary reduction agreement and use the money to purchase an annuity or to invest in a mutual fund.

Also, such arrangements may be made arbitrarily, without concern for discrimination. The essential requirement is that the employer must be approved as a tax-exempt organization or be a public school.

A 20% rule provides that the maximum amount the employee can exclude from compensation in any given year is to be determined by multiplying the years of prior service by 20% of current compensation, and then deducting all amounts previously excludable that were used to purchase retirement benefits.[57] This exclusion generally cannot exceed the overall $30,000 or 25% of pay limitation on contributions to a qualified contribution plan,[58] or the limits on elective deferrals. This limit is generally an adjusted $7,000, but for 403(b) annuities it is $9,500.[59]

The employee begins to pay income tax when the annuity proceeds are received. Upon death, as much as $5,000 of the proceeds to a survivor may be excludable as a death benefit.

Thus, a professor employed by a college or university (or any other employee of a charitable, religious, scientific, or educational nonprofit organization) can arrange to have a substantial part of compensation excluded from income by directing the employer to purchase annuities or mutual funds.

Recipients of distributions from these tax-sheltered annuities, except for distributions required by law, can roll over the otherwise taxable portion to an IRA in the same manner as distributees of other plans.[60] Thus, they can avoid current taxation while changing the form of their retirement investment. Distributions not rolled over are eligible for the five-year forward averaging treatment mentioned earlier.

18.8 State and Local Government, and Tax-Exempt Organization Employees

Employees of state and local government units and tax-exempt organizations can defer up to

[54]IRC Sec. 408(b).

[55]These plans are sometimes called "salary reduction agreements" because the employee agrees to have salary reduced by a specified amount. The employer agrees to pay that amount into the fund rather than to the employee. The employee's W-2 form reflects the lower amount as salary.

[56]IRC Sec. 403(b)(1).

[57]IRC Sec. 403(b)(2).

[58]IRC Sec. 414(c)(4).

[59]IRC Sec. 402(g)(4).

[60]IRC Sec. 403(b)(8).

$7,500, but not more than one-third of compensation, by electing to defer both receipt of the money and its taxation until the earlier of termination of employment or occurrence of an unforeseeable emergency.[61] These deferrals often do not earn income and are not funded—the employing unit and the employee have merely agreed that payment will be made at a later date. However, if the deferral does earn income, taxation of those earnings is also deferred until distributed.

18.9 Social Security Integration

For 1990, the social security tax is imposed upon the first $51,300 of wages or salary.[62] Many qualified plans are "integrated" with social security coverage or benefits in some fashion.[63] This is not considered to be discriminatory under the tax law, subject to some limitations:

1. If the plan is a defined contribution plan, the integration of the plan with social security is based on contributions. Integration will be considered nondiscriminatory if total contributions (*including* the employer's portion of social security) for each participant bear a uniform relationship to the participant's total compensation, or basic rate of pay.[64] These rules also apply to self-employed persons.

For example, assume that a corporation has two employees, one who owns all of the stock and one who is not a shareholder. The salary of the owner is $55,000 per year and the other employee earns $20,000. The FICA tax will be paid on the entire $20,000 for the other employee, but on only the first $51,300 of the owner's salary. The corporation could have a plan to which it would contribute the social security percentage of the remaining $3,700 of the owner's salary and half of that percentage of the first $51,300 of compensation. Since the other employee earns less than the maximum amount to which the social security tax applies, there is no discrimination. The social security tax rate has been applied uniformly to the total compensation.[65]

Although, as mentioned earlier, there is a general prohibition against discrimination in favor of officers, employees who are stockholders, and highly paid employees, some degree of favoritism is thus allowed, particularly where "other" employees are paid smaller salaries.

2. If the plan is a defined benefit plan, the benefits under the plan can be reduced by a portion of the eligible benefits to be received under social security. This is then reflected in the calculation of the employer contribution, thus reducing the amount necessary to fund the plan.

The rationale of this approach is that the employer and the employee are already paying for the social security benefits,[66] so it is only equitable that earnings not covered by social security get a differential advantage.

18.10 Credit for the Elderly

Retirement benefits received under either social security or the Railroad Retirement System are generally exempt from income tax, except as explained below. The person who receives these benefits never paid any tax on the *employer's* contribution, which is equal to the amount withheld from the employee's wages.[67] On the other hand, persons who provide for their own retirement without the benefit of social security find their retirement income (rents, dividends, interest, and the includable portion of pensions and annuities) fully subject to income tax.

To put these self-providers and social security recipients on a more comparable basis, Congress could have taxed social security payments the same as other pensions. That is, the law could allow the annuitant a tax-free recovery of the contribution to the plan, taxing amounts received in excess of amounts paid in. Instead, Congress provided a tax credit for the self-providers,[68] although the credit in most cases will be very small or zero.

Eligibility requirements for the credit are as follows:

1. The taxpayer must be over age sixty-five, or retired under a public retirement plan. The rules are slightly different in the latter situation.
2. The taxpayer must not be a nonresident alien.

Details of this credit were discussed in Chapter 4.

18.11 Taxation of Social Security Benefits

Social security benefits escaped taxation as income from the start of program payments in 1936

[61]IRC Sec. 457.

[62]A rate of 7.65% applied to the employer and employee alike for 1990. The amount to which the tax applies is scheduled to increase annually by a cost-of-living factor. Where a person is an employee and is also self-employed, the combined earnings are used for purposes of the "base" limitation.

[63]Integration can take several forms. In general, however, an integrated plan refers to one in which the social security system is viewed as part of the retirement plan.

[64]The employer's portion of social security consists of two parts—the old-age portion and the hospital portion. The two together make up the FICA tax

[65]IRC Sec. 401(l).

[66]A self-employed person pays social security tax, but the rates are different. For 1990, the effective rate is 15.3%.

[67]The employee's half of the total social security payment is not a deduction to the employee for federal income tax purposes.

[68]IRC Sec. 37(a).

through 1983. But a perceived crisis in financing social security led to re-examination of some of the basic assumptions that had produced nontaxability. As a result, social security annuitants with substantial income from other sources now find up to as much as 50% of their social security benefits included in their regular taxable income.

Most affected taxpayers start with their adjusted gross income. To that, they add any amounts they have received of tax-exempt interest. (Note that it was in connection with this calculation that individuals first had to report tax-exempt interest on their federal income tax returns.) If the resulting total exceeds $32,000 for a married couple filing jointly, or $25,000 for unmarried persons, then 50% of the excess (but not more than 50% of social security benefits received) will be included in taxable income.[69]

> **Example:** Jack and Mary Cline receive $10,000 of social security benefits. Their adjusted gross income is $29,000, but they also have $6,000 of tax-exempt municipal bond interest. They thus have $35,000 for purposes of this calculation. This exceeds $32,000 by $3,000, and thus $1,500 of their social security benefits will be includible in taxable income.
>
> Comments—

1. In a sense, part of the tax advantage of investing in municipal bonds is lessened for the Clines. They might conclude that $3,000 of their municipal interest is being taxed at one-half their marginal tax rate.
2. If Jack and Mary would receive the same social security benefit amounts whether or not married to each other, they could avoid the tax on the $1,500 by getting divorced and thus having $25,000 each of income, $50,000 in total, before the social security taxation provision came into play.
3. Taxability of social security benefits, unlike taxation of other annuity programs, allows no deduction against the amount to be taxed for the contribution to purchase the social security that was made with nondeductible dollars by the retired person. Instead, not more than 50% of the social security is ever subject to tax.

18.12 Incentive Stock Options

Incentive stock options represent a tax advantage to employees that may or may not be related to their retirement plans. As the name implies, the purpose of such a plan is generally to provide an incentive for employees to work harder and smarter in an attempt to increase their own personal wealth. We include the topic in this chapter because of the relationship to overall employee compensation.

An incentive stock option is a plan whereby an employee is allowed to purchase stock of the employer corporation without recognition of any income at the time the option is granted or at the time it is exercised, and with capital gain treatment at the time of sale, provided that certain holding period and other requirements are satisfied.[70]

The option must be one that meets the following requirements:

1. The plan must specify the number of shares to be issued under the plan.
2. The employees or groups of employees who are eligible to receive stock options must be identified.
3. The stockholders of the corporation must approve the plan.[71]
4. The option must be granted within ten years.[72]
5. The employee must exercise the option within ten years of the date it was granted.
6. The option price must be equal to or greater than the fair market value of the stock at the time the option was granted.
7. The terms of the option must provide that the option is exercisable only by the employee and is transferable only upon the employee's death.
8. Prior to granting the option, the employee must not own more than 10% of the voting power of the corporation's stock. (This requirement does not apply if the option must be exercised within five years and if the option price is at least 110% of the fair market value of the stock at the time the option was granted.)
9. The option must not be exercisable while any other incentive stock option is outstanding to that employee.
10. The total fair market value of stock optioned to an employee for any one year may not exceed $100,000.

As mentioned above, the employee will not have any gross income at the time the option is granted or at the time it is exercised, if the conditions above are satisfied. If the employee holds the stock for at least one year *and* at least two years elapse between the time the option is granted and the time the

[69]IRC Sec. 86.

[70]IRC Sec. 422A.

[71]The approval must be within twelve months before or after the plan is adopted.

[72]The ten-year period begins to run on the date of adoption of the plan or the date the plan is approved by the shareholders, whichever is earlier.

stock is sold, there will be long-term capital gain.[73] If these conditions are satisfied, the employer corporation will not get any deduction. In other words, the corporation will treat the sale of stock to the employee just the same as any sale of stock to a new or existing stockholder. For example, assume that Billy Barnes receives an incentive stock option. The option price is $100 per share, and at the date of grant of the option the stock has a fair market value of $95 per share. Later, when the stock is valued at $120 per share, Billy exercises the option and buys 1,000 shares at $100. After both the one-year-following-purchase and two-years-following-date-of-option have passed, Billy sells the stock for $150 per share. The result is $50 per share of long-term capital gain for Billy and no deduction for the corporation.

Suppose that in the example above, Billy had held the stock for more than one year after purchase, but there had been less than two years between the date of granting of the option and the date of sale of the stock. There would be the following tax results:

1. Billy would have *ordinary income* of $20 per share (the difference between the option price and the value at the time the option was exercised).
2. The employer corporation would get a deduction for $20 per share, an amount equal to the ordinary income recognized by Billy.
3. Billy's long-term capital gain would be $30 per share (the total amount of the gain less the amount which is treated as ordinary income).

If Billy had not satisfied either the one-year or the two-year period, the result would be the same except that the capital gain would be short term rather than long term.

18.13 Restricted Property

In Chapter 2 we mentioned the general rule that where an employer sells property to an employee at less than its "regular" price, the bargain portion of the sale will be compensation to the employee. The same rule will apply, for example, where a corporate employer sells its stock to an employee at a reduced price. Thus, if Billy Barnes, an employee of ABC corporation, purchased 100 shares of ABC stock from the corporation for $20 per share, at a time when the fair market value of ABC stock was $25 per share, Billy would have $500 of additional compensation. However, a special rule applies if the stock, or other property for that matter, is subject to a "substantial risk of forfeiture."[74] This means that the person's rights to the full enjoyment of the property are conditioned upon the performance of substantial services in the future. We will use the term "restricted property" to designate such property. Although the rules apply to nonemployees as well as employees, an example of an employee will illustrate the rules and the related decisions that must be made.

Assume that Billy Barnes, employed by ABC corporation, was granted an option in 1989 to purchase 100 shares of ABC stock for $20 per share. The stock was then trading for $25 per share. One of the conditions of acquiring full title to the stock, however, was that Billy must remain employed by ABC for five more years. Should employment stop, for any reason, Billy will not acquire the stock and will not receive a refund of the $20 per share. However, Billy believed that the offer is sound and paid ABC the necessary $2,000. The projection is that after five years the stock will be worth $70 per share.

The rule is that Billy will have gross income when the stock becomes "substantially vested" (in this case, after five years) but there is an election to be made, called the 83(b) election.[75] The results are as follows (assuming that the stock is worth $70 per share in 1994 when full title is acquired):

If the election is not made:

1. Billy had no gross income in 1989;
2. Billy has $5,000 of ordinary income in 1994, when the restrictions are satisfied and full ownership of the stock is acquired;
3. Billy's basis for the stock is $7,000.

If the election is made:

1. Billy had $500 of ordinary income in 1989;
2. Billy has no income in 1994 when the restrictions lapse and the stock is acquired;
3. Billy's basis for the stock is $2,500 (the amount paid plus the amount included in gross income in 1989).

Assume that the stock continues to increase in value so that in 1996 it is worth $80 per share and Billy sells it for $80.

If the election was not made: Billy has $1,000 of long-term capital gain ($8,000 selling price less $7,000 basis).

[73]The holding period begins to run on the date the employee takes possession of the stock, which can be later than the date the option was exercised.

[74]IRC Sec. 83.

[75]The taxpayer has only thirty days from the date of transfer of the property within which to make the election.

If the election was made: Billy has $5,500 of long-term capital gain ($8,000 selling price less $2,500 basis).

Why make the election? (1) It *can* result in converting what would otherwise be ordinary income into capital gain; (2) it can result in the deferral of gain recognition until the date the property is sold rather than the date the restrictions lapse.

What are the risks of making the election? (1) If the property is forfeited because of not fulfilling the restrictions, only the amount paid for the property is deductible, not the discount portion which was included in gross income; (2) if the property does not increase in value as expected, the long-term capital gain will not result.

18.14 Conclusion

Taxation is a patchwork quilt as it relates to retirement plans and retirement income. Almost any person who is gainfully employed can obtain some sort of tax-sheltered vehicle to help provide for ultimate retirement. There are many special rules, qualifications, and limitations which must be postponed for advanced study in tax. The fundamentals discussed in this chapter are only a beginning.

TRUE-FALSE QUESTIONS

State whether each of the following statements is true or false. For each *false* answer, reword the statement to make it *true.*

T F 1. If an employee is not required to include a retirement plan contribution as a part of gross income, the employer may not take a deduction.

T F 2. As a general rule, income earned by the principal of a qualified retirement plan trust is not subject to income tax until a beneficiary (retiree) receives payment.

T F 3. A defined benefit plan is one in which an employee's benefits under the plan will be determined in advance, with contributions to the plan being sufficient to provide funds for those benefits to be paid.

T F 4. A defined contribution retirement plan is one in which the amount which is paid into the plan is fixed or determinable, but the amount of the benefits which will be paid from the plan will depend upon unknown future events.

T F 5. A noncontributory pension plan is one that is funded entirely by the employee.

T F 6. An individual may not qualify for both an H.R. 10 plan and an IRA for the same taxable year.

T F 7. For a defined contribution retirement plan, it is not necessary to consider the life expectancies of the employees when calculating the amount of the contribution to the fund.

T F 8. "Past service credit" is the term used to refer to the amounts that an employer should contribute to a retirement plan for the years of service by employees prior to the time the retirement plan was adopted.

T F 9. A "money-purchase pension plan" is one form of a "defined contribution plan."

T F 10. The maximum amount which a person may contribute, and deduct, for an IRA is 25% of earnings, or $2,000, if less.

T F 11. Under a profit-sharing plan, an employer can contribute to the plan and take a deduction for an amount up to 15% of compensation paid to covered employees.

T F 12. Under an incentive stock option, the option price of the stock must be equal to or larger than the fair market value of the stock as of the date the option is granted to an employee.

T F 13. An employee stock ownership plan is a trust designed primarily for corporations that are entirely owned by the employees.

T F 14. If an employee receives within one year the total balance due from a retirement plan, because of death or retirement, there will be no taxable gain.

T F 15. Where a lump-sum distribution from a retirement fund is received by an employee because of termination of employment, the employee can invest the proceeds in an individual retirement account without paying any tax.

T F 16. Depending upon the amount of other income which a person receives, including tax-exempt state and local government bond income, up to one-half of the amount of social security receipts may be subject to federal income tax.

T F 17. An IRA plan is a retirement plan available only to a self-employed person.

T F 18. Under an H.R. 10 plan, a taxpayer can transfer money to a trust and take a deduction from adjusted gross income.

T F 19. The advantages of both an H.R. 10 plan and an IRA are threefold: a deduction for the contribution to the plan, no current tax on the earnings of the plan, and the earnings of the plan are not taxed until paid out to the beneficiary.

T F 20. Under an individual retirement account, a married couple with only one spouse employed can contribute money to an Individual Retirement Account for both the employed and the unemployed spouse, and the limit is $2,250 instead of $2,000.

PROBLEMS

Problem 18-1. Harvey McAllister is single and is employed by a company that has no retirement plan. During the current year, his salary was $14,000. His only other income consisted of interest of $180 and dividends of $250.

(a) Is Harvey eligible to set up an H.R. 10 plan? Explain.

(b) Is Harvey eligible to set up an IRA? Explain. What are the tax advantages?

(c) Assuming that Harvey wants to contribute to a fund for his eventual retirement, how much can he contribute?

(d) Assume that Harvey is married and his wife is not employed. Is there a way for Harvey and his wife to contribute to a retirement plan for her? Explain.

Problem 18-2. The Maxwell Company is a small wholesale business with six full-time employees plus the owner, Mr. Charles Maxwell. Mr. Maxwell has been thinking about a profit-sharing or pension plan of some kind for his employees, all of whom are over age twenty-five and have over three years of service.

(a) Can he create an IRA for these employees? If so, what are the requirements? What are the advantages to him?

(b) Can Mr. Maxwell create an H.R. 10 plan for himself without including his employees? Discuss.

(c) Can Mr. Maxwell create an IRA plan for himself without including his employees? Discuss.

Problem 18-3. What is meant by the term "discrimination" as it applies to pension plans? Discuss.

Problem 18-4.

(a) If an employer has two employees in 1990, one who receives a salary of $35,000 and one who receives a salary of $10,000, and an amount equal of 10% of salary is contributed to a pension plan, is there discrimination in favor of the person receiving the $35,000 salary? Explain.

(b) Are the nondiscrimination provisions of the tax rules limited to the amount or percentage that is contributed to a pension plan? Explain.

(c) Explain how a pension plan contribution can be integrated with social security.

Problem 18-5.

(a) Distinguish between retirement plan tax deductions and retirement plan funding. Give an example of each.

(b) How does this difference relate to "past service credits"?

Problem 18-6.

(a) Distinguish between "defined contribution plan" and "defined benefit plan."

(b) Give two examples of each.

(c) From a management point of view, which is simpler to operate? Discuss.

Problem 18-7. The Armadillo Shell Company has been in operation for fifteen years. It began with three employees, including the owner. Twelve years ago, when there were six employees, the business was incorporated. Now there are twenty-two full-time employees. Twenty of those have over three years of regular employment. The twenty range in age from twenty-two to fifty-two. The company has never had a retirement, pension, or profit-sharing plan.

A retirement plan that is currently being considered involves the following considerations:

(a) No employee would be eligible to participate in the plan until he or she had *both* reached the age of twenty-five and had a minimum of three years of full-time service as an employee of Armadillo.

(b) After becoming eligible, each employee would have 100% vesting in the plan. (Vesting refers to nonforfeitability of benefits by an employee.)

(c) Any employee who was 100% vested and who died prior to retirement age of sixty-five would receive a death benefit of $25,000 in lieu of benefits that might otherwise be paid.

(d) Each employee, upon reaching retirement age of sixty-five, could receive monthly retirement benefits equal to 70% of the average monthly pay for the twelve months of full-time service immediately prior to retirement.

(e) Any eligible employee could retire at age sixty-two or thereafter with benefits equal to 65% of the benefits that would be received if he or she were age sixty-five.

(f) Upon death of a retired employee, his or her spouse will continue to receive 75% of the retirement benefits.

(i) Ignoring the problems associated with "prior service credit," prepare a list of the variables that should be considered in determining the current cost of the proposed retirement plan. Include a reason why each variable should be considered.

(ii) Which of those variables can be ignored if the retirement plan provides that 18% of the employer's profits will be paid into a retirement fund each year with each employee to receive a lump-sum retirement bonus based upon his or her years of employment as a percentage of years of employment for all employees.

Problem 18-8. Larry Hutton had been employed by Erck Corporation for twenty-five years as a draftsman. During that time he was covered by a qualified pension plan. The plan was a noncontributory plan. Erck Corporation terminated business this year and Larry received a lump-sum distribution of $35,000 from the plan. Of that amount, $20,000 is attributable to benefits accrued before 1974 and $15,000 is attributable to benefits accrued after 1973.

(a) How will the $35,000 be treated as far as Larry's income tax liability is concerned?

(b) Larry is age forty-eight and has already obtained new employment. He would prefer to avoid paying tax on the lump-sum distribution, if possible. He would like to invest the proceeds for his eventual retirement. Is there a way for Larry to do both? Explain.

Problem 18-9. Chester Frame is single and age sixty-seven. During the year, his income consisted of the following:

Dividends from stock	$1,200
Interest	900
Wages	1,500
Social security benefits	3,200

(a) Compute Chester's retirement income credit. (Refer back to Chapter 4 for an example.)

(b) Would it make any difference if Chester's social security benefits were $1,000?

Problem 18-10. At the end of 1990, Peter Sims has agreed to manage the ABC Realty partnership. As part of his compensation package, the partnership transferred him a 10% partnership at the end of 1990. It is valued at $15,000. Peter is not allowed to sell the interest for two years. In addition, Peter is required to forfeit the partnership interest if certain revenue goals are not achieved during 1991 and 1992. All of the restrictions on the partnership interest lapse on January 1, 1993.

(a) Is Peter required to include in his 1990 taxable income the transfer of the partnership interest?

(b) Assume the year is 1993 and the value of the partnership interest on January 1, 1993, was $25,000. What are the tax consequences to Peter and ABC Realty as a result of the expiration of the restrictions on Peter's interest in the partnership?

(c) May Peter include the transfer of the partnership interest in his 1990 taxable income? If so, how much must be included?

PROBLEMS WITH AN ASTERISK REQUIRE ADDITIONAL RESEARCH.

Problem 18-11.* What is meant by the term "vesting" as it applies to pension plans? Discuss. What does it mean if an employee is 40% vested?

Problem 18-12.* In late January, Bob Davison, age forty, was computing his tax for the previous year. He discovered that he had been more successful financially than he had thought, and that his tax was going to be more than he had planned. Bob is a self-employed piano instructor, giving private lessons to gifted children. Bob's only deductions are business-related routine expenses. He is a very careful record keeper and is sure that he has not overlooked any expenditures that could be deducted. Bob has paid the maximum FICA tax and understands that he will get no deduction for that expenditure. He has no other retirement plan.

(a) Is it too late for Bob to make arrangements for a self-employed retirement plan for last year? If not, how much may he contribute to the plan and deduct on his tax return?

(b) Would it make any difference if Bob were married and his wife was employed?

(c) Would it make any difference if Bob were an employee, had no self-employment income, and was not covered by a plan of his employer's? Advise Bob.

Problem 18-13.* Betty Lewis, who is single, earned $12,000 last year. She was eligible for an IRA, which she created. She contributed $1,000 to the plan.

(a) How much may Betty deduct on her tax return as the result?

(b) How much could Betty have contributed to the plan and deducted from gross income?

(c) What difference would it make if Betty were self-employed?

19

tax practice and procedure

19.1 Tax Administration

This chapter is devoted to the interface between the taxpayer and the government in getting returns filed and processed and in settling disputes. Chapter 19 covers tax research, which will include the origin of the law, and how and by whom it is shaped and interpreted.

Tax administration is primarily in the hands of the U.S. Internal Revenue Service, which is a part of the U.S. Department of the Treasury. The IRS is headed by an appointed Commissioner of Internal Revenue. It interprets the tax laws, answers taxpayer inquiries, collects the tax, audits tax returns, initiates legal action, and designs the tax forms. Its nearly 125,000 permanent employees include accountants, attorneys, and many clerical staff persons.[1]

19.2 Filing Requirements

The U.S. federal income tax is essentially a self-assessment system. That is, the taxpayer initiates the filing of an income tax return, as contrasted to systems in which the government proposes an assessment or obtains revenue through a system of taxes collected at the time of a transaction. Sales taxes (imposed by all except five states)[2] and real estate taxes are examples of an approach different from self-assessment. The sales tax is paid at the time of making a purchase, and the taxpayer cannot easily avoid it. Real estate taxes are typically based upon valuations determined by assessors, from whose appraisals a taxpayer can usually appeal.

For most individuals, the income tax return is due on April 15 for the prior calendar year.[3] The exceptions are those few individuals who are on a fiscal year (i.e., a year ending on the last day of a month other than December). Their returns are due the fifteenth day of the fourth month following the end of the fiscal year.

Three types of extensions of time are available:

1. Automatic extensions are granted, without any action being taken to obtain them, for those taxpayers who are outside the United States (with Puerto Rico treated as part of the United States) on the return filing date. This extension is for two months (i.e., to June 15 for most taxpayers) and extends the time for payment as well as for filing.[4]
2. Automatic four-month extensions are available to individuals who file a Form 4868. This extension will postpone the return filing date to August 15 but will not extend the time for payments unless at least 90% of the tax shown as due on the return has been paid prior to or with the extension application.[5]
3. Discretionary extensions of time may be granted by the IRS, but all extensions combined cannot exceed a maximum of six months, unless the

[1] *1988 Annual Report of the Internal Revenue Service.*

[2] Alaska, Delaware, Montana, New Hampshire, and Oregon. The District of Columbia also imposes a sales tax.

[3] IRC Sec. 6072(a).

[4] Treas. Reg. 1.6081-2. However, interest is charged on any unpaid tax from April 15.

[5] Treas. Reg. 1.6081-4.

taxpayer is outside the United States.[6] The IRS generally will require a taxpayer to obtain an automatic extension before considering an additional extension request—and generally grants extensions only for periods of sixty days or less. Form 2688 is commonly used for these extension requests, although a letter can be used.

4. A person who is outside the U.S. and is in the process of satisfying the requirements for the foreign income exclusion (see Chapter 2) can get an extension by filing Form 2350. Generally, the extension will be for thirty days beyond the date the taxpayer qualifies for the foreign income exclusion.

Partnership and fiduciary returns have the same due dates as individual returns.[7] Corporate returns, however, are due on March 15, or the fifteenth day of the third month following the end of a fiscal year.[8] Corporations can get an automatic six-month extension by filing a Form 7004.[9] Further extensions are discretionary with the IRS.

19.3 Prepayment Requirements

While the U.S. income tax system is one of self-assessment, the prepayment requirements tend to reinforce the necessity for filing returns and provide some discipline toward getting the tax paid.

Salary and wage payments to individuals are subject to withholding of both income tax and social security tax. The employer is required to withhold and make payment to the IRS, with certain penalties for noncompliance.[10] Where an individual has social security tax withheld on more than the social security wage base ($51,300 in 1990) because of having two or more employers during the year, the excess social security tax is treated as additional withholding tax for income tax purposes.[11] See line 60 of Form 1040 [Appendix 1-D(b)].

Amounts of income tax withheld from a given amount of salary or wages depend primarily on the number of exemptions. Employers are furnished tables, or can use a formula approach to determine the correct amount.[12] Employees can voluntarily authorize increased withholding, such as to cover tax that will be due on other income that is not subject to withholding. In the other direction, an employee who would have too much withheld because of exceptionally large deductions or credits, may claim additional withholding allowances; one who will only be employed during part of the year can request a special calculation; and one who had no tax liability last year and expects none this year can execute an exemption certificate and avoid any withholding.[13]

Payments to persons who are not employees, but are independent contractors of the payor, are not subject to withholding. However, there are certain reporting requirements with which the payor must comply.[14] Generally, this means that the payor prepares a Form 1099 at the end of the year and reports to both the payee and the IRS the amount of the payment. Payors of interest, dividends, rents, and other nonemployee compensation may be required to make "backup withholding" of 20% of the payment. This is required where the payee has failed to report such receipts in income in prior years or has failed to supply appropriate information so that the payor can file the Form 1099 correctly.[15]

Since many individuals, and all corporations, have income that is not subject to withholding tax, a system of estimated tax payment requirements provides a rough equivalent of withholding. Individuals with such income are required to make quarterly estimated tax payments so that at least 90% of the amount of tax that is finally determined to be due is prepaid.[16] The first estimated tax payment is due on April 15 of the year for all calendar-year taxpayers, and on the fifteenth day of the fourth month for fiscal-year taxpayers.[17] No extensions of time are granted for estimated tax payments. The second payment is due June 15; the third on September 15; and the fourth on January 15 of the following year.

Appendix 19-A is a worksheet for calculating the amount of estimated income tax for 1990. Quarterly payments are made with a declaration

[6] IRC Sec. 6081(a) and Treas. Reg. 1.6081-1.

[7] Partnerships generally have a calendar year because the partners use a calendar year. IRC Sec. 706. See the discussion in Chapter 10. Fiduciaries are more likely to have a fiscal year.

[8] IRC Sec. 6072(b).

[9] IRC Sec. 6081(b).

[10] IRC Sec. 3402 requires the withholding. IRC Secs. 6651–6661 impose various penalties for noncompliance. Here, Sec. 6656 would probably be the relevant statute, but see also Sec. 7215 for criminal penalties.

[11] Treas. Reg. 31.6413(c)-1.

[12] IRC Sec. 3402(c)–(q).

[13] IRC Sec. 3402(n) and Treas. Reg. 31.3402(n). This is done on a Form W-4. Students with part-time jobs, for example, may not have enough income for the year to owe any tax. Execution of this form will eliminate the withholding, resulting in the receipt of more wages currently rather than waiting to file the tax return and getting the refund of withheld taxes several months later.

[14] IRC Sec. 6041A. An "employee" is defined by IRC Sec. 3401(c).

[15] IRC Secs. 6051–6053. "Backup withholding" is in IRC Sec. 3406.

[16] IRC Secs. 6015 and 6017. Payment is required by IRC Sec. 6153. Penalties are imposed by IRC Sec. 6654.

[17] IRC Sec. 6073.

FIGURE 19-1 Estimated tax payments required by corporations

If Filing Requirements Are First Met		*Percentage of Estimated Taxes Payable on 15th Day of:*			
After	*Before*	*4th Month*	*6th Month*	*9th Month*	*12th Month*
	4th month	25%	25%	25%	25%
3rd month	6th month		33⅓%	33⅓%	33⅓%
5th month	9th month			50%	50%
8th month	12th month				100%

voucher (Form 1040ES), which is shown in Appendix 19-B. One such voucher is required with each payment. The one illustrated is for the fourth payment, due Jan. 15, 1991. Self-employed persons pay their estimated social security tax along with their estimated income tax in this manner. (See line 11 in Appendix 19-A.)

The penalties for substantially underestimating tax are calculated as of each of the quarterly estimated tax payment dates. They are at the same rate as interest paid on tax deficiencies, but are not deductible (while interest sometimes is). Penalties can be avoided by relying on one of two exceptions:[18]

1. Relying on the tax liability for the prior year as the estimate of current year's tax.
2. Paying as of each quarterly due date 90% of the tax that would be due if the income for the year to date were annualized.

Corporations are required to make deposits of estimated taxes to a Federal Reserve bank or authorized commercial bank. The estimated tax is the excess of the expected tax liability less any credits. Deposits are required as shown in Fig. 19-1.[19]

Corporations with $1 million or more of taxable income in any of the three previous taxable years are required to pay an estimated tax of 90% of the current year tax ultimately shown on this return and cannot avoid penalty by basing their estimate on the prior year tax, except for their first quarterly estimated payment of each year.[20]

Rules for other corporations and for trusts are similar to those for individuals.[21]

19.4 Tax Return Audits

Office audits are conducted in the local IRS office and are usually initiated by a notification letter to the individual taxpayer. A tentative appointment date and time are set, which the taxpayer can change to suit his or her convenience. The letter will usually indicate the type of information in which the IRS auditor is interested. Returns for office audit are selected mainly through a random sampling process, although unusual items of income or deduction increase the probability of selection. The office audit is handled by IRS people who audit mostly individual taxpayers. Although an office audit is not restricted to such matters, a typical audit is concerned with such things as itemized deductions, exemption amounts, and some of the deductions for AGI, such as alimony, employee business expenses, and IRA contributions. Normally, an office audit does not deal with some of the more sophisticated matters of business or corporate returns.

A taxpayer who has support in the tax law for the positions taken on the return, and who can document the facts involved, will usually fare well in an office audit. Adverse decisions of the office auditor can be appealed to the IRS's Appeals Division, subject to the same rules and in the same manner as discussed below for field audits.

19.5 Field Audits

Generally, the taxpayer will receive a notice that a tax return is to be examined, accompanied by the suggestion that either the taxpayer or a representative call to schedule the time, date, and place of the audit. The notice will designate the year or years to be examined.

If the examination of a business return is to be conducted in the taxpayer's office, some responsible employee should be designated as liaison with the revenue agent. The employee should be instructed not to attempt to deal with technical questions but should be prepared to explain the flow of information into the books of entry. The agent should be requested to prepare a list of any questions, or a list of supporting documentation which is desired. Furthermore, the agent should be requested not to raise questions, except those that are obviously routine, with the taxpayer or employees, but to save them for the taxpayer's representative, if one is involved.

[18] IRC Sec. 6654(d).
[19] IRC Sec. 6154(b).
[20] IRC Sec. 6655(i).
[21] IRC Sec. 6655.

19.6 Negotiating with the Field Agent

Once the agent has concluded the examination, the taxpayer and/or his or her representative will be given the opportunity to discuss the findings.

While agents are basically fact-finders, like other professionals they pride themselves on having acquired sufficient technical understanding of the subject matter to reach reasonable conclusions based upon not only the facts but also the law. Although efforts should be directed principally to supporting the facts that favor the taxpayer, discussion of the applicable law may prove helpful. The agent may then find it necessary to do some research before discussing the issue further.

If the agent has taken an adverse position and has not modified it after discussion, the taxpayer may prepare a written memorandum. Many times an agent will adopt some of the arguments made by the taxpayer in the report that he or she must prepare. If a representative prepared the return under examination, certain questions that the agent might raise may have been foreseen, and the representative will be prepared to answer them.

19.7 Requests for Technical Advice

In many instances, part of a disagreement between an agent and a taxpayer lies in their differing views of the facts and the issues, not merely on what interpretation should be given to them. Here technical advice can be of great advantage.

During either an examination or at the Appeals Office conference, the taxpayer has the right to request that an issue be referred to the National Office of the IRS for technical advice. One of three reasons should be given when the request is made:

1. Within the IRS, lack of uniformity exists as to disposition of the issue;
2. the issue is unusual; or
3. the issue is complex.

This type of appeal will generally be used only in situations in which there is a question as to how the law applies to a particular factual situation. It also has value where someone knows of an unpublished IRS position that the agent will not apply to the taxpayer.[22]

Although the district office is not required to grant the request, relatively few such requests appear to be denied. If the request is denied, the taxpayer may appeal to the District Chief, Audit Division, within ten days. An adverse decision here cannot be appealed. The National Office, however, will, if the taxpayer requests, review the file. It may disapprove of denial and authorize the request for technical advice.[23]

If technical advice is to be requested, an attempt is made to prepare a statement of facts and issues on which the agent and the taxpayer can agree. In the process of trying to reach agreement on such a statement, the taxpayer and the agent often come to see their positions more clearly and find they have a basis for a settlement without recourse to the National Office. If agreement cannot be reached, then separate statements by each party may be filed with the National Office.

In either event, the taxpayer's position on the issues may be explained in a statement submitted to the National Office. Also, an oral conference to be held in Washington, D.C. can be requested if it appears that the National Office position will be adverse to the taxpayer. Such a request *must* be made when the matter is first being referred to the National Office, or a conference may not be offered.

Once the National Office advice has been obtained, the likelihood of settling the case in a manner contrary to that advice is fairly remote, short of docketing the case with the Tax Court. Therefore, requests for advice should normally be a last resort, to be used when the taxpayer feels reasonably sure that all basis for compromise is gone. However, in some types of cases, the preparation of a statement of facts and issues creates a climate in which compromise is possible.

19.8 Settling with the Agent

When the agent has prepared the report on his or her conclusions relative to the audit, the taxpayer will receive a copy, together with a Form 870, Waiver of Restrictions on Assessment of the agreed deficiency.

A Form 870 (Appendix 19-C) is the method by which the taxpayer notifies the district director of agreement with the findings of the agent. The signing of a Form 870 is not, however, binding on the IRS or on the taxpayer. The taxpayer, by signing the Form 870, waives the right to any further hearings before paying the tax. (See the discussion later of the ninety-day letter.) If the taxpayer intends to contest the deficiency before paying, the Form 870 is not signed.

A taxpayer signing an *unconditional waiver* of

[22]Private letter rulings which are issued to a taxpayer are available as public information (with the taxpayer's identity removed). These sources of information are, however, considered unpublished and unofficial except as applicable to *the* taxpayer to whom originally issued.

[23]Rev. Proc. 89-2.

assessment will stop the running of interest on the deficiency on the thirtieth day after the waiver is filed with the IRS, and assessment may be made at such time. A taxpayer signing a *conditional waiver* of assessment will stop the running of interest on the thirtieth day after the waiver becomes effective.

The IRS may reopen the case even after the deficiency has been paid, when there has been fraud, malfeasance, collusion, concealment, misrepresentation, or substantial error, or where failure to reopen would be a serious administrative omission. Furthermore, cases closed by the use of Form 870 or by a letter informing the taxpayer that the case is closed ("agreed cases") may be reopened by postreview in Washington. Cases in which a refund or credit in excess of $200,000 is allowed are automatically postreviewed in Washington, except where the refund or credit is due to overpayment of estimated tax or where a foreign tax credit is allowed.

The taxpayer may (after executing the Form 870 and paying the tax deficiency) file a refund claim or sue for a refund. In a hardship case, even before paying the tax, the taxpayer can offer to pay a lesser sum in compromise of the deficiency.

At any stage of the proceeding, the taxpayer may be requested by the IRS to execute a Form 872 (Appendix 19-D), Consent to Extend the Time to Assess Tax. The request to sign the Form 872 will usually be made when the expiration of the statutory period for assessment appears imminent. Normally, a request for the execution of a Form 872 will be made within six months of the expiration of the statute of limitations, in order to give both the government and the taxpayer time to arrive at a proper conclusion.

Should the taxpayer refuse to execute the Form 872, the Treasury will usually issue a statutory ninety-day letter (discussed in Section 19.12) almost immediately. Generally, a Form 872 is signed by the taxpayer in order to prevent immediate issuance of a ninety-day letter and to leave the avenues of appeal open, but reasons for not signing the Form 872 may be:

1. The taxpayer feels settlement is impossible at the agent or Appeals office levels.
2. Negotiation could best be conducted after the issuance of a ninety-day letter.
3. There is insufficient time for the IRS to conduct an examination, as the statute of limitations is about to expire.[24]

[24]It is possible to grant a *selective* extension of the statute of limitations. In such a case only the issues mentioned in the extension will be open and the statute of limitations will apply to all other issues. Statute of limitations is covered by IRC Secs. 6501–6521.

In cases in which it appears the agent is obviously in error, and in the rare case in which the agent refuses to adjust the erroneous position or is prolonging the audit unnecessarily, a request to speak to the agent's supervisor is proper. This procedure cannot be expected to be fruitful, however, if a technical point is involved. The agent's supervisor is usually thoroughly familiar with the technical issues, having discussed them with the agent as the audit proceeded, and it is rare for the agent to take a position different from that of the supervisor.

19.9 Appeals Office

To secure an Appeals Office conference where the dispute is for less than $10,000 or an office audit is involved, the taxpayer need only send a letter to the district director within thirty days of the date on which the thirty-day letter (see below) was mailed. The letter merely requests a conference. If the dispute concerns a field audit and involves more than $10,000, a formal written protest must be filed.

The conference is conducted in a rather informal atmosphere. The agent will not be present. Witnesses may be brought to the conference, but this is seldom done, as written affidavits are usually sufficient. Furthermore, the taxpayer's inexperience with matters of this type may hamper what should be a rather simple method of disposing of the controversy; thus, having a CPA or attorney handle the matter is usually best. Most representatives prefer that the taxpayer not be present during the process.

The IRS has taken the position that taxpayers are not entitled to a conference as a matter of right. For example, where failure or refusal to comply with the tax laws is due to moral, religious, political, constitutional, conscientious, or similar ground, a conference may be denied.

19.10 The Thirty-Day Letter

The thirty-day letter is an administrative letter advising the taxpayer, after review is completed, that the agent has proposed a deficiency and that the taxpayer must either expect to pay the deficiency or take certain administrative steps to have the proposed deficiency abated. If the taxpayer fails to take either step within the thirty-day period, a statutory ninety-day letter will be issued.

There are, as previously noted, two different types of responses to the thirty-day letter, depending upon the amount of the proposed deficiency.

If the amount in dispute is less than $10,000, the letter advises the taxpayer that a written protest is unnecessary. The taxpayer can request a conference with the Appeals Office. A written memorandum of the taxpayer's position may be sent if the taxpayer wants to do so.

If the amount in dispute is more than $10,000, a written protest is necessary. The letter suggests that the taxpayer seek a conference with the Appeals Office.

The taxpayer should follow the instructions of the thirty-day letter.

19.11 Appeals Office Conference

The Appeals Office of the Regional Commissioner's Office is the only IRS organization that has true settlement authority.

After the taxpayer has carefully evaluated the basic issues in the case, the taxpayer or his or her representative may decide that the case can best be settled by considering the "hazards of litigation" as opposed to only the factual matters involved.

In order to proceed to the Appeals Office, if over $10,000 is involved, a written protest must be filed in duplicate, specifically identifying the issues to which the taxpayer takes exception. No particular form is required, but it should contain the information required by the instructions in the thirty-day letter and IRS Publication 5. A properly drafted protest will represent a major plus in settlement negotiations. After presenting the facts, the protest should include an analysis of the issues raised by the agent in the report. Authoritative support, such as cases and rulings favoring the taxpayer's position, should be cited. The taxpayer should not discuss issues not raised by the agent. If new issues are brought up, the IRS conferee will request supplementary memoranda.

A taxpayer does not proceed to the Appeals Office without some risk. The conferees are experienced IRS personnel and can raise more sophisticated arguments or even, on occasion, bring up new issues.

A careful evaluation of issues must thus be made prior to the appeal conference. Timing items (such as asset depreciation lives and overaccruals) are generally far less significant than permanent items (such as capital loss versus ordinary loss). Those issues that are material and that warrant litigation should be segregated. The ability to trade issues in the most beneficial way is a major factor in these negotiations.

The preparation of a protest and the overall preparation necessary for the conference will probably represent a substantial investment in professional time. The taxpayer needs to view the situation from a dollars-and-cents standpoint. The costs incurred for professional counsel must be measured against the amount of tax in controversy.

If settlement does not appear possible, thought should be given to retaining legal counsel. Getting the client's lawyer involved with the protest will ensure that counsel has familiarity with the issues and can most effectively coordinate what is done at the Appeals level with the litigation that is to follow. The attorney will then be in a much better position to help the client decide whether to go the Tax Court route or pay the tax and sue for a refund in the District Court or U.S. Claims Court.

Settlement at the Appeals Office level is usually executed on a Form 870AD (see Appendix 19-E). The conferee will send the appropriate form along with instructions for its execution. The settlement agreed upon at the Appeals Office will not be upset by IRS postreview unless there has been fraud, malfeasance, or a material misrepresentation of fact. However, the legal effect of a Form 870AD remains to some degree unclear. The IRS position is generally that the taxpayer is barred from later filing a refund claim, while the courts would reject a taxpayer refund suit if the claim is filed after the statute has run on IRS assessing the deficiency.

19.12 The Ninety-Day Letter

A taxpayer can request a ninety-day letter at any time after the agent has submitted the report. The ninety-day letter is the "statutory notice of deficiency" that is required before a deficiency can be assessed and collected. The assessment itself is then the recording of the deficiency on the summary record of assessment maintained by the district director or the director of a regional service center, which step initiates the collection process.

The ninety-day letter states that if within ninety days (150 days if the letter is mailed to a taxpayer outside the United States), the taxpayer does not file a petition with the Tax Court, the tax will be assessed.

A ninety-day letter is issued

1. at the request of a taxpayer who desires to file a petition with the Tax Court,
2. by the district director when the taxpayer has failed to file a protest from the thirty-day letter, or
3. by the Appeals Division upon failure to reach a settlement. The office of the regional counsel of the IRS will be requested to concur in the issuance of a ninety-day letter at this level, as that office will have to represent the IRS should the case go to Tax Court.

FIGURE 19-2 Appeals available to the taxpayer

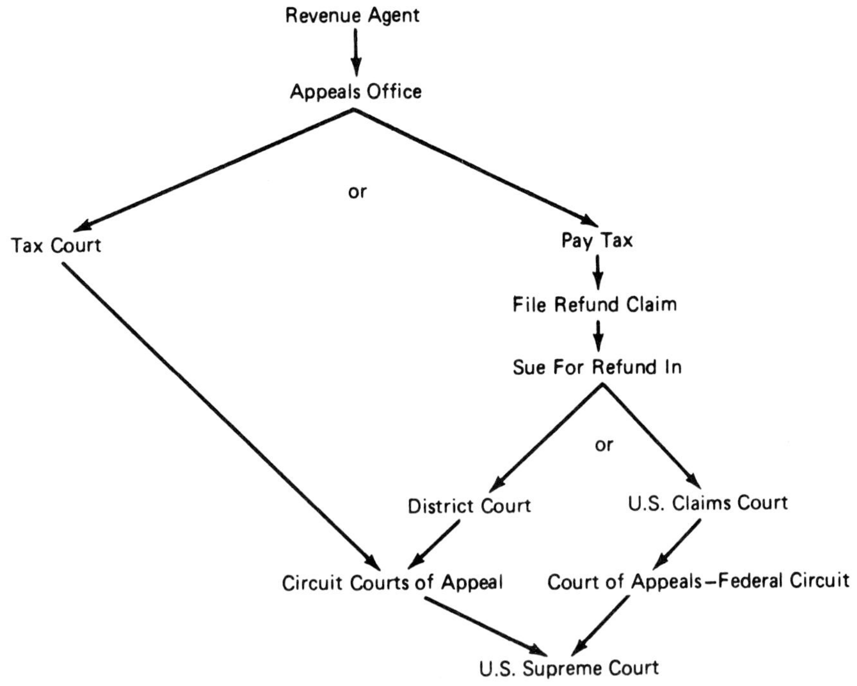

When the taxpayer has received the ninety-day letter, the following alternatives are available:

1. File a petition with the Tax Court.
2. Pay the deficiency, file a claim, and then sue for refund in either the District Court or the U.S. Claims Court.[25]
3. Allow the IRS to assess the deficiency, at which time the normal collection procedures will begin.
4. Negotiate with the IRS for the rescission of the 90-day letter by mutual agreement.

Once the taxpayer has received the ninety-day letter, he or she can pay the tax and still go to the Tax Court; but without paying the tax and filing a refund claim, access cannot be obtained to either a District Court or the U.S. Claims Court.

19.13 The Litigation Process

In reviewing the judicial authorities applicable to a case, the taxpayer should be mindful that a forum must be chosen if settlement cannot be achieved within the IRS. The immediate avenues of appeal are the Tax Court, the District Court, and the U.S. Claims Court. The District Court and the Claims Court, however, are available only if the deficiency is paid and a refund action instituted.

Figure 19-2 shows the appeals available to the taxpayer.

[25]Of course, if the taxpayer has decided that the dispute will not be won, the deficiency can be paid with no further action to continue the case.

More cases go to the Tax Court than go the refund claim route. Decisions of all three of the trial courts can be appealed to the appropriate Circuit Court of Appeals.[26] Since there are twelve Circuit Courts of Appeal, the taxpayer must carefully review the decisions in similar cases of the specific Circuit Court to which appeal will be made if the Tax Court or District Court renders an adverse decision.

The Tax Court has a small-tax-disputes procedure for cases in which the amounts involved are less than $10,000. Litigation under this procedure is at the option of the taxpayer. Generally, the process is more informal. *Decisions in these small cases cannot be appealed.*

While the District Court is bound by the decisions of the Circuit Court in the same geographic area, the Tax Court has not always been so restricted. After taking a position on a particular issue, the Tax Court, until 1970, applied its rule to all taxpayers on a national basis. A taxpayer would then have to appeal to the Circuit Court to have a decision reversed. A reversal by the Circuit Court of Appeals was not binding in the Tax Court, which in subsequent similar cases could again render a decision based upon its own position, forcing the taxpayer to appeal.

The Tax Court now has a different policy. It will follow decisions of a Circuit Court of Appeals

[26]Obviously, an appeal is only made by the party who loses. An appeal does not occur if the losing party is convinced that there is nothing to be gained from the appeal or that the cost (legal fees, etc.) is too high.

for cases arising in that court's geographic jurisdiction even if the Tax Court disagrees. When it does disagree, it will issue a decision based on the appellate court's rule and will state its own disagreements. If a similar case arises in a different geographic area under the jurisdiction of a different Appeals Court that has not ruled on the problem, the Tax Court will follow its own view despite its earlier contrary decision that followed a Circuit Court view.

By resorting to the Tax Court, a taxpayer forgoes the possibility of a district court or claims court refund suit. Thus, there is no looking back to bemoan, "If only I had gone to District Court instead of Tax Court." A jury, which will act as fact-finder, is forgone in Tax Court, since a jury trial is available only in District Court.

The IRS is represented by its own attorneys in matters before the Tax Court; it is represented by attorneys from the Tax Division of the Justice Department in cases before the District Courts and the Claims Court. Justice Department attorneys also handle all appeals cases for the IRS.

The U.S. Claims Court and the Court of Appeals—Federal Circuit have only been in existence since October 1, 1982, although there was a predecessor, the U.S. Court of Claims. Both the U.S. Claims Court and the related Court of Appeals—Federal Circuit are national in jurisdiction. Therefore, the possibility of having those courts render different decisions in different geographic regions is removed, as contrasted with the Circuit Courts of Appeal mentioned earlier.

It is not the purpose of this chapter to detail the procedural and/or theoretical problems involved in choosing one court in preference to another. What should be clear is that the decision is not an easy one. The taxpayer initially has the choice between courts, but it is not one that can be *reversed* at the whim of the taxpayer or representative. The decision as to which route to go should be made by the taxpayer only after considering the views of an attorney. However, there are situations in which the taxpayer has no practical choice but to go to the Tax Court. For example, the taxpayer may not be able to pay the proposed deficiency. In other situations, such as payroll and most excise tax matters, the taxpayer cannot go to the Tax Court and so must seek an alternative.

19.13.1. The Taxpayer versus the Government

What if taxpayers decide to fight what they regard as unwarranted assessments and to protest occasional high-handed behavior by revenue agents? Does it pay off?

The results are interesting. For the fiscal year ending September 30, 1988, for example, cases disposed of (settled or by trial) that were docketed before the Tax Court involved $4.3 billion in proposed deficiencies. The taxpayers wound up having to pay only $1.3 billion or about 30% of the amounts proposed. (Too much should not be made of these numbers. Many controversies involve *when*, not *whether*, something should be taxed or deducted.)

In District Court suits, for the same year, taxpayers obtained refunds in 18.5% of the cases. In the Court of Claims (now the U.S. Claims Court), taxpayers obtained refunds in only 6.6% of the cases.

More cases go the Tax Court route than the refund claim route. Decisions of the Tax Court or of the District Court can be appealed to the appropriate Circuit Court of Appeals. Out of 293 such appeals decided, the government won 222. Decisions of the courts of appeal can be appealed to the United States Supreme Court.[27] The Supreme Court declines to hear many tax cases. During fiscal year 1988, it handed down decisions in three tax cases, two of which the government won.[28]

The pattern of tax controversy is thus one of substantial compromises achieved at the administrative level; IRS dominance over the taxpayer by a slight margin at the trial court level; and government dominance over the taxpayer when appeals are taken from lower-court decisions.

19.14 Rulings

Upon request, the IRS will consider issuing an interpretation of a *prospective transaction*, setting forth what the tax effects will be. These are called letter rulings. Almost 30,000 are issued in a typical year. Where substantial amounts of money are involved and the tax results are uncertain, many tax practitioners consider obtaining a letter ruling to be inexpensive insurance. Although a letter ruling is not legally binding upon the IRS, by long-established policy such a ruling will be followed for the taxpayer *to whom the ruling is furnished*. Unfortunately, many taxpayers have found to their sorrow that such rulings are not necessarily effective when applied to other taxpayers.

The ruling process is not without its critics. The IRS, with minor exceptions, is not directed by law to furnish any rulings. Thus, in general, the IRS views the issuance of a letter ruling as a favor to a taxpayer rather than an obligation. The result

[27]All statistics from Internal Revenue Service, *1988 Annual Report* (Washington, D.C.: U.S. Government Printing Office), 1988, Publication 55.

[28]Statistics are for the fiscal year ending September 30, 1988.

is that there are many types of transactions on which the IRS is unwilling to issue rulings. Some people contend that any taxpayer should be able to obtain a binding advance ruling on *any* proposed transaction that involves a substantial (to the taxpayer) amount of money. In fact, there are situations where a taxpayer can appeal to the courts from an unfavorable IRS ruling or from a refusal of the IRS to rule. These include the tax-exempt status of employee benefit plans and certain nonprofit organizations and the status of certain municipal bond issues.[29] Copies of rulings, and requests for technical advice, are now generally available to other taxpayers—with taxpayer identifying data removed to protect privacy.

19.15 The Taxpayer's Burden of Proof

In contesting a tax deficiency, the taxpayer has one great advantage and one great disadvantage. The existence of the first is the rationale for the second.

The advantage is that the taxpayer controls most of the evidence and can preserve and produce the evidence most favorable to his or her version of what happened. To offset this rather substantial advantage, the tax law attaches a presumption of correctness to the determinations made by the IRS, whether or not supported by any evidence.

Thus, if a revenue agent proposes a $1,000 deficiency in taxes on the grounds that the taxpayer claimed charitable contributions that should be disallowed as deductions, the government need not prove that the taxpayer did not make the contributions, or that the organizations to which the contributions were made were not tax-exempt. The taxpayer has the burden of proving *both* that the contributions were made and that the receiving organizations were of the type that justify a deduction under Sec. 170 of the Internal Revenue Code.

This burden of proof on the taxpayer will vary, depending on the person with whom the taxpayer is dealing. Some revenue agents seem to want proof beyond the shadow of any doubt. Others are satisfied with almost anything tending to support the deduction claimed. This "human element" is perhaps unavoidable and makes tax work all the more interesting.

The Tax Court tends to take the position that the burden of proof is more a burden of going forward with the evidence; therefore, a taxpayer's unsubstantiated but credible (and unrefuted) testimony may be all that is needed on certain types of issues.

In a suit for refund in a district court, on the other hand, the exact burden of proof that is imposed may vary with the judge, if the trial is without a jury. As noted earlier, a jury trial is only available in district court.

19.16 Civil Penalty Provisions in the Tax Law

Arguing with the government may pay off, but the taxpayer may well wonder what risks are involved. As long as neither fraud nor negligence is involved, the taxpayer who loses will be charged interest on any deficiencies in tax. The interest runs from the date the tax payment was due. The interest cost of this type of "borrowing" from the government may or may not be less than that of "borrowing" from alternative sources. To the extent that the interest is deductible, the after-tax cost becomes less as the taxpayer's tax bracket gets higher.[30] Amounts paid for tax advice in preparing a return or in connection with tax controversies may also be deductible. For individuals, such costs are miscellaneous itemized deductions subject to the 2% "floor." (See Chapter 3.)

A charge is also made for substantial underpayment of estimated tax. This charge is not interest and is never deductible.

These two charges (interest on deficiencies and underpayments of estimates) are subject to adjustment to keep them in line with prevailing interest rates. The rate has ranged from 9% to 20% in recent years. On March 31, 1990, it was 11%. Under present rules, the interest rate can change every three months.[31]

Filing a return late will result in a penalty of 5% a month, up to a maximum of 25% of the tax, unless reasonable cause can be shown for failing to file the return on time.[32] Because it costs the IRS approximately $75 to identify a taxpayer who fails to file a return, Congress enacted a minimum penalty to apply where a taxpayer does not file within sixty days of the due date (including extensions). The minimum penalty will be the lesser of the amount of tax due or $100. Advice of a competent tax adviser that no return was necessary is usually reasonable cause. Where a return cannot be filed on time because of illness, inability to obtain necessary information in time to prepare

[29]IRC Secs. 7428 and 7476–7478.

[30]To a corporation, interest paid to the government on tax deficiencies is treated just like any other interest on borrowed money (e.g., it is deductible). Tax deficiency interest is personal interest to an individual, and nondeductible after 1991. (See Chapter 3.) Penalties, on the other hand, are designed to punish the taxpayer for wrongdoing and are not deductible.

[31]IRC Sec. 6621. The rate of interest is the federal short-term rate plus three points for deficiencies and one point less for refunds (i.e., if 9% for deficiencies, then 8% for refunds).

[32]IRC Sec. 6651. The rate is applied to the additional tax which is due.

the return, or other acceptable reasons, an extension of time for filing the return can be obtained, as previously discussed.

Where any part of a deficiency in tax is deemed to have been caused by negligence or intentional disregard of the tax rules, an additional penalty of 20% of the tax can be imposed.[33] Also, there is a penalty for overvaluation of property. The purpose of this penalty is to discourage taxpayers from overvaluing property that was donated to charity (see Chapter 3 for discussion of charitable contributions) or involved in tax shelters, but the penalty is not restricted to those problems. A valuation overstatement occurs when a taxpayer claims a value for that property on the tax return which is 200% or more of the correct amount, and the result is underpayment of tax of at least $5,000 ($10,000 for most corporations). The amount of the penalty is dependent upon the percentage of overvaluation:[34]

Valuation Overstatement	*Penalty*
200% or more but less than 400% of the correct valuation	20% of the underpayment of tax
At least 400% of the correct valuation	40% of the underpayment of tax

Failure to file the information returns, discussed earlier, on dividend income, interest income, income tax withheld, and other required information returns also incurs a penalty. The general rule is that the penalty is $50 per failure, up to a maximum penalty of $250,000 per calendar year. Where the failure was the result of intentional disregard of the requirements, the penalty will be the greater of $100 per failure or a specific percentage of the total amounts not reported (generally 5% or 10%). There is also a $50-per-failure penalty for not supplying a taxpayer's identification number unless there is reasonable cause. The maximum for that is also $100,000.[35]

There is also a penalty of 20% of certain substantial understatements of tax. For the penalty to apply, the understatement must be at least the greater of 10% of the correct tax or $5,000 for an individual (or $10,000 for a corporation). Interest on tax shelter deficiencies in excess of $1,000 is at 120% of the rate otherwise charged. If a tax shelter is not involved, this 20% penalty can be avoided by either sufficient disclosure of the matter in the tax return or by having "substantial authority" for the tax position taken.[36]

[33]IRC Sec. 6662(b).
[34]The same penalty structure applies to substantial estate or gift-tax undervaluations.
[35]IRC Secs. 6721 and 6722.
[36]IRC Sec. 6662(d)(2).

Finally, there is a *civil fraud* penalty that applies if any part of a deficiency is due to fraud. This penalty is 75% of the deficiency attributable to fraud.[37]

As noted, penalties, unlike interest, are never deductible.

19.17 The Statute of Limitations

In general, the IRS has three years from the date a tax return is due (or the date filed, if filed after the due date) within which to audit the return and assess any deficiencies.[38] The taxpayer has the same period within which to file a claim for refund if it is believed that too much tax was paid.

There is an exception when any part of the deficiency was due to fraud.[39] There is no time limit on assessment of a deficiency if the taxpayer committed fraud. The burden of showing, by a preponderance of the evidence, that there was fraud rests upon the government.

Criminal fraud is different from civil fraud. Penalties for criminal fraud are not based on the amount of tax involved; they consist of fines and/or imprisonment. The government must prove its case in a criminal tax matter beyond a reasonable doubt, as in any other criminal proceeding. Accusations of criminal fraud are very serious and require the attention of competent legal defense counsel. Criminal fraud penalties can run as high as $100,000 ($500,000 for a corporation), depending upon the offense, *and* up to five years in jail.

The statute of limitations on these is normally six years from the date of commission of the criminal act.[40] In a tax offense, this would commonly mean six years from the date of the filing of the return.

There are some exceptions to the general three-year tax deficiency rule. A six-year statute of limitations applies if the taxpayer fails to report 25% or more of gross income.[41] It matters not that the omission was completely innocent. If the taxpayer's return is fraudulent, there is no statute of limitations on assessing deficiencies. In 1949, the government assessed a deficiency (plus interest, plus a 50% civil fraud penalty) on a 1924 return when it was able to show that part of the deficiency was due to fraud.[42]

A taxpayer may have to pay additional tax after filing the return—usually as the result of an

[37]IRC Sec. 6663(b).
[38]IRC Sec. 6501(a).
[39]IRC Sec. 6501(c).
[40]IRC Sec. 6531.
[41]IRC Sec. 6501(e).
[42]*Reuben D. Silliman* (CA2 1955), 47 AFTR 300, 55-1 USTC 9290.

IRS audit. At that time, only a little of the three-year period may remain, since the time is measured from the date the tax return was filed. If the deficiency is paid, there may be only a short time to file a claim for refund. Consequently, the taxpayer is allowed to file a claim for refund at any time within two years from the date of paying the tax, regardless of the other three-year statute of limitations.[43]

When either the taxpayer or the government adopts an inconsistent position, resulting in an item being twice taxed, twice deducted, or something similar, a special exception to the statute of limitations may be invoked.

19.18 Preparer Responsibilities and Penalties

The federal government does not license people who prepare tax returns for others, although at least two states (California and Oregon) do. It does recognize certain individuals (CPAs and attorneys by virtue of their professional status, and "enrolled agents" by virtue of either their IRS experience or passage of a special examination) as being qualified to represent taxpayers before the IRS in connection with the audit of tax returns.[44]

For return preparers who are paid for their services, the tax law provides certain requirements applicable to all, whether CPA, attorney, enrolled agent, or completely unlicensed.[45] Penalties are provided for failing to sign a return properly as preparer,[46] for failing to provide the taxpayer with a copy of the return prior to his signing it,[47] for failure to retain a copy of the return or a list of clients,[48] and for negligence in preparing returns or willful disregard of rules and regulations.[49] The penalties range from $25 each for failing to sign a return or furnish the taxpayer with a copy to $1,000 for a willful attempt to under-state tax.[50] A preparer who misrepresents his qualifications, guarantees refunds, or is negligent in his or her work may be the subject of a court-issued injunction barring such person from further misconduct or even prohibiting future preparation of income tax returns.[51]

Anyone who participates in providing tax return information that he or she knows will result in an understatement of tax may be subject to a $1,000 civil penalty ($10,000 if the taxpayer is a corporation) in addition to possible criminal penalties.[52]

It may thus be understandable why tax return preparers demonstrate some conservatism in their dealings with the IRS. At the same time, there is a sharp difference between "negligence" and merely disagreeing with the IRS. A preparer who has "reasonable" support for the advice given to a taxpayer relative to a position taken on a tax return should be able successfully to resist imposition of any penalties.

In the next two chapters, the concern will be with tax research and the use of that research to solve tax problems and to provide "reasonable support" and "substantial authority" for positions taken on returns.

19.19 Conclusion

The tax controversy process is an essential part of the ongoing evolution of the U.S. tax law. That IRS agents frequently assert larger deficiencies than are ultimately determined to be due, or that tax deficiencies are asserted on a majority of returns audited, is not an indictment of the IRS, of taxpayers, or of the system. It is only after controversy that the exact application of the whole of the tax law to one specific factual situation can sometimes be determined. The right to take even the government to court is dear to the traditions of this country. The maintenance of that right is essential to the credibility, viability, and effectiveness of the tax system.

[43]IRC Sec. 6511.
[44]Representing taxpayers before the IRS does not include representation of taxpayers as an advocate in Tax Court proceedings. Attorneys can do the latter, as can others who pass a special examination given by the Tax Court.
[45]IRC Sec. 7701(a)(36) defines an "income tax return preparer."
[46]IRC Sec. 6695(b). Signing properly includes providing an appropriate identification number.
[47]IRC Sec. 6695(a).
[48]IRC Sec. 6695(d).
[49]IRC Sec. 6694. Negligence includes taking an undisclosed position for which there is not a realistic possibility of sucess in the event of a controversy. See IRS Notice 90–20 and Rev. Proc. 90–16.
[50]IRC Sec. 6694(a).
[51]IRC Sec. 7407.
[52]IRC Sec. 6701.

TRUE-FALSE QUESTIONS

State whether each of the following statements is true or false. For each *false* answer, reword the statement to make it *true*.

T F 1. The administration of the income tax laws for the United States is the responsibility of the Department of Justice.

T F 2. For most individuals, the federal income tax is due on April 15 each year.

T F 3. Individuals who are out of the United States on the date when their tax return would normally be due are eligible for an automatic six-month extension for filing and paying the tax.

T F 4. A person who is not outside the United States on the tax return due date can receive a four-month extension for filing and paying the tax by filing a Form 4868 by the regular due date.

T F 5. The IRS can grant extensions of time for filing, with a maximum of six months, where the taxpayer has a good reason for the extension.

T F 6. Corporate income tax returns are due on the fifteenth day of the third month following the end of a fiscal year.

T F 7. Persons who are self-employed are required to make monthly prepayments of their estimated federal income tax.

T F 8. If a person is an employee, had no tax liability for last year, and expects no tax liability for the current year, he or she can file an exemption certificate so that the employer will not withhold any federal income tax from the salary or wages.

T F 9. An office audit is normally conducted in the IRS office nearest to the taxpayer.

T F 10. Tax returns are selected for audit entirely on the basis of random samples.

T F 11. An IRS field audit is conducted at the taxpayer's home or place of business and the taxpayer has no appeal from the auditor's conclusion regarding the correctness of the return.

T F 12. A request for technical advice is a procedure whereby the taxpayer requests the National Office of the IRS for an informal determination as to the applicability of tax law to a particular factual situation.

T F 13. A "thirty-day letter" is the term given to a notice which is sent to a taxpayer advising that the agent has proposed a deficiency which is to be paid or appealed within thirty days.

T F 14. A "ninety-day letter" is a statutory notice of deficiency which must be appealed within ninety days unless the taxpayer wants to agree to the deficiency and pay the tax.

T F 15. After a taxpayer receives a "ninety-day letter" the only course of action to take is to file a petition with the Tax Court.

T F 16. If a taxpayer decides to go to court and wants a jury trial, the suit must be brought in a federal district court.

T F 17. If a taxpayer litigates a case in Tax Court and loses, an appeal may be made directly to the Supreme Court of the United States.

T F 18. The Tax Court has a small-case procedure for disputes of less than $10,000 and there is no appeal from the decision reached in that forum.

T F 19. If a taxpayer files a tax return late, without reasonable cause for doing so, the penalty will be an additional 25% of the amount of tax owed.

T F 20. The penalty for civil tax fraud is an amount equal to 50% of the tax deficiency.

PROBLEMS

Problem 19-1. Betsy Rains is self-employed. Her taxable income fluctuates widely from year to year, and is very difficult to estimate in advance. She wants to be sure to avoid any interest or penalties for failure to pay an adequate amount of estimated income tax and self-employment tax. Advise Betsy of an approach which will assure her of prepaying a sufficient amount to avoid any interest or penalty.

Problem 19-2. Omar McFee has just had his tax return audited by the IRS. The auditor wants to assess $2,000 of additional tax because Omar claimed home office expenses even though his employer had provided an office at the employer's premises. Outline the steps that might be followed in an attempt to settle the dispute in his favor.

Problem 19-3. Betsy Allen failed to file a tax return on April 15. She did not file a request for extension. She finally got around to sending all of the necessary forms, properly completed, to the appropriate IRS office on November 20. She had no good reason for the delay except that she is a habitual procrastinator.

Her tax return, as filed, showed that she owed an additional tax of $500. She sent a check for $500 with the return.

(a) Will Betsy have to pay any interest as the result of this late filing? If so, is the interest deductible on her income tax return for the year it was paid?

(b) Will Betsy incur any penalty for the late filing? If so, how much? Is it deductible?

(c) Assume that Betsy had a refund of $100 coming on her taxes. Would there be a penalty for late filing? Explain.

Problem 19-4. James Callahan is a self-employed bookstore operator. He understands the procedures for withholding social security and income tax for employees. Since he withdraws $800 from the business each month for personal and living expenses, he wonders if he should treat himself as an employee.

(a) Explain the procedure for paying his taxes in advance.

(b) How would the filing and payment procedures differ if James were to incorporate the business?

Problem 19-5. The U.S. federal income tax system is called a self-assessment system. What does that mean? How does the system differ from alternative systems that are not self-assessment systems?

Problem 19-6. Edna Quasar expects to be traveling on business in Europe from April 1 until July 15. Normally, her tax return would be due on April 15. Edna does not believe that she can have all of the information gathered together for proper filing of her return before April 1. Explain what Edna should do, if anything, to postpone the filing date until after her return. Explain how she can avoid any penalties.

Problem 19-7. The Ace Roofing Company, a corporation, has a fiscal year that ends May 31.

(a) Barring any extensions, when is the tax return due for the corporation?

(b) Is the corporation eligible for an automatic extension? If so, for how long and how may it be obtained?

Problem 19-8. Gil and Mary Boston operate an unincorporated furnace and air-conditioning business. Gil takes care of all installations and repairs. Mary runs the office, makes appointments, and does all of the correspondence and bookkeeping. Last year they estimated their total tax liability, including social security tax, to be $8,000. Consequently, they made four quarterly estimated tax payments of $2,000 each. Upon completing their income tax return in April of this year, they determine that the total tax is $10,500, so they owe an additional $2,500.

(a) Assuming that they are not eligible for any of the exceptions for waiver of the underpayment penalty, what is the amount of their underpayment which will be used to calculate a penalty?

(b) How much would have been required for each quarterly installment to avoid any underpayment penalty, again assuming that none of the other exceptions will apply?

(c) Assume that the tax liability for the previous year had been $7,500. Would a penalty for underpayment be assessed? Explain.

Problem 19-9. You have just received a phone call from your tax client, Mr. Carter. He has received a notice that his tax return for the year before last will be audited. Not having seen the letter of notice, you are not certain if the audit is a field audit or an office audit.

(a) What difference does it make?

(b) Would the preparation for the audit be any different for one than the other?

Problem 19-10. For the following statements, determine whether they apply to the various levels of courts by choosing one or more of the following numbers: (1) Tax Court, (2) District Court, (3) U.S. Claims Court, (4) Circuit Court of Appeals, and (5) Supreme Court.

(a) Is a (are) court(s) of original jurisdiction.

(b) Must pay tax deficiency before going to this court(s).

(c) May elect to have a small-tax-disputes procedure for cases involving less than $10,000.

(d) A jury is available only in this court.

(e) This court hears only a few tax-related decisions each year.

PROBLEMS WITH AN ASTERISK REQUIRE ADDITIONAL RESEARCH.

Problem 19-11.* Your client, Ms. Shady, has just called you with the following question. "Last year I paid $800 each to several different people to perform odd jobs in my business. I wrote checks to them, so I feel that I have the documentation to support taking a deduction on my federal income tax return. However, I attended a business luncheon yesterday and the speaker was talking about an 'information return' which should be filed with the IRS where a person makes payments to a non-employee. Will you tell me more about this, including the circumstances under which I must make such a reporting and any penalties imposed if I do not comply." You look in your file for Ms. Shady and find that her business is a proprietorship, she files a Schedule C with her personal income tax return, and uses a calendar taxable year. The current date is March 10. The payments which she referred to in her question to you were for last year. Advise Ms. Shady.

APPENDIX 19-A

Amended Estimated Tax Schedule (Use if your estimated tax changes during the year.)

1	Amended estimated tax	1	
2a	Amount of 1989 overpayment chosen for credit to 1990 estimated tax and applied to date (2a)		
b	Estimated tax payments to date (2b)		
c	Add lines 2a and 2b	2c	
3	Unpaid balance (subtract line 2c from line 1) (see instructions D.1 and E on pages 1 and 2)	3	

1990 Estimated Tax Worksheet (Keep for Your Records—Do Not Send to Internal Revenue Service)

1	Enter amount of adjusted gross income you expect in 1990	1	
2	If you plan to itemize deductions, enter the estimated total of your deductions. If you do not plan to itemize deductions, see **Standard Deduction for 1990** on page 4. Enter your standard deduction here	2	
3	Subtract line 2 from line 1. Enter the result here	3	
4	Exemptions. Multiply $2,050 by the number of personal exemptions. If you can be claimed as a dependent on another person's 1990 return, your personal exemption is not allowed	4	
5	Subtract line 4 from line 3	5	
6	Tax. Figure your tax on line 5 by using the 1990 Tax Rate Schedules on page 4. DO NOT use the Tax Table or the Tax Rate Schedules in the 1989 Form 1040 Instructions	6	
7	Enter any additional taxes (see line 7 instructions)	7	
8	Add lines 6 and 7	8	
9	Credits (see line 9 instructions)	9	
10	Subtract line 9 from line 8. Enter the result, but not less than zero	10	
11	Self-employment tax. Estimate of 1990 net earnings from self-employment $ __________________ ; if $51,300 or more, enter $7,848.90; **if less, multiply the amount** by .153 (see line 11 instructions)	11	
12	Other taxes (see line 12 instructions)	12	
13a	Add lines 10 through 12	13a	
b	Earned income credit and credit from **Form 4136**	13b	
c	Total estimated tax. Subtract line 13b from line 13a. Enter the result, but not less than zero	13c	
14a	Enter 90% (66 ⅔% for farmers and fishermen) of line 13c (14a)		
b	Enter 100% of the tax shown on your 1989 tax return (14b)		
c	Enter the **smaller** of line 14a or 14b. This is your required annual payment	14c	
	Caution: Generally, if you do not prepay at least the amount on line 14c, you may be subject to a penalty for not paying enough estimated tax. To avoid a penalty, make sure your estimate on line 13c is as accurate as possible. If you are unsure of your estimate and line 14a is **smaller** than line 14b, you may want to pay up to the amount shown on line 14b. If you prefer, you may pay 100% of your estimated tax (line 13c). For more information, get Pub. 505.		
15	Income tax withheld and estimated to be withheld (including income tax withholding on pensions, annuities, certain deferred income, etc.) during 1990	15	
16	Subtract line 15 from line 14c. (**Note:** If line 13c minus line 15 is less than $500, you are not required to make estimated tax payments.) If you are applying an overpayment from 1989 to 1990 estimated tax, see instruction C.2 on page 1	16	
17	If the first payment you are required to make is due April 16, 1990, enter ¼ of line 16 (minus any 1989 overpayment that you are applying to this installment) here and on line 1 of your payment-voucher(s). You may round off cents to the nearest whole dollar	17	

APPENDIX 19-B

Form **1040-ES**

Department of the Treasury
Internal Revenue Service

1990
Payment-Voucher

Return this voucher with check or money order payable to the Internal Revenue Service. Please write your social security number and "1990 Form 1040-ES" on your check or money order. Please do not send cash. Enclose, but do not staple or attach, your payment with this voucher.
File only if you are making a payment of estimated tax.

OMB No. 1545-0087

(Calendar year—Due Jan. 15, 1991)

1 Amount of payment $ ____________ 2 Fiscal year filers enter year ending ____________ (month and year)	Please type or print	Your first name and initial	Your last name	Your social security number
		(If joint payment, complete for spouse) Spouse's first name and initial	Spouse's last name if different from yours	If joint payment, spouse's social security number
		Address (number and street)		
		City, state, and ZIP code		

For Paperwork Reduction Act Notice, see instructions on page 1.

APPENDIX 19-C

Form 870 (Rev. December 1983)	Department of the Treasury – Internal Revenue Service **Waiver of Restrictions on Assessment and Collection of Deficiency in Tax and Acceptance of Overassessment**	Date received by Internal Revenue Service

Names and address of taxpayers *(Number, street, city or town, State, ZIP code)*	Social security or employer identification number

Increase in Tax and Penalties

Tax year ended	Amount of tax	Penalty
	$	$
	$	$
	$	$

Decrease in Tax and Penalties

Tax year ended	Amount of tax	Penalty
	$	$
	$	$
	$	$

(For any remarks, see back of form)

Instructions

General Information

If you consent to the assessment of the deficiencies shown in this waiver, please sign and return the form in order to limit any interest charge and expedite the adjustment to your account. Your consent will not prevent you from filing a claim for refund *(after you have paid the tax)* if you later believe you are so entitled It will not prevent us from later determining, if necessary, that you owe additional tax; nor extend the time provided by law for either action.

We have agreements with State tax agencies under which information about Federal tax, including increases or decreases, is exchanged with the States. If this change affects the amount of your State income tax, you should file the required State form.

If you later file a claim and the Service disallows it, you may file suit for refund in a district court or in the United States Claims Court, but you may not file a petition with the United States Tax Court.

We will consider this waiver a valid claim for refund or credit of any overpayment due you resulting from any decrease in tax and penalties shown above, provided you sign and file it within the period established by law for making such a claim.

Who Must Sign

If you filed jointly, both you and your spouse must sign. If this waiver is for a corporation, it should be signed with the corporation name, followed by the signatures and titles of the corporate officers authorized to sign. An attorney or agent may sign this waiver provided such action is specifically authorized by a power of attorney which, if not previously filed, must accompany this form.

If this waiver is signed by a person acting in a fiduciary capacity *(for example, an executor, administrator, or a trustee)* Form 56, Notice Concerning Fiduciary Relationship, should, unless previously filed, accompany this form.

Consent to Assessment and Collection

I consent to the immediate assessment and collection of any deficiencies *(increase in tax and penalties)* and accept any overassessment *(decrease in tax and penalties)* shown above, plus any interest provided by law. I understand that by signing this waiver, I will not be able to contest these years in the United States Tax Court, unless additional deficiencies are determined for these years.

Signatures			
▶			Date
▶			Date
▶	By	Title	Date

Form 870 (Rev. 12-83)

Form 872 (Rev. January 1981)	Department of the Treasury — Internal Revenue Service **Consent to Extend the Time to Assess Tax**	In Reply Refer To: SSN or EIN

____
(Name(s))

taxpayer(s) of ____
(Number, Street, City or Town, State, ZIP Code)

and the District Director of Internal Revenue or Regional Director of Appeals consent and agree to the following:

(1) The amount of any Federal _______________ *(Kind of tax)* tax due on any return(s) made by or for the above taxpayer(s) for the period(s) ended ____

____,

may be assessed at any time on or before _______________ *(Expiration date)*. However, if a notice of deficiency in tax for any such period(s) is sent to the taxpayer(s) on or before that date, then the time for assessing the tax will be further extended by the number of days the assessment was previously prohibited, plus 60 days.

(2) This agreement ends on the earlier of the above expiration date or the assessment date of an increase in the above tax that reflects the final determination of tax and the final administrative appeals consideration. An assessment for one period covered by this agreement will not end this agreement for any other period it covers. Some assessments do not reflect a final determination and appeals consideration and therefore will not terminate the agreement before the expiration date. Examples are assessments of: (a) tax under a partial agreement; (b) tax in jeopardy; (c) tax to correct mathematical or clerical errors; (d) tax reported on amended returns; and (e) advance payments. In addition, unassessed payments, such as amounts treated by the Service as cash bonds and advance payments not assessed by the Service, will not terminate this agreement before the expiration date.

This agreement ends on the above expiration date regardless of any assessment for any period includible in a report to the Joint Committee on Taxation submitted under section 6405 of the Internal Revenue Code.

(3) The taxpayer(s) may file a claim for credit or refund and the Service may credit or refund the tax within 6 months after this agreement ends.

(SIGNATURE INSTRUCTIONS AND SPACE FOR SIGNATURE ARE ON THE BACK OF THIS FORM) Form 872 (Rev. 1-81)

MAKING THIS CONSENT WILL NOT DEPRIVE THE TAXPAYER(S) OF ANY APPEAL RIGHTS TO WHICH THEY WOULD OTHERWISE BE ENTITLED.

YOUR SIGNATURE HERE → ______________________________ ______________________ *(Date signed)*

SPOUSE'S SIGNATURE → ______________________________ ______________________ *(Date signed)*

TAXPAYER'S REPRESENTATIVE SIGN HERE → ______________________________ ______________________ *(Date signed)*

CORPORATE NAME → ______________________________

CORPORATE OFFICER(S) SIGN HERE
→ ______________________ ____________ *(Title)* ______________________ *(Date signed)*
→ ______________________ ____________ *(Title)* ______________________ *(Date signed)*

______________________________ **DISTRICT DIRECTOR OF INTERNAL REVENUE**

______________________________ **REGIONAL DIRECTOR OF APPEALS**

BY ______________________________ *(Signature and Title)* ______________________ *(Date signed)*

Instructions

If this consent is for income tax, self-employment tax, or FICA tax on tips and is made for any year(s) for which a joint return was filed, both husband and wife must sign the original and copy of this form unless one, acting under a power of attorney, signs as agent for the other. The signatures must match the names as they appear on the front of this form.

If this consent is for gift tax and the donor and the donor's spouse elected to have gifts to third persons considered as made one-half by each, both husband and wife must sign the original and copy of this form unless one, acting under a power of attorney, signs as agent for the other. The signatures must match the names as they appear on the front of this form.

If this consent is for Chapter 41, 42, or 43 taxes involving a partnership or is for a partnership return, only one authorized partner need sign.

If this consent is for Chapter 42 taxes, a separate Form 872 should be completed for each potential disqualified person, entity, or foundation manager that may be involved in a taxable transaction during the related tax year. See Revenue Ruling 75-391, 1975-2 C.B. 446.

If you are an attorney or agent of the taxpayer(s), you may sign this consent provided the action is specifically authorized by a power of attorney. If the power of attorney was not previously filed, please include it with this form.

If you are acting as a fiduciary (such as executor, administrator, trustee, etc.) and you sign this consent, attach Form 56, Notice Concerning Fiduciary Relationship, unless it was previously filed.

If the taxpayer is a corporation, sign this consent with the corporate name followed by the signature and title of the officer(s) authorized to sign.

Form **872** (Rev. 8-81)

APPENDIX 19-E (a)

Form 870-AD (Rev. December 1986)	DEPARTMENT OF THE TREASURY — INTERNAL REVENUE SERVICE OFFER OF WAIVER OF RESTRICTIONS ON ASSESSMENT AND COLLECTION OF DEFICIENCY IN TAX AND OF ACCEPTANCE OF OVERASSESSMENT	
SYMBOLS	NAME OF TAXPAYER	SSN or EIN

Pursuant to the provisions of section 6213(d) of the Internal Revenue Code of 1986, or corresponding provisions of prior internal revenue laws, the undersigned offers to waive the restrictions provided in section 6213(a) of the Internal Revenue Code of 1986, or corresponding provisions of prior internal revenue laws, and to consent to the assessment and collection of the following deficiencies with interest as provided by law. The undersigned offers also to accept the following overassessments as correct:

DEFICIENCIES (OVERASSESSMENTS)

YEAR ENDED	KIND OF TAX	TAX				
		$	$	$		
		$	$	$		
		$	$	$		
		$	$	$		
		$	$	$		
		$	$	$		

SIGNATURE OF TAXPAYER		DATE
SIGNATURE OF TAXPAYER		DATE
BY	TITLE	DATE

FOR INTERNAL REVENUE USE ONLY	DATE ACCEPTED FOR COMMISSIONER	SIGNATURE
	OFFICE	TITLE

(SEE REVERSE SIDE)

Form 870-AD (Rev. 12-86)

APPENDIX 19-E (b)

This offer is subject to acceptance for the Commissioner of Internal Revenue. It shall take effect as a waiver of restrictions on the date it is accepted. Unless and until it is accepted, it shall have no force or effect.

If this offer is accepted for the Commissioner, the case shall not be reopened in the absence of fraud, malfeasance, concealment or misrepresentation of material fact, an important mistake in mathematical calculation, deficiencies or overassessments resulting from adjustments made under Subchapters C and D of Chapter 63 concerning the tax treatment of partnership and subchapter S items determined at the partnership and corporate level, or excessive tentative allowances of carrybacks provided by law; and no claim for refund or credit shall be filed or prosecuted for the year(s) stated above other than for amounts attributed to carrybacks provided by law.

NOTE.—The execution and filing of this offer will expedite the above adjustment of tax liability. This offer, when executed and timely submitted, will be considered a claim for refund for the above overassessments, as provided in Revenue Ruling 68-65, C.B. 1968-1, 555. It will not, however, constitute a closing agreement under section 7121 of the Internal Revenue Code.

If this offer is executed with respect to a year for which a **JOINT RETURN OF A HUSBAND AND WIFE** was filed, it must be signed by both spouses unless one spouse, acting under a power of attorney, signs as agent for the other.

If the taxpayer is a corporation, the offer shall be signed with the corporate name followed by the signature and title of the officers authorized to sign.

This offer may be executed by the taxpayer's attorney or agent provided this action is specifically authorized by a power of attorney which, if not previously filed, must accompany the form.

Form **870-AD** (Rev. 12-86

20

tax research

There are many types of tax research. Research done in the U.S. Treasury Department may involve mathematical models of the U.S. economy. These are put together with the goal of projecting how the U.S. economy will react to different possible changes in the tax law. A different kind of research is done by a taxpayer's attorney in preparing a brief for the Tax Court. Still another type of research is done by a Ph.D. candidate who wants to impress the dissertation committee with scholarly achievement. There is the research done by a CPA to answer a tax question for a client. This can vary depending upon whether the question centers around planning for future events or is a matter of filing a tax return for last year. Also, there is research that a taxpayer may do in order to handle tax affairs more effectively.

In a way, all of these types of research deal with the same subject matter. This chapter will describe the source material used in tax research where the purpose is tax compliance and tax planning. For these purposes, it is usually necessary to focus on the tax law and its interpretation by taxpayers and the government.

20.1 The Statute

Appendix 20-A sketches the history of the U.S. income tax. There, the Sixteenth Amendment to the Constitution is pointed out as the starting point for the income tax that exists today. This amendment permitted Congress to levy a broad-based federal income tax. There have been many major changes since it began in 1913.

The U.S. tax law today is often referred to as the "Internal Revenue Code of 1986, as amended." It is one *title* in a comprehensive multivolume set of laws called the U.S. Statutes at Large. In 1954, the tax law was completely renumbered and revised. Since then, in lieu of rewriting the law as a whole, Congress has added, deleted, and changed the law within the framework of the structure created in 1954. In 1986 the Code was revised so much that Congress renamed the Code as the Internal Revenue Code of 1986.

The Code itself is subdivided as follows:

Subtitles (such as Subtitle A, Income Taxes, and Subtitle B, Estate and Gift Taxes).

Chapters (such as Chapter 1, Normal Taxes and Surtaxes).

Subchapters (such as Subchapter S, Tax Treatment of S Corporations and Their Shareholders).

Parts (such as Part II of Subchapter P, which discusses treatment of capital losses).

Subparts (such as Subpart F of Part III of Subchapter N of Chapter I of Subtitle A, which deals with controlled foreign corporations).

Sections (such as Sec. 1221, which defines a capital asset).

While subchapters, subparts, and so on, may be discussed in the literature, the basic unit of the Internal Revenue Code for research and citation purposes is the section. The other subdivisions are referred to as a shorthand way to cover a group of related sections. Thus, a reference to *Subchapter S* is an abbreviated way of referring to Secs. 1361 through 1379. If a tax question deals with the tax that an S corporation pays on passive income,[1] the reference or citation would be to Sec. 1375 of the Internal Revenue Code (sometimes abbreviated to IRC Sec. 1375), with no mention of Subchapter S (or Chapter 1). If a person wanted to refer to some specific part of Sec. 1375 as authority for a specific statement, that subunit of the section would be cited.[2]

Figure 20-1 is the full and complete Sec. 1375 as it existed at the time this book went to press. The arrow in the left margin has been added for purposes of the following example.

Assume that a person wanted to cite the authority for the following statement: "An S corporation will pay no tax on passive income at the corporate level if it has a loss for the year." Section 1375 does provide that rule, but the whole section takes an entire page. (Some IRC sections take far more space.) Merely to cite "IRC Sec. 1375" would assume that anyone wanting to find that specific portion of Sec. 1375 would be energetic and astute enough to read the entire page carefully. Such an assumption is neither prudent nor good tax scholarship. Tax citations should always attempt to lead the reader to the exact place where the writer wants the reader to look. Thus, a better citation would be "IRC Sec. 1375(b)(1)(B)." That portion of subsection (b) contains the loss rule. However, it, in turn, requires that you also look at other provisions, such as Sec. 63(a) and Sec. 248.

20.2 Regulations

Many tax questions can be resolved by reading the Internal Revenue Code. Its language is often a marvel of precision. However, there are times when the language is not clear. At such times, it may be possible to find an answer in the Regulations. Sometimes, Congress has delegated the specific rule making to the Treasury Department. The statute will simply read, "pursuant to regulations to be issued by the Secretary."[3] This refers to the Secretary of the Treasury, under which name regulations are issued.

Like the IRC, which is just the Internal Revenue title in the U.S. Code, the Treasury Department Regulations are one part of a multivolume set called the Code of Federal Regulations. The concern here, of course, is only with regulations dealing with tax matters.

Regulations sometimes are described as being "interpretative" or "legislative." The interpretative regulations cover those IRC provisions which the Treasury Department (of which, remember, the IRS is a subunit) feels need clarification, interpretation, or elaboration in order to be better understood by taxpayers and IRS personnel.[4]

The "legislative" regulations are those which Congress has directed the Treasury Department to issue.[5] Unless clearly contrary to the underlying statute, such regulations tend to have the force and effect of law itself, hence the appellation "legislative." Interpretative regulations carry great weight in determining what the law means, but lack the finality of the statute or the legislative regulations. Taxpayers have, on occasion, been successful in challenging such regulations in the courts.[6]

Regulations are cited by section number. In general, the numbering of regulations will include the number of the IRC section to which they apply. A regulation corresponding to IRC Sec. 1502 is Reg. 1.1502-44. It is reproduced in Fig. 20-3. The prefix (1.) means that this is a regulation dealing with *income tax.* The numbers immediately following the prefix (1502) will always correspond to the statute number to which they relate—but it will only be coincidental if the following subsection numbers correspond to subsection numbers of the Code. Therefore, the balance of the regulation number (-44) does not relate to any particular number contained in the numbering system of the statute.

IRC Sec. 1501 permits an affiliated group of corporations to file a consolidated income tax return. As noted above, Sec. 1502 (Fig. 20-2) is the congressional mandate to the Treasury Department to prepare regulations to explain how taxpayers should comply. Figure 20-3 illustrates Reg. 1.1502-44(a) and (b). There the subject is the treatment of the percentage depletion deduction and the related limitation upon that deduction for the members of the consolidated group. Note that it was necessary for the regulations to contain a definition of "adjusted consolidated taxable income," which is in Reg. 1.1502-44(b). Note that the words used in Sec. 1502 clearly delegate the rule-making authority to the "Secretary." Thus, there is a substantive difference between such legis-

[1]This is the subject of Chapter 11.
[2]References throughout are to the Internal Revenue Code sections.
[3]For example, see IRC Sec. 1502 (Fig. 20-2). Instead of writing rules for consolidated income tax returns in the Code, Congress delegated that responsibility to the Treasury Department.

[4]For example, the deduction for the exemption amount is allowed by IRC Sec. 151 and dependents are defined by IRC Sec. 152. The statute contains rather detailed rules. Nevertheless, the regulations contain some further definitions, such as for "student." See Treas. Reg. 1.151-3(b).
[5]For example, the consolidated return regulations mentioned in footnote 3.
[6]See, *e.g.*, the Supreme Court decision in *U.S.* v. *Vogel Fertilizer Co.*, 49 AFTR2d 82-491, 82-1 USTC 9134, holding Treasury Regulations Section 1.1563-1(a)(3) invalid.

FIGURE 20-1

IRC §1375. TAX IMPOSED WHEN PASSIVE INVESTMENT INCOME OF CORPORATION HAVING SUBCHAPTER C EARNINGS AND PROFITS EXCEEDS 25 PERCENT OF GROSS RECEIPTS.

(a) General Rule.—If for the taxable year an S corporation has—

(1) subchapter C earnings and profits at the close of such taxable year, and

(2) gross receipts more than 25 percent of which are passive investment income, then there is hereby imposed a tax on the income of such corporation for such taxable year. Such tax shall be computed by multiplying the excess net passive income by the highest rate of tax specified in section 11(b).

(b) Definitions.—For purposes of this section—

(1) Excess net passive income.—

(A) In general.—Except as provided in subparagraph (B), the term "excess net passive income" means an amount which bears the same ratio to the net passive income for the taxable year as—

(i) the amount by which the passive investment income for the taxable year exceeds 25 percent of the gross receipts for the taxable year, bears to

(ii) the passive investment income for the taxable year.

→ (B) Limitation.—The amount of the excess net passive income for any taxable year shall not exceed the amount of the corporation's taxable income for [1]such taxable year as determined under section 63(a)—

(i) without regard to the deductions allowed by part VIII of subchapter B (other than the deduction allowed by section 248, relating to organization expenditures), and

(ii) without regard to the deduction under section 172.

(2) Net passive income.—The term "net passive income" means—

(A) passive investment income, reduced by

(B) the deductions allowable under this chapter which are directly connected with the production of such income (other than deductions allowable under section 172 and part VIII of subchapter B).

(3) Passive investment income; etc.—The terms "subchapter C earnings and profits", "passive investment income", and "gross receipts" shall have the same respective meanings as when used in paragraph (3) of section 1362(d).

(4) Coordination with section 1374.—Notwithstanding paragraph (3), the amount of passive investment income shall be determined by not taking into account any recognized built-in gain or loss of the S corporation for any taxable year in the recognition period. Terms used in the preceding sentence shall have the same respective meanings as when used in section 1374.

(c) [2]Credits Not Allowable.—No credit shall be allowed under part IV of subchapter A of this chapter (other than section 34) against the tax imposed by subsection (a).

(d) Waiver of Tax in Certain Cases.—If the S corporation establishes to the satisfaction of the Secretary that—

(1) it determined in good faith that it had no subchapter C earnings and profits at the close of a taxable year, and

(2) during a reasonable period of time after it was determined that it did have subchapter C earnings and profits at the close of such taxable year such earnings and profits were distributed.

the Secretary may waive the tax imposed by subsection (a) for such taxable year.

FIGURE 20-2

[¶34,365] CODE SEC. 1502. REGULATIONS.

The Secretary shall prescribe such regulations as he may deem necessary in order that the tax liability of any affiliated group of corporations making a consolidated return and of each corporation in the group, both during and after the period of affiliation, may be returned, determined, computed, assessed, collected, and adjusted, in such manner as clearly to reflect the income-tax liability and the various factors necessary for the determination of such liability, and in order to prevent avoidance of such tax liability.

FIGURE 20-3

Reg. §1.1502-44 Percentage depletion for independent producers and royalty owners. (TD 7725, filed 9-30-80.)

(a) In general. The sum of the percentage depletion deductions for the taxable year for all oil or gas property owned by all members, plus any carryovers under section 613A(d)(1) or paragraph (d) of this section from a prior taxable year, may not exceed 65 percent of the group's adjusted consolidated taxable income (under paragraph (b) of this section) for the consolidated return year.

(b) Adjusted consolidated taxable income. For purposes of this section, adjusted consolidated taxable income is an amount (not less than zero) equal to the group's consolidated taxable income determined without—

(1) Any depletion with respect to an oil or gas property (other than a gas property with respect to which the depletion allowance for all production is determined pursuant to section 613A(b)) for which percentage depletion would exceed cost depletion in the absence of the depletable quantity limitations contained in section 613A(c)(1) and (6) and the consolidated taxable income limitation contained in paragraph (a) of this section,

(2) Any consolidated net operating loss carryback to the consolidated return year under §1.1502-21, and

(3) Any consolidated net capital loss carryback to the consolidated return year under §1.1502-22.

lative regulations and interpretative regulations.[7] The complete Sec. 1502 regulations contain approximately 80 pages.

20.3 Rulings

Regulations are issued by the Treasury Department. A subunit, the IRS, also interprets the IRC and the regulations. The IRS usually finds it necessary to make interpretations of the statute before Treasury has even proposed regulations.[8] The IRS must design tax forms, audit tax returns, and settle tax controversies within certain time constraints. Also, specific, detailed questions and problems arise from the day-to-day administration of the tax law.[9] To help with these situations, the IRS issues *Revenue Rulings* to guide both taxpayers and IRS personnel. Revenue Rulings usually involve an interpretation of the law and/or application of the rules to a specific set of facts. A typical Revenue Ruling is reproduced as Appendix 20-B. *Revenue Procedures,* on the other hand, usually deal with administrative or procedural questions, such as due dates, applicable forms, which IRS office to send certain forms, etc. A typical Revenue Procedure is reproduced as Appendix 20-C. In Chapter 19 we discussed the procedure of seeking technical advice from the IRS. When advice is sought in connection with a pending transaction rather than in connection with an audit, the IRS may issue a "letter ruling." These are binding only upon the taxpayer to whom they are issued, hence they are "private," although they are published after removal of the taxpayer's identity. An example of such a ruling is shown in Appendix 20-D.

Various forms of *Information Releases* are also issued from time to time as the need arises. The IRS also announces, periodically, which of the "regular" Tax Court decisions it will follow (called *acquiescence*) and which decisions it will not follow (called *nonacquiescence*).[10] It does not announce a position in all cases, however.

The Revenue Rulings tend to be based upon private rulings or technical advice previously issued, but are given more attention and review for policy implications at higher levels within IRS. They appear in the *Internal Revenue Bulletin* (a weekly publication of IRS) together with a notice that they do not have the force and effect of Treasury Regulations.[11]

Rulings are relied upon, of course, because they do represent the considered opinion of the policymaking people within the IRS. In dealings with lower-level personnel in the IRS, Revenue Rulings and Revenue Procedures are given as much weight as though they were the statute itself.

[7]Note, however, that regulations are never labeled with these terms. A researcher must discern from the language of the Code which of these apply in a given situation.

[8]Regulations on a new statute are usually issued in a *proposed* form first. This gives the public, tax practitioners, taxpayers, and interested groups an opportunity to respond, giving the Treasury Department their point of view. When regulations become "final," they are considered a more permanent part of the body of law than are Revenue Rulings or other pronouncements of the IRS.

[9]Sometimes questions and problems arise which were not foreseen by the writers of regulations. Therefore, there is a further need for a procedure, such as the issuance of Revenue Rulings, to provide official guidance on such matters. However, rulings do not have as much authority as the regulations.

[10]The IRS is not obligated to follow decisions of the Tax Court *in other similar cases.* It must, of course, abide by the Tax Court's decision in that specific case, although an appeal might be made to the Circuit Court. An *acquiescence* or *nonacquiescence* serves as a public, official announcement of the IRS's position. This is important to taxpayers and tax practitioners because it serves notice that the IRS will or will not follow the decision in subsequent (although similar) circumstances.

[11]The *Internal Revenue Bulletin* is published weekly as a pamphlet. A subscription can be purchased from the U.S. Government Printing Office.

Further, in determining whether a taxpayer or the preparer of a taxpayer's return has been negligent in taking a position, the IRS will treat one of its own rulings as a statement of the tax law unless some reasonable support can be produced for an opposing position. However, as mentioned in the Chapter 19 discussion of tax controversy, the Appeals Office has a tendency, unless there are policy considerations to the contrary, to look to the litigating chances of the taxpayer's position and not just to the positions set forth in IRS rulings.

An example of a citation to a Revenue Ruling is: "Rev. Rul. 77-271, 1977-2 CB 116." This means Revenue Ruling number 271 issued in 1977. (The numbers begin with number one at the beginning of each year.) The remainder of the citation indicates where the ruling can be found. It was published in Vol. 1977-2 of a Government Printing Office publication called *Internal Revenue Cumulative Bulletin,* at page 116. The *Cumulative Bulletin* (abbreviated *CB*) is published two or three times each year.[12] It is a hardback volume for permanent reference. If a ruling is cited before the *CB* volume has been printed, the corresponding Government Printing Office publication citation might be "IRB 1977-32, 10." This means that Revenue Ruling 77-271 was published in the weekly *Internal Revenue Bulletin,* Number 32 for 1977, at page 10. The *Cumulative Bulletin* consolidates the weekly bulletins for the time period that it covers (usually six months) and is thus the preferred citation whenever possible. Many libraries destroy the weekly bulletins, which do not have a hard cover, after the related *CB* has been published.

20.4 Court Decisions

There are many courts that may try a tax dispute. The Tax Court, federal District Courts, and U.S. Claims Court are all courts of original jurisdiction.[13] In addition, Circuit Courts, the Court of Appeals—Federal Circuit, and the Supreme Court may hear cases on appeal. (See Fig. 19-2.)

All court decisions, except the small claims division of the Tax Court, become a matter of public record and a part of our tax laws. It is frequently important to refer to the text of a court decision to learn how the court interpreted various parts of the tax statute and applied the law to particular facts.

For purposes of the following discussion, the court decisions have been divided into three groups:

1. Bound volumes of "regular" Tax Court decisions.[14] These are published by the Government Printing Office (GPO). A Tax Court decision will usually be cited with the name of the taxpayer, the volume of the GPO Tax Court reports in which it appears, and either the number of the case or the page in that volume where the case starts, or both. Thus, *John F. Nutt Est.,* 52 TC 484, can be found in Volume 52 of *Tax Court Reports* published by the Government Printing Office, at page 484. The index to Volume 52 in either P-H's or CCH's loose-leaf Tax Court report would cross-reference the case in those respective volumes, also.
2. Tax Court decisions that the Court does not deem to have much precedential value are issued as Memorandum decisions and are not published by the Government Printing Office.[15] They are commonly cited as TC Memo, with the year and case number. Thus, *Louise Owen,* TC Memo 1950-300, means that the *Owen* case was a memo decision in 1950, and was number 300 that year. Both P-H and CCH publish bound volumes of Tax Court Memo decisions. They both index *Owen* with a paragraph reference (the P-H reference being 50,300). They would also show the Tax Court decision number so that a researcher could find the case in either of their volumes with the number 1950-300.
3. All other court decisions in federal tax matters are contained in either *American Federal Tax Reports* (AFTR) and *American Federal Tax Reports,* Second Series (AFTR2d), published by Prentice-Hall, or *United States Tax Cases* (USTC), published by Commerce Clearing House. Tax cases can also be found, together with federal nontax cases, in other law book series, primarily those published by West Publishing Co. The details of those citations will not be covered here.

A proper citation should always include the court that rendered the decision. The citation 52 TC 484 requires no further indication because such a reference is for a Tax Court decision. But the citation 41 AFTR2d 78-604 reveals only that it was not issued by the Tax Court. It does not indicate that it was decided by the U.S. District Court for the Middle District of Alabama, Southern Division. A more complete cite would be *Enterprise Banking Company* v. *U.S.* (DC. Ala 1977),

[12]A subscription to the *IRB,* mentioned in footnote 11, does not include a copy of the *CB,* which may also be purchased from the GPO. Revenue Rulings, Revenue Procedures, and other IRS announcements will also be received weekly by subscribers to a commercial tax service such as P-H *Federal Taxes* or CCH *Standard Federal Tax Reporter.*

[13]See the discussion in Chapter 19.

[14]A "regular" decision is one that covers some aspect of the law not previously covered by the Court in depth. They are contrasted to "memorandum" decisions, discussed shortly. Note that prior to 1943 the Tax Court was called the Board of Tax Appeals (BTA).

[15]A case may be deemed to have little precedential value, for example, if it deals with some issue not generally applicable to other taxpayers, such as where the issue was whether a taxpayer had sufficient evidence or documentation to support some itemized deduction.

41 AFTR2d 78-604.[16] Technically, this is both the *name* and the citation for the case. The name alone might permit a researcher to find the case *if* the appropriate index volume were at hand. Sometimes it is not. Also, a case may appear in more than one printed volume. A researcher having a series other than AFTR2d might have difficulty. Therefore, citations to more than one series are not uncommon. If a writer is trying to persuade someone, the citations used should be to publications available to the reader whenever possible.

For example, *Corn Products Refining Co.* v. *Comm.* (S. Ct. 1955), 350 U.S. 46, 76 S. Ct. 20, 100 L. Ed. 29, 47 AFTR 1789, 55-2 USTC 9746 is a complete name and citation. From it, the following is revealed:

1. The taxpayer was *Corn Products Refining Co.* Sometimes it is appropriate to use a short name for the case (e.g., *Corn Products*), since in tax litigation the other party is always the government. (Here, "Comm." refers to the Commissioner of IRS.)
2. The case may be found in five different places:
   a. Volume 350 of the *United States Supreme Court Reports* (published by the Government Printing Office) at page 46;
   b. Volume 76 of the *Supreme Court Reporter* (published by West Publishing Co.) at page 20;
   c. Volume 100 of the *Lawyers' Edition* (published by Lawyers' Co-operative Publishing Co.) at page 29;
   d. Volume 47 of *American Federal Tax Reports* (published by Prentice-Hall) at page 1789; and
   e. Volume 55-2 of *United States Tax Cases* (published by Commerce Clearing House) at paragraph 9746.
3. The case was decided by the Supreme Court in 1955.[17]

20.5 Tax Treatises

Tax treatises are scholarly works dealing with the tax law. Authors analyze and interpret the tax law. Generally, such works contain only a minimum of primary source data.[18] Some of the leading treatises include[19]

Bittker and Eustice, *Federal Income Taxation of Corporations and Shareholders*, 3rd ed. (Boston: Warren, Gorham & Lamont, 1979).

Rhoades, *Income Taxation of Foreign Related Transactions* (New York: Matthew Bender & Co.).

Merten's Law of Federal Income Taxation (Wilmette, Ill.: Callaghan & Co.).

Willis, Pennell, and Postlewaite, *Partnership Taxation*, 3rd ed. (Colorado Springs: Shepard's—McGraw-Hill, 1983).

20.6 Tax Services

All of the primary source material—statute, regulations, rulings, cases—plus editorial interpretation and information retrieval indexing are pulled together in a unique tax tool, the tax service. Three standard tax services are published by, respectively, Prentice-Hall (P-H), Commerce Clearing House (CCH), and Research Institute of America (RIA).[20] These are kept current through an ingenious system of weekly replacement and addition pages. Kept up to date and used properly, such services can provide answers to most routine tax problems. The tax services differ, but there are some common materials included in all.

First, there is the full text of the Internal Revenue Code, in a separate volume. The Regulations, on the other hand, are scattered through the volumes of the services. Indexed like an encyclopedia, the services contain in one place an integration of Internal Revenue Code, Regulations, rulings, court decisions, and editorial comment. Usually, the rulings and court decisions are merely listed as items relevant to a particular topic. At best, they are only summarized briefly rather than reported in full text.

The key to effective use of a tax service is a methodical approach to a research problem:

1. Consult the topical index.
2. Read the paragraphs referred to by the index.
3. Refer to new developments by cross-referencing the paragraph number to the New Matters volume.[21]

Sometimes a little imagination may be required to find the index heading under which a problem may be listed. This relates partly to one's

[16]There is an advantage to having the year of the decision shown as part of the citation. Here, the reference to 41 AFTR2d 78-604 does mean that the decision will be found in the bound volume for the year 1978. However, the decision was rendered on December 5, 1977. Inclusion of the date, which does not require much space, can be helpful to the researcher by providing some immediate indication of how old or new the case may be.

[17]Sometimes the court and date will be printed immediately following the name of the case, and sometimes after the last citation. Either method is acceptable.

[18]Primary sources in tax law are the Code, Regulations and other IRS announcements, and court cases.

[19]There are annual or more frequent supplements to these works.

[20]P-H: *Federal Taxes 2nd;* CCH: *Standard Federal Tax Reporter;* RIA: *Tax Coordinator—2nd.* These are not the only tax services available, but are those most likely to be in a college or business library.

[21]Admittedly, this is an oversimplification. Many leading universities with graduate degree programs in accounting and/or tax devote an entire course to tax research.

ability to think in tax terms—an ability that is developed with experience.

In addition to the topical index and the cross-reference table to current developments,[22] a tax service usually has other indexes.

1. There is a list of court decisions by name, indicating the paragraph number of the service in which the decision is mentioned or discussed, as well as the citation for the decision. If the name of a decision is known but not the citation, this index can save a great deal of time in searching.
2. There are finding lists for code sections, regulations, and rulings. In tax administration and in tax articles, a ruling may be cited without specific reference. It may be desirable to find the ruling, plus an editorial discussion of its meaning and use. A finding list will help a researcher to find the ruling more quickly. One advantage of a tax service is that *all* rulings on a particular point are likely to be included. Therefore, a researcher may find rulings contrary to one cited by an author or an adversary in a tax dispute in the same general location as the one being cited.
3. Finally, there is an index to tax articles. This is arranged by the same paragraph numbers as the text of the service. Frequently, a well-researched and well-written article on a topic may greatly help to clarify a problem of current concern.

Another important advantage of the loose-leaf tax services is that each contains editorial commentary. Reading of a statute, regulation, ruling, or case usually will not result in specific *planning* ideas being identified. Editorial commentary, on the other hand, frequently does suggest alternative strategies for planning financial activity, or alternative explanations or interpretations of the various rules.

20.7 Tax Handbooks

A tax service encompasses many volumes. All three of the services mentioned here (P-H, CCH, RIA) annually publish paperback condensations of the text material in the larger services. These can be useful tools for both the tax specialist and the neophyte. They are well indexed, so that a problem often can be clarified merely by finding the handbook discussion. They are also cross-indexed to the larger tax service, so that the handbook discussion will cite the paragraph number in the larger service where a more exhaustive analysis can be found.

Assume that a person wanted to know more about gambling loss deductions. The index of the P-H (1990) *Federal Tax Handbook,* under "Gambling" lists "losses" at paragraph 2211.[23] Turning to that paragraph reveals a short statement on the deduction. Included in that statement, however, are footnote references to the P-H *Federal Taxes* service. Footnote number 15 refers the reader to paragraph 1655.501 for a discussion of gambling losses. If the question involved the effect of a gambling loss upon a net operating loss carryback for a professional gambler, footnote number 16 refers the reader to paragraph 1725.09 of the larger service. There the reader will find references to Revenue Rulings and court decisions on that topic. Hence, a comprehensive discussion of the topic can be obtained using the *Handbook* as a starting point.

20.8 Beyond the Basic Service

Comprehensive though it is, a basic tax service can go only so far in a subject with such varied factual patterns as federal taxes. Beyond the basic service, a researcher still needs the *Cumulative Bulletins,*[24] the cases, a record of changes in the Internal Revenue Code, and a citator.[25]

20.9 Code Changes

The record of changes in the Internal Revenue Code is handled by a specialized Prentice-Hall service, with the appropriate title of *Cumulative Changes in the Internal Revenue Code and the Regulations.* It is sufficient here to mention this work only and leave a detailed consideration of its use to advanced study.

20.10 Citator

The *Prentice-Hall Citator* is a separate service, consisting of bound volumes plus a loose-leaf volume maintained on a current basis. Cases reported by Prentice-Hall are divided into the issues involved. The citator listing for a case is likewise divided by the issues involved. Thus, the case of *Bingham's Trust* v. *Commissioner,* 33 AFTR 842, which was decided by the Supreme Court in 1945, involved fifteen separate issues. In researching

[22]"Current developments" include not only the most recent rulings and court decisions, but proposed legislation. For taxpayers engaged in planning future transactions, particularly of a long-term nature, it is wise to consider possible changes in the statute that have been proposed by the Treasury Department, or others, and may be in congressional committee.

[23]The CCH handbook is called the *Master Tax Guide.* The RIA handbook is entitled *Master Federal Tax Manual.*

[24]The tax services only provide the full text of Revenue Rulings for the current year. Previous rulings are only summarized. The *CBs* are necessary for the full text of rulings of prior years.

[25]A citator is a list of cases plus subsequent litigation on the same point. See the discussion following.

that case, a person might be interested only in issue number 10. The *Prentice-Hall Citator* will list separately all those cases involving issue number 10 in which *Bingham* v. *Comm.* has been cited. For each case, it will indicate, with letter keys, the nature of the citation (whether the case cited was followed, distinguished, reversed, etc.). The listing for each case will be to the page in that opinion in which *Bingham* v. *Comm.* was mentioned. Obviously, the *Prentice-Hall Citator* makes it possible to do a thorough research job, even given a limited amount of time, because only the court decision related to the issue in question need be read.

The *CCH Citator* is part of the CCH regular service and cites cases without any identification of issues or information regarding whether the case was later followed, reversed, distinguished, etc. It consists of a complete list of all tax cases in alphabetical sequence, with citations and cross references.

In any event, no serious tax researcher should rely on a case or a ruling that has not been checked through the citator for current developments. From the citator, with one case as a starting point, dozens or even hundreds of cases pertinent to a specific issue can often be found, including perhaps one that will help dispose of the problem at hand.

20.11 Other Tax Publications

Tax magazines, proceedings of tax institutes and meetings, and similar publications allow access to the research and experience of others. The American Institute of CPA's *Tax Adviser,* the American Bar Association's *Tax Lawyer,* and *The Journal of Taxation* are three leading periodicals of this sort.

20.12 Computerized Tax Research

PHINET is a computerized tax research system developed and offered by subscription by Prentice-Hall. The computer data base includes the full Prentice-Hall Federal Tax Service plus the text of the Code, Regulations, Rulings, and cases. By a skillful use of selected words and phrases, a researcher can query the computer. For example, if a person were interested in knowing if there had ever been any cases involving taxpayers who claimed a deduction for payments to an astrologer for investment advice, the computer could be asked. (The last time we checked, there were none, but it could happen in the future if the stars are right.) This extremely powerful research tool is increasingly being used. It is enough for this introductory course that you know of its availability.

Lexis is a similar service offered by Mead Data Central. Westlaw is a similar computerized tax (and legal) research tool developed by West Publishing Co. Thus, on-line computer access to a full range of tax research materials is being achieved. It provides faster and more comprehensive access to basic source material. Some of the computerized systems are updated daily.

20.13 How to Evaluate Cases

The Internal Revenue Code is the basic source of the rules of tax accounting. Yet with its thousands of words there are more questions raised than answers provided. The Regulations are the Treasury Department's attempt to provide these answers. Some Regulations do an admirable job, some produce other results. For most tax research purposes, the Regulations and the Code constitute basic authority. Employees of the IRS will follow the Regulations, if they appear to be clear on a particular point, until the Treasury Department changes them.

Revenue Rulings also constitute basic authority within the Treasury Department. If a Ruling is "on all fours" with a situation, it is unlikely that Treasury Department personnel will ignore it.

The same is not necessarily true for court cases, however. Cases get to court in the first place only as the result of a dispute between a taxpayer and the Treasury Department. Where there is a constant stream of cases on the same basic issue (such as capital gain versus ordinary income on the sale of realty), there is apparently a prevailing policy in the Treasury Department that encourages such litigation.

In dealing with the IRS prior to litigation, the cases that furnish the most assistance are Tax Court cases in which the IRS has formally acquiesced. The congressional committee reports are of very little use unless the disagreement involves part of the statute not yet covered by Regulations. Tax Court cases in which the IRS has nonacquiesced are of no use to a taxpayer at the audit level and may indicate a Treasury Department desire for more litigation on a particular subject.

Where the Commissioner of IRS has neither acquiesced nor nonacquiesced in a Tax Court decision, IRS personnel will normally follow the case if the facts are nearly the same. District Court decisions, on the other hand, usually carry very little weight, unless the dispute involves a refund claim and the discussion is at the Appeals Office level. If the decision is from the local U.S. District Court, it may dispose of the argument. District Court decisions can also be useful to the taxpayer if they are the only ones on a particular point, and no Regulation or Ruling covers that precise point.

Decisions of the U.S. Claims Court (Court of Claims before 10-1-82) are not always given the weight they may deserve. This is because tax cases tried by this court are relatively few and many persons do not understand the function of this special court. However, in some areas, such as capital gains on realty, the U.S. Claims Court may have such carefully developed opinions that their decisions carry weight simply from the persuasive power of the reasoning.

The decisions of the U.S. Circuit Courts of Appeal carry substantial weight. This is especially true for circuit court decisions in the same circuit as the taxpayer who has a disagreement with IRS. Finally, of course, the decisions of the U.S. Supreme Court are the law of the land.

Unfortunately for the researcher, decisions do not always come in the fashion most useful for analysis. Tax Court and U.S. Claims Court decisions usually include a fairly comprehensive factual background of the dispute and a detailed court opinion. District Court decisions, on the other hand, vary considerably. If a jury verdict was involved, all that may be available might be the charge to the jury and a statement of the verdict. This is usually of limited value. Circuit Court and U.S. Supreme Court decisions are usually very comprehensive both with regard to the relevant facts and analysis of the law.

Since the objective in analyzing cases will usually be, in part, to find similarities between a taxpayer's facts and the favorable decisions, and differences between a taxpayer's facts and the unfavorable decisions, careful analysis of the facts becomes all-important. It also must be determined whether the applicable law was the same,[26] and whether subsequent cases might have criticized or even overruled the particular decision in question.

In reading a trial court decision, it is important to distinguish between those decisions where the applicable law was relatively clear but the taxpayer was unable to prove sufficient facts to bring the situation within it, and those cases where the facts were relatively clear and the argument was over the law. Thus, in *Sterno, Inc.* (TC Memo 1959-241), the Tax Court held that commissions that were paid by one corporation to a related sales corporation were not deductible to the extent that they exceeded the amount of salaries, commissions, and expenses paid out by the sales corporation. This case was decided on the basis that the taxpayer had not carried the burden of proving that the determination of the IRS was wrong. But for a later year (in TC Memo 1965-23), the same taxpayer was able to satisfy its burden of proof and the sales commission payments *were* allowed as a deduction.

A refund claim was then filed by the taxpayer who had received the payments in the year for which the Tax Court disallowed a portion of them for deduction purposes; the taxpayer (the sales corporation) argued that the amounts received were not compensation for services rendered but were dividends. The difference is substantial, inasmuch as a corporation receiving a commission includes 100% of the amount in its income, whereas a corporation receiving a dividend gets a dividends-received deduction. Thus, the parent corporation would have been entitled to a substantial refund. However, the U.S. Claims Court denied the refund claim. It said that the Tax Court's decision had merely concluded that the paying corporation had not proved that the payments were reasonable—the Tax Court had not determined that the payments were dividends. [*Sterno Sales Corporation* v. *U.S.* (1965), 15 AFTR2d 979.]

It is also important to read decisions of Courts of Appeal with care. A Court of Appeals normally will not find that a lower court's findings of fact should be reversed unless a very clear error was made by the lower court. Thus, an appeals court often affirms a lower-court decision on the basis that the factual determinations of the lower court were not clearly erroneous. On the other hand, an appeals court takes a different attitude about the way a lower court applies the law. If the appeals court disagrees with the lower court as to the application of the law, it will reverse without the necessity of finding the lower-court decision clearly erroneous. It is quite possible for two very similar cases to be decided differently by trial courts based upon their peculiar facts, and for both decisions to be affirmed by the appeals court involved. Appeals court decisions are most valuable when they deal with questions of law and are probably least valuable in tax situations where they deal only with the question of whether the trial court made erroneous findings of fact.

20.14. Tax Law Evolution

The statute, the regulations, and the court decisions all interact with a constantly changing world to produce change in the tax law. Perhaps an illustration will clarify how this process works.

[26]This is where the *Cumulative Changes in the Internal Revenue Code and the Regulations* can be helpful. If Congress has changed the applicable statute between the time of a case and the present, the applicability of the case obviously can change dramatically.

20.14.1. The Professional Corporation Hassle

For over a decade prior to 1962, a concerted drive had been aimed at Congress to obtain for self-employed persons, particularly professionals who then could not operate in corporate form, the pension and profit-sharing benefits available to employees. The complaint was simple. Most proprietorships and partnerships could conduct their businesses in corporate form. Since 1958 and the advent of the small business corporation,[27] these people could even obtain the benefits of being corporate employees without incurring the disadvantage of paying the corporate income tax.

Not so for the psychiatrist, physician, dentist, lawyer, CPA, and so on. State law and/or the rules of their professional bodies prohibited practice in corporate form. As proprietors or as partners in a partnership, they could set up employee benefit plans for their employees. Most were in relatively high tax brackets. They could obtain no aid in the form of tax concessions to help provide for their own eventual retirement. Compared with their colleagues employed by corporations, universities, and foundations, they felt that they were being discriminated against.

The Treasury Department fought the proposed pension legislation vigorously. The bill got through the House many times, only to flounder in the Senate. Finally, in 1962, a much-watered-down bill passed and became law. It is known as Keogh or H.R. 10 and has been changed several times since 1962. Its present version is discussed in Chapter 18.

While legislation was struggling along, however, another line of attack was being pursued, spearheaded by physicians. In a series of court cases, especially the landmark *Kintner* decision, they established the proposition that a medical clinic could be a partnership under state law but a corporation for federal income tax purposes.[28] Although they achieved success in specific cases, the doctors found that the Internal Revenue Service was unwilling to concede. The Treasury Department issued regulations purportedly designed to implement the *Kintner* decision, except that application of the regulations produced a result that was the opposite of that which the court had reached.[29] Unable to obtain favorable administrative rulings and faced with recurrent and expensive court battles, the doctors tried a new approach. They tackled the state legislatures. In most states, they were joined by the other professions. By 1970, forty-eight states had enacted some sort of bill that at least purported to set up professional corporations for the practice of one or more professions. During the sixties, the Treasury had responded with more regulations explaining why professional service organizations could never be corporations for tax purposes.

Although the Internal Revenue Service continued to force taxpayers into court, the courts without exception upheld the validity of professional corporations. The finale came on Aug. 8, 1969, when the Internal Revenue Service ruled that "in response to recent decisions of the Federal Courts . . . that organizations of doctors, lawyers, and other professional people organized under state professional associations acts will, generally, be treated as corporations for tax purposes."[30]

Once professional corporations had been accepted, the tax controversy battlefield shifted. Some professionals formed one-person corporations which became partners in professional partnerships. By so doing, the professional could set up a generous pension plan in the corporation but would not be required to provide comparable benefits to the partnership's employees (the receptionist, the nurse, etc.). The IRS was unsuccessful in court cases challenging this practice, and therefore Congress enacted legislation to end it.[31] Concern still existed, however, over the tax avoidance potential of the one-person professional corporation, and therefore the 1982 tax law enacted still more legislation giving the IRS the power to reallocate income from the professional corporation to the individual stockholder if necessary to prevent abuses.[32] The 1986 and 1987 tax legislation further reduced the advantage of corporate professional practice. Professional corporations generally can no longer use fiscal years, offset passive losses against active income, or take advantage of the graduated tax-rate structure available to other corporations.

Other parts of the tax law as it exists at any moment have similar antecedents.

20.15 Conclusion

Technical tax research, of the sort discussed in this chapter, is interesting and challenging. People who dislike it seldom make good tax practitioners. However, tax practice goes considerably beyond capability at research. In the last analysis,

[27] Now called S corporations. See Chapter 11.
[28] *U.S.* v. *Kintner et al.* (CA9 1954), 216 F.2d 418, 46 AFTR 995, 54-2 USTC 9626.
[29] Treas. Reg. 301.7701-2(h) (1969).
[30] TIR 1019 (August 8, 1969). This announcement was repeated in Rev. Rul. 70-101, 1970-1 CB 278.
[31] IRC Sec. 414(m), enacted in 1980.
[32] IRC Sec. 269A.

tax consulting is a subset of business consulting, just as controlling tax expense and liability is a subset of financial management. The really great tax person is the one who can come up with innovative ways of solving practical business problems with maximum positive tax results. If tax research is thought of as the art of answering tax questions, then tax planning should be viewed as the ability to ask the questions that lead to answers that make good sense from both a business and a tax perspective.

In Chapter 21, tax planning will be explored in more detail.[33]

[33]Additional material on tax research can be obtained from Prentice-Hall, CCH, and RIA.

TRUE-FALSE QUESTIONS

State whether each of the following statements is true or false. For each *false* answer, reword the statement to make it *true*.

T F 1. The federal income tax was enacted by the Sixteenth Amendment to the Constitution.

T F 2. The Internal Revenue Code of 1986 is so named because 1986 was the last time the entire income tax law was rewritten and reorganized.

T F 3. The Internal Revenue Code is a part of the U.S. Code.

T F 4. The basic segment that is used as reference to the Internal Revenue Code is the Subchapter.

T F 5. The citation "IRC 1.562-1" refers to a portion of the statute.

T F 6. Regulations are issued by the Treasury Department for the sole purpose of interpreting the statutes enacted by Congress.

T F 7. The Regulations generally carry the same numbering system as the IRC except for a prefix (1.), which indicates that the Regulation deals with income tax.

T F 8. Sometimes Congress authorizes the Treasury Department to write rules dealing with a certain aspect of the tax laws, in which case the resulting regulations are called legislative regulations.

T F 9. Internal Revenue Rulings are issued by the Internal Revenue Service for the purpose of explaining the official position relative to a given set of facts and the applicable tax law.

T F 10. The Internal Revenue Service publishes a weekly bulletin for official announcements called the *Cumulative Bulletin.*

T F 11. If the Internal Revenue Service disagrees with a Tax Court decision, it may issue a public acquiescence for the case.

T F 12. All court decisions on tax litigation, except for the small tax division cases in the Tax Court, are published in bound volumes either by the Government Printing Office or one of the commercial publishers.

T F 13. The citation Rev. Rul. 79-91, IRB 1979-11, 9, should be read as Revenue Ruling number 91 for 1979, which can be found in the eleventh issue of the *Internal Revenue Bulletin* for 1979 at page 9.

T F 14. All Tax Court decisions are published by the Government Printing Office.

T F 15. AFTR and AFTR2d are abbreviations for two series of published tax cases issued by Prentice-Hall.

T F 16. A proper citation to a tax case should include a reference to the court that issued the decision.

T F 17. A tax service is an editorial commentary on the tax law, organized by subject rather than Code section.

T F 18. If Regulations have not been issued relative to a particular section of the IRC, congressional committee reports can be helpful in determining how the law should be applied.

T F 19. Tax Court Memorandum decisions are issued by the Tax Court in those situations where the court believes the decision will not have much precedential value.

T F 20. A citator is a list of court decisions arranged in chronological order.

PROBLEMS

Problems 20-1 through 20-5 require the use of the P-H *Federal Tax Handbook.*

Problem 20-1.

(a) Mr. Tiller, who is a farmer, has asked you if the cost of purchasing commercial lime, which is to be applied to his fields, will be a deduction in the year he pays for it. He uses the cash method of accounting. Is it?

(b) What Treasury Regulation covers this question? How is this reference noted in the *Handbook?*

(c) Would it make any difference if Mr. Tiller's farm were part of a "syndicate"? Explain.

(d) Where would you expect to find more detailed rules on what constitutes a farming syndicate?

Problem 20-2. The life expectancy or cost recovery period which has been assigned to various assets has been changed several times over recent years by Congress. It is not uncommon, therefore, to have to refer to a chart or table in order to determine the proper amount of depreciation deduction for property even if it is ACRS or MACRS property.

(a) In the *Handbook* where is the table which shows the proper amount of ACRS depreciation for a piece of 15-year ACRS real estate which is now in its fourth year of use? (The property is not low income housing.)

(b) In the *Handbook* where is the table which shows the proper amount of ACRS depreciation for a piece of 19-year ACRS real estate for which an optional 35-year straight-line method has been elected and which was first placed in service in August 1986 by a calendar year taxpayer?

(c) In the *Handbook* where is the explanation of the proper amount of depreciation (MACRS) deduction for a business automobile which was placed in service in September, 1988, and which is now in its third year of business use?

(d) In the *Handbook* where is the explanation of the proper amount of depreciation (MACRS) deduction for a business automobile which was placed in service in February, 1989, and which is now in its second year of business use?

Problem 20-3.

(a) In the securities market, bonds are normally quoted at a price that does not include interest. It is understood that when a person buys a bond, the total price will be the quoted amount *plus* any accrued interest. When the bonds are sold at a set price that includes both principal and interest, it is said that the bonds are bought "flat." If Ms. Greentree purchased such bonds, how will she go about dividing the purchase price between principal and interest? Explain the research steps taken.

(b) Does it make any difference if interest is in arrears at the date of purchase?

(c) Where can further discussion of this topic be found?

Problem 20-4.

(a) Assume that Mr. Barker has just hired an employee in his small dry-cleaning business. He has never had an employee before. The weekly rate of pay is $175. Mr. Barker wants to know how much should be withheld for income tax purposes. The employee is single and has no dependents. Determine the amount of withholding. Explain the research steps taken.

(b) May the amount determined in part (a) be rounded? Explain.

(c) Where could instructions be found for withholding on amounts paid to an employee which are not related to time periods, such as sales commissions?

Problem 20-5.

(a) Mr. and Mrs. Holiday are in the process of getting a divorce. Mr. Holiday will pay all of the legal fees and has asked you if he can get a tax deduction. Prepare an answer, including the steps you take to look it up in the *Handbook.*

(b) What if Mr. Holiday paid you for consultation relative to the tax effects of the divorce, including advice to him on alimony, property settlements, child support, and his income-tax-filing status? Would he be able to deduct such a fee? Explain. Where is more detailed information available?

(c) What section(s) of the IRC govern(s) this question?

Problems 20-6 through 20-10 require the use of the CCH *Master Tax Guide* (*MTG*). For each of Problems 20-1 through 20-5 (except 20-3), substitute *MTG* where the problem reads *Handbook.*

Problem 20-6. Answer Problem 20-1 using the *MTG* as the source.

Problem 20-7. Answer Problem 20-2 using the *MTG* as the source.

Problem 20-8. Murphy Randolph purchased a retirement annuity for $15,000. Under its terms, Murphy is to receive $2,280 per year (payable monthly at the rate of $190) for the remainder of his lifetime.

(a) In this text, annuities were discussed in Chapter 2. Where are they discussed in the *MTG?*

(b) Where are the annuity tables?

(c) Assuming that Murphy is single and age sixty-five at the date the annuity payments begin, how much does the table provide as the expected receipts for Murphy's lifetime?

(d) What is the annuity exclusion ratio for Murphy?

(e) Assume all of the same facts except that the taxpayer is Madilyn Randolph. What is her exclusion ratio?

Problem 20-9. Answer Problem 20-4 using the *MTG* as the source.

Problem 20-10. Answer Problem 20-5 using the *MTG* as the source.

Problems 20-11 through 20-15 require the use of the P-H *Federal Taxes.*

Problem 20-11. Assume that someone has told you that the tax problem you are working on may have an answer in Revenue Ruling 77-452. (Explain the research steps taken.)

(a) Find the proper citation to this Revenue Ruling.

(b) Find a summary of the ruling. Where is it?

(c) Where could you find the full text of the ruling?

Problem 20-12.

(a) Assume that you have been referred to the Supreme Court decision of *Comm.* v. *W. O. Culbertson, Sr.,* but you were not given a citation. Using Vol. 1 of P-H *Federal Taxes,* find the citation.

(b) Where in *Federal Taxes* is there a reference to this case?

Problem 20-13.

(a) Look in Vol. 1 of the 1989 edition P-H *Federal Taxes* and see if there have been any periodical articles written on the topic "Illegal Bribes and Kickbacks." (*Hint:* The relevant IRC Section is 162.)

(b) If you did not know that the applicable IRC Sec. was 162, how could you find it?

Problem 20-14. Marty Horn is one of your clients and has been claiming a home office deduction for several years. He is employed by the Podunk Philharmonic Orchestra which has concerts three nights a week at the Podunk activity center. Since the activity center is used for a wide range of activities, the orchestra is allowed to use it for practice only three hours prior to each performance. As a result, Marty must practice playing the French horn in a sound proof room in his house. He practices at home about 25 hours per week. The IRS has disallowed the home office deduction on the grounds that no revenue is earned at home and the activity center is Marty's principal job location. Marty has asked you to research this issue and determine whether it would be worthwhile to challenge the IRS in court on this matter.

Problem 20-15.

(a) Given the facts concerning your own expenses in connection with college courses (i.e., housing, tuition, books, transportation, supplies), do you qualify for an educational expense deduction?

(b) List the steps in the research process. Cite all authorities used.

Problems 20-16 through 20-20 require the use of the CCH *Standard Federal Tax Reporter* (*SFTR*).

Problem 20-16. Answer Problem 20-11 using the CCH *SFTR.*

Problem 20-17. Answer Problem 20-12 using the CCH *SFTR.* Instead of Vol. 1, the index is called an "Index" volume. Note that the CCH service also contains a volume called the Citator.

Problem 20-18. Answer Problem 20-13 using the CCH *SFTR.*

Problem 20-19. Answer Problem 20-14 using the CCH *SFTR.*

Problem 20-20. Answer Problem 20-15 using the CCH *SFTR.*

Problem 20-21. What is the full meaning of each of the following, including the full meaning of all abbreviations:

(a) Rev. Rul. 78-356, 1978-39 *IRB* 19.

(b) Rev. Rul. 72-359, 1972-2 *CB* 478.

(c) *Arnold L. Santucci,* ¶ 73,178 P-H Memo TC.

(d) *Walter R. Crabtree,* 20 TC 841.

(e) *Martin* v. *U.S.* (DC Ga. 1954), 119 F. Supp. 468, 45 AFTR 734.

(f) *KPV Southerland Paper Co.* v. *U.S.* (Ct. Cl. 1965) 15 AFTR2d 919, 344 F.2d 377, 170 Ct. Cl. 215.

(g) *Jean Conrad,* 27 BTA 741.

(h) *Malat* v. *Riddell* (S. Ct. 1966), 17 AFTR2d 604, 383 U.S. 569, 16 L. Ed. 2d 102, 86 S. Ct. 1030.

(i) *Mirro-Dynamics Corp.* v. *U.S.* (CA9 1967), 19 AFTR2d 1029, 374 F.2d 14.

Problem 20-22. What are the differences between a "regular" tax court decision and a "memorandum" decision?

Problem 20-23. Where is a "regular" tax court decision published?

Problem 20-24. Where is a "memorandum" tax court decision published?

Problem 20-25. What is the meaning of "acquiescence" as that term is used in taxes?

Problem 20-26. If a taxpayer wants to appeal a decision from the Tax Court, where does the appeal take place?

Problem 20-27. Is it possible to have a jury trial in the Circuit Court of Appeals? Explain.

Problem 20-28. Is the IRS required to follow a decision of a federal District Court in a later situation where the facts are exactly the same as those in the previously litigated case? Explain.

APPENDIX 20-A

A Concise History of the Income Tax

Income has been a base for the imposition of tax for almost as long as recorded history. Elementary roots of the income tax have been traced back to the Roman Empire. Some scholars have suggested that the tax imposed by Caesar Augustus at the time of the birth of Christ may have been a form of income tax (see Edwin R. A. Seligman, *The Income Tax,* Macmillan, 1914).

The Florentine Republic in Italy in the fourteenth and fifteenth centuries imposed a property tax which evolved into an income tax. This tax later fell into disfavor because of administrative difficulties, and was replaced by taxes that more closely resembled the present-day sales or value added taxes.

The New Plymouth colony had a tax based on a person's "faculties" in 1643. Historical records do not reveal much about the tax, but it appears that it was to be applied to a person's abilities. How else to measure that than by income? The Massachusetts Bay Company enacted a tax in 1646 on the gains of tradesmen and artisans. A century later the colonies were still collecting a tax on the "faculties" of citizens, with the measure of the tax being based on a person's ability to pay as reflected by income. Nevertheless, these early income taxes were only supplements to the primary tax base, property. By 1850 some of the southern states were using income as a tax base, following English rules which had been adopted in 1799.

In an attempt to raise more revenue to finance the Civil War, the United States enacted a tax on income in 1861 and 1862. By 1864 the rates were as high as 10% on income over $10,000. Apparently the collection of the tax was never carried out with much vigor, and the income tax was repealed in 1872, when the need to finance the war was eliminated. Nevertheless, the tax had been challenged in the courts, and the Supreme Court found that a federal tax on income was not in violation of the constitutional prohibitions on any "direct" tax (Article I, Section 9, Clause 4, of the Constitution). Therefore, when Congress again felt a need to collect more taxes it incorporated the language of the 1864 Revenue Act into the statute passed (without President Cleveland's signature) in 1894, believing that if the tax had been declared constitutional once it would surely pass the test again. But such was not to be the case.

A Mr. Pollock objected to a corporation, of which he was a shareholder, paying the tax. This time the Supreme Court reversed its earlier interpretation and decided that such a tax was unconstitutional (*Pollock* v. *Farmers' Loan and Trust Co.,* 1895, 157 U.S. 429 and 158 U.S. 601).

Political commentary was hot and heavy on both sides of the question. There were those who saw a pressing need for more federal government funds and an income tax as the only sensible and equitable way to finance the government. Others were convinced that such a tax would rend the country asunder, pitting geographic region against geographic region and rich against poor. If there was to be such a tax levied at the national level, an amendment to the Constitution was a prerequisite. Finally, in 1909, Congress passed a joint resolution to amend the Constitution. The states began a ratification process similar to that currently under way for the Equal Rights Amendment. On February 25, 1913, the necessary two-thirds majority had been obtained. The Sixteenth Amendment provides that "The Congress shall have power to lay and collect taxes on incomes, from whatever source derived, without apportionment among the several States, and without regard to any census or enumeration."

In the early summer of 1913 Congress enacted such a tax under the newly granted authority, making the effective date retroactive to March 1, 1913. Even so, the judicial battles were not quite over. The progressive rates were challenged as an arbitrary abuse of power. The Supreme Court disposed of that argument in 1916 (*Brushaber* v. *Union Pacific Railroad Co.,* 240 U.S. 1), and there has not been a serious general threat to the income tax since.

Before 1939, Congress enacted tax laws without any overall plan or organization. It was necessary with each Revenue Act to repeat the language of earlier statutes. The country had been through World War I, the go-go years of the 1920s, and the economic turmoil of the 1930s. Although only about 6% of the population was required to pay income tax under the rules in effect at that time, the Department of Justice and the Bureau of Internal Revenue expressed a desire to have the laws better organized. In 1939 Congress enacted the Internal Revenue Code of 1939, which was the first overall revision coupled with a codification of the rules.

Both the rates and the number of people impacted by the income tax increased dramatically during the years of World War II. In addition, a change in philosophy occurred. No longer was the tax law viewed as just a means of collecting revenue; now it was seen as a vehicle for accomplishing social and economic goals. One of the complaints often heard today is that the tax laws are too complex. One reason for this complexity is the variety of incentives and deterrents incorporated into the tax laws. Another reason is the attempt to create equity, a difficult task when the law applies to over 200 million individual situations.

In 1954 Congress again enacted a comprehensive revision, restructuring, and renumbering of the rules. Among the landmark changes that have occurred since 1954 are the investment credit provisions, which began in 1962. In 1964 and 1965, some general tax reductions were enacted, as well as some specific liberalizations such as income averaging. The Tax Reform Act of 1969 was a monumental change in many of the detailed rules, particularly those affecting businesses. The Tax Reform Act of 1976 made significant changes in the gift and estate taxes. The Revenue Act of 1978 made history with a liberalization of the treatment of capital gains, among other changes. The Economic Recovery Tax Act of 1981 made very far reaching modifications, including a liberalization of depreciation and investment tax credit and a general overhaul of the estate and gift tax rules. The Tax Reform Act of 1986 (enacted in October 1986) made some of the most far reaching changes in tax rules which we have ever experienced. The Tax Law of 1987 (enacted in December 1987) and the Technical and Miscellaneous Revenue Act of 1988 (enacted in October, 1988) made further sweeping changes, particularly upon businesses. The Omnibus Budget Reconciliation Act of 1989 (enacted in December, 1989) made a very large number of technical changes and corrected many of the errors and oversights of prior legislation. Some of these most recent changes have been pointed out from time to time throughout this text, particularly where a change in law created new planning implications.

Today the federal income tax is ingrained in the very fabric of our society. Perhaps only a hermit, panning for gold in the distant mountains, can escape its impact—and then only so long as he does not find what he seeks. All of us must live, work, and die with the tax laws as much a part of the environment as the air we breathe.

APPENDIX 20-B

Rev. Rul. 85-12, 1985-1, CB 181

DEPLETION—Percentage depletion of oil and gas wells. Where none of producer's production is sold through related retailer and producer has no direct or indirect ownership interest in retailer, producer isn't precluded from taking percentage depletion under Sec. 613A(c) or from being an independent producer for purposes of windfall profit tax under Sec. 4987(b)(2).

Issue. Is a corporation, an oil and gas producer, precluded from taking the percentage depletion deduction as provided by section 613A of the Internal Revenue Code or claiming the reduced rates of the Crude Oil Windfall Profit Tax provided to independent producers by section 4987(b)(2) of the Code because a related sister corporation, through which the producer does not sell its production, is a retailer as defined in section 613A(d)(2) of the Code?

Facts. *X*, a wholly owned subsidiary of *Y* corporation, is the owner of various working and royalty interests in oil and gas leases located throughout the United States. All of *X*'s sales of produced oil and gas are made at or near the wellhead to unrelated parties. It acts neither as a refiner nor a retailer, and standing on its own, *X* would be entitled to claim percentage depletion under section 613A(c) of the Code and would be classified as an independent producer for windfall profit tax purposes under section 4992 of the Code.

Z is also a wholly owned subsidiary of *Y*, and a sister company to *X*. *Z* has engaged in marketing of petroleum and petroleum products for the past several years. It purchases petroleum or derivative products from unrelated third parties, and resells such products at a profit through retail outlets. Sales by *Z* to end users exceed $5,000,000 annually or $1,250,000 per quarter.

X and *Z*, along with other subsidiaries of *Y*, join together in the filing of a consolidated U.S. Corporate Income Tax Return.

Law and Analysis. Section 613A(a) of the Code provides that, except as otherwise provided in section 613A, the allowance for depletion under section 611 with respect to any oil or gas well shall be computed without regard to section 613, which provides the allowance for percentage depletion.

Section 613A(c) of the Code provides that, except as provided in section 613A(d), the allowance for depletion under section 611 shall be computed in accordance with section 613 with respect to so much of the taxpayer's average daily production of domestic crude oil as does not exceed the taxpayer's depletable oil quantity; and so much of the taxpayer's average daily production of domestic natural gas as does not exceed the taxpayer's depletable natural gas quantity; and the applicable percentage (determined in accordance with the table contained in paragraph (5)) shall be deemed to be specified in subsection (b) of section 613 for purposes of subsection (a) of that section.

Section 613A(d)(2) of the Code provides that section 613A(c) shall not apply in the case of any taxpayer who directly, or through a related person, sells oil or natural gas (excluding bulk sales or such items to commercial or industrial users), or any product derived from oil and natural gas through any retail outlet operated by the taxpayer or a related person or to any person (i) obligated under an agreement or contract with the taxpayer or a related person to use a trademark, trade mark, or service mark or name owned by such taxpayer or related persons, in marketing or distributing oil or natural gas or any product derived from oil or natural gas, or (ii) given authority, pursuant to an agreement or contact with the taxpayer or a related person, to occupy any retail outlet owned, leased, or in any way controlled by the taxpayer or a related person.

Section 613A(d)(2) of the Code further provides that such limitation upon the allowance for percentage depletion does not apply in any case where the combined gross receipts from the sale of oil, natural gas, or any product derived from oil and gas for the tax year of all retail outlets do not exceed $5,000,000.

Section 613A(d)(3) of the Code provides that a person is a related person with respect to the taxpayer if a significant ownership interest in either the taxpayer or such person is held by the other, or if a third person has a significant ownership interest in both the taxpayer and such person. For purposes of the preceding sentence, the term "significant ownership interest" means, with respect to any corporation, 5 percent or more in value of the outstanding stock of such corporation.

Section 4992(b) of the Code provides that for purposes of the windfall profit tax, with respect to any quarter, a person to whom section 613A(c) does not apply by reason of section 613A(d)(2) relating to certain retailers is not an independent producer. For the purposes of defining an independent producer section 4992(b)(2) provides that section 613A(d) is to be applied by substituting "quarter" for "taxable year" each place it appears in paragraph 613A(d)(2) and by substituting $1,250,000 for $5,000,000 in section 613A(d)(2). Thus, a "retailer" is also prohibited from utilizing the reduced rates on independent producer oil provided in section 4987(b)(2).

Where none of a producer's production is sold through a related retailer, the producer does not lose the benefit of the section 613A(c) exemption if an owner of 5 percent or more of its stock is a retailer because the producer does not benefit from the retailer's retail sales of oil and gas. The producer, *X*, has no direct or indirect ownership interest in the retailer, *Z*, and thus, does not benefit from the retail sales. Although the two corporations *X* and *Z* are related persons for purposes of section 613A(d) by virtue of the provisions of section 613A(d)(3), none of *X*'s production is, in form or substance, sold through *Z*. Thus, *X* is not precluded from taking percentage depletion under section 613A(c) or from being listed as an independent producer for purposes of the windfall profit tax under section 4987(b)(2).

Holding. Corporation *X* is not precluded from taking the percentage depletion deduction as provided in section 613A of the Code, or claiming the reduced rates of windfall profit tax provided by section 4987(b)(2) by virtue of the fact that a related sister company, *Z*, through which *X* does not sell its production, is a retailer as defined in sections 613A(d)(2) and 4992(b).

APPENDIX 20-C

Rev. Proc. 77-35, 1977-2 CB 568

26 CFR 601.105: Examination of returns and claims for refund, credit or abatement; determination of correct tax liability.

(Also Part I, Sections 43, 6201, 6211, 6213, 6401; 1.43-1, 301.6201-1, 301.6211-1, 301.6213-1, 301.6401-1.)

Rev. Proc. 77-35

SECTION 1. PURPOSE

The purpose of this Revenue Procedure is to provide guidance for uniform treatment of adjustments that decrease the earned income credit allowed by section 43 of the Internal Revenue Code of 1954.

SEC. 2. BACKGROUND

Inquiries concerning the appropriate handling of adjustments that decrease the earned income credit indicate a need for clarification.

SEC. 3. PROCEDURES

.01 When there is a deficiency as defined in section 6211 of the Code, the notice of deficiency will include the earned income credit adjustment.

.02 In agreed cases or cases involving only the earned income credit adjustment, the correction will be made in the same manner as an adjustment of a prepayment credit. In unagreed cases, the taxpayer will be offered a district conference.

SEC. 4. EFFECTIVE DATE

The procedures set forth in Section 3 of this Revenue Procedure are effective October 3, 1977, the date of publication in the Internal Revenue Bulletin.

APPENDIX 20-D

Private Letter Ruling 8143107

LOSSES—Abandonment or loss of useful value—goodwill, customer's list and related items; Theft or embezzlement losses—what is a deductible theft—elements of theft in general. Loss deduction denied on purchase of accounting practice that had fewer clients than represented and which included worthless covenant not to compete. Because client list is considered unitary asset under RevRul 69-311, 1969-1 C.B. 62, there could be no deductible loss unless there had been a closed and completed transaction with respect to client list as a whole. Since loss of individual clients wasn't such a disposition, no deduction was allowed. Similarly, there hadn't been closed or completed transaction indicating that covenant not to compete had been discarded or practice had been discontinued. IRS wouldn't issue ruling on factual issue of whether theft loss had occurred. Ref. ¶14,250(5); (60); 14,407(10). Sec. 165.

Ltr Rul 8143107

This is in reply to your request for a ruling that you have sustained a deductible loss in connection with the purchase of an accounting practice.

We understand the facts to be substantially as follows. On September 20, 1980, you entered into a written contract to buy an accounting practice, including the seller's list of clients. You completed paying the purchase price on October 16, 1980. Upon taking over the practice, you discovered that some of the seller's representations concerning the practice were not true. You learned that the seller did not have all the clients named in the list of clients attached to the contract, had not been doing all the work he represented he was doing for the clients he did have, and had been doing substandard work.

You did not contact any of the clients before paying the purchase price. When you did contact them, you found that most of them were looking for a new firm to handle their business because they were dissatisfied with the seller's services. Consequently, you were able to retain only some of the clients that the seller had been serving at the time of your purchase.

Although you purchased accounts of specific clients, you did not evaluate each account individually. You determined the purchase price for the entire practice by capitalizing the previous year's purported earnings.

As part of the contract, the seller covenanted not to compete for a period of five years. You did not, however, allocate a specific value to the covenant in the contract. You believe that the covenant is worthless because you believe that the seller is not competent enough to compete.

Because you paid for a covenant you believe to be worthless and clients that the seller did not have, you ask whether you may deduct as a loss the difference between what you paid for the practice and what you believe it was actually worth.

Section 165(a) of the Internal Revenue Code allows a deduction for losses. In the case of an individual taxpayer, section 165(c) limits the deduction to losses incurred in a trade or business, losses incurred in any transaction entered into for profit, and losses arising from fire, storm, shipwreck, or other casualty, or from theft.

The term "other casualty" has been held to mean an event of a sudden, unusual, or unexpected nature that is similar to fire, storm, or shipwreck. See RevRul 72-592, 1972-2 C.B. 101.

Section 1.165-8(d) of the Income Tax Regulations provides that "theft" includes, but is not limited to, larceny, embezzlement, and robbery. Under RevRul 72-112, 1972-1 C.B. 60, a taxpayer claiming a theft loss must show that the loss resulted from the taking of property that was illegal under the law of the state where it took place and that the taking was done with criminal intent.

Criminal intent, and therefore theft, involve determinations of fact. Under section 4.021 of RevProc 80-22, 1980-1 C.B. 654, the Service will not ordinarily issue a ruling on any matter in which the determination requested is primarily one of fact. In general, whether there had been a theft loss must be determined initially by the taxpayer, who should be prepared to substantiate the loss in the event of examination of the return claiming the loss by the appropriate district director.

Because the Service is generally precluded from ruling on theft losses and no casualty is involved in your request, this ruling addresses only whether there has been a loss incurred in a trade or business or transaction for profit.

Section 1.165-1(b) of the regulations provides that to be deductible a loss must be evidenced by closed and completed transactions, fixed by identifiable events. Under Carnrick v. Commissioner, 21 B.T.A. 12 (1930), a purchase of property for more than it is worth does not produce a deductible loss.

Section 1.165-2(a) of the regulations provides that a loss incurred in a business or in a transaction for profit and arising from the sudden termination of the usefulness of any nondepreciable property, in a case where such business or transaction is discontinued or where such property is permanently discarded from use, shall be allowed as a deduction. Under section 1.167(a)-3, goodwill is nondepreciable.

In Golden State Towel and Linen Service, Ltd. v. United States, 373 F.2d 938 (Ct.Cl. 1967), the court adopted the rationale that customer lists are either coextensive with or at least included in goodwill.

A covenant not to compete may be part of goodwill or a separate depreciable asset, depending on circumstances. See Forward Communications Corp. v. United States, 608 F.2d 485 (Ct.Cl. 1979). Section 1.167(a)-8 of the regulations concerns gains or losses on the permanent withdrawal of depreciable property from use. Examples of withdrawal are sale or exchange, abandonment, or placing in a supplies or scrap account. Section 1.167(a)-9, concerning obsolescence of depreciable property, is cross-referenced to section 1.167(a)-8 for rules governing allowance of losses upon obsolescence.

RevRul 69-311, 1969-1 C.B. 62, discusses whether a taxpayer who purchased an accounting practice may deduct as a loss the value attributable to accounts that are terminated. In disallowing a loss deduction, the revenue ruling holds, in part, that client accounts constitute a single unitary asset whose basis is taken into account in determining gain or loss upon disposition of the business. Loss of individual clients does not affect the indefinite useful life of the asset.

Metropolitan Laundry Co. v. United States, 100 F.Supp. 803 (N.D. Cal. 1951), is an exception to the rule in RevRul 69-311. In that case the taxpayer lost all its customers in San Francisco due to seizure of its facilities in 1943 for war use, but retained all its customers in Oakland. When it regained its facilities after the war, it tried to reestablish its customer structure in San Francisco but was completely unsuccessful. In allowing the taxpayer a loss deduction, the court reasoned that the taxpayer had permanently lost a substantial, identifiable, vendible portion of a unitary asset, and the value of the portion could be measured with certainty.

In Sunset Fuel Co. v. United States, 519 F.2d 781 (9th Cir. 1975), a taxpayer purchased a list of customers in connection with the acquisition of a fuel oil distributorship. The taxpayer allocated four cents per gallon of fuel oil purchased by the customers during the previous year as the value for each customer on the list. The court held that the allocation formula was arbitrary and the purchase price was negotiated with respect to the whole list as a single asset. Consequently, the taxpayer could not rely on the formula to justify loss deductions for terminated accounts.

Based solely on the facts represented in your ruling request, we conclude as follows.

You purchased the client list as a unitary asset. No facts indicate that you evaluated each account individually, even by an arbitrary formula such as that in Sunset Fuel Co. Rather, you determined what the purchase price of the accounting practice should be by capitalizing earnings. No facts indicate a situation similar to that in Metropolitan Laundry Co. Because there has not been a disposition of the business, under RevRul 69-311 there is no closed and completed transaction with respect to the client accounts you paid for.

With respect to the covenant not to compete, there is also no closed end completed transaction. Assuming without determining that the covenant is a nondepreciable asset separate from goodwill or the client accounts, no facts indicate that the covenant has been discarded or the accounting practice to which it relates discontinued, as illustrated in section 1.165-2(a) of the regulations. Alternatively, assuming without determining that the covenant is a separate depreciable asset, no facts indicate any withdrawal from use, as illustrated by section 1.167(a)-8.

Accordingly, the instant situation is governed by Carnrick, and no loss deduction is allowable with respect to either the client accounts or the covenant not to compete.

Except as specifically provided above, no opinion is expressed as to the federal income tax consequences of the transaction above under any other provision of the Internal Revenue Code.

This ruling is addressed only to the taxpayers who requested it. Section 6110(j)(3) of the Code provides that it may not be otherwise used or cited as precedent.

21

analyzing tax-planning opportunities

21.1 Tax Research in Tax Planning

Research is the testing of hypotheses. A hypothesis is an assumption about the nature of reality—a tax hypothesis, therefore, is an assumption about the nature of a tax reality. It may start out as a guess.

A woman is in the process of getting a divorce from the man who she put through graduate school. She gave up part of her career-preparation years to invest in his career. They agree that she is entitled to some sort of rehabilitative or transitional alimony—perhaps $15,000 per year for the five years that it will take her to get her own professional life back on stream. She assumes that the alimony he will pay her will not be taxable to her. This is an assumption, or a hypothesis.

The hypothesis can be tested. The index to the P-H *Federal Tax Handbook*[1] will lead to Par. 1322, which contains a discussion of alimony as gross income.[2]

Alimony payments must be made in cash, must end with the payee's death, and alimony payments in excess of $10,000 per year must continue for at least three consecutive years in order to be deductible. The divorce or separation agreement must not state that the payment is not to be taxed as alimony.[3] While $15,000 is more than $10,000, five years is more than three. Thus the woman has a problem with her assumption that what she would receive would be tax-free to her. Her husband has already stated his opposition to any statement in the divorce decree that the payments would not be deductible to him. If she insists that the payments not terminate upon her death, however, she can keep them tax-free. Most state laws, absent anything to the contrary in the divorce decree awarding the alimony, do provide for termination upon the payee's death. The 1986 tax law changes, which reduced to only three years the prior requirement of payments continuing for six years if they were to be taxable to the wife, also eliminated the requirement that the decree specifically provide for termination of the payments on death.

What are the woman's alternatives?

1. Provide in the agreement that the husband will not take a deduction.
2. Make explicit in the decree that payments will not terminate with her death. That eliminates taxability to her.
3. Explore the value of the deduction to the man. If she has income, he will have a deduction. They talk about it. On $15,000, her marginal tax rate will be 15%, and part of the $15,000 won't be taxed at all because of the personal exemption and the standard deduction. He is likely to be in a 33% tax bracket for the full $15,000. They agree that he can have the alimony deduction, by providing the payments terminate on her death—but with

[1]The reader may use a different tax research source. Most contain a detailed index that can be used much the same as any encyclopedia. Most will refer to the IRC, which is the primary source for all of the tax law provisions. References to *Federal Taxes* are contained in the footnotes of the *Handbook*. References in brackets in the text of the *Handbook* discussion are to other paragraphs of the *Handbook* or to the IRC.

[2]IRC Secs. 61(a)(8) and 71 provide that alimony is includable in gross income. The deduction is authorized by IRC Sec. 215.

[3]IRC Secs. 71(b)(1)(D) and 71(f)(1).

the alimony being $17,500 instead of $15,000. This gives her $16,000 after tax, at an after-tax cost to him of $11,725.

What use was the research? We were able to restate our original hypothesis of nontaxability to read: Payments of more than $10,000 per year can only be excludable from income if for less than three consecutive years, or if they do not terminate on death of the payee, or if the agreement provides that they are not to be taxed. With that clearer understanding, the woman was able to evaluate her alternatives. Then she and her husband were able to come to a win-win decision that will return her more after tax than the $15,000, but cost him less after-tax than $15,000. All it required was a change in one fact, termination upon death. If she is in good health, she can take out a five-year term insurance policy to cover the alimony she won't receive in the event of death. Such a policy should cost less than $100 per year.

How does tax research relate to tax planning? Planning is the formulation of courses of action aimed at solving problems or creating opportunities. Tax research involves testing the tax assumptions implicit in those plans. From the interaction of the two come changes in what is to be done, further testing of the tax assumptions in those changes, modifications to plans, reflecting all of the risks and trade-offs involved, and finally adoption of plans in which optimum results are achieved.

Is tax planning merely tax research? Decidedly not! Being able to ask pertinent questions, to think of new approaches to the business or the tax side of the situation, and to stick with a problem until answers are reached that make both business sense and tax sense—that is what tax planning is all about.

21.2 The Arithmetic of Tax Planning and Controversy

The Internal Revenue Code specifically allows taxpayers to deduct expenses in connection with the determination, collection, or refund of any tax.[4] The effect of a provision of this sort is to encourage tax planning and controversy—with the encouragement increasing as the tax bracket rises.

Assume that a taxpayer is in a 28% tax bracket. A transaction that has about a 50% chance of being upheld for tax purposes is being contemplated. The cost that will be incurred if the transaction is undertaken will be $10,000. The after-tax cost will be only $7,200, because 28% of the $10,000 will be recovered as a tax deduction. How much potential saving is needed before the transaction appears justified?

The "value" of the tax plan will be one-half the total possible saving, since the probability of actually attaining the saving is 0.5. Algebraically, it can be written: $0.5x = \$7{,}200$. The potential tax saving has to be at least $14,400. It makes no sense with these facts to spend an after-tax $7,200 to save less than an after-tax $14,400.

If the taxpayer is in a 15% tax bracket, the after-tax cost of $1,000 spent seeking tax savings is $850. Assuming the same 0.5 probability of actually getting the saving, the taxpayer would have to be able to save $1,700 to have a chance to break even.

Some general rules can be stated, but there will be exceptions. In general, the higher the taxpayer's tax bracket, the greater the likelihood that tax plans involving a high risk of tax controversy will appear justified; the lower the taxpayer's tax bracket, the less likelihood that tax plans involving a risk of controversy will appear warranted. This was part of the rationale behind the Tax Reform Act of 1986 and its attempt to reduce the benefit of tax shelters. Lower tax rates make an investment made primarily for tax reasons far less attractive.

These generalizations are supported by an analysis of the income sources and deductions of taxpayers in various tax brackets. The higher the tax bracket, the greater the proportion of income from sources that possess some tax savings potential. The higher the tax bracket, the greater the probability that deductions will be itemized. At the other extreme, the opportunities for tax savings are slim for a taxpayer whose sole source of income is wages subject to withholding and who uses the standard deduction.

21.3 How to Analyze Tax Planning Problems

Some tax planning problems have a single solution; others can be solved in one of several ways, with varying tax and business results. In some problems, the facts initially available may be insufficient. In a real-world situation, most of the unknown facts may be ascertained once their importance is realized.

The first step, therefore, is to focus on the problem. There may be a business objective to be achieved with a minimum of tax expense. There

[4] IRC Sec. 212(3). Such expenses may be part of the miscellaneous itemized category, which must exceed 2% of AGI to result in a deduction. But note that penalties, such as the 25% substantial understatement penalty of IRC Sec. 6661, are *not* deductible.

may be a situation where a tax benefit is available through taking some sort of action.

Once the problem is at least tentatively defined, as much data as possible should be gathered. This mainly involves seeing what facts are relevant, what facts (if any) must be obtained or assumed, and what applicable tax provisions deal with the situation.

Only a limited number of tax factors can be involved in any given situation. If income tax minimization is to be achieved, the options are to (1) avoid the recognition of income, (2) increase deductible expenses, (3) reduce the applicable tax rates (directly or by obtaining a credit or special deduction), or (4) affect the timing of items of income or expense by deferral or acceleration.

Avoiding the recognition of income can be illustrated by structuring a transaction so that it is an exchange of property for property, rather than an exchange of property for property plus cash.[5] Deductible expenses can be increased, for example, by leasing land rather than owning it. One way of reducing applicable tax rates may be to operate a business in a corporate form rather than as a sole proprietorship, taking advantage of the lower rates for income below $75,000. Reporting a sale on the installment basis is one of innumerable examples of minimizing taxes by affecting the timing of reporting items.

One or more of the four factors will be involved in any income tax plan. In addition, of course, a tax plan must be fully documented so that the taxpayer can prove that what was purported to have been done was in fact done. The plan should make business sense, should be adaptable to possible future changes in the taxpayer's situation, and should not expose the taxpayer to unbearable risks.

A few examples will help illustrate how tax planning works.

Example 1. Two individuals, each owning 50% of the stock of a corporation and desiring to split the one corporation into two separate corporations, one owned by each, need to be very careful. They have a sound business purpose, but there is a risk that the attempt to split the business might result in having the value of at least one of the resulting corporations taxed to the shareholder as a dividend. Such an outcome could result in very high taxes—with the proceeds of liquidating the corporation perhaps not even being enough to pay the taxes.

Alternative ways in which the problem can be handled or the situation disposed of must be identified. Here is where imagination comes into play. Some of the alternatives dreamed up in a brainstorming session may be ridiculous. These can be eliminated quickly as the next step is taken—critical evaluation of the alternatives.

Based on the facts and what can be determined about the tax rules, each alternative should be analyzed with the question: "What would happen if this were done?" Reference books may have to be consulted a number of times to clarify vague points. The final plan will probably involve some sort of divisive reorganization under IRC Sec. 355—and the two individuals would probably be well advised to get a private ruling from IRS on the tax effect of the transaction.

Example 2. An individual has been offered 50% of the stock of an S corporation engaged in the land development business. The corporation has but one project, consisting of 250 acres. Zoning changes have been obtained, subdivision plats have been recorded, and streets and other amenities have been installed. The existing two shareholders have invested $100,000 in their stock, and the corporation has borrowed another $500,000. Tax basis of the only corporate asset, the subdivision, is $500,000, but its present fair market value is estimated to be $2 million.

The individual would be paying $1.5 million to the corporation for previously unissued stock which will then give him 50% of the stock outstanding. With the money, the corporation can finish developing and marketing the subdivision. It is estimated that within five years, the subdivision can be sold out and the corporation liquidated.

The individual is satisfied with the business aspects of the transaction. The other shareholders have agreed that he can force a corporate liquidation at any time, and to the extent possible will get cash back instead of land in any such liquidation. His CPA is, however, concerned about the tax side.

While the individual is paying $1.5 million for his stock, the profit of the corporation as it sells the land will not be based on the agreed-upon $2 million valuation for the land. Instead, the corporation will report income based on the $500,000 tax basis. Thus, the individual will actually pay tax on $750,000 (50% of the $1.5 million appreciation in value of the land) which represents to him part of the cost of his stock.

This can be seen most easily by assuming that the corporation would liquidate shortly after the individual acquires his stock. The distribution of the land to the shareholders in liquidation would create ordinary income of $1.5 million to the corporation. Of this, $750,000 would be income to the shareholder. He would receive back $1.5 million.

But notice his tax result! He has $750,000 of ordinary income. This increases the tax basis of his S corporation stock to $2.25 million. He receives $1.5 million cash in the liquidation. This creates a

[5] Nontaxable exchanges were the subject of Chapter 6.

short-term capital loss (assuming the liquidation is less than one year after the stock was acquired; otherwise, the loss would be long term, but the difference is irrelevant here.)

The same type of tax result will occur at the end of the corporation's life, when the subdivision has been sold out. Over the years, he will realize as taxable income the $750,000 that represents his half of the difference between tax basis and the agreed value when he bought his stock. This will increase his tax basis. The cash he withdraws will reduce it. When all the land is sold and all the cash is gone, he will have stock with a $750,000 tax basis in a corporation that has no assets. Since capital losses are of limited tax use for most individuals, this is hardly a desirable state of affairs.

What to do?

"An S corporation is like a partnership," says the CPA. "A partnership could deal with this by making an election under section 754. This allows someone who purchases a partnership interest to have a special basis, based on the purchase price, for the partnership assets." But his research discloses that no such election is available to one who purchases S corporation stock. (In fact, such an election is not available to one who acquires a partnership interest by making a contribution to the partnership, either, but is only available when a partnership interest is acquired from an existing partner.)

One possibility would be to have the corporation liquidate now, which would step-up the tax basis of the land to its $2 million current value. The S corporation shareholders reject that idea, however, when they discover that it will cost them current tax on the liquidation. Their reason for selling the S corporation stock is to raise money to finish developing and selling the land.

"Perhaps a joint venture would do the job," suggests the CPA. "A new partnership is formed, with the S corporation as a 50% partner and the individual as a 50% partner." The parties all agree that this is really the same as what they had intended. To cover possible liability exposure problems, the investor suggests that maybe his 50% interest could be held through an S corporation that he would create for the purpose. The CPA agrees that this would be fine.

At first blush, of course, this joint venture approach would not really appear to solve the underlying problem. The land contributed to the partnership by the original S corporation will still have as its tax basis to the partnership the same $500,000 that has caused the tax problem. But IRC Section 704(c) not only allows, but actually requires, that the taxable income from the sale of the land that was contributed to the partnership be allocated among the partners so as to take account of the difference between tax basis and fair market value at the time of the contribution. The partnership agreement for the joint venture will provide for such a special allocation. Thus, the individual, after liquidation of the joint venture, should have no unused tax basis, and during the life of the joint venture should only be paying tax on income calculated on the basis of the value of the land for which he paid coming into the joint venture.

Example 3. The taxpayer is the Billy Barnes Corporation. A $30,000 equipment item with a 5-year life was purchased late in the year. Of that amount, $10,000 can be expensed, under the election provided by IRC Sec. 179. If that election is used, the remaining $20,000 will be depreciated under the ACRS rules which provide for 20% to be written off for the year of purchase, 32% the following year, 19.2% in the third year, 11.52% in the fourth and fifth year, and a final 5.76% in the sixth year. The corporation is in the 15% bracket currently, with or without the $10,000 being treated as an expense. It expects to be in a 25% bracket in future years.

Traditionally, tax advice might have been to make the election and get the extra $10,000 deduction for the current year. The deduction, at a 15% tax rate, would result in tax savings of $1,500. This alternative should be compared with other alternatives. If the election to expense under Sec. 179 is made, the depreciation deduction for the year will be $10,000 plus the regular depreciation on $20,000. Thus, there are two choices, summarized as follows:

A: Use Sec. 179.

B: Do not use Sec. 179.

Table 21-1 examines each of the options, where *cy* = current years.

The above analysis, extended as it is, is not complete. To answer the question properly, the future tax savings from the depreciation deductions should be converted into present-value numbers. This is done in Table 21-2, assuming that the appropriate discount rate is 10%. Thus, option B has the highest present value.

Example 4. A star tennis player, age twenty, earns $500,000 to $600,000 a year. Being realistic, he knows that the big money cannot continue forever. He would like to invest as much of it as possible on a tax-sheltered basis. The tax shelter investments that have been investigated so far have been either confusing or scary. What are the alternatives?

1. He can pay taxes, spend what is left, and at age thirty be burned out and settle down to selling life insurance or real estate.
2. He can invest in a tax shelter such as oil and gas wells. Tax benefits subsidize 28% (because he is in the 28% bracket) of the dollars put in, while the income, if any, will have some shelter from percentage depletion.
3. Since he is a self-employed person engaged in a trade or business, with no employees, he can contribute $30,000 a year to a Keogh plan (see

TABLE 21-1

Option	cy	cy+1	cy+2	cy+3	cy+4	cy+5
A						
Section 179 deduction	$10,000	-0-	-0-	-0-	-0-	-0-
"Regular" ACRS write-off:						
20% ($20,000)	4,000					
32% ($20,000)		$6,400				
Years 3–6 ($20,000)			$3,840	$2,304	$2,304	$1,152
Total deduction	$14,000	$6,400	$3,840	$2,304	$2,304	$1,152
Tax rate	15%	25%	25%	25%	25%	25%
Total tax reduction	$ 2,100	$1,600	$ 960	$ 576	$ 576	$ 288
B						
Section 179 depreciation	-0-	-0-	-0-	-0-	-0-	-0-
"Regular" ACRS write-off:						
20% ($30,000)	$ 6,000					
32% ($30,000)		$9,600				
Years 3–6 ($30,000)			$5,760	$3,456	$3,456	$1,728
Total deduction	$6,000	$9,600	$5,760	$3,456	$3,456	$1,728
Tax rate	15%	25%	25%	25%	25%	25%
Total tax reduction	$ 900	$2,400	$1,440	$ 864	$ 864	$ 432

TABLE 21-2

	Tax Savings from Option *A*	*B*	*P.V. Factor*	*P.V. of Tax Savings* *A*	*B*
cy	$2,100	$ 900	1.00000	$2,100	$ 900
cy+1	1,600	2,400	0.90909	1,454	2,182
cy+2	960	1,440	0.82645	793	1,190
cy+3	576	864	0.75132	433	649
cy+4	576	864	0.68301	393	590
cy+5	288	432	0.62092	179	268
Total				$5,352	$5,779

Chapter 18), which can be invested and accumulate tax-free.

4. He can adopt a pension plan and set age thirty, rather than sixty-five, as the normal retirement age for this particular occupation. A *defined benefit* pension plan's deductible contribution, remember, is the amount needed to fund benefits provided for in the plan.[6] If the pension plan has only ten years (from now until age thirty), rather than forty-five years (from now until age sixty-five) to accumulate a retirement fund, a lot more money will be required each year for each dollar of benefits to be paid. If he is going to retire and start drawing benefits at age thirty, rather than at age sixty-five, the fund is going to be paying out these benefits for a much longer time. Treasury Reg. 1.72-9 provides that the life expectancy at age thirty is over fifty-two years, whereas at age sixty-five is twenty years! Again, that means that the fund has to be much larger per dollar of benefits. If payments are going to start thirty-five years sooner, the money put in will have far fewer years to grow through reinvested earnings.

If the plan in alternative 4 fixes thirty as the retirement age, the limit on maximum retirement benefits (discussed in Chapter 18) will need to be adjusted. Recall that the normal limit is the smaller of $90,000 or the average of the past three years' earnings.[7] With retirement age under the plan less than sixty-five, those ceilings need to be adjusted to the actuarial equivalent of a $90,000 benefit beginning at age sixty-five. If the proper actuarial calculations are made, an age thirty retirement can be funded, though with a benefit substantially less than $90,000.

Assume that his CPA firm's actuary calculates the maximum equivalent retirement benefit as $19,000 per year. Depending upon the actuarial assumptions being made, about all he would get from this would be a tax deduction for $25,000 per year.

[6]See the discussion in Chapter 18.

[7]IRC Sec. 415(b)(2).

Since this is less than the $30,000 per year that could be contributed to a defined contribution plan, as in (3) the defined benefit plan currently appears less advantageous.

Using a conservative 6% return on the plan investments in alternative (3) would mean that the retirement fund would grow to $395,000 by the time he is thirty. If he were to incorporate himself, earnings of the corporation after salary, pension plan contribution, and other expenses can be allowed to accumulate in the corporation. With the fund investing conservatively in bonds, and the corporation investing its retained earnings (after paying a tax of 34%) in dividend-paying stocks on which it pays very little tax because of the 70% dividends received deduction, he could probably accumulate another $250,000 in the corporation by the time he reaches age thirty. That will give him a total of almost $650,000 to work with, or fall back on, for a new career after "retirement." An added benefit of the corporation may be the ability to take a deduction for disability insurance premium payments covering his inability to play tennis due to injury or illness.

21.4 Conclusion

The first requirement for tax planning, or any other kind of planning, is some reasonable understanding of the present situation and of the possible answers to the question, "Where do we go from here?" Thus, tax planning, like war, is too important to be left to the professionals (whether they be generals, in the case of war, or CPAs or lawyers, in the case of tax planning). At the same time, the tax consequences may be so important an element of every possible alternative that it is impossible to think creatively about the different approaches without obtaining constant input from someone knowledgeable in tax matters. Tax people, as a result, tend to get intimately involved in the business and personal planning of their clients, and tend to become sophisticated business and financial planners as a result of their experience. By the same token, successful business people and investors find some basic tax knowledge indispensable in order to make even tentative plans or to know how to use the tax assistance of professionals most effectively.

The tax system is a reality. It is not the only reality. Successful planning must deal with the tax reality and with all other significant and pertinent realities. Planning that makes tax sense but not business sense is probably neither good business planning nor good tax planning.

PROBLEMS

Problem 21-1. James and Wanda Page have three children, ranging in age from seven to twelve. James is a partner in a local CPA firm. His earned income is approximately $80,000 per year. In addition, the Pages have investment income, mostly dividends but some interest, of about $8,000 per year. This is from securities that Wanda inherited four years ago. They own all of the securities jointly. Itemized deductions will be $12,000. They own a small rental house which Wanda manages. The property generates an additional $2,000 per year net income.

(a) What is their tax liability for the year? (Use 1990 rates.)

(b) Assume that they were to create a trust for the benefit of the children. It would be irrevocable, and would accumulate income for later distribution to the children. The trust corpus would consist of all of the securities. What would be the taxable income for them and for the trust? (Assume that the trust can be managed by someone who will not charge a management fee.)

(c) Explain the difference in tax which would result from one child being age 14.

(d) Could the rental property be put into trust with any resulting tax savings? Explain.

(e) What general principles of tax planning are reflected by the foregoing set of questions and the answers? Explain. Suggest other ideas for tax savings.

PROBLEMS WITH AN ASTERISK REQUIRE ADDITIONAL RESEARCH.

Problem 21-2.* Dr. Paine, a local dentist, has called you for a conference. She wants some information about her financial record keeping and tax returns.

Since opening her practice seven years ago, her accountant has kept both books and tax records under the accrual method. She thinks it would be helpful to change to the cash method for tax purposes, but to continue to use the accrual method for business records. She has just returned from a conference with other dentists and discovered in conversations with them that almost all used the cash method for tax purposes. Upon returning home, she asked the accountant for the records and was astonished to find that at the beginning of the current year accounts receivable were $12,000. "It's bad enough to pay tax on money I receive, but to pay tax on money I haven't received, and may not receive is too much. There has got to be a better way," was her remark to you. You have found that accrued expenses at the beginning of this year were $3,200.

What tax planning opportunities exist for your client? Include in your discussion consideration of the following:

(a) Advantages of remaining on the current system.

(b) Requirements for a change; that is, will the IRS have to approve? What adjustments might be required?

(c) Can the cash method be used for tax purposes and the accrual method for book purposes? What advantages are there to be gained from using the accrual method for book purposes?

Problem 21-3.* Four individuals, A, B, C, and D, own the stock of two corporations in the following ratios:

Shareholder	*Corporation X*	*Corporation Y*
A	38%	40%
B	25%	21%
C	37%	10%
D	0	29%

None of the shareholders is related to any other shareholder. Corporation X has taxable income of $78,000 for the current year. Corporation Y has taxable income of $43,000 for the current year. What is the amount of the tax liability for each corporation for the year? What is the least change in stock ownership that would cut the combined tax bill of X and Y?

Problem 21-4.* Your client, Professor Smith, is a university professor. In addition, he is an active inventor and designer. From time to time over the years he has been able to acquire a patent on his inventions, but he does not consider himself to be involved enough in such activities to have a trade or business. Also, he can clearly establish that these activities are not a hobby. He spends several hundred dollars of his own money each year for research and development in connection with activities that could lead to a patentable device.

(a) Are these expenditures deductible?

(b) What is the distinction between expenditures that are deductible as research and development costs and those which would have to be capitalized?

(c) Your research should result in some questions that you would like to ask Professor Smith. Prepare a list of them along with an explanation of why each question is important.

Problem 21-5.* The Terrific Manufacturing Co. is being audited by the IRS. The company manufactures electronic parts for the mass communication industry. It is a closely held corporation. All of the stock is owned by three brothers, each owning one-third of the stock.

During a plant visit, an IRS auditor noted that there were three expensive boats stored in the corporation's warehouse. Two were inboard motor boats, large enough for sleeping six or eight persons. The third was a sailboat, large enough to sleep four to six persons. All three were on trailers. The IRS agent discovered that one boat belonged to each of the three brothers. However, each had purchased his boat with personal funds, and no corporate funds were ever used for the purchase, maintenance, or operating expenses. There had never been any deduction claimed on any of their personal tax returns for any expenses in connection with the boats or any use of the boats. The agent did discover that the boats were stored in the corporation's warehouse during the winter months because they would be safe from vandalism and theft. The stockholders paid no rent to the corporation for the storage space.

The agent proposes to impute rental income to the corporation for the fair rental value of the space occupied by the boats. Also, the three stockholders should report additional imputed dividend income as the result of this "fringe benefit," of free boat storage.

(a) Research the question of additional imputed income to the corporation from the three individuals who have their boats stored by the corporation. What would be some of the arguments (pro and con) as to whether this is (or is not) income to the corporation? (Cite any authority relied upon.)

(b) Research the question of imputed dividend income to the three shareholders. Explain why they might (or might not) have such income. (Cite any authority relied upon.)

Problem 21-6.* Stronghold Federal Savings and Loan Association (Stronghold) is a federally chartered mutual savings and loan association. As such, it has no capital stock. Rather, it is "owned" by the depositors. Votings rights exist for various groups as follows: Holders of savings account deposits: 1 vote per $100 (or fractional part thereof) on deposit. Maximum number of votes per person: 400. Borrowers: 1 vote per person.

The following constitute the relevant operating policies of Stronghold:

1. Net earnings are distributed semiannually to savings account holders on a pro rata basis.
2. Upon liquidation or dissolution, savings account holders would be entitled to a pro rata distribution of all assets.
3. Account holders are entitled to withdraw any or all funds upon thirty-day notice. Stronghold may, at its option, grant withdrawals sooner than the thirty days.
4. Stronghold may, at any time, close a holder's account by paying such holder the total balance of his or her account.

Weakkneed Savings and Loan Association (Weakkneed) was a stock savings and loan association chartered by the state of Maine. It was authorized to do the following:

1. Offer various classes of savings accounts.
2. Issue guaranty stock.
3. Make loans.

As regards voting matters, each person who had done business with Weakkneed in any of the capacities above, was entitled to vote as follows:

1. Persons holding a savings account were entitled to one vote per $100 (or fraction thereof) on deposit.
2. Persons holding stock were entitled to one vote per share held.
3. Persons who were borrowers were entitled to one vote each.

The following were the operating policies of Weakkneed, pursuant to state law:

1. The guaranty stock was the fixed capital, and was not subject to withdrawal by the owner or owners thereof.
2. Holders of guaranty stock were entitled to elect a majority of the board of directors.
3. Holders of guaranty stock were deemed to have a proprietary interest in the business, and thus would be entitled to the residual of assets in the event of dissolution or liquidation.

Early in 1990, Weakkneed was merged into Stronghold under a plan whereby the shareholders of Weakkneed forfeited their shares for one of the following alternatives:

1. For each share of Weakkneed, a holder received a $12 deposit in a Stronghold passbook account. There was a restriction that such deposits could not be withdrawn for at least twelve months following the merger;
2. For each share of Weakkneed, a holder received a $12 deposit in a Stronghold time certificate of deposit in Stronghold ranging in maturity dates from one to ten years.

Robert Johnson exchanged 7,000 shares of Weakkneed stock for $84,000 in passbook saving accounts. His basis in the stock was $8 per share, resulting in a realized gain of $28,000.

Does the transaction constitute a statutory merger under Sec. 368(a)(1)?

Problem 21-7.* Your client owns and operates an air-conditioning and heating installation and repair service. There are two employees besides himself. Assets total approximately $20,000. They have been depreciated rapidly but are in excellent working condition. The business is operated from a building that is leased on a long-term basis. The lease is subject to transfer should the business be sold.

Your client is thinking of selling the business. There have been some preliminary inquiries, mostly about the profitability of the business. Tax returns for recent years indicate taxable income of approximately $60,000 per year. Since the business is not incorporated, that figure is after itemized deductions and exemptions, which have been about $10,000 each year. Thus, Schedule C income has been about $70,000 per year.

Preliminary indications are that a prospective buyer might offer about $200,000 for the business. Your client has asked that you prepare a memo for him which will advise him of the various options that he might have available in connection with the sale of the business. He has said that the $200,000 selling price looks attractive, but he wants to be sure that the income tax bite is as little as possible.

(a) Prepare a list of items that should be taken into consideration when selling a business such as this.

(b) Prepare a list of additional information that you would need in order to advise your client satisfactorily. (Do not concern yourself with the *detailed* dollar amounts of such things as asset cost or accumulated depreciation.)

Problem 21-8.* Jake Turner, your client, has some stock that has appreciated in value. He wants to sell it, and would have a long-term capital gain of $50,000. Jake is somewhat familiar with the rules for basis and holding period of gift property and has proposed the following. Jake will make a gift of the stock to his minor child. The child will then sell the stock, with Jake acting as the child's custodian. The income tax that the child will incur will be substantially less than what Jake would incur, because the child has no other income and is over age 14.

Jake expects to have about $100,000 of taxable income for the year without this transaction. He estimates that even if he were to incur a gift tax liability, the income tax savings would still be far greater than the gift tax.

(a) Research this question and prepare an answer for Jake. (*Hint:* Consider "step transaction doctrine" and "form versus substance.")

(b) Keep a careful record of all of your research steps and authorities which you find.

Problem 21-9.* Mr. Harcourt, your client, owns 100% of the outstanding stock of a small manufacturing corporation. He has been negotiating with a potential buyer of the business and has reached some tentative terms. He is to sell the stock of the corporation. Payments will be made over a period of five years. During the current year he will receive a cash payment of $100,000. In each of the next four years he will receive an amount that will be determined under a formula which takes into consideration the amount of profit generated by the corporation which is the buyer. However, Mr. Harcourt will not receive less than $125,000 each year for four years.

Mr. Harcourt has asked you if the arrangement, which he finds otherwise satisfactory, would permit him to use the installment method for reporting his substantial gain. If so, he wonders how to calculate the profit ratio since he expects to receive substantially more than the minimum.

(a) Research this question for Mr. Harcourt, and prepare an answer to him based upon your findings.

(b) Keep a careful record of your research steps and authorities that you have relied upon.

Problem 21-10.* Mrs. Frank is a widow, age 54. She will not be 55 until next taxable year. Her husband died earlier this year. They had lived in the same residence, which was their only home, for the past ten years. Her basis in the house is $55,000 and it is currently worth approximately $145,000. While Mr. Frank was alive they had never made use of the Sec. 121 exclusion on the sale of a residence. She would like to sell the residence this year and use the Sec. 121 exclusion. She reasons that the residence would have been sold by her and her husband if he had lived and they would have been able to use the exclusion since he was age 57. Since this year is the year of his death, she will file a joint federal income tax return as a "surviving spouse." Can she sell the house and use the Sec. 121 election to have nonrecognized gain?

EPILOGUE

tax reform

Tax reform is not only a current issue but an ancient problem. How ancient? We read in I Kings 12, of Rehoboam, the son of Solomon. Of him the people demanded a lighter tax burden. Rehoboam responded, "My father made your yoke heavy, but I will add to your yoke." He raised taxes rather than lowering them. The result? The Kingdom was split by a tax revolt into Israel and Judah, with Rehoboam losing Israel and retaining only Judah. But politicians never learn. In 1984, Democratic presidential candidate Walter Mondale declared that it was necessary to raise taxes—and carried only one state and the District of Columbia. In 1988, Bruce Babbitt declared new tax revenues were essential—and finished next to last in the Democratic caucuses in Iowa and in the Democratic primary in New Hampshire. George Bush promised, "no new taxes," and was elected President.

What is the purpose of the U.S. tax system?

It is possible to conceive of that purpose as being solely the collection of revenue. A tax law based on such a purpose would provide a minimum of special benefits and incentives. Any such would be difficult to get into the law and more difficult to keep in the law. A revenue-only tax law would seldom change in essence, although it might frequently change its rates. It would be relatively simple and its impact would be relatively predictable, because past experience with the very same law would help predict the effect of altering those few variables such as rates which would be changed from time to time.

Such a tax law would attempt to be neutral, in that it would have as one of its goals a minimum of either incentive or penalty. Transactions that would seem advantageous relative to other transactions absent a tax law would still seem as advantageous after reflecting the impact of the tax law. Property values would be affected only minimally by tax law changes, since all types of property would be affected about the same.

That is not, of course, the present tax law in the United States. Congress estimates that special incentives, relief provisions for various categories of taxpayers, and attempts to provide equity and social insurance cost over $300 billion annually before the 1986 Tax Reform Act through what are called "tax expenditures."[1] Constant tinkering with the law contributes to an adversary climate in tax administration which partly causes uncertainty as to what particular tax provisions actually mean. It also costs both taxpayers and government additional scores of millions for lawyers, accountants, crowded courts, and complex administrative procedures.

One school of critics of the present U.S. tax system would simplify the system by eliminating most or all nonbusiness itemized deductions of individuals, doing away with special incentive provisions, and then lowering the rate of tax on what would then be a much larger base of income. Some of this thinking is reflected in the 1986 Tax Reform Act.

Another school focuses on the lack of operational progressivity revealed by tax statistics as compared to the apparent progressivity of the tax

[1]Joint Committee on Taxation, "Estimate of Federal Tax Expenditures for Fiscal Years 1984–1989," JCS-39-84 (Washington, D.C.: U.S. Government Printing Office, 1984).

rate tables. Especially if the burden of all taxes is analyzed, there is relatively little progressivity[2] in the combined federal, state, and local tax structures in the U.S. This is offensive to many people on ideological grounds, and these people would also advocate doing away with itemized deductions, special credits, and other incentives—but with primary focus on those of major benefits to upper-income taxpayers.

And then there are the defenders of the *status quo.* They would point out that the U.S. income tax system has evolved over a period of seventy-five years to its present status, and that it provides a tool for fiscal and economic fine-tuning that has become increasingly important as government has played a larger and larger role in the U.S. economy. One does not simply abandon such a tax system on theoretical and ideological grounds. As the tax law changes, each new status quo acquires its own advocates.

Thus, the answers to questions of tax reforms are not answers that can be provided by specialists in public finance, or economists, or CPAs, or lawyers, or by any group of technicians. They are answers that come from the values and perceived self-interest of the various groups and individuals concerned about tax reform—or, to be even more precise, from the perception by those involved in enacting tax laws as to the values and the self-interest of their particular constituencies.

Throughout this book, different tax reform issues have been discussed in the context of the provisions involved. Often, the evolutionary nature of U.S. tax provisions has been stressed. However, we have not tried to evaluate these provisions. The sort of standards or principles which would serve as a starting point for such an evaluation would likely include:

1. ***Equity:*** Every practicable effort should be made to treat all persons who are in the same economic situation, for example, those with the same annual income, in the same way (sometimes referred to as "horizontal equity"). Also, appropriate and fair distinctions should be made in the treatment of those who are in different economic circumstances (sometimes referred to as "vertical equity" or "progressivity"). The most common illustrative example of progressivity is a graduated tax whose rates increase as the level of income increases, thus relating the tax to the taxpayer's presumptive ability to pay.
2. ***Moral Integrity:*** In structure, administration, and enforcement, the tax system should foster honest and conscientious self-assessment. Integrity of the system—an understanding that it operates as intended, fairly toward all—will tend to produce integrity in the taxpaying public. Under this criterion, emphasis is also placed on the taxpayer's being treated fairly and with dignity in the administration of the tax rules. The privacy of tax returns is of importance to the taxpayer and should be protected. The relationship between the government tax-collecting agency and the taxpayer should not *ipso facto* be an adversary one. The rules by which administrative proceedings are conducted should not assume wrongful intent or behavior by the taxpayer.
3. ***Simplicity:*** The tax system should be made as simple as practicable so that taxpayers, tax administrators, and legislators all can understand the rules and confidently apply them or comply with them. Simple provisions and rules are more likely to be uniformly applied, and the results of such uniform application are less likely to be affected by individual judgment, interpretation, or circumstances.
4. ***Consistency Over Time:*** It is very frustrating, even to full-time practicing professionals, to have to deal with constant changes in rules. Over the past half-dozen years or so, there have been substantial changes, sometimes more often than annually (e.g., the "luxury car" limitations on investment credit and depreciation). While change is necessary and perhaps inevitable, many have argued that confidence in the system erodes, and efficiency is reduced, when the rules change sometimes before taxpayers have had time to digest the former rules, or certainly before they have had time to make adjustments in financial plans taking tax provisions into consideration.
5. ***Efficiency:*** A good tax system should contribute to, or at least not hinder, the economy's obtaining from its limited resources the highest possible output not only of goods and services but also of those intangibles making up the "quality of life."
6. ***Political Acceptability:*** Political acceptability, as used here, refers more to acceptance by the electorate than it does to feasibility of passage by the legislature. A tax system would not be acceptable, but would be rejected, evaded, or ignored, if the public perceived it to be unfair, overly complex, or inefficient in operation. Included in political acceptability is not only the concept and general effect of the tax, but its implementation and administration, as well.
7. ***Flexibility:*** The tax laws should have built-in provisions for their periodic legislative review. This is especially desirable if the tax system is to be used to accomplish economic and social objectives as well as to raise revenues.

   Laws enacted to solve the problems of a given time period tend to become obsolete. Tax laws are no exception. The criterion of flexibility is intended to make the revenue-raising mechanism,

[2] Joseph A. Pechman and Benjamin A. Okner, *Who Bears the Tax Burden?* (Washington, D.C.: The Brookings Institution, 1974).

and the law itself, responsive to and reflective of changing economic and social priorities.

These criteria conflict with each other. For example, equity often is achievable only with a loss of simplicity, while too heavy-handed an emphasis on moral integrity may lead to a zealousness that threatens political acceptability. There must inevitably be some trading-off.

The nature of the U.S political process is such that total scrapping of the present system and substitution of a philosophically coherent approach (e.g., elimination of all incentive provisions, itemized deductions for individuals, and lowering of tax rates) is not politically likely. Each provision in the tax law has its own constituency. Its proposed repeal generates heated opposition, regardless of what else is being done to any other provisions. Politicians don't like heated opposition, so legislation tends to focus on specific tax provisions, and on their modification rather than their abolition.

For example, when the use of accelerated depreciation on business real estate was criticized as creating excessive tax benefits, a first response was to provide for a partial recapture, as ordinary income, of some part of the gain on disposition of the realty that would otherwise be capital gain. Originally, holding the property for at least ten years eliminated entirely this ordinary income recapture of part of the excess of accelerated over straight-line depreciation. Later, property was categorized (low-income housing, other residential, and commercial) and different holding periods were required in order to avoid any ordinary income upon sale. The ability to eliminate ordinary income by a long-enough holding period was then abolished for all but low-income housing. In 1981, all depreciation taken on commercial realty, not just the excess of accelerated over straight line, was made subject to ordinary income recapture if accelerated depreciation was elected. Determining the tax effects of a 1989 sale of realty that has been held for some time is now quite complicated, since each of the changes except the last treats differently the depreciation taken before and after a cutoff date. In addition, since the ordinary income portion of the gain is usually based on the excess of accelerated over straight-line depreciation, the passage of time affects the calculation inasmuch as there comes a point in the depreciation of the realty where the "accelerated" method is producing less than the straight-line would have, and thus the potential ordinary income is being reduced year by year.

However, Congress was not content with this rather complicated approach to this particular tax question. Along the line, it also decreed the annual excess of accelerated over straight-line depreciation on realty would constitute a tax preference item. In 1986 it went further and mandated straight-line depreciation for all real property placed in service after 1986. Going even further, real property will be depreciated for alternative minimum tax purposes over longer lives.

The history of other tax provisions could be similarly sketched. The result is a mosaic of rules, exceptions to the rules, special provisions, exceptions to the special provisions, etc. Powers and interests are not so much balanced as placated, while the costs and effects of changes are not only misunderstood by the citizenry but are often incomprehensible to the legislators and technicians who formulate the statutory provisions and to the lawyers and CPAs who attempt to counsel taxpayers on their impact.

There are many consequences to such a state of affairs. Such confusion is wastefully expensive, requiring the efforts of thousands of people; it has a devastating impact on people's perception of their ability to cope with the demands of their society, which in turn may have a detrimental impact on their willingness to comply with the rules; it contributes to governmental corruption in tax legislation and administration. As to balancing powers and interests, confusion and complexity of the magnitude of the present federal income tax law puts increasing power into the hands of legislators, congressional staff people, and special interest groups, without any balancing force capable of dealing adequately with how that power is exercised.

Complexity warps the perception of the taxpayer. Add to complexity, tax rules that seem to be in a constant state of change, and many average taxpayers recognize that efforts to control income tax liability may be at least as important to after-tax economic well-being as are the efforts made to earn the income. So taxpayers may conclude that the capriciousness, complexity, and constant change of the tax law justify taking any action or making any claim which would be unlikely to result in criminal charges. They may rationalize that "everyone's doing it," and so join the insistent clamor for tax benefits and privileges for whatever groups they identify with. Can they be fairly criticized for all this? They are behaving as the system assumes they will behave and encourages them to behave.

Abstractly, however, this is "bad." It is the essence of the just society that it encourage good rather than evil, selflessness rather than selfishness, cooperation rather than destructive aggrandizement. Thus, complexity and constant change must be viewed as not being in the public good, all ot things being equal. But, of course, all other things are seldom equal.

Thus, in spite of the negative aspects of the present system, there are some positive arguments for the retention of its essential features.

1. ***A Tax Incentive Is Not an Expenditure:*** A tax incentive is not the same thing as a governmental expenditure. A tax incentive allows people to retain what they already have, and there is a subtle difference between keeping what you have and benefiting from a program of governmental subsidy. There is probably less damage done to our society if taxpayers get to keep too much of their own money than if a governmental program funnels funds to the wrong recipients, or squanders money in bureaucratic foolishness, or is "taken" by chiselers.

   Some would also argue that equating tax incentives and governmental expenditures requires the presumption that the federal government has an ownership claim to income superior to that of the taxpayer who is actually receiving or earning that income. While the ability to levy an income tax probably encompasses the legal power to tax 100% (or even more) of income, there is probably substantial agreement that even if such a power exists, its exercise would be unconscionable, and that an individual's right to his or her income is a property right that should be jealously and zealously safeguarded. An analogy is sometimes drawn between the government and an armed robber. The robber may have the *power* to take your money, but that does not mean he has the *right* to do so. The government may have the power to take 100% of your income, but doing so would not be right.

   There is also the measurement problem. In the context of equating tax expenditures with incentives, the impossibility of accurately measuring the cost of tax incentives tends to make much of the discussion difficult. However, even if tax expenditures could be measured with high accuracy, the measurement would suffer from the *ceteris peribus* (all other things being equal) problem. For example, the tax expenditure for charitable contributions is estimated on the assumption that all other tax system elements would be the same without the tax provision as with it. But that is patently, although unmeasurably, absurd. If the incentive does encourage contributions, then eliminating the deduction will reduce the contributions. Charitable organizations will have less to spend, fewer employees, etc., and their employees and suppliers will thus have less taxable income and pay less tax, buy less from their suppliers, and so on.

   Finally, there are real legal differences between what can be done with appropriations as compared to tax incentives. For example, the charitable contribution deduction can provide a tax incentive for contributions to religious organizations, while a direct money appropriation from the federal government would violate the constitutional separation of church and state.

2. ***Tax Incentive Advantages:*** Tax incentives are simpler, speedier, more direct, and more efficiently administered than are other incentive programs. Although it could stand improvement, the Internal Revenue Service administers an apparatus that has great flexibility, at low administrative cost per dollar involved, whereas other incentive programs generally lead to expansion of governmental agencies and are frequently accompanied by long time delays in field implementation as well as substantial overall inefficiency in accomplishing their objectives.
3. ***Tax Incentives Conform to Human Nature:*** There is the belief that taxpayers will try to lessen or avoid taxes no matter what the tax system, and therefore the natural human game-playing tendency should be channelled into socially desirable activity. If people will do things to cut their taxes anyway, let them do socially desirable things (like putting their money into residential housing). Related to this is the belief that in many areas of economic behavior, a tax incentive may have more impact than a cash subsidy (i.e., a dollar saved may be worth more than a dollar earned, if the dollar saved is a tax dollar).
4. ***Tax Incentives Have a Built-in System of Checks and Balances:*** Many believe that the intimate involvement of most citizens with the federal income tax process leads to a relatively high level of knowledge of tax incentives as compared to the public knowledge of other types of incentive programs. This, in turn, results in a built-in contribution to the system of checks and balances comparable in its effect to the safeguards built into the appropriation process.

Given such an environment, what are some of the key tax reform issues as we approach the 1990s?

DOUBLE TAXATION OF CORPORATIONS

Who bears the burden of an income tax imposed on business? The economics and the politics of taxation are affected by one's perception of the answer to this question. Since business entities are merely conduits, the answer has to be that the burden of the corporate income tax falls on the corporate shareholder, the worker, and the consumer. The proportion that each pays varies, of course, among industries as well as during different periods of time.

Coupled with an apparent upcoming shortage of investment capital, the reality of double taxation leads many to conclude that elimination of the double taxation would help solve the capital shortage. Elimination would probably involve one or a combination of both:

1. allowing corporations a deduction for dividends paid, or

2. taxing corporate income to shareholders as earned rather than as distributed, with the shareholder getting a credit for the income tax paid as a deposit by his corporation.

The probable direct effect of either approach would seem, in part, to be the shift of the tax impact to the shareholders. Alternative 1 presumably would force corporations to pay most of their current earnings in dividends, subjecting these dividends to tax in the hands of taxpaying shareholders and sending the corporations back to the equity markets to get the cash they now obtain through retaining earnings.

In the second approach, corporate cash flows would not change, but investors in marginal tax brackets higher than the corporation would find their after-tax return decreased. Under the 1986 tax rate changes, there now are few such investors.

Pension funds, churches, and other tax-exempt investors likely would benefit from the first alternative as their cash flow from dividends was increased, and also would benefit from the second alternative if their dividend credit could produce a cash refund. But the net impact, because of the tax exempt shareholders, would be to reduce total income tax receipts. That reduction would have to be balanced by tax increases somewhere. Only when the question is answered as to where those tax dollars will come from can the ultimate impact of eliminating double taxation be evaluated.

U.S. TAXATION OF FOREIGN INCOME

U.S. taxpayers are allowed to take a credit against their U.S. tax for foreign income taxes paid. Presumably, the U.S. taxpayer is indifferent as to whether he pays a dollar of tax to the United States or to a foreign country, so long as the foreign tax rate does not exceed the amount for which he can obtain a credit. The rationale for the foreign tax credit is equity to the taxpayer and neutrality of the tax system in making international investment decisions.

From the standpoint of the U.S. national interest, some contend, there is a great difference between a dollar in taxes paid to a foreign country and the same dollar paid to the United States. U.S. investment should be discouraged from going abroad, it is argued, if U.S. unemployment is to be minimized. In fact, though, since the use of foreign corporations allows U.S. persons to defer tax on foreign earnings, there is in the present system a positive incentive for U.S persons to invest abroad in countries where the income tax rate is substantially less than the U.S. income tax rate.

Which viewpoint a particular individual may adopt will likely depend on whether he believes that the U.S. tax loss is more than made up by the advantage to U.S. national interests of having U.S. business actively engaged around the world.

CREDITS INSTEAD OF DEDUCTIONS

If tax rates rise as income rises, then the value of a tax deduction will be greater, in terms of after-tax dollars, to someone with higher income. A credit, by contrast, is worth the same dollars to all taxpayers with a tax liability against which the credit will apply. If the credit is refundable (i.e., if the credit exceeds the tax liability, the government writes the taxpayer a check), then truly all taxpayers, even those who have no tax to pay, are being treated alike.

One deduction often proposed for change to credit status is the personal exemption. By definition, every person is entitled to at least one exemption amount deduction, so that it is the most universal tax deduction in the system. A major argument for changing it to a credit is that the exemption amount is the community's way of sharing or subsidizing the cost of people supporting themselves and others who are dependent upon them. Therefore, why should the community subsidize one human being more heavily than another merely because of a higher income level? In fact, from the standpoint of community concern for the individual, why not subsidize on a basis where the subsidy declines as the income rises? In fact, the personal exemption does phase out at higher income levels under the 1986 Tax Reform Act.

It is possible, though, to view the exemption amount differently. Instead of focusing on how taxpayers at different income levels are treated, think of the exemption amount in terms of the taxation of taxpayers having the same adjusted gross income. If, as discussed briefly in Chapter 3, some concept of "disposable income" seems to influence the tax deduction allowed individuals, then exemptions can be viewed as a way of adjusting a given level of income for some minimal amount of annual expense that needs to be incurred for each person who must be supported out of that income. Only after such an adjustment has been made can disposable income properly subject to income tax be determined. Would it be fair to impose the same income tax on a single person with $20,000 of income as a family of eight with $20,000?

CAPITAL RECOVERY ALLOWANCES

As can be demonstrated,[3] expensing capital investments at the time made would produce an after-tax rate of return on those investments equal to the before-tax rate of return, *all other things being equal.* Making the investment nondeductible forever, by contrast, would reduce the after-tax return on investment to the same percentage of the before-tax as the complement of the tax rate.

Some types of investments (e.g., research and development expenditures) can be charged to expense when incurred. Others (e.g., purchased goodwill) are never deductible. Most are recovered over some period of time (e.g., ACRS life) and in some pattern (e.g., straight-line).

The issue is whether incentives are needed for business to make investments. One argument points out that businesses will not, in fact, make investments unless they perceive potential profits. Hence, it is concluded that tax incentives are not as useful in stimulating investment when consumer demand is weak as they are in changing the perceived profitability of different competing investments when consumer demand is strong.

A contrary argument points to the infinite complexity of the world economy. Projects compete with projects, but the dollars also compete with the costs of financing and the returns on passive as well as active investment in all corners of the globe. Hence, anything that will improve the perceived profitability of investments which, for instance, create jobs in the United States, should be good for the U.S. economy in the long run.

There is also the question of business "climate." It is argued that regardless of actual effect, policies (e.g., the restoration of the investment credit, which increases the perceived profitability of a project by lowering the after-tax investment) which show business that government is cooperative and supportive increase the likelihood of investments being made by apparently reducing uncertainty and risk as to unfavorable future tax legislation.

NEGATIVE INCOME TAX

Properly speaking, the negative income tax proposal is a social welfare proposal and not a tax matter at all. But the tax law is concerned with all sorts of matters, as has been frequently pointed out, so it is not *just* a tax law anyway.

At the extreme if fully implemented, the negative income tax would result in every person (or at least every family group) either writing checks to the IRS or getting checks from the IRS. Those who have positive taxable income would write checks, while those with negative taxable income would receive them. Instead of making payments on estimated taxes, those with negative taxable income would receive estimated tax refund checks.

The argument is that the tax collecting and administration structure is much more efficient than the multitude of welfare agencies and programs now in operation. Thus, the costs of welfare per dollar distributed could be dramatically slashed. Beyond that, the negative income tax proposal represents an acceptance of the proposition that solely by virtue of being a U.S. resident a person has a right to some minimum level of income regardless of the reasons why he or she has no more income.

The opposition to this approach to welfare includes people of several different viewpoints. One viewpoint is that without controls over the use of funds, persons being subsidized will be victimized (by their own weaknesses and through being exploited by others) so that there will still be a need for special programs to look out for, e.g., dependent children, and thus many of the anticipated savings will not materialize.

Some are concerned that the magnitude of a negative income tax program would swamp the IRS, leading to a decline in the efficiency and effectiveness of its overall program. If forced to deal with "welfare chiselers," would IRS inherit all the problems of administration of present programs, so that rather than create efficiency in welfare the change would produce chaos in tax collection?

CAPITAL GAIN PROVISIONS

Some argue that capital gains should be taxed no differently than any other form of income. Others argue that they should not be taxed at all. Still others would index capital assets and thus not tax any gain reflecting only price-level changes. With the Tax Reform Act of 1986, Congress moved away from giving special treatment to capital gains. As of early 1990, there seemed to be a likelihood that Congress would again provide special treatment for capital gains.

To some, the significance of the special tax treatment of capital gains lies in the importance of wide participation in the securities markets of the United States. Rather than seeing the states use lotteries and casino gambling to raise revenues, they would prefer to see tax exemption or tax

[3]Wm. L. Raby and Paul M. Loveday, "Depreciation and Economic Life, 39 *Taxes*, 684 (August 1961).

shelter accorded security profits to provide a continuing stimulant to small investor participation in the U.S. system of financing business. Business expansion, it is argued, would lead to higher levels of tax collection, more than offsetting the modest revenue losses from not taxing security gains.

ADAPTING TO INFLATION

A tax law with dollar amounts specified as limits or floors for many items, with a progressive rate structure, and with a variety of objectives inevitably is subjected to stresses and strains during inflation. Is a $1,080 (1986) exemption amount adequate? Is $2,000 (1989)? Why do people who have not had an increase in real income nevertheless pay sharply higher income taxes? Should not depreciation allowances be adjusted for changes in the value of the dollar so that we are not taxing capital and destroying the ability of business to replace its plant and equipment?

The attempt to maintain relative equities during inflation can only serve to complicate an already complicated law. Yet failure to do some things will be perceived by the voters as callous indifference to their problems. The real answer would be to continue to keep inflation under reasonable control, and thus eliminate the problem. Failing that, there is some support for the idea that key elements in the individual tax structure, and capital recovery in the business area, might be linked to price indexes so as to automatically mirror inflation. The tax law's existing indexing, on the other hand, is attacked annually.

RELIANCE ON OTHER TAXES

In the past, it was believed that tax reductions and incentives did not cost tax revenue in the long run because of their stimulating effect on the economy. Increased income meant that lower tax rates produced more dollars.

Now there is less faith in the growth potential of the U.S. economy. Where do the dollars come from to reduce the deficit, let alone support expanding governmental expenditures, if not from the income tax? Where do the dollars come from to support a reduction in income taxes?

A prime candidate is some form of excise or sales tax. Many feel that the European experience with the value-added tax (VAT) has been favorable, and that such a tax is the logical next step for the United States as well. Property taxes create administrative problems, but excise taxes fit into an existing framework and are relatively easy to implement. Main arguments against excise taxes (including VAT) reflect their lack of progressivity, in the sense that ability-to-pay is not a direct factor, contribution to inflation, and invasion of a revenue source widely used by the states. Selective excise taxes can partially overcome the regressivity complaint (e.g., retail sales taxes that exempt basic necessities). Some observers see substantial gasoline tax increases (e.g., perhaps of $1 a gallon) as both a way of raising revenue and reducing our dependence on imported oil. Others would impose a tax on all energy consumption (based on BTUs).

CONCLUSION

Tax reform is obviously not a simple black and white, good or bad, problem. It does not start with a clean slate, but rather deals with the world as it is at a given moment. Tax incentives are valuable, and tax reforms inevitably take from some and give to others. Perhaps that is why major reform is discussed so much, and done so little; and perhaps that is why what tax reform legislation there is tends to be painfully complex. There is pro and con to almost every tax issue, but there may be more con to tax reform than so-called pros are willing to admit.

INDEX